23/11/15

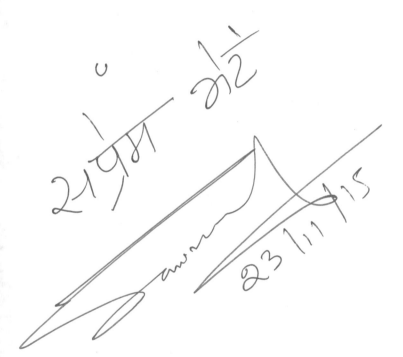

1081

II Oṁ Śrī Paramātmane Namaḥ II

Śrīmad Bhagavadgītā

Sādhaka-Sañjīvanī [with Appendix]-Vol. II
Commentary

By Swami Ramsukhdas

[With Sanskrit text, Transliteration and English Translation]

(Translated into English by S. C. Vaishya)
Revised by R. N. Kaul & Keshoram Aggarwal

tvameva mātā ca pitā tvameva
tvameva bandhuśca sakhā tvameva
tvameva vidyā draviṇaṁ tvameva
tvameva sarvaṁ mama devadeva

Gita Press, Gorakhpur, India

Eleventh Reprint 2014 3,000
Total 43,800

❖ **Price : ₹ 100**

(One Hundred Rupees only)

Printed & Published by :

Gita Press, Gorakhpur—273005 (INDIA)

(a unit of Gobind Bhavan-Karyalaya, Kolkata)

Phone - (0551) 2334721, 2331250; Fax - (0551) 2336997
e-mail : **booksales@gitapress.org** website : **www.gitapress.org**

॥ Shri Hari ॥

Contents

Seventeenth Chapter

Śraddhātraya (Threefold Faith)-Vibhāga Yoga

|| Shri Hari ||

Ninth Chapter

INTRODUCTION

In the seventh chapter, Lord Kṛṣṇa was unfolding to Arjuna knowledge (wisdom) with realization (real knowledge of manifest Divinity). But in between, Arjuna at the beginning of the eighth chapter, raised seven questions. So Lord Kṛṣṇa, by answering the first six questions, in brief, answered, in detail the seventh question—"How are you to be known at the time of death by the self-controlled?"

Now, the Lord starts the same topic of Knowledge (Jñāna), with Realization (Vijñāna), in the ninth chapter.

श्रीभगवानुवाच

इदं तु ते गुह्यतमं प्रवक्ष्याम्यनसूयवे।
ज्ञानं विज्ञानसहितं यज्ज्ञात्वा मोक्ष्यसेऽशुभात्॥ १॥

śrībhagavānuvāca

idaṁ tu te guhyatamaṁ pravakṣyāmyanasūyave
jñānaṁ vijñānasahitaṁ yajjñātvā mokṣyase'śubhāt

The Blessed Lord said:

To you who is free from the carping spirit I shall now unfold the most mysterious knowledge (Jñāna), along with realization (Vijñāna) by knowing which, you will be released from evil i.e., the evil of worldly birth and death. 1

Comment:—

'Idaṁ tu te guhyatamaṁ pravakṣyāmyanasūyave'—Lord Kṛṣṇa, has used the term 'Idam' (this), to highlight the topic, which he wants to unfold. To state its merit, He has used the superlative form, of the adjective—'Guhyatamam' (most profound). It means, that this knowledge combined with realization, is most profound. It has been called, a 'sovereign secret', in the second verse, and 'the greatest secret', in the sixty-fourth verse of the eighteenth chapter.

Here, in this chapter, first He used the expression 'Guhyatamam' (the most profound), and later (in 9/34) used 'Manmanābhava' (fix your mind on Me), while, in the eighteenth chapter, first He used the expression 'Sarvaguhyatamam' (the most secret of all), and then (in 18/65) said 'Manmanābhava' (fix your mind on Me). It means, that the same topic has been explained here, as well as, there.

This most profound secret cannot be disclosed to all, because the Lord has described His own merit, in it. One who possesses a critical spirit, in the least, can take the contrary meaning, that Lord Kṛṣṇa, is boasting of His own merits. The Lord wants to say to Arjuna, that he is devoid of a carping spirit. So He, will unfold the most profound knowledge, along with realization to him viz., He will explain the 'Tattva' and also the methods for its realization.

Secondly, He means to say, that every human being is eligible to take refuge in Him. Even the vilest sinner, belonging to any caste, creed, country and colour, deserves to seek refuge, in Him. So, by taking refuge in Him, he can attain Him. Hence He wants to disclose this secret.

The Lord uses the term 'Tu' (indeed), as He could not say, in the seventh chapter, all that He wanted to say. So, He declares, that He will amplify the same topic again.

'Jñānaṁ vijñānasahitam'—The belief, that the Lord is the root of the universe, is 'Jñāna' (Knowledge), and the realization that in the universe, there is nothing besides the Lord is 'Vijñāna' (real knowledge of manifest Divinity). In the first half, of the preceding verse, the Lord has eulogized 'Knowledge along with Realization', by the terms 'Idam' and 'Guhyatamam'.

Knowledge and Realization

"By having this knowledge, combined with realization, you will be freed from evil. This knowledge is a sovereign science, and a sovereign secret etc. Men, devoid of faith in this Dharma (Duty), revolve in the path of the mortal world" (9/1—3). By saying so the Lord explained 'Knowledge'. "All this universe is pervaded, by Me in My unmanifest form i.e., in this universe, there is nothing else besides Me" (9/4—6). By saying so He explained 'Vijñāna'.

"All beings compelled by their own nature go into My Prakṛti (the prime cause), at dissolution and at the beginning of creation, I bring them forth again. But these actions, do not bind Me. With Me as a supervisor, nature brings forth, the whole creation. Fools, not knowing My supreme nature, think low of Me. Senseless persons with vain hopes, vain actions and vain knowledge, have embraced a nature, which is fiendish, demoniacal and delusive. Great souls, possessing divine nature, knowing Me as imperishable and prime cause of creation, worship Me constantly, with an undivided mind. Others, through their offering of knowledge, worship Me as their very self etc." (9/7—15). By saying so, the Lord explained the term 'Knowledge'. "I am a Vedic ritual, I am sacrifice, I am an offering to the departed (ancestors), I am a medicinal herb etc., and I am, a being as well as, non-being, i.e., I am everything" (9/16—19). By saying—so He explained, 'Vijñāna'. "Those who worship Me through sacrifice, to seek access to heaven, having enjoyed the vast world of heaven, return to the world of mortals, on the exhaustion of their merit. To those, who worship Me with exclusive devotion, I attend to their needs and preserve what is already possessed, by them. These devotees, who endowed with faith, worship other gods, worship Me ignorantly. Those who do not know Me, as the Enjoyer and Lord of all sacrifices, fall. Those who offer Me with devotion a leaf, a flower, a fruit or even water etc., and all their actions, are freed from the bondage of actions" (9/20—28). By saying so, He explained, 'Knowledge'. "I am equally present in all beings; there is none hateful or dear, to Me. But, those who worship Me with devotion, are in Me and I am in them" (9/29). By saying so, He explained, 'Vijñāna'. In the next five verses (from 9/30—34) 'Vijñāna' has further been explained.*

'Yajjñātvā mokṣyaseśubhāt'—Affinity with unreal, is an evil which is the cause of birth in good and evil wombs. This affinity, is not natural and real, it is merely assumed, by error. So, a man can be liberated from this assumed affinity, by not strengthening it. Actually man (soul) is an eternal fraction of the Lord, but assumes its affinity of 'I'ness and 'Mineness', with the body and the world, and thus dies and is, reborn. When he realizes reality or he is inclined towards God, then he is released from the evil of worldly, birth and death.

Appendix—The world is manifest. Karmayoga (performance of action in a disinterested manner) being unmanifest is secret. Being more secret than Karmayoga, Jñānayoga (knowledge of the self) is more secret. Being more secret than even Jñānayoga, Bhaktiyoga is the most secret. The secret (guhya) and the more secret (guhyatara) are worldly but the most secret (guhyatama) is unworldly.

All worlds, from the abode of Brahmā downwards, being subject to rebirth, are evils (Gītā 8/16). Having known the most profound topic, a man is totally liberated from the evil of worldly birth and death. A man is liberated from this evil by Karmayoga and Jñānayoga also but here liberation from the evil means—there should not be any other entity in the least besides God and there should not remain even the subtle iota (trace) of

* It does not mean that Jñāna and 'Vijñāna' are water tight compartments and they don't include each other.

ego which causes philosophical differences.

'To know the self' is 'Jñāna' and 'to know God in full' is 'Vijñāna'. Within 'nirguṇa' (attributeless God), 'saguṇa' (God in full) is not included but within 'Saguṇa', 'nirguṇa' is included, therefore the knowledge of 'Saguṇa' is 'Vijñāna' viz., special 'Jñāna'.

Link:—In the next verse, Lord Kṛṣṇa mentions, the merits of Knowledge with Realization.

राजविद्या राजगुह्यं पवित्रमिदमुत्तमम्।
प्रत्यक्षावगमं धर्म्यं सुसुखं कर्तुमव्ययम्॥ २॥

rājavidyā rājaguhyaṁ pavitramidamuttamam
pratyakṣāvagamaṁ dharmyaṁ susukhaṁ kartumavyayam

This knowledge (Jñāna) with realization, is the sovereign of sciences, and mysterious, and is, supremely holy, most excellent, directly realizable (attendant with virtue) very easy to practise and is imperishable. 2

Comment:—

'Rājavidyā'—This knowledge with Realization, is a sovereign science, after knowing which, nothing remains to be known.

At the beginning of the seventh chapter, Lord Kṛṣṇa said, "After knowing My entire form, nothing else remains to be known." He declared at the end of the fifteenth chapter, "The undeluded person who knows Me, beyond perishable Matter and superior to the imperishable soul, knows all i.e., nothing else remains to be known to him."

So it seems that greater importance has been attached to the Lord Who is endowed with attributes and form in comparison to other forms whether manifest or unmanifest, attributeless or with attributes.

'Rājaguhyam'—This is a sovereign secret, because in the

world there is nothing more secret, than this.

As an actor, in a play conceals his original identity, similarly, the Lord is not manifest to all (Gītā 7/25), because men devoid of devotion have a critical spirit. But, He becomes manifest to His loving devotees. To disclose his identity is something very secret.

'Pavitramidam'—This science is supremely holy and is a purifier. By this science, even the vilest sinner becomes instantly virtuous viz., holy and secures, lasting peace (9/31).

In the tenth chapter, Arjuna addressed Lord Kṛṣṇa, as the greatest purifier (10/12); in the fourth chapter, Lord Kṛṣṇa declared, that in the world there is no purifier like knowledge (4/38), and here He declares Knowledge with Realization, (by using eight adjectives) as a purifier. It means, that the Lord and His name, form, sport, place, thought, utterance, loud-chanting, meditation and knowledge etc., are holy and purify i.e., everything of the Lord is a great purifier, which purifies all beings.

'Uttamam'—This science, is super-excellent, because it makes My devotees, the most noble. One becomes so noble, that I obey him. About those devotees, the Lord declares, "They abide in Me and I abide in them" (9/29) i.e., by being absorbed in Me, they become one, with Me.

'Pratyakṣāvagamam'—It is directly realizable. The more one knows it, the more uncommon, he becomes. As soon as, he knows it, he secures lasting peace. Thus it is directly realizable.

'Dharmyam'—It is virtuous. All the actions performed, for God-realization without a desire for fruit, are included in virtuous actions.

In the second chapter, Lord Kṛṣṇa said to Arjuna, "There is nothing more welcome for a man of the warrior class, than a righteous war" (2/31). It means, that all actions performed according to one's caste and stage (order) of life, sanctioned by scriptures, are virtuous. Besides these, all the means for God-realization and all divine traits, have also been called immortal Dharma (Righteousness), (Gītā 12/20).

'Avyayam'—It is imperishable. The Lord has also said, that His devotee never perishes (9/31).

'Kartuṁ susukham'—It is very easy to practise. How easy it is to offer a leaf, a flower, a fruit or water etc., to God, by regarding them as His (9/26)! If a devotee offers somethings to God, thinking these as his own, the Lord reciprocates them, an infinite times, more. But, if he offers them, to Him regarding them as His, He offers Himself to him. How easy it is! By doing so, He has only to rectify his error.

The Lord, is easily attainable, because He pervades everywhere, every time, in all the persons and things etc. Whatever is seen, heard and grasped therein, He pervades. All men are His, and He is theirs. But, they without realizing this real affinity attach importance to Matter and thus follow, a cycle of birth and death. If they pay a little attention to Him, they will perceive a singularity in Him, and will realize that they have no affinity with nature, but they have very innate relationship, with God.

Appendix—Karmayoga and Jñānayoga is 'rāja-vidyā' (sovereign science) and Bhaktiyoga is 'rāja-guhya' (sovereign secret). In the fourth and fifth verses of this chapter 'rāja-vidyā' and in the thirty-fourth verse 'rāja-guhya' has been specially mentioned.

'Pratyakṣāvagamam'—It bears direct fruit. Peace is attained by Karmayoga, salvation is attained by Jñānayoga and love (devotion) is directly attained by Bhaktiyoga. By taking refuge in God, a man directly becomes free from fears, sorrows, worries and doubts. The realization of the self which is truth, consciousness is also direct. 'Dharmyam'—It is not devoid of virtues, but it is virtuous, it is imbued with virtues. Having known it, the human life becomes successful viz., nothing remains to be done, nothing remains to the known and nothing remains to be attained.

'Susukhaṁ kartum'—It is very easy to practise because God is naturally attained. All is God— it needs no labour, it is mere acceptance. From the view point of Karmayoga, if the things, which are not ours but which are of others, are used is rendering service to others, what force is needed in it! From the view point of Jñānayoga, if we get established in the self, what force is needed! From the view point of Bhaktiyoga, if we surrender ourselves to God, what force is required! All these disciplines culminate easily.

'Avyayam'—In fact this is the imperishable and final entity beyond which there is nothing else.

Link:—When it is very easy to practise and is also a sovereign science, why do people not avail themselves of it? The answer comes:

अश्रद्दधानाः पुरुषा धर्मस्यास्य परन्तप।
अप्राप्य मां निवर्तन्ते मृत्युसंसारवर्त्मनि ॥ ३ ॥

aśraddadhānāḥ puruṣā dharmasyāsya parantapa
aprāpya māṁ nivartante mṛtyusaṁsāravartmani

People devoid of faith in this Dharma, fail to reach Me, O oppressor of the foes, and they whirl in the path of the world of death i.e., they remain caught up in the recurring cycle of births and deaths. 3

Comment:—

'Aśraddadhānāḥ puruṣā dharmasyāsya parantapa'—'Dharma', is of two types—'Svadharma' and 'Paradharma'. Ever existent self is, 'Svadharma', and nature and its evolutes, is 'Paradharma'. In the preceding two verses, the Lord promised to explain Knowledge with Realization, and eulogized it by assigning eight merits. This is mentioned here, as 'Dharma'. People devoid of faith, are those, who are absorbed in worldly perishable things, by regarding these as real.

What a wonder it is, that men have faith in bodies, families, wealth and property etc., which are kaleidoscopic and depend, on them! They do not reflect, how long they will remain with bodies, and how long those bodies will remain, with them. They should depend on the self, or on God.

'Aprāpya māṁ nivartante mṛtyusaṁsāravartmani'—The Lord says that He is present in all climes, times, things and persons and He is ever attained. Those who have faith in the mundane instead of attaining Him, whirl in the path of birth and death. If they are born, they have to die; if they die, they are to be born. To whatever species, they go, they assume affinity with those species. Actually their connection with those bodies, is constantly severing. This affinity, cannot last long. Such people, revolve in the path of the mortal world. Even after reaching higher regions, as the abode of Brahmā etc., they have to return (8/16,25; 9/21). It means, that there is rebirth, so long as they do not attain God.

The Lord, while using the expression 'Mṛtyusaṁsāravartmani', means that they revolve in the path of the mortal world. In the seventh verse of the twelfth chapter, the world has been called, an ocean of birth and death.

God by his grace, suspending the fruit of actions, bestows this human body, so that men may attain salvation. But, by seeing those who, by missing this golden opportunity for salvation, follow a cycle of birth and death. God pities them and repents His action because those fools, without attaining Him, descend into a still lower plane (Gītā 16/20).

'Aprāpya mām'—This expression, shows that a man has got a right to realize God. In the twentieth verse of the sixteenth chapter, also Lord Kṛṣṇa expresses His view that even a demoniac-natured man can, attain Him. So the Lord declares, "Even the vilest sinner, can become virtuous and secure, lasting peace" (9/30-31) and "Even the most sinful of all sinners, can cross all sins by the raft of Knowledge" (4/36).

There was a city, surrounded by high walls, having an exit. A blind man with the help of a stick, wanted to grope his way out of the city. But, as soon as he neared the exit, he had an itching sensation. So, he began to scratch his skin, and he missed the exit, and went ahead. This routine continued, and he could not go out. Similarly, this soul revolves in heaven, hell and eighty-four lac forms of lives, but is unable to be liberated. So, the Lord by this grace, bestows this human body, so that he may be freed from the cycle of birth and death. But he suffers from itch, for pleasure, and by hankering after prosperity and pleasures, he dies and follows, the cycle of birth and death.

This soul is an eternal fraction of the Lord, and He is its real, abode. So, after attaining Him, there is no return, as has been declared in the Gītā, time and again: "One who knows My birth and activities divine, does not take birth again, but attains Me" (4/9); "Those who merge in Him, have no return" (5/17); "Those who attain the Supreme Abode, don't return" (8/21); "Having reached which, one never returns" (15/4); "Having reached which, men don't return" (15/6). The Śrutis, also declare the same.

An Exceptional Fact

Generally, people think that they are worldly, and so birth and death, is a natural process. But, it is perfectly wrong. A man is a fraction of God, and so he belongs to God's Abode. He is eternal and sentient, while the world is kaleidoscopic, perishable and insentient. So, he has no real affinity with the world, but he has assumed his affinity with it. The bodies, come back, again and again (8/19) while his self remains, the same.

He can never, have union, with the world and disunion from God. He may go to heaven, hell, eighty-four lac forms of lives, or through a human life, he cannot be separate, from God. But, in other births, besides the human birth, he cannot recognize God, because his discrimination is not aroused. In this human life, he has got an opportunity to recognize Him, because He by His grace has bestowed upon him the power of discrimination, that he could recognize Him and attain Him. But it is very surprising and indeed shocking, that he instead of attaining Him, circulates, in the path of the mortal world.

We have come to this human world, to attain salvation. But, we get attached to bodies, families, wealth, property etc., which are not ours, and forget that we belong to God, and to His Abode. So, we think, that it is very difficult, to attain Him. The fact is, that it is very easy to attain Him, because He pervades everytime, everywhere, all things, men, incidents and circumstances etc., and all are, in Him. So, we are ever with Him and He is ever with us. We cannot be separate, from Him and He cannot be separate, from us.

It means, that we do not belong to this mortal world, and this mortal world (including men, things, bodies etc.,) does not belong to us. We are only God's, and only God is, ours.

Appendix—People devoid of faith in the glory of 'Jñāna' with 'Vijñāna' mentioned in the preceding verse, don't derive benefit from it but remain engrossed in perishable pleasures by attaching importance to them. Therefore they, instead of attaining God, follow the cycle of birth and death; having renounced the natural path of immortality, whirl in the path of death.

The expression 'aprāpya mām' means that in human body there was an opportunity to attain God. The man was in close vicinity to God-realization but devoid of faith, he, instead of attaining God, goes on whirling in the world. He instead of believing the ever present entity, believes in the unreal which does not stay even for a moment. His heart is so impure that he, having perceived the direct influence of God, has no faith in Him. As having perceived the direct benefit in the association with the good and in loud chanting of the holy names of God etc., he is not specially engaged in them. At the sudden death of some near and dear one or in any other sudden sad occurrence, he develops temporary dispassion but does not remain constant in it. On 21st September, 1995 in the entire world the idols of Lord Gaṇeśa drank milk and the people saw this incident with their own eyes. But several people who regard themselves as intelligent (wise) didn't believe in this incident and contradicted it by the medium of newspapers and T.V. etc. In the assembly of Kauravas when Duḥśāsana made an effort to make Draupadī naked by pulling her Sārī, by God's grace there was a heap of Sārīs and Duḥśāsana's all efforts failed. Having seen such a miracle before their own eyes,, the Kauravas didn't come to their senses. Therefore those whose intellect is Tāmasika (of the nature of ignorance) and impure, they are not influenced by such unique incidents. They don't believe in such incidents. They see all things perverted (Gītā 18/32). Such people devoid of faith, by renouncing the path of immortality, follow the path of death in which there is nothing but death. They follow the path by which they may never attain God.

By being attached to aparā, a man whirls in the path of death. If he, instead of being attached to aparā, is attached to God, the master of that aparā, he will be liberated from the wheel of birth and death forever. A man can be liberated in this life and can even attain God's love (devotion) which is far superior to salvation. But having possessed such a high qualification, eligibility and competence, he follows the path of death. Therefore the Lord with pity utters—'aprāpya māṁ nivartante mṛtyusaṁsāravartmani' and 'māmaprāpyaiva kaunteya tato yāntyadhamāṁ gatiṁ' (Gītā 16/20). It proves that now there is the golden opportunity to attain salvation. If a man himself is engaged in attaining salvation, then dharma, the scriptures, the exalted souls, the world and God—all help him.

Link:—In the next two verses, there is description of the sovereign science, which is mentioned, in the first two verses.

मया ततमिदं सर्वं जगदव्यक्तमूर्तिना।
मत्स्थानि सर्वभूतानि न चाहं तेष्ववस्थितः॥ ४॥
न च मत्स्थानि भूतानि पश्य मे योगमैश्वरम्।
भूतभृन्न च भूतस्थो ममात्मा भूतभावनः॥ ५॥

mayā tatamidaṁ sarvaṁ jagadavyaktamūrtinā
matsthāni sarvabhūtāni na cāhaṁ teṣvavasthitaḥ
na ca matsthāni bhūtāni paśya me yogamaiśvaram
bhūtabhṛnna ca bhūtastho mamātmā bhūtabhāvanaḥ

All this universe is pervaded by Me in My unmanifest form. All beings abide in Me, but I do not abide in them. Nor does the whole creation vest in Me; look at My divine Yoga (power). Being the creator and sustainer of beings, I, do not in reality, dwell in them. 4-5

Comment:—

'Mayā tatamidaṁ sarvaṁ jagadavyaktamūrtinā'—The Lord's manifest form (Sākāra) is that which is perceived by mind, intellect and senses, while His unmanifest form (Nirākāra) is that, which is not known by mind, intellect and senses. Here, the Lord by the term 'Mayā' (by Me), has explained His manifest form, while by 'Avyaktamūrtinā', His unmanifest form. It means, that He exists, in both the forms. The Lord, here wants to express the forms in entirety. The difference in His forms, is according to sects and creeds. In fact He is the same, though He is called by different names and attributes.

In the Gītā, wherever there is a description of the real and the unreal, for the real (soul) it is mentioned "By which all this is pervaded" (2/17) because, being a portion of the Lord, like Him, it pervades everything. Where, there is description of worship, of the Lord endowed with attributes and formless, there it is mentioned as "By whom all this is pervaded" (8/22). Where, there is description of worship, of the Lord through performance of duty, there also, it is mentioned, "By whom all this is pervaded" (18/46). For making synchronous adjustment with these statements, He declares, "All this universe, is pervaded by Me."

'Matsthāni sarvabhūtāni'—All beings abide, in Me i.e., all this universe in the form of higher and lower nature, abides in Me because all emanate, from Me, abide in Me and also merge, in Me.

'Na cāhaṁ teṣvavasthitaḥ'—Now the Lord, makes a contradictory statement, by saying that, He does not abide in them. The reason is, that if He had abode in them, with their decay and death, He would also have decayed and died. But it is not so, because the worldly bodies and things are kaleidoscopic and perishable, while in Him, there is not even the slightest modification. He remains detached, from them, established, in His Own Self.

When He declares, that He abides in them, He means that they seem to exist, because of His existence.

'Na ca matsthāni bhūtāni'*—He again declares, that the beings do not dwell, in Him. The reason is, that if the beings had dwelt in Him, like Him they would not have undergone any change in them, and they would not have perished. It proves, that they do not dwell in Him.

Now, the contradictory statements are further explained, by means of an illustration. The Lord, abides in the world and the world abides in the Lord; the Lord does not abide in the world, and the world does not abide in the Lord. Waves, are in water and water is in waves, but waves have no existence of their own, besides water. Similarly, the world has no existence of its own, besides the Lord, because like waves, the world (beings)

* It may also mean that beings don't accept that they are established in God, they accept them to be established in Nature so they are not established in him.

emanates, from the Lord, dwells in Him and merges in Him. Thus the Lord abides in the world, and the world abides in the Lord.

But, if we do not accept the independent existence of waves, because they have no existence, besides water, there is neither water in waves, nor waves in water, there remains only water, which appears as waves. Similarly, neither God abides in the world, nor does the world abide in God; the world has no existence of its own, besides the Lord, "All this is God" (7/19).

All the earthenware vessels, are of nothing, besides clay. So, there is clay in these and they are in clay. But actually, it is not so. If there had been clay in earthenware vessels, with the destruction of the earthenware vessels, clay would have been destroyed. But it is not so. Similarly, if earthenware vessels, had been in clay, they would remain safe forever, like clay. But it is not so. It means, that earthenware vessels, are not in clay. In the same way, neither God dwells in the world, nor does the world dwell, in God. If God dwelt in the world, He would die, with the death of the world. But, He does not die. It means, that He does not dwell in the world. He is established in His own self. Similarly if the world dwelt in God, the world would continue to exist, with the existence of God. But as the world perishes, so the world does not dwell, in God.

When a man, from a distance thinks of the Ganges and its bank, at Haridvāra, he forms an image of the scene, of devotees bathing, fish jumping and the clock tower etc., but actually these do not exist there. Similarly, this world, is a manifestation of the Lord's, pursuit of mind. But, when He renounces this pursuit of mind, there is no world, there is only God.

Thus, if we accept the existence, of the world, God dwells in the world and the world dwells, in God. But if we realize reality, there is neither God, in the world nor is the world, in God, there is only God. This is the view, of liberated souls and perfect devotees.

'Paśya me yogamaiśvaram'*—The Lord's divine power, is that, though He dwells in the entire world and the entire world dwells in Him, He does not dwell in the world, and the world does not dwell, in Him i.e., He being detached from the world, is established in Him. It means, being manifold, He is One and there is nothing in the universe, besides Him.

The term 'paśya' means to 'know' and 'to see'. Here it means 'to know', while in the eighth verse of the eleventh chapter it means, 'to see'.

'Bhūtabhṛnna ca bhūtastho mamātmā bhūtabhāvanaḥ'—The Lord, is the creator and the sustainer of all beings, but He does not dwell in them i.e., He does not depend on them, and is not attached to them. The same fact, has been pointed out by Him, in the seventeenth verse of the fifteenth chapter, when he declares, "The Supreme Person, is distinct from both the perishable (world) and the imperishable (soul), He is called the Supreme Soul and He pervades and sustains, the three worlds."

He means, that as He in spite of being the creator and sustainer of the world, remains detached, free from egoism and excessive fondness, a striver, should bring up his family and manage other affairs, by remaining free from attachment, without I, mine and egoism etc. A striver, should behold the world, as Lord's manifestation and its affairs, as the sport of the Lord, and should ever remain satisfied, and pleased.

A Vital Fact

If a striver, tries to understand, he can realize, 'All this is God.' The criterion is, that he remains equanimous, in favourable

* Here the term 'Yoga' is made from the root of the verb 'Yuj saṁyamane' because the Lord controls the whole universe. The god of death also controls the beings according to their virtuous and evil actions but his control is confined to the mortal world, while God controls infinite worlds as well as the gods of death appointed in those worlds. This power of His control is called 'Yoga'.

and unfavourable circumstances, regard and disregard, and praise and reproach etc. Other people, may criticize his principles and beliefs, and say, that his belief that in the world there is nothing besides God, is merely a fancy. He should not feel any deficiency in his belief; he should remain, unaffected and unperturbed. He should not seek arguments and illustrations, to prove his point. His realization, should be constant and natural. A striver, may not have to give a thought, to that.

Appendix—'Mayā tatamidaṁ sarvam'—this expression means that as in snow there is only water, similarly God alone pervades the entire universe as equanimous, quiet, truth-knowledge-bliss solidified. The world which is perishing every moment, has no independent existence. The world which seems to exist out of ignorance, is also because of the existence of God. When there is one indivisible existence (Is) in all forms, then how can there be four divisions as 'I', 'you' (thou), 'this' and 'that'? How can there be egoism and mineness? How can practice be done to wipe out the unreal which has no existence?

The Lord has used the expression 'na ca matsthāni bhūtāni' for 'matsthāni sarvabhūtāni' and He has used the expression 'na cāhaṁ teṣvavasthitaḥ' for 'mayā tatamidaṁ sarvaṁ jagadavyaktamūrtinā'. So long as a striver holds that God and the world are two or different from each other, he should understand that there is the world in God and God is in the world (Gītā 6/30). But when he holds that there is only one entity instead of two, then there is neither the world in God nor is God in the world.

The man himself has accepted the independent existence of the world—'yayedaṁ dhāryate jagat' (Gītā 7/5). The world seems to have independent existence because of egoistic notion, the sense of mine and desire. Therefore so long as a striver has egoism, mineness and desire, there is the world in God and God is in the world. But when egoism, the sense of mine and desire are wiped out, then from the view-point of a God-realized soul, neither there is the world in God nor is God in the world viz., only God remains—'Vāsudevaḥ sarvam'.

There is the world in God, and God is in the world—this is 'Jñāna' and there is neither the world in God nor God in the world viz., there is nothing else besides God—this is 'Vijñāna'

In Śrīmadbhāgavata it is mentioned that so long as a striver holds that there is independent existence of the world, he should worship God by regarding the beings as the manifestation of God by his dealings.* But when from his view-point, the world does not exist any more, only God remains, then he should be indifferent even to the thought—'all is God'.† 'Bhūtabhṛnna ca bhūtastho mamātmā bhūtabhāvanaḥ'—God is the origin of the whole creation—'ahaṁ sarvasya prabhavaḥ' (Gītā 10/8), 'ahaṁ kṛtsnasya jagataḥ prabhavaḥ' (Gītā 7/6). God also sustains these beings—'yo lokatrayamāviśya bibhartyavyaya īśvaraḥ' (Gītā 15/17). Though God is the origin of all beings and also sustains them, yet He does not get tainted, is not attached to them and does not depend on them. As God does not abide in those beings, therefore by being attached to those beings and objects, God is not attained.

In fact there is no entity of matter besides the divine entity alone—'nāsato vidyate bhāvo nābhāvo vidyate sataḥ' (Gītā 2/16). The world seems to exist, it is valued and we are attached to it because of the desire for pleasure. Therefore so long as there is desire for pleasure, the world seems to exist.

Those who behold the world in God viz., behold the world,

---

* yāvat sarveṣu bhūteṣu madbhāvo nopajāyate
tāvadevamupāsīta vāṅmanaḥkāyavṛttibhiḥ

Upto the time a striver beholds Me viz., God in all beings, he should worship Me with all the activities (dealings) of his mind, speech and body.

† Sarvaṁ brahmātmakaṁ tasya vidyayā'tmamanīṣayā
paripaśyannuparamet sarvato muktaśaṁśayaḥ

(Śrīmadbhā. 11/29/18)

not as the manifestation of God, but as the material world, are atheists. But those who behold God in the world viz., don't behold the world as the world but behold it as the manifestation of God, are believers (theists).

Link:—Now, the Lord explains by an illustration how the beings dwell in Him.

यथाकाशस्थितो नित्यं वायुः सर्वत्रगो महान्।
तथा सर्वाणि भूतानि मत्स्थानीत्युपधारय॥ ६॥

yathākāśasthito nityaṁ vāyuḥ sarvatrago mahān
tathā sarvāṇi bhūtāni matsthānītyupadhāraya

Just as the mighty wind, moving everywhere, ever rests in ether, likewise know that, all beings vest in Me. 6

Comment:—

'Yathākāśasthito nityaṁ vāyuḥ sarvatrago mahān'—As the mighty wind, moving everywhere, ever rests in ether, as breeze, air or wind, similarly, all beings animate or inanimate, revolving in the three worlds, and fourteen spheres, dwell in the Lord.

The Lord, has used the term, 'Matsthāni', from the fourth verse to the sixth verse, three times. It means, that all the beings rest in Him, they cannot be separated from Him, even though they accept their affinity with matter (nature) and its evolutes, and bodies etc.

Just as, wind is born of ether, remains in ether, and merges in ether, man (soul) emanates, from the Lord, dwells in Him, and merges into Him. When wind merges in ether, it has no existence of its own, only ether remains. Similarly when the soul merges, into the Lord, only He remains.

Unlike wind, this soul, does not move everywhere. But, when it accepts its affinity of 'I'ness and 'Mineness' with this body, the movement of the body seems to it as its own movement, though it always rests in the Lord. Therefore, the Lord, in the twenty-fourth verse of the second chapter, has declared the soul to be eternal, omnipresent, immovable, constant and everlasting. Here it has been called 'all-pervading', because of the movement of the body, otherwise it is immovable and constant. So, the Lord declares, that all beings, rest in Him immovably and constantly.

It means, that beings of all the world, have no independent existence of their own, they ever rest, in the Lord. But, they do not realize this fact, because they assume their affinity, with the body. If they renounce this assumed affinity of 'I'ness and 'Mineness' with the body, they can secure infinite bliss. So, the Lord by warning human beings, declares that they ever rest in Him, so no labour or time is required, to attain Him. The only obstacle is, that they do not realize the fact.

'Iti upadhāraya'—A striver, should know the fact, that all beings totally rest in Him. By knowing this fact, he will have a disinclination for the world, and then realize Him. To realize Him, a striver should assume, with determination, that the Lord, Who pervades everywhere, in all the things and persons etc., is his, and he is His, while neither things and men etc., are his, nor he is theirs.

An Important Fact

All beings rest, in the Lord. But, the bodies are born, they live and die, because, they are transitory, while the soul undergoes, no change. This soul, has its identity with God, but when it assumes, its identity with the body, by having a disinclination for God, it becomes conscious of its separate entity, as 'I am a body'. This 'I'ness consists of two fragments—the self, and non-self, or it is called the embodied soul. In this 'I'ness, the fragment of non-self, is naturally attracted towards nature. Having identity with, a fragment of nature, the embodied soul, mistakes this attraction of nature towards Nature, as its own and thinks, 'I should get riches, pleasures and worldly enjoyments.' Thus, he has disinclination towards God, to a great extent. It accepts the body's death, as its own. Actually this soul, is an eternal portion of the Lord, but by having affinity with the world, it wants to enjoy worldly pleasures, and to maintain the body forever. Actually, this desire is to remain with God forever because, he has his real affinity, with Him. However he (embodied soul) may identify himself, with the body, yet his affinity and attraction towards God, can neither vanish nor is there is any possibility of their vanishing. 'I should ever live; I should ever be happy; I should attain supreme joy'—in this form, attraction for God, subsists in him. But he commits a blunder, that he wants to attain this supreme joy, through worldly objects. By an error, he has a desire for pleasure, which are transitory. If he realizes the reality, that all worldly pleasures are perishable, and sources of pain, then his desire for them perishes, and his desire to attain eternal bliss is aroused. The more this desire, (want) is aroused, the more disinclination, a striver has for perishable objects etc. When he has a total disinclination, for them, he realizes that he has rested in the Lord, since time immemorial.

Appendix—As the wind is born of ether, stays in ether and merges into ether viz., the wind has no independent existence besides ether, similarly all beings are born of God, abide in God and merge into God viz., beings have no independent existence besides God—if a striver accepts this fact firmly, he will realize the reality—'all is God'.

In order to understand this verse the idea of cause and effect is more apt than 'Vivartavāda'. 'Vivartavāda' means opposite appearance. The thing which actually does not exist but seems to exist, as the appearance of a snake in a rope—this is Vivartavāda. In Vivartavāda two entities are necessary; as the rope and the snake which appears—both are separate entities (one real and the other merely appearance). But in this verse there is the example of ether and the wind (air), both have the same entity. It means that just like the snake in the rope, the wind in ether is not merely an appearance but air is the effect of ether. The effect has its identification with the cause viz., the effect and the cause—both have one entity as gold and ornaments (effect) made of gold are the same. As gold and ornaments—in both there is only gold, similarly God and all beings—in both there is only God. This idea has been mentioned in the Gītā by the expressions 'Vāsudevaḥ sarvam' (7/19) and 'sadasaccāham' (9/19) which is the chief principle of the Gītā. Vivartavāda is not a principle but is a means to be free from the wrong notion of regarding the world as real (existent).

If there is pulsation (movement) in air, then there is air in ether and ether is in air. If there is no pulsation in air, there is neither air in ether nor ether in air viz., there is only ether. In other words, so long as there is assumption of the independent existence of air, there is air in ether and ether in air. But if we see from the realistic point of view, there is neither air in ether nor ether in air viz., there is only ether. Similarly from the realistic point of view, there are neither beings in God nor God in beings, only God exists viz., all is God (Gītā 9/4-5).

In this verse for air (wind) two adjectives 'sarvatragaḥ' and 'mahān' have been used. By this it should be understood that the soul also from the worldly point of view (because of attachment with Prakṛti) is 'sarvatragaḥ' as it wanders in eighty-four lac wombs, three worlds and fourteen spheres. The term 'mahān' should mean the beings (group of beings) of infinite universes. As wind always stays in the sky viz., wind has its eternal relationship with ether, similarly the beings have their eternal relation (eternal union) with God.

Link:—In the previous verse, Lord Kṛṣṇa explained, that all beings dwell in Him. But He did not explain, their new creation and final dissolution, which are going to be explained, in the next two verses.

सर्वभूतानि कौन्तेय प्रकृतिं यान्ति मामिकाम्।
कल्पक्षये पुनस्तानि कल्पादौ विसृजाम्यहम्॥ ७॥

sarvabhūtāni kaunteya prakṛtiṁ yānti māmikām
kalpakṣaye punastāni kalpādau visṛjāmyaham

All beings, O Kaunteya, merge into My Prakṛti (the prime cause), at the end of a Kalpa and I myself create them again, at the beginning of the next Kalpa. 7

Comment:—

'Sarvabhūtāni kaunteya prakṛtiṁ yānti māmikām kalpakṣaye'— All beings, are God's fragments, and ever rest in Him. But, they identify themselves with Nature and its evolutes, body etc., by having an affinity of 'I'ness and 'Mineness'. So, these are born and die, again and again. At the time of final dissolution, when Brahmā, the creator's life period of a hundred years, is over, the entire creation goes into an unmanifest state, with their actions.

'Punastāni kalpādau visṛjāmyaham'—When actions of those beings, become mature, to bear fruit, the Lord has His pursuit of mind, to become manifold from, one. This, is the beginning of a new creation. It has been mentioned, in the third verse of the eighth chapter, as follows—"This resolve, which brings forth the existence of beings, is called Ādikarma (Action)." In the fourteenth chapter, it is mentioned "I place the seed" (14/3) and "I am the seed-giving, Father" (14/4).

It means, that at the beginning of a new creation, when Brahmā emanates from the Lord, the Lord according to the actions of the beings, brings them forth, again. The Lord declares, it in the thirteenth verse of the fourth chapter, "The fourfold caste was created by Me, according to their qualities and actions."

Brahmā's day is called a 'Kalpa', which extends for a thousand fourfold Yugas (ages). His night, is also of the same duration. Brahmā, lives for a hundred years. When Brahmā's, life period is over, he merges into the Lord, which is called the end of a Kalpa, and when he emanates from the Lord, that is the beginning of a new Kalpa.

Here, it is mentioned that all beings go into His prakṛti, at the end of a Kalpa, but He generates them again at the beginning, of the next Kalpa. It means, that prakṛti being active, when it gets tired, merges into God itself, and beings having affinity with prakṛti also merge in it at the time of final dissolution. But at the time of a new creation, the Lord brings forth those beings, who had affinity with prakṛti again, by giving them the fruit of their mature actions, in order to, purify them. As a person, builds a house, but it slowly gets destroyed by itself whole, the Lord brings forth beings, but they die themselves. In the same way, a man (soul) being a portion of the Lord, has natural inclination for the Lord, but he has a fall himself, by having desires and attachment for the perishable body, and world. So, a striver by attaching importance to discrimination, by renouncing desires and attachment, should be inclined, towards the Lord.

Appendix—In the entire universe there are three important factors—origin, state of existence and dissolution. A striver has an eye only on the state of existence of the world, so the Lord in the preceding verse having described the existence, now in this verse mentions the origin, and dissolution. It means that the origin, existence and dissolution—all the three spring from the entire form of God.

In fact there is no state of existence of the world but the flow of its origin and dissolution is said to be the state of existence. If we perceive from the real point of view we find that there is not even the origin of the universe, but there is only dissolution viz., it has no existence. Therefore in the world dissolution, non-existence or disunion is only predominant—'nāsato vidyate bhāvaḥ' (Gītā 2/16).

प्रकृतिं स्वामवष्टभ्य विसृजामि पुनः पुनः।
भूतग्राममिमं कृत्स्नमवशं प्रकृतेर्वशात्॥ ८॥

prakṛtiṁ svāmavaṣṭabhya visṛjāmi punaḥ punaḥ
bhūtagrāmamimaṁ kṛtsnamavaśaṁ prakṛtervaśāt

By use of My Nature (prakṛti), I bring forth, again and ever again, this whole multitude of creations, subject however to the influence of their, own nature. 8

Comment:—

'Bhūtagrāmamimaṁ kṛtsnamavaśaṁ prakṛtervaśāt'—Here, the term 'prakṛti', stands for individual prakṛti. At final dissolution, all beings merge in individual Nature (causal bodies) and individual Nature merges into Cosmic Nature and Cosmic Nature, merges into the Lord. But, at the beginning of a creation when actions of those beings become mature to bear fruit, the Lord, thinks to become manifold from one. So, there is commotion in nature. When curd is churned, butter and butter-milk become separate. Out of this, butter flows over butter-milk. Here, butter is sāttvika, butter-milk is tamas and the action of churning is, Rajas. Similarly, from the commotion in prakṛti (Nature), also the three attributes (qualities)—goodness, activity (passion) and inertia (ignorance), are born. Out of the three modes, the heaven, this mortal world and the underworld, are born. In these three worlds, beings are born according to their actions, and nature. This description, is also given in the third and fourth verses of the fourteenth chapter. Where 'prakṛti' has been called 'Mahadbrahma', and 'the Lord's pursuit of mind to become manifold' has been declared, as 'placing the seed of all life.'

At dissolution the soul submerges into God, but it does not

attain emancipation, because it submerges being associated with modes of nature. Had it renounced its association with modes, it might have emancipated forever, and would not have undergone, the wheel of birth and death.

Attachment to these modes, is the cause of beings' birth, in good and evil bodies. So, a being remains under its control. In the nineteenth verse of the eighth chapter, there is a description of a being who remains under the control of his own individual nature. In the fifth verse of the third chapter, there is description of helplessness, under one's nature after birth. A being, is tied by these Nature-born modes, in all the three worlds, as is also described in the fifth verse of the fourteenth chapter.

'Prakṛtim svāmavaṣṭabhya'—Prakṛti (Nature) is an uncommon power of the Lord, which can neither be called different from Him, nor one with Him. The Lord, as its supervisor, keeping Nature under control, brings forth beings, at the beginning of creation, because all changes take place in nature, not in the Lord. It does not mean, that God Himself is incapable, dependent and weak, to do so.

As a man, performs actions by controlling his mind and senses etc. (But when he comes under the sway of mind and senses etc., he instead of being their master becomes, a slave to them), the Lord brings forth beings, by keeping Nature under control, without getting entangled in her.

'Visṛjāmi punaḥ punaḥ'—The Lord, brings forth, this whole multitude of beings in different moving and unmoving species, and different bodies. In physical bodies of some of the species, there is preponderance of the earth element, in some, of fire element, in some of the air element. Thus, the Lord creates many forms, of bodies.

Here, one point needs to be understood. The Lord, brings forth only those beings, who have become slaves to their nature, by having the affinity, of 'I' and 'mine', with personal nature (body). On being a slave, to his personal nature, one becomes a slave to the Cosmic Nature. In case, he is not a slave to such Nature, he is not reborn at the cosmic dawn.

Appendix—In reality Prakṛti is not different from God. Therefore God in His integral form comprises Prakṛti. To regard God without Prakṛti is to have unipresent view of God and it is not possible.

'Avaśaṁ prakṛtervaśāt'—Parā prakṛti viz., the self is totally independent (established in the self). By being connected with the alien Aparā Prakṛti, the self has become dependent (established in prakṛti), otherwise it can never be dependent. Attachment to the modes is its dependence—'kāraṇaṁ guṇasaṅgo'sya sadasadyonijanmasu' (Gītā 13/21).

God creates only those beings again and again who are under the sway of prakṛti (their individual nature). Those who are not under the control of prakṛti (nature) are not created (born)—'sarge'pi nopajāyante pralaye na vyathanti ca' (Gītā 14/2).

Link:—A man is bound by actions, when either he is attached to them or accepts himself as the doer. But, the Lord is, not bound by actions. Why? The clarification, comes in the next verse.

न च मां तानि कर्माणि निबध्नन्ति धनञ्जय।
उदासीनवदासीनमसक्तं तेषु कर्मसु॥ ९॥

na ca māṁ tāni karmāṇi nibadhnanti dhanañjaya
udāsīnavadāsīnamasaktaṁ teṣu karmasu

O Dhanañjaya (Arjuna), those actions, however, do not bind Me, who remains like one unconcerned with, and unattached, to such actions. 9

Comment:—

'Udāsīnavadāsīnamasaktaṁ teṣu karmasu'—The Lord, is not attached to the action which He performs, in bringing forth the whole multitude of beings, because He remains like one unattached and indifferent. He is not happy at creation and sad, at dissolution. Why has the Lord said, that He remains like one unattached and indifferent? The term 'like' has been used because, God knows the fact that actions etc., have no existence of their own besides Him, so how can He remain unconcerned and unattached to His own self? One remains unconcerned and indifferent to a thing only when he accepts its independent existence otherwise he is like unconcerned and indifferent.

'Na ca māṁ tāni karmāṇi nibadhnanti'—In the preceding verse, the Lord declared, "I bring forth beings, repeatedly. Such activities have been termed here, as 'Tāni karmāṇi' (those actions). The Lord is not bound by the actions because, He has not the least affinity, with actions and their fruit. The Lord, by saying so, advises human beings, that they will also not be bound by actions, if they perform these, without attachment for them and their fruit. Otherwise, they would be bound and must follow, the wheel of birth and death. How surprising it is, that a man gets himself bound by having affinity with those actions, and their fruits, things and men etc., that perish! Mundane objects perish but affinity with them, persists. Men die, but affinity with objects remains." How foolish of man!

Appendix—A man is bound by actions (karmaṇā badhyate jantuḥ)—from this worldly point of view the Lord declares that He is not bound by actions (Gītā 4/14); because He is neither attached to actions nor to the fruit of actions nor He has the sense of doership. But if we perceive the reality, actions have no independent existence at all. The action in the form of the creation of the world is only God's manifestation—'te brahma tadviduḥ kṛtsnamadhyātmaṁ karma cākhilam' (Gītā 7/29), 'bhūtabhāvodbhavakaro visargaḥ karmasañjñitaḥ' (Gītā 8/3). It means whatever is being done such as the origin, existence and dissolution of the universe, is being done only by God and is His manifestation. He who creates and whatever is created, He who sustains and whatever is sustained, He who destroys and whatever is destroyed—all these are organs (manifestation) of only one entire God—'ahaṁ kṛtsnasya jagataḥ prabhavaḥ pralayastathā' (Gītā 7/6).

When all is God and there is no one else besides Him, then with whom should He be indifferent? Therefore the Lord has said to Himself 'udāsīnavat' 'as if I am unconcerned (indifferent)'.

Link:—After describing, detachment and indifference, in the previous verse, Lord Kṛṣṇa now describes, how He is a non-doer, a supervisor.

मयाध्यक्षेण प्रकृतिः सूयते सचराचरम्।
हेतुनानेन कौन्तेय जगद्विपरिवर्तते॥ १०॥

mayādhyakṣeṇa prakṛtiḥ sūyate sacarācaram
hetunānena kaunteya jagadviparivartate

O son of Kuntī, under My supervision, Nature brings into being the whole creation, both animate and inanimate; thus the world, undergoes various changes. 10

Comment:—

'Mayādhyakṣeṇa prakṛtiḥ sūyate sacarācaram'—The Lord, animates nature, to bring forth the whole creation. As different machines, such as refrigerators, heaters, trains, lifts, televisions and X-rays etc., function with the power of electricity; so, creation, preservation, destruction and all the mundane activities, are performed by nature with the power of God, Who animates Nature but Himself, remains as a supervisor. It means, that as electric power manifests itself through machines, the Lord's power, manifests itself, through Nature.

The Lord, is an actionless supervisor, while the world revolves i.e., the world undergoes changes. These changes, will continue to occur, so long as, beings have their affinity of 'I'ness and 'Mineness' for Nature, and its evolutes—bodies. Thus they will go on revolving, in the path of the mortal world. It means, that without God-realization they cannot rest permanently, anywhere. Nature, whirls them, in the path of birth and death (Gītā 9/3).

All beings, are established in God, and so God is attainable to them, but they assume their affinity of 'I'ness and 'Mineness' with Nature, and so Nature brings them forth and merges them in her, under the supervision of the Lord. In fact, Nature has no power to bring them forth and to merge them, because it is insentient. They cannot die and take birth, because they, being a portion of the Lord, are imperishable, sentient and unaltered. But, by assuming their affinity, of 'I'ness and 'Mineness' with objects and persons born of Nature, they have to take birth, and have to die.

All actions, of the entire universe, such as creation, preservation and dissolution are performed by nature, in nature and are of nature. But nature, derives the power of action from God, Who remains actionless. As all actions, approved and disapproved by scriptures are performed, in the light of the sun, these actions result, in favourable and unfavourable circumstances for beings. But the sun and its light, remain the same, without undergoing any change; similarly there is a lot of modification in the world, but the Lord and His portion (i.e.,) soul, remain the same. There is no change, ever possible in the self (soul). A man thinks, that there is a change in him but actually there is no change in him. Change is in his body etc. But this change to him appears in himself, because he identifies himself with a body and the world. If he accepts, his true affinity with God (which is natural), his true love for God, will be spontaneously aroused.

Appendix—Nature brings into being the whole creation, both animate and inanimate by receiving power from God viz., nature undergoes all changes, there is no change in God. So long as beings are attached to prakṛti (nature), they under the control of prakṛti, undergo different changes viz., they don't remain at rest anywhere but they whirl in the wheel of birth and death.

Prakṛti under the control of God, creates the entire universe but the embodied soul being controlled by one's own prakṛti, whirls in the circle of birth and death. It means that God is independent, but His fragment, the self becomes dependent because of the desire for pleasure.

In essence God (the powerful) and prakṛti (His power)—both are one but the Lord in order to explain it to people, declares that prakṛti plays the predominant role in the creation of the universe. In fact neither prakṛti nor actions have independent existence.

If we perceive God and His prakṛti different, then prakṛti is the material cause and God is the instrumental cause; because God is not transformed into the world but it is prakṛti which is transformed. But if we perceive God and His prakṛti as one (which really are one), then He alone is the material cause and as well the instrumental cause.

At the beginning of the seventh chapter the Lord described the nature of parā and aparā prakṛtis and here (at the beginning of the ninth chapter) He is describing their evolutes (origin, state of existence and dissolution) which is the Lord's drama (play) of human semblance. It means that in the seventh chapter there is predominantly the description of parā and aparā and here is predominantly the description of the master of parā and aparā (God). In this chapter there is elaborate description of the Lord's pastime, influence and glory, by which a striver may develop his love (devotion) for God, lest he may rest content merely at salvation.

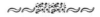

Link:—The ignorant people, who without having an inclination

for the Lord under whom the whole world is revolving, follow the opposite path, have been described in the next two verses.

अवजानन्ति मां मूढा मानुषीं तनुमाश्रितम्।
परं भावमजानन्तो मम भूतमहेश्वरम्॥ ११॥

avajānanti māṁ mūḍhā mānuṣīṁ tanumāśritam
paraṁ bhāvamajānanto mama bhūtamaheśvaram

Fools disregard Me on My taking on a human form, not knowing My supreme nature, as the Great Lord of beings. 11

Comment:—

'Paraṁ bhāvamajānanto mama bhūtamaheśvaram'—The Great Lord, is He, Who is ruler, patron, director and supervisor of nature, from Whom, Nature derives power to create, preserve and destroy, the animate and inanimate beings, and Who is the master of the gods, who control their own worlds, to which different beings go, according to their actions. Without His will, not even a leaf of a tree moves. This, is His lordliness. This has been described here, by the expression, 'Bhūtamaheśvaram'.

By 'Paraṁ bhāvam', He means, that fools do not know His supreme nature, that He is free, to make any drastic change. They do not know, that He transcends the perishable Matter, is also superior to the imperishable soul, and He, is known as the Supreme Person, in the Vedas (Gītā 15/18). So they ignore Him by taking Him as an ordinary mortal, in human form.

'Mānuṣīṁ tanumāśritam'—They, treat the Incarnation of the Lord, as an ordinary human being. As a common man, by identifying himself with the body, thinks that the family, honour or dishonour, is his own, and gain and loss of property etc., is also, his own. As common beings, were not manifest before birth and will not be manifest after death, they are manifest, only in the interim (2/28), and deluded persons, treat Him as a common man. They regard Him, as a slave to the human body, like a common man.

The human body of the Lord, is not the fruit of any action. He incarnates by His own free-will (Śrīmadbhāgavata 10/33/35) as a fish, a tortoise, or a boar etc., He does not depend on a body, but the body, an evolute of Nature, depends on Him, because He manifests Himself, keeping His Nature under control (Gītā 4/6).

Fools, treating the Lord as an ordinary being, do not seek refuge in Him, because they do not know, His divine play, rather, they consider Him, as a slave to a body. The same fact, has been pointed out, in the twenty-fourth and twenty-fifth verses of the seventh chapter, when the Lord declares, "Not knowing My unsurpassable and undecaying supreme state, these ignorant folk, do not recognise Me, as the unborn and imperishable Supreme Spirit." So, they instead of taking refuge in the Lord, seek refuge, in other gods (Gītā 7/20).

'Avajānanti māṁ* mūḍhā'—Fools disregard the Lord, under Whose supervision Nature brings forth and merges infinite universes, Who controls the activities of the universes and Who by His grace has bestowed, this human body. They think, lowly of Him, by regarding Him, as a common earthbound man, and attaching importance to mundane prosperity and pleasure.

Appendix—In this verse the Lord's glory has been described specially. There is no greater lord than God, He is the 'Supreme' (superior to all). But the ignorant don't know Him in His true nature. They instead of regarding Him as unworldly (superhuman) regard Him as a worldly common man.

Some people hold that Lord Kṛṣṇa was not God, but He was a yogī. There are eight limbs of Yoga—yama (five great vows), niyama (canons of conduct), āsana (posture), prāṇāyāma (restraint of breath), pratyāhāra (withdraw of the senses), dhāraṇā (concentration), dhyāna (meditation) and samādhi (trance)

* Here the term 'Mām' has been used for the same Lord (God) Who has been described from the fourth verse to the tenth verse of this chapter.

(Yogadarśana 2/29). Out of these eight, the first one is Yama. Yamas are five—ahiṁsā (non-violence), truthfulness, continence, non-stealing and non-acquisition (Yogadarśana 2/30). Therefore he who is a yogī, will certainly follow 'Yamas' viz., he will speak the truth only. If he tells a lie he can't be a yogī because he has not even observed the first rule 'Yama' of Yoga. In the Gītā Lord Kṛṣṇa has called Himself several times the Lord (Īśvara).* Therefore if He is a Yogī, then He speaks the truth and if He speaks the truth, then He is God in full (entirety)—this will have to be accepted.

Link:—In the next verse, the Lord describes the ways of those fools, who are not able to understand the Divinity, in the Incarnation, of the Lord.

मोघाशा मोघकर्माणो मोघज्ञाना विचेतसः।
राक्षसीमासुरीं चैव प्रकृतिं मोहिनीं श्रिताः॥ १२॥

moghāśā moghakarmāṇo moghajñānā vicetasaḥ
rākṣasīmāsurīṁ caiva prakṛtiṁ mohinīṁ śritāḥ

Those fools, with their vain hopes, futile actions and fruitless knowledge, have adopted a nature, which is fiendish, demoniacal and delusive. 12

Comment:—

'Moghāśā'—The hopes of those people, who by having a disinclination for God, have a desire for pleasure and heaven, are vain, because it is not a rule that such hopes must be fulfilled. Even, if these are fulfilled, they perish, after bearing fruit. Therefore, until a man attains God, all his hopes and desires are in vain,

* 'Bhūtānāmīśvaro'pi san' (4/6), 'Sarvalokamaheśvaram' (5/29), 'mattaḥ parataraṁ nānyatkiñcidasti' (7/7), 'mayā tatamidaṁ' sarvaṁ jagadavyaktamūrtinā (9/4), 'yo māmajamanādiṁ ca vetti lokamaheśvaram' (10/3), 'sarvasya cāhaṁ hṛdi sanniviṣṭaḥ' (15/15) etc.

because they with their fruit, are perishable (Gītā 7/23).

'Moghakarmāṇo'—The actions of the people, who have a disinclination for God, are vain, because if they perform actions approved by scriptures for their fruit, they with their fruit, will perish. Their fruit, would carry the people, to higher regions, from where, they will have a return. Thus, they waste their time, energy and intellect in vain, they remain blank, being deprived of the real gains of human life.

It means, that man, being a portion of God, is eternal, while actions and their fruits, are perishable. So, he will gain nothing besides pain and disquietude by performing actions for their fruit, unless and until, he attains God. On the other hand, actions that are performed for God, to please Him and are offered to Him, are not perishable, but real (Gītā 17/27).

In the twenty-eighth verse of the seventeenth chapter also, Lord Kṛṣṇa declares "Sacrifice, gift and penance and anyother action, performed without faith, is declared as unreal (non-existent). It is of no use, here or hereafter." It means, that a man having disinclination for God, by performing actions such as sacrifice, gift and penance etc., cannot realize God. So his actions are in vain.

'Moghajñānāḥ'—Knowledge of languages, scripts, arts, literature and the universe etc., of those people, who have a disinclination for God, is in vain, because that knowledge cannot lead them, to salvation, they cannot be free, from the bondage of birth and death. By having a disinclination for God, even after acquiring a lot of knowledge, they will follow a wrong course, in the same way, as an accountant cannot maintain accounts correctly if there is an error in any figure in the accounts. Thus, they will have a fall.

'Vicetasaḥ'—They are senseless (fools), because, they cannot discriminate between the real and the unreal, gain and loss, and bondage and liberation etc.

'Rākṣasīmāsurīṁ caiva, prakṛtiṁ mohinīṁ śritāḥ'—Such senseless persons, having a disinclination for God, embrace a nature which is fiendish, demoniacal and delusive.

Persons, with demoniacal nature, are those who without caring, for the pain and loss of others, are ever engaged in their selfish motives, in fulfilling their desires and hoarding money, for the enjoyment of their sensual pleasures etc.

Persons, with a fiendish nature, are those who become angry with those whom they think as obstacles, to the fulfilment of their desires, and so they harm and ruin them, for their own selfish motive.

Persons, possessing a delusive nature, are those, who without a rhyme or reason, trouble others. (They shoot flying birds and hit a sleeping dog and are pleased.)

Out of all the abovementioned, three natures, the basic nature, is demoniacal. This demonical nature is of three types. Demonical nature, is of those in whom desire predominates; fiendish are those, in whom anger predominates and delusive, those in whom delusion predominates. It means, that desire is the root of demoniacal nature. If desire is not fulfilled, anger is born (Gītā 2/62), and from anger, ensues delusion (2/63). This delusion, is born of greed and folly, also.

Appendix—In this verse there is mention of the demoniacal nature which has been described with its fruit in detail in the sixteenth chapter by the Lord. The fruit of the people's demoniacal nature is that they are hurled into eighty-four lac wombs and hells (Gītā 16/19-20). The people of demoniacal nature don't get the fruit which they desire (moghāśāḥ), but they reap the unpleasant fruit (punishment) of their action certainly. They commit sins in order to derive pleasures but instead of having pleasures they have to suffer pain certainly. They look down upon God and its fruit is their own loss, what difference does it make in God?

Link:—After describing the ways of the fools, in the eleventh and twelfth verses, now the Lord describes, the ways of devotees.

महात्मानस्तु मां पार्थ दैवीं प्रकृतिमाश्रिताः ।
भजन्त्यनन्यमनसो ज्ञात्वा भूतादिमव्ययम् ॥ १३ ॥

mahātmānastu māṁ pārtha daivīṁ prakṛtimāśritāḥ
bhajantyananyamanaso jñātvā bhūtādimavyayam

But great souls, (mahātmā) who possess divine nature, knowing Me as the sole and prime cause of creation; and as eternal, worship Me, constantly with an undivided mind. 13

Comment:—

'Mahātmānastu māṁ pārtha daivīṁ prakṛtimāśritāḥ'—Here, the term 'Tu' (But), has been used to explain singularity of the devotees, possessing divine nature, which runs counter to delusive and demoniacal nature, mentioned in the previous verse.

'Daivīṁ prakṛtim'—Here, 'Daiva' stands for God (Paramātmā), and 'prakṛtim' stands for nature. God is 'Sat' (Real). So all the good qualities and conduct, are included, in divine nature.

The divine traits (Gītā 16/1—3) are common and everyman, has a full claim over them. It all depends upon him, whether he possesses them or not. Those, who by possessing these, have an inclination for God, attain salvation.

One is discovery, while the other is creation or compound. Discovery relates to the eternal entity which is ever-existent, and creation or compound relate to the things which are born and are perishable. Divine traits, belong to God and so they are, divine property. A human being, being a fragment of God, has these divine traits, as they are his inherent possession. This is discovery. They are not born, they are not his personal property.

Divine traits, are natural. If a man, thinks that he has cultivated these traits, with his effort, he feels proud of them. But, if he feels that they are natural divine gift, he is not proud. A man's pride, is aroused only in imperfection. When a man has pride, by saying, "I always speak the truth", it means, that sometimes he tells a lie also, otherwise he cannot be proud of that.

A man, may possess divine traits, only when his sole aim is to attain God. By depending on those traits, to realize God, he can have an inclination for Him, and then instead of having pride, he possesses politeness, simplicity and modesty, and has an ever enhancing zeal, in spiritual discipline.

Men, who having a disinclination for God, are engaged in perishable pleasures and prosperity, are small souls or deluded persons, while those, who have an inclination for God and depend only on Him, are great souls.

'Bhajantyananyamanaso jñātvā bhūtādimavyayam'—The Lord is imperishable, and is the prime cause of creation. He is without a beginning and an end. Infinite universes, emanate from Him, remain established in Him, and merge in Him, but He remains the same, without any change.

Out of worldly things, if a portion is taken out, it becomes less. For example, if an ornament is made out of a lump of gold, or a utensil from a lump of clay, the lump becomes smaller. But there is no change, in the Lord, even though infinite universes emanate, from Him, because He is the imperishable seed (Gītā 9/18). Those, who know Him as imperishable and the prime cause of creation, worship Him constantly, with undivided mind.

The more merits a man knows of something, the more devoted he is to it. Those, who come to know, that the Lord is the supreme, their minds are so much engrossed in Him, that they never think of pleasures, either of this world or the next. Their minds, are not attracted towards anything or anyone, besides the Lord. So they adore Him, with an undivided mind.

Worship of the Lord, in anyway is fruitful. But a devotee, who worships Him with exclusive devotion, by having affinity

'I am only God's and only God, is mine' is immensely benefited. A devotee, is engaged in worship for a few hours. His relationship with God, remains as long as he is, engaged in worship. But an other devotee, regards himself as God's and God as his. His relationship with God, is everlasting, because this eternal relationship is real and eternal. Whatever actions, mundane or spiritual, he performs with his body, senses, mind and intellect, are to please the Lord and so are different forms of worship, to Him. This is adoration with an undivided mind, which has been described in the Gītā, time and again (8/14; 9/22; 12/6; 14/26 etc.).

Appendix—In the preceding verse the Lord having described the ways of the worldly people, which lead them to ruin, now describes the ways of the uncommon devotees who have devotion for God. 'Daivī prakṛti' means—Divine nature.

The people depending on the demoniac nature neither believe in God nor follow His teachings (Gītā 3/32). But the people depending on the divine nature, believe in God and follow His teachings (Gītā 3/31).

'Jñātvā bhūtādimavyayam'—God is the imperishable seed of infinite universes (Gītā 7/10, 9/18)—this firm assumption is to know God the prime cause of the creation and also to know Him imperishable. 'Firm assumption' is similar to 'knowing'. God is the origin (prime cause) of the entire creation and He is imperishable—this has been described from the fourth verse to the eleventh verse of this chapter.

Link:—Having described His devotees, in the preceding verse, the Lord in the next verse, describes, how they worship Him.

सततं कीर्तयन्तो मां यतन्तश्च दृढव्रताः ।
नमस्यन्तश्च मां भक्त्या नित्ययुक्ता उपासते ॥ १४ ॥

satataṁ kīrtayanto māṁ yatantaśca dṛḍhavratāḥ
namasyantaśca māṁ bhaktyā nityayuktā upāsate

Constantly chanting My names and glories, striving firm in vow, prostrating before Me, they worship Me with devotion, ever steadfast. 14

Comment:—

'Nityayuktāḥ'—A man, can remain always steadfast, only in worshipping God, not in mundane pleasures and accumulation of prosperity, because he gets disgusted with pleasures and loses taste for accumulation sometimes. But his determination and aim, of God-realization, ever remain the same.

Man (soul) being a portion of God, has real affinity for Him. So long as, a man does not recognize that affinity, he has a disinclination for the Lord, and assumes that he is separate from Him. But, when he recognizes his eternal affinity for Him, he is inclined towards Him, and cannot remain separate from Him.

The natural affinity of a man with God, 'I am God's and God is mine', ever remains steadfast, in wakefulness, sleep, sound sleep; in loneliness, during worship and in company, while performing different actions. As a man always remembers that he is the son of Mr. X, so a striver accepts his affinity, with the Lord that He, Who is the prime cause of creation, the Imperishable, the Supreme Lord is his and he is His, and thus he, ever remains steadfast.

'Dṛḍhavratāḥ'—The worldly people, who are engaged in pleasure and prosperity, cannot be firm in spiritual vows (Gītā 2/44). But those, who have removed a sense of 'I'ness from their hearts, by accepting the fact 'We are God's and God is ours', they resolve "We are not of the world, and the world is not ours." So, we have not to hanker after, worldly pleasures and prosperity, but we have to serve others, by regarding them as God's.

Thus, they remain steadfast in their resolution, and never

deviate from it, because their aim is God-realization, and they are, His fragments.

'Yatantaśca'—As worldly people, nourish their family with attachment, and strive for pleasure and prosperity, so do devotees strive, for God-realization ardently. Efforts of such devotees, seemingly mundane are not really mundane, as their aim is God. So their activities, are directed towards God.

'Bhaktyā kīrtayanto mām'—Devotees, sometimes chant the names and glories of the Lord, sometimes read scriptures and sometimes give divine talks, or hold divine discourses and so on. All of these are as hymns of the Lord.

'Namasyantaśca'—They prostrate before the Lord, by having the feeling that whatever divine traits they possess, and whatever spiritual inclination they have, is only by His grace. They hold that their promptness and inclination towards God, is not the result of their own efforts. Virtues and good conduct, have been developed in them, by His grace. So, they merely prostrate.

'Satataṁ māṁ upāsate'—The devotees, having undivided devotion, perform all actions, whether spiritual or even mundane, such as eating, drinking, sleeping, waking, business and farming etc., only for Him, to please Him.

Appendix—Whatever a devotee utters, that is 'Kīrtana' viz., loud chanting of the holy names of God and of His glories; and whatever action he does, that is service to God* (Gītā 9/27).

---

* Kāyena vācā manasendriyairvā buddhyā'tmanā vānusṛtasvabhāvāt
karoti yad yat sakalaṁ parasmai nārāyaṇāyeti samarpayettat
(Śrīmadbhā. 11/2/36)

"Whatever a man does with his body, speech, mind, senses, intellect and ego according to his nature which he has formed, surrender (offer) it to God with the feeling that it is only for God."

Sañcāraḥ padayoḥ pradakṣiṇavidhiḥ stotrāṇi sarvā giro
yadyatkarma karomi tattadakhilaṁ śambho tavārādhanam
(Śivamānasapūjā)

Devotees are 'nityayukta' (ever united with Me) because they have renounced affinity with the transitory world.

Link:—Strivers are of several kinds. Strivers, who follow the Discipline of Devotion, have been described, in the previous two verses. Now, He describes, the other strivers.

ज्ञानयज्ञेन चाप्यन्ये यजन्तो मामुपासते।
एकत्वेन पृथक्त्वेन बहुधा विश्वतोमुखम्॥ १५॥

jñānayajñena cāpyanye yajanto māmupāsate
ekatvena pṛthaktvena bahudhā viśvatomukham

Others worship Me (as the One, Undivided Pure-Consciousness) through their offering of Knowledge (Jñāna-yajña); while still others worship Me in My Universal Form, taking Me to be different in dissimilar celestial forms. 15

Comment:—

[As hunger of the hungry persons, is the same and similar is the satisfaction, after having meals, but their relish is different. Similarly strivers have the same need to realize God, and they attain the same Lord, but according to their faith, interests and taste, their methods of worship are different. However, there is one important difference. Those who want to seek satisfaction in perishable and worldly things, are never satisfied. Those who having a disinclination for the world, are inclined towards spiritualism, are perfectly satisfied, after attaining God, and then, for them nothing remains—to be done, to be known, and to be achieved.]

'Jñānayajñena cāpyanye yajanto māmupāsate ekatvena'—Several strivers, following the Discipline of Knowledge, by renouncing the unreal, through discrimination, worship His

'O Lord Śiva! my walk and movement etc., is your circumambience and all words are your hymns. Whatever actions I perform, all that is your worship.'

attributeless formless aspect, and regarding the pure consciousness, as his very self.

They regard, the kaleidoscopic world, as non-existent, because it neither existed in the past, nor will exist in future and at present, also it is continuously perishing. So, it seems to exist, in the light of the Lord, Who really exists. So they behold the cosmic consciousness, constantly.

Here the term 'Yajantaḥ', means that they have reverence only for God—this is their worship.

'Pṛthaktvena bahudhā viśvatomukham'—Some strivers, following the Discipline of Action, regarding themselves as servants, and the world as an Universal Form of the Lord, serve it with their bodies, senses, minds, intellects, possessions, resources and actions. They, ever serve the Lord, in the form of common men and by God's grace, attain perfection.

Appendix—All strivers according to their tastes, ability, faith and belief, following their spiritual disciplines, whomsoever they worship, that is the worship of the entire form of God. In this chapter from the sixteenth verse to the nineteenth verse there is the description of the Lord's entire form.

Link:—How can, the divergent and conflicting forms of worship, reach the same Lord? The Lord, gives the answer, in the next four verses.

अहं क्रतुरहं यज्ञः स्वधाहमहमौषधम्।
मन्त्रोऽहमहमेवाज्यमहमग्निरहं हुतम्॥ १६ ॥*
पिताहमस्य जगतो माता धाता पितामहः।
वेद्यं पवित्रमोङ्कार ऋक्साम यजुरेव च॥ १७॥

---

* The Lord from the seventh to the twelfth chapter while describing divergent forms of worship, has used the term 'I' again and again. In the sixteenth verse He has used the term eight times, more than in any other verse.

गतिर्भर्ता प्रभुः साक्षी निवासः शरणं सुहृत्।
प्रभवः प्रलयः स्थानं निधानं बीजमव्ययम्॥ १८॥

aham kraturaham yajñaḥ svadhāhamahamauṣadham
mantro'hamahamevājyamahamagniraham hutam
pitāhamasya jagato mātā dhātā pitāmahaḥ
vedyam pavitramoṅkāra ṛksāma yajureva ca
gatirbhartā prabhuḥ sākṣī nivāsaḥ śaraṇam suhṛt
prabhavaḥ pralayaḥ sthānam nidhānam bījamavyayam

I am the Vaidika ritual, I am the sacrifice, I am the offering to the departed, I am medicinal herb, I am the sacred formula, I am the clarified butter, I am the sacred fire and I am the act of offering oblation into the fire. I am the knowable, the purifier, the sacred syllable Om, and the three Vedas—Ṛk, Sāma and Yajus. I am the father, sustainer, mother, grandfather, goal, supporter, Lord, witness, abode, refuge, disinterested friend, origin, end, resting place, storehouse and the imperishable seed, of this universe. 16—18

Comment:—

[When a devotee according to his faith and reverence establishes his affinity with the Lord, in His manifold aspects, his affinity, is with the real, because in the universe, there is no existence besides the Lord. He should admit this fact, without having any doubt, that in the universe, apart from God, there is no object, no thought and no act. Similarly, the Lord is manifest in diverse entities—there is no doubt about it. If a doubt lurks, in mind how all objects can be the manifestation of God, this doubt, deprives the striver of emancipation. Rather, it puts him into trouble. Therefore, it should be accepted firmly, that in gross or subtle form, or as effect and cause, whatever is seen, heard, grasped or assumed, is only God. This all-pervasiveness of God, has been described, from the sixteenth to the nineteenth verse.]

'Aham kraturaham yajñaḥ svadhāhamahamauṣadham'— 'Kratu' is a Vedic ritual, while 'Yajña' denotes, sacrificial worship. The offerings made to the manes is 'Svadhā'. Vegetables, food and medicinal herbs, such as seeds of the sesame plant, rice, barley etc., are 'Auṣadha'. The Lord Himself, is everyone of the above-mentioned things.

'Mantro'hamahamevājyamahamagniraham̐ hutam'—He is, the sacred formula which is chanted, at the time of sacrificial worship. He is the clarified butter, the sacred fire and the act of offering oblation, into a fire.

'Vedyam̐ pavitramoṅkāra ṛksāma yajureva ca'—The Lord, is the knowledge, of the method of sacrificial worship, which should be performed systematically, in order to satisfy desires or to get rid of them.

Acts of sacrifice, rewards and penance, are purifying to the wise (Gītā 18/5). In them the articles of oblations, which are offered without expecting a fruit and the action, which is performed without expecting its fruit, are also purified. That purity, is the Lord's manifestation.

Act of sacrifice, gifts and penance, as enjoined by scriptures, are always begun, with the utterance of the sacred syllable, 'Om̐' (Gītā 17/24). So the Lord is, Om̐.

The Vedas, deal with methods of Vedic rituals, and sacrificial worship etc. The Ṛgveda, is the collection of aphorisms of sacred formulas, with a regular order of words, the Sāmaveda, is a collection of sacred formulas, and prayers, which are sung with a rhythm during sacrifices, and the Yajus, consists of sacred formulas with irregular order of words. All the three, are forms of the Lord.

'Pitāhamasya jagato mātā dhātā pitāmahaḥ'—The Lord, creates the entire universe. So, He is called the source and dissolution of the whole universe (Gītā 7/6). He also protects the universe, so He is father, as is also mentioned in the forty-third verse of the eleventh chapter.

The Lord, sustains the whole universe, in all respects.

He decides the destiny of all beings. Therefore, He is the sustainer.

The Lord, gives birth to beings, in different bodies according to fruit of their actions. So, He is the mother of the entire creation.

He, is the grandfather, because Brahmā, the creator of the world, is the father of the world, in common knowledge, and Brahmā is born of Him. From this angle, He is the father of Brahmā. Arjuna, has also called Him the Primal Cause of Brahmā, (Gītā 11/37).

'Gatirbhartā prabhuḥ sākṣī nivāsaḥ śaraṇaṁ suhṛt'—The Lord, is the Supreme Goal of beings. He is the supporter of beings because, all sustenance comes from Him. He, is the owner and Lord, of the universe. He is witness because He knows all beings, all the time, very well. He is the 'Abode' (Nivāsa), because beings, rest in Him. He gives shelter, to beings, so He is refuge. He is a disinterested friend, because He is their well-wisher, without expecting any reward.

'Prabhavaḥ pralayaḥ sthānaṁ nidhānaṁ bījamavyayam'—The entire universe, emanates from Him and again merges in Him. So, He is the origin, (the material cause and the efficient cause) and end, of the entire universe (Gītā 7/6).

He is the resting place (Sthāna),* of the universe, because at the time of final dissolution, the entire universe (including Nature), merges in Him and rests in Him.

He is the storehouse (Nidhāna), because in all the states of creation and dissolution, etc., nature, the universe, soul and everything else, reside, in Him, only.

The Lord, is the imperishable seed, because an ordinary seed is born of a tree and then it perishes, when the plant sprouts up.

* 'Nivāsa' (Abode) is the place where beings reside during the span of creation while 'Sthāna' (resting place) is the place where the universe (including Nature) remains merged in the period of dissolution.

But, the Lord after creating infinite universes, remains the same, and is without origin and end. He can never perish.

Appendix—As from the view point of discipline of knowledge 'modes are acting on the modes' (Gītā 3/28), similarly from the view-point of a devotee, only God's objects are being offered to God. As a person worships the Ganges with Ganges-water, worships the sun with a lamp, worships the earth with flowers, similarly God is being worshipped by God's objects. The fact is that He Who is worshipped is God, the material for worship is also God, the act of worship is also God and the worshipper is also God.

The worldly seed is produced by farming but the unworldly seed in the form of God, is not a born one (produced), therefore the Lord in the seventh chapter declares Himself to be the eternal seed—'bījaṁ māṁ sarvabhūtānāṁ viddhi pārtha sanātanam' (7/10). Here the Lord declares that He is the imperishable seed—'bījamavyayam'. The reason is that the worldly seed perishes, when the plant sprouts up, but the unworldly seed in the form of God by producing infinite universes, remains the same, there is not the least modification in the seed. It means that God exists at the beginning of the entire creation and also exists at the end of it. The entity which exists at the beginning and at the end also exists in the mid-state—this is the principle. As several earthen wares are made of clay, remain in clay and at last merge into clay, similarly all the seeds of the entire universe are born of God, abide in God and at last merge into God (Gītā 10/39). It means that the worldly seed perishes when it sprouts up but the imperishable seed in the form of God ever remains the same at the beginning, in the middle and at the end. Therefore at present only God manifests Himself as the world. There is nothing else besides Him.

तपाम्यहमहं वर्षं निगृह्णाम्युत्सृजामि च।
अमृतं चैव मृत्युश्च सदसच्चाहमर्जुन॥ १९॥

tapāmyahamahaṁ varṣaṁ nigṛhṇāmyutsṛjāmi ca
amṛtaṁ caiva mṛtyuśca sadasaccāhamarjuna

Arjuna, for the welfare of the world I as the sun, radiate heat, withhold and send forth, rain. I am immortality, as well as, death; I am also being and non-being, both. 19

Comment:—

'Tapāmyahamahaṁ varṣaṁ nigṛhṇāmyutsṛjāmi ca'—The Lord, in the form of the sun, cures ailments of beings, by drying impure and dirty materials, which cause ailments, on the earth. As the sun, the Lord radiates heat to dry the poisonous matter of medicinal herbs and other vegetations. He dries water, to make it pure and sweet, and then sends it back as rain, for the welfare of beings.

'Amṛtaṁ caiva mṛtyuśca sadasaccāhamarjuna'—The Lord, is immortality, as well as, death. He is immortality—it means that all beings live by sustaining their life-breath, (they do not die). He is death, as it means the departure of life-breath from the body, of all beings (their death). He is being, as well as non-being, the cause as well as, effect. It means, that as a great soul regards that, all is God, in the view of the Lord also, He is all, though a common man views death and immortality, being and non-being; gross and subtle, sattva, rajas and tamas; cause and effect; water and ice etc., different. But, in fact, the world is a manifestation of the Lord. As in clothes made of yarn, there is nothing besides yarn, in so too things, actions, incidents, circumstances and men etc., there is nothing else, besides God.

Appendix—God existed before the creation of the universe and in the end God will remain, then in the mid-state who else can be there besides God? Therefore immortality is a form of God and death is also a form of God. The real (parā prakṛti) is a form of God and the unreal (aparā prakṛti) is also a form of God. As the food offered to God becomes 'prasād' (a gift or blessing) from God and it includes both sweet food such as 'rasagullā' and 'gulābajāmuna' and also bitter vegetables such as 'karelā' (bitter gourd) and 'methī'. Similarly the favourable as well as unfavourable circumstances—all are the manifestations of God. The Lord as the sun withholds water and then sends forth rain—these two opposite activities (withholding and sending back) are performed by God. Not only this but the water which is withheld is God, the rain which is sent forth is God and the action of raining is also God. 'Sadasaccāhamarjuna'—In the entire universe there is nothing besides 'sat' (parā) viz., the real and 'asat' (aparā) viz., the unreal. The world is unreal and the Lord Who resides in it, is real. The body is unreal and the soul which resides in it, is real. The body and the world are kaleidoscopic while the soul and God are free from modifications. The body and world are perishable, while the soul and God are imperishable (Gītā 2/12). The Lord declares that He is changeable and is also unchangeable, He is perishable and is also imperishable. It means that all is God, there is nothing else besides God (Gītā 7/7).

In 'nāsato vidyate bhāvo, nābhāvo vidyate sataḥ' while differentiating 'Sat' from 'Asat' there is discrimination but in 'sadasaccāham' there is no need of any discrimination but there is faith (belief) required. All is God—this belief is more powerful than discrimination. The reason is that discrimination is useful when both the real and the unreal are distinguished. But when the unreal does not exist at all, then what is the use of discrimination? If we assume the entity of the unreal, then there is need for discrimination; but if we don't assume the entity of the unreal, then there is belief. In discrimination there is division between the real and the unreal but in belief or faith all being God there is no division at all. In faith there is only the real viz., only God.

In the Discipline of knowledge, there is predominance of discrimination while in the Discipline of Devotion, there is predominance of belief and love (devotion). In the Discipline of knowledge, discrimination between the real and the unreal, the self and the non-self, the eternal and the transient is important; so there is duality—'dvaita', but in the Discipline of Devotion, belief in God is important, so there is non-dualism—'advaita'. It means that in fact there is real non-dualism in devotion as there are no two entities.

In the Discipline of Knowledge a striver negates the unreal. By negation, the entity of the unreal can persist. The more emphasis a striver lays on the negation of the unreal, the more the assumption of the entity of the unreal is strengthened. Therefore 'to negate the unreal', is not so good as is 'to be indifferent to it'. Better than indifference to it is the notion—'all is God'. Therefore a devotee neither negates the unreal nor is indifferent to it, but he beholds God in all—the real and the unreal because in fact all is God.

The Lord declares—

ahamevāsamevāgre nānyad yat sadasat param
paścādahaṁ yadetacca yo'vaśiṣyet so'smyaham

(Śrīmadbhā. 2/9/32)

'Before the creation I was present, there was noting else besides Me and after the creation whatever this world appears, I am also that. The real, the unreal and that which can be beyond both the real and the unreal, I am that also, and when the creation is destroyed, whatever remains, I am also that.'

The body, senses, mind, intellect and ego etc., all is God. For example if we think of Haridwāra (with the mind), the mind appears as the immovable objects such as 'Hari kī paiḍī' and the clock tower etc., and the mind appears as the movable objects such as the Ganges, the sailing fish and the bathing persons, viz., the mind became both—the movable and the immovable objects.

Similarly the real is God and the unreal is also God.

From our point of view there are two divisions—the real and the unreal, therefore the Lord has used the expression—'sadasa ccāham' in order to explain it to us, otherwise from the Lord's point of view, there is nothing else besides Him. If we perceive even from the topmost philosophical point of view, we find that there is only one entity. Two entities are not possible at all. A man is deluded when he accepts the other entity (Gītā 7/13). Attachment and aversion also ensue by assuming (accepting) the other entity.

Link:—After describing, the ways of fools and devotees, now in the next two verses, the Lord, describes the ways of enjoyment-seekers, who having a disinclination for God, perform sacrifice etc., to reap their fruit. Therefore, they repeatedly come and go.

त्रैविद्या मां सोमपाः पूतपापा
यज्ञैरिष्ट्वा स्वर्गतिं प्रार्थयन्ते।
ते पुण्यमासाद्य सुरेन्द्रलोक-
मश्नन्ति दिव्यान्दिवि देवभोगान्॥ २०॥

traividyā māṁ somapāḥ pūtapāpā
yajñairiṣṭvā svargatiṁ prārthayante
te puṇyamāsādya surendraloka-
maśnanti divyāndivi devabhogān

Those who perform rituals with some interested motive as laid down in the three Vedas, and drink the juice of soma plant, and thus having purged themselves of sin, worship Me as Indra, by sacrifices, praying to seek access to heaven, attain Indra's paradise, as the result of their good deeds, and they enjoy, the celestial pleasures of the gods. 20

Comment:—

'Traividyā māṁ somapāḥ pūtapāpā yajñairiṣṭvā svargatiṁ

prārthayante te puṇyamāsādya surendralokamaśnanti divyāndivi devabhogān'—Worldly people, are generally engaged, in worldly pleasure. There are others, who attach value to perishable objects, aspire for heavenly pleasure and so perform actions with a selfish motive, as laid down in the three Vedas for them. The term 'Traividyā', has been used, for such people.

Soma is a plant about which it is said, that in the bright half of a lunar month, everyday, on it one leaf sprouts forth and upto the full-moon-day there are fifteen leaves, while in the dark half of a lunar month, everyday one leaf falls, and in fifteen days all the leaves fall.* Those who perform religious sacrifice, purify the sap of soma-plant with Vedic sacred formulas and then drink it. Thus, they are purged of sins which are obstacles, to heavenly enjoyment.

The Lord, in the preceding verse declared, that He is, being and non-being, both. So here, the term 'Mām' has been used for Indra, the lord of the gods, because when He is, being and non-being, both, He is also Indra. Moreover, persons who perform sacrifice, in order to reach heaven, worship Indra, and pray to him to grant them, an access to heaven.

With the view to attain heaven, they sing hymns in praise of Indra, and beg of him, residence in heaven—both for these are prayers. As a reward of the performance, of Vedic and Paurāṇika

* The Soma plant which has fifteen leaves, whose shape is like a serpent, whose knots are red from where the leaves sprout forth, with the five parts (root, branch, leaves, flower and fruit) brought on the full-moon-day binds mercury. The Soma tree also with five organs (root, bark, leaves, flower and fruit) binds mercury and makes its ash and so on. Out of the Soma climber and Soma tree the Soma climber possesses more properties. In the dark fortnight each day one leaf falls from this part while in the light fortnight each day one leaf sprouts forth. Thus this climber plant grows. If the root-fruit (Kanda) of this plant is taken out on the full-moon-day, it is very useful. The mercury bound in this root-fruit with thorn-apple makes the body iron-like strong and it has a hundred thousand times-more effect i.e., its one particle changes a hundred thousand particles of iron into gold. This Soma climber plant is very rarely found.

rituals, they are granted celestial enjoyments. Those heavenly pleasures, are far more attractive and singular, than those of the mortal world. There, they enjoy five sense-objects of sound, touch, form, taste and smell. Moreover, they also enjoy other luxuries, honour and glory etc.

Appendix—Here is the description of such people who strongly believe in the existence of the world and who value it and whose worship to God is a mistaken approach (Gītā 9/23). The fruit of the worship of such people is perishable (Gītā 7/23). Because of being within the entire form of God, all is God; therefore here for Indra (the lord of gods) the term 'mām' has been used. The term 'puṇyam' has been used for Indra's paradise because it is purer than the human world.

ते तं भुक्त्वा स्वर्गलोकं विशालं
क्षीणे पुण्ये मर्त्यलोकं विशन्ति।
एवं त्रयीधर्ममनुप्रपन्ना
गतागतं कामकामा लभन्ते॥ २१॥

te taṁ bhuktvā svargalokaṁ viśālaṁ
kṣīṇe puṇye martyalokaṁ viśanti
evaṁ trayīdharmamanuprapannā
gatāgataṁ kāmakāmā labhante

Having enjoyed, the extensive heavenly world, they return to the world of mortals when they, exhaust their merit. Thus, taking recourse to action with interested motive, enjoined by the three Vedas, and seeking worldly enjoyments, they repeatedly come and go. 21

Comment:—

'Te taṁ bhuktvā svargalokaṁ viśālaṁ kṣīṇe puṇye martyalokaṁ viśanti evaṁ trayīdharmamanuprapannā gatāgataṁ kāmakāmā labhante'—The heavenly world, has been called extensive, because it is vast, there age is longer, and pleasures are, in abundance.

Those who want to go to heaven, instead of depending on God, rely on actions with interested motive, enjoined by the three Vedas. They go to heaven and are obliged to return to this world, after their merits run out. Here again, they acquire merits and thus, the wheel of going and coming back, revolves.

If the meaning of 'Pūtapāpā', of the previous verse, is taken, as those who are purged of all sins and the meaning of 'Kṣīṇe puṇye', is taken as those whose merits are destroyed, it means, that being free from all sins and merits, they should have been liberated from bondage. But they do not attain liberation, they, rather go and come. So the terms, mean that they are purged of only those sins which are obstacles to go to heaven; and their merits are exhausted after enjoying, heavenly pleasures. Therefore, reference is not, in context of the exhaustion of all their sins and merits.

Link:—But, what about those, who depend only on the Lord? Their position is explained, by the Lord, in the next verse.

अनन्याश्चिन्तयन्तो मां ये जनाः पर्युपासते।
तेषां नित्याभियुक्तानां योगक्षेमं वहाम्यहम्॥ २२॥

ananyāścintayanto māṁ ye janāḥ paryupāsate
teṣāṁ nityābhiyuktānāṁ yogakṣemaṁ vahāmyaham

To those men, who worship Me alone, thinking of none but Me, who are ever-devout, I provide them gain and security. 22

Comment:—

'Ananyāścintayanto māṁ ye janāḥ paryupāsate'—Those, who admit, that the entire universe is the Lord's manifestation, and all the activities and changes are His sport, and do not attach importance to anything else, besides the Lord, because everything except the Lord, is perishable. They have no desire, even for the maintenance of their bodies. So, they have exclusive devotion, for Him. Whatever action, moving, eating, drinking or talking etc., they perform, is in order to, please God. By regarding the Lord, as loving and glorious, the memory, of the Lord in devotees, is constant and natural. These devotees are called 'Ananya' (exclusively devoted), because for them, the Lord is both the means and an end. They have a firm conviction, that they have to take refuge in God only, they have to adore and think of Him only, and they have to attain Him, only. They do not harbour any other desire, except that of the Lord.

'Teṣāṁ nityābhiyuktānām'—'Nityābhiyuktānām' (of those ever united), are those, who having undivided devotion, think of Him and perform all actions, to please Him. They, have a disinclination for the world, an inclination for the Lord, and perform actions by depending on Him. In other words, their disinclination for the world, is their 'Ananyatā' (exclusive devotion), their inclination for the Lord is their 'Cintana' (constant memory), and in all active and inactive conditions, circumstances whatever, he does, is their 'Upāsanā' (worship). Those devotees, who possess these three traits, are 'Nityābhiyuktā' (ever devout).

'Yogakṣemaṁ vahāmyaham'—'Yoga' means, the provision of the means required, and 'Kṣema' means, security of what has been gained.

But, the fact is that 'Yoga' means, either to attend or not to attend to the needs of devotees, because the Lord is a disinterested friend, of devotees, so He remains engrossed, in their welfare. He provides only those means, which are useful, for their welfare. Similarly, He protects what has been provided, only if its security, is a means in their spiritual progress. Otherwise, He will destroy it. Destruction of harmful things, is 'Kṣema' (security). Therefore, His devout devotees, remain pleased and satisfied, in all circumstances, because they believe that those circumstances have been created by God's will, and so they will enable them to attain, salvation. They, become puppets in the hands of the Lord, and God's will, becomes their will.

In fact 'Yoga' means, affinity with God and 'Kṣema' means salvation. From this view-point, the Lord strengthens a devotee's affinity with Him, and tries to lead him to salvation. Therefore, Lord Kṛṣṇa, in the forty-fifth verse of the second chapter, orders Arjuna. "Don't worry about 'Yoga' and 'Kṣema". It means that a devotee should be free, from any care for gain and security.

'Vahāmyaham'—It means, that as a mother, looks after her small son and provides him cheerly with all necessities, similarly the Lord provides, all the means required by the devotees.

Appendix—The Lord here mentions the superiority of His devotees to those, who perform actions with interested motive, enjoined by the Vedas as described in the preceding verse, and also to those who worship other gods. The devotees, who have exclusive devotion for God, neither believe in Indra, who has been described in the preceding verse nor believe in other gods as is described in the next verse. Those who worship Indra etc., reap the limited fruit for their worship, according to their desire. But the worshippers of God receive limitless fruit. The worshippers of gods are like paid labours (servants) while the worshippers of God are like the members of the family. If a labour works, he is paid the limited amount of money as wages according to his labour (work), but if a member of the house works, he is the master of the entire wealth (money) of the family.

The 'ananya bhaktas' (devotees with exclusive devotion) are those who hold that there is no other entity besides God—'Uttama ke asa basa mana māhīṁ, sapanehů̐ āna puruṣa jaga nāhīṁ' (Mānasa, Araṇya 5/6).

'Yogakṣemaṁ vahāmyaham'—The Lord provides the devotee all the necessary means required by him and provides security of what has been gained—this is the Lord's 'yogakṣemaṁ vahāmyaham'. Though the Lord provides gain and security to

अजामिल उद्धार

Redemption of Ajāmila

पत्र, पुष्प, फल, जलका ग्रहण

Accepting of leaf, flower, fruit and water

भगवान् वेदव्यास

Sage Vedavyāsa

कौरव-सभामें विराट् रूप The cosmic form in Kaurava court

उद्धारकर्त्ता भगवान् श्रीकृष्ण

The liberating Lord Kṛṣṇa

चार अवस्थाएँ Four stages

संसार-वृक्ष **The world in the form of Aśwattha tree**

भजन करनेवाले भक्त

Devotees—Performers of Bhajana

all strivers, yet he specially provides gain and security to those devotees who have exclusive devotion for Him in the same way as a mother brings up her loving child herself instead of leaving it under the care (supervision) of a servant

As a devotee attains bliss by serving God, similarly God takes delight in serving His devotee—'ye yathā māṁ prapadyante tāṁstathaiva bhajāmyaham' (Gītā 4/11).

Link:—After explaining the position of those devotees who depend only on the Lord, He describes in the next verse those devotees who worship other gods.

येऽप्यन्यदेवता भक्ता यजन्ते श्रद्धयान्विताः।
तेऽपि मामेव कौन्तेय यजन्त्यविधिपूर्वकम्॥ २३॥

ye'pyanyadevatā bhaktā yajante śraddhayānvitāḥ
te'pi māmeva kaunteya yajantyavidhipūrvakam

O son of Kuntī, even those devotees who, with faith, worship other gods, in reality worship Me also though not with a proper approach. 23

Comment:—

'Ye'pyanyadevatā bhaktā yajante śraddhayānvitāḥ'—These devotees, who have not realized, that the Lord is all-being and non-being, (Gītā 9/19) worship other gods, because they think that other gods are apart from and independent of Him, and that by their grace they will gain everything.

'Te'pi māmeva kaunteya yajantyavidhipūrvakam'—Devotees, who worship other gods, actually worship Him, because, in the whole universe, there is nothing besides, Him. Therefore, their worship to other gods is worship to Him, only, but that is a mistaken approach. The Lord, by the expression 'Yajantyavidhipūrvakam', does not mean that they do not possess knowledge—what sort of worship—materials, what sacred text, should be used, and what sort of worship, should be done. But, it means, that they regard other gods separate, from the Lord. They worship other gods, because their wisdom has been led astray, by desires (Gītā 7/20). But the fact is, that whatever power, the other gods have, has come to them, from the Lord, and so it is only, His power.

It means that, if a devotee worships any deity, regarding him as the Lord, without having any desire for fruit, that will be worship to God, and it will lead him to God-realization. Secondly, if he worships the Lord, with a desire, he will be regarded as a devotee—a seeker of worldly objects, a sufferer etc., whom the Lord has called noble, (Gītā 7/18).

In fact, all is God. So every kind of worship, service and good, offered to others, is only an offering to God. As rain-water, in the form of a stream, river and waterfall etc., flows into the sea (because that water comes from the sea and belongs to the sea), whomsoever, a devotee worships, he worships, only God.

Appendix—'Traividyā mām' (9/20), 'Ananyāścintayanto mām' (9/22) and 'te'pi māmeva' (9/23)—the Lord has used the term 'mām' in these three verses which means that all is God, therefore the Lord knows all as His manifestation. If a striver has no desire and beholds God in all, he may worship anyone, that is indeed the worship to God. It means that if he has the disinterested motive and regards other gods as the manifestation of God, then his worship to gods will not remain the mistaken approach but will be worship to God only.

In the seventh chapter the term 'devayajaḥ' was used (7/23), the same has been mentioned here as 'yajante'.

Link:—But why is their worship not with a proper approach? The explanation follows.

अहं हि सर्वयज्ञानां भोक्ता च प्रभुरेव च।
न तु मामभिजानन्ति तत्त्वेनातश्च्यवन्ति ते॥ २४॥

ahaṁ hi sarvayajñānāṁ bhoktā ca prabhureva ca
na tu māmabhijānanti tattvenātaścyavanti te

I am verily the recipient and Lord of all sacrifice (Yajña), but they do not know My essence (tattva), and hence they have a fall. 24

Comment:—

[In the second chapter, Lord Kṛṣṇa declares, "Those who are deeply attached to pleasures and prosperity, cannot attain the determinate intellect, concentrated on God" (2/44). In God-realization, there are two obstacles—to have a sense of enjoyership, and to, have the possessive spirit. These two pervert the intellect, of a man. They force a man, to have a disinclination for God. In childhood, a person depends on his mother, and cannot live without her. But when he grows up and is married, he becomes a husband to his wife and does not like his mother much, he rather, becomes indifferent to her. Similarly, when this (soul), gets entangled in worldly pleasures and prosperity, it forgets the Lord, who is the enjoyer and the Lord of all sacrifices etc., and thus man has a fall. But, when he realizes, that God is the real enjoyer of all the things, and He is the only Lord, he comes to the right path and does not fall.]

'Ahaṁ hi sarvayajñānāṁ* bhoktā ca prabhureva ca'—The Lord, is the enjoyer of all virtuous actions, such as sacrifice, charity, penance, pilgrimage etc., which are performed, according to the ordinance of scriptures and according to one's, caste and stage (order) of life etc., because, all ordinances have been made only by Him, so that beings, remaining detached from actions and

* Though the term 'Yajñānām' used in the plural number includes all actions (duties) yet the term 'Sarva' means to show that no scriptural or physical or practical duty has been excluded.

their fruits, may not deviate, from the self and may worship Him, with exclusive devotion. As He, is the enjoyer of all sacrifice, He is also the Lord of all the worlds, things, men, incidents, circumstances, actions and beings, including their senses, bodies, minds and intellects, as the entire universe, has emanated from Him and so, He is their Lord.

An Important Fact

The Lord is the enjoyer. What does it mean?

The Lord has declared, "A great soul realizes, that all this is, God" (Gītā 7/19) and "In my view, I am being and non-being, both" (Gītā 9/19). It means, that when a devotee performs virtuous actions, such as sacrifice, charity, penance or provides food to the hungry, helps the destitute, waters plants, feeds dogs and birds etc., all of these are enjoyed by the Lord, because it is He Who has manifested Himself, in different forms.* Thus a devotee, serves the Lord only, with all these articles offered to the hungry, the needy, and to anyone else, in His universal form. The Lord, is the enjoyer of all, whatsoever, is offered to Him, in diverse forms.

How is, He the Lord?

Devotees regard God, as the Lord of the higher and the lower nature. He is the master of the entire universe, and so He is free in creating, preserving, destroying, conducting, and enjoying this entire universe, and also in bringing about, any change in it. Thus He is the Lord.

* There is an anecdote. Once the saint named Nāmadeva went for pilgrimage. There he cooked food and went to take clarified-butter. In the meanwhile a dog came there and ran with a loaf of bread. Saint Nāmadeva ran after him with clarified-butter-pot and said, "O Lord, I wanted to offer this loaf of bread with clarified-butter to You. Why are You running away?" As soon as he uttered these words, the Lord manifested Himself because in the form of that dog there was no one else besides the Lord. Thus whatever is offered to anyone, is offered only to God.

'Na tu māmabhijānanti tattvenātaścyavanti te'—In fact, the Lord is the real, and the unreal; the sentient and the insentient, all. So, He is the enjoyer and the Lord of all, the things etc. But those, who do not know this fact, think that if they offer food or water to creatures, it is received by them, and so they are enjoyers. But, actually the real enjoyer is the Lord. So, without perceiving the Lord, in different manifestations, they fall. Therefore, every person should regard the Lord, as the enjoyer. Thus, whatever is offered to anyone, should be offered only to Him, knowing it to be His.

Secondly, all the worldly pleasures and prosperity, are the Lord's and are for the service of the Lord, Who has manifested Himself, in the form of the universe. But, people attached to pleasures and prosperity, by considering these their own, think that they are their master, but actually they become slaves to them. By depending on them, they regard these as part and parcel of their life, while they are really different, from them. Thus they have a fall. But if they know the fact, that God is the enjoyer and the Lord of, all the sacrifices, they are liberated.

'Cyavanti' (fall) means, that without attaining God, they fall. By performing virtuous actions, they go to higher regions, such as heaven etc., but having enjoyed heavenly pleasures, they have to return to the world of mortals (Gītā 9/21). Thus, instead of attaining salvation, they have to follow the wheel of birth and death. This is their fall.

Appendix—In the end of the fifth chapter the Lord declared, 'I am the enjoyer of all sacrifices and austerities'—'bhoktāraṁ yajñatapasām' (5/29). There the Lord declared in an affirmative way that he who has realized Him as the enjoyer of all sacrifices attains peace; and here by negative inference He declares that these, who don't know Him as the enjoyer (recipient) of all sacrifices, have a fall. When a man himself becomes the enjoyer, he has a fall. If he regards the Lord as the enjoyer of all virtuous actions, he no longer remains an enjoyer, and his desire for pleasure is wiped out, and without the desire for pleasure he attains peace.

In fact only God is the ultimate doer and ultimate enjoyer of all actions. But in spite of being a doer and an enjoyer, He remains untainted viz., He has no sense of doership or enjoyership (no desire for the fruit of action)—'tasya kartāramapi māṁ viddhyakartāramavyayam' (Gītā 4/13), 'na māṁ karmāṇi limpanti na me karmaphale spṛhā' (Gītā 4/14).

Link:—The Lord, in the next verse, describes the relative end of different devotees who worship, other deities with an interested motive.

यान्ति देवव्रता देवान्पितॄन्यान्ति पितृव्रताः।
भूतानि यान्ति भूतेज्या यान्ति मद्याजिनोऽपि माम्॥ २५॥

yānti devavratā devānpitṝnyānti pitṛvratāḥ
bhūtāni yānti bhūtejyā yānti madyājino'pi mām

Those who worship the gods, with self-interest, go to gods, after death, those who worship the manes come to the manes, those who adore the evil-spirits, join the evil-spirits. But, those who worship Me, attain Me, alone. 25

Comment:—

[In the preceding verse, the Lord declared, that He is the enjoyer of all sacrifices, and the Lord of the entire universe. But, those who instead of, regarding Him as the enjoyer and the Lord, themselves become enjoyers and the Lord, have a fall. Now, in this verse, He explains, how they fall.]

'Yānti devavratā devān'—Those, who do not know reality, about the Lord, but hanker after worldly pleasures and prosperity, worship other gods, and follow rites, relating to them (Gītā 7/20). Those gods, carry their devotees to their abodes, but they have to return from there, because all the worlds from the abode of Brahmā downwards, are subject to return (Gītā 8/16).

In the twenty-third verse, the Lord declares, that those devotees who worship other gods, also worship Him alone, though not with a proper approach. It means, that those devotees do not know, that all is God. Their aim of worship, is to get worldly pleasures and prosperity, so they fall. If they had worshipped, either the Lord or even gods, without having any desire, they instead of attaining the gods, would have attained, the Lord. Had they not desired anything, from the gods (as manifestation of the Lord), and the Lord and even if the Lord and the gods had offered them, they should have declined the offer. They should have rather responded, "O Lord! You are ours, and we are Yours. Had the worldly things (pleasures and prosperity) been more valuable than this affinity with You, we would have desired or begged of You. But there is nothing more valuable, than this affinity. So why should we beg?" Having such sentiments, they would have become a source of bliss to Him, and they would not have attained, the perishable and inferior, celestial world.

'Pitṝnyānti pitṛvratāḥ'—Those, who want their desires to be satisfied, worship the manes, by regarding them as their favourite deity. But the greatest desire, that can be satisfied by the manes, is that they can take their devotees, to their abode.

'Bhūtāni yānti bhūtejyā'—Persons possessing the mode of ignorance (darkness), worship the spirits and ghosts, to fulfil their worldly desires. They worship spirits at night, on the cremation ground with meat, wine and incantations etc. The maximum benefit they can get is that those evil-spirits, can fulfil their worldly desires. But after death, they go to the spirits i.e., become evil-spirits.

'Yānti madyājino'pi mām'—Those, who think of Me and worship Me, with exclusive devotion, attain Me, certainly.

An Important Fact

Those, who worship other gods, manes and spirits etc., for worldly pleasures and prosperity, have to go to hell or to follow, the cycle of birth and death in eighty-four lac forms of lives. In human birth, by having affinity of love with God, they could be a source of bliss to Him. But being engrossed in cheap worldly desires, they adore petty gods, manes and evil-spirits, and thereby get entangled in a vicious circle. Therefore, they should devote themselves only to God, very cautiously. If they worship the Lord, they can attain Him. Or if they worship others regarding them as manifestation of the Lord, without a desire for the fruit of worship, they can attain Him. Regarding them, as separate from the Lord, and having a desire for fruit, these are the two causes of downfall.

Birth as an evil-spirit is very bad, impure and so, is their, worship. So those who worship spirits, have a sure downfall, because, they can never behold them as a manifestation of God,* nor can serve them, without a selfish motive.

Here is an anecdote. There was a man, who worshipped a female spirit, called 'Karṇa' (she when under the control of someone, is said to, reveal to him all secrets). When anyone went to him, to get an answer for his question, he could know the question, and would answer it. He earned a lot of money. Someone wanted to learn his secret. He said, that he applied excreta to his ear and with the help of 'Karṇa' a female spirit, he come to know, the question and answer into my ear. But at the time of his death he wanted to run to the bank of the river Narmadā, so that he could attain salvation. But that female evil-

* If a devotee regards an evil-spirit as the manifestation of God, the evil-spirit attains emancipation and the devotee has a vision of God. Once the devotee, Nāmadeva saw an evil-spirit of a very big size. Nāmadeva prayed to it by regarding it as his favourite deity with the result that the evil-spirit attained emancipation and God revealed Himself to him.

spirit presented herself, as a female hog, and killed him. Thus, she took him to her abode. So, the worship of spirits, is forbidden.

But strivers, can offer oblations of food and water, to evil-spirits and ghosts, so that they may be liberated, from the life of evil-spirits. Even, saints and great souls, have done so.

Appendix—The term 'Vrata' mean precept (rule). Therefore the term 'devavrata' means—to follow precepts relating to the worship of gods (Gītā 7/20). By taking refuge in God, performance of action for Him is 'worship to God'—'Svakarmaṇā tamabhyarcya siddhiṁ vindati mānavaḥ' (Gītā 18/46).

If all actions are offered to God, it is worship to God (Gītā 9/27). If actions are performed in a disinterested manner and they are offered to God, then no forbidden action can be performed because it is due to desire only that forbidden actions are done (Gītā 3/36-37).

In fact all is the manifestation of God. But he who assumes (accepts) any other entity besides God, does not attain salvation. Even if he goes to the highest worlds, he has to return from there to this mortal world (Gītā 8/16).

Link:—An idea may come to the mind of people, that when access even to the minor gods, is not easy, access to the Lord should be, very difficult. The Lord clarifies the point now.

पत्रं पुष्पं फलं तोयं यो मे भक्त्या प्रयच्छति ।
तदहं भक्त्युपहृतमश्नामि प्रयतात्मनः ॥ २६ ॥

patraṁ puṣpaṁ phalaṁ toyaṁ yo me bhaktyā prayacchati
tadahaṁ bhaktyupahṛtamaśnāmi prayatātmanaḥ

Whoever, offers Me with devotion, a leaf, a flower, a fruit or even water, I accept these devout offering of a devotee, with love. 26

Comment:—

[All the things and actions, belong to the lower nature, of the Lord. But, a man by identifying himself with these becomes their enjoyer, and lord. Actually the Lord is their enjoyer and master. So, the Lord, orders devotees, to offer all things and actions to Him (9/27). By doing so, they will be free, from bondage forever (9/28).]

Secondly, in the worship of gods several ordinances etc., are to be observed, but in attaining Him, there are no rules and regulations, because a man (soul) being His fraction has natural affinity, with him. So he can attain the Lord, without any formalities with firm feelings of affinity with Him, in the same way, as a child can go to the lap of its mother, without any formality.

'Patraṁ puṣpaṁ phalaṁ toyaṁ yo me bhaktyā prayacchati'—A Devotee, who offers, with love a leaf (basil leaf etc.,) a flower, a fruit or even water, the Lord, appears in person and accepts the article offered, by him, with love. The Lord, satisfied the three worlds by demanding a leaf from Draupadī, and by eating it. He liberated, the elephant who offered Him a flower. He relished the fruit offered by Śabarī so much, that he could never forget it and always praised, her hospitality. When Rantideva offered water, to the Lord Who came as a person of low-caste, he had His vision.

When a devotee, is absorbed in devotion, he forgets what he is offering, to the Lord. Similarly, the Lord is also so much absorbed in love, that He takes no heed, of what He is eating. The Lord, ate the rind of the bananas, offered by Vidura's wife, with love.

'Tadahaṁ bhaktyupahṛtamaśnāmi prayatātmanaḥ'—The Lord, not only accepts the offering of devotees, but also eats it. As a flower, is to be smelt but the Lord eats it, because it was offered by a devotee, with love. It means that if a devotee wants to offer food to the Lord, He immediately, feels hungry.

'Prayatātmanaḥ' stands for the devotee, whose heart remains engrossed in God, and who totally depends only on Him. The Lord, partakes the articles offered, by such a loving devotee.

Here, a leaf, flower, or fruit and water denote all things. The reason is, that a leaf, a flower, and a fruit are the effects, of the cause of water, as all the three are born, of water. So all objects (things) of the entire universe, are denoted by them, as all are the result of water. So all things should be offered, to the Lord.

In this verse, the term 'Bhakti' (Devotion), has been used, two times. 'Bhaktyā', shows devotion of a devotee, while 'Bhaktyupahṛtam', is an adjective, for the thing offered with devotion. It means, that when a devotee offers a thing with devotion, it becomes a symbol of devotion (love), and so the Lord, eats it because He has a craving for love.

An Important Fact

In this verse, there is stress on devotion (love), rather than of objects, as the Lord, has a thirst for loving sentiment, not for objects. As a chaste wife, and an obedient disciple, feel highly delighted by serving her husband and the preceptor respectively, a devotee is very much delighted by offering a thing to the Lord, because he feels that the Lord by His special grace, has given him an opportunity to serve Him, with a thing, which is actually His.

The Lord, eats the thing, offered with devotion. There is an anecdote in this connection. There was a priest who offered almonds, walnuts, cashew nuts and pistachio nuts etc., to the Lord in the temple, from the Dīwālī festival to the Holī festival. But, when these nuts became costly, he began to offer ground nuts. One day, the priest had a vision of the Lord, in his dream. The Lord said, "My dear, you have started to offer, only ground nuts." The priest again started to offer almond etc. The priest was convinced, that the Lord ate the things offered, to Him.

It is said, by saints that things offered to the Lord, with devotion, become unusual in smell, and taste etc., and are not spoiled, with passage of time. This is not a hard and fast rule, but it depends upon, the devotion of a devotee.

When articles are offered as oblation, into fire, it is sacrifice; when they are offered to others, it is called charity. When by abstinence, they are not used for one's ownself, it becomes austerity; and when these are offered to God, which lead to union with Him—all these are different names, of renunciation.

Appendix—In order to worship the gods, several rules have to be observed (followed) (Gītā 7/20), but in the worship of God there is no rule. In the worship of God there is predominance of love (devotion) and one's regarding Him as one's own, rather than of any method—'bhaktyā prayacchati', 'bhaktyupahṛtam'.

As an innocent (simple hearted) child puts into its mouth whatever comes to its hand, similarly the Lord by becoming simple hearted eats whatever is offered to Him by the simple hearted devotee—'ye yathā māṁ prapadyante tāṁstathaiva bhajāmyaham' (Gītā 4/11); as Vidurānī offered the peel of a banana to Lord Kṛṣṇa, He ate it with a great relish.

The expression 'bhaktyā prayacchati' means that a devotee offers a thing to God with love (devotion), not with a desire. In the worship of gods certain things are necessarily required but in the worship of God nothing particular is required, but only love or devotion is required.

Link:—A man has a downfall, if he is attached, either to things or actions. In the previous verse, it was mentioned that things should be offered, to the Lord. In the next verse, He explains that actions, should also be offered, to the Lord.

यत्करोषि यदश्नासि यज्जुहोषि ददासि यत्।
यत्तपस्यसि कौन्तेय तत्कुरुष्व मदर्पणम्॥ २७॥

yatkaroṣi yadaśnāsi yajjuhoṣi dadāsi yat
yattapasyasi kaunteya tatkuruṣva madarpaṇam

O son of Kuntī, whatever you do, whatever you eat, whatever you offer in sacrifice, (yajña) whatever you bestow as a gift, whatever you do, by way of penance, dedicate it all to Me. 27

Comment:—

[It is a policy of the Lord, that howsoever men approach Him, even so does, He seek them (Gītā 4/11). When a devotee offers his things, to the Lord, the Lord also responds with His gift. The things offered by a devotee are limited, while those granted by the Lord, are limitless. If a devotee offers himself to the Lord, the Lord also offers Himself to him. Actually, the Lord has already offered Himself, to the universe (Gītā 9/4) and also has offered freedom, to them. So, if they offer the freedom bestowed by Him to Him, He will also offer, His freedom to them, and thus depend on them. Therefore, Lord Kṛṣṇa orders Arjuna to offer that freedom to Him.]

'Yatkaroṣi'—This expression, includes all scriptural, physical, vocational, social, spiritual and mundane, actions. Lord Kṛṣṇa orders Arjuna, to offer all actions to Him. If he offers himself to Him, all his actions will be spontaneously offered, to Him. Now, Lord Kṛṣṇa divides those actions, into different parts.

'Yadaśnāsi'—This expression, includes all the physical actions, as taking meals, drinking water, taking medicines, wearing clothes, walking, sleeping, waking, bathing etc.

'Yajjuhoṣi'—This expression includes, all the sacrificial actions, such as arrangement of material for sacrifice, burning fire, chanting sacred formulas, and offering oblation, to the sacred fire.

'Dadāsi yat'—This expression includes, gift, presents and help he offers, to others.

'Yattapasyasi'—It includes all actions that a devotee performs, by way of penance: such as control over sense-organs, discharging duty, facing unfavourable and favourable circumstances happily, pilgrimage, fasting, adoration, meditation, chanting and trance etc.

'Tatkuruṣva madarpaṇam'—It means, that by offering every action, to the Lord, the devotee becomes free from the feeling of 'I'ness and 'Mineness', which binds him, and he attains perfection, having attained which, he does not reckon any other gain greater than that, and established in which he is not moved even by great sorrow, and which is free, from the contact of pain (Gītā 6/22-23).

In this verse, 'Yat' (whatever) has been used five times, which means that the offer of each of the actions, is of great merit. But how much more meritorious it will be, if all actions, are offered to Him.

An Important Fact

In the twenty-sixth verse, Lord Kṛṣṇa said, that a devotee should offer a leaf, a flower, a fruit or even water, to Him. All these things are easily available, but they require a little effort. In the twenty-seventh verse, He said that whatever action a devotee performs he should offer it to, God. It means, that there is nothing new, whether an article or action should be offered to God. But a devotee, should offer himself to, God. By doing so, all his actions will be automatically offered, to the Lord. As a mother, is pleased with different actions, such as jumping, running, playing, smiling etc., of a child, so the Lord is pleased with different actions of a devotee, as he becomes His.

But, it does not mean, that forbidden actions are to be offered to the Lord. The Lord is offered only things and actions that are sanctioned by scriptures. As, a thing which suits a saint is given to him, a thing or action which suits the Lord, is offered to Him.

Now, if anyone offers forbidden actions, such as theft etc., to the Lord, according to the scriptures, he will acquire its manifold fruit, i.e., he will be be severely punished.

Appendix—To offer something honourably to the person to whom it belongs is called 'arpaṇa' (to dedicate). The Lord has used the term 'prayacchati' for offering things and has used the term 'arpaṇam' for dedicating actions in the expression 'tatkuruṣva madarpaṇam' because actions are not given.

A Jñānayogī renounces the assumed affinity with the world but a devotee does not assume any other entity besides God. In other words a Jñānayogī renounces the sense of 'I' and 'mine' and a devotee accepts 'thou' and 'thy'. Therefore a Jñānayogī renounces objects and actions and a devotee dedicates objects and actions to God viz., without having the sense of possession over those objects and actions, regard them as God's and the manifestation of God.

When a man regards a thing as real and values it, it is very difficult to renounce it, by regarding it as unreal; but it is easy to offer the same thing to any other person, to render service to him with it. Then if it is offered (dedicated) to the most venerable, the most beloved God, how easy it is! Secondly the person who renounces a thing may he proud of his renunciation but he who dedicates it to God, can't be proud of his dedication, because if the thing which belongs to God, is dedicated to Him, how can the devotee be proud of it? 'Tvadīyaṁ vastu govinda tubhyameva samarpaye'. All objects (the entire universe) belong to God from time immemorial. 'Dedicating them to God' means to rectify the mistake of regarding them as his own. When a mistake rectified, a man is not proud of his such act of rectification; rather he gets pleased at the removal of the mistake.

When a striver regards the world as God's, his affinity with the world is renounced viz., the world disappears, the independent existence of the world does not persist any more (which really does not exist) but only God remains (Who really exists). Therefore a devotee needs no discrimination in order to renounce affinity with the world. He does not renounce affinity with the world but regards the world as God's or as God's manifestation because the 'aparā prakṛti' (lower nature) also belongs to God (Gītā 7/4).

Link:—In the previous two verses the Lord said that a devotee should offer all things and actions to Him. In the next verse He describes the good that accrues from offering everything and every action to Him.

शुभाशुभफलैरेवं मोक्ष्यसे कर्मबन्धनैः।
सन्न्यासयोगयुक्तात्मा विमुक्तो मामुपैष्यसि॥ २८॥

śubhāśubhaphalairevaṁ mokṣyase karmabandhanaiḥ
sannyāsayogayuktātmā vimukto māmupaiṣyasi

With your mind firmly set on the Yoga of renunciation i.e., by dedicating all actions to Me, you will be free from the bondage of actions having good and bad results; and freed from them, you yourself having completely surrendered shall attain Me. 28

Comment:—

'Śubhāśubhaphalairevaṁ mokṣyase karmabandhanaiḥ'— By offering all things and actions i.e., by offering himself, a devotee, becomes free from good and bad results, of actions performed in innumerable births. In human life, such a man does not perform evil actions. All his actions, are performed in accordance with the ordinance of scriptures and saints. But, by chance, if a forbidden action is performed by him, the Lord who is installed in his heart, destroys it.

All actions performed, with body, mind, intellect and senses etc., are external, and so their good or bad result, in the form of favourable or unfavourable circumstances, is also external. But if a man by error accepts his affinity with those circumstances, and thus feels happy and sad, the feeling of sadness and happiness, is bondage which leads him, to the wheel of birth and death. On the other hand, a devotee, in all the favourable and unfavourable circumstances, regarding them as God's will, feels God's grace and becomes free from bondage.

'Sannyāsayogayuktātmā'—It means, that a devotee should offer all his actions to God. Here 'Saṁnyāsa', does not stand for the Discipline of Knowledge. It means, surrender to God, as is mentioned in 18/57 also.

As a Sāṅkhyayogī rests happily in the self, or in God, mentally relegating all actions to the body with nine doors (Gītā 5/13) a devotee, offers all his actions of innumerable births and their fruits, to God.

'Vimukto māmupaiṣyasi'—A devotee after becoming free, from bondage, attains God.

An Important Fact

What is, bondage of good* and evil actions?

Every action, whether good or evil, has a beginning and an end. Similarly, there is connection and disconnection of circumstances, as fruit of actions. It means, that if an action and its fruit are transitory, how can affinity with them, be lasting? But, when the eternal self assumes affinity with actions, he is connected with their fruits. Though his affinity with actions and their fruits, is not possible, yet he assumes this affinity. He (self) is eternal. So his assumed affinity, which he accepts in himself, also appears to be eternal.

He feels happy when good actions, bear fruit, in the form of favourable circumstances. But, this happiness does not persist

* As evil actions lead to bondage, so do good actions lead to bondage. As shackles whether of gold or iron bind a man, so do both virtuous and evil actions lead to bondage as they conduce a man to rebirth.

for a long time. So he has a desire for happiness. This desire, is the root of all sorrow. Before happiness, there was sorrow and again it will end in sorrow. It means, that so long as, he has a desire for happiness, he cannot escape sorrow.

When he surrenders himself to God, he realizes his real identity with God, (because he as a fraction of the Lord) and his assumed affinity, with the body perishes. Actually, he already had his identity with God, but he did not realize it because he performed actions with a selfish motive. But, when he offers actions, as well as himself to God, he attains His love, naturally. In that state, he feels the Lord's grace, in both the favourable and unfavourable circumstances. As a kind mother, shows her affection in rearing, as well as, in scolding a child, so does the Lord, by sending favourable and unfavourable circumstances to shower His grace, on devotees. A devotee,without paying any heed to favourable and unfavourable circumstance, meditates only on, God.

Appendix—The Lord, by the expression 'yānti madyājino'pi mām' (9/25) (those who worship Me, attain Me alone) whatever started saying, while concluding the same, He declares, "By dedicating all actions and objects to Me, you will be free from the bondage of actions, having good and bad result; and freed from them, you yourself having completely surrendered to Me, shall attain Me."

Actions are also good and bad and their fruit (result) is also good and bad. Actions which are done for the welfare of others, are good; and which are done for one's own self, are bad. Favourable circumstance is the good result and unfavourable circumstance is the bad result. A devotee of God dedicates good actions to God, he does not do bad actions and is not happy and sad in good and bad result viz., in favourable and unfavourable circumstances. His 'sañcita' (accumulated) actions of infinite lives are burnt to ashes in the same way as a burning piece of grass burns the heap of grass to ashes.

By dedicating the actions, objects and the self to God, affinity (attachment) with the world is renounced and there remains relationship with only God, which has naturally ever been there—'mamaivāṁśo jīvaloke jīvabhūtaḥ sanātanaḥ' (Gītā 15/7). By regarding the mundane, which is not ours, as ours, we are ensnared in bondage. By regarding the things as ours, only bondage persists, the things don't persist. A devotee has no sense of mine (possession) with any object, person or action, so he is freed from the bondage.

Here 'Samarpaṇayoga' has been called 'Sannyāsayoga'.

The term 'māmupaiṣyasi' means that the devotee becomes 'abhinna' (one) with God, he loses his independent identity viz., he becomes verily the Lord's own self—'jñānī tvātmaiva me matam' (Gītā 7/18). This is called 'premādvaita' (non-dualism of devotion or love).

Link:—Now a doubt arises, that the Lord frees those from bondage, who surrender themselves to Him, it means that he does not free others, and so He is not gracious, and equanimouts to all. The Lord clarifies this point.

समोऽहं सर्वभूतेषु न मे द्वेष्योऽस्ति न प्रियः ।
ये भजन्ति तु मां भक्त्या मयि ते तेषु चाप्यहम् ॥ २९ ॥

samo'haṁ sarvabhūteṣu na me dveṣyo'sti na priyaḥ
ye bhajanti tu māṁ bhaktyā mayi te teṣu cāpyaham

I am the same to all beings; as such to Me there is none hateful, nor dear. But, those who worship Me with devotion, are in Me and I am also, in them.* 29

---

* In the first part of this verse there is the description of all beings while in the second part of those who worship the Lord.

Comment:—

'Samo'haṁ sarvabhūteṣu'—The Lord, pervades the whole universe (Gītā 9/4) and He is a disinterested friend, of all beings (Gītā 5/29).

The Lord pervades everywhere, equally from a small ant, to a big elephant and from the vilest sinner, to the most virtuous saint, because all souls are His fragments of His own Self. So they cannot be separated from Him, and He cannot be separated, from them. The beings can be different by birth, by actions, by circumstances, by incidents and by union and disunion etc., but He always and equally, pervades all of them.

'Na me dveṣyo'sti na priyaḥ*'—The Lord, has neither attachment for the virtuous persons, nor aversion to, the evil ones. He loves, all beings equally. But, the virtuous people, desiring fruits for their virtuous actions, go to higher regions, while evil-doers go to hell, and pass eighty-four lac forms of lives.

The Lord, provides earth, water, fire, air and ether, equally to all beings because these are His portion. As a man, has neither attachment to a healthy limb, nor aversion for a diseased one, the Lord, has neither attachment for the virtuous persons, who follow His precepts, nor aversion to the evil-doers as also, His critics because, He is the same, to all beings. He has no partiality. It is partiality, from which attachment and aversion, evolve.

'Ye bhajanti tu māṁ bhaktyā mayi te teṣu cāpyaham'—Those, who worship the Lord with devotion, without having any attachment for the world, and work to please Him, are in Him and He is in them (Gītā 9/14; 10/9).

It does not mean, that other beings are not in Him, but it means that they do not accept this fact, they think that they are

* Here the term 'Priyaḥ' stands for attachment not for loving because all beings are loving to the Lord as they are born of him (Mānasa 7/85/2). The Lord always emphasizes the fact that one should be free from attachment and aversion. So here the term has been used for attachment.

worldly and so they remain established, in the world, and a body, which are transitory. But those, who regard the Lord, as pervading everywhere, all the time, in all things, incidents, circumstances and beings, are specially, in Him and He is specially, in them.

Secondly, those who have this affinity, that they are the Lord's and He is theirs, they become so much intimate, that they become one. So they are in Him, and He is in them.

Thirdly, their 'I'ness comes to an end. So they dwell, in Him.

Now a question arises here that it might mean, the Lord is not the same, for all beings. He loves His devotees, more than He loves other beings. So He is not just. The answer is, that the Lord has declared, "Howsoever men approach Me, even so, do I seek them" (Gītā 4/11). Therefore, though the Lord is the same, and just, for all beings, yet it is the devotion of devotees, which attracts the Lord, towards them. If He is not attracted towards them, it means that He is ungrateful and unjust.

As a son, is called worthy or unworthy, because of his virtuous and evil actions, so a louse like insect, sucks blood, instead of milk from the udders of a cow, and as with the same electricity, in a refrigerator water is frozen to ice, while in a heater fire is burnt, because of their different characteristics. Similarly, persons because of their different characteristics, have different grasping capacity, to receive His grace. As a good conductor of heat, or electricity, conducts heat or electricity, but some other substances, do not conduct, at all. The defect does not lie, with the source of energy, but with an instrument. Similarly, God's grace or His sameness is equal, to all. But evil-doers, because of their ignorance do not realize His grace, and equivalence. The Lord's grace, manifests itself among His devotees, according to their devotion, while it is not revealed, among those, who have no devotion, and who are non-believers.

It means, that men because of their worldly attachment, think that they are worldly. If they start worshipping the Lord, their attachment is wiped out and they start feeling, that they are in God and God is in them. Actually, they are ever in God and God is ever, in them, but the reality, is veiled by attachment.

The Lord, has used the term 'Ye' (who), which means, that whosoever worships Him with devotion, is in Him and He is in His devotee; he may be of any caste, creed, colour and country etc.

Appendix—'Samo'haṁ sarvabhūteṣu'—A man (the self) may or may not dedicate (offer) his actions and objects to God, it does not make any difference in God. He ever remains the same. The Lord is not at all touched by any particular 'Varṇa' (order of life), particular āśrama (stage of life), particular caste, particular action and particular ability etc. Therefore a person of every Varṇa, Āśrama, Caste etc., can have an inclination to Him, can be a devotee to Him and can attain Him.

'Na me dveṣyo'sti na priyaḥ'—From the view-point of God, there is no one else besides Him, then how can the question arise of His being hateful or dear to anyone? A man (the self) is bound by having attachment and aversion to good and bad actions and their fruit; and by renouncing attachment and aversion, he is liberated viz., he attains salvation. Therefore only the individual self, not God is bound and liberated. The self has partiality; in God there is no partiality at all, He ever remains the same to all beings.

In the eleventh verse of the fourth chapter the Lord declared—'ye yathā māṁ prapadyante tāṁstathaiva bhajāmyaham', the same notion has been expressed here by the expression 'ye bhajanti tu māṁ bhaktyā mayi te teṣu cāpyaham'. God pervades all beings equally, He has no partiality. But those who worship God with devotion, they are in God and God is in them viz., God is specially revealed in them. As in the earth, water pervades everywhere, but it is specially revealed in a well, similarly God in spite of pervading the entire universe, is specially revealed in devotees. This speciality is the fruit of God's grace because devotees worship God with wholehearted devotion. As ghee (clarified butter) present in the body of the cow, is of no use to the cow, but the ghee extracted from her milk (curd) is of use to her, similarly people are not purged of their sins by God merely by His pervasion in the entire universe but only those, who have an inclination to God and worship Him with devotion, are purged of their sins.* Common people in spite of being within God, don't behold Him, but devotees behold God everywhere (Gītā 6/30). Devotees love God and God loves His devotees—'priyo hi jñānino'tyarthamahaṁ sa ca mama priyaḥ' (Gītā 7/17). Therefore the devotees are in God and God is in devotees—'mayi te teṣu cāpyaham'. It means that there is no partiality in God but the people who have disinclination for God, have developed partiality.

In essence (reality) God is 'samo'haṁ sarvabhūteṣu'—(I am the same to all beings); but the devotees realize 'mayi te teṣu cāpyaham'—(they are in Me and I am in them). It means that though the Lord equally pervades all beings, yet only the devotees realize this fact; other beings don't realize it. In fact this power of realization has been bestowed upon people by God only. The only duty of a man is to turn towards God.

In Rāmacaritamānasa it is mentioned—

sātavă̐ sama mohi maya jaga dekhā
moteṁ saṁta adhika kari lekhā

(Mānasa, Araṇya 36/2)

It means that God equally pervades all beings, He equally loves them, equally showers His grace on them and has very close intimacy with them but His love, grace and intimacy etc., specially appear in devotees. These special traits are bestowed upon devotees by His grace and by God only, when devotees love God. Other people don't get engrossed (absorbed) in God

* sanamukha hoi jīva mohi jabahīṁ
janma koṭi agha nāsahiṁ tabahīṁ (Mānasa 5/44/1)

and they don't love Him so much as devotees do. Therefore devotees are also loving to God. The natural love between God and a devotee has been mentioned by the expression, 'mayi te teṣu cāpyaham' (devotees are in Me and I am in them).

Link:—Now, in the next verse the Lord expounds the greatness of devotion and devotees.

अपि चेत्सुदुराचारो भजते मामनन्यभाक् ।
साधुरेव स मन्तव्यः सम्यग्व्यवसितो हि सः ॥ ३० ॥

api cetsudurācāro bhajate māmananyabhāk
sādhureva sa mantavyaḥ samyagvyavasito hi saḥ

Even if the vilest sinner worships Me with exclusive devotion, he should be considered a saint, for he has rightly resolved to be My devotee. 30

Comment:—

[If a multimillionaire says, that he will help anyone, whosoever seeks his help with money, his charity will be testified when he actually helps the man who is his enemy. To prove the veracity of His statement here, the Lord first mentions the vilest sinner.]

'Api cet'—In the seventh chapter, the Lord declares, "Evil-doers do not worship Me" (7/15) but here He declares, "The vilest sinners worship Me." There seems, to be a contradiction in these two statements. To remove this doubt, the Lord has used the terms 'Api cet' (even if). It means, that in the seventh chapter, the Lord has described their evil nature. Swayed by that nature, they generally do not take refuge in God. But it does not mean, that there is any restriction imposed by the Lord upon the sinners, that they should not worship, Him. If they want to worship Him, they can. The Lord, has no ill-will against, any being.

'Sudurācāro bhajate mām ananyabhāk'—Even the sinners of the worst conduct, by worshipping the Lord with exclusive devotion, attain salvation. Even, at present, sins may be committed sometimes by them, because of their past influences. But, they are firmly determined with exclusive devotion, to attain the Lord. Now, they do not aim at riches, honour, respect, happiness and comforts etc. Their only aim, is exclusive devotion.

Now a question arises, how the vilest sinner can worship, the Lord. The answer is that, there can be several reasons:

(i) When, in adversity, he gets no worldly support from any quarter, he surrenders himself, to the Lord.

(ii) The atmosphere and the company of saints convert him.

(iii) Any past virtuous influence, may be aroused somehow or the other, as was aroused in Bālmīki, Ajāmila and Sadana the butcher etc., who were converted, into devotees though they were sinners.

(iv) If a person, escapes some mortal danger somehow or the other, he may start believing in the Lord's, singular power.

(v) By beholding saints and by the grace of saints, like Vālmīki and Ajāmila, may start worshipping the Lord.

Several thieves, robbers, murderers and other vilest sinners, became devout devotees, of the Lord.

Now a doubt arises, how can the vilest sinner worship the Lord, continuously, when even the devotees, who have been engaged in the worship of God for several years, cannot worship Him continuously. Here, importance has been attached, to exclusive and undivided devotion, rather than continuous devotion. As a chaste wife, has her relationship only with her husband, that sinner has his affinity, only with God.

'Ananyabhāk'—A person, can have exclusive devotion, by admitting his relationship with the Lord i.e., by changing his egoism. He should admit, that He is the Lord's and the Lord is his. He is more purified, by changing his egoism, than by performing action, such as sacrifice, charity, penance and chanting the Lord's name etc.

There are three factors in connection with, changing egoism:—

(i) To root it out:—A devotee, following the Discipline of Knowledge, realizes that his self is different from egoism, and so he remains established in the self. Thus, his ego is eliminated.

(ii) To purify it:—By following the Discipline of Action, a devotee discharges his duty for others, without expecting any fruit for his duty. For example, a son should discharge his duty towards his father, without bothering whether the father treats him as a son or not, or whether he troubles him. He should discharge his duty under all circumstances, without laying any claim on him. He should not expect his father, to be favourable to him. He should cherish no desire, for his own comfort or gain. Thus, having no desire of his own, his egoism is purified.

(iii) To change it:—In the Discipline of Devotion, ego is changed. For example—a chaste wife by changing her ego, becomes only of her husband. She regards her husband's house, as hers, his Gotra as hers, and she does not regard her relation with parents, in-laws and children. But she does serve all of them, for the sake of her husband. Similarly, the ego of a devotee changes. By following the Discipline of Devotion, just like a chaste wife, who becomes only her husband's, a devotee becomes God's and only God becomes his. Thus, he changes his egoism. This change of egoism, is denoted by the expression, 'Ananyabhāk'.

'Sādhureva sa mantavyaḥ'—He should be considered a saint. This is the Lord's, special behest. Though he does not possess all the virtues of a saint, yet he should be regarded as a saint, because he has admitted that he is only God's and only God is his. Thus by changing his egoism, he will become a saint, in no time.

Now the question arises why the Lord has to say, that he should be considered a saint. The answer is, that generally, people judge a man by his actions. Where saintliness is not manifest, and some trace of poor conduct is observed, then only it is said, that he should be considered a saint. With change of ego, he has accepted himself as God's. Therefore, his feelings and conduct will become pure, in no time. So, the Lord says, that such a person should be considered, a saint.

A man is a devout devotee, but if any day, he is seen with a prostitute, people regard him as immoral, though he may have gone there to reform her. Similarly, a sinner, may be regarded religious-minded and virtuous, if he is seen by people, counting the beads of a rosary, on the bank of the Ganges. Worldly people, generally, view actions of other people. But the Lord instead of paying heed to their actions, pays attention to their, feelings.

'Samyagvyavasito hi saḥ'—In the second chapter of the Gītā in connection with the Discipline of Action, the Lord says that in this path the intellect is determinate, while here He says that, he himself has rightly resolved. There, the determination is by intellect, while here he himself is determined. Whatever, is determinded by one-self is permanent, while that what is determined by intellect, is shortlived, because intellect can be attracted towards worldly pleasures etc., when one does not live in spiritual atmosphere, as that of listening to divine discourses, or studying the scriptures.

As a girl, after her marriage changes her egoism, and becomes her husband's and she even without making any effort, always remembers that she is her husband's, a devotee, after becoming the Lord's once, becomes His, forever, because he has rightly so resolved. So the Lord says, that he should be considered, a saint. By doing so, he speedily becomes virtuous (Gītā 9/31).

A person, may be evil and a sinner so long as, he has a disinclination for the Lord, but when he has an inclination for the Lord, by having exclusive devotion to Him, all his evils and sins, are rooted out.

Appendix—In Jñānayoga and Karmayoga there is predominance of intellect 'eṣā te'bhihitā sāṅkhye buddhiryoge tvimāṁ śṛṇu'

(Gītā 2/39). Therefore the intellect of a Jñānayogī and a Karmayogī is determinate 'vyavasāyātmikā buddhirekeha' (Gītā 2/41), 'vyavasāyātmikā buddhiḥ' (Gītā 2/44). But in Bhaktiyoga there is predominance of one's own, therefore a devotee himself is determined viz., he has rightly resolved—'Samyagvyavasito hi saḥ'.

Whatever is determined by mind and intellect, can be forgotten but whatever is determined by the self, can't be forgotten. The reason is that the mind and intellect don't stay with us always, in sound sleep we realize that they don't stay with us viz., we lack them, but the self ever exists. Whatever happens in the self, that remains permanent. Therefore the acceptance 'I am God's and God is mine' is one's own, not of the mind and intellect. Once there is this acceptance, then it does not change into non-acceptance because the self, at the root being a fragment of God, is inseparable from God. But by mistake the self accepts its affinity with Prakṛti (Gītā 15/7). Therefore in fact only the mistake is rectified. As soon as the mistake is rectified, the eternal union with God is naturally manifested 'naṣṭo mohaḥ smṛtirlabdhā' (Gītā 18/73). The acceptance of affinity with others was the mistake, it was the delusion.

Link:—In the next verse the Lord declares the result of right resolution.

क्षिप्रं भवति धर्मात्मा शश्वच्छान्तिं निगच्छति।
कौन्तेय प्रतिजानीहि न मे भक्तः प्रणश्यति॥ ३१॥

kṣipraṁ bhavati dharmātmā śaśvacchāntiṁ nigacchati
kaunteya pratijānīhi na me bhaktaḥ praṇaśyati

Speedily he becomes virtuous and secures lasting peace, O Kaunteya, and take a vow, that My devotee is never destroyed. 31

Comment:—

'Kṣipraṁ bhavati dharmātmā'—Speedily, he becomes virtuous and pure because, being a portion of the Lord, he is virtuous but by having his affinity with the world, he became a sinner, which was a transitory phase of his life. As soon as, he changes his egoism and becomes God's, his affinity with the world is wiped out, and he realizes that he is virtuous, because all the evils are the product of attaching importance, to the world. But, as soon as, a striver attaches importance only to God, rather than to the world, he becomes virtuous. So long as, he has sinful feelings, he cannot resolve, that he is God's—this is correct. But it does not mean, that a past sinner cannot thus resolve. Being a fragment of God, he is ever sinless. But due to his attachment to the world, sins visit him. In case, he starts hating sins and resolves, that he has to adore God only, he can be instantly, virtuous. In ego, where there is desire, for the world, there is inclination to God, also. If this inclination to God is strengthened, desire for the world, is wiped out and God-realization takes no time.

A Vital Fact

It is a rule, that if a man changes his egoism, his actions are automatically changed. If a man, by performing virtuous actions, wants to be virtuous, it will take a long time. But, if he changes his egoism he will become virtuous and his actions will change, automatically. Similarly if a sinner, changes his egoism and admits that he is God's and God is his, he speedily becomes virtuous. It means, that when man desires worldly pleasures, by having an affinity of 'I'ness and 'Mineness', with the body and the world, he becomes full of desires (Gītā 2/43) but when by renouncing his affinity with the world, he realizes his real affinity, with the Lord, he becomes virtuous.

Generally, people have a misconception, that a man becomes truthful by speaking the truth, and a thief by committing theft. But this is not true. When a man accepts himself as truthful, then he always speaks the truth, and by speaking the truth, his spirit of truthfulness, is strengthened. Similar is the case, with a thief. It proves, that as doer, so his activities, and his activities strengthen, his assumption "I am truthful or I am a thief."

It means, that as a person is, so are his actions. When even a sinner, becomes God's, not worldly, his actions are, virtuous.

'Śaśvacchāntiṁ nigacchati'—One who through spiritual activities, tries to become virtuous, can acquire enjoyment and prosperity, due to his latent desire for these objects. But he can not attain, everlasting peace. When the vilest sinner, changes his egoism and becomes the Lord's, he cannot have desires and cannot attach importance, to the unreal. So, he attains lasting peace.

Secondly, being a portion of the Lord, he possesses lasting peace, but by having his affinity with the world he cannot realize, that lasting peace. Only by having his affinity with the Lord, he realizes that lasting peace.

'Kaunteya pratijānīhi na me bhaktaḥ praṇaśyati'—Here, the Lord asks Arjuna to promise; and He Himself does not promise. The reason is, that a promise of the Lord, can be broken but one made by a devotee, is maintained by the Lord. As Lord Kṛṣṇa's oath, of not holding a weapon, is broken by Him, because His devotee, Bhīṣma swears that he will force Him, to hold a weapon.

The Lord declares, "My devotee never falls." By this declaration, He means to say that when a person has total inclination, to God, he has not the least possibility, to fall. The reason is, that it was his assumed affinity with the body, which led him to a fall. When he, having renounced this affinity has an exclusive inclination to God, how can there be any possibility, of his fall?

Now a doubt arises, that when even the vilest sinner can become virtuous, a virtuous person can also become, a vile sinner again. But Lord Kṛṣṇa declares, that a devotee can never fall i.e., he cannot become a sinner again. It shows that the Lord is not only just, but also gracious. It is His grace, which enables a devotee never to fall.

Appendix—As a patient gets connected with the physician, similarly when a man believes in his weakness and in the Lord's omnipotence, then he gets connected with God. It means that when a man is distraught with the worldly sufferings and finds himself helpless (weak) in getting rid of them, and has a belief in God, that by the omnipotent God's grace, he can get rid of this weakness and can escape the worldly sufferings, then he immediately becomes a devotee—'kṣipraṁ bhavati dharmātmā'. If a hungry person gets food, will he delay in taking that food?

So long as a man perceives some power, ability and speciality in him, he can't be 'ananyabhāk' (with exclusive devotion). He worships God with exclusive devotion only, when he finds no helping hand to remove his sufferings. By having exclusive devotion he becomes 'dharmātmā' (virtuous) viz., a devotee of God

A devotee has no downfall because he depends on God viz., his means and end both are only God, he has no power of his own but he depends totally on God's power. Here a doubt may arise, if a devotee has no downfall, then why did the Lord say to Arjuna in the eighteenth chapter "If from egoism, thou wilt not listen to Me, thou shalt perish"—'Atha cettvamahaṅkārānna śroṣyasi vinaṅkṣyasi' (18/58) while the Lord regards him as His devotee 'bhakto'si me sakhā ceti' (Gītā 4/3). The clarification is that a devotee can perish only, when he instead of depending on God, depends on egoism—'ahaṅkārānna śroṣyasi'. So long as he depends on God, he can't have a downfall viz., can't perish.

A devotee is like a child and a Jñānī is like a grown up boy. As a mother loves all her sons equally, yet she looks after the child specially, not the grown up sons. The reason is that the child totally depends on its mother, therefore it needs more care than the grown up sons need. Similarly the Lord takes special care of His devotee who depends on Him and He provides him gain and security—'yogakṣemaṁ vahāmyaham' (Gītā 9/22). But who will provide gain and security to a Jñānī? Therefore a striver following the discipline of knowledge can fall from Yoga but a devotee can't fall from Yoga.

The gods such as Brahmā etc., say to the Lord—

ye'nye'ravindākṣa vimuktamāninastvayyastabhāvādaviśuddhabuddhayaḥ
āruhya kṛcchreṇa paraṁ padaṁ tataḥ patantyadho'nādṛtayuṣmadaṅghrayaḥ

(Śrīmadbhā. 10/2/32)

'O Lotus-eyed! The people who don't take refuge in Your holy feet; and without having devotion in You, their intellect has not been purified, they assume that, they are liberated but in fact they are certainly bound. If by taking pains in their spiritual practice they may attain the highest rank (goal), yet they fall from there.'

tathā na te mādhava tāvakāḥ kvacid bhraśyanti mārgāttvayi baddhasauhṛdāḥ
tvayābhiguptā vicaranti nirbhayā vināyakānīkapamūrdhasu prabho

(Śrīmadbhā. 10/2/33)

'But O God! Those, who are Your devotees and who have true love in Your holy feet unlike the Jñānī's who are proud of themselves, never fall from their spiritual practice. O Lord! They because of the protection provided by You, move about fearlessly by putting their feet on the heads of the chief of the army which may obstruct their progress, no obstacle can obstruct their path.'

The Vedas, eulogizing the Lord, say—

je jñāna māna bimatta tava bhava harani bhakti na ādarī
te pāi sura durlabha padādapi parata hama dekhata harī
biswāsa kari saba āsa parihari dāsa tava je hoi rahe
japi nāma tava binu śrama tarahiṁ bhava nātha so samarāmahe

(Mānasa, Uttara. 13/3)

If a striver following the Discipline of knowledge lacks something viz., he has any flaw, he may have a downfall, but if there is a flaw in a striver following the path of Devotion, he does not have a downfall. Therefore the Lord declares—

bādhyamāno'pi madbhakto viṣayairajitendriyaḥ
prāyaḥ pragalbhayā bhaktyā viṣayairnābhibhūyate

(Śrīmadbhā. 11/14/18)

"O Uddhavajī! My devotee, who could not control his senses totally so far, and the objects of senses, time and again obstruct him and attract towards them, even then because of his devotion which increases every moment, he generally is not overpowered by sense-objects."

na vāsudevabhaktānāmaśubhaṁ vidyate kvacit

(Mahābhārata, Anu. 149/131)

'The devotees of God never and nowhere meet with evil.'

sīma ki cẳpi sakai kou tāsū, baRa rakhavāra ramāpati jāsū

(Mānasa, Bāla. 126/4)

'Kaunteya pratijānīhi'—The Lord asks Arjuna to take a vow because even the Lord Himself can't break the vow (promise) of a devotee who becomes submissive to the Lord. Therefore the Lord by addressing Durvāsā, declares—

ahaṁ bhaktaparādhīno hyasvatantra iva dvija
sādhubhirgrastahṛdayo bhaktairbhaktajanapriyaḥ

(Śrīmadbhā. 9/4/63)

'O twice born! I am totally dependent on devotees, I am not free. My devotees are very loving to Me. They have full authority over My heart.'

'Kaunteya pratijānīhi na me bhaktaḥ praṇaśyati'—By this expression a striver should have a firm belief that he can never have a downfall because he is only God's.

Link:—In this context, Lord Kṛṣṇa explains seven kinds of persons, even they can seek devotion to the Lord. Out of them, a sinner has been explained, in the preceding two verses. Now in the next verse, He explains the other four kinds of people. The remaining two will be explained, in the thirty-third verse.

मां हि पार्थ व्यपाश्रित्य येऽपि स्युः पापयोनयः ।
स्त्रियो वैश्यास्तथा शूद्रास्तेऽपि यान्ति परां गतिम् ॥ ३२ ॥

māṁ hi pārtha vyapāśritya ye'pi syuḥ pāpayonayaḥ
striyo vaiśyāstathā śūdrāste'pi yānti parāṁ gatim

O Pārtha, womenfolk, Vaiśyas, Śūdras and even those,

that are born of sinful wombs taking refuge in Me, attain the Supreme God. 32

Comment:—

'Māṁ hi pārtha vyapāśritya ye'pi syuḥ pāpayonayaḥ striyo vaiśyāṣtathā śūdrāste'pi yānti parāṁ gatim'—The Lord, has called the man, who has been immoral, in this human birth, a sinner (9/30). But 'Pāpayonayaḥ' (born of the womb of sin), are those who were sinners in the previous birth, and are born of sinful wombs, as the fruit of their previous actions. The sinful-womb, is a very wide term, which includes demons, devils, animals, and birds etc.* Sage Śāṇḍilya declares, "As men, deserve virtues such as, kindness, forgiveness, generosity etc., the beings, from the lowest womb to the highest womb can seek devotion, to the Lord" (Śāṇḍilya-Bhaktisūtra), because all of them, being a fraction of the Lord, are His, and so they are free, to have an inclination for Him. Therefore, even those, who are born of a womb of sin, by taking refuge in Him, attain Him.

Actually, a man becomes impure, by having a disinclination for the Lord. As coal, loses its lustre and becomes black, after leaving a fire and brightens again in the fire, the soul being a portion of the Lord, becomes impure by losing its lustre due to its disinclination from the Lord, but when it has inclination for the Lord, its impurity is wiped out, and it becomes so pure, that the Lord makes soul a jewel of His crown.

Capability and incapability, are judged in worldly life. But, in having affinity with God, these are not significant. Only he, who desires Him from his heart, is most capable, as for as, the Lord is concerned. For instance, a child serves his mother well, she loves it. Another child, does nothing but wails and invokes the mother's help, feeling afflicted. The mother, does not care, that it does nothing, how she should take the child in her lap. She can't bear affliction. Her heart melts. She takes the child into

---

* Cowherdesses, cows, trees, animals, snakes and other foolish creatures by having exclusive devotion suddenly attained Me (Śrīmadbhā. 11/12/8).

her lap, without caring for its purity or impurity. Similarly, when a sinful man possessing the worst conduct, being afflicted, wails and invokes God, God's heart melts and He accepts him as His, and loves him without paying attention, to his sinful conduct. It proves, that the present sins of a person who becomes a devotee, are not obstacles to God-realization. Then, how can sins of previous birth, be an obstacle, because these can bear fruit in the form of birth in low wombs, and under unfavourable circumstances? Only, they cannot create an obstacle, in adoration of God.

By the term womanfolk, He means that women of all castes, creeds, colours, classes, countries etc., by taking refuge in Him, become pure and attain Him. Devahūti, Śabarī, Kuntī, Draupadī, Vraja's cowherdesses of the past, and Mīrā, Karamaitī, Karamābāī, Pḥūlībāī of the present, are women-devotees. Similarly, Samādhi and Tulādhāra, among Vaiśyas and Vidura, Sañjaya and Niṣādarāja Guha, among Śūdras, are examples of devotees.

An Exceptional Fact

The term 'Pāpayonayaḥ' (born of the womb of sin), is not an adjective qualifying womanfolk, Vaiśyas and Śūdras. If it qualifies womanfolk, it is unjustified, because women of the three castes Brāhmaṇa, Kṣatriya and Vaiśya, are authorized to perform Vedic actions, such as oblation etc., with their husbands.

The Lord, has mentioned womanfolk separately, besides the four castes. It means that they independently also, by taking refuge in Him, can attain Him. So, they should take refuge only in Him, without seeking help of any individual.

If it qualifies Vaiśyas, it is also unjustified because, they are fully authorized to study the Vedas and perform Vedic actions, such as oblation etc.*

If it qualifies Śūdras, it is also not reasonable, because they are included, among the people of the four castes. So, only people

* Those possessing good conduct are born as Brāhmaṇas, Kṣatriyas and Vaiśyas but those of bad conduct are born of the wombs of bitches, pigs and pariahs.

of inferior birth such as Yavana, Hūṇa and Khasa etc., should be included, among those born of a womb of sin. There is no restriction, for any being to have an inclination to Him, because he is an integral part of Him. Moreover, animals, birds, trees and plants etc., can also be included among those, even thought they have no discrimination to move towards Him, but, if because of past influence or any other reason, they have an inclination for Him, they can become devotees, like 'Gajendra', the elephant and 'Jaṭāyu', the bird.

A Vital Fact

Feelings, play a more important role, than birth, in the field of spiritualism. A man, born in a high family or caste, may be proud of his birth, because of his affinity with the body. But, actually he, being a fraction of the Lord, is His, and is different from a body. So, when he renounces his affinity with the body, he becomes one with Him, or attains Him. Similarly, a 'Jīva' is not converted into Brahma. But Brahma Himself realizes, Brahma. In Brahma, there is never such assumption—"I am the embodied soul," while an embodied soul, is not Brahma. Due to affinity with vital force, a being, is called a 'Jīva'. In Brahma, there is no such vital force. Therefore, Brahma realizes Brahma. It means, 'I am limited'—this feeling is being destroyed and Brahma is realized.

A man, is different from the body. So long as, he identifies himself with a body, he remains, a slave to this body, which is an instrument made of flesh and bones, and to produce excrement and urine. This identification with a body, is the result of lack of discrimination. Without discrimination, a man can follow, neither the Discipline of Devotion, nor that of Action. So a devotee, who wants to attain devotion or salvation, should have a clear conception, that he is different from his body. He has identity with the Lord, while the body has its identity, with the world. So long as, he identifies himself with the body, he does not deserve, either devotion or knowledge. A devotee through devotion, remains engrossed in the Lord and so automatically, he has no identity with body and thus sex, caste, creed and colour etc., do not remain obstacles, to God-realization. Similarly, a person following the Discipline of Knowledge, by applying his discrimination, realizes that he is different from the body, and thus he also attains the Lord and any distinction of caste, creed, colour, class and country etc., does not debar, a devotee from realizing God.

Appendix—These who don't take refuge in others besides God, their such exclusive refuge (dependence) here has been called 'vyapāśraya' viz., special refuge in God.

The sinner in this birth is more guilty than the sinner of the previous birth. Therefore the Lord first (in the thirtieth and thirty first verses) mentions the sinner of this birth and now in this verse He mentions the sinner of the previous birth—'ye'pi syuḥ pāpayonayaḥ'.

Link:—In the next verse, Lord Kṛṣṇa describes the two kinds of persons, who are fully qualified to attain Him.

किं पुनर्ब्राह्मणाः पुण्या भक्ता राजर्षयस्तथा।
अनित्यमसुखं लोकमिमं प्राप्य भजस्व माम्॥ ३३॥

kiṁ punarbrāhmaṇāḥ puṇyā bhaktā rājarṣayastathā
anityamasukhaṁ lokamimaṁ prāpya bhajasva mām

No wonder then, that the holy Brāhmaṇas and devout Kṣatriya saints, should attain Him. Therefore, having obtained this transient and unhappy body, do continually worship Me. 33

Comment:—

'Kiṁ punarbrāhmaṇāḥ puṇyā bhaktā rājarṣayastathā'— When, even the vilest sinners and beings born of the womb of sin, as well as womenfolk, Vaiśyas and Śūdras by taking refuge in Him, attain Him, no wonder then, that the holy Brāhmaṇas and Kṣatriyas by taking refuge in Him should attain Him i.e., they will attain Him, certainly.

The term 'Puṇya' (holy), used here is antonym to the term 'Durācārī' (sinner), used in the thirtieth verse, while the term 'Brāhmaṇāḥ' is antonym to the term 'Pāpayonayaḥ', used in the thirty-second verse. It means, that Brāhmaṇas are holy, both by actions and birth. Similarly, for the Kṣatriyas the terms 'Ṛṣi' (saint) and 'rāja' (royal), have been used to denote their purity of birth and actions.

The term 'Bhaktāḥ', has been used to emphasize the fact, that those Brāhmaṇas and Kṣatriyas having a virtuous conduct, in the previous birth, as well as in this birth, through devotion attain Him, without any doubt. Moreover, 'Puṇyā brāhmaṇāḥ' and 'Rajarṣayaḥ', these two terms, denote external purity of actions and birth, while 'Bhaktāḥ' denotes internal purity, because a devotee takes refuge in the Lord, from his heart.

'Anityamasukhaṁ lokamimaṁ prāpya bhajasva mām'—This human birth, is the last of all births, because it destroys all the innumerable, future births. A man, can be a source of bliss to the Lord Himself, by being an ardent devotee. This birth is sacred, but is transient. The body may die any moment. So, a man should attain salvation, as soon as possible. This body is joyless, there is no happiness in it. In the fifteenth verse of the eighth chapter it has been called, the 'abode of pain'. Therefore, a man should not hanker after worldly pleasures, during this human life and waste his precious time.

Here, the expression 'Imaṁ lokam', stands for human body, of whitch the only aim is God-realization, as according to the ordinance of the Lord, this is the last of all births. If, in this life he does not attain God, he misses a golden opportunity, which will not be available to him, in other species. So He advises men to worship Him, without aiming at perishable objects and without attaching any value to them. The Lord's exhorting a devotee, to worship Him does not mean, that this worship will be of any benefit to the Lord, it will benefit the devotee only.

A Vital Fact

The man (soul), being a fraction of the Lord, is pure, sentient and imperishable. Then, by having affinity with transient evils, how can he himself be sinful and how can the Lord regard Him, as sinful? Being attached to the transient body and the world, he gets engaged in evils and sins. So, as soon as, he renounces that affinity of 'I'ness and 'Mineness' with the body and the world, he comes to know that he is pure. Similarly, animals, birds and pariah etc., born of the womb of sin, become free from sinful actions performed, in the previous birth. So, they by taking refuge in the Lord, can also attain Him. Thus the Lord, has referred to sinners of this birth and of the previous birth.

Then, the Lord describes, those who are mediocre. First, He talks about women, including, those of Brāhmaṇas and Kṣatriyas. Then, He talks about the twice-born viz., Vaiśyas, who are not so virtuous, as Brāhmaṇas and Kṣatriyas. Then, He describes, Śūdras who are inferior to the twice-born viz., Vaiśyas. So, He declares, that even women, Vaiśyas, and Śūdras taking refuge in Him, attain Him. Thus there is no wonder that those Brāhmaṇas and Kṣatriyas, who are holy by birth and actions, should attain Him.

The Lord here (9/30—33) has mentioned seven kinds of persons even they can seek devotion to God. They are, the vilest sinners, those born of a womb of sin, womenfolk, Vaiśyas, Śūdras, Brāhmaṇas and Kṣatriyas. Lord Kṛṣṇa, should have described the holy Brāhmaṇa or Kṣatriya, first, but first of all, He mentions the vilest sinner. The reason is, that the lower a person, the more loving he is to the Lord, because he is not proud, of his virtues. He naturally, considers himself lower and inferior. So the Lord, names him first. In the twelfth chapter also, He declares that devotees who have attained perfection, are dear to Him while, strivers, are extremely dear to Him (Gītā 12/13—20).

Here, a point needs attention. The Lord, has divided persons, into seven categories according to their caste, (Brāhmaṇa, Kṣatriya, Vaiśya and Śūdra); conduct, (vilest sinner and that born of womb of sin) and sex (womanfolk), to emphasize the fact, that beings belonging to any caste, having any sort of conduct and of any sex, by, worshipping God, can attain Him as they are all fractions of God. They have become extraordinary, not because of their caste, conduct and sex, but because of their devotion, to the Lord.

In the seventh chapter, the Lord has divided devotees into four groups according to their attitudes, and here He has divided them into seven groups according to their caste, conduct and sex, in order to explain that all devotees, without any distinction of caste, creed, conduct and sex etc., are deserving of God-realization. So, no one should lose heart, as far as devotion and God-realization, are concerned. If they have a disinclination for Him. So they themselves can develop inclination for Him as well. They are free to and capable of doing so.

Appendix—The Lord from the thirtieth verse to the thirty-third verse mentioned seven kinds of persons who are qualified (eligible) for devotion and God-realization—they are the vilest sinners of this birth, sinners of the previous birth, womenfolk, Vaiśyas, Śudras, Brāhmaṇas and Kṣatriyas. No person remains out of these seven kinds of persons. Every human being is eligible for God-realization without any distinction of his birth, caste; and even if he committed so many sins in his previous birth. Brāhmaṇa, Kṣatriya, Vaiśya and Śūdra—all the four Varṇas have been mentioned in this verse. Anyone may not think that only men have been included, so the Lord has also mentioned the womenfolk. The persons such as Yavana, Hūṇa, Khasa etc., who are below the people of the four Varṇas in rank have been included in 'Pāpayoni' (born of sinful wombs). Besides human beings other beings (birds and beasts etc.,) can also be included in 'Pāpayoni' because every living being is a fragment of God and therefore there is no bar for anyone from the side of God that one can't turn towards God.

He who is committing sins at present is a 'durācārī' and

he who because of being a sinner in the previous birth, is born of sinful womb is a 'Pāpayoni'. It means that even the vilest sinner and the one born of the most sinful womb, is entitled to God-realization. Therefore a man by taking into consideration his caste and conduct, should not get disappointed as far as God-realization is concerned. Caste and conduct are transient and unreal but a man's affinity with God is eternal and real. Therefore God accepts the relationship of devotion, not of caste and conduct—

kaha raghupati sunu bhāmini bātā, mānaů eka bhagati kara nātā
jāti pẳti kuḷa dharma baRāī, dhana bala parijana guna caturāī
bhagati hīna nara sohai kaisā, binu jala bārida dekhia jaisā

(Mānasa, Araṇya. 35/2-3)

The worldly people see the outward caste, conduct, rather than the inward reality; but God sees the reality that a man (the self) is His fragment.

In the sixteenth verse of the seventh chapter, the Lord according to the inner feelings of devotees, has divided them into four kinds—'Arthārthī' (seeker of wealth) 'Ārta' (afflicted), 'Jijñāsu' (seeker of knowledge) and 'Jñānī' (wise devotee); and here according to their outward assumption (caste and conduct) from the worldly point of view, He has mentioned seven kinds. In the seventh chapter there is description of those devotees who are engaged in the worship of God and here is the description of those persons who can divert themselves towards God. It means that in spite of the distinction of 'Varṇa' (order of life), 'Āśrama' (stage of life), dress, castes and sects etc., all the people can become devotees of these four kinds—arthārthī, ārta, jijñāsu and jñānī and can attain God. As far as God-realization is concerned, in it all are one, no one is low (inferior) or high (superior). A being may be born of any womb, he is neither disqualified for God-realization, nor was, nor will be nor can be disqualified.

'Kiṁ punarbrāhmaṇāḥ puṇyā bhaktā rājarṣayastathā'—The purpose of using the term 'bhaktāḥ' in the middle of the half verse is that there is not the glory of the holy Brāhmaṇas and Kṣatriya-saints but there is glory of their devotion. It means that the Lord is neither (envious of) impartial to sinners of the worst conduct and to these who are born of sinful wombs nor He is partial to the holy Brāhmaṇas and Kṣatriya saints. He is the same to all beings (Gītā 9/29). But he who worships God with love (devotion), he may be of any region, guise, varṇa, āśrama, caste, creed etc., he has his intimate relationship with God—'mayi te teṣu cāpyaham' (Gītā 9/29). Therefore the sinners of the worst conduct, these born of sinful wombs, womenfolk, Vaiśyas, Śūdras, Brāhmaṇas and Kṣatriya, all the seven become one as far as devotion is concerned, no difference remains in them. Therefore the Lord orders Arjuna to worship Him—'bhajasva mām'. 'Bhajana' (worship) means—to be inclined to God, to love God (to have one's ownship with God) and to aim at God-realization. To render service to others by regarding them as the manifestation of God, to offer things to others in disinterested manner and to help the needy and scarcity-stricken people—this is also worship.

'Anityamasukhaṁ lokamimaṁ prāpya bhajasva mām'—Having obtained the transient and joyless human life viz., we may live alive and enjoy pleasures—having renounced such desires, we should worship God. The reason is that there is no joy in the world, there is mere illusion of joy. Similarly there is the illusion of living. We are actually not living but we are dying every moment.

In the twenty-ninth verse of this chapter the Lord declared, "Those who worship Me with devotion, are in Me and I am also in them." Therefore here Lord Kṛṣṇa orders Arjuna to worship Him—'bhajasva mām'.

Link:—Lord Kṛṣṇa, from the twenty-ninth to the thirty-third verses, has described devotion and worship. How to worship Him, is made clear, in the next verse.

मन्मना भव मद्भक्तो मद्याजी मां नमस्कुरु ।
मामेवैष्यसि युक्त्वैवमात्मानं मत्परायणः ॥ ३४ ॥

manmanā bhava madbhakto madyājī māṁ namaskuru
māmevaiṣyasi yuktvaivamātmānaṁ matparāyaṇaḥ

Fix your mind on Me, be devoted to Me, adore Me, prostrate to Me, thus making yourself steadfast in Me, and entirely surrendering to Me, you will, reach Me. 34

Comment:—

[The Lord discloses His secret to His devotee Arjuna who is devoid of a carping spirit, and who has devotion for Him.]

'Madbhaktaḥ'—Lord Kṛṣṇa, asks Arjuna, to be devoted to Him. He should realize his real relationship with Him, that he is His and He is his. He should renounce, the assumed relationship, that he belongs to a particular caste, creed and country etc.

'Manmanā bhava'—The mind, is fixed on a person or a object, that a person loves and likes. So Lord Kṛṣṇa, reminds Arjuna that his affinity with Him is eternal, because he is His fraction. The Lord cannot forget this affinity, but Arjuna can forget it. So He exhorts him, to fix his mind on Him, by loving and liking Him.

'Madyājī'—The Lord, asks him to perform all actions, such as eating, drinking, sleeping, moving and his profession etc., as an adoration to Him.

'Māṁ namaskuru'—However, agreeable or disagreeable, an incident may happen to a devotee and he may be aware of it through his senses, but to him in reality, it is divine grace, only. If something very unfavourable happens, the devotee should regard it as a special divine grace, as it is not according to the devotee's own will, but, it is according to Lord's own sweet will. If something favourable happens, with what proportion of the devotee's consent? In that proportion, the divine grace is lesser. But in an unfavourable incident, the devotee should feel highly blissful, as it is destined, purely by God. It means, that a devotee should bow to Him and His will. He should remain satisfied and happy, in favourable and unfavourable circumstances, by regarding these as the Lord's gift, because He is all merciful and is a disinterested friend, of all beings. Nothing, can happen against, His will.

A devotee surrenders himself to the Lord, without having any desire of his own and always remains satisfied with, what the Lord does; and he addresses the Lord, "O Lord! In which birth, in what circumstances, whatever action helplessly, I have done; to neutralize those actions, and make me pure, whatever dispensation, you are making, I shall accept with much pleasure, because, they are conducive to my salvation. Why should I brood over them?" Thus, he thinks, that whatever is done by Him, is for his welfare.

'Māmevaiṣyasi yuktvaivamātmānaṁ matparāyaṇaḥ'—The term, 'Madbhaktaḥ' signifies, self-surrender, the term 'Manmanā' signifies, surrender of the inner sense and 'Madyājī' signifies, that all his activities become worship-material. The expression 'Māṁ namaskuru' signifies, surrender of the body at the Lord's feet. It means, that a devotee, by surrendering his actions, things, body, mind and himself to the Lord, attains Him.

The expression 'Yuktvaivamātmānam' means, that a devotee by changing his egoism, that he is only the Lord's, surrenders himself to the Lord. In that case, all the actions performed with senses, mind and intellect etc., will be directed towards Him and he will desire nothing else, besides the Lord. By doing so, he will attain God, without any doubt.

The term 'Matparāyaṇaḥ' means, that he should become a puppet in the hands of the Lord, by wholly depending on Him. He should have, not even a trace of thought to do anything, against, the Lord's will.

An Important Fact

(1) A devotee, by fixing his mind on Him, by being devoted to Him, by adoring Him, and by bowing down to Him, surrenders

himself to Him. Out of these four factors, the most important is, that he becomes a devotee of the Lord and then all the perishable worldly things to which he was attached, become His. Thus a devotee, should admit the reality, that he is only the Lord's. Thus his 'mineness' is gone. This notion of mineness, was wrong. It is corrected.

(2) A man, by identifying himself with a body and the world, cannot know the reality, about them. If he as a spectator, by isolating himself from them, beholds them, he comes to know the reality, that he, as a portion of the Lord is eternal, while they are perishable. But, those who surrender themselves to God and become one with Him, without having any separate entity of their own, know the Lord. In them, not only 'I'ness and 'mineness' are gone, but also there should be left not even a trace of these.

When, a man identifies himself with a body, he feels the pleasure and pain of the body as his own, and cannot realize, that he is different from the body. Similarly, when a man realizes, that being a portion of the Lord, he is one with Him, he is not, at all affected, by any change, which happens either, in the body or the world. His actions, are automatically performed by God's will. He becomes one with the Lord. As Rādhājī, is one with Lord Kṛṣṇa, both of them are one and the same, but to exchange love, the Lord has manifested Himself, in two forms. This is His sport of union and disunion. In their union, there is a feeling of disunion and in their disunion, there is a feeling for union. Thus, union and disunion strengthen each other, and in this process there is enhancement of spiritual love, which cannot be, expressed in words. This state of enhancement, of indescribable spiritual love, is God-realization.

Harmony of the Topic, in the Seventh and the Ninth Chapters—

At the beginning of the seventh chapter, Lord Kṛṣṇa declared, that He would teach Arjuna, knowledge (wisdom) with realization (real knowledge of manifest Divinity) (7/2). The flow of the Lord's gospel, was interrupted when Arjuna, put questions at the beginning of the eighth chapter. So, when the eighth chapter was over, Lord Kṛṣṇa, at the beginning of the ninth chapter, restarted the same topic, of the seventh chapter Himself, by declaring, "To you, who do not cavil, I shall now unfold the most profound Knowledge with Realization" (Gītā 9/1). The topic, which was explained, in thirty verses in the seventh chapter, continued in thirty-four verses of the ninth chapter, and first eleven verses of the tenth chapter. Arjuna was very much influenced by Lord Kṛṣṇa's gospel, and so he recalls the Lord's glories, from the twelfth to the eighteenth verses, of the tenth chapter. It means, that the topic mentioned in the seventh chapter, has also been explained in the ninth chapter.

The topic, which was explained in the first verse of the seventh chapter by the terms, 'With the mind attached to Me' in brief, has been explained in detail, in the thirty-fourth verse of the ninth chapter by the terms, 'Fix your mind on Me' etc.

In the second verse of the seventh chapter, the Lord declared, "I shall unfold to you in full, this knowledge combined with realization, having known which, nothing else, remains to be known." The same statement, has been made by Him, in the first verse of the ninth chapter, when He declares, "I shall unfold this knowledge with realization, by knowing which, you will be released from evil." By being released from evil, nothing remains, to be known. Thus, the Lord unfolded the knowledge with realization, and its fruit.

In the third verse of the seventh chapter the Lord, declared, "Among thousands of men, scarcely one strives for perfection, and of those who strive, scarcely one knows Me, in truth." Why does, scarcely one know Him, in truth? The answer comes, in the third verse of the ninth chapter, "Men having no faith in Dharma (Knowledge with Realization), failing to reach Me, whirl in the path of mortal world."

In the sixth verse of the seventh chapter and in the eighteenth verse of the ninth chapter, He declared, "I am the origin and the end, of the entire world."

In the tenth verse of the seventh chapter, He declared, "I am the eternal seed of all beings." In the eighteenth verse of the ninth chapter He declared, "I am the imperishable seed."

In the twelfth verse of the seventh chapter, by declaring, "Neither I exist in them, nor do they exist in Me" the Lord described in brief, the sovereign science, which has been described in detail, in the fourth and fifth verses of the ninth chapter.

In the thirteenth verse of the seventh chapter, the Lord declared the whole of the creation, to be deluded by objects evolved from the three modes of Nature, while in the eighth verse of the ninth chapter, He declared the whole multitude of beings helpless under the regime of Nature.

In the fourteenth verse of the seventh chapter, the Lord declared, "Those who take refuge in Me alone, cross this divine illusion, of Mine." In the twenty-second verse of the ninth chapter, He declared, "Those who worship Me alone, thinking of no one else, who are ever devout, I provide gain and security."

In the fifteenth verse of the seventh chapter, He declared, "The evil-doers, the deluded, do not worship Me", while in the eleventh verse of the ninth chapter He declared, "Fools do not know, My supreme nature."

Again, in the fifteenth verse of the seventh chapter, He declared, "They have embraced the demoniac nature" while in the twelfth verse of the ninth chapter, He declared, "Those senseless persons have embraced a demoniacal nature."

What, in the sixteenth verse of the seventh chapter, has been called 'virtuous', the same in the thirteenth verse of the ninth chapter, has been called a 'great soul'.

In the seventh chapter from the sixteenth to the eighteenth verses, there is description of four types of virtuous men, while in the ninth chapter from the thirtieth to the thirty-third verse, there is explanation of seven types of devotees, according to their caste, conduct and sex.

In the nineteenth verse of the seventh chapter He declared, "The man of realization, realizes, that all this is God," while, in the nineteenth verse of the ninth chapter, He declared, "I am being and non-being, both."

A devotee having a disinclination for the Lord, worships the gods either, because he wants his desires to be fulfilled by them, or he does not know, the Lord in reality. In the twentieth verse of the seventh chapter, there is a description of those whose discrimination has been carried away by various desires, and so they worship other gods, while in the twenty-third verse of the ninth chapter, there is description of those, who worship other gods, because they don't recognize (know) the Lord, in reality.

In the twenty-third verse of the seventh chapter, there is description of those who by worshipping other gods, craving for some worldly fruit, gain perishable fruit, while in the twenty-first verse of the ninth chapter, there is the description of those who as a result of their deeds, enjoy celestial pleasures in heaven, and then return to this world of mortals, when their merits are exhausted.

In the twenty-third verse of the seventh chapter, the Lord declared, "The worshippers of gods, attain the gods, whereas My devotees, attain Me alone." The same fact, has been pointed out, in the twenty-fifth verse of the ninth chapter.

In the first part of the twenty-fourth verse of the seventh chapter, the Lord declared, "Men of poor understanding think of Me, the unmanifest, as having manifestation and take me as an ordinary human being not knowing my supreme Nature" while, in the first part of the eleventh verse of the ninth chapter, He declared, "Fools don't know My higher nature, as the Great Lord of beings." Similarly, in the second part of the twenty-fourth verse of the seventh chapter, the Lord declared, "Men of poor understanding don't know My supreme state, immutable and unsurpassed", while in the second part of the eleventh verse of the ninth chapter, He declared, "Fools don't know My supreme nature, as the great Lord of beings."

In the twenty-seventh verse of the seventh chapter, the Lord said, "All beings are subject to illusion at birth", while, the same fact has been pointed out by Him, in the third verse of the ninth chapter, when He declared, "Men return to the path of the mortal world."

In the thirtieth verse of the seventh chapter, the Lord has laid special emphasis on the knowing Him in entirety while, in the thirty-fourth verse of the ninth chapter, He has laid special emphasis on the fact, that one should entirely depend on Him, (surrender one self to Him).

Appendix—In this verse the important point is 'the change of ego'. A devotee changes his ego by accepting the fact 'I am God's' and connects the self with God. He instead of depending on his spiritual practice, depends on God. Therefore he has not to renounce attachment to the world, but it is naturally renounced. The reason is that 'Varṇa' (order of life), 'Āśrama' (stage of life), caste, ability, right (authority), action and qualities etc., to which he is attached may be different but they are all transient, they appear and disappear but affinity of God with the self is not transient but it is beginningless, eternal and axiomatic.

ॐ तत्सदिति श्रीमद्भगवद्गीतासूपनिषत्सु ब्रह्मविद्यायां योगशास्त्रे श्रीकृष्णार्जुनसंवादे राजविद्याराजगुह्ययोगो नाम नवमोऽध्यायः ॥ ९ ॥

oṁ tatsaditi śrīmadbhagavadgītāsūpaniṣatsu brahmavidyāyāṁ yogaśāstre śrīkṛṣṇārjunasaṁvāde rājavidyārājaguhyayogo nāma navamo'dhyāyaḥ

Thus reciting Oṁ, Tat, Sat, the names of the Lord, in the Upaniṣad of the Bhagavadgītā, the knowledge of Brahma, the Supreme, the scripture of Yoga and the dialogue between

Śrī Kṛṣṇa and Arjuna, this is the ninth designated discourse: "The Yoga of Sovereign Science and Sovereign Secret."

Words, letters and Uvāca (said) in the Ninth Chapter—

(1) In this chapter in **'Atha navamo'dhyāyaḥ'**, there are three words, in **'Śrībhagavānuvāca'**, there are two words in verses, there are four hundred and forty-six words and there are thirteen concluding words. Thus the total number of words, is four hundred and sixty-four.

(2) In **'Atha navamo'dhyāyaḥ'** there are seven letters, in **'Śrībhagavānuvāca'**, there are seven letters, in verses, there are one thousand, one hundred and twelve letters, and there are fifty-one concluding letters. Thus, the total of letters, is one thousand, one hundred and seventy-seven. Out of the thirty-four verses of this chapter, the twentieth and the twenty-first verses, are each of forty-four letters, while each of the remaining thirty-two verses, is of thirty-two letters.

(3) In this chapter there is one **'Uvāca'** (said) **Śrībhagavānuvāca'.**

Metres Used in the Ninth Chapter

In this chapter, out of the thirty-four verses, in the twentieth and twenty-first verses, there is **'Upajāti'** metre. Out of the remaining thirty-two verses in the first quarter of the first verse 'bha-gaṇa' and in the third quarter 'na-gaṇa', being used, there is **'saṅkīrṇavipulā'** metre; in the first quarter of the second verse, 'ra-gaṇa' being used, there is **'ra-vipulā'** metre; in the first quarter of the third, and tenth verses 'bha-gaṇa' being used, there is **'bha-vipulā'** metre; in the first quarter of the seventeenth verse and in the third quarter of the thirteenth and twenty-sixth verses 'na-gaṇa' being used, there is **'na-vipulā'** metre. The remaining twenty-five verses, are possessed of the characteristics of right **'pathyāvaktra'** Anuṣṭup metre.

II Shri Hari II

Tenth Chapter

INTRODUCTION

In the seventh chapter, Lord Kṛṣṇa while clarifying knowledge with realization actually He was unfolding the secrets of His heart. But Arjuna put some questions, in between. So the Lord answered his questions and then reverted to the previous topic in the ninth chapter, and concluded it, by advising exclusive surrender, to the Lord. But He was not satisfied with what He had already said to Arjuna. As a devotee wants to know of His glories in detail (Gītā 10/18), He also wanted to say something secret to His loving devotee, Arjuna. So, by His grace without being asked by Arjuna, He starts the topic, in the tenth chapter.

श्रीभगवानुवाच

भूय एव महाबाहो शृणु मे परमं वचः।
यत्तेऽहं प्रीयमाणाय वक्ष्यामि हितकाम्यया॥ १॥

śrībhagavānuvāca

bhūya eva mahābāho śṛṇu me paramaṁ vacaḥ
yatte'haṁ prīyamāṇāya vakṣyāmi hitakāmyayā

The Blessed Lord said:

Once again, O mighty-armed, listen to My supreme word, which I shall convey to you, who are so loving, and out of solicitude for your welfare. 1

Comment:—

'Bhūya eva'—The knowledge of glories of the Lord, promote devotion. So the Lord by His grace, in the seventh chapter (from the 8th to the 12th verses) mentioned, His seventeen glories and in the ninth chapter (from the 16th to 19th verses) mentioned His thirty-seven glories. Here, in order to tell some more glories* and to supplement the glory of devotion mentioned (in Gītā 8/14 and 9/22, 34) the Lord uses the expression 'Bhūya eva' (Again verily) to explain His devotion in a special way.

'Śṛṇu me paramaṁ vacaḥ'—The Lord wants to narrate His supremacy and glories to Arjuna, because he is His devout devotee. So He asks him, to listen to His supreme word.

Secondly, whenever Lord Kṛṣṇa wants to disclose His secret to Arjuna, He uses such terms, as 'supreme words' etc., as in the third verse of the fourth chapter, he said, "This secret is supreme" because He who taught the immortal Yoga to the sun-god was sitting before him and was driving his horses, and also, in the sixty-fourth verse of the eighteenth chapter, He says to Arjuna, "Listen again to My supreme word" and His supreme word is "Surrendering all duties to Me, seek refuge in Me alone. I shall liberate you from all sins; grieve not" (Gītā 18/66). Here, in this context, the Lord says that diverse feelings of creatures, emanate from Him alone and His devotees, such as the seven great seers, four Sanaka etc., and fourteen Manus were born of His will i.e., He, is the root of all of them.

While talking about knowledge (wisdom), in the thirteenth chapter, He continues the same topic, in the fourteenth chapter; similarly explaining the topic of knowledge with realization, in the seventh and ninth chapters, He continues, it in the tenth chapter. At the beginning of the fourteenth chapter He declares, that He shall impart to him once more, supreme knowledge, the best of all forms of knowledge, while at the beginning of the tenth chapter here, He says to Arjuna to listen to His supreme word, which means that in the Discipline of Knowledge, there

* In the tenth chapter the Lord has mentioned His forty-five glories from the fourth to the sixth verses.

is Predominance of discrimination, while in the Discipline of Devotion, there is predominance, of reverence and faith.

'Yatte'haṁ prīyamāṇāya vakṣyāmi hitakāmyayā'—If a listener has reverence and faith, in the speaker and the speaker has a feeling for the welfare of the listener, whatever he says, sinks down in, the mind of the listener. Thus, the listener's devotion to the Lord, grows.

Now, a doubt arises, that the Lord, again and again, has laid emphasis on rooting out desires, but here, He Himself has a desire. The clarification is, that when a person has desire for his pleasures and prosperity etc., that is called a desire and is harmful. But when there is a desire to do good to others, that is not desire, that is renunciation (i.e.,) the means, to root out a desire. Therefore, the Lord, teaches a lesson to the beings, that as He is engrossed, in the welfare of all beings, they should also have dealings with others, for their welfare. By doing so, their desires are easily wiped out, and they attain Him. "Those who are engaged in the welfare of all beings, come unto Me (Who is endowed with attributes)" (Gītā 12/4). "Those who are actively engaged in the welfare of all beings, attain the Beatitude of Brahma" (Gītā 5/25).

Appendix—Arjuna, after coming to the battlefield, instead of desiring victory, wants to attain salvation, therefore he has been addressed as 'mahābāho'. This vocative denotes Arjuna's superiority, ability to grasp the Lord's gospel and his right to grasp it.

'Paramaṁ vacaḥ'—The Lord's word is 'parama' viz., supreme because it leads beings to salvation. The Gītā is loving and adorable to the entire universe because it enables the people to attain salvation.

'Vakṣyāmi hitakāmyayā'—Arjuna is a representative of all beings and he wants to attain the highest good (bliss).* Therefore

* 'yacchreyaḥ syānniścitaṁ brūhi tanme' (Gītā 2/7)
'tadekaṁ vada niścitya yena śreyo'hamāpnuyām' (Gītā 3/2)
'yacchreya etayorekaṁ tanme brūhi suniścitam' (Gītā 5/1)

the Lord utters supreme word for the welfare of all the people. There is no other good for human beings besides salvation. The Lord's utterance leads people to salvation and their aim is also to attain salvation. Therefore the Lord's utterances are imbued with the supreme good of human beings. No one can do as much good to mankind as God can—

umā rāma sama hita jaga māhīṁ,
guru pitu mātu bandhu prabhu nāhīṁ.

(Mānasa, Kiṣkindhā 12/1)

There are differences of opinions as far as the utterances of others are concerned, but the utterances of the Lord are universal truth. The Lord is preaching the gospel of the Gītā being established in Yoga*. Therefore His utterances are specially benedictory. What is God's establishment in Yoga? Generally God is the Supreme disinterested friend of all beings, but when a person keenly eager, takes refuge in Him, then a tide of emotions for his welfare surges up in Lord's mind—this is the Lord's establishment in Yoga.† Even as the udder of the cow gets wet with milk out of affection for her calf on seeing it before her.

'Yatte'haṁ prīyamāṇāya vakṣyāmi hitakāmyayā'—In this expression the Lord says to Arjuna, "You love Me by heart and I have the feeling for your welfare from the core of My heart, therefore I shall again unfold to you 'Jñāna' with 'Vijñāna' which I have already unfolded to you in the seventh and in the

---

* na śakyaṁ tanmayā bhūyastathā vaktumaśeṣataḥ
paraṁ hi brahma kathitaṁ yogayuktena tanmayā

(Mahābhārata Āśva. 16/12-13)

"The Lord said to Arjuna—The repetition of whole gospel of the Gītā in the same way is out of My power. At that time I described the divinity (Godhood) by getting established in Yoga."

† brūyuḥ snigdhasya śiṣyasya guravo guhyamapyuta (Śrīmadbhā. 1/1/8; 10/13/3)

'The preceptors disclose even the most profound secret to their loving disciple.'

'gūḍhau tattva na sādhu durāvahiṁ, ārata adhikārī jahā̐ pāvahiṁ.

(Mānasa, Bāla. 110/1)

ninth chapters." It proves that the Lord in the seventh, ninth and tenth—these three chapters has outpoured his heart for the welfare of all beings.

Link:—Why does the Lord Himself declare His supreme word? The clarification is.

न मे विदुः सुरगणाः प्रभवं न महर्षयः।
अहमादिर्हि देवानां महर्षीणां च सर्वशः॥२॥

na me viduḥ suragaṇāḥ prabhavaṁ na maharṣayaḥ
ahamādirhi devānāṁ maharṣīṇāṁ ca sarvaśaḥ

Neither gods (devatā) nor the great sages (ṛṣis) know the secret of My origin; for I am the prime cause, in all respects of gods, as well as, the great sages. 2

Comment:—

'Na me viduḥ suragaṇāḥ prabhavaṁ na maharṣayaḥ'—Though, bodies, intellects, worlds and materials of the gods, are divine, yet they do not know, the Lord's origin, of His incarnations and His divine glories etc. They are unable to know Him, in His entire form; and His vision is difficult, for them. They are, always eager to behold His form (Gītā 11/52).

Even seers or liberated souls, possessing uncommonly divine powers, who have risen above the world, don't know, the secret of His origin, completely.

Here the Lord has mentioned gods and great seers, having divine experience, because the gods, hold the highest rank next to the Lord, and great seers possess, the highest knowledge. They do not know Him, because whatever power, intellect, resources, they have at their disposal, have been given by the Lord and so, these are limited. So, how can the limitless Lord, be known by limited power and resources etc.? As the birth and marriage of a mother, remains beyond the access of a son, the gods and the seers, who emanate from the Lord, don't know Him, who is their cause. The effect can merge in the cause, but cannot know it. Similarly, seers cannot know Him, their cause. They can merge in Him. The whole universe including the gods and the seers, emanates from Him, and merges into Him.

Gods and sages cannot know the beginning, the end and the interim (the present), of the Lord and how He is and in how many forms, He has manifested Himself. They cannot know His dimensions and limits. The reason is, that He was the same, when they were born and He will remain the same when they merge or die. So, how can they, whose bodies are born and die, know the beginningless, endless and limitless God, with their limited intellect, ability and power etc. How can the limitless be confined to a limited intellect?

In the fourteenth verse of this chapter, also the Lord declares, that neither the gods nor the demons know His manifestation, because the gods are ever engaged in enjoying heavenly pleasures, while demons in knavery and beguilement. Thus, gods have no time to know, Him and demons cannot know Him, by their knavery and beguilement.

Appendix—Whatever the Lord declared in the third verse of the seventh chapter by the expression 'manuṣyāṇāṁ sahasreṣu', He declares the same here by the expression 'na me viduḥ'. Why do they not know God? The reason is that He is the prime cause, in all respects of gods, as well as of the great sages. In the twenty-sixth verse of the seventh chapter also the Lord declared, "I know the created beings of the past, the present and the future but no one knows Me." Therefore Arjuna also in the fourteenth and fifteenth verses says, "Neither the gods nor the demons know You but You alone know Yourself by Yourself."

In this verse the Lord has disclosed His sovereign secret. The Lord is not known by knowledge, intellect, ability and power etc., but He is known by the faith and belief of the inquisitive devotee and by His own grace.

Link:—In the previous verse, it has been mentioned that neither gods nor great sages, know the secret of His origin, How then, can an ordinary striver, know Him and attain salvation? The Lord answers.

यो मामजमनादिं च वेत्ति लोकमहेश्वरम्।
असम्मूढः स मर्त्येषु सर्वपापैः प्रमुच्यते॥ ३॥

yo māmajamanādiṁ ca vetti lokamaheśvaram
asammūḍhaḥ sa martyeṣu sarvapāpaiḥ pramucyate

He who knows Me as unborn and without a beginning, as the Great Lord of the world, he, undeluded among men, is purged of all sins. 3

Comment:—

'Yo māmajamanādiṁ ca vetti lokamaheśvaram'—Though, a striver cannot know the Lord in His entirety, yet he can know Him so much, that he can attain salvation. His knowledge about Him is that he can assume that the Lord is unborn, without beginning and He is the Lord of all the lords, of the different worlds. The Lord, is beyond time. The time which is referred in the world by days and months etc., is ordinary time, while the Lord is beyond time. This time rests in the Lord. The Lord is, eternal time. Such firm assumption removes, all doubts about His glories.

'Asammūḍhaḥ sa martyeṣu sarvapāpaiḥ pramucyate'—The Lord, is birthless, beginningless and is the Lord of all the lords. It means, that He is imperishable and the supreme sovereign, of the world. So, He pervades everywhere, everytime, all things and is the Lord of everyone. It means, that He is here, now, in him and his Lord also, while the world, is perishing every moment. Thus knowing the reality about the Lord, and the world, one renounces his affinity with the world (including the body) and becomes free from the feeling of, 'I'ness and 'Mineness'. Thus, knowing the truth, he is no more deluded and by becoming free, from the feeling of 'I'ness and 'Mineness', he has affinity with the Lord, and becomes free from all sins, of the present and the past. Mere learning of affinity with God, will not serve the purpose. It is to be given a practical shape.

What is delusion? Delusion means, lack of knowledge, about reality. What is reality? The reality is, that a man cannot be identified with, the world and the body, while he cannot be separated, from the Lord. The man, who is free from this delusion can know Him, endowed with attributes and without attribute, endowed with form and formless in reality, and has not the least doubt, about His different forms, sports, secrets and glories etc.

Appendix—In the twenty-fourth verse of the ninth chapter the Lord by the negative inference said, "He who does not know Me, has a fall." Here by the positive inference He says, "He who knows Me, is purged of all sins."

Here the term 'vetti' means—'to accept firmly and undoubtedly' because God cannot be known by senses, mind and intellect (Gītā 10/2). Therefore God is not to be known but He is to be believed and realized. When even prakṛti cannot be known, then how can God, Who is beyond Prakṛti, be known? Realization means—to merge the self into God and to be one with Him by losing his independent identity. By becoming 'abhinna' God can be known, because in fact he (the self) is not apart from Him, he is 'abhinna' with Him. Similarly the world can be known by becoming detached from the world because in fact he is detached from it.

The great sages don't know the secret of His origin but they do know that the Lord is unborn and without a beginning. The self, being a fragment of God, is also unborn and without a beginning. Therefore when he knows the Lord as unborn and without a beginning, he will know the self also the same (unborn and without a beginning) because the self by becoming identified (abhinna) with God knows God. By knowing the self as unborn and without a beginning, he becomes undeluded, then how will sins stay in him? The reason is that sins have accrued afterwards, the self is unborn and without beginning from time immemorial. 'Sarvapāpaiḥ pramucyate' means—to be free from attachment to the modes. So long as a man is attached to the modes, he can't be purged of sins because attachment to the modes is the root of sins.

In the verses fourth to sixth ahead there is discussion on non-delusion in which the Lord has declared Himself to be the origin of all. The Lord Himself is without beginning and is the origin of diverse feelings and great sages.

Link:—The Lord, in the next three verses, explains His supreme word, which He mentioned in the first verse.

बुद्धिर्ज्ञानमसम्मोहः क्षमा सत्यं दमः शमः ।
सुखं दुःखं भवोऽभावो भयं चाभयमेव च ॥ ४ ॥
अहिंसा समता तुष्टिस्तपो दानं यशोऽयशः ।
भवन्ति भावा भूतानां मत्त एव पृथग्विधाः ॥ ५ ॥

buddhirjñānamasammohaḥ kṣamā satyaṁ damaḥ śamaḥ
sukhaṁ duḥkhaṁ bhavo'bhāvo bhayaṁ cābhayameva ca
ahiṁsā samatā tuṣṭistapo dānaṁ yaśo'yaśaḥ
bhavanti bhāvā bhūtānāṁ matta eva pṛthagvidhāḥ

Intellect, wisdom, non-delusion, forgiveness, truth, self-restraint (control over the mind and the senses), joy (pleasure), and sorrow (pain), evolution and dissolution, fear and fearlessness, non-violence, equanimity, contentment, austerity, charity, fame and disrepute—these diverse feelings of creatures, emanate from Me alone. 4-5

Comment:—

'Buddhiḥ'—It is the faculty, of deciding something, with an aim.

'Jñānam'—It is discrimination, between the real and the unreal, the proper and the improper, the imperishable and the perishable etc. This discrimination, has been bestowed upon every human being, by God.

'Asammohaḥ'—It is non-delusion. To have a feeling of 'I'ness and 'Mineness', with a perishable body and the world, is delusion and its absence, is non-delusion.

'Kṣamā'—Whatever harm, a man may cause, if we bear it in spite of possessing power, to punish him and we have a sentiment, that he should not be punished by God, here or hereafter. This sentiment is called 'Kṣamā'.

'Satyam'—Truth, is the accurate presentation for the welfare of all of what one has heard, seen and known, without selfishness and pride.

'Damaḥ śamaḥ'—By having, the aim of God-realization, control over senses is called 'Damaḥ' and control over the mind, so that it may not think of mundane pleasures is called 'Śamaḥ'.

'Sukhaṁ duḥkham'—Feelings of pleasure in favourable circumstances, is 'Sukham', and feelings of pain, in unfavourable circumstances, is 'Duḥkham'.

'Bhavo'bhāvaḥ'—'Bhava', means birth or evolution of a thing, being and incident etc., while 'Abhāva', means their death or dissolution.

'Bhayaṁ cābhayameva ca'—A feeling of possibility of some undesired result as a fruit of actions, against the saints, scriptures or the social customs is 'Bhaya' (Fear), and lack of fear is 'Abhaya' (Fearlessness).

'Ahiṁsā'—To hurt others, with body, mind and speech etc., in all climes, times and circumstances, is violence and absence of violence is 'Ahiṁsā' (Non-violence).

'Samatā'—Evenness of mind or temper, in favourable and unfavourable circumstances, is 'samatā' (equanimity).

'Tuṣṭiḥ'—Contentment, in all circumstances, is 'Tuṣṭiḥ'.

'Tapaḥ'—To bear all circumstances happily while performing one's duty is 'Tapaḥ', (austerity). To observe a fast on 'ekādaśī' etc., is also, austerity.

'Dānam'—It is a gift of objects or money, earned by honest means, which is made to a deserving person happily, without having any desire, for the fruit of action (Gītā 17/20).

'Yaśo'yaśaḥ'—Fame, that a man receives as an outcome of his good qualities, feelings and actions, is 'Yaśa' while 'Ayaśaḥ' is ill-fame or disrepute, that a man acquires as outcome of his bad conduct, feelings and deeds.

'Bhavanti bhāvā bhūtānāṁ matta eva pṛthagvidhāḥ'— Diverse feelings, of creatures emanate, from the Lord i.e., He is the base and the root, of all of them.

Here 'Mattaḥ', stands for Lord's power and influence, while 'Pṛthagvidhāḥ' stands, for His divine glories.

One who knows, that all of the good or bad actions and feelings, in the world are nothing but the sport of the Lord gets firmly established in Him, (Gītā 10/7).

Out of the twenty diverse feelings mentioned here, twelve have been called as single and they are all born in the mind. Besides these fearlessness, which makes a pair with fear, is also born in the mind. The remaining seven feelings, are contradictory. Out of these evolution and dissolution, fame and disrepute—these four are fruits of previous actions, while pleasure, pain and fear—these three, are an outcome of folly. A man, is free in wiping out this folly.

The Lord, is the base and root of all these twenty feelings. In the twelfth verse of the seventh chapter also, He declares that whatever entities there are born of sattva (goodness), of rajas (passion) and tamas (ignorance), know them all, as evolved from Him, alone.

Therefore, the purpose of the Lord is to draw attention towards Him, Who is the source of all divine glories and feelings.

An Important Fact

Whatever a striver, beholds in the world, is the Lord's manifestation, and His sport. His sport, includes His pranks of boyhood at Ayodhyā where He incarnates as Rāma, there He is loved by His father, mother and other people. He is received and shown hospitality, by His father-in-law and mother-in-law, and other people of Janakapurī. Then, His sport continues in the woods, where He comes across, both devotees and demons. Afterwards, in Laṅkā his sport, includes battle and bloodshed. Thus, all these sport have been included in the Rāmāyaṇa. Similarly, all the feelings, actions, whether similar or dissimilar, are the sports of the Lord. So a striver should always behold him, only in various persons, things, incidents and feelings etc., because, He is at the root of all of them.

Appendix—From the point of view of knowledge, all feelings emanate from prakṛti, but from the view-point of devotion, all feelings emanate from God. If these feelings are regarded of the self, the self being the 'parā prakṛti' (higher nature) of God, is inseparable (one) with God, therefore these feelings are also of God only. In God these feelings ever persist but in the self they appear and disappear because of its attachment to the aparā (lower nature). As these feelings emanate from God, so they are all the manifestations of God.

'Pṛthagvidhāḥ'—This expression means that as a hand is one but in it there are different fingers, similarly God is one but the feelings, which emanate from Him, are different. Though the

Lord is the same yet different types of opposite feelings persist simultaneously in Him.

महर्षयः सप्त पूर्वे चत्वारो मनवस्तथा।
मद्भावा मानसा जाता येषां लोक इमाः प्रजाः ॥ ६ ॥

maharṣayaḥ sapta pūrve catvāro manavastathā
madbhāvā mānasā jātā yeṣāṁ loka imāḥ prajāḥ

The seven great seers, the more ancient four Sanaka etc., and fourteen Manus, who are all devoted to Me, are born of My will and all the creatures forming the world, have come forth from them. 6

Comment:—

[In the previous verses, the Lord mentioned His twenty glories, in the form of feelings. Now in this verse, He mentions His twenty-five divine glories, in the form of persons, who are administrators, of the entire creation.]

'Maharṣayaḥ sapta'—The seven great seers, are those who possess seven qualities—they are long lived, they have revealed sacred formulas, they are glorious, they possess divine vision, they are learned, they have realized righteousness, and they are inventors of 'Gotras' (sub-castes). These seven seers are—Marīci, Aṅgirā, Atri, Pulastya, Pulaha, Kratu and Vasiṣṭha. They know Vedas, and are reputed as annotators of the Vedas. They are administrators, of creation and are appointed to help Brahmā, the creator, in his work.

'Pūrve catvāraḥ'—Sanaka, Sanandana, Sanātana and Sanatkumāra, were the first to be born, of the mind of Brahmā, after he did penance. They are manifestations of the Lord. They always remain, children of five years. They wander in the three worlds, to promulgate devotion, knowledge (wisdom) and dispassion. They always utter the words 'Hari Śaraṇam' (Refuge in the Lord). They love divine discourses, and so one of them holds divine discourses and the other three, listen to him.

'Manavastathā'—In a day of Brahmā, which consists of 43,20,000,000 years of mortals, there are fourteen Manus. They are Svāyambhūva, Svarociṣa, Uttama, Tāmasa, Raivata, Cākṣuṣa, Vaivasvata, Sāvarṇi, Dakṣasāvarṇi, Brahmasāvarṇi, Dharmasāvarṇi, Rudrasāvarṇi, Devasāvarṇi and Indrasāvarṇi.* They are creators and activators of the world, by carrying out Brahmā's orders.

'Mānasā jātāḥ'—They are born of the mind of Brahmā, in order to create the universe. So they can be called, Brahmā's sons. They can also be called the Lord's sons, because the Lord manifested Himself as Brahmā, in order to create the world. The whole creation, is the product of the Lord's mind.

'Madbhāvā'—They are all devoted to the Lord.

'Yeṣāṁ loka imāḥ prajāḥ'—There are two types of creatures, in the world—those born of the contact of the male and female, and those born of word (sacred word or text) or preaching. The former, are called 'Binduja' while the latter are called 'Nādaja'.

All the great saints and souls of the past, the present and the future, following the path of renunciation, as well as Sanaka etc., who were not married, belong to the latter type, while the off-springs born of seven great sages and fourteen Manus, who were married, belong to the former category.

Appendix—The seven great sages, four Sanakas etc., and fourteen Manus— they are all born of the Lord's mind and therefore are inseparable (one) with God.

Link:—After mentioning His divine glories, in the form of feelings and persons, from the fourth verse to the sixth verse,

* A day of Brahmā consists of a thousand fourfold ages. Out of it one Manu rules over more than seventy-one fourfold ages. Now Brahmā is running in his fifty-first year in which the seventh Manu named Vaivasvata is ruling over.

now in the next verse, the Lord explains the fruit of knowledge, of divine glories.

एतां विभूतिं योगं च मम यो वेत्ति तत्त्वतः।
सोऽविकम्पेन योगेन युज्यते नात्र संशयः॥७॥

etāṁ vibhūtiṁ yogaṁ ca mama yo vetti tattvataḥ
so'vikampena yogena yujyate nātra saṁśayaḥ

He who knows, in reality, this divine glory and power of Mine, is endowed with unfaltering Yoga of devotion; of this there is no doubt. 7

Comment:—

'Etāṁ vibhūtiṁ yogaṁ ca mama'—'Etāṁ', stands for 'the near most'—His divine glories and Yoga power, described from the fourth to the sixth verses. 'Vibhūti', stands for His divine manifestations in the form of feeling and persons, glories and 'Yoga', stands for His singular infinite power. All His divine glories, are born of Him. Through the power with which these manifestations take place is His divine Yoga (Gītā 9/5). The same has been called, His supreme Yoga (Gītā 11/8) while, the Lord shows His macrocosmic form to Arjuna.

An Important Fact

When a man enjoys worldly pleasures, his power is mitigated, and the things are destroyed. Thus, there is a double loss. But, if he uses the things without deriving pleasure out of them, his power is not mitigated. Actually, there is no real joy, in enjoying sense-objects. Real joy, comes out of restraint. This self-control, can be classified into two kinds (i) Control over others (ii) Self-control. The first means, that the sorrows of others may be annihilated and they may become happy—with this sentiment to direct them, towards a virtuous path by deviating them from a wrong path. The second one, means, to renounce selfishness and pride, totally and not to enjoy pleasures, in the least. This twofold self-control, is known as 'Yoga' or 'power'. This Yoga or power, is innate in the Lord, while in other creatures, it is a result of practice.

When a man controls others, with egoistic and selfish feelings, he experiences a sort of joy. In this joy, his power is mitigated and he, whom he controls, becomes a slave. Therefore, instead of this control, there should be such control, in which there is no selfish or egoistic feeling, it involves welfare of others and their freedom from suffering since eternity and attainment of supreme bliss—this is excellent and is supreme control. At the top of it, stands the Lord's control, and that is called 'Yoga'.

The term 'Yoga', also stands for equanimity, union with God and power. The Lord is all-powerful. All power, comes from Him only. This power is partly revealed in man, if he becomes desireless. On having desires, the power decreases, and on effacement of desires, power is accumulated. By working continuously, this power is exhausted and by repose, it is gained, as a man gets tired, by speaking continuously, he regains power by silence. Power is lost in creation, and gained, in dissolution. It means, that power is mitigated by affinity with Nature, and regained by renunciation.

'Yo vetti tattvataḥ'—A discerning man, knows that whatever singularity is seen in the universe, is the power and glory of the Lord. As a goldsmith, while making ornaments of different kinds, always keeps in mind, that in them there is nothing besides gold, a striver should behold every person, object or action, as a manifestation of the Lord, because all persons and objects etc., are kaleidoscopic and perishable; so they have no singularity of their own. Whatever, singularity is seen in them, is the reflection of the Lord, Who is eternal and imperishable. Therefore, an onlooker should behold the Lord everywhere. This is real knowledge.*

* In this context of devotion 'Tattvataḥ vetti' (Knows in truth) should mean 'Assumption (Supposition) in truth.' When a man assumes that he belongs to a

'So'vikampena yogena yujyate'—He is endowed with, unfaltering devotion to the Lord i.e., he is attracted only towards, the Lord.

'Nātra saṁśayaḥ'—There is no doubt. It means, that after knowing the Lord in reality, a striver instead of paying attention to the divine glory and power, etc., beholds these only as a manifestation of the Lord i.e., he beholds only God. No worldly grandeur, can influence him. Thus, it fosters his devotion, to Him.

Appendix—Whatever singularity (speciality) is observed in the world, that is all the Lord's yoga viz., Lord's uncommon influence and power. The speciality which evolves from that uncommon influence, is 'vibhūti' (manifestation)—thus he who knows, in reality, this divine glory and power of God, is endowed with unfaltering devotion, of this there is no doubt. 'There is no other existence at all besides God'—this firm and doubtless acceptance is 'to know God in reality'. The Lord has called such a man, who knows in reality the divine glory and power of God, the man of wisdom viz., 'Jñānavān' (Gītā 7/19).

The Lord by the expression 'Avikampayoga' means to say that this 'Bhaktiyoga' neither shakes itself, nor anyone can shake it, because in it there is nothing else besides God.

All things can be bought by paying money—by thinking so, a common man values money and so he is attracted towards money. Similarly when a man holds that whatever majesty or value appears, that is all only God's, he is naturally attracted toward God and is endowed with unfaltering devotion for God.

The expression 'nātra saṁśayaḥ' means that when there is no other entity at all besides God, then how can there be any doubt in it? There is no room for doubt at all because a doubt

---

particular caste his assumption continues so long as he does not renounce it. That assumption is not true because that depends on affinity with the body and so can perish. But the assumption that the Lord is the root and origin of the entire universe is real. So it can never perish but changes into knowledge.

can arise only when there are two entities. When there is no one else besides God, then where will a striver have his inclination, why will he have it, in whom will he have it and how will he have it? Therefore the striver is endowed with unfaltering devotion in God—there is no doubt about it.

Link:—In the previous verse, Lord Kṛṣṇa explained that he who knows in reality His divine glory and power, is endowed with unfaltering Yoga of devotion. What is meant by unfaltering Yoga of devotion? The answer comes in the next verse.

अहं सर्वस्य प्रभवो मत्तः सर्वं प्रवर्तते।
इति मत्वा भजन्ते मां बुधा भावसमन्विताः॥ ८॥

ahaṁ sarvasya prabhavo mattaḥ sarvaṁ pravartate
iti matvā bhajante māṁ budhā bhāvasamanvitāḥ

I am the cause of the whole creation; from Me all things move. The wise knowing this and full of faith and devotion, continually worship Me viz., they take refuge in Me alone. 8

Comment:—

[Whatever, was said in the previous verse, that what is seen, heard and known is nothing besides the divine glory, of the Lord, is repeated in this verse. The power through which their manifestations appear is His divine yoga. It is expressed through the word Mattaḥ. Whatever, has been said in the seventh, eighth and ninth chapters, has been condensed in the first line of this verse.]

'Ahaṁ sarvasya prabhavaḥ'—The Lord is the material and efficient cause of all creatures, born through mind, word, semen, earth, womb, egg, sweat viz., He is the origin of the whole creation, sentient or insentient, moving or unmoving.* He is

* As the Lord has declared in the sixth verse of the seventh chapter that He is the source of the entire creation and in the fourth verse of the fourteenth

the material cause, as well as the efficient cause, of the entire creation. It means, that He has manifested Himself, in the form of the entire creation.

'Mattaḥ sarvaṁ pravartate'—Everything, in the world moves, because of the Lord. As electricity manifests itself, in various forms in instruments suited to those forms, the Lord, is the root of all the worldly actions.

'Ahaṁ sarvasya......pravartate'—The Lord says that a striver, instead of paying attention to various feelings, actions, things and persons etc., should behold the Lord, Who is the origin of all of them.

The Lord, uses the term 'Mattaḥ' (from Me), again and again, as in the seventh and the twelfth verse of the seventh chapter and fifth and the eighth verse of the tenth chapter, to emphasize the fact that all feelings, actions and creatures etc., emanate from Him, remain established in Him, and merge into Him. So if a striver, either knows or assumes this fact, that in the entire universe, there is nothing else, besides the Lord, he will have unwavering unity (Yoga), with Him.

Here, by giving the word 'Sarva' (All), two times, the Lord means to say that, only He is the creator and conductor, of the entire universe.

'Iti matvā bhāvasamanvitāḥ'—When strivers assume, that the Lord is the creator and conductor of the entire creation, and He is the supreme Lord and none is equal to Him, none will be equal to Him, and none can be equal to Him, they place their faith and devotion, in Him and their attention, never deviates from Him. In those devotees, who entirely depend on Him, divine traits such as equanimity, fearlessness, truthfulness etc., grows naturally. The reason is, that where there is Divinity, there are divine traits.

---

chapter that He is the seed giving father. Here He declares that He is the origin of the whole creation.

'Budhā'—They are wise because they behold the Lord, as the origin of entire creation. The same fact, has been pointed out, by the Lord in the eighteenth and the nineteenth verses of the fifteenth chapter, when He declares, "One who knows Me beyond perishable Matter and superior to the imperishable soul, knows Me, in reality and worships Me, with all his heart" (Gītā 15/18-19).

'Māṁ bhajante'—Uttering and loud chanting, of the name of the Lord, thinking of the Lord, meditation, listening to divine discourses, study of scriptures, such as the Gītā, the Rāmāyaṇa etc., all this is, worship. But the real worship is that in which a devotee, likes and loves nothing, besides the Lord. Forgetfulness of the Lord, is repugnant to their nature. Such absorption in God, is real worship.

An Important Fact

Every striver, should know that the Lord is the origin and the source of power, of all things, objects, creatures and persons. So the only aim of the life, should be God-realization. The Lord mentions His divine glories and power, in order to attract the attention of the strivers, towards Him. This fact, has been mentioned in the Gītā, several times—'He from whom is the emanation of all beings, by Whom all this is pervaded, should be worshipped through the performance of one's duty' (18/46). "The Lord Who dwells in the hearts of all beings and Who is the source of inspiration for them, they should seek refuge in Him alone, with all their heart" (18/61-62) etc.

The Disciplines of Action, Knowledge and Devotion are various disciplines for different strivers, according to their tastes and interests, but the above-mentioned knowledge, is very necessary, for all the strivers.

Appendix—People attach importance to money because things can be acquired (gained) by paying money. Things are gained by paying money but they don't evolve, but from God all things evolve and are also gained. Therefore those who realize God's glory instead of getting entangled in the greed for petty money, worship God—'sa sarvavidbhajati māṁ sarvabhāvena bhārata' (Gītā 15/19).

The Lord declares that all objects and persons emanate from Him (ahaṁ sarvasya prabhavaḥ) and He is the root of all actions (mattaḥ sarvaṁ pravartate). But a man (the self) by having affinity with objects and actions, by assuming them as his and by becoming their enjoyer and doer, gets bound. When he becomes the enjoyer of objects, the objects lead him to bondage, and when he becomes the doer of actions, the actions lead him to bondage. If he neither becomes an enjoyer nor a doer, there is no bondage for him.

Whatever glory is seen in the world is emanating from God. The fact has been mentioned in Gītā by the Lord by the term 'mattaḥ' several times as—

'mattaḥ parataraṁ nānyatkiñcidasti' (7/7)

"of this world there is no other cause or effect besides Me."

'matta eveti tānviddhi' (7/12)

'These (Sāttvika, Rājasa and Tāmasa) modes are evolved from Me—know them so.'

'bhavanti bhāvā bhūtānāṁ matta eva pṛthagvidhāḥ' (10/5)

'These diverse feelings (intellect, wisdom, non-delusion etc.,) of creatures emanate from Me alone.'

'mattaḥ smṛtir jñānamapohanaṁ ca' (15/15)

'I am the source of memory, knowledge and reasoning faculty.'

Link:—In the next verse, the Lord mentions the way of the worship, of those devotees.

मच्चित्ता मद्गतप्राणा बोधयन्तः परस्परम्।
कथयन्तश्च मां नित्यं तुष्यन्ति च रमन्ति च॥ ९॥*

* In this verse there are six points. A devotee has to do the first two

maccittā madgataprāṇā bodhayantaḥ parasparam
kathayantaśca māṁ nityaṁ tuṣyanti ca ramanti ca

With their minds fixed on Me, with their lives surrendered to Me, enlightening each other about My excellences and greatness and ever speaking of Me, they always remain contented and delighted with Me. 9

Comment:—

[Those who have realized, that the Lord is the origin and source of inspiration of all things and creatures, for them nothing remains to be done, to be known and to be acquired. They have ever, to be engrossed in Him. The same fact, has been explained in this verse.]

'Maccittā'—Their minds are fixed on the Lord. There are two things—one is the fixation of the mind on the Lord, and the second is fixation of the self on the Lord. When a devotee, by admitting the fact that he is the Lord's, is absorbed in Him, his mind, intellect etc., are automatically absorbed in Him, because, these organs depend on the doer. So, if a devotee worships the Lord and wants to fix his mind on Him, by thinking, that he is a worldly householder, it is very difficult for him to fix his mind. It means, that if he himself remains devoted to the world, and attempts to absorb his mind in God, it is practically impossible.

Secondly, a person can fix his mind on what he likes the most, and he likes the most a thing or person with whom he has affinity. So, a devotee should admit the fact, that he is only the Lord's and the Lord is only, his. The body and the world, are not his. So he surrenders himself to Him and His will, becomes his will. Such devotees, are said to have fixed their minds on God.

---

things himself—to fix his mind on Him and to surrender himself to Him. The next two points—enlightening each other and ever speaking of Him, occur when two devotees meet and the last two—contentment and the delight are the fruits of the first four.

In the Gītā 'Mana' and 'Citta', have been used in different senses (6/14) as well as, in the same sense. Here, it has been used in the same sense as in 7/4. It means that it includes both 'Mana' and 'Citta'.

'Madgataprāṇā'—They surrender their life and actions, spiritual as well as mundane to the Lord. Just like cowherdesses, they surrender their lives to Him. They are not attached to their vital force. They have, neither a desire to live, nor are afraid of death, because they know that they are different, from life and have no affinity with it, while their affinity with the Lord is axiomatic. So, a striver's only aim, should be to realize God without caring for favourable and unfavourable circumstances, such as health and sickness, respect, insult and pleasure and pain etc.

'Bodhayantaḥ parasparam'—When two devotees meet, they talk about the sport, secrets, qualities and glories of the Lord. Thus, they share His devotion, with each other and are more absorbed in Him.* They are enlightened, with the help of each other, in the same way, as darkness is dispelled from under two lighted earthen lamp, if they are placed, facing each other. Such devotion and enlightenment is not possible while concentrating alone.

'Kathayantaśca mām'—When they meet, any devotee who is interested in listening to, a divine discourse, they hold the discourse. As Sanaka etc., all the four hold divine discourses, and also listen to them. One of them, becomes a speaker and the other three become, the listeners. But the speaker is not proud of his talent, and the listener is not ashamed of his becoming, a listener.

Nityaṁ tuṣyanti ca'—Thus the exchange of those divine

* It is the nature of devotees that their organs of speech, ears and minds are applied respectively in uttering, hearing and thinking of the Lord's sports only. As lustful men relish sex talks, so do devotees relish the Lord's sports and stories (Śrīmadbhā. 10/13/2).

discourses relating to various sports, qualities, glories and secret etc., of the Lord, creates contentment. They get contentment, only in Him.

'Ramanti ca'—They take delight in him. In that state, they become one with Him, there is no difference in them. Sometimes, a devotee has devotion to the Lord, while at times the Lord, becomes a devotee to His own devotee. In this way, the sport of love, between the Lord and his devotee, continues for infinite ages and this love, enhances every moment.

Thus a striver should direct all his feelings and actions, towards the Lord.

Appendix—Here the Lord describes the unfaltering Yoga of devotion described in the seventh verse. The mind of devotees ever remains absorbed in God, it does not wander anywhere. From their view-point, when there is no other entity besides God, then where will their mind wander, how will it wander and why will it wander? Those devotees live alive only for God and all their actions are also surrendered to God. If anyone wants to listen to the Lord's qualities, glories, life history and sports etc., they narrate the extraordinary facts of the Lord's life to him, being absorbed in them (glories etc.,) and if anyone is interested in narrating them, the devotees listen to him by getting engrossed in them in a loving manner. In it neither the narrator nor the listener is contented. There is no contentment—this is disunion; and there is even new relish—this is union. Because of this disunion and union, the love is enhanced every moment. In the 'Nāradabhaktisūtra' it is mentioned—

'Kaṇṭhāvarodha romāñcāśrubhiḥ parasparaṁ lapamānāḥ pāvayanti kulāni pṛthivīṁ ca' (68)

'Such devotees having exclusive devotion, with choking throat, being thrilled, eyes filled with tears, talking about the glories of the Lord, sanctify their families and the entire earth.'

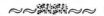

Link:—By explaining the way of the worship of devotees in the previous verse, now in the next two verses the Lord explains how He responds to devotional activities, of the devotees.

तेषां सततयुक्तानां भजतां प्रीतिपूर्वकम्।
ददामि बुद्धियोगं तं येन मामुपयान्ति ते॥ १०॥

teṣāṁ satatayuktānāṁ bhajatāṁ prītipūrvakam
dadāmi buddhiyogaṁ taṁ yena māmupayānti te

Upon them, ever devout and worshipping Me always with love, I confer that Yoga of wisdom (equanimity), by which they attain Me. 10

Comment:—

[A devotee of the Lord, has no desire to gain wisdom or equanimity or anything else, besides the Lord.* They ever remain absorbed in Him. So, their whole responsibility devolves on the Lord, they become mere instruments in His hands. So the Lord confers, the Yoga of wisdom, on them.]

'Teṣāṁ satatayuktānām'—'Ever steadfast', are those whose (according to the ninth verse), minds are fixed on Him, whose lives are surrendered to Him, who talk about the sport, secret, qualities and glories of the Lord and exchange these with one another, and who ever remain contented, and delighted, in Him.

'Bhajatāṁ prītipūrvakam'—Not to speak of, mundane pleasures and prosperity and occult powers, those devotees do not have a desire even for spiritual knowledge and dispassion. They always remain absorbed, in the Lord, without thinking of anything else, even in a dream.

'Dadāmi buddhiyogaṁ tam'—The Lord, confers on them the Yoga of wisdom viz., equanimity, by which they remain the

* The devotee, who has surrendered himself to Me, has no desire either for the posts of Brahmā, the creator and Indra, the king of the gods, or the kingdoms of the earth and the underworld or all the accomplishments of Yoga and even emancipation (Śrīmadbhā. 11/14/14).

same in favourable and unfavourable circumstances, profit and loss, honour and dishonour, praise and blame, and they think of equanimity as the Lord's gift, not their own achievement.

'Yena'—The devotees, by that equanimity, which is conferred on them by the Lord, attain Him.

'Māmupayānti te'—Those devotees, who surrender themselves to Him and remain contented and delighted in Him, attain Him i.e., they attain a state of perfection. Whatever deficiency they felt, is overcome.

Appendix—So long as attachment and aversion persist, only the world appears, the Lord is not visible. The Lord transcends the pairs of opposites. As long as there are pairs of opposites in the form of attachment and aversion, two entities instead of one appear. But when attachment and aversion are wiped out, then nothing is seen besides God. It means when attachment and aversion are wiped out and equanimity is attained, then 'all is God'—this is realized.' Therefore the Lord confers on His devotees equanimity. This equanimity is 'buddhiyoga' viz., Karmayoga—'samatvaṁ yoga ucyate' (Gītā 2/48). In the Gītā Karmayoga has been called 'buddhiyoga' as 'dūreṇa hyavaraṁ karma buddhiyogāddhanañjaya' (2/49), 'buddhiyogamupāśritya maccittaḥ satataṁ bhava' (18/57). Having attained buddhiyoga' (equanimity), a devotee by sharing the sorrows of others, tries to comfort (console) them.

One sort of reflection (thinking) is done intentionally and the other occurs naturally. Whatever reflection or adoration is done that is unnatural and which automatically occurs is natural. The reflection which is done, does not ever persist but the reflection which occurs, like breathing, ever persists continuously without any break—'satatayuktānām'. If a striver loves his body and is attached to it, he has to think of (reflect upon) God and the thoughts pertaining to body crop up automatically. But when there is true love for (one's ownness with) God, one has not to worship God but there is automatic worship which he can't escape. Therefore here is mention of worship with love—'bhajatāṁ prītipūrvakam'.

तेषामेवानुकम्पार्थमहमज्ञानजं तमः ।
नाशयाम्यात्मभावस्थो ज्ञानदीपेन भास्वता ॥ ११ ॥

teṣāmevānukampārthamahamajñānajaṁ tamaḥ
nāśayāmyātmabhāvastho jñānadīpena bhāsvatā

In order to bestow My grace upon them, I, dwelling in their self, destroy their darkness, born of ignorance, by the luminous lamp of wisdom. 11

Comment:—

'Teṣāmevānukampārthamahamajñānajaṁ tamaḥ'—Those devotees, have no desire to gain any mundane pleasure or prosperity etc. They do not even aspire, for salvation. They worship the Lord, with devotion without a desire for fruit. The Lord, is very much pleased with their devotion and His heart melts, with compassion. So, He wants to confer something on them. But they have no desire. So, by His grace He destroys their ignorance-born darkness, and enables them to attain perfection. He removes, all their deficiencies.

'Ātmabhāvasthaḥ'—Generally, people identify themselves, with their bodies, and consider the change of their bodies, as their own change. Actually, the self is different from the body. The Lord dwells, in that self.

'Bhāsvatā jñānadīpena nāśayāmi'—The Lord, destroys the ignorance-born darkness, by a luminous lamp of wisdom. It means, that He enables a devotee to realize the self, or to behold the Divine Presence, within himself. The devotee has not to practise, any spiritual discipline like hearing, thinking and assimilation etc. He has not to make any efforts, for Self-realization.

An Important Fact

When a devotee remains absorbed, only in the Lord, the Lord confers on him equanimity, as well as supremely holy Self-realization. It means, that the devotee has not to make efforts, either for equanimity or Self-realization,* because where, there is a mother in the form of devotion, there are as children dispassion and knowledge (Self-realization). It means, that the perfection attained by the aspirant, may have some deficiency. But the perfection conferred by the Lord, has not even a trace of imperfection.

As the Lord, provides gain and security to those devotees who worship Him, alone (Gītā 9/22), He confers equanimity and Self-realization to those devotees, who entirely depend on Him, though they have no desire. And even, by conferring equanimity and Self-realization, He remains a debtor to them. As the Lord, Himself declares in the Bhāgavata about the cowherdesses—"I can't pay the debt of the chaste cowherdesses, even by having the long age of the gods, because they broke the chain of domestic affinity, which even great seers and sages don't break, easily" (10/32/22).

The devotees, are so much absorbed in devotion for the Lord, that they are surprised to perceive equanimity and Self-realization in them. Moreover, they pray to God, that they should not feel any singularity in them, by having His gifts given to them by His grace, but they ever want to remain absorbed in devotion to Him. Even if, they are vouchsafed the power to emancipate the world, they don't feel elevated in anyway, and keep always absorbed, in God.

Appendix—Though Karmayoga and Jñānayoga—both these disciplines are the means while Bhaktiyoga (the Discipline of Devotion) is the end, yet the Lord confers on His devotees

* My devotees, besides service to Me, don't ever aspire for five kinds of salvation.

Karmayoga (equanimity)—'dadāmi buddhiyogaṁ tam' and also confers Jñānayoga—'jñānadīpena bhāsvatā'. Aparā (the lower) and parā (the higher)—both these prakṛtis (natures) are God's. Therefore the Lord by showering His grace, confers on His devotee Karmayoga in which there is predominance of aparā and also Jñānayoga in which there is predominance of parā. Therefore a devotee easily attains 'niṣkāmabhāva' (selflessness) which a Karmayogī wants to attain; and also Self-realization which a Jñānayogī wants to attain. Having attained Karmayoga, good to the world is done by a devotee and having attained Jñānayoga, the devotee's (self's) identification with the body is annihilated.

A devotee remains contented and engrossed in thinking of God and in loving Him. He neither feels that he lacks anything nor he feels that he needs to gain anything. As a child totally depends on its mother, it does not think of its needs. The mother fully takes care of it, she bathes it, she changes its clothes when they are dirty. Similarly when a devotee surrenders himself totally to God by holding, 'As I am, I am God's and only God is mine', he does not think of himself. Therefore the Lord, dwelling in his self, destroys his darkness, born of ignorance, by the luminous lamp of wisdom. A child is specially stupid (deluded) while a devotee is specially discriminative.

The main duty of a devotee is to assume the Lord as his own. When a devotee discharges his duty, the Lord also discharges His duty, and without the demand, without the desire of the devotee, of His own accord, confers on him the power of both—Karmayoga and Jñānayoga so that he may not lack anything.

In Karmayoga there is Bliss in the form of peace, in Jñānayoga there is constant Bliss (akhaṇḍarasa) and in Bhaktiyoga there is infinite (endless) Bliss (anantarasa). In 'śāntarasa' and 'akhaṇḍarasa'—'anantarasa' is not included but in 'anantarasa' both—'śāntarasa' and 'akhaṇḍarasa' are included.

Karmayoga and Jñānayoga are 'laukika' (worldly) disciplines but Bhaktiyoga is 'alaukika' (unworldly) discipline. Having attained the 'alaukika' by God's grace the 'laukika' is naturally attained but having attained the 'laukika' the 'alaukika' is not attained. The reason is that the 'laukika' is included in the 'alaukika' but in 'laukika' 'alaukika' is not included.

A jñānī can be devoid of devotion, but a devotee can't be devoid of knowledge (Self-realization).* The Gopīs did not study the Vedas, nor did they have association with the enlightened exalted souls nor did they observe fast (vows) and austerities etc.,† yet they possessed extraordinary knowledge‡. It means that a devotee realizes the self. He has already realized 'All is God'—'Vāsudevaḥ sarvam'.

'Ātmabhāvasthaḥ'—God abides in the self because the self is a fragment of God. In fact God has revealed Himself in the form of the soul (self) because being the parā prakṛti of God, the self is inseparable with God. In the Upaniṣad it is mentioned that the Lord having created the bodies, entered these bodies—'tatsṛṣṭvā tadevānuprāviśat' (Taittirīya. 2/6).

---

* mama darasana phala parama anūpā, jīva pāva nija sahaja sarūpā.

(Mānasa, Araṇya 36/5)

† te nādhīta śrutigaṇā nopāsitamahattamāḥ, avratātaptatapasaḥ satsaṅgānmāmupāgatāḥ. (Śrīmadbhā. 11/12/7)

"They neither studied the Vedas, nor had they methodical association with the exalted souls. Similarly they neither observed fasts (vows) such as kṛcchra-cāndrāyaṇa etc., nor did they undergo any austerity. But it was because of their satsaṅga (true love) for Me that they attained Me."

‡ na khalu gopikānandano bhavānakhiladehināmantarātmadṛk
vikhanasārthito viśvaguptaye sakha udeyivān sāttvatāṁ kule

(Śrīmadbhā. 10/31/4)

Gopīs say to Lord Kṛṣṇa—'O friend! you are decidedly not only the son of Yaśodā, but you are the witness of the innerself (soul) of all beings. Having heard the prayer of Brahmājī, You have manifested Yourself in Yadukula for the protection of the universe.'

Link:—After listening to the words of the Lord, pertaining to His uncommon grace, Arjuna being influenced by His grace, praises Him, by using several adjectives, in the next four verses.

अर्जुन उवाच

परं ब्रह्म परं धाम पवित्रं परमं भवान्।
पुरुषं शाश्वतं दिव्यमादिदेवमजं विभुम्॥ १२॥
आहुस्त्वामृषयः सर्वे देवर्षिर्नारदस्तथा।
असितो देवलो व्यासः स्वयं चैव ब्रवीषि मे॥ १३॥

arjuna uvāca

paraṁ brahma paraṁ dhāma pavitraṁ paramaṁ bhavān
puruṣaṁ śāśvataṁ divyamādidevamajaṁ vibhum
āhustvāmṛṣayaḥ sarve devarṣirnāradastathā
asito devalo vyāsaḥ svayaṁ caiva bravīṣi me

Arjuna said:

You are the Supreme Brahma (eternal) (pure-consciousness), the Supreme Abode, the Supreme Purifier, the Eternal Divine Person, the Prime Deity, the Unborn, the Omnipresent. Likewise all the sages, have acclaimed You, as also the celestial sage Nārada, so also Asita, Devala and Vyāsa; and You Yourself, also have proclaimed, this to me. 12-13

Comment:—

'Paraṁ brahma paraṁ dhāma pavitraṁ paramaṁ bhavān'— Arjuna, while praising Lord Kṛṣṇa, says to Him, that He is the Supreme Imperishable Brahma, as He said to him in response to his question (Gītā 8/3), He is the Supreme Abode in Whom the entire universe rests (Gītā 9/18). And He is the most sacred.

'Puruṣaṁ śāśvataṁ divyamādidevamajaṁ vibhum āhustvāmṛṣayaḥ sarve devarṣirnāradastathā asito devalo vyāsaḥ svayaṁ caiva bravīṣi me'—In the holy books, such as the

Mahābhārata etc., the sages,* celestial sage Nārada,† other sage Asita and his son, sage Devala‡ and also great sage Vyāsa$ have acclaimed Him as Eternal, Divine Person, Primeval God, Unborn and Omnipresent.

As soul, He is eternal (Gītā 2/20), as formless and having attributes, He is Divine Person (Gītā 8/10), as the source of gods and great seers, He is the Prime Deity (Gītā 10/2). The ignorant folk do not recognize Him, as the unborn (Gītā 7/25) while the undeluded know Him, as unborn (Gītā 10/3). All the universe, is pervaded by Him, in His unmanifest form (Gītā 9/4) and He Himself declares, that He is Omnipresent in this verse.

Appendix—Having used the expression 'paraṁ brahma' for attributeless and formless, Brahma, 'paraṁ dhāma' for God endowed with attributes and formless and 'pavitraṁ paramaṁ bhavān' for God endowed with attributes and form, Arjuna seems to say to Lord Kṛṣṇa that He is God in full (samagra) (Gītā 7/29-30, 8/1—4).

---

* Sage Mārkaṇḍeya has said, "Lord Kṛṣṇa is the religious sacrifice of all the religious sacrifices, austerity of austerities and He is present, past and future" (Mahā. Bhīṣma. 68/3). Sage Bhṛgu declares that He is God of the gods and He is the supreme aboriginal Lord Viṣṇu (Mahā. Bhīṣma. 68/4).

Sage Aṅgirā declares, "He is the creator of all beings" (Mahā. Bhīṣma. 68/6). Sanatkumāra etc., have said, "The sky and the earth exist by His forehead and arms respectively. All the three worlds are situated in His stomach. He is the Eternal Person. A striver can know, Him by purifying his heart through austerity. He is superior even to the seers who are satisfied by realizing God. He is the Supreme Goal of the generous royal sages who never flee battlefield" (Mahā. Bhīṣma. 68/8—10).

† Celestial sage Nārada declares—"Lord Kṛṣṇa is the creator of all the worlds and knower of all feelings. He is the Lord of the lords, of deities and the gods" (Mahā. Bhīṣma. 68/2).

‡ Asita and Devala sages declare—"Lord Kṛṣṇa is the only creator of Brahmā and all the worlds" (Mahā. Vana. 12/50).

$ Great sage Vyāsa declares—"You are the Lord of the Vasus (a class of gods). You have conferred power on Indra, the king of the gods and You are the Supreme Lord of the gods" (Mahā. Bhīṣma. 68/5).

He who Himself is pure (holy) and also sanctifies others is 'parama pavitra' (most sacred). God Himself is the most sacred and His name and form etc., are also the most sacred. In the thirty-eighth verse of the fourth chapter also Jñāna (knowledge) has been declared to be the purest (most sacred)—'na hi jñānena sadṛśaṁ pavitramiha vidyate'. But that knowledge is also within the entire form of God. Therefore the Lord is more sacred than even knowledge.

सर्वमेतदृतं मन्ये यन्मां वदसि केशव।
न हि ते भगवन्व्यक्तिं विदुर्देवा न दानवाः ॥ १४ ॥

sarvametadṛtaṁ manye yanmāṁ vadasi keśava
na hi te bhagavanvyaktiṁ vidurdevā na dānavāḥ

I accept as true, all that You tell me, O Keśava. Neither the gods nor the demons, O blessed Lord, know your manifestation. 14

Comment:—

'Sarvametadṛtaṁ manye yanmāṁ vadasi keśava'—'K' stands, for Brahmā, the creator, 'A' stands for, Lord Viṣṇu, the preserver, 'Īśa' stands for, Lord Śaṅkara, the destroyer and 'Va' stands for 'Vapu' the body. So 'Keśava' stands for the trinity of Brahmā, Viṣṇu and Śaṅkara. It means, that He is the creator, preserver and destroyer, of the entire creation.

By using the term 'Yat' (which), Arjuna means that whatever the Lord has said to him, from the seventh to the ninth chapters, he holds as true. By 'Etat' (this), he means to say, that he also believes as true, whatever He has said, in the tenth chapter about His divine glories and power. It means, that He is the creator, conductor and the supreme Lord, of the entire creation, without any doubt.

In the Discipline of Devotion, importance is attached to faith. Lord Kṛṣṇa, in the first verse of this chapter ordered Arjuna to listen to His supreme word. So Arjuna, expresses his faith in

His words by using the term, 'Ṛtam' (True).

'Na hi te bhagavanvyaktiṁ vidurdevā na dānavāḥ'—O Lord, You declared (in Gītā 4/5), "Arjuna, you and I, have passed through many births. I know them all, while you don't." Similarly, You declared (in Gītā 10/2), "Neither the gods nor the great sages, know the secret, of My birth." Thus, Arjuna believes as true, whatever the Lord declared about His manifestation. Though the gods, possess divine power, yet that power is perishable. So the gods cannot know, His manifestation. As far as, demons are concerned, they possess uncommon magical and fraudulent power, by which they cannot know the Lord's manifestation, because He, being eternal and limitless, cannot be known by perishable and limited power, of demons. It means, that the Lord cannot be known, by the power of men, gods and demons, because their power belongs to matter, while He is beyond Matter. Renunciation, dispassion, austerity and study of the scriptures etc., can purify the mind, but cannot enable a man, to know the Lord. The Lord, can be known, by His grace to the devotee who having exclusive devotion, depends on Him, only.

Appendix—No one can know God through his own endeavours, but He can be known only by His own grace—

'soi jānaī jehi dehu janāi,
jānata tumhahi tumhai hoi jāī.
tumharihi kṛpā̐ tumhahi raghunandana,
jānahiṁ bhagata bhagata ura candana. (Mānasa 2/127/2)

God is beyond the reach of miracles and occult powers and also scientific inventions.

स्वयमेवात्मनात्मानं वेत्थ त्वं पुरुषोत्तम।
भूतभावन भूतेश देवदेव जगत्पते॥ १५॥

svayamevātmanātmānaṁ vettha tvaṁ puruṣottama
bhūtabhāvana bhūteśa devadeva jagatpate

You alone know Yourself by Yourself, O Supreme Person, O creator of beings, O Lord of creation, O God of gods, O Lord of the universe. 15

Comment:—

'Bhūtabhāvana bhūteśa devadeva jagatpate puruṣottama'— Being the origin, of all beings even through His thought, He is 'Bhūtabhāvana', being the Lord of beings He is Bhūteśa; being the Lord of the gods, He is 'Devadeva'; being the preserver of the universe He is 'Jagatpate', and being supreme, of all the persons He is known as 'Puruṣottama', in the world, and in the Vedas (Gītā 15/18).

In this verse, five vocatives have been used for the Lord. In no other verse, in the Gītā, so many vocatives have been used, at a time, because, he is enraptured by listening to His divine glories and His grace for the devotees.*

'Svayamevātmanātmānaṁ vettha tvam'—He knows Himself, by Himself, without any external help of instruments etc. This knowledge, is beyond instruments. It is transcendental, and comes not through, instruments.

A conclusion, from the verse can be drawn, that as the Lord knows Himself by Himself, the soul, a fragment of the Lord should also know itself, by itself, because it cannot be known, by senses, mind and intellect etc.

Appendix—'You alone know Yourself by Yourself'—it means that You are the knower, You are the entity to be known and You are also the act of knowing viz., You are all. When there is no one else besides You, then who should know and to whom should he know?

If an effort is made to know the Supreme Reality (Divinity),

---

* Here 'Bhūtabhāvana', 'Bhūteśa', 'Devadeva', 'Jagatpate' and 'Puruṣottama' can denote the sun, Lord Śiva, Lord Gaṇeśa, Durgā and Lord Viṣṇu, the five great deities of the rank of the Lord. By using those five terms Arjuna means to say that He has manifested Himself as these five deities.

we are distanced from that reality because when a striver holds that there is some entity to be known, then he wants to know it. That Divinity is the knower of all, He is not to be known. No one can be the knower of the Lord Who is the knower of all.* As with the eye everything can be seen but the eye can't be seen with the eye, because the power of seeing of the eye is not the sense-object viz., powers of senses themselves are beyond the reach of senses.† Therefore God Himself is known by Himself.

Link:—The Lord declared, "He who knows in reality this glory and power of Mine, gets established in Me, through unwavering devotion" (Gītā 10/7). So Arjuna, in the next three verses, requests Lord Kṛṣṇa to tell him of His divine glories in detail.

वक्तुमर्हस्यशेषेण दिव्या ह्यात्मविभूतयः ।
याभिर्विभूतिभिर्लोकानिमांस्त्वं व्याप्य तिष्ठसि ॥ १६ ॥

vaktumarhasyaśeṣeṇa divyā hyātmavibhūtayaḥ
yābhirvibhūtibhirlokānimāṁstvaṁ vyāpya tiṣṭhasi

You alone, can describe in full Your divine glories, by which You remain, pervading these worlds. 16

Comment:—

'Yābhirvibhūtibhirlokānimāṁstvaṁ vyāpya tiṣṭhasi'—The Lord, in the seventh verse declared, that he who knows in reality His glory and power, gets established in Him, through unfaltering devotion. So, Arjuna wants to know His glories and power, so

---

* 'nānyo'to'sti draṣṭā' (Bṛhadāraṇyaka. 3/7/23)

'There is no one else the seer (onlooks) besides Him.'

Vijñātāramare kena vijānīyāt (Bṛhadāraṇyaka 2/4/14)

'How to know the knower of all?'

† 'It is the mind, not the senses, which sees the senses. It is intellect, not the mind, which sees the mind. It is ego, not intellect, which sees the intellect. It is the self, not ego which sees the ego. It is only the self which sees the self.'

that his devotion for Him, may be aroused. Arjuna wants to attain salvation, through devotion. So, he wants to know, in full His divine glories, which cannot be described by anyone else, beside Him.

'Vaktumarhasyaśeṣeṇa'—Arjuna, tells Lord Kṛṣṇa, that He spoke of His glories (in seventh, ninth chapters and also at the beginning of the tenth chapter). He also explained, that he who knows His glories is endowed, with unfaltering devotion. So Arjuna prays to Him, to describe His glories in full, so that he may know them and be endowed with unfaltering devotion, as this is an easy way for obtaining it.

'Divyā hyātmavibhūtayaḥ'—Arjuna, calls the glories of the Lord, as divine, because, whatever singularity is seen in the universe, is only the Lord's. So a striver should think that whatever singularity or attraction is seen, in the universe, is not of the universe, but only of the Lord. Therefore, to see anything charming in the world, is sense-enjoyment while to see the glory of the Lord is 'Vibhūti', and is also, 'Yoga'.

Appendix—Arjuna says to Lord Kṛṣṇa, "You alone, can describe in full your divine glories because You alone know Yourself by Yourself" (10/15). "Anyone else may know You—it is not possible" (10/2, 14). "Therefore You alone can narrate your total divine glories that I may be endowed with unfaltering devotion."

कथं विद्यामहं योगिंस्त्वां सदा परिचिन्तयन्।
केषु केषु च भावेषु चिन्त्योऽसि भगवन्मया॥ १७॥

kathaṁ vidyāmahaṁ yogiṁstvāṁ sadā paricintayan
keṣu keṣu ca bhāveṣu cintyo'si bhagavanmayā

How may I realise You, O Master of Yoga, by constant meditation on you? In what various aspects are You, O blessed Lord, to be meditated upon by me? 17

Comment:—

'Kathaṁ vidyāmahaṁ yogiṁstvāṁ sadā paricintayan'— The Lord, in the seventh verse of this chapter, said that he who knows Him in reality, gets established in Him, through unwavering devotion. So Arjuna asks Him, how he may know Him, by constant meditation.

'Keṣu keṣu ca bhāveṣu cintyo'si bhagavanmayā'—The Lord, in the fourteen verse of the eighth chapter, declared, "I am easily attainable to the ever steadfast Yogī, who constantly thinks of Me, with undivided mind." Again, He declared, in the twenty-second verse of the ninth chapter, "To those devotees who constantly think of Me, and worship Me alone, who are ever-devout, I provide gain and security." So Arjuna asks Him, in what various aspects He is to be thought of, by him. [Here meditation (thought), is the means, while Knowledge about Him, is the end.]

Arjuna asks Lord Kṛṣṇa, "In what things, persons, places etc., are You to be thought of, by me?" Lord Kṛṣṇa, will further reply, "There is no creature animate or inanimate which can exist, without Me. I stand holding the entire universe, with a single fragment of Myself." It means, that He pervades everywhere, all things, creatures and incidents etc. So, whatever glory, brilliance, beauty, prosperity or power etc., he thinks of, he should think it only of the Lord and thus, instead of thinking of the universe, he will think only, of Him.

Appendix—Arjuna's question means, 'O Lord! In which forms have You revealed Yourself so that I may think of You in those forms?' Arjuna's this question aims at easy realization of God. Arjuna is a representative of all strivers, therefore his question is useful for all strivers. Arjuna knew Lord Kṛṣṇa but he did not know Him in His entire form. He had inquisitiveness (curiosity) to know the Lord's entire form. So he asks Lord Kṛṣṇa. "How should I know You in Your entire form and in what different forms should I think of You?" It proves that the

Lord's divine glories are not of secondary importance but they are very important as they are the means for God-realization. The Lord has revealed Himself in the form of His divine glories. So long as a striver does not know God in reality, he has the notion of primary or secondary importance. But when he knows God in reality, then he has no notion of primary or secondary importance because when there is no other entity besides God, then what is the question of primary or secondary importance? It means that there are the primary and the secondary, from the view-point of a striver, not from the view-point of God and of an enlightened soul.

विस्तरेणात्मनो योगं विभूतिं च जनार्दन।
भूयः कथय तृप्तिर्हि शृण्वतो नास्ति मेऽमृतम्॥ १८ ॥

vistareṇātmano yogaṁ vibhūtiṁ ca janārdana
bhūyaḥ kathaya tṛptirhi śṛṇvato nāsti me'mṛtam

Tell me again in detail, O Janārdana, Your power of Yoga and Your manifestations; for I am not yet satiated even after hearing your sweet words like nectar. 18

Comment:—

'Vistareṇātmano yogaṁ vibhūtiṁ ca janārdana'—Lord Kṛṣṇa, explained the topic of knowledge (Wisdom) with realization, in the seventh and the ninth chapters, in detail, but He was not satisfied. So He Himself started the topic again, in the tenth chapter, by asking Arjuna to listen to His supreme word. Arjuna's attention was drawn particularly towards the Lord's grace, and His glories. So he requests Him to tell him further in detail, of His glories and His power of Yoga, so that he may be endowed, with unfaltering devotion to Him

'Bhūyaḥ kathaya tṛptirhi śṛṇvato nāsti me'mṛtam'—Arjuna wants to know what is decidedly good for him (Gītā 2/7; 3/2; 5/1)

and Lord Kṛṣṇa has declared, that he who knows in reality, His divine glory and power, is endowed with unfaltering devotion (Gītā 10/7). So Arjuna thinks, that it is an easy means, to be endowed with unfaltering devotion, by knowing of His divine glories, so that, unfaltering devotion will lead him to salvation. Then he requests Him to advise him of His divine glories in detail once again.

As a person, while taking a meal requests for a tasty dish, again and again, while taking meals the taste suffers either owing to not getting the food in plenty or on stomach being full, but such is not the case in divine glories as they are infinite and there is no satiety while hearing them. Arjuna wants to listen to the Lord's nectarean words again, because His glories are numberless and Arjuna knows no satiety, in hearing them.

Appendix—As a hungry man relishes food and a thirsty man relishes water, similarly the Lord's utterances seem very extraordinary to inquisitive Arjuna. The more extraordinary the Lord's utterances appear to Arjuna, the more devotional feelings are welling up (aroused) in him for the Lord.*

Link:—In response to Arjuna's request Lord Kṛṣṇa tells him His divine glories.

श्रीभगवानुवाच

हन्त ते कथयिष्यामि दिव्या ह्यात्मविभूतयः।
प्राधान्यतः कुरुश्रेष्ठ नास्त्यन्तो विस्तरस्य मे॥ १९॥

śrībhagavānuvāca

hanta te kathayiṣyāmi divyā hyātmavibhūtayaḥ
prādhānyataḥ kuruśreṣṭha nāstyanto vistarasya me

*Vide 'Gītā-Darpaṇa' (article 12) 'Gītā meṁ bhagavānkā vividha rūpoṁ meṁ prakaṭa honā.

The Blessed Lord said:

Now I shall tell you of My divine glories in brief, O best of the Kurus, for there is no end, to the details of My manifestation. 19

Comment:—

'Hanta te kathayiṣyāmi divyā hyātmavibhūtayaḥ'—Arjuna, requests Lord Kṛṣṇa, to tell him more of divine glories and power. So Lord Kṛṣṇa starts talking of His divine glories here, (He will speak of His power in the forty-first verse).

By the term 'Divyā' (Divine), the Lord says, that whatever singularity is seen in the universe, is of the Lord. Therefore, a striver, should behold the Lord everywhere, in all the things and person etc.

'Prādhānyataḥ kuruśreṣṭha nāstyanto vistarasya me'—Arjuna requests Lord Kṛṣṇa to tell him His divine glories in detail. Lord Kṛṣṇa tells him that He will explain His divine glories in brief, because there is no end to the details. But, in the eleventh chapter when Arjuna hesitatingly says to Lord Kṛṣṇa, "If You consider me capable of beholding Your Cosmic Form, O Lord of Yoga, show me, Your Eternal self." Lord Kṛṣṇa asks him to behold His hundreds and thousands of divine forms. How surprising!* It is surprising, because a person can

---

* By the ear we come to know of the things visible as well as invisible (heaven, hell etc.). In the process of theology 'hearing' occupies the first position. In devotion also 'hearing' occupies the first position. We come to know of Pure-Consciousness by hearing and then by assumption or knowledge we attain salvation or God-realization.

When a man sleeps, his senses being contracted merge in the mind, the mind merges in intellect, the intellect merges in ignorance. Thus in his sleep his senses are not active. But if a man at that time is called by his name, he wakes up because of a lot of power in the words. Thus the words have an access not only to the ear but to the self.

Eyes can see the form or colour. But their power is limited and is less than that of ears.

The senses can perceive their own objects only. They can't perceive the

hear more than, he can see. The power of vision, is limited and less than that of hearing. Then why does the Lord say so? The reason is, that by listening to the gospel of Gītā, Arjuna comes to know of the Lord's power, more and more. In this chapter, when the Lord declares that there is no end to the details of His manifestations, Arjuna comes to know of his endlessness. He thinks that his knowledge about the Lord, is very meagre. So he becomes cautious and requests the Lord hesitatingly, to show him His Cosmic Form. The Lord by His grace bestows upon him, divine eyes and directs him to behold His, hundreds and thousands of, divine forms.

Secondly, when a listener asks a speaker something, having pride of his own, he cannot get a satisfactory answer. But when he puts a question politely, modestly and innocently, he gets a satisfactory answer. In this chapter, Arjuna wants to know of His glories, in order to know, His limit. So the Lord declares that there is no end or limit to, His glories. So He will be brief. But, in the eleventh chapter, he prays to Him politely and hesitatingly, to show him His Universal Form, the Lord confers on him, divine eyes and enables him to behold His Cosmic Form. So, a striver, by renouncing his pride should totally depend on God, in order to gain infinite bliss.

Appendix—God is infinite; therefore His divine glories are also infinite. Therefore the details of the Lord's divine glories can neither be narrated nor be heard. If they can be narrated and heard, how will they remain endless? Therefore the Lord declares that He will tell His divine glories in brief.

The Lord addresses Arjuna as 'kuruśreṣṭha'—by this He means

Cosmic Soul (Pure-Consciousness). The Pure-Consciousness can be known by one's own self. So Arjuna said, "You alone know Yourself by Yourself' (Gītā 10/15). In the second chapter the Lord declared, "When a man thoroughly abandons all desires, he is satisfied in the self through the self" (Gītā 2/55). It means that the self can't be perceived by the senses. So the self can't be perceived by eyes; but the ear by perceiving it transmits it to the self.

that he is noble because he has got a desire to know Him.

Link:—The Lord, from the twentieth verse to the thirty-ninth verse, describes His eighty-two divine glories.

अहमात्मा गुडाकेश सर्वभूताशयस्थितः ।
अहमादिश्च मध्यं च भूतानामन्त एव च ॥ २० ॥

ahamātmā guḍākeśa sarvabhūtāśayasthitaḥ
ahamādiśca madhyaṁ ca bhūtānāmanta eva ca

I am the self, O conqueror of sleep, seated in the hearts of all beings. I am the beginning, the middle and also, the end of all creation. 20

Comment:—

[The Lord can be thought of, in two ways (1) As of one's favourite Deity only. In case the mind deviates, it should again be fixed on God. (2) Whatever thought, comes to the mind, should be considered as His manifestation. With this second view-point the Lord, is describing His divine glories.]

'Ahamādiśca madhyaṁ ca bhūtānāmanta eva ca'* —Here, by saying that He is the beginning, the middle and the end of all beings, the Lord has given the gist of His divine glories. As in ornaments made of gold, there is nothing but gold, though in between they may have different names and shapes, as ornaments, in the same way, all beings are born of Him, they live in Him, in different forms and they merge in Him.

* Here the term 'Ādi' (Beginning) and 'Anta' (End) are used in masculine gender while the term 'Madhyam' (Middle) is used in common gender. It means that at the beginning He remains 'I am the prime cause of the gods and great seers, (Gītā 10/2) and at the end also He remains (Śrīmadbhāgavata 10/3/25). But in the middle at the time of creation persons, creatures and objects etc., of masculine, feminine and common gender live in the universe. Thus the common gender includes all the three genders. Therefore the Lord here as well as in the thirty-second verse has used the term 'Madhya' in common gender.

It means, that there is nothing else, at the beginning, in the middle and at the end, besides the Lord. The Lord pointed out this fact, first in the twentieth verse then in the middle in the thirty-second verse and at last in the thirty-ninth verse, by declaring Himself as the seed of all beings. It means, that all is God (Gītā 7/19). He has also declared that He becomes manifold in different forms (Chāndogya. 6/2/3) and He remains at the end, also (Śrīmadbhā. 10/3/25). It means that He is in the middle also. In this verse, in the thirty-second and thirty-ninth verses, the Lord has mentioned His main glories, referring to Himself. In other verses, His glories have been mentioned as the head of a class, the controller of the group, or due to some special characteristic of that glory. So, a striver should always think, that all the divine glories are nothing, besides manifestations of the Lord. He should behold only God, in all of these, because Arjuna put the question, "In what aspects are You to be thought of, by me" (Gītā 10/17).

'Ahamātmā guḍākeśa sarvabhūtāśayasthitaḥ'—How should a striver make use, of these divine glories? A striver, should think, that the Lord has manifested Himself in all beings. He is the beginning, the middle and the end of the whole universe. He is the seed of all of them. It means, that in the whole universe there is nothing, besides Him.

Appendix—God is the beginning, the middle and the end of all beings—it means that there is nothing else besides God viz., all is God.

Lord Kṛṣṇa is entire and the soul (self) is His divine glory. The soul is the Lord's 'parā prakṛti' and 'antaḥkaraṇa' (internal instrument viz., mind) is the Lord's 'aparā prakṛti' (Gītā 7/4-5). Parā and Aparā—both are inseparable with God.

आदित्यानामहं विष्णुर्ज्योतिषां रविरंशुमान्।
मरीचिर्मरुतामस्मि नक्षत्राणामहं शशी॥ २१॥*

* In these divine glories the sixth inflexion has been used. This inflexion is

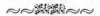

ādityāṇāmahaṁ viṣṇurjyotiṣāṁ raviraṁśumāṇ
marīcirmarutāmasmi. nakṣatrāṇāmahaṁ śaśī .

I am Viṣṇu among the twelve sons of Aditi; and the radiant sun among the luminaries; I am the glory of the Maruts, and the moon, among stars. 21

Comment:—

'Ādityānāmahaṁ viṣṇuḥ'—Vāmana (Viṣṇu) is the most important son, of all the twelve sons of Aditi. As an incarnation of Vāmana, He got the property of demons, as charity, and gave it* to the sons of Aditi viz., to the gods.

'Jyotiṣāṁ raviraṁśumān'—Among the luminaries, such as the moon, stars and fire etc., the Lord is the the radiant sun, by whose light, all of them are illuminated.

'Maricirmarutāmasmi'—The Lord, is the glory of the forty-nine Maruts (wind-gods), It is because of that glory, that Indra, the king of the gods, split the foetus of Diti into forty-nine parts, but the foetus instead of being destroyed, was turned from one to forty-nine.

'Nakṣatrāṇāmahaṁ śaśī'—Lord Kṛṣṇa, is the lord named moon of twenty-seven stars, such as Aśvinī, Bharaṇī and Kṛttikā etc.

Whatever distinction there is in those divine glories, is of the Lord.

[In this context there is a description of the Lord's divine glories, rather than His incarnations as "I am Viṣṇu among Aditi's sons" (10/21). "Among wielders of weapon I am Rāma" (10/31), "Among the members of the Vṛṣṇi clan, I am Kṛṣṇa and among the Pāṇḍavas, I am Arjuna" (10/37).]

---

used to point out the important thing out of many and to show their affinity. In the first part of the verse it has been used for importance while in the second part for affinity.

* The sun of the month 'Kārtika' is also known as Viṣṇu.

वेदानां सामवेदोऽस्मि देवानामस्मि वासवः।
इन्द्रियाणां मनश्चास्मि भूतानामस्मि चेतना॥ २२॥

vedānāṁ sāmavedo'smi devānāmasmi vāsavaḥ
indriyāṇāṁ manaścāsmi bhūtānāmasmi cetanā

Of the Vedas, I am the Sāmaveda; I am Vāsava (Indra) among the gods; of the senses, I am the mind and of living beings, I am consciousness. 22

Comment:—

'Vedānāṁ sāmavedo'smi'—Of the four Vedas, Sāmaveda is the most suitable for music. In it, there is the description of the Lord's glory in the form of Indra's glory. So, Sāmaveda is the divine glory of the Lord.

'Devānāmasmi vāsavaḥ'—Of all the gods, Indra is the chief one, the lord of the gods. So Lord Kṛṣṇa, has mentioned him, as His divine glory.

'Indriyāṇāṁ manaścāsmi'—The five senses function, properly, only if the mind remains with them. If it wanders away, they cannot function properly. So the mind, is reckoned, as the Lord's divine glory.

'Bhūtānāmasmi cetanā'—The difference, between a living person and a dead person, is that the former has consciousness (life, energy), while the latter has no consciousness. So this consciousness, is the Lord's divine glory.

Whatever distinction is there, in the divine glories, is the Lord's.

रुद्राणां शङ्करश्चास्मि वित्तेशो यक्षरक्षसाम्।
वसूनां पावकश्चास्मि मेरुः शिखरिणामहम्॥ २३॥

rudrāṇāṁ śaṅkaraścāsmi vitteśo yakṣarakṣasām
vasūnāṁ pāvakaścāsmi meruḥ śikhariṇāmaham

Among the Rudras, I am Śaṅkara; among the Yakṣas (genies), and Rākṣasas (Demons), I am Kubera. Among the Vasus (a class of the gods), I am the god of fire, and of the mountains, I am Meru. 23

Comment:—

'Rudrāṇāṁ śaṅkaraścāsmi'—Śaṅkara is the lord of all the eleven Rudras, named Hara, Bahurūpa and Tryambaka etc. They are the bestowers of beatitude, to others. So Śaṅkara is said to be the Lord's divine glory.

'Vitteśo yakṣarakṣasām'—Kubera, is the lord of genies and demons. He is also the lord of fabulous wealth, so he is called a Lord's divine glory.

'Vasūnāṁ pāvakaścāsmi'—The god of fire, is the lord of eight Vasus, named Dhara, Dhruva and Soma etc. The god of fire, is said to be the mouth of the Lord through which oblation reaches the deities. So he is a Lord's divine glory.

'Meruḥ śikhariṇāmaham'—Of all the mountains, having mounts of gold, silver and copper etc., the golden Meru mountain, is the most important. It is the storehouse of jewels and diamonds. So, this mountain is, His glory.

Whatever distinction, these divine glories have, is the Lord's. So only He, should be thought of, in all these glories.

पुरोधसां च मुख्यं मां विद्धि पार्थ बृहस्पतिम्।
सेनानीनामहं स्कन्दः सरसामस्मि सागरः॥ २४॥

purodhasāṁ ca mukhyaṁ māṁ viddhi pārtha bṛhaspatim
senānīnāmahaṁ skandaḥ sarasāmasmi sāgaraḥ

Among priests, O Pārtha, know Me to be their chief, Bṛhaspati; among the generals I am Skanda; of the mass of water, I am, the ocean. 24

Comment:—

'Purodhasāṁ ca mukhyaṁ māṁ viddhi pārtha bṛhaspatim'—

Bṛhaspati, is the best of all the priests, and he is superior to others, in learning and wisdom. He is the preceptor of Indra, the lord of the gods, and is the priest of the gods. So, he is a divine glory of the Lord.

'Senānīnāmahaṁ skandaḥ'—Skanda (Kārtikeya), is the son of Lord Śaṅkara. He, is said, to have six faces and twelve arms. He is the general of the gods. So he is a Lord's divine glory.

'Sarasāmasmi sāgaraḥ'—Of the mass of water, the ocean is the biggest, is very deep and remains within limits. So it is called a Lord's divine glory.

After beholding these distinctions in the Lord's glories, a striver should think only, of God.

महर्षीणां भृगुरहं गिरामस्म्येकमक्षरम्।
यज्ञानां जपयज्ञोऽस्मि स्थावराणां हिमालयः॥ २५॥

maharṣīṇāṁ bhṛgurahaṁ girāmasmyekamakṣaram
yajñānāṁ japayajño'smi sthāvarāṇāṁ himālayaḥ

Among the great seers I am Bhṛgu, of speech I am the monosyllablic 'Oṁ'; of sacrifice (yajña), I am the Japa yajña, the constant repetition of the Lord's name; and of the immovable, the Himālaya. 25

Comment:—

'Maharṣīṇāṁ bhṛgurahaṁ'—Among the great seers, Bhṛgu is a great devotee, possessing wisdom and glory. It was he who by testing the trinity, proved Lord Viṣṇu superior to Brahmā and Maheśa. Lord Viṣṇu holds the mark of his foot on His chest. So, the Lord's glories, are revealed through him.

'Girāmasmyekamakṣaram'—First the monosyllable 'Oṁ', was revealed. Then 'Gāyatrī' (a Vedic metre), was revealed from Oṁ; then the Vedas were revealed from Gāyatrī; and other scriptures and Purāṇas etc., are based on the Vedas. So the Lord has declared

'Oṁ', His divine glory. The Lord has also declared it in 7/8 "I am the sacred syllable 'Oṁ', in all the Vedas" and in 8/13 "He who leaves the body and departs, reciting the one-syllabled 'Oṁ', and dwelling on Me in My absolute aspect, attains the "supreme state," and also in 17/24 "Acts of sacrifice, gift and penance, as enjoined by scriptures, are always undertaken, with the utterance of 'Oṁ' by followers of the Vedas."

'Yajñānāṁ japayajño'smi'—In other sacrifices, certain rules and ordinances, are to be observed and in performing these any error may be committed, which may result, in harm. But, in the constant repetition of the Lord's name, there is no question of any harm and it can be performed at anytime without any hard and fast rules. The Hindus, Muslims, Buddhas and the Jains etc., all believe, that it is a very good means, to attain salvation. So the Lord has named it, as His divine glory.

'Sthāvarāṇāṁ himālayaḥ'—Among the mountains, the Himālaya is the highest and the greatest. Moreover, being the abode of seers, for the performance of penance, it is very sacred. The sacred rivers, such as the Ganges and the Yamunā etc., emanate from it. Even, in these days great seers and saints, meditate on the Lord, in the caves of the Himālayas. The sages, named Nara-Nārāyaṇa are performing penance there, for the salvation of the beings, of the world. It is said, to be the abode of Lord Śaṅkara's-in-laws. Lord Śaṅkara also resides on one of its mounts, named Kailāsa. So it is called, the Lord's divine glory.

Whatever distinction or attraction, is seen in the universe, is of the Lord, but a man by thinking of that distinction or attraction of the world, gets entangled in it and thus he has a downfall. If he knows the reality, that the distinction is of the eternal Lord, not of the perishable world, he will think of, only the Lord and he will develop love, for Him.

अश्वत्थः सर्ववृक्षाणां देवर्षीणां च नारदः।
गन्धर्वाणां चित्ररथः सिद्धानां कपिलो मुनिः॥ २६॥

aśvatthaḥ sarvavṛkṣāṇāṁ devarṣīṇāṁ ca nāradaḥ
gandharvāṇāṁ citrarathaḥ siddhānāṁ kapilo muniḥ

Of all trees I am Aśvattha (the holy pīpala tree); among the celestial sages, Nārada; among the Gandharvas (celestial musicians), I am Citraratha; among the siddhas (the perfect), the sage Kapila. 26

Comment:—

'Aśvatthaḥ sarvavṛkṣāṇām'—Aśvattha, is the pīpala or holy fig tree. Every other tree can grow under it. It can grow, even on very hard surface, such as a roof or a wall or on a mountain. It has always been associated with worship of the Divine. In Āyurveda, it is said to be a cure, for several diseases. So, it is recognized as, Lord's divine glory.

'Devarṣīṇāṁ ca nāradaḥ'—The celestial sage, named Nārada, always works according to Lord's will. He becomes an instrument, in the Lord's sport. He always sings of the Lord's glories and virtues, on his harp. He inspired the sages Vālmīki and Vyāsa, to write the scriptures, such as the Rāmāyaṇa and the Bhāgavata. Men, gods, demons etc., all have faith in him, and so they consult him and do according to his advice. Therefore, he is a glory of the Lord.

'Gandharvāṇāṁ citrarathaḥ'—The celestial songsters and musicians, are called Gandharvas, Citraratha is the most prominent of all of them. He was a friend of Arjuna who learnt music, from him. So the Lord claims him, as His divine glory.

'Siddhānāṁ kapilo muniḥ'—The Siddhas (the perfect ones) are of two types—those who have attained perfection, by spiritual discipline and those who have been endowed with perfection, since birth. Sage Kapila, belongs to the second type. He emanated from the womb of Devahūti, the wife of sage Kardama. He is the author of the Sāṅkhya system of philosophy and the Lord of those, who attained perfection. So the Lord has claimed him, as His divine glory.

A striver, should always behold the Lord, as all the divine glories, are His.

उच्चैःश्रवसमश्वानां विद्धि माममृतोद्भवम्।
ऐरावतं गजेन्द्राणां नराणां च नराधिपम्॥ २७॥

uccaiḥśravasamaśvānāṁ viddhi māmamṛtodbhavam
airāvataṁ gajendrāṇāṁ narāṇāṁ ca narādhipam

Among horses, know Me to be Uccaiḥśravā, begotten of the churning of the ocean for nectar; of lordly elephants Airāvata (Indra's elephant); among men, a king. 27

Comment:—

'Uccaiḥśravasamaśvānāṁ viddhi māmamṛtodbhavam'—When the ocean was churned, fourteen jewels came out of it. Out of these, one of the jewels was Uccaiḥśravā. He is Indra's vehicle, and is the king of horses. So the Lord, has claimed him as His divine glory.

'Airāvataṁ gajendrāṇām'—Airāvata is the best of all the elephants. He was also born of the ocean, when it was churned. He is also, Indra's vehicle. So the Lord claims him, as His divine glory.

'Narāṇāṁ ca narādhipam'—A king, is regarded as the best among men, because he fosters, preserves and rules over the subjects. Moreover, he is regarded as possessing more divine power than other human beings. So, he is called Lord's divine glory.*

A striver, should think of the Lord, because all of them, are His divine manifestations.

* Here Manu (the progenitor of the human race) of the present Manvantara (the fourteenth part of a day of Brahmā) can also be regarded as the king.

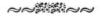

आयुधानामहं वज्रं धेनूनामस्मि कामधुक् ।
प्रजनश्चास्मि कन्दर्पः सर्पाणामस्मि वासुकिः ॥ २८ ॥

āyudhānāmahaṁ vajraṁ dhenūnāmasmi kāmadhuk
prajanaścāsmi kandarpaḥ sarpāṇāmasmi vāsukiḥ

Of weapons, I am the Vajra (thunderbolt); of cows, I am the celestial cow Kāmadhenu. I am Kāma, the sexual desire responsible for procreation; of serpents, I am Vāsuki. 28

Comment:—

'Āyudhānāmahaṁ vajram'—Of all the weapons, the thunderbolt, which was made of the bones of sage Dadhīci, who gave up his body, is the best one. It involved the willing self-sacrifice of sage Dadhīci. So, the Lord has named the thunderbolt as His glory.

'Dhenūnāmasmi kāmadhuk'—The celestial cow Kāmadhenu came out of the ocean while churning it. This cow has the power to supply all the requirements of the gods and men. So she is said to be the Lord's divine glory.

'Prajanaścāsmi kandarpaḥ'—Kandarpa is Cupid, the god of sexual urge in beings. Progeny is possible because of this urge. This progenitive instinct is to be revered if it is utilized for progeny by renouncing the sensuous pleasures. This urge is His divine glory. In the eleventh verse of the seventh chapter also the Lord declared, "I am sexual desire not in conflict with virtue or scriptural injunction."

'Sarpāṇāmasmi vāsukiḥ'—Vāsuki is the lord of all serpents and is a devotee of the Lord. It was used as the rope to rotate the Mount Meru in the act of churning the ocean. So the Lord speaks of this serpent as His divine glory.

The singularity seen in these divine glories is the Lord's.

अनन्तश्चास्मि नागानां वरुणो यादसामहम्‌।
पितॄणामर्यमा चास्मि यमः संयमतामहम्‌॥ २९॥

anantaścāsmi nāgānāṁ varuṇo yādasāmaham
pitṝṇāmaryamā cāsmi yamaḥ saṁyamatāmaham

Of the Nāgas (water-snakes) I am Ananta (the serpent-god); of aquatic creatures and water-gods, I am Varuṇa, among the manes I am Aryamā; and among regulators of life I am Yama, the god of death. 29

Comment:—

'Anantaścāsmi nāgānām'—The 'Nāgas', are the snakes living in water. 'Ananta' is the lord of the snakes, with thousand hoods. It offers comfort to the Lord by acting, as His bed. It joined the Lord's sport several times, when He was incarnated. So, the Lord speaks of it as His divine glory.

'Varuṇo yādasāmaham'—Varuṇa, is the lord of the aquatic creatures and water-gods, and is a devotee of the Lord. So, he is a divine glory of the Lord.

'Pitṝṇāmaryamā cāsmi'—Aryamā, is the presiding deity, over all the seven manes such as Kavyavāha, Anala and Soma etc. So he is a divine glory of the Lord.

'Yamaḥ saṁyamatāmaham'—Yama is the lord of death. He purifies the beings, by enabling them, to reap the fruit of their virtuous and evil actions. He is very just, and righteous. He is a devotee of the Lord and a lord of his region. Therefore, he is a divine glory of the Lord.

The uniqueness in these glories, is not personal, which has emanated, only from the Lord. Therefore a striver, should think of the Lord, when he thinks of His divine glories.

प्रह्लादश्चास्मि दैत्यानां कालः कलयतामहम्‌।
मृगाणां च मृगेन्द्रोऽहं वैनतेयश्च पक्षिणाम्‌॥ ३०॥

prahlādaścāsmi daityānāṁ kālaḥ kalayatāmaham
mṛgāṇāṁ ca mṛgendro'haṁ vainateyaśca pakṣiṇām

Among the demons I am Prahlāda; among reckoners of existence I am Time; among beasts, I am the lion; and among birds, Garuḍa, (the vehicle of Lord Viṣṇu). 30

Comment:—

'Prahlādaścāsmi daityānām'—'Daitya' (Demons), were those who were born of Diti. Among the demons, Prahlāda was the chief demon. He showed great devotion for the Lord, without having any desire for the fruit. So, he is called a divine glory of the Lord.

The Lord in the case of Prahlāda, has used the present tense, because His devotees never die. They can be ever beheld by believers. Even when, they merge into the Lord, if a person wants to behold them, the Lord appears, in their form.

'Kālaḥ kalayatāmaham'—Time, is the reckoner of the appearance, stay and disappearance of things and beings, in the universe. Therefore it is called a glory of the Lord.

'Mṛgāṇāṁ ca mṛgendro'ham'—The lion is the lord of beasts. He is more powerful and courageous, than other wild beasts, such as tiger, panther, leopard and bear etc. So, he is a glory of the Lord.

'Vainateyaśca pakṣiṇām'—Garuḍa, the son of Vinatā, is the lord of birds and God's devotee. He is the vehicle of Lord Viṣṇu. When he flies the sound of the hymns of Sāmaveda, is produced with his wings. So he is the Lord's divine glory.

The distinction in all these glories, is the Lord's. So a striver while thinking of them should think of the, Lord only.

पवनः पवतामस्मि रामः शस्त्रभृतामहम्।
झषाणां मकरश्चास्मि स्रोतसामस्मि जाह्नवी॥ ३१॥

pavanaḥ pavatāmasmi rāmaḥ śastrabhṛtāmaham
jhaṣāṇāṁ makaraścāsmi srotasāmasmi jāhnavī

Among purifiers, I am the wind; among warriors, I am Rāma. Among fish, I am an alligator; and among rivers, I am the Ganges. 31

Comment:—

'Pavanaḥ pavatāmasmi'—Wind is capable of purifying all things. It makes bodies healthy, so it reveals Lord's glory.

'Rāmaḥ śastrabhṛtāmaham'—Though Rāma, is an incarnation of God, yet as far as the wielders of weapon, are concerned, Rāma is the best of all of them. So the Lord has mentioned, Rāma, as one of His divine glories.

'Jhaṣāṇāṁ makaraścāsmi'—Among fish, the alligator is most powerful. Therefore the Lord names it as His divine glory.

'Srotasāmasmi jāhnavī'—Among rivers, streams and waterfalls etc., the Ganges, is the most sacred. Its water is holy, because it flows from the feet of Lord Viṣṇu. Believers by beholding or touching it, or drinking its water or bathing in, attain salvation. If a dead man's bones are dropped into her, she leads him to salvation. So she is the Lord's divine glory.

A striver instead of attaching importance to the Lord's divine glories, should attach importance to Him.

In the seventeenth verse of this chapter, Arjuna put two questions to Lord Kṛṣṇa "How may I know You," and "In what aspects are You to be thought of, by me?" The answer is, that he should think of the Lord, in all His divine glories. The result of that thinking will be, that he will come to know that, He is the root or origin, of all the divine glories. Thus, he will come to know the reality, about Him.

When a man, beholds any distinction, singularity or beauty in the universe, he gets entangled in it. But if he regards it as the Lord's, he will think only of Him, and thus will come to know the reality, about Him. By knowing the reality, of His glory and power, one is endowed with unwavering devotion, to Him (Gītā 10/7).

सर्गाणामादिरन्तश्च मध्यं चैवाहमर्जुन।
अध्यात्मविद्या विद्यानां वादः प्रवदतामहम्॥ ३२॥

sargāṇāmādirantaśca madhyaṁ caivāhamarjuna
adhyātmavidyā vidyānāṁ vādaḥ pravadatāmaham

Arjuna, I am the beginning, the end and also the middle of all creation. Of sciences, I am the science of the self (soul); in debates I am logic. 32

Comment:—

'Sargāṇāmādirantaśca madhyaṁ caivāham'—The Lord Himself, is the beginning, the middle and the end of all creatures. It means, that He is in all. So, while beholding the universe, or the beings, one should think of the Lord.

'Adhyātmavidyā vidyānām'—The science which leads a man to salvation, is called Adhyātmavidyā.* All other sciences, (learnings) are imperfect. Something remains to be known, after knowledge gained from these. But this science, is perfect. After knowing it, nothing else remains to be known. So it is Lord's divine glory.

'Vādaḥ pravadatāmaham'—Debates are of three types—(1) Supporting one's point and opposing other's points, in order to gain victory over an opponent. (2) Only to oppose others. (3) Brushing aside all prejudices, debating by reason faithfully, to know reality. This third one, is reason (logic) which is superior,

* There is a difference between 'Adhyātmavidyā' (the science of the self) and 'Rājavidyā' (Sovereign science). In the former importance is attached to the attributeless Lord while in the latter to the Lord endowed with attributes i.e., the Lord Who pervades everywhere and everytime, all things, creatures etc.

to the first two. So it is the Lord's divine glory.

Appendix—Of all the worldly sciences 'adhyātmavidyā' viz., science of the self (soul) is the best. The same science in the colophon at the end of the chapters of the Gītā, has been called 'brahmavidyā'

The Lord calls 'adhyātmavidyā' viz., the science of the self as His divine glory because it is the simplest, easiest and is directly realizable to all. In practising it, in understanding it and in attaining it, there is no difficulty. Practice, understanding and attainment are not applicable to it at all. The reason is that it is ever attained and in all the states—wakefulness, sleep and sound sleep etc., it ever remains the same. The science of the self is as much evident as evident even this world is not there. It means that we can realize the science of the self very clearly, but we can't realize the existence of the world so clearly. We should understand this fact in this way. If we think of our childhood and see our present state, we find that now the body is not the same, habits are not the same, language is not the same, behaviour is not the same, place is not the same, time is not the same, companions are not the same, actions are not the same, ideas are not the same, all these have changed but our entity viz., the self has not changed, so we say, "I am the same who was in childhood''. It means that whatever has changed is of a different nature and whatever has not changed is of a different nature. What has not changed is the self (soul) and whatever has changed is the body. This is science (knowledge) of the self viz., 'ātmajñāna'.

अक्षराणामकारोऽस्मि द्वन्द्वः सामासिकस्य च।
अहमेवाक्षयः कालो धाताहं विश्वतोमुखः॥ ३३॥

akṣarāṇāmakāro'smi dvandvaḥ sāmāsikasya ca
ahamevākṣayaḥ kālo dhātāhaṁ viśvatomukhaḥ

Of letters, I am 'A'; of word-compounds I am the dual (Dvandva) the copulative. I am verily the endless Time; I am the sustainer of all, having My face, on all sides. 33

Comment:—

'Akṣarāṇāmakāro'smi'—'A' is the first letter of alphabet. It occupies an important place in both vowels and consonants. The consonants cannot be pronounced, without this letter. So it is Lord's glory.

'Dvandvaḥ sāmāsikasya ca'—Out of the four important word-compounds, while both the words in compounding themselves retain equal importance, they are called the dual or 'dvandva'. In it because, each word maintains its individuality, the Lord has named it as His divine glory.

'Ahamevākṣayaḥ kālaḥ'—Time in itself, is beginningless and endless, and is called the Lord. In final dissolution, when even the sun merges into the Lord, time is counted or measured through the Lord (Paramātmā).* So the Lord is eternal time.

Time passes every moment. But here the Lord, Who is endless time, remains the same without any modification and change. The same endless Time, is a Lord's divine glory. In the eleventh chapter, the Lord has said that He is the mighty world-destroying, Time (Gītā 11/32).

'Dhātāhaṁ viśvatomukhaḥ'—Having His face on all sides, the Lord sees all the creatures. So He sustains all of them, very generously. Thus He has described Himself, in the form of His divine glory.

मृत्युः सर्वहरश्चाहमुद्भवश्च भविष्यताम्।
कीर्तिः श्रीर्वाक्च नारीणां स्मृतिर्मेधा धृतिः क्षमा ॥ ३४ ॥

* In final dissolution Brahmā, the creator also merges into the Lord. So time (of final dissolution) is measured by the eternal and endless Lord.

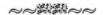

mṛtyuḥ sarvaharaścāhamudbhavaśca bhaviṣyatām
kīrtiḥ śrīrvākca nārīṇāṁ smṛtirmedhā dhṛtiḥ kṣamā

I am, the all-destroying Death. I am the origin of future beings. Of females, I am Kīrti, Śrī, Vāk, Smṛti, Medhā, Dhṛti and Kṣamā (the goddesses), presiding over the qualities, fame, fortune, speech, memory, intelligence, steadfastness and forgiveness, respectively. 34

Comment:—

'Mṛtyuḥ sarvaharaścāham'—Death, has such an uncommon power that after death, everything is destroyed and nothing remains, in memory. Actually it is not death's power, it is the Lord's power.

Had death, not possessed the power of forgetfulness, a man would have been very much worried, about the relatives of previous births and he might also have been attached to persons and things, with whom he had affinity, in the previous births.

'Udbhavaśca bhaviṣyatām'—As the Lord, is the sustainer of all beings, He is the source of future beings. It means, that it is He, Who creates the universe, sustains and destroys it.

'Kīrtiḥ śrīrvākca nārīṇāṁ smṛtirmedhā dhṛtiḥ kṣamā'—These seven females are considered, the best of all women in the world. Out of them Kīrti, Smṛti, Medhā, Dhṛti and Kṣamā, are daughters of Prajāpati Dakṣa, Śrī is the daughter of sage Bhṛgu, and Vāk is Brahmā's daughter. Fame, prosperity, speech, memory, intelligence, steadfastness and forgiveness are also, the seven most known, female qualities.

A person achieves fame, because of virtues. Prosperity, can be wealth, property and cattle, such as cows, horses, camels and elephants etc.

Speech, enables a man to be called a learned person. Remembrance of something is memory.

Intelligence, enables a man to fix something in the mind. Steadfastness means, not to deviate from one's principles, and beliefs etc.

Forgiveness, is the quality of forgiving an offender, by forgetting the wrong done, in spite of having the capacity and opportunity, to avenge the wrong done.

The first three, of these qualities are revealed outwardly, while the next four are revealed from inside the beings. The Lord, has named these as His divine glories.

So, if these qualities are seen anywhere, in any being, a striver should think of the Lord, by thinking these qualities as of the Lord. If a striver, finds them in himself, he should think them, as Lord's, and not as his own, because they are divine traits, which emanate only from the Lord. If a person, considers them his own, he feels proud of himself; and pride is a demoniac propensity, which leads one to a fall.

Strivers, should regard these excellent qualities, as the Lord's, just like Kākabhuśuṇḍi, who by sage Lomaśa's curse, was turned from Brāhmaṇa (the priest class) to an untouchable bird, a crow. But, he was neither afraid nor displeased; he was rather pleased because, he thought that it was the Lord's will (Mānasa 7/113/1). Thus, if a striver, starts beholding the Lord, in all things, incidents, circumstances and creatures etc., it will lead him, to bliss.

बृहत्साम तथा साम्नां गायत्री छन्दसामहम्।
मासानां मार्गशीर्षोऽहमृतूनां कुसुमाकरः ॥ ३५ ॥

bṛhatsāma tathā sāmnāṁ gāyatrī chandasāmaham
māsānāṁ mārgaśīrṣo'hamṛtūnāṁ kusumākaraḥ

Of the Sāma hymns, I am Bṛhatsāma; of the Vedic metres, I am Gāyatrī. Of the twelve months of the Hindu calendar, I am Mārgaśīrṣa, and of seasons, I am the flowery spring. 35

Comment:—

'Bṛhatsāma tathā sāmnām'—Bṛhatsāma, is a psalm in the

Sāmaveda, devoted to the praise of God, under the name of Indra. In 'Atirātrayāga' it is a 'Pṛṣṭhastotra' (endorsed hymn). It is regarded as the most prominent and best of psalms, in the Sāmaveda. So the Lord speaks of it, as His divine glory.*

'Gāyatrī chandasāmaham'—The Gāyatrī, is the most important of all the metres, contained in the Vedas. The Gāyatrī, is said to be the mother of the Vedas, because the Vedas have emanated from it. It consists of the trio of God—His form, His prayer and meditation on Him. Therefore, its chanting leads a striver to God-realization. So the Lord, speaks of it, as His very self.

'Māsānāṁ mārgaśīrṣo'ham'—The crop, which supplies food to the people is harvested in the month of Mārgaśīrṣa. Religious sacrifice, is also performed with the newly harvested crop, in this month. In the days of Mahābhārata, the new year commenced with this month. Hence the Lord declares it to be, His divine glory.

'Ṛtūnāṁ kusumākaraḥ'—In the spring season, the plant kingdom gets reanimated with fresh leaves and flowers, even without water. The weather is neither too hot nor too cold. So the Lord declares it, to be His divine glory.

Whatever excellence is observed in these divine glories is the Lord's. So a striver, should think only of the Lord, in all divine glories.

द्यूतं छलयतामस्मि तेजस्तेजस्विनामहम्।
जयोऽस्मि व्यवसायोऽस्मि सत्त्वं सत्त्ववतामहम्॥ ३६॥

dyūtaṁ chalayatāmasmi tejastejasvināmaham
jayo'smi vyavasāyo'smi sattvaṁ sattvavatāmaham

I am the dicing of those that cheat; I am, the glory of the glorious. I am, the victory of the victorious, the resolution, of the

* In the twenty-second verse the Lord declared Sāmaveda to be His divine glory while here He declares Bṛhatsāma to be His divine glory.

resolute; the goodness, of the good. 36

Comment:—

'Dyūtaṁ chalayatāmasmi'—The game of chance played for money, property or kingdom etc., is called gambling. The Lord has called it His divine glory.

Question:—If gambling is the Lord's divine glory, it means that there is no harm in gambling and then it should be justified. But then why is it forbidden, according to the ordinance of scriptures?

Answer:—In this context, there is description of the Lord's divine glories, not of sanction and prohibition. Arjuna put the question, "In what various aspects are you to be thought of, by me?" So the Lord is answering his question by telling him, that he should think of Him only, whatever he beholds in the form of His divine glories, because He declares, "All this universe is pervaded by Me" (Gītā 9/4).

Suppose a striver, in the past had the habit of gambling. Now he is busy with adoration. By chance, he is reminded of gambling. So he should think of God in it. Thus by beholding the Lord in gambling, and the loss and gain involved in it, a striver, will think only of the Lord.

The man (soul), is a fragment of the Lord but by error he has assumed his affinity with the body and the world. If he notices the excellences and the glories in the world, as the Lord's and thinks of Him, it will lead him to God-realization (Gītā 8/14). On the other hand, if he regards the glories as belonging to the world and thinks of the world, it will lead him to complete ruin (Gītā 2/62-63). These glories have been described so that a striver by thinking of the Lord, may know Him, in reality.

'Tejastejasvināmaham'—Tejas, is the glory or splendour of great souls, who possess divine traits. In front of great men who possess this glory, even sinners hesitate to commit sins. So it has been considered as the Lord's divine glory.

'Jayo'smi'—Everyone, likes victory. So, victory is the glory of the Lord.

A striver should not enjoy the pleasure of his victory by regarding it, as the manifestation of his power, but he should regard it, as the manifestation of the Lord.

'Vyavasāyo'smi'—Resolution or determination, is the Lord's divine glory. A lot of importance, has been attached to it in the Gītā, "The determination is one pointed" (2/41); "Those who are deeply attached to pleasure and worldly prosperity do not have the determinate intellect" (2/44); "Even, if the vilest sinner worships Me, with exclusive devotion, he should be considered a saint for he has rightly resolved" (9/30).

A striver, should not regard this resolution (determination), as his virtue but should consider it as Lord's glory, which he could cultivate only by, His grace.

'Sattvaṁ sattvavatāmaham'—The goodness of good persons, is Lord's glory. The quality of sattva (goodness) which prevails, suppressing rājasa (passion) and tāmasa (ignorance), should not be regarded, by a striver, as his own, but as the Lord's.

All virtues and achievements, such as glory, victory, resolution and goodness, really belong to the Lord. So a striver, instead of considering these his own, should consider them as the Lord's, and so he should think of Him, only.

वृष्णीनां वासुदेवोऽस्मि पाण्डवानां धनञ्जयः ।
मुनीनामप्यहं व्यासः कवीनामुशना कविः ॥ ३७ ॥

vṛṣṇīnāṁ vāsudevo'smi pāṇḍavānāṁ dhanañjayaḥ
munīnāmapyahaṁ vyāsaḥ kavīnāmuśanā kaviḥ

Among the members of the Vṛṣṇī clan (yādavas), I am Kṛṣṇa; among the Pāṇḍavas, Dhanañjaya; among the sages, I am Vyāsa

and among the knowing seers, I am the sage, Śukra. 37

Comment:—

'Vṛṣṇīnāṁ vāsudevo'smi'—Here, there is no reference to Lord Kṛṣṇa, as an incarnation, but as the best member of the Vṛṣṇi clan. All the divine glories in this chapter, have been described from the worldly view-point. In fact they are all manifestations of, the Lord.

'Pāṇḍavānāṁ dhanañjayaḥ'—Whatever distinction Arjuna, the Lord's dear friend possesses, is the Lord's. So the Lord declares him to be His very self.

'Munīnāmapyahaṁ vyāsaḥ'—It was sage Vyāsa, who compiled the Vedas, and divided them into four parts. The Mahābhārata, the eighteen celebrated Purāṇas and other scriptures were written by him. He is known, as the guide to modern authors. Any new treatise is said to be a polluted one. It means, it contains some portion which has already been included, in Vedavyāsa's works. Being the most important of all sages, he has been declared by the Lord as, His divine glory. So a striver, should think of the Lord because all this distinction in him, is the Lord's.

'Kavīnāmuśanā kaviḥ'—The term 'Kavi', stands for the learned men who know the scriptural principles well. Śukrācārya, was the foremost of the learned. He was an expert, in the science of reviving the dead. He is known for his science of ethics. Because, of his virtues and learning, he has been declared to be the very self, of the Lord.

Whatever distinction a striver, comes across should be regarded as the imperishable Lord's, not of the perishable world.

दण्डो दमयतामस्मि नीतिरस्मि जिगीषताम्।
मौनं चैवास्मि गुह्यानां ज्ञानं ज्ञानवतामहम्॥ ३८॥

daṇḍo damayatāmasmi nītirasmi jigīṣatām
maunaṁ caivāsmi guhyānāṁ jñānaṁ jñānavatāmaham

I am the authority of those who punish as rulers; I am righteousness, in those who seek victory. Of secrets, I am silence and I am wisdom, of the wise. 38

Comment:—

'Daṇḍo damayatāmasmi'—Just punishment is necessary, for a convict to deter him, from sinful behaviour and to enable him to follow the right conduct. So the Lord has declared it to be, His divine glory.

'Nītirasmi jigīṣatām'—It is righteousness by which, one gains victory, and again it is righteousness, which makes a victory everlasting. So, the Lord declares it to be, His divine glory.

'Maunaṁ caivāsmi guhyānām'—Out of all the secrets, silence is most important, because every person cannot know the feelings of those, who keep silent. So the Lord speaks of it as, His divine glory.

'Jñānaṁ jñānavatāmaham'—Whatever knowledge or wisdom, the wise have, is the Lord's divine glory.

So, whatever distinction, is perceived anywhere is not personal, but divine. So a striver, should always behold the Lord, in all the divine glories.

यच्चापि सर्वभूतानां बीजं तदहमर्जुन।
न तदस्ति विना यत्स्यान्मया भूतं चराचरम्॥ ३९ ॥*

yaccāpi sarvabhūtānāṁ bījaṁ tadahamarjuna
na tadasti vinā yatsyānmayā bhūtaṁ carācaram

* The Lord from the twentieth verse to the thirty-ninth verse has described His eighty-two divine glories—four in each of twentieth, twenty-first, twenty-second, twenty-third verses, three in the twenty-fourth verse, four in the twenty-fifth, four in the twenty-sixth, three in the twenty-seventh, four in each of the twenty-eighth, twenty-ninth, thirtieth and thirty-first verses, five in the thirty-second, four in the thirty-third, nine in the thirty-fourth, four in the thirty-fifth, five in the thirty-sixth, four in the thirty-seventh, and thirty-eighth each and one in the thirty-ninth verse.

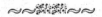

O Arjuna, I am the seed of all beings. There is no creature, animate or inanimate, that can exist without Me. 39

Comment:—

'Yaccāpi sarvabhūtānāṁ bījaṁ tadahamarjuna'—Here the Lord gives a gist of all His divine glories, by declaring that He is the seed or the cause of the entire, animate or inanimate creation. By the term 'seed', He means that He is efficient cause, as well as the material cause, of the entire creation. In other words, it can be said that He Himself is the creator, as well as, the creation.

In the tenth verse of the seventh chapter, the Lord declares Himself as 'the eternal seed', in the eighteenth verse of the ninth chapter, 'the imperishable seed' and in this verse only 'seed'. It means, that He in spite of remaining the same, manifests Himself as the entire universe; and in spite of His manifestation, in the form of the world, He remains, the same.

'Na tadasti vinā yatsyānmayā bhūtaṁ carācaram'—In the universe, whatever creature, animate or inanimate, moving or unmoving, are seen these cannot exist, without, the Lord. All of them, originate from Him i.e., He is manifest, in all of them. By knowing this fact, a striver should think of God alone in whatever, he sees and whatever comes to his mind, and intellect.

Here, the Lord declares, that there is no creature, animate or inanimate, that can exist without Him, while in the fortieth verse of the eighteenth chapter, He declares that there is no existence, which is free from the three modes (sāttvika, rājasika and tāmasika), born of matter (nature). The reason is, that here the context is of the Discipline of Devotion. Arjuna, put the question, "By what various aspects, are You to be thought of, by me?" The Lord answers, "I exist in all the forms, which come to your mind." But (in 18/40) in the context of the Discipline of Knowledge, in which, a striver should discriminate between Matter (Prakṛti) and soul. A striver, should renounce his core affinity with matter. The entire universe, consists of three modes, born of matter (nature). So the Lord, declares that there is no existence, which is free from the three modes, born of matter (Nature).

An Important Fact

In this chapter, the Lord has recounted His eighty-two divine glories, from the tenth to the thirty-ninth verses. His purpose in describing these is, not to mention that they are superior, mediocre or inferior, rather He wants to draw attention of the devotees, to the fact, that whatever comes to their sight or mind, they should think of, God only. The Lord, while describing his eighty-two glories, means to say, that a striver, should think of God only, whatever thing, circumstance or person he comes across,* because, Arjuna put the question as to which aspect He was to be thought of, by him (Gītā 10/17). So the Lord, has described His divine glories, in brief here. Similarly, in the Śrīmadbhāgavata also, (in the sixteenth chapter of the eleventh canto), Lord Kṛṣṇa has described, His divine glories to Uddhava. Some of the divine glories described, in the Gītā and the Śrīmadbhāgavata, are similar while some of them are not. In the Gītā, He declares that among priests, He is Bṛhaspati (10/24), while in the Bhāgavata He states that among priests, He is Vasiṣṭha (11/16/22). Now the question rises, why the same speaker, Lord Kṛṣṇa makes this distinction. The answer is, that Lord Kṛṣṇa while describing His divine glories, does not mean to attach importance to a thing or a person etc., but He wants to say that a striver, should think only of the Lord, whatever thing or person he comes across, physically or mentally. Therefore, whatever distinction appears in any object or person, should be regarded only, as the Lord's.

---

* Lord Nārāyaṇa pervades the entire universe, which is seen or heard, externally and internally.

Appendix—All beings are born in four different ways—

(1) Jarāyuja—born with amnion from the womb as men, cows, buffaloes, sheep and goats etc. (2) aṇḍaja—born from eggs as birds, snakes, squirrels and lizards etc., (3) Udbhijja—sprouting up from the earth as trees, creepers, grass, corn etc., (4) svedaja—born of sweat as louse and tiny whitish louse etc., as well as those born from the earth in rainy season such as earthworms etc. From these four sources eighty-four lac forms of lives are born. Out of these there are two kinds—immovable and movable. Trees, creepers, grass and vegetation etc., are immovable while men, beasts and birds etc., are movable. Out of these beings some live in water, some fly in the sky and some others live on the earth. Besides them there are several other forms of lives such as gods, manes, gandharvas (celestial singers and musicians), ghosts, evil spirits, devils, demons, 'pūtanā' and 'bālagraha' etc. God is the seed viz., the root cause of all these beings. It means that there are infinite beings in infinite universes but the seed of all of them is only one. Therefore only God has manifested Himself in all these forms—'Vāsudevaḥ sarvam'.

As seed is the origin of agriculture (farming), so is God the origin of the entire universe. As from millet there is production of millet; from wheat there is production of wheat; from an animal, animals are produced; from men, men are produced; similarly from God, only God emanates viz., the Lord is revealed in the form of the world. As in ornaments made of gold there is only gold, in the tools made of iron there is only iron, in the earthen-wares made of clay there is only clay, in the cloths made of cotton there is only cotton, similarly the world emanating from God is the manifestation of only God.

From the worldly seed, only one type of crop is grown. As from the seed of wheat, only wheat is produced, other crops such as millet, green lentil (mūṁga) and 'moṭha' etc., are not produced. Their seeds are different. But God is such a seed from

Whom different kinds of beings are born (Gītā 14/4); and in spite of giving birth to the entire creation, there is no modification or diminution in Him, He remains immutable because He is the imperishable seed (Gītā 9/18) and He is the eternal seed (Gītā 7/10).

Link:—Now in the next verse, Lord Kṛṣṇa concludes the topic by revealing, that there is no end, of His divine glories.

नान्तोऽस्ति मम दिव्यानां विभूतीनां परन्तप।
एष तूद्देशतः प्रोक्तो विभूतेर्विस्तरो मया॥ ४०॥

nānto'sti mama divyānāṁ vibhūtīnāṁ parantapa
eṣa tūddeśataḥ prokto vibhūtervistaro mayā

O harasser of foes, there is no end of My divine glories; this is only a brief description by Me, of the manifestation of My glories. 40

Comment:—

'Mama divyānāṁ* vibhūtīnām'—The term 'Divya', stands for singularity or uncommonness. If a striver, thinks of the Lord only, in whatever circumstances he is or wherever he is, that singularity or divinity, is revealed to him, because there is none else, as singular and divine, as the Lord. The gods who are called divine, are also always eager to behold, the Lord (Gītā 11/52). It proves that the Lord is the most divine. So His glories, are also divine. But the divinity of these glories, is revealed to a striver, only when he has the sole goal, to realize God and he, being free from attachment and aversion, thinks entirely of Him, in order to know the reality of Divinity.

* Arjuna first asked Lord Kṛṣṇa to tell him His divine glories (11/16). So Lord Kṛṣṇa while starting the description said that He would tell him His divine glories (10/19) and while concluding the topic he again tells Arjuna that there is no end of His divine glories (10/40). Thus the term 'divine' has been used in the question as well as in the beginning and conclusion of the answer.

'Nānto'sti'—There, is no end of the Lord's, divine glories. As the Lord himself, is endless, so are His glories, virtues, sport and discourses etc. Therefore, the Lord, while beginning His divine glories and concluding them, has said, that there is no end of His divine glories. In the Śrīmadbhāgavata also, about His glories, He says that He can count the number of atoms with the passage of time, but He, Who has created millions of universes, cannot count, His divine glories.

The Lord is endless, limitless and bottomless i.e., He is beyond the limit of time, and space.

'Eṣa tūddeśataḥ prokto vibhūtervistaro mayā'—The Lord, describes His divine glories, in detail from the view-point of Arjuna. But, from His view-point, this description is very brief, because His glories are endless.

[In this chapter some of the glories of the Lord, have been described. There may be other glories, which have not been described here, but they can be related to strivers. Therefore, whatsoever attracts the mind of a striver, should be regarded as the Lord's divine glory, whether it has been described here or not, and he should think only, of Him.]

Appendix—In the Gītā the Lord has mentioned His seventeen divine glories in the form of cause (7/8—12), thirty-seven divine glories in the form of effect and cause (9/16—19), twenty-five divine glories in the form of persons (10/6), eighty one glories in the form of principal and in the form of the ruler (10/20—38), one divine glory in the form of essence (10/39) and thirteen divine glories in the form of His influence (15/12—15). All this means that there is nothing else besides God. In all forms, God has manifested Himself. All this is the entire form of God. The unreal is kaleidoscopic while the real is immutable. These—the real (parā) and the unreal (aparā)—both are the Lord's divine glories—'Sadasaccāhamarjuna' (Gītā 9/19). It means that only God has manifested Himself in the form of divine glories. Therefore whatever attracts us, that is only the Lord's attraction. But we want to enjoy pleasures, so that attraction instead of changing into love (devotion) for God, is changed into desire and attachment which bind us to the world.

In the Gītā the Lord has called Brahma also 'mām' (His own self) (8/13). He has also said 'mām' to gods (9/23), He has also said 'mām' to Indra (9/20) and He has also said 'mām' to Uttamagati (supreme goal) (7/18), He has also said 'mām' to 'kṣetrajña' (the self) (13/2), He has also called the indwelling God as 'mām' (16/18) and He has also said the seed of all beings as 'mām' (7/10) and so on. It means that God, Who is endowed with attributes and is also attributeless; Who is endowed with form and is also formless; as well as men, gods, beasts, birds, gods, evil spirits and devils etc.,—all combined together is the entire form of the Lord viz., all are the divine glories of God, all is His majesty.* All these divine glories are imperishable.

Here a doubt arises, when the entire universe is the manifestation of God, then what is the purpose of the description-repetition of His divine glories? The explanation is that the question of Arjuna was, "In what various aspects should I think of You?" (10/17). In fact all is the entire form of God but the thing in which a man sees some speciality, it is easy to behold God and to think of Him in that thing, because mind is naturally attracted towards the thing whose speciality is marked in the mind. Therefore the Lord has described His divine glories. While describing His prominent divine glories the Lord declared, "I am the beginning, the middle and the end of all beings and of the

---

* sarve ca devā manavassamastāssaptarṣayo ye manusūnavaśca
indraśca yo'yaṁ tridaśeśabhūtọ viṣṇoraśeṣāstu vibhūtayastāḥ

(Viṣṇu Purāṇa 3/1/46)

'All gods, Manu, seven great sages, Manu's son and gods' king, Indra etc., as well as whatever is there besides them—all of them are Lord Viṣṇu's divine glories.'

entire creation" (10/20, 32), "I am the seed of all beings. There is no creature, animate or inanimate, that exists without Me" (10/39), and "I stand holding the entire universe in a fragment of My body" (10/42), then what remains besides God? Nothing remains. It means that all is God—'Vāsudevaḥ sarvam' (Gītā 7/19).

In the Gītā the description of the divine glories of God is not of secondary importance but it is an important means for God-realization which leads to 'Vāsudevaḥ sarvam.' The reason is that if any speciality appears in the world and we regard it as the Lord's speciality, naturally we shall be attracted towards God rather than towards that thing or person. Attraction or attachment to matter leads to bondage—'kāraṇaṁ guṇasaṅgo'sya sadasadyonijanmasu' (Gītā 13/21). Therefore the purpose of the description of the divine glories is that a striver may get rid of the notion of the existence of the world, the value of the world and the lovability of the world and may realize 'Vāsudevaḥ sarvam' which is the main aim of the gospel of the Gītā.

Existence of the world, its value and attachment to it, lead a men to bondage. If a man instead of being attracted towards the world, and instead of having the notion to enjoy pleasures out of it, regards it as the manifestation of God, then the assumption of the existence of the world, its value and attachment to it, will be renounced and he will accept the existence of God, he will value Him and will be attached to Him viz., will love Him.*

Link:—In the eighteenth verse, Arjuna requested Lord Kṛṣṇa, to describe His glories and power of Yoga. Having described

* nareṣvabhīkṣṇaṁ madbhāvaṁ puṁso bhāvayato'cirāt
spardhāsūyātiraskārāḥ sāhaṅkārā viyanti hi

(Śrīmadbhā. 11/29/15)

'When a devotee regards all men and women as My manifestation viz., beholds Me in them, then soon he gets rid of evils such as envy, fault-finding, contempt etc., with egoistic notion totally.'

His divine glories, now, He describes His power of Yoga, in the next verse.

यद्यद्विभूतिमत्सत्त्वं श्रीमदूर्जितमेव वा।
तत्तदेवावगच्छ त्वं मम तेजोंऽशसम्भवम्॥ ४१ ॥

yadyadvibhūtimatsattvaṁ śrīmadūrjitameva vā
tattadevāvagaccha tvaṁ mama tejoṁ'śasambhavam

Every such thing that is glorious, brilliant or powerful, know that, to be a manifestation, of a spark of My splendour. 41

Comment:—

'Yadyadvibhūtimatsattvaṁ śrīmadūrjitameva vā'—Whatever glory, brilliance, power, beauty or any other singularity, appears in animate or inanimate things, and persons etc., should be known as a manifestation, of a spark of the Lord's splendour—**'tattadevāvagaccha tvaṁ mama tejoṁ'śasambhavam'**. Without Him, there is no singularity, anywhere.

Therefore, whatever speciality a person observes, he should regard it, as the Lord's and so think of Him, only. If he thinks, that the speciality is of a person or a thing etc., he has a fall. If a chaste wife observes, something special in any other person, except her husband, her chastity gets polluted. Similarly if a devotee, perceives any singularity anywhere else except in God, his exclusive devotion, is affected.

Whatever beauty, glory or attraction, power or any other quality, appears in an object or a being, it is only the Lord's. How? If it had been, of a person or a thing, it might have remained there forever. But that is not so. Then, whose is it? It is of the Lord, Who is the illuminator, the origin and the base of all of these. One, who regards it as of a person or thing, gets entangled in the world, and gains nothing. But if he, after a serious thought comes to know the fact, that objects and persons that are perishable, cannot possess those qualities, they are only the Lord's, he attains bliss.

As electric current, works our radio but an ignorant person may regard the sound coming only from the radio, without attaching any importance to the electric current, while a person having knowledge of it knows, that the radio works by electric power. Similarly, an ignorant person, may regard the speciality of a person and an object as theirs, but a wise man treats it as, the Lord's.

In the eighth verse of this chapter, the Lord declared that, He is the source of all the creation and from him all things evolve. It means, that whatever glory, brilliance, power or any other speciality, is seen, is of the Lord. Once, a saint heard a prostitute singing a song with a melodious voice. He cried, "Oh! What a melody bestowed upon her, by the Lord!" Thus the saint instead of paying attention to the prostitute, paid attention to the glory, of the Lord. Therefore, wherever any beauty, excellence, quality or speciality appears, should be regarded as that of the Lord. But it does not mean, that we should not feel thankful, to those who have done good to us, with their qualities. We should be grateful to them, and we should render service, to them. But we should not get entangled in the world, by regarding these as belonging to them.

An Important Fact

While describing His divine glories, from the twentieth verse to the thirty-ninth verse, the Lord has used the term 'Asmi' (I), several times, to lay emphasis on the fact, that He is the origin of all divine glories. He has used the term 'Viddhi' (Know), two times, once in the twenty-fourth verse, and the second time in the twenty-seventh verse and 'Avagaccha' (Know), in the forty-first verse.

The term 'Viddhi' (Know), has been used to make us cautious. A man becomes cautious, by knowledge and by a ruling power. A preceptor, imparts knowledge, while a king rules with his authority. In the twenty-fourth verse, the Lord mentions the name of preceptor, Bṛhaspati. It means, that people should know the reality, about His divine glories, through a preceptor. That knowledge will lead them to, unwavering devotion (Gītā 10/7). In the twenty-seventh verse, the Lord by mentioning the king as His divine glory, means to convey that we through the ruling power of a king, should follow the right path viz., make our life virtuous. To bring home something, a preceptor applies his love, while a king applies his power. A preceptor wants his disciple to attain salvation, while a king wants his subjects, to obey the rules of the country.

The terms 'Uccaiḥśravā' and 'Airāvata', in the twenty-seventh verse, denote prosperity of the king. So the term 'Viddhi' (Know), in this verse, specially seems to be used, for the king.

The term 'Avagaccha' (Know), used in this verse, means to know the reality that whatever distinction is observed in the universe, is only the Lord's.

Thus, by giving the term 'Viddhi', two times and 'Avagaccha' once, the Lord means that, so long as, a person does not carry out the orders of the preceptor, and the king and try to understand reality, the knowledge imparted by the preceptor and the authority of the king, will be of no avail, for him. If, he himself carries out their orders, and knows the reality, then and then only, it can be useful for him.

Appendix—Besides the divine glories already mentioned, if a striver is attracted towards any person or thing, there he should behold God viz., he should firmly hold that that speciality is not of a person or a thing but that is only God's. When he firmly believes that there is only God, the world will disappear in the same way as when we hold that in ornaments made of gold, there is nothing else besides gold, then existence of the ornaments is lost; when we think that in the toys made of sugar, there is nothing else besides sugar, then toys vanish. The reason is that in fact the world has no existence. Only the man (self) because of his attachment and aversion, has sustained the world 'yayedaṁ dhāryate jagat' (Gītā 7/5). The gist of all this is that a striver has to attain the goal—'Vāsudevaḥ sarvam' (all is God). Therefore the Lord according to 'Arundhatīnyāya' has described His divine glories so that strivers may realize 'Vāsudevaḥ sarvam' because when a striver beholds God in divine glories, then God will be seen everywhere viz., there will be no attraction for things, but there will be attraction for God only because God has manifested Himself as things.

Whatever speciality or remarkability is possessed by man, that is bestowed upon him only by God. If God had not possessed that speciality or remarkability, how would He have bestowed it upon the man? How can there be any speciality in the fragment (aṁśa) which is not in the whole (aṁśī)? A man commits an error that he, by regarding the speciality as his own, gets proud of it and does not pay attention to God, the origin (source) of the speciality.

All things, persons etc., of the creation are perishing every moment. The speciality in the form of beauty and power etc., which is perceived also vanishes. Therefore everything of the universe is preaching us the practical sermon, "Don't look at me, I'll not stay forever but look at my maker Who has manifested Himself in different forms and Who will stay forever. Whatever beauty or power or remarkability is being perceived in me, that is not mine but that is only His." Having realized this fact, we shall have no attraction for things and persons etc., but we shall behold God in them. Thus there will not be 'Bhoga' viz., enjoyment of pleasures but naturally there will be 'Yoga' (viz., natural eternal union with God).

God is the remarkable storehouse of all powers, arts and sciences etc. Powers can't stay in the inert Prakṛti (matter) but can stay in divine Godhood only. How can the knowledge, by which all actions are being performed, stay in matter? If it is assumed that there are all powers in Prakṛti, even then it will have to be accepted that Prakṛti has no ability to reveal those powers and to use those powers (for the creation of the universe etc.). As a computer in spite of being inert, works wonders but it is made and conducted by the sentient viz., man. It can't work without being constructed, guided and conducted (directed) by man. A computer has no independent existence but it is man-made, while God exists by itself.

Had God not possessed special traits, how would have they been inherited by beings? A particular trait of the seed is found in that tree which grows from that seed. How will any special trait, which is not in the seed, be possessed by the tree? The poetic talent of a poet comes from God, the power of oration of an orator comes from God, the power of charity in a donor comes from God. He is the origin of all these powers. Salvation, knowledge and love etc.—all have been bestowed upon us by God. This is not the evolute of nature. If 'I am an embodiment of salvation'—this is true, then how was I bound, when was I bound and why was I bound? If 'I am knowledge personified'—this is true, from where was ignorance emanated, how was it emanated, when was it emanated and why was it emanated? How can the darkest night of 'amāvasya' stay in the sun? In fact knowledge is the possession of God, but a man has assumed it as his own, thus ignorance has evolved.* 'I am knowledge personified, knowledge is mine'—This 'I' and 'mine' (egoism and the sense of possession) (ahaṁtā-mamatā) is ignorance†. When we are not inclined towards the Lord Who has bestowed upon us salvation, knowledge and love, then it appears that salvation is

---

* Knowledge or the power of knowing is not there in prakṛti. Prakṛti never remains uniform but it is kaleidoscopic. If there is knowledge in Prakṛti, that knowledge also instead of being uniform, will be kaleidoscopic. The knowledge which is born, will not stay forever but will be transient. If anybody holds that there is knowledge only in prakṛti, we call that prakṛti God, there is difference only in words. It means that there is no knowledge in prakṛti, if there is, then that (prakṛti) is God.

† maiṁ aru mora tora taiṁ māyā,
jehiṁ basa kīnhe jīva nikāyā. (Mānasa, Araṇya 15/1)

mine, knowledge is mine, love is mine. This is the singularity of the Lord that He has endowed us with the things in such a way that we think that they are ours. This singularity of God is an example for strivers which they should follow. A man commits a blunder that he assumes the thing, which has been bestowed upon him by God, as his own; but he does not cast a glance on the most gracious giver. He sees the thing received but he does not see the giver. He perceives the action but he does not perceive the cause by whose power the action could be done. In fact the thing is not one's own, but the giver is one's own.

A man becomes a Karmayogī with the power conferred on him by God, he becomes a Jñānayogī with the knowledge bestowed upon him by God and He becomes a Bhaktiyogī by possessing the devotion (love) showered on him by God. Whatever singularity or speciality is observed in a man, that is all the gift from God. Having given all the things to him, He does not reveal the fact—this is His nature.

Link:—Having answered Arjuna's question, in the next verse, the Lord Himself reveals an important fact.

अथवा बहुनैतेन किं ज्ञातेन तवार्जुन।
विष्टभ्याहमिदं कृत्स्नमेकांशेन स्थितो जगत्॥ ४२॥

athavā bahunaitena kiṁ jñātena tavārjuna
viṣṭabhyāhamidaṁ kṛtsnamekāṁśena sthito jagat

Or what need is there, for you O Arjuna, of detailed knowledge? I stand supporting the entire universe, with a single fragment, of Myself. 42

Comment:—

'Athavā'—This term suggests something different, from what has been stated already. By this term, the Lord means to say, that He has already answered the question. Now, He wants to tell him something remarkable, of His own accord.

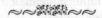

'Bahunaitena kiṁ jñātena tavārjuna'—Lord Kṛṣṇa says, "O brother Arjuna! What need is there, to know all this in detail? Though I am sitting before you as a chariot-driver, with the horses' bridle and a whip, in My hands, to carry out your order, yet I hold countless universes, in both the states of new creation and final dissolution, in a fragment of My body."

'Viṣṭabhyāhamidaṁ kṛtsnamekāṁśena sthito jagat'—The Lord, means to say, that He stands holding the countless universes, in a fragment of His body, through His Yogic power. But it does not mean that, that fragment is occupied by countless universes, and so that fragment is not empty. That fragment is still empty. As, with our intellect, we know several languages, scripts and art etc., but it does not mean, that there is no more room in it, to know more languages and scripts etc. We can learn, several other languages, scripts and arts etc., with it. When even our intellect, a small fragment of matter, is not filled with the knowledge, of different languages etc., how can a fragment of the Lord, Who is transcendental, endless, limitless and bottomless, be filled with, countless universes?

Appendix—This verse means that God has manifested Himself in the form of the world because He is the pervaded as well as the pervader. He is subtle as well as great, He is real as well as unreal. He is infinite, therefore he stands holding the countless universes in a fragment of His body—'ekāṁśena sthito jagat'.

The Lord wants to draw attention to the fact that Only He is all. If a striver pays attention to Him, then he need not know and think of any divine glory. The Lord means to say, "When I, Who am the base, support, illuminator and seed (root) of all divine glories, am sitting before you, then what is the need of thinking of My divine glories?"

ॐ तत्सदिति श्रीमद्भगवद्गीतासूपनिषत्सु ब्रह्मविद्यायां योगशास्त्रे श्रीकृष्णार्जुनसंवादे विभूतियोगो नाम दशमोऽध्यायः॥ १०॥

oṁ tatsaditi śrīmadbhagavadgītāsūpaniṣatsu brahmavidyāyāṁ yogaśāstre śrīkṛṣṇārjunasaṁvāde vibhūtiyogo nāma daśamo'dhyāyaḥ

Thus with the words Oṁ Tat, Sat, the names of the Lord, in the Upaniṣad of the Bhagavadgītā, the knowledge of Brahma, the Supreme, the scripture of Yoga and the dialogue between Śrī Kṛṣṇa and Arjuna, this is the tenth designated discourse : "The Yoga of Divine Glories."

Words, letters and Uvāca (said) in the Tenth Chapter

(1) In this chapter in **'Atha daśamo'dhyāyaḥ'**, there are three words, in **'Arjuna Uvāca'** etc., there are six words, and in verses, there are five hundred and fifty-six words, and thirteen concluding words. Thus, the total number of words, is five hundred and seventy-eight.

(2) In **'Atha daśamo'dhyāyaḥ'** there are seven letters, in **'Arjuna Uvāca'** etc., there are twenty letters, in verses one thousand three hundred and forty-four letters, and there are forty-six concluding letters. Thus the total letters are one thousand, four hundred and seventeen. Each of the verses, in this chapter consists of thirty-two letters.

(3) In this chapter, there are three **'Uvāca'**—two **'Śrībhagavānuvāca'** and one **'Arjuna Uvāca'**.

Metres Used in the Tenth Chapter—

In this chapter, out of the forty-two verses, in the first quarter of the second and twenty-fifth verses, 'na-gaṇa' being used, there is **'na-vipulā'** metre; in the first quarter of the seventh verse, and third quarter of the fifth and thirty-second verses, 'ma-gaṇa' being used there, is **'ma-vipulā'** metre; in the first quarter of the eighth verse and third quarter of the twenty-sixth verse 'bha-gaṇa' being used there is **'bha-vipulā'** metre; in the first quarter of the sixth verse, 'ra-gaṇa' being used there is **'ra-vipulā'** metre. The remaining thirty-six verses, have the characteristics of right **'pathyāvaktra'**, Anuṣṭup metre.

|| Shri Hari ||

Eleventh Chapter

INTRODUCTION

At the end of the tenth chapter, Lord Kṛṣṇa graciously said to Arjuna, "I hold countless universes in a fragment of My body and yet I am sitting before you as a chariot-driver, with horses' bridle and a whip in My hands and carrying out your wishes I am the core of all the divine glories and Yoga (influence) and when I am sitting before you, what need is there for you to have detailed knowledge of My divine glories"? After listening to the statement of Lord Kṛṣṇa, Arjuna thinks of His special grace and being wonder-struck, speaks.

अर्जुन उवाच

मदनुग्रहाय परमं गुह्यमध्यात्मसञ्ज्ञितम्।*
यत्त्वयोक्तं वचस्तेन मोहोऽयं विगतो मम॥ १॥

arjuna uvāca

madanugrahāya paramaṁ guhyamadhyātmasañjñitam
yattvayoktaṁ vacastena moho'yaṁ vigato mama

Arjuna said:

By this, profound discourse of spiritual wisdom that you have delivered, out of compassion for me, my darkness has been dispelled. 1

Comment:—

'Madanugrahāya'—The Lord, out of grace declared, "Out

---

* After thinking of the unusual grace of the Lord on him Arjuna was overwhelmed with joy. So without keeping in mind the rule he spoke this verse of thirty-three letters instead of thirty-two because when a man is beside himself, he is likely to forget the rule.

of compassion, for those who worship Me, I destroy their ignorance—born of darkness" (Gītā 10/11). Arjuna, was very influenced by His statement. So he offered praises to Him (10/12—15) and told Him, that it was only out of compassion, that He revealed to him His closely guarded secret.*

'Paramaṁ guhyam'—The Lord, after describing His important divine glories, at the end of the tenth chapter, told him of his own accord, that He stood supporting the whole universe, with a single fragment of his Self (10/42). Arjuna regards this fact, as the supreme secret.

'Adhyātmasañjñitam'—In the seventh verse of the tenth chapter, the Lord declares, that he who knows, in reality His divine glories and Yoga-power (viz., He is the origin of all divine glories and again those divine glories, merge in Him), he is endowed with unfaltering Yoga of devotion. This has been called by Arjuna 'Adhyātmasañjñitam' (spiritual wisdom)†.

'Yattvayoktaṁ vacastena moho'yaṁ vigato mama'—Arjuna's delusion, was that he did not know that the Lord holds the entire universe, in a fragment of His body. But, when the Lord explained the fact to him, he came to know His uniqueness that though countless universes emanate from a fragment of His body, they remain established in it, and again merge in it, yet He remains, the same. Arjuna said that his delusion‡ was dispelled, but the Lord knew that his delusion was not totally dispelled. So again,

---

* Whatever Lord Kṛṣṇa explained to Arjuna in the Gītā from the beginning to this stage was out of compassion only because all His actions are full of His grace but a man does not realize this fact. When a man realizes His grace, he attains Divinity very easily and quickly. When Arjuna realizes His grace, he being overwhelmed with joy tells Him that it is by His grace that his delusion is destroyed.

† Whatever has been said by the Lord about devotion so far, is the supreme-secret-spiritual gospel.

‡ A man does not know delusion so long as he has it. But he knows it only when it is dispelled.

in the forty-ninth verse, the Lord says to Arjuna, "Be neither perturbed nor deluded."

Appendix—Arjuna says to Lord Kṛṣṇa, "Your utterance, which You have made, is out of compassion for me rather than to show Your learning. In it there is no other motive except Your grace alone."

'I am the beginning, the middle and the end of all beings' (10/20), 'I am also the seed of all beings' (10/39), 'Everything which is glorious, brilliant and powerful know that to be a manifestation of a spark of My splendour' (10/42), 'I stand supporting the entire universe with a single fragment of Myself (10/42)—having heard these words Arjuna felt that his delusion was destroyed. But in fact his delusion was partly destroyed, it was not destroyed totally.

Link:—How Arjuna's delusion was dispelled, is explained by him, in the next verse.

भवाप्ययौ हि भूतानां श्रुतौ विस्तरशो मया।
त्वत्तः कमलपत्राक्ष माहात्म्यमपि चाव्ययम्॥ २॥

bhavāpyayau hi bhūtānāṁ śrutau vistaraśo mayā
tvattaḥ kamalapatrākṣa māhātmyamapi cāvyayam

From You, O lotus-eyed, I have heard in detail, an account of the origin and dissolution of creation and also of Your immortal glory. 2

Comment:—

'Bhavāpyayau hi bhūtānāṁ śrutau vistaraśo mayā'—The Lord declared, "I am the origin (source) of the entire creation, and in Me again, it dissolves. There is no other source, besides Me" (Gītā 7/6-7); "Whatever beings, there are, born of sattva, of rajas or of tamas, know them all, as evolved from Me alone" (7/12); "Diverse feelings, of creatures emanate, from Me alone" (10/4-5);

"I am the source of all creation; everything in the world, moves because of Me" (10/8); "I am the beginning, the middle and also the end, of all beings" (10/20); and "I am the beginning and the end and also the middle of all creation" (10/32). So, Arjuna says that he has heard in detail, an account of the origin and dissolution of beings. He means that all the beings evolve from Him, live in Him and merge in Him i.e., He is all in all.

'Māhātmyamapi cāvyayam'—Arjuna wants to say, that he also heard of His immortal glory, as explained by Him, in the seventh verse of the tenth chapter, that he who knows in reality, His divine power and glory, is endowed with unfaltering Yoga of devotion.

The Lord's glory, has been called immortal, because after knowing His divine glory and power in reality, one is endowed with devotion, which is immortal, because the Lord Himself is immortal, so devotion for Him, should also be immortal.

Appendix—In this verse Arjuna from his point of view tells the reason how his delusion was dispelled. 'Māhātmyamapi cāvyayam'—Here by the term 'api' it is interpreted that Arjuna heard the Lord's perishable glory and also heard His imperishable glory. 'Bhavāpyayau hi bhūtānām'—this is God's perishable viz., changeable glory. A man may be connected with God in any way—this will lead him to salvation—this is God's imperishable viz., immutable glory. It means that the real as well as the unreal, all is only God—'sadasaccāham' (Gītā 9/19).

Link:—In the next two verses, Arjuna requests Lord Kṛṣṇa, to vouchsafe a vision of His Cosmic Form.

एवमेतद्यथात्थ त्वमात्मानं परमेश्वर।
द्रष्टुमिच्छामि ते रूपमैश्वरं पुरुषोत्तम॥ ३॥

evametadyathāttha tvamātmānaṁ parameśvara
draṣṭumicchāmi te rūpamaiśvaraṁ puruṣottama

O Lord Supreme, You are precisely what You have declared Yourself to be. But, I long to see Your cosmic divine form, O greatest of persons. 3

Comment:—

'Puruṣottama'—Arjuna addresses the Lord, as the best (Supreme) person, because no other person is equal to Him. The same fact, has been pointed out by the Lord Himself in the fifteenth chapter when He declares, "I am beyond perishable matter, and superior to the imperishable soul. Therefore, I am known in the world and in the Vedas, as the Supreme Person" (15/18).

'Evametadyathāttha tvamātmānam'—Arjuna says, that whatever has been spoken by the Lord about His virtues, glories and divine powers, (from the seventh to the tenth chapters), is wholly true, without any doubt.

The Lord declares, "I am the origin of the entire creation and in Me again it dissolves" (7/6), "It has no other source, besides Me" (7/7), "All is God" (7/19), "I am Brahma (the Infinite), Adhyātma (Self), action, Adhibhūta (Matter), Adhidaiva (Brahmā, the creator) and Adhiyajña (the Unmanifest Divinity)" (7/29-30). "I am the Supreme Person, attainable by exclusive devotion" (8/22), "All this universe, is pervaded by Me, but I don't dwell in the beings, nor do the beings, dwell in Me" (9/4-5); "I am, being and non-being, both" (9/19); "I am the source of all creation and everything in the world moves, because of Me" (10/8) and "I support the whole universe with a single fragment of Myself" (10/42) etc. Arjuna says, that whatever has been said, by Him is wholly true.

'Parameśvara'—Arjuna heard Lord Kṛṣṇa says, "I am Lord of all beings" (4/6); "I am the Supreme Lord of all the worlds" (5/29). So Arjuna addresses Him, as the Lord Supreme, because He is the Supreme Lord, of the entire creation.

'Draṣṭumicchāmi te rūpamaiśvaram'—Arjuna tells Lord Kṛṣṇa, that after hearing of His immortal glory, he has a firm belief in

His words; and after hearing the words, that He supports the entire universe with a single fragment of His self, he has developed an irresistible yearning, to see His Cosmic Form.

Secondly, Arjuna says that though He is the Supreme Ruler of all the universes, yet it is very kind of Him to love him so much, to act as he wishes and to answer whatever, he asks. It is, because of His extraordinary kindness to him, that he has developed an irresistible yearning to see that form, in whose single fragment He supports the entire universe.

In the sixteenth verse of the tenth chapter, Arjuna requested Lord Kṛṣṇa to describe in full, His divine glories. In response to his question, Lord Kṛṣṇa while describing His divine glories, in the beginning and at the end, told him that there was no end to His divine glories (10/19,40). So, He gave only a brief description. But, here Arjuna requests Him to show him His divine form (only one), but Lord Kṛṣṇa says to him, "Behold in hundreds and thousands, My multifarious divine forms" (11/5). As in this mortal world, if a greedy person demands a lot, from a donor, he gets only a little; but if he demands a little hesitatingly, the donor gives more. Similarly, first Arjuna requested the Lord to describe His divine glories in detail, so He described in brief. But, here Arjuna becomes cautious and hesitatingly prays to Lord Kṛṣṇa, to reveal that form to him, if He deems it fit. The Lord, is influenced by this hesitating mood and asks him to behold His multifarious divine form, in hundreds and thousands.

Also Lord Kṛṣṇa while sitting in a part of Arjuna's chariot said, "In a part of this body of Mine, the entire creation (having infinite universes) pervades." So Arjuna, developed an irresistible yearning to see that form of His.

Appendix—Arjuna means to say to the Lord, "O Lord! Having heard Your words, I have understood You well and there is no doubt about it. Only You are all—this is exactly the same. Now only Your cosmic divine form is left to be seen."

The gospel can be preached in two ways—by utterance and by demonstration. In the tenth chapter the Lord described His entire form and declared, "I stand supporting the entire universe with a single fragment of Myself". Now in this chapter Arjuna requests Lord Kṛṣṇa to show him His cosmic form.

मन्यसे यदि तच्छक्यं मया द्रष्टुमिति प्रभो।
योगेश्वर ततो मे त्वं दर्शयात्मानमव्ययम्॥ ४॥

manyase yadi tacchakyaṁ mayā draṣṭumiti prabho
yogeśvara tato me tvaṁ darśayātmānamavyayam

O Lord if You, think that this cosmic form could possibly be seen by me, then, O Lord of Yoga, reveal to me that imperishable form. 4

Comment:—

'Prabho'—The term 'Prabho', means Omnipotent. Arjuna uses this vocative 'Prabho', for Lord Kṛṣṇa to indicate, that He is Omnipotent. So, even if he is not agreeable, the Lord, by His grace and power could enable him, to have a vision of His divine form.

'Manyase yadi tacchakyaṁ mayā draṣṭumiti'—Arjuna says to Lord Kṛṣṇa, that even if He does not reveal His divine form to him, he will believe His words, that His form is the same as He has described, but he is not qualified and deserving to behold it. Thus, Arjuna does not doubt the Lord's statement in the least, rather he has full faith in it. So he prays to Him, to reveal to him His divine form, if He thinks it possible for him, to see it.

'Yogeśvara'—By using the address 'Yogeśvara', Arjuna says that He is the Lord of all Yogas (Disciplines), such as the Disciplines of Devotion, of Action, of Meditation, of Knowledge etc. So by His power, He could enable him, to behold His divine Cosmic Form.

Arjuna, in the seventeenth verse of the tenth chapter, used the term 'Yogin' but now he uses the term 'Yogeśvara' (the Lord of Yoga) i.e., the Master of all the Yogas, because now there is a lot of change in his attitude, towards the Lord.

'Tato me tvaṁ darśayātmānamavyayam'— Arjuna prays to Lord Kṛṣṇa, to reveal to him His imperishable form, from which infinite universes emanate, in which they remain established, and in which they again merge.

Appendix—The cosmic form of the Lord has been called 'avyaya' (imperishable) which proves that the entire universe is the Lord's manifestation. Being imperishable it does not cease to be totally (Gītā 15/1). In fact the mutable (the unreal) and the immutable (the real)—both combinedly is the entire form of God—'sadasaccāhamarjuna'. Insentience appears because of one's own attachment and ignorance.

Link:—After listening to Arjuna's humble prayer, the Lord asks him to behold His Cosmic Form.

श्रीभगवानुवाच

पश्य मे पार्थ रूपाणि शतशोऽथ सहस्रशः।
नानाविधानि दिव्यानि नानावर्णाकृतीनि च॥ ५॥

śrībhagavānuvāca

paśya me pārtha rūpāṇi śataśo'tha sahasraśaḥ
nānāvidhāni divyāni nānāvarṇākṛtīni ca

The Blessed Lord said:

Behold My forms, O Pārtha (Arjuna), hundreds and thousands, multifarious and divine, of various colours, sizes and shapes. 5

Comment:—

'Paśya me pārtha rūpāṇi śataśo'tha sahasraśaḥ'—Listening to the humble and hesitating prayer of Arjuna, the Lord, was very much pleased with him. So He addressing him as 'Pārtha' (the son of Pṛthā, Kuntī), asks him to behold His forms, by hundreds and thousands i.e., innumerable forms. Thus, the Lord explains that as His divine glories are infinite, so are His forms.

'Nānāvidhāni divyāni nānāvarṇākṛtīni ca'—Now, the Lord describes the characteristics of those forms. They were heterogenious in character, consisting of different shapes, colours and sizes.

As a particle of the earth, is earth in miniature, this world, being, a fragment of the Lord having a Cosmic Form, is nothing besides the Lord. But, it is not manifest to all, in its divine form, it is manifest only in its worldly form. It is so, because a man, instead of beholding the Lord, see only, the perishable world. As the Lord, even in an incarnation, is not manifest to all (Gītā 7/25), He appears, only, as a common man, to all; similarly, the universal form of the Lord is seen as of the world, by a common man. Here, the Lord by revealing Himself in His divine imperishable Cosmic Form, calls upon Arjuna to behold, His divine forms.

Appendix—Arjuna, regarding himself as incapable (undeserving) requests the Lord to show him His cosmic divine form if He so wills. But the Lord asks him to behold His hundreds and thousands forms. It proves that, if something is left at God's will, it is more beneficial than what is desired with one's own will, and expected with one's own intellect. The reason is that a man may learn several sciences, arts and crafts etc., study several scriptures, yet his intellect is meagre and limited. The more simple (innocent), helpless and free from pride a striver is, the more he will know about God. Pride is an obstacle in the way of knowing God. The more sensible a man thinks himself to be, the more insensible he remains. By assuming himself sensible, he becomes a slave to sensibility. The more free from the pride of sensibility he is, the more sensible he is.

Link:—In the previous verse, the Lord called upon Arjuna to behold His Cosmic Form, of various colours and shapes. Now in the next verse, He asks Arjuna to behold the gods and other wonders, in His body.

पश्यादित्यान्वसून्रुद्रानश्विनौ मरुतस्तथा।
बहून्यदृष्टपूर्वाणि पश्याश्चर्याणि भारत॥ ६ ॥

paśyādityānvasūnrudrānaśvinau marutastathā
bahūnyadṛṣṭapūrvāṇi paśyāścaryāṇi bhārata

Behold in Me, O Bhārata, the twelve sons of Aditi, the eight Vasus, the eleven Rudras (gods of destruction), the two Aśvinīkumāras (the twin physicians of gods) and the forty-nine Maruts (wind-gods) and many more marvels, never revealed before. 6

Comment:—

'Paśyādityānvasūnrudrānaśvinau marutastathā'—The twelve sons of Aditi are—Dhātā, Mitra, Aryamā, Śakra, Varuṇa, Aṁśa, Bhaga, Vivasvān, Pūṣā, Savitā, Tvaṣṭā and Viṣṇu (Mahā. Ādi. 65/ 15-16).

The eight vasus are—Dhara, Dhruva, Soma, Ahaḥ, Anila, Anala, Pratyūṣa and Prabhāsa (Mahā. Ādi. 66/18).

The eleven Rudras are—Hara, Bahurūpa, Tryambaka, Aparājita, Vṛṣākapi, Śambhu, Kapardī, Raivata, Mṛgavyādha, Śarva and Kapālī (Harivaṁśa. 1/3/51-52).

Aśvinīkumāras, are the twin born physicians of gods. The forty-nine Maruts (wind-gods) are—Sattvajyoti, Āditya, Satyajyoti,Tiryagjyoti, Sajyoti, Jyotiṣmān, Harita, Ṛtajit, Satyajit, Suṣeṇa, Senajit, Satyamitra, Abhimitra, Harimitra, Kṛta, Satya, Dhruva, Dhartā, Vidhartā, Vidhāraya, Dhvānta, Dhuni, Ugra, Bhīma, Abhiyu, Sākṣipa, Īdṛk, Anyādṛk, Yādṛk, Pratikṛt, Ṛk, Samiti, Saṁrambha, Īdṛkṣa, Puruṣa, Anyādṛkṣa, Cetasa, Samitā,

Samidṛkṣa, Pratidṛkṣa, Maruti, Sarata, Deva, Diśa, Yajuḥ, Anudṛk, Sāma, Mānuṣa and Viś (Vāyupurāṇa 67/123—130).

The Lord, calls upon Arjuna to behold them all, in His Cosmic Form.

These thirty-three varieties of gods, are the principal ones. The forty-nine Maruts (wind-gods), are regarded as separate from the thirty-three varieties of gods, because they were transformed from demons to gods. So the Lord, has separated them from other gods, by using the term 'tatha' (and) (also).

'Bahūnyadṛṣṭapūrvāṇi paśyāścaryāṇi bhārata'— The Lord, asks Arjuna to behold such marvels in those forms, which he might have neither seen, nor heard of nor imagined, nor thought of. After beholding such forms, a person is wonder-struck and left aghast.

Appendix—In the preceding verse the Lord asked Arjuna to behold His forms of various kinds, colours, sizes and shapes in His cosmic form; now in this verse He mentions the same in detail.

The Lord means to say that all gods are His manifestations only viz., He has revealed Himself in the forms of those gods (Gītā 9/23).

Link:—After hearing the Lord's order to behold His cosmic form, Arjuna may be curious to know where to behold it. So the Lord declares.

इहैकस्थं जगत्कृत्स्नं पश्याद्य सचराचरम्।
मम देहे गुडाकेश यच्चान्यद्द्रष्टुमिच्छसि॥ ७॥

ihaikasthaṁ jagatkṛtsnaṁ paśyādya sacarācaram
mama dehe guḍākeśa yaccānyaddraṣṭumicchasi

O conqueror of sleep Arjuna, now behold within this body of Mine, the entire universe consisting of both animate and inanimate

beings and whatever else you wish to see. 7

Comment:—

'Guḍākeśa'—Arjuna is addressed as 'Guḍākeśa because he was the conqueror of sleep. The Lord by addressing Arjuna as Guḍākeśa, invites him to observe His cosmic form, attentively giving up indolence.

'Ihaikasthaṁ jagatkṛtsnaṁ paśyādya sacarācaram mama dehe'—At the end of the tenth chapter, the Lord declared, that He supports the whole universe, with a single fragment of His self. So, Arjuna developed a desire to see his cosmic form. Therefore, the Lord calls upon Arjuna to behold, within a part of His body the entire creation, consisting of both animate and inanimate beings, while He is sitting in front of him with the horses bridle and a whip, in His hands. The Lord says that in His body, wherever he looks, he will see, infinite universes. The word 'Cara' stands for all creatures possessing mobility, such as men, gods, genies, demons, ghosts, beasts and birds etc., while 'Acara', denotes things devoid of motion, such as trees, plants and hills etc., and 'Adya', here means now. The Lord means to say, that there is no reason for any delay, for Him to reveal His cosmic form. So He reveals it, the moment Arjuna expresses his earnest desire to behold it.

'Yaccānyaddraṣṭumicchasi'— By this expression, Lord Kṛṣṇa wants to convey to Arjuna, that he can perceive, not only the incidents relating to the present, but also of the past, and the future. Moreover, Arjuna had a doubt, whether they would win the war or the Kauravas, would (Gītā 2/6). So Lord Kṛṣṇa asks him to perceive at that moment, in a part of His body, a scene of his own victory, and his enemy's defeat.

An Important Fact

The Lord, in the seventh verse of the tenth chapter, declared, "He who knows in reality, the divine glory and power of Mine, is endowed with, unfaltering Yoga of devotion. "Hearing this statement, Arjuna by offering praise and prayer to Him, requested Him to describe His divine glories. Similarly, by hearing the Lord's statement, that He stands supporting the whole universe with a single fragment of His self, Arjuna prays to the Lord to reveal to him, His cosmic form. If the Lord had not made this statement, Arjuna would have not prayed to Him, to reveal His cosmic form. It means, that the Lord by His own grace, wants to reveal to him His cosmic form.

A similar incident occurred, when Arjuna asked Lord Kṛṣṇa to place his chariot, between the two armies. Lord Kṛṣṇa placed the chariot between the two armies in front of Bhīṣma and Droṇa and said, "Arjuna, behold these Kauravas" (1/25). It indicates, that the Lord wanted to preach the gospel, of the Gītā. If the Lord, had not said so, and Arjuna had not seen his kinsmen, he might not have grieved, and the Lord might not have preached the gospel of the Gītā. It means, that the Lord by His grace, has preached the gospel of Gītā, of His own accord.

Appendix—The Lord orders Arjuna to behold the entire universe in a single fragment of His body. It proves that Lord Kṛṣṇa is entire and in a fragment of His body He holds the entire universe.

'roma roma prati lāge koṭi koṭi brahmaṇḍa'—

(Mānasa, Bāla 201)

The Lord is clearly showing this fact. When the Lord holds the entire universe in a fragment of His body, then what remains besides Him? All is only God. Therefore the Lord says to Arjuna, "Whatever you want to see, all this you can see in My cosmic form." Arjuna wanted to know the result of the war, which he saw in the cosmic form of the Lord (the chief warriors were rushing head long into the Lord's fearful mouths) (Gītā 11/26-27).

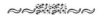

Link:— The Lord, in the previous three verses, called upon Arjuna to behold His cosmic form, four times by using the term 'Paśya' (see). But Arjuna in spite of his best efforts could behold nothing. So the Lord (knowing the cause of Arjuna's failure to see that form), bestowing upon him a gift of divine vision, for him, to behold His cosmic form.

न तु मां शक्यसे द्रष्टुमनेनैव स्वचक्षुषा।
दिव्यं ददामि ते चक्षुः पश्य मे योगमैश्वरम्॥ ८॥

na tu māṁ śakyase draṣṭumanenaiva svacakṣuṣā
divyaṁ dadāmi te cakṣuḥ paśya me yogamaiśvaram

But you cannot view Me, with these human eyes of yours; therefore I grant you divine vision with which, behold My divine power of Yoga. 8

Comment:—

'Na tu māṁ śakyase draṣṭumanenaiva svacakṣuṣā'—Lord Kṛṣṇa, knew that His transcendent form, could not be seen, with ordinary human eyes, because their power is very poor and limited, and these can see, only the objects of nature such as men, beasts and birds etc., but cannot behold His form, which is beyond the reach of senses, mind and intellect.

'Divyaṁ dadāmi te cakṣuḥ paśya me yogamaiśvaram'— By His power of Yoga, the Lord bestowed upon Arjuna the divine faculty, in order to enable him to have a vision of the spiritual objects, beyond the reach of sense-organs, as well as, His cosmic form, with his human eyes.

The term, 'Paśya', has two meanings—to see with intellect (discrimination), and to see with one's eyes. In the verse of the ninth chapter, it is related perceiving with intellect, while here, the context is of seeing with eyes.

An Important Fact

Suppose the word 'Gītā', is written somewhere. An illiterate person, just notices black marks, a man having knowledge of letters, can see the letters, but an educated person who is a scholar, and who has studied the Gītā, thoroughly, after having a look at the word 'Gītā', thinks of its chapters, verses and its gospel etc. Similarly, when the Lord bestowed upon Arjuna divine eyes, he could see the uncommon cosmic form of the Lord and its divinity, which are beyond the power, of ordinary intellect.

Now, a doubt, arises, when Arjuna said to Lord Kṛṣṇa, in the fourth verse, "If you think that it can be seen by me, then reveal to me, Your imperishable form", the Lord should have said as in the eighth verse, "You can't see Me with your human eyes, therefore, I give you divine eyes." But, the Lord ordered him to behold His cosmic form. When he was unable to behold that form, the Lord bestowed upon him divine eyes. Why?

The Lord has done so, in order to indicate how His grace extends to strivers, by degrees. Actually, the Lord is very much gracious. He showers His grace, upon His devotees, in various strange manners. In the Gītā the Lord, through his preachings by changing his attitude, towards his duty, described His divine glories, and aroused curiosity, in Arjuna. So by Lord's inspiration, Arjuna prayed to Him, to tell him once more, in detail, His power of Yoga and His glories, for he knew no satisfaction in hearing His sweet words. Having described His glories, the Lord announced that He stood holding the entire universe with a single fragment of His self. So Arjuna, prayed to Him to reveal to him His cosmic form, with infinite universes. Thus the Lord revealed His cosmic form, and ordered Arjuna again and again, to behold it. But, when Arjuna was unable to view the cosmic form, the Lord bestowed upon him divine eyes. It means that, when a devotee takes refuge, in the Lord, He shoulders the whole responsibility, of meeting all needs of the devotee.

Appendix—The verb 'paśya' has two meanings—'to know' and 'to see.' In the fifth verse of the ninth chapter this term in the expression 'paśya me yogamaiśvaram' has been used in the sense 'to know' and here the expression 'paśya me yogamaiśvaram' this term means 'to see' the cosmic form of the Lord. It means that whatever is to he known, is God, and whatever is to be seen, is also God. There is nothing else besides God. In this chapter there is singularity of seeing the Lord's divine form rather than its description. Therefore Sañjaya at the end of the Gītā mentioned the singularity of the dialogue and also the singularity of the Lord's cosmic form (18/76-77).

The Lord's cosmic form was divine, therefore the Lord endowed Arjuna with divine eyes to behold His divine form.

Link:—In the next verse, Sañjaya describes to Dhṛtarāṣṭra the nature of the divine cosmic body, revealed by the Lord of Arjuna.

सञ्जय उवाच

एवमुक्त्वा ततो राजन्महायोगेश्वरो हरिः ।
दर्शयामास पार्थाय परमं रूपमैश्वरम् ॥ ९ ॥

sañjaya uvāca

evamuktvā tato rājanmahāyogeśvaro hariḥ
darśayāmāsa pārthāya paramaṁ rūpamaiśvaram

Sañjaya said:

O King, having spoken thus, the Supreme Lord of Yoga, Hari (Kṛṣṇa), showed to Pārtha (Arjuna) His supremely divine form (Viśwarūpa).* 9

Comment:—

'Evamuktvā tato..........rūpamaiśvaram'—'Evamuktvā', denotes the topic of the preceding verse, when the Lord declared, "You

* Sañjaya was bestowed upon the divine vision by Vedavyāsa. So he also beheld the Lord's cosmic form (Gītā 18/77). Now Sañjaya, describes this cosmic form to Dhṛtarāṣṭra.

can't see Me with your human eyes, therefore I give you divine eyes. With these behold My divine power, of Yoga."

In the fourth verse, Arjuna addressed Lord Kṛṣṇa as the Lord of Yoga, while here Sañjaya addresses Him as the Supreme Lord of Yoga. It means, that the Lord revealed His hundreds and thousands of multifarious divine forms, while Arjuna wanted to behold only one. If a devotee, has a little inclination towards the Lord, He by His limitless power, enhances that inclination.

The form, which was called by Arjuna, in the third verse, as divine, has been called by Sañjaya here, as supremely divine. It means that the Lord Kṛṣṇa, the great Lord of all the Yogas, reveals such an uncommon, singular, and wonderful cosmic form, that even such a valiant, steady and self-controlled warrior, as Arjuna, who has been granted divine vision by the Lord, has to say it is hard to gaze at (11/17), 'My mind is tormented by fear' (11/45), and the Lord had to console him by asking him to be free from fear (11/49).

Appendix—Sañjaya calls Lord Kṛṣṇa 'mahāyogeśvara' by which he means that Lord Kṛṣṇa is the Lord of all Yogas. There is no Yoga whose lord He is not. All Yogas are within Him.

Arjuna called Lord Kṛṣṇa 'Yogeśvara' (11/4), but Sañjaya calls Him 'mahāyogeśvara'. The reason is that Sañjaya already knew Lord Kṛṣṇa really and more deeply than Arjuna knew. More than Sañjaya the Lord was known to Vedavyāsajī. It was by the grace of Vedavyāsajī that Sañjaya heard the dialogue between Lord Kṛṣṇa and Arjuna—'vyāsaprasādācchrutavānetadguhyamahaṁ param' (Gītā 18/75). More than Vedavyāsajī, the Lord knew Himself by Himself (Gītā 10/2, 15).

Link:— Sañjaya describes the Lord's supreme divine form in the next two verses.

अनेकवक्त्रनयनमनेकाद्भुतदर्शनम् ।
अनेकदिव्याभरणं दिव्यानेकोद्यतायुधम् ॥ १० ॥

दिव्यमाल्याम्बरधरं दिव्यगन्धानुलेपनम्।
सर्वाश्चर्यमयं देवमनन्तं विश्वतोमुखम्॥ ११ ॥

anekavaktranayanamanekādbhutadarśanam
anekadivyābharaṇaṁ divyānekodyatāyudham
divyamālyāmbaradharaṁ divyagandhānulepanam
sarvāścaryamayaṁ devamanantaṁ viśvatomukham

That Supreme Deity of countless mouths and eyes, presenting many a wonderful sight, decked with unlimited divine ornaments, wielding many divine weapons, wearing divine garlands and clothes, besmeared all over with divine perfumes, all wonderful and infinite with faces on all sides. Such a divine cosmic form, the Lord revealed to Arjuna. 10-11

Comment:—

'Anekavaktranayanam'—All the mouths and eyes of the Supreme Deity, were divine. The mouth, eyes, arms and legs etc., of other beings, seen in his cosmic body were also His, because He had revealed Himself, as the Supreme Deity is His cosmic form.

'Anekādbhutadarśanam'—In the cosmic body of the Lord, innumerable, unusual and marvellous forms, shapes and colours, were beheld by Arjuna.

'Anekadivyābharaṇam'—All the ornaments of diverse forms on hands, feet, ears, noses and necks in the cosmic body of the Lord, were divine, because the Lord revealed Himself in ornaments.

'Divyānekodyatāyudham'—The Lord held, in His raised hands, many divine weapons, such as discus, club, bow, arrows and spear etc.

'Divyamālyāmbaradharam'—The Lord in his cosmic form, had many divine garlands of flowers, gold, silver, pearls, gems etc., around His neck, and was clad in various kinds of divine costumes of red, yellow, green, white, brown, and many other colours.

'Divyagandhānulepanam'—The Lord in his cosmic form, was besmeared with divine fragrances, such as musk, sandal and vermilion pastes on His face, head, as well as, all over his body.

'Sarvāścaryamayaṁ devamanantaṁ viśvatomukham'— The cosmic body, revealed by the Lord, was infinite and unbounded by space and the innumerable faces, forming part of that body covered all sides. Everything in the cosmic form, was wondrous.

If a man thinks that he is bathing in the Ganges at Haridvāra, though there is neither Haridvāra nor the Ganges, yet his mind forms different images of Haridvāra, the Ganges, bridge and people bathing there, similarly, the Lord manifested Himself in numberless forms, with ornaments, weapons, garlands, clothes and perfumes etc.

It is mentioned in the Śrīmadbhāgavata, that when Brahmā, the creator, stole some calves and the cowherds of Lord Kṛṣṇa, the Lord manifested Himself, not only as calves and cowherds, but also as canes, horns, flutes, clothes and ornaments (Śrīmadbhā. 10/13/19).

Appendix—In the second chapter there is mention of the marvellous nature of the soul which is a fragment of God (Gītā 2/29). Here is the mention of the wondrous (marvellous) form of the Lord. The more the Lord is beheld, the more singularity is perceived in Him. The singularity of the Lord is infinite (endless).

Link:—In the next verse, Sañjaya describes the effulgence, of the Lord's cosmic form.

दिवि सूर्यसहस्रस्य भवेद्युगपदुत्थिता।
यदि भाः सदृशी सा स्याद्भासस्तस्य महात्मनः॥ १२॥

divi sūryasahasrasya bhavedyugapadutthitā
yadi bhāḥ sadṛśī sā syādbhāsastasya mahātmanaḥ

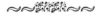

If the effulgence of a thousand suns blazed forth all at once in the sky, that would hardly match the radiance of the mighty Lord. 12

Comment:—

'Divi sūryasahasrasya bhavedyugapadutthitā yadi bhāḥ sadṛśī sā syādbhāsastasya mahātmanaḥ'—As the light of thousand stars, twinkling together in the sky, cannot be compared with the light of the moon, and as the light of a thousand moons, cannot be compared with the light of the sun, similarly, the splendour of a thousand suns shining all at once, in the sky, cannot be like that of the cosmic form, of the Lord. It means that the splendour of the Lord was incomparable. The reason is, that the effulgence of the sun is material, while the splendour of the Lord was divine. So, the splendour belonging to two different categories, cannot be compared, only an indication can be given. Therefore, by referring to the brilliance of a thousand suns, Sañjaya is, hinting at the effulgence of the cosmic form.

Appendix—The light (splendour) of a thousand suns shining all at once in the sky, can't match the radiance of the Lord because the radiance present in the sun has also emanated from God (Gītā 15/12). There may be the light of thousands of suns, but that light is material while the Lord's light is not material but divine.

Link:—After describing the Lord's cosmic form, and its splendour, Sañjaya, in the next verse, describes that Arjuna beheld the universe, in the cosmic form of the Lord.

तत्रैकस्थं जगत्कृत्स्नं प्रविभक्तमनेकधा।
अपश्यद्देवदेवस्य शरीरे पाण्डवस्तदा॥ १३ ॥

tatraikasthaṁ jagatkṛtsnaṁ pravibhaktamanekadhā
apaśyaddevadevasya śarīre pāṇḍavastadā

Then Arjuna, saw unfolded in that Supreme Deity, the whole

universe with its many divisions concentrated at one place. 13

Comment:—

'Tatraikasthaṁ jagatkṛtsnaṁ pravibhaktamanekadhā'— Arjuna with divine eye, beheld the entire univese with its manifold divisions, such as the gods, human beings, beasts, birds, earth, ocean, sky and stars etc. It means, that Arjuna in a part of the body of the Lord, beheld the entire universe, with animate and inanimate beings, divided into different worlds, as a world of the gods, and a world of human beings, and so on.*

'Apaśyaddevadevasya śarīre pāṇḍavastadā'—'Tadā' means that Arjuna saw Lord Kṛṣṇa's cosmic form, as soon as, He revealed it. 'Apaśyat' means, that Arjuna saw the same form, which the Lord revealed to him by bestowing upon him divine vision. Arjuna, saw the same cosmic form, as has already been described by Sañjaya.

As the world of the gods, is superior to the mortal world, so is the Lord far superior to the world of the gods, as all the worlds including the paradise, the world of the gods are of matter, while the Lord is beyond Matter. So God, is the Lord of the gods.

Appendix—Arjuna beheld in the body of the Lord, the whole universe with its many divisions concentrated at one place—creatures born from the womb, creatures born from eggs, vegetation sprouting up from the earth, louse etc., born of sweat, immovable and movable creatures, birds etc., which

* In Śrīmadbhāgavata there is an anecdote. Once Yaśodā beheld the Lord's cosmic form in Kṛṣṇa's small mouth. Think over it that out of infinite universes there is one universe in which there is India. In India there is Vraja zone. In Vraja zone there is Nandagaon. In Nandagaon there is Nanda's house. In Nanda's house the child Kṛṣṇa is standing. Kṛṣṇa's mother named Yaśodā threateningly asked Him why He had eaten dust and ordered Him to open His mouth. When He opened His mouth, Yaśodā beheld the entire world, Nandagaon, Nanda's house and also herself (Śrīmadbhāgavata 10/8/39). Similarly Arjuna also beheld the entire universe in a part of the Lord's body.

fly in the sky, creatures which live in water and creatures that live on the earth. The universe may seem to be endless but it is held in a fragment of the Lord's body (Gītā 10/42). In whatever part of the Lord's body, Arjuna had a look, he saw the infinite universes there.

Link:—Sañjaya in the next verse, describes how Arjuna felt, after beholding the cosmic form of the Lord.

ततः स विस्मयाविष्टो हृष्टरोमा धनञ्जयः।
प्रणम्य शिरसा देवं कृताञ्जलिरभाषत॥१४॥

tataḥ sa vismayāviṣṭo hṛṣṭaromā dhanañjayaḥ
praṇamya śirasā devaṁ kṛtāñjalirabhāṣata

Then Dhanañjaya, struck with wonder and his hair standing on end, bowed before the divine Lord, and with joined palms, addressed Him, thus. 14

Comment:—

'Tataḥ sa vismayāviṣṭo hṛṣṭaromā dhanañjayaḥ'—Arjuna was overwhelmed with wonder, at the sight of the cosmic form of the Lord, because he had not even dreamt of, such a form. His joy, knew no bounds after thinking of the Lord's grace, and his hair stood on an end.

'Praṇamya śirasā devaṁ kṛtāñjalirabhāṣata'—After perceiving the Lord's uncommon grace, Arjuna felt highly grateful to Him, and he was so much inspired with a feeling of deep reverence, for the Lord that he bowed his head with utmost reverence, to the Lord. He thought, that he could do nothing more than, bowing his head i.e., surrendering himself to Him. So, he with joined palms, laying his head at the feet, of the Lord began to offer his praises, to the Lord's cosmic form.

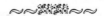

Link:—Arjuna overwhelmed with joy and wonder, and describing the sight, which he saw in the Lord's cosmic form, makes a rapturous utterance, offering his praise, to Him, in the next three verses.

अर्जुन उवाच

पश्यामि देवांस्तव देव देहे
सर्वांस्तथाभूतविशेषसङ्घान्।
ब्रह्माणमीशं कमलासनस्थ-
मृषींश्च सर्वानुरगांश्च दिव्यान्॥ १५॥

arjuna uvāca

paśyāmi devāṁstava deva dehe
sarvāṁstathābhūtaviśeṣasaṅghān
brahmāṇamīśaṁ kamalāsanastha-
mṛṣīṁśca sarvānuragāṁśca divyān

Arjuna said:

O Lord, I see within Your body all the gods and multitude of different beings; observe Brahmā seated on His lotus-seat, Śiva and all the sages and celestial serpents. 15

Comment:—

'Paśyāmi devāṁstava deva dehe sarvāṁstathābhūtaviśeṣa-saṅghān'—With divine eyes, Arjuna, was able to behold not only multitude of beings, but also paradise, the abode of the gods, and also the entire universe with Brahmā, the creator, Viṣṇu, the preserver and Maheśa, the destroyer.

'Brahmāṇamīśaṁ kamalāsanastham'—Arjuna says, that he beheld Brahmā seated on a lotus-seat. This lotus-seat is the one that sprang from the navel of Lord Viṣṇu. It means, that Arjuna saw the stalk of the lotus and also the place, from where the lotus sprang up. It shows that he had a vision of Viṣṇu, the progenitor of Brahmā. He also saw Lord Śiva, sitting in his abode, under the banyan tree, on mount Kailāsa.

'Ṛṣīṁśca sarvānuragāṁśca divyān'—Arjuna, beheld the sages, living on the earth and divine serpents, living in the underworld.

In this verse, Arjuna's statement affirms that he beheld, the three worlds—the earth, the paradise and the underworld, in Lord Kṛṣṇa's body, with three division concentrated at one place (Gītā 11/13). Besides them, he also beheld the abodes of Brahmā, Viṣṇu and Maheśa, as well as, those three chief deities. This is all due, to the glory of the divine eyes, bestowed by the Lord.

An Important Fact

When Lord Kṛṣṇa declares, that He holds the entire universe in a limb of his body, Arjuna prays to Him, to reveal His divine form to him. So Lord Kṛṣṇa asks him to behold the entire universe, in His one limb (11/7). Sañjaya who was offered divine vision by Vedavyāsa, also declares that Arjuna saw in the person of that Supreme Deity, comprised in one limb, the whole universe, with its manifold divisions (11/13). But Arjuna, here (in 11/15) declares that he beholds multitudes of different beings; he does not use the expression 'Ekastham' (resting at one place). The reason, is tnat wherever Arjuna saw, he beheld, only His cosmic form. At that time, Arjuna did not look at the Lord, Who was acting as his chariot-driver. So he beheld only, his cosmic form. But the Lord revealed the entire universe in his one limb, and Sañjaya also beheld the Lord sitting as a chariot-driver, in the chariot as well as, His cosmic form. So, both of them, use the term, 'Ekastham' (concentrated at one place).*

Now a question arises, in which limb according to Lord Kṛṣṇa, as well as Sañjaya, Arjuna, beheld the cosmic form.

* The term 'Ekastham' (concentrated at one place) has been used both by the Lord and by Sañjaya. So it should be assumed that Arjuna also beheld the cosmic form in a limb of the Lord.

The answer is, that it is very difficult to mention a particular limb, because millions of universes, are held in a pore of His body. It means, that He holds infinite universes, in each of His limbs.*

Appendix—Arjuna in the cosmic form of God sees gods, living beings, Brahmājī, Lord Viṣṇu, Lord Śaṅkara, sages, celestial serpents and the multitude of different beings. It means that Arjuna, while sitting in the mortal world, sees the abode of gods, the abode of Brahmā, the abode of Lord Viṣṇu, Kailāsa, the abode of Lord Śiva and the world of celestial serpents etc. Therefore whatever is said and heard, all that is held in a fragment of God. God may be endowed with form or He may he formless, He may be the biggest or the smallest, He remains endless. The entire creation is born of Him, resides in Him and merges into Him, but He ever remains the same.

अनेकबाहूदरवक्त्रनेत्रं
पश्यामि त्वां सर्वतोऽनन्तरूपम्।
नान्तं न मध्यं न पुनस्तवादिं
पश्यामि विश्वेश्वर विश्वरूप॥ १६॥

anekabāhūdaravaktranetraṁ
paśyāmi tvāṁ sarvato'nantarūpam
nāntaṁ na madhyaṁ na punastavādiṁ
paśyāmi viśveśvara viśvarūpa

O Lord of all universe, I behold You, endless in forms on all sides, with numerous arms, bellies, faces, and eyes. O Universal Form (Viśwarūpa), I see, neither Your beginning nor middle nor end. 16

---

* Infinite universes rise up from each of your pores and fall down again in the same way as particles of dust appear flying in the rays of the sun coming through a window screened with netting (Śrīmadbhā. 10/14/11).

Comment:—

Arjuna uses, two vocatives 'Viśvarūpa' (Universal Form), and 'Viśveśvara' (Lord of the universe), to convey that this universe is nothing but His manifestation, and that He is also the Lord of the entire universe. The body of a human being, is insentient, while its master, the soul is sentient. But, there is no such distinction in the cosmic form of the Lord. In this form, everything is sentient. By the vocative 'Viśvarūpa', Arjuna declares, that He is the body and by the vocative 'Viśveśvara' Arjuna means, to say that He is the master of the body.

'Anekabāhūdaravaktranetram'—Arjuna saw the Lord, with countless arms, bellies, mouths (faces) and eyes.

'Paśyāmi tvāṁ sarvato'nantarūpam'—Arjuna, saw His innumerable forms, extended on all sides.

'Nāntaṁ na madhyaṁ na punastavādim'—The cosmic body, as was revealed to Arjuna, was infinite, on all sides. Arjuna could know neither its beginning, nor middle, nor end, because there was no limit in it.

Arjuna, first used the term 'end', because he wanted to see the end of His body, on all sides, to know His stature. But, when he was unable to see it, he tried to see the middle and then the beginning, but it was of no avail. The order in which Arjuna viewed cosmic form is related here by this expression.

Appendix—Here is the description of the endlessness of the Lord's cosmic form. Even His fraction is also infinite. As in ink, is there any place where there is no script? In gold, is there any place where there are no ornaments? Similarly what is not there in God viz., naturally all is there in God.

किरीटिनं गदिनं चक्रिणं च
तेजोराशिं सर्वतो दीप्तिमन्तम्।

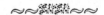

पश्यामि त्वां दुर्निरीक्ष्यं समन्ता-
द्दीप्तानलार्कद्युतिमप्रमेयम् ॥ १७ ॥

kirīṭinaṁ gadinaṁ cakriṇaṁ ca
tejorāśiṁ sarvato dīptimantam
paśyāmi tvāṁ durnirīkṣyaṁ samantā-
ddīptānalārkadyutimaprameyam

I see You, wearing a diadem, holding a mace and discus, a mass of effulgence, shining alround having a brilliance like the blazing fire and sun, dazzling and boundless on all sides. 17

Comment:—

'Kirīṭinaṁ gadinaṁ cakriṇaṁ ca'—The Lord's cosmic form, retained the famous emblems, club, discus and also diadem. Here the term 'Ca' (and), should denote conch and lotus. Thus Arjuna could behold the four-armed Lord, also in that cosmic form.

'Tejorāśim'—The cosmic form of the Lord, was a mass of splendour i.e., there was unlimited glitter in that form. Sañjaya also, described His splendour in these words, "If there were the effulgence of a thousand suns blazing forth, all at once in the sky, that would hardly be, like that of the mighty Lord" (11/12).

'Sarvato dīptimantam'—Being effulgence incarnate, the Lord was shining everywhere, on all sides.

'Paśyāmi tvāṁ durnirīkṣyaṁ samantāddiptānalārka-dyutimaprameyam'—This brilliance of the cosmic form, of the Lord, was like that of blazing fire and sun. As brilliance of sun, dazzles the eyes, the lord's also dazzled the eyes; the eyes could not bear its sight. [Here it is surprising that though Arjuna was blessed with divine eyes, to behold that form, yet it dazzled him, because of its most wonderful effulgence.]

The splendour and effulgence, of the Lord, was limitless and immeasurable on all sides, and no other splendour can stand comparison with it.

Appendix—'Aprameyam'—All the forms of God, whether

endowed with attributes or attributeless, whether endowed with form or formless, are boundless and His fragment, soul is also boundless—'anāśino'prameyasya' (Gītā 2/18). God is not an object to be known because He is the knower of knowledge even—'vedāntakṛdvedavideva cāham' (Gītā 15/15).

'Durnirīkṣyam'—Though Arjuna was blessed with divine sight by God, yet Arjuna was not fully capable to see the cosmic form of the Lord. It proves that God cannot be known even by the power bestowed upon a man by God. Even God doesn't know Himself completely, if He knows Himself, how will He remain infinite?

त्वमक्षरं परमं वेदितव्यं
त्वमस्य विश्वस्य परं निधानम्।
त्वमव्ययः शाश्वतधर्मगोप्ता
सनातनस्त्वं पुरुषो मतो मे ॥१८॥

tvamakṣaraṁ paramaṁ veditavyaṁ
tvamasya viśvasya paraṁ nidhānam
tvamavyayaḥ śāśvatadharmagoptā
sanātanastvaṁ puruṣo mato me

You are I recognise, the Imperishable, the Supreme Being (Akṣara) to be realized; You are the ultimate refuge of this universe; the protector of eternal Dharma (duty and righteousness) and You are the eternally imperishable Being. 18

Comment:—

'Tvamakṣaraṁ paramaṁ veditavyam—The Lord is the imperishable Supreme Being, who is attributeless and formless, and Who has been described in the scriptures, as the absolute or Brahma, and Who is realized by liberated souls.

'Tvamasya viśvasya paraṁ nidhānam'—Arjuna says, that the Lord is the ultimate resort or support, of the entire universe. At final annihilation, the entire universe merges in Him and at the beginning of new creation, it emanates again from Him. Thus He is the final resort (abiding place), of the entire universe. (Here Arjuna offers praises to the Lord, Who is formless, and is endowed with attributes.)

'Tvam śāśvatadharmagoptā'—Arjuna says, that when there is, a decline of righteousness and rise of unrighteousness, the Lord by an incarnation, destroys the evil and protects 'Sanātana Dharma', the Dharma that has existed, since time immemorial and shall exist forever. [Here Arjuna offers praises, to the Lord, endowed with attributes and form.]

'Avyayaḥ sanātanastvaṁ puruṣo mato me'—Arjuna assumes that the Lord is the eternal, imperishable Being, the almighty God, Who remains imperishable, even when the entire universe, perishes.

Appendix—Here the expression 'tvamakṣaraṁ paramaṁ veditavyam' denotes attributeless and formless Brahma; the expression 'tvamasya viśvasya paraṁ nidhānam' denotes God endowed with attributes and formless; and the expression 'tvam śāśvatadharmagoptā' denotes God endowed with attributes and form. It means that 'nirguṇa-nirākāra, 'saguṇa-nirākāra' and 'saguṇa-sākāra'—these all joined together, is the entire form of God, having known which nothing remains to be known (Gītā 7/2) because there is nothing else besides Him.

Link:—After describing the wonderful cosmic form of the Lord from the fifteenth verse to the eighteenth verse Arjuna in the next two verses describes fierceness, terror and power of the cosmic form.

अनादिमध्यान्तमनन्तवीर्य-
मनन्तबाहुं शशिसूर्यनेत्रम्।

पश्यामि त्वां दीप्तहुताशवक्त्रं
स्वतेजसा विश्वमिदं तपन्तम्॥ १९॥

anādimadhyāntamanantavīrya-
manantabāhuṁ śaśisūryanetram
paśyāmi tvāṁ dīptahutāśavaktraṁ
svatejasā viśvamidaṁ tapantam

I see You, without beginning, middle or end, infinite in power, of infinite arms, the sun and the moon being Your eyes, the blazing fire Your mouth; warming the universe, withYour radiance. 19

Comment:—

'Anādimadhyāntam'—Arjuna saw the Lord, without a beginning, middle or end i.e., He had no limits.

In the sixteenth verse, Arjuna also said, "I see, neither Your beginning, nor middle, nor end." This statement conveys the infinitude of the cosmic body i.e., infinitude in space, while in the nineteenth verse, it is in the context of the infinitude of time. It means, that the Lord, is beyond limits of time, space and causation. All, the space, time and causation, are within Him. Then how can He be encompassed by space, time and causation. In other words, He cannot be measured, by space, time and causation.

'Anantavīryam'—Arjuna, wants to convey, that the Lord's power, strength, glory and energy, are unlimited.

'Anantabāhum'*—The Lord is endowed, with numberless arms.

'Śaśisūryanetram'— The sun and the moon, which illuminate the entire universe, are the Lord's eyes. Thus, the universe is illuminated by His light.

'Dīptahutāśavaktram'—The Lord's mouth, is the blazing fire,

* In the sixteenth verse Arjuna said that the Lord had numerous arms while here he says that He is endowed with infinite arms. It seems that there is repetition. But actually it is not so. There is the description of the divine (mild) form of the Lord while here is the description of His fierce and terrible form.

which receives various articles offered, when religious sacrifice, is performed.

'Svatejasā viśvamidaṁ tapantam'—The Lord warms the universe, with His radiance. It means, that persons, things and incidents etc., that create unfavourable and undesirable circumstances, to torture beings, and those who are affected by those circumstances are, fragments of the cosmic form, of the Lord.

Appendix—This verse means that God is endless in all ways. The universe, which is scorched by the Lord's blazing fire is not different from Him. Therefore He, Who scorches with the blazing fire, and the universe, which is scorched with that blazing fire—both are the manifestations of God.

द्यावापृथिव्योरिदमन्तरं हि
व्याप्तं त्वयैकेन दिशश्च सर्वाः।
दृष्ट्वाद्भुतं रूपमुग्रं तवेदं
लोकत्रयं प्रव्यथितं महात्मन्॥ २०॥

dyāvāpṛthivyoridamantaraṁ hi
vyāptaṁ tvayaikena diśaśca sarvāḥ
dṛṣṭvādbhutaṁ rūpamugraṁ tavedaṁ
lokatrayaṁ pravyathitaṁ mahātman

The space between the heaven and earth and all the spheres is pervaded by you, alone. Seeing this marvellous and frightening form of Yours, O Great-Soul, the three worlds feel greatly alarmed. 20

Comment:—

'Mahātman'—By this address, Arjuna means to say, that His self is the greatest of all. None can equal it.

'Dyāvāpṛthivyoridamantaraṁ hi vyāptaṁ tvayaikena diśaśca

sarvāḥ'—The entire space, between heaven and earth, is filled, with the Lord.

The Lord is all-pervading, He pervades all the ten quarters—east, west, north, south, east-north, north-west,west-south, south-east, upward and downward.

'Dṛṣṭvādbhutaṁ rūpamugraṁ tavedaṁ lokatrayaṁ pravyathitam'—[Arjuna having described the frightening form of the Lord, in the nineteenth verse and in the first half of the twentieth verse, now starts describing the result of beholding this form.] Seeing, a dreadful, uncommon, marvellous and resplendent form, of the Lord, all the beings inhabiting the heaven, the earth and the netherworld, are greatly alarmed and are trembling with fear.

Though Arjuna has mentioned of the heaven and the earth, yet he has used the expression, 'the three worlds,' which may include the netherworld, also. The reason, is that Arjuna did not behold these systematically one after the other. He saw the heaven, the earth and the netherworld etc., altogether and so he is describing these in the same manner, in which he beheld.

Now a doubt arises, why were the three worlds greatly alarmed and trembling with fear? Did the beings of the three worlds, also behold, the cosmic form? And if they beheld, it then how?

The clarification is, that Arjuna beheld those three worlds within the cosmic body of the Lord. Those three worlds, were greatly alarmed and were trembling with fear, after noticing the terrible beasts, such as lions, tigers, snakes, as well as, death in His cosmic body.

A Vital Fact

In fact, the entire universe is a fragment of the cosmic form, of the Lord. The transience and modifications that appear in the universe, are nothing but, the sport of the Lord. The Lord, as well as his cosmic form, has His independent existence, while the universe has no independent existence of its own. Arjuna saw the cosmic form of the Lord, with divine eyes, while devotees perceive this universe, as the manifestation of the Lord.

A passionate person, seeks pleasures in the universe, while a devotee who has nothing to do with mundane pleasures, beholds it as Lord's manifestations. As a child, regards the same woman as its mother, a father, as his daughter, a husband as his wife, and a lion as his prey, similarly the world, appears true with human eyes, transitory, with discriminating eyes, and divine with emotional eyes, and a fragment of the cosmic form seen with divine eyes.

Appendix—The term 'tvayaikena' used in this verse means "only You have revealed Yourself in numberless forms—'Vāsudevaḥ sarvam'. No one can count Your numberless forms but in all of them only You prevail."

In God there are several kinds of wonders. He is endless from different view-points such as space, time, thing, person, form, knowledge and Yoga etc. Whichever we have neither seen nor heard, nor known nor understood and which is beyond our imagination—all that is within the Lord's cosmic form.

Link:—In the next two verses, Arjuna describes the scene of heaven, which he beheld in the Lord's, cosmic form.

अमी हि त्वां सुरसङ्घा विशन्ति
केचिद्भीताः प्राञ्जलयो गृणन्ति।
स्वस्तीत्युक्त्वा महर्षिसिद्धसङ्घाः
स्तुवन्ति त्वां स्तुतिभिः पुष्कलाभिः ॥ २१ ॥

amī hi tvāṁ surasaṅghā viśanti
kecidbhītāḥ prāñjalayo gṛṇanti

svastītyuktvā maharṣisiddhasaṅghāḥ
stuvanti tvāṁ stutibhiḥ puṣkalābhiḥ

Those multitudes of gods merge in You; some in awe with folded hands are chanting Your names and glories; bands of great sages and Siddhas (emancipated souls) cry "Hail Highest Majesty", and shower praises on You with excellent hymns. 21

Comment:—

'Amī hi tvāṁ surasaṅghā viśanti'—When Arjuna went to heaven, he became familiar with the gods there. So Arjuna says, that these gods were entering the Lord's frightening form. All of the gods, are born of Him, remain established in Him, and again merge, in Him.

'Kecidbhītāḥ prāñjalayo gṛṇanti'—Hosts of gods, were entering the Lord's terrible form. The remaining gods, were much afraid of meeting the same fate. With joined palms, therefore, they began to utter the Lord's names, glories and praises.

Though the gods, being afraid of death, viewing the man-lion incarnation (which was within the cosmic form), were singing praises of the Lord. But to Arjuna, it seemed that these gods being terrified of the cosmic form, were resorting to praising the Lord, in His cosmic form.

'Svastītyuktvā maharṣisiddhasaṅghāḥ stuvanti tvāṁ stutibhiḥ puṣkalābhiḥ'—The group of seven principal sages, the sages living in the abode of gods and other great sages, such as Sanaka and Sanandana etc., as well as the gods, were extolling the Lord by means of sublime hymns.

Appendix—Deities (gods), sages and emancipated souls etc., all are the organs of the Lord's cosmic form. Therefore those who are entering the Lord's form, those who are terrified, those who are chanting the Lord's names and glories, are none else but God; and also He in Whom they are entering, by Whom they are terrified, Whose names and glories they are chanting is also only God. This is the speciality of the Lord endowed with attributes.

रुद्रादित्या वसवो ये च साध्या
विश्वेऽश्विनौ मरुतश्चोष्मपाश्च।
गन्धर्वयक्षासुरसिद्धसङ्घा
वीक्षन्ते त्वां विस्मिताश्चैव सर्वे॥ २२॥

rudrādityā vasavo ye ca sādhyā
viśve'śvinau marutaścoṣmapāśca
gandharvayakṣāsurasiddhasaṅghā
vīkṣante tvāṁ vismitāścaiva sarve

The (eleven) Rudras, (twelve) Ādityas, (eight) Vasus, (twelve) Sādhyas, (ten) Viśvedevas, (two) Aśvinīkumāras, (forty-nine) Maruts, manes, hosts of Gandharvas, Yakṣas, Asuras and Siddhas—they all, gaze at You, in amazement. 22

Comment:—

'Rudrādityā vasavo ye ca sādhyā viśve'śvinau marutaścoṣmapāśca'—Brief notes, on eleven Rudras, twelve Ādityas, eight Vasus, two Aśvinīkumāras, and forty-nine Maruts, have already been given, in the explanation of the sixth verse of this chapter. The names of the twelve Sādhyas are—Mana, Anumantā, Prāṇa, Nara, Yāna, Citti, Haya, Naya, Haṁsa, Nārāyaṇa, Prabhava and Vibhu (Vāyu Purāṇa 66/15-16).

The ten, Viśvedevas are—Kratu, Dakṣa, Śrava, Satya, Kāla, Kāma, Dhuni, Kuruvān, Prabhavān and Rocamāna (Vāyu Purāṇa 66/31-32).

The seven manes are—Kavyavāha, Anala, Soma, Yama, Aryamā, Agnisvātta and Barhiṣat (Śiva Purāṇa, Dharma. 63/2). They are called 'Ūṣmapā, because they eat hot food.

'Gandharvayakṣāsurasiddhasaṅghā'—The Gandharvas, are said to be born of Kaśyapa's three wives, named Muni, Prādhā and Ariṣṭā. They are experts in the art of different melodies and music. They are musicians, of the heaven.

The Yakṣas, are said to be born, of Kaśyapa's wife Khasā.

The 'Asuras' (Demons), are the 'Daityas, Dānavas and Rākṣasas,' who are sworn enemies* of Devas (the gods), Kapila etc., are known as Siddha.

'Vikṣante tvāṁ vismitāścaiva sarve'—All, the above-mentioned gods, manes, Gandharvas, Yakṣas, were gazing at the Lord, in amazement. All of them, were limbs, of the cosmic form, of the Lord.

Appendix—Rudra, Āditya, Vasu, Sādhyas, Viśvedeva etc., all are the organs of the entire form of God. Therefore the onlooker and also the objects to be seen—all are none else beside God.

Link:—Arjuna, in the next three verses, while describing the fearful cosmic form, of the Lord, explains its effect, on the universe.

रूपं महत्ते बहुवक्त्रनेत्रं
महाबाहो बहुबाहूरुपादम्।
बहूदरं बहुदंष्ट्राकरालं
दृष्ट्वा लोकाः प्रव्यथितास्तथाहम्॥ २३॥

rūpaṁ mahatte bahuvaktranetraṁ
mahābāho bahubāhūrupādam
bahūdaraṁ bahudaṁṣṭrākarālaṁ
dṛṣṭvā lokāḥ pravyathitāstathāham

O mighty-armed, seeing Your immeasurable and frightening form with numerous mouths, eyes, arms, thighs, feet, bellies and fearful teeth, the worlds are terror-stricken, and so am I. 23

* When the gods and the demons are described together, the term 'Asura' (Demon) stands for those who are the sworn enemies of gods.

Comment:—

[In the Lord's cosmic form, from the fifteenth verse to the eighteenth verse, there is a description of the Lord's divine form, from the nineteenth verse to the twenty-second verse, of his terrible form and from the twenty-third verse to the thirtieth verse, of His very dreadful form.]

'Bahuvaktranetram'—The Lord's, mouths and eyes in His dreadful cosmic form, were of various sizes, shapes and expressed different moods.

'Bahubāhūrupādam'—The arms, thighs and feet, were also of different sizes, shapes and colours etc., and their movements were also unusual.

'Bahudaṁṣṭrākarālaṁ dṛṣṭvā lokāḥ pravyathitāstathāham'—After beholding the terrible teeth, in the Lord's mouths, the worlds were terrified, and Arjuna also was terror-struck.

Arjuna had already described, numerous arms, eyes, bellies, faces of the Lord's cosmic body, and also the terror in the three worlds, after beholding these. Then why is He repeating it?

There are several reasons for doing so.

(1) Arjuna beholds a novelty and singularity, in each phase, of the cosmic form.

(2) After having a vision of the Lord's cosmic form, Arjuna was so much confused and alarmed, that he did not remember what he had already described, and so he repeated it.

(3) First, he spoke of the three worlds, feeling greatly alarmed after beholding the terrible form of the cosmic body. But, here he says that he was also terrified at the sight of the Lord's, terrible cosmic form.

(4) When a man is overwhelmed with emotions of fear or joy, of sorrow or surprise, he repeats, a word, a phrase or a sentence several times. After seeing, a cobra, a man being afraid of it cries, 'A cobra! A cobra! A cobra!' Similarly, a person

left alone, on an island, may describe his loneliness by saying, "Alone! Alone! All alone," and so on. Thus Arjuna has repeated the words out of fear, joy and surprise etc. Arjuna admits this fact, when he says, "Having seen Your form which was never seen before, I feel delighted and my mind is distressed with fear" (11/45). It means, that this is no mere, repitition.

Appendix—Those who are beholding and those who are being beheld, those who are terrifying and those who are being terrified—all those beings and also Arjuna himself are within the cosmic form of God.

नभःस्पृशं दीप्तमनेकवर्णं
व्यात्ताननं दीप्तविशालनेत्रम्।
दृष्ट्वा हि त्वां प्रव्यथितान्तरात्मा
धृतिं न विन्दामि शमं च विष्णो॥ २४॥

nabhaḥspṛśaṁ dīptamanekavarṇaṁ
vyāttānanaṁ dīptaviśālanetram
dṛṣṭvā hi tvāṁ pravyathitāntarātmā
dhṛtiṁ na vindāmi śamaṁ ca viṣṇo

When I see Your form, touching the sky, effulgent in many colours, with mouths wide open, with large shining eyes, my heart trembles with fear, I lose courage and find no peace, O Viṣṇu. 24

Comment:—

[In the twentieth verse, Arjuna described the Lord's height and breadth, while here he describes His tremendous height, only.]

'Viṣṇo'—Arjuna says that it was the all-pervading Lord Viṣṇu Himself, Who incarnated as Kṛṣṇa, in order to lighten the burden of the earth.

'Dīptamanekavarṇam'—The Lord's terrible cosmic form, was multicoloured and effulgent.

'Nabhaḥspṛśam'—His form was so tall, that it was touching the sky. It means, that as far as Arjuna could see he beheld the cosmic form of the Lord meeting the sky. It indicates, that even divine sight could not have access to the end, of the limitless cosmic form of the Lord.

'Vyāttānanaṁ dīptaviśālanetram'— Just like a wild beast, the Lord's mouth was wide open, to ingest the entire universe.

His eyes were large, shining and fiery.

'Dṛṣṭvā hi tvāṁ pravyathitāntarātmā dhṛtim na vindāmi śamaṁ ca viṣṇo'— Arjuna says, that he was very much frightened at the sight of the Lord's cosmic form, and he lost his courage, self control and peace of mind.

Here a question arises, that Arjuna besides being a valiant warrior of extraordinary calibre, was blessed with divine eye by the Lord, yet he trembled with fear, while beholding the Lord's cosmic form, but Sañjaya was not terror-struck. Why?

The answer is, that saints say that Bhīṣma, Vidura, Sañjaya and Kuntī, knew the Lord in reality, while Arjuna did not know Him fully. Arjuna's, delusion was not completely destroyed (11/49). So, he trembled with fear. But Sañjaya, knew the reality, about the Lord viz., he had delusion. So Sañjaya was not terror-struck.

It proves, that the Lord and saints, shower their grace, even on unqualified and undeserving persons, but qualified and deserving persons, know the reality about Him, in the same way, as a mother loves her innocent child more than she loves a grown up son, while the grown up son knows her and her loving nature more than an innocent child. The Lord, loved the simple and innocent cowherds, cowherdesses and cows, more than He loved the liberated souls, though the latter knew His true self. Similarly, Sañjaya deserved to have a vision of the Lord's cosmic form, and so he could behold, it without requesting the Lord, while the Lord Himself had to arouse curiosity in Arjuna, and revealed to him this cosmic form, as Arjuna regarded the Lord as his friend, not as the Lord. So the Lord, was more gracious to Arjuna and it was by His grace, that Arjuna's delusion was destroyed (Gītā 18/73). It proves, that the Lord by His grace, destroys the delusion, of His devotees.

Appendix—Here the term 'nabhaḥspṛśam' denotes the infinity of God's cosmic form. As far as Arjuna's eye can reach, he sees only the cosmic form—'sā kāṣṭha sā parā gatiḥ' (Kaṭha. 1/3/11) viz., that God is the last limit and the supreme goal.

दंष्ट्राकरालानि च ते मुखानि
दृष्ट्वैव कालानलसन्निभानि।
दिशो न जाने न लभे च शर्म
प्रसीद देवेश जगन्निवास॥ २५॥

daṁṣṭrākarālāni ca te mukhāni
dṛṣṭvaiva kālānalasannibhāni
diśo na jāne na labhe ca śarma
prasīda deveśa jagannivāsa

Seeing Your mouths, with fearful teeth, resembling the raging fires at the time of universal destruction, I know not, the cardinal directions, nor do I find peace. Therefore, be kind to me, O Lord of the gods and the shelter, of the universe. 25

Comment:—

'Daṁṣṭrākarālāni ca te mukhāni dṛṣṭvaiva kālānalasannibhāni'—Arjuna says, that seeing the Lord's frightful faces on account of their terrible teeth, and flaring like the raging fire at the time of universal dissolution, he was terror-stricken.

'Diśo na jāne na labhe ca śarma'—Beholding, such a terrible form of the Lord, Arjuna, could not know, even the four quarters of the world. The quarters, are discerned with the help of, sunrise and sun-set. But the sun was shining, the Lord's eye, situated within His cosmic form. Moreover, the splendour of the Lord, was more than even the effulgence of a thousand suns, blazing forth, all at once (11/12). So, he knew not the four cardinal directions. So being utterly amazed and confused, he lost happiness and peace.

'Prasīda deveśa jagannivāsa'— He is the Lord of the gods and Abode of the entire universe. So the gods and men etc., being terrified, invoke the Lord only. After beholding the frightening form of the Lord, being terror-struck, Arjuna thought, that the Lord was displeased and angry. So he prayed to Him, for His pleasure and kindness.

Appendix—The Lord, being pleased with Arjuna, is showing him His cosmic form (Gītā 11/47), but having seen the terrible and frightening form of the Lord, Arjuna has the false notion that the Lord is displeased with him. So he prays to Him to be pleased with him.

Link:—Arjuna in the next two verses describes that the chief warriors were rushing headlong into the Lord's fearful mouths.

अमी च त्वां धृतराष्ट्रस्य पुत्राः
सर्वे सहैवावनिपालसङ्घैः ।
भीष्मो द्रोणः सूतपुत्रस्तथासौ
सहास्मदीयैरपि योधमुख्यैः ॥ २६ ॥
वक्त्राणि ते त्वरमाणा विशन्ति
दंष्ट्राकरालानि भयानकानि ।
केचिद्विलग्ना दशनान्तरेषु
सन्दृश्यन्ते चूर्णितैरुत्तमाङ्गैः ॥ २७ ॥

amī ca tvāṁ dhṛtarāṣṭrasya putrāḥ
sarve sahaivāvanipālasaṅghaiḥ
bhīṣmo droṇaḥ sūtaputrastathāsau
sahāsmadīyairapi yodhamukhyaiḥ

vaktrāṇi te tvaramāṇā viśanti
daṁṣṭrākarālāni bhayānakāni
kecidvilagnā daśanāntareṣu
sandṛśyante cūrṇitairuttamāṅgaiḥ

All the sons of Dhṛtarāṣṭra, with hosts of kings of the earth, Bhīṣma, Droṇa, Karṇa, with the chief warriors on our side as well, are rushing headlong into Your mouths with terrible teeth and fearful to look at. Some of these are seen sticking in the gaps between the teeth, with their heads crushed. 26-27

Comment:—

'Bhīṣmo droṇaḥ sūtaputrastathāsau sahāsmadīyairapi yodhamukhyaiḥ'—Arjuna says, that the chief warriors on their side, such as Dhṛṣṭadyumna, Virāṭa and Drupada etc., believed in righteousness and were prepared to wage the war, regarding it as their duty. All these warriors, as well as Bhīṣma, Droṇa, Karṇa were rushing headlong into the Lord's mouth. Arjuna mentions these three names, of the rival army, to explain that they also joined the army, as a part of their duty.*

* Bhīṣma—Bhīṣma is a very well-known figure in the history of the world for his vow of life long celibacy and renunciation of his claim to his father's throne in order to facilitate his father's marriage with Satyavatī. He was so firm in his vow that he fought against his preceptor Paraśurāma. Lord Kṛṣṇa had vowed that he would remain unarmed. But when Bhīṣma vowed that he would compel Lord Kṛṣṇa to be equipped with weapon, He had to take up arms, once a whip and the second time a disc and run towards Bhīṣma.

Droṇa—Droṇa ate Duryodhana's food. So it was incumbent upon him to fight, thus he joined the battle regarding it as his duty. But at last listening to the gods he withdraws himself from the battle thinking of his duty as a Brāhmaṇa (a member of the priest class). He was so impartial that he taught his own son, Aśvatthāmā how to set Brahmāstra (a weapon or missile which caused infallible destruction and was used and withdrawn by chanting sacred formulas) in motion only while to his disciple Arjuna he taught both how to set it in motion and how to withdraw it.

Karṇa—Being a bosom friend of Duryodhana, he fought on his side. Even when Lord Kṛṣṇa disclosed to him that he was Kuntī's son, he refused to give up the cause of Duryodhana. Moreover he asked Lord Kṛṣṇa not to disclose the

'Amī ca tvāṁ dhṛtarāṣṭrasya putrāḥ sarve sahaivāvanipāla-saṅghaiḥ'—Those kings who were well-wishers of Duryodhana, and were ready to fight on his side, as well as Dhṛtarāṣṭra's hundred sons—Duryodhana and Duḥśāsana, etc., were rushing headlong, into the Lord's mouths, having terrible teeth.

'Kecidvilagnā daśanāntareṣu sandṛśyante cūrṇitairutta-māṅgaiḥ'—Some warriors were ingested by the Lord, but some of them were seen sticking in the gaps between the teeth, with heads crushed.

Here a doubt arises, as to how, Arjuna saw the warriors rushing headlong into the mouth of the Lord's cosmic form, when they were arrayed alive, on the battlefield? The clarification is, that the Lord asked Arjuna to behold whatever else he desired to see, in His cosmic form (11/7). Moreover, Arjuna had a doubt whether they or their enemies would win (2/6). So Arjuna, could foresee their own victory, in the Lord's cosmic body. The same fact, will be pointed out by the Lord, in response to Arjuna's question (11/32—34).

Appendix—Arjuna, in the cosmic form of the Lord, is beholding the imminent future. The Lord is beyond the limit of time, so in Him the past, the future and the present—the three are only present (Gītā 7/26).

Link:—In the next verse, Arjuna describes those notable

---

secret to Yudhiṣṭhira otherwise he, regarding him as his elder brother, would handover the kingdom to him and who would hand it over to Duryodhana. So the Pāṇḍavas would lead a miserable life forever.

His charities were imcomparable. One day Indra, the king of the gods, in Arjuna's interest, begged him to make a gift of his natural armour and earrings attached to his body. With great delight he tore his armour and earrings from his body and gave them away. Kuntī asked him not to kill anyone of her sons in the war. He promised not to kill her four sons but he would fight against Arjuna who could either be killed or would kill him. Even if Arjuna died, she would have five sons (including him viz., Karṇa).

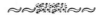

warriors who were striving for God-realization, and took up arms, regarding it as their duty, by giving the illustration of rivers.

यथा नदीनां बहवोऽम्बुवेगाः
समुद्रमेवाभिमुखा द्रवन्ति।
तथा तवामी नरलोकवीरा
विशन्ति वक्त्राण्यभिविज्वलन्ति॥ २८॥

yathā nadīnāṁ bahavo'mbuvegāḥ
samudramevābhimukhā dravanti
tathā tavāmī naralokavīrā
viśanti vaktrāṇyabhivijvalanti

As diverse torrents of rivers rush towards an ocean, so do these warriors of the mortal world, enter into Your blazing mouths. 28

Comment:—

'Yathā nadīnāṁ bahavo'mbuvegāḥ samudramevābhimukhā dravanti'—The source of the water of a river is, ocean. Water evaporates from the ocean, falls as rain, on the earth and shapes as rivers. So, rivers have a natural tendency to flow towards the ocean and finally lose their names and identity, by merging with an ocean. In fact, they had no identity of their own, even in the past, but they merely appeared separate, in the form of the flow of rivers.

'Tathā tavāmī naralokavīrā viśanti vaktrāṇyabhivijvalanti'—Just like, rivers, all the creatures rush towards the Lord, to attain eternal bliss. But, some of them by identifying themselves with the perishable and unreal body, are engaged in worldly pleasures and prosperity, and thus by error, accept their separate existence. But there are other valiant devotees who, not taking any heed for pleasures and prosperity, march towards God, in order to, attain the goal of human life. Bhīṣma and Droṇa etc., were such valiant warriors, who entered the Lord's mouths, blazing with the fire of knowledge, and thus they became fiery themselves, by attaining oneness with Him.

The term 'Amī (those), has been used to denote, the small number and significance of devotees who strive for, God-realization.

Link:— Arjuna, in the next verse, describes those warriors who being engaged in worldly pleasures and prosperity, joined the war in order to gain praise and kingdom, illustrated by moths.

यथा प्रदीप्तं ज्वलनं पतङ्गा
विशन्ति नाशाय समृद्धवेगाः ।
तथैव नाशाय विशन्ति लोका-
स्तवापि वक्त्राणि समृद्धवेगाः ॥ २९ ॥

yathā pradīptaṁ jvalanaṁ pataṅgā
viśanti nāśāya samṛddhavegāḥ
tathaiva nāśāya viśanti lokā-
stavāpi vaktrāṇi samṛddhavegāḥ

As moths out of their folly rush headlong into the burning fire for destruction, even so, do these people, hurriedly speed into Your mouths for their annihilation. 29

Comment:—

'Yathā pradīptaṁ......samṛddhavegāḥ'—Moths, living in green grass, in the dark night of rainy season, being enamoured of blazing fire, in order to get light, rush into the blazing fire, for their destruction. If a person, out of pity extinguishes the fire, they feel very sad, because they foolishly think, that they have been deprived of a great gain.

'Tathaiva nāśāya viśanti lokāstavāpi vaktrāṇi samṛddhavegāḥ'— Worldly people, generally hanker after worldly pleasures and prosperity and they also think of these. Such warriors were Duryodhana, his co-warriors and such other kings, who were entering the Lord's blazing mouths, for their destruction i.e., they were paving their way, for eighty-four lac forms of life, and hell. It means, that generally people, hanker after worldly pleasures, prosperity, praise, honour and rest etc. In order to, gain these they have to bear insult, dishonour, loss, worry and internal burning sensation etc., yet they yearn for these.*

Appendix—In the preceding verse there is the illustration of rivers and in this verse there is the illustration of moths. Moths out of their folly, being enamoured of blazing fire, themselves rush into the blazing fire in order to enjoy light, but rivers flow towards the ocean in order to merge in it and to lose their separate identity. Therefore those men who have a desire 'to take' are like moths and the men who have a desire 'to give' are like rivers. The feeling 'to take' is insentience (matter) and the feeling 'to give' is sentience (consciousness). When a man has the notion 'to take' from others, then forbidden actions are performed by him but when a person has the notion 'to give' to others, then virtuous actions are done by him. He, who has a desire 'to take', goes to heaven (paradise) while he who has a desire 'to give' attains salvation. The reason is that the feeling of 'getting' from others leads to bondage while the feeling of 'giving' to others leads to salvation.

Link:—Having described, the entry of the warriors into the Lord's mouths, Arjuna, now in the next two verses, describes the Lord's terrible form, and the process of their destruction.

लेलिह्यसे ग्रसमानः समन्ता-
ल्लोकान्समग्रान्वदनैर्ज्वलद्भिः ।

*A moth out of ignorance falls on the burning lamp and so does fish devour bait on a fish-hook out of ignorance. But people in spite of knowing the disastrous consequences of desires don't renounce them. How tempting this delusion! (Bhartṛhari Vairāgyaśataka)

तेजोभिरापूर्य जगत्समग्रं-
भासस्तवोग्राः प्रतपन्ति विष्णो॥ ३०॥

lelihyase grasamānaḥ samantā-
llokānsamagrānvadanairjvaladbhiḥ
tejobhirāpūrya jagatsamagraṁ-
bhāsastavogrāḥ pratapanti viṣṇo

Devouring all the worlds through Your flaming mouths, and licking them on all sides, Your fiery rays, fill the whole world with radiance, and heat it, O Viṣṇu. 30

Comment:—

'Lelihyase grasamānaḥ samantāllokānsamagrānvadanair-jvaladbhiḥ'—The Lord was devouring the beings of all the worlds through His burning mouths, and was licking them, with His tongue lest anyone of them, should escape.

'Tejobhirāpūrya jagatsamagraṁbhāsastavogrāḥ pratapanti viṣṇo'—The Lord's brilliance was very frightening and it was burning and tormenting the entire universe.

Appendix—Here the Lord by using the terms 'lokānsamagrān' (all the worlds) and 'jagatsamagraṁ' (insentient and sentient, unmoving and moving beings of the world) means to say that all these are within the entire form of God.

In the Gītā, God has been called 'samagra'—'asaṁśayaṁ samagraṁ māṁ' (7/1), actions have been called 'samagra'—'yajñāyā-carataḥ karma samagraṁ' (4/23) and in this verse the world has been called 'samagra'. It means that all are the manifestations of God.

Link:—Having viewed the Lord's cosmic form, in its most terrible phase, in which warriors were rushing headlong for their destruction, Arjuna was terrified and also filled with curiosity, to know Who Śrī Kṛṣṇa really was, and what He proposed to do. So he put a question.

आख्याहि मे को भवानुग्ररूपो
नमोऽस्तु ते देववर प्रसीद।
विज्ञातुमिच्छामि भवन्तमाद्यं
न हि प्रजानामि तव प्रवृत्तिम्॥ ३१॥

ākhyāhi me ko bhavānugrarūpo
namo'stu te devavara prasīda
vijñātumicchāmi bhavantamādyaṁ
na hi prajānāmi tava pravṛttim

Tell me, who You are, so fierce in form. I bow deeply to You, O Supreme Deity, be kind. I wish to know You, the Primal One, in your essence (tattva), for I do not understand Your objective. 31

Comment:—

'Ākhyāhi me ko bhavānugrarūpo namo'stu te devavara prasīda'—Arjuna says, that the Lord revealed Himself in His divine form, as well as the fearful form, and Arjuna, could not know the reality about Him. So, he asked Him, who He was. Beholding such a terrible form, what could he do, but bow down his head? So he bowed deeply to Him. Having a vision of His terrible form, licking the people on all sides, Arjuna prayed to Him, to be merciful to him.

'Vijñātumicchāmi bhavantamādyaṁ na hi prajānāmi tava pravṛttim'—The Lord, first of all incarnated Himself, in his cosmic form (in the form of the world). So he has been addressed as the Primal One. Arjuna could not know the Lord's motive, in revealing that divine form, as well as the terrible form, in His cosmic body. So he wanted to know, His motive in that revelation and also what He wanted to do, afterwards.

Now a question arises, that the Lord's first incarnation was in the cosmic form (in the form of the universe), and here Arjuna beheld His cosmic form, in a limb of His body. Are both of His forms the same or are different? The answer is, that it is only the Lord who knows the reality; yet after reflection, it seems that the universe was also within the cosmic form, which Arjuna beheld. When it is said, that the Lord pervades everywhere, it means that he pervades the infinite universes, within and without, this universe. All these universes, are held, in one of His limbs.

Appendix—Having seen the grand terrible form of the Lord, Arjuna is so much terrified and perturbed that he asks his friend Śrī Kṛṣṇa Who He is!

Link:—In the next verse, the Lord answers Arjuna's question.

श्रीभगवानुवाच

कालोऽस्मि लोकक्षयकृत्प्रवृद्धो
लोकान्समाहर्तुमिह प्रवृत्तः।
ऋतेऽपि त्वां न भविष्यन्ति सर्वे
येऽवस्थिताः प्रत्यनीकेषु योधाः॥ ३२॥

śrībhagavānuvāca

kālo'smi lokakṣayakṛtpravṛddho
lokānsamāhartumiha pravṛttaḥ
ṛte'pi tvāṁ na bhaviṣyanti sarve
ye'vasthitāḥ pratyanīkeṣu yodhāḥ

The Blessed Lord said:

I am the mighty world-destroying kāla now engaged in wiping out the world. Even without you the warriors arrayed in the hostile army will not survive. 32

Comment:—

[After reflection, the Lord's cosmic form, seems very extraordinary, because even for Arjuna, possessing the divine eyes it was hard to look at (11/17). Being terrified, Arjuna asked him Who, He was. It seems, that if Arjuna had not put this question to Him, He might have continued to reveal Himself, to him. But when Arjuna, questioned Him, He ceased revealing Himself and answered his question.]

'Kālo'smi lokakṣayakṛtpravṛddhaḥ'—In the preceding verse, Arjuna asked the Lord, Who He was. So the Lord replied, that He was the mighty world-destroying Time.

'Lokānsamāhartumiha pravṛttaḥ'—Arjuna, said to the Lord, that he did not know His purpose, what He wanted to do. So the Lord answered, that He wanted to exterminate, the warriors of the two armies.

'Ṛte'pi tvāṁ na bhaviṣyanti sarve ye'vasthitāḥ pratyanīkeṣu yodhāḥ'—Arjuna had said that he would not fight (2/9). So Lord Kṛṣṇa says, that even without him, the warriors arrayed in the hostile army will not survive, because He Himself is bent upon their destruction, and their chances for survival, are nil. Moreover, he himself has seen that the warriors of both the armies were rushing headlong, into His terrible mouths.

Here a doubt arises, that Arjuna saw the warriors of both the armies, rushing headlong into the Lord's mouth, why does the Lord, refer only to the warriors of the hostile army that they will not survive, even without him? The clarification is that Arjuna while fighting, was going to kill the warriors of the hostile army. So, the Lord says that even if he does not kill the warriors of the hostile army, they will not be spared; their destruction is inevitable.

Now, another doubt arises as to why warriors such as Aśvatthāmā etc., were saved. The clarification is, that the Lord talks only about those warriors, who would be killed by Arjuna. The Lord means to say to Arjuna, that the destruction of those warriors of his hostile army, who would be killed by him, is inevitable because they have already been slain by Him, he should become, merely an instrument (11/33).

Link:—In the above verse, the Lord declared, that even without Arjuna, the warriors of his hostile army would not survive. Why then should Arjuna at all engage himself, in this carnage? The answer is given, in the next two verses, by the Lord.

तस्मात्त्वमुत्तिष्ठ यशो लभस्व
जित्वा शत्रून्भुङ्क्ष्व राज्यं समृद्धम्।
मयैवैते निहताः पूर्वमेव
निमित्तमात्रं भव सव्यसाचिन् ॥ ३३ ॥

tasmāttvamuttiṣṭha yaśo labhasva
jitvā śatrūnbhuṅkṣva rājyaṁ samṛddham
mayaivaite nihatāḥ pūrvameva
nimittamātraṁ bhava savyasācin

Therefore, arise and win glory in conquering the foes, and experience the pleasure of the affluent kingdom. These warriors stand already slain by Me; and you are merely an instrument, O Savyasācin (Savyasācin—One who can shoot arrows with the left hand also). 33

Comment:—

'Tasmāttvamuttiṣṭha yaśo labhasva'—The Lord, says to Arjuna that he himself has beheld, that his rivals will be inevitably slain. So he should, gird up his loins and win glory and fame. But, he should not regard the victory as the fruit of his efforts, as he will be bound (Gītā 5/12) because profit and loss, fame and defame etc., are destined, by the Lord. So a man, should not get entangled in them.

The expression 'Yaśo labhasva' does not mean, that he should get elated by winning fame through victory. He should rather think, that his opponents had already been killed by the Lord, so fame was gained, as was destined. It was not the result of his efforts, otherwise he would be bound.

'Jitvā śatrūnbhuṅkṣva rājyaṁ samṛddham'—An affluent

kingdom, involves two factors (i) There should be no enemy or rival. (ii) It should be rich and prosperous. The Lord, says to Arjuna that after getting victory over his enemies, he will enjoy such an affluent kingdom. To enjoy the affluent kingdom does not mean that he should enjoy riches. But it means, that the kingdom to which ordinary men are attracted, can be acquired by him easily.

'Mayaivaite nihatāḥ pūrvameva'—The warriors of Arjuna's hostile army, have already been slain by the Lord, because their days are numbered.

'Nimittamātraṁ bhava savyasācin'—Arjuna, was called 'Savyasācī' because he could shoot arrows with his left hand, also. Addressing him by this term, the Lord asks him to shoot arrows with both of his hands i.e., he should fight heart and soul with full courage, valour and intelligence, carefully by becoming merely His instrument and he should not feel proud of his victory because, they have already been slain by Him.

A striver, should also apply his intellect and power etc., for God-realization. But he should not be proud, of his resources and devotion etc. He should think, that he will attain Him only, by His grace. The Lord declares, it in the Gītā, "A devotee performing all actions, by My grace, attains the eternal, imperishable Abode" (18/56); "Fixing your mind on Me, you will by My grace, overcome all obstacles" (18/58). Thus a striver, without having any pride, by His grace, attains Him. Every person, while performing his duty, should try his best but he should not be proud of his success, in the least. When Lord Kṛṣṇa, raised the Govardhana, he asked the cowherds also to support it, with their sticks. The cowherds thought that their sticks were supporting the Govardhana, but actually it was the nail of the little finger of the Lord's left hand, which supported the Govardhana. When they felt proud, the Lord moved his finger a little downward, and the Govardhana began to slip downward. So, all of them cried, "O brother Kṛṣṇa, help us." The Lord, asked them to apply their full strength. But, when they found their efforts futile,the Lord raised the mount up, with His finger. So, if a man by becoming an instrument in the Lord's hands, without having pride of his power, and without having a desire for the fruit of his actions, performs his duty, he may attain salvation. A striver, meets with failure, due to his pride. If he does not have pride, he can attain salvation, instantly. The pride in his efforts, is a stumbling block to his attainment. Therefore, the Lord advises Arjuna, not to feel proud, but regard it as His grace. Whatever is to happen will certainly, happen. It cannot be checked by a man, with his power. So, he should remain equanimous, in whatever happens, as a result of his actions. By doing so, he will attain salvation, because bondage, damnation to hell and degradation, to eighty-four lac species, is the result of misdeeds, whereas salvation, liberation, beatitude and divine love etc., are natural and self-evident.

Appendix—'Nimittamātraṁ bhava savyasācin'—By this expression the Lord does not mean that Arjuna should perform actions nominally but it means that he should apply his full power but he himself should not take the credit of his victory viz., he should make the best efforts but he should not feel proud of his achievement. Whatever power, knowledge and capability have been bestowed upon a striver by God, he should fully apply them but he can't attain God by applying his power. He will be attained by His grace only.

God is showering His grace most graciously on us. As a calf draws milk only from one udder of the cow, but God has provided her with four udders. Similarly God is showering His grace from the four sides. We have to become merely an instrument in His hand. Arjuna had to fight in the war, therefore the Lord asks him to fight by merely becoming an instrument and he will get victory. Similarly we have the world before us, if we practise spiritual discipline by becoming merely an instrument, we shall get victory over the world.

द्रोणं च भीष्मं च जयद्रथं च
कर्णं तथान्यानपि योधवीरान्।
मया हतांस्त्वं जहि मा व्यथिष्ठा
युध्यस्व जेतासि रणे सपत्नान्॥ ३४॥

droṇaṁ ca bhīṣmaṁ ca jayadrathaṁ ca
karṇaṁ tathānyānapi yodhavīrān
mayā hatāṁstvaṁ jahi mā vyathiṣṭhā
yudhyasva jetāsi raṇe sapatnān

Slay, Droṇa, Bhīṣma, Jayadratha, Karṇa and other brave warriors who are already doomed to be killed by Me. Be not afraid. Fight, and you will conquer your enemies, in battle. 34

Comment:—

'Droṇaṁ ca bhīṣmaṁ ca jayadrathaṁ ca karṇaṁ tathānyānapi yodhavīrān mayā hatāṁstvaṁ jahi'—Lord Kṛṣṇa, exhorted Arjuna to fight by giving up fear, because Droṇa, Bhīṣma, Jayadratha, Karṇa and such other valiant warriors,* however formidable they might be, they stand already slain by Him. So he should get victory over them, without being proud of his victory.

'Mā vyathiṣṭhā yudhyasva'—Arjuna considered it sinful, to kill his preceptor, Droṇa and patriarch Bhīṣma. So the Lord asks him not to be distressed with fear of violence. He should perform, his duty of waging war, as he is a warrior belonging to the warrior class.

* Bhīṣma, Karṇa and Droṇa were well-known for the bravery throughout the world. So it was diffficult to get victory over them. Jayadratha was not such a valiant warrior, but he was armoured with the boon that he who dropped his severed head on the ground, would have his own head smashed into a hundred pieces.

'Jetāsi raṇe sapatnān'—Arjuna, was not sure whether they would win the war, or they would be vanquished by the enemy (Gītā 2/6). So the Lord, while revealing His cosmic form to him, said to him, "Behold within this body, whatever else you desire to see" (11/7). He saw scenes of his victory and the enemy's defeat. Arjuna, also beheld Bhīṣma, Droṇa and Karṇa, the valiant warriors of the hostile army rushing headlong into the Lord's body. So, He declares, that he will conquer, his enemies in battle.

An Important Fact

A striver, gets discouraged when he finds himself incapable of controlling worldly temptation and removing evils. So, the Lord encourages him, by declaring, "Be not distressed with fear. Fight, you will conquer, your enemies." So a striver, having no pride of his own, by depending on the Lord, should perform his duty. If he is worried about the enemies, it means, that he has pride of his own. Moreover, he should not be worried about evil thoughts, if these come to his mind, because they are all perishable, and have been destroyed, by the Lord. So a striver, should not attach importance to them.

"Kill those, who stand already killed, by Me"—this statement of the Lord arouses a doubt, that if someone kills a person it means, that he is killed only by the Lord. Thus, does the murderer incur no sin? The answer is, that no one is authorized to slay others, or to trouble them. He has a right, only to serve others, and give comfort to them. If one had the right to kill others, there would not be any value, of a sanction and prohibition. So, a person, who murders others or tortures them, certainly incurs, sin. But a member of the warrior class, who by giving up pride and selfishness, joins a battle, as sanctioned by scriptures, incurs no sin, because it is his duty.

Appendix—Lord Kṛṣṇa says to Arjuna that all the valiant warriors have already been slain by Him. This should mean that a striver's attachment and aversion, desire and anger etc., have already been destroyed viz., they have no existence. We ourselves have given them existence, have valued them and have accepted them in ourselves. In fact they have no independent existence at all—'nāsato vidyate bhāvaḥ' (Gītā 2/16).

Link:—Beholding the very terrible cosmic form of the Lord, Arjuna asked Him, in the thirty-first verse, who He was and what He wanted to do. In the thirty-second verse, the Lord answered, that He was the mighty Time, and came to destroy the world. Then in the thirty-third and thirty-fourth verses, the Lord asked him to fight, consoling him that he would win, because his enemies had already been killed by Him. Sañjaya, now reveals to Dhṛtarāṣṭra, Arjuna's reaction to the Lord's exhortation.

सञ्जय उवाच

एतच्छ्रुत्वा वचनं केशवस्य
कृताञ्जलिर्वेपमानः किरीटी।
नमस्कृत्वा भूय एवाह कृष्णं-
सगद्गदं भीतभीतः प्रणम्य॥ ३५॥

sañjaya uvāca

etacchrutvā vacanaṁ keśavasya
kṛtāñjalirvepamānaḥ kirīṭī
namaskṛtvā bhūya evāha kṛṣṇaṁ-
sagadgadaṁ bhītabhītaḥ praṇamya

Sañjaya said:

Having heard these words of Lord Keśava, the crowned one (Arjuna), with folded hands, trembling, prostrating himself over again overwhelmed with fear addressed Lord Kṛṣṇa, in a choked voice, after bowing down. 35

Comment:—

'Etacchrutvā vacanaṁ keśavasya kṛtāñjalirvepamānaḥ kirīṭī'—Arjuna, was terror-struck, after beholding the Lord's terrible cosmic form. He was more terrified when the Lord declared, that He was the mighty Time, Who would destroy all the warriors. So, he began to tremble and bowed to Him, with joined palms.

Arjuna helped Indra, the king of the gods, by killing demons Kāla and Khañja etc. As a token of his pleasure, Indra placed a divine diadem (Kirīṭa), possessing the brilliance of sun, on his head. So Arjuna is called 'Kirīṭī' viz., the crowned one. Here, the same Arjuna, who helped Indra by killing huge demons, was trembling with fear.

'Namaskṛtvā bhūya evāha kṛṣṇaṁsagadgadaṁ bhītabhītaḥ praṇamya'—Time, is Lord's destroying power, which always keeps on devouring all beings without exception. When Arjuna, beheld the terrible form of the Lord, he thought that Lord Kṛṣṇa is the master of that Time (Death), which devours the entire universe. So, except Him, there was no saviour, to protect him, from the clutches of Time (Death). So Arjuna, bowed deep to Him, again and again.

'Bhūya'—By this term, Sañjaya means to say, that from the fifteenth verse to the thirty-first verse, Arjuna offered praises to the Lord and bowed to Him, and now again he begins to offer his praises to Him and bows to Him.

Voice, gets faltered and choked, out of fear, as well as joy. If Arjuna had been too much terrified, he could not have uttered any words. It shows, that Arjuna was not, too much terrified.

अर्जुन उवाच

स्थाने हृषीकेश तव प्रकीर्त्या
जगत्प्रहृष्यत्यनुरज्यते च।

रक्षांसि भीतानि दिशो द्रवन्ति
सर्वे नमस्यन्ति च सिद्धसङ्घाः ॥ ३६ ॥

arjuna uvāca

sthāne hṛṣikeśa tava prakīrtyā
jagatprahṛṣyatyanurajyate ca
rakṣāṁsi bhītāni diśo dravanti
sarve namasyanti ca siddhasaṅghāḥ

Arjuna said:

O Omniscient Lord, it is but apt that the universe exults, and is filled with love by chanting Your names and glory; terrified demons are fleeing in all directions, and all the hosts of Siddhas (perfected souls) are bowing to you. 36

Comment:—

[It is observed, that a man being overwhelmed with terror, cannot speak. But Arjuna though terrified is offering praises to the Lord, from the thirty-sixth verse to the forty-sixth verse. How? The answer is, that after beholding the cosmic form of the Lord, Arjuna was terrified, as well as delighted, as he himself says, "I feel delighted, that I have seen what was never seen before; at the same time, my mind is confounded with fear" (11/45). It proves that Arjuna was not so much overwhelmed with terror, that he could not offer praises, to the Lord.]

'Hṛṣīkeśa'—'Hṛṣīka' means senses and 'Īśa' means master, so 'Hṛṣīkeśa' means the Lord of the senses viz., God. It means, that the Lord is the conductor of senses and mind etc.

'Tava prakīrtyā jagatprahṛṣyatyanurajyate ca'—People of the world, by having a disinclination for the world, chant the names and glory of the Lord, narrate His activities and listen to these. By doing so, they are delighted. It means that people, by having an inclination for the world, develop attachmemt, aversion and burning sensation etc., while, by chanting the Lord's names and glories, they attain peace and delight.

When the Lord incarnates, all the sentient and insentient beings, such as gods, human beings, sages, birds, beasts, trees, plants, rivers and streams etc., are delighted. Similarly, all of them are delighted, by chanting the Lord's names and glories. When they get delighted, by chanting His name and glories i.e., their minds get engrossed in Him, then they develop devotion for Him.

'Rakṣāṁsi bhītāni diśo dravanti'— All the demons, giants, ghosts and evil-spirits, etc., flee in different directions, out of fear when, Lord's names and glories, are chanted.* They flee, due to their own sins, not due to hearing of the Lord's names and glories.

It is because of their sins, that their ears cannot hear most pious, auspicious names and glories, of the Lord. But, if they stay there and listen to His names and glories, they become free, from their base life and attain salvation.

'Sarve namasyanti ca siddhasaṅghāḥ'—The perfected souls, saints and strivers, by chanting the Lord's names and glories and listening to His sports, bow to Him.

All these scenes and sports are being revealed by the Lord, in His divine cosmic form.

'Sthāne'—Arjuna, shows propriety of the above-mentioned actions of beings, because an inclination for the Lord, leads to peace and bliss, while disinclination for Him, leads to disquietude and distresses. It means, that a being (spirit) is a portion of the Lord, and so he is delighted by having an inclination for Him, and such qualities as peace, forgiveness and politeness, are revealed in him. But if he goes astray, he

---

* The places, where people don't chant and listen to the Lord's names, glories and sports which dispel fear of demons, are haunted by ogresses (Śrīmadbhā. 10/6/3).

has to face adversity, which is natural.

The man (soul), is a fragment of the Lord. But, having an inclination for matter, he has a desire for prosperity and pleasure. The more, he tries to gain these, the more entangled, he gets in disquietude, adversity and in burning sensation etc. But, when by having disinclination for the world, he starts moving towards the Lord, he starts attaining bliss, and his sorrows diminish.

Appendix—Here the term 'sthāne' should be understood for both the preceding verses and the succeeding verses to this verse. Whatever the Lord said in the thirty-second, thirty-third and thirty-fourth verses and whatever has been said in this verse for that Arjuna says, "O Lord! You said that the warriors of the hostile army have already been slain and I should merely become an instrument— in this way whatever You said is quite proper. The world is delighted by chanting Your names and glories, and the demons, being terrified, are fleeing—whatever is happening is proper. All this human-drama is being staged by You, not by me."

Link:— Arjuna justifies the propriety of the term 'Sthāne', used in the preceding verse, in the next four verses, and offers repeated salutations to the Lord.

कस्माच्च ते न नमेरन्महात्मन्
गरीयसे ब्रह्मणोऽप्यादिकर्त्रे।
अनन्त देवेश जगन्निवास
त्वमक्षरं सदसत्तत्परं यत्॥ ३७॥

kasmācca te na nameranmahātman
garīyase brahmaṇo'pyādikartre
ananta deveśa jagannivāsa
tvamakṣaraṁ sadasattatparaṁ yat

O Great Soul, why should they not bow to You, the greatest

of all, the progenitor, even of the Brahmā? O Infinite one, O Lord of the gods, O Abode of the universe, You are eternal. You are the being (real), the non-being (unreal), and that, which is beyond, both being and non-being viz., the Imperishable Brahma. 37

Comment:—

'Kasmācca te na nameranmahātman garīyase brahmaṇo-pyādikartre'—The Lord, is the progenitor not only of the universe, but of Brahmā Himself, who created it. Thus, being the greatest and the best of all the worldly things and persons etc. He deserves the homage of all. Homage, is paid to two kinds of persons (i) Preceptors (ii) Parents, grand-parents and elders. The Lord, is the preceptor* and father of Brahmā, the creator of the universe.

'Ananta'—The Lord, is infinite, because He transcends time, space and intellect etc. He has no beginning and no end. His forms and glories, are also infinite.

'Deveśa—He is the Lord of all the gods, who are known, such as Indra, the king of the gods and Varuṇa, the deity of the waters etc., as well as, those who are unknown; their destiny, is shaped by Him and He controls all of them.

'Jagannivāsa'—The Lord, is the Abode of the infinite universes, because all of them are held in one of His limbs. In spite of it, that limb is not fully occupied, it still remains vacant.

'Tvamakṣaraṁ sadasattatparaṁ yat'—The Lord, is Imperishable.† He is the real, which never ceases to be and He is also the unreal, which has no existence, and He is also, the Absolute, the Transcendental, Who is beyond the power of senses, mind and intellect and cannot be described, in anyway.

---

* Sage Patañjali has said, "The Lord is the preceptor of even Brahmā who emanated from Him first of all" (Yogadarśana 1/26).

† In the first verse of the eighth chapter Arjuna asked, "What is Brahma?" The Lord answered, "The Supreme Imperishable is Brahma." Similarly Arjuna called Him the Imperishable in (11/18) and also in this verse.

It means, that He is the best, the greatest and the most Supreme Being. So it is proper to pay obeisance to You.

Appendix—By the expression 'Sadasaccāham' (9/19) and by the expression 'sadasattatparaṁ' used here the infinitude and entirety of the Lord endowed with attributes are proved.

The real and the unreal are relative terms, so they are earthly (worldly) but He Who is beyond them, having independent existence, is unearthly (divine). Both the mundane and the divine are the manifestations of the entire God. The higher and lower nature of God are not beyond the real and the unreal but God transcends the real and the unreal also—'mattaḥ parataraṁ nānyatkiñcidasti dhanañjaya' (Gītā 7/7).

Within 'saguṇa' (entire form of God), 'nirguṇa' can be included, but within 'nirguṇa', 'saguṇa' cannot be included. The reason is that in 'saguṇa' there is no negation of 'nirguṇa', but in 'nirguṇa' there is negation of 'saguṇa'. Therefore 'nirguṇa' is unipresent (finite) viz., within it all is not included. But within 'saguṇa' (entire form) all is included, nothing is left out. Therefore, Arjuna by the expression 'sadasattatparaṁ yat' seems to say, "You are the real, You are the unreal and You are also the entity beyond these two, which we can imagine. From the view-point of knowledge You are also the indescribable entity which can be called neither real (existent) nor unreal (non-existent)—'na sattannāsaducyate' (Gītā 13/12). It means that there neither has been, nor is, nor will be, nor can be anyone else besides You viz., You and only You exist."

त्वमादिदेवः पुरुषः पुराण-
स्त्वमस्य विश्वस्य परं निधानम्।
वेत्तासि वेद्यं च परं च धाम
त्वया ततं विश्वमनन्तरूप॥ ३८॥

tvamādidevaḥ puruṣah purāṇa-
stvamasya viśvasya paraṁ nidhānam
vettāsi vedyaṁ ca paraṁ ca dhāma
tvayā tataṁ viśvamanantarūpa

You are the Primeval God, the primordial spirit. You are the ultimate shelter of the universe, you are the knower, the knowable and the Supreme Abode. This universe is fully pervaded by you, Being of infinite forms. 38

Comment:—

'Tvamādidevaḥ puruṣaḥ purāṇaḥ'—The Lord, is the Primal Deity, because He is the source of everything sentient and insentient. He is called the most ancient Person, because He is the source of the entire creation and is eternal.

'Tvamasya viśvasya paraṁ nidhānam'—He is the ultimate resort of the universe, because the entire universe emanates from Him, abides in Him and merges in Him.

'Vettāsi'—It is He, Who possesses real and full knowledge of the past, the present and the future, and there is none who can be equal to Him in knowledge.

'Vedyam'—He is the only knowable by the scriptures and the saints and His knowledge, is the highest goal of human life.

'Paraṁ dhāma'—He, is the Supreme Abode, attaining Whom, there is no return and nothing remains to be done, to be known, and to be acquired. This Supreme Abode, is also called salvation or the Supreme State etc.

'Anantarūpa'—His forms, which He revealed in His cosmic body, are infinite.

Tvayā tataṁ viśvam'—The entire universe, is pervaded by Him, He permeates every particle, of the universe.

Appendix—In this verse Arjuna is repeating the utterances of the Lord by the term 'ādideva' which was expressed by the Lord by the expression 'ahamādirhi devānāṁ maharṣīṇāṁ ca sarvaśaḥ' (10/2). Though Prakṛti is also beginningless—'prakṛtiṁ puruṣaṁ caiva viddhyanādī ubhāvapi' (13/19), yet prakṛti depends on God. The reason is that prakṛti is the kaleidoscopic power of God but God is not anyone's power and He is the master of the power.

'purāṇaḥ'—The Lord mentioned it by the term 'purāṇam' (8/9). No one is more ancient than God because He is beyond time.

'paraṁ nidhānam'—It was mentioned by the Lord by the term 'nidhānam' (9/18). The universe is endless but it abides in a fragment of God.

'vettā'—This was mentioned by the Lord by the expression 'vedāhaṁ samatītāni' etc. (7/26).

'vedyam'—This was mentioned by the Lord by the term 'vedyam' (9/17).

'paraṁ dhāma'—The Lord mentioned it by the expression 'yaṁ prāpya na nivartante taddhāma paramaṁ mama' (8/21).

'tvayā tataṁ viśvam'—The Lord mentioned it by the expressions 'yena sarvamidaṁ tatam' (8/22) and 'mayā tatamidaṁ sarvam' (9/4).

वायुर्यमोऽग्निर्वरुणः शशाङ्कः
प्रजापतिस्त्वं प्रपितामहश्च।
नमो नमस्तेऽस्तु सहस्रकृत्वः
पुनश्च भूयोऽपि नमो नमस्ते॥ ३९॥

vāyuryamo'gnirvaruṇaḥ śaśāṅkaḥ
prajāpatistvaṁ prapitāmahaśca
namo namaste'stu sahasrakṛtvaḥ
punaśca bhūyo'pi namo namaste

You are the God of wind, God of death (yama), God of fire and water, the moon-god, Prajāpati, and the great grandfather of

beings. Salutations to You, salutations a thousand time and again salutations to You. 39

Comment:—

'Vāyuḥ'—The Lord, is the Wind-god who gives life-breath and energy, to all beings.

'Yamaḥ'—The Lord is the god of death, and the entire universe, is controlled by Him.

'Agniḥ'—He is the Fire-god, who gives light, fire and heat and digests food as the gastric fire.

'Varuṇaḥ'—The Lord is the god of water, without which life is impossible.

'Śaśāṅkaḥ'—The Lord is the moon, which nourishes plants, herbs and vegetation.

'Prajāpatiḥ'—He is Dakṣa Prajāpati, who created the universe.

'Prapitāmahaḥ'—Brahmā is the grandfather of all beings, because he is the father of Dakṣa Prajāpati who created the universe. God is the creator of Brahmā. So, He is the great grandfather of all beings.

'Namo namaste'stu sahasrakṛtvaḥ punaśca bhūyo'pi namo namaste'—The Lord, Himself is god Indra and He is also other gods. He possesses infinite forms. How can Arjuna describe His merits and glories? He can do nothing, besides bowing to Him again and again.

A striver, is responsible for performing his duty, only so long as he depends on his power i.e., he is proud of his power. But, when he is unable to perform it, he only bows to the Lord i.e., he surrenders himself to the Lord, and then the full responsibility goes to the Lord, and he then performs the duty, only as His instrument, without having any responsibility, of his own.

नमः पुरस्तादथ पृष्ठतस्ते
नमोऽस्तु ते सर्वत एव सर्व।
अनन्तवीर्यामितविक्रमस्त्वं
सर्वं समाप्नोषि ततोऽसि सर्वः॥ ४०॥

namaḥ purastādatha pṛṣṭhataste
namo'stu te sarvata eva sarva
anantavīryāmitavikramastvaṁ
sarvaṁ samāpnoṣi tato'si sarvaḥ

O Lord of infinite prowess, my salutations to You from the front, the rear and from all sides. O All in all! You, who possess limitless might, and pervade the world, You are omnipresent. 40

Comment:—

'Namaḥ purastādatha pṛṣṭhataste namo'stu te sarvata eva sarva'—Being horror-struck, Arjuna is unable to think what to say, and so he bows to the Lord, and offers Him salutations from all quarters.

'Anantavīryāmitavikramastvam'—The Lord, possesses infinite prowess and might, which is beyond the conception of any mortal.

'Sarvaṁ samāpnoṣi tato'si sarvaḥ'— He pervades the entire universe, there is no atom in the universe, which is devoid of Him.

Arjuna, beholds that the Lord pervades infinite universes and infinite universes, abide in one of His limbs.

Appendix—Having seen the divine cosmic form of the Lord, Arjuna said, "You are scorching the universe with your radiance"—'svatejasā viśvamidaṁ tapantam' (11/19), then He who was scorching and also the universe which was being scorched—both are the organs of the Lord's cosmic form. Seeing the frightening form of the Lord, the three worlds are greatly alarmed—'lokatrayaṁ pravyathitaṁ mahātman' (11/20), the world which is greatly alarmed is also an organ of the Lord's cosmic form. Having seen God, the gods being terrified, are uttering the Lord's glories—'kecidbhītāḥ prāñjalayo gṛṇanti' (11/21) and 'terrified demons are fleeing in all the ten directions'—'rakṣāṁsi bhītāni diśo dravanti' (11/36)—thus the terrified gods and demons are also the organs of the cosmic form of the Lord. The reason is that these gods and demons etc., were not present in Kurukṣetra, but they were seen by Arjuna in the cosmic form of God.

Brahmā, Viṣṇu, Śiva, Rudras, Ādityas, Vasus, Sādhyas, Viśvedevas, Aśvinīkumāras, Maruts, manes, celestial serpents, Gandharvas, Yakṣas, Asuras, great sages, Siddhas, Wind-god, Yama (god of death), god of fire, god of water, the moon, the sun etc., and besides them Bhīṣma, Droṇa, Karṇa, Jayadratha etc., all the kings are the organs of the Lord's divine cosmic form. Not only this but Arjuna, Sañjaya, Dhṛtarāṣṭra and the armies of Kauravas and Pāṇḍavas are also the organs of that cosmic form—'sarvaṁ samāpnoṣi tato'si sarvaḥ.'

It means that whatever insentient or sentient, unmoving or moving is being seen, heard and thought of, that is all only imperishable God. In order to realize it, a striver should have a firm belief that whether he understands it or not, he realizes it or not, he accepts it or not, but this is a verity. As water-element equally pervades, whether it is a drop of water or a big ocean, similarly God pervades everywhere from the tiniest to the biggest objects—by having this belief, a striver should do obeisance mentally every time to all persons and objects etc. Whatever objects such as trees, rivers, mountains, stones and walls etc., are seen, by beholding his favourite God in them he should pray to them, 'O Lord! Bestow your love upon me. I do obeisance to You'. By doing so God will be visible to him everywhere because in fact 'All is God'.

Link:—Arjuna in the next two verses prays to the Lord to

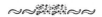

forgive him for the offences committed by him because he did not know Him in His true perspective.

सखेति मत्वा प्रसभं यदुक्तं
हे कृष्ण हे यादव हे सखेति।
अजानता महिमानं तवेदं
मया प्रमादात्प्रणयेन वापि॥४१॥
यच्चावहासार्थमसत्कृतोऽसि
विहारशय्यासनभोजनेषु।
एकोऽथवाप्यच्युत तत्समक्षं
तत्क्षामये त्वामहमप्रमेयम्॥४२॥

sakheti matvā prasabhaṁ yaduktaṁ
he kṛṣṇa he yādava he sakheti
ajānatā mahimānaṁ tavedaṁ
mayā pramādātpraṇayena vāpi
yaccāvahāsārthamasatkṛto'si
vihāraśayyāsanabhojaneṣu
eko'thavāpyacyuta tatsamakṣaṁ
tatkṣāmaye tvāmahamaprameyam

Whatever I may have said due to carelessness or love, addressing You as "O Kṛṣṇa, O Yādava, O Friend", thinking of You only as a friend ignorant of Your greatness; and the way in which I may have shown any disrespect to You in jest, while playing, reposing, sitting or dining, either alone or in company—I crave forgiveness from You, Who are infinite, O infallible Lord. 41-42

Comment:—

[Having seen the terrible form, of the Lord, when Arjuna is terror-struck, he forgets that He is Śrī Kṛṣṇa, and so he asks Him Who He is. But, when he regains his memory, he comes to know, that He is the same Lord Kṛṣṇa, his friend. So he prays to Lord Kṛṣṇa, to forgive him for any of his past offence.]

'Sakheti matvā prasabhaṁ yaduktaṁ he kṛṣṇa he yādava he sakheti ajānatā mahimānaṁ tavedaṁ mayā pramādātpraṇayena vāpi'—Those, who are venerable do not, called by personal names. They are addressed as your highness, your honour, or sire or sir, etc. Arjuna, did not pay due regard and reverence to Kṛṣṇa, Who was no other than the Lord, Himself. He did not know Him and His glory, in reality. So, he instead of addressing Him, as sir or sire etc., addressed Him in a familiar and friendly way, as 'Kṛṣṇa' or 'friend', due to carelessness or love. Arjuna, knew the Lord's real self and His glories, to some extent, because he rejecting the powerful Nārāyaṇī army (consisting of 1,09,350 foot-soldiers, 65,610 horses, 21,870 chariots and 21,870 elephants) and opted for Him, Who would remain unarmed in the war. But, he did not know, that the Lord holds infinite universes, in one of His limbs and His glories, are infinite. So he realized that he was an ordinary mortal, while the Lord is the greatest master of even gods, and His merits, are numberless. In fact, no one can know the glory of the Lord, in its entirety. It is infinite. In case, it is known, it becomes finite. When even glories emanating from His power, are countless, how can His own glories be finite, and be counted and grasped?

'Yaccāvahāsārthamasatkṛto' si vihāraśayyāsanabhojaneṣu eko'-thavāpyacyuta tatsamakṣaṁ tatkṣāmaye tvāmahamaprameyam'—Arjuna, realized that he by regarding the Lord as his equal and friend, had slighted and shown disrespect to Him, the Infinite, in jest, while playing, reposing, sitting or dining, either alone or in company, and it was quite improper and unseemly, on his part, to do so. So, he humbly sought His pardon, for his past misbehaviour.

Arjuna and Lord Kṛṣṇa were, indeed very intimate friends. Both of them were very frank with each other, while playing, bathing, reposing, sitting or dining etc. So, Arjuna might not have behaved with decorum and poked fun at him. Arjuna addressed the Lord as infinite, because He was beyond the limit, of even divine eyes.

Appendix—Arjuna regarded Lord Kṛṣṇa as his friend but having seen the Lord's glory, he forgets the notion of friendship with Him and he is surprized and terrified. He could never think of such a grandeur of the Lord.

Link:— In the next two verses, Arjuna describing His glories, pleads for forgiveness again.

पितासि लोकस्य चराचरस्य
त्वमस्य पूज्यश्च गुरुर्गरीयान्।
न त्वत्समोऽस्त्यभ्यधिकः कुतोऽन्यो
लोकत्रयेऽप्यप्रतिमप्रभाव ॥४३॥

pitāsi lokasya carācarasya
tvamasya pūjyaśca gururgarīyān
na tvatsamo'styabhyadhikaḥ kuto'nyo
lokatraye'pyapratimaprabhāva

You are the Father, also the Great Teacher of this animate and inanimate creation and are supremely adorable. O Lord, manifesting incomparable glory, in all the three worlds, there is none equal to You; who could then possibly excel You? 43

Comment:—

'Pitāsi lokasya carācarasya tvamasya pūjyaśca gururgarīyān'—He, is the father of human beings, birds, beasts and all other animate and inanimate beings, in infinite universes, because all the beings emanate from Him, and are sustained by Him. He is also the greatest teacher, because He is adored, even by gods and teachers, and is the source of all knowledge.

'Na tvatsamo'styabhyadhikaḥ kuto'nyo lokatraye'pyapratima-

prabhāva'—There, neither is, nor can be, anyone equal, to the Lord. The Lord's power is incomparable. Then how could any one excel him?

Appendix—Arjuna from the worldly point of view, by regarding the world as existent, says "There is none equal to You; who could then possibly excel You?" But in fact, when there is none else besides God, then no question arises of being equal to Him or to excel Him.

तस्मात्प्रणम्य प्रणिधाय कायं
प्रसादये त्वामहमीशमीड्यम्।
पितेव पुत्रस्य सखेव सख्युः
प्रियः प्रियायार्हसि देव सोढुम्॥४४॥

tasmātpraṇamya praṇidhāya kāyaṁ
prasādaye tvāmahamīśamīḍyam
piteva putrasya sakheva sakhyuḥ
priyaḥ priyāyārhasi deva soḍhum

Therefore, O adorable Lord, bowing deeply and prostrating before You, I implore You to forgive me. Bear with me, O Lord as a father with a son, as a friend with a friend, or as a lover with his beloved, and forgive my faults. 44

Comment:—

'Taṣmātpraṇamya praṇidhāya kāyaṁ prasādaye tvāmahamīśa-mīḍyam'—He, is the Lord of infinite universes, possessing infinite attributes and glories. Arjuna says to Lord Kṛṣṇa, when even great sages, saints and gods, who always offer praises to Him, cannot know His infinite glories, how can he offer praises to Him? So, he can merely bow down, and prostrate his body, at His feet, in order to please Him.

'Piteva putrasya sakheva sakhyuḥ priyaḥ priyāyārhasi deva soḍhum'—Three factors are responsible for insulting a person

(i) carelessness (ii) Fun (iii) Intimacy. As a child out of ignorance sitting on the lap of its father, pulls the beard and the moustache of its father, and even slaps him, yet the father, is pleased with it. He has not the least feeling, that the child, is slighting and insulting him. A friend, is very frank with his intimate friend and insults him, in jest, while playing, reposing, sitting or dining etc., his friend, takes it lightly treating it, as fun. A husband, condones the lapses of his wife, because of their intimacy. So Arjuna, prays to Lord Kṛṣṇa to forgive all his faults, in the same way, as a father or a friend or a husband, does for his son, friend, or wife.

In the forty-first and forty-second verses, Arjuna explained that carelessness, intimacy and fun, are three factors, which contribute to a feeling of a slight. So, here by citing the examples of father and son, husband and wife, friend and friend, Arjuna clarifies the above three factors, respectively.

Eleven kinds of sentiments, in the eleventh chapter

In the eleventh chapter, there is description of eleven sentiments. In the Lord's divine form there is a sentiment of serenity (11/15—18), in the cosmic form there is a sentiment of wonder, (11/20); in the fearful form, in which people are being destroyed, there is a sentiment of wrath (11/30—32); in the vast and terrible form having fearful teeth resembling a raging fire, there is a sentiment of disgust (11/23—25); when Lord Kṛṣṇa asks Arjuna to arise for battle, there is a sentiment of bravery (11/33); when Arjuna bows down and prostrates his body, there is a sentiment of service (11/44); when Arjuna beholds warriors, entering the Lord's mouth, with great rapidity for destruction, there is a sentiment of pity (11/28-29); when Arjuna prays to Lord Kṛṣṇa, to forgive his faults, by giving illustrations of a father, a friend and a husband, these are sentiments, of affection, friendship and conjugal love, respectively (11/44) and when Arjuna thinks of the way, in which he might have insulted Lord Kṛṣṇa in jest, there is the sentiment of humour (11/42).

Link:—Arjuna, in the next two verses, prays to the Lord to reveal His four-armed form.

अदृष्टपूर्वं हृषितोऽस्मि दृष्ट्वा
भयेन च प्रव्यथितं मनो मे।
तदेव मे दर्शय देवरूपं
प्रसीद देवेश जगन्निवास॥ ४५॥

adṛṣṭapūrvaṁ hṛṣito'smi dṛṣṭvā
bhayena ca pravyathitaṁ mano me
tadeva me darśaya devarūpaṁ
prasīda deveśa jagannivāsa

I rejoice that I have witnessed what was never revealed before, but my mind is confused with fear. Reveal to me kindly that divine form (the placid form of Viṣṇu), O Lord of the gods, O Abode of the universe. 45

Comment:—

[When Arjuna prayed to the Lord, to reveal His cosmic form to him He revealed it to him. So having faith in His grace, he prays to him to reveal to him, His divine form.]

'Adṛṣṭapūrvaṁ hṛṣito'smi dṛṣṭvā bhayena ca pravyathitaṁ mano me'—When Arjuna, had a vision of the Lord's cosmic form, his joy knew no bounds, and he considered himself very fortunate, because the Lord by His infinite compassion, had revealed to him that form. But, when he beheld the fearful phase, of that cosmic form, he trembled with fear.

'Tadeva me darśaya deva rūpaṁ prasīda deveśa jagannivāsa'—The term 'Tat' (that), denotes that Arjuna in the past, had a vision of that divine form, which is now out of sight. When Arjuna, saw the Lord's cosmic form, he saw Brahmā seated on the lotus-seat (11/15). It indicated that he also beheld Lord Viṣṇu, from whose navel, the divine lotus sprang. Then Arjuna, in the seventeenth verse, said, "I see you with a diadem, club, discus ('Ca' denotes conch and lotus)". It shows, that Arjuna had a vision of the divine form* (four-armed Lord) also, within that cosmic form.

The term 'Deva rūpam', refers to the four-armed divine form, which he saw within the Lord's cosmic form. Secondly, in the fifteenth verse, Arjuna addressed the Lord as 'Deva' (God) (Divinity), which means that Arjuna prayed to Him, to reveal to him neither the cosmic form nor the human form, but the four-armed form.

'Prasīda devesa jagannivāsa'—Here the term 'Jagannivāsa', denotes the cosmic form, while 'Ḍeveśa, refers to His four-armed form. Arjuna by using the term 'Jagannivāsa', means to say that His cosmic form, which is the abode of the universes, has already been seen by him, and he is still beholding it. But he prays to Him, to reveal to him His divine form (Deveśa) viz., the Lord of the gods).

An Important Fact

The cosmic form of the Lord, is divine, imperishable and eternal. In this form, there are infinite universes; and Brahmā, Viṣṇu and Śiva, who create, preserve and destroy these universes, which are also infinite. Infinite universes, emanate from this form and again merge into it, yet, it remains, the same without any modification. It is so unusual that the effulgence of a thousand suns blazing forth all at once, cannot be compared with, its splendour (11/12). This form, can be seen only with divine eyes. With an eye of knowledge, one perceives existence of the Lord,

* The Lord in the forty-ninth verse by the term 'Punaḥ' (again) and 'Tadeva' (even that) and Sañjaya in the fiftieth verse by the term 'Bhūyaḥ' (again) mention the same divine four-armed form (seen in the cosmic form).

Who is the origin of the universe; with an emotional eye, one sees the universe, as manifestation of the Lord, but one cannot have a vision of the cosmic form, of the Lord with human eyes. As far as human eyes, are concerned, with these one can perceive, the universe neither, as originated from the Lord, nor as His manifestation, nor His cosmic form, because eyes being evolutes of matter cannot perceive, objects, beyond it.

Various forms of the Lord, whether they are two-armed, four-armed or a million-armed, are divine and imperishable and the same, is the case, whether He is formless, attributeless or with form and attributes etc.

In His sport of love, the Lord possesses only two-arms, but when He wants to reveal his glory, He reveals his cosmic form to a devotee, as He revealed to Arjuna, in a limb of his human body.

The Lord, possesses infinite divine virtues, such as glory, beauty, generosity and grace etc., and He reveals Himself with those virtues, to His devotees in His cosmic form. The Lord, bestows divine eyes upon His devotees, and enables them to behold different aspects, of His form, according to their tastes and eligibility. In the eleventh chapter, also the Lord revealed, first His gentle divine form (11/15—18), then, the fearful form (11/19—22) and then the most terrible form (11/23—30). When Arjuna, was terrified by having a vision of His most fearful form, the Lord, ceased revealing other aspects of His cosmic form. It means, that the Lord revealed to Arjuna, aspects of His cosmic form, according to his need and eligibility.

किरीटिनं गदिनं चक्रहस्त-
मिच्छामि त्वां द्रष्टुमहं तथैव।
तेनैव रूपेण चतुर्भुजेन
सहस्रबाहो भव विश्वमूर्ते॥ ४६॥

kirīṭinaṁ gadinaṁ cakrahasta-
micchāmi tvāṁ draṣṭumahaṁ tathaiva
tenaiva* rūpeṇa caturbhujena
sahasrabāho bhava viśvamūrte

I wish to see You as befere, crowned, holding a mace and a discus in two of Your hands, in Your former state only, having four-arms, O thousand-armed, O Universal Manifestation. 46

Comment:—

'Kirīṭinaṁ gadinaṁ cakrahastamicchāmi tvāṁ draṣṭumahaṁ tathaiva'—Arjuna, desired to see the Lord crowned, holding a mace and a discus i.e., the Lord's four-armed divine form.

By using the term 'Tathaiva', Arjuna means to say, that when he expressed his wish to see His cosmic form, He revealed that form to him (11/3). So, now he wants to see His four-armed divine form only which he saw in His cosmic form.

'Tenaiva rūpeṇa caturbhujena sahasrabāho bhava viśvamūrte'—The term 'Eva' (only), has been used, for the negation of cosmic form, mentioned in the fifteenth and the seventeenth verses, the expression 'Tena caturbhujena rūpeṇa', for the four-armed form and the term 'Bhava' for 'be' or 'appear'. In the previous verse, the term, 'Tadeva', and in this verse, the terms 'Tathaiva' and 'Tenaiva', indicate that Arjuna was very much terrified, of the cosmic form and so he uttered the term 'Eva' (only),three times to express his desire to have a vision of His four-armed form only. Arjuna, did not want to see the four-armed form, in the cosmic form.

* The terms 'Idam' denotes nearness, 'Etat' denotes much nearness, 'Adas' denotes distance and 'Tat' denotes invisibility (out of sight). For the Lord's cosmic form the term 'Idam' has been used in the eighteenth and the nineteenth verses for Bhīṣma and Droṇa etc., who were very near, the term 'Etat' has been used in the thirty-third verse for the gods etc., seen in the cosmic body at a far distance, the term 'Adas' has been used in the twenty-first, twenty-sixth and twenty-eighth verses and for the four-armed form of Lord Viṣṇu seen in the first phase of the cosmic form (being out of sight at that time) the term 'Tat' has been used.

Arjuna addresses the Lord as 'Sahasrabāho' (a thousand-armed), to pray Him to withdraw that cosmic form, and become only four-armed, while the vocative 'Viśvamūrte' (Universal Form), indicates that Arjuna wanted the Lord to withdraw His cosmic form, and become a four-armed Viṣṇu.

Appendix—Though in this verse there is mention of a mace and a discus which the Lord holds but because here it has been mentioned that He is four-armed, so in the other two arms, he is holding a conch and a lotus—it should be understood.

Link:— In the thrity-first verse, Arjuna asked Lord Kṛṣṇa Who He was, so fierce in form. Lord Kṛṣṇa replied that He was the mighty world-destroying Kāla, then engaged in wiping out the world. Hearing this reply and beholding the Lord's terrible cosmic form. Arjuna thought, that He was very angry. So Arjuna prayed to Him again and again, to be pleased with him.The Lord, in the next verse comments in order to remove his misconception.

श्रीभगवानुवाच

मया प्रसन्नेन तवार्जुनेदं
रूपं परं दर्शितमात्मयोगात्।
तेजोमयं विश्वमनन्तमाद्यं
यन्मे त्वदन्येन न दृष्टपूर्वम्॥ ४७॥

śrībhagavānuvāca

mayā prasannena tavārjunedaṁ
rūpaṁ paraṁ darśitamātmayogāt
tejomayaṁ viśvamanantamādyaṁ
yanme tvadanyena na dṛṣṭapūrvam

The Blessed Lord said:

Arjuna, being pleased with you, I have shown you through My

power of Yoga, this supreme, shining primal and infinite Universal Form, which none but you, has ever seen. 47

Comment:—

'Mayā prasannena tavārjunedaṁ rūpaṁ darśitam'— O Arjuna! You are time and again, saying "Be kind to me" (11/25, 31, 45). But I have neither revealed to you this terrible cosmic form out of anger, to frighten you nor because of your qualifications, deserving nature, or devotion. It was because of your desire to behold My universal form, that I by My grace bestowed upon you divine eyes to have a vision of this form. It means, that it was only out of compassion, that being pleased with you, I enabled you to behold My cosmic form. Your desire was merely an instrument.

At the end of the tenth chapter in the forty-first verse, I told you wherever any excellence is seen, that is My glory. Thus, I completed My reply to your question. In the last verse of the tenth chapter, of my own initiative I told you, "You need not know much, whatever is seen or heard or grasped in the world, that comes from within a fragment of My body." Further, I told you, "You need not know My glories and divine power, when the base of all glories and divine power, I Myself am standing before you." I told you all these things, out of My special divine grace. Then you expressed your desire, to behold the cosmic form and I revealed it to you, by blessing you with divine eyes. This is out of My pleasure and grace only. Therefore you need not fear at all.

'Ātmayogāt'—I have revealed to you this universal form, through My own power of Yoga.

'Param'—This cosmic form is supreme.

'Tejomayam'—This form is glittering and effulgent. So, you said that it was hard to look at, even with divine eyes (11/17).

'Viśvam'—This universal form of Mine is all-pervading and you yourself have addressed Me as 'Viśvarūpa' and 'Viśvamūrte' (Universal Form).

'Anantamādyam'—This universal form of Mine, is without beginning and an end, because it is primal and without cause.

'Yanme tvadanyena na dṛṣṭapūrvam'—None, besides you has ever seen this universal form. Now a question arises why, the Lord has made this remark, when this form was revealed to Rāma's mother, Kausalyā, Kṛṣṇa's mother Yaśodā and also Bhīṣma, Droṇa, Sañjaya, Vidura etc., in the court of the Kauravas, by Him. The answer is, that the cosmic form revealed to Arjuna was very frightening and many valiant warriors and commanders etc., were entering the Lord's blazing mouths headlong and therefore it was quite different from, what the Lord had revealed to Kausalyā, Yaśodā and also, in the court of the Kauravas.

Secondly, on the battlefield it was inevitable to reveal such a fearful cosmic form, to the warrior, Arjuna, while there was no need to reveal such a form to Yaśodā and Kauśalyā etc., nor were they capable, of beholding that form.

The Lord declared, that none, besides him had ever seen His universal form, but He did not say that none besides Arjuna, was beholding that form at that time, because Sañjaya was also beholding that form. Therefore he declares, "Recalling that wondrous cosmic form of Lord Kṛṣṇa, great is my wonder and I rejoice again and again" (18/77).

An Important Fact

Lord Kṛṣṇa declared, "O Arjuna, being pleased with you, I have shown you this universal form." It shows that the Lord is much more gracious, than a striver regards Him to be. His grace is infinite, while a man's power to admit His grace is limited.

Generally a striver, in favourable circumstances thinks that the Lord is gracious to him, and he becomes pleased. But the fact is, that the Lord showers His grace equally on a striver, in favourable, as well as unfavourable circumstances. So, one should perceive His grace, in all the circumstances and should, neither limit it to favourable circumstances, nor enjoy it.

Attachment to happiness, also binds a striver (Gītā 14/6), because it is an obstacle to attainment of the state, which transcends the three Guṇas (modes of nature). So a striver, should not enjoy happiness, which is derived out of spiritual discipline. He should rather remain engaged, in the discipline scrupulously. By doing so, in the course of time, he will have disinclination for that happiness. But, if a striver cautiously remains detached from that happiness, he can attain the Supreme Bliss instantly.

Link:— In the next verse, the Lord explains, that besides His grace, there is no other means, to have a vision of His cosmic form.

न वेदयज्ञाध्ययनैर्न दानै-
र्न च क्रियाभिर्न तपोभिरुग्रैः।
एवंरूपः शक्य अहं नृलोके
द्रष्टुं त्वदन्येन कुरुप्रवीर॥ ४८॥

na vedayajñādhyayanairna dānai-
rna ca kriyābhirna tapobhirugraiḥ
evaṁrūpaḥ śakya ahaṁ nṛloke
draṣṭuṁ tvadanyena kurupravīra

Arjuna, in this mortal world, I could not be seen in this form, by anyone, other than you, either through the study of the Vedas, or of rituals, or by gifts, sacrifices or austere penances. 48

Comment:—

'Kurupravīra'—The Lord, addresses Arjuna as 'Kurupravīra' (great hero of the Kurus), because among all the Kurus, he was the noblest, as it was only he, who was curious to listen to the gospel of the Gītā, to have a vision of His cosmic form and to know Him, in reality. One who wants to see Him, and to know Him is noble.

'Na vedayajñādhyayanairna dānairna ca kriyābhirna tapobhirugraiḥ'—The study of the Vedas, the performance of sacrifice with due ceremony, enjoined by the scriptures, offering charity, observing fasts, undergoing severe bodily and mental suffering as austere penances, etc., cannot enable a man, to behold the Lord's cosmic form, because all of these have a beginning and an end. Thus, their fruit is also perishable. How then, can they enable a man, to behold the Lord's cosmic form, which is infinite, imperishable, eternal and divine? The eternal form can be beheld, only by His grace, because His grace is also eternal.

In the Gītā there is a general description of sacrifice, charity and penance. In the twenty-eighth verse of the eighth chapter and in the fifty-third verse of this chapter, there is description of the study of the Vedas, performance of sacrifice, offering charities and undergoing penance. In addition, to these four, in this verse, there is description of actions also. In the twenty-eighth verse of the eighth chapter, there is the use of seventh inflexion and plural number, in other cases, generally there is the use of first inflexion and plural number, while in this verse, there is use of third inflexion and plural number, which means, that the practice of each of the above-mentioned methods or even all the means together made time and again cannot be conducive, to the vision of the Lord's cosmic form. The reason is, that the vision of His cosmic form, is not the fruit of any action.

As by these meritorious deeds, a man cannot be qualified to have a vision of the Lord's cosmic form, similarly His four-armed form, cannot seen by these means, (11/53), it can be seen only by exclusive devotion (11/54). Even the gods, are always eager to behold it. But there is a difference between the two forms. By having a vision of the four-armed form, a devotee can develop love and devotion for the Lord, but by beholding the cosmic form he is scared and so he cannot develop love and devotion. Therefore, the four-armed form, can be seen by unswerving devotion, while the cosmic form can be beheld only by His grace.

'Evaṁrūpaḥ śakya ahaṁ nṛloke draṣṭuṁ tvadanyena'— It does not mean, that Arjuna could view the cosmic form of the Lord, by any means, such as study of the Vedas or by rituals or by gifts, sacrifice or austere penance. But it menas, that this form can be seen, only by His grace.

Sañjaya, had also a vision of the Lord's cosmic form, but that was possible by divine vision, offered to him by sage Vyāsa's grace. It means, that the grace of the Lord, saints and devotees, is more significant than the meritorious acts, of strivers. They shower their grace, on all of us without any motive.

Some people, have a misconception that the Lord did not reveal, His cosmic form to Arjuna, but He only told him that infinite universes, vast in a limb of His cosmic body. But actually it is not so. The Lord, Himself asked Arjuna, "Behold within this cosmic body of Mine, the entire creation" (11/7). When Arjuna in spite of his best efforts, could not behold it, Lord Kṛṣṇa said to him, "You cannot see Me, with these gross eyes of yours; therefore I vouchsafe to you divine eyes" (11/8). Then the Lord, by bestowing upon Arjuna divine eyes, revealed to him His cosmic form. Sañjaya also said, "Arjuna saw in the body of that Supreme Deity, held in one limb, the whole universe with its manifold divisions" (11/13). Arjuna also having a vision of the Lord's cosmic form, said, "I behold, in Your body all the gods and multitudes of different beings, Brahmā perched on his lotus-seat, Śiva, all the sages and celestial serpents" (11/15). Thus, we see that Lord Kṛṣṇa, by granting divine eyes, revealed to Arjuna His cosmic form. It was not by the eye of wisdom, that Arjuna perceived Him (Gītā 13/34;15/11), it was only by divine eyes, that he beheld Him. The reason is, that by an eye of wisdom, one can distinguish the real from the unreal, but it is only by the divine eye that one could behold Him.

Link :—Lord Kṛṣṇa in the next verse orders Arjuna to behold His divine gentle form in order to remove his fear.

मा ते व्यथा मा च विमूढभावो
दृष्ट्वा रूपं घोरमीदृङ्ममेदम्।
व्यपेतभीः प्रीतमनाः पुनस्त्वं
तदेव मे रूपमिदं प्रपश्य॥४९॥

mā te vyathā mā ca vimūḍhabhāvo
dṛṣṭvā rūpaṁ ghoramīdṛṅmamedam
vyapetabhīḥ prītamanāḥ punastvaṁ
tadeva me rūpamidaṁ prapaśya

On seeing such a frightening form of Mine, be neither afraid nor bewildered. With a fearless and complacent mind, behold once again the same four-armed form of Mine. 49

Comment:—

'Mā te vyathā mā ca vimūḍhabhāvo dṛṣṭvā rūpaṁ ghoramīdṛṅmamedam'— Lord Kṛṣṇa, says to Arjuna that seeing His dreadful form, with mouths terrible with teeth, in which the chief warriors are rushing headlong, and some are seen sticking in the gaps between the teeth, with their heads crushed, and He, devouring all the worlds with His flaming mouths, licking them on all sides, he should neither be afraid nor bewildered, and he should rather be pleased. It means, that it was proper on his part to feel delighted, as he had felt (11/45) by thinking of the grace, instead of being bewildered.

Arjuna had said 'I am terror-struck' (11/23) and 'I am terrified at heart' (11/24). So in response to Arjuna's feeling of terror, Lord Kṛṣṇa says, "Don't be terrified."

The Lord, revealed to him His cosmic form by being kind to him, so he should not be bewildered. Secondly, He was already pleased with him, so his request to seek His pleasure, was nothing else besides delusion; he should renounce this delusion. Thirdly, he said that his delusion had disappeared (11/1) but actually it had not disappeared. So he should renounce his delusion, and being fearless and pleased, should behold His divine form. As, there was no change* in Him, in all the circumstances, while driving his horses, or talking or revealing the cosmic form, he should also, not undergo any change, after beholding His cosmic form.

The Lord, further said to Arjuna that he was terrified and bewildered, because of his egoism, and mineness. It was sheer foolishness. So, he should be free from this foolishness. It is because of these wicked traits, a man wants to maintain perishable things and persons etc. But those having a spiritual inclination, behold the Lord pervading everywhere and so become fearless. Beholding the Nṛsiṁha (head of a lion and the body of a man) incarnation of the Lord, when even gods were terrified, Prahlāda, was not afraid because he beheld Him, pervading everywhere. So he fell at His feet and He took him to His lap, and began to lick him.

'Vyapetabhīḥ prītamanāḥ punastvaṁ tadeva me rūpamidaṁ prapaśya'—Arjuna, in the forty-fifth verse said, "My mind is confused by fear." So the Lord says to him, "Be fearless and have a complacent mind."

The Lord uses the term 'Punaḥ' (again), asking Arjuna to behold again, the same four-armed form, which he had seen in His cosmic body, and by the term 'Tadeva' and 'Idam' Lord indicates as you do not want to see this form alongwith the

* Though Arjuna finds change in him yet he thinks that the Lord is uniform and never undergoes any change. So he addresses Him as 'Acyuta' in the beginning, the middle and the end (Gītā 1/21, 11/42 and 18/73).

Brahmā, Śiva and frightful cosmic form therefore I manifest Myself in that four-armed form only and he should behold, that very form, very carefully.

How long did Sañjaya and Arjuna have that divine vision?—

Sañjaya was offered divine vision* by sage Vyāsa, when the war was going to be waged so that he could communicate the details of the war to Dhṛtarāṣṭra. But, when at the death of Duryodhana, Sañjaya was overwhelmed with grief, he lost his divine vision.†

When Arjuna requested Lord Kṛṣṇa, to reveal to him, His cosmic form, He bestowed upon him divine eyes (11/8) and Arjuna had a vision of His divine form and fearful form in His cosmic body. But beholding His malevolent form, Arjuna was terrified and offering his praises to Him, he said that he was affected by fear and so prayed to Him, to reveal to him his four-armed form. Then, He revealed to him first, His four-armed form and then the two-armed, human form. It proves, that Arjuna possessed divine vision upto the forty-ninth verse, because Arjuna in the fifty-first verse, says to Lord Kṛṣṇa, "Seeing this gentle human form of Yours, O Janārdana, I am now composed, and restored to my usual nature.

Now a doubt arises as to why Arjuna did not lose the faculty of divine vision, when he had been frightened and terrified (11/23-24). The clarification is, that by then Arjuna, was not too frightened to lose his divine vision. But, he is much frightened now and so being terrified, he bows to the Lord again and again, and prays to Him to reveal to him the divine form, with

* O king! Sañjaya will relate to you the details of the war. Everything of the battlefield will be visible to him. Sañjaya endowed with divine vision will become omniscient and will tell you the incident of the war (Mahā. Bhīṣma. 2/9-10).

† O sinless king! I am overwhelmed with grief at your son's departure to the heavenly abode and I have lost my divine vision bestowed upon me by sage Vyāsa (Mahā. Sauptika. 9/62)

four-arms (11/45). It is here, that he loses divine vision.

Secondly, Arjuna had a keen desire to see His cosmic form (11/3). So Lord Kṛṣṇa vouchsafed divine vision to Arjuna but here he had no longing to behold His cosmic form, but being terrified, he longs to see His divine form, so there is no need of the divine eye. Thus, he loses divine vision.

If Sañjaya and Arjuna, had not been overwhelmed with grief and fear, they would have continued to possess the divine vision and seen more details. But, it was because of their grief and terror, that they lost their divine vision. Similarly, when a man out of delusion is attached to the world, he loses discrimination. As a greedy man, by losing discrimination commits deadly sins, such as thefts, robberies and even murders, but if he without being deluded, attaches due importance to discrimination, he himself will attain salvation, and will lead the world to salvation.

Appendix—Arjuna being non-plussed, humbly sought the Lord's pardon for his past misbehaviour—'tatkṣāmaye tvāmahamaprameyam' (11/42), so here the Lord says, "I may appear either in My serene form or frightening form, after all I am your friend. You were terrified, it was your delusion, it was a lack in friendship. All that is seen is My pastime. What is there to be terrified? In friendship, who is the high and who is the low."

God has revealed Himself in the form of the universe, therefore this universe is said to be the first incarnation at the beginning of the creation—'ādyo'vatāraḥ puruṣaḥ paraśya' (Śrīmadbhā. 2/6/41). As God has incarnated Himself as Rāma and Kṛṣṇa, so has He incarnated Himself as the universe. It has been called incarnation because in it God is objectively seen. At the time of incarnation though He seems to be worldly, yet He remains unworldly (divine) (Gītā 4/6). But He seems to be earthly to the ignorant people because of their own attachment and aversion (Gītā 7/24-25, 9/11).

It is God's will whether He reveals Himself in serene form or terrific form. If the scene is beautiful, where flowers are blooming and the atmosphere is full of fragrance, that is also the manifestation of God; and on the other hand if there is the scene where flesh, bones and waste matter are lying and that garbage is giving out stench—that is also the manifestation of God. There is nothing else besides God. God revealed Himself as Rāma and Kṛṣṇa and He also revealed Himself as a fish, a tortoise and a wild boar. He may assume any form but He is certainly God. Whatever person or object is seen, that is the form of God and whatever action takes place, that is His pastime. If any person commits a sin or does injustice to other, it means that He is staging the human drama of Kali age. He plays according to the semblance he assumes.* If He assumes the form of an idol (arcāvatāra), He like an idol, acts by remaining immovable. It is not befitting for Him to perform an action as an idol but it is proper for Him not to perform any action, otherwise how will He remain an incarnation in the form of an idol? While assuming the form of a wild boar, He acts like a wild boar and when He incarnates as a man, He acts (behaves) like a man†. He may assume any form and may act accordingly but it does not affect devotees' hearts because they hold that there neither is, nor was, nor will be nor can be any other entity besides God.

The universe which we (the worldly people) see is not the cosmic form of God because the cosmic form is divine and imperishable while the universe which we see is material and perishable. As we see the material Vṛndāvana but within it don't see the divine Vṛndāvana, similarly we see the material (physical) universe, but within it the divine universe (cosmic form) is not seen to us. It's reason is the desire for pleasure. It is because of this desire for pleasure that inertness, materialism and impurity

* jathā aneka veṣa dhari nṛtya karai naṭa koi
soi soi bhāva dekhāvai āpuna hoi na soi (Mānasa, Uttara. 72 b)

† Vide the appendix to the fourth verse of the ninth chapter.

have prevailed in the universe. It is because of the desire for pleasure that there is attraction for the world. If this attraction is wiped out, then the whole world is divine cosmic form only.

On Self-realization the universe appears divine to a Jñānī, but it seems sweet (loving) to a devout devotee. Having seen it in the form of 'mādhurya' (sweet), as a man naturally loves his body, so does a devotee naturally loves all beings. But Arjuna saw the Lord's divine (glorious) cosmic form because he wanted to see the same form—'draṣṭumicchāmi te rūpamaiśvaraṁ puruṣottama' (11/3). In 'mādhurya' there is special lovingness and in 'aiśvarya' (glory) there is special influence. It means that the divine cosmic form in spite of being one, appears in numerous forms, according to the sentiment of a devotee and in spite of appearing in numerous forms, it remains one. Diversity is unity and unity is diversity is the Lord's singularity, unworldliness (divinity) and peculiarity.

Link:—In the next verse, Sañjaya described the Lord's four-armed divine form, which was revealed to Arjuna, as was promised to him, by the Lord, in the previous verse.

सञ्जय उवाच

इत्यर्जुनं वासुदेवस्तथोक्त्वा
स्वकं रूपं दर्शयामास भूयः।
आश्वासयामास च भीतमेनं
भूत्वा पुनः सौम्यवपुर्महात्मा॥५०॥

sañjaya uvāca

ityarjunaṁ vāsudevastathoktvā
svakaṁ rūpaṁ darśayāmāsa bhūyaḥ
āśvāsayāmāsa ca bhītamenaṁ
bhūtvā punaḥ saumyavapurmahātmā

Sañjaya said:

Having spoken thus to Arjuna, Lord Vāsudeva, showed again His usual four-armed form and assumed the two-armed gentle appearance, thus the great soul gave solace to Arjuna, who was frightened. 50

Comment:—

'Ityarjunaṁ vāsudevastathoktvā svakaṁ rūpaṁ darśayāmāsa bhūyaḥ'— The expression 'Ityarjunaṁ vāsudevastathoktvā', denotes that, when Arjuna prayed to Lord Kṛṣṇa to reveal to him, His four-armed divine form, He asked him not to be terrified of His cosmic form, and behold His divine form, with a complacent mind.

The term 'tathā' means, as the Lord only out of grace revealed to Arjuna His cosmic form, so did He reveal His four-armed divine form, to him, this vision was not due to possession of extraordinary spiritual qualifications by Arjuna but due to divine grace only.

By the term 'Bhūyaḥ' Sañjaya means to say that the Lord revealed to Arjuna the same divine form which he had beheld within the cosmic body of the Lord (11/15,17) and for which he prayed to Him (11/45-46).

'Āśvāsayāmāsa ca bhītamenaṁ bhūtvā punaḥ saumyavapurmahātmā'—Lord Kṛṣṇa revealed to Arjuna his four-armed form and then He assumed two-armed human form in order to console Arjuna who was frightened.

Now a question arises whether the Lord was four-armed or two-armed. The answer is that He remained two-armed for carrying on His human sport, but revealed His four-armed form sometimes, when He thought it proper.

In the tenth chapter, the Lord described his divine glories and in the eleventh chapter He has revealed, His cosmic form. Thus a devotee comes to know His usual power and influence. If a person, knows Him in reality, or has faith in Him, he may be freed, from the bondage of birth and death, forever.

How gracious the Lord was to Arjuna, that first He revealed His cosmic form, then divine form, and finally assumed His two-armed form! Moreover, He has also showered His grace on all of us, that we should think of the Lord, whenever and wherever, our mind is attracted towards any person, object or glory or merit etc. All of us, have got the same golden opportunity of listening to His divine glories, and thinking of and recollecting His cosmic form, which was available to a few persons, such as Arjuna and Sañjaya. So we should not miss such an opportunity.

Link:— When the Lord by assuming the human form, consoled Arjuna, the latter said.

अर्जुन उवाच

दृष्ट्वेदं मानुषं रूपं तव सौम्यं जनार्दन।
इदानीमस्मि संवृत्तः सचेताः प्रकृतिं गतः ॥ ५१ ॥

arjuna uvāca

dṛṣṭvedaṁ mānuṣaṁ rūpaṁ tava saumyaṁ janārdana
idānīmasmi saṁvṛttaḥ sacetāḥ prakṛtiṁ gataḥ

Arjuna said:

Having seen this gentle human form of Yours, I am now composed and am restored to my normal nature. 51

Comment:—

'Dṛṣṭvedaṁ mānuṣaṁ rūpaṁ tava saumyaṁ janārdana idānīmasmi saṁvṛttaḥ sacetāḥ prakṛtiṁ gataḥ'—Arjuna says to Lord Kṛṣṇa, that having seen His human form, which He assumes as a sport, even cows, beasts, birds, trees and creepers etc., are thrilled, with delight (Śrīmadbhā. 10/29/40). Having beheld that human form, he is also composed and is his normal self again.

The terror which was caused by beholding the Lord's cosmic form, has disappeared altogether. By the term 'Sacetāḥ', Arjuna means to say, that when he diverted his attention towards the Lord's grace, he realised that he was a pigmy before the wonderful cosmic form, of the Lord and it was only out of grace, that He revealed to him His cosmic form, divine form and finally assumed the human form though he did not deserve it.

Appendix—Arjuna has called the Lord's form as human because it was gentle two-armed form. Lord Kṛṣṇa was two-armed. In Brahmavaivartapurāṇa it is mentioned—

tvameva bhagavānādyo nirguṇaḥ prakṛteḥ paraḥ,
arddhāṅgo dvibhujaḥ kṛṣṇo'pyarddhāṅgena caturbhujaḥ.

(Prakṛti. 12/15)

'You, O God, are the origin of all, You are attributeless, You transcend prakṛti, You have revealed Yourself as two-armed Kṛṣṇa, with half part; and with the other half part, You have revealed Yourself as four-armed Viṣṇu.'

dvibhujo rādhikākānto lakṣmīkāntaścaturbhujaḥ,
goloke dvibhujastasthau gopairgopībhirāvṛtaḥ.
caturbhujaśca vaikuṇṭhaṁ prayayau padmayā saha,
sarvāṁśena samau tau dvau kṛṣṇanārāyaṇau parau.

(Prakṛti 35/14-15)

'Two-armed Kṛṣṇa is Rādhikā's husband and four-armed Viṣṇu is Lakṣmī's husband. Kṛṣṇa surrounded by Gopas (cowherds) and Gopikās (cowherd women) live in Goloka, and Viṣṇu with Lakṣmī (as well as His councillors) reside in Vaikuṇṭha. Both of them (Kṛṣṇa and Viṣṇu) are the same in everyway viz., both are one only.'

It means that two-armed Kṛṣṇa, four-armed Viṣṇu and the Lord with thousands of arms (cosmic form)—all the three are the manifestations of the entire-God (God in full).

Link:—Lord Kṛṣṇa, supporting Arjuna's view, expressed in the above verse, explains the rarity of the vision, of His four-armed divine form.

श्रीभगवानुवाच

सुदुर्दर्शमिदं रूपं दृष्टवानसि यन्मम।
देवा अप्यस्य रूपस्य नित्यं दर्शनकाङ्क्षिणः॥५२॥

śrībhagavānuvāca

sudurdarśamidaṁ rūpaṁ dṛṣṭavānasi yanmama
devā apyasya rūpasya nityaṁ darśanakāṅkṣiṇaḥ

The Blessed Lord said:

It is exceedingly difficult to observe this form of Mine which you have seen. Even, the gods are always, keen to behold it. 52

Comment:—

'Sudurdarśamidaṁ rūpaṁ dṛṣṭavānasi yanmama'—Here, the form of the Lord which has been delineated is the four-armed one, because even the gods cannot think of the cosmic form; and as far as the human form, is concerned, how can it be difficult for the gods to see it, when even a man can behold it? So here reference is to His four-armed divine form, which has already been mentioned as 'divine form' (11/45) and 'His own form' (11/50).

'Devā apyasya rūpasya nityaṁ darśanakāṅkṣiṇaḥ'—The Lord, has declared here, that it is exceedingly difficult to see His four-armed divine form. In the fifty-third and fifty-fourth verses, He says that neither by the study of Vedas, nor by penance, by charity, nor by ritual can, He be seen, in this form. Then, He declares that He can be seen in this form, by unswerving devotion. Now a doubt arises, why the gods cannot see Him, when they are always eager to behold Him. The answer is that their eagerness does not involve, exclusive devotion. Their aim is to enjoy heavenly pleasure which they hanker after. Their eagerness, is just like worldly human beings, who want to behold the Lord, while hankering after worldly pleasure and prosperity. If a traveller while travelling, finds a jewel, and gets lost in, it without reaching the destination, the gods attach secondary importance to salvation, and so they cannot behold the Lord, as they are too much entangled in pleasure.

The gods cannot behold the Lord, by having eagerness, because they are proud of the high status of their divine abode, bodies and pleasures etc. Therefore, Arjuna, in the fourteenth verse of the tenth chapter, said, "O Lord, neither the gods nor demons know Your manifestation." Thus Arjuna, has taken both of them as belonging to the same category. It means, that as the gods possess prosperity, the demons possess magical power. But, prosperity or power is not conducive, to the Lord's vision. He, can be seen by exclusive devotion (11/54), both by the gods and human beings.

By the expression 'Devā api, the Lord means to say, that virtuous actions can lead to higher regions, rather than to God-realization.

Appendix—Though the bodies of gods are heavenly, yet God's body is more singular (more divine) than gods' bodies. The bodies of gods are material, effulgent while God's body is divine. God's body is truth-knowledge-bliss solidified, eternal, unearthly and very divine.* Therefore even gods are always been to behold God. As common people are fond of visiting new places, so are gods fond of beholding God but they have no love (devotion) for Him. It means that as devotees want to behold God by unswerving devotion, the gods don't want to behold Him in this way. Therefore God is subservient to His

* cidānandamaya deha tumhārī, bigata bikāra jāna adhikārī.

(Mānasa, Ayodhyā. 127/3)

loving devotees, but He is not subservient to gods.

Link:—The Lord, clarifies the same point, which has already been described, in the preceding verse.

नाहं वेदैर्न तपसा न दानेन न चेज्यया।
शक्य एवंविधो द्रष्टुं दृष्टवानसि मां यथा॥५३॥

nāhaṁ vedairna tapasā na dānena na cejyayā
śakya evaṁvidho draṣṭuṁ dṛṣṭavānasi māṁ yathā

Neither by the study of Vedas, nor by penance, nor charity, or ritual could I be viewed in this form, as you have. 53

Comment:—

'Dṛṣṭavānasi māṁ yathā'—The Lord, says to Arjuna, that he has seen His four-armed divine form, only by His grace. He seeks to convey that a devotee, can have His vision, only by His grace, not by any other qualification.

'Nāhaṁ vedairna tapasā na dānena na cejyayā śakya evaṁvidho draṣṭum'—A man can buy an article for a hundred rupees, only if its cost to the shopkeeper is less than a hundred rupees. Similarly, if the Lord can be bought by means of Vedas, or penance or charity or ritual, it means that He is cheaper than these meritorious deeds. But, actually it is not so, all these meritorious acts, cannot equal the Lord, in cost. He is far superior, to all merit and deed. How can, He be bought by a human being, or an object resting in a negligible fragment of the universe, created by Him? He can be attained, only by His grace. The Lord showers His grace, on a person, when he, renouncing his pride of his possessions and resources, surrenders himself to Him. In that case, the Lord reveals Himself immediately. Till a man attaches importance to material things, ability, power and understanding etc., and relies upon these, the Lord remains, afar in spite of, being the nearest.

Here, the vision of the Lord's four-armed form, rather than the cosmic form, has been declared as rare, because the cosmic form has already been glorified in almost identical words, in the forty-eighth verse. If we take it as praise of the cosmic form, it means that we expose the Lord to a charge of repetition. Also in the next verse the Lord Himself explains, that He can be seen in this form by exclusive devotion. The cosmic form cannot be viewed by exclusive devotion, because how can a devotee have exclusive devotion, for His cosmic form, when even the valiant devotee Arjuna, was terrified of that form, while having divine vision?

Link:—When the Lord cannot be seen by any meritorious deed, how can He be seen then? Lord Kṛṣṇa, suggests the means, in the next two verses.

भक्त्या त्वनन्यया शक्य अहमेवंविधोऽर्जुन।
ज्ञातुं द्रष्टुं च तत्त्वेन प्रवेष्टुं च परन्तप॥५४॥

bhaktyā tvananyayā śakya ahamevaṁvidho'rjuna
jñātuṁ draṣṭuṁ ca tattvena praveṣṭuṁ ca parantapa

By unswerving devotion only can I be seen in this form (with four-arms) and known in its essence and even its merger, O scorcher of foes. 54.

Comment:—

'Bhaktyā tvananyayā śakya ahamevaṁvidho'rjuna'—Here, the term 'Tu' (Indeed), has been used, to emphasize the point that the four-armed form, holding a conch, a disc, a mace and a lotus each in one of the hands, cannot be seen by any meritorious deeds, but only by exclusive devotion.

Exclusive devotion means, dependence on God only, without

having the least dependence on one's own ability, power, intellect or resources etc. This exclusive devotion, is not determined either by the mind or intellect or senses etc., but by one's own self. Restlessness for a vision of the Lord, is specially contributory to the attainment of divine vision. One cannot feel at ease, without His vision, even for a moment. One should become restless, for beholding the Lord. That restlessness for the Lord, burns the sins of infinite births. For such devotees, who have an exclusive devotion, for the Lord, He declares, "He who always and constantly thinks of Me with exclusive devotion, to that Yogī always absorbed in Me, I am easily attainable" (Gītā 8/14); and "To those, who worship Me alone, thinking of none else, who are ever devout, I provide, gain and security" (Gītā 9/22).

Exclusive devotion also means, no dependence on adoration or meditation or spiritual discipline, for God-realization. Then why to worship the Lord and meditate on Him? These are the means, to do away one's pride. When pride is destroyed, the Lord's grace, manifests itself and it is by His grace, that a devotee attains Him.

'Jñātuṁ draṣṭuṁ ca tattvena praveṣṭum'—The Lord, can be known, seen and attained, by exclusive devotion.

The Lord, can also be known in reality, and attained through knowledge (wisdom) (Gītā 18/55) but He cannot be forced to reveal Himself, to such a devotee.

'Jñātum' (to be known), means, that a devotee knows the Lord in reality, that all is God (Gītā 7/19) and He is, being and non-being, both (Gītā 9/19). It does not mean, that the Lord is encompassed by the devotee's intellect, but He penetrates his intellect fully.

'Draṣṭum' means, that a devotee can behold the Lord in any form, such as Lord Viṣṇu, Lord Rāma or Lord Kṛṣṇa.

'Praveṣṭum' means, that a devotee realizes his identity,

with the Lord or he enters the sport of the Lord. To enjoy His sport the desire of the devotee, and the will of the Lord, are the chief factors.

In that case, though all his desires are destroyed, yet the Lord fulfils, not only his spiritual desire, but also mundane desire, if any. Before beholding the Lord, Dhruva and Vibhīṣaṇa, both had a desire to rule over the kingdoms. Their worldly desires, were satisfied by the Lord. It means that the Lord, first satisfies the desire of a devotee, and then by His own sweet will enables, him to attain perfection. In that case, nothing remains to be known, to be done and to be acquired by him.

An Important Fact

The keen desire of a devotee for God-realization, rouses the desire, in the Lord to meet His devotee. None can create, any hurdle in the Lord's desire, to meet His devotee. Then, He removes all obstacles of a devotee, by His grace and reveals Himself to him, without consideration of his eligibility.

Appendix—Where the Lord has mentioned the Supreme State of Knowledge (Jñāna), there by knowledge, a striver knows Him in essence (tattva) and merges unto Him—thus there are two attainments; but here by devotion a striver knows him in essence, sees Him and merges into Him—there are three attainments. By devotion God can also be seen—this is the special feature of devotion, while having attained even the Supreme State of Knowledge, God is not seen. Therefore there is special glory of devotion. By devotion God in His entire form is attained.

In the attainment of Brahma (the Absolute)—'knowing' and 'entering'—there are two attainments but in the attainment of 'Samagra' (entire God) 'knowing', 'entering' and 'seeing'—there are three attainments. The reason is that in the finite, there is finitude and in the entire there is entirety.

मत्कर्मकृन्मत्परमो मद्भक्तः सङ्गवर्जितः ।
निर्वैरः सर्वभूतेषु यः स मामेति पाण्डव ॥ ५५ ॥

matkarmakṛnmatparamo madbhaktaḥ saṅgavarjitaḥ
nirvairaḥ sarvabhūteṣu yaḥ sa māmeti pāṇḍava

O Pāṇḍava (Arjuna), he who acts for My sake, depends on Me, is devoted to Me, has no attachment and is free from malice, towards all beings, reaches Me. 55

Comment:—

[The five points mentioned in this verse, can be divided into two parts (i) Attachment to the Lord (ii) Detachment from the world. The first part includes, the first three points 'works for Me', 'depends on Me' and is 'devoted to Me', while the second part, includes the last two points—'no attachment' and 'freedom from malice'.]

'Matkarmakṛt'—It means, that all the spiritual pursuits, such as utterance of the Lord's name, loud chanting, meditation, good company and study of the sacred books, as well as, performing mundane duties, according to one's caste, creed and stage (order) of life, should be performed, for the Lord's sake.

Actually, the division of actions into spiritual ones and mundane ones, is external. All the actions, whether spiritual or mundane, should be performed for the Lord's sake, only because the body, senses, mind and intellect etc., with which one performs actions, have been given to him by God, and they are His. So he should perform actions, with the power given by Him, according to His ordinance, in order to please Him, by becoming merely an instrument in His hands.

'Matparamaḥ'— 'Matparamaḥ', is he who regarding the Lord as the Supreme, depends, only on Him.

'Madbhaktaḥ'— He is devoted to the Lord i.e., he has admitted his relationship with the Lord, that only He is his and he only is His. This relationship, develops devotion for Him.

Such a devotee, beholds the Lord pervading everywhere, all the time in all persons, things and his own self. From the angle, that God is everywhere, He is also here. Being at all times, He is now. Pervading all beings and things, He is also in him. As He belongs to all, He is also his. He, who has such a belief, is the Lord's devotee.

'Saṅgavarjitaḥ nirvairaḥ sarvabhūteṣu yaḥ'—The devotee, who works for the Lord's sake, depends on Him and is devoted to Him, he becomes free from attachment and desires.

Further, when a devotee realizes, that he is a fragment of the Lord, his devotion for Him is aroused, and then he becomes free from attachment. Having detachment and conviction, that God pervades all beings, he becomes free, from malice towards all of them, even on his receiving the worst treatment. He beholds the Lord's will and grace, in every dealing. Thus, his affinity with the world, is renounced and he attains God.

'Sa māmeti'—This expression, includes the three points—to know Him in reality, to behold Him, and to attain Him; as explained in the preceding verse. It means, that he attains the object of human life, by reaching Him.

An Important Fact

The Lord, at the end of the ninth chapter, said to Arjuna, "Fix your mind on Me, be devoted to Me, adore Me, bow down to Me, thus making yourself steadfast in Me, and entirely depending on Me, you will come to Me" (9/34).

After disclosing this secret, Lord Kṛṣṇa, wanted to reveal more secrets to his devotee Arjuna and so He revealed these, in the tenth and the eleventh chapters.

If man, depends on the perishable and kaleidoscopic, matter (prakṛti) and its evolutes, the body and the world, he has disinclination, for the imperishable and eternal Lord. The tenth and the eleventh chapters aim, at removing this disinclination and conducing one towards the Lord.

A man possesses two kinds of power—of thinking, and of beholding. Both of these are to be utilized for devotion to God. So Lord Kṛṣṇa, preached, in the tenth chapter, that whatever speciality or merit or glory a person perceives, in a thing or a being, and when a thought comes to his mind, he should think of the Lord, only.

In the eleventh chapter, He, by revealing His cosmic form to Arjuna, means to preach that a devotee should behold Him pervading everywhere, in different forms and names etc., because this entire universe is a part of His cosmic form.

Arjuna, prayed to Lord Kṛṣṇa, two times. In the seventeenth verse of the tenth chapter, he asked, "In what various aspects are you to be thought of, by me?" So, the Lord mentioned His divine glories, that he could think of Him, in those glories.

At the beginning of the eleventh chapter Arjuna, said, "I want to see Your divine form." So the Lord revealed to Arjuna, His cosmic form by offering him divine vision.

It means, that a striver should think only of the Lord, and should behold everyone and everything, as the manifestation of the Lord, only.

Appendix—The nature of the devotion, by which the four-armed God can be beheld, is that a striver having renounced attachment to the world should totally depend on God. The expression 'matkarmakṛt' means dependence on God with the gross (physical) body; 'matparamaḥ' means—dependance on God with the subtle and the causal bodies and 'madbhaktaḥ' means dependence of the self on God, because 'I am God's and God is mine'—this acceptance is through the self itself. 'Sa māmeti'—this expression means attainment of the entire form of God.

ॐ तत्सदिति श्रीमद्भगवद्गीतासूपनिषत्सु ब्रह्मविद्यायां योगशास्त्रे श्रीकृष्णार्जुनसंवादे विश्वरूपदर्शनयोगो नामैकादशोऽध्यायः ॥११॥

oṁ tatsaditi śrīmadbhagavadgītāsūpaniṣatsu brahmavidyāyāṁ yogaśāstre śrīkṛṣṇārjunasaṁvāde viśvarūpadarśanayogo nāmaikādaśo'dhyāyaḥ

Thus with the words Oṁ, Tat, Sat, the names of the Lord, in the Upaniṣad of the Bhagavadgītā, the knowledge of Brahma, the Supreme, the scripture of Yoga and the dialogue between Śrī Kṛṣṇa and Arjuna, this is the eleventh designated discourse: 'The Yoga of the vision of the Cosmic Form."

Words, letters and Uvāca (said) in the Eleventh Chapter—

(1) In this chapter in '**Athaikādaśo'dhyāyaḥ**' there are three words, in '**Arjuna Uvāca**' etc., there are twenty-two words, in verses there are eight hundred and fifty-one words, and there are thirteen, concluding words. Thus the total number of the words, is eight hundred and eighty-nine.

(2) In this chapter in '**Athaikādaśo'dhyāyaḥ**' there are seven letters, in '**Arjuna Uvāca**' etc., there are seventy letters, in verses there are two thousand, one hundred and ninety-three letters and there are fifty concluding words. Thus the total of the letters, is two thousand three hundred and twenty. In this chapter, out of fifty-five verses, in the first verse there are thirty-three letters, in each of the verses from the fifteenth to the fiftieth, there are forty-four letters and there are thirty-two letters, in each of the remaining eighteen verses.

(3) In this chapter the term '**Uvāca**' has been used eleven times— four times '**Arjuna Uvāca**', four times '**Śrībhagavānuvāca**' and three times '**Sañjaya Uvāca**'.

Metres Used in the Eleventh Chapter

Out of the fifty-five verses, in this chapter, there is **'anuṣṭup'** metre, in nineteen verses; **'upendravajrā'** metre, in three verses, and **'upajāti'** metre, in thirty-three verses.

Out of the nineteen verses, having **'anuṣṭup'** metre; in the first quarter of the first and fifty-fifth verses 'bha-gaṇa' being used there is **'bha-vipulā'** metre; in the first quarter of the eleventh and fifty-third verses 'na-gaṇa' being used there is **'na-vipulā'**, metre, and in the first quarter of the tenth verse 'na-gaṇa', and in the third quarter 'bha-gaṇa' being used there is **'saṁkīrṇa-vipulā'**, metre. The remaining fourteen verses (2/9, 12—14, 51-52, 54) possess the characteristics, of right **'pathyāvaktra'** Anuṣṭup metre.

Out of the remaining thirty-six verses, the twenty-eighth, twenty-ninth and forty-fifth verses have **'upendravajrā'** metre, while the remaining thirty-three verses (15—27, 30—44, 46—50) have the characteristics of right, **'upajāti'** metre.

॥ Shri Hari ॥

Twelfth Chapter

INTRODUCTION

Lord Kṛṣṇa, in the thirty-third and the thirty-fourth verses of the fourth chapter, explained the superiority of the path of knowledge (wisdom), and exhorted Arjuna to gain knowledge. Then He explained, the glory of knowledge. After that, He explained the importance of worship of the Supreme, Who is attributeless and formless, in the sixteenth and the seventeenth verses, and from the twenty-fourth to the twenty-sixth verses of the fifth chapter, from the twenty-fourth to the twenty-eighth verses of the sixth chapter and from the eleventh to the thirteenth verses of the eighth chapter.

In the forty-seventh verse of the sixth chapter, He explained the glory of a devotee. From the seventh chapter to the eleventh chapter, He time and again through the terms 'Aham' (I) and 'Mām' (me) specially, laid emphasis on the importance of worship of God, Who is endowed with attributes and form, and also is endowed with attributes, but is formless. At last, in the fifty-fourth and fifty-fifth verses of the eleventh chapter, He glorified exclusive devotion, and its fruit.*

---

* Before this chapter in the following verses, there is a description of the devotees who worship the Lord, with form.

6/47—He full of faith worships Me with his inner self abiding in Me.

7/1—The mind intent on Me, practising Yoga and taking refuge in Me.

7/29-30—They strive taking refuge in Me of steadfast in mind.

8/7—With mind and intellect fixed in Me.

8/14—He constantly remembers Me with single-minded devotion.

9/14— They firm in vows worship Me with steadfast devotion.

9/22— They worship Me alone thinking of no one else.

9/30—Worship Me with exclusive devotion.

Having heard the above description, Arjuna had a curiosity to know, which of the devotees—of those who worship God with attributes, or those who worship the unmanifested, attributeless Brahma, is better. So he puts the question—

अर्जुन उवाच

एवं सततयुक्ता ये भक्तास्त्वां पर्युपासते।
ये चाप्यक्षरमव्यक्तं तेषां के योगवित्तमाः ॥ १ ॥

arjuna uvāca

evaṁ satatayuktā ye bhaktāstvāṁ paryupāsate
ye cāpyakṣaramavyaktaṁ teṣāṁ ke yogavittamāḥ

Arjuna said:

Those devotees who, ever steadfast, thus worship Thee (Saguṇa) and those again, who worship only the Imperishable and the Unmanifest (Nirguṇa) which of them are better versed in Yoga? 1

Comment:—

'Evaṁ satatayuktā ye bhaktāḥ'—The expression 'Ye bhaktāḥ'

10/9—With their mind and their life wholly absorbed in Me, enlightening each other.

11/55—He performs all actions for Me, he is devoted to Me and he depends on Me.

In the following verses before this chapter there is the description of the devotees who worship formless God.

4/34—Know that (knowledge of the self) by prostration, by question, by service.

4/39—The man who is full of faith obtains that knowledge.

5/8—Sāṅkhyayogī who knows the truth (reality) thinks, " I do nothing at all."

5/13—Neither acting nor causing others to act.

5/24-26—Attains Brahma Nirvāṇa (beatitude of God).

6/25—Having established the mind in the self or in God.

8/11—The Supreme Being who is declared Imperishable by those who know to the Vedas.

8/13—Uttering the mono-syllabled Oṁ, the Brahma and remembering Me.

9/15—Others worship Me in My absolute formless aspect.

(those devotees) stands, for the same striver for whom 'Yaḥ' (who) and 'Saḥ' (he) terms, have been used by the Lord in the fifty-fifth verse of the eleventh chapter. Such strivers, worship God, Who is endowed with attributes and form.

Here the term 'Evam', directs towards the fifty-fifth verse of the eleventh chapter.

'Satatayuktā (ever steadfast), is he who believes 'I am only God's.'

The strivers (devotees), who have full faith in God, have the only aim of God-realization. Therefore while undertaking, either spiritual activities, such as adoration and meditation etc., or mundane activities, such as business or service or earning their livelihood, such devotees ever remain steadfast in Him, by thinking of Him i.e., they have their affinity only for Him.

A striver, commits an error if while performing spiritual activities, he thinks that he has affinity for God, and while performing mundane actions, he believes that he has affinity for the world. The reason is, that he has not fixed God-realization, as the only aim of his life. If he realizes that the only aim of human life is, God-realization, and sticks to it, all his activities will conduce him to God-realization.

If an aspirant thinks of the Lord, at the beginning of an activity and at its end, it means, that he has thought of the Lord, even during the performance of the activity, in the same way as a businessman while making entries in his account book, gets so much absorbed in it, that he even forgets who he is, and why he is making those entries and calculations. Though it seems forgetfulness, yet it is not forgetfulness because he has his aim in his mind. Similarly a striver, always believes that he is only God's and whatever action he performs, is only for Him. Therefore while engaged in performing duties his apparent forgetfulness of God is not in fact forgetfulness of God as he has no doubt in his conviction that he is only God's and working only for God.

'Tvāṁ paryupāsate'—Here, the term 'Tvām'—should be interpreted in a wider sense, covering all the forms with attributes assumed by Him during His various incarnations, as well as the form with which He resides in His Divine Abode, and also He, Who is called by different forms and names, according to, the beliefs of devotees.

The term 'Paryupāsate' means, 'to worship well.' As a chaste wife through her body serves her husband, thinking of him in his absence and serves his parents and performs all household duties, only to please and serve him, so does a striver, being engrossed in Him, by chanting His names, through thinking and meditation, by rendering service to beings and through the performance of mundane duties, worships Him alone, without attaching the least importance to perishable objects and actions.

'Ye cāpyakṣaramavyaktam'—The term 'Ye', stands for the strivers, who worship attributeless and formless, God.

The term 'Akṣaram', stands for the Imperishable Brahma, Who is all Truth, all Consciousness and all Bliss consolidated, (it will be explained in the third verse of this chapter).

The term 'Avyaktam', stands for the Unmanifested, Who is incomprehensible to the senses. Here, the use of two adjectives 'Akṣaram' (imperishable) and 'Avyaktam' (Unmanifest), has been made for attributeless and formless Brahma (It will also be explained in the third verse of this chapter).

It seems, that the Lord by using the term 'Api' (only), wants to compare the devotees who worship the Lord endowed with form, with those devotees who worship only the formless Absolute (Brahma), by regarding Him, superior.

'Teṣāṁ ke yogavittamāḥ'—Here the term 'Teṣām', stands for both the devotees—those who worship God with attributes, and also those, who worship attributeless God. In the fifth verse of this chapter, this term has been used for devotees who worship attributeless, God, while in the seventh verse, it has been used for devotees, who worship God with attributes. So Arjuna wants to ask, which of the two, is better.

If we give a serious thought to the answer offered by the Lord to Arjuna's question, we come to realise the importance of Arjuna's question.

From the second verse of this chapter to the twentieth verse of the fourteenth chapter, Lord Kṛṣṇa went on speaking continuously. This is the only occasion when Lord Kṛṣṇa, spoke continuously for such a long time, by uttering seventy-three verses. It shows that, Lord Kṛṣṇa wants to clarify many vital points. He wants to explain the identity of the Lord, Who is endowed with form, with Brahma, Who is formless; the means of attaining the two, and the marks of perfect devotees (Gītā 12/13—19) and the wise (Gītā 14/22—25) and how they may realize the importance of renouncement, of attachment to the world.

It means, that the supreme word, the most secret of all, for the supreme good of all beings, which the Lord wanted to announce, for the welfare of them, was disclosed in response to Arjuna's question inspired by Lord Kṛṣṇa.

Appendix—The Gītā being a 'Yogaśāstra', in it 'Yoga' is important. Therefore who is a real Yogavettā?—This is Arjuna's question. There are three categories of Yogavettās—(i) Yogavit viz., Yogī, (ii) Yogavittara viz., better of the two Yogīs, (iii) Yogavittama viz., the best of all Yogīs. Arjuna has no doubt about 'Yogavit' and 'Yogavittara' but he has doubt about 'Yogavittama'.

Link:—The Lord, answers Arjuna's question, in the next verse pertaining to the superiority of worshippers who worship God with attributes, and those who worship, attributeless God.

श्रीभगवानुवाच

मय्यावेश्य मनो ये मां नित्ययुक्ता उपासते।
श्रद्धया परयोपेतास्ते मे युक्ततमा मताः॥ २॥

śrībhagavānuvāca

mayyāveśya mano ye māṁ nityayuktā upāsate
śraddhayā parayopetāste me yuktatamā matāḥ

The Blessed Lord said:

Those who, fixing their mind on Me, worship Me ever steadfast and are endowed with supreme faith, are the most perfect Yogīs, in My opinion. 2

Comment:—

[Lord Kṛṣṇa explained this fact of his own accord without being asked in the forty-seventh verse of the sixth chapter, but Arjuna could not understand it (verdict). So he put this question, in the first verse of this chapter. Similarly, strivers on account of not having keen desire and curiosity do not understand the spiritual teaching imparted in religious discourses by the saints and the scriptures as it was told in a general way not as an answer to a specific question. Therefore they disregard them though general impression remains but if they have a keen desire to know it, they pay special attention and listen to it, with faith and also study the scriptures carefully. Therefore, strivers should listen to religious discourses and study the scriptures carefully, considering these as meant for them and translate those teachings into practice.]

'Mayyāveśya mano ye māṁ nityayuktā upāsate'—When a person's mind, is concentrated, he thinks automatically of persons or object he loves.

The expression 'Nityayuktāḥ (ever steadfast or earnest), means that the striver himself should remain absorbed in God, by thinking, "only God is mine and I am only of God." When a striver has a firm resolve (aim), to realize God, his mind and intellect automatically, get absorbed in Him. On the other hand, if his aim is not God-realization, his mind and intellect cannot be absorbed in Him, in spite of, his best efforts. Mind and intellect, are the instruments which remain under the control, of the agent. So, when a striver himself gets absorbed in Him, the mind and the intellect, automatically get absorbed in Him.

A striver, commits an error, when he instead of getting absorbed himself practises to concentrate his mind and intellect on Him. So, there is a general complaint, that strivers' mind and intellect do not get absorbed in Him. Through the concentration of mind and intellect he can attain the state of a trance, but he cannot realize God. God-realization is possible only, if he himself, gets absorbed in Him.

Real worship, consists in surrendering oneself to God and believing, "I am only God's and only God is mine." When a man surrenders himself to God, all prescribed actions, including chanting His name, thinking, meditation, service and adoration etc., are performed, only for Him.

A body, is a fragment of prakṛti (nature), while the soul (self), is a fragment of God. But the self having forgotten the real affinity for God, assumes affinity for nature and its evolute i.e., body, senses, mind and intellect etc. As soon as, he (the self), renounces this assumed affinity, his real and eternal affinity for God is manifested, and his memory is regained—"Destroyed is my delusion, as I have gained my knowledge (memory)" (Gītā 18/73).

It is because of man's (soul's), inclination to matter (nature), i.e., by deriving pleasure out of it, that he assumes his affinity for it, i.e., he assumes, "I am body." Because of this assumed affinity for the body, he holds that he belongs to a particular caste, creed, colour, profession, order of life and regards the self, rather than the body, as at a stage of boyhood, youth and old age etc., viz., he does not regard the self, as different from the body.

This assumed affinity for the alien body, and the world, becomes so firm, that he remembers it without making any effort. If he realizes his real affinity, for the sentient and eternal Lord, he can never forget Him, and while performing all actions, such as sitting, eating, drinking, sleeping and waking etc., he automatically will think of Him.

A striver, whose only aim, instead of hankering after worldly pleasures and prosperity, is God-realization, it means, that he has started realizing his real affinity, for God. When he fully realizes this real affinity, he has not the least desire, to hanker after worldly pleasure and prosperity, through his mind, intellect, senses and body etc.

The self (soul), in spite of being a fragment of God, assumes Its affinity for nature, because it wants to derive pleasure out of it. So a striver, having a disinclination for the world, should realize his real affinity for God, and should have an inclination for Him, only.

'Śraddhayā parayopetāste me yuktatamā matāḥ'—A striver, has faith in a thing or person etc., whom or what he considers as the best and then he follows the principle, decided upon by him, without deviating from it.

A person's mind, is fixed on the object or person he loves, and his intellect is fixed on the object or person in whom he has faith. If he is a lover, he seeks company of the beloved, but if he has faith, he ever remains ready to carry out, the wishes of the adored one.

He, who loves only God, ever realizes his affinity for Him, and never feels any separation from Him. Therefore, such devotees, are the most perfect in Yoga, in the Lord's opinion.

The fact, which has been pointed out here, by using a plural number in the expression 'Te me yuktatamā matāḥ (they are the best in Yoga in My opinion), has already been explained, in the singular number by the Lord in the forty-seventh verse of the sixth chapter, by the expression 'Sa me yuktatamo mataḥ' (he is considered by Me, to be the best Yogī).*

Appendix—'Sa yogī paramo mataḥ' (Gītā 6/32), 'sa me yuktatamo mataḥ' (Gītā 6/47), 'te me yuktatamā matāḥ' (Gītā 12/2)—Thus the Lord has mentioned the Supreme (the most perfect) Yogī; it means that a striver may practise anyone of the paths such as Karmayoga, Jñānayoga etc., but he is the best (Supreme) who has attained devotion. A Karmayogī and a Jñānayogī finally attain devotion but a Bhaktiyogī from the outset remains absorbed in devotion (which is the fruit of Karmayoga and Jñānayoga), therefore he is the best of all.

Knowledge and devotion—both are equal as far as the freedom from sufferings is concerned, but devotion is more glorious than knowledge, because in knowledge there is 'akhaṇḍa' (integral) relish (bliss) but in devotion there is infinite relish. Infinite relish increases every moment, in it there are waves of singular bliss which make it unique. As in the world when we come to know that 'this is a paper currency' or 'this is a watch' etc., our ignorance in regard to that is wiped out, similarly by Self-realization, ignorance of the self is removed. When ingorance is removed, a man is delivered from sufferings, fear and bondage of birth and death etc. But love (devotion) is more singular than

* In the fifty-fourth verse of the eleventh chapter the Lord has declared, "By single-minded devotion I can be known and seen in reality and also entered into." But in the fifty-fifth verse of the eighteenth chapter the Lord declares for the devotees who woship the attributeless Absolute (Brahma), "He, having known Me in truth, forthwith enters into Me." Here He does not declare that he can see Him. Thus only the devotees who worship the Lord with attributes can see Him. This is a singularity of such devotee.

The Lord in the forty-seventh verse of the sixth chapter has declared the striver full of faith in His form with attributes the best Yogī. Thus such a striver (devotee) is very loving to Him.

knowledge. Knowledge has no access to God but devotion has. Knowledge is realized by the Self but love is relished by God and He is the knower of love. God is not hungry for knowledge but He is hungry for love. Having attained salvation, a Jñānayogī is satisfied with the self and content in the self (Gītā 3/17), but having attained devotion, a devotee is not satisfied but his bliss is enhanced more and more. Therefore the last stage is love, not salvation.

As 'this is a paper currency'—it is known, then ignorance of it is removed but if there is greed to get more and more money, the money provides a special taste (relish). Similarly in devotion there is a singular relish. It means that in the world as greed for money has attraction for a man, similarly love for God has attraction for a devotee, but knowledge has no such attraction. Greed for wealth causes downfall but love elevates a devotee to a higher peak of devotion than knowledge does. There is not that relish in an object and in the knowledge of that object as is in the attraction for that object.

In the Path of Discrimination (Jñānayoga) there is assumption of both the real and the unreal together, so a trace of subtle ego persists for a long time. This subtle ego viz., the trace of ego persists even on having attained salvation. This subtle ego does not lead to the cycle of birth and death but it is a stumbling block to have 'abhinnatā' (intimate love or inseparation) with God. Therefore by following the path of discrimination, the wise men (Jñānīs) or philosophers can attain salvation; but they may become 'abhinna' with God viz., they may have true devotion (love) for God—this is not the rule. It is because of the subtle ego that there are differences of opinions among philosophers and their philosophical thoughts. But in the path of faith (Bhaktiyoga), a devotee from the outset, does not assume any other independent existence besides God. Therefore God and he become inseparable (abhinna). Both being inseparable viz., with the dawn of sincere love, the subtle ego and all philosophical differences of opinions evolving from the subtle ego are totally wiped out* viz., dvaita, advaita, dvaitādvaita, viśiṣṭādvaita etc.—all become the manifestation of God which is a reality. Therefore the devout devotee who has realized 'Vāsudevaḥ sarvam' (All is God), does not insist on a particular sect (opinion) but respects all sects equally. As he does not insist on any sect, so he never disrespects any sect. It means that unity by virtue of love is superior to the unity through knowledge. In knowledge distance and distinction are wiped out, but intimacy (Abhinnatā) is not developed. But in love distance, distinction and separation—all the three come to an end. Therefore in love (devotion) there is real non-dualism. In love there is so much power that by it a devotee becomes the favourite deity of even God. The strivers following the path of knowledge, regard salvation the Supreme, then how can they realize the glory of love or devotion (premābhakti or parābhakti). (Parābhakti is the Supreme devotion in which a devotee has a unique attraction for God which increases every moment?) In salvation there is 'akhaṇḍa ānanda' viz., constant bliss (relish) but in love there is endless bliss which increases every moment. This 'Premamukti' is far superior and is the more advanced stage to salvation, Self-realization, realization and 'Kaivalya' etc.†

Karmayoga and Jñānayoga—these two are the worldly paths (Gītā 3/3). But Bhaktiyoga is not the worldly path viz., is not the path followed by human beings. He who remains absorbed in God is 'bhagavanniṣṭha' (dependent on God and His grace) viz., his state is unearthly. His means and end—both are only God. Therefore Bhaktiyoga is the means and

---

* prema bhagati jala binu raghurāī, abhiantara mala kabahum̐ na jāī.
(Mānasa, Uttara 49/3)

† śravaṇaṁ kīrtanaṁ viṣṇoḥ smaraṇam pādasevanam
arcanaṁ vandanaṁ dāsyaṁ sakhyamātma nivedanam
(Śrīmadbhā. 7/5/23)

also the end; so it has been declared—'bhaktyā sañjātayā bhaktyā' (Śrīmadbhā. 11/3/31) viz., devotion evolves from devotion. Śravaṇa, kīrtana, smaraṇa, pādasevana, arcana, vandana, dāsya, sakhya and ātma-nivedana—this is nine types of 'Sādhanabhakti' (devotion as a means)* and then is the devotion as an end which is called 'premalakṣaṇābhakti' (Sādhyabhakti) (the Supreme devotion) which is the aim to be attained by all the disciplines such as Karmayoga and Jñānayoga (Gītā 18/54). This devotion as an end (aim), is the Supreme essence which is to be attained.

In Jñānayoga a striver, by attaching importance to the discrimination between the real and the unreal, renounces the unreal. By renouncing the unreal, the entity of the renouncer as well of the thing renounced, remains for a long time, therefore in Jñānayoga, the total renunciation of the unreal is very much delayed. In Karmayoga, a striver renders service to others with the things he has. The worthless things of inferior quality are renounced easily but it is difficult to renounce things of Superior quality. But if those things are used in rendering service to others, the unreal is easily and quickly renounced. In Bhaktiyoga a devotee regards the world as God's or as God's manifestation, and thus the world (the unreal) is extinguished and God remains. Therefore by Karmayoga the unreal (inert) is more quickly renounced than by Jñānayoga and by Bhaktiyoga it is more quickly renounced than by Karmayoga, because in devotion the unreal does not persist at all—'Sadasaccāham' (Gītā 9/19). Therefore Karmayoga is Superior to Jñānayoga—'tayostu karmasannyāsāt karmayogo viśiṣyate' (Gītā 5/2) and Bhaktiyoga is Superior to Karmayoga—

* dvaitaṁ mohāya bodhātprāgjāte manīṣyā,
bhaktyarthaṁ kalpitaṁ (svīkṛtaṁ) dvaitamadvaitādapi sundaram.

(Bodhasāra, Bhakti. 42)

Dualism before Self-realization causes delusion but after Self-realization the accepted-dualism for devotion is superior to the non-dualism of Jñānayoga.

yogināmapi sarveṣāṁ madgatenāntarātmanā
śraddhāvānbhajate yo māṁ sa me yuktatamo mataḥ

(Gītā 6/47)

Link:—In the preceding verse, the Lord declared the worshippers of God, with form and attributes, to be the best Yogīs. So a question arises, whether worshippers of attributeless Absolute (Brahma), are not the best Yogīs. The Lord, answers the question, in the next two verses:—

ये त्वक्षरमनिर्देश्यमव्यक्तं पर्युपासते।
सर्वत्रगमचिन्त्यं च कूटस्थमचलं ध्रुवम्॥ ३॥
सन्नियम्येन्द्रियग्रामं सर्वत्र समबुद्धयः।
ते प्राप्नुवन्ति मामेव सर्वभूतहिते रताः॥ ४॥

ye tvakṣaramanirdeśyamavyaktaṁ paryupāsate
sarvatragamacintyaṁ ca kūṭasthamacalaṁ dhruvam
sanniyamyendriyagrāmaṁ sarvatra samabuddhayaḥ
te prāpnuvanti māmeva sarvabhūtahite ratāḥ

But those, who worship the Imperishable (Akṣara), the Undefinable, the Unmanifest, the Omnipresent, the incomprehensible, the Unchanging and the Immobile, the constant, by restraining all the senses, being even-minded everywhere, engrossed in the welfare of all beings, also come to Me. 3-4

Comment:—

The term 'Tu' (but), shows that worshippers of the formless Brahma, are different from those, who worship the Lord with form.

'Sanniyamyendriyagrāmam'—Having given the term 'Sanniyamya', with two prefixes 'Sam' and 'Ni' the Lord, lays emphasis on full control over all senses. If they are not fully controlled, there is difficulty in the worship of attributeless Absolute. The senses of devotees who worship the Lord with attributes, are fixed on Him and so there is not much need of controlling the senses, as for devotees who worship attributeless Brahma. Such devotees, having no base for thought, without controlling the senses, can think of the objects of senses, and thus can perish (Gītā 2/62-63). Therefore, for devotees who worship the attributeless God, it is necessary to control, not only the senses fully, but also the mind, because so long as, there is attachment of the mind with the objects of senses, the Absolute (Brahma), cannot be attained (Gītā 15/11).

In the Gītā, control over senses has been considered very essential, in the Disciplines of Knowledge and Action. There is no such stress in the Discipline of Devotion.

'Acintyam'—The term stands for the Absolute, Who is beyond the reach of senses and mind, because they being evolutes of prakṛti cannot even know and think of prakṛti; then how can they know and think of God, Who transcends prakṛti (Nature)? God can be known, only by the self.

'Sarvatragam'— God is all-pervading and limitless. So, he cannot be attained, by limited mind, intellect and senses.

'Anirdeśyam'— 'Anirdeśyam', is that which cannot be defined, through language or speech. Only that, which is accompanied by caste, quality, action and is confined through space, time, thing and individual can be defined, or hinted at. How can the all-pervading and sentient God, be defined or hinted at, by insentient language?

'Kūṭastham'—This term, stands for the Absolute, Who while pervading all space, time, things and individuals, remains unvitiated and uncontaminated. He always remains uniform and unaltered, without undergoing any change, at all. On a 'Kūṭa' (anvil), different instruments and ornaments etc., are shaped, but it ever remains, the same. Similarly, in spite of birth, existence and destruction of different beings and objects, God pervading them, remains the same. He is not affected by, their birth, existence and destruction.

'Acalam'—Brahma, is totally immovable and free from change, while prakṛti (nature), is movable.

'Dhruvam'—The Absolute, Who is certain and eternal is called 'Dhruva'. Out of all the eight adjectives used for Him, this one is the most important, otherwise people may misunderstand, whether He exists or not, as all the other adjectives, are in the negative. He ever exists and never ceases to be, in the least, "The world seems to exist, because of His existence or light" (Mānasa 1/117/4).

'Akṣaram'—The Absolute, Who is Truth, Consciousness and Bliss, solidified, is never destroyed. He is imperishable. He does not suffer, any diminution.

'Avyaktam'—He is unmanifested, He is incomprehensible to the mind and senses, and He is also devoid of any form or shape.

'Paryupāsate'—The term, here stands for real worship of devotees, who worship the attributeless, Brahma. Real worship, consists in remaining established in God, by identifying the self with Him, without any desire and egoistic notion.

He, Who is denoted by these eight adjectives, is an imperfect form of Brahma, because Brahma is incomprehensible, even to the intellect. But worship, which is offered with these eight adjectives, is the worship of attributeless Brahma, and this worship results, in the attainment of attributeless Brahma. He cannot be an object of intellect. Keeping in view these eight adjectives, of the absolute, the adoration made, is called 'Paryupāsate.' This is real worship of the Absolute, and it results, in merging with the Absolute.

An Important Fact

In order to explain the existence of God, two kinds of adjectives—in the negative and in the positive, have been given. The negative adjectives, imperishable, indefinable, unmanifest, unthinkable, immovable, unlimited, show that God is different from prakṛti (nature), while the positive adjectives, such as omnipresent, uniform, eternal, and nouns—truth, consciousness and bliss, show the Lord's, independent existence.

Innate, Inactive, Absolute, beyond the states of activity and non-activity, is the illuminator, of activity and non-activity. The different adjectives, have been used, so that the intellect may have a conception about Him, and so it may reflect upon, that Absolute.

In the Gītā, the description of God and the soul (self), is almost the same. The adjectives, which have been used here, for God have been used for the soul—as in the twenty-fourth and the twenty-fifth verses of the second chapter, 'omnipresent', 'immovable', 'unmanifest' and 'unthinkable' etc., and in the sixteenth verse of the fifteenth chapter, 'unchangeable' and 'imperishable' have also been used, for the soul. Similarly, in the twenty-fifth verse of the seventh chapter, the adjective imperishable has been used for God, while in the fifth verse of the fourteenth chapter, it has been used for soul.

Both God and the soul, pervade everywhere. 'The whole world is pervaded by God (The Supreme Person)' (8/22, 18/46) and 'all this world is pervaded by Me' (9/4). Similarly, in the seventeenth verse of the second chapter, it is said about the soul also, "All this is pervaded by the soul."

As the sight of two eyes does not clash nor sounds in spite of being wide-spread do not conflict with the ears, so does (according to the dualistic principle) the all-pervasiveness of God, not strike against the all-pervasiveness of the soul, both being without form or shape.

'Sarvabhūtahite ratāḥ'—In the Discipline of Action, renouncement of attachment, a sense of mine, desire and selfishness, is very important. When a person, uses objects such as the body, riches and property, in rendering service to others, without regarding them as his and for him, his attachment, a sense of mine, desire and selfishness, are naturally renounced. When a body is used, in rendering service to others, egoism is renounced, and when objects are used for others, a sense of mine, is renounced. A striver following the Discipline of Action, considers the objects in his possession as the objects of those people, to whom he renders service. So it is indispensable for a 'Karmayogī', to remain engrossed in the welfare of all beings. But in this verse as well as in the twenty-fifth verse, of the fifth chapter, the Lord declares that the 'Jñānayogīs' (the followers of the Discipline of Knowledge) remain engrossed in the welfare of all beings. It proves that the path of action, is necessary even in the path of knowledge, in order to renounce affinity, for actions totally.

Here, a point needs attention. The service rendered with the body, objects and actions is limited, because all objects and actions, are limited. But, he who has a feeling for the welfare of all beings, renders unlimited service, because there is no limit of the feeling. Therefore, a striver, should use the objects for the welfare of all beings, by regarding these as theirs, without attachment. Because of unlimited feeling, when a striver renounces his affinity for matter totally, he realizes the unlimited Essence, i.e., God. When a person, regards objects as his own, he has an egoistic notion, as well as, unevenness of mind. But, when he uses these for others, by regarding these as theirs, his egoistic feelings and unevenness of mind, come to an end. On the other hand, a common person may use every object of his own, in rendering service to his kith and kin, but because of his attachment and a sense of mine for them (limited feeling), he cannot realize, the limitless God. So, in order to attain, the limitless God, a striver should possess limitless feelings, of the welfare of all beings.

A striver, following the Discipline of Knowledge, because

of lack of dispassion cannot renounce worldly objects, by considering these as illusory, so long as he attaches importance to perishable objects. But a striver, following the Discipline of Action, can renounce these easily, by using these in rendering service, to others. The former, can renounce objects only, if he has a keen dispassion, while the latter can renounce these with a little dispassion, because he uses them for the welfare of others. Thus affinity, for matter is renounced easily, by being engrossed, in the welfare of all beings, and the path of action, is an easier one.

Devotees, who worship an attributeless Absolute, specially hold two views, (i) Whatever appears in the form of insentient or the sentient, and moving or the unmoving, is soul or Brahma (the Absolute). (ii) Whatever appears, is perishable, transitory and unreal. Thus, realizing the seen, as unreal, and whatever remains, is soul or Brahma.

A striver, following the path of knowledge, cannot attain perfection, merely by learning 'All is Brahma', so long as he has attachment in his mind i.e., he possesses evil propensities, such as desire (lust), and anger etc. So, like a Karmayogī, it is necessary for him to remain engrossed, in the welfare of all beings, to attain perfection, by renouncing attachment.

Those strivers, who having assumed the world, as unreal, meditate on God in solitude, their physical renouncement of actions, proves useful, in their spiritual path. But, by mere renunciation, they do not attain to perfection (Gītā 3/4). For attaining perfection, dispassion for pleasure and detachment from the body, senses, mind and intellect, are very essential, and for dispassion and detachment, they should remain engrossed, in the welfare of all beings. When they lead a lonely life, away from the world, they have an egoistic notion, which can be removed by being engrossed, in the welfare of all beings.

A striver, should not only be detached from the world, but

also from the body, because the body is also a part of the world. So long as, he identifies himself with the body, and remains attached to it, even by living in loneliness, he cannot attain his aim. In order to, efface egoism and attachment, he must be engrossed, in the welfare of all beings.

Also it is not possible for a striver, ever to remain in solitude, because he has to come into contact with society, for the maintenance of his body. Moreover, if he is not completely dispassionate, because of his pride, in dealing he may be harsh, and so his egoistic notion, does not come to an end. Therefore, he cannot achieve his aim. In order to get rid of this harshness, he should remain engrossed, in the welfare of all beings. A striver, following the Discipline of Knowledge may not render service, on a large scale but the Lord declares, that he will attain Him, as he is intent on the welfare, of all beings.

It is necessary for both the strivers, whether they worship God with attributes, or God without attributes to, remain engrossed in the welfare, of all beings. When a striver thinks that his own welfare, is different from the welfare, of all beings, it means that he has egoistic feelings which is a stumbling block to God-realization. When a striver, performs all actions (eating, drinking, sleeping etc., as well as chanting His name, meditation, study of the scriptures etc.,) for the welfare of the world, his egoism, comes to an end and God's power, which is ever engaged in the welfare of all beings, supports him.

Real service, does not consist in offering objects and in bodily service, but in thinking of the welfare, of all beings without any selfish motive or reward. One should serve them, as he serves the limbs of his body, without expecting any fruit.

As a common man, without receiving any moral teaching, serves his body very scrupulously, without being proud of the act, so does a God-realized soul, remain engrossed in the welfare, of all beings, through the likeness of the self (Gītā 6/32) without having the least pride or egoism. A striver, should ever follow the foot steps of such a God-realized soul, scrupulously.

'Sarvatra samabuddhayaḥ'—Devotees, who worship attributeless and formless Brahma, have evenness of mind in all persons and objects, because they therein behold only Him who is equally pervading in all of them (Gītā 5/19).

The Lord, wants to explain, that devotees following the path of knowledge, besides thinking of God in solitariness, should also be even-minded, in practical life. Secondly, in loneliness,they cannot remain totally lonely, because, the body is also a part of the world. When a striver beholds the world, and the body as one, it means that he is even-minded. But, if he views the body and the world, as separate, it is uneven-mindedness. Real loneliness, consists in beholding only God everywhere, and in remaining established in Him, and having renounced egoism, attachment for the body, senses, mind and intellect etc., totally. Such a striver is really, even-minded.

In the Gītā, 'evenness of mind' means beholding the same Lord, pervading everywhere, rather than the same dealings with everyone. The Lord, in the eighteenth verse of the fifth chapter, mentions five beings in this regard—a learned and humble Brāhmaṇa, a cow, an elephant, a dog and a pariah. None, can have the same dealings, with all of them. The similar dealings are not possible. One should not resort to any such dealings. A striver beholds God, in all of them. As in different ornaments made of gold, there is nothing but gold, so does a striver, have equal vision as he heholds God, everywhere.

A liberated soul, has equal vision, as he beholds God, everywhere. Such liberated souls, are models for strivers. A striver has no equanimity, because he accepts the existence of worldly objects. When he ceases to accept, their existence, he attains, equanimity.

A striver tries to behold God everywhere, while for God-realized souls, there is nothing but, God. They are even-minded, because they behold only God, everywhere. This natural state, of a realized soul, is an ideal for strivers. They aim at it. In what proportion, the independent existence of non-self, the strivers accept, in that proportion they are not, even-minded. The lesser the independent existence, in their mind, the more even-minded, they become. Strivers try to see the Absolute, everywhere. But the intellect of the God-realized soul, is naturally influenced by the Absolute.

'Te prāpnuvanti māmeva'—The Lord declares, that devotees who worship the attributeless God, also attain Him. It means, that He, is in no way different, from the attributeless Brahma (Gītā 9/4; 14/27). He is both endowed with attributes and also, attributeless.

In these two verses, the Lord has mentioned four factors pertaining to the worshippers of attributeless Brahma—(1) The conception of attributeless Absolute, (2) condition of the striver, (3) the nature of worship, (4) what the striver, attains.

(1) In response to Arjuna's question, which he put in the second half of the first verse, using two adjectives, imperishable and unmanifested, pertaining to the attributeless Absolute, the Lord, in order to, give a more detailed description, uses five adjectives in the negative (imperishable, indefinable, unmanifest, unthinkable and immovable), and three in the positive (omnipresent, fixed and eternal) forms.

(2) Such strivers, behold the attributeless Absolute, everywhere, all the time, in all objects and persons etc. It is, on account of body consciousness and acceptance of the separate existence of worldly objects, there is desire to enjoy sense-objects and thus sense-objects are enjoyed. Strivers of the Absolute do not regard, any independent existence of anything, except God. So they do not attach any importance, to worldly pleasure and do not want to enjoy, these because, for them such pleasure has no separate existence. Such strivers, being even-minded, remain engrossed,

in the welfare of all creatures.

(3) His worship, is that he has a constant eye, on the attributeless Absolute.

(4) The Lord declares, that those who worship attributeless God, also attain Him. It means, that God with attributes, and God, Who is attributeless, are one and the same.

Appendix—Whatever the characteristics of Brahma (incomprehensible, changeless, immobile, imperishable, unmanifest) the Lord has mentioned here, the same characteristics have been stated of the soul as—'incomprehensible' (2/25), 'changeless' (15/16), 'immobile' (2/24), 'imperishable' (5/16,18), 'unmanifest' (2/25) etc. The purpose of stating the same characteristics is that the Soul and Brahma (the Absolute) are the same in nature. If the Soul assumes its affinity for the body, it becomes 'Jīva' (the embodied Soul), but the same Soul, having renounced its affinity for the body, is Brahma viz., the Self having identification with the body is different from Brahma otherwise it is Brahma. Therefore having attained Brahma, the worshipper merges into the Being of the worshipped—'idaṁ jñānamupāśritya mama sādharmyamāgatāḥ' (Gītā 14/2). 'Te prāpnuvanti māmeva'—God whether He is 'saguṇa' (with attributes) or 'nirguṇa' (attributeless) is the same, therefore the devotees who worship attributeless Brahma, also attain God. The Lord means to say that His attributeless and formless entity is not different from His entire form.

'Sarvabhūtahite ratāḥ'—The world, the Soul and God—from all the three points of view all of us are one. It means that all the bodies are one as they are all within 'aparā prakṛti' (lower nature) and all the Souls are one as they are within 'parā prakṛti' (higher nature). Therefore when a striver becomes evenminded in all beings—'sarvatra samabuddhayaḥ' and he looks on all as one, like his own body—'ātmaupamyena sarvatra samaṁ paśyati yo'rjuna' (6/32), then he develops the feeling of remaining engrossed in the welfare of all beings. The reason is that when he regards all the bodies as his own body, he neither thinks anyone evil nor wishes anyone evil nor does anyone evil. Thus having renounced evil, welfare of others is naturally done by him. Not only this but he even does not think of doing evil to the person who does him evil because he regards all beings as his own; in the same way as if there is a sudden cut on the tongue with one's own teeth, one, by being angry, does not break one's own teeth—'umā santa kai ihai baḍāī, manda karata jo karai bhalāī.' (Mānasa, Sundara. 41/4).

The service, which is rendered to others by renouncing evil, can't be done by offering the biggest charity and by performing the most virtuous actions. Therefore renunciation of evil is the root of good (virtue). He who has renounced evil, can be 'sarvabhūtahite ratāḥ' (engrossed in the welfare of others).

Link:—In response to Arjuna's question, the Lord in the second verse, declared devotees who worship the Lord, with attributes the most perfect in Yoga, while in the third and the fourth verses, He declared, "The devotees who worship attributeless God attain, Me." The Lord in the next three verses, describes the difficulty and ease, of the two kinds of worship.

क्लेशोऽधिकतरस्तेषामव्यक्तासक्तचेतसाम् ।
अव्यक्ता हि गतिर्दुःखं देहवद्भिरवाप्यते ॥ ५ ॥

kleśo'dhikatarasteṣāmavyaktāsaktacetasām
avyaktā hi gatirduḥkhaṁ dehavadbhiravāpyate

The difficulty in following their discipline of those whose minds are attached to the Unmanifest is greater, for the Unmanifest is hard to reach, by the body-conscious beings. 5

Comment:—

'Kleśo'dhikatarasteṣāmavyaktāsaktacetasām'—Strivers whose thoughts are set on the Unmanifest, are those who regard the worship of the attributeless Absolute as superior but whose minds have not entered the attributeless Absolute. In order to enter the Absolute, a striver should possess three qualities—interest (inclination), faith and qualification. Such strivers, having heard the glory of the Absolute, develop a bit of inclination and having faith, start the spiritual discipline; but because of identification of the self, with the body and because of lack of dispassion, their minds, do not comprehend the Absolute.

The Lord, in the twenty-seventh and the twenty-eighth verses of the sixth chapter, explains that a Yogī who has become one with God, experiences easily infinite bliss, viz., the Eternal (Brahma). But here, by the terms 'greater difficulty' He explains, that the minds of these strivers, unlike those, who have become one with God, have not got absorbed, in the Eternal. Their minds, are only attached to the Absolute. It means, that these remain attached to the bodies, but having heard the glory of worship of the Unmanifest, and regarding this worship as superior to others, they get attached to it. But attachment is always to the body not to the Unmanifest. It is atonement with the manifest or absorption in which involvements strain for such body-centred people.

In the fifth verse of the thirteenth chapter, as well as, in several other verses, the term 'Avyaktam' (unmanifest), has been used for Prakṛti (nature), while here in this verse, it stands for Brahma (the Eternal or the Absolute) Who is attributeless and formless. The reason is, that Arjuna, in the first verse of this chapter, put the question pertaining to the worship of God with attributes and form and also of Brahma the Imperishable and the Unmanifest. So here, it stands for the Eternal or the Absolute, rather than nature, because object of worship is God, not Nature.

In the fourth verse of the ninth chapter, the expression 'Avyaktamūrtinā, has been used, for the unmanifested form with attributes. So, a question may arise, that in this verse also, the expression 'Avyaktāsaktacetasām' may stand, for those whose minds are set on God, Who is unmanifest and endowed with attributes. But this interpretation is, also not proper, because in the first verse, the term 'Tvām', stands for God, Who is endowed with attributes and form while the term 'Avyaktam' and 'Akṣaram' stand, for the attributeless and formless Eternal (Absolute). What is Brahma? The Lord, has already answered the question in the third verse of the eighth chapter, by declaring that Brahma (the Absolute), is the Imperishable. There also, the term 'Imperishable' has been used for God, Who is attributeless and formless. Therefore, in response to Arjuna's question, in which he used the term 'unmanifest' and 'imperishable' the Lord answered, by using the term 'unmanifest' which stands for God, Who is attributeless and formless.

The expression 'Kleśo'dhikataraḥ', (difficulty is greater) primarily shows, that the imperishable (formless) Brahma, is very hard to reach, by those who are attached to their bodies.* Further, it shows, that all devotees, worshipping the attributeless Absolute, have to face great difficulty, than those who worship God with attributes, from the first stage, to the last one.

An Important Fact

Now, it is explained how the worship of God, Who is endowed with attributes, is easy, while the worship of attributeless God, is difficult.

Worship of God with attributes—

1. Such a striver can easily concentrate his senses and mind, on God, because He is with form and attributes. He can think of Him, listen to His life-story and pastimes and can adore Him

* Strivers are mainly of two types:—

First are those strivers who are inclined to the spiritual practice after listening to religious discourses, having good company and studying the scriptures. Such strivers face greater difficulty in spiritual practice.

easily, (Gītā 8/14). Therefore, there is less possibility of his dwelling on worldly objects.

2. It is attachment to the world, which causes difficulty in the spiritual path. Such a striver depends totally on God, as a kitten depends on its mother. For such a striver, God secures what is not already possessed, and preserves what he already possesses (Gītā 9/22). In the Mānasa also, it is mentioned that God, like a mother who looks after a child, cares for devotees, who worship Him and depending only on Him (3/43/2-3). So, they easily get rid of worldly attachment.

3. Such strivers, attain the Lord, quickly (without delay) (Gītā 12/7).

4. The Lord, Himself, destroys the darkness born of ignorance, of such strivers (Gītā 10/11).

5. The Lord, straightway delivers them from the ocean of death-bound existence (Gītā 12/7).

6. If devotees, take refuge in Him alone, the Lord by His grace, releases them from any subtle vice, if it subsists in them (Gītā 18/58, 66).

7. They have full faith in the Lord, Who pervades everywhere. It is because of their faith, that they take refuge in Him, and the Lord grants them the Yoga of Discrimination i.e., wisdom by which, they attain Him (Gītā 10/10).

8. They believe, that the Lord, is most gracious to all beings. So by His grace, they cross all obstacles and they quickly attain Him (Gītā 18/56—58).

9. No one can, ever remain even, for a moment, without doing work (Gītā 3/5). So a devotee has to offer those actions, to God. By doing so, he is easily liberated, from the bondage of actions (Gītā 18/46).

10. Such a striver, can easily renounce objects, by rendering service to others. He can renounce these more easily, if they are

offered to deserving persons, and much more easily, if they are offered to God.

11. Such a striver, needs love and faith, more than discrimination and dispassion. As Draupadī, had a feeling of enmity, towards the Kauravas, yet because of her faith in the Lord, He manifested Himself, before her, when she invoked Him.* The Lord, pays attention to the devotion and faith, of His devotees, rather than their defects. Everyone, can accept his affinity, for Him.

Worship of attributeless God—

1. For such a striver, it is extremely difficult to control a fickle and restless mind, and senses, on the attributeless and formless, Absolute. Because of the lack of any base and because of the lack of dispassion, there is greater possibility for a striver, to think of the sense-objects.

2. The difficulty is greater, for a striver who is attached to body. A striver, worshipping the attributeless Absolute, wants to get rid of this attachment, through discrimination, by depending upon his power, like a baby-monkey, which (by depending upon its strength) catches hold of its mother, in order to protect itself (Gītā 18/51—53). Therefore, in the Mānasa, the Lord compares the wise with an adult son, while a devout devotee, with a small son (3/43/4). Thus, by depending on his strength he is not free from attachment, easily.

3. In the Gītā, in the thirty-ninth verse of the fourth chapter, the term 'Acireṇa', refers to attainment of peace, after having gained Self-realization. It does not declare, that Self-realization is instantly, possible.

4. Devotees of the attributeless Absolute, attain to Him,

---

*This factor applies to those devotees who have a exclusive devotion to the Lord and depend only on Him. He manifests Himself before them as soon as they call Him. Moreover He shoulders their responsibility to remove their defects also.

with their own effort (Gītā 13/34).

5. They, themselves attain to His being (Gītā 5/24).

6. Such strivers, come to know their defects late, and they realize these with difficulty. But, having realized these properly, they can also remove them.

7. In the thirty-fourth verse of the fourth chapter and the seventh verse of the thirteenth chapter, the Lord has advised such devotees, to receive instructions, from a teacher, through devotion. In this discipline, a preceptor, is a must. Not being fully aware, of the perfection of a preceptor or the preceptor not being perfect, it becomes very difficult for strivers, to maintain their faith. Thus, it involves delay.

8. They cannot realize His grace, because they regard Him attributeless, formless and indifferent. So they don't realize His grace, and they have to overcome obstacles, by their own effort. Thus, Self-realization may be delayed.

9. A Jñānayogī, also offers his actions to Prakṛti. But, it can be done only, if his discrimination is fully aroused, otherwise he will be bound to action, by having a pride of doership.

10. It is very difficult, for such a striver to renounce objects, by regarding these as illusory, so long as, he has attraction for them, and has egoism and attachment for the so-called his body, and name.

11. Such a striver, attains the Absolute, only when he becomes qualified and deserving, by possessing discrimination and a burning dispassion, which cannot be cultivated, so long as, a devotee is attached to the world.

'Avyaktā hi gatirduḥkhaṁ dehavadbhiravāpyate'— Generally, the terms 'Dehī' and 'Dehabhṛt', stand for the embodied beings. They also stand, for the soul or self. Here, the term 'Dehavadbhiḥ*,

* Here according to the Pāṇini formula 'Matupa' is the prefix is Tadasāsyas minniti matup' (5/2/94). The term 'Dehavadbhiḥ' stands for those who have identified themselves with their bodies.

stands for those who identify themselves with their bodies, because in the first half of this verse the expression 'Avyaktāsaktacetasām' (whose minds are set on the unmanifested), has been used for strivers who worship the attributeless Brahma (the Absolute). It shows, that they regard worship of the attributeless Absolute, as superior to other worships, but their minds have not entered the Absolute, because of their identification with the bodies. It is because of their identification with their bodies, that they have to face greater difficulty.

In the worship of the attributeless Absolute, the main obstacle, is that a devotee identifies himself, with the body. So the term 'Dehavadbhiḥ' has been used. In order to, remove this identification, the Lord has given his guidance in the thirteenth and the fourteenth chapters, though Arjuna did not put the question. The Lord, clearly explains, that a body (field), is different, from the soul (knower of the field) in the first verse of the thirteenth chapter, in order to remove the identification with body.

Here, the expression 'Avyaktā gatiḥ, has been used, to attain the goal, the attributeless and unmanifested Brahma. Common people, identify themselves, with bodies. So they face greater difficulty, in reaching the Unmanifested. If they cease to identify themselves with bodies, they can attain the goal of the Unmanifested, very easily and quickly.

Appendix—In the worship of the attributeless Brahma, the worshipper who identifies himself with the body is Jīva (the embodied Soul), and if he renounces this identification, he is the worshipped one (Brahma). The assumed affinity with the body is the main obstacle in the identification of the Self with Brahma. Therefore for the body-conscious beings, the allurement with the attributeless Absolute is difficult and is delayed. But in the worship of God endowed with attributes, disinclination for God, rather than identification with the body, is the obstacle. Therefore the striver, who worships God endowed with attributes, having a disinclination for the world, inclines to God and instead of depending on the spiritual practice, depends on God. Therefore God delivers him quickly from the ocean of birth and death (Gītā 12/7, 8/14). This is the singularity of the worship to God endowed with attributes.

In this worship to God endowed with attributes, a devotee does not attach importance to the renunciation of the world, by regarding it as unreal, because he holds the insentient and the sentient, the real and the unreal—All is God only—'sadasaccāhamarjuna' (Gītā 9/19). Therefore worship of God endowed with attributes is the worship of entire God. In the Gītā, God endowed with attributes, has been regarded as 'samagra' (entire) and Brahma, Jīva, Karma, Adhibhūta, Adhidaiva and Adhiyajña—they are all within the entire God (Gītā 7/29-30). Therefore by reflecting upon the Gītā, it seems that worship of the attributeless Absolute (Brahma) is the worship of a fragment of entire God, and worship of God endowed with attributes (saguṇa) is the worship of entire God—'tvāṁ paryupāsate' (Gītā 12/1), 'māṁ dhyāyanta upāsate' (12/6).

He, who worships a fragment of the entire (God), also finally attains the entire—'te prāpnuvanti māmeva' (Gītā 12/4), 'tato māṁ tattvato jñātvā viśate tadanantaram' (18/55). Therefore those who want to worship the attributeless (Absolute), may worship Brahma, but they should not slight God endowed with attributes. It is very dangerous (harmful) for the worshipper of attributeless God to slight, to blame and to refute saguṇa (attributes) viz., it is an obstacle for attaining perfection. The reason is that 'aparā prakṛti' belongs to God, therefore to blame it, means to blame God. By refuting the attributes, he accepts the existence of attributes, which is an obstacle, because without accepting their existence, what will be refuted? Therefore if a striver, without blaming and slighting the other strivers, practise spiritual discipline promptly, at last (finally) all strivers, become one because the Divinity is one.* If a striver remains indifferent to 'saguṇa', he can attain salvation, but the differences in opinions cannot be wiped out. But if he pays heed to 'saguṇa', all differences come to an end and a striver attains the entire form of God.

ये तु सर्वाणि कर्माणि मयि सन्न्यस्य मत्पराः ।
अनन्येनैव योगेन मां ध्यायन्त उपासते ॥ ६ ॥

ye tu sarvāṇi karmāṇi mayi sannyasya matparāḥ
ananyenaiva yogena māṁ dhyāyanta upāsate

But those, who worship Me, surrendering all action to Me, regarding Me as the supreme goal, meditating on Me, with single-minded devotion. 6

Comment:—

[In the fifty-fifth verse of the eleventh chapter, out of the five marks of a devotee, having single-minded devotion, there are three expressions (Matkarmakṛt, Matparamaḥ and Madbhaktaḥ), in the positive and two (Saṅgavarjitaḥ and Nirvairaḥ) in the negative aspect. Here also, the same expressions have been used, in a different manner, in this verse—

(1) The expression 'Sarvāṇi karmāṇi mayi sannyasya,' stands for 'Matkarmakṛt'.

(2) The term 'Matparāḥ', stands for the term 'Matparamaḥ', (looks on Me as Supreme God).

(3) The expression 'Ananyenaiva yogena', denotes 'Madbhaktaḥ', (devoted to Me).

---

* vadanti tattattvavidastattvaṁ yajjñānamadvayam
brahmeti paramātmeti bhagavāniti śabdyate

(Śrīmadbhā. 1/2/11)

'The enlightened exalted souls call the Divinity, which is knowledge personified and unparalleled, by these three names—Brahma, Paramātmā and Bhagavān.'

(4) Those devotees, who remain absorbed in Him with single-minded devotion, become 'Saṅgavarjitaḥ' (free from attachment).

(5) When, they become free from attachment, they become 'Nirvairaḥ' (without enmity), and also free from other evils such as envy, jealousy etc. In order to attach importance to this feeling of 'freedom from enmity' the Lord while describing the marks of devotees who have attained perfection, in the thirteenth verse, first of all mentions 'Adveṣṭā' (freedom from ill-will or hatred). Therefore, a striver should not bear the least ill-will to anyone].

'Ye tu sarvāṇi karmāṇi mayi sannyasya'—The term 'Tu' (but), has been used, in order to emphasize the fact that worship of the Lord with attribute, is easier than that of the attributeless Absolute.

Though the term 'Karmāṇi' (actions), is in plural, and so it stands for all actions, yet the adjective 'Sarvāṇi' has been used so that all actions—mundane (for the maintenance of the body and of earning livelihood), as well as spiritual (adoration and meditation etc.,) and other prescribed actions performed through body, speech and mind may be included (Gītā 9/27).

Here, by the expression 'Mayi sannyasya', the Lord does not mean to say, that actions should be physically renounced, because none can ever remain, for even a moment without performing action (Gītā 3/5; 18/11). Also, abandonment of action, sanctioned by scriptures, or out of delusion, is declared to be 'tāmasī' (of the nature of ignorance) (Gītā 18/7), and if it is abandoned, because it is painful i.e., from fear of physical suffering, this abandonment is 'rājasika' (passionate) (Gītā 18/8). In this way, affinity for actions cannot be renounced. In order to be liberated, from the bondage of actions, it is necessary to renounce the sense of mine, attachment and the desire for their fruit, because these three bind him.

When a striver aims at God-realization, he has no desire to acquire objects; and by thinking himself of God, he instead of being attached to the body etc., is attached, only to God. When he surrenders himself to God, all his actions, are also surrendered to God.

In the Gītā, actions which are surrendered to God, have been called 'Madarpaṇakarma', 'Madarthakarma' and 'Matkarma'.

1. 'Madarpaṇakarma', are those actions, which were started with any other aim but are surrendered to God, either during their performance or after.

2. 'Madarthakarma', are actions which are performed only for God, from the very beginning. They are performed by obeying Him, in order to please and realize Him.

3. 'Matkarma' are all mundane actions (business and service etc.,) and spiritual actions (adoration and meditation etc.,) which are performed, for the sake of God by regarding them as God's.

In fact, all actions should be performed, with the only aim, of God-realization.

A devotee, who performs actions, in the above-mentioned three ways, in order to attain perfection, has not the least affinity for actions, because he has neither desire for fruit nor a sense of doership nor attachment to objects, body, senses, mind, intellect and other actions etc. Actions of a perfect soul, are naturally, surrendered, while a striver, performs actions with the aim of surrendering these to God.

As a Bhaktiyogī, is liberated from the bondage of actions, by surrendering his actions to God, so does a 'Jñānayogī, get liberated, being detached from actions by believing that they are performed by prakṛti (nature).

'Matparāḥ'—It means 'surrender to God, by regarding Him, as most adorable and supreme'. Such a devotee, who adores God with attributes, becomes merely an instrument in His hands.

Therefore, he regards virtuous actions as performed by God. Moreover, he has no desire for worldly pleasures, because it is not his aim. Thus, being free from desires, evil actions, are not performed by him.

'Ananyenaiva yogena māṁ dhyāyanta upāsate'—This expression, means that such a striver adores God, with a single-minded (exclusive) devotion and he wants to attain Him, by depending on Him only. For God-realization they give more rather all importance to Divine grace not to their efforts or discipline. It means that He is both the end and the means of the devotee. Such a devotee chants His name and glory and meditates on Him by having the only aim of God-realization.

तेषामहं समुद्धर्ता मृत्युसंसारसागरात्।
भवामि नचिरात्पार्थ मय्यावेशितचेतसाम्॥७॥

teṣāmahaṁ samuddhartā mṛtyusaṁsārasāgarāt
bhavāmi nacirātpārtha mayyāveśitacetasām

To those whose mind is fixed on Me, I straightway deliver them from the ocean of the death-bound world, O Pārtha (Arjuna). 7

Comment:—

'Teṣāmahaṁ samuddhartā mṛtyusaṁsārasāgarāt bhavāmi nacirātpārtha mayyāveśitacetasām'—'Mayyāveśitacetasām', are those strivers, whose aim is only God-realization, whose minds are exclusively set on Him, and who themselves remain absorbed in Him.

As an ocean consists of nothing but water, so there is nothing, but death in the world. Nothing in the world is immune, from the buffets of death. Everything is perishing (dying) all the time. So the world has been called an ocean of death-bound existence.

In his daily life man, is bound to face both desirable and undesirable circumstances. Feelings of agreeableness and disagreeableness towards him are inherent in a man. Through such feelings he develops for attachment and aversion, for them. Thus he gets bound (Gītā 7/27). Even strivers, become a prey to attachment and aversion, by being attached to their own sects and saints, and by having aversion to the other sects and saints and so they cannot cross the ocean of death-bound existence, quickly. Partiality to sects, is delusion, which binds a man. So the Lord, has laid special emphasis on the freedom from pairs of opposites time and again.*

A striver, whose all likes are centred in God has exclusive devotion in God; and all his dislikes are centred in the world viz., by rendering selfless service, he renounces the desire for favourable circumstances, he can be very easily liberated, from the bondage, of the world.

The Lord rewards, men in whatever way, they approach Him (Gītā 4/11). So He declares, that He is same to all beings (Gītā 9/29). But to those, who love him only, who perform all actions, only for Him and who looking upon Him, as the supreme goal, ever remain absorbed in chanting His name, thinking of Him, and meditating on Him, He straightway delivers, them from the ocean of death-bound existence.†

Appendix—In the fifth verse of the sixth chapter the Lord stated for a common striver that he should emancipate himself by his ownself—'uddharedātmanātmānaṁ' but here He declares, "I emancipate them from the ocean of death-bound

---

* Free from dualities (2/45) (5/3); freed from the delusion of dualities (7/28); liberated from dualities (15/5); neither an aversion to disagreeable action nor an attachment to an agreeable one (18/10); casting aside attraction and aversion (18/51).

† The terms 'Samuddhartā bhavāmi' also include the ideas that a devotee who worships God with attributes, crosses (overcomes) all obstacles by His grace and attains Him (Gītā 18/56—58); God takes up all the burdens and cares of His devotees (Gītā 9/22); "Out of compassion for them, I, dwelling within their Self, destroy the darkness born of ignorance" (Gītā 10/11); "I liberate them from all sins" (Gītā 18/66).

world"—'teṣāmahaṁ samuddhartā'. It means that first a striver starts his spiritual practice himself. Out of those strivers he, who depends on God, God liberates him from the bondage because he has this faith in God, that He would liberate him. He without worrying for his emancipation, remains engrossed in adoring God. His means and end—both are only God. But the striver, who follows the Discipline of Knowledge, he himself is responsible for his emancipation.

On Self-realization, devotion is attained—this is not the rule; but having attained devotion, the self is certainly realized. Therefore the Lord declares—

mama darasana phala parama anūpā
jīva pāva nija sahaja sarūpā

(Mānasa, Araṇya. 36/5)

God confers on his devotees both Karmayoga (equanimity) and Jñānayoga viz., destroys their ignorance—born of darkness (Gītā 10/10-11) because God designated as Bhagavān is entire by nature.

Because of body-consciousness the striver, who follows the path of knowledge, his mind is attached to the Unmanifest—'avyaktāsaktacetasām' (Gītā 12/5). But a devotee's mind is fixed on (Bhagavān) God—'mayyāveśitacetasām'. In the Path of Knowledge, discrimination is important while in devotion for faith (belief) is important. In the Path of Knowledge 'aparā prakṛti' is to be renounced, while in devotion it is the manifestation of God itself.

Link:— In the second verse,the Lord declared that the devotees who worship God with attributes, are the most perfect in Yoga, while in the sixth and the seventh verses He declared that, He delivers such devotees from the ocean of death-bound existence. Therefore, the Lord now commands Arjuna to become perfect in

Yoga, by fixing his mind and intellect on Him, as He describes, in the eighth verse; or through practice of concentration, or through performance of actions for His sake, or through the renouncement of fruit of actions, as He describes, in the ninth, the tenth and the eleventh verses, respectively.

मय्येव मन आधत्स्व मयि बुद्धिं निवेशय।
निवसिष्यसि मय्येव अत ऊर्ध्वं न संशयः॥८॥

mayyeva mana ādhatsva mayi buddhiṁ niveśaya
nivasiṣyasi mayyeva ata ūrdhvaṁ na saṁśayaḥ

Fix thy mind on Me alone and fix thy intellect on Me alone; there upon thou shalt live in Me entirely. There is no doubt, about it. 8

Comment:—

'Mayyeva mana ādhatsva mayi buddhiṁ niveśaya'—According to the Lord, only those persons are most perfect in Yoga, who have realized their eternal union, with God. In order to make strivers perfect in Yoga, the Lord orders them through Arjuna, to fix their minds and intellects on Him, by regarding Him, as the most loving and supreme Goal.

We have our eternal union with God, but we do not realize it, because we do not fix our mind and intellect, in Him. Therefore, the Lord directs us, to fix our mind and intellect in Him, and then we shall realize that we live in Him i.e., we are established in Him.

'Fix thy mind on Me'—it means, that the mind should be diverted from the thought of the world, to God. 'Fix thy intellect in Me'—it means, that the striver, should have a firm resolve, that he is only God's, only God is, his and He is the Supreme, to be attained. By doing so, he will cease thinking of the world and his attachment to it will come to an end, and he will have affinity, only for God.

Fixation of intellect, is more important than, fixation of mind. If one has, a firm resolve, with his intellect, his mind will also accept, that resolution. If a person's aim, is not God-realization, he may attain accomplishment (Siddhis), but he will not realize God. Therefore, a striver should have a firm resolve, that he has to realize God. Desire for pleasure and prosperity, is the greatest obstacle to this firm resolve. It is the desire, for mundane pleasures which induces him to acquire money, honour and praise etc. Thus the intellect of the irresolute, is scattered and endless (Gītā 2/41). But, if he has the resolve only to realize God, this resolve is so sacred and powerful, that the Lord becomes ready to account, even a most sinful one, righteous. It is merely through his resolve, that he soon becomes righteous and attains eternal peace (Gītā 9/30-31).

'I am only God's and only God is mine'—this resolve, to a striver seems to have appeared in the intellect. But, in fact, he is already established in God, even though he may not know this. The criterion is that this affinity for Him, is never forgotten. A striver, never forgets 'I am', in the same way, as he never forgets that he is married or he is a disciple, of a particular preceptor. This resolve, remains established in his inner self, without practice. This affinity, remains fixed in remembrance, as well as in forgetfulness, because this resolve of affinity, is in 'I'ness. When, even this assumed affinity remains fixed, both in remembrance as well as in wakefulness, how can the real and eternal affinity for God, be forgotten? Therefore, when the self gets fixed in God, the mind and the intellect, automatically get fixed in Him, and the self merges in Him.

An Important Fact

A Common man, identifies the self with the body and assumes his affinity for the body, mind and intellect etc. But, everyone can realize the fact, that he is the same, from the childhood to the present time while his body, senses, mind and intellect etc., have changed. He should firmly believe this fact, at the present moment (a common man tries to understand this fact with his intellect, while this is something which is to be known, by the self).

Everyone knows, that the self has not changed and believers assume, that God has also, not changed. It means, that God and the self, belong to one class. On the other hand, a body, senses, mind and intellect, have changed and the world is also changing. Thus this kaleidoscopic world and body, belong to another similar class. An uniform and permanent self, and God, are not seen in their manifested form, while a kaleidoscopic body and the world, are seen in their manifested form. When, the self identifies itself, with the mind, intellect, senses and body etc., it thinks, that it is undergoing change, while It being a fragment of God, never undergoes any change.

We do not know—'What is I?' But we know, 'I am', without any doubt. We also know, the world is never uniform, it constantly undergoes change. It means that 'I'(the real self), is different from the world. If one of the two is known, in its right perspective, the other will be automatically known, this is a rule. The real self which is the substratum, and the illuminator of 'I', is sentient and eternal. It has no affinity with, the transitory world. But, it has its natural affinity, for God. This is Self-realization. On such realization one's mind and intellect, are automatically fixed in Him.

'Nivasiṣyasi mayyeva ata ūrdhvaṁ na saṁśayaḥ'—The expression 'Ata ūrdhvam' means, that as soon as mind and intellect, totally get fixed in God i.e., a striver, is not at all attached to the mind and intellect, he will realize God.

The Lord declares, "Having fixed thy mind and intellect in Me alone, thou shalt live in Me, undoubtedly." It shows that Arjuna had some doubt. So, the Lord uses the expression

'Na saṁśayaḥ' (no doubt). What is doubt? Generally, people think that God can be realized only, if they perform virtuous actions, have good conduct, they meditate on God by leading a secluded life, and so on. In order to, remove this doubt, the Lord declares, that all these means joined together are not so valuable as fixation of the mind and intellect in Him, and by having God-realization as the aim; and by doing so, they will realize Him, undoubtedly (Gītā 8/7).

So long as, the intellect attaches importance to the world, and the mind thinks of the world, a man should think that (in spite of being established in God, naturally) he is established, in the world. This establishment or attachment to the world, leads him to the cycle of birth and death.

Therefore, by removing his doubt, the Lord exhorts Arjuna not to worry about his situation, after he has fixed his mind and intellect in Him. As soon as, his mind and intellect are fixed in Him alone, he will undoubtedly, reside in Him.

A striver's, only duty is to fix his mind and intellect, in God. When his mind is fixed on God, he will not think of the world, and when his intellect is fixed in God, he will not depend on the world. Thus, without thinking of the world and without depending on it, he will think of God and depend on Him and it will lead him, to God-realization.

Here Citta (the faculty of cognition), should also be included in the 'mind', and 'egoism', should be included in 'intellect', because without fixing Citta (the faculty of cognition) and egoism, it cannot be said, "Thou shalt live in Me alone."

The soul is a fragment of God, Who is the only master of the entire universe. But, It attracts, a fragment of the world, (body, senses, mind and intellect etc.,) towards It, by regarding them as Its own (Gītā 15/7) i.e., It becomes their master. It forgets, that being a fragment of God It always remains fixed in Him, but It has accepted Its separate existence, in the same way, as a foolish son in spite of being, an heir to his multi-millionaire father's entire property and riches, by being separate from him, regards a flat of a huge building, as his own. But, when the son, realizes his mistake, he comes to know the reality that he is the heir to his father's entire property. So the Lord declares, that as soon as, he surrenders the so-called mind and intellect, to Him (which are really His as He is the owner of the entire universe, including the mind and intellect), he, being free from attachment to the mind and intellect, will live in Him, undoubtedly (because in fact he being His fragment, already lives in Him).

The Lord, in the fourth verse of the seventh chapter, described the earth, water, fire, air, ether—these five subtle elements, mind, intellect and egoism, the eightfold division of His nature, which is lower nature (Aparā Prakṛti), while in the fifth verse He described His higher nature, the soul (Parā Prakṛti). Though both these natures, belong to God, yet the latter being a fragment of God, is superior to the former (Gītā 15/7). But the higher nature (soul), by an error regards the lower nature as Its own, and for Itself, and is thus bound i.e., becomes the cause of Its birth, in good and evil wombs (Gītā 13/21). Therefore, the Lord exhorts Arjuna, to offer the so-called his mind and intellect, the lower nature to God (which are really His). By doing so, his affinity for the mind and intellect, which he has assumed by an error, will be renounced, and he will realize his true affinity for God, which is eternal and axiomatic.

An Important Fact Pertaining to God-realization

God cannot be realized, by a particular method, such as meditation etc., because those who depend on such methods, depend on the body, mind, senses and intellect etc., which are insentient. God, Who is sentient cannot be bought, through objects which are insentient, because all these objects cannot be equivalent to Him.

Worldly objects, are acquired through performance of actions (efforts). So, a striver thinks, that God can also be realized through actions, such as spiritual practice etc.

His belief is confirmed, when he studies the life-stories of Manu-Śatarūpā and Pārvatī etc., who realized God, through penance. But in fact, it is not so. God is realized only, when the assumed affinity for the insentient (Matter), is totally renounced. This fact, applies in those cases also, where it seems that they have realized Him, through penance. In fact, He is ever-realized to everyone, but He is veiled when a person accepts his affinity for the insentient. As soon as, he renounces this assumed affinity, God is revealed to him. Therefore, those strivers, who hold that they can realize Him, through spiritual practice are in the wrong. Spiritual practice, is useful only in renouncing the assumed affinity for the unreal i.e., insentient (Matter). Without understanding this secret, if a striver depends on spiritual discipline, and is attached to it, his affinity with matter persists. Till the least value, is attached to matter, God-realization is difficult. As soon as, it is renounced, He is realized. So a striver, should renounce his affinity totally, for matter, through spiritual practice. This affinity, for matter is easily renounced, when spiritual discipline, is practised only with the aim of God-realization.

Appendix—Mind and intellect are God's 'aparā prakṛti' (Gītā 7/4-5). Inspite of being God's prakṛti viz., nature, the 'aparā prakṛti' possesses a different nature (inert and kaleidoscopic) from that of God. But 'parā prakṛti' is not of a different nature from that of God. Therefore 'aparā prakṛti' is not uniform and untainted like God but the self is such 'mama sādharmyamāgatāḥ' (Gītā 14/2). Mind and intellect belong to the class of 'aparā prakṛti' viz., they are fragments of Prakṛti but we (the Self) are the fragments of God. Therefore the Self belongs to a different class from mind and intellect. There is attraction and union in the entities belonging to the same class, rather than to those belonging to different classes—This is the rule. Therefore mind and intellect can't be merged in God, only the Self can be merged in God. A striver commits an error that he, by assuming the independent existence of mind and intellect, by keeping the Self aloof, tries to merge his mind and intellect in God. But the reality is that only the self is merged in God, mind and intellect are not merged. When the Self merges in God, the mind and intellect lose their existence, and only God remains. The reason is that in fact mind and intellect have no existence of their own, the self has given them existence 'yayedaṁ dhāryate jagat' (Gītā 7/5), 'manaḥṣaṣṭhānīndriyāṇi prakṛtisthāni karṣati' (Gītā 15/7). Therefore in the Gītā, where there is the description of fixing the mind on God by the expressions 'mayyāsaktamanāḥ' (7/1), 'manmanā bhava' (9/34, 18/65), 'mayyāveśya mano ye mām' (12/2), 'mayyeva mana ādhatsva mayi buddhiṁ niveśaya' (12/8), 'maccittaḥ satataṁ bhava' (18/57) and so on, that is indeed the method of fixing the Self on God. When a striver tries to fix the mind and intellect on God, they are not fixed but the Self is fixed—'nivasiṣyasi mayyeva'. The reason is that a man's (self's) nature is that he gets fixed where his mind and intellect are fixed. As in the direction in which the needle moves, so does the thread follow it, similarly where the mind and intellect are fixed, the Self is also fixed there. By assuming the existence of the world, by valuing it and by being attached to it, the mind and intellect are fixed on the world and by their fixation, the Self is also fixed on the world; therefore the Lord orders to fix the mind and intellect on Him so that the Self may have disinclination for the world. As when a goldsmith heats up gold in the fire in order to purify it, then the adulterated metal is removed and pure gold remains, similarly when mind and intellect are fixed on God, they are separated from God and the Self merges into God viz., only God remains. In the Śrīmadbhāgavata the Lord declares—

viṣayān dhyāyataścittaṁ viṣayeṣu viṣajjate
māmanusmarataścittaṁ mayyeva pravilīyate

(11/14/27)

'By thinking of the sense-objects, the mind gets entangled in sense-objects, and by thinking of Me the mind gets absorbed in Me viz., the mind ceases to exists.'

It means that when a striver tries to fix the mind and intellect on God, they instead of being fixed, are merged into Him because at the root, the Aparā Prakṛti is God's nature only. When the mind and intellect are steeped in God, they have no independent existence but only God exists—'Vāsudevaḥ sarvam'. In other words the mind and intellect are diverted from the world but they cannot grasp God, therefore they lose their independent existence and only God remains.

In the Path of Knowledge the Self is important while in devotion God is important. Therefore a Jñānī gets established in the Self—'samaduḥkhasukhaḥ svasthaḥ' (Gītā 14/24), while a devotee gets established in God—'nivasiṣyasi mayyeva'. By getting established in the Self, constant (akhaṇḍa) bliss is relished and by getting established in God infinite (endless) bliss is relished which increases every moment. By getting established in God, a devotee beholds God everywhere (Gītā 6/30) because he has already had the feeling that God is omnipresent.

In this verse the fixation of the mind, the intellect and the Self is in sequence. When the Self is fixed, ego is wiped out.

In love (devotion), the mind is fixed; in faith, the intellect is fixed. 'Fixation of the mind and intellect on God' means to love God and to have esteemed belief in God viz., having renounced lovingness and value for the world, only to love and value God.

अथ चित्तं समाधातुं न शक्नोषि मयि स्थिरम्।
अभ्यासयोगेन ततो मामिच्छाप्तुं धनञ्जय॥ ९॥

atha cittaṁ samādhātuṁ na śaknoṣi mayi sthiram
abhyāsayogena tato māmicchāptuṁ dhanañjaya

If thou art unable to fix thy mind steadily on Me, then repeatedly try to reach Me by the constant practice of (Yoga) Divine Name etc., having God as its aim O winner of wealth (Arjuna). 9

Comment:—

'Atha cittaṁ samādhātuṁ na śaknoṣi mayi sthiram abhyāsayogena tato māmicchāptuṁ dhanañjaya'—Though the term 'Mana' stands, only for the mind, yet being related to spiritual discipline mentioned in the preceding verse here, it is proper to take it both for the mind and the intellect.

The Lord, says to Arjuna, if he is unable to fix his mind on Him, he should seek to reach Him by constant practice of Yoga.

'Abhyāsayoga' is a compound word in which 'Abhyāsa', means fixation of the mind on something repeatedly, while 'Yoga' stands for equanimity. Thus, repeated (constant) practice by having equanimity is 'Abhyāsayoga'. Adoration and chanting of the Lord's name etc., performed with the aim of God-realization, is also 'Abhyāsayoga'.

Only constant practice without 'Yoga' (union with God or equanimity) will induce, a striver, to have several mundane desires about wife, sons, riches, honour, praise, health and other favourable circumstances etc., because many diverse and endless, are the thoughts of the irresolute (Gītā 2/41). Therefore, actions of such a person, will not lead to 'Yoga'. 'Yoga' is only possible, when the aim of every action, is only God.

When a striver, having the aim of God-realization, practises chanting of His name, etc., different thoughts come to his mind. Therefore, a striver, having a firm resolve that he has only to realize God, should become, indifferent to all other thoughts.

Here, by the expression 'Māmicchāptum', the Lord declares that he should seek to reach Him, by constant practice, while in the preceding verse, He exhorted Arjuna to surrender his mind and intellect to Him. So a striver, may think that mind and intellect can be surrendered to Him (fixed on Him), through practice of concentration and then God, will be realized. But the Lord does not mean it so. He means to explain, that a striver can realize God through practice, if he has a firm resolve, only to realize Him.

When a striver, practises repeatedly chanting His name, adoration and learning the scripture etc., his mind is purified, and the desire for God-realization, is aroused. When he remains equanimous, in success and failure, desire becomes keen. This keen desire, makes him restless. This restlessness for God-realization, destroys the mundane attachment, as well as, sins of infinite births. Then he develops an exclusive devotion to Him, and so separation from God becomes unbearable for him. If he cannot live, without Him, He also cannot live without him, and so he attains Him.

A striver, does not attain Him, immediately, because he bears his separation, from Him. As soon as, this separation from Him, becomes unbearable, God is attained because He pervades, everywhere. The only weakness of a striver is, that he has not a burning desire and so he cannot attain Him, immediately. It is because of his sensual desire, that he thinks that he will be able to realize Him, only in future. As soon as, there is restlessness and a burning desire for God-realization, the desire for sensual pleasures, will come to an end and God will then be realized, without any delay.

If a striver, in the beginning resolves, that he has to realize only God, whatsoever may happen in the worldly sphere, he can very quickly realize God, by anyone of the paths of action, of knowledge or of devotion.

Appendix—In the twenty-sixth verse of the sixth chapter, there was mention of 'abhyāsa' (practice), but here is mention of 'abhyāsayoga' which leads to salvation. If there is only practice, but there is no Yoga, a state will be formed which will not lead to salvation.

To control the mind or to concentrate it on God again and again is 'abhyāsa'. In 'abhyāsayoga', the mind is not controlled, but the mind is detached from the Self—'samatvaṁ yoga ucyate' (Gītā 2/48).

अभ्यासेऽप्यसमर्थोऽसि मत्कर्मपरमो भव।
मदर्थमपि कर्माणि कुर्वन्सिद्धिमवाप्स्यसि॥ १०॥

abhyāse'pyasamartho'si matkarmaparamo bhava
madarthamapi karmāṇi kurvansiddhimavāpsyasi

If you are unable to practise as above said, be thou intent on performing ordained actions for Me; and thus doing selfless actions for My sake, thou shalt achieve perfection. 10

Comment:—

'Abhyāse'pyasamartho'si matkarmaparamo bhava'—Here the term 'Abhyāse', stands for 'Abhyāsayoga', described in the preceding verse. In the Gītā, the topic of preceding verse, is described in brief, in the next verse. The topic of fixing the mind on Him, and the intellect in Him, described in the eighth verse, was mentioned in the ninth verse, by the expression 'to fix the mind', which also includes intellect. In the same way the term 'Abhyāse', (in the tenth verse), has been used for 'Abhyāsayoga' as in the ninth verse.

The Lord declares, that if he is unable to practise as described, in the preceding verse, he should work for His sake. It means, that all actions (according to one's caste, order of life, for earning livelihood and for maintenance of the body, as well as, adoration, meditation and chanting of His name, and other spiritual activities) should, instead of being performed for mundane pleasure and prosperity, be performed, only for God-realization. Actions which are performed, for God-realization according to His direction, are called 'Matkarma', and a striver who is intent on performing actions, for His sake, is 'Matkarmaparama'. Such a striver, should have his affinity, only for God, and his activities should also be performed, only for God.

When a striver, ceases to hanker after mundane pleasure and prosperity, the forbidden actions, are totally renounced by him, because it is desire which tends a man, to perform forbidden actions (Gītā 3/37). Therefore, when a striver decides on God-realization, as the aim, all his actions are in accordance with, scriptural injunctions and they are performed for the sake of God, only.

'Madarthamapi karmāṇi kurvansiddhimavāpsyasi'—Whatever has been said, in the first half of the verse by the expression 'Matkarmaparamo bhava', has been repeated in the second half. When a striver, performs actions only for His sake, he attains, perfection or God-realization.

As the Lord, in the eighth verse, explained fixation of the mind on Him, and the intellect in Him, the independent means of God-realization, and, in the ninth verse, the constant practice of divine name etc., the independent means to realize Him, so does He mention here the performance of actions for His sake, as the independent means to realize him.

As profit in business acts, as an encouragement to a businessman, and he tries to earn more and more money, and more enthusiastically, so, when all actions are performed for God's sake, a striver, develops a keener desire for, God-realization and also practises spiritual discipline, more enthusiastically. When he has such a burning desire, that he cannot bear separation, from the all-pervading God, God does not remain veiled, but by His grace He is attained, by him. If a striver's only aim is God-realization, and he performs all actions only for His sake, it means, that he has invested his intellect, ability, time and resources, in God-realization by considering them as the Lord's. What more can he do than this? The Lord, does not expect anything more, from him. So He enables him, to realize Him.

Appendix—Performance of actions for God's sake is easier than practice. The reason is that practice being new has to be done but actions are performed naturally as a man is so habituated. A man gets bound by performing actions for himself—'karmaṇā badhyate jantuḥ'. Therefore by offering actions to God, a man easily attains God (Gītā 9/27-28).

'Madarthamapi'—this expression means that actions should be done only for God's sake from the beginning.

अथैतदप्यशक्तोऽसि कर्तुं मद्योगमाश्रितः।
सर्वकर्मफलत्यागं ततः कुरु यतात्मवान्॥ ११॥

athaitadapyaśakto'si kartuṁ madyogamāśritaḥ
sarvakarmaphalatyāgaṁ tataḥ kuru yatātmavān

Resorting to Yoga if thou art unable to do even this (the discipline mentioned in the preceding verse) then subduing your mind, senses and intellect etc., (equanimity) and renounce the fruit, of all actions. 11

Comment:—

'Athaitadapyaśakto'si kartuṁ madyogamāśritaḥ'—In the preceding verse, the Lord declared, "Thou shalt attain Me by performing actions, for My sake" while, here He declares, "Thou shalt attain Me, by renouncing the fruit of all actions." The former, can be called the path of devotion, while the latter, the path of action. Both of these are independent means, of God-realization.

In this verse, it seems proper that the expression 'Madyogamāśritaḥ' (resorting to union with Me), is related with

'Athaitadapyaśakto'si' (if you are unable), because if it is taken to be related with 'Sarvakarmaphalatyāgaṁ kuru' (do renouncing the fruits of all actions), because of prominence of dependence on God, it will become, the path of devotion. Thus, it will not be different from the path of devotion described, in the tenth verse, while the Lord wants to explain the path of devotion in the tenth verse, and the path of action, in the eleventh verse.

Also in this verse, the Lord has used the expression 'Yatātmavān' (subduing mind, senses and intellect), which is more important in the path of action, because without it, renouncement, of the fruit of actions, is impossible.

If a striver, does not believe in God so much but he does social service, and he cannot surrender all actions to Him, but renounces the fruit of action, which is beyond his power (Gītā 2/47), his affinity, for the world, is renounced.

'Sarvakarmaphalatyāgaṁ tataḥ kuru yatātmavān'—For a person, who wishes to attain to Yoga, action (without attachment) is said to be the means (Gītā 6/3). It is attachment, to the fruit of action, which binds a man. So if a striver, subdues his senses, mind and intellect, he can easily renounce, the fruit of action. If a striver does not control his mind, intellect and senses etc., he will naturally think of sense-objects and then he will be attached to them, and thus he may perish (Gītā 2/62-63). If a striver's aim, is to renounce the fruit of action, he can easily control his mind and senses.

Here the expression 'Sarvakarma', stands for religious sacrifice, charity, penance, service, and means of livelihood, according to one's caste and order of life, as well as, all other prescribed actions. 'Renouncement of the fruit of actions', does not mean, physical renouncement but the renouncement of the sense of mine, attachment and desire etc., for the fruit, of actions.

A striver, following the path of action, should not remain inactive, by thinking that there is no need for the performance of action, when he does not want to reap its fruit. Therefore, the Lord warns the strivers, "Let thy attachment not be to, inaction" (Gītā 2/47).

In the ninth verse of the eighteenth chapter, also the Lord while describing the marks of the 'Sāttvika tyāga', explained renouncement of the attachment to the fruit of actions as the 'Sāttvika tyāga'.

When actions are performed, having renounced attachment, to the fruit of actions, the impetus to act, calms down and old attachment perishes. Without the desire for fruit of actions, affinity for actions, is totally renounced and new attachment does not arise. Then, nothing remains to be done for a striver, because it is attachment, desire, a sense of mine for action, and desire for fruit, which force, him to act. He may, physically restrain himself, from performing actions, for a short time. But so long as, he has attachment and aversion, his nature forces him, to act. The impetus to act, calms down only when actions are performed, without any selfish motive, having renounced attachment and aversion etc.

This means (of the renouncement of the fruit of action), is very useful for those strivers, who have no natural reverence or devotion to words of God, with attributes and form, but have a natural inclination to do good, to others.

Where the Lord, advises to renounce desire for the fruit of action, He emphasizes, that it also implies renunciation of attachment, because with total renunciation of both, desire and attachment, we are liberated from the bondage of action (Gītā 18/6).

Renouncement of fruit (desire for fruit), of actions, is an independent means of God-realization. When, desire for the fruit of actions is renounced, attachment for the sense-objects, perishes and one attains peace (happiness, of the mode of goodness). If he does not enjoy that peace, he attains perfection or God-realization i.e., he becomes one, with Him.

In the fifty-fifth verse of the eleventh chapter, the Lord mentioned, 'freedom from attachment' as one mark, out of five, of a striver-devotee. In this verse, He mentions the renouncement of the fruit of actions, which is possible only, when there is renouncement of attachment, to the world. The renunciation of fruit of action, as described in the twelfth verse of the chapter, immediately leads to the attainment of Supreme Peace or God-realization. It means that total renunciation of attachment, immediately leads to Supreme Peace.

Appendix—If a striver is unable to perform actions for God's sake, he should perform actions by renouncing the desire for fruit, because it is the desire for fruit which paves the way to bondage—'phale sakto nibadhyate' (Gītā 5/12).

Link:—The Lord, from the eighth verse to the eleventh verse, recommended four methods, one after another, in the event of Arjuna's failure to adopt anyone. So a doubt may arise, whether the fourth, means 'renunciation of the fruit of action', is an inferior means to the other three, as the Lord described it as the last one, and moreover He did not mention its fruit. In order to, remove this doubt the Lord glorifies renunciation and also mentions about its fruit.

श्रेयो हि ज्ञानमभ्यासाज्ज्ञानाद्ध्यानं विशिष्यते।
ध्यानात्कर्मफलत्यागस्त्यागाच्छान्तिरनन्तरम्॥ १२॥

śreyo hi jñānamabhyāsājjñānāddhyānaṁ viśiṣyate
dhyānātkarmaphalatyāgastyāgācchāntiranantaram

Better, indeed, is knowledge than practice, better in turn is meditation, better still is renunciation of fruit of action; Supreme Peace immediately follows such renunciation. 12

Comment:—

[The Lord, from the eighth verse to the eleventh verse, recommended four alternative means, in the event of Arjuna's failure to adopt the one—fixation of the mind and intellect in Him, practice, of divine name etc., performance, of action for His sake and renunciation, of the fruit of actions. So a person, may think that they have been mentioned, in the descending order of merit. Moreover, in the first three means, there is mention that these will attain Him, while in the last one, there is no mention of it. So they may think, that the discipline mentioned in the eleventh verse, is inferior to the other means.

In order to, remove this doubt the Lord in the twelfth verse, declares that renunciation of action is an excellent means, which provides Supreme Peace, immediately. So this method is, in no way, inferior to the other three. All the four means, are independent, to realize God. A striver can follow, anyone of these, according to his inclination, faith and qualifications etc.

The other three means, of God-realization are very well-known. But the last one, that God can be realized by renunciation of the fruit of actions, is not so common and familiar. Therefore, the Lord, in order to, declare its superiority, to the other three disciplines and to signify its reward, has added the twelfth verse. So the Lord makes the position clear, in the twelfth verse.]

'Śreyo hi jñānamabhyāsāt'—According to the great sage Patañjali 'Abhyāsa', consists in making effort, again and again, to be concentrate on something (Yogadarśana 1/13).

Here this term 'Abhyāsa', does not stand for 'Abhyāsayoga', it refers to practice only, because in this practice (breath restraint or control of the mind) there is no requirement of scriptural knowledge, meditation or renunciation of desire for the fruit of actions. There is 'Yoga' (union with God) only, when affinity for matter is renounced, while in such practice, there is dependence on matter (the body, senses, mind and intellect).

Here the term 'Jñāna', stands for the knowledge of scriptures, rather than Self-realization, because Self-realization, is the fruit of all spiritual disciplines. This knowledge, is better than practice, in which there is neither knowledge of the scriptures, nor meditation, nor renunciation of fruit of action.

Spiritual knowledge, which is gained through the study of scriptures and through the discourses of saints, but not translated into practice, is 'Jñāna', which is mentioned here. This knowledge, has been called, better than practice, because practice without knowledge of scriptures, is not so useful for God-realization, as is knowledge without practice. Because through knowledge, the desire for God-realization is aroused, and so a striver, can transcend the world, more easily than he can by above referred practice.

'Jñānāddhyānaṁ viśiṣyate'—Here the term 'Dhyāna', stands for meditation or concentration of mind, rather than 'Dhyānayoga', which involves the knowledge of scriptures and renunciation of fruit of action. Such meditation, is better than knowledge, which does not involve practice, meditation and renunciation of fruit of action. Mind is controlled by meditation, rather than by mere spiritual knowledge. Through meditation, there is accumulation of energy, which is not possible, through knowledge.

If a striver, utilizes that energy for spiritual progress, he can advance very quickly, which is not possible through knowledge. Besides, it a striver, through meditation (if he studies scriptures) can gain true knowledge, more easily, while a striver who studies scriptures, faces difficulty in meditation, because of volatility of mind. [In these days also, it can be seen that there are so many people who study scriptures, but there are only a few, who practise meditation.]

'Dhyānātkarmaphalatyāgaḥ'—Renunciation of fruit of action, without knowledge and meditation, is better than meditation without knowledge and renunciation, of fruit of action. This expression does not stand for the physical renunciation, of fruit of actions, but it relates to renunciation of a sense of mine, attachment and desire for actions and their fruits. Attachment, to all perishable objects, which are the fruits of actions, is to be renounced.

Attachment to actions and desire for fruits, lead a man to bondage, otherwise he is easily liberated, from worldly bondage.

The body, senses, mind, intellect, ability, power and other objects, which a man possesses, have been acquired from the world. So a 'Karmayogī', without regarding these as his, and for him, utilizes these in rendering service to the world, without any selfish motive. Thus their flow is towards the world and then having renounced affinity totally for the world, he realizes, his natural affinity for God, which is eternal. So a Karmayogī, need not meditate on God. Moreover, if he wants to practise meditation, he can do it very easily, as he has no mundane desires, while a striver, with desire, faces difficulty in meditation.

In the sixth chapter, (in the topic of meditation) the Lord explains, that when the mind restrained by the practice of meditation, gets established, in the Supreme Self and it becomes free from all desires. The mind being matter cannot grasp sentient, God. Therefore, on its affinity being cut asunder from the self, he (the self) gets established in God, (Gītā 6/18, 20), while a Karmayogī, having renounced all desires, immediately gets established in God (Gītā 2/55). The reason is, that in meditation, the mind is concentrated on God, therefore, due to dependence on the mind (matter) he (the self), has affinity for matter, for a long time. But in Karmayoga, desire and attachment (matter), are renounced and so attachment for the mind, is also naturally renounced, and he attains Him, very easily and quickly. Thus Karmayoga, is better than meditation.

'Nothing is mine, nothing is required for me, and nothing is to be done for me'—this is the gist of Karmayoga, and so it is superior, to other paths (Gītā 5/2).

'Tyāgācchāntiranantaram'—Here the term 'Tyāgāt', has been used, for the renunciation of fruit of action. It is very necessary to understand, the true nature of renunciation. The self cannot be renounced by us, nor can anything which is not ours, be renounced. For example the light and heat of the sun, cannot be separated from it, nor can it be said that dark and cold, are separated from the sun, because they are ever separate. Therefore, only whatever is not ours, but we have assumed it as ours, by an error, is renounced.

The soul is sentient and imperishable, while the world is insentient and perishable. But the soul (having forgotten God, Whose fragment It is) accepts the world as Its. Therefore, there is need for renouncing the assumed affinity, for the world.

Affinity with the worldly objects, is limited, because these objects, are limited. But their renunciation is limitless. Renunciation immediately leads to God-realization, because God is also limitless, as He knows no limit of clime, time, objects and individuals. The limitless Lord, is not realized because of our attachment for limited objects.

By renunciation of fruit of action, the assumed affinity for the world is renounced. Therefore, the true nature of renunciation, is the renunciation of the assumed affinity for actions, and their fruits.

Even the fruit of such spiritual activities such as adoration, meditation and trance etc., should be renounced, because so long as, these are done for one's self, the individuality subsists. Thus one suffers delay, in being free from bondage. Real renunciation, consists in renouncing affinity, even for the propensity of renunciation. Here the term 'peace', stands for Supreme Peace or God-realization.

Renunciation of fruit of action, is better than practice or knowledge, or meditation. So long as, a striver remains attached to fruit of action, he (because of the dependence on matter) cannot be liberated (Gītā 5/12).

Therefore, renunciation of fruit of action, is necessary in practice, knowledge and meditation also. It is attachment for perishable objects, which is the root of disquietude. In Karmayoga, attachment to actions and their fruits, is abandoned from the very beginning (Gītā 5/11). So Karmayogī, having no affinity for matter (insentient), attains, eternal peace (Gītā 5/12), in the form of God-realization.

An Important Fact Pertaining to the Renunciation of the Fruit of Action

'Karmaphalatyāga' (renunciation of the fruit of action), is another name for 'Karmayoga' (the discipline of action), because in the discipline of action, only renunciation of fruit of action, is important. This Yoga, was lost to the world, long before the incarnation of Lord Kṛṣṇa (Gītā 4/2). The Lord by His grace, revealed this Karmayoga again, by making Arjuna an instrument (Gītā 4/3), to human beings, in order to encourage them to attain salvation, which is generally considered impossible without leading a secluded life, or having renounced actions, objects and kith and kin etc. The Lord, means to explain, that a person can attain salvation or God-realization, in all circumstances, by performing his duties, in a detached way.

In Karmayoga, renunciation of attachment, for the fruit of action is important. Actions bear fruit, in the form of favourable and unfavourable circumstances, such as, health and sickness, riches and poverty, honour and dishonour, praise and blame, and so on. If a person has an attachment or aversion for them, he can never realize, God (Gītā 2/42—44).

Perishable things, are fruit of action, such fruit, being perishable cannot be everlasting. Action, is also not everlasting. Then how can the fruit of action, be everlasting, when its cause, i.e., the action, is perishable. So, it is an error to be attached to perishable fruit, or to desire it. Renunciation of attachment, for the fruit of action, is the seed of, Karmayoga.

It seems difficult to renounce attachment for actions, and their fruit, while performing actions, in Karmayoga. But actually, it is not so. It seems difficult, when a man regards the objects (body etc.,) required for performance of actions, as his and for him. But, when he regards these, as of the world, because they have been acquired from the world, and he performs his duty, his attachment is renounced, and he realizes God (Gītā 3/19). In fact, it is not actions which lead to bondage, but it is desire and attachment for the fruit of actions, which lead to bondage. When desire and attachment for the fruit of actions, are renounced, all actions change into inaction (Gītā 4/19—23).

The Lord, declares the unselfish performance of actions, better than their physical renunciation (Gītā 5/2). According to the Lord, a Sannyāsī is not he, who does not perform actions, but he, who performs actions (duty) without depending on their fruit (Gītā 6/1). A Karmayogī, being free from attachment and having renounced all thoughts, easily attain to Yoga (Gītā 6/4). On the other hand, those, who, having regarded actions and their fruits as theirs and for them, hanker after pleasures, verily ingest sin (Gītā 3/13). Therefore, in the world it is attachment for the fruit of action, by which a man is bound (Gītā 5/12). He, who relinquishes the fruit of action, is a man of renunciation (Gītā 18/11).

In the Gītā, there is a greater emphasis on the renunciation of the attachment to the fruit of actions, than any other means, of God-realization. Actions should be performed, renouncing attachment and desire for fruits (Gītā 18/6). A striver should be attached, neither to virtuous or extraordinary actions, nor should he have an aversion for evil or ordinary actions, because actions will be over, but attachment and aversion will continue and these will lead him to bondage. On the other hand, he, who performs actions, being free from egoism, attachment and aversion, though he slays people, he really slays not, nor is he bound (by his actions) (Gītā 18/17). Therefore, the Lord declares, that renunciation of fruit of action, is better than penance, knowledge, action, practice and meditation etc. Other means, outwardly seem excellent, but these do not prove much useful, and moreover involve labour. Renunciation of attachment to the fruit of actions, leads a striver to salvation very easily, in the same circumstances, he is placed in, and without changing his place or order of life etc.

In fact, God is not acquired, but is realized. He is realized, by renouncing the sense of 'I' and 'mine', attachment and desire, for the body, mind, senses and objects etc., rather than, by practising spiritual disciplines. As soon as, affinity for matter is renounced, through knowledge, practice, meditation, penance etc., a striver, realizes God, Who is ever-realized. This affinity for matter, is renounced, more easily by renouncing fruit of action, than by knowledge, practice, meditation and penance etc., because in all these means, a striver has affinity with matter (body, mind, intellect and senses etc.,) and as he regards the body as his and the means for him. If such a striver, has the aim of God-realization, and he wants to realize Him, by these means, he realizes Him, with delay and difficulty, at last. But in Karmayoga, he renounces his affinity, for matter from the very beginning and so he realizes God, Who is ever-realized quickly and easily. This affinity, is the main stumbling block to God-realization—this fact does not become clear to a striver, when he follows other means.

When a striver, resolves that he has not to perform forbidden actions, such as theft, falsehood, infidelity, violence, fraud, forgery and eating forbidden food etc., under any circumstances, even by thought and speech, then only prescribed actions, are automatically performed, by him.

A striver, should resolve to relinquish, forbidden actions,

rather than perform prescribed actions, otherwise he will feel proud of performing prescribed actions, and his egoism will be maintained. Because of his pride, forbidden actions will be performed by him. But if he resolves that he will not perform forbidden actions, he will not feel proud, because he is not doing anything creditable, which requires any ability or power. In this relinquishment, also he may feel proud out of folly. Then, he should think, that there is nothing to feel proud of, as he is doing nothing special, in renouncing what should be renounced. A man, has normal desire to reap the fruit of action, only when some action is performed. If no action, has been performed, only forbidden action, has been renounced,* why can he have a desire, for the fruit of action? When a person, has no sense of doership, attachment for fruit of action, is automatically, renounced. This renouncement, naturally, leads him to peace, which is axiomatic.

An Important Fact Pertaining to Spiritual Discipline

The three means (constant practice of divine name etc., performance of action for the Lord and renunciation of the fruit of actions), of God-realization, have been described in the ninth, the tenth and the eleventh verses. Out of the three (except the renunciation of the fruit of action), if a thought is given seriously, each means, includes the other two, also as (1) In the constant practice, adoration and chanting the name etc., actions are done for the Lord and there is no desire for fruit. (2) In the performance of actions, for the Lord, there is practice and there is no desire for fruit of actions.

* If a person resolves not to perform forbidden actions, he will either perform prescribed actions or will not perform actions at all. Prescribed actions purify the mind and total non-performance of actions conduces a man to God-realization. Total non-performance of actions means the state of freedom from lust rather than the state of inactivity or laziness because laziness etc., are also forbidden actions.

First of all, a striver should fix his aim of God-realization. Then he should, realize his real affinity, for God. After that anyone of the three means, will lead him to God-realization.

The ease or difficulty, of means depends, on the inclination and aim of a striver. If he has only the inclination and aim of God-realization, the means becomes easy, otherwise difficult.

As food stuff, may be different according to the taste of hungry persons, but hunger before and satisfaction after, eating the food, are the same; so do strivers have different means according to their interests, beliefs and qualifications, but pain of non-realization of God, and the desire (hunger), for God-realization, are the same for all the strivers. Every striver, belonging to any class attains the same bliss (satisfaction), in the form of God-realization.

Here, the Lord has mentioned four means of God-realization by making Arjuna, a questioner:—

(1) Path of Surrender (2) Path of Practice (3) Performance of Actions, for God (4) Renunciation of fruit of Actions.

All the four paths, are equally independent and noble, and all of these, lead to God-realization. A striver, can adopt anyone of them, according to his inclination, faith and qualification, by regarding it, as the best.

He should never, consider the means (spiritual discipline), followed by him to be inferior to other paths and should never lose heart, so far as God-realization is concerned. If the only aim of a striver is God-realization, the means (spiritual discipline), followed is according to his inclination, faith and qualification, and it is practised to the best of his capacity and with promptness having a burning desire for God-realization, his path will lead him to that goal, without any doubt. The reason is, that God is omniscient; He having known the striver's intention and efforts etc., by His grace influences him towards God-realization.

Every human being has God-realization as its birth right

because the Lord by His grace, has bestowed upon man this human body, so that he may realize Him. No two persons, can possess the worldly materials equally, because they acquire these according to their fate. But everyone, can realize God equally, because He is not realized only through actions.

Dispassion for the world, and a keen desire for God-realization, are two important factors for the same. Though anyone of these two, can induce a striver, to God-realization, yet, a keen desire is a more powerful means, than dispassion.

Out of the four paths mentioned above, the first three specially arouse desire for God-realization, while the fourth-one (renunciation of the fruit of action) attracts a striver to renounce affinity, for the world.

When a striver, feels that mundane pleasures are painful, and he renounces these from his heart, then having his aim of God-realization, he will automatically progress, towards spiritualism, and realize Him, by His grace.

Similarly, as God is most loving to him and he cannot bear separation, from Him, his unbearable restlessness, will also lead him to God-realization.

Appendix—Practice, knowledge of scriptures and meditation—these three means are 'karaṇasāpekṣa' (dependent on instruments), but renunciation of the fruit of action is 'karaṇanirapekṣa' (independent of instruments). The reason for declaration that the renunciation of the fruit is better, is that people regard it as inferior to other spiritual disciplines. It does not mean that renunciation of the fruit is superior to the other three means. But in fact all the four means are highly good and are for those strivers who aim at renunciation.

In the four means mentioned in this verse, the means 'madarthamapi karmāṇi' (performance of actions for God's sake) mentioned in the tenth verse, has not been included. The reason is that in 'madarthamapi karmāṇi' the spiritual discipline culminates in devotion. Therefore devotion and renunciation—both are highly good means.

Here the renunciation of the fruit of action should mean renunciation of the desire for the fruit of action. Desire is internal while renunciation of the fruit of action is external. Even when the fruit for action is renounced, the desire within may linger. Therefore a striver should aim at the renunciation of the desire for the fruit of action. When the desire is renounced, the striver is delivered from the wheel of birth and death. Salvation is not attained by renouncing things but it is attained by renouncing desires.

Link:—The Lord, out of the devotees who worship attributeless and formless Brahma, and those who worship God with attributes, declared the latter to be most perfect in Yoga, and ordered Arjuna, to follow the latter path. Then pertaining to the latter worship, He explained the four means of God-realization, from the eighth verse to the eleventh verse. Now in five groups, from the thirteenth verse to the nineteenth verse, He describes the marks of His loving devotees, who have attained perfection. In the first group, consisting of the thirteenth and the fourteenth verses, He mentions, twelve marks.

अद्वेष्टा सर्वभूतानां मैत्रः करुण एव च।
निर्ममो निरहङ्कारः समदुःखसुखः क्षमी॥ १३॥
सन्तुष्टः सततं योगी यतात्मा दृढनिश्चयः।
मय्यर्पितमनोबुद्धिर्यो मद्भक्तः स मे प्रियः॥ १४॥

adveṣṭā sarvabhūtānāṁ maitraḥ karuṇa eva ca
nirmamo nirahaṅkāraḥ samaduḥkhasukhaḥ kṣamī
santuṣṭaḥ satataṁ yogī yatātmā dṛḍhaniścayaḥ
mayyarpitamanobuddhiryo madbhaktaḥ sa me priyaḥ

He, who has no ill-will for any being, who is friendly

and compassionate to all, who is free from the sense of mineness and egoism, and is even-minded in pleasure and pain, forgiving, ever content, self-controlled, unshakable in determination, with mind and intellect dedicated to Me—a Yogī, My devotee, is dear to Me. 13-14

Comment:—

'Adveṣṭā sarvabhūtānām'—A person, can bear ill-will to another person, in two ways— (1) By creating, an obstacle, to the acquirement of something desirable, such as wealth, honour, praise etc. (2) By creating, undesirable objects, actions, persons and incidents etc. A devotee, bears no ill-will, in the least, to anyone, even though, they may act against his principles, become an obstacle to his progress and may harm him physically, economically or mentally as he beholds his own favourite Deity, abiding in them (Mānasa 7/112 b).

Not only this, but he beholds and feels the gracious sweet will of God, in the actions of those, who bear ill-will to him.

Every being (soul), is a fragment of God. So if a striver, bears ill-will to any being, it means that he bears, ill-will to God. Such a person bearing ill-will, to anyone can neither be identified with God, nor can he have exclusive devotion to Him. When a devotee becomes totally free, from ill-will, he can be fully devoted, to God. Therefore, a devotee is free from malice, for each and every being.

'Maitraḥ karuṇa eva ca'*—A devotee, is not only free from malice, for every being but he is also friendly and compassionate, to all beings, because he beholds that all beings are His manifestations. 'The Lord, is a disinterested friend of all beings' (Gītā 5/29), (Śrīmadbhāgavata 3/25/21). The Lord's

* The marks of a devotee described here are greater in number and also more singular than the marks of the liberated soul who has attained perfection by transcending the modes of nature (Gītā 14/22—25), 'Maitraḥ' (friendly) and 'Karuṇaḥ' (compassionate) these words have been used only here, not there.

nature, descends on His devotees and therefore, he is friendly and compassionate to all beings, without any selfish motive (Mānasa 7/47/3).

He is friendly, even to those who harm him, because he holds, that whatever is done, is meant for his welfare, by the sweet will of God. Moreover, he thinks that those who are harming him, deserve special respect, because they are destroying his past sin, by becoming an instrument.

Every striver, thinks and he should also think, that those who are doing wrong or those who harm him, are purifying him of the sins of the past. When even a common striver, is friendly and compassionate, to those who bear ill-will to him, a devotee who has attained perfection must be very much more friendly and compassionate, to them.

In the 'Pātañjalayogadarśana', four factors have been mentioned, to purify the mind.

'Friendship, to those who are happy, compassion to those, who are sad, a feeling of pleasure to those, who are virtuous, and indifference to those, who are sinners' (1/33).

But here Lord Kṛṣṇa, has included the four factors in two—friendship and compassion. It means, that a perfect devotee is friendly to the happy and the virtuous, and compassionate, to the sad and the sinful.

A striver, instead of being indifferent to a sinner should be compassionate to him, because the striver, who is suffering is being purified of his old sins by reaping fruit of his sinful actions of the past, while the sinner, who is inflicting pain on a striver, is committing a new sin. So, he specially deserves, compassion.

'Nirmamaḥ'—Though a devotee is naturally friendly and compassionate to all beings, yet he has no sense of mine, with anyone. It is mineness with beings, and objects, which binds him. He is totally free from a sense of mine, even with his so-called body, senses, mind, and intellect. A striver, commits an error that he tries to be free from mineness with beings and objects, but he does not pay proper attention to the point, that he has to be free from mineness, with his body, mind, intellect and senses, also.

'Nirahaṅkāraḥ'—A person, has egoistic feelings by identifying, the self with the body and senses etc. If a devotee, has no egoism, but he realizes his true affinity for God, noble, divine and unique traits, are revealed in him. But he, knowing those traits (virtues) as divine, regards them as of God, not of his own. So, he becomes free from egoism.

'Samaduḥkhasukhaḥ'—A devotee, remains even-minded in pleasure and pain, favourable and unfavourable circumstances, without having attachment and aversion, for them.

Favourable and unfavourable circumstances, by making a man happy and sad, bind him. A devotee, knows of favourable and the unfavourable circumstances, but he remains even-minded, he feels neither happy nor sad.

'Kṣamī'—The Lord, in the thirteenth verse of this chapter, by the term 'Adveṣṭā', declared that His devotee does not bear any malice, towards those people who bear animosity, with him. Here, by the term 'Kṣamī', the Lord says that he is forgiving even to those, who do wrong to him without having the least desire, to punish them. He wants them not to be punished by God or anyone else, for the wrong done to him. This is an excellence of a devotee.

'Santuṣṭaḥ satatam'*—Generally, a being, is content in favourable circumstances, but he loses his calm, in undesirable circumstances. This contentment is not eternal, because he wants to derive satisfaction out of perishable persons and objects etc. He

* In the Bhāgavata there is description of such a man who is ever content. As a person wearing shoes has no fear of pebbles and thorns, so is a man, who is content ever and everywhere, happy without any trace of sadness.

(the self), being eternal can attain real and permanent contentment, only by realizing God, Who is eternal.

Having realized God, a devotee ever remains content, because he has neither disunion from Him, nor does he need the perishable world. Therefore, there is no reason for his discontent. It is because of contentment, that he does not attach importance, to any mundane being or object, in the least.*

The term 'Satatam', with the term 'Santuṣṭaḥ' shows, that a devotee ever remains content and that contentment never undergoes any change, nor is there any possibility, of any change in it. A perfect soul, always remains content, whether he has attained perfection through the paths of action, or knowledge or devotion.

'Yogī'—Here the term 'Yogī', stands for a devotee, who has realized God (who ever remains united with Him), through the path of devotion.

In fact, no person can ever be disunited from God. He, who has realized this fact, is a Yogī.

'Yatātmā'—He, who has fully controlled his body, including the mind, intellect and senses, is 'Yatātmā'. A God-realized devotee has not to control his mind, and intellect etc. These are naturally, under his control. So, in him there is no possibility of any evil, born of contact of senses, with sense-objects. In fact, the mind, intellect and senses should follow a right path. But, these deviate from the right path, because a person is attached, to the world. A devotee's mind, intellect and senses, remain under his control, because he is not in the least, attached to the world, and so his actions are exemplary.

The senses of virtuous and righteous persons, never deviate

* Saint Kabīra declares:—

All the riches in the form of cows, elephants, horses and jewels stand nowhere before the wealth of contentment.

from the right path. King Duṣyanta got attached towards Śakuntalā; so he had full confidence that she must belong to a Kṣatriya family, rather than a Brāhmaṇa. According to the poet Kālidāsa, in case of doubt, the inclination of a virtuous person, is testimony of the right path (Abhijñāna Śākuntalam 1/21).

How can, the mind, intellect and senses of a perfect devotee, deviate from the right path, when the snses of even, a righteous person do not deviate?

'Dṛḍhaniścayaḥ'—An enlightened soul, has a firm determination that the world has no independent existence, while God never ceases to be, and his affinity for Him is eternal. An ignorant person, considers the world as real, and attaches importance to it, while a perfect devotee, does not believe in the existence of the world, for him only, God exists.

In that firm determination, only existence of God, remains. Actually this determination is not of the intellect, it is of the self. But it is reflected, in the intellect.

Conceding the independent existence of the world and assuming affinity with it, doubt and contrary feeling arise in the intellect. Such intellect never becomes steady. The intellect, of a perfect soul remains without any doubt, while that of the ignorant remains, doubtful. The intellect of the ignorant, attaches value to the world and accepts its existence. But the intellect of a perfect soul does not accept existence of anything else, except God. His intellect is totally free from doubt and contrary feeling, and is steadfast, in God only.

'Mayyarpitamanobuddhiḥ'—When a striver resolves, that he has to realize God only, and he becomes God's (which he really is), his mind and intellect, are naturally dedicated to Him. Then, why should the mind and intellect of a perfect devotee, not remain dedicated to Him?

Naturally, a person's mind, is fixed on the object or person he loves, and his intellect is fixed, in the object or person he considers, the best. For a devotee none is more loving and better, than God. So his mind and intellect are naturally, dedicated to Him.

'Yaḥ madbhaktaḥ sa me priyaḥ'*—God loves all, but a devotee loves only God. So according to His promise, "As men approach Me, so do I accept them" (Gītā 4/11), He loves devotees.

Appendix—In the Gītā the marks of a Karmayogī have been stated (2/55—72, 6/7—9), the marks of a Jñānayogī have been stated (14/22—25) and the marks of a devotee have been stated (12/13—19). But while stating the marks of a devotee, the Lord has declared—'adveṣṭā sarvabhūtānāṁ maitraḥ karuṇa eva ca'. The marks 'friendly' and 'compassionate' have been mentioned only in a devotee, not in a Karmayogī nor in a Jñānayogī. A Karmayogī and a Jñāṇayogī are equanimous but are not friendly and compassionate. But a devotee possesses the feelings of friendship and compassion from the beginning.

A devotee holds that all beings, being the fragments of entire-God, are none but God, then who should be at enmity, with whom should he be at enmity and why should he be at enmity?—'nija prabhumaya dekhahiṁ jagata kehi sana karahiṁ birodha' (Mānasa, Uttara. 112 b). For example a devotee loves Rāma, another Kṛṣṇa and the third one Śiva. In spite of their deities being different they can have oneness among themselves but all Jñānayogīs can never be so. If a devotee and a Jñānayogī happen to meet each other, the devotee will pay more respect to the Jñānayogī than the Jñānayogī will pay to the devotee. Therefore the mark of devotees has been mentioned—'sabahi mānaprada āpu amānī' (Mānasa, Uttara. 38/2).

---

* Lord Rāma declares that the entire universe is equally loved by Him because it has been created by Him. But those who having renounced their egoism and hypocrisy adore Him with mind, speech and action, they may be men, women or impotent persons are most loving to Him (Mānasa, Uttara. 87/4, 87 A).

At the beginning of the Rāmacaritamānasa, Goswāmī Tulasīdāsajī Mahārāja does obeisance to the wicked persons besides the gentle ones and does it with sincere feelings—'bahuri bandi khala gana satibhāeṁ̐' (Mānasa, Bāla. 4/1). Only a devotee can do so, a Jñānayogī can't. Though a Jñānayogī does not bear malice to anyone in the least, yet naturally he remains indifferent and neutral. In the path of discrimination (knowledge), there is predominance of detachment (Vairāgya) and 'Vairāgya' (renunciation) is dry. Therefore though a Jñānayogī is not hard hearted, yet he seems hard hearted outwardly because of his dispassionate and indifferent nature.

He who takes joy from others is hard at heart and he who gives joy to others, is soft at heart. A Jñānayogī rejoices having attained salvation, so he remains hard at heart. But a devotee has the notion to give joy to others from the beginning, so he is soft at heart. A devotee bears no malice even to the enemy. A Jñānayogī is like father and a devotee is like mother, therefore a devotee is more compassionate than a Jñānayogī.

'Eva'—This term means that a devotee is devoid of malice—not only this but he is friendly and compassionate also to others.

'Nirmamo nirahaṅkāraḥ'—It is inevitable for every striver to be free from the sense of mine and egoism; therefore in the Gītā the Lord, in Karmayoga, Jñānayoga and Bhaktiyoga—all the three, has mentioned the strivers to be free from them—in Karmayoga 'nirmamo nirahaṅkāraḥ sa śāntimadhigacchati' (2/71), in Jñānayoga 'ahaṅkāraṁ........vimucya nirmamaḥ śānto brahmābhūyāya kalpate' (18/53) and in Bhaktiyoga 'nirmamo nirahaṅkāraḥ sama duḥkha sukhaḥ kṣamī' (12/13). In this connection, a point needs special attention that in fact the self is free from the sense of mine and egoism. Egoism (I'ness) and sense of possession (mineness)—both are assumed in the Self, they are not real. Had they been real, we could have never been free from the sense of mine and egoism and the Lord would have also not ordered Arjuna to be free from the sense of mine and egoism. But we can be free from the sense of mine and egoism, therefore the Lord states so.

In Karmayoga, first 'desire' is renounced, then a Karmayogī naturally becomes free from the 'sense of mine' and 'egoism' (Gītā 2/71). In Jñānayoga, first 'egoism' is renounced, then a Jñānayogī naturally becomes free from the 'sense of mine' (Gītā 18/53). In Bhaktiyoga, a devotee dedicates himself to God, then by God's grace, he naturally is freed from the 'sense of mine' and 'egoism'.

'Mayyarpitamano buddhiryo madbhaktaḥ sa me priyaḥ'—Here the expression 'mayyarpitamano buddhiḥ' stands for the person who has dedicated himself to God. When the self in dedicated, then mind and intellect are naturally dedicated. When the self is dedicated, then mind and intellect are naturally dedicated. When the self is dedicated, then nothing remains at all. The reason is that the self is primary (viz., of the first importance) while the body, mind and intellect etc., are of secondary importance. A devotee is a devotee first while as a human being he is second. When a devotee dedicates himself to God, his mind and intellect are also dedicated and then mind and intellect lose their independent existence but only God remains.

God is equally related with both prakṛtis—'parā' and 'aparā' but the self (parā) is not related with 'aparā'. The reason is that the self is superior to 'aparā prakṛti' and is a fragment of God. Therefore the self has affinity with God. The expression 'mayyarpitamanobuddhiḥ' means that the self should not assume the 'aparā prakṛti' (minds-intellect) as its own but should assume God as its own.*

God is knowledge-personified and is ever perfect in itself.

* Here within 'mana' (mind), 'citta' and within 'buddhi' (intellect), 'aham' (ego) should be included.

Therefore He has no hunger (inquisitiveness) for knowledge, but He has certainly a hunger for love. Therefore the Lord declares that the devotee, who has dedicated his mind and intellect to Him, is loving to Him. No one else at all can be loving to God besides such a devotoe.

Suppose a Prince being the son of the King begs alms from others, it incurs displeasure of the king, similarly if the self, being a fragment of God and an embodiment of truth-knowledge-bliss solidified, cherishes desire of receiving something from the unreal, inert world, the abode of sorrows, it displeases God, it is unpleasant to God because it is much harmful for that being. Only the devotee, who entertains no such hope from anyone else besides Him and which involves his great welfare, is loving to Him—

eka bāni karunānidhana kī, so priya jākeṁ gati na ānakī.

(Mānasa, Aranya. 10/4)

Link—In the second group, consisting of the next verse, the Lord describes six marks of perfect (enlightened) devotees.

यस्मान्नोद्विजते लोको लोकान्नोद्विजते च यः।
हर्षामर्षभयोद्वेगैर्मुक्तो यः स च मे प्रियः॥ १५॥

yasmānnodvijate loko lokānnodvijate ca yaḥ
harṣāmarṣabhayodvegairmukto yaḥ sa ca me priyaḥ

He by whom no being gets agitated and who is not agitated by any being and who is free from joy, anger (envy), fear and perturbation, he is dear to Me. 15

Comment:—

'Yasmānnodvijate lokaḥ'—A devotee beholds his most loving Lord, everywhere and in all. Therefore, all the activities undertaken by him, with his mind, speech and body are only, to please God (Gītā 6/31). Then, how can he agitate anyone?

Even then, the life- story of devotees shows, that some people, bear ill-will to them and oppose them, without any reason merely having heard their glory or action or sometimes even seeing his gentle countenance.

A devotee, never hurts anyone because he realizes, that all is God (Gītā 7/19). All his activities, are naturally for the welfare of all beings. He does not annoy anyone even by an error. People may get annoyed with him, because of their satanic nature. How, can a devotee be blamed, for this satanic nature?

Bhartṛhari declares—"Deer, fishes, and gentle persons live on straw, water and contentment respectively; but hunters, fishermen and vile persons, are at enmity with them without any rhyme or reason."

In fact, no person can be agitated by devotees. Even vile persons who bear envy for devotees, in the company of saints by beholding and touching them, by talking to them and even by thinking of them, abandon their hellish traits and become devotees. It is because of their generous nature, that even vile persons renounce their evil nature, and become devotees.

Lord Śiva in the Mānasa also declares, "It is because of virtue that a saint, returns good for evil" (Mānasa 5/41/4).

But, it is not a rule, that all persons who bear envy to devotees, should be benefitted.

If it is believed that no one, is agitated by devotees, nor does anyone act against them, nor have they, any enemy or friend, how can it be said, these (as is said in the eighteenth and nineteenth verses) that they are, alike to foe and friend, honour and dishonour, praise and blame etc.? It means, that it is because of their wicked nature, that vile people can be shaken by virtuous actions of devotees, and can act against them and regard them as their foes, while devotees do not regard anyone as their enemy, nor do they upset anyone.

'Lokānnodvijate ca yaḥ'—A devotee, is also not agitated by any being because of two factors—

(1) A devotee may have to face unfavourable circumstances, but having known the reality and because of great devotion for God, he remains so much engrossed in his devotion, that he beholds God, everywhere in every being, object and action etc. So he beholds the Lord's pastime only. Thus, he is not agitated by any action.

(2) A man is agitated only when someone does anything against his desire or belief etc. But as a devotee has no desire, he is not at all excited.

'Harṣāmarṣabhayodvegairmukto yaḥ sa ca me priyaḥ'—When the Lord declares, that a perfect devotee is free from joy, He means to say, that he remains free from evil or modifications, such as Rājasika or Tāmasika joy etc. But it does not mean, that he is free from joy but it means that his joy is eternal, uniform and unique. His joy does not undergo any modification, when he either acquires perishable mundane objects or loses them. He ever feels happy, after beholding, God and His pastime.

A common man, is envious of other persons' good fortune, wealth, knowledge, glory and honour etc. Sometimes even strivers are envious, of other strivers' spiritual progress. But a perfect devotee, is totally free from this evil, because for him in the entire universe, there is no independent existence of any being, except of God.

If a striver, after thinking of the spiritual progress of other strivers, thinks that he should also progress in the sameway, it is useful for him. But, if he is envious of others' progress, he has a downfall.

A person, can be full of fear, because of two factors—(i) External, such as a lion, a snake, a thief or a robber etc., and anyother, worldly loss (ii) Internal reasons, such as the thought and performance of evil and forbidden deeds, including theft, falsehood, fraud and adultery etc.

A man, is in the greatest fear, of death. Even a wise man, is generally, in fear of death. Sometimes, a striver is also afraid of the fact that his body will become weak, by spiritual practice, such as adoration and meditation etc., and how, he would be able to maintain his body and look after the family, if he become fully dispassionate. A common man, is afraid of a rival, who is stronger than he. A man, has to remain in fear of all of them, because he depends on matter (body etc.,). When he totally depends on God's feet, he becomes free from fear, forever.

As an enlightened devotee always beholds the pastime of his loving Lord, only, how can he be full of fear?

The Lord, has used the term 'Udvega' (agitation), three times in the verse. No being is agitated by a devotee, he is not agitated by any being. Thirdly, He has used this term, to show that a man may also be agitated in other cases, as he may not be able to complete a piece of work, in spite of his best efforts, he may not be able to reap, the fruit of action, there may occur undesirable incidents, such as earth-quake and flood etc. But, as far as a perfect devotee, is concerned, he remains free from all such excitement.

A man, is agitated because of his desire born of ignorance, and his hellish nature. A devotee, has no desire, because he is totally free from ignorance. As far as, his demoniac nature is concerned, it perishes during the course of his spiritual practice. As he has no independent will, and God's will is his will, he ever remains pleased, in desirable, as well as, undesirable circumstances, by thinking of God's grace, in them. So, there is a total lack of agitation in him.

An enlightened devotee, remains free from agitation, joy, envy and fear etc., because, from his view-point they have no independent existence, except of God. He does not attach any importance to these, and so he is not affected by them.

When a person, is proud of his virtues, it means that he has inculcated an evil propensity of pride, while a divine trait can never give birth, to a demoniac trait, because "the divine nature is deemed conducive to liberation" (Gītā 16/5). So, in this verse, the term 'Muktaḥ' (liberated or free) instead of 'Bhaktaḥ' (devotee), has been used because a devotee, ever remains free from all evils. The evil, of pride gives birth to several other evils, as all evils depend, on the evil of pride.

An enlightened devotee, does not even know, that he possesses any virtue. If he finds any virtues appearing in him, he regards it as God's, not, as his. Thus, having no pride of virtue, a devotee remains free, from all evils. God is loving to devotees, therefore devotees, are loving to God (Gītā 7/17).

Appendix—When a man cognises existence of any other entity besides God, then agitation, envy and fear etc., emanate. From the view-point of a devotee, there is no other existence besides God, then whom should he agitate, envy and frighten and why?—'nija prabhumaya dekhahiṁ jagata kehi sana karahiṁ birodha' (Mānasa, Uttara. 112 b).

Link:—In the third group, which consists of the next verse, the Lord describes six marks of, perfect devotees.

अनपेक्षः शुचिर्दक्ष उदासीनो गतव्यथः।
सर्वारम्भपरित्यागी यो मद्भक्तः स मे प्रियः॥ १६॥

anapekṣaḥ śucirdakṣa udāsīno gatavyathaḥ
sarvārambhaparityāgī yo madbhaktaḥ sa me priyaḥ

He, who has no expectation, is internally and externally pure, skilful, unconcerned and untroubled, renouncing all new action for pleasure and prosperity, he, My devotee is dear to Me. 16

Comment:—

'Anapekṣaḥ'—A devotee, considers God the noblest. He thinks that there is no greater gain, than God-realization. So, he is not in the least, attracted towards any worldly object. He is not even attached to his so-called body, senses, mind and intellect, because he regards these as God's, as they really belong to Him. He is not even worried, how he will maintain his body. He is, totally free from desires.

A devotee, is not shaken even by the greatest sorrow, because he remains absorbed in the Lord's pastime, even in most unfavourable circumstances. He, does not desire favourable circumstances, of any kind.

Such a devotee, knows that all mundane objects are perishable, while he (the self), can never be separated from God. Having known this reality, he has no desire to acquire, these perishable objects.

It is not a rule, that by mere desire a man, can get necessary material for maintenance of life, and without having desire, he does not. He naturally, acquires necessary objects to maintain his body, because arrangement for necessary materials for the maintenance of the body, has already been made, by God. If he has keen desire to acquire any mundane objects, he creates an obstacle to the acquisition of objects, as desire does not spread and go to others. So, other people, are not inspired to offer such objects to him. It is generally seen, that no one wants to offer any object to those (thieves etc.,) who have a keen desire to acquire these. On the other hand, people want to offer objects to dispassionate ascetics and innocent children etc., who do not desire them. Arrangements are made, happily by others, for the maintenance of their bodies. It proves, that necessities of life are provided for those, who have no desire for them. Therefore, it is nothing but a folly, to desire required objects, because desire is an invitation to suffering. An enlightened devotee, does not even expect to maintain his body.

Some devout devotees, do not even desire, to behold God. They totally depend upon His sweet will and remain absorbed in Him, by thinking of His boundless grace. The Lord, follows such devotees, so that the dust of their feet may touch Him so that He may be sanctified (Śrīmadbhā. 11/14/16).

A devotee, who adores God, to reap the fruit of devotion in the form of worldly objects, is really a devotee to the objects, rather than to God, as he desires objects, rather than God. But, He is so generous, that He accepts him as His devotee (Gītā 7/16), because he wants his desire to be fulfilled, by Him only. The Lord, shows not only this favour, but also changes seekers of wealth, such as Dhruva, into men of wisdom, having fulfilled their desire.

'Śuciḥ'—The body of a devotee, becomes very much pure, because he has neither egoism nor a sense of 'mine'. His mind also, becomes very pure, because his mind is free from attachment and aversion, pleasure and pain, desire and wrath and such other evils. Such a devotee, because of his external and internal purity, sanctifies other people who behold him, touch him, talk to him and think of him. Places of pilgrimage, sanctify all people, while devotees provide pilgrimage to those places, which places, are sanctified by a touch of their feet (but devotees are not proud of it). Such devotees, sanctify even the pure and they move from one place of pilgrimage to another, by making these as great places of pilgrimage (Śrīmadbhāgavata 1/13/10).

King Bhagīratha, says to Ganges:—"O mother, those who have renounced all mundane and spiritual desires, who having a disinclination; for the world, are calm in themselves, are devoted to Brahma (the Absolute), and purify the worlds, such saintly souls, will destroy all sins with their touch, because God Who destroys all sins, resides in their hearts."

'Dakṣaḥ'—'Dakṣaḥ' (clever) is he, who has attained the aim of this human life i.e., God-realization. The Lord, in the Śrīmadbhāgavata declares, "The limit of the wisdom of the wise and the skill of the skilful, consists in attaining the Imperishable and the Real, through this perishable and unreal, body" (12/29/22).

In fact, worldly skill is not real skill, it is a kind of a blot because it induces a man, to attach more importance to matter, which leads him to a downfall.

An enlightened devotee, is also skilful in mundane affairs. But, it is an insult to him if his skill in mundane affairs, is regarded as a touchstone of his progress, in the spiritual sphere.

'Udāsīnaḥ'—An enlightened devotee, remains indifferent, to whatever happens. He remains detached from all incidents and circumstances etc., in the same way, as a man standing on the top of a high mountain, is unaffected by fire or flood, on the earth. He remains alike, to a friend and a foe, from his heart though his dealings, outwardly may seem different. He is ever impartial, because he regards the entire universe including the body, as God's.

'Gatavyathaḥ'—He remains, free from affliction and worries. He is not troubled by favourable and unfavourable circumstances, attachment and aversion, pleasure and pain and such other, evils.

'Sarvārambhaparityāgī'—Performance of new actions for pleasure and prosperity, is known as 'Ārambha', such as accumulation of new articles and starting new business etc., to hoard money. A devotee, renounces all initiative in action, for pleasure and prosperity etc.

A person, who hankers after worldly pleasure and prosperity, and who is proud of himself because of his caste, creed, order of life, learning, intellect, ability, position and authority etc., is not a devotee. A devotee, is he who is devoted to God. He surrenders his body, senses, mind, intellect, actions and their rewards etc., to God, because He is their real owner. He regards prakṛti (Nature) and its evolute, as God's. Therefore, a devotee regards no one else, except God, as his. He, instead of performing actions for himself, performs these to please, God. He never performs action to gain wealth or property, comfort or luxury, honour or praise etc. He does not perform any action, for pleasure or prosperity, because he has a true desire for God-realization.

'Yo madbhaktaḥ sa me priyaḥ'—The Lord, has so much of attraction, that a devotee is automatically attracted towards Him, and he becomes devoted to Him.

"The sages, who are satisfied in the self, and who out of wisdom, have renounced their affinity for matter (insentient), adore God, without expecting any reward, because He possesses such virtues which attract people, towards Him" (Śrīmadbhā. 1/7/10).

Now a question can arise, as to why all persons are not attracted towards God and become devoted to Him, if He has so much of attraction.

In fact, a person (the self) is naturally attracted, towards Him, because he is His fragment. But, it is because of his attachment to the body, senses, mind, intellect, family and worldly objects etc., that he has a disinclination for God, Whose fragment he is. God pervades everywhere, but He is not revealed to man, because of his attachment to sense-objects i.e., mundane pleasures. When a man, renounces his attachment to perishable pleasures, he is naturally attracted towards God, and becomes devoted to Him. The Lord, calls such a devotee who has an exclusive devotion to Him 'Madbhaktaḥ', and he is loving to Him.

Appendix—'Anapekṣaḥ'—A devotee has no expectation even for the so-called necessities of life. A devotee holds that 'All is God' and than what should he expect? 'śuci'—Even the vision, touch and the discourse of a devotee saint sanctifies others. Even the wind by contact with his body becomes pure.

Though a Jñānayogī, an exalted soul also possesses such purity, yet a devotee remains specially obsessed in the welfare (because of his friendly and compassionate nature) of all beings from the very beginning, so he is specially pure (holy). 'Dakṣa'—A devotee is wise because he has achieved the aim of human life viz., for him nothing remains to be done, nothing remains to be known and nothing remains to be attained.

'Sarvārambha parityāgī'—This expression has also been used, for the person who has transcended the three guṇas, in the twenty-fifth verse of the fourteenth chapter 'sarvārambha parityāgī guṇātītaḥ sa ucyate'. An exalted soul who has transcended the three guṇas, being free from the sense of doership, is 'sarvārambhaparityāgī' viz., he abandons all new undertakings for pleasure and prosperity. For a devotee nothing remains to be done at all for himself, then what activity should he do? He may undertake an activity but he remains free from attachment, desire for its fruit and any insistence on its doing etc., it may be undertaken or not, it does not make any difference to him. He remains equanimous in both the states.

Link:—The Lord, in the fourth group, which consists of the next verse, mentions the five marks of a perfect devotee.

यो न हृष्यति न द्वेष्टि न शोचति न काङ्क्षति।
शुभाशुभपरित्यागी भक्तिमान्यः स मे प्रियः॥ १७॥

yo na hṛṣyati na dveṣṭi na śocati na kāṅkṣati
śubhāśubhaparityāgī bhaktimānyaḥ sa me priyaḥ

He, who neither rejoices nor hates, neither grieves nor desires, and who has renounced attachment and aversion in good and evil, deeds, he who is thus devoted, is dear to Me. 17

Comment:—

'Yo na hṛṣyati na dveṣṭi na śocati na kāṅkṣati'—There are four important demerits—(1) attachment, (2) aversion (hate), (3) rejoicing and (4) grief. An enlightened devotee, is free from these four evils. He realizes that the world, being perishable has no independent existence. He (the self), being a fragment of God, is imperishable. So, he instead of having his affinity, for the changing world, accepts his affinity for God, which is eternal.

Thus, his mind is totally free from such evils, as attachment and aversion etc.

During spiritual practice, the more one advances towards spiritualism, the less attachment and aversion, he has. When he attains perfection, these evils perish totally.

A common man, rejoices when he acquires desirable objects and gets rid of undesirable ones, while he grieves when he gets undesirable objects or is likely to get them, or loses desirable ones. An enlightened devotee, remains even-minded and free from evils, such as attachment and aversion etc.

At night, in the dark, a person wishes to light a lamp and he feels happy having lighted it. He hates a person or becomes angry with him, who extinguishes the light, and is worried as to how to light it again. But, at noon, when the sun shines brightly, he has neither a desire to light the lamp, or is rejoiced having lighted it, nor is angry with a man, who extinguishes it nor is worried how to light it again. Similarly, when a man has a disinclination for God and inclination for the world he desires favourable circumstances, to maintain his body etc., he is rejoiced having acquired these, hates those or is angry with those, who are an obstacle to their acquisition and is worried how to acquire them again if these are not acquired. But, he who (like the sun at noon) has attained perfection, becomes free from these evils. He has no desire at all, and so he has no need for the world.

'Śubhāśubhaparityāgī'—All actions, of a devotee, change into inaction, because he is free from a sense of mine, attachment, and desire for fruit. So, his good actions, also change into inaction. Evil actions, are not performed by him, because he is totally free, from attachment, aversion and desire etc., which influence a man to perform evil actions.

He is neither attached to good actions, nor has an aversion for evil ones. Only virtuous actions, prescribed by scriptures are performed, by him while forbidden actions, are renounced by him, without having any attachment or aversion for them. A real renouncer, is he who has totally renounced attachment and aversion for them.

It is not actions, but attachment and aversion, which bind a man. As a perfect devotee, is free from attachment and aversion, he is said to have renounced good and evil deeds.

It may also mean, he is a renouncer of the fruit of good and evil, actions. But this idea has already been expressed in the first half of this verse, when the Lord declares, "He neither rejoices nor hates, neither grieves nor desires." If this meaning is taken, then there is a repetition, of the same idea. Therefore, here it should mean, renouncement of attachment and aversion for good and evil actions.

'Bhaktimānyaḥ sa me priyaḥ'—A devotee loves God, very much and so he naturally thinks of Him, remembers Him and adores Him. Such a devotee has been called a 'Bhaktimān' (full of devotion).

A devotee, has an exclusive devotion for God, therefore he is loved by Him.

Appendix—Joy (hṛṣyati) and grief (śocati), attachment (kāṅkṣati) and aversion (dveṣṭi)—these are dualities (pairs of opposites). A devotee remains free from these dualities. In 'Nārada bhaktisūtra' it is mentioned—'yatprāpya na kiñcidvāñchati na śocati na dveṣṭi na ramate notsāhī bhavati' (5).

'Having attained devotion, a devotee neither desires anything nor grieves nor hates nor is attached to anything and having obtained a thing, he is not encouraged (rejoiced).'

Link:—In the fifth and last group, which consists of the next two verses, the Lord mentions ten marks, of a perfect devotee.

समः शत्रौ च मित्रे च तथा मानापमानयोः।
शीतोष्णसुखदुःखेषु समः सङ्गविवर्जितः॥ १८॥

तुल्यनिन्दास्तुतिर्मौनी सन्तुष्टो येन केनचित्।
अनिकेतः स्थिरमतिर्भक्तिमान्मे प्रियो नरः ॥ १९ ॥

samaḥ śatrau ca mitre ca tathā mānāpamānayoḥ
śītoṣṇasukhaduḥkheṣu samaḥ saṅgavivarjitaḥ
tulyanindāstutirmauni santuṣṭo yena kenacit
aniketaḥ sthiramatirbhaktimānme priyo naraḥ

He who is, alike to foe and friend, in honour and dishonour, also who is alike, in cold and heat, (favourable and unfavourable circumstances, in pleasure and pain, who is free from attachment, who holds blame and praise equally, who is thoughtful, contented with any means of subsistence, who has no attachment to his body and his abode and is firm in mind, that man full of devotion, is dear to Me. 18-19

Comment:—

'Samaḥ śatrau ca mitre ca'—Being free from attachment and aversion, a perfect devotee, is even-minded, towards foe and friend, equally. Not to talk of common men, even strivers, are swayed by feelings of enmity and friendship, towards an enlightened devotee. But, he ever remains even-minded, to foe and friend.

If there is a quarrel between two persons, over division of property, one of them has a feeling of enmity, towards a devotee, while the second person has a feeling of friendship, for him. In sitting over judgment, a devotee, will allow a little more, to the former and a bit less, to the latter. It seems, that the judgment of the devotee is not just, but the former will feel, that the judgment is right. Such a judgment, will create a feeling of equanimity, even in the person who regards the devotee, as his enemy.

An enlightened devotee, is alike to foe and friend. It means, that people regard him, as a foe or a friend. So he has in reality not been without foe and friend, but he has been called to be alike, to both of them.

'Tathā mānāpamānayoḥ'—A man, feels honoured or dishonoured, when he identifies the self with body. A devotee, has neither egoistic feelings, with his body nor a sense of mine. So, if his body is honoured or dishonoured, his mind, does not undergo any modification (happiness or sadness). He always remains established, in equanimity.

'Śītoṣṇasukhaduḥkheṣu samaḥ'—An enlightened devotee's equanimity, has been described here, in the two pairs of opposites—

(1) He is equanimous in cold and heat i.e., there is no modification in his mind, even when there is contact of the senses, with sense-objects.

(2) He has equanimity, in pleasure and pain, i.e., his mind remains the same in gain and loss, of riches and materials etc.

'Śītoṣṇa', stands for cold and heat i.e., a sense of touch only, but here it stands for all other senses also. When senses, are in contact with their sense-objects, a perfect devotee, knows of favourable and unfavourable circumstances, but he remains equanimous, while a common man feels happy or sad, and has an attachment and aversion for those circumstances.

In the Gītā, 'to remain even in pleasure and pain' and 'to be devoid of pleasure and pain' both, are used in the same sense. The favourable (happy) and unfavourable (sad) circumstances, are inevitable. So, it is not possible to be devoid of them, but an enlightened devotee, remains the same (even) without feeling, either happy or sad. One can be devoid of pleasure and pain, which arise from favourable and unfavourable circumstances. In the Gītā, where there is mention of being even in pleasure and pain, it means, that one is equable, in favourable and unfavourable circumstances. And, where there is mention of absence of pleasure and pain, it means pleasure and pain, arising from these circumstances.

'Saṅgavivarjitaḥ'—The term 'Saṅga', means, both affinity (union) and attachment. It is not possible for a person, to be disunited physically, from the body, mind, senses and intellect, so long as, he remains alive. He can physically renounce, objects other than the body. But real renouncement, consists in renouncing attachment for objects and beings, rather than their physical renouncement. Had physical renouncement, led a person to salvation, every person after death, would have attained salvation, as he abandons even his body. If he is attached to beings and objects etc., even after death, he is in bondage, because it is attachment, rather than physical renouncement, which leads to bondage.

Physical renouncement, can also be a means, to renounce attachment, but attachment, should be renounced from the heart. If there is the least attachment to the world, a person, will certainly think of it. Then attachment, will give birth to desire, anger and delusion respectively, and may lead him to ruin (Gītā 2/62-63).

The Lord, in the fifty-ninth verse of the second chapter, by using the expression 'Paraṁ dṛṣṭvā nivartate', declared, "Even the taste for the objects of sense, turns away when the Supreme is seen." It means that attachment is totally renounced, after God-realization. But, it does not mean that attachment, cannot be totally renounced, during spiritual practice. When the soul of a striver, is no longer attached to external contacts (objects), even during spiritual practice, he immediately attains undying bliss or God-realization (Gītā 5/21; 16/22).

Attachment, abides neither in the soul (self), which is a pure sentient fragment of God, nor in matter (prakṛti). It retains in the ego, of the embodied soul, and it seems to reside in the mind, intellect, senses and sense-objects. When a striver, ceases to identify himself with body and has no attachment for it, his attachment for objects etc., will totally perish. This attachment, originates out of ignorance (lack of discrimination). A man, is attached to persons, and objects etc., because, he does not attach importance to, discrimination. A perfect devotee, has no ignorance, therefore he is totally free, from attachment.

A person, by an error having a disinclination for God, Whose fragment he (the self) is, is attached to the world, by regarding it as, his. When this assumed affinity, for the world is renounced, he becomes, even-minded. This even-mindedness, naturally leads him to, detachment.

A Vital Fact

In fact a being, has a natural inclination (devotion) to God. But, because of his assumed affinity with the world, this inclination (love) to God, is not revealed. This inclination for the Lord, appears as attachment, for the world. In spite of this attachment, to the world, love towards God, is not totally, effaced. But, as soon as a striver, is inclined towards Him, this attachment for the world, perishes in the same way as darkness disappears with sun-rise. Similarly, the more he is detached from the world, the more, he is inclined to God. After rooting out, attachment, detachment, also perishes, in the same way as fire also perishes after having burnt pieces of wood. With the disappearance of attachment and detachment, there is natural and effortless flow of devotion, to God. Then, the devotee surrenders himself to God, and all his actions are performed, in order to please Him. Being pleased with him, God offers love (devotion) to him. The devotee, offers devotion, again to God. It pleases the Lord much, and He again offers love (devotion), to him. Again, the devotee returns it, to Him. In this way, this pastime of give and take, of ever-enhancing love, goes on.

Tulyanindāstutiḥ'—Praise or censure, is generally concerned, with one's name. This is, done by others. People praise or blame, a devotee by his name. A devotee, has neither egoistic feelings, nor a feeling of 'mine, in his name and body. So he remains totally unaffected, by praise or blame. He has neither attachment for a person, who praises him nor aversion for a person, who blames him.

Common people, feel elated by praise or pained by blame, while strivers, blush from praise, and become cautious by blame. But an enlightened devotee, remains equanimous, in praise and blame, though for the good of others sometimes, he may behave, like strivers, blushing on hearing praise and being cautious on being blamed.

A devotee, beholds God, everywhere. So he remains unaffected by praise and blame, and does not make any distinction, between those who praise him and those who blame him. Moreover, he does not perform forbidden (evil) actions, and as far as, good actions are concerned, he thinks that it is He, Who was making him an instrument, performs them. So he remains even-minded, in praise and blame.

Maunī—An enlightened devotee, is called 'Maunī' (thoughtful), because he naturally thinks of God. He beholds God, in every thought that comes to his mind (Gītā 7/19). He constantly thinks of Him, only.

Here the term 'Maunī' (silent), cannot be taken for a person, who is restrained in speech, because by doing so, devotees who propagate devotion, and divine discourse, through speech, will not be called, devotees. Moreover, if silence (restraint in speech) had made a person a devotee, it would have been very easy, for anyone to become a devotee, merely by becoming silent and there would have been innumerable devotees, though only a few devotees exist. Besides, even a hypocrite, can remain silent. So, here the term 'Maunī, stands for an enlightened soul, who thinks of God.

'Santuṣṭo yena kenacit'—Other people, hold that a devotee is content, with bare means of bodily maintenance, but in fact, he is not content with mundane objects and circumstances. He is content constantly, as he remains engrossed, in devotion to God. So, he remains even-minded, in favourable and unfavourable circumstances, by regarding these as happenings of His sweet will.

'Aniketaḥ'—'Aniketaḥ', is not he who is homeless, but one who is not attached, to a fixed abode, whether he is a householder, or an ascetic. A devotee, is not at all attached to his dwelling place, to his body (gross, subtle and causal), and has not the least, sense of mine, with these.

'Sthiramatiḥ'—A devotee, has neither any doubt nor contrary feeling, about the existence and form of God. He remains firm in mind, about it without any proof, such as scriptures etc., because, he always naturally remains engrossed in Him.

Desires, are stumbling blocks of steady-mindedness (Gītā 2/44). Therefore, when a man completely casts off desires, he is called, 'steady in mind' (Gītā 2/55). When a person, has desire to derive pleasure, out of contact of senses with sense-objects, he is attached to the world. This attachment, to the world is not renounced, even by regarding the world, as unreal in the same way, as a person gets attached to cinema, even by regarding the scene (persons and objects) as unreal or fake, or he is reminded of old scenes, by thinking of them, though he knows that they do not exist, at that time. Therefore, so long as a man has desires, from the heart for worldly pleasures, his worldly attachment, cannot be renounced, even by considering the world false or fake. Attachment, strengthens the independent existence of the world. When desire for mundane pleasures, is renounced, attachment for the world automatically perishes, and then the independent existence of the world, ceases to be, and the mind gets fixed on God.

'Bhaktimānme priyo naraḥ'—In the term 'Bhaktimān', there is suffix 'Matup', in the word 'Bhakti', which shows that a person, naturally has devotion (love for God). But he commits an error that instead of having devotion to God, he develops devotion for the world. So he cannot relish devotion for God, and his life becomes dull and insipid. An enlightened devotee, ever remains engrossed in sentiments of devotion. So he is called Bhaktimān (full of devotion). Such a man, full of devotion, is loving to Him.

The Lord, by the term 'Naraḥ', means that, only he who has attained the aim of his life by realizing God, deserves to be called a 'Naraḥ' (man). He, who hankers after mundane pleasure and prosperity, does not deserve, to be called a man.

[In these two verses, there is description of a perfect devotee, who remains established in equanimity, in the five pairs of opposites such as friend and foe, honour and dishonour, cold and heat, pleasure and pain, praise and blame. When a striver, attains equanimity in these five pairs, he attains total equanimity.]

An Important Fact Pertaining to This Topic

The Lord, in this topic from the thirteenth verse to the nineteenth verse, by using the expression 'Me priyaḥ' (loving to Me), four times and 'Priyo naraḥ' (that man is loving to Me) the fifth time, divided the topic of marks of his enlightened devotees, into five groups—the first group, consisting of the thirteenth and the fourteenth verses, the second group, consisting of the fifteenth verse, the third group, of the sixteenth verse, the fourth group, of the seventeenth verse, and the fifth and last group, of the eighteenth and the nineteenth verses. It means, that there are five different groups of signs of enlightened devotees, rather than one, otherwise the Lord might not have repeated the expression, 'Me priyaḥ,. (loving to Me), four times and 'Priyo naraḥ', the fifth time.

All groups of these signs of enlightened devotees, include the absence of attachment and aversion, pleasure and pain. In the first group, the terms 'Nirmamaḥ' and 'Adveṣṭā' respectively, stand for freedom from attachment and aversion, while the expression 'Samaduḥkhasukhaḥ' stands for freedom from (balanced in), pleasure and pain. In the second group, the expression 'Harṣāmarṣabha-yodvegaiḥ', stands for freedom from attachment and aversion, pleasure and pain. In the third group, the term 'Anapekṣaḥ' stands for freedom from attachment, the term 'Udāsīnaḥ' stands, for freedom from aversion while 'Gatavyathaḥ' stands for freedom from pleasure and pain. In the fourth group, the expressions 'Na kāṅkṣati', 'Na dveṣṭi', 'Na hṛṣyati' and 'Na śocati' respectively, stand for, freedom from attachment, aversion, pleasure and pain. In the last group, the expression 'Saṅgavivarjitaḥ' stands, for freedom from attachment, the term 'Santuṣṭaḥ' stands, for contentment in only God i.e., freedom from aversion while the expression 'Śītoṣṇasukhaduḥkheṣu samaḥ' stands, for freedom from pleasure and pain. Thus, there are clearly five different groups, otherwise the Lord, might have not made needless repetition of words.

As there are, five different groups, so a person who possesses the marks of anyone of the groups, is a loving devotee, of God. The Lord, while explaining the different marks of enlightened devotees, in each group, wants to mention that their virtues may slightly differ, according to their spiritual practice, fate, caste, order of life, circumstances and temperaments etc., but all of them, are totally free from attachment and aversion, pleasure and pain and such other defects; and they are even-minded and remain engrossed, in the welfare of all beings, equally.

A striver, by following the signs of anyone of the five groups, according to his inclination, faith, ability and temperament, should try to inculcate them, in him. He should not lose heart, certainly he will be successful.

Appendix—In these two verses the Lord has mentioned

such cases where it is difficult to be equanimous. If a striver becomes equanimous in such cases, it will not be difficult for him to be equanimous in other cases. To remain unaffected is 'samatā' (equanimity).

Though from the viewpoint of a devotee, there is no entity besides God, yet from the viewpoint of other people a devotee appears to be alike to foe and friend. Inspite of having the knowledge of friendship and enmity, he remains even minded.

'Śītoṣṇa sukha duḥkheṣu'—A devotee remains equanimous in favourable and unfavourable circumstances pertaining to the body, the senses, the mind, the intellect and also to opinions and principles etc. He is neither attached to the favourable circumstances nor has an aversion to the unfavourable ones.

'Yo madbhaktaḥ sa me priyaḥ', 'bhaktimānme priyo naraḥ'—These expressions mean that they are loving to God because of their devotion for Him, not because of virtues (marks). Virtues are not significant but his devotion is significant.

Link:—In the preceding seven verses the Lord mentioned thirty-nine marks of enlightened devotees. Now in the next verse He answers Arjuna's question clearly.

ये तु धर्म्यामृतमिदं यथोक्तं पर्युपासते।
श्रद्दधाना मत्परमा भक्तास्तेऽतीव मे प्रियाः ॥ २० ॥

ye tu dharmyāmṛtamidaṁ yathoktaṁ paryupāsate
śraddadhānā matparamā bhaktāste'tīva me priyāḥ

And those, who with faith, hold Me as their supreme goal, and follow this nectar of wisdom (law or doctrine), such devotees, are exceedingly dear to Me. 20

Comment:—

'Ye tu'—The term 'Ye' (who), has been used for those

devotees, about whom the question was put, in the first verse by Arjuna. In response to his question, the Lord in the second verse, declared the worshippers of the Lord, with attributes, to be the most perfect, in Yoga. Then, He explained the means to perform that worship, and afterwards having explained the marks of enlightened devotees, now He concludes, the topic.

Here, the term 'Ye', stands for those strivers, who having supreme faith in God, depend on Him and follow spiritual practice, by treating the marks of enlightened devotees, as model virtues.

The term 'Tu', has been used to show the distinction, between enlightened devotees and devotees, who are on the way to, God-realization. By the use of this term, it appears as if the Lord, loves the striver devotees, more than perfect devotees.

'Śraddadhānāḥ'—In the marks of the perfect devotees, there is no mention of faith, because faith is required, only so long as a striver, does not realize God. Therefore, the term stands for, strivers who have faith in God, and who try to translate immortal wisdom (which has been preached by Him from the thirteenth to the nineteenth verses), into practice, in order to realize God.

Though, in the path of devotion, there is importance of faith and love (devotion), while in the path of knowledge, there is importance of discrimination, yet it does not mean, that there is no importance of discrimination, in the path of devotion and no importance of faith, in the path of knowledge. In fact, faith and discrimination, play an important role, in all spiritual paths. Discrimination enhances devotion. Similarly, faith in God and in scriptures induces a striver, to follow the path of knowledge. Therefore, faith and discrimination, are helpful in both the paths, of devotion and knowledge.

'Matparamāḥ'—Strivers, following the path of God-realization, regard the Lord as their supreme goal, in order to, cultivate model virtues of enlightened devotees. Thus by thinking of Him, and by depending upon Him, all those virtues are, naturally, cultivated in them.

This fact, of regarding the Lord as the supreme goal, has already been pointed out, in the fifty-fifth verse of the eleventh chapter, and in the sixth verse of the twelfth chapter. In this verse, it has been repeated again. It proves, that it plays an important role, in the path of devotion. When a striver, regards the Lord, as the supreme goal, by God's grace, he is naturally inspired to practise spiritual discipline, and all the stumbling blocks, to his spiritual progress vanish.

'Dharmyāmṛtamidaṁ yathoktam'—The five groups, consisting of thirty-nine marks, of enlightened devotees, are full of righteousness or wisdom, having no trace of unrighteousness. Such a, discipline is like nectar. So it has been called 'Dharmyāmṛta' (the nectar of wisdom). But, this path can be followed only, when a striver has the only aim of God-realization, without hankering after riches, honour, praise, prosperity and pleasure etc.

In every group, all the marks are full of nectar of wisdom. So a striver, can follow anyone of the groups, by regarding those virtues, as model.

Every striver, possesses these virtues partly, and he also possesses, evils. Every being possesses both virtues and vices. One can renounce vices totally, but it is not possible for him to renounce virtues, totally. An enlightened soul, possesses only virtues, according to his spiritual path and temperament. So virtues, have been divided into five groups. But vices are to be renounced totally, so these are not divided, into groups.

A striver, keeps good company, but he does not totally avoid, bad company. He has self-control, but he also, loses it. He practises spiritual practice, but also indulges in, anti-spiritual activities. So he does not attain perfection, he remains, like common mundane people. Moreover, so long as, he possesses vices also, with virtues, he is proud of virtues; and pride, is the root of wicked nature. Therefore, a striver should follow this nectar of wisdom, by renouncing all vices, otherwise he will not realize, God. He should try his best, to do away with evils. If he finds himself unable, to get rid of these, he should pray to God, with restlessness.

All the virtues and virtuous feelings, are born by having affinity for the real (God), while all the vices and evil feelings come from affinity, for the unreal world. Even the vilest person, cannot totally lack virtues, because he has affinity for the real (God), whose fragment he is. So, he possesses virtues and virtuous feelings, to some extent or the other. When he realizes God, his affinity for the unreal, is totally renounced and then all his vices and evil feelings, vanish.

Virtues are a divine endowment. The more, a striver is inclined to God or he holds Him, as supreme goal, the more, the virtues and good feelings, are revealed in him and the vices and evil feelings, vanish. When he realizes God, his affinity for the unreal is renounced, and all vices and evil feelings, totally go away.

Attachment and aversion, pleasure and pain, desire and wrath, are modifications of the mind, they are not permanent features, (Gītā 13/6), like the heat in the sun. The heat cannot be separated, from the sun and so, affinity between the sun and the heat, is eternal and imperishable, while modifications, such as desire and anger do not remain permanently, even in common men these decrease in strivers and are totally absent in enlightened souls. Had these modifications, been innate, they would have remained uniform and would not have vanished, till the inner sense remained. Therefore, they are not innate, and rather come and go. The more a striver, advances towards his destination, of God-realization, the evils such as attachment and aversion become less and less and when God is realized, and these totally disappear.

The Lord, in the Gītā time and again, has exhorted Arjuna to renounce attachment and aversion, (3/34, 2/64, 18/51) totally. It means, that they can be renounced, otherwise the Lord would not direct Arjuna, to renounce them.

In the Gītā, there is also mention, that an enlightened soul, is totally free from evils, such as attachment and aversion etc. These evils are transitory. Had these not been transitory, how could one have been free from them? In this chapter, from the thirteenth verse to the nineteenth verses, the Lord, has explained time and again, that enlightened devotees, are totally free from evils, such as attachment and aversion etc., because they have total disinclination, for the unreal. The Lord, has mentioned this nectar of wisdom, so that strivers, may follow this by regarding the enlightened devotees, as their model.

'Paryupāsate'—Strivers have great reverence, for enlightened devotees. Because, of their natural attraction (devotion) for God, enlightened devotees, are naturally endowed with divine traits. But, strivers follow perfect devotees, in order to cultivate their virtues by totally renouncing evils. They, may not be able to cultivate all their virtues, but whatever virtue is cultivated, should be created thoroughly and with faith. No opposite tendency should be allowed to stay. For instance, strivers may not be compassionate, thoroughly, but they should not have cruelty, towards anyone. Strivers, do not possess these virtues completely, so they have been asked to follow these virtues (nectar of wisdom), as described, from the thirteenth to the nineteenth verses of this chapter, with faith. This is the meaning of 'Paryupāsate'. If they possess, all virtues of anyone of the five contents, they will attain, the status of perfect devotees.

When a striver, has a burning desire and restlessness, for God-realization, all his evils get destroyed, because desire and restlessness destroy those evils. Then, he practises spiritual discipline, naturally and realizes God, quickly and easily.

'Bhaktāste'tīva me priyāḥ'—Here, the term 'Bhaktāḥ' stands, for strivers who follow the path of devotion, by depending on God.

The Lord, in the fifty-third verse of the eleventh chapter, having declared that He cannot be seen, either by the study of Vedas or austerity or charity or sacrifice, in the fifty-fourth verse, mentioned that He can be known and seen by a single-minded devotion. In the fifty-fifth verse, He explained the form of single-minded devotion, by mentioning the marks of his devotees. Then, in the first verse of this chapter, Arjuna asked, "Those devotees who, ever earnest, worship Thee and again, those who worship the Imperishable and the Unmanifested—which of them are better versed in Yoga?" The Lord, in the second verse, answered the question, "Those who fixing their mind, on Me, worship Me, ever earnest and endowed with supreme faith, are the most perfect in Yoga." Here, while concluding the topic, the Lord uses the term 'Bhaktāḥ', for those strivers.

The Lord, calls such strivers exceedingly dear to Him, while He calls enlightened devotees only dear to Him. Why?

(1) The enlightened devotees, have attained perfection or God-realization; but strivers even without realizing Him, hold Him as their supreme goal.

(2) Perfect devotees, are like His grown up (wise) sons, while strivers are like His small innocent sons, (Mānasa 3/43/4).

As a baby is loving to everyone, so is a striver, loving to God.

(3) The Lord, becomes free from the debt of perfect devotees, by enabling them to have His vision, while He holds that He is

indebted to the strivers, because He has not yet enabled, them to behold Him. So, He declares, that they are exceedingly dear, to Him.

Appendix—Duty is called 'dharma'. Not to deviate from dharma is called 'dharmya' 'All is God'—No other principle can be equal to this principle, therefore this is 'dharmya' (Gītā 9/2).

A striver keeps faith. But a God-realized soul needs no faith as he has a direct experience that there is no other entity besides God. When all is God, then who should have faith and in whom? A striver holds that there is another entity, so he follows the virtues possessed by God-realized devotees but he has also the feeling that if there is anything else besides God, that is His pastime.

In spite of the assumption of the other entity, a striver depends on God, and none else but God is his beloved, therefore he is exceedingly dear to God. Until he realizes 'All is God', God Himself feels indebted to him.

In Śrīmadbhāgavata the Lord declares—

yāvat sarveṣu bhūteṣu madbhāve nopajāyate
tāvadevamupāsīta vāṅmanaḥ kāyavṛttibhiḥ

(11/29/17)

Until a devotee really holds that all beings are God's manifestations viz., 'All is God', he should worship Me with all the activities (dealings) of his mind, speech and body.

sarvaṁ brahmātmahaṁ tasya vidyayā''tmamanīṣayā
paripaśyannuparamet sarvato mukta saṁśayaḥ

(11/29/18)

'The devotee by following the above mentioned discipline becomes determined—'All is God'. Then he by this spiritual knowledge, being free from all doubt beholding God everywhere, should become calm viz., he should not even think of 'All is God', but he should have a clear vision of God'.

ॐ तत्सदिति श्रीमद्भगवद्गीतासूपनिषत्सु ब्रह्मविद्यायां योगशास्त्रे
श्रीकृष्णार्जुनसंवादे भक्तियोगो नाम द्वादशोऽध्याय:॥ १२॥

oṁ tatsaditi śrīmadbhagavadgītāsūpaniṣatsu brahmavidyāyāṁ yogaśāstre śrīkṛṣṇārjunasaṁvāde bhaktiyogo nāma dvādaśo'dhyāyaḥ

Thus with Oṁ, Tat, Sat the names of the Lord, in the Upaniṣad of the Bhagavadgītā, the knowledge of Brahma, the supreme, the scripture of Yoga and the dialogue between Śrī Kṛṣṇa and Arjuna, this the twelfth discourse is designated: **"The Yoga of Devotion."**

In this chapter, the Lord, having described devotion to God with different means to realize Him, has mentioned the marks of enlightened devotees. Moreover, this chapter begins with devotion and also ends with devotion. In the third, the fourth and the fifth verses, there is description of the Discipline of Knowledge, in order to prove the superiority of devotion to knowledge, by comparing them. So the chapter has been entitled "The Yoga of Devotion."

Words, letters and Uvāca (said) in the Twelfth Chapter—

(1) In this chapter, in **'Atha dvādaśo'dhyāyaḥ'** there are three words, in **'Arjuna Uvāca'** etc., there are four words, in verses, there are two hundred and forty-four words and there are thirteen concluding words. Thus the total number of words, is two hundred and sixty-four.

(2) In this chapter in **'Atha dvādaśo'dhyāyaḥ'** there are seven letters, in **'Arjuna Uvāca'** etc., there are thirteen letters, in verses, there are six hundred and forty letters and there are forty-five concluding letters. Thus the total number of letters,

is seven hundred and five. In this chapter in each verse, there are thirty-two letters.

(3) In this chapter the term **'Uvāca'** (said) has been used twice **'Arjuna Uvāca'**, once and **'Śrībhagavānuvāca'**, once.

Metres Used in the Twelfth Chapter—

Out of the twenty verses of this chapter, in the third quarter of the ninth verse 'bha-gaṇa', being used there is **'bha-vipulā'** metre; in the third quarter of the nineteenth verse 'na-gaṇa' being used there, is **'na-vipulā'** metre; in the first quarter of the twentieth verse 'na-gaṇa' and in the third quarter 'bha-gaṇa', being used there, is **'saṁkīrṇa-vipulā'** metre. The remaining seventeen verses are possessed of the characteristics of right **'pathyāvaktra'**, Anuṣṭup metre.

|| Shri Hari ||

Thirteenth Chapter

INTRODUCTION

At the beginning of the twelfth chapter Arjuna asked Lord Kṛṣṇa, "The devotees who, with their minds constantly fixed in You, adore You, as possessed of form and attributes, and those who adore only the Imperishable, the Unmanifest—which of these two are better?" The Lord, responded, "I consider those the best, who endowed with supreme faith, having fixed their mind on Me, worship Me." Further, He explained, "Those who adore only the Imperishable, the Unmanifest also attain Me, but greater is their difficulty, because they are centred in the body." Then He described the former type of worship, in detail. Now He starts the thirteenth chapter in order to explain the latter kind of worship in detail and in order to remove the main obstacle in this worship in the form of the identification of the body, with the self.

First the Lord starts the topic of discrimination between Kṣetra (Body) and Kṣetrajña (Soul) (Spirit).

श्रीभगवानुवाच

इदं शरीरं कौन्तेय क्षेत्रमित्यभिधीयते।
एतद्यो वेत्ति तं प्राहुः क्षेत्रज्ञ इति तद्विदः ॥ १ ॥

śrībhagavānuvāca

idaṁ śarīraṁ kaunteya kṣetramityabhidhīyate
etadyo vetti taṁ prāhuḥ kṣetrajña iti tadvidaḥ

The Blessed Lord said:

**Body pointed out as 'this' (as distinct from the Self), O

Kaunteya, is termed as Kṣetra, the field and he, who knows it, as such, is called, Kṣetrajña, by the sages. 1

Comment:—

'Idaṁ śarīraṁ Kaunteya Kṣetramityabhidhīyate'—A man addresses all the material objects as 'this beast', 'this bird', 'this tree' etc., (meaning thereby that they are distinctly separate from him), but sometimes he calls this body as 'I' or sometimes as 'My'. The fact is that the body which is said to be 'I' or 'My' is also 'this' i.e., separate from the Self. Gross, subtle and causal—all the three bodies are to be called as 'this' or 'these'.

The gross (physical) body, consists of five elements—earth, water, fire, air and ether. It is made of mother's ovum and father's sperm. It is also called 'Annamayakośa' because it is born of evolute of food and is sustained by it. It is known as 'Idam' (this), because it is known by senses.

The subtle body, consists of five sense-organs, five organs of action, five life-breaths, mind and intellect. It is called 'Prāṇamayakośa' (sheath of life-breath), because of the predominance of life-breath, 'Manomayakośa' because of the predominance of mind and 'Vijñānamayakośa', because of the predominance of intellect. This subtle body, is also called 'Idam', because it is known by the inner sense.

Ignorance, is called the causal body. A man's knowledge can have an access upto intellect only. Whatever is beyond intellect, is not open to knowledge. So, it is called ignorance. This ignorance being the cause of all bodies is called causal body—'Ajñānamevāsya hi mūlakāraṇam' (Adhyātma., Uttara. 5/9). This causal body, is also called personal nature and also 'Ānandamayakośa' (sheath of bliss). In wakeful state, there is predominance of gross body and it is accompanied by subtle body, and causal body as well. In dream there is predominance of subtle body, which is accompanied by causal body. In sound sleep, there is predominance of causal body, and a person is neither, aware of the gross body, which is 'Annamayakośa' nor of subtle body which is 'Prāṇamayakośa', 'Manomayakośa' and 'Vijñānamayakośa' viz., intellect merges in ignorance. Therefore, sound sleep is a state of causal body. In wakefulness and sleep, a man feels pleasure and pain, but in sound sleep, no pain is felt, there is only bliss. Therefore, the causal body is called 'Ānandamayakośa' (sheath of bliss). The causal body is also called 'Idam', because it is known by the self.

All the three bodies, are called 'Śarīra', because they decay every moment. (The root of Śarīra is 'Śṝ hiṁsāyām'.) As the cover (made of leather) of a sword, is called 'sheath', similarly, the three bodies of the embodied soul, in which it resides and which it assumes as its own, are denoted by a sheath. The body is called a field (Kṣetra), because it is subject to constant decay (the root of Kṣetra is Kṣi, which means decay).

As seeds, sown in a field yield the corresponding crop in course of time, even so seeds of actions, which a man performs by having feelings of egoism and attachment, yield their fruit, at an appointed time and thus, one is born, a god, a bird, a beast or an insect, etc., according to his actions, and then dies. So it is called a 'Kṣetra' (field).

The body is different from the self, but a man identifies himself with it, and thus he gets entangled. He himself, being a portion of the Lord is sentient and great, but he considers himself great, by possessing wealth and property etc. If he regards himself, as great because of his wealth and property, it means that wealth and property, are superior to him. Thus he degrades himself by attaching too much importance to these and identifying with them. Therefore Lord advises to view the body etc., as different from the self by this expression.

'Etadyo vetti'—The soul, knows this body, it is the knower of the body, senses, mind, intellect and life-breath. But, sometimes it identifies itself with the body and says 'I am the body', while sometimes it assumes its affinity of 'mineness' with the body and says, "This body is mine."

In the first half of this verse, the body has been mentioned by the term 'Idam', while in the second half, it has been referred to as the term 'Etat', yet the 'Etat' denotes more nearness, than the 'Idam'. Therefore, the term 'Idam' stands for the body, while 'Etat' means 'I'ness in the body.

'Taṁ prāhuḥ kṣetrajña* iti tadvidaḥ'—As in the sixteenth verse of the second chapter, those who know the truth about real and unreal, are called seers, here those who know the reality about Kṣetra (Body) and Kṣetrajña (Soul), are called sages. The soul is called Kṣetrajña, because it assumes its identity or affinity, with the body, otherwise it is Supreme Soul, Paramātmā (Gītā 13/31).

A Vital Fact

There is bondage for a man if he has assumed his affinity of 'I'ness, and 'mineness', with the body. But, actually he is different from the body. So, if he realizes the truth, that the body being 'Idam' (this), is different from him, he is emancipated. This knowledge, about the body that this is different from the self, is significant, not only for strivers, but also for all human beings, because all of them are eligible for attaining salvation, or emancipation. So the Lord, has made this distinction, between the self and the body, just at the beginning of the gospel.

The body, is seen distinct from the self. Therefore, it is called 'Idam'. The physical body, consisting of earth, water, fire, air and ether which is ever-changing is 'Idam' (this). Change in the body, is perceived by five sense-organs—ear, eye, skin, tongue and nose. Changes in sense-organs are perceived, by the mind. The change of mind (its fixity or volatility), is perceived by intellect. The change in the intellect (full understanding, partial

* The term 'Kṣetrajña' being the object of the verb—'Prāhuḥ' should have the second inflexion but because of the word 'Iti' there is first inflexion.

understanding, no understanding), is known by the self, which ever remains unchanged. Thus the self is a real onlooker, which can perceive and know others independently, but can never be known or seen, by anyone.*

Senses can know their objects, but objects cannot know senses (which are subtler than and superior to, objects and their illuminator). Similarly, senses and sense-objects cannot know the mind; the mind, senses and sense-objects cannot know the intellect, while intellect, mind, senses and sense-objects cannot know, the self. The reason is that senses, mind and intellect, are not an independent knower. Each can know objects of grosser form than it, while the self is an independent knower, because it is far subtler than and superior to a body, senses, mind and intellect.

Though, it has been mentioned that sense-organs, mind and intellect are also perceivers (onlookers), yet the fact is, that these can perceive, only when they are accompanied by the self, because the mind and intellect etc., being evolutes of matter (Prakṛti)—(Nature) cannot be independent onlookers. The self, is the real onlooker.

Now a question arises, as to how the soul which is sentient, becomes an onlooker of the insentient intellect etc., because the onlooker can see objects of its own class? The answer is, that the soul identifies itself, with the insentient matter and accepts its own separate entity as 'I am'. This 'I' is neither insentient, nor sentient. By identifying itself with matter, it (man) says, "I am rich or I am learned." By giving high value to embodiment of consciousness (self), it says, "I am Brahma'. Thus this 'I', is the soul seated in Nature, which is the cause of his birth, in good

* First of all the eye is the onlooker while the form is the object to be seen. Then mind is the onlooker while the senses such as eyes are the objects to be seen. Then intellect is the onlooker and the mind is the object to be seen. At last the soul is the onlooker of the dispositions of the intellect but the soul can't be seen by anyone.

and bad wombs (13/21). Thus, the embodied soul, has both the portions, the sentient, as well as the insentient. The sentient portion, attracts him towards the Lord, while the insentient portion because of identity with matter, attracts him towards matter, and thus he becomes an onlooker of intellect, mind, senses, sense-objects and body etc. This assumed identity, or affinity, is the root cause of all evils.

Appendix—The term 'Idam' (kṣetra), comprises infinite universes. In infinite universes, in all the beings 'parā' (the Self) is 'kṣetrajña' and 'aparā' (the world) is 'kṣetra'. A striver (the Self) is the knower of the world and he believes in God. The knower is more pervading. Therefore there are infinite universes, in a fragment of Kṣetrajña—'yena sarvamidaṁ tatam' (Gītā 2/17). A striver should know that he is not kṣetra but he is kṣetrajña, the knower of kṣetra.

The objective world is in a fragment of the seer (onlooker). As all objects are seen with the eye, but it does not mean that the eye can't see more objects. Therefore the eye is bigger than the objective world. We may know innumerable facts with the intellect but it does not mean that intellect has no further power to know more. In it there is further scope to know more, therefore intellect is more extensive than the innumerable facts known with it. The origin, existence and dissolution of Brahmā are also within the knowledge of our intellect. All the bodies—gross, subtle and causal are the entities to be perceived. The whole phenomenal existence is in a fragment of the seer (kṣetrajña).

A man is called 'wealthy' because he possesses wealth, but if he has no wealth, the person remains but he is no more called 'wealthy'. Similarly the self is called 'kṣetrajña' by having affinity with 'kṣetra' but when affinity with 'kṣetra' is renounced, the self remains but it is no more called 'kṣetrajña'. It means that the same pure-consciousness (from the view-point of understanding) is called 'kṣetrajña' by having affinity with 'kṣetra', is called imperishable by having affinity with the perishable, is called—'śarīrī' (embodied soul) by having relation with 'śarīra' (body), is called 'draṣṭā' by being related with 'dṛśya', is called 'sākṣī' (witness) by having connection with 'sākṣya' (object to be witnessed) and is called a doer (kartā) by being connected with instruments (karaṇa). In fact that entity is nameless. That is mere awareness.

Link:—In the next verse, the Lord explains what that Kṣetrajña is.

क्षेत्रज्ञं चापि मां विद्धि सर्वक्षेत्रेषु भारत।
क्षेत्रक्षेत्रज्ञयोर्ज्ञानं यत्तज्ज्ञानं मतं मम॥ २॥

kṣetrajñaṁ cāpi māṁ viddhi sarvakṣetreṣu bhārata
kṣetrakṣetrajñayorjñānaṁ yattajjñānaṁ mataṁ mama

Know Me as the knower of self (Kṣetrajña) in all the bodies (Kṣetras), Arjuna. The Knowledge of Kṣetra and Kṣetrajña, is considered true knowledge, by Me. 2

Comment:—

'Kṣetrajñaṁ cāpi māṁ viddhi sarvakṣetreṣu bhārata'—In all Kṣetras (fields or bodies), 'I am', consists of two parts 'I', and 'am'. In 'I am' 'I' is Kṣetra (which has been mentioned as 'Etat', in the preceding verse), while 'am', the knower of 'I'ness, is Kṣetrajña (which has been called the knower, by the term, 'Yaḥ vetti'. It is called 'am', because of the use of the word 'I'. If it is not used with 'I', it will not remain 'am', but it will remain 'Is'. The reason is that, 'Is' is called 'am' because of its use with 'I'. Therefore, in fact, 'Kṣetrajña' (am), has its affinity with God (Is). So the Lord declares, "Know Me, as Kṣetrajña, in all Kṣetras."

The object, known is called 'Jñeya', and that 'Jñeya' is known, through an organ. There are two types of organs—outer and inner. A man, knows objects with outer organs (ears, eyes etc.,) and knows the outer organs with inner organs (mind, intellect etc.).

The inner organ, has four faculties—mind, intellect, cogitation and ego. Out of these ego is the subtlest. Ego is known by luminous 'Kṣetrajña'. This 'Kṣetrajña', is an embodiment of God.

Here the Lord, uses the term 'Viddhi' (know), to impress upon Arjuna, that he should know that he has his identity with Him, not with the body. As he identifies himself, with the body and regards the body as his own, so should he identify himself with Him (oversoul), and regard Him, as his own. As the self (soul), and the Lord, have been identified here, they have also been identified in the seventeenth verse of the second chapter, when the Lord declares, for the soul, "Know that to be imperishable, by which all the universe is pervaded" and in the fourth verse of the ninth chapter, when He declares for Himself, "All this universe is pervaded by Me." Thus the Lord, identifies the Kṣetrajña (His portion), with Himself. Further in the thirty-fourth verse of this chapter, he explains the identity of bodies and world (the evolutes of prakṛti), with prakṛti (matter). The Lord, exhorts Arjuna to have a disinclination for the body, which is a portion of prakṛti and an inclination instead for Him, because he is His portion.

In fact, a body has its identity with the world, while the soul (Kṣetrajña), has its identity with the Lord. But the man (soul), by assuming his identity with the body, regards himself as separate, from the Lord. So the Lord, wants Arjuna to know the truth, about the body and the soul.

By the term 'Api' (also), the Lord emphasizes the significant fact, that in the scriptures He is described as, all pervasive. No doubt, an all pervasive God, He is. But, in different bodies as different souls also is He. The gist of this comment is, that the individual soul, is not different from, the oversoul. The individual soul is He Himself, and one should realize his identity, with Him.

Man, himself is different from the world, but he has his identity, with the Lord. So, he can know the world in reality, when he observes the world, being detached from it. But, he can have a true knowledge of the Lord, by identifying himself, with Him.

'Kṣetrakṣetrajñayorjñānaṁ yattajjñānaṁ mataṁ mama'—The Kṣetra (body), has its identity with the world, while the Kṣetrajña (Soul) has its identity with the Lord—this is true knowledge. By the expression 'Mataṁ mama', He wants to lay emphasis upon the point that knowledge of several languages, scripts, arts and sciences etc., and even, of the whole world, is not, true knowledge, because this knowledge, entraps a man into the world, though it may be useful. True knowledge, enables him to renounce his affinity with the body, and be free, from the cycle of birth and death. The self, is different from the body and one, with the cosmic soul. This is true knowledge.

Appendix—Kṣetrajña (soul) and Brahma (the Absolute) are one. Having relationship with one 'kṣetra', this soul is called 'kṣetrajña' and when it is free from the relationship of all 'kṣetras', it is 'Brahma'.

'idaṁ śarīraṁ kaunteya kṣetram'—This expression proves that there is identification of the body (kṣetra) with infinite universes (the entire creation) and the expression 'kṣetrajñaṁ cāpi māṁ viddhi' proves that the Self is identified with the endless, boundless and limitless God. Therefore anything which is farthest from us (the Self) is the body and any entity which is nearest is God. It means that the body and the world are one and the Self and God are one (Gītā 15/7). This is knowledge.

The term 'mām' has been used for Brahma which means that Brahma and God are not two but only one—'mayā tatamidaṁ sarvaṁ jagadavyaktamūrtinā' (Gītā 9/4) 'all this universe is pervaded by Me in My unmanifest form'. The Supreme Reality, which pervades endless universes without being tainted, is Brahma and He, Who is the master of endless universes, is God.

Link:—In the preceding verse, the Lord said that knowledge of Kṣetra and Kṣetrajña, is true knowledge. In the next verse, He further explains the distinction, between the two and asks Arjuna to listen to Him.

तत्क्षेत्रं यच्च यादृक्च यद्विकारि यतश्च यत्।
स च यो यत्प्रभावश्च तत्समासेन मे शृणु॥ ३॥

tatkṣetraṁ yacca yādṛkca yadvikāri yataśca yat
sa ca yo yatprabhāvaśca tatsamāsena me śṛṇu

What is that Kṣetra, what is it like, what are its modifications, whence comes out of what, and also, who that Kṣetrajña is, and what its glory is; hear briefly from Me. 3

Comment:—

'Tatkṣetram'—The term 'Tat' (that), denotes, first the topic discussed earlier, and secondly, it denotes distance. What has been termed 'Idam', in the first verse of this chapter, has been termed 'tat', here. Kṣetra does not pervade everywhere nor does it remain forever and it is decaying every moment, even now—it shows its distinctiveness and distance from the self.

'Yacca'—'What is that Kṣetra, is described, in the fifth verse of this chapter.

'Yādṛkca'—'What is it like', has been described in the twenty-sixth and twenty-seventh verses, as emanated and perishable (liable to appear and disappear).

'Yadvikāri'—Though being evolutes of prakṛti, twenty-three elements, have also been called modifications, yet here, the term, refers to modifications, such as desire and aversion etc., which have been enumerated, in the sixth verse and which are born of assumed affinity, between Kṣetra and Kṣetrajña.

'Yataśca yat'—'Whence is what'—This expression, conveys the intention of the Lord, to trace the origin of this Kṣetra, and it has been described, in the second half of the nineteenth verse.

'Sa ca'—'Sa' (that), denotes Kṣetrajña, mentioned in the second half of the first verse, and we are advised to listen to the Lord, regarding that Kṣetrajña.

'Yaḥ'—The term 'Yaḥ' (Who), conveys the intention of the Lord, to reveal its true character, as has been enumerated in the second half of the twentieth verse, and also in the twenty-second verse.

'Yatprabhāvaśca'—The power (glory), of the soul, has been described, in the verses thirty-first to thirty-third of the chapter.

'Tatsamāsena me śṛṇu'—The term, 'Tat', here stands both for Kṣetra and Kṣetrajña. So the Lord asks Arjuna to hear from Him, the description of four points about Kṣetra, and two points about Kṣetrajña.

In the first two verses of this chapter, there is a brief description of Kṣetra and Kṣetrajña, which has been called 'knowledge', by Him. But detailed description starts, from the third verse, and so Lord Kṛṣṇa asks Arjuna, to listen to what, He says on Kṣetra and Kṣetrajña.

In this verse, the Lord orders Arjuna, to hear the four points regarding Kṣetra while only two points—who that Kṣetrajña is and what his powers (glories) are, regarding Kṣetrajña. Now a doubt arises, why the Lord has not discussed the powers (glories), of Kṣetra and why He has not described the nature of Kṣetrajña, its modifications, and origin. The explanation is, how Kṣetra which decays every moment, can have any glory. Worldly people, out of ignorance attach importance to riches. Actually, it has no power or glory. So the Lord has not described it. The Lord has started that the Kṣetrajña, is imperishable, therefore, his nature is also imperishable. So, there is no need to describe his nature, separately, the nature is included in, 'who that Kṣetrajña is'. Kṣetrajña, does not undergo any modifications, the modifications such as desire and aversion etc., appear in him, because of his assumed affinity with Kṣetra. So, there is no question of describing his modifications, as Kṣetrajña is immutable or without modifications. Kṣetrajña is non-dual, beginningless and eternal. As, he has no origin, so no question arises of describing from whom, he has originated.

Appendix—The Lord by the expression 'tatsamāsena me śṛṇu' means to say that a striver need not know more and more. In knowing more, more time will be spent but less spiritual discipline will be practised.

Link:—Where have the Kṣetra and the Kṣetrajña been described in detail? The answer is given, in the next verse.

ऋषिभिर्बहुधा गीतं छन्दोभिर्विविधैः पृथक्।
ब्रह्मसूत्रपदैश्चैव हेतुमद्भिर्विनिश्चितैः॥४॥

ṛṣibhirbahudhā gītaṁ chandobhirvividhaiḥ pṛthak
brahmasūtrapadaiścaiva hetumadbhirviniścitaiḥ

The truth, about the Kṣetra and Kṣetrajña, has been sung by the seers in manifold ways; it has been stated separately in different Vedic chants and also in the conclusive and reasoned texts of the Brahmasūtras, clearly. 4

Comment:—

'Ṛṣibhirbahudhā gītam'—The ancient seers, to whom the Vedic chants have been revealed, and who are authors of scriptures, jurisprudence and other religious texts, have expounded in detail, the true meaning of 'Kṣetra' and 'Kṣetrajña', by the terms, the insentient and the sentient, the unreal and the real, the body and the soul, and the perishable and imperishable, etc.

'Chandobhirvividhaiḥ pṛthak'—The term 'Chandobhiḥ' (Vedic chants), with the adjective 'Vividhaḥ' (Various), refers to the four Vedas—Ṛk, Yajuḥ, Sāma and Atharva, including their Saṁhitā (Hymnical texts), as well as Brāhmaṇa (the theological portion of the Vedas) and Upaniṣads (the portions of the different branches of the Vedas which contain discourses on Divine knowledge), these have described the Kṣetra, and the Kṣetrajña, separately.

'Brahmasūtrapadaiścaiva hetumadbhirviniścitaiḥ'—There is also a reasoned exposition, of the truth about Kṣetra and Kṣetrajña, in the Brahmasūtras.

The Lord, means to say, that He is describing the Kṣetra and Kṣetrajña, in brief. But if anyone wants to go into details, he should consult the above-mentioned sacred scriptures.

Link:—In the third verse, Lord Kṛṣṇa ordered Arjuna to listen to the six points on Kṣetra and Kṣetrajña. Out of those six points, He describes the two points on Kṣetra 'What that Kṣetra is' and 'what its modifications are', in the next two verses.

महाभूतान्यहङ्कारो बुद्धिरव्यक्तमेव च।
इन्द्रियाणि दशैकं च पञ्च चेन्द्रियगोचराः॥५॥

mahābhūtānyahaṅkāro buddhiravyaktameva ca
indriyāṇi daśaikaṁ ca pañca cendriyagocarāḥ

The five great elements, and the ego, the intellect, the Primordial Matter (Nature), the ten senses, the mind and five objects of senses (this is Kṣetra, which includes twenty-four elements). 5

Comment:—

'Avyaktameva ca'—Here, the term 'Avyakta', stands for Primordial Matter, (Nature). Primordial Nature, being the cause of cosmic intelligence and being the evolute of none, is only 'prakṛti'.

'Buddhiḥ'—This term, stands for cosmic intelligence. It is 'prakṛti' as it gives birth to ego, and being an evolute of Primordial Nature, it is 'Vikṛti'. It means, that this cosmic intelligence is, 'Prakṛti-Vikṛti'.

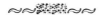

'Ahaṅkāraḥ'—This term, stands for the cosmic ego. Being the cause of five subtle elements, it is 'prakṛti' and being an evolute of intelligence, it is 'Vikṛti'. So it is 'Prakṛti-Vikṛti'.

'Mahābhūtāni'—The five great (subtle) elements, are—ether, air, fire, water and earth. These are of two kinds—mixed and unmixed. If each of the elements is divided into five parts, and then one part of each is mixed, that is a mixed element.* If they remain separate, they are called unmixed. Here, the five elements, are unmixed. The five elements, are also known as, subtle elements (sūkṣma mahābhūta) and subtle forms of matter (tanmātrās).

These elements, being the cause of ten senses, one mind and five objects of senses, are called prakṛti while being the evolute of ego they are Vikṛti. Thus these elements are 'Prakṛti-Vikṛti'.

'Indriyāṇi daśa'—The tongue, hands, feet, the generative organ and the organ of defecation—these are, the five organs of action; while senses of hearing, touch, sight, taste and smell, constitute the five senses of perception. Being the effect of five subtle elements but being the cause of none, these are 'Vikṛti.'

'Ekaṁ ca'—The term 'Ekam', stands for the mind. It, being the evolute of five elements and being cause of none, is 'Vikṛti'.

'Pañca cendriyagocarāḥ'—Sound, touch, colour, taste and smell, the objects of five senses of perception being the effects, not the cause, are 'Vikṛti'.

Thus, the five subtle elements, ego and intellect—these seven are Prakṛti-Vikṛti, the Primordial Matter, is Prakṛti and ten senses, mind, and five objects of senses—these sixteen are Vikṛtis. These twenty-four elements, constitute the Kṣetra. A meagre portion of this Kṣetra, is this human body, which has been termed as 'Idaṁ śarīram' (this body), in the first and 'tat-kṣetram', (that Kṣetra), in the third verse.

---

* Ether is divided into two parts, out of the two parts one part remains as ether while the other half is divided into four parts and each of the parts is given to air, fire, water and earth. Other four elements are also divided in the

इच्छा द्वेषः सुखं दुःखं सङ्घातश्चेतना धृतिः।
एतत्क्षेत्रं समासेन सविकारमुदाहृतम्॥ ६॥

icchā dveṣaḥ sukhaṁ duḥkhaṁ saṅghātaścetanā dhṛtiḥ
etatkṣetraṁ samāsena savikāramudāhṛtam

Desire and aversion, pleasure and pain, the body and consciousness (life-breath), firmness: these comprise the Kṣetra, with its modifications, described briefly. 6

Comment:—

'Icchā'—This term, denotes a passionate longing, for the acquisition of an object, a person or circumstances etc. First of all, the Lord mentions the evil in the form of desire, because this longing (desire) is the root of all evils, pains and sins.

'Dveṣaḥ'—Unfulfilment of desire and hurt to one's pride leads to anger. A subtle form of anger, is aversion. Thus the term 'aversion' includes, jealousy and anger etc.

'Sukham'—A feeling of pleasure aroused in the mind, by the appearance of agreeable circumstances, is called 'Sukha'.

'Duḥkham'—Agony, caused in the mind, by disagreeable circumstances, is 'Duḥkha'.

'Saṅghātaḥ'—This term, stands for a physical body consisting of twenty-four elements. After being born, the seeming existence of this body, is a modification and its constant change, is also a modification (Vikāra).

'Cetanā'—The term, refers to life-breath. It undergoes modifications. It remains calm in sattva mode but is disturbed when a man is overwhelmed with grief, worry and fear etc. This life-breath ever decays. Therefore, it is a modification.

Common people, call the creature having life-breath, as

---

same way. Half of each remains the same and the remaining half is divided into four parts and each of the parts is given to the other four elements. Thus the mixture of all the elements is known as the mixed element.

'Cetana' and without life-breath as 'Acetana'. Therefore, life-breath, is called 'Cetanā'.

'Dhṛtiḥ'—'Dhṛti', denotes firmness. It undergoes modifications. A man deviates from firmness, in unfavourable circumstances. Sometimes, he is firm, while other times he deviates from firmness. Sometimes he is more firm, sometimes less. Sometimes he holds virtues, sometimes vice. Being subject to change, it is modification of Kṣetra.

[This firmness of three modes viz., sāttvika, rājasika and tāmasika, has been described, from the thirty-third verse to the thirty-fifth verse of the eighteenth chapter. Sāttvika firmness, is very necessary, for spiritual progress.]

'Etatkṣetraṁ samāsena savikāramudāhṛtam'—As, in the first verse of this chapter, the expression 'Idaṁ śarīram', was used to show a distinction, between the self and the body, similarly the term 'Etat', has been used to prove the distinction of the seer (self), from the seen (Kṣetra, and its modification).

In the fifth verse, the Lord described the Kṣetra, in the form of the world, while in this verse, He describes, it as a body with its modifications. Actually, the world and the body are one, and the same, as these belong to the same class. As, in the second verse of this chapter, the Lord described His identity with Kṣetrajña (soul), here he describes the identity of the body along with its modifications, with the world. In the twenty-first verse, instead of saying that the spirit is seated in the individual body, He declares, the spirit to be seated in cosmic Matter. This proves, that if a man assumes his identity with an individual body, he, automatically gets connected with cosmic matter, as the micro and macro parts are, one and the same. As a matter of fact, there is no micro (individual), only macro (cosmos), is there. The conception of individuality is a mistake. It means, that an individual body, and cosmic Matter, are the same. As waves of an ocean, are not different from the ocean, so is the individual body, not different from the world. Therefore, the notion that individuality, is separate from cosmos, is a mistake.

An Important Fact

When the Kṣetrajña (spirit), out of ignorance, assumes its affinity with Kṣetra (body), evils such as desire and aversion etc., are born, in the Kṣetra. In fact, Kṣetrajña by nature, is totally free, from all kinds of evils and modifications. It is affinity, between the two which is responsible, for all evils and modifications. If a striver, realizes that he is different from the body, and he has his identity with the Lord, he becomes free, from all evils and modifications.

On Self-realization, desire and aversion, are totally annihilated. Such a realized soul, is conscious of pleasure and pain viz., or favourable and unfavourable circumstances. But these do not cause any modification in mind viz., he does not feel, happy and sad.*

The body of a liberated soul, becomes supremely holy and pious, and he has no affinity of 'I' and 'mine', with the body. His body remains alive, according to his destiny. Till the body lives, life-breath also lives. On working hard, life-breath becomes turbulent, otherwise, it is calm. The Sāttvika, firmness which subsisted during practice, remains even, on Self-realization. But on realization, the liberated soul has no affinity with modifications—'Cetanā' and 'Dhṛti', as he has no identity with the inner sense.

It means that four evils—desire, aversion, pleasure and pain—which were due to his identification with the body, are totally destroyed, on Self-realization. Three modifications—'Saṅghāta', 'Cetanā' and 'Dhṛti', remain in his life, but they do not affect him.

* Knowledge of anything is not defective (as while having meal a man may know the taste of a dish) but attachment or aversion to it is defective.

Appendix—When the Self has affinity with kṣetra, evils such as desire, aversion; pleasure, pain etc., arise in kṣetrajña—'puruṣaḥ sukhaduḥkhānāṁ bhoktṛtve heturucyate' (13/20). All evils such as desire and aversion etc., abide in the ego (knot between the sentient and the insentient). In ego also these evils abide in the insentient fragment only.

Here the Lord has called the body consisting of twenty-four elements and its seven modifications as 'etat' (this)—'etatkṣetram'. It means that the Self is not identified with kṣetra but is totally different. The three bodies—gross, subtle and causal being within the term 'etat' are not the Self. Here a point needs special attention that when even 'mahattattva' (cosmic intelligence) and 'mūla prakṛti' (Primordial Matter) have been mentioned as 'etat', then 'ego' is certainly included in 'etat', there is no doubt about it. Nearer than 'ego' to the self is 'Cosmic intelligence' and nearer than 'Cosmic intelligence' is 'Prakṛti', that Prakṛti is also included in 'etatkṣetram'. It means that 'ego' is not 'the Self' at all. The man, who discerns the Self and ego (kṣetra) as separate entities, is not born again and he realizes God (Gītā 13/23).

Link:—When a man identifies himself with the body, evils such as desire and aversion, are born and they affect him. Therefore, the Lord, in the next five verses under the name of 'Jñāna' (Wisdom), enumerates twenty virtues to do away, with the assumed identity.

अमानित्वमदम्भित्वमहिंसा क्षान्तिरार्जवम्।
आचार्योपासनं शौचं स्थैर्यमात्मविनिग्रहः ॥ ७ ॥

amānitvamadambhitvamahiṁsā kṣāntirārjavam
ācāryopāsanaṁ śaucaṁ sthairyamātmavinigrahaḥ

Absence of pride, freedom from hypocrisy, non-violence,

forgiveness, straightforwardness, service to the teacher, purity of body and mind, steadfastness, and self-control. 7

Comment:—

'Amānitvam'—Absence of pride is known as 'Amānitva'. It is the superiority complex, because of one's possessions, of arts, virtues, wealth, ability etc., that engender, conceit or pride. One possesses a superiority complex, because of his identity, with the body. It means, that he attaches too much importance to matter and so he cannot, know the truth. The less proud a man is, the lesser importance he attaches to matter. The less importance he attaches to matter, the lesser proud, he is, and the more speedily, he follows spiritual discipline.

Remedy:—A striver, should keep company with devout devotees, saints and liberated souls. Their company frees him, not only from pride, but also from many other evils.

Saints honour others, but themselves remain free, from the desire of honour (Mānasa 7/38/2). Similarly, a striver in order to be free from pride, should have the habit to offer honour, respect and praise etc., to others. He can form this habit, only when he regards others superior, to him in any sphere. It is a rule, that every person has some speciality. This may be due to his caste (order of life), stage of life, learning, intelligence and rank etc. Therefore, a striver should offer respect, to others keeping their uniqueness, in mind. When, it becomes his habit, his desire to covet honour is gradually wiped out. He must be cautious, that while offering honour to others, he should not expect honour, in return.

An Important Fact

Out of all the divine traits, the Lord has mentioned, fearlessness as the first one (16/1) and absence of pride (16/3) the last, in the Discipline of Devotion. But in the Discipline of Knowledge, He has given priority to absence of pride (13/7) and referred to fearlessness, at the end—'Perception of God' (the object of true knowledge) (13/11). It means, that a devotee, like Prahlāda beholds the Lord pervading everywhere, and so becomes, fearless at the beginning. He offers regard, honour and praise etc., to others, without having any pride. At last, his assumed affinity with the body perishes, and he becomes totally free, from pride. But a striver, following the Discipline of Knowledge, does not assume his identity with the body, at the very beginning (13/1) and so, has no pride. At last he realizes the self as pervading everywhere and becomes fearless.

'Adambhitvam'—Hypocrisy, means putting on a pretence or false appearance, of virtue or goodness, for the sake of honour, prestige and worship etc. If a sinner, in the company of virtuous persons, exhibits himself as a devotee, a righteous or a charitable person, he is a hypocrite. Similarly, if a striver, is engaged in adoration and prayer etc., in loneliness, and is feeling drowsy, but he becomes alert, as soon as he hears the footsteps of someone coming, it is also a subtle hypocrisy. There is also, hypocrisy when a pious and virtuous person, in the company of bad persons renounces his piety and virtues, and poses himself as others are, as can be seen in clubs and hotels etc. Absence, of this sort of hypocrisy, is 'Adambhitva.'

Remedy:—A striver, should fix the goal of human life, that he has to realize God, and that he should ever be engaged in adoration, and other spiritual practices, without caring for, what the people think of him and say, about him.

'Ahiṁsā'—Non-violence, means total absence of violence. It consists in inflicting no pain, on anyone, through a body, speech or mind. Pain or injury, can be inflicted in three ways—by one's own self, getting it inflicted by others, and by abetting it. Violence is inflicted, either out of anger, greed or delusion. Thus, violence is of nine kinds. Again, the nine kinds can be divided according to quantity, in three parts—a little, more, much more. Thus, the types of violence, come to twenty-seven. These twenty-seven kinds, of violence, can be inflicted through body, speech and mind. In this way, violence can be inflicted, in eighty-one ways.

Non-violence, can also be divided into four categories, according to place, occasion, time and person. A man may observe non-violence, in places of pilgrimage and temples, on occasions, such as on festivals, on days, such as a birthday and death anniversary etc., and to a person etc., such as cows, deer, preceptor, parents and children etc.

Total abstention from violence, or inflicting pain on any creature, at any place and time through speech, body or mind, is called universal non-violence.

Remedy:—A striver, should regard comfort, welfare and service of others, as his own, because the self, in every person is the same. By arousing this sort of discrimination, how can a person, inflict pain or injury on anyone? A feeling of non-violence, automatically develops, in him.

'Kṣāntiḥ'—'Kṣānti', means forbearance i.e., forgiveness. He, who has developed this feeling, never thinks of punishing an evil-doer, either himself or having him punished by others, in anyway. Even in having power, he does not nurse any thought of revenge, upon him.

Remedy:—(1) Forgiveness in the self, is self-evident, because the self is free, from all modifications and evils. So a striver, should have a firm belief, that he remains unaffected, by evil and wrong done to him. This belief, naturally, develops forgiveness.

(2) He beholds the self, present in all beings (6/29). If while having a meal the tongue is chewed, a person is not angry with his teeth, because the tongue and the teeth, both are his own parts, similarly, the same self, abides in all the beings. So a person, possessing the virtue of forgiveness, never entertains,

the idea of punishing a wrong-doer.

'Ārjavam'—It means, straightforwardness of body, mind and speech. No sense, of ornamentation, in the body. Simplicity in living, natural straightforwardness, in behaviour, absence of arrogance—this is straightforwardness of body. Absence of crookedness, deceit, envy and aversion etc., and serenity, benevolence and compassion, these include straightforwardness of mind. Absence of taunt, censure, malicious gossip and pinching, harsh language and use of simple, true, aggreable and wholesome language—this is straightforwardness of speech.

Remedy:—A man by assuming his affinity, with the gross, subtle and causal bodies, regards himself superior to others. So he does not possess straightforwardness, of mind, speech and behaviour. If he renounces this assumed affinity with the body, and has an eye on the self, he becomes straightforward.

Ācāryopāsanam'—A teacher, who imparts knowledge and teaches good precepts, is called an Ācārya. If anyone serves, such a type of teacher, he is benefitted. But here the term 'Ācārya', denotes a liberated soul. Bowing to him, paying reverence to him, and serving him with body, mind and speech, in order to make him happy—this is service, to him. But real service, consists in translating his principles into practice. The service rendered to the body, of a conscious man is regarded as service to him. But, to render service to the body of a realized soul, is not service, in its real sense. It is only partial service.

In the Discipline of Devotion, there is not so much need of a preceptor, as in the Discipline of Knowledge, because a devotee, following the path of devotion, entirely depends on God. So the Lord by his grace, provides gain and security (9/22), removes all difficulties and obstacles (18/58) and enables him to behold the Divine presence, within himself (10/11). But, in the Discipline of Knowledge a striver depends on his spiritual practice, which has some defects, such as follows—

(1) A striver, having received knowledge through scriptures and saints, assumes that he is different from the body and so he attains peace, and he thinks, that he has realized the self. But, when he comes across favourable and unfavourable circumstances, he feels pleasure and pain. It means, that he has not realized, the self.

(2) When anyone calls him by his name, he thinks, he is that person. It means, that he is still established, in the body.

(3) An emancipated soul, has natural discrimination between the sentient and the insentient. But a striver, discriminates the real from the unreal, during wakefulness and he forgets it, during sleep. He gets hold of this discrimination again, while he awakes from sleep.

(4) When a striver, serves saints and preceptors and takes an active part in good company, he thinks, that he should be considered superior, to others by the saints and preceptors.

Thus a striver, regards his imperfect knowledge, as perfect. So the Lord by the term 'Ācāryopāsanam', wants to emphasize the fact, that a striver, following the path of knowledge, should practise spiritual discipline, under the guidance of a teacher. In the thirty-fourth verse of the fourth chapter also, Lord Kṛṣṇa said to Arjuna, "Go to the liberated souls, prostrate yourself at their feet, render them all forms of service, and question them with a guileless heart, then they will unfold knowledge to you." In this way, wise men remove the defects of a striver, which he himself does not know, easily, and enable him to realize, the Lord.

A striver, should go to such a preceptor, who according to him is endowed with, the following traits.

1. He should be a liberated soul.

2. He should know, the Disciplines of Action, Knowledge, and Devotion etc., in the right perspective.

3. His company and words, remove doubts even without being referred.

4. His company, gives solace and peace.

5. His relationship with a striver, is only for his welfare, without having any selfish motive.

6. He does not expect anything, of the striver, in the least.

7. All his activities are directed, towards the welfare of strivers.

8. His company, enhances the spiritual inclination, of strivers.

9. His company, sight, discourses and remembrance, remove wicked traits and develop divine traits, in the strivers.

10. He is uncommon, and singular and has, no equal.

So a striver, should serve and obey such a preceptor, with faith and reverence. He should live with a preceptor, only for his emancipation. He should not worry about, what his preceptor does and what he does not do, and why he does so, and so on. He should depend on his preceptor, and act according to his behest, and hints. If such a preceptor, does not accept a striver as his disciple formally, the striver should not insist on it. He should accept him, as his preceptor by heart.

If such a liberated soul, is not available, a striver should take refuge, in the Lord. By doing so, either the Lord Himself guides him as a preceptor, or makes a preceptor available.

Remedy:—A striver who aims at God-realization, should serve the saints from his heart, because their grace, bears quick fruit. He should, have this conviction and act accordingly.

An Important Fact

A disciple, should serve his teacher. If a disciple performs his duty, scrupulously, his affinity with the world is renounced, and he gets identified with, the truth in teacher viz., virtues of his teacher develop in him. Having renounced affinity, with the world, he attains salvation and having identified himself with the truth in teacher, he develops devotion. With this identification he does not remain a disciple, and he is not controlled by scriptures etc. But if a disciple, does not perform his duty, scrupulously, he will remain only a nominal disciple, not a real one. Without remaining a real disciple, his affinity with the world will not be renounced, and he will not get identified, with the teacher. Thus, he will remain a slave, to the world.

If a disciple expects of his teacher to lead him alone to salvation—'It is also a bondage, for the disciple. A disciple, should surrender himself to his preceptor, without having any will of his own. He should become a yesman, to his preceptor's will.

It is the foremost duty of a preceptor, to emancipate his disciple. If he does not perform his duty, he is a nominal preceptor. If he has a desire to receive anything (money, respect, praise etc.,) from his disciple, he is not a teacher but he is a slave, to the disciple.

'Śaucam'—'Śaucam', means external and internal purity. The body, is purified by cleaning it with water and earth etc., while the mind is purified by having divine traits, such as mercy, forgiveness and generosity etc.

Remedy:—The body, is made of filthy materials. It may be cleaned again and again, yet it contains filth. By knowing the fact, that it is full of filth, a striver becomes indifferent and detached to it.

Earning money by truthful and honest means, according to one's caste and stage of life, without laying claim to others' property, etc., and purity of diet, purify the mind.

'Sthairyam'—It denotes steadfastness or firmness. A striver, should be firm, in his aim of God-realization, in the face of difficulties, dangers and obstacles.

Remedy:—(1) People attached to worldly pleasures and prosperity, cannot have their determinate intellect, concentrated on God (Gītā 2/44). So a striver, should renounce this attachment, to worldly pleasures and prosperity.

(2) A striver, should remain firm, in whatever he decides, even on insignificant tasks. By doing so, he forms a habit of being firm, in other spheres also.

(3) The more faith a striver has, in saints and scriptures, the more firm, he is.

'Ātmavinigrahaḥ'—Here, the term 'Ātmā', stands for the mind, and control over the mind is 'Ātmavinigrahaḥ'. Some thoughts, come to the mind and these disappear quickly. They are called 'Sphuraṇās', (fleeting thoughts). But, when the mind is attached, to that thought, it becomes a 'Saṅkalpa' (pursuit or projection of the mind). 'Sphuraṇā', is just like an image in the mirror, the mirror does not catch the image, while 'Saṅkalpa' is like a film in a camera, which catches the image. A man, is attached to the thoughts, by having, attachment and aversion, for them. Fleeting thoughts, are destroyed by practice, while pursuits of the mind, are destroyed by dispassion. Thus the mind, can be controlled by practice, and dispassion (Gītā 6/35).

Remedy:—(Refer to the explanation of the twenty-sixth verse of the sixth chapter, for controlling the mind.)

Appendix—The Lord enumerates the virtues under the name of 'Jñāna' (wisdom) in order to do away with the assumed identity of the Self with the kṣetra. These virtues are helpful in renouncing this identification.

इन्द्रियार्थेषु वैराग्यमनहङ्कार एव च।
जन्ममृत्युजराव्याधिदुःखदोषानुदर्शनम् ॥८॥

indriyārtheṣu vairāgyamanahaṅkāra eva ca
janmamṛtyujarāvyādhiduḥkhadoṣānudarśanam

Dispassion towards the objects of senses and absence of egoism; constant perception of evil and misery in birth, death, old age and disease. 8

Comment:—

'Indriyārtheṣu vairāgyam'—It denotes, absence of attraction and attachment, for all the objects of senses, of this world as well as the next, in the form of sound, touch etc., which are enjoyed by senses. For the maintenance of his life, a striver should not have attachment and passion etc., with sense-objects, even during physical contact with them.

Remedy:—(1) Attachment to the objects of senses, develops a sense of importance for them, which leads to sins and deprives a striver, of God-realization. Only, by effacing attachment, we can get established in God. This conviction, develops detachment from sense-objects.

(2) Even great kings and emperors, could not enjoy sensual pleasures forever. Their bodies, decayed and they died. This thought, develops dispassion.

(3) Sensual enjoyments, lead persons to grief and worry, only. Sense enjoyment does not bless, one with any eminence and singularity. This thought also develops dispassion.

'Anahaṅkāra eva ca'—Everyone, feels, 'I am'. Identification of 'I', with that, body, gives birth to, 'I am body'. The feeling 'I am body', gives birth to, egoism. This identification of the self with body, is the cause of a man's birth, in good and evil bodies (Gītā 13/21). Actually, this egoism has no existence of its own, but it emanates from the identification of the self, with a body. But when a striver, distinguishes the sentient from the insentient, his egoism disappears. Thus strivers, can be free from this feeling of egoism. An affinity with worldly objects and a feeling of superiority, because of one's renunciation, dispassion etc., give birth to pride. Here, the term 'Anahaṅkāra', denotes absence of pride and egoism both.

When a man awakes from his sleep, he first of all knows, 'I am'. Then he believes that he belongs to a particular caste or creed etc. This is a routine process to realize the ego. Similarly there is an order for freeing oneself from a feeling of egoism. First, a striver, renounces the pride of wealth etc., which he has, because of assumed affinity with, the gross body. Secondly, his pride of doership, because of affinity with organs of actions, is destroyed. Then the pride of knowership, because of the predominance of intellect, perishes. At last, his egoism disappears. Then, only the Self, which is Truth, Knowledge, and Bliss, remains.

Remedy:—(1) Superiority complex, leads to pride. So a striver, instead of finding fault with others, should find fault with himself, and try to get rid of his faults.

(2) A striver, should realize that the same soul pervades, all the bodies. So, he is in no way different, from other persons. Through ignorance, taking the all-pervading soul, as confined to the body only, he becomes one, with the body. As, by having affinity with time, intellect and speech, he regards himself, 'I am here', 'I am wise', 'I am a preacher'. To deny this affinity, is a remedy, to be free from egoism.

(3) In the scriptures, the Lord has been referred to as Truth, Consciousness (Knowledge) and Bliss. These are three names of the Lord. They do not denote three different entities. Keeping the goal in view, denoted even by anyone of these three names, a striver, can be free from all worldly thoughts. Being free from thoughts, he can realize his automatic identity, with the Absolute and be free from, egoism.

(a) **'Sat' (Truth or Reality):**—The Lord, had been, always has been, and remains, forever. He, is neither born, nor destroyed. He, neither increases nor decreases. He always, remains the same. Reflecting this way through intellect, one can become free from worldly thoughts. Thus, being free from thoughts, a striver, snaps his ties with, intellect and realizes, his axiomatic identity, with the self. On such realization, pride goes away.

(b) **'Cit':**—As 'I' is an illuminator and a body, senses etc., are illumined, so is Knowledge Absolute the illuminator and I, thou, this and that, are illumined.* These are quite distinct, from an illuminator. So 'I', 'thou', 'this', and 'that', are quite distinct from the oversoul. In this way, getting established in that Knowledge Absolute, the self is realized and egoism, is destroyed.

(c) **'Ānanda' (Bliss)**—Intellect, can know the Matter (insentient world) only. It has no access beyond it. In order to, know the divine, it is indispensable to renounce, affinity with intellect. Establishment of the self, in the Supreme, is a means to renounce this affinity. Then, only the supreme in the form of 'Bliss' remains, Who is also 'Knowledge' and 'Truth'. Thus a striver, is freed from egoism.

'Janmamṛtyujarāvyādhiduḥkhadoṣānudarśanam'—As a pitcher, is baked in a potter's kiln, a helpless child, burns within the womb of a mother. During the process of birth, it has to bear unbearable pain, while coming out of the womb. A striver, should constantly think of the trouble of pain on birth.

No one, can escape death, it is inevitable for one, who is born. When a man under compulsion, has to leave a body, residence and wealth etc., which he regarded as his own, throughout life, but he never hopes to regain, then due to attachment, he undergoes a lot of suffering. Moreover, when a man dies, he suffers as much pain, as he suffers when thousands of scorpions sting him, all at once. Thus, a striver, should perceive evil, in death.

In old age, the body and the limbs, become feeble, the man cannot move easily. He cannot digest food. The members of his family insult him. He is reduced, to a helpless state. He is very much sad by memories of his glorious past. Thus, the problems of old age, should be perceived.

---

* A businessman heard that in one firm there was profit while in the other one there was loss. Thus profit and loss are different but there is no difference in the knowledge about the two, knowledge is the same. Similarly 'I', 'You', 'This' and 'That' are different but their illuminator (knowledge) is the same. In that light of knowledge all the actions in 'I', 'You', 'This' and 'That' are performed.

This body, is an abode of various diseases, which are very painful. So, there should be constant perception of troubles caused by diseases.

By perceiving evil in them, he should think, that they are a result of his past sins and evil actions. By thinking so, he develops dispassion for the perishable things, objects and bodies etc. It means, that perception of evil in life, death, old age and disease etc., leads to dispassion, because attachment to sensual pleasures i.e., contact with these Guṇas (Qualities or modes) is responsible for birth of a soul, in good and evil wombs ((Gītā 13/21) and rebirth, is an abode of pain (Gītā 8/15).

Affinity with Matter (Nature), and attaching importance to it, is the root of all evils. The soul being a portion of the Lord, is pure by nature while evils are impure. So these belong to two different classes. Thus, an embodied soul, is oppressed by evils which are his own creation. It is also declared, in the Mānasa, that the soul is sentient, pure and naturally a lot of bliss (Mānasa 7/117/1). So evils and pains, are not pleasing. But, by identifying itself, with a body, it always suffers. Therefore, the Lord emphasizes, to wipe out the assumption of identity of the self, with a body, by viewing evil in birth and death etc.

Appendix—One is 'bhoga' of sufferings, while the other is the effect of sufferings. To feel sad in sufferings and to desire pleasure is 'bhoga' of sufferings and by finding out the cause of suffering, to wipe it (the cause) out, is the influence of sorrow. Here the effect of sorrow has been expressed by the expression 'duḥkhadoṣānudarśanam'.

By being sad in suffering, discrimination disappears. But because of the influence of suffering, discrimination does not disappear but by applying his discrimination, a man discovers the reason for suffering and then wipes out the cause of suffering. Desire for pleasure is the root of all sufferings. When the root is weeded out, its effect is naturally wiped out; therefore when the desire for pleasure is wiped out, all sorrows get destroyed.

असक्तिरनभिष्वङ्गः पुत्रदारगृहादिषु।
नित्यं च समचित्तत्वमिष्टानिष्टोपपत्तिषु॥ ९॥

asaktiranabhiṣvaṅgaḥ putradāragṛhādiṣu
nityaṁ ca samacittatvamiṣṭāniṣṭopapattiṣu

Non-attachment, non-identification of the self with son, wife, home and the like and equanimity in all desirable and undesirable, happenings. 9

Comment:—

'Asakti'—Attachment to perishable worldly objects, persons and circumstances etc., is 'Sakti'. Absence of that attachment is called, 'Asakti'. A man, is attached to them, to seek pleasure, from them. He feels pleasure, while there is contact. But real joy, reveals itself, with termination of the contact (Gītā 6/23). So, it is indispensable to renounce, attachment for the mundane for a striver.

Remedy:—Pleasure, which is derived from the contact of senses, with their objects, seems like nectar at first, but is like poison in the end (Gītā 18/38). One, who enjoys pleasures born of contact, has to bear suffering. So, by thinking of their result a striver, is not attached to them.

'Anabhiṣvaṅgaḥ putradāragṛhādiṣu'—Close association with one's sons, wife, house, wealth and cattle etc., is really assumed. A man, is so much identified* with them, that he regards their sickness and death etc., as his own. So, a man should not identify himself, with them.

Remedy:—Render service, to your kith and kin, without expecting any service or reward in return. If they take pleasure, in

* Proper dealings and rendering of service to sons and wife is not identification, it is rather non-attachment which leads to immortality.

serving you, accept their service, without deriving any pleasure, out of it.

'Nityaṁ ca samacittatvamiṣṭāniṣṭopapattiṣu'—Absence of joy and attachment, in the favourable circumstances and absence of grief and aversion, in unfavourable circumstances, is equanimity. In that state a striver, remains unaffected by all desirable and undesirable, happenings. In 2/48, the Lord has called it 'Equanimity' (Evenness of mind), in success and failure.

Remedy:—A striver, should utilize desirable happenings and circumstances, to render service to the beings of the world, without any selfish motive. Similarly, in undesirable happenings and circumstances, he should renounce the desire to receive favourable circumstances. He, should feel, neither happy in agreeable circumstances, nor sad, in disagreeable ones.

He should have a firm belief, that the desirable, as well as the undesirable circumstances, are a means to realize God. So, he has to transcend these and thus a striver attains equanimity.

मयि चानन्ययोगेन भक्तिरव्यभिचारिणी।
विविक्तदेशसेवित्वमरतिर्जनसंसदि ॥१०॥

mayi cānanyayogena bhaktiravyabhicāriṇī
viviktadeśasevitvamaratirjanasaṁsadi

Unswerving devotion to Me with sole dependence on God, inclination for solitary places, and dislike for the worldly people. 10

Comment:—

'Mayi cānanyayogena bhaktiravyabhicāriṇī'—Having dependence, on the world a striver's body-consciousness, remains intact. This 'ego' is the main hurdle to Self-realization. To remove this hurdle the Lord, declares that exclusive devotion is a means to Self-realization. In simple words it means, that through devotion, ego is easily wiped out. Total dependence only on Him and His grace, is called wholehearted discipline.

Having consummate and unadulterated love for God, is unswerving devotion to Him. It means, that He is both the means and the end. This is unswerving devotion with wholehearted, devotion.

A striver, following the discipline of Knowledge also, having an aptitude for devotion, by depending on the Lord, attains, Self-realization. The Lord, mentioned this unswerving devotion, as a means to transcend the three Guṇas—(qualities) (Gītā 14/26).

Doubt:—Here, the Lord has mentioned devotion, as a means for Self-realization, while in the fifty-fourth and fifty-fifth verses of the eighteenth chapter, He refers to knowledge, as a means to attain devotion, why?

Answer:—Devotion, is of two kinds—as a means, and as an end; so is knowledge of two kinds—as a means and as an end. Both, in the end, are one and the same, like the two faces of the same coin. In the end, both (as means) are methods to attain devotion and knowledge, (as an end). Therefore, both the statements—devotion, as the means for Self-realization and knowledge, as the means to attain devotion, are justified. Therefore, a striver, according to his past and present propensities, should follow anyone of the Discipline of Action, Knowledge or Devotion. He, should be very cautious, that His only aim is God-realization, not the world. With this aim, he attains God, with his own discipline.

Doubt:—Why has the Lord mentioned His devotion, as a virtue, which makes for Jñāna (wisdom)? Does a striver, following the Discipline of Knowledge, practise devotion?

Answer:—Strivers following the Discipline of Knowledge, are of two kinds—those having predominance of feelings (devotion), and others having predominance of knowledge.

(1) The striver who has predominance of devotion, wants to

know the reality, by depending upon God (7/6; 13/18). The terms 'Mām' (Me) and 'Mama' (My), in the second verse; Me (from Me) in the third verse; 'Mayi' (to Me) in this tenth verse and 'Madbhaktaḥ' (My devotee) and 'Madbhāvāya' (to My being) in the eighteenth verse of this chapter, denote that upto the eighteenth verse, it is related to a striver, in whom devotion predominates. But, from the nineteenth to the thirty-fourth verses, no such word as 'I', 'Me', or 'My' etc., has been used, which indicates that, it describes a striver, in whom knowledge predominates. So here, devotion is a means for Self-realization.

Further, as butter or milk, with other ingredients of sāttvika food, or alone, promotes strength and health, similarly devotion to the Lord, with the Discipline of Knowledge, or alone, makes a striver eligible for God-realization and by itself also induces him, to transcend the three modes (Gītā 14/26). According to Śrī Patañjali, devotion is one of the eight yogic practices, and an independent means for God-realization. Thus devotion, occupies an important place, even in the Discipline of Knowledge.

(2) A striver, having predominance of knowledge, is one, who endowed with discrimination and dispassion, distinguishing the real (spirit) from the unreal (Matter), wants to know the truth (Gītā 13/19—34).

Today, because of excessive attachment to sensual pleasures, a striver, following the Discipline of Knowledge is rare, indeed. So the Discipline of Devotion, is very useful for them. Thus, here the description of devotion is appropriate and reasonable.

Remedy:—By having affinity, with the Lord and depending on Him, utterance of His name, loud chanting, meditation and adoration etc., are easy means, to develop devotion, for Him.

'Viviktadeśasevitvam'—A lonely and holy place, free from hustle, bustle and disturbances, is suitable for meditation, adoration, study of sacred books and other spiritual practices. So, it is proper for a striver, to carry on his spiritual practice for

God-realization, in a lonely woodland or temple etc. But if he is unable to find such a lonely and holy place, he need not lose heart, in the least. He should realize, that he (Spirit) is different from the body (Matter). Even in a lonely woodland or temple or the bank of the Ganges, if he identifies himself with body, it means that he identifies himself with the world and, so there is not much use of a lonely place.

Real loneliness is that state in which the striver beholds nothing else, but the Lord or the self, and he realizes that he has no identity with the body, mind and senses etc., because these are evolutes of matter, while the self (Spirit), transcends matter (nature).

'Aratirjanasaṁsadi'—A striver, should have no inclination for worldly affairs. If anybody wants to discuss with us spiritual subjects, the desire to meet him is not, 'Aratirjanasaṁsadi'. The company of men, attached to worldly enjoyment, is an obstacle to spiritual life, while the company of saints, exalted souls and strivers for God-realization, is helpful to spiritual practice. So, the former, not the latter, should be disliked and discarded, the latter is indispensable for spiritual progress. It has been said—a man should not keep company with attachment, but if detachment is not possible, he should keep company of noble persons, because, their company, is a good remedy for attachment. By their company, a striver develops detachment.

अध्यात्मज्ञाननित्यत्वं तत्त्वज्ञानार्थदर्शनम्।
एतज्ज्ञानमिति प्रोक्तमज्ञानं यदतोऽन्यथा॥ ११॥

adhyātmajñānanityatvaṁ tattvajñānārthadarśanam
etajjñānamiti proktamajñānaṁ yadato'nyathā

Constancy, in the knowledge of the Supreme Spirit, in seeing God everywhere as the object of true knowledge—all

this is declared to be knowledge (jñāna), and what is contrary to it, is called ignorance (ajñāna). 11

Comment:—

'Adhyātmajñānanityatvam'—All scriptures direct men towards God. With this point in view, a striver should dwell upon God to the best of his understanding. From arguments and counter arguments it is proved, that God exists at all times, while the world does not exist, at anytime. Every moment it is decaying. The Self or the Supreme Spirit, is eternal and imperishable, while the world is transitory, perishable and is subject to modifications. The world, actually has no existence of its own, besides the Lord. The world, appears to exist, in the light of the Self or God. Thus, to dwell upon the negation of independent existence of the world, and ever-existence of God, is 'Adhyātmajñānanityatvam'.

Remedy:—Study of the sacred texts, listening to the divine discourses, and inquiries, constitute the remedy.

'Tattvajñānārthadarśanam'—'Tattvajñāna' means, God. Constantly beholding Him, pervading everywhere is 'seeing God, as an object of true' knowledge. A striver, should behold nothing else, besides the Lord, as He pervades everywhere, everytime, every person, thing, incident or circumstance. To have such a constant perception, is 'Tattvajñānārthadarśanam'.

'Etajjñānamiti proktamajñānaṁ yadato'nyathā'—The twenty virtues, mentioned from 'Amānitvam' (absence of pride) in the seventh verse to 'Tattvajñānārthadarśanam' (beholding the Lord) in this verse, are all conducive to God-realization by wiping out a striver's identification, with the body. So these have been named, (true) knowledge. The opposites of these virtues are—pride, hypocrisy and violence etc. Such wicked propensities, are conducive to disinclination for God-realization, as well as, identification of the self, with a body. So they are named, ignorance.

An Important Fact

If a striver, by developing acute discrimination, can renounce his assumed affinity with a body, all these virtues get naturally revealed, in him. Then he need not inculcate separate virtues, in him. A striver, should know the distinction between the real (Spirit), and the unreal (body). By knowing this distinction, his assumed affinity with body, is renounced. Secondly, he should have only an aim for God-realization.

This is everybody's experience that the body has changed but 'I' remain the same and implication of the body with the Self is not real but a false notion. Only by having this belief, his spiritual practice begins. The aim for God-realization arouses discrimination, which leads to dispassion. The Lord, has described these twenty virtues, to strengthen discrimination, and dispassion. With this aim, the evils are rooted out, whether a striver, realizes it or not. As leaves, on the branches of a tree, even when rooted out, remain green for a few days, so the evils of a striver, are rooted out, as soon as he fixes his goal, to realize God. In the beginning a striver, does not realize this fact, because evils appear in him. But gradually he realizes, that he is free from all those, evils.

During spiritual practice, a striver sometimes feels the presence of evils, in him. Actually, at that time, the evils make their exit. During spiritual practice, if the number of evil propensities increases, it means, that these are making their entry. But, if they are decreasing, it means that they are making their exit, and so they will vanish, altogether. Under such circumstances, a striver should not lose heart, he should be whole-heartedly engaged, in spiritual practice. By doing so, all his evils, totally disappear.

Appendix—These twenty virtues have been called 'Jñāna' (wisdom) because they enable us to know the difference between 'kṣetra' and 'kṣetrajña'. Whatever opposite to it is 'Ajñāna' (ignorance). Without following the spiritual discipline (these virtues), a man may learn facts pertaining to knowledge but he can't realize the reality. Therefore without spiritual practice, ignorance (to perceive 'kṣetra' and 'kṣetrajña' alike) prevails, and so long as ignorance prevails, if a man having learnt the difference between 'kṣetra' and 'kṣetrajña', discusses it, then in fact he strengthens 'dehābhimāna' (identification of the Self with the body). But he who practises these virtues, he becomes able to distinguish between 'kṣetra' and 'kṣetrajña'.

Link:—The Lord in the next verse, describes that the Knowable Who, ought to be known.

ज्ञेयं यत्तत्प्रवक्ष्यामि यज्ज्ञात्वामृतमश्नुते।
अनादिमत्परं ब्रह्म न सत्तन्नासदुच्यते॥१२॥

jñeyaṁ yattatpravakṣyāmi yajjñātvāmṛtamaśnute
anādimatparaṁ brahma na sattannāsaducyate*

I shall describe at length that which is fit to be known, and by knowing which, one attains immortality. It is the supreme Brahma Who is without beginning and Who is said to be, neither existent nor non-existent. 12

Comment:—

'Jñeyaṁ yattatpravakṣyāmi'—The Lord, promises that He will describe at length that Brahma or God, for Whose realization this human body has been bestowed, and Who has been described in the scriptures.

By the term 'Jñeyam' He means that having known all other subjects, sciences and arts of the world, something else remains,

* In this verse the Lord by the term 'Pravakṣyāmi' made a promise to describe that which is to be known; by 'Amṛtamaśnute' the result of that knowledge, by 'Anādimat', its mark, by 'Parama Brahma' its (His) name and by 'Na sattannāsaducyate' its (His) description have been given.

to be known. Moreover, worldly knowledge cannot make one free from the cycle of birth and death. But, by knowing God, nothing else remains to be known, and the cycle of birth and death, also comes to an end. Therefore, in the world, there is nothing worth knowing, except God.

'Yajjñātvāmṛtamaśnute'—By knowing God, one attains immortality, and then nothing remains to be known, to be done and to be acquired.

In fact, a man (self) is immortal, but by assuming his identity with a body, he regards the death and birth of the body, as his own birth and death. By knowing the Lord, this error is rectified, and he realizes the self or his immortality.

'Anādimat'—The entire universe, emanates from the Lord, remains established in Him, and merges in Him, while He remains the same. So He is called, without beginning.

'Paraṁ brahma'—Prakṛti (matter), as well as Veda is called Brahma, but 'Parama Brahma', is the Absolute, formless Brahma, or God Who is all-pervading and ever remains, the same. None is superior to Him in pervasiveness, purity and eternity. He is called 'Parama Brahma'.

'Na sattannāsaducyate'—God, cannot be called, either existent or non-existent. He cannot be called existent, because something can be existent, in relativity with something else, which is non-existent. The word day, is used only in relation with, night. But, if there is no night, a day cannot be called, a day. He cannot be called non-existent, because He surely exists. The fact is, that words cannot describe the real character of God, either by the positive or negative method. As the sun, is different from both the night and the day, so is God different from, both, the existent (Sat) and the non-existent (Asat). 'Sat' or 'Asat' is determined through intellect. This is 'Sat' and that is 'Asat'—it is in the realm of the world, which is a subject of mind, speech and intellect. But, He is beyond, not only of speech, but also of mind and intellect. So He cannot be called, either existent (being) or non-existent (non-being).

Appendix—God has been called 'Jñeya' because He is to be known, he should be known and He can be known. In fact He is not to be known with the help of Prakṛti bacause Prakṛti can't have an access to Him as He transcends Prakṛti. But He can be known by the Self.

Prakṛti (matter) and Puruṣa (the Self)—both have been called eternal (Gītā 13/19); therefore being the master of the two, God has been called here 'anādimat'.* In the fourth and fifth verses of the seventh chapter the Lord, having stated the 'aparā prakṛti' as 'itīyaṁ me' and 'parā prakṛti' (soul) as 'me parām', has mentioned that both are dependent upon Him; therefore the master of the two is only God.

In the Upaniṣad it is mentioned—

kṣaraṁ pradhānamamṛtākṣaraṁ haraḥ kṣarātmānāvīśate deva ekaḥ'

(Śvetāśvatara. 1/10)

Prakṛti is perishable (kaleidoscopic) and its enjoyer, Puruṣa (the soul), is immortal, imperishable (unchangeable). God keeps these two (prakṛti and puruṣa) under His control.

In the Gītā entire-God has been described in three ways—

(i) God is real (existent) and also unreal (non-existent)—'sadasaccāham' (9/19).

(ii) God is real, also unreal and is also beyond the two—'sadasattatparaṁ yat' (11/37).

(iii) God is neither real nor unreal—'na sattannāsaducyate' (13/12).

It means that in fact there is nothing else besides God. He is totally beyond the access of mind, intellect and speech, so He

* 'Anādimatparaṁ brahma'—This expression may also mean 'anādi, matparaṁ brahma' viz., brahma depends on Me—'brahmaṇo hi pratiṣṭhāham' (Gītā 14/27).

cannot be described but He can be attained.

In fact God cannot be described in words. But He is called real in relativity with the unreal, immutable in relativity with the mutable and omnipresent in relativity with the unipresent but in fact the terms real, immutable and omnipresent are not applicable to Him. The reason is that all the terms are used in relativity and in having affinity with Prakṛti; but the Divinity is independent and transcends Prakṛti. A name is given in relation to space, time, thing, person, state and quality etc. God transcends all limits of space and time etc., then how can He be addressed by particular names? Therefore it is mentioned here that God can't be called either real (existent) or unreal (non-existent).

There is no beginning of God. How can there be the beginning of God Who is eternal viz., from time immemorial? All are within limits but He is beyond limits. He is neither real nor unreal. With beginning-beginningless, within limits and beyond limits, real and unreal—these differences are there because of affinity with Prakṛti. The Supreme Reality transcends all restrictions such as with beginning-beginningless, within limits and beyond limits and real and unreal. Thus whatever has been said about the description of God, Who is to be known, is in fact no description but it is to draw attention towards the aim. It means that God is not merely to be described but this description draws a striver's attention towards the knowable. Therefore a striver should not merely learn facts but should reflect upon them with a view to have an insight into it.

Link—In the preceding verse, Lord Kṛṣṇa described the attributeless-formless Brahma, the Absolute, Who is worth knowing, by saying that He is neither existent nor non-existent. In the next verse, He describes the reality of what is worth knowing (Jñeya) viz., God as formless and endowed with attributes.

सर्वतःपाणिपादं तत्सर्वतोऽक्षिशिरोमुखम्।
सर्वतःश्रुतिमल्लोके सर्वमावृत्य तिष्ठति॥१३॥

sarvataḥpāṇipādaṁ tatsarvato'kṣiśiromukham
sarvataḥśrutimalloke sarvamāvṛtya tiṣṭhati

With hands and feet all over, with eyes, hands, mouth and with ears everywhere, He stands pervading all. 13

Comment:—

'Sarvataḥpāṇipādaṁ tat'—As there are, various scripts in ink and various ornaments in gold, the Lord has His hands and feet everywhere. Therefore, He accepts all offerings from all quarters made to Him physically, or mentally. Moreover, His hands are ever ready to protect devotees, from all the dangers everywhere. He has his feet everywhere, and so he accepts the sandal-paste, flowers and prostrations etc., offered by devotees, according to their feelings. If thousands and lacs of devotees, adore the Lord's feet, separately at a time, the Lord's feet are present then and there, according to the sentiments of devotees.

'Sarvato'kṣiśiromukham'—Wherever, devotees wave lamp to God and offer homage to Him with kindled lamps, there are God's eyes to see these. He has eyes, everywhere. It means, that no activities are hidden from Him. He beholds the devotees, wherever they perform actions, such as a dance, meditation, prayer and various spiritual practices. It means, that he who beholds the Lord, present everywhere, He is never out of his sight (Gītā 6/30).

He has His head everywhere and therefore, sandal-paste and flowers etc., offered to Him, as a mark of reverence, reach His head. Having His mouth everywhere, He accepts the articles of food offered by His devotees, everywhere (Gītā 9/26).

'Sarvataḥśrutimat'—The Lord, hears the loud, slow and silent (mental) prayer, of His devotees.

The Lord, unlike men has all His limbs, everywhere. It

means, he can hear, speak or accept the articles offered, with His eyes. Similarly, He can perform all actions with anyone of his sense-organs. He has all the sense-organs, in each of the smallest limbs.

By this statement, that He has His limbs everywhere, He means that he pervades all the time, all places, persons, incidents and circumstances etc. So He is not away, from anyone, He is close at hand, for everyone. Saints, have also declared, the same.

As a man, leading a mundane life, beholds the universe everywhere, a devout devotee, beholds the Lord, pervading everywhere.

'Loke sarvamāvṛtya tiṣṭhati'—The Lord, stands pervading the infinite universes, because, in the forty-second verse of the tenth chapter also, He declares that He stands, holding the entire universe, with a single fragment of His.

Appendix—In God everywhere there is everything. As in a pen and ink, which script is not there? A man having knowledge of different scripts can write them with the same pen and ink. In a lump of gold, which ornament is not present? A goldsmith out of that lump prepares several ornaments such as bangles, necklaces and nose rings etc., similarly in iron which arm or weapon or instrument is not there? Which idol is not present in clay and stone? Similarly in God what is not there? The entire universe is born of God, stays in Him and at last merges into Him. When He is at the beginning, He is at the end, then Who else can be there in the mid-state? If a striver accepts this fact firmly that God pervades everywhere, God will be seen to him because only He exists, there is no other existence besides Him. The Lord declares—

ahamevāsamevāgre nānyad yat sadasat param
paścādahaṁ yadetacca yo'vaśiṣyeta so'smyaham

(Śrīmadbhā. 2/9/32)

'I was present before the universe was created, there was

nothing else besides Me; and after the creation whatever the world appears, that is also I. The real, the unreal and any other entity which can be imagined beyond the real and the unreal, that is also I. If there is anything else besides the creation that is also I; and at the destruction of the creation, whatever remains, that is also I.'

It means that there is only one existence and that is not realized because we remain entangled in the pairs of opposites.

Link:—Describing the Lord, as formless and endowed with attributes, in the preceding verse, in the next three verses, there is a description of His singularity (transcendent character), all-pervasiveness and omnipotence.

सर्वेन्द्रियगुणाभासं सर्वेन्द्रियविवर्जितम्।
असक्तं सर्वभृच्चैव निर्गुणं गुणभोक्तृ च॥ १४॥

sarvendriyaguṇābhāsaṁ sarvendriyavivarjitam
asaktaṁ sarvabhṛccaiva nirguṇaṁ guṇabhoktṛ ca

He (God), though without all senses, is the perceiver of all sense-objects, unattached yet sustains all, unpossessive of guṇas (attributes), yet enjoys them. 14

Comment:—

'Sarvendriyaguṇābhāsaṁ sarvendriyavivarjitam'—There is pre-existence of God; then there is His power, prakṛti (matter). The evolute of matter is Mahattattva (Cosmic intelligence), an evolute of cosmic intelligence, is cosmic ego, and the evolutes of ego, are five gross elements, while the evolutes of five gross elements, are mind and ten senses. The evolutes of ten senses, are five objects of senses—all these are the evolutes of cosmic Nature. But God transcends, prakṛti and its evolutes, whether He is attributeless or endowed with attributes, whether He is formless, or with form. He transcends prakṛti, even when He incarnates. In that case, He manifests Himself, keeping prakṛti under His control.

How can God, be bound by guṇas (modes) (attributes), when even an embodied soul, by attaining God transcends guṇas? He is ever transcendent in character, He has no hands, feet, eyes etc., like other living beings, but He is capable of perceiving the objects of senses.* He listens to the call of His devotees, even without ears, embraces His devotees without skin, beholds beings without eyes, tastes articles of food, offered by His devotees, without tongue, runs to help His devotees, without feet and so on.

'Asaktaṁ sarvabhṛccaiva'—God loves, all beings, without having attachment for them, unlike worldly parents, who support their family with attachment, He supports and nourishes all the beings, throughout the entire universe, either on the earth, in the ocean or in ether or in heaven, in a better way without any attachment and provides necessities for them. Being a disinterested friend, He purifies all of them, destroying their good deeds and sins, through favourable and unfavourable, circumstances.

'Nirguṇaṁ guṇabhoktṛ ca'—Though God is devoid of guṇas, yet He enjoys. It means, that the Lord is pleased seeing all the actions performed, by His devotees, in the same way, as parents are pleased seeing activities of their children and thus He is an enjoyer.

Appendix—In spite of the predominance of Brahma (the Absolute) in this topic, now in this verse there is the description of entire God. This entire form is the Reality to be known. Therefore there is the predominance of the entire form both in knowledge and devotion—'Vāsudevaḥ sarvam' (Gītā 7/19), 'sarvaṁ khalvidaṁ brahma' (Chāndogya. 3/14/1).

This verse means that there is no other existence at all

* He (God) grasps and rapidly moves without hands and feet; He sees without eyes and hears without ears (Mānasa 1/118/3-4).

besides God. Whatever we'll say, is not different from God. He is devoid of all and He comprises all.

बहिरन्तश्च भूतानामचरं चरमेव च।
सूक्ष्मत्वात्तदविज्ञेयं दूरस्थं चान्तिके च तत्॥ १५॥

bahirantaśca bhūtānāmacaraṁ carameva ca
sūkṣmatvāttadavijñeyaṁ dūrasthaṁ cāntike ca tat

He exists, without and within, all beings and constitutes the moving and also the unmoving creation; because He is subtle, He is incomprehensible. He is near and stands afar, too. 15

Comment:—

[In the six verses, from the twelfth to the seventeenth, there is a description of the Knowable. Out of those six verses, this is the fourth verse which also includes the idea of the preceding three verses, and the next two verses. Therefore, this verse contains a gist of the topic of, the Knowable.]

'Bahirantaśca bhūtānāmacaraṁ carameva ca'—In a block of ice, immersed in the sea, there is water within and without and there is nothing else, besides water. Similarly all the moving and unmoving beings, are pervaded, both inside and outside by God. It means, that the entire moving and unmoving creation, is nothing else besides, God. The same, has been described by the Lord, from the angle of a realized soul as, 'Vāsudevaḥ sarvam' and from His angle He is describing 'Sadasaccāham'. Thus, the experience of God and of realized souls, is the same.

'Dūrasthaṁ cāntike ca tat'—A thing can be near or far, from three view-points—space, time and thing. God, is nearest as well as, farthest, from all the three view-points. He pervades everywhere, is close at hand and afar too.* He existed in the

* Water is far from the earth, fire is far from water, air is far from fire, ether is far from air, cosmic intelligence is far from ether, Matter (Prakṛti)

past, exists now, and will exist, in future; He existed before, all things came into existence, He will exist, when the things perish and He exists now, in the form of things. Though the Lord, is the nearest, yet He is far away, from those who hanker after worldly pleasures and prosperity. But, He is the nearest for those, who have an inclination for Him. So a striver, renouncing the desire for pleasures and prosperity, should arouse a yearning, only for God-realization. By doing so, he will realize his eternal union, with God.

'Sūkṣmatvāttadavijñeyam'—God, being subtle, is beyond senses and mind. He cannot be known, through senses and mind, by people. Now, a question arises that, when he cannot be known, he must be non-existent. But, He is not a naught. As molecules of water, existing in the sky are not seen, but they are perceived in the form of rain, or hail, God being subtler, than molecules of water, is incomprehensible, by senses, mind and intellect etc.

People do not know God, because of their ignorance. As an illiterate person cannot read the word 'Gītā', but a learned person in Saṁskṛta, can read the word, and know its contents, and one who is well-versed in the Gītā, its deep thoughts come to his mind. Similarly, an ignorant person cannot know God, but one who has known Him, in reality, beholds nothing else, besides Him.

God is worth-knowing (13/12, 17). He can be known by the self, so he is called 'Jñeya', but He cannot be known, by senses, mind and intellect, so He is called 'Avijñeya'. In order to know

---

is far from cosmic intelligence and God (Paramātmā) is far from Matter. Thus God is the farthest. Though He is the farthest, yet He pervades all because He is their cause, all are born of Him.

Gross body is nearer than Matter (Prakṛti); subtle body is nearer than the gross body; causal body is nearer than the subtle body; ego is nearer than the causal body; God is nearer than ego. Thus God is the nearest.

Him, a striver, should believe that He pervades everywhere. By having this belief, he will be able to behold Him, everywhere because He in reality exists, everywhere. This belief (assumption) is, also a discipline. It has its own glory, and will lead to God-realization.

Appendix—In the twelfth verse, God has been called 'Jñeya' (worth knowing). But in this verse He has been called 'Avijñeya' (can't be known) which means that God is not known like the world. As the world is known through senses, mind and intellect, God in not known through senses, mind and intellect. Senses, mind and intellect are the evolutes of Prakṛti while God is beyond Prakṛti. The evolutes of Prakṛti can't know even Prakṛti completely, then how can they know God Who transcends prakṛti? One has to accept the existence of God by faith in Him. As acceptance is done by the Self itself, not by sense-organs etc., (mind, intellect and senses).* The Self has its identity with God, therefore God is also attained by acceptance, not by thinking, reflection and description. The Self has never been identified with the body and the world, nor is identified, nor will be identified nor can be identified. The Self has neither been, nor is, nor will be nor can be separate from God.

अविभक्तं च भूतेषु विभक्तमिव च स्थितम्।
भूतभर्तृ च तज्ज्ञेयं ग्रसिष्णु प्रभविष्णु च॥ १६॥

avibhaktaṁ ca bhūteṣu vibhaktamiva ca sthitam
bhūtabhartṛ ca tajjñeyaṁ grasiṣṇu prabhaviṣṇu ca

He is undivided and yet He seems to be distributed over all beings. He who is the only object worth knowing is the creator,

* There is acceptance in the Self, therefore whatever is accepted is not forgotten; as 'I am a Brāhmaṇa'; 'I am married' etc. But whatever is decided through the mind or intellect is forgotten. There remains no doubt, there is also not the opposite feeling in the acceptance by the Self.

sustainer and the destroyer of all beings. 16

Comment:—

'Avibhaktaṁ ca bhūteṣu vibhaktamiva ca sthitam'— Actually, there is one indivisible existence, (God) pervading in all diverse forms. Division, is a mere appearance. Just as space, though really one and indivisible, appears divided into innumerable forms; so God though really undivided, seems to be spread over beings. In the twenty-seventh verse of this chapter also, the Lord declares, "A seer beholds the Supreme Lord, abiding equally in all perishable beings." Similarly, in the twentieth verse of the eighteenth chapter also, while describing Sāttvika knowledge, He declares, "The knowledge by which the one Imperishable Being, is seen in all existences is Sāttvika."

'Bhūtabhartṛ ca tajjñeyaṁ grasiṣṇu prabhaviṣṇu ca'—The Almighty God, Who should be known (13/2) and Who is worth knowing (13/12) has been described as the sustainer (Lord Viṣṇu), the destroyer (Lord Śiva) and creator (Lord Brahmā). The same Lord, as Brahmā with the predominance of 'rajoguṇa' (activity) creates the universe, as Viṣṇu with the predominance of 'sattvaguṇa' sustains it and as Śiva with the predominance of 'tamoguṇa' destroys it, yet He remains untainted by these guṇas (modes) having full control over them.

Appendix—In this verse there is the description of the entire form of God. As the world from the material point of view is one, so is also the Real Entity (God) one and undivided. As the world consisting of the five elements, in spite of being one, appears in the form of different objects, persons (insentient-sentient, unmoving-moving) etc., similarly God in spite of being one, appears in different forms. It means that God in spite of being one, exists in several forms; and in spite of existing in several forms, is one. The Real Entity can never be two because if they are two, it means that the unreal is included in it.

He Who creates is God and He Who is created is also God.

He Who sustains is God and He Who is sustained is also God. He Who destroys is God and He Who is destroyed is also God.

Link:—In the previous verse, the Lord said that He who is worth knowing, is the creator, sustainer and destroyer of the entire universe. In the next verse, it is explained that He is the light of all lights.

ज्योतिषामपि तज्ज्योतिस्तमसः परमुच्यते।
ज्ञानं ज्ञेयं ज्ञानगम्यं हृदि सर्वस्य विष्ठितम्॥ १७॥

jyotiṣāmapi tajjyotistamasaḥ paramucyate
jñānaṁ jñeyaṁ jñānagamyaṁ hṛdi sarvasya viṣṭhitam

That supreme soul is said to be, the light of all lights, entirely beyond darkness (ignorance). He is knowledge (jñāna), the knowable (jñeya) the goal of knowledge and is vested in the hearts of all. 17

Comment:—

'Jyotiṣāmapi tajjyotiḥ'—The sun, the moon, the stars, fire and electricity, are illuminators (light), of physical objects. The five sense-organs—ear, eye, skin, tongue and nose are, the illuminators (light) of sound, sight (colour), touch, taste and smell. The sense-organs can perceive the objects of sense, if the mind, remains with them. So mind, is the light (illuminator) of senses. Similarly, intellect is the light of the mind, as it guides and distinguishes, the real from the unreal. Self is the light of the intellect, because if a man does not attach importance, to the real and does not translate reality into practice, there is not much utility, of intellectual knowledge. The self is a fragment of the Lord, and so He is the light (Illuminator), of the self. So He is the light of all lights, and is self-effulgent but He is illuminated by, none.

As an examinee, can see other examinees who are sitting

on the front benches, but cannot see those, who are sitting at his back, similarly ego and intellect etc., can perceive mind and senses etc., but cannot perceive God, Who sees all of them, Who is their illuminator and Who is not illuminated by, anyone. He equally illuminates the entire world, moving or unmoving (Śrīmadbhā. 10/113/55). In Him, there is no trio of an illuminator, illumination and the illumined.

'Tamasaḥ paramucyate'—The Supreme Lord, is entirely beyond darkness or ignorance. It means, that He is totally untainted and detached. Senses, mind, intellect and ego, can be tainted by ignorance and knowledge, but He is beyond ignorance, in the same way as, the sun is beyond the reach of darkness.

'Jñānaṁ jñeyaṁ jñānagamyam'—God is knowledge Himself, free from ignorance. All beings, receive knowledge from Him. He is worth knowing (knowable), because nothing remains to be known, after knowing him. Worldly knowledge, is no doubt useful, but it is not a must, as it is not perfect in itself. After possessing it, something else remains, to be known. In fact, it is only the Lord, who is to be known certainly. Lord Kṛṣṇa, in the fifteenth chapter, declares, "I am worth knowing through the Vedas" (15/15) and "He who knows Me, knows all" (Gītā 15/19).

Virtues, such as absence of pride, freedom from hypocrisy, and non-violence etc., which have been described, from the seventh verse to the eleventh verse of this chapter, have been declared to be (true) knowledge. By that knowledge, renouncing the unreal, the Lord, can be known in reality. So the Lord has been called the goal to be attained by this knowledge.

'Hṛdi sarvasya viṣṭhitam'—Though God pervades everywhere, He is particularly seated, in the hearts of all.

How to realize the presence of God in the heart?

(1) A striver, should realize the difference between, the real and the unreal. He should know, that there are different states, such as wakefulness, sleep, and sound sleep; childhood,

youth and old age, but he himself remains, the same. Pleasant and painful, favourable and unfavourable circumstances, appear and disappear, but he remains the same. There is contact, with things, persons etc., and then there is separation, from these, but he remains the same. It means that he is different from, all of them. By knowing this truth in reality, he will realize the presence of God in his heart, because he himself, being a fraction of the Lord, has identity with Him.

(2) As a starving person, becomes uneasy without food and a thirsty man without water, a striver, should become uneasy for God-realization. Then, he will realize that He is seated in his heart. By this realization, he will understand that God is all-pervading. This is true realization.

Appendix—The Knowable entity, which has been described from the twelfth verse to the seventh verse, is only the entire form of God ('Vāsudevaḥ sarvam'). The reason is that in it attributeless-formless (twelfth verse), God endowed with attributes—formless (thirteenth verse) and God endowed with attributes and form (sixteenth verse) all the three have been described.

'Jñānagamyam'—God can be known by spiritual realization, not by actions and objects etc. There is no other method besides spiritual realization to know Him. A man may know God by any spiritual discipline such as Karmayoga, Jñānayoga, Dhyānayoga etc., in fact He will be known only by Spiritual realization. If He is known by faith, belief, devotion and God's grace etc., then also He is known by Spiritual realization only. The reason is that 'knowing' is done by knowledge.

Here the term 'jñānagamyam' may also mean that He is attained by twenty virtues which have been mentioned from the seventh verse to the eleventh verse of this chapter.

Link:—Having given a brief description of Kṣetra (Body),

knowledge and the knowable (worth knowing), from the first verse to the seventeenth verse, the Lord now concludes, the topic, in the next verse, by pointing out the reward of knowing this topic.

इति क्षेत्रं तथा ज्ञानं ज्ञेयं चोक्तं समासतः।
मद्भक्त एतद्विज्ञाय मद्भावायोपपद्यते ॥ १८ ॥

iti kṣetraṁ tathā jñānaṁ jñeyaṁ coktaṁ samāsataḥ
madbhakta etadvijñāya madbhāvāyopapadyate

Thus the Kṣetra (body), knowledge (jñāna) and the object of knowledge (the knowable) have been briefly described; and knowing this in reality, My devotee reaches Me. 18

Comment:—

'Iti kṣetraṁ tathā jñānaṁ jñeyaṁ coktaṁ samāsataḥ'—The Kṣetra, has been described, in the fifth and sixth verses of this chapter; the twenty virtues which have been mentioned, from the seventh verse to the eleventh verse, have been declared knowledge and God, Who is the object of knowledge, has been discussed, from the twelfth verse to the seventeenth verse. Thus they have been briefly described, by the Lord.

'Madbhakta etadvijñāya madbhāvāyopapadyate'—A devotee, having known the Kṣetra, knowledge in the form of twenty virtues, and the knowable (God) in reality, attains the Lord or realizes his identity with Him. His assumed affinity, with the Kṣetra (body) is renounced, by knowing the true nature of Kṣetra, his sense of individuality vanishes, by having a deep insight into knowledge, consisting of the twenty virtues, and he attains God viz., realizes his identity with Him, by knowing the Knowable.

Link:—In the first and the second verses, the Kṣetra and the Kṣetrajña, were described in brief. The Lord reverts to the same topic, and describes these in detail under the name of prakṛti (Matter) and 'Puruṣa' (Spirit).

प्रकृतिं पुरुषं चैव विद्ध्यनादी उभावपि।
विकारांश्च गुणांश्चैव विद्धि प्रकृतिसम्भवान्॥ १९॥
कार्यकरणकर्तृत्वे हेतुः प्रकृतिरुच्यते।
पुरुषः सुखदुःखानां भोक्तृत्वे हेतुरुच्यते॥ २०॥

prakṛtiṁ puruṣaṁ caiva viddhyanādī ubhāvapi
vikārāṁśca guṇāṁścaiva viddhi prakṛtisambhavān
kāryakaraṇakartṛtve hetuḥ prakṛtirucyate
puruṣaḥ sukhaduḥkhānāṁ bhoktṛtve heturucyate

Know that prakṛti (matter) and 'Puruṣa' (Spirit) are both eternal and know also, that all modifications and guṇas (modes) are born of prakṛti. Prakṛti is, said to be, the cause of all activities of the body (Kārya) and external and internal organs, while Puruṣa is said to be, the cause of experiencing pleasure and pain. 19-20

Comment:—

[In the third verse, Lord Kṛṣṇa ordered Arjuna to hear from Him, what the Kṣetra is, what it is like, what its modifications are, and whence is what. Out of these four, the first and the third were, described in the fifth and the sixth verses, respectively. The second, will be described in the twenty-sixth and twenty-seventh verses. Now, while describing 'Whence is what' He says that all modifications and guṇas are born of prakṛti. Modifications were described, in the sixth verse. Here in this verse, He explains that guṇas are born of prakṛti—this is something new.

From the twelfth to eighteenth verses, there is a description of the knowable (God), while here, from the nineteenth to the thirty-fourth verses, there is a description of 'Puruṣa' (Kṣetrajña). There, all are mentioned to be within God, while here all are mentioned to be within spirit. It means, that essentially God and individual spirit, are not two, but only one.]

'Prakṛtiṁ puruṣaṁ caiva viddhyanādī ubhāvapi'—The term, 'Prakṛtim' stands for 'Primordial Matter', the cause of the entire Kṣetra (universe). Seven prakṛti-vikṛti (Five elements, ego and cosmic intelligence) and sixteen vikṛtis (ten senses, mind and five objects of senses)—all these are the evolutes of Matter and Prakṛti is their cause.

The term 'Puruṣam', here stands for 'Kṣetrajña', which has been called a knower of the Kṣetra, in the first verse of this chapter.

As the spirit, being a fraction of the Lord, is without beginning, so is Matter. But the spirit and matter, are different in other aspects. Matter is endowed with attributes, while the spirit is attributeless; Matter undergoes modifications, while the spirit, is free from modifications, Matter is the cause of the universe, while the spirit is the cause of nothing. There is a relationship of cause and effect, in Matter and its evolutes while the spirit is free from, this relationship.

The expression, 'Ubhāvapi' denotes that Prakṛti and Puruṣa, both are different. As both of them are beginningless the difference between them is also eternal.

As the terms 'Kṣetra' and 'Kṣetrajñaḥ', used in the first verse of this chapter, stand for the individual body and the individual soul respectively. Here 'Prakṛti', stands for 'Primordial Matter' and its evolutes, while 'Puruṣam' stands for all 'Kṣetrajña' (Spirit).

The term 'Viddhi', in the second verse of this chapter, was used to know the identity of the individual soul, with the cosmic soul while here, points out that the two—'body' and 'spirit' or 'Prakṛti' (Primordial Matter) and 'Puruṣa' (spirit), are different. So the Lord advises Arjuna, to understand it well, that the two, are quite different, because a common man identifies, the body with self.

'Vikārāṁśca guṇāṁścaiva viddhi prakṛtisambhavān'—Know the seven modifications—desire, aversion, pleasure, pain, body, life-breath and firmness, as well as the three Guṇas—sattva, raja and tama are born of prakṛti. It means, that Puruṣa is free from modifications and modes. In the seventh chapter, the Lord mentioned the guṇas to be evolved from Him, while here He says, that these are born of 'prakṛti'. There, because of the context of devotion, the Lord mentioned them to be evolved from Him, and He also explained that His wonderful divine potency of His, consisting of the three Guṇas can be overcome by taking refuge, in Him. But here, there is the context of knowledge, so the guṇas are said to be born of prakṛti. A striver, should not assume his affinity, with them. Thus he can get rid of them.

'Kāryakaraṇa.... prakṛtirucyate'—Ether, air, fire, water, earth and sound, touch, sight, taste, smell—these ten, are prakṛti's evolutes. Mind, intellect, ego, ear, skin, eye, tongue, (the sense of taste), nose, tongue (the organ of speech), hands, feet, generative organ and anus—these thirteen are included in the term, 'Karaṇa' (instruments). Prakṛti alone, is the cause of activities effected by all of them. Whatever is born, is called 'Kārya' (evolute), and the means by which the activities are performed, is called 'Karaṇa' (instrument). These instruments are of three types—1. Organs of action 2. Sense-organs 3. Mind, intellect and ego. The organs of action, are gross, the sense-organs are subtle, and the mind, intellect and ego are, very subtle. The organs of action and the sense-organs, are external instruments and mind, intellect and ego, are internal instruments. Actions are performed by organs of action, while mind, intellect and ego, control the organs of actions, as well as, sense-organs. It means, that the sense-organs control, the organs of action, the mind controls, the sense-organs, intellect controls, the mind and ego controls, the intellect. The organs of action and the sense-organs do not function, without mind, intellect and ego. When the mind is connected with sense-organs, then the sense-objects are perceived. The intellect decides, which sense-objects, are approved (sanctioned) and which are improper (prohibited). Ego, controls the intellect.

Ego is of two kinds—1. Ego as Vṛtti and ego, as a doer.

The disposition of ego, is not defective. But, when a man (the self), identifies himself with this ego, being deluded he becomes the doer (agent) (Gītā 3/27).

Cosmic intelligence, is an evolute of Prakṛti, while ego is the evolute of intelligence, but a man by identifying himself with the ego, becomes the master i.e., becomes a doer and an enjoyer (Gītā 13/21). However when he realizes the self, he is neither a doer, nor an enjoyer (Gītā 13/31). The performance of these actions, have been mentioned in the Gītā in several ways as "All actions are performed by Nature alone" (13/29); "All actions are performed by the modes of Nature" (3/27); "The modes are acting on the modes" (3/28); "There is no agent, other than the modes" (14/19); "Senses move among the sense-objects" (5/9) etc. It means, that all actions performed by the external and internal instruments, are performed by Prakṛti (Nature).

'Puruṣaḥ sukhaduḥkhānāṁ....heturucyate'—It is the Puruṣa, that experiences, pleasure and pain; Prakṛti being insentient cannot experience, pleasure or pain. The Puruṣa, experiences these only, by being pleased and displeased, in favourable and unfavourable circumstances. If he is not pleased and displeased, in favourable and unfavourable circumstances, he can never be an enjoyer, of pleasure and pain.

In the fourth and the fifth verses of the seventh chapter, the Lord has described His lower (insentient) and higher (sentient), natures. Both natures are portions of God. So, they are naturally flowing towards God. The embodied soul, a fragment of God, has a natural inclination, to Him. But, being attracted by worldly enjoyments, he identifies himself with the body. Thus he creates his own distinct existence (Gītā 13/21). This is denoted as, 'I am'. It consists of two aspects—consciousness incarnate and inertness. Pleasure and pain, affect only the inert portion (Matter or body). But because of affinity with Matter, he assumes pleasure and pain, in the self. He feels 'I am happy', 'I am sad'. Thus a businessman, regards loss in business, as his own loss. Similarly, when a body suffers from fever, he thinks that he suffers from fever. If the self, suffered once, it would continue suffering. It means that the self, neither suffers loss nor suffers, from fever.*

A man (spirit), wants to be emancipated from pleasure and pain, because he assumed his identity with Matter, otherwise he himself being a portion of the Lord, always remains the same, without undergoing any modifications, in the form of pleasure and pain etc. It means, that in this identification of the self, with the body, the self has a desire for emancipation, while the body, has desire for worldly enjoyments. So at last, the sentient self, is emancipated, rather than the inert body.

All modifications are always in the non-self, not, in the self. So, to be an experiencer of pleasure and pain, is not natural, in the self. Being attached to the non-self, an embodied soul, becomes the experiencer of pleasure and pain. It means, that the pure self, can never experience pleasure and pain. The pure self cannot have two contrary states, because it is always changeless, uniform and constant. There can be two states, in the changing non-self. The self in spite of being uniform, having affinity with the changing non-self, thrusts upon itself, changes and modifications, which take place in the non-self. This is a common experience, that we remain the same, in pleasure and pain, we do not change. Pleasure and pain, are different from each other, but we ever remain, uniform. But by assuming relationship, with pleasure, we become happy, and by assuming relationship with pain, we become sad. In reality, we are neither happy, nor sad.

Appendix—The Lord describes the distinction between 'Kṣetra' and 'Kṣetrajña' now by the names 'Prakṛti' and 'Puruṣa'. The description of 'Kṣetra' and 'Kṣetrajña' is from the individual point of view while that of 'Prakṛti' and 'Puruṣa' is from the

* If a man realizes that he is the self, why should he suffer from the fever or desire or craving?

collective point of view.

There are two divisions—one is of 'Prakṛti' while the other is of 'Puruṣa'. The body and the world are included in the Prakṛti division while the Self and God are included in the Puruṣa division. As 'Prakṛti' and 'Puruṣa' are beginningless, so is the knowledge of the distinction between the two viz., discrimination beginningless. Therefore from the discrimination point of view, these two divisions are totally unrelated with each other. Prakṛti is unreal, inert and embodiment of sufferings while Puruṣa is truth, consciousness and embodiment of bliss. Prakṛti is perishable, mutable and active while Puruṣa is imperishable, immutable and actionless. With Prakṛti there is ever disunion while with Puruṣa there is ever union. At the beginning of the Gītā the Lord has described this division between the body and its possessor by the terms—'śarīra-śarīrī', 'deha-dehī', the real and the unreal etc.* Therefore it is very essential for every striver to understand this division and it quickly leads to Self-realization. The reason is that identification of the Self with the body is bondage and the realization that the two are totally different from each other, is salvation.

Prakṛti is God's potency and God is its master.† From the knowledge point of view potency and its master—both are different because there is change (increase and decrease) in potency but God remains the same. But from the devotion point of view both are one because potency can't be separated from its possessor viz., potency has no independent existence without its master. In order to support the two views of knowledge and devotion, the Lord has neither stated Prakṛti as 'endless' nor 'an ending one' but has only stated it as 'beginningless'. The reason is

* 'Puruṣa' on the acceptance of 'ego' is named 'jīva, kṣetrajña, śarīrī' and 'dehī' etc.

† 'māyāṁ tu prakṛtiṁ vidyānmāyinaṁ tu maheśvaram' (Śvetāśvatara. 4/10).

that if Prakṛti is said to be endless (eternal), then the discipline of knowledge will be refuted because from that point of view Prakṛti has no existence at all—'nāsato vidyate bhāvaḥ' (Gītā 2/16). If Prakṛti is stated to be 'an ending one' (transient), the principle of devotion will be refuted because from the devotion point of view, Prakṛti being the potency of God is inseparable with Him—'sadasaccāham' (Gītā 9/19). If we perceive from the real point of view, it is clear that though the nature of Prakṛti is different from that of Puruṣa, yet both are integral.

In fact the form (nature) of God is 'entire'. It is not possible that there is no potency in God. If God is regarded to be totally powerless, then God will be proved to be unipresent. In Him power may change its form or may remain unmanifest but there can never be negation of power. Power abides in Him in its causal form, otherwise where will potency (Prakṛti) abide besides God? Therefore here both Prakṛti and Puruṣa have been called 'beginningless'.

Link:—In the preceding verse, the Lord mentioned the Puruṣa, as the cause of the experience, of pleasure and pain. The question arises, how the Puruṣa, is the cause. The answer follows.

पुरुषः प्रकृतिस्थो हि भुङ्क्ते प्रकृतिजान्गुणान्।
कारणं गुणसङ्गोऽस्य सदसद्योनिजन्मसु॥ २१॥

puruṣaḥ prakṛtistho hi bhuṅkte prakṛtijānguṇān
kāraṇaṁ guṇasaṅgo'sya sadasadyonijanmasu

When the spirit (puruṣa) seated in matter (prakṛti) enjoys the modes born of prakṛti (matter), attachment to the modes becomes the cause of its birth, in good and evil bodies. 21

Comment:—

'Puruṣaḥ prakṛtistho* hi bhuṅkte prakṛtijānguṇān'—In

* Here the term 'Prakṛtistha' (seated in the Matter) denotes 'Śarīrastha'

fact, the spirit is not seated in Matter (body). But because of its identification with a body, it assumes the body as 'I', and 'Mine', and is thus said to be seated in the body. Such a spirit, experiences pleasure and pain, in agreeable and disagreeable circumstances. This is said by the way that the spirit enjoys the modes born of Matter.

As in a bus accident, the bus driver is held responsible for an accident because of his attachment (responsibility) to the bus, and so he is punished. It is because of the spirit's attachment to the body, that it (the spirit) enjoys the fruit of action performed by the body. If it is not attached to a body and it feels all actions to be performed by Prakṛti alone, (Gītā 13/29), it will not have to accept the fruit of actions.

'Kāraṇaṁ guṇasaṅgo'sya sadasadyonijanmasu'—Good wombs are those, in which there is abundance of pleasure, while bad ones are those, that bear much pain. The spirit, takes birth in good and evil wombs, because of its attachment to the modes, born of Prakṛti.

The three modes—Sattva, Rajas and Tamas, are born of Prakṛti. All the worldly objects and actions, are born of the modes of Prakṛti. When the spirit attaches itself, to these modes, it has to take birth in good or bad wombs. If it is not seated in the body and has no feeling of 'I'ness and 'Mine'ness in this body, but remains established in the self, it will not be an enjoyer of pleasure and pain. It will become equanimous in pleasure and pain i.e., will become 'Svastha', (Gītā 14/24). It can establish a relationship with Nature, or it can get fixed in the oversoul. It cannot merge in the non-self, because non-self (Matter) is perishable, while the self is eternal. Both, belong to two different

---

(seated in the body). Here is the context of 'Puruṣa and Prakṛti'. So the Puruṣa is said to be seated in Prakṛti. In fact the spirit is not seated in the body, but by not realizing its situation in the self, it assumes its identification with the body.

classes. But its getting established in the oversoul, is axiomatic, as both are of the same class. Bondage is unnatural to it, while identity with the oversoul is natural to it. Bondage is painful to it, while merger in the oversoul is pleasant to it.

In the ego of the self, where there is discriminative faculty, to know a distinction between, Prakṛti and Puruṣa, there only exists ignorance to assume identity, with Prakṛti. By assuming identity, this Puruṣa, is called 'Prakṛtistha' (seated in Nature), and the sense of 'I' and 'mine' increases. This is attachment, to the modes of Prakṛti. This attachment binds him (Puruṣa) (Gītā 14/5) and therefore, he meets with destiny, according to predominance of the modes, of Nature (Gītā 14/18).

Appendix—The Lord in the second half of the nineteenth verse and in the first half of the twentieth verse has described 'Prakṛti', and in the second half of the twentieth verse and here in this verse, He has described 'Puruṣa'.

Attachment to objects, persons and actions is 'guṇasaṅga' (attachment to modes) which is the cause of birth and death. Attachment to the modes is transient while detachment from the modes is eternal. Detachment is nature of the Self—'asaṅgo'hyayaṁ puruṣaḥ' (Bṛhadā 4/3/15). If we are not attached to the transient or the modes, we can't follow the wheel of birth and death.

'I' is inert (non-self) (Prakṛti) and 'am' is sentient (self) (Puruṣa) and 'I am'—this is the identification of the Self with the non-Self. In 'I am' there is the sense of doership and enjoyership. If 'I' does not remain, then 'am' will not remain but 'is' will persist. As there is no identification of a lump of iron with fire, so the lump of iron remains lying on the earth, while fire from this hot lump of iron merges into the formless fire-element, similarly 'ego' perists in Prakṛti and 'am' (being a form of 'is') merges into 'is'. In 'is' there is neither doership nor enjoyership. It means that 'am' is attracted towards pleasures, 'is' is not attracted; 'am' becomes the doer and enjoyer, 'is' does not become the doer and enjoyer. Therefore a striver instead of assuming 'am' should assume only 'is' viz., he should realize it.

Everyone realizes that pleasures and pains appear and disappear while the Self ever remains the same. Even the most sinful person realizes this fact. In spite of realizing this fact, a man feels happy and sad with the fleeting pleasures and pains. The reason is that attachment to pleasure and fear of pain do not let him realize that he is different from pleasure and pain—this discrimination does not work. In fact a man (the Self) does not feel happy and sad at all but he, identifying the Self with the body, assumes himself to be happy and sad. It means that pleasure (happiness) and pain (sadness) are based on his indiscriminative assumption only.

Link:—In the preceding three verses, Prakṛti (Matter) and Puruṣa (Spirit), were described. In the next verse, there is a description of Puruṣa, in particular.

उपद्रष्टानुमन्ता च भर्ता भोक्ता महेश्वरः।
परमात्मेति चाप्युक्तो देहेऽस्मिन्पुरुषः परः॥ २२॥

upadraṣṭānumantā ca bhartā bhoktā maheśvaraḥ
paramātmeti cāpyukto dehe'sminpuruṣaḥ paraḥ

The Soul (Puruṣa) having been vested within the body is called a 'witness', because he gives consent, he is called a 'permitter'; as he assumes that he sustains the body, he is called a 'sustainer'; as he experiences pleasure and pain, he is called 'experiencer'; being the master of the body he is 'Great Lord' (Maheśvara). Really speaking, this Puruṣa by his own nature is the Supreme Soul. In spite of, His residence in the body; he is untainted and unattached. 22

Comment:—

'Upadraṣṭānumantā ca bhartā bhoktā maheśvaraḥ'—The

Puruṣa (spirit), is eternal, all-pervading, immovable, constant and everlasting (Gītā 2/24). As the Puruṣa, observes the body, an evolute of prakṛti, He becomes a witness.

He, is the permitter, because He gives advice and permission, in the performance of actions.

He, by identifying himself with the individual body, sustains the body by providing food, water and other necessities, and protects it from cold and heat etc. So, He is the sustainer.

By identifying Himself with the body, He undergoes all sorts of experiences. He experiences pleasure and pain, in favourable and unfavourable, circumstances. So, He is the experiencer.

He regards Himself, as the Lord of the body, senses, mind, intellect, wealth and property etc. So He is called the Great Lord.

'Paramātmeti cāpyukto dehe'sminpuruṣaḥ paraḥ'—The Spirit, dwelling in this body, is really the same, which has been termed as the 'Supreme Soul', in the scriptures. In spite of its residence, in the body, it has no affinity with it. Though it dwells in the body, it neither acts, nor is tainted (13/31).

In this verse, the Spirit dwelling in the body, has been called by different names, as a man is called by different names (such as father, uncle, brother and grandfather etc.,) according to the relationship it bears, though it is the same.

Appendix—In fact the Puruṣa (spirit) is transcendental (untainted and unattached) but having relationship with others, he becomes a witness, a permitter etc. As a man becomes a father by having relationship with a son, he becomes a son by bearing relationship with the father, he becomes a husband by bearing relationship with the wife and he becomes a brother by bearing relationship with a sister. All these relations are in order to perform one's duty, rather than to have the sense of mine (possession). The real Self is totally unattached and untainted.

Here the purpose of giving several epithets such as 'upadraṣṭā' (witness), 'anumantā' (permitter) etc., is to express unity that the Self is only one. In the topic of knowledge the description of both Prakṛti and Puruṣa is important. Therefore here all the terms such as 'upadraṣṭā', 'anumantā' and 'īśvara' etc., are to be taken to stand for (denote) Puruṣa.

Link:—Having described 'Prakṛti' and 'Puruṣa', from the nineteenth verse to the twenty-second verse, the Lord in the next verse, declares the reward of knowing the two, in reality.

य एवं वेत्ति पुरुषं प्रकृतिं च गुणैः सह।
सर्वथा वर्तमानोऽपि न स भूयोऽभिजायते॥ २३॥

ya evaṁ vetti puruṣaṁ prakṛtiṁ ca guṇaiḥ saha
sarvathā vartamāno'pi na sa bhūyo'bhijāyate

He who thus knows Puruṣa (Spirit) and prakṛti (nature) together with its modes, though he acts in everyway (whatever state of life he may be in), he is not born again. 23

Comment:—

'Ya evaṁ vetti puruṣaṁ prakṛtiṁ ca guṇaiḥ saha sarvathā vartamāno'pi na sa bhūyo'bhijāyate'—Here the term 'Evam' (thus), denotes that the Spirit is different from, the body. He who knows this difference in reality, while performing his duty according to his caste, creed, stage of life and circumstances etc., is not reborn. He knows that prakṛti with its evolutes, modifications and instruments etc., which appears in the form of universe, is different from the Self. So he is not born again, because attachment to the modes of nature, is the cause of its birth (Gītā 13/21).

Here, the expression 'Sarvathā vartamāno'pi' (acts in anyway), does not involve forbidden actions, because he who knows prakṛti, with its modes as different from the self, can have no desire to gain the unreal. When he has no desire, forbidden actions cannot be performed by him, because desire is the only cause of forbidden actions (Gītā 3/37).

The Lord, exhorts a striver, to know the self in reality and that there is no action, in the self. So he can be neither an agent, nor an experiencer. When he realizes, that he is not an agent (doer), his pride of doership comes to an end, and so he has no desire for fruit of action, which are naturally performed by him according to the ordinance of the scriptures. Having transcended the guṇas, (modes of nature), he is not born again.

Appendix—The expression 'dehe'smin puruṣaḥ paraḥ' used in the preceding verse is explained in this verse. He whose discrimination has been aroused viz., 'dehe'smin puruṣah paraḥ' has been realized, he, in spite of performing his duty according to his order—stage of life (varṇāśrama), remains untainted. In fact a man (the Self) is untainted, but being attached to the modes, he gets tainted and follows the cycle of birth and death (13/21). The modes are related with Prakṛti, not with Puruṣa (13/19-20).

The term 'api' used in the expression 'sarvathā vartamāno'pi' means that he, in spite of acting in everyway, like the person who is attached to the world, remains unaffected (Gītā 3/25).

'Na sa bhūyo'bhijāyate'—As butter once churned out of the curd does not become curd by mixing it with whey again, similarly having renounced relationship with the modes born of Prakṛti, a man is not bound by modes again. He merges into Brahma viz., as Brahma is free from birth and death, so does he become free from the cycle of birth and death.

In the thirty-first verse of the sixth chapter the expression used is 'sarvathā vartamāno'pi sa yogī mayi vartate', while here the expression is 'sarvathā vartamāno'pi na sa bhūyo'bhijāyate'. In the expression 'sa yogī mayi vartate', the words used in the sixth chapter, are in the context of attainment of love, while in the expression 'na sa bhūyo'bhijāyate' the words used here, are in the context of Self-realization. In both states of love and

Self-realization, there is no attachment to modes. The difference in the two is that in Self-realization, there is emancipation from birth and death but in love besides emancipation (salvation), the devotee attains oneness with God.

Link:—In the preceding verse, the Lord explained that the true knowledge of prakṛti and Puruṣa, is the means of being free, from rebirth. Now, curiosity arises, whether there is any other means also to be free from rebirth i.e., to attain salvation. So, the Lord mentions four means, in the next two verses.

ध्यानेनात्मनि पश्यन्ति केचिदात्मानमात्मना।
अन्ये साङ्ख्येन योगेन कर्मयोगेन चापरे॥ २४॥

dhyānenātmani paśyanti kecidātmānamātmanā
anye sāṅkhyena yogena karmayogena cāpare

Some perceive God in their own self by the self through meditation; others by the discipline of knowledge, and still others by the discipline of action. 24

Comment:—

'Dhyānenātmani paśyanti kecidātmānamātmanā'—Strivers, by meditation on the Supreme Soul, Who is formless and attributeless, as well as, endowed with attributes and form etc., (as described in the twenty-seventh and twenty-eighth verses of the fifth chapter, from the tenth to the twenty-eighth verses of the sixth chapter and from the eighth to the fourteenth verses of the eighth chapter), according to their faith and taste, realize, the self or God.

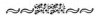

As by knowledge of the distinction between, Prakṛti and Puruṣa, one's affinity with Prakṛti is eliminated, so is this affinity, discarded by meditation. No meditation is possible, when mind is either in a deluded state, or in the volatile state. Meditation begins, in the non-volatile state. When the mind is concentrated in the self, that is the state of trance, in which there is no thought, of the world, body or any inclination etc. Then a Dhyānayogī, by perceiving the self in the self, by the self gets self-satisfied (Gītā 6/19-20).

'Anye sāṅkhyena yogena'—'Several strivers realize, the self by the self, through the Discipline of Knowledge, as has been described (from the eleventh to the thirtieth verses of the second chapter, from the thirty-third to the thirty-ninth verses of the fourth chapter, in the eighth and ninth verses as well as from the thirteenth to the twenty-sixth verses of the fifth chapter and in the fourth and fifth verses etc., of the twelfth chapter).

Here, the Discipline of Knowledge, stands for discrimination. A devotee, following the Discipline of Knowledge, discriminates between the real and the unreal. The real is eternal, all-pervading, unchanging, immovable, unmanifest and unthinkable, while the unreal is transitory, kaleidoscopic, movable and it always, undergoes modifications. Thus a devotee following this discipline, by discriminating the real from the unreal, isolates himself from prakṛti and its evolutes and realizes, the self in the self, by the self.

'Karmayogena cāpare'—Some strivers, attain the Supreme, through the Discipline of Action, as has been mentioned (from the forty-seventh to the fifty-third verses of the second chapter, from the seventh to the nineteenth verses of the third chapter, from the sixteenth to the thirty-second verses of the fourth chapter, in the sixth and seventh verses etc., of the fifth chapter). A devotee following the Discipline of Action, performs all his duties as well as religious sacrifice, charity, penance and pilgrimage etc., for the welfare of others. By doing so, his affinity with things, objects and persons etc., is renounced and he realizes the Supreme.

A man, has assumed his identification with the body. In order to do away with the assumption, he should assume his identification with the Lord, as he identified himself with the body. This identification with the Lord is not through senses etc. In knowing, the oversoul through instruments, dependence on matter subsists. Unless, affinity with Prakṛti is renounced, he cannot get himself established, in the Supreme Soul. Therefore,

Self-realization is beyond instruments.

Appendix—As in the preceding verse the Lord stated that attaching importance to discrimination is a means for salvation, similarly here in this verse He mentions others means such as meditation etc., to attain salvation. In the Gītā, God-realization has been mentioned—by meditation in the twenty-eighth verse of the sixth chapter, by Jñānayoga (Sāṅkhyayoga) in the fifteenth verse of the second chapter and by Karmayoga (Discipline of Action) in the seventy-first verse of the second chapter. All these are independent means for God-realization.

अन्ये त्वेवमजानन्तः श्रुत्वान्येभ्य उपासते।
तेऽपि चातितरन्त्येव मृत्युं श्रुतिपरायणाः ॥ २५ ॥

anye tvevamajānantaḥ śrutvānyebhya upāsate
te'pi cātitarantyeva mṛtyuṁ śrutiparāyaṇāḥ

Others ignorant of this (Discipline of Meditation, Knowledge and Action) hearing from others, celebrated souls worship; and they too go beyond death, by their devotion, to what they have heard. 25

Comment:—

'Anye tvevamajānantaḥ śrutvānyebhya upāsate te'pi cātitarantyeva mṛtyuṁ śrutiparāyaṇāḥ'—Strivers, who have a keen desire but who cannot understand in full, anyone of the Disciplines of Meditation, Knowledge or Action, by listening to liberated souls, and by obeying them promptly, realize the self. As a poor man, receives money from rich people, by carrying out their wishes, a devotee, receives divine knowledge, by obeying great souls. But the difference is, that money is gained when a rich man offers it, and obedience to great souls naturally, leads a man to realize God, Who is automatically attained, as payment of the money, depends on a rich man and his will, but God-realization does not depend, on anyone.

A man regards the body's death as his own by identifying himself with his body. Those, who rely on the advice of saints and great souls, and act according to it, their assumed affinity, with the body is renounced. So, they go beyond death i.e., they become free from the assumption, by which they regarded the death of a body, as their own death.

Such strivers, who rely on the advice of great souls, are divided into three categories:—

(1) Those, who do not desire worldly enjoyment, but have only yearning for God-realization; and the great soul they depend on, is really exalted, they attain God-realization, quickly.

(2) Those who have a desire for God-realization, but their mundane desires have not perished, by obeying great souls, first they will be free from worldly desires, and then will attain God.

(3) Strivers who only aim at God-realization, even though, the saints whom they obey, are not exalted souls, will realize God, by His grace, because He being omniscient, knows all beings.

Actually, great souls transcend virtues and vices. If a striver finds fault with them, he will behold the reflection of his own vices, because they have no vices, at all. So a striver, need not watch their actions and behaviour. He should draw spiritual inspiration from them. He should neither speak ill of them, nor find fault with them, otherwise he cannot progress spiritually.

Appendix—The people who have no ability to understand the scriptures and whose discriminative power is weak but have a burning desire to go beyond death, such people also by obeying the liberated exalted souls, go beyond death.

In the Upaniṣad, there is an anecdote. Satyakāma, the son of Jabālā went to sage Gautama so that Gautama might preach him the gospel. The sage gave him four hundred lean and feeble cows and ordered him to tend them. Satyakāma enthusiastically said, "I shall return only when their number increases to a thousand." Having said this, he carried them to the forest and began to rear them there. After several years when their number was increased to a thousand, then a bull said to him, "Our number has increased to a thousand, therefore you should take us back to the preceptor (teacher)." Having said this, the bull preached him the gospel of the first pāda of Brahma. The next day Satyakāma started for the seminary with the cows. On the way Agni preached him the gospel of Brahma's second pāda; Haṁsa preached him the gospel of Brahma's third pāda and Madgu (an aquatic bird) preached him the gospel of the fourth pāda of Brahma. Thus on the way having gained knowledge of the Supreme, he came back to sage Gautama. When the teacher asked him, he narrated the whole anecdote and requested the teacher to preach him the gospel in his own words. Then Sage Gautama preached him the gospel (Chāndogya. fourth chapter, fourth to ninth khaṇḍa) (portions). In this way only by obeying an enlightened liberated exalted soul, Satyakāma attained Self-realization.

Link:—In the preceding verse, the Lord declared that those strivers who worship after hearing from others too, go beyond death. Now a question arises, what causes death? The Lord answers the question.

यावत्सञ्जायते किञ्चित्सत्त्वं स्थावरजङ्गमम्।
क्षेत्रक्षेत्रज्ञसंयोगात्तद्विद्धि भरतर्षभ॥ २६॥

yāvatsañjāyate kiñcitsattvaṁ sthāvarajaṅgamam
kṣetrakṣetrajñasaṁyogāttadviddhi bharatarṣabha

Whatever being is born, moving or unmoving, O best of the Bharatas (Arjuna), know it all as emanated from the union of the field (kṣetra) and knower of the field (kṣetrajña). 26

Comment:—

'Yāvatsañjāyate kiñcitsattvaṁ sthāvarajaṅgamam kṣetrakṣetrajña-saṁyogāttadviddhi bharatarṣabha'—The unmoving creation, such as trees, plants, creepers, grass and mountains etc., and moving beings, such as human beings, gods, beasts, birds, insects and fishes etc., (living on the earth, in the water and the sky)—all are born, of the union of Kṣetra (field), and Kṣetrajña (knower of the field).

All the perishable objects, which appear and disappear, are included in 'Kṣetra', which the knower of this Kṣetra, ever remaining the same, is Kṣetrajña. Affinity of the Kṣetrajña (Spirit), with Kṣetra (body), in the form of 'I'ness and 'Mine'ness, is the union of the spirit and the body. It is because of this assumed union, that the spirit has to be born, as moving and unmoving beings. This union has been called, 'attachment to the modes of nature', in the twenty-first verse. It means, that the eternal spirit by identifying itself with the kaleidoscopic prakṛti and its evolutes, body etc., assumes itself as perishable.

[The birth of moving, as well as, unmoving beings, has been denoted by the term 'Sañjāyate' (Is born) and the death will be denoted by the term 'Vinaśyatsu' (perishing), in the next verse.]

'Tadviddhi bharatarṣabha'—Lord Kṛṣṇa, exhorts Arjuna to know the fact that the contact (identification) of the spirit with the body, is responsible for its rebirth. So, if it does not assume its identification, with the body, it will not be reborn.

Appendix—Here within the expression 'yāvatsañjāyate' all the creatures born from the womb, born from an egg, sprouting from the ground, born of perspiration, water creatures, sky creatures (birds) and land creatures, men, gods, manes, ghosts, evil spirits and devils etc., should be included. The same fact has been pointed out in the sixth verse of the seventh chapter by the expression 'etadyonīni bhūtāni'.

In the topic of devotion, the Lord, having stated the twofold prakṛti—'parā' and 'aparā' as His, declared, "All beings have evolved from this twofold prakṛti and I am the origin of the entire creation and it dissolves in Me" (Gītā 7/6). But here in the topic of knowledge, the Lord declares that all beings are born of the union of 'Kṣetra' and 'Kṣetrajña'. It means that in the topic of devotion He draws a devotee's attention towards Him because a devotee has firm faith in Him. God is his means as well as end. But in the topic of knowledge the Lord draws attention towards the 'Kṣetrajña' (Self) that identification of 'Kṣetrajña' with 'Kṣetra' has led the man to the bondage of birth and death. Here the question arises that there is attraction and union between the objects of the same class, then how has there been a union of 'Kṣetrajña' (the Self) with the inert (the non-Self)? The answer is that as there can't be union of day and night, similarly there can't be union of 'Kṣetrajña' and 'Kṣetra'. But being a fragment of God, 'Kṣetrajña' has this power that it can draw an object belonging to a different class and can assume its affinity with that object. God has bestowed this freedom upon this being. But he has misused this freedom viz., he instead of assuming his affinity with God, has assumed his affinity with the world and has thus got entangled in the wheel of life and death (Gītā 13/21).

Link:—In the preceding verse, the Lord explained that the identification of the spirit with the body, leads the spirit to birth and death. Now, the question arises what should a man do, to be free from the cycle of birth and death. The Lord answers the question, in the next verse.

समं सर्वेषु भूतेषु तिष्ठन्तं परमेश्वरम्।
विनश्यत्स्वविनश्यन्तं यः पश्यति स पश्यति॥ २७॥

samaṁ sarveṣu bhūteṣu tiṣṭhantaṁ parameśvaram
vinaśyatsvavinaśyantaṁ yaḥ paśyati sa paśyati

He alone truly sees God who perceives the Supreme Lord, as imperishable and abiding equally, in all perishable beings. 27

Comment:—

'Samaṁ sarveṣu bhūteṣu'—It means, that the Lord abides equally in all beings, moving or unmoving, of various sizes, colours and forms, endowed with Sattva, Raja and Tama, modes of nature.

The Lord, in the second verse of this chapter declared, "Know Me as the Knower of the field (Kṣetrajña) in all fields (Kṣetras)". As the Lord identifying Himself with the spirit (Kṣetrajña), there said, that He is the spirit in all the bodies, here also points out that He abides, equally in all beings.

'Tiṣṭhantam'—All beings undergo birth, life and dissolution; they are born in the cosmic dawn and dissolve in the cosmic night. They are born in various species. In other words, they are always circulating. They do not remain constant, even for a moment. But the Lord remains constant, uniform and the same, in all these revolving beings.

'Parameśvaram'—God, is the Supreme Lord, of all beings who regard themselves as the Lord of someone or the other. He is the supreme Lord, of the entire creation, sentient or insentient.

'Vinaśyatsvavinaśyantaṁ yaḥ paśyati sa paśyati'—He truly sees, who perceives the imperishable Supreme Lord, the same, without any modifications, in all perishable beings. It means, that he who sees his own self, identified with a body does not see truly, while he who sees his self, identified with the Lord, sees truly.

In the second verse of this chapter, the Lord declared, "It is the knowledge of Kṣetra (prakṛti or matter) and Kṣetrajña (Puruṣa or Spirit), which I regard as true knowledge." The same fact, has been mentioned by the Lord here, when He declares, "He alone truly sees, who realises the Supreme Lord, as imperishable and abiding equally, in all perishable beings." It means, that in the union of Kṣetra (Matter) and Kṣetrajña (Spirit), Kṣetra ever undergoes modifications, while Kṣetrajña always remains the same. Similarly, all beings are born and then their bodies perish, but the Supreme Lord, ever remains the same, in all conditions and circumstances.

In the preceding (twenty-sixth) verse, the Lord explained that whatever being is born, know it as emanated, from the union of Kṣetra, and Kṣetrajña. Out of the two the Kṣetra ever undergoes modification, while there is no modification at all in the Kṣetrajña. So a striver, should realize this fact, that matter is constantly separating, from the self. In this verse, the Lord explains, that a striver should realize his identity with the Supreme Lord, Who is imperishable and Who abides, equally in all perishable beings.

Appendix—As in the sky sometimes there is light of the sun, sometimes it is dark, sometimes there is a cloud of smoke, sometimes the sky is overcast, sometimes there is lightning and thundering, sometimes it rains, sometimes it hails and sometimes different kinds of sounds are produced, but the sky does not undergo any change; it remains the same—untainted, unaffected and immutable. Similarly in the omnipresent Entity sometimes there is new creation and final annihilation, sometimes there is creation and annihilation, sometimes there is birth and death, sometimes there is famine, sometimes there is flood, sometimes there is an earthquake, sometimes there is a terrifying war but there is no difference in that Entity. There may be a lot of topsyturvydom but that Entity ever remains the same—untainted and immutable. This immutability is natural while modifications (attachment) are unnatural and assumed. A person may be bound or liberated, he may be sinful or virtuous, this immutable Entity prevails equally in both of them.

As the Ganges flows continuously but the bedrock, over which it flows, ever remains fixed. Sometimes the water of the Ganges is pure and clean, sometimes it is mixed with dust; sometimes water is lessened while sometimes it is in flood, sometimes the water becomes warm, sometimes it is cool; sometimes the speedy flow of water causes sound, sometimes it becomes calm. But the bedrock remains as if is, it does not undergo any change. Similarly sometimes there are fish in water, sometimes creatures such as snakes etc., come flowing, sometimes planks or beams come swimming, sometimes flowers appear flowing, sometimes rubbish, filth and dung etc., appear flowing, sometimes a dead body seems floating and sometimes a living person comes swimming. They all appear and disappear but the foundation stone remains the same fixed, unaffected and immutable. Similarly space, time, objects, persons, actions, states, circumstances and incidents etc., are continuously changing but the Self (divine Entity) ever remains immovable. All changes and destruction occur in space and time etc., but not in the self.

'Yaḥ paśyati sa paśyati'—This expression in the fifth verse of the fifth chapter has been used about the means and here in this verse it has been used for the end (perfection). The same fact will be pointed out ahead in the sixteenth verse of the eighteenth chapter by the negative inference that he who looks upon the pure Self as the doer, that man of perverse understanding, does not see right—'na sa paśyati durmatiḥ'.

Link:—In the next verse, the Lord declares the reward of the vision of a person, who sees the Lord, as imperishable and abiding, equally in all beings.

समं पश्यन्हि सर्वत्र समवस्थितमीश्वरम्।
न हिनस्त्यात्मनात्मानं ततो याति परां गतिम्॥ २८॥

samaṁ paśyanhi sarvatra samavasthitamīśvaram
na hinastyātmanātmānaṁ tato yāti parāṁ gatim

He who sees the Lord present, equally everywhere, realising this he does not destroy himself by the self, therefore, he reaches the Supreme Goal. 28

Comment:—

'Samaṁ paśyanhi sarvatra samavasthitamīśvaram'—The person who beholds the Lord, pervading the entire universe, the sentient and the insentient, the moving and the unmoving beings i.e., he realizes his identity with Him, does not kill the self, by the self i.e., does not follow a cycle of birth and death.

On the other hand, a person, who by identifying himself

with a body regards its fitness, sickness, birth and death etc., as his own, destroys the self by the self i.e., leads the self, to the cycle of birth and death. It means, that identity of the self, with the body, leads a person to a downfall and he has to follow, the cycle of birth and death.

In fact nobody can kill himself, as the self is indestructible. Moreover, nobody wants to make himself non-existent. In fact, to assume identity with the body, is to commit suicide; to degrade himself and put himself into the cycle of birth and death.

'Tato yāti paraṁ gatim'—A person (self), who by identifying himself with the body, had to take birth in good and evil bodies, by realizing his identity with the Supreme Lord, attains the Supreme Goal, viz., the Supreme Lord, Who is ever attained.

A Vital Fact

The Lord, pervades everywhere, every time, every person, thing, incident, circumstance or action, equally. If He is hard to be attained, what is easy to be attained? We can attain Him, wherever we desire. In fact, the seemingly existent world, does not stay even, for a moment. In the world, there is nothing but change. It is a mass of change only. As, when an electric fan moves speedily, it seems like a circle and its blades appear like the circle and they go out of sight, similarly, the world seems to exist and the Lord like the blade Who really exists is not seen. Actually it is only God who exists.

Did these bodies, which appear today, exist, a hundred years ago? Will they exist after a hundred years? If the answer is 'No', it means that they do not exist at present, also. The reason is that, whatever does not exist at the beginning, and at the end, has no existence in the middle also. But God, existed even before creation, will exist after dissolution and also exists now. Thus, the world is actually non-existent, while God exists always. But the world seems to exist, by ignorance, because of God, who is existent.

If delusion perishes, the world will not appear to exist, only the Lord will be seen—'The Supreme is all' (Gītā 7/19). As in different ornaments made of gold, there is nothing else, besides gold, in the entire universe there is nothing else, but the Lord. The Lord, existed in the past, He exists now and He will exist in future. The only aim of human life, is to realize Him.

If a person instead of realizing God, gets entangled in the world, it is not human, it is beastly. This beastliness, is to be renounced. So a striver, should behold the imperishable Lord, in all the perishable beings. If he beholds the perishable and not the imperishable, he commits suicide.

In the Mahābhārata also, it is mentioned that he who in spite of being imperishable, holds the spirit as perishable, which of the sins has not been committed, by such a suicidal thief?

He, who beholds the Lord, pervading the entire universe equally, does not commit suicide but realises the Supreme Goal. But, he who, instead of beholding the Lord pervading the entire universe, beholds the universe and the body only, commits suicide, and instead of attaining the Supreme Goal, follows, a cycle of birth and death. So a man, should lift himself by himself, he should not degrade, himself (Gītā 6/5).

As a face, reflected in the looking glass, and an elephant, seen in a dream are not real, this universe in spite of, having no existence of its own, seems to exist. If a striver, has a belief that the Lord exists, and the universe only seems to exist, he will realize the fact, in the course of time. When a striver is at Vṛndāvana, he has not to remember this fact or he has not to fix it in his mind by constant repetition, but he has not the least doubt, about it. Similarly, if a striver assumes the existence of the Lord firmly, even though he may not see Him now, he will realize His existence, because the unreal has no existence and the real cannot remain concealed, for a long time.

Appendix—In fact in the twenty-seventh and twenty-eighth verses there is description of the Self (Soul) but because of the use of words 'Parameśvara' (Supreme Lord) and 'Īśvara' (Lord) in these verses, the Supreme Lord has been described in the explanation (comment) because the Self is identical with the Supreme Soul (Gītā 13/22).

Link:—In the twenty-sixth verse, the Lord talked about the union of Kṣetra (Matter) and Kṣetrajña (Spirit). There are two ways to be free from this union—realizing one's identity with the Lord, and renouncing one's assumed affinity with Prakṛti (Body). The former, has been discussed in the preceding two verses. Now He explains the latter, in the next two verses.

प्रकृत्यैव च कर्माणि क्रियमाणानि सर्वशः ।
यः पश्यति तथात्मानमकर्तारं स पश्यति ॥ २९ ॥

prakṛtyaiva ca karmāṇi kriyamāṇāni sarvaśaḥ
yaḥ paśyati tathātmānamakartāraṁ sa paśyati

He who sees that all actions are performed only by nature (prakṛti), and that the self (ātmā) is not the doer, he verily sees reality. 29

Comment:—

'Prakṛtyaiva ca karmāṇi kriyamāṇāni sarvaśaḥ'—In fact, the self or the Absolute, is equanimous, tranquil and devoid of modifications, while His potency, prakṛti, is full of activities. Though prakṛti is also said to be devoid of activity, at the time of dissolution, yet on reflection, it becomes clear that it starts its activity in subtle form, towards the creation, at that time, also. That subtle activity, is known as non-activity, because in that state, there is no activity of the creation of the universe. From the beginning of the creation, to its middle, prakṛti moves towards creation, while after its middle, it starts moving towards dissolution. If prakṛti is said to be inactive, during dissolution and final dissolution, how can there be beginning, middle and end of dissolution, and final dissolution? It means, that activity goes on in subtle form, even during dissolution. During a state of creation, there is more activity, while during the state of dissolution, there is less activity.

The sun rises in the morning. Its light increases from morning to noon, and decreases, from noon to evening. From evening to midnight, it grows darker, while from midnight to morning, darkness decreases. Actually the juncture of light and darkness is noon, and midnight, nor morning and evening. Thus the process of light and darkness, goes on continuously. Similarly, Prakṛti undergoes activity, during creation as well as dissolution, new creation, as well as, final dissolution.*

When a man (Spirit) identifies himself, with active prakṛti, the activities performed by the body seems to him, to be his own activities.

'Yaḥ paśyati tathātmānamakartāraṁ sa paśyati'—All the actions, such as eating, drinking, walking, moving, rising, sitting, sleeping, waking, meditating and trance etc., which go on in the gross, subtle and causal bodies, are performed by prakṛti, not by the self, because the self is without action. He who intuits this reality, realizes that he himself, is a non-doer.

Here, the activities are said to be performed by Prakṛti, while in other verses, they are said to be performed by the modes of Prakṛti, or by senses. These statements, though apparently different, are basically the same. Prakṛti is the cause of guṇas and senses. Guṇas are the evolutes of prakṛti and senses are the evolutes of guṇas. So all actions performed by prakṛti or guṇas (Modes of Prakṛti) or senses are performed, by Prakṛti.

Appendix—All actions are performed by Prakṛti, not by the Self. In the Gītā the actions, performed by 'Prakṛti', have been described in several ways such as—actions performed by the modes of nature and actions performed by senses etc., as all actions are performed by the modes of nature—'prakṛteḥ

* The duration of the new creation is measured by the sun. But at the time of final dissolution when even the sun is merged, time is measured by the only means, the eternal, imperishable Lord.

kriyamāṇāni guṇaḥ karmāṇi sarvaśaḥ' (3/27); the modes are acting on the modes—'guṇā guṇeṣu vartante' (3/28); there is no doer other than the modes—'nānyaṁ guṇebhyaḥ kartāraṁ yadā draṣṭānupaśyati' (14/19); Senses move among the Sense-objects—'indriyāṇīndriyārtheṣu vartante' (5/9) etc. It means that all actions are performed by 'Prakṛti' only. Therefore Prakṛti is never inactive in the least, while in the Self there is never any activity in the least. Therefore in the Gītā, it is mentioned that the Sāṅkhyayogī, who knows the truth, believes that he does nothing at all—'naiva kiñcitkaromīti yukto manyeta tattvavit' (5/8); he neither acts himself nor causes others to act—'naiva kurvanna kārayan' (5/13); the Self in spite of dwelling in the body neither acts nor is tainted—'śarīrastho'pi kaunteya na karoti na lipyate' (13/31); he who assumes the Self as the doer, that man of perverse understanding does not see right because his mind is impure (untrained)—'tatraivaṁ sati kartāramātmānaṁ.............' (18/16) etc.

यदा भूतपृथग्भावमेकस्थमनुपश्यति।
तत एव च विस्तारं ब्रह्म सम्पद्यते तदा॥ ३०॥

yadā bhūtapṛthagbhāvamekasthamanupaśyati
tata eva ca vistāraṁ brahma sampadyate tadā

When he realizes, that the manifold state of beings is centred in prakṛti, and evolve from that prakṛti alone, then he attains Brahma. 30

Comment:—

[Prakṛti can be seen in two forms—actions and things (objects). In the twenty-ninth verse, there is mention of how to renounce affinity with actions, while in this verse there is description of how to renounce, affinity with objects.]

'Yadā bhūtapṛthagbhāvamekasthamanupaśyati tata eva ca vistāraṁ brahma sampadyate tadā'—When a striver, realizes the whole variety of beings, whether born from the womb or egg and ground or sweat, with gross, subtle and causal bodies, as centred in Prakṛti, he attains Brahma.

The bodies, names, shapes, forms, mental projections, qualities, modifications, birth, sustenance and, death, of all beings of the three worlds, are born of prakṛti. The bodies of all beings, evolve from prakṛti, rest in prakṛti and merge in it. He, who realizes this fact, attains Brahma i.e., he realizes the Self or the Absolute. Actually, Brahma is already attained, it was only the affinity with Prakṛti, which was an obstacle to this attainment. When he realizes, that all beings rest in Prakṛti, and are born of Prakṛti, he realizes, the axiomatic self.

All the moving and unmoving bodies, born of the earth, rest on the earth, undergo changes and activities*, on the earth and merge in the earth. It means, that they are nothing else, besides the earth. Similarly, all bodies of beings, are born of Prakṛti, rest in it and merge in it. So, they are nothing else, besides prakṛti. In the same way, the self always rests, in the Supreme Soul. Though it undergoes modifications, because of its assumed affinity with prakṛti; yet really, it is unattached. If a person, realizes this fact, he attains, Brahma.

Attachment and aversion, are born out of affinity with prakṛti. A man, perceives virtues in others, if he has attachment for them, but perceives vices, out of aversion. So, this veil of attachment and aversion, conceals reality. But, when a striver, realizes that his so-called, gross, subtle and causal bodies, as well as the bodies of other beings, emanate from prakṛti, rest in it, and merge in it, then he realizes the negation of the three bodies in the self, the veil of attachment and aversion is removed, and he realizes God, Who is ever realized.

Appendix—In the preceding verse there is mention of the

* There are two kinds of activities—those which happen (occur) and those which are performed. The growth of a boy to youth and old age are the activities which happen while eating and drinking etc., are the activities which are performed. All these activities take place in bodies.

person while in the verse there is mention of time.

In the topic of devotion, the Lord declares that diverse feelings of creatures emanate from Him alone—'bhavanti bhāvā bhūtānāṁ matta eva pṛthagvidhāḥ' (10/5); but here in the topic of knowledge, He declares that diverse feelings of creatures are centred in 'Prakṛti'. It means that where there is the distinction between the real and the unreal, there all the feelings are centred in the unreal but where there is the description of the entire form of God, there all feelings emanate from Him. In the entire form, the real and the unreal—'All is God'—'sadasaccāham' (9/19).

Link:—In the next verse, the Lord describes the self, to whom Brahma is attained, which has been mentioned in the preceding verse, and which in the twenty-second verse of this chapter, has been described, as detached from the body.

अनादित्वान्निर्गुणत्वात्परमात्मायमव्ययः ।
शरीरस्थोऽपि कौन्तेय न करोति न लिप्यते ॥ ३१ ॥

anāditvānnirguṇatvātparamātmāyamavyayaḥ
śarīrastho'pi kaunteya na karoti na lipyate

O Kaunteya, the self being without beginning and without attributes, is imperishable Paramātmā (Supreme Soul), though dwelling in the body, it neither acts, nor is tainted. 31

Comment:—

'Anāditvānnirguṇatvātparamātmāyamavyayaḥ'—As has been mentioned in the nineteenth verse also, the self is without beginning. But there prakṛti has also been called, beginningless. So what is the difference between the two? In response to this question, the Lord explains, that the self is without attributes (guṇas), and their evolutes, while prakṛti, is full of three guṇas and modifications. The self, being free from guṇas and modifications, is the imperishable and untainted Supreme Soul.

'Śarīrastho'pi kaunteya na karoti na lipyate'—The self, in spite of dwelling in a body, neither acts nor is tainted, it remains detached, from prakṛti and is attributeless and imperishable. It is, neither a doer, nor an enjoyer. But, when It identifies Itself with a body, It assumes, that It is a doer as well as, the enjoyer of pleasure and pain. But, actually It is only an illuminator and spectator, It is never tainted, because of being a portion of the Lord. It ever rests in Him. The illuminator, here means, illumination incarnate. It is not an illuminator, in relation to the illumined.

Here the term 'Api', signifies that every embodied being, from an ant to Lord Brahmā since eternity, has been unattached and untainted, by its own intrinsic nature. He had never any identity with a body, as the two belong to two different classes. The body, being an evolute of prakṛti, remains seated in Matter, while the self being a fragment of God remains, identical with the Lord. However he may seem to be mixed up, with the body and feel identified with the body, his untaintedness, is never affected. He, ever remains untainted. He may not realize this fact, yet he undergoes no modifications. The self, did nothing, does nothing, was neither contaminated, nor gets contaminated.

Though the self, seated in prakṛti, becomes a doer and an enjoyer, yet in the twenty-first verse, the Lord announced, that the spirit seated in prakṛti, experiences pleasure and pain. While, here He declares, that the self (Spirit) in spite of dwelling in the body, is neither a doer nor an experiencer. Actually prakṛti and its evolute, body—both are one and the same. Actually, the self has no connection, either with the individual body, or the collective prakṛti. But, it assumes itself, as a doer and an experiencer, by identifying itself with a body, otherwise it is neither a doer, nor an enjoyer.

Appendix—The self is without beginning while the body has a beginning. The self is without 'guṇas' (attributes) while the body is an evolute of 'guṇas'. The self is the Supreme Soul but the body is the non-self. The self is imperishable while the body is perishable. Therefore though an ignorant person holds that the self dwells in the body but in fact it does not rest in the body viz., it is totally detached from the body—'na karoti na lipyate'. The reason is that the body is related with the world but the self is related with the Supreme Soul (God). Therefore the self can never abide in the body. But without paying attention to this fact, a man assumes the self to be abiding in the body.

'Nirguṇatvāt'—Though the self is devoid of guṇas, yet it is bound by being attached to 'guṇas' (Gītā 13/21). Outwardly it appears that bondage is natural and salvation will be attained by making efforts. But the fact is that salvation is natural and a person himself paves the way to bondage. Guṇas are not at all related with the self but they are related with 'Prakṛti' (Gītā 13/23). Therefore the self is without beginning, without attributes, is the Supreme Soul, is imperishable and it neither acts nor is tainted—all this is quite natural. A striver has to realize this naturality of one's own.

As while residing in a house, we are different from the house, so are we (the self) assuming to be dwelling in the body, different from the body.

'Na karoti na lipyate'—The self neither acts nor is tainted—this fact is not a result of any spiritual practice, but it is so by nature. It means that in the self there is no doership-enjoyership—it is self-evident. It needs no effort viz., nothing is to be done for it. It means that doership and enjoyership are not to be wiped out but they are not to be accepted in the self; but a striver has to realize their absence because in fact they are not in the self. Therefore a striver should realize that he is neither a doer nor an enjoyer. Realization of freedom from doership and enjoyership in the self (disinterestedness and freedom from the sense of mine) is liberation from the worldly bondage. In the Gītā, this point has been declared in this way that the memory is gained—'naṣṭo mohaḥ smṛtirlabdhā' (18/73).

If the self is not the doer and enjoyer, then who is the doer and enjoyer? Let us reflect upon it. First think over—who is a doer? The body is not the doer because it is perishing every moment. Mind, intellect, citta (faculty of reflection) and ego—these four are instruments which are called internal instruments (antaḥkaraṇa). This 'antaḥkaraṇa' is also not the doer because the instrument depends upon the doer but the doer is independent—'svatantraḥ kartā' (Pāṇi. chap. 1/4/54). An instrument is very helpful in the accomplishment of an action (task)—'sādhakatamaṁ karaṇam' (Pāṇi. chap. 1/4/42). Therefore without the instrument an action is not accomplished at all. As a pen does not write independently but that is merely an instrument for writing which depends upon the writer (doer). Therefore an instrument is not a doer and a doer is not an instrument. Secondly if there is doership in the instrument, why does the self feel happy and sad? If the instrument is happy and sad, what harm does it cause us? The true self is also not the doer because 'I'ness is the evolute of 'Prakṛti', then how is this 'I'ness possible in the self which transcends 'Prakṛti'? Had there been doership in the self, it would have never been destroyed because the self is imperishable. Therefore here the Lord negated doership in the self—'na karoti'.

In the eighteenth chapter also the Lord declares, "He who assumes the self as the doer, that man of perverse understanding does not see right because his mind is not pure" (Gītā 18/16). In fact he who is an enjoyer (experiencer) (who becomes happy and sad) is a doer.

Now let us reflect upon—who is an enjoyer? The enjoyer is neither real nor unreal. The real can't be an enjoyer because the real lacks nothing—'nābhāvo vidyate sataḥ'; while the enjoyership comes to an end—'na lipyate'. The unreal can also not be an enjoyer because the unreal has no existence—'nāsato vidyate bhāvaḥ'. In the unreal there is no consciousness. Therefore in the unreal there can't be even an imagination of enjoyership. It means that doership and enjoyership are neither in the real nor in the unreal. In the union of the real and the unreal also there is neither doership nor enjoyership; because as the union of the day and the night is impossible, so is the union of the real and the unreal impossible. Therefore doership and enjoyership are merely assumed—'kartāhamiti manyate' (3/27). When a striver discriminately, totally renounces attachment to the body viz., wipes out the sense of 'I' and 'mine' (which is actually not there), then he remains neither a doer nor an enjoyer but only a divine entity remains. In this way a striver, having realized the absence of doership and enjoyership in him, is liberated viz., he does not remain a doer or an enjoyer (experiencer) but remains the Pure Self (Divine Entity).

'Na karoti na lipyate'—The Lord has explained and discussed this expression in the thirty-second and thirty-third verses of this chapter.

Link:—How is the self dwelling in the body, not tainted? The answer ensues:—

यथा सर्वगतं सौक्ष्म्यादाकाशं नोपलिप्यते।
सर्वत्रावस्थितो देहे तथात्मा नोपलिप्यते॥ ३२॥

yathā sarvagatam saukṣmyādākāśam nopalipyate
sarvatrāvasthito dehe tathātmā nopalipyate

As the all-pervading ether is not tainted because of being subtle, so the self (ātmā) permeated everywhere in the body, is not tainted. 32

Comment:—

[In the previous verse, the Lord explained by the expression 'Na karoti' (neither acts), that the self is a non-doer, while by the expression 'Na lipyate' (nor is tainted), He explained that the self, is not an experiencer. But here in this verse, first He explains, how the self, is a non-experiencer, while in the next verse, He will explain how the self, is a non-doer. Why has He changed the order? The answer is, that a man performs actions in order to, receive its fruit. So, first he thinks of the reward, and then performs actions. Thus, the Lord asks a striver, not to be an enjoyer. By renouncing the fruit of action, doership, is automatically renounced.]

'Yathā sarvagataṁ saukṣmyādākāśaṁ nopalipyate'—Ether equally, pervading the air, fire, water and earth is not tainted by their qualities and modifications, because of its subtle character.

'Sarvatrāvasthito dehe tathātmā nopalipyate'—As ether, equally pervading the gross elements, such as air etc., is not tainted, so the Self pervading, all bodies is not tainted, because it is eternal, omnipresent, immovable, constant, everlasting, unmanifest, unthinkable and immutable (Gītā 2/24-25) and the entire universe, is pervaded, by the imperishable Self (Gītā 2/17).

Appendix—Consciousness is one but because of ego, it appears diverse. The soul is called a fragment because it has identified itself with ego, a fragment of 'aparā prakṛti' (lower nature)—'mamaivāṁśo jīvaloke jīvabhūtaḥ sanātanaḥ' (Gītā 15/7). If it does not identify itself with ego, there is only one consciousness. Besides that entity all is illusion. That divine entity is the base, support, illuminator and refuge of all illusions. That divine entity is not unipresent but that pervades everywhere. The entire creation (actions and objects) are within that entity. The creation is born and perishes but that entity remains the same. It means that the divine entity neither dwells in the body nor in prakṛti only but like the ether pervades everywhere within and without the entire creation including all the bodies. That all pervading entity is the self and that is Godhood. It means that the omnipresent entity is only one. That is Yoga of the Yogīs, that is wisdom of the wise and that is God of devotees. A striver should always aim at attaining that entity.

That entity seems to be unipresent because of ego. That ego is based on the desire for pleasure. While practising the spiritual discipline also, a striver starts enjoying pleasures—'sukhasaṅgena badhnāti' (Gītā 14/6). This desire for pleasure lingers till a striver transcends the three guṇas (modes). Therefore a striver should be very cautious in order to ward off the desire for pleasure.

Link:—In the preceding verse, the Lord explained that the Self is not tainted i.e., the Self is not an enjoyer. In the next verse, He will explain, how the Self is not a doer.

यथा प्रकाशयत्येकः कृत्स्नं लोकमिमं रविः ।
क्षेत्रं क्षेत्री तथा कृत्स्नं प्रकाशयति भारत ॥ ३३ ॥

yathā prakāśayatyekaḥ kṛtsnaṁ lokamimaṁ raviḥ
kṣetraṁ kṣetrī tathā kṛtsnaṁ prakāśayati bhārata

O scion of the Bharata (Arjuna), as the one sun, illumines the entire universe, so does the Lord of the Kṣetra (spirit) light up, the whole Kṣetra (field). 33

Comment:—

'Yathā prakāśayatyekaḥ kṛtsnaṁ lokamimaṁ raviḥ'—One sun, illumines the entire universe, and all activities are performed in its light, but it has no feeling of doership. A learned Brāhmaṇa, studies the Vedas in the light of the sun, while a hunter shoots animals in the same light, but the light is not held responsible, for the study of the Vedas or for hunting.

Here the term 'Loka', stands for the entire universe (fourteen worlds), because all objects (moon, stars, fire, jewels and herbs etc.,) are, illumined by the sun.

'Kṣetraṁ kṣetrī tathā kṛtsnaṁ prakāśayati bhārata'—Like the sun, one Kṣetrī (Kṣetrajña or spirit), illumines the entire field (bodies) i.e., all actions are performed in the light of the spirit (self), yet the self, neither performs actions nor, does it cause them to be performed.

The sun, illumines the gross universe only i.e., actions of the gross universe, are performed in the light of the sun, while the self (spirit), illumines the gross, subtle and causal, all the three kinds of bodies, i.e., in its light, all actions of the three kinds of bodies, are performed.

As the sun, has no pride of doership of illumining the entire universe, nor is it tainted by the ẹvil of partiality, the self also remains untainted, unattached, impartial and uniform, without having a pride of doership of infusing the light of life, and activity into the entire universe. It is the self, which is the base and illuminator, of all actions, things and appearances etc., because, nothing can exist without a base, and nothing can be illumined, without an illuminator.

Appendix—As the sun illumines the entire universe and in its light all the good and evil actions are performed but the sun is neither the doer nor the enjoyer of those actions. Similarly the self illumines all the bodies of the entire universe viz., provides existence and agility to them, but in fact it itself neither does any action nor is tainted viz., it is neither a doer nor an enjoyer. It means that the pure self takes no pride in illumining the bodies of the entire universe.

Only one, who can do a work, is responsible to do it. As however expert a painter may be, he can't make a painting without the material (colour and brush etc.,) similarly the self can do nothing without the help of 'Prakṛti', therefore the self cannot be responsible at all to do any action. This is everyone's experience that we can do nothing without the body. Therefore the body is of use only, if we want to do an action with it. If we don't want to do any work, then what is the use of the body? It is of no use. If we don't want to see any object, what is the utility of the eye for us? If we don't want to hear, what is the use of the ear to us? In the performance of physical actions, the physical (gross) body is used. In reflection and meditation, the subtle body is used. In trance, the causal body is used.* If we do nothing with these three bodies, what is their use to us?

* Trance and relapse (deviation)—both occur in the causal body. When

The body and the actions performed with the body are useful for the world. The self is a divine entity, therefore the body and the actions performed with the body are of no use for the self. The self lacks nothing, it is self sufficient, therefore we need nothing for ourselves. Besides the divine entity (self), there is none else because the reality can be only one, not two. Therefore we need no companion. Thus when we have no affinity with any action (doership), nor we have any relation with the thing to be acquired through desire, nor have we any affinity with the possessions (sense of mine), the identification with 'Prakṛti' will be cut asunder. With the breach of identification with 'Prakṛti', the activity will take place but there will be no one as doer or an enjoyer (Gītā 13/29).

Link:—Now the Lord winds up the topic of Kṣetra (Field, body), and Kṣetrajña (knower, self), by mentioning the reward of fully grasping the difference, between the two.

क्षेत्रक्षेत्रज्ञयोरेवमन्तरं ज्ञानचक्षुषा।
भूतप्रकृतिमोक्षं च ये विदुर्यान्ति ते परम्॥ ३४॥

kṣetrakṣetrajñayorevamantaraṁ jñānacakṣuṣā
bhūtaprakṛtimokṣaṁ ca ye viduryānti te param

Those, who with the eyes of wisdom, perceive the difference between Kṣetra (Field) and Kṣetrajña (the knower of the field) and between prakṛti along with its evolutes and the self (ātmā), attain the Supreme. 34

Comment:—

[The Discipline of Knowledge, begins with discrimination, and ends in real discrimination (knowledge). Discrimination, enables a man to renounce his affinity, with prakṛti and leads him to God-realization. This fact, is mentioned here.]

---

affinity is renounced with the causal body, that is the natural state of Self-realization (Sahaja Samādhi or Sahajāvasthā).

'Kṣetrakṣetrajñayorevamantaraṁ jñānacakṣuṣā'—Here, the expression 'Jñānacakṣuṣā' (eye of wisdom), denotes discrimination between the real, and the unreal, Kṣetra and Kṣetrajña. The Kṣetra, (Field) ever undergoes modifications, but the Kṣetrajña (spirit) (the knower of the field), always remains the same and no modification, is ever possible in it.

'Bhūtaprakṛtimokṣaṁ ca ye viduryānti te param'—Discrimination, enables a man to renounce his connection with prakṛti, and its evolutes. When a striver realizes, that he (self), is different from prakṛti, he attains God.

This God-realization, has been explained by the Lord, by different expressions (in the fourth verse of the twelfth chapter, in the eighteenth and twenty-third verses as well as in this verse of the thirteenth chapter).

In the Discipline of Knowledge, identification of the self with the body, is the main obstacle to God-realization. So, in the first and the second verses, the Lord discussed that the spirit (self) is different from the body (Kṣetra) (field). Then, He described in several ways, that Kṣetrajña is different from Kṣetra. Here, He is concluding the topic by declaring, that those who perceive the difference between Kṣetra and Kṣetrajña properly, their affinity, with Kṣetra, is totally renounced.

Kṣetrajña, has accepted its separateness from God, by having a disinclination for Him, while it has assumed its identity with Kṣetra by having an inclination for it. So, the Lord declares, both the facts—that it has its identity with God, while, it is totally distinct, from Kṣetra. The Lord, in the second verse of this chapter, declared its identity with God, while here He is explaining that Kṣetra has its identity, with the world. Both the statements, mean that Kṣetrajña, has its identity, with God.

Into a pitch dark house, no one dares to go, after hearing that it is inhabited by scorpions, snakes and thieves etc., and is also haunted by ghosts and evil spirits. But, when a courageous person, enters the house with a lamp, all kinds of fears are removed, because he finds nothing of that sort in the house. Similarly, by having disinclination for God, Who pervades everywhere, in the form of light, the world, appears to exist to him, and he is haunted by several kinds of fear. But when he realizes the reality, he comes to know, that the world has no existence, and all his fears, are removed. Then he beholds only God, Who pervades every person, thing and circumstance, all the time. A lamp, has to be brought, in order to remove darkness, but this light (God), is not to be brought from, anywhere. Therefore, a striver, by renouncing totally his affinity, with the world, naturally realizes the Supreme.

Appendix—The knowledge of the distinction between 'Kṣetra' and 'Kṣetrajña' is called 'discrimination'. The strivers who having attached importance to this discrimination, perceive the difference between 'Kṣetra' and 'Kṣetrajña' in right perspective, and realize 'Prakṛti' and its evolute (body) totally different from the self, attain God. From their view-point nothing else remains besides the Pure Consciousness.

The Lord by the expression 'madbhāvāyopapadyate' (13/18) mentioned the attainment of God endowed with attributes, while here by the expression 'ye viduryānti te param' He mentions the attainment of attributeless God (the Absolute). In fact the attainment of 'madbhāva' and 'param' is one and the same (Gītā 8/21, 14/27).

ॐ तत्सदिति श्रीमद्भगवद्गीतासूपनिषत्सु ब्रह्मविद्यायां योगशास्त्रे
श्रीकृष्णार्जुनसंवादे क्षेत्रक्षेत्रज्ञविभागयोगो नाम त्रयोदशोऽध्यायः॥१३॥

oṁ tatsaditi śrīmadbhagavadgītāsūpaniṣatsu brahmavidyāyāṁ yogaśāstre śrīkṛṣṇārjunasaṁvāde kṣetrakṣetrajñavibhāgayogo nāma trayodaśo'dhyāyaḥ

Thus with Oṁ, Tat, Sat, the names of the Lord, in the Upaniṣad of the Bhagavadgītā, the knowledge of Brahma, the

Supreme, the scripture of Yoga and the dialogue between Śrī Kṛṣṇa and Arjuna, this is the thirteenth discourse designated: "The Yoga of Discrimination, between the Kṣetra and the Kṣetrajña."

In this chapter, there is description of the distinction between, Kṣetra (Field, Prakṛti) and Kṣetrajña (Knower of the field, spirit). When a striver realizes, that the Kṣetra, is different from the Kṣetrajña, he realizes his union, with God. So the chapter has been entitled "Kṣetrakṣetrajñavibhāgayoga."

Words, letters and Uvāca (said) in the Thirteenth Chapter—

(1) In this chapter, in **'Atha trayodaśo'dhyāyaḥ'** there are three words, in **'Śrībhagavānuvāca'**, there are two words, in verses, there are four hundred and eight words, and there are thirteen concluding words. Thus the total number of words is four hundred and twenty-six.

(2) In this chapter in **'Atha trayodaśo'dhyāyaḥ'**, there are eight letters, in **'Śrībhagavānuvāca'** there are seven letters, in verses, there are one thousand and eighty-eight letters, and there are fifty-two concluding letters. Thus the total number of letters, is one thousand one hundred and fifty-five. In this chapter, there are thirty-two letters, in each verse.

(3) In this chapter there is one **'Uvāca'** (said)—**'Śrībhagavānuvāca'.**

Metres Used in the Thirteenth Chapter

In this chapter, out of thirty-four verses, in the first quarter of the first verse and the third quarter of the eighteenth verse, 'ma-gaṇa' being used there is **'ma-vipulā'** metre; in the third quarter of the seventeenth verse and first quarter of the thirty-first verse, 'ra-gaṇa' being used there is **'ra-vipulā'** metre; and in the first quarter of the twenty-third verse 'na-gaṇa' being used there is **'na-vipulā'** metre. The remaining twenty-nine verses possess the characteristics, of right **'pathyāvaktra'**, Anuṣṭup metre.

|| Shri Hari ||

Fourteenth Chapter

INTRODUCTION

At the end of the thirteenth chapter, Lord Kṛṣṇa said that he, who with an eye of wisdom, perceives the difference between Kṣetra and Kṣetrajña, attains the Supreme. Now a question arises as to what that wisdom (Jñāna) is, what its value or glory is and how it is easily gained? The Lord, starts the fourteenth chapter, in order to answer these questions.

Connection with prakṛti and its evolutes, leads to bondage. The Lord, in the thirteenth chapter, explained how to renounce connection with prakṛti. Now, He starts the fourteenth chapter, in order to explain the method of renouncing the link with its evolutes, the Guṇas. In the first two verses, He glorifies wisdom.

श्रीभगवानुवाच

परं भूयः प्रवक्ष्यामि ज्ञानानां ज्ञानमुत्तमम्।
यज्ज्ञात्वा मुनयः सर्वे परां सिद्धिमितो गताः ॥ १ ॥

śrībhagavānuvāca

paraṁ bhūyaḥ pravakṣyāmi jñānānāṁ jñānamuttamam
yajjñātvā munayaḥ sarve parāṁ siddhimito gatāḥ

The Blessed Lord said:

I shall once again explain to you that supreme wisdom (Jñāna), the best of all wisdoms by knowing which, all sages have attained the highest perfection, and were liberated, from this mundane existence. 1

Comment:—

'Paraṁ bhūyaḥ pravakṣyāmi jñānānāṁ jñānamuttamam'—The

expression 'Bhūyaḥ pravakṣyāmi', denotes the Lord's declaration to explain the knowledge (Jñāna) (discrimination) of Kṣetra and Kṣetrajña, prakṛti (Matter) and Puruṣa (Spirit), as described in the eighteenth, twenty-third and thirty-fourth verses of the thirteenth chapter.

This wisdom (Jñāna) is the supreme of all other knowledge—spiritual as well as mundane, of arts, sciences, languages and scripts etc., because other knowledge leads to bondage, while it leads to God-realization. Here, the Lord has used, two terms 'Uttama' and 'Para', which mean the same 'Supreme' or 'the best'. The term 'Uttama' (best) denotes that this knowledge is the best, as it is conducive to renouncement of connection between the body and the world, while the term 'Para' (Supreme) denotes that this knowledge, tends to God-realization.

'Yajjñātvā munayaḥ sarve paraṁ siddhimito gatāḥ'—By knowing, i.e., realizing that supreme wisdom all great sages who attained God-realization, and being liberated, from mundane existence, without any exception.

A muni (Sage), is he, who renounces his affinity, with the body. The expression, 'Paraṁ siddhim' denotes, that all the mundane perfections including the Siddhis, such as, Aṇimā, Mahimā and Garimā etc., gained, by the Yogīs are merely imperfections, because all of these lead to bondage, and the cycle of birth and death and are obstacles to God-realization. The highest perfection, is God-realization because it frees a man from the cycle of birth and death.

Appendix—(This fourteenth chapter is an appendix to the thirteenth chapter.) This wisdom of the division between 'Kṣetra' and 'Kṣetrajña' is superior to all other earthly and unearthly wisdoms and is the Supreme. This wisdom is an unerring device for God-realization, therefore having realized this wisdom, all strivers attain God viz., are liberated from mundane existence.

'Jñānānāṁ jñānamuttamam'—This expression means that this wisdom is superior to Sāttvika, Rājasa and Tāmasa knowledge and also to the earthly as well as unearthly knowledge and is the Supreme. No other wisdom besides this can lead a striver to the attainment of the highest perfection. There is nothing else besides God—this realization is the attainment of the highest perfection. It means that for the man who has attained the highest perfection, actions and objects lose their existence totally and nothing remains in his view except that divine entity which really exists.

इदं ज्ञानमुपाश्रित्य मम साधर्म्यमागताः।
सर्गेऽपि नोपजायन्ते प्रलये न व्यथन्ति च॥ २॥

idaṁ jñānamupāśritya mama sādharmyamāgatāḥ
sarge'pi nopajāyante pralaye na vyathanti ca

Those, who having taken refuge in this wisdom and have merged into My Being, are not born again, at the time of a new creation, nor do they suffer, at the time of final dissolution. 2

Comment:—

'Idaṁ jñānamupāśritya'—In the preceding verse, the term 'wisdom' was qualified by the adjectives, supreme and best. Having acquired that wisdom, a man's doubts perish, and he becomes, an embodiment of wisdom.

'Mama sādharmyamāgatāḥ'—Having acquired that wisdom, people enter into the Lord's Being i.e., they become free from doership and enjoyership, like the Lord and realize that they are uniform and untainted, like Him.

The wise, become uniform and untainted, like the Lord, but they cannot create, sustain and destroy the universe, like Him. Some of the Yogīs by the practice of Yoga, acquire some exceptional power, but that cannot be on a par with, the Lord's power, which is but natural. The power of a Yogī, is limited, while that of the Lord is unlimited, as He is, omnipotent.

'Sarge'pi nopajāyante'—Here, the term 'api' (also), denotes that the wise are not born, even at the time of creation, when different worlds come into existence, and their masters or officers are born. Those wise men, being free from contact with the Guṇas, are not born, because it is contact with the Guṇas which determines, one's birth.

'Pralaye na vyathanti ca'—At the time of final dissolution, all beings are scorched or drowned by floods. There is commotion and lamentation in the entire universe. But, those wise men are not tormented, they do not undergo any commotion or lamentation.

They are neither born, at the time of new creation, nor are tormented at the time of final dissolution, because their contact with Prakṛti and its Guṇas, which is the cause of birth, death and lamentation etc., is totally, renounced.

Appendix—Till affinity with the causal body, persists in mediation, a striver attains 'nirvikalpa sthiti' (a state of trance) and when this affinity goes away, then there is natural transcendental awareness—'nirvikalpa bodha'. There is relapse from the 'nirvikalpa sthiti' but from 'nirvikalpa bodha' there is no such relapse. It means that there is deviation in 'nirvikalpa sthiti' but there is never any such deviation at all in 'nirvikalpa bodha'; this transcendental awareness ever remains the same. This fact has been pointed out here by the expression 'sarge'pi nopajāyante pralaye na vyathanti ca'.

There are new creation and final dissolution in 'Prakṛti'. Having attained God, Who transcends 'Prakṛti', there is no effect of the new creation and final dissolution because that God-realized soul has no affinity with 'Prakṛti'. That state, when there is no affinity with 'Prakṛti', is also called 'ātyantika pralaya'. It means that when a man has affinity with the body, the evolute of 'Prakṛti', he becomes dependent* and follows the cycle of birth and death; but having totally renounced affinity with the evolute of 'Prakṛti', he becomes independent, unconcerned and is freed from birth and death forever.

'Mama sādharmyamāgatāḥ'—This expression means that as God is Truth-Consciousness-Bliss solidified, so do the self-realized exalted souls become Truth-Consciousness-Bliss solidified.

Link:—Those who have become one with God, are not born again, at the time of creation. But, what about those who are born? The process of their emanation, is described, in the next verse.

मम योनिर्महद्ब्रह्म तस्मिन्गर्भं दधाम्यहम्।
सम्भवः सर्वभूतानां ततो भवति भारत॥ ३॥

mama yonirmahadbrahma tasmingarbhaṁ dadhāmyaham
sambhavaḥ sarvabhūtānāṁ tato bhavati bhārata

My primordial matter (prakṛti), known as the great Brahma, is the womb of all creatures; in which, I place the seed of all life. The birth of all beings, follows from this combination of matter and Spirit. 3

Comment:—

'Mama yonirmahadbrahma'—Here, the primordial Matter (Prakṛti), has been called 'Mahad Brahma', because of the following factors:—

(1) The Lord is beyond the great and the small, therefore, He is the subtlest, as well as the grossest. In the entire universe, besides the Lord the largest entity, is the primordial matter. So, the primordial matter (mūla Prakṛti), has been called 'Mahad Brahma'.

(2) The primordial matter is called 'Mahad Brahma', because

* 'Kāryate hyavaśaḥ karma sarvaḥ prakṛtijairguṇaiḥ' (3/5)
'Avaśaṁ prakṛtervaśāt' (9/8)
Rātryāgame'vaśaḥ pārtha prabhavatyaharāgame' (8/19).

it is, in between 'Mahat' (Mahattattva i.e., cosmic intelligence), and 'Brahma' (God).

(3) In the preceding verse, the terms 'Sarga' and 'Pralaya' respectively, may be misinterpreted, as Brahmā's day and night. So, 'Mahad Brahma' has been used, to denote new creation (revelation of Brahmā) and final dissolution (dissolution of Brahmā). It means, that a liberated soul's affinity, is renounced with the primordial Matter. So it is, neither born, at the time of new creation, nor are tormented at the time of, dissolution.

The primordial matter, being the birth abode of all beings, is called a womb. Infinite universes, emanate from it, and again merge into it. It is the cause of all mundane powers, and energies.

This primordial matter is called 'mama' (my), because it is the Lord's, it functions under His control, only. Without His will, it cannot do anything, through its own power. "With Me as the supervisor, prakṛti brings forth, the whole creation" (Gītā 9/10). The Lord has used the expression 'Mama mahadbrahma' in order to explain, that He is superior to prakṛti.

The spirit in spite of, being a fraction of the Lord, establishes its contact not only with prakṛti, but also with its evolutes, the three Guṇas and their evolute, the body, having a disinclination for the Lord thus gets bound. So, the Lord, wants to emphasize the fact, that affinity of the spirit is, with God, Who is superior to His Prakṛti, as the spirit, is His portion (Gītā 15/7). Therefore, the spirit should not degrade itself, by assuming affinity with prakṛti.

'Tasmingarbhaṁ dadhāmyaham'—Here the term 'Garbham' (seed), stands for totality of beings, with their actions and past influences (latencies). The Lord, does not place any new seed. The beings, who are following the cycle of birth and death, since time immemorial, merge in Prakṛti, at the time of final dissolution (Gītā 9/7). When their actions, having become mature, are inclined to bear fruit, the Lord at the time of new creation, brings them into further contact with prakṛti (this contact was already there, with the causal body). This further gross contact is what, He means by placing the seed.

'Sambhavaḥ sarvabhūtānāṁ tato bhavati bhārata'—After the Lord, has placed the seed in prakṛti, all beings with their gross and subtle bodies, are reborn. The birth of beings, at the time of creation, is called the discharge of spirits (Visarga), which also goes by the name of primeval action (Karma). So, it is the primeval action, or primeval idea of the Lord, which brings forth, the existence of beings (Gītā 8/3).

[So long as the spirit (Embodied Soul), is not emancipated, it continues to have its affinity with prakṛti and its portion, the causal body. So, at the time of final dissolution, the spirit with the causal body, merges in prakṛti.]

Appendix—The Lord means to say that though the self has got entangled in the cycle of birth and death, yet it is His fragment. The soul is identical in attributes with Him, not with the body.

Link:—In the preceding verse, there was description of the birth of all beings, in totality. Now, He describes the birth of all beings individually, in the next verse.

सर्वयोनिषु कौन्तेय मूर्तयः सम्भवन्ति याः ।
तासां ब्रह्म महद्योनिरहं बीजप्रदः पिता ॥ ४ ॥

sarvayoniṣu kaunteya mūrtayaḥ sambhavanti yāḥ
tāsāṁ brahma mahadyoniraham̐ bījapradaḥ pitā

Of all the bodies that take birth from different wombs, this Primordial Matter (Brahma or Prakṛti) is the Mother, while I am the seed-giving, Father. 4

Comment:—

'Sarvayoniṣu kaunteya mūrtayaḥ sambhavanti yāḥ'—All beings born from a womb, such as men and animals etc., born from eggs, such as birds and snakes etc., born from sweat, such as louse etc., and sprouting forth from the earth, such as plants and vegetation etc., having different shapes and of different species, including the gods, manes, devils, ghosts and other evil spirits etc., are included, in the term 'Sarvayoniṣu mūrtayaḥ', (all the species).

A poet, has rightly said, that a turban, luck, speech, personal nature, shape, sound, thoughts and writing, are not similar, even of two persons. In eighty-four lac species, so many beings since eternity have taken birth, but their shapes are different from one another.

'Tāsāṁ brahma mahadyoniraham bījapradaḥ pitā'—The primordial Matter, is the Mother of all beings, that take birth from different sources, as mentioned above, while God is the seed-giving father. The bodies, of different colours and shapes, are constituted of matter, while the spirit dwelling in them, is a portion of the Lord. The Lord Himself, declares, "Know Myself to be the Kṣetrajña (Spirit), in all the Kṣetras (bodies)" (Gītā 13/2). This can be clarified, by giving an illustration of a piece of cloth, which is wet. In the piece of cloth there are many minute holes. If it is soaked in, water it permeates, all the holes, equally. In this illustration, the piece of cloth denotes matter (Prakṛti), each of the holes denotes a body and the water, which permeates the holes and the cloth denotes God. It means, that God permeates all bodies and the entire, universe. Though in different bodies He seems different like water in holes.

Appendix—Eighty-four lac wombs, gods, manes, celestial singers, ghosts, evil spirits, demons, devils, moving and unmoving creatures, water creatures, land creatures, birds, creatures born from the womb, creatures born from eggs, plants etc., sprouting from the ground, creatures born of perspiration etc.,—all should be included within the term 'sarvayoniṣu'. The same fact has been mentioned in the sixth verse of the seventh chapter by the expression 'etadyonīni bhūtāni sarvāṇītyupadhāraya' and in the twenty-sixth verse of the thirteenth chapter by the expression, 'yāvatsañjāyate kiñcitsattvaṁ sthāvarajaṅgamam'.

Here the term 'mūrti' means body. Within this concrete-abstract, manifest-unmanifest—both kinds of bodies should be included. The earth, water and fire are manifest. Air and ether are unmanifest. The bodies of ghosts, demons and evil spirits etc., are also unmanifest as in their bodies there is predominance of air.

The Lord in the first and the second verses declared that if a man (the Self) has no affinity with 'Prakṛti', he is free from birth and death and in the third and the fourth verses He declared that by having affinity with 'Prakṛti', he has to follow the cycle of birth and death. The same fact (mentioned in the third and fourth verses) has been described in detail ahead from the fifth verse to the eighteenth verse.

Link:—In the next verse, the Lord explains how the guṇas (modes of nature), evolved from prakṛti, bind the spirit.

सत्त्वं रजस्तम इति गुणाः प्रकृतिसम्भवाः।
निबध्नन्ति महाबाहो देहे देहिनमव्ययम्॥ ५॥

sattvaṁ rajastama iti guṇāḥ prakṛtisambhavāḥ
nibadhnanti mahābāho dehe dehinamavyayam

Sattva, rajas and tamas—these guṇas (modes) born of prakṛti, bind the imperishable spirit to the body, O mighty-armed. 5

Comment:—

'Sattvaṁ rajastama iti guṇāḥ prakṛtisambhavāḥ'—The three guṇas—sattva, rajas and tamas are born of prakṛti (primordial matter), which has been called 'Mahad Brahma', in the third and the fourth verses.

Here the term, 'Iti' (these) denotes, that these guṇas (attributes or qualities) out of which infinite universes evolve, and innumerable beings, diverse in character, are born, are neither more or less, than three in number.

'Nibadhnanti mahābāho dehe dehinamavyayam'—These three guṇas, bind the imperishable spirit, to the body. The fact is, that these guṇas do not bind the spirit, but it is the spirit, which is bound by assuming its affinity with the guṇas and their evolutes—(objects, wealth, family and body etc.,). The spirit identifies itself, with the body and is attached to other persons and wealth etc. So in spite of being imperishable, it regards diseases and death of the body, as its own and also the loss of other persons and wealth etc., as its own.

It is a great wonder that the spirit in spite of being imperishable, immovable and uniform, being overpowered by guṇas and their propensities, itself becomes sāttvika, rājasa and tāmasa. Gosvāmī Tulasīdāsajī also declares in 'the Mānasa' that the spirit being a portion of the Lord, is imperishable, sentient, pure and naturally a mass of bliss (7/117/1).

Actually, the spirit is never bound by guṇas but when it assumes its affinity of 'I'ness, 'Mineness' and 'for me', with the body, it gets bound and the Lord seems to be attained with difficulty by it (Gītā 12/5). Due to body consciousness, bound by the three Guṇas, it cannot realize its immortality, which is beyond the three Guṇas. The embodied soul, in spite of, being bound by three guṇas in fact remains as it is. It means, that it does not decay. So it is called 'Avyayam'.

With the sense of 'I' and 'mine', in the body, these three guṇas, bind the soul in the body. In the absence of a sense of 'I' and 'mine' it is only God Himself.

An Important Fact

The spirit, assumes its affinity with the body, in two ways.

(i) I am the body—sense of egoism.

(ii) The body is mine—sense of mineness.

Thus, the spirit, by having links of egoism and a sense of mine, is bound by, the three guṇas.

Though a married person is linked with all members of the family of his wife, yet he regards necessities of his wife as his own, so the spirit having assumed its affinity with the body, regards the latter's necessities as its own. Moreover, in spite of being imperishable, it is afraid of death and has a desire to live. If it renounces its affinity with the body, it will have no desire to live, nor will it be afraid of death. Therefore, so long as, it has a desire to live, and is afraid of death, it means, that it is bound by guṇas.

The spirit is uniform and imperishable, while the body being kaleidoscopic and perishable, is decaying every moment. So, if a striver, does not attach importance to what is decaying and perishing every moment, he will realize automatically the imperishable and transcendental self.

Appendix—Being born of Prakṛti, Sattva, Raja and Tama—these three guṇas (modes) are in the 'Prakṛti' division. But a man (the self) assumes his relationship (of 'I' and 'mine') with the body, so these guṇas bind the imperishable self to the perishable inert body viz., 'I am the body and the body is mine'—this identification is caused. It means that all modifications emanate by having affinity with prakṛti. In the self there is no modification at all—'asaṅgo hyayaṁ puruṣaḥ' (Bṛhadāraṇyaka. 4/3/15), 'dehe'sminpuruṣaḥ paraḥ' (Gītā 13/22). It is because of these modifications that he has to be born and to die.

In fact the guṇas don't bind the individual self but this self by being attached to guṇas is bound (Gītā 13/21). If the guṇas bound the self, then a person could never be liberated from those guṇas, till they persisted, viz., he could not attain salvation.

Link:—In the preceding verse, the Lord explained that the three guṇas bind the spirit to a body. Now, in the next verse, he explains the essential character of sattva and the way in which, it binds the spirit.

तत्र सत्त्वं निर्मलत्वात्प्रकाशकमनामयम्।
सुखसङ्गेन बध्नाति ज्ञानसङ्गेन चानघ॥ ६॥

tatra sattvaṁ nirmalatvātprakāśakamanāmayam
sukhasaṅgena badhnāti jñānasaṅgena cānagha

Of these, Sattva, being pure illuminates and is flawless. It binds, (O sinless one) by creating attachment for happiness and knowledge. 6

Comment:—

'Tatra sattvaṁ nirmalatvāt'—In the preceding verse, the Lord described the three guṇas. Out of these three, Sattva is stainless and so it is conducive to, the knowledge of God-realization.

'Prakāśakam'—Sattva being stainless and pure is illuminating, and free from morbidity, of any kind. As in light, all objects are clearly visible, with the predominance of Sattvaguṇa, all the propensities of Rajoguṇa and Tamoguṇa, are clearly seen. Desire, anger, greed, pride and envy etc., which evolve from Rajoguṇa and Tamoguṇa, are clearly seen in that light. With the predominance of Sattva, the senses become animated and the mind, works more promptly in understanding mundane, as well as, the spiritual, topics.

The quality of Sattva (mode of goodness) can be divided into two parts—(i) Pure Sattva (ii) Impure Sattva. The former aims at God-realization, while the latter at mundane pleasures and prosperity.*

With the predominance of the mode of pure Sattva, a striver,

* The impure Sattva is called so because it does not aim at God-realization. This impure Sattva has 'Rājasa' in it.

having the aim of God-realization, has a natural inclination for spiritual progress, while a person possessing the mode of impure Sattva, hankers after worldly pleasures and prosperity, which lead him to bondage. Even in the impure Sattva the intellect scans and grasps worldly objects properly and minutely. Having this mode, scientists make inventions, but having no aim for God-realization, because of their pride of success and desire for praise and money etc., get bound.

'Anāmayam'—In fact, the quality of Sattva is not totally flawless, but it is more flawless than either Rajoguṇa or Tamoguṇa. Only the Lord, or the self, is totally flawless, but Sattvaguṇa has been called flawless, because, it is conducive to God-realization.

'Sukhasaṅgena badhnāti jñānasaṅgena cānagha'—Due to predominance of Sattva, a striver experiences, joy and peace. He is attached, to joy and peace, and he does not want to be deprived of these. This attachment, leads him to bondage.

During this period, his faculty of knowledge develops. He comes to know, several wonderful facts and topics, never known before. So he is attached to this knowledge, and he has a desire to maintain it forever. This attachment is the cause of his bondage. Moreover, his pride of superiority, that he knows more than others, also leads him to bondage. Thus he cannot transcend, the three guṇas. This attachment, is the quality of Rajas, which binds a striver (Gītā 13/21). If the striver, is not attached to joy and knowledge, he transcends, the three guṇas, including the Sattvaguṇa and realizes, the self.

A striver, should not enjoy that pleasure and knowledge, nor should he aim at them. He should think, that they are not conducive to attainment of his goal. Moreover, he has to attain that goal, which is an illuminator of pleasure and knowledge. Knowledge and pleasure, are mental projections during the preponderance of Sattva. These wax and wane, they come and go, while the self remains uniform, and constant. It knows no increase or decrease. Therefore, a striver should remain quite unconcerned and indifferent, to these modifications. He should not enjoy them. Thus he will not get entangled, in pleasure and knowledge, the evolutes of Sattva. If he is not attached to them, he realizes, God quickly. Even if he does not renounce this attachment, by having an aim of God-realization, in course of time, he develops a disinclination for pleasure and knowledge, and then he attains, God.

Appendix—Here the Lord has declared that Sattvaguṇa is flawless—this is singularity of Sattvaguṇa. The reason is that Sattvaguṇa is very close to the transcendental position (state). Though Sattvaguṇa is flawless, but because of attachment it becomes full of flaws—'sukhasaṅgena badhnāti jñānasaṅgena cānagha'; because attachment is the nature of Rajoguṇa—'rajo rāgātmakaṁ viddhi' (Gītā 14/7). Happiness and knowledge are not obstructive to the transcendental position. But attachment to them is obstructive. Attachment means to assume them one's own. In fact Sattvaguṇa is not one's own, but it is of 'Prakṛti'.

A man has the predominance of Rajoguṇa—'rajasi pralayaṁ gatvā karmasaṅgiṣu jāyate' (14/15), 'madhye tiṣṭhanti rājasāḥ' (14/18). Therefore so long as attachment persists, salvation is not attained; the Real Self being totally detached, complete detachment is essential for salvation.

The Lord has said Sattvaguṇa 'anāmaya' (free from blemish or flaw) and also the Supreme State as 'anāmaya'—'padaṁ gacchantyanāmayam' (2/51). By this it should be understood that Sattvaguṇa is relatively flawless while the Supreme State is absolute flawless.

Though all the three modes are born of 'Prakṛti', yet Rajoguṇa evolves from longing and attachment and Tamoguṇa is born of ignorance (14/7-8), but Sattvaguṇa is born only of 'Prakṛti'. It means that 'Sattvaguṇa' is born of 'Prakṛti' but it does not evolve from any flaw. Therefore it has said to be 'anāmaya'.

Sāttvika happiness and Sāttvika knowledge are also not the nature of the self but being born of 'Prakṛti', are of others (alien) viz., are dependent. Sāttvika happiness is dependent, it is not one's own nature, it is not bliss of the self.

Difference between Sāttvika knowledge and divine knowledge (self-realization)—In Sāttvika jñāna "I am Jñānī (wise)"—this attachment persists but 'Tattvajñāna' is totally free from attachment viz., on self-realization, wisdom persists, but 'I am wise'—this (sense) does not remain. In Sāttvika knowledge the onlooker remains and he is conscious of his speciality but in 'Tattvajñāna' there is no spectator, the self-realized soul becomes perfect but he is not conscious of his speciality because he loses his individuality. This consciousness of speciality is attachment. When he accepts 'I am wise', then he is conscious of his speciality. On self-realization, the self-realized soul realizes the bliss in the self. In the twenty-seventh verse of the thirteenth chapter, there is the description of 'Sāttvika jñāna' and in the twenty-eighth verse of the same chapter, there is description of self-realization.

Link—In the next verse the Lord describes the characteristic of rajoguṇa and shows how, it binds, the spirit.

रजो रागात्मकं विद्धि तृष्णासङ्गसमुद्भवम्।
तन्निबध्नाति कौन्तेय कर्मसङ्गेन देहिनम्॥ ७॥

rajo rāgātmakaṁ viddhi tṛṣṇāsaṅgasamudbhavam
tannibadhnāti kaunteya karmasaṅgena dehinam

Know rajas to be of the nature of passion, the source of longing and attachment. It binds the spirit through attachment to action, O son of Kuntī. 7

Comment:—

'Rajo rāgātmakaṁ viddhi'—This quality of rajas, manifests itself in the form of passion or attachment to persons, things and actions etc.

The Lord by the term 'Rāgātmakam' means to say that as in ornaments made of gold, there is nothing else besides gold, in Rajoguṇa there is nothing besides, attachment.

In the philosophy of sage Patañjali 'Rajoguṇa' has been manifested as 'activity' (action). But in the Gītā, the Lord (in spite of accepting activity, as the secondary characteristic of Rajoguṇa), declares attachment, as the main characteristic, of Rajoguṇa.* Therefore, the Lord exhorts Arjuna to perform actions, renouncing attachment (2/48). Performance of actions without attachment, leads a man to attain the Supreme (3/19). In the twenty-second verse of this chapter, the Lord while giving the marks of him, who has risen above the three guṇas, declares that he neither hates activity when present, nor longs for it when, absent. It means, that such a soul performs actions, without attachment. Thus, it is attachment only, which leads to bondage.

At the time of new creation, the Lord's resolve of becoming manifold from one, is translated into practice. In the Gītā, it is called karma (action) (8/3). When curd is churned, butter and butter-milk, are separated. Similarly, at the time of creation, with the rajoguṇī resolve, there is commotion in prakṛti (matter) and

*This is the singularity of the Gītā that without refuting a sect or an opinion, it expresses its view. In the Gītā on the one hand undertaking of an action is Rajoguṇa (14/12) while the action performed without attachment etc., is said to be Sāttvika (18/23). It means that actions do not lead to bondage, but it is attachment to them and the desire for their fruit which lead to bondage. A man free from attachment is not bound by actions (4/19). They do not lead the liberated souls to bondage (14/22). The Lord also performs actions at the time of the creation of the universe and also when He incarnates. But the actions do not bind Him because He remains unattached to them (9/9).

In the twenty-third, twenty-fourth and twenty-fifth verses of the eighteenth chapter the Lord has described three kinds of actions—Sāttvika, Rājasika and Tāmasika. Had all the actions been included in Rajoguṇa, they might have not been called Sāttvika and Tāmasika. It means that only attachment is Rajoguṇa.

then Sattvaguṇa, in the form of butter, and Tamoguṇa, in the form of butter-milk, are separated. By the Sattvaguṇa inner sense (mind), and senses; by Rajoguṇa, life-breath and organs of action; and by Tamoguṇa, gross objects and bodies etc., are created. Other things and objects, are created by the three guṇas. Thus the Lord creates, the entire universe Himself, being totally free from attachment (Gītā 4/13).

'Tṛṣṇāsaṅgasamudbhavam'—'Tṛṣṇā' is thirst or desire for hankering after things etc., not yet acquired of and maintaining these having acquired them. This desire, leads to attachment for those things and persons etc. This expression 'Tṛṣṇāsaṅgasamudbhavam', according to Sanskrit grammar has a double meaning—(1) It is the source of thirst (desire) and attachment. (2) It evolves from thirst and attachment. As a seed sprouts up into a tree, and a tree produces, several seeds, similarly rajoguṇa enhances desire, and attachment, while desire and attachment enhance rajoguṇa. It means, that they nourish each other. Thus, both the meanings are appropriate.

'Tannibadhnāti kaunteya karmasaṅgena dehinam'—Rajoguṇa binds the spirit, through attachment to actions. With the predominance of Rajoguṇa there is enhancement of desire and attachment, which induce a man, to perform actions. When he starts actions, he is more and more entangled in their thought, as well as in thoughts of new actions. Thus a man, does not get an opportunity, to attain salvation. He, because of desire and attachment for actions is bound and follows a cycle of birth and death. So a striver, should perform actions without having a desire for their fruit, according to the circumstances available, but should not begin new actions, for prosperity and pleasure.

Here the term 'Dehinam' (spirit) denotes that Rajoguṇa binds through attachment to actions that spirit alone which assumes its affinity with the body. A man feels happiness in even performing actions with a selfish motive.

A man is also bound, when he has a desire to enjoy, the fruit of actions. Thus a man is bound by attachment to actions, and the fruit of actions.

In order to be free, from this attachment a striver, should always think of the kaleidoscopic nature of persons, things, incidents and circumstances etc. All of these are decaying and dying every moment. Even kings and emperors with all their luxuries, such as riches, palaces and attendants etc., have met, the same fate. Man should think, that he is going to meet the same fate. So, he should not waste his energy, intellect and time, by having attachment for actions and their fruit. This attachment, will lead him to a cycle of birth and death, and he will be deprived of the real attainment of human goal. Therefore, instead of performing new actions for prosperity and pleasure, he should do his prescribed duty, according to available circumstances, without having any attachment for it. Such thoughts, influence a striver, for detachment, from actions.

Appendix—Rajoguṇa binds a man (the Self) through attachment to actions. Therefore even Sāttvika actions, because of attachment, lead to bondage. If there is no attachment, the actions don't bind him (Gītā 18/17). Therefore by Karmayoga a striver attains salvation because in Karmayoga there is attachment neither to actions nor to their fruit (Gītā 6/4).

Link:—In the next verse, the Lord describes the characteristic of Tamoguṇa (darkness attribute or the Principle of Inertia), and the way in which, it binds the spirit.

तमस्त्वज्ञानजं विद्धि मोहनं सर्वदेहिनाम्।
प्रमादालस्यनिद्राभिस्तन्निबध्नाति भारत॥ ८॥

tamastvajñānajaṁ viddhi mohanaṁ sarvadehinām
pramādālasyanidrābhistannibadhnāti bhārata

But, know Tāmasa (mode of darkness or ignorance) born of ignorance, deludes all embodied beings. It binds the spirit, O Bhārata, through inattention, indolence and sleep. 8

Comment:—

'Tamastvajñānajaṁ viddhi mohanaṁ sarvadehinām'—Here the term 'tu' (but), has been used to denote that Tamoguṇa is far inferior to Sattvaguṇa and even, Rajoguṇa.

It is born of ignorance or folly, and it deludes embodied beings i.e., those, who regard the body, as their self. It enshrouds discrimination and so they cannot discriminate, between the real and the unreal; and the proper and improper. It does not allow to enjoy even Rājasika pleasure and prosperity. Then there is no question of the safety of Sāttvika happiness.

The Lord means to say, that human beings are deluded of Tamoguṇa, but He has used the expression 'Sarvadehinām' (all embodied beings), to denote that human beings, who lack discrimination are like other deluded beings, such as birds and beasts etc., that eat, drink, sleep and produce young-ones.

'Pramādālasyanidrābhistannibadhnāti bhārata'—This Tamoguṇa, binds embodied beings through heedlessness, indolence and sleep.

'Pramāda'—(Heedlessness), is of two kinds—(1) Heedlessness by which one does not discharge one's duty which is conducive to one's own welfare, as well as, to the welfare of others. (2) Heedlessness, by which one performs futile actions, which are of no use either to him or to others. Futile actions, can further be divided into two categories.

(i) Extravagance, on smoking, drinking and movies etc.

(ii) Playing cards and backgammon etc., shooting birds and beasts etc., and destroying plants etc.

Indolence, is also of two kinds—(1) In this state of indolence a man remains idle, sleeps more than is required and ever postpones his work. This indolence, leads a man to bondage. (2) In the second kind of indolence, a person feels drowsy after the day's hard, mental and physical work. That sort of sleep is inevitable. This indolence is not a defect.

Sleep can also be divided into two parts—(1) Sleep which is necessary, for a healthy body and a healthy mind. It is regulated and is helpful in the practice of Yoga (Gītā 6/17). (2) Unnecessary sleep—One sleeps too much. It is a stumbling block to the practice of Yoga and so it is to be discarded (Gītā 6/16).

Thus Tamoguṇa (mode of ignorance), binds a man through heedlessness, indolence and sleep i.e., which are stumbling blocks, to his mundane and spiritual progress.

An Important fact

Sattva (mode of goodness), Rajas (mode of passion) and Tamas (mode of ignorance) bind a man (spirit). Out of the three, Sattva binds by attachment to happiness, and to knowledge, Rajas binds by attachment to actions, but in Tamas there is no need for any attachment, it automatically binds a man.

If a striver, is not attached to happiness, and is not proud of knowledge, his happiness and knowledge, will lead him to a state, which transcends the three guṇas. Similarly, actions and their fruit without attachment, will lead to attainment of the Supreme (Gītā 3/19).

The three guṇas (modes) are evolutes of prakṛti (nature) and he (the self), is free from nature and its modes. But, he is bound, because of his contact, with these modes. So, if he realizes this fact, he could be free from them.

Link:—In the next verse, the Lord describes the natural function of the three guṇas (modes), before these bind the spirit.

सत्त्वं सुखे सञ्जयति रजः कर्मणि भारत।
ज्ञानमावृत्य तु तमः प्रमादे सञ्जयत्युत॥ ९॥

sattvaṁ sukhe sañjayati rajaḥ karmaṇi bhārata
jñānamāvṛtya tu tamaḥ pramāde sañjayatyuta

The mode of goodness (Sattva) sways one towards happiness, passion Rajas towards action, O Bhārata, while ignorance, veiling knowledge, leads one to, negligence and inattention (Tamas). 9

Comment:—

'Sattvaṁ sukhe sañjayati'—A striver, is attached to happiness and thus he is bound. Because of this attachment, he does not make any further spiritual progress, and transcend the three guṇas.

In the sixth verse of this chapter, the Lord declared that the mode of goodness, binds by attachment to happiness and knowledge. But here He refers to only attachment for happiness. It means, that pride of knowledge, also provides happiness which binds a striver. So, He describes, only happiness.

'Rajaḥ karmaṇi bhārata'—As a child, takes pleasure in moving his arms and legs etc., so a man feels happy while performing actions. As he is attached to actions, this attachment overpowers him. He pays attention to the Lord's words 'You are not entitled to the fruit of action' (Gītā 2/47), but he does not pay attention to the fact, that he should not be attached, to actions. He goes through the Lord's declarations such as, "Your right is to perform your duty; let your attachment, not be to inaction" and "Action is said to be the means of the sage who wishes to attain to Yoga" (Gītā 6/3). So he thinks, that he must perform actions. Thus, by performing actions he is attached to them. So the Lord warns him, that he should beware of attachment to actions, which binds him. A striver, should discharge his duty promptly by performing actions, but should not get attached to them (Gītā 6/4).

'Jñānamāvṛtya tu tamaḥ pramāde sañjayatyuta'—The mode of ignorance covers a man's discrimination and he cannot distinguish, between the real and the unreal, right and wrong. So he is engaged, in idle pursuits, and does not discharge his duty, promptly.

Two characteristics of the mode of goodness, are—knowledge (discrimination), and illumination (light). The mode of ignorance, by covering discrimination, misleads a man to heedlessness and by covering light (purity of senses and mind), misleads him to indolence and sleep. So he cannot know reality in spite of reading and listening about it.

Appendix—Sattvaguṇa does not bind a striver merely by happiness but it binds by attachment to happiness—'sukhasaṅgena badhnāti' (Gītā 14/6). Similarly Rajoguṇa binds through attachment to action—'tannibadhnāti kaunteya karmasaṅgena dehinam' (14/7). But Tamoguṇa by its nature binds a man, in it there is no need for attachment. Therefore in Tamoguṇa the term 'saṅga' (attachment) has not been used.

'I am happy'—this is attachment to happiness; and 'I am doer of virtuous actions, my actions are very good'—this is attachment to actions. A man is bound only, when he gets attached viz., accepts his affinity with happiness or actions etc.

Link:—In the next verse, the Lord describes how these guṇas (modes) act, one over the other.

रजस्तमश्चाभिभूय सत्त्वं भवति भारत।
रजः सत्त्वं तमश्चैव तमः सत्त्वं रजस्तथा॥ १०॥

rajastamaścābhibhūya sattvaṁ bhavati bhārata
rajaḥ sattvaṁ tamaścaiva tamaḥ sattvaṁ rajastathā

Goodness (Sattva) prevails, over passion (Rajas) and ignorance (Tamas), O Bhārata. Passion overpowers goodness and ignorance and ignorance predominates, goodness and passion. 10

Comment:—

'Rajastamaścābhibhūya sattvaṁ bhavati bhārata'—Goodness prevails, overpowering passion and ignorance. This mode develops illumination, purity, dispassion, generosity and detachment etc., overpowering, Rajoguṇa viz., greed, activity, disquietude and craving for worldly pleasure and prosperity etc., and Tamoguṇa viz., heedlessness, indolence, unnecessary sleep and delusion etc.

'Rajaḥ sattvaṁ tamaścaiva'—Passion prevails overpowering, goodness and ignorance viz., greed, activity, disquietude and craving for worldly pleasure and prosperity prevails over the propensities of Tamoguṇa and the quality of Sattva, mentioned above.

'Tamaḥ sattvaṁ rajastathā'—The mode of ignorance viz., heedlessness, indolence, excessive sleep and delusion etc., overpower, the traits of Sattvaguṇa and Rajoguṇa.

The order of describing should be that one of the modes, prevails overpowering the other two modes, and it binds a man. Here (from the sixth to the tenth verse), the Lord has reversed the order as the discussion relates as to how, it binds a man, how he is attached, and finally how, one of the modes prevails over the other two. This order is justified. The Lord, in the second verse of this chapter, explained that those who have renounced their connection with prakṛti, are not born at the time of creation, nor are they tormented at the time of dissolution. But those who are linked with prakṛti, get bound (14/5). Now a question arises, how they bind a man? The Lord, from the sixth to the eighth verse has explained how the three kinds of modes bind a man (spirit). Then, the question arises as to what they do before binding, the spirit. In response to this the Lord explains that they drive him to, happiness, to actions and to heedlessness (14/9). Again, the question arises how they drive him, so the Lord answers, that one of them prevails over the other two, (14/10). Thus the order kept by the God is justified.

Appendix—The mode (guṇa) which increases becomes predominant while the other two guṇas become subdued. This is the nature of modes.

Link:—When one of the modes, prevails over the other two, what are the marks of that prepondering mode? The Lord first delineates the marks of the predominance, of the mode of goodness.

सर्वद्वारेषु देहेऽस्मिन्प्रकाश उपजायते।
ज्ञानं यदा तदा विद्याद्विवृद्धं सत्त्वमित्युत॥ ११॥

sarvadvāreṣu dehe'sminprakāśa upajāyate
jñānaṁ yadā tadā vidyādvivṛddhaṁ sattvamityuta

When the vents of the body (senses and mind) are illumined by light (purity) and knowledge, then it may be said, that Sattva (goodness) is dominant. 11

Comment:—

'Sarvadvāreṣu dehe'sminprakāśa upajāyate jñānaṁ yadā'—When the mode of goodness prevails, overpowering the modes of passion and ignorance, all the senses and the mind, are illuminated. As, in the light of the sun, the objects are seen clearly, one perceives things, in the right perspective. The mind thinks properly.

When the senses and the mind, are cleansed, one can distinguish between the real and the unreal, right and wrong, good and bad and what ought to be done and what ought, not to be done.

By using the term 'Dehe'smin', (in this body), the Lord wants to emphasize the importance of human birth. It is only in this birth, that one can develop the mode of goodness i.e., purity and discrimination. The Lord, has used the expression 'Sarvadehinām' (Gītā 14/8), for all embodied beings, who are bound by the mode of ignorance. It means, that the modes of ignorance and passion, develop in other bodies also, but the mode of goodness can develop, only in the human body. So, a man by overpowering the modes of passion and ignorance, should transcend even the mode of goodness, in order to attain the goal of human life. The Lord, by His grace has given us power and freedom in this human body, to prevail over these three modes.

'Tadā vidyādvivṛddhaṁ sattvamityuta'—When a striver's mind, is illumined and discrimination is aroused, he should know that the mode of goodness, has prevailed by overpowering, the modes of passion and ignorance. So he should not feel proud of his achievement, regarding discrimination and illumination, as his own. He should regard these, as marks, of the mode of goodness.

The expression 'Iti vidyāt' (thus may be known), denotes that only a man can know, that the modes, not the self, undergo modifications. But a man, by assuming his identification with the three modes of nature, assumes himself as Sāttvika (good), Rājasika (passionate) and Tāmasika (ignorant). So, by attaching importance to his discrimination, he should regard himself free, from all flaws and modifications.

These modes undergo modifications, but he is an onlooker who observes all the modifications. If he himself, had undergone changes, who could have observed, the modifications?

With the predominance of the mode of goodness, the senses and mind, become cleansed, discrimination is aroused, dispassion takes the place of attachment, quietude displaces disquietude, and generosity displaces greed. All actions, are performed as a duty, without desire for their fruit (Gītā 18/9). The person possessing this mode, does not attach importance to worldly pleasure and prosperity, but only makes both ends meet. With the development of intellect and discrimination, all actions are performed very carefully and promptly, and one can distinguish between right and wrong. So, when there is predominance of the mode of goodness, a striver, should be particularly engaged in adoration and meditation etc., because, even a little spiritual practice at that time, is very useful.

Appendix—There is a difference between 'prakāśa' (light) and 'jñāna' (knowledge). 'Prakāśa' means wakefulness in senses and mind viz., when there is absence of the world of fancy (greed, unrest, craving etc.,) born of Rajoguṇa; and also absence of sleep, indolence and heedlessness born of Tamoguṇa, but there is purity. 'Jñāna' means discrimination between the real and the unreal, the eternal and the transient, what ought to be done and what ought not to be done, what should be accepted and what should be rejected and so on.

Link:—In the next verse, the Lord describes the marks, when there is an increase, in the mode of passion.

लोभः प्रवृत्तिरारम्भः कर्मणामशमः स्पृहा।
रजस्येतानि जायन्ते विवृद्धे भरतर्षभ॥ १२॥

lobhaḥ pravṛttirārambhaḥ karmaṇāmaśamaḥ spṛhā
rajasyetāni jāyante vivṛddhe bharatarṣabha

Greed, activity, inclination to act with interested motives, unrest and craving—these spring up, Oh best of the Bharatas, when there is an increase in the mode of passion (Rajas). 12

Comment:—

'Lobhaḥ'—Greed, is the lust for multiplying wealth and possessions. But, if wealth increases without illegal means through one's own profession or business, though one has no craving, it is not greed.

'Pravṛttiḥ'—The urge, to undertake various form of activities is 'Pravṛtti'. Activity free from attachment and aversion, is not harmful, because even great souls, who have transcended the three modes of nature, are engaged in activity (Gītā 14/22). But it is harmful, if it is performed with attachment and a desire for its fruit.

'Ārambhaḥ karmaṇām'—These actions are undertaken, in order to gain wealth, name, fame and praise etc. Performance of new actions, for worldly pleasure and prosperity, is the undertaking of actions viz., 'Ārambha' while one's profession or an activity according to circumstances or need of the hour, is a 'Pravṛtti'.

The goal of human life, is not worldly pleasure or prosperity but God-realization. So, in the Disciplines of Devotion and Knowledge, emphasis has been laid on giving up all initiative, for Ārambhaḥ action with interested motive (12/16, 14/25). In the Discipline of Action, acts are performed without desires and self-centred projections (Gītā 4/19). Without actions, a striver, following the Discipline of Action cannot attain equanimity, (Gītā 6/3). So a striver, should be engaged in action, according to the circumstances available, without having any attachment. By doing so, his urge for action, comes to an end. Thus, undertaking of actions, turns into activity.

'Aśamaḥ'—Unrest or dissatisfaction in the mind, is called 'Aśama'. Unfulfilled desires cause unrest. If desires are renounced; there is no, restlessness.

'Spṛhā'—Desire for bare necessities of life, is 'Spṛhā. A striver, should renounce this desire, because nothing can be gained, merely by desire. It is not an evil to be aware of hunger, thirst and cold, but desire for getting food, water and cover is an evil.

'Rajasyetāni jāyante vivṛddhe bharatarṣabha'—When, there is an increase in the mode of passion, a striver, should think that his life is running smoothly. Then desire for more, is mere stupidity. By such thinking, he should do away with, this mode and become, indifferent to it.

Appendix—When there is an increase in Rajoguṇa, light and knowledge, the qualities of Sattva, are subdued. 'Rajoguṇa' is opponent of detachment—'rajo rāgātmakaṁ viddhi' (14/7). It is because of attachment to actions and objects that this (Rajoguṇa) does not let a man attain Yoga. The reason is that a man attains Yoga only when he is detached from actions and objects (Gītā 6/4).

Link:—In the next verse, the Lord describes the symptoms when there is an increase, in the mode of ignorance.

अप्रकाशोऽप्रवृत्तिश्च प्रमादो मोह एव च।
तमस्येतानि जायन्ते विवृद्धे कुरुनन्दन॥ १३॥

aprakāśo'pravṛttiśca pramādo moha eva ca
tamasyetāni jāyante vivṛddhe kurunandana

O Son of Kuru, when there is an increase in the mode of ignorance, darkness, inactivity, inattention (negligence) and delusion, are manifested. 13

Comment:—

'Aprakāśaḥ'—When the mode of ignorance prevails, overpowering the mode of goodness, the senses and mind, are not pure and discrimination, disappears. This is in contrast with 'Prakāśa'.

'Apravṛttiḥ'—When the mode of ignorance prevails, overpowering the mode of passion, a person, has no inclination to discharge, even his obligatory duties. He wants to remain idle.

'Pramādaḥ'—It means, neglect of duties, which are conducive to mundane as well as, spiritual progress, and addiction to idle pursuits, such as smoking, playing cards and gammon etc., and going to movies etc.

'Mohaḥ'—When there is an increase in the mode of ignorance, delusion is aroused and discrimination is obscured, then a man, has no ability to endeavour to perform his duties for material and spiritual progress.

'Eva ca'—This expression, includes frivolous pursuits, such as excessive sleep and waste of time and money etc.

'Tamasyetāni jāyante vivṛddhe kurunandana'—These, are the symptoms of an increase, in the mode of ignorance. When there are non-illumination (indiscrimination) and inactivity etc., it means, that the mode of ignorance has prevailed, overpowering the modes of goodness and passion.

The three modes—of goodness, of passion and of ignorance being subtle, are beyond the access of senses and mind. So, they are not clearly perceived, they can be perceived only by their marks or symptoms. The Lord has discussed their marks, in the eleventh, twelfth and thirteenth verses, so that a striver may develop, the mode of goodness by prevailing over, the modes of passion and ignorance.

A Vital Fact

A striver, observes that the three modes of goodness, of passion and of ignorance are born, they perish and they undergo modifications, while he himself remains the same. The marks of the three modes, are perceived while he himself is an onlooker, so he is different from them. But, by assuming his identification with them, he acquires flaws, such as lust and anger etc. It is an invitation, to these flaws. While he becomes angry, he justifies his anger, by thinking that everybody, gets angry. At other times, he regards himself as a man with anger, even when he is not angry. Thus, this anger gets rooted in his ego, and it becomes difficult for him to get rid of it. Actually, these flaws do not abide in him, because he is permanent and flawless, while these flaws stay in the mind and intellect, temporarily as these appear and disappear. So a striver, without identifying himself with the mind and intellect, should have a firm faith, that there are no flaws in him. By doing so, the flaws, such as anger etc., totally perish gradually.

The Lord, while discussing the marks of the three modes of nature, warns a striver, to be aware of the fact, that the modes and their traits, being the evolutes of nature, undergo changes, while he himself being a fraction of the Lord is imperishable and does not undergo any change. By thinking so, the mode of goodness naturally develops, and overpowers, the modes of ignorance and passion. Attachment for happiness , relating the mode of goodness, is also a stumbling block to the attainment of a transcendental state. So a striver, should not be attached to happiness born of the mode of goodness, because such attachment, is a mark of the mode of passion. From attachment, arises desire, and from desire (unfulfilled) ensues, anger. Delusion, arises from anger. This delusion, misleads a person from the mode of passion, to the mode of ignorance, and he has a fall (Gītā 2/62-63).

Appendix—Darkness and inactivity are opponents to Sattvaguṇa and Rajoguṇa; and heedlessness and delusion are Tamoguṇa's own symptoms.

Link:—In the next two verses, the Lord points out the destiny, which awaits a man, who dies during the predominance of one of the modes of nature.

यदा सत्त्वे प्रवृद्धे तु प्रलयं याति देहभृत्।
तदोत्तमविदां लोकानमलान्प्रतिपद्यते ॥ १४ ॥

yadā sattve pravṛddhe tu pralayaṁ yāti dehabhṛt
tadottamavidāṁ lokānamalānpratipadyate

When a man dies during the predominance of Sattva (guṇa), he obtains the pure worlds attained by men of noble deeds. 14

Comment:

'Yadā sattve pravṛddhe tu pralayaṁ yāti dehabhṛt tadottamavidāṁ lokānamalānpratipadyate'—A man, may be naturally established in anyone, of the three guṇas (modes)—Sattva,

Rajas or Tamas. Sattvaguṇa, in its nature is immaculate. He who dies during the predominance of Sattva (goodness), he attains to the pure worlds of those, who perform noble deeds.

The term 'Uttamavidām', denotes the knower of the highest (great sages), having lofty feelings, possessing true knowledge and performing pious, actions. A person, who dies in the mode of goodness, which may be a temporary phase of his life, is elevated, to the worlds, where great sages and saints live. It means, that good traits born of the modes of nature, are as good as, are pious actions. From this view-point, there is greater importance of feelings (modes), in actions, than inactions themselves, which are sanctioned by scriptures. Therefore, the mode of goodness, occupies a very high place. Out of the objects, actions, modes and aim, actions are superior to objects, modes are superior to actions, and aim is superior, to the modes.

The mode of goodness, is more subtle and widespread, than the modes of passion and ignorance. In the world, also the diet of subtle beings, is less than of gross ones, as the gods being subtle, are satisfied only with fragrance. But, as far as, power is concerned, the power of the subtle, is more than, the gross. So persons having predominance of the subtle mode (feelings) of goodness, attain to the higher world.

Now a doubt arises as to how a person, who dies during the predominance of the Sattva (goodness), which may be a temporary phase of his life, attains to the higher worlds, attained by those, who perform virtuous actions, throughout their life. The answer is, that there is a special concession from the Lord that at the time of death, by thinking of whatever object that, one leaves the body, that and that alone, he attains (Gītā 8/6). So a person, dying during the predominance of the mode of goodness, attains to the higher pure worlds, there is no doubt, about it.

Appendix—'Tadottamavidāṁ lokānamalān'—The people who possess discrimination, are discerning persons. If they by regarding the Sattvaguṇa as their own, don't take delight in it, and have an inclination to God, then they by being detached from (transcending) Sattvaguṇa, will attain the Supreme Abode of God, otherwise having affinity with Sattvaguṇa, they will attain to the higher worlds, upto the Abode of Brahmā.

'Amalān'—In the higher worlds upto the Abode of Brahmā, there is relative purity but in the Supreme Abode of God, there is absolute purity.

रजसि प्रलयं गत्वा कर्मसङ्गिषु जायते।
तथा प्रलीनस्तमसि मूढयोनिषु जायते॥१५॥

rajasi pralayaṁ gatvā karmasaṅgiṣu jāyate
tathā pralīnastamasi mūḍhayoniṣu jāyate

When one dies, in the preponderance of mode of passion, he is born among those attached to action; and when he dies in the preponderance of the mode of ignorance, he is born in the wombs of the deluded. 15

Comment:—

'Rajasi pralayaṁ gatvā karmasaṅgiṣu jāyate'—When a person, dies during predominance of the mode of passion, when propensities such as greed, activity, unrest and craving etc., increase, he is born among those human beings, who are attached to action.

He, whose conduct has been good, throughout his life and who has performed good actions, if he dies, when the mode of passion, is predominant, is born as a human being with good conduct and emotion and performs, good actions. If a person possessing no virtues, dies when there is predominance of the mode of passion, with propensities such as greed etc., he is born as a man, who is attached to objects, persons and actions etc. He, who dies during the predominance of the mode of passion and whose life has been full of evil propensities, such as greed and anger etc., is born, as a human being, possessing the demoniac traits. It means, that even as human beings, they are born of three kinds of traits according to those of the previous life. But, all of them possess discrimination, bestowed upon them, by the Lord. By attaching importance to this discrimination, every human being through spiritual practice, good company and study of the scriptures etc., can realize God, because they are eligible for God-realization.

'Tathā pralīnastamasi mūḍhayoniṣu jāyate'—The person, who dies during the predominance of the mode of ignorance, when there is an increase in propensities, such as negligence, delusion and unillumination etc., is born, in the wombs of the deluded (senseless) creatures, such as beasts, birds, moths, insects, trees and creepers etc. Out of those deluded ones, trees and creepers etc., are more deluded, than birds and beasts etc.

If a person, performs good actions, but at the time of death has a predominance of the mode of ignorance and is born in the womb of deluded one, then also, he maintains his virtues, good conduct and nature. As the sage, named Bharata died during the predominance of the mode of ignorance, by thinking of the deer, to whom he was much attached, so, he was born a deer. But, because of renunciation and penance of his previous human births, he did not live with his mother and instead of eating green leaves, he ate only dry leaves. He possessed so much of carefulness, during his life as a deer, as is rarely possessed, even by human beings.

Appendix—In Rajoguṇa attachment, rather than action, binds a man and leads him to birth and death. It is because of attachment that it has been said that he is born among those attached to action—'karmasaṅgiṣu jāyate'. In the form of action, Rajoguṇa remains even in the person who has transcended the guṇas—'prakāśaṁ ca pravṛttiṁ ca' (Gītā 14/22). If a person is attached to any object, action or person, he will be born among those persons who are attached to action. A man is by nature attached to action because only a human being has the right of performing new actions—'karmānubandhīni manuṣyaloke' (Gītā 15/2).

Link:—Why does the predominance of the three modes, at the time of death yield different results? The answer follows:—

कर्मणः सुकृतस्याहुः सात्त्विकं निर्मलं फलम्।
रजसस्तु फलं दुःखमज्ञानं तमसः फलम्॥ १६॥

karmaṇaḥ sukṛtasyāhuḥ sāttvikaṁ nirmalaṁ phalam
rajasastu phalaṁ duḥkhamajñānaṁ tamasaḥ phalam

The fruit of good actions is said to be Sāttvika (goodness) and pure, the fruit of Rajas is pain, while the fruit of Tamas (guṇa) is ignorance. 16

Comment:—

[Actually, actions are neither Sāttvika, nor Rājasa nor Tāmasa. Actions performed by Sāttvika, Rājasa and Tāmasa doers, are called Sāttvika, Rājasa and Tāmasa respectively.]

'Karmaṇaḥ sukṛtasyāhuḥ sāttvikaṁ nirmalaṁ phalam'—Sattvaguṇa (the mode of goodness) is pure and flawless. Action performed by the Sāttvika doer (agent), is also Sāttvika, because the doer is reflected in his activity; and the fruit of that action, is also pure and pleasant.

So long as, a doer has his connection with the Sattvaguṇa (the mode of goodness), even though he has no desire for fruit of action, he is said to be a Sāttvika doer, and his actions, bear fruit. But when his connection with the mode is renounced, he is no more called a Sāttvika doer, and his actions bear no fruit, they turn into inaction.

'Rajasastu phalaṁ duḥkham'—Rajoguṇa, is full of attachment. Actions performed by a Rājasika doer, are Rājasika and so, is their fruit. It means, that Rājasika actions, are performed with the view of getting, pleasures, comforts, luxuries, respect and praise etc., here and hereafter. But these pleasures born of contacts (with objects), are verily sources of pain (sorrow), (Gītā 5/22). These lead to the cycle of birth and death. So the Lord, has declared the fruit of Rājasa action is pain.

Rajoguṇa (the mode of passion), gives birth to sin and pain. A person, possessing the mode of passion, performs sinful actions, which bear painful fruit. In the thirty-sixth verse of the third chapter, Arjuna asked Lord Kṛṣṇa, "By what, is a man impelled to commit sin, as if by force, even against his will?" The Lord answered, "It is craving (desire), born of the mode of passion, which impels a man, to commit sin."

'Ajñānaṁ tamasaḥ phalam'—Tamoguṇa is full of delusion. Actions by a Tāmasika person, are performed without thinking of their fruit, in the form of violence and loss etc., out of delusion. So such a person, is reborn after death, in the species of silly creatures such as beasts, birds, moths, insects, trees and creepers etc.

This verse, can be summed up as follows. The Sāttvika person in all the circumstances, is happy, the Rājasika one, is sad, while the Tāmasika, is ignorant, having no discrimination.

So long as, a person is attached to actions, and modes of nature, he cannot be happy, because his actions, bear different kinds of fruit, in the form of modes and circumstances. But, when he renounces his attachment to actions and modes, he cannot be sad and bound.

The thought, at the time of one's death, is the root of a being's rebirth. The predominance of anyone of the modes, is the root of that thought. The predominance of a mode, depends upon actions. It means, that a person performs actions, according to the mode and those actions, strengthen the mode and he thinks at the time of death, according to that mode of nature. Thus, the thought at the last moment, mode of nature and actions all the three are responsible, for a person's rebirth, in good and bad species.

Appendix—Attachment is the very nature of Rajoguṇa and that attachment is verily the cause of pain (sorrow)—'rajasastu phalaṁ duḥkham'. Attachment is the root of all worldly sufferings and sins. Attachment gives birth to desire—'kāma eṣa krodha eṣa rajoguṇasamudbhavaḥ' (Gītā 3/37).

'Ajñānaṁ tamasaḥ phalam'—Tamoguṇa (mode of ignorance) obstructs knowledge, illumination and discrimination, because Tamoguṇa gives birth to ignorance and is also born of ignorance (Gītā 14/8, 17).

Link:—In the preceding verse, the Lord explained the fruits of predominance of the three guṇas (modes) of a person while dying. Now, in the next verse, He explains how the guṇas, activate their respective actions.

सत्त्वात्सञ्जायते ज्ञानं रजसो लोभ एव च।
प्रमादमोहौ तमसो भवतोऽज्ञानमेव च॥१७॥

sattvātsañjāyate jñānaṁ rajaso lobha eva ca
pramādamohau tamaso bhavato'jñānameva ca

From Sattva (the mode of goodness) arises knowledge, from Rājasa (the mode of passion) arises greed and from Tāmasa (the mode of ignorance), arise heedlessness, delusion and ignorance. 17

Comment:—

'Sattvātsañjāyate jñānam'—Sattva, awakens knowledge or discrimination. That discrimination, enables a man to perform only good actions, which bear Sāttvika and pure fruit.

'Rajaso lobha eva ca'—Rajoguṇa gives birth to greed etc. Actions of a greedy person, bear painful fruit.

Greed, is the lust for multiplying possessions. Greed can manifest itself, in two forms—not to incur proper expenditure and to accumulate wealth etc., by foul means. If a person, does not spend money according to the need of the moment, because of greed, he loses his peace of mind. If he accumulates and hoards money, by foul means, he incurs sins, which lead him to hell and eighty-four lac forms of lives, which are full of suffering.

'Pramādamohau tamaso bhavato'jñānameva ca'—Heedlessness, delusion and ignorance arise, from Tāmasa. A Tāmasika man, thinks of wrong as right, and regards, all things contrary (Gītā 18/32).

In this verse, it is mentioned that ignorance arises from Tāmasa, while in the eighth verse of the chapter Tāmasa, has been said to be born of ignorance. It means, that as a seed is born of a tree and a tree is born of the seed, ignorance, is born of Tāmasa and Tāmasa is born of ignorance.

In the eighth verse, the Lord explained heedlessness, indolence and sleep, as the three propensities of Tāmasa, while in the thirteenth verse as well as in this verse, there is mention of heedlessness, and there is no mention of sleep. It indicates, that necessary sleep is neither Tāmasa nor forbidden, nor leads to bondage, but is a necessity for a Sāttvika person, as well as a transcendental person (who has transcended the three modes of nature). It is only excessive sleep, which is Tāmasa and which binds a person, because it makes him lazy, idle and a lot of his time, is wasted

An Important Fact

The soul (spirit), in spite of being a fragment of the Lord, assumes its affinity, with matter (nature) and its modes. Those modes, give birth, to the propensities in the mind. Those propensities, force a person to perform the same sort of actions. The fruit of those actions, causes a person to be born in good and evil bodies. It means, that during life, those actions bear fruit, in the form of favourable and unfavourable circumstances.

While after death, they cause his birth in good and evil wombs. But in fact it is the propensities of modes, at the root of actions, which conduce him to have his birth in good and evil bodies (Gītā 13/21). It means, that attachment to modes of nature is not weaker than actions. As actions bear good and bad fruit, attachment to modes of nature also bears good, and bad fruit (Gītā 8/6). So in the context of fourteen verses from the fifth to the eighteenth, the Lord, first in the fourteenth and the fifteenth verses, explained the destiny which awaits a man who dies during the predominance of one of the modes of nature; then in the sixteenth verse He explained the fruit of the actions in the form of favourable and unfavourable circumstances and finally in the eighteenth verse He explains the different destinies, awaiting those who are established in the three guṇas. Thus, different propensities arise, from these guṇas (modes) and these force a person, to perform the same sort of actions, as has been described in this verse. In this topic, the chief characteristic of the modes, has been mentioned.

A person, whose aim is God-realization, not mundane pleasures and prosperity, does not remain established in prakṛti (matter). So, he is not controlled, by the modes of nature. Through spiritual practice, when his egoism changes and he has a firm resolve to attain his aim, he realizes the self, which transcends the three modes. This is called wisdom (knowledge), of the self which has been delineated by the Lord, in the first and the second verses of this chapter, and also in the description of the marks and the conduct of the person, who has transcended the three modes, in the five verses from the twenty-second to the twenty-sixth. Thus the Lord in this chapter, has explained how a person can realize, the self or Him, by transcending the three guṇas.

Appendix—Knowledge (discrimination) emanates from Sattvaguṇa (mode of goodness), and if a striver is not attached to it, it gets enhanced and leads him even to salvation viz., it is transformed into Self-realization. But when there is an increase in greed, heedlessness, delusion and ignorance, then he can escape no loss, no suffering, no womb of the deluded and no hell viz., he has to face them all.

Link:—In the fourteenth and the fifteenth verses, the Lord indicated the destiny, which awaits a man dying during the predominance of one of the modes of nature. Now in the next verse, He explains the different destinies awaiting those dying who are established, in the three guṇas (modes of nature).

ऊर्ध्वं गच्छन्ति सत्त्वस्था मध्ये तिष्ठन्ति राजसाः।
जघन्यगुणवृत्तिस्था अधो गच्छन्ति तामसाः॥ १८॥

ūrdhvaṁ gacchanti sattvasthā madhye tiṣṭhanti rājasāḥ
jaghanyaguṇavṛttisthā adho gacchanti tāmasāḥ

Those, who are established in the mode of goodness rise high, those in the mode of passion, remain in the middle (regions); and those in the mode of ignorance sink low. 18

Comment:

'Ūrdhvaṁ gacchanti sattvasthā'—Sattvasthā (who are established in the mode of goodness), are those who have the predominance of the mode of goodness, and who because of that mode, observe self-control and fast, offer charity, and perform virtuous actions, such as running of cowpens and water huts, construction of roads, plantation of trees and supply of food free of cost etc. Such people, after giving up these physical body, go upwards to regions higher than the earth, viz., heaven etc., referred to in the fourteenth verse of the chapter, as the pure worlds of those, who know the Highest. Those persons who go to higher regions, have predominance of the fire element in their bodies acquired there.

'Madhye tiṣṭhanti rājasāḥ'—'Rājasāḥ' (who are established in the mode of passion), are those who have predominance of passion and attachment, and who are engaged in pleasure and prosperity, without going against the ordinance of scriptures. Such persons, are reborn on the earth, as human beings, in whom there is predominance of the earth element.

The term 'tiṣṭhanti' (dwell), denotes that they dwell in the middle region i.e., they are reborn as human beings on the earth, because of their attachment to things and persons etc., while their conduct is in accordance with the ordinance of scriptures.

'Jaghanyaguṇavṛttisthā adho gacchanti tāmasāḥ'—Persons having predominance of the mode of ignorance, being overpowered by heedlessness, indolence and sleep, waste their time and money, on trifles and futile pursuits. They do not discharge their duties sincerely, they think ill of others and they perform evil actions, such as theft, robbery and fraud etc. Such persons, die in the predominance of 'Tamoguṇa', go downhill, and degrade themselves.

They go downwards in two ways—lower births and lower regions. They are either reborn, in lower species such as beasts, birds, moths, insects, snakes, scorpions and evil spirits etc., or they undergo terrible suffering and torture in the infernal regions, known as Vaitariṇī, Asipatra, Lālābhakṣa, Kumbhīpāka, Raurava and Mahāraurava etc. Those who in spite of having modes of goodness and passion, in their life, die during the predominance of the mode of ignorance, take birth in the womb of deluded (Gītā 14/15) while, those who have the predominance of the mode of ignorance throughout their life, after death, fall into a foul hell (Gītā 16/16). It means, that a person takes rebirth according to thoughts at the last moment, but gets pleasures or pains in that life, according to actions performed, in the previous birth. For example, if a man has performed good actions in his life, but if at the last moment he thinks of a dog, he will be reborn as a dog, but he will get comforts and luxuries. On the other hand, if a person has performed evil actions, but if he thinks of a man at the time of death, he will take rebirth as a man, but he will be deprived even of the bare necessities of life, and will ever suffer, from diseases.

In order to develop the mode of goodness (Sāttvikaguṇa) a striver, should study the scripture, keep company of noble persons, reside in holy places of pilgrimages, devote mornings and evenings, the most suited time, to devotion and meditation, and discharge his duty according of his caste, creed, stage of life and the ordinance of scriptures. He should meditate on God and chant the sāttvika sacred formulas. In Śrīmadbhāgavata, there are ten factors, which influence in acquiring the guṇas (modes). These are—scriptures, water (diet), subjects (company), place, time, actions, birth, sacred formula, (mantra) and past influences (Saṁskāra). They develop Sāttvika, Rājasika and Tāmasika guṇas, according to their own nature.

An Important Fact

A person, having predominance of the mode of passion (Rajoguṇa), at the time of death, is reborn in the mortal world, as a human being (14/15) and a person established in the mode of passion, is also reborn as a human being (14/18). It means, that all human beings have only the mode of passion, they have neither the mode of goodness (Sattvaguṇa) nor the mode of ignorance (Tamoguṇa). But actually it is not so, because the Lord Himself declares, that when a man dies, during the predominance of Sattva (goodness), he attains to the pure worlds (14/14) and when he dies, being established in the mode of goodness, he goes to higher regions (14/18). Similarly, He declares that if a person dies, during the predominance of Tamas (ignorance), he is born in the womb of the deluded (14/15) and if he dies when he is established in the mode of ignorance, he sinks downwards (14/18). The three modes (guṇas) of goodness (Sattva), passion

(Rajas) and ignorance (Tamas) bind, the imperishable spirit to the body (14/5). The whole world, is deluded by the threefold modes, of nature (7/13). The doers are said to be, of three types—Sāttvika, Rājasika and Tāmasika (18/26—28). There is no being, in the entire universe, which is free, from the three modes born of nature (18/40).

Those who go to higher regions, have predominance of the mode of goodness, while the modes of passion and ignorance, occupy a secondary place. Those who are born in the mortal world as human beings, have predominance of the mode of passion, while the mode of goodness occupies, a subsidiary place and the mode of ignorance, occupies a third place. Those, who sink downwards have predominance of the mode of ignorance, while the modes of passion and goodness respectively, occupy the second and third place. Thus, when there is predominance of one of the modes in a person, he also possesses the other two modes, to a certain extent. Thus, with the predominance of anyone of the modes, every being has a different nature.

As the Lord, in spite of performing the Sāttvika, Rājasika and Tāmasika actions, remains, above these threefold modes of nature (4/13), similarly, great men who transcend the modes of nature, remain unaffected by the reactions of the Sāttvika, Rājasika and Tāmasika, propensities (14/22). Therefore, adoration to the Lord and company of the transcendental souls, are helpful, for a striver in transcending, the modes of nature.

Appendix—If there is a little increase in Tamoguṇa, then a man is reborn in the womb of the stupid creatures and if there is much increase in Tamoguṇa, he is hurled into hells.

Link:—Having discussed the three modes of nature, from the fifth to the eighteenth verses, now the Lord, in the next two verses, discusses the means of rising above, the three guṇas (modes) as well as, its reward.

नान्यं गुणेभ्यः कर्तारं यदा द्रष्टानुपश्यति।
गुणेभ्यश्च परं वेत्ति मद्भावं सोऽधिगच्छति॥ १९॥

nānyaṁ guṇebhyaḥ kartāraṁ yadā draṣṭānupaśyati
guṇebhyaśca paraṁ vetti madbhāvaṁ so'dhigacchati

When the seer beholds no doer other than the modes, and knows the self beyond the modes, he attains to My Being. 19

Comment:—

'Nānyaṁ guṇebhyaḥ kartāraṁ yadā draṣṭānupaśyati guṇebhyaśca paraṁ vetti madbhāvaṁ so'dhigacchati'—There is no agent, other than the guṇas (modes) i.e., the modes alone, are responsible for all actions and modifications. The self, the illuminator of the modes, is an observer, who is in no way contaminated, by the modes and who has no connection with, the modes and actions, because they ever undergo modifications, while there is no modification, at all in the self. The thoughtful striver, who attains knowledge of the self, attains to the Lord's Being i.e., becomes identical with Him. It means, that the striver (self) who assumed his affinity with the guṇas (modes) by error, that assumption is wiped out and he realizes his natural identity with the Lord.

Appendix—'Guṇebhyaśca paraṁ vetti'—It means that the striver realizes that he is established in the illuminator by which the modes are illumined (Gītā 13/31).

'Madbhāvaṁ so'dhigacchati'—This expression means that he attains My Being viz., he attains Brahma. The same fact has been mentioned in the second verse by the expression 'mama sādharmyamāgatāḥ'.

A discriminative striver beholds no doer other than the modes and realizes himself to be detached from the modes viz., from actions and objects. Being detached from actions and objects, he attains Yoga (becomes Yogārūḍha)—'yadā hi nendriyārtheṣu ....' (Gītā 6/4). Having attained Yoga, he attains peace and if he is not arrested there in other world, if he does not take delight in that peace, he attains God.

गुणानेतानतीत्य त्रीन्देही देहसमुद्भवान्।
जन्ममृत्युजरादुःखैर्विमुक्तोऽमृतमश्नुते ॥२०॥

guṇānetānatītya trīndehī dehasamudbhavān
janmamṛtyujarāduḥkhairvimukto'mṛtamaśnute

When the embodied soul (wise) rises above these three guṇas (modes) out of which the body is evolved, he is freed from birth, death, old age and pain and he achieves immortality. 20

Comment:—

'Guṇānetānatītya trīndehī dehasamudbhavān'—Though a thoughtful person (soul), has no connection with the body, yet people think him dwelling in the body. So he has been termed as 'Dehī' (Embodied Soul).

A body is evolved out of these modes. A man (soul), assumes his affinity with these modes. Attachment to these modes, is the cause of his birth, in good and evil wombs (Gītā 13/21). A thoughtful person rises above the three modes, which have been discussed, from the fifth to the eighteenth verses of this chapter i.e., he renounces his assumed affinity with them, because he clearly perceives that he (self), is distinct from the guṇas, having no connection at all, because the self undergoes no change while, the guṇas always undergo modifications. The self, has no connection even with, prakṛti (matter), from which these modes evolve. Then how could he (self), have any affinity with guṇas?

'Janmamṛtyujarāduḥkhairvimukto'mṛtamaśnute'—When a striver, rises above these three modes, he becomes free, from the sufferings of birth, death and old age, because attachment to these modes, is the cause of his birth etc. These modes, appear and disappear, and they also undergo modifications, in their forms—Sāttvika, Rājasa and Tāmasa, while he (the self), ever remains detached and so undergoes no modifications in the form of birth, death and old age. It is because of his attachment, to the guṇas, that he suffers the pangs of birth, death and old age. One, who realizes the self, totally detached from these modes, attains immortality, which is natural.

A man (soul), by his identification with a body, regards its death as his death. He being a portion of the Lord, is immortal but, being attached to pleasure and prosperity, and having a desire to maintain the decaying and dying body, he does not realize his immortality. A thoughtful person, applying his discrimination, comes to know that he is different from the body, and thus realizes, his immortality.

Attainment of His Being, as described in the preceding verse and attainment of immortality, described in this verse, are one and the same.

In verses 7/29, 13/8 and 14/20, there is mention only of old age, there is no mention of childhood and youth. Why? The reason is, that a person does not suffer so much, in these two stages, as he suffers in old age, because in old age he becomes feeble and has not much physical power.

At the time of death, also he suffers a lot of afflictions. But, he who rises above the three guṇas, becomes free from the pain of birth, death and old age forever.

He, who realizes the true nature of the self, is not reborn. During his life he will pass through the stages of old age and death, but these will not give him pain.

A man (the self), by his identification with a body is reborn, and assumes the body's old age and pain etc., in him. The body is evolved, out of the three modes. A transcendental great person, being free from the three modes, becomes free from all the pains, which he bore, because of his assumed identification, with the body.

Therefore, every person should realize his transcendental self, before death. When he transcends the three guṇas (modes), he is freed from all the sufferings, of old age and death, and he realizes his immortality, and is not reborn.

Appendix—Every human being has the feeling that he should live alive and never die. He wants to be immortal. His desire for immortality proves that in fact he is immortal. Had he (the self) not been immortal, he would have not desired to be immortal. For example if a person feels hungry and thirsty, it proves that there are such things (food and water) by which his hunger and thirst may be satisfied. If there had not been food and water, he would have not felt hungry and thirsty. Therefore immortality is self-evident—'bhūtagrāmaḥ sa evāyaṁ' (Gītā 8/19). When a man (the self) in spite of being immortal, ignoring his discrimination, assumes his identification with the body viz., he assumes "I am the body", then he is in dread of death and desires to be immortal. But when he attaches importance to his discrimination and accepts the fact "I am not the body because the body is ever mortal while I am ever immortal," then he realizes his axiomatic immortality. The Self, ever being uniform, perceives the modifications and changes of the body. Therefore a striver instead of attaching importance to modifications and changes, should attach importance to the beingness of the Self (which is ever existent) and to his immortality.

This verse is the gist of the fourteenth chapter.

Link:—Having heard from Lord Kṛṣṇa, the truth that the embodied soul, transcending the three guṇas, attains to immortality, Arjuna became curious to know the characteristics and conduct, of such a person, who has transcended the three guṇas and also the means of rising above these, and so he puts the question:—

अर्जुन उवाच

कैर्लिङ्गैस्त्रीन्गुणानेतानतीतो भवति प्रभो।
किमाचारः कथं चैतांस्त्रीन्गुणानतिवर्तते॥ २१॥

arjuna uvāca

kairliṅgaistrīnguṇānetānatīto bhavati prabho
kimācāraḥ kathaṁ caitāṁstrīnguṇānativartate

Arjuna said:

What are the marks of him, who has transcended the three guṇas (modes), O Lord? What is his conduct like? How does he transcend, the three modes? 21

Comment:—

'Kairliṅgaistrīnguṇānetānatīto bhavati prabho'—O Lord, I want to know the characteristics of a person, who has transcended the three modes of nature. What are the symptoms of such a person, by which he can be distinguished, from other common people?

'Kimācāraḥ'—What is his conduct, what is his daily routine, how does he live and what are, his activities? Are they regulated or nonregulated? How are they different, from those of common men?

'Kathaṁ caitāṁstrīnguṇānativartate'—What is the means, by which one, can transcend the three modes?

Link:—In response to Arjuna's first question, the Lord explains the marks of a person who has transcended the three guṇas (modes), in the next two verses:

श्रीभगवानुवाच

प्रकाशं च प्रवृत्तिं च मोहमेव च पाण्डव।
न द्वेष्टि सम्प्रवृत्तानि न निवृत्तानि काङ्क्षति॥ २२॥

śrībhagavānuvāca

prakāśaṁ ca pravṛttiṁ ca mohameva ca pāṇḍava
na dveṣṭi sampravṛttāni na nivṛttāni kāṅkṣati

The Blessed Lord said:

O Pāṇḍava, he does not hate illumination, activity and delusion when those are abundantly present, nor does he long for them, when all absent. 22

Comment:—

'Prakāśaṁ ca'—Purity of the senses and mind, is called 'Prakāśa', or illumination. It means, that illumination is the power, which enables the senses to perceive the five objects of senses, the mind, to think and the intellect, to judge.

The Lord (in 14/11) explained two marks of the mode of Sattva (goodness)—illumination (purity) and knowledge. Out of the two, only illumination has been mentioned here because in the mode, of goodness illumination occupies a predominant place. Unless there is illumination (purity) in the senses, mind and intellect, discrimination, is not aroused. Illumination arouses knowledge. So knowledge should be included within, illumination.

'Pravṛttiṁ ca'—So long as, a person is attached to the modes of nature, the propensities, such as greed, activity, undertaking of actions, unrest and craving, of the mode of passion arise. But when a man rises above, the three guṇas (modes), the propensities of the mode of passion, do not spring up, but there is activity free from attachment and desire. Thus, the activity of the transcendental person, is flawless.

The mode of passion, has two forms—attachment and actions. Out of the two, attachment is the root cause of all suffering. A transcendental person, is free from attachment. But he performs actions, without having any desire, for the fruit of actions. These actions denote 'Pravṛtti' (Activity).

'Mohameva ca pāṇḍava'—Delusion, can be of two kinds

(i) absence of discrimination, between the real and the unreal or between what ought to be done, and what ought not to be done. (ii) Error, in practical life. As far as the first kind of delusion, is concerned, a transcendental soul, is totally free from it. But, as far as, an error in practical life is concerned, even a transcendental person, may commit it. He may have an optical illusion, and may take a rope for a snake and a shell, as a piece of silver, by error.

'Na dveṣṭi sampravṛttāni na nivṛttāni kāṅkṣati'—Illumination is the effect of Sattva, activity of Rajas and delusion of Tamas. A transcendental person, does not hate illumination, activity and delusion, when these are present, nor does he long for them, when they are absent. It means, that he does not hate them by thinking why they have evolved, and that they should disappear, nor does he desire, that they should continue or they should evolve, again. A person, who has transcended the three modes of nature, remains indifferent, to them.

An Important Fact

One thing, arises as 'cropping up of thoughts' while another is, 'to be engaged in thoughts' (have feelings of attachment and aversion). There is a world of difference, between the two. The former is cosmic, while the latter is personal. We are not responsible for what happens in the world, but we are held responsible, for what we do. Moreover, by having attachment and aversion for worldly activities, we assume our affinity with them i.e., we become a doer and so we have to get the fruit. If we do not assume our affinity, with these, we cannot be responsible for them, and we will not, have to reap their fruit (because they are performed by the body, a fragment of the world) in the same way, as we are not held responsible for the numberless actions, which are performed, in the world, through cosmic power. So a striver, should have neither attachment nor aversion to good and evil propensities, evolved from the three modes of nature i.e., he should not assume affinity with them.

These propensities, appear in the mind, of even transcendental souls. They appear and again disappear. But, he has neither attachment nor aversion for them, he does not even perceive them, as such because he beholds, nothing else besides the Lord, in the entire universe.

One is to perceive, while the other is automatically seen. 'To see' comes within 'doing' and 'automatically seen' comes, within 'what happens.' A fault lies in 'seeing', not in 'what is automatically seen.' A striver, should not feel perturbed, even if he perceives the worst propensity, in his mind. He should have, neither attachment nor aversion to it. He commits an error, that he is either attached to those propensities, or has an aversion to them, and so he is entangled. Lord Rāma says to His younger brother, Bharata in the Rāmacaritamānasa:—

"O dear! There are innumerable virtues and vices evolved, by the deluding potency of the Lord. Discrimination, consists in their non-perception while ignorance consists in their perception" (7/41).

A striver, should think seriously, that dispositions appear and disappear, but he (the self) remains the same. The changeable cannot see the changeable, only the changeless can see, the changeable. This is a rule. It proves, that the self is an observer, while the dispositions, are to be observed. So, he is different from them. So he should not assume his affinity with them, he should, neither be pleased nor displeased with, the appearance and disappearance of the kaleidoscopic, mutable and perishable, dispositions. He should ever remain fixed, in his real self, which is non-changing, immutable and imperishable.

Appendix—The man, who transcends guṇas, desires neither the favourable circumstances to continue nor the unfavourable ones to disappear. Having realized his immutability, he has the knowledge of the desirable and the undesirable circumstances, but he (the Self) is not affected by them. The propensities of the mind change but he himself remains untainted. The striver should not be affected by dispositions because the transcendental soul is the ideal for a striver and the striver is his follower.

It is inevitable for every striver that he should not identify the Self with the body. The dispositions are there in the mind, not in the Self. Therefore a striver should regard these dispositions neither as good nor bad nor in the Self. The reason is that these propensities are fleeting but the Self ever remains the same. Had these propensities been in us (the Self), they would have persisted, so long as the Self exists. But this is every one's experience that we ever exist but the propensities appear and disappear. These propensities are evolute of prakṛti, while we (the Self) are identified with God. Therefore the Self, who experiences the modifications apart from the Self, remains uniform.

उदासीनवदासीनो गुणैर्यो न विचाल्यते।
गुणा वर्तन्त इत्येव योऽवतिष्ठति नेङ्गते॥ २३॥

udāsīnavadāsīno guṇairyo na vicālyate
guṇā vartanta ityeva yo'vatiṣṭhati neṅgate

He who like one unconcerned, is not moved by the modes of nature and established in the self remains apathetic without wavering, knows, that it is only the modes, that act. 23

Comment:—

'Udāsīnavadāsīnaḥ'—When two persons fight, he who sides with either is called, partial. He who is just, to both is a mediator, while 'Udāsīna' is he, who sees the two but has an attitude of indifference, towards either of the two. From the view point of a realized soul, who has risen above the three guṇas, there is no existence of the world, except God. He himself has merged in God. So to whom should he be indifferent? Therefore, no question of his being indifferent, arises. But to common people, he seems indifferent to the world. That state is described as 'Udāsīnavat'.

'Guṇairyo na vicālyate'—The propensities of modes of goodness, passion, and ignorance, appear in his mind but he is not moved, by these. He is unconcerned, as he remains when those propensities come to the minds of others, because he perceives that nothing exists, besides the Lord.

'Guṇā vartanta ityeva yo'vatiṣṭhati'—He remains, fixed in the self, by understanding that it is the modes, which are acting, on the modes (Gītā 3/28).

'Neṅgate'—A person, who rises above the three modes of nature, does not perform any action himself, because in the imperishable pure self, there is no activity.

[In the above-mentioned two verses, the Lord has described the attitude of indifference and untaintedness of the person, who has transcended, the modes of nature.]

Appendix—'Na vicālyate', 'avatiṣṭhati' and 'neṅgate'—in fact these three expressions have the same meaning. But the purpose of giving these three expressions is that the transcendental exalted soul remains fixed (established) in the Self. He neither wavers himself nor can be moved by anyone else.

'To do', 'to be or to occur' and 'is'—there are these three states. If 'to do' is changed into 'to be' and 'to be' is changed into 'is', then ego is totally wiped out. A worldly minded person (not a striver) holds, "I am doing actions"—'ahaṅkāravimūḍhātmā kartāhamiti manyate' (Gītā 3/27). He, who becomes a doer, has to become an enjoyer also. The striver with the predominance of discrimination, realizes that 'actions are occurring'—'guṇā guṇeṣu vartanta' (Gītā 3/28) viz., 'I do nothing'—'naiva kiñcitkaromīti' (Gītā 5/8). But he who has realized the Self, such an enlightened exalted soul realizes only an entity ('is')—'yo'vatiṣṭhati neṅgate'. That divine entity equally pervades all actions. Actions come to an end but the consciousness remains the same. An exalted soul, instead of having an eye on actions, has an eye only on the conscious entity ('is').

Link:—In the next two verses, the Lord answers Arjuna's second question, "What is his conduct?"

समदुःखसुखः स्वस्थः समलोष्टाश्मकाञ्चनः ।
तुल्यप्रियाप्रियो धीरस्तुल्यनिन्दात्मसंस्तुतिः ॥ २४ ॥
मानापमानयोस्तुल्यस्तुल्यो मित्रारिपक्षयोः ।
सर्वारम्भपरित्यागी गुणातीतः स उच्यते ॥ २५ ॥

samaduḥkhasukhaḥ svasthaḥ samaloṣṭāśmakāñcanaḥ
tulyapriyāpriyo dhīrastulyanindātmasaṁstutiḥ
mānāpamānayostulyastulyo mitrāripakṣayoḥ
sarvārambhaparityāgī guṇātītaḥ sa ucyate

He regards pain and pleasure alike, dwells in his own self, views a clod of earth, a stone and gold alike, remains equable amidst the pleasant and the unpleasant, is firm and views blame and praise alike; he equates honour and dishonour and is the same to friends and foes, he has abandoned all activities—such a man is said to have risen above, the three modes of nature. 24-25

Comment:—

'Dhīraḥ samaduḥkhasukhaḥ'—A person, having transcended the modes of nature, discriminates the real from the unreal, and remains firm (fixed), in the self.

He remains the same, in desirable and undesirable circumstances viz., pleasure and pain, which appear as the fruit of his past actions. They cannot make him happy and sad.

'Svasthaḥ'—In the self, there is neither pleasure nor pain. The self, is their illuminator. He remains established in the self.

'Samaloṣṭāśmakāñcanaḥ'—He has neither attachment nor aversion, to a clod of earth, a piece of stone and a piece of gold. He makes proper use of these but remains alike, in their gain and loss. Not to know the distinction between a clod of earth, a stone and gold is not, even-mindedness. Having known their distinction, not to have attraction and aversion for them, is even-mindedness. The knowledge of their distinction is not a fault, but to be affected by these is an evil.

'Tulyapriyāpriyaḥ'—He remains alike, in success and failure, which he gets, as the fruit of his actions.

'Tulyanindātmasaṁstutiḥ'—Praise and blame, mainly relate to name. The man beyond guṇas has no connection at all, with the name. He is neither pleased, when he is praised, nor displeased when he is blamed. He has neither attachment for those, who praise him nor aversion to those, who blame him. It is a common trait, that a man likes praise but dislikes blame. He who rises above guṇas, knows the two, but he treats both of these alike. He remains established, in the self, where praise and blame, have no access.

Both praise and blame, are activities done by others. To be pleased or displeased with these is a mistake. Whatever one's nature is, and whatever his conviction is, he will speak, accordingly. It is not just if a striver, expects of others, that they should not censure him. It is rather unjust, if he compels other persons to praise him, and not to blame him. He should be pleased, when someone blames him, because in that case his sins are wiped out and he is purified. When someone praises him, then his virtues are destroyed. So, he should not be pleased, with praise, because it involves danger.

'Mānāpamānayostulyaḥ'—A person, regards honour and dishonour of a body or a name as his own, when he identifies himself, with the body. But the person, who has transcended the modes, having snapped his connection with the body, is neither pleased with honour nor displeased with dishonour, because he remains established in the self, which is free from all alterations and modifications. So he feels neither happy when he is honoured, nor sad, when he is dishonoured. He remains alike. To have knowledge of honour and dishonour, is not an evil. But to be happy and unhappy, is an evil. Both are modifications of nature.

'Tulyo mitrāripakṣayoḥ'—He entertains no feeling of friendship or enmity, towards anyone. But, people find their own sentiments of friendship or enmity, reflected in him. So, even by knowing the fact that some other persons, regard him as their friend or enemy, he maintains an attitude of impartiality, towards them.

If he has to divide a thing, between two—one, who regards him as a friend and the other, who regards him as an enemy, he gives a bit less to the former, than to the latter, because he is generous to the latter, even in judgement. This is also, equanimity or even-mindedness.

'Sarvārambhaparityāgī'—He abandons all new undertakings for pleasure and prosperity. He performs actions, according to circumstances, being free from feelings of egoism, attachment, having no desire for their fruit, and abandons these, without having any desire for praise and honour etc.

'Guṇātītaḥ sa ucyate'—Such a person, is said to have risen above, the three guṇas (modes of nature).

In fact, the person, who has transcended the three modes of nature, cannot, have any marks. Marks vest in the modes of prakṛti or in prakṛti. How can he, who has marks, transcend guṇas? Arjuna, has inquired of the marks, of such a person. The Lord has described those marks. In fact, these are marks of his so-called inner sense, and body. These marks, are only hints about such a person. They cannot describe him. The modes, are the evolutes of nature, while a body. senses, mind and intellect, are the evolutes of modes. So the senses, mind and intellect cannot even, fully describe the modes which are, their cause. How can these describe prakṛti, the cause of modes? Then, how is it possible for these to describe the one, who has transcended the modes?

Here the Lord, has mentioned four pairs of opposites—pleasure and pain, pleasant and unpleasant, praise and blame and honour and dishonour, to denote that one who becomes equanimous in them, he becomes equanimous in other pairs of opposites, also easily. A person, having transcended the three modes, regards these pairs alike. He always remains balanced, and his peace, is never disturbed.

[In the twenty-fourth and the twenty-fifth verses, the Lord has described equanimity, of a great person, who has transcended the three modes of nature.]

Appendix—Flaws such as attachment and aversion neither abide in the non-Self nor in the Self nor they are the intrinsic characteristic of the mind but they abide in the ego (identification of the Self with the body). In fact there is no real identification but it is merely assumed out of indiscrimination. It means that there are no flaws in the Self but a man assumes them in the Self because of indiscrimination. He realizes that flaws appear and disappear, while the Self ever exists as it is; but he does not attach importance to this realization. If he discriminately realizes that the Self is free from these flaws, he will not become their experiencer (happy and sad).

Link:—Now, the Lord, in the next verse, answers Arjuna's third question—"How does he transcend, the three modes?"

मां च योऽव्यभिचारेण भक्तियोगेन सेवते।
स गुणान्समतीत्यैतान्ब्रह्मभूयाय कल्पते॥ २६॥

mām ca yo'vyabhicāreṇa bhaktiyogena sevate
sa guṇānsamatītyaitānbrahmabhūyāya kalpate

He who worships Me with unadulterated devotion, rises above the three modes and becomes eligible, for attaining Brahma. 26

Comment:—

[Though the Lord, discussed the means of rising above the

modes, in the nineteenth and the twentieth verses of this chapter, yet Arjuna, in the twenty-first verse again asked the question: What is the means of attaining to the transcendental position? It means, that Arjuna wants to know of any other means, besides the one, already discussed. Therefore, the Lord regarding Arjuna as eligible for devotion, explains the path of devotion.]

'Māṁ ca yo'vyabhicāreṇa bhaktiyogena sevate'—In this clause the term 'Yaḥ' (Who), denotes the server (worshipper), the term 'Mām' (Me), denotes the worshipped and the expression 'Avyabhicāreṇa bhaktiyogena sevate', denotes exclusive devotion (worship). In exclusive devotion—a devotee, without depending either on the world or even on the Discipline of Knowledge, and devotion, etc., depends only on God, and takes refuge only in Him.

'Sa guṇānsamatītyaitān'—He, who worships the Lord, with exclusive devotion, has not to rise above the three modes, but by the Lord's grace the modes are automatically transcended, by him (Gītā 12/6-7).

'Brahmabhūyāya kalpate'—Having transcended the modes, he becomes eligible for attaining, Brahma. Here the Lord, has talked about devotion. So He should have said, that the devotee becomes eligible for attaining Him, instead of saying that he becomes eligible for attaining Brahma. The reason is, that Arjuna asked the means of transcending the modes (attainment of Brahma, the Absolute). So, the Lord answered accordingly.

Also in the scriptures it is mentioned, that he who worships the Lord, with exclusive devotion, has not to adopt any other means, even in the Discipline of Knowledge, for becoming eligible to attain Brahma. He automatically, becomes eligible to attain Brahma. But a devotee is not satisfied with this attainment, he wants to please the Lord. He regards the Lord's pleasure, as his own pleasure. It means, that one who surrenders himself to the Lord, becomes eligible, for attaining Brahma, automatically. This is something different, whether he attaches importance to this attainment, or not.

The Absolute, Who is attained by the Disciplines of Knowledge and Action etc., is also attained, by the Discipline of Devotion. The means to attain Him, may be different, but what is attained, is the same Absolute.

Appendix—Whatever a striver wants to attain that is all attained by devotion. The striver who predominantly wants to attain Brahma viz., salvation or enlightenment, he attains Brahma by devotion because God is the abode of Brahma (Gītā 14/27). Brahma is an integral part of the entire form of God (Gītā 7/29-30). In the tenth verse of the thirteenth chapter also the Lord has declared that exclusive devotion is a means to Self-realization.

In Śrīmadbhāgavata the worship of God Who is endowed with attributes, has been mentioned 'nirguṇa' (transcending the modes); as—'manniketaṁ tu nirguṇam' (11/25/25), 'matsevāyāṁ tu nirguṇā' (11/25/27) etc. Therefore he, who worships God endowed with attributes, transcends the three guṇas (modes). God endowed with attributes is not dependent on attributes but attributes are dependent on Him. He who is swayed (controlled) by Sattva-Raja-Tama, is not 'Saguṇa' (God endowed with attributes), but Saguṇa is He Who is endowed with endless divine qualities such as limitless grandeur, sweetness, loveliness and generosity etc. Sāttvika, Rājasa and Tāmasa actions can be performed by God but He is not controlled by those modes.

A dovotee by having an inclination to God, naturally and easily transcends the modes of nature. Not only this, he also comes to know the entire form of God.

Link:—How does a devotee, who worships the Lord, become eligible for attaining Brahma? The Lord, answers the question, in the next verse.

ब्रह्मणो हि प्रतिष्ठाहममृतस्याव्ययस्य च।
शाश्वतस्य च धर्मस्य सुखस्यैकान्तिकस्य च॥ २७॥

brahmaṇo hi pratiṣṭhāhamamṛtasyāvyayasya ca
śāśvatasya ca dharmasya sukhasyaikāntikasya ca

For, I am the abode of Brahma, the Immortal and the Imperishable, of eternal Dharma (Law or righteousness) and of absolute bliss. 27

Comment:—

'Brahmaṇo hi pratiṣṭhāham'—When Lord Kṛṣṇa declares, that He is the abode of Brahma, He means to say, that He has His identity, with Brahma. As burning fire which is seen, and fire present in a piece of wood which is not seen, are one and the same, similarly the Lord is the same, as endowed with form and also, without form. As the nose smells the same food, while the tongue tastes it, similarly the same Lord is Brahma, for a devotee following the Discipline of Knowledge, and Lord Kṛṣṇa for a devotee of devotion.

In fact Lord Kṛṣṇa and Brahma, are one and the same. The Lord has used the term 'Brahma', for Himself in 5/10 and also 'unmanifested form' in 9/4. So He is both with form and without form.

'Amṛtasyāvyayasya ca'—The Lord, is Immortal and imperishable. It means, that the Immortal and the Imperishable are not two different entities, but one and the same. The same immortality, has been described in 13/12 and 14/20.

'Śāśvatasya ca dharmasya'—Lord Kṛṣṇa, is the abode of eternal Dharma, and eternal Dharma, is the abode of the Lord. It means that the Lord and eternal Dharma, are one and the same.* In

*There are four important Dharmas (Religions) in the world. They are Hindū (Sanātana or Eternal), Bauddha, Christian and Muslim. The founders of Bauddha, Christian and Muslim religions are Buddha, Jesus Christ and Mohammada respectively. But the Sanātana Dharma was not originated by anyone, it is eternal and beginningless like the Lord. This is a discovery by high sages. What is discovered, has its own pre-existence. The methods of God-realization described in other Dharmas are also the gift of 'Sanātana Dharma'.

the Gītā, Arjuna has addressed Lord Kṛṣṇa, as the guardian of the eternal Dharma (law) (11/18). God also incarnates, for the establishment of the Sanātana Dharma (4/8).

'Sukhasyaikāntikasya ca'—Lord Kṛṣṇa, is the abode of absolute bliss, and absolute bliss, is the abode of the Lord. The same absolute bliss, has been called eternal bliss (5/21), supreme bliss (6/21) and infinite bliss (6/28).

In this verse, in the expression 'Brahmaṇaḥ' and 'Amṛtasya', like the expression 'Rāhoḥ śiraḥ', the sixth inflexion has been used, which means that 'Rāhu' and 'Śiraḥ' (head), are not two different entities, but both are, one and the same. Similarly, here Brahma, the Immortal, the Imperishable, is Lord Kṛṣṇa and Lord Kṛṣṇa is Brahma, the Immortal, the Imperishable. In this verse, emphasis has been laid on the identity of Lord Kṛṣṇa, with Brahma, the Imperishable and the Eternal Dharma etc. All of them, in spite of being called, by different names, are one and the same. Thus, a devotee, who worships Lord Kṛṣṇa, attains Brahma.

Appendix—'I am the abode of Brahma and imperishable immortality'—this statement pertains to the Absolute Who is attributeless and formless, and to the path of knowledge; 'I am the abode of eternal Dharma'—this statement pertains to God endowed with attributes and form and to Karmayoga; and 'I am the abode of Absolute Bliss'—this statement pertains to God endowed with attributes and form and to Karmayoga; and 'I am the abode of Absolute Bliss'—this statement pertains to God endowed with attributes and formless and to the path of meditation. It means that he, who worships God endowed with

---

When there is a decline of this Dharma, the Lord incarnates Himself for the establishment of Dharma (Gītā 4/7-8). So the Lord establishes it, He does not found it. Actually all the other religions are the product of Sanātana Dharma. So if their principles are obeyed without any desire for their fruit, they will lead to salvation undoubtedly. A deep thought for salvation as is described in Sanātana Dharma is not available in other religions. The principles of Sanātana Dharma (Hindū Dharma) are totally scientific and they lead to salvation.

attributes and form and depends on Him, attains the aim which is attained by Jñānayoga, Karmayoga and Dhyānayoga. By all the three Yogas, the same God Who is called 'entire' is attained.

All the divine glories are God's grandeur. Brahma is also one divine glory (grandeur) of God. Therefore here the Lord has declared—'brahmaṇo hi pratiṣṭhāham'. In the Padma Purāṇa it is mentioned that 'Brahma' is a ray of Lord Kṛṣṇa's nail.

yannakhendurucirbrahma dhyeyaṁ brahmādibhiḥ suraiḥ
guṇatrayamatītaṁ taṁ vande vṛndāvaneśvaram

(Pātāla. 77/60)

Lord Śaṅkara says—'I do obeisance to Vṛndāvaneśvara Lord Kṛṣṇa Who transcends the three modes and gods meditate upon Brahma who is the ray of Lord Kṛṣṇa's nail—moon.'

ॐ तत्सदिति श्रीमद्भगवद्गीतासूपनिषत्सु ब्रह्मविद्यायां योगशास्त्रे
श्रीकृष्णार्जुनसंवादे गुणत्रयविभागयोगो नाम चतुर्दशोऽध्यायः ॥१४॥

oṁ tatsaditi śrīmadbhagavadgītāsūpaniṣatsu brahmavidyāyāṁ yogaśāstre śrīkṛṣṇārjunasaṁvāde guṇatrayavibhāgayogo nāma caturdaśo'dhyāyaḥ

Thus with the words Oṁ, Tat, Sat, the names of the Lord, in the Upaniṣad of the Bhagavadgītā, the knowledge of Brahma, the Supreme, the science of Yoga and the dialogue between Śrī Kṛṣṇa and Arjuna, this the fourteenth discourse is designated:

"The Yoga of the Division of the three guṇas (modes)."

In this chapter, sattva (goodness), raja (passion) and tama (ignorance), the three modes of nature, have been described. The person, who transcends this three modes, realizes his eternal union with the Lord. So the chapter, has been entitled 'Guṇatrayavibhāgayoga' (Division of the three modes of nature).

Words, letters and Uvāca (said) in the Fourteenth Chapter:

(1) In this chapter in **Atha caturdaśo'dhyāyaḥ'** there are three words, in **'Śrībhagavānuvāca'** etc., there are six words, in verses,

there are three hundred and twenty-two words, and there are thirteen concluding words. Thus the total number of words is three hundred and forty-four.

(2) In this chapter in **'Atha caturdaśo'dhyāyaḥ'** there are eight letters, in **'Śrībhagavānuvāca'** etc., there are twenty letters, in verses, there are eight hundred and sixty-four letters and there are fifty-one, concluding letters. Thus the total number of the letters is nine hundred and forty-three. In this chapter there are thirty-two letters, in each verse.

(3) In this chapter the term **'Uvāca'** (said) has been used thrice—**'Śrībhagavānuvāca'** twice and **'Arjuna Uvāca'** once.

Metres Used in the Fourteenth Chapter—

Out of the twenty-seven verses, of this chapter, in the first quarter of the fifth verse 'na-gaṇa' being used there is **'na-vipulā'** metre; in the first quarter of the sixth and tenth verses 'ra-gaṇa' being used there is **'ra-vipulā'** metre; in the third quarter of the fifteenth and seventeenth verses 'bha-gaṇa', being used there is **'bha-vipulā'** metre; in the first quarter of the nineteenth verse 'ma-gaṇa' being used there is **'ma-vipulā'** metre; in the first quarter of the ninth verse 'bha-gaṇa' and in the third quarter 'na-gaṇa' being used there is **'saṁkīrṇa-vipulā'** metre. The remaining twenty verses have the characteristics of right **'pathyāvaktra'**, Anuṣṭup metre.

|| Shri Hari ||

Fifteenth Chapter

INTRODUCTION

In response to Arjuna's question, "Those devotees who worship Thee with attributes and those who worship the Absolute (the Imperishable and the Unmanifested)—which of them are better versed in Yoga?" The Lord declared the former to be superior to the latter. In the fifth verse, the Lord while comparing the two declared, "The difficulty of those whose thoughts are set, on the Unmanifested is greater, for the goal of the Unmanifested, is hard to reach by the embodied beings." How to overcome this difficulty of body consciousness—this topic, as well as, the description of the Absolute has been given, in the thirteenth and the fourteenth chapters.

In the twenty-first verse of the fourteenth chapter Arjuna asked, "What are the marks and conduct of him, who has transcended the three modes (guṇas) and how does he transcend them?" In response to this, the Lord after discussing the marks and conduct of the person who has transcended the three modes, in verses twenty-second to the twenty-fifth, in the twenty-sixth verse He explained unadultered devotion, as the means to transcend, the three modes, for the devotees who worship God with attributes. It means, that devotee who has exclusive devotion to God (who totally depends upon Him) transcends the three modes easily. The expression 'Avyabhicāreṇa bhaktiyogena', stands for devotion free from dependence on the world, the term 'Yaḥ' stands for the embodied soul, while the term 'Mām' stands for God. In the fifteenth chapter these very three subjects have been described in detail which are referred in brief just above.

Man (soul) being a fragment of God, is transcendental but he is bound because of his identification with, and attachment to the body (world)—the evolute of the modes. He is not liberated from these modes, so long as he does not know the glory of the Lord, the transcendental one. Therefore, the Lord, introduces the fifteenth chapter in order, to explain His glory and secret, to enable a striver to cultivate unswerving devotion.

A man (soul), is a fragment of God (Gītā 15/7) and so he has his affinity, only for God. But by error, he assumes his affinity for the body, senses, mind and intellect, etc., which are evolutes of Nature, by regarding them as 'I', or 'mine', or for me. This is the main stumbling block, to exclusive devotion. In order to remove this stumbling block, the Lord in the first five verses of the fifteenth chapter, having described the universe as a Pīpala tree, exhorts Arjuna, to cut it down with an axe of dispassion.

श्रीभगवानुवाच

ऊर्ध्वमूलमधःशाखमश्वत्थं प्राहुरव्ययम्।
छन्दांसि यस्य पर्णानि यस्तं वेद स वेदवित्॥ १॥

śrībhagavānuvāca

ūrdhvamūlamadhaḥśākhamaśvatthaṁ prāhuravyayam
chandāṁsi yasya parṇāni yastaṁ veda sa vedavit

The Blessed Lord said

He who knows the Pīpala tree which is said to be imperishable, as having its root above and branches below, and whose leaves are the Vedas, is the knower of the Vedas. 1

Comment:—

'Ūrdhvamūlamadhaḥśākham'— [Like the first two verses of the thirteenth chapter, here in the first verse of the fifteenth chapter also the Lord presents a view of all the topics of the entire chapter. The expression 'Ūrdhvamūlam' denotes God; the expression 'Adhaḥśākham' denotes Brahmā, the representative of all beings while the term 'Aśvattham' denotes the world. He who knows the omnipotent Lord (the root of the Pīpala tree in form of the universe) in reality has been called 'Vedavit' (knower of the Vedas).

Generally trees have their roots below and branches above. But this tree in the form of the universe is strange as it has its root above and branches below. The supreme abode of God from where there is no return is above all the other worlds. Brahmā is the main branch (stem) of the tree in the form of the world as he emanates first of all. The abode of Brahmā is lower than that of God. Brahmā is lower than God in position, virtues, rank and age etc., so he is called 'Adhaḥ'.* As the root is the foundation (support) of the entire tree, so is God the origin of the entire universe. Brahmā, the creator is born of Him and he has been described by the expression 'Adhaḥśākham' (branches below).

God is the illuminator and base of the entire creation and He is superior to everyone in everyway. "There is none equal to Thee, how could then there be one superior to Thee in the three worlds" (Gītā 11/43)†? Being the base and the support of the entire universe He is called 'Ūrdhvamūlam' (root above).

The term 'Mūla' stands for the root or the base. The universe is born of Him and is preserved by Him. He is eternal, infinite and the base of the entire creation. He resides in His eternal abode, which is situated above all the worlds in His manifested form with attributes. So He is known as 'Ūrdhva'. This world is born of Him and therefore it is called 'Ūrdhvamūla' having its root above.

As trunks, branches and tendrils sprout from the root of the tree, so does the entire universe emanate from God. It is expanded by Him, it remains established in Him and it is by His power that beings act‡. Having taken refuge in such Lord,

* The expression 'Adhaḥśākham' includes all creatures from Brahmā to insects.

† No one appears either to be superior or equal to Him (God).

‡ This fact has been mentioned in the Gītā when Lord Kṛṣṇa declares, "I am the source and dissolution of the entire universe" (7/6), "I am the origin,

a person is satisfied forever (the Lord talks of taking refuge in Him in the fourth verse).

At the time of creation Brahmā, the creator accepts Prakṛti but he remains liberated from it as he has no attachment to it. Except Brahmā all the other beings having affinity of 'I'ness and 'mineness' for Prakṛti (nature) and its evolute body etc., are bound and take birth and then die again and again i.e., their branches spread downward. The three kinds of birth because of the three modes of goodness, of passion and of ignorance are included in the expression 'Adhaḥśākham (Gītā 14/18).

'Aśvattham'—The term 'Aśvattham' has two meanings—(1) That which may not last even by tomorrow i.e., kaleidoscopic* and (2) Pīpala tree.

According to the first interpretation the universe does not remain fixed even for a 'Kṣaṇa'† (moment), it is kaleidoscopic, the seen is changing into the unseen. It seems to exist like a mirage. The mere change appears as creation, existence or dissolution. It is because of its kaleidoscopic nature, that it is called 'Aśvattham'.

According to the second interpretation the universe has been called a Pīpala tree. In the scriptures, this tree has been glorified very much. The Lord, declares while describing His divine manifestations, 'Among all the trees I am the 'Aśvattha' (Pīpala)' (Gītā 10/26). If the plants of Pīpala, myrobalan and

---

the dissolution, the formation, the treasure house and the imperishable seed of the universe" (9/18), "I am the source of all; from Me everything evolves" (9/10), "The ancient activity or energy streamed forth from Him" (15/4), "From Him all beings have evolved" (18/46).

* The term 'Śvaḥ' stands for tomorrow. That which continues by tomorrow is 'Śvattha' and that which does not last even by tomorrow is 'Aśvattha'.

† The philosophers have explained the term 'Kṣaṇa' (moment) in the following way—a needle pricks the lotus leaf in three moments—touch in the first moment, making the hole in the second moment, and palling the other side of the leaf in the third moment.

basil, are worshipped by regarding them as divine, their worship becomes, worship of God.

God is the root of the universe, and therefore this Pīpala tree, in the form of the universe, being a manifestation of God, deserves to be worshipped. The worship of Pīpala tree, in the form of universe is to render service to it, without having any desire to derive pleasure, out of it. This world is a manifestation of God, for those who do not desire to derive pleasure out of it—All is God (Gītā 7/19). But this world, is the abode of sorrow, for those who desire to derive pleasure out of it, because they (the self), are imperishable, while the world is perishable, transitory or kaleidoscopic. Therefore, the objects of the world cannot satisfy the self, and the people have to follow a cycle of birth and death. So everyone, should render service to the world, without expecting any reward from it.

'Prāhuravyayam'—This tree, in the form of the world, is called imperishable, because in spite of being perishable, its beginning and end, are not known, its flow is continuous (eternal), and its root is imperishable God. As the water of sea evaporates, with the heat of sun, changes into a cloud, falls on the ground in the form of rain, and flows into the sea again, in the form of a stream or a river and the process continues endlessly, so does the cycle of the world go on, without any end. This cycle moves so rapidly, that just like a movie in spite of, being kaleidoscopic, it seems fixed.

This tree in the form of this world, is called imperishable, but in fact, it is not so. Had it been imperishable, the Lord, in the third verse of this chapter, would not have declared, "Its form is not perceived here, as it is said" nor would He have inspired Arjuna to cut off this firm rooted Pīpala tree, with a strong axe of non-attachment.

'Chandāṁsi yasya parṇāni'—The Vedas, are the leaves of this tree, in the form of the universe. Here, the Vedas, mean the portion of the Vedas which deal with rituals and their performance, for the fruits.* As trees, with flowers and leaves without bearing any fruits cannot satisfy people, so can mundane pleasure and prosperity, looking beautiful outwardly, like flowers and leaves, not provide imperishable bliss.

Virtuous actions performed, in order to attain, heaven are better than forbidden actions, but they cannot lead to salvation as those people having enjoyed the vast heaven, enter the world of mortals, when their merit is exhausted (Gītā 9/21). Thus, such actions and their fruits—both are perishable. Therefore, a striver, should realize God, by becoming detached from both of them.

Leaves are born of the branches of a tree, and they protect and nourish it. They beautify it and strengthen it (the movement of leaves strengthen its root, stem and branches). The Vedas, are also born of Brahmā, the main branch of this tree, in the form of the world and actions sanctioned by the Vedas, nourish and protect the world. So, the Vedas, have been called leaves. When actions, are performed with a desire for fruit, these lead him to heaven. This is nourishment of the tree. In heaven, there are celestial damsels and gardens etc. This is the beauty of that tree.

The performance of actions for their fruit leads to the cycle of birth and death—this is strengthening of this tree.

Here the Lord means to say, that a striver, instead of getting entangled in the leaves, in the form of performance of actions for their fruit, should depend only on God, the root of the tree. Having depended on God, he realizes the reality about the Vedas, which deal with the Supreme Being, rather than the world or heaven (Gītā 15/15).†

*In the Vedas the number of the hymns which deal with the fruit of actions, is eighty thousand while the number of the hymns which lead to salvation, is twenty thousand. Out of these twenty thousand hymns, there are four thousand on the path of knowledge, and sixteen thousand, on the path of devotion.

†The Vedas ascertain the Supreme Person Who is the supreme goal.

'Yastaṁ veda sa vedavit'—He who knows this tree, in the form of the universe, knows the reality, about the Vedas. The real knowledge of the world, consists in knowing the world, as kaleidoscopic and also having no desire of deriving any pleasure out of it. When a man realizes, that the world is transitory (unreal), he cannot derive any pleasure out of it. While enjoying the sense-objects, he does not realize the world, to be transitory. A man depends on the world and has a desire to derive pleasure, out of it only by regarding the worldly beings and objects, as real. When he realizes, its true character he has a disinclination for the world, and an inclination to God, and he realizes his identity, with God. Such a person, is a knower of the Vedas. The person who has only studied the Vedas, may be a scholar, but he has not really known, the Vedas. The real knower of the Vedas, is he who having renounced his affinity, for the world, has realized God.

The Lord in the fifteenth verse of this chapter, has declared that He Himself is the knower of the Vedas. Thus the Lord identifies, such a man, who knows the reality about the world, with Him by calling him a knower of the Vedas. It means, that discrimination bestowed upon human beings, is so glorious that a person having known the reality about the world can become the knower of the Vedas, like God.*

The man (soul), being a fragment of God, has only affinity, for God. He has assumed his affinity for the world by an error. He, who through discrimination having rectified this error i.e., having renounced his assumed affinity, for the world, has realized his self-evident identity, with God, knows the reality about the tree in the form of the world, and he has been called 'Vedavit' (the knower of the Vedas), by the Lord.

Appendix—The world, the Soul and the Supreme Soul—all the three are only God—'Vāsudevaḥ sarvam'. It has been described

*The same fact has been pointed out by the Lord when He declares, "They have attained unity with Me" (Gītā 14/2).

here in the form of a tree.

In spite of being kaleidoscopic, the purpose of calling the world 'avyaya' (imperishable) is that though the world undergoes changes constantly, yet nothing is spent out of it viz., it does not know any diminution. As in the sea, several waves appear to rise and there are tides also, but water of the sea remains the same, it neither decreases nor increases. Similarly though it appears that the world constantly undergoes changes, yet it remain. 'avyaya' (unspent). The reason is that the kaleidoscopic world also being the evolute of God's power 'aparā prakṛti' is the manifestation of God—'sadasaccāhamarjuna' (Gītā 9/19). Both—the kaleidoscopic 'aparā prakṛti' (lower nature) as well as the unchangeable 'parā prakṛti' (higher nature) is God's manifestation. This world is in the form of waves in God-ocean. As in the ocean, the waves appear rising outwardly only; inside the ocean, there are no waves, the ocean remains calm and uniform, similarly outwardly the world appears to be kaleidoscopic, yet within it, there is God Who is ever calm and uniform (Gītā 13/27). It means that the world as the world is not imperishable but it is imperishable as the manifestation of God. A glimpse of God appears in the form of the world. A striver instead of catching that glimpse (world), should be inclined to God. To cognise the reality of that glimpse, to value it and to be attached to it lead to bondage.

Another purpose of using the term 'avyaya' is that the person who gets attached to the world, his cycle of birth and death will also be imperishable viz., will never come to an end. The long path can come to an end but how can be round path end? As a bullock used in a crusher goes on moving round and round without an end, similarly the person attached to the world will go on following the cycle of birth and death endlessly.

The world is 'avyaya' because the seed of the world is 'avyaya'—'bījamavyayam' (Gītā 9/18).

Link:—The Lord in the next verse, describes the tree of creation, described in the preceding verse, in more detail along with its parts.

अधश्चोर्ध्वं प्रसृतास्तस्य शाखा
गुणप्रवृद्धा विषयप्रवालाः ।
अधश्च मूलान्यनुसन्ततानि
कर्मानुबन्धीनि मनुष्यलोके ॥ २ ॥

adhaścordhvaṁ prasṛtāstasya śākhā
guṇapravṛddhā viṣayapravālāḥ
adhaśca mūlānyanusantatāni
karmānubandhīni manuṣyaloke

Its branches nourished by the modes, with sense-objects for its buds (twigs) extend below and above and the roots which bind the soul according to its actions in the human body stretch forth in all regions higher or lower. 2

Comment:—

'Tasya śākhā guṇapravṛddhāḥ'—Brahmā, is the main branch of the tree of creation. All beings such as the gods, men and other lower species, are born of Brahmā, the Creator. So, all the worlds from the abode of Brahmā, down to the nethermost-region and all the beings, such as the gods, persons and germs etc., living in them, are branches of that tree of creation. As branches of tree spread, when they are watered, so do the branches of creation spread, by attachment to the modes which are responsible for one's birth in good, medium and evil bodies (Gītā 13/21; 14/18). In the entire creation, there is no place, object or person, that is free from the three modes of nature (Gītā 18/40). It is because of attachment for the modes that the world, seems to exist. The modes can be experienced by inclination and objects, born of the modes. Therefore, the Lord by using the expression 'Guṇapravṛddhāḥ', wants to explain, that so long as, a man is attached to the modes, in the least, the branches of tree of creation, will go on extending. So, in order to, cut off this tree, a striver, should not be at all attached, to the modes, otherwise he cannot renounce his attachment, to the world.

'Viṣayapravālāḥ'—The inclinations of the modes as well as all palpable objects are included in 'Viṣayapravālāḥ' (sense-objects as buds). As a stem grows from the root, branches from the stem and buds from the branches, and again, branches extend from, buds, so are sense-objects, buds of this tree of universe. A person, thinks of the sense-objects, because of the three modes. As water in the form of modes nourishes, and extends the branches of the tree of creation, so does it nourish and extend, the buds of sense-objects. As buds, are seen but water which pervades these is not seen, so, are the objects of the senses with their characteristics of sound etc., seen, but the modes are not seen, they are known by the sense-objects.

The expression 'Viṣayapravālāḥ' means that a man cannot renounce attachment for the world, so long as, he thinks of sense-objects (Gītā 2/62-63). "Thinking of, whatever being, a person, at the end gives up his body to that being does he attain" (Gītā 8/6). So if he thinks of sense-objects, the thought, will lead him to bondage. This birth is like sprouting of buds.

Like buds, sense-objects also appear beautiful, so a man is attracted to them. A striver, by applying his discrimination, can easily renounce those objects, by knowing these as transitory and sources of sorrow (Gītā 5/22). It is because of attachment to them, that they appear beautiful and attractive; in fact they are not so. Therefore, renouncement of attachment for them is real renouncement. As a person, has not to work hard, in destroying soft buds, so should a striver, not think it difficult to renounce, these sense-objects. They are just like poisonous sweet-dishes, which may appear sweet and attractive but are deadly.* So a

* Sense-objects are more poisonous than a cobra because poison kills a

striver, should totally renounce thinking of sense-objects, and enjoying them, in order to cut off this tree of creation.*

'Adhaścordhvaṁ prasṛtā'—Here, the term 'Ca' (and), should mean the middle world i.e., mortal, human world (as described by the expression 'Manuṣyaloke karmānubandhīni' in this verse). The term 'Ūrdhvam', stands for the abode of Brahmā, where one can go by two paths—the northern path (the path of light known as Devayāna), and the southern path (the path of darkness known as Pitṛyāna), described as light and dark paths, in twenty-fourth and the twenty-fifth verses of eighth chapter. The term 'Adhaḥ', stands for hells which are also of two kinds—by birth and by place.

This expression, explains that branches of the tree of creation, having its root in God above, extended in all directions, below, above and in the middle. Out of these the main branch is human life, in which a human being is authorized to perform new actions, while in other births, he has to reap the fruit of his past actions. In human life, he can either, rise above (to upper region) or go below (to the lower region—hell) or even attain God, the highest state, by cutting off the tree of creation. It depends upon him, whether he attains God, by attaching importance to discrimination, or paves the way to hell, by enjoying pleasure foolishly. Therefore, saint Tulasīdāsa in the Mānasa declares, "This human life is a ladder, either to hell or heaven or to attain salvation, and it endows us with knowledge, dispassion and devotion, which lead to benediction" (7/121/5).

'Adhaśca mūlānyanusantatāni karmānubandhīni manuṣyaloke'—All the other lives, except human life, are to reap the fruit of past actions in the form of pleasure and pain. A man, has to

---

man when it enters his body while sense-objects affect him when he merely sees them.

*If you want to attain salvation, you should renounce sense-objects from a distance regarding them as poisonous.

take birth in good and evil wombs, in order to reap the fruit of his virtues and evil actions. In human life, he can perform either virtuous or evil actions, or may attain salvation, by being free from virtues and evils.

Here the term 'Mūlāni', stands for the root in the form of ego, attachment and desire, rather than for God. A man, identifies the self with the body, is attached to body etc., and has desire for family, prosperity, name and fame etc. He wants his memorial, even after giving up this mortal body. Other species, also possess these desires to some or more extent, but they bind a being only in human life.* When a person performs actions, inspired by

*These three (1) The desire to have a vision of God (God-realization) or devotion to God (2) The desire for Self-realization and (3) The desire to render selfless service to others, are not desires because the self and God are ever attained, and are one's own. As taking money from one's own pocket is not theft, so is the desire for Self-realization or God-realization not a desire. Similarly, the desire to use the worldly objects in rendering service to the world, is renunciation rather than, desire. The desire for attaining what is one's own and imperishable, is a necessity (hunger), while the desire to give those objects, which are others' and perishable to them, is renunciation. As desire for food, is a necessity for the body, rather than a desire, so is desire of God to satisfy the hunger of the self not a desire. There is a desire for the insentient (Matter), while there is necessity (hunger) for the sentient. A desire is never satisfied, it is rather enhanced and so it is to be renounced, while necessity is satisfied (fulfilled) by anyone of the three paths—of action, of knowledge and of devotion. A man become, a slave to the world, by regarding worldly persons and objects, as his. If he has the aim of using them in rendering service to others, by regarding them as theirs, he will be liberated from slavery (dependence)—This is path of action. The soul is a fragment of God, but It being attached to the perishable objects, has deviated from Him. If a person renounces his attachment to perishable persons and objects, he will realize the self—this is known as path of knowledge. By having inclination for the world, he has a disinclination for God. If he accepts the fact that he is only God's and only God is his, devotion to God will be aroused in him—This is path of devotion. It means, that a man being attached to the perishable world, has become a slave to the world, has deviated from the self and has a disinclination for God. If he does not accept the world as his (which is not really his), he will cease to be a slave to the world, will realize the self and will attain God-realization, or devotion to Him.

desires, impressions of these actions, accumulate in his mind and induce him to the cycle of birth and death. A man, has to reap the fruit of actions performed, during this life, here, as well as hereafter (Gītā 18/12). So a man, cannot be free from the bondage of actions, so long as he has identity with body and he is attached to the world and cherishs desires. A striver, has to cut off identity, attachment and desire, and has to depend on God, Who is the creator and base of the universe. The same, has been described in fourth verse of this chapter, by the expression "I seek refuge in the Primal Person." As a man, is bound in this human life, so can he be free in this life in the same way, as a knot can be untied, at a point at which it is tied.

The roots of the tree of creation in the form of ego, attachment and desire extend below and above, in all the worlds, among all beings. Birds and beasts, also have identity with their bodies, are attached to their offspring and have a desire, to eat delicious food when hungry. Similarly, the gods have identity with their divine bodies, are attached to heavenly pleasure and have a desire to acquire, more and more pleasure. Thus, all beings have identity, attachment and desire in one form or the other. But they do not bind other beings, except mankind. Though other beings, such as the gods etc., also possess discrimination, yet they do not use it, because overwhelmed by pleasures in abundance and their enjoyment. So they cannot realize that they (the self) are devoid of those evils while a man can realize that he (the self) is different from or devoid of all such defects as, ego, attachment and desire.

A man possesses the ability of realizing the bad consequences of the enjoyment of pleasure. The man who enjoys pleasures without thinking of their consequences is worse than a beast, because a beast paves the way to human life by reaping the fruit of its past actions, while a man is paving the way to birth in the womb of beasts, by enjoying forbidden pleasures.

Link:—In the next verse, the Lord explains the purpose of the description of the tree of creation, mentioned in the preceding two verses.

न रूपमस्येह तथोपलभ्यते
नान्तो न चादिर्न च सम्प्रतिष्ठा।
अश्वत्थमेनं सुविरूढमूल-
मसङ्गशस्त्रेण दृढेन छित्त्वा॥ ३॥

na rūpamasyeha tathopalabhyate
nānto na cādirna ca sampratiṣṭhā
aśvatthamenaṁ suvirūḍhamūla-
masaṅgaśastreṇa dṛḍhena chittvā

Its (of the world) real form is not perceived, neither its end or its origin, nor its foundation (resting place); so having cut off this firm and deep-rooted Pīpala tree, with a strong sword of non-attachment. 3

Comment:—

'Na rūpamasyeha tathopalabhyate'—In the first verse of this chapter, the tree of creation, has been called imperishable, and in the scriptures also, it is mentioned, that persons who perform virtuous actions, in order to reap their fruit, enjoy mundane and heavenly pleasure, in abundance. Having heard such statements, a person, feels that the human world and paradise, are pleasant and permanent. So he desires sense-objects, and is filled with insatiable desires, he holds that there is nothing else, beyond sensual enjoyments (Gītā 2/42; 16/11). An ignorant person, has this feelings so long as, he has ego, attachment and desire with the world or body. But the Lord declares, that when a striver, perceives it, by separating the self from the world i.e., by renouncing his affinity for it, he does not perceive it as imperishable and pleasant, but he perceives it as perishable and unpleasant.

'Nānto na cādirna ca sampratiṣṭhā'—The world, has neither its end or origin nor, in space and time. As a person, while visiting an exhibition, being enamoured of its objects, does not know its beginning and end, without going out of it, so does a person not know the origin and end of the world, by having attachment to it.

All the means (senses, mind and intellect), to perceive the origin and end of the world, are fragments of the world. So they cannot know the world, in the same way as a jar of clay, cannot absorb the earth, within it. Therefore, when a man (the self), separates himself from the world (mind, intellect and sense), he knows the world, in reality.

In fact, the world has no independent existence. It is only a process of birth and death. This process, appears as its existence. If a further thought, is given to it, it will be experienced, that there is no birth, there is only decay. When it does not stay, in one form even for a moment, how can it be called existent? It seems to exist, because of a striver's attachment, to the world. As soon as, this attachment is renounced, the seeming existence, disappears and a striver realizes the self or God.

An Important Fact

No scientist has perceived the beginning, the middle and the end of universe, till today, nor can he perceive it. If a person, having attachment to the world and enjoying mundane pleasure, wants to perceive the beginning, middle and end, of it all, his efforts, are in vain.

In fact, there is no need to perceive the beginning, the middle and the end of this universe, there is need to renounce, the assumed affinity, for it.

Philosophers differ in their opinions, whether the universe is without beginning and perishable, or beginningless and infinite or illusory, but all of them agree, that our affinity for it is unreal (assumed), which must be, renounced.

An easy way to renounce this assumed affinity, for the world is that materials (mind, intellect, senses, body, riches and property etc.,) acquired from the world, should be used in rendering service, to the world.

All mundane materials, such as women, sons, honour, praise, wealth, property, long life, good health and abundant pleasure cannot satisfy a person, because he (the self), is imperishable, while all the mundane pleasures are perishable. How can the imperishable be satisfied, by the perishable?

'Aśvatthamenaṁ suvirūḍhamūlam'—It is because of ego, attachment and desire with it that the universe (having no foundation), seems firm rooted.

Attachment and senses of mineness to beings, objects and actions etc., strengthens worldly bondage. Because of his attachment one identifies himself, with them. After amassing riches he thinks "I am very rich" but when his wealth is lost he holds that he has been ruined. Out of greed, he performs forbidden actions and commits sins, in order to, hoard money. Then he has a conviction that he cannot earn money without foul means, as falsehood, fraud and dishonesty etc. He ceases to think, that the money earned by foul means, will have to be left behind it while evils, such as falsehood, fraud and dishonesty etc., will accompany him, to the next world* and will lead him to a miserable life, here as well as, hereafter. Not only this, but he also instigates other people, to earn money by foul means, calling it a business by justifying falsehood and fraud etc., for it. This evil feeling (faith), is a firm root of the branches of, ego, attachment and desire. This evil feeling (faith), makes him evil,

* When a person gives up his body, the wealth remains lying in shelves, animals remain tied here and there, his wife accompanies him to the gate, sons go upto the cremation ground, the body to the pyre while it is only one's righteousness (Dharma) which accompanies him to the next world.

because the Lord declares, "What a man's faith is, that verily, He is" (Gītā 17/3).

The branches of ego, attachment and desire, are so firmly rooted, that they cannot be, totally rooted out, through study of the scriptures, or by listening to divine discourses and thinking. Strivers, while listening to religious discourses, think of renouncing these evils, but in practical life they find themselves, unable to renounce these. The reason is, that they want to renounce these as well as enjoy mundane pleasures, from persons and objects etc., like a greedy person, who wants to relish a sweet dish mixed with poison and yet escape from poison. But it is impossible. When a striver, has no desire at all to derive any kind of pleasure from the world, this firm rooted tree of the universe is naturally rooted out.

Further, a striver believes that it is very difficult to get rid of these evils, of identification, attachment and desire. But the fact, is that these defects automatically, vanish, they cannot stay, as these are by nature transient. So a striver should never think that it is difficult to renounce, them.

'Asaṅgaśastreṇa dṛḍhena chittvā'—The Lord declares, that though the tree of creation is firm rooted, it can be cut off with a strong sword (axe) of non-attachment. A man may be attached to a place, person, object or circumstance etc., because of their attraction, and because of the desire to derive pleasure out of these. Absence of attachment, is non-attachment or dispassion. This dispassion, can be of two kinds (i) Common (ii) Strong. Strong dispassion is also called 'Uparati' (indifference) or 'Para vairāgya'.

An Important Fact Pertaining to Dispassion

A man, may abandon his house and property physically, but if he attaches importance to them, from his heart or if he feels proud that he is a renouncer, it means that he is not dispassionate.

When he has not the least attachment to them, and he has no attraction towards them—this is dispassion.

Secondly, he should be detached from his so-called parents, wife, sons, brothers and friends etc. He should accept his affinity, for them in order to render service to them, rather than to have a desire to acquire anything from them for his selfish motive.

Thirdly, there is detachment from the body. This is real detachment. If there is attachment for the body, it means that there is attachment for the entire universe, because the body is the seed, of the entire universe. Absence of identification with the body, is detachment (dispassion), from the body.

In order to renounce this identification with the body (egoism), first a striver, should renounce the desire for honour, praise and riches etc. Even when a striver, renounces the desire for honour, praise and fame etc., here, because of his subtle desire, he wants his name and fame to be maintained, through memorials etc., after his death. All these desires must be renounced. Sometimes a striver, is envious or jealous of others. That envy or jealousy should also be renounced.

Even when, these desires are renounced, a man may remain attached to his body, even after he has given up the body. So the bones of the dead body are immersed into the Ganges, after the body is burnt, so that one may meet with a good fate. When a man through discrimination, realizes, that the sentient soul is different, from the insentient body, his attachment or sense of 'mine', is renounced. When both desire and attachment are renounced, ego almost vanishes i.e., it remains, only in its, subtle form. It totally perishes, when a devotee attains God-realization or real exclusive devotion, to God.

When a man realizes, 'I am neither body nor the body is mine,' desire, attachment and identification—the three perish. This is real detachment or dispassion.

All desires (lusts) perish, from the inner sense of the striver, who is dispassionate, from within. A devotee possessing strong dispassion, having no affinity for the insentient objects, such as the body, senses, mind and intellect etc., wishes everyone to be happy, free from disease and suffering and to attain benediction.

'I' is the knower and the onlooker, while the entire universe, including the gross, subtle and causal bodies, to be known and seen. 'I', is imperishable, while the universe and the body, are perishable. He who realizes this distinction, cuts off this tree of creation, with a strong axe of non-attachment. When a man, does not attach importance to this discrimination, the tree of creation, seems to be firm-rooted.

Worldly objects cannot be totally destroyed, but attachment to these can be totally, renounced. This detachment, is known as cutting of this tree.

The universe ceases, to be, when attachment to it, is renounced. Only a thing or person, we have no real affinity for, can be renounced (cut off). A man (the self), is sentient and imperishable, while the universe is insentient, and perishable. So his affinity for the universe is unreal, it is assumed, by an error. He, who is really detached, gets detached. We should accept the fact, that we have no attachment for the universe. Howsoever, firm-rooted the world may be, if we do not accept our affinity for it, it is naturally cut off, because this affinity, is merely assumed. So a striver, should doubtlessly believe,that he has no affinity at all for the world, even though he may not perceive it, in practical life.

A man, himself has accepted this affinity for the body, and the world. So, it is his responsibility, to cut it off. Therefore, the Lord is exhorting us, to cut it off.

Some Easy Means of Renouncing this Affinity for the World

(1) Render service to the world, with the material acquired

from the world, without any selfish motive.

(2) Renounce desire, for mundane pleasure and prosperity.

(3) Renounce dependence, on the world totally.

(4) Renounce a sense of 'I' and 'mine, with the body and the world.

(5) Stick firmly to reality, "I am God's; God is mine."

(6) Have a resolve, "I have to realize God."

(7) Perform your duty, sanctioned by the scriptures scrupulously (Gītā 18/45).

(8) Attach importance, to your own experience, that your body, circumstances, strength, ability etc., are not the same, as they were, in your childhood, they have all changed, while you are the same.

(9) Do not accept your assumed affinity, for the world.

Appendix—The Lord has declared about Himself—"I am the beginning, the middle and also the end of the entire creation" (Gītā 10/20, 32) and here about the world He declares, "It has neither its end nor origin nor existence." It means that God exists in the beginning, in the middle and in the end of the creation while the world has no existence either at the beginning or in the middle or in the end viz., the world does not exist—'nāsato vidyate bhāvaḥ' (Gītā 2/16). Therefore there is nothing else besides God.

'Asaṅgaśastreṇa dṛḍhena chittvā'—Here the term 'chittvā' does not mean 'to cut' or 'to destroy' but it means 'to be detached'. The reason is that this world being God's 'aparā prakṛti' is imperishable. The Self is detached—'asaṅgo'hyayaṁ puruṣaḥ' (Bṛhadā. 4/3/15). The Self is free from attachment to the modes. Attachment to the modes is the root of birth and death—'kāraṇaṁ guṇe saṅgo'sya sadasadyonijanmasu' (Gītā 13/21). Therefore having realized the detached, untainted, undecaying and immortal nature of the Self, getting established in it, is 'to cut off the world-tree'.

The world seems to exist owing to attachment. The thing, to which a man is attached, seems to be existing and valuable. Without attachment, the world may appear to exist but it is not of any value. Therefore the expression 'asaṅgaśastreṇa dṛḍhena chittvā' means—to wipe out attachment to the world totally viz., not to be attached to anyone else besides God and not to assume anything of the entire creation as one's own and for one's own self. In fact the existence of the world does not lead to bondage but attachment to the world leads to bondage. Existence is not an obstacle but attachment is the obstacle. Therefore other philosophers call the world real or unreal etc., but the Lord says that attachment to the world should be renounced. Having given up attachment to the world, the world in its seeming form disappears and it is revealed as the manifestation of God—'Vāsudevaḥ sarvam'.

Link:—In the next verse, the Lord explains what a striver should do, after cutting off the tree of creation.

ततः पदं तत्परिमार्गितव्यं
यस्मिन्गता न निवर्तन्ति भूयः।
तमेव चाद्यं पुरुषं प्रपद्ये
यतः प्रवृत्तिः प्रसृता पुराणी॥ ४॥

tataḥ padaṁ tatparimārgitavyaṁ
yasmingatā na nivartanti bhūyaḥ
tameva cādyaṁ puruṣaṁ prapadye
yataḥ pravṛttiḥ prasṛtā purāṇī

Then that supreme goal (God), should be sought after having reached which none returns again, saying, "I seek refuge, in that Primal Person, from whom has originated this ancient creation of the world." 4

Comment:—

'Tataḥ padaṁ tatparimārgitavyam—In the preceding verse,

the Lord talked of cutting off the tree of creation, while here, He speaks of, seeking God. It proves, that it is inevitable to renounce affinity, for the world, before seeking God. The reason is, that He pervades equally, every object, person, incident, circumstance etc., all the time, but when a person accepts his affinity for the universe, he cannot realize Him. The spiritual practice of chanting, and study of the scriptures etc., does not prove much fruitful, because of his affinity for the world. So a striver, should attach, first and foremost importance, to renouncement of affinity, for the world.

The man (soul) (self), is a fragment of God, but he forgets his eternal affinity for Him, when he accepts his affinity for the world in error. When this error is rectified, he gains recognition (memory) of the reality, that he is God's. Therefore, the Lord declares, that he has had already his affinity for the supreme goal (God), only He is to be sought for.

When a striver, accepts the world as his, the ever-attained Lord, seems to be unattained and the world which is never attained, seems to be attained. Therefore, the Lord by using the term 'Tat' (that), exhorts Arjuna, to seek Him, Who is ever attained.

Only that is sought, which already exists. God is without beginning and He pervades, everywhere and so He is not to be sought after by applying, any particular means. But, it means that a striver, instead of depending on the world (body, family and wealth etc.,) which is never his, should depend on God, Who is always, his, Who is in him and Who exists, even now. In this way, a striver should seek Him.

A striver, should perform spiritual practice, certainly, because there is no activity superior to it. But he should not think that God will be realized by spiritual practice, because by thinking so, he will be proud and pride is a stumbling block, to God-realization. He can be realized, by His grace, He cannot be bought, by any means (spiritual practice). Spiritual practice, roots out evils of attachment and desire, for the world, which are obstacles to, God-realization. These obstacles, have been created by the striver himself. Therefore, when a striver wants to root out these evils, from his heart, by God's grace, they are rooted out.

Generally strivers assumes that God can be realized (through the purification of the mind), in the same way by making efforts, as worldly objects, are acquired. But in fact, it is not so, because even the most virtuous actions such as penance etc., are transitory, and have a beginning and an end. So, how can the perishable bear an imperishable fruit? Through penance and renunciation etc., the assumed affinity, for Matter, (the world and the body), is renounced. Having renounced this assumed affinity, ever-attained God, Who ever pervades everywhere is realized—memory for him is aroused and recognition is gained.

Having listened to Lord's gospel, Arjuna says, 'Recognition (memory) is gained' (Gītā 10/73). Though forgetfulness, is also without beginning, yet it can come to an end. There is a vast difference,between the memory of the world and that of God. Of the world's memory, forgetfulness is possible, as a person suffering from paralysis could forget the knowledge, acquired earlier through study. But if God's memory, is once gained there is never forgetfulness (Gītā 2/72, 4/35).

Even while suffering from paralysis he never forgets his existence (I am), because he can never have his real affinity for the world, and his real affinity for God, can never be renounced. He who has realized the fact, that he has no affinity for the body and the world, has in fact cut off this tree of creation; and he who has realized the truth that he (the self), is a fragment of God, has sought God. As soon as a striver renounces his affinity for the world, he realizes (attains) God, Who is ever-attained.

'Yasmingatā na nivartanti bhūyaḥ—The term 'Yasmin', used here stands for God, Who has been described in the first verse by the expression 'Ūrdhvamūlam' (root above), and in this verse by the expression 'Ādyaṁ puruṣam' (Primal Person), and Who is going to be described in more detail, in the sixth verse ahead.

As a drop of water, after merging in the ocean cannot be separated from it, so the soul (the self), a fragment of God, having attained God, cannot be separated from Him, i.e., from His abode, there is no return. It is attachment to nature, or to its modes, which is the cause of a soul's birth in good and evil wombs (Gītā 13/21). Therefore, when a striver cuts off the attachment to the modes, with a strong axe of non-attachment, no question arises of his rebirth, anywhere.

'Yataḥ pravṛttiḥ prasṛtā purāṇī'—God is the creator of the entire universe (creation), and also its base and illuminator. A man, out of delusion is attracted towards the world, created by Him, because of its sensual pleasure and forgets the Creator. When the world, created by God, seems so charming and loving, how much charming and loving, should He be? Though in the world created by Him, attraction towards the world, is in fact attraction to Him, because it is a manifestation of His fragment (Gītā 10/41), yet, out of ignorance, a person assumes that there is attraction because of the glory of the world, rather than that of God, and so he gets entangled, in the world.

Every being's, nature is that (it or) he depends upon the object or person etc., he considers it superior to all others and from which he expects to receive some pleasure or satisfaction. Worldly people, hanker after wealth, because they think that they can acquire all the necessities as well as luxuries of life, and honour and praise etc., by money (wealth). So, they do not hesitate to commit sins and doing injustice, while earning money. They even do not give proper rest to their, bodies because they remain engaged in earning money,which according to them is superior, to all other attainments. Similarly, when a striver, comes to know that God is the Supreme Being, and having realized Him, one attains such a bliss, which is superior to all mundane pleasures, all sensual pleasures, become insipid before that bliss (Gītā 6/22) and then he starts worshipping Him, with all his being (heart) (Gītā 15/19).

'Tameva cādyaṁ puruṣaṁ prapadye'—A striver, should seek refuge in the Primal Person, Who is the source of all beings (Gītā 10/2). If he takes refuge, in other perishable worldly, persons and objects, they will ruin him, in the same way as a crocodile devours a person who takes refuge, in it. Therefore, he should take refuge, only in the imperishable Lord, rather than, in the perishable world.

When a striver, fails in getting rid of his defects, by applying all his power, he gets disappointed. In such circumstances, if he seeks refuge only in God, by His grace he totally becomes free from evils, and realizes Him. Therefore a striver, should never lose heart, as far as God-realization, is concerned. Having taken refuge in Him, he should become free from all fears and worries, because by doing so, by His grace all obstacles are overcome and God is realized (Gītā 18/58,62).

As a striver, has to renounce his attachment for the world, so has he also to renounce attachment to non-attachment, because by being detached he may still have egoism in its subtle form, by thinking "I am detached." But, when he takes refuge in Him, this subtle egoism can perish, easily. When he seeks refuge in Him, he surrenders his so-called body, senses, mind, intellect, egoism ('I'ness), riches, property and family to Him i.e., he has no feelings of possession, over them.

The devotee, who takes refuge in God, thinks 'I am God's' and 'I am for Him' and 'God is mine' and 'He is for me.' Out of these two thoughts, the former 'I am God's and for Him' is superior, to the latter, because in the former thought, he has no desire of his own, he remains satisfied and happy with God's will. So, he desires, neither to do nor to acquire, anything for himself. In this way, his undefinable and singular devotion to God, is aroused.

In devotion, there is limitless bliss and it provides bliss, even to God, Who is the storehouse of bliss. In this devotion, meeting with the Lord, does not satisfy a devotee, this devotion does not decrease in separation, but it is enhanced, every moment. Devotion (love), which is attained after Self-realization, is also attained, through surrender (refuge).

The term 'Eva' means, total dependence on God, only, having renounced all other supports. The same idea, has been expressed in the Gītā, in the expression., "Those who take refuge in Me alone" (7/14), "Seek refuge in Him alone" (18/62) and "Take refuge in Me alone" (18/66).

The term 'Prapadye', means 'I seek refuge.' Here a doubt may arise, whether the Lord, also seeks refuge and in whom He seeks refuge? The clarification is, that the Lord does not seek refuge in anyone, because He is the Supreme Lord of the entire creation. In order to set an example to the people He explains it to a striver, by speaking in his language, that he should think, "I take refuge."

'God is' and 'I am' in both these one divinity exists in the form of 'is'. When the self assumes Its affinity, for the body, senses, mind and intellect etc., there cannot be unswerving devotion, or total surrender, to God.

But 'is' is changed into "am' due to 'I'. If individuality of 'I' is merged into cosmos 'is' then only 'is' will remain, there will be no 'am'. Being a fragment of God, the self always depends on God, but by an error, It having a disinclination for God, depends on the perishable world. So It has to suffer, because of Its dependence on the perishable. Therefore a striver, having realized his true affinity, for God depends only on Him i.e., seeks refuge only in Him.

Appendix—The world is perishing every moment, therefore it is renounced—'asaṅgaśastreṇa dṛḍhena chittvā', and God is ever-attained, so He is to be sought for (discovered)—'tataḥ padaṁ tatparimārgitavyam'. There is a difference between 'production' and 'discovery'. The thing which does not exist, is produced, while the thing, which already exists, is discovered. God is ever-attained and self-evident, so He is searched out, He is not produced. When a striver accepts the existence of God, he discovers Him. There are two ways of discovery—the first one is that as we forget a necklace by placing it somewhere and then we search it here and there; and the second is that the necklace is worn round the neck but we have the false notion that the necklace is lost, we search it here and there. The discovery of God is like the discovery of the necklace worn round the neck. In fact God is not lost. But because of attachment to the world, we have not an eye on Him, so He appears to be lost to us. It means that God, Whom we want to attain and Whom we seek, is constantly present in us. So He is discovered on being sought. But the world can never be gained, because it is not in us, as actually it does not exist.

God has neither been unattained, nor is unattained, and His unattainment is in fact impossible. He has not been unattained but there has been forgetfulness. This forgetfulness is without beginning but it comes to an and. As two persons are unfamiliar with each other and the third persons asks them, "How long have you been unfamiliar with each other?" No one can answer it. Similarly suppose we don't know Sanskrita language, then how long has this ignorance of ours been? We can't tell it. It means that the existence of the persons, our existence and the existence of Sanskrita language, have already been there, but their familiarity is not there. Similarly at the time of forgetfulness also the existence of God remains the same. God is ever-attained but we are forgetful of Him, viz., we have no eye on Him, we have disinclination for Him, we are unfamiliar with Him and we have the wrong notion that He is unattained to us. On the discovery of God, this forgetfulness is gone and He is attained. The method to discover Him is to get detached from (renounce) that which is non-existent—'asaṅgaśastreṇa dṛḍhena chittvā'. Renunciation means to be disconnected with it and to reject it by assuming that it has no existence, no value. Therefore detachment from the world implies the discovery of God. In Śrīmadbhāgavata it is mentioned—'atattyajanto mṛgayanti santaḥ' (10/14/28).

'Tameva cādyaṁ puruṣaṁ prapadye'—Having renounced affinity with the world, a striver gets established in the Self and he is liberated. Having attained liberation (salvation), the desire for the world is wiped out but hunger for love is not satisfied. In Brahmasūtra it is mentioned 'muktopasṛpyavyapadeśāt' (1/3/2). 'That Lord, Who is an embodiment of love, is attainable even for the liberated souls'. It means that the perfection of human life lies in attaining the love for God Whose fragment the Self is. In Self-realization, there is bliss of the Self, while in God there is Supreme Bliss (endless Bliss). He, who is not satisfied with salvation, attains love (devotion) which enhances every moment—'madbhaktiṁ labhate parām' (Gītā 18/54). Therefore the Lord has mentioned that a striver, having renounced attachment to the world, viz., having attained salvation, and then having sought God, should seek refuge in Him.

Link:—The Lord in the next verse, points out the marks of those devotees, who attain the supreme goal (God) by taking refuge, in the primal Being (God).

निर्मानमोहा जितसङ्गदोषा
अध्यात्मनित्या विनिवृत्तकामाः।
द्वन्द्वैर्विमुक्ताः सुखदुःखसञ्ज्ञै-
र्गच्छन्त्यमूढाः पदमव्ययं तत्॥५॥

nirmānamohā jitasaṅgadoṣā
adhyātmanityā vinivṛttakāmāḥ

dvandvairvimuktāḥ sukhaduḥkhasañjñair-
gacchantyamūḍhāḥ padamavyayaṁ tat

Free from vanity and delusion, victorious over the evil of attachment, dwelling constantly in the self or God, with desires completely stilled, liberated from the dualities,(known as pleasure and pain), such highly placed undeluded strivers reach, the Eternal Goal. 5

Comment:—

'Nirmānamohā'—When a person, has a sense of 'I' and 'mine' in the body, he has a desire to win, honour (respect) etc. He, by identifying the self, with a body, regards the honour of the body, as honour of the self, and he gets entangled. But those devotees, who regard only God, as theirs, have no sense of egoism and possession in the body, and so they do not get pleased, by honour (respect), of the body. Having taken refuge only in God, they are not attached to a body and so they have no desire, for honour (respect).

Having only the aim of God-realization and by depending on God only, those devotees, develop a disinclination, for the world. They become detached, from the world. So, they become free from worldly delusion.

'Jitasaṅgadoṣā'—Attraction towards God, is called devotion (love), and attraction towards the world, is called attachment. It is because of attachment, that evils such as a sense of possession, desire, lust and hope etc., arise. It is by taking refuge in God, that a striver gets victory over, all these evils.

A man, can be attached to both the objects acquired, as well unacquired. But, there is desire, only for unacquired ones. So the expression 'Vinivṛttakāmāḥ' (desires completely stilled), has been used separately.

'Adhyātmanityāḥ'—When a devotee, takes refuge in God, his egoism changes.* He believes that he is God's and not of

* Though all beings constantly dwell in the omnipresent Lord who is

the world. Thus, he constantly dwells in Him. As a person, according to his birth, accepts that he is a Brāhmaṇa or Vaiśya and he always remains, assured of it, even without, remembering it, so, do the devotees, who accept their affinity, for God, always dwell in Him.

'Vinivṛttakāmāḥ'—A man, desires mundane objects and favourable circumstances, only when he aims at mundane pleasure and prosperity. But those devotees, whose aim, is not to acquire mundane objects, become totally free, from desires.

It is sense of mineness in the body, which gives birth to desires. When a man is thus attached to a body, he wants it to be healthy and strong. So is the case with, other mundane objects and riches etc. As a devotee, is not attached to a body and the world, all his desires are stilled. He thinks that his so-called body, senses, mind, intellect and egoism ('I'ness), are only God's, and only God is his. The desires of such a devotee, are totally silenced.

An Important Fact

In fact, this body is constantly decaying (perishing). A striver, has to accept this reality, in a practical way. All desires are born of having contact with perishable objects, such as body etc. One day this process of decay, will be over, and then it will be said, that the body has decayed (died). But actually, the body has not died today. The process of constant decay has completed today. Therefore, in order to be free from desires, a striver should realize this fact, that mundane objects, such as the body etc., are not, his, because these are transient while he (the self) is permanent and eternal.

---

the illuminator of the entire creation yet they by an error assume that they dwell in the world as "I belong to a particular caste or creed or sect etc." It is because of this contrary assumption (belief) that they are bound and are born in good and evil wombs.

In fact, desires are never satisfied. When a desire seems to be satisfied, another one appears, and so a person tries to satisfy that one. The more, they are satisfied, the more they arise. All persons and objects of the world cannot satisfy desires, of even a single person, so if a person desires limited objects of the world, in order to derive pleasure out of them, it is an error on his part one who entertains desires, cannot attain peace (Gītā 2/70). Therefore, renouncement of desires, is a means of attaining, supreme peace. So a striver, should renounce desires, instead of trying to satisfy them.

The belief, that mundane objects, provide pleasure, gives birth, to desire. The keener the desire, to acquire an object, the greater the pleasure, a person derives out of that object. But, the fact is, that it is not the object which provides pleasure, as it is renouncement of attachment of that object, which gives pleasure. This renouncement occurs, when he acquires, the object. If he renounces the desire to acquire the object he cannot feel happy on getting the object or sad on not getting that object.

In fact, mundane objects have no independent existence, as they are perishing all the time. So how the desire for such transitory objects can remain lasting? Thus all strivers, can be freed from desires.

'Dvandvairvimuktāḥ sukhaduḥkhasañjñaiḥ'—Devotees are liberated from contrary experiences, known as pleasure and pain, attachment and aversion, because according to them, all the favourable and unfavourable circumstances, are regarded as God's gift, presented to them, by Him. They have an eye on God's grace, rather than on desirable or undesirable circumstances. So they are easily liberated from the pairs of opposites.

God is a disinterested friend, of all beings (Gītā 5/29). So He never think, of evil of His fragment, the soul (self). Whatever, He does, is only for the welfare, of beings. So devotees, ever remain pleased, with His will. Though their senses, mind and intellect, know of desirable and the undesirable circumstances, yet they themselves, are free from the pairs of opposites.

An Important Fact

This contrary experience (of attachment and aversion etc.,) is the root of sins. In order, to renounce such experience a striver, should not attach importance to perishable objects. This opposite feeling is of two kinds—

(1) Gross (practical) contrary experience between pleasure and pain, a agreeable and disagreeable etc. Beings, including men, birds, beasts and even trees etc., desire the agreeable and have an aversion for the disagreeable.

(2) Subtle (Spiritual) opposite feelings. It is essential and useful, to regard one's own way of adoration, and one's own favourite Deity, as supreme. But the sentiment in which a striver, honours and praises his method of worship, and his favourite deity, regarding them as superior, to the worship and deity of others whom he discredits and blames, by considering them, inferior, is harmful for a striver.

In fact, all spiritual practices, aim at a total renouncement of affinity, for the world. Spiritual practices (disciplines), may differ according to tastes, faiths, beliefs and qualifications of each devotee but their aim is the same. So a striver, instead of having an eye on, the difference of spiritual practices, should have an eye on the aim and be devoted to his spiritual practice. By doing so his subtle opposite feeling comes to an end.

In the Gītā, the gross is called 'Mohakalilam' (mire of delusion) (2/52) while subtle is called 'Śrutivipratipannā (bewildered by the Vedic text)* (2/53). So long as a striver, is

* Śrutivipratipannā means that the person remains in a dilemma and cannot take the decision which of the paths as mentioned in the scriptures of knowledge, of action, of devotion, of dualism, of non-dualism, of pure non-dualism, of dualism-non-dualism, of action for reward or action without

attached to the world or attaches importance, to the world, this opposite experience exists. So it is necessary to root out this.

So long as, there is delusion, contrary experiences exist? He who perceives pair of opposites in the self is deluded. This contrary experience of attachment and aversion, pleasure and pain, happiness and sadness etc., abides in the mind rather than in the self. The mind is insentient, while the self is sentient and is an illuminator of the insentient. Therefore, the self has no affinity for the mind, this affinity is merely assumed.

Everybody knows, that he remains the same, in the pairs of opposites, such as pleasure and pain etc. But out of delusion, by identifying the self with these, he becomes happy and sad. If he remains established in the self, whichever remains, the same without assuming that the pairs of opposites (such as pleasure and pain) are in him, he will be liberated from the duality of pleasure and pain etc.

The Lord, has pointed out an easy way, to be liberated from the dualities of attachment and aversion etc., by declaring "Attachment and aversion of man abide in sense objects through the feeling of pleasantness and unpleasantness; let, none come under their sway" (Gītā 3/34). It means, that a striver, should not act by coming under their sway, because they are strengthened by doing so.

'Gacchantyamūḍhāḥ padamavyayaṁ tat'—He, who desires perishable objects, who makes efforts to acquire them, and feels happy or sad by acquiring them, or without acquiring them, is deluded. In fact, the world is kaleidoscopic while God is eternal, and it is because of His existence that the world, seems to exist. He, who accepts the existence of the world, is deluded.

As a deluded person, perceives the world clearly, so does

reward is better. Similarly he cannot decide which of the deities—Lord Viṣṇu, Lord Rāma, Lord Kṛṣṇa, Lord Śiva, Lord Gaṇeśa or Goddess Durgā should be worshipped.

an undeluded great soul, perceive God clearly. He, who accepts the existence of the world, is deluded, while he who accepts it as kaleidoscopic, is undeluded. The undeluded one, is not affected by pleasure and pain, and he, who remains the same, in pleasure and pain is fit, for attaining Immortality (Gītā 2/15). Therefore, here in this verse, the Lord has laid emphasis two times, on the renouncement of delusion, by using the expression 'Nirmānamohāḥ', and also the term Amūḍhāḥ'.

Delusion can be of two kinds—(1) inclination to the world, rather than to God, (2) not to know the reality about God. In this verse, the expression 'Nirmānamohāḥ' stands for, freedom from delusion of the world, while the term 'Amūḍhāḥ'* stands for true knowledge about God.

God, Who has been mentioned by the expression 'Ūrdhvamūlam' (root above), in the first verse, Who has been called, the Supreme Goal, which should be sought in the fourth verse, and Who has been glorified in the sixth verse, the same supreme abode has been called here, 'Avyayam padam' (the Eternal Goal). Strivers who have become totally free from evils, such as honour, delusion and attachment etc., attain the Eternal Goal, from where, there is no return.

In fact, Eternal Goal, is naturally ever-attained by every human being but a man does not realize this fact as he has turned his eye away from that Goal (God). This can be explained by an illustration. When our train stops at a station, an other train suddenly starts moving, our eye being on the moving train we feel as if our train has started moving. But we come to know the reality, when we look out at the station. Similarly, when a person is attached to the world, he finds himself moving (kaleidoscopic). But, when he looks at the self, he realizes that he (the self), is

* As the devotee who knows attributeless God becomes undeluded (5/20) so does the devotee who worships the Lord endowed with attributes and form also becomes undeluded (10/3;15/19).

the same (uniform), it is not kaleidoscopic.

Appendix—Within Jñānayoga and Karmayoga, devotion is not included but within devotion both Jñānayoga and Karmayoga are included (Gītā 10/10-11). So here the term 'adhyātmanityāḥ' may mean 'Jñānayoga' and the term 'vinivṛttakāmāḥ' may mean 'Karmayoga'.

Link:—The Lord in the next verse, describes the characteristics of the Eternal Goal (Abode) referred Which is attained by the devotees in the preceding verse.

न तद्भासयते सूर्यो न शशाङ्को न पावकः ।
यद्गत्वा न निवर्तन्ते तद्धाम परमं मम ॥ ६ ॥

na tadbhāsayate sūryo na śaśāṅko na pāvakaḥ
yadgatvā na nivartante taddhāma paramaṁ mama

Neither doth the sun illumine that (Eternal Goal), nor the moon, nor the fire; having gone thither, they (who reach there) return not; that is My Supreme Abode. 6

Comment:—

[The sixth verse, is the link between the fifth verse and the seventh verse. In this verse the Lord declares, that the Eternal Goal is His Abode, Which has identity with Him, in the same way as His fragment, the soul, has identity with Him. Therefore, the soul has also identity with that Abode (Eternal Goal), i.e., the soul, has eternal union with that Abode.

Though this verse, is closely related with the twelfth verse, yet it has been introduced here to link the fifth and the seventh verses. In this verse the Lord makes two important points (1) The sun etc., cannot illumine that Abode. The reason for it has been explained in the twelfth verse and (2) Those, who reach His abode do not return to the world (the cause has been explained by the Lord in the seventh verse of this chapter.)]

'Na tadbhāsayate sūryo na śaśāṅko na pāvakaḥ'—When,

even the sun which is matchless in brilliance and effulgence and which illumines the entire universe cannot illumine, that Supreme Abode, how can the moon and fire, illumine that? The Lord in the twelfth verse of this chapter declares, "That light of the sun, which illumines the world, that which is in the moon and in the fire—know that light to be Mine."

So, how can the sun, the moon and the fire, illumine the Supreme Abode (God), when they receive light from Him?* It means, that God is sentient, while the sun, the moon and the fire are insentient (matter) and these three illumine respectively, the eye, the mind and the tongue, which are also insentient. So God can neither be seen with eyes, nor be thought of with mind, nor be described in words. How can sentient (God) be illumined by the insentient? God, the illuminator of all pervades, all of them, without being proud of His illuminating light.

The self, being a fragment of God is also an embodiment of that light, and therefore, it can also not be illumined by insentient objects, (mind, intellect and senses etc.). These objects, should be utilized to render service only to others (considering them as God's) in order to renounce, affinity for them.

Here, a point needs attention, that the sun, has not been regarded here as sun-god, or a god, but as the source of light. It means, that the sun is superior to other sources of light, and so there is mention of the moon and fire also, in the same way, as mentioned (in Gītā 10/37) by Himself as Vāsudeva, a noble person among the Vṛṣṇis (Yādavas, the descendents of Yadu), rather than as Lord Vāsudeva (Kṛṣṇa).

'Yadgatvā na nivartante taddhāma paramaṁ mama'—The self,

* (1) When neither the sun illumines that God, nor do the moon, the stars and the electricity illumine Him, how will fire illumine Him? This entire universe is illumined by that God.

(2) Lord Rāma is the illuminator Who illuminates the universe (Mānasa 1/117/4).

is a fragment of God, So long as, it does not atttain its source God, it cannot be liberated, from the cycle of birth and death. It attains real and permanent peace, only when it attains God, Whose fragment It is, in the same way, as water of a river gets lost after merging in an ocean, whose fragment it is. In fact, the self has its identity with God, but because of Its attachment with matter (which is assumed), it has to take birth in good and evil wombs.

Here the term 'Paramadhāma', stands both for the abode of God, as well as, for God. This Supreme Abode, is the embodiment of light. As the sun in spite of remaining fixed, at its particular position, pervades everywhere, in the form of light i.e., the sun and its light are one and the same, so are the Supreme Abode and all-pervading God, one and the same.

According to the beliefs of devotees, the same Supreme Abode, which is sentient, embodiment of knowledge, embodiment of light and embodiment of God, is known by different names, as Brahmaloka, Sāketaloka, Goloka, Devīdvīpa, and Śivaloka etc.

This imperishable Supreme Goal, pervades everyone, in the form of the self. So, all of us, dwell in that Supreme Goal, but we do not realize this fact, because of our identity with and attachment and desire, for the matter (body etc.,).

Appendix—We are fragments of God—'mamaivāṁśo jīvaloke' (Gītā 15/7). Therefore the Lord's Abode is also our abode. This is the reason that having attained that Abode, there is no return to this world. So long as we don't attain that Abode, we like a passenger, will go on wandering in several wombs and in several worlds and will not be able to stay anywhere. Even if we reach the Abode of Brahmā, the highest plane of existence, we have to return—'ābrahmabhuvanāllokāḥ punarāvartino'rjuna' (Gītā 8/16). The reason is that the entire universe is a foreign land, not our own land; it is the abode of others, not ours. Our roaming and going astray will come to an end only, when we reach our Real Abode.

Having attained the Lord's Supreme Goal (Abode), there is no return—this has been mentioned in the Gītā in the following three verses—

1. Yaṁ prāpya na nivartante taddhāma paramaṁ mama (8/21).

2. Tataḥ padaṁ tatparimārgitavyaṁ yasmingatā na nivartanti bhūyaḥ (15/4).

3. Yadgatvā na nivartante taddhāma paramaṁ mama (15/6).

The Lord in the path of knowledge has declared the state from which there is no return—'gacchantyapunarāvṛttiṁ jñānanirdhūtakalmaṣāḥ' (Gītā 5/17), but in the path of devotion there is attainment of God's Supreme Abode—this is the speciality of devotion. In the Abode of God, love is specially relished.

The Supreme Goal can neither be illumined by 'ādhibhautika light' (sun, moon etc.,) nor by 'ādhidaivika light' (eye, mind, intellect and speech etc.,). The reason is that it is Self-effulgent. In it there is no distinction between the illuminator and the illumined.

In 'gatvā' there is 'gati', not 'pravṛtti' because the fragment naturally moves towards the whole, in it there is no 'pravṛtti'. 'Pravṛtti' is intentionally done while 'gati' is spontaneous and automatic.

'Gati' (motion) and 'pravṛtti' (activity)—'Gati' is natural which involves no labour, no effort and no doership. But 'pravṛtti' is unnatural, needs labour and effort and involves doership. There is 'pravṛtti', when the person has the egoistic notion but there is 'gati', when there is no egoism. Therefore 'gati' is towards the Self, while 'pravṛtti' is towards the non-Self. 'Gati' is towards God, while 'pravṛtti' is towards the world. 'Gati' is towards the sentience while 'pravṛtti' is towards the insentience. 'Gati' leads towards the limitless while 'pravṛtti' leads towards the limited. 'Gati' paves the way to independence while 'pravṛtti' paves the way to dependence. When a man hankers after pleasures and prosperity, there is 'pravṛtti' and when he provides comfort to others, there is 'gati'.

The origin of 'gati' is 'the real' while the origin of 'pravṛtti' is 'the unreal'. As the origin of the Ganges is Gaṅgotrī, if by keeping back the water of the Ganges, a dam is built which is of a greater height than the height of Gaṅgotrī, then naturally the water of the Ganges will flow back to its origin, Gaṅgotrī. Thus the flow of the Ganges towards its origin is 'gati'. Therefore there is 'gati' in two ways—to have a disinclination for the world (pleasures and prosperity) and to have an inclination to God Who is to be attained. If the assumption of the unattainment of the ever-attained Lord is wiped out, it is also 'gati' (motion) towards God. In 'gati' the assumed distance from God comes to an end and the real unity with God is revealed.

If a striver feels that his feelings and conduct are better than they were several years ago, this is a striver's 'gati'. In the 'gati', during the course of spiritual practice, there may be a subtle ego; but having attained salvation, the 'gati' that is there towards the ever-increasing love, is totally free from the subtle ego. The reason is that the more disinclination a man has for God, the more egoistic, he becomes. Even by getting established in the Self, the subtle ego may linger which is not an obstacle to salvation but it causes differences of opinions among philosophers. By becoming 'abhinna' (inseparable) or one with God, the ego is totally effaced.

Link:—In the preceding verse, the Lord declared, "That is My Supreme Abode, from which those who reach it, never return." In the next verse, He explains why the soul, Which is a fragment of God, and Which (like the Supreme Abode), has identity with Him, is unable to realize him.

ममैवांशो जीवलोके जीवभूतः सनातनः।
मनःषष्ठानीन्द्रियाणि प्रकृतिस्थानि कर्षति॥७॥

mamaivāṁśo jīvaloke jīvabhūtaḥ sanātanaḥ
manaḥṣaṣṭhānīndriyāṇi prakṛtisthāni karṣati

An eternal fragment of My own self having become an embodied soul, in the world of life, draws to itself the (five) senses with the mind for the sixth, which are abiding in nature. 7

Comment:—

'Mamaivāṁśo jīvaloke jīvabhūtaḥ sanātanaḥ'—The term, 'Loka' stands for Nature and its evolutes, which have no identity with the soul (self). The term 'Jīvaloke', stands for all the bodies, in the three worlds and the entire universe, which the soul, acquires.

The soul, is a fragment of God, but having assumed Its affinity for a body, senses, mind and life-breath etc., which are the evolutes of Nature, It has become an embodied-soul—'Jīvabhūtaḥ', which is artificial, not real, like an actor in a play.

The Lord in the seventh chapter declared, "This world is sustained by My higher Nature, which is the soul" (7/5) i.e., though the soul, has no real affinity for the lower Nature (world), yet It has assumed its affinity, for it.

As the soul is a fragment of God, so He always thinks of Its welfare. As a lion-cub having joined a flock of sheep, considers that he is a sheep and not a lion-cub, though even by mixing with them, he is not converted into a sheep, so does the soul, identifying Itself with the body etc., forget Its real identity. As a lion, makes the lion-cub aware of his identity by showing him that he is the same, in shape, nature and roar etc., as the former, so does the Lord, make the man (soul) aware, that he is His fragment, having no affinity for Nature. He had neither any affinity with Nature, in the past, nor will have in future, nor can he have it any time.

Out of all the means (disciplines) of God-realization, the means of changing 'egoism' ('I' ness) and 'sense of mineness' is, easy and good. A striver's egoism and sense of mineness determine his feelings and actions. A striver should believe that he is only God's and only God, is his.

Everyone knows that a person, acts according to his assumption of particular caste, creed and order of life. But this assumption, that he is a Brāhmaṇa or an ascetic, is a temporary phase of life, in order to perform his duty, like an actor in a play. But a man (soul), is a fragment of God—this is a permanent reality. He regards, the mind, senses, intellect, body, riches and property as his own, by an error, but they never regard him, as theirs while God, the creator of the entire universe declares, that the soul is His fragment.

What a blunder, we commit when we regard the objects, such as the body etc., as ours! Can we change them, as we desire? Can we possess them as long as we desire? Can we maintain them, and carry them with us?

My mind, intellect, senses and body, are different today, from what they were in childhood, while I am the same, without undergoing any change. He, who perceives changes, himself remains changeless. Worldly objects and persons, are not my lasting companions. I am an onlooker of the changing scene.

When a striver holds 'I am God's', it means that he is absorbed in God. A striver, commits an error, that he instead of getting the self absorbed in God, tries, to engage his mind and intellect, in Him. So, he finds it difficult to control his mind, and it takes a lot of time. So long as, a striver having forgotten the fact 'I am God's assumes 'I am a Brāhmaṇa or an ascetic', and tries to engage his mind and intellect in God, he will not be so much successful, as he can be when he accepts the fact that 'I am God's.' Therefore, when the Lord in the fourth verse of this chapter, exhorts Arjuna to seek refuge in Him, He means to say, that the self should be, engaged in Him. Gosvāmī Tulasīdāsa also declares, "If a person by becoming God's, follows spiritual practice, such as name chanting etc., his spoiled life of innumerable births, can be improved, today and even now" (Dohāvalī 22).

It means that if a striver, himself gets absorbed in Him, his mind and intellect get easily absorbed in Him. As Meghanāda, while declaring that he is the son of Rāvaṇa in a play, and also performing his part scrupulously, from within does not believe that he is Meghanāda, so should a striver, while performing his duties on the stage of this world, think that he is God's, not of the world.

An embodied soul, has been of God since time immemorial. God has never abandoned it, nor has had a disinclination for it. The soul can also not renounce Him, but in having misused Its freedom it has developed a disinclination for God, by an error. As ornaments made of gold cannot be separate from gold, so can, the embodied soul never be separate from God.

A so-called, wise man commits a blunder, that he has a disinclination for God, Whose fragment he is. He does not pay attention to the fact, that God being a disinterested friend of all beings, is very benevolent and noble and His benevolence and love, is beyond description. So it is an utter folly on his part, to regard perishable objects, as his, sacrificing the all-benevolent, and all-merciful Lord.

When a man performs his duty, by obeying Him, He liberates him from the bondage of birth and death, forever. But, if he however by error performs forbidden actions, He warns him through sufferings that he is suffering, because of his past evil actions and so he should not perform forbidden actions, again. Moreover, He purifies him of his past sins, by forcing him to reap the fruit of his past actions and prevent him from committing new sins.

God, regards a man (the soul) as His fragment, whether he is in hell or in heaven, in human-womb (life), or in animal-womb. How benevolent, generous and great He sees the downfall of men, and feels sad, He declares, that being qualified and deserving to attain Him, they do not attain Him, but go down to the lowest state (Gītā 16/20).

God attracts him towards Him, in all circumstances, by creating pleasant and unpleasant, favourable and unfavourable circumstances. So a striver, should ever remain pleased and satisfied by thinking of His grace, because it is He, Who does not let him remain, in the same condition forever, otherwise he may forget Him.

It is not at all difficult, for a man (the self), being a fragment of God, to realize Him. It is because of his disinclination for Him, and inclination for mundane objects, such as a body etc., that he feels it difficult, to attain Him quickly. He is already attained. As soon as, a striver, has an inclination towards Him by having a disinclination for the world, he realizes Him. It is not an adventure on his part, to acquire mundane riches and property etc., because all of these are perishable. But it is an achievement to realize God, Who is imperishable and eternal.

The more importance a man, attaches to perishable objects, the more, fall he has, but the more importance he attaches to the imperishable Lord, the higher he rises, because he is a fragment of God.

A man, can never attain greatness by acquiring perishable mundane materials, though by a perverted outlook he may think so. But in fact, by thinking so, he is deprived of real greatness (God-realization). The greatness attained by acquiring mundane materials, is unreal and transient, while the greatness attained by God-realization, is real and eternal. Even gods honour, such a God-realized soul, and desire his arrival in their abode. Not only this, but even God becomes his subservient.

'Manaḥṣaṣṭhānīndriyāṇi prakṛtisthāni karṣati'—The soul, being a fragment of God abides in Him, while senses and mind, being a fragment of prakṛti (nature), ever abide in it. But the self, regards the mind and senses, as Its own, and it thus attracts the mind and senses.

Here the term 'Mana', stands both for the mind and the

intellect. Similarly, the five organs of action and five life-breaths, should also be included, in the five senses. The Lord declares, that the soul being His fragment and abiding in Him, by an error, regards It as abiding in body, mind and senses, and forgets its real abode. But actually, It can never be separate from Him.

The Lord, mentions the five senses and the mind, in order to point out the fact, that a man (the soul) by being attached to senses and mind, is bound. Therefore a striver, should surrender the body, senses, mind and intellect to the world, by rendering service with these to the world, and surrender himself to God.

An Important Fact

(1) A man feels unhappy, because by an error he regards his body, family, property, honour and praise, as his and for him. Moreover, it is very mean of him, that he regards himself as great, because of prosperity and pleasure, while he becomes a slave to them. In fact, the objects, which we regard as necessities of life, and to which we attach importance, become superior to us, whether we know or we do not know that fact.

But if a person becomes a slave to God, God becomes his slave and makes him a jewel of His crown. But mundane objects, never make anyone a jewel of their crown, even when he becomes a very devoted slave, to them. In fact he becomes great, by taking refuge in Him. About such a devotee, the Lord declares, "O twice-born, I am not independent, I depend on My devotees. They are very loving to Me, they have a full right over My heart" (Śrīmadbhā. 9/4/63). Can mundane persons and objects, attach so much of importance, to us? Never.

This man (soul), in spite of being a fragment of God, being attached to prakṛti (nature) has a downfall. If he does not become a slave, to mundane objects, such as body, senses and mind etc., he becomes beloved of Him (Gītā 18/64). The Lord, calls those devotees who have attained Him, dear to Him (Gītā 12/13—19) while He calls strivers, who have not attained Him, but want to attain Ḥim, exceedingly dear to Him (Gītā 12/20). How much stupidity it is of man who does not regard the most benevolent Lord, Who calls strivers exceedingly dear, and enlightened souls, only dear, as his!

(2) The body, is a fragment of the world, while the selt (soul) is a fragment of God. A striver, commits an error, that he in spite of being a fragment of God, gets attached to the world, and wants the world as well as, God to be favourable to him. He should rectify this error. It can be rectified by moulding himself, according to God. It means, that he should leave the body at the will of the world, and leave the self at the will of God.

Offering a gift of the world to the world, and offering the gift of God to God, is honesty. This honesty, is called salvation or emancipation. But if the gifts presented by the world and God, are not given back to them, it is dishonesty. This dishonesty is called bondage.

Having offered the gift of the world to the world and having offered the gift of God to Him, he should be free from all worries. He should be a slave to His will, having no desire of his own, either to live or to die or to have favourable circumstances. Having surrendered himself to God, he should pray to Him, to enable him not to forget Him, in whatever circumstance he is placed by Him—on the earth, or in heaven or in hell; in childhood, in youth or in old age; honoured or dishonoured; happy or sad.

A man is worried only about his limited property, riches and the family which he regards as his own, but he is not worried about a lot of property, riches and millions of families which he does not regard as his own. Thus, he is liberated or emancipated from most of them. Only a little bondage is there. If he ceases to regard the limited as his own, he will be emancipated, from these also.

We should give a serious thought to the topic that a few persons and a little property which we regard as our own are sure to vanish but if we do not discard our supposed relationship with them, they will lead us to bondage, of birth and death. Therefore, a striver, should surrender his body and objects to the world—which is a path of selfless action: or he should distinguish the self, from the world including the body—this is a path of knowledge; or he should surrender himself to God—this is the path of devotion. A striver, may follow anyone of the three paths—each will bear the same fruit.

Appendix—Here the Lord has mentioned that the soul is His fragment; the same soul in the fifth verse of the seventh chapter has been said to be His 'parā prakṛti' (higher Nature) (Gītā 7/5). Therefore in both the cases the term 'Jīvabhūta' (embodied soul) has been used—'jīvabhūtaḥ', 'jīvabhūtām'. 'Parā' and 'Aparā'—both are God's powers (Gītā 7/4-5). Since 'parā' instead of having an inclination to God, started having an inclination towards 'aparā', it (parā) started following the cycle of birth and death. This fact has been mentioned by the expression 'yayedaṁ dhāryate jagat' in the seventh chapter and by the expression 'manaḥṣaṣṭhānīndriyāṇi prakṛtisthāni karṣati' here.

Though 'aparā' is also God's, yet its nature is different (kaleidoscopic). Therefore the Lord declares, that he transcends the 'aparā'—'yasmātkṣaramatīto'ham' (Gītā 15/18). But 'parā' and God are of the same nature (immutable). Therefore by the term 'eva' in the expression 'mamaivāṁśaḥ' the Lord means to say that the soul is only His (God's) fragment, in it there is not the least trace of 'prakṛti'. As the body is the fragment of both mother and father, the Self is not the fragment of God and 'prakṛti', but it is only God's fragment. Therefore the Self has affinity only with God, not with 'prakṛti'. But it itself gets attached to 'prakṛti'—'manaḥṣaṣṭhānīndriyāṇi prakṛtisthāni karṣati'.

'Aparā Prakṛti' belongs to God but the man (the soul) assumed it as his own and began to derive pleasure out of it, so he is bound. As the things don't belong to him (the Self), so they don't stay with him nor does the pleasure stay with him.

A man assumes his affinity with the gross, the subtle and the causal bodies, which is the root of all calamities. The Self attracts the body towards itself viz., assumes the body as its own but does not accept God as its own Who is really its own. This is the main error committed by it (the Self).

The Self is not a fragment of Brahma (attributeless) but is a fragment of God (endowed with attributes)—'īsvara aṁsa jīva abināsī' (Mānasa 7/117/1). The reason is that Brahma is merely Pure Consciousness. Therefore in Brahma there can't be a fragment and the whole. The Soul is identical with Brahma viz., the entity, which is the soul in diverse forms, is Brahma in one form. If the Self is attached to the body, it is embodied Soul (Jīva), and if it is not attached to the body, it is Brahma. Therefore in fact both Jīva and Brahma are fragments of the entire form of God. So the Lord has declared that He is the base of Brahma—'brahmaṇo hi pratiṣṭhāham' (14/27) and also declared that Brahma is a fragment of His entire form—'te brahma tadviduḥ..........' (7/29-30).

The mind and senses are the fragments of 'prakṛti' and so they abide in 'prakṛti'—'prakṛtisthāni'. Therefore a man (the Self) should learn this lesson that he should have his affinity with the Entity Whose fragment he is. He himself will have to form this connection with God, no one else will form it. The reason is that he himself has accepted the connection with the world and he himself is disinclined to God. The world is not responsible for his inclination (attachment) to the world and God is not responsible for his disinclination for Him but in both cases, the Self is responsible. The Self being the fragment of God, is independent but it has misused this independence. Therefore the Self will have to make the proper use of this independence—'uddharedātmanātmānam' (Gītā 6/5).

The affinity of the mind and senses with 'prakṛti' is eternal and real but their affinity with the Self is transient and assumed. Transient affinity never remains permanent but it goes on changing and perishing. But the relationship of the Self with God is immutable and imperishable. But having accepted the transient affinity, the Self develops a disinclination for God, which he does not realize.

'Mamaivāṁśo jīvaloke'—This expression reveals the feeling that we assume God as ours but God knows us as His own. When a man (the Self) takes refuge in God, then he also comes to know that the Lord is his—'māmeva ye prapadyante māyāmetāṁ taranti te' (Gītā 7/14).

A man (the Self) is an eternal fragment of God; therefore his real valour consists in accepting his affinity with God viz., in assuming God as his own. In physical valour an action is important which is performed only for the world because the body is a fragment of the world. But in the valour of the Self, the feeling is important. Therefore freedom from evils, detachment, and the sense of mine with God—these are valorous feelings of the Self. By being free from evils, a man becomes useful for the world. By being detached from the body and the world, he becomes useful for himself. If he assumes God as his own, he proves useful for God. Without being free from evils, a man can't be useful for the world. Without being detached from the body and the world, a man can't be useful for himself. Without having the sense of mine with God, a man can't be useful for God.

I should be free from evils, I should be detached, I should be a lover of God—the realization of such necessity is a man's valour. But first of all a striver should accept that he can be free from evils, he can be detached and he can be a lover of God. For that a striver should know that from the view-point of the world all beings are one, from the view-point of the soul also all are one and from the view-point of the Lord also all are one. Therefore as we have the feeling for the welfare of our body, similarly we should have the feeling to promote the welfare of all bodies; or as we remain untainted and unconcerned with other bodies, so should we remain unconcerned with this body also. If we assume the identity of this body with all other bodies, we can be free from evils. Having renounced attachment to all bodies including our body, we can be detached (established in the Self). Having renounced attachment to all bodies as well as to the world, we can be the lovers of God.

Being fragments of God, we have our affinity with God—'mamaivāṁśo jīvaloke', therefore we abide in God. But the body, senses, mind and intellect have their affinity with 'prakṛti', so they abide in 'prakṛti'—'prakṛtisthāni', 'vikārāṁśca guṇāṁścaiva viddhi prakṛtisambhavān' (Gītā 13/19). There has neither been, nor is, nor will be, nor can be our union with the body; while we have neither been, nor are, nor will be nor can be separate from God. If anything is at the farthest from us, it is the body; and if anyone is nearest to us, it is God. But because of desire—the sense of mine—identification, we see things in a perverted way viz., the body appears near while God appears far away, the body seems to be attained while God seems to be unattained.

In order to renounce the assumed affinity with the body, a striver should accept three facts—1. The body is not mine because it is beyond my control. 2. I need nothing. 3. I have to do nothing for myself. So long as a striver assumes his affinity with the three bodies—the gross, the subtle and the causal, the actions performed with the gross body, reflection done with the subtle body and trance attained with the causal body—all the three bind him. But when he renounces affinity with the three bodies, then actions, reflection and trance don't bind him viz., he becomes detached from them.

In order to arouse (realize) his eternal affinity with God, a striver should accept three facts—1. God is mine, 2. I am God's, 3. All is God's. When his eternal affinity with God is aroused, a striver attains love (devotion) to God. Attainment of devotion to God is the acme (or accomplished state) of human life.

A man has three desires—desire for pleasures, eagerness for enlightenment (Self-realization) and a yearning for love. The desire for pleasure is related with the body, eagerness for enlightenment is related with the Self and the yearning for love is related with God. It is an error to assume the body as one's own because the body is a fragment of 'prakṛti'. Therefore desire for pleasure is not of the Self; but the assumption that it is of the Self, is an error. But eagerness for enlightenment and yearning for love, are one's own, there is no error in it. Therefore by applying the body in the service of the family, the society and the world in a disinterested manner, or by intensifying the eagerness for enlightenment, this error is rectified. With the rectification of this error, the desire for pleasure is wiped out. With the destruction of the desire for pleasure, the eagerness for enlightenment is satisfied and the striver realizes the Self viz., he attains enlightenment and he becomes a liberated soul. Then in a man (the Self) who is a fragment of God, the yearning to love God is intensified. All beings are fragments of God, therefore their final aim is to love God. Yearning for love is the universal yearning. Having attained love, human life becomes perfect and then nothing remains to be done, to be known and to be attained.

Link:—Due to assuming the mind and senses as Its own, the soul accompanied with them wanders in innumerable wombs. This is described in the next verse by the Lord by means of an illustration.

शरीरं यदवाप्नोति यच्चाप्युत्क्रामतीश्वरः।
गृहीत्वैतानि संयाति वायुर्गन्धानिवाशयात्॥८॥

śarīraṁ yadavāpnoti yaccāpyutkrāmatīśvaraḥ
gṛhītvaitāni saṁyāti vāyurgandhānivāśayāt

As the wind wafts scent from its base, so does the Jīvātmā (embodied soul), assuming itself as the lord of body etc., take the senses along with the mind from the body, which it leaves behind, and migrate to the body, which it acquires. 8

Comment:—

'Vāyurgandhānivāśayāt'—Just as, the wind carries away scent (perfume) from a perfume box, but this perfume does not stay permanently in the wind, because the wind has no eternal affinity for the scent. So does the individual soul, carrying the senses,. mind, intellect and natural instincts etc., (subtle and causal—both bodies) by assuming them as Its own, migrate to the body, which It acquires.

As essentially the wind is unconnected with the smell (scent), so is the soul unconnected with the mind, senses and body etc., but, by assuming these as Its own, attracts them towards it.

As wind in spite of being an evolute of ether, carries smell (perfume) a fragment of the earth, so does the soul in spite of being a fragment of God, carrying the transitory body, an evolute of Nature, migrate to different wombs.The wind being matter (insentient), does not possess discrimination, that it should not take scent from its base. But an embodied soul has the discrimination and power, to renounce affinity for the body. Every human being, has been bestowed independence, by which he can either get attached to an insentient body etc., or renounce this attachment. In order to, rectify the error, he should accept the reality, by changing the assumption, that he (the soul) has no affinity for the physical, the subtle and the causal bodies, as fragment of Nature. Then, he can be easily liberated, from the bondage of birth and death.

In this illustration the Lord has used three words—(1) Wind (2) Scent (perfume) (3) Seat. Here, the seat stands for physical body. As wind carries scent from a perfume box and the box is left behind, so does the soul carry the subtle and causal bodies, while the physical bòdy is left behind.

'Śarīraṁ yadavāpnoti yaccāpyutkrāmatīśvaraḥ gṛhītvaitāni saṁyāti'—Here the term 'Īśvaraḥ', stands for the embodied soul. This soul, commits three errors—(1) It regards Itself as the master of mind, intellect and body etc., but actually, becomes their slave. (2) It having become the master of insentient objects, forgets Its real master, God. (3) It does not renounce Its assumed affinity for the insentient objects, though It is free in renouncing them.

God has given independence to the embodied soul, to make proper use of objects, such as a body etc., in order to, attain salvation, rather than to become their master. But by an error, It instead of properly utilizing these, regards Itself as their master and really becomes their slave.

It can renounce this assumed affinity, only when it comes to know, that It has become a slave, to mundane objects, such as body etc., whose master, It regards Itself. By doing so, he (the soul) feels a shortage of mundane objects and feels itself as an orphan.

One who is fond of becoming a master, cannot attain God, because he forgets the real master. A child in childhood cannot live without his mother, but when it grows into a youth and as a householder, becomes a master of his sons and wife etc., he forgets his mother; so does the soul forget Its real master, when It becomes the master of insentient objects, such as the body etc. So long as, this forgetfulness continues i.e., It has a disinclination for God, and It will go on suffering.

The term 'Api',with the term 'Īśvaraḥ', has been used to denote, that this lord i.e., the individual soul is not powerless, insentient and dependent, like wind. It has capability and discrimination, to renounce the assumed affinity for the world and realize Its true affinity for God. But, it is because of Its yearning for sensual pleasures, that it neither renounces nor does It want to renounce, Its assumed affinity for the world. As soon as, It renounces this affinity, it cannot carry bodies (like the scent) with It i.e., he becomes free from birth and death.

A man (soul), has got two kinds of power (i) Life-breath power (ii) Power of desire. The life-breath power, decays every moment and when it comes to an end, that is called death. Attachment to the insentient, leads a man, to have desire to act and to acquire. If this desire to act and to acquire is wiped out, while possessing life-breath power, a man is emancipated. But, if he gives up the body while possessing desire, he has to be reborn. On account of desires of the previous birth, he receives new life-breath to fulfil them.

The life-breath power, should be spent in removing desires. Desire can be easily wiped out by being engrossed in the welfare of all beings, without any selfish motive.

The term 'Gṛhītvā' means to make attachment and accept them as mine which are not ours. It takes them with It by regarding them as Its, while these never regard It, as theirs nor are they controlled by It. This error of attachment and assumed affinity binds It.

Whether a thing is acquired or not, whether it is superior or inferior, whether it is being used by us or not, whether it is far or near, if we regard it as ours, our attachment to it, subsists.

A man (the self), remains attached to mundane objects, such as a body etc., even after giving up the body. Therefore, the bones of a dead body are immersed into the Ganges, so that the man (self or soul) may attain salvation. We are free and powerful enough, to renounce this assumed affinity (attachment).

If we renounce it during this life, we may attain salvation in this very life.

This inclination towards, mundane objects which are not ours and disinclination for God, Who is ours, are great stumbling blocks in spiritual progress.

The term 'Etāni', stands for the mind and the five senses, referred to in the seventh verse. Here it denotes mind, intellect, five senses, five organs of action and five life-breaths—the aggregate of seventeen elements of the subtle body, as well as the causal body. The embodied soul, taking all of these migrates to the body, which it acquires. Just as a person, casts off worn-out clothes and puts on new ones, so does an embodied soul, cast off worn-out bodies and enter others, which are new (Gītā 2/22).

In fact, it is not possible for the pure sentient soul, to renounce a body and to migrate to another body, because It is immobile and pervading everywhere (Gītā 2/17,24). But when It identifies Itself with a body, an evolute of Nature i.e., It is seated in Nature, It gives up, one body and acquires, another body. When the soul ceases to identify Itself with the bodies, (physical, subtle and causal), It is not reborn, because assumed identification with a body, becomes the cause of Its birth in good and evil wombs.

Appendix—In the preceding verse the term 'Karṣati' has been used while in this verse the term 'gṛhītvā' has been used. 'Karṣati' means 'to attract' and 'gṛhītvā' means 'to catch' viz., 'to identify'. The purpose of the Lord in giving the illustration of the wind is that the Soul, like the wind, remains untainted. In spite of dwelling in the body, in fact the Self's untaintedness never suffers—'śarīrastho'pi kaunteya na karoti na lipyate' (Gītā 13/31). Perfume does not stay permanently in the wind, it disappears automatically; but attachment to the mind, intellect and senses is not renounced, unless the individual Self renounces it. The reason is that the Self itself has caught them viz., has been attached to them—'gṛhītvaitāni'; therefore he will be detached from them only, when he renounces attachment to them.

There is a natural distaste for every sensual pleasures—this is everyone's experience. Inclination to pleasures is unnatural but disinclination is natural. A man (the Self) develops taste, but distaste is natural. As a smoker while smoking a cigarette, breathes in the smoke but it breathes out naturally. If the mouth is shut, it is breathed out through the nose. This smoke does not stay, but he forms the bad habit of smoking and gets addicted to it. Similarly pleasures don't stay but the pleasure-seeker gets into the bad habit of enjoying pleasures. Objects of pleasures disappear naturally and there is natural disinclination for them but because of bad habit, he gets attached to the pleasures and actually being independent, he feels that he is dependent upon them. In spite of being engrossed in pleasures, in fact his untaintedness is not wiped out but he does not take any heed of it and doesn't attach importance to it. He in spite of having no affinity with the body, having assumed affinity with it, derives pleasure from it. Affinity is transient while disunion is eternal. The body being of the class of the world (inert and kaleidoscopic), is different from the category of the Self. It is not possible to have relationship with the thing which is alien. Being a fragment of God, the soul and God are of the same nature. Therefore he (the Soul) has his natural affinity with God. If a person (the Self) by having faith in utterances of Saints, God and the scriptures, accepts his affinity with God, he will realize his natural affinity with God. But he attaches importance to objects. Unless he accepts his affinity with God, God does not let him have his affinity with any other thing but breaks it off. A man in spite of applying his full force, can't maintain his relationship with the world permanently.

Link:—Now, the Lord explains the expression 'Manaḥ-ṣaṣṭhānīndriyāṇi', used in the seventh verse.

श्रोत्रं चक्षुः स्पर्शनं च रसनं घ्राणमेव च ।
अधिष्ठाय मनश्चायं विषयानुपसेवते ॥ ९ ॥

śrotraṁ cakṣuḥ sparśanaṁ ca rasanaṁ ghrāṇameva ca
adhiṣṭhāya manaścāyaṁ viṣayānupasevate

It (the individual soul), enjoys the objects of senses using the sensations of hearing, sight, touch, taste and smell, as well as, the mind. 9

Comment:—

'Adhiṣṭhāya manaścāyam'—Several (good or bad) projections and distractions, appear and disappear in the mind, while the self (sentient soul) ever remains unaffected. Being transcendental in nature it is quite apart from it the insentient body, senses, mind and intellect and it is their base and illuminator.

The self joining with the mind, experiences (enjoys) the objects of the senses, such as form (colour), touch, sound, taste and smell. It cannot experience pleasure or pain with the senses, without mind. It is only through the mind, that the embodied soul, enjoys sense-objects.

'Śrotraṁ cakṣuḥ sparśanaṁ ca rasanaṁ ghrāṇameva ca'—

Ear, the sense of hearing has the power of hearing.* Till

---

* The thoughts that come to the mind are projections and distractions. During sleep, these appear as dream. We do not express every thought, nor do we act according to this thought, because we apply our own intellect. Expression of every thought, and translating it into practice is nothing but insanity. Thus projections, distractions, dream and insanity, are one and the same.

Through ears we get two kinds of knowledge (i) of sound (ii) of subject. So, the sense of hearing plays an important role in both the paths of knowledge and of devotion, though through the sense of seeing (eye) also the subject can be known by studying the scriptures, but that is also the power of sound, in written form. When we start studying, first we gain knowledge through hearing. The sound has such power which cannot be thought of. The sense of hearing, only can receive, that power not the other senses.

today, we have heard words favourable (praise, honour, blessing, melody, music etc.,) and unfavourable (blame, dishonour, curse, abuse etc.,) but have they affected the self in anyway? No.

A person, hears happy news of the birth of his grandson and sad news of the death of his son, at the same time. Thus he has knowledge of two news. But, is there any difference in that knowledge, or in the self?

We have seen many pleasant and unpleasant (horrible) scenes, with our own eyes. But have they affected the self, in anyway?

We have touched many soft or hard, hot or cold objects, but is there any difference, because of the touch, in the self?

We have tasted bitter, pungent, sweet, astringent sour and saltish food, but have these left any effect, on the self?

Similarly, we have experienced different kinds of good and bad scents. But is there any difference in the self, because of those different scents?

An Important Fact

The five senses of hearing, sight, touch (skin), taste and smell, have affinity respectively, for five organs of actions—tongue, feet, hands, genital organ and anus. If one who is deaf, is also dumb; oil rubbed on the sole of his feet, has a healthy effect on his sight; hands can be used to touch an object, because of skin; control over the tongue, controls the genital organ; smell makes its entrance through nose, while it makes its exit through anus.

The five sense-organs, the five organs of action and the five senses, are formed respectively,out of portion of the mode of goodness, the mode of passion and the mode of ignorance, of each of the five subtle elements.

Five subtle Elements	Portion of the mode of goodness (Sattva)	Portion of the mode of passion (Rajas)	Portion of the mode of ignorance (Tamas)
Ether	Ear	Tongue (the organ of speech)	Sound
Air	Skin	Hands	Touch
Fire	Eye	Feet	Sight (colour)
Water	Tongue (for taste)	Genital organ	Taste
Earth	Nose	Anus	Smell

The mind and the intellect, are made of the Sāttvika portion, the life-breath is made of the Rājasika portion while the body is made of the Tāmasika portion of the mixed five elements.

'Viṣayānupasevate'—If a businessman, stops his business at one place and starts it at another due to some reason, so does soul migrate, from one body to another, and It starts enjoying the objects of senses, in the new body also, as it did in the first body, because of Its past habit. Thus an embodied soul, has to be born in good and evil wombs, because of its attachment, to sense-objects.

God has bestowed this human body upon us, to enable us to attain salvation, rather than to enjoy pleasure or to experience pain. As we can feed a cow which is given to a Brāhmaṇa as a charity, but we cannot lay claim to its milk, so can we make proper use of the body bestowed upon us by God, but we cannot enjoy, the objects of senses with it.

An Important Fact

The more the embodied soul enjoys, the objects of senses, the more It is attached, to them. This attachment leads it to rebirth and all sorrows. In fact, the pleasure born of contact with objects of senses is illusory and source of sorrow, but these seem pleasant in the beginning out of ignorance, (Gītā 18/38).

Had there been happiness in sense-objects, prosperous persons possessing all the luxuries would have been happy, but they also undergo sufferings and disquietude. Enjoyment of pleasure, results in loss of wealth, health, quietude, patience, happiness and honour etc.*

As thirst is not quenched by drinking water in a dream, so can a man not attain peace, by enjoying objects of senses. A man thinks, that he will attain peace through prosperity and pleasure. But the more prosperity he acquires and the more pleasure he enjoys, the keener desire he has, to acquire and enjoy these†. "All the riches of the world, all beautiful women, all excellent objects cannot satisfy a man even if he acquires all of them" (Viṣṇupurāṇa 4/10/24; Mahā. Ādi. 85/13). Because the soul, is a fragment of God and is sentient, while sense-objects, are fragments of prakṛti (Nature) and are insentient. So how can insentient and perishable, satisfy the sentient and imperishable? As thirst cannot be quenched, even by the most delicious dishes without water, so can, the thirst for God-realization, not be quenched by insentient mundane objects. The more he possesses them, the more hungry, he feels.

If a striver, has a resolve this very day, that he has not to enjoy objects of senses. Then the thought of these ceases to come to his mind, and it leads him to be pure and evenminded. Those, who gain equanimity of mind, naturally realize God (Gītā 5/19), because He is ever-attained. But He remains veiled, because of a striver's attachment, to objects of senses.

---

*We have not enjoyed pleasures (the objects of senses). The objects of senses have enjoyed us; we have not performed penances, penances have burnt us; time has not been spent, we have been spent; desire has not decayed but we have decayed.

†Desire is never satisfied after enjoying the sensual pleasures but it is rather strengthened in the same way as fire burns up when clarified ghee is added to it (Manu. 2/94).

Not to talk of God-realization, even firm determination to turn only towards God cannot be had, by those who are attached to pleasure and prosperity (Gītā 2/44).

Gosvāmī Tulasīdāsa, in the Rāmacaritamānasa prays that as a voluptuary loves a woman and is attracted towards her, because of her beauty and as, a greedy person hankers after riches and hoards these, so should he be attracted towards Raghunātha's handsome form, and treasure the divine name (Lord Rāma) by continuously repeating it. Mundane pleasure and prosperity, are not ever dear, even to a worldly person, but the form and chanting of the name of Lord Rāma, are always dear to devotees.

Appendix—By enjoying sense pleasures, the Self becomes secondary while the body and the world become prominent. Therefore the Self is termed as 'Jagat' (world) (Gītā 7/13).

Link:—In the preceding three verses, there is description of the soul (embodied or individual soul). While concluding the topic the Lord, in the next verse, describes who knows this soul, and who does not?

उत्क्रामन्तं स्थितं वापि भुञ्जानं वा गुणान्वितम्।
विमूढा नानुपश्यन्ति पश्यन्ति ज्ञानचक्षुषः ॥ १० ॥

utkrāmantaṁ sthitaṁ vāpi bhuñjānaṁ vā guṇānvitam
vimūḍhā nānupaśyanti paśyanti jñānacakṣuṣaḥ

The duped do not know the soul having identified itself with three guṇas departing from, or dwelling in the body, or enjoying the objects of senses, but they, who possess the eye of wisdom, behold It. 10

Comment:—

'Utkrāmantam'—The soul (self), while giving up a physical body, departs taking the subtle body and the causal body with It. So long as, the heart beats, the soul dwells, in that body. Even when the heart stops beating, the soul may stay for sometime. In fact, the soul being immovable and sentient, does not migrate, it is the life-breath, which migrates. But, It is said to migrate, because of its attachment, for the subtle body and the causal body.

The term "Utkrāmati", used for the Jīvātmā, (embodied soul) which assumes itself, as the lord, as mentioned in the eighth verse, has been called here 'Utkrāmantam' (depart).

'Sthitaṁ vā'—As a camera takes a picture of an object as it is reflected, so is the subtle body formed, according to the thought which a person has at the time of death. As the process of making photograph takes sometime, so the physical body to be prepared according to the thought of the last moment takes sometime.

The term, which has been described as Yadavāpnoti, in the eighth verse has been called 'Sthitam', here.

'Api bhuñjānaṁ vā'—When a man enjoys objects of senses, of sound, touch, form, taste and smell, he thinks that he is very careful, he knows the objects of senses well, and enjoys them, carefully. But in fact, he is deluded, as their enjoyment leads him to hell and evil wombs.

Philosophers and scriptures have different opinions about God, the soul and the world. But all of them agree, that the soul, suffers because of Its attachment to the world and attains bliss, by having affinity for God.

The deluded hear, study and also declare, that the world is transient and kaleidoscopic, yet they assume it as permanent, because they cannot enjoy the objects of senses without regarding these as real or permanent. A voluptuary, becomes so much deluded that he regards gratification of lust, as his highest aim (Gītā 16/11). So his eyes of wisdom ever remain shut. People know, that they have to die, because they are living in a world of mortals, yet they want to live, in order to enjoy sense-objects.

The term 'Api', denotes that when soul having given up one

body, migrates (with subtle body and causal body) to another, to acquire it and enjoys the objects of senses, It in spite of appearing attached to the modes, actually remains detached. In fact, the soul (self), neither departs, nor stays, nor enjoys, Itself.

The expression 'Viṣayānupasevate' used in the preceding verse, has been termed here as 'Bhuñjānam'.

'Guṇānvitam'—It means, that it is because of assumed contact of the soul with the modes, that activities of departure, stay and enjoyment, appear in It.

In fact, the soul has no affinity for modes, but by an error It assumes Its affinity for them, in order to derive pleasure out of the world, and so It has to take birth in high and low bodies.

A man, in order to derive pleasure, out of the world, assumes his affinity for persons and objects of the world. An orator regards an audience as his, a person having no son, adopts a boy as his son, he who has no real brother, or sister, assumes relationship of a brother or a sister, with someone else, and so on. The Lord declares, that the embodied soul, in spite of being transcendental (beyond guṇas), in its intrinsic nature, by assuming relationship with guṇas (space, time, individual, object), gets into bondage.

The expression 'Prakṛtisthāni', used in the seventh verse stands for the expression 'Guṇānvitam', used here.

A Vital Fact

So long as, a man is in the least attached to prakṛti (nature) and its evolute, the modes, he is made to act helplessly, by the modes of nature (Gītā 3/5). If he (the sentient self) depends on insentient nature, he suffers from the evil of impurity. Even when, he totally becomes free from modes of Nature, but relishes this freedom (because of the trace of egoism), the evil of egoism persists. But, when he ceases to relish it, his evil egoism comes to an end, and his devotion accelerates, continuously. The supreme aim of a man, is to attain this devotion. Having attained this devotion (love), a devotee attains perfection. The Lord, having bestowed upon His devotee this unique devotion, gets pleased and considers him the most devout, among all the Yogīs (Gītā 6/47).

A man, transcends the three modes of Nature by practising the spiritual disciplines through his discrimination, but having transcended the three modes of Nature, he attains devotion (love) to Him through His grace only.

'Vimūḍhā nānupaśyanti'—As, we remain the same, while performing different actions, so does the self (soul), remain the same while giving up one body, acquiring another body and enjoying the objects of senses. But he, who having identified the self with the body, thinks he is a doer (3/27) is a deluded one, who does not behold reality.

The deluded are so much attached to pleasure and prosperity that they do not realize the fact, that mundane objects, such as body etc., are perishable. Moreover, they do not think, that sensual pleasures, are sources of sorrow. While describing the food of three kinds in the seventeenth chapter, which are dear to the good, the passionate and the ignorant, the Lord, first has given the effect of food liked by the good (Sāttvika), the effect of the food liked by the passionate (Rājasika), has been given afterwards, while no remark has been given, of the food, which is dear to the ignorant (Tāmasika) (Gītā 17/8—10). Why? The reason is, that a good person thinks of the fruit, before performing an action, the passionate first performs the action and then reaps its fruit, while the ignorant person, does not think of the result at all. So the Lord here, means to say, that the deluded (delusion is a trait of the ignorant) while enjoying objects of senses, do not think, of the result, of sensual enjoyment. They remain, engrossed in pleasure and prosperity. Their knowledge remains veiled, by the mode of ignorance and therefore they cannot distinguish, the soul from the body.

'Paśyanti jñānacakṣuṣaḥ'—All the beings, objects, incident and circumstances, are kaleidoscopic i.e., the seen, is changing, into the unseen. This is known as beholding with an eye of wisdom. The unchanging (permanent), can perceive the changing.

A wise man, also give up a physical body, but he neither acquires another body nor does he enjoy the objects of senses, with attachment. The Lord, in the thirteenth verse of the second chapter, declares, "Just as, in this body the embodied (soul) passes through childhood, youth and old age, so also, does It pass into another body. But the wise man, is not deluded (perplexed) by this." The reason is, that a wise man beholds, with an eye of wisdom, that all activities, such as birth or death etc., or modifications occur, in the kaleidoscopic body, rather than, in the uniform self. The self, ever remains free, totally from all modifications. It is because of identification with a body and because of the desire to derive pleasures out of it, that a man feels modification, in him (the self). The deluded, behold the soul connected with the modes, while the wise behold It, in reality, free from contact, with modes.

Appendix—A man (the Self) by assuming his identity with the guṇas (modes) becomes 'guṇānvita'. If he does not assume his affinity with the modes, he is nirguṇa (free from the three modes)—'anāditvānnirguṇatvāt' (Gītā 13/31). It means that attachment to the modes causes his birth and death (Gītā 13/21). Though no one wants his degradation (downfall), yet because of his attachment to sense pleasures, he does not know the means of his progress. He sees his progress in acquiring perishable objects but the result is his much degradation.

Departing from one body, dwelling in the other body and enjoying the sense-objects—these are three different activities but the Self dwelling in them is the same—in spite of this clear fact an indiscriminative person does not know it viz., he does not pay attention to his experience and does not attach importance to his experience. Being deluded by the three modes, he remains unconscious (Gītā 7/13). The Self does not stay with any state continuously—this is everyone's experience. Its untaintedness is self-evident.

The Lord in the preceding verse mentioned five actions—hearing, seeing, touching, tasting and smelling, while in this verse He has mentioned three actions—departing from one body, dwelling in the other body and enjoying the sense-objects. Out of these eight, no action persists continuously, but the Self ever remains the same. Actions are eight in number but in all of them the Self remains only one. Therefore everyone knows their presence and disappearance, their beginning and end. But the person (the Self) who knows the beginning and the end, is eternal.

There is supposed union and gradual disunion of the body, objects and every pleasure. The Self remains one in all the states and in spite of being one, passes through several states. Had the Self not remained one and the same, who would have known the different states? Though this fact is quite clear, yet the deluded people don't perceive (realize) the reality, but the Yogīs who possess the eye of wisdom, perceive this reality.

Link:—The Lord, in the next verse, describes characteristics of those who perceive (behold) Him, by striving and also the deficiency of those, who do not behold Him, even by striving.

यतन्तो योगिनश्चैनं पश्यन्त्यात्मन्यवस्थितम्।
यतन्तोऽप्यकृतात्मानो नैनं पश्यन्त्यचेतसः॥ ११॥

yatanto yoginaścainaṁ paśyantyātmanyavasthitam
yatanto'pyakṛtātmāno nainaṁ paśyantyacetasaḥ

The Yogic aspirants perceive Him, as established in the self, but the unintelligent and the unenlightened, who have not purified their hearts, even though striving, do not behold Him. 11

Comment:—

'Yatanto yoginaścainaṁ paśyanti'—Here the term 'Yoginaḥ', stands for those strivers following the path of knowledge, whose only aim is God-realization.

The term 'Yatantaḥ, here stands for 'striving', with a firm determination from the heart.

Strivers whose only aim is God-realization, become automatically free from attachment, a sense of mine and the desire for fruit. They strive with exclusive devotion, and so yearning, promptness, restlessness and thoughtfulness, are naturally revealed, in them. This is all included in the term 'Yatantaḥ', used here. Such strivers, who strive with exclusive devotion and firm determination, having a disinclination for the world, perceive Him established in the self. The term 'Paśyanti', stands for this perception.

Such strivers, who want to attain the real (God-realization), and renounce the unreal (world), perceive Him, as established in the self, when their discrimination, is fully aroused.

'Ātmanyavasthitam'—God (The Supreme Being) always equally pervades everywhere. He is the self, seated in the hearts of all beings, (Gītā 10/20). Therefore, the Yogīs (sages) realize (behold) Him, in the self.

Existence is of two kinds—(1) That which undergoes modifications or changeable (2) Axiomatic (self-evident). The existence, which has its appearance after being born, is called changeable existence, while existence which is never born, but which exists eternally, and remains as it is, in a uniform way, is called, axiomatic existence. The world and the bodies, undergo modifications, while God and the soul are self-evident. It is an error, to identify the self, with the body.* When a striver

* A man identifies the self with the body and has egoistic notion. Similarly he regards the body as 'mine'. It is because of his egoistic notion that the body seems real to him and it is because of the sense of mine with the body that he is attached to it.

renounces, this identity as well as a sense of mine, he gets established, in the self.

When a man does not attach importance to discrimination, bestowed upon him by God, he is bound through egoism, and a sense of 'mine'. This affinity is so much strengthened, that it continues even after death, and it is also so brittle, that it can be broken anytime and a man is free, in maintaining it or renouncing it. By misusing this freedom, he creates affinity with body, etc., which does not belong to his class.

When a man does not attach importance to discrimination, it is veiled and then the body seems real. But, by good company and the study of the scriptures etc., as this discrimination is unveiled, the assumed affinity for the body, is renounced. When discrimination is fully unveiled (aroused), a striver realizes that he is naturally established, in the self. This is what the Lord means by the expression, 'Ātmani avasthitam'.

Egoism is born by the attachment of a man (the self), to the world. Egoism can be of two kinds—(1) Through hearing from others— 'I am' Mohana or Śyāma and 'I' am Brāhmaṇa or Kṣatriya (2) Through the performance of actions—'I' am an orator, a teacher or a physician, through speech, teaching and treating patients. But this egoism, is a temporary phase. When it is renounced, a striver realizes, that he is established, in the self which is self-existent.

A Vital Fact

(1) God in the form of 'Is', Who pervades everywhere, as the illuminator and base of 'I', 'you', 'this' and 'that'. These four ever undergo changes, while He (Is) never undergoes, any change. Moreover, it is because of his egoistic notion, that a man feels, that he is different from others i.e., he has to use 'am', because he says 'I', otherwise there is only 'Is'.

Till, 'I'ness persists, there is individuality or finiteness. On its effacement only 'Is' i.e., the Absolute, remains.

'Ātmani avasthitam'—means that there is, 'Is' in 'Am' and 'Am' in 'Is'. In other words, there is macro in micro and micro in macro. An individual and the society cannot be separated from each other, in the same way, as the waves and the sea, cannot be separated from each other. But, as in the element water, neither the sea nor the waves are there, so is God free, from an individual or society. When a striver, realizes this fact, he realizes, that He is established, in the self.

A man cannot realize, that He is established in the self, because of his attachment to the world, to derive pleasure out of it and because of his disinclination for Him. So long as it is not realized that the self is God, we feel God as separate and away from us and we have to make efforts to achieve God and there separation is a must when he renounces attachment to the body, he realizes (beholds), that He is established, in the self and does not suffer pain of separation, from Him.*

He who beholds God, in the self, does not support the opinion, that God is different from the self. It is the sense of 'I' ness, which separates the self from God. In fact, the self has no evil, such as 'I'ness or dependence or shortage or ignorance etc. But, by an error a man (the self), assumes that they are in him. In order to remove these evils, he should behold Him, in the self. When he beholds Him, in the self, he becomes free from all evils, because in Him, there is no evil.

As the world is kaleidoscopic, so is 'I', because it is a fragment of the world, as "I am a boy", "I am young", "I am old", "I am sick", "I am healthy" and so on.† Both the world and

* Only wise who constantly behold God in the self attain eternal bliss (Kaṭha. 2/2/13).

† Here a doubt may arise that the states of boyhood and youth etc., change but 'I' remains the same. The explanation is 'I' seems the same because of

'I', are perishable, while the self and God are imperishable. As the world has no existence, so does 'I' also, have no existence.

Saint Sundaradāsa declares, "We see what does not exist, but we do not see what exists." The reason is, that instruments such as, the mind, intellect and senses etc., with which we see, also do not exist. So the unreal can be seen, with the help of the unreal, the real cannot be seen, with the help of unreal.

Moreover, the unreal seems to exist, in the light of the real. The real is the illuminator, and the base, of the unreal. As we can see the world, with the eye, but we cannot see the eye with it, so how can God, Who is the knower of all, be known by them? How can the unreal, which is illumined by the real, illumine the real?

The self, can be realized by the self, rather than by senses, mind and intellect etc. Similarly God, Who is established in the self, can also be realized by the self, rather than through discourses or through intellect or through hearing* as the senses, the mind and the intellect etc., are evolutes of Nature. How can He, Who transcends Nature, be known by the evolutes of Nature? Therefore, when a striver, renounces his affinity for nature, he realizes Him, in the self.

A striver, commits an error, that he wants to know God, in the same way, as he knows the world. But the methods of knowing the two, are contrary to each other. The world can be known by medium (means), such as senses, mind and intellect etc., while God cannot be known by them, because He is beyond

its identity with the reality (sentient). In fact the illuminator of 'I' (i.e., the self) remains the same while there is a subtle change in 'I'. 'I' is not the same in youth as 'I' was in boyhood. Similarly there is change in 'I' when the soul passes into another body though the self remains the same (Gītā 2/13).

*(1) God can be realized neither through discourses, nor through intellect nor through much hearing (Kaṭha. 1/2/23).

(2) God can be realized neither through speech nor through mind nor through eyes (Kaṭha. 2/3/12).

their access, as He is transcendental.

The sentient, cannot be realized, by depending on, the insentient. Those who, having depended on Matter, or the insentient (physical, subtle and causal bodies), want to realize God, cannot realize Him, even through trance, because a trance also depends, on the causal body.*

The wise, who know that God is theirs, and they are God's, with the eye of wisdom, having separated the self, from the body, senses, mind and intellect etc., realize him. But those unwise and unenlightened people, who regard the body as theirs, and who consider themselves of the body, even though striving, do not, realize God, Who is established, in the self.

(2) **'Ātmani avasthitam'**—The Lord has declared, that He is established in the self, of all beings (i.e., He pervades everywhere). In order to realize this fact, a striver should believe in the following four points:—

1. God is, here.
2. God is, now.
3. God is, in me.
4. God is, mine.

As God pervades everywhere, He is also here. As He existed in the past, exists at present and will also exist in future, He

---

* A man acts with the physical body, thinks with the subtle body and experiences trance with the causal body.

The causal body and the trance experienced with it in spite of being superior to wakefulness, sleep and sound sleep are in their subtle form constantly active. When a person transcends the causal body, only the self remains. This is the constant trance of the self, which transcends both activity and inactivity i.e., when a man realizes the self there is neither activity nor inactivity. There is deviation from the trance of the causal body. But in the trance of the self viz., on Self-realization there is neither trance nor deviation. This is known as 'seedless trance' because in it the connection (seed) with the world is totally destroyed. This is also known as 'Sahajāvasthā' (innate or natural condition) though it transcends all conditions.

is also, now. As He pervades all, He also pervades me, and as He is everyone's, He is also, mine. From these facts it is very obvious—

1. As God is here, we need not go anywhere, to realize Him.

2. As God is present now, we need not wait, for future.

3. As He is in me, I need not search Him, anywhere outside.

4. As He is mine, I need not regard, others as mine. He is also very loving to me, because He is mine.

These four points are very significant and useful, for all strivers. This realization is the quintessence of all spiritual practices. It needs no qualification, no practice, no ability and no virtue. Everyone is qualified, deserving and able, in believing it. The only condition is, that he should have only the desire for God-realization.

'Yatanto'pyakṛtātmāno nainaṁ paśyantyacetasaḥ'— 'Akṛtātmānaḥ' are those unrefined people, who have not purified their mind, they have been called 'Acetasaḥ' (unintelligent), because they do not discriminate, the real from the unreal.

Those, who regard mundane objects, such as the body and also persons as theirs, and expect to derive pleasure, out of them, by attaching importance to them, are unintelligent and unrefined. Such people, also want to realize God, but they want to realize Him, with the help of insentient objects, such as body, mind and intellect etc. As He cannot be realized with their help, He can be realized, by renouncing attachment, to them.

In this verse the term 'Yatantaḥ', has been used twice, in order to explain that the wise perceive Him by striving, while the unintelligent do not behold Him, even by striving. It means, that so long as, a man is attached to worldly objects, he cannot realize God, with body, senses, mind and intellect, though these are useful, in making effort to attain Him. How can those, who have an eye on the unreal (mundane pleasures and prosperity), behold Him?

Unrefined and unintelligent people, also meditate on God, study scriptures and chant His name, but they cannot behold Him, because they attach importance, to mundane objects (pleasures and prosperity). Though their efforts are not in vain, yet they cannot realize Him, at the present moment. He can be realized immediately, if a striver renounces attachment to the insentient, totally.

A striver cannot renounce attachment to insentient body, mind and intellect etc., so long as, he depends upon them. Moreover, he possesses egoism, in its subtle form, if he practises spiritual discipline with the help of mind and intellect etc. He can be free, from this subtle egoism by renouncing attachment, to the insentient. This attachment, can be easily renounced, when a striver totally depends on God i.e., he firmly believes and accepts the reality 'I am God's and God is mine'. It needs, neither effort nor practice.

Appendix—Neither pleasure nor prosperity stays permanently with us—a man naturally has this discretion. But the people, who in spite of studying the scriptures, keeping good company and practising spiritual discipline, don't pay attention to their discretion and don't realize that they are different from pleasures and prosperity, are 'akṛtātmā' viz., they have not purified their hearts. Such people in the sixteenth verse of the eighteenth chapter have been called 'akṛtabuddhi' (of impure or untrained mind) and 'durmati' (of perverse understanding). Though God-realization is not difficult, yet in spite of practising the spiritual discipline, they don't know God because of their attachment and desire for worldly pleasures. The reason is that discretion does not stick in those people who hanker after pleasures and prosperity.

In the preceding verse the people who have been called

'vimūḍhāḥ' (deluded), here have been called 'acetasaḥ' (unintelligent). Being deluded by modes, they neither know the division of sense-objects nor that of the Self viz., they don't know that the Self is different from pleasures of which there is supposed union and gradual disunion with it.

In this topic from the seventh verse to the eleventh verse, the Lord wants to explain that His fragment, the Soul, is totally different from the materials (bodies, objects and actions) which by an error he regards as his own—these materials are evolutes of prakṛti—'prakṛtisthāni'. Both are totally different in the same way as are the sun and the darkest night of amāvasyā (last day of the dark half of a month). Their union is impossible. He who perceives that the sentient and the insentient are totally different from each other, is wise and is a Yogī (sage). But he who perceives the sentient (the Self), identified with the insentient (matter), is ignorant and a 'bhogī' (voluptuary).

Link:—In the fifteenth chapter, there are four topics, each consisting of five verses. This is the third topic of five verse, from the twelfth to the fifteenth verses, as well as the sixth verse. This topic specially deals with His glory, virtues and divinity. The topic (how the sun, the moon, the fire cannot illumine, that Eternal Goal) which was not very clear, there, in the sixth verse, is explained, in the next verse.

यदादित्यगतं तेजो जगद्भासयतेऽखिलम्।
यच्चन्द्रमसि यच्चाग्नौ तत्तेजो विद्धि मामकम्॥ १२॥

yadādityagataṁ tejo jagadbhāsayate'khilam
yaccandramasi yaccāgnau tattejo viddhi māmakam

The light (coming from Me) of the sun that illumines the whole world, and which is in the moon and in the fire—know, that light to be Mine. 12

Comment:—

[It is a man's nature, that he is attracted towards a thing, which he feels as, significant. He is attached to material objects (body, wife, son and riches etc.,) by regarding these as significant. Therefore the Lord, in order to, efface the influence of worldly objects from the mind of the embodied soul, discloses the secret, that whatever significance or splendour there is, of those material objects, that is really (basically) His, as all of these are illumined, by His light as He is supremely glorious.]

'Yadādityagataṁ tejo jagadbhāsayate'khilam'—As the Lord (in 2/55) declares, that desire resides in the mind so does He here declare, that light (splendour) resides in the sun. It means that as desires appear in the mind though they are not of the mind, so does the light appear that it is of the sun, though it is not, it comes from God.

The light (splendour), of the sun illumines the whole world, but that light is really God's, though it appears to be of the sun, as the sun cannot illumine God or His Supreme Abode. The great sage Patañjali, declares—

"God is the preceptor of the ancestor of all beings, because He transcends the limit of time" (Yogadarśana 1/26).

How much influential and unique, God must be when His light (splendour), is so unique, that with it the sun illumines the world and the same light is reflected in the moon, the fire, the stars and the lightning (electricity) etc.! By thinking so, a man is naturally attracted towards Him.

The sun is the presiding deity of eyes. Therefore, light (power of sight) in eyes, should also be regarded as God's (coming from Him).

'Yaccandramasi'—As the illuminating power, as well as, the burning power in the sun, is God's, so is illuminating power or the cooling power, as well as, the nourishing power, in the moon, is

God's; because, in the moon the light of the sun, is reflected.

Here, the moon also denotes, stars and planets.

The moon is the presiding deity of the mind. Therefore, light (power of thought), in the mind should also be regarded, as transmitted in succession from God.

'Yaccāgnau'—As the sun's light, is reflected in the fire, so is the fire's illuminating power, as well as, the burning power God's; rather than of the fire.

The fire, also denotes lightning (electricity), a lamp and fire-flies.

Fire, is the presiding deity of speech. Therefore, the light (power of explanation) in the speech, should also be regarded as God's.

'Tattejo viddhi māmakam'—The light, which resides in the sun, the moon and the fire and which illumines, other objects (stars, planets, lightning and fire-fly etc.,) should be regarded, as God's.

The Lord means, that whatever being or object there is glorious or splendid, and to which, a man is attracted, is a manifestation of a part, of His splendour (Gītā 10/41). As in sweetmeats, there is sweetness of sugar, so is the light (splendour), in the sun, the moon and the fire of God's. The whole world, is illumined by His light. He is the light, of all lights (Gītā 13/17).

The sun, the moon and the fire, are the presiding deities and illuminators respectively, of the eye, the mind and speech. A man, in order to express his thoughts or feelings and in order to understand them, has to use his eyes, mind and tongue. These three sense-organs, are more useful than other organs, in order to gain knowledge. Out of these three, the eye and the tongue, are external organs, while the mind is an internal one. These three instruments, (organs) can illumine only worldly objects. They cannot illumine God, because the light residing in them, is not theirs but is God's.

Appendix—God is the source of all powers. In this connection there is an anecdote in the Kenopaniṣad. Once God got victory over demons for gods. But the gods became proud of their power for this victory. They thought that they could get victory over demons with their own power. In order to destroy their false pride, God revealed Himself before them as a 'Yakṣa' (demigod). Having seen the 'Yakṣa' the gods were surprised and began to think who he was? The gods sent the Fire-god to him so that they could know who he was. Yakṣa asked the Fire-god who he was? The Fire-god said, "I am the famous Fire-god named 'Jātavedā' and I can burn everything on the earth to ashes, if I so wish." Then the demigod put a straw before him and asked him to burn it. The Fire-god made the best possible efforts but he could not burn it. Being ashamed of his failure, he returned to the gods and said that he could not know who that demigod was. Then the Wind-god approached him to know who he was. The demigod asked the Wind-god who he was. The Wind-god said, "I am the famous Wind-god named 'Mātariśvā' and if I wish, I may blow off everything which is there on the earth." Then the demigod put a straw before him and asked him to blow it off. The Wind-god could not blow it off in spite of applying his full power. Being ashamed of his failure, he returned to the gods and said that he could not know who the demigod was. Then gods commissioned Indra to Yakṣa in order to know who he was. As soon as Indra reached there, the demigod disappeared and in place of the demigod, Umādevī, the daughter of Himācala appeared. Having been asked by Indra, Umādevī replied that God revealed Himself in the form of a Yakṣa in order to crush their pride. It means that in the entire universe whatever power or speciality or singularity is perceived that has emanated only from God (Gītā 10/41).

Link:—Having explained His light (splendour), in all the seen objects, in the preceding verse, in the next verse, He explains how His energy is energizing cosmic life.

गामाविश्य च भूतानि धारयाम्यहमोजसा।
पुष्णामि चौषधीः सर्वाः सोमो भूत्वा रसात्मकः॥१३॥

gāmāviśya ca bhūtāni dhārayāmyahamojasā
puṣṇāmi cauṣadhīḥ sarvāḥ somo bhūtvā rasātmakaḥ

Entering the earth, I support all beings by My energy, and having become the sapid moon, I nourish all vegetation. 13

Comment:—

'Gāmāviśya ca bhūtāni dhārayāmyahamojasā'—The Lord, permeating the earth, supports all beings moving and unmoving. It means, that the movable as well as immovable beings, are supported not by the power of the earth, but by the power of God.*

Scientists also agree, that on this globe, water level is higher than the land, and there is much more water, than land†, yet the earth does not submerge. It is because of the Lord's supporting power, that the earth does not submerge. The production power, as well as the attraction power, of the earth should also be regarded as God's.

'Puṣṇāmi cauṣadhīḥ sarvāḥ somo bhūtvā rasātmakaḥ'—The moon, has two kinds of power—the illuminating and the nourishing. Having described the illuminating power, in the preceding verse, here He describes, its nourishing power, He

* All—the heaven, the sun, the moon, the sky with stars, the ten directions, the earth and the ocean are supported by the power of God (Mahābhārata, Anu. 149/134).

He Who, having resided the earth, controls it but is not known by the earth; He Who is declared by the verse of the Vedas as the embodiment of purity, the Lord, the controller, the Destination and the Deity of the universe, Who is said to offer salvation to men and sages—that Lord Kṛṣṇa Candra, the Master of the entire universe, the affectionate of those who seek refuge in Him, be the subject of my eyes.

† On this globe (earth) water occupies seventy-one percent part while the land occupies only twenty-nine percent part.

declares, that it is He, Who through the medium of the moon, nourishes all plants.

The moon, in the bright half of the lunar month nourishes vegetation, while in the dark half it withers it. In the bright half, the sweet rays of the moon, nourish all herbs and plants, by infusing sap into them. A child in the womb of its mother, also grows in the bright half of a lunar month.

Here the term 'Somaḥ', stands for the 'Candraloka' (the lunar world), rather than only the moon. The moon, has not only the illuminating power, but also the power to create nectar. Nectar first comes to the moon from the lunar world, and then it comes to the earth, from the moon.

Here the term 'Auṣadhīḥ' stands for different kinds of corn, such as wheat and gram etc. The moon nourishes all herbs, plants and vegetables. All beings, such as men, birds and beasts etc., are nourished by the corn, nourished by the moon. That nourishing power of the moon, is in fact of God, rather than its own. The moon is merely an instrument on His hands.

Appendix—The earth and the moon etc.,—all is the Lord's lower nature (Gītā 7/4). Therefore only God is its supporter, producer, sustainer, protector and illuminator etc.,—all. Aparā Prakṛti (lower nature) being the power of God, is inseparable with Him.

Here the term 'Soma' stands for 'Candraloka' (the lunar world) which is above the Sun.*

Link:—Having explained how He is the source of energy of the cosmic life, in the preceding verse, in the next verse, He explains how He digests food, through the gastric fire.

---

* na viduḥ soma te māyāṁ ye ca nakṣatrayonayaḥ
tvamādityapathādūrdhvaṁ jyotiṣāṁ coparisthitaḥ
(Padmapurāṇa, Sṛṣṭi. 41/128)

अहं वैश्वानरो भूत्वा प्राणिनां देहमाश्रितः।
प्राणापानसमायुक्तः पचाम्यन्नं चतुर्विधम्॥ १४॥

ahaṁ vaiśvānaro bhūtvā prāṇināṁ dehamāśritaḥ
prāṇāpānasamāyuktaḥ pacāmyannaṁ caturvidham

As the fire of life, in the bodies of living creatures and united with the Prāṇa and Apāna breaths, I digest, the four kinds of food. 14

Comment:—

'Ahaṁ vaiśvānaro bhūtvā prāṇināṁ dehamāśritaḥ'— Having described the light in the fire as His light, in the twelfth verse, here in this verse He describes, the gastric fire, that digests the four kinds of food.* It means, that it is by God's power, that the fire illumines objects and also digests food. This fire, digests food of immovable creation such as plants, trees and creepers, of movable beings such as birds and beasts etc., as it digests, the food of human beings and enables them to grow. It means, that God in the form of gastric fire, nourishes the bodies of beings.

'Prāṇāpānasamāyuktaḥ'—In the body, there are five primary vital airs, known as 'Prāṇa', 'Apāna', 'Samāna', 'Udāna' and 'Vyāna' and there are five secondary vital airs known as 'Nāga', 'Kūrma', 'Kṛkara', 'Devadatta' and 'Dhanañjaya'.† In the verse, the Lord

---

* The fire that abides in the stomach is called Vaiśvānara and it digests the food which is eaten.

† The functions of these ten vital airs are as follows:—

(1) Prāṇa:—It resides in the heart. It exhales air, digests the food and so on.

(2) Apāna:—It resides in anus. It inhales air, excretes waste matter and throw out the foetus from the womb.

(3) Samāna:—It resides in the navel. It circulates the essence of the digested food in all the limbs.

(4) Udāna:—It abides in the throat. It separates the solid and the liquid portions of food. It separates the subtle body from the physical body and transmigrates it to another body or to the world.

describes, only two main kinds of vital air— Prāṇa and Apāna which fan the fire, that abides in the stomach and also circulate the essence of the digested food, to every part of the body.

'Pacāmyannaṁ caturvidham'—Beings, eat four kinds of food—

(1) Bhojya:—That which is eaten, having been chewed with teeth, such as bread and sweet cake etc.

(2) Peya:—That which is swallowed, as milk and juice etc.

(3) Coṣya:—That which is sucked, such as sugarcane and mango etc. The immovable beings, such as tree etc., receive food, in this way.

(4) Lehya:—That which has to be licked such, as sauce and honey etc.

These four kinds, can further be divided into many other sub-kinds. The Lord, declares that it is He, Who digests the four kinds of food, by becoming gastric fire. No food, can be digested without His power.

Appendix—Entering the earth to support all beings, becoming the moon to nourish all vegetation, and becoming the gastric fire to digest the food in the living creatures—all these activities are carried out by God's power. But a man by regarding them to be done by himself, feels proud for nothing—'ahaṁ karomīti vṛthābhimānaḥ'; as a dog, which moves under the bullock-cart in its shade, thinks that it itself alone drives the bullock-cart.

---

(5) Vyāna:—It abides in whole of the body. It shrinks and expands the body and its parts.

(6) Nāga:—It's function is belching.

(7) Kūrma:— It's function is shutting and opening the eyes.

(8) Kṛkara:—It's function is sneezing.

(9) Devadatta:—It's function is yawning.

(10) Dhanañjaya:—It abides in the body even after death and puffs out the dead body. In fact, only one vital air is differentiated according to its various functions.

Link:—Having described His illuminating, nourishing and digesting powers, in the preceding three verses, the Lord in the next verse, while concluding the topic, declares that He is the only object, worth knowing.

सर्वस्य चाहं हृदि सन्निविष्टो-
मत्तः स्मृतिर्ज्ञानमपोहनं च।
वेदैश्च सर्वैरहमेव वेद्यो-
वेदान्तकृद्वेदविदेव चाहम्॥ १५॥

sarvasya cāhaṁ hṛdi sanniviṣṭo
mattaḥ smṛtirjñānamapohanaṁ ca
vedaiśca sarvairahameva vedyo
vedāntakṛdvedavideva cāham

I am seated in the hearts of all; I am the source of memory, knowledge and the reasoning faculty. It is verily 'I' known by all the Vedas; I am indeed, the author of the Vedānta and correct interpreter and knower of the Vedas too. 15

Comment:—

'Sarvasya cāhaṁ hṛdi sanniviṣṭaḥ*'—Having described His illuminating, nourishing and digesting powers, in the preceding verses, the Lord discloses the secret, that He is lodged in the hearts of all beings. Though He remains pervaded everywhere, such as in the body, senses, mind and intellect etc., yet, He specially resides, in the heart.

The heart, is an important part of the body. All the feelings arise in the heart. Feelings occupy an important place in all actions. Pure feelings purify all objects and actions etc., and therefore, are very important. The heart is an evolute, of the mode

* The two birds named the soul and God live together with friendly feeling for each other by depending on the same tree i.e., body. Out of the two one (the soul) enjoys the fruits of that tree (action) by relishing them while the other one (God) does not enjoy them but merely remains a spectator (Muṇḍaka 3/1/1).

of goodness; therefore, the Lord is specially lodged, in the heart.

As the Lord dwells in the hearts of all men, no striver, should lose heart, as far as God-realization is concerned. Every person, whether he is sinful or virtuous, foolish or wise, poor or rich, sick or healthy or whether she is a woman, without any distinction of caste, creed, colour, order of life, is fully qualified for and deserving of God-realization, under all circumstances. But he or she, should possess such a burning desire or restlessness, that he or she may not remain, without realizing Him.

Though God, being omnipresent, pervades equally everywhere, in the sun, the moon, the fire, the earth and the gastric fire etc., yet He is particularly seated in the heart, in the same way, as milk can be available from the udders of a cow, though it pervades her entire body or as water, is available from a well, though it permeates the entire earth (Gītā 13/17; 18/61).

An Important Fact Pertaining to God

In fact, God is already attained to all human beings, as He dwells in their hearts, but they do not realize His existence, in their hearts because of their assumed affinity (attachment) for Matter, (the world). As soon as, there is total renouncement of this affinity for Matter, they automatically, realize Him.

When a person performs virtuous actions for Him, talks of Him and thinks of Him, he has to depend on Matter (the insentient and the unreal), because performance of actions or talking or thinking of Him is not possible, without depending on the insentient (gross, subtle and causal bodies). So these should induce a man, to renounce his affinity for the world, and that is possible only when these (virtuous actions, talking of God and thinking of Him) are done, for the welfare of the world only, rather than, for one's own self.

Those, who think that God can be realized, through spiritual practice or virtues or qualifications etc., are wrong. A thing, that is acquired by making some payment, for it, is of lesser value, than that payment (price). So if God is attained by certain spiritual practice or virtues or qualifications etc., it means, that He is less valuable than those means, while there is none even equal to Him, so how can anyone or anything be superior (of more value) to Him, (Gītā 11/43)? Moreover, if He is secured (realized) for some money (by any means), it means, that there is not much use in realizing Him, because we already possess something more valuable, than He.

As God-realization, is not the fruit of actions, so he cannot be achieved through actions like other objects. Every action, is born of egoistic notions while God is realized when egoism is renounced. So how can He, be realized through actions? It means that God cannot be realized, through actions. It means that God cannot be realized, through insentient objects, such as the body, senses, mind and intellect etc., but, He can be realized by renouncing affinity (attachment), for them. So long as a striver, depends upon them, he cannot realize God. God can be realized, through mind and intellect etc.,—this belief is a blunder. But, as soon as, he depends only on Him, without depending on any other object, He is attained, without delay.

'Mattaḥ smṛtirjñānamapohanaṁ ca'—Smṛti, means the recollection of an object or incident etc., which was perceived in the past, by a person, but which he forgot. There is difference between 'Smṛti' (recollection) and 'Cintana' (thinking). There is 'Smṛti' of something of the past, while there is 'Cintana' of something new. So there is 'Smṛti' of God, while there is 'Cintana', of the world, because the world did not exist before, while God has existed, since time immemorial. There is not so much power in 'Cintana, as is there in 'Smṛti'. In 'Smṛti' there is less sense of doership, while in 'Cintana', there is more sense of doership. This recollection can be of two kinds—natural and by effort. The former is automatically remained in the self, while the latter is made by intellect.

Memory is of two types—One is resorted to, while the other is automatic (natural). The former is through intellect, while the latter is, through the self. Natural recollection aids a man, to renounce his affinity for the world, instantly. So, the Lord declares that He is a source of this natural recollection (memory).

What is the memory? Memory is that the soul in spite of being a fragment of God, by an error, has an inclination for the world and a disinclination for God. But when a man rectifies this error, and realizes that he is only God's, and not of the world, it is called 'Smṛti' (memory or recollection) (Gītā 18/73). In memory, no new knowledge or experience, is gained. There is only a revelation of a fact, which he forgot, that a person, has his real affinity for God.

A man (the soul) is naturally endowed with, selflessness (Karmayoga), Self-realization (Jñānayoga or the path of knowledge) and Devotion to God, (Bhaktiyoga or the path of devotion). But, he has forgotten these since time immemorial. Once he regains this memory, he never loses it, because it is regained (aroused) in the self, rather than in the intellect. The memory of the intellect, can be lost, when intellect becomes dull.

Knowledge of a subject is called 'Jñāna'. All the mundane, as well as, spiritual knowledge, is merely a reflection of God, Who is an embodiment of knowledge. In fact, real knowledge is known by the self. There is no doubt or confusion (illusion) in this knowledge, as it is infinite, perfect and eternal, while knowledge of senses and intellect is limited, imperfect and changeable, as such, there is doubt or confusion (illusion) in it. The sun, in spite of being large looks small, it means that knowledge of senses, is imperfect. Similarly, what is felt justified by the undeveloped intellect, may be unjustified, when intellect is developed or purified. Thus, knowledge gained by senses and mind, is limited and imperfect. This imperfect knowledge is called ignorance, while knowledge of the self, is perfect. In fact, the knowledge of senses and intellect is illumined, by knowledge of the self i.e., the former, comes into existence, by the latter.

Removal of doubt, confusion, illusion, misapprehension and fallacious judgment, etc., is, 'Apohana'. The Lord declares, that these are removed, by His grace.

Are the scriptures true or false? Who has seen God? The world is real. Such types of doubts, confusion and illusions, are removed by God's grace. The misapprehension that the world, is real or mundane objects provide real joy, is also removed, by His grace. At the end of the gospel of the Gītā Arjuna also declares, "I have gained my knowledge (memory), my delusion (doubt), is destroyed through Your grace" (Gītā 18/73).

'Vedaiśca sarvairahameva vedyaḥ'—Here the term 'Sarvaiḥ', stands for the Vedas and the scriptures, which help a man, to acquire true knowledge of God, and enable him to realize Him.

Here the Lord explains, that Vedas aim to enable a striver, to realize God, rather than to acquire, mundane pleasures. There is a description of the performance of actions for their fruits in the Vedas, because most of the people perform actions, for their fruits. Therefore, the Vedas, (being the mother of all beings) also nourish them.

It is verily He, who is to be known by all the Vedas, because without knowing Him, knowledge is imperfect.* Arjuna had a keen desire to know God. Therefore, the Lord declares that He, Who is to be known by all the Vedas, and scriptures, is sitting before him.

'Vedāntakṛt'—The Vedas, were created by Him (Gītā 3/15; 17/23). Therefore, He can explain the principles of the Vedas and can reconcile the contradictions, that appear to exist, in them. So He

* Having studied the Vedas thoroughly the fool who does not know God is merely the bearer of the load of the Vedas.

(Mahābhārata, Śānti. 318/50)

declares, that He is the real knower of Vedas, and can give correct interpretation removing all doubts, pertaining to Vedas.

'Vedavideva cāham'—It is He, who knows the correct intention of Vedas, because these have been created by Him.

Even scholars find themselves at their wits end, in giving a right judgment, on contradictions, in the Vedas, (Gītā 2/53). They can know Vedas, in the right perspective and be free from contradictions, only by depending on God.

The Lord, in the first verse of this chapter declared, "He who knows this imperishable Pīpala tree, is the knower of the Vedas." But here, He declares, that He is the knower of the Vedas. It means, that the great soul who knows the reality about the world, becomes identified with God. The reality, about the world, is that the world has no existence of its own, only God exists. Having learned this fact, he renounces his assumed affinity, for the world and dependence on it, and he realizes his real affinity for God and depends on Him.

An Important Fact Pertaining to the Topic

The Lord, has described His manifestations, in the different forms, in four chapters—

In the seventh chapter from the eighth verse to the twelfth verse, the Lord has mentioned His seventeen manifestations, by declaring that He is the cause of important objects of the universe. Thus, He has proved His omnipresence, in different forms.

In the ninth chapter from the sixteenth verse to the nineteenth verse, He, having described His thirty-seven manifestations in actions, sentiments and objects etc., in the form of effect and cause, has explained His omnipresence, and all pervasiveness.

The tenth chapter is designated, as the Yoga of Divine manifestation. In the fourth and the fifth verses, He has mentioned twenty qualities, as His manifestation, while in the sixth verse, He has mentioned His twenty-five manifestations, in the form of great persons. Then, from the twentieth verse to the thirty-ninth verse, He has particularly mentioned, His eighty-two exceptional manifestations.

In this fifteenth chapter from the twelfth to the fifteenth verses, the Lord has mentioned His thirteen manifestations, in order to show His glory.*

The purpose of describing His manifestation, in four chapters is to make the striver, realize that all is God (Gītā 7/19). Therefore, while describing His manifestations, He has specially proved, His omnipresence as—

"There is no other cause of this universe higher than Me" (7/7).

"I am existence and non-existence, O Arjuna" (9/19).

"I am the source of all; from Me, everything moves" (10/8).

"There is no being, whether moving or unmoving, that can exist without Me" (10/39) i.e., all the beings, whether moving or unmoving, are His manifestations.

Thus while concluding the description of His manifestation, in this fifteenth chapter, He declares:—

"I am seated in the hearts of all" (15/15).

It means, that all beings and objects exist, because of the existence of God; these have no independent existence, of their own.

In the absence of light i.e., in darkness no object is visible. When we see an object, first we see light, and then the object i.e., every object is seen, within the light, but we instead of having our eye on the light, have it on the object. Similarly, we gain knowledge of all objects, actions and feelings etc.,

* The thirteen manifestations described in this chapter are as follows:—

(1) The light (splendour) in the sun (2) The light in the moon (3) The light in the fire (4) The supporting energy of the earth (5) The nourishing power of the moon (6) The gastric fire (7) He is lodged in hearts (8) Memory (9) Knowledge (10) Ratiocinative faculty (11) He Who is to be known by the Vedas (12) The author of the Vedānta (13) The knower of the Vedas.

within the unique and permanent Light (Knowledge), Who is the illuminator and base of all of them. Therefore, when we behold worldly objects, first the illuminator of those objects (God), is seen, but because of our attachment to the world we do not perceive Him.

In fact, the world has no independent existence. But, it seems to exist, because of our attachment to beings and objects, and because of desire to derive pleasure out of them. As soon as, this attachment for them and the desire to derive pleasure out of them, are renounced, God's existence, will be realized. Therefore, the Lord, while describing His manifestations, aims at explaining that a striver, should behold God in every being or object, he looks at, or thinks of, (Gītā 10/41).

At present, people attach too much importance to riches, and regard themselves as superior to others, because of their wealth.* But in fact, wealth by itself cannot be used. It is the things bought with that wealth, that are used. Thus a man, who attaches too much importance to wealth, cannot attach importance, to God. Then, how can a burning desire for God-realization grow in him? Such a man, cannot even resolve, to realize God. He cannot even understand, that life can run smoothly, without wealth.

As a businessman, during a transaction thinks in terms of money only, so does a striver, having the aim of God-realization, behold God only, in every object and activity etc. He comes to realize, that there neither is, nor can be, any other entity besides God.

A Vital Fact

Arjuna, in the fourteenth chapter asked Lord Kṛṣṇa, the method of transcending the three modes of nature. It is attachment, to these modes, which entangles a man. Therefore the Lord has

* The man who regards himself as superior or inferior to others because of his wealth, degrades himself. A wealthy man becomes proud of his wealth and pride is the root of demoniac endowment. All the evils and sins are born of pride.

mentioned his manifestations, in order to stress upon strivers that He, is superior to all the modes of nature i.e., to the world and His glory, is greater than any other glory.

In order to explain His glory, the Lord (from the twelfth to the fifteenth verses of the chapter), describes that it is He, Who illumines the entire world; Who entering the earth supports all beings; who nourishes all herbs and plants (corn etc.). Again it is He, Who digests food, by becoming gastric fire, and it is He, Who is the source of memory, knowledge and the ratiocinative faculty. It means, that all the activities of the world from the beginning to the end, whether these are individual or social, are undertaken within Him, by His power only. A man, because of his egoism, becomes the doer of actions and thus gets himself in bondage.

Appendix—Whatever the Lord said in the first verse of this chapter, He concludes it in this verse.

In the preceding three verses the Lord described His divine glories in the form of His impact and activities but in this verse He describes Himself. It means that in this verse there is His own description; 'ādityagata' (residing in the Sun), 'candragata' (residing in the Moon), 'agnigata' (residing in the Fire) or 'vaiśvānaragata' (residing in the gastric fire)—this is not God's own description. Though at the root there is only one Reality (Tattva), there is difference only in the description.

The expression 'mamaivāṁśo jīvaloke' proves that God is 'ours', while here the expression 'sarvasya cāhaṁ hṛdi sanniviṣṭaḥ' proves that God is 'in the Self'. If we regard the Lord as ours, then there will be spontaneous love for Him and if we accept Him 'in the Self', then there is no need to go anywhere else to attain Him.

The term 'apohanam' means 'apagata ohanam' viz., removal of doubt. The term 'vedānta' means the end of the Vedas viz., the gist of the Vedas—'ubhayorapi dṛṣṭo'ntaḥ' (Gītā 2/16).

The Lord declares that the Vedas are several but out all of them, it is only He Who is to be known and He is also their knower. It means that only He is all.

Link:—The Lord, in this chapter from the first verse to the fifteenth verse (in three sub-topics), has described the tree of creation i.e., the world, the embodied soul and God, in detail. While concluding the topic, He in the next two verses, describes them respectively in explicit words as Kṣara, Akṣara and Puruṣottama.

द्वाविमौ पुरुषौ लोके क्षरश्चाक्षर एव च।
क्षरः सर्वाणि भूतानि कूटस्थोऽक्षर उच्यते॥ १६॥

dvāvimau puruṣau loke kṣaraścākṣara eva ca
kṣaraḥ sarvāṇi bhūtāni kūṭastho'kṣara ucyate

There are two kinds of Puruṣas in the world, the perishable (Kṣara) and the imperishable (Akṣara). All bodies of beings are said to be perishable and the unchanging Jīvātmā is called imperishable. 16

Comment:—

'Dvāvimau puruṣau loke kṣaraścākṣara eva ca'—Here, the term 'Loke', stands for the entire world. In the seventh verse of this chapter the term 'Jīvaloke', also stands for the world.

The world is divided into two aspects (categories), the perishable objects, such as the body etc., (the insentient), and the imperishable soul (the sentient), which resides in the body. It is because of the soul, that the life-breath and the body function. As soon as, life-breath within the soul, leaves the body, it stops functioning, and it starts to rot. People burn a dead body, because it is useful, only so long as, the soul resides in it. It means that it is the soul, rather than the body, which is significant.

All the objects, such as the body etc., made of the five gross elements—earth, water, fire, air and ether, are insentient and perishable. The physical body, has its identity with physical world; the subtle body consisting of the ten senses, five vital airs, the mind and the intellect (these seventeen), has its identity with the subtle world, while the causal body (nature, impressions of the actions, ignorance), has its identity with causal world (nature). They are called 'Kṣara', because they are perishable.

In fact, there is nothing as individual; but when a person regards a little portion of the world, as his own, he says that it is individual. The body and other objects, seem different from the world, because of a man's attachment, a sense of mineness to them, otherwise they are one, and the same. In fact, all objects and actions, belong only to Nature.* Therefore, all actions with the physical, subtle and causal bodies, are to be performed for the welfare of the world only, not for one's own self.

The term 'Akṣaraḥ', stands for the imperishable soul, which never undergoes any modification.† Nature is insentient, (matter), while the soul, being a fragment of God, is sentient.

---

* If a striver regards the objects and actions as the world's, it means he follows the path of action; if he regards them as Nature's, he follows the path of knowledge; if he regards them as God's, it means he follows the path of devotion. They may be of the world or of Nature, or of God, in no case they are not one's own.

† In the Gītā the perishable (Kṣara), the imperishable (Akṣara) and the Supreme Person (Puruṣottama) have been described by different names as follows:

Chapter-Verse	Kṣara (perishable)	Akṣara (imperishable)	Puruṣottama
7/4—6	Aparā prakṛti (lower Nature)	Parā prakṛti (higher Nature)	Aham (I)
8/3-4	Adhibhūtaḥ (elements); Karma (action)	Adhyātmaḥ (Self); Adhidaiva (Self)	Brahma (the Supreme) Adhiyajña (the Lord)
13/1-2	Kṣetra (field)	Kṣetrajña (knower of the field)	Mām (Me)
14/3-4	Mahadbrahma (Nature); Yoni (womb)	Garbha (germ)(seed); Bīja (seed)	Aham (I); Pitā (father)

The term 'Kṣaraḥ', used in the verse stands for the Pīpala tree in the form of the world, which should be cut, as is mentioned in the third verse, while 'Akṣaraḥ' is the soul, a fragment of God, as is described in the seventh verse.

In Gītā, for each of the Kṣara, Akṣara and Puruṣottama, different words belonging to the three genders, have been used on different occasion. It means, that Nature, the soul, and God are neither female, nor male nor a hermaphrodite. They are free from the restrictions of gender.*

In order to, show the superiority of 'Puruṣottama' (the Supreme Person), the Lord has used, for both 'Kṣara' (perishable) and Akṣara (imperishable), the term 'Puruṣa' (person).

'Kṣaraḥ sarvāṇi bhūtāni'—Here, the term 'Kṣara', stands for a tree in the form of universe, as described at the beginning of the universe, which is without end, or origin or foundation, and which according to the Lord, should be cut with a strong axe, of non-attachment.

Here the term 'Bhūtāni', stands for all the three physical, subtle and causal bodies, because, bodies rather than the soul, are perishable.

'Kūṭastho'kṣara ucyate'— The Lord, here has called the soul 'Akṣara' (imperishable), while in the seventh verse, He called It, His eternal fragment.

---

* In the Gītā the perishable (Kṣara), the imperishable (Akṣara) and the Supreme Person (Puruṣottama) have been used in all the three genders. For example—

(1) Kṣara—	Kṣaraḥ (15/16)— masculine gender
	Aparā (7/5)—feminine gender
	Mahadbrahma (14/3-4)—neuter gender
(2) Akṣara—	Jīvabhūtaḥ (15/7)—masculine gender
	Jīvabhūtām (7/5)— feminine gender
	Adhyātmam (8/3)— neuter gender
(3) Puruṣottama—	Bhartā (9/18)—masculine gender
	Gatiḥ (9/18) —feminine gender
	Śaraṇam (9/18) —neuter gender

The soul, may acquire anybody or may go to any world, but ever remains uniform, without undergoing any modifications (Gītā 8/19; 13/31). Therefore, It has been called 'Kūṭastha', (immutable or unchanging).

In the Gītā, both God and the soul, have been described as possessing the same characteristics. God (in 12/3) has been called 'Kūṭastha' (unchanging) and (in 8/4) 'Akṣara' (imperishable), while here, the soul has been described as 'Kūṭastha' (unchanging), and 'Akṣara' (imperishable). Both of these have identity in essence and character.

The soul, is ever-uniform and according to non-dualistic principle, is the same as God, but becomes the embodied soul by identifying Itself with Nature, and its evolute body etc.

Appendix—In the sixth verse and from the twelfth verse to the fifteenth verse the Lord described the divine entity that has its independent existence, while the earthly entity has no independent existence. The earthly entity seems to exist because of the divine entity. The earthly entity is illumined by the unearthly (divine) entity only. Whatever influence is perceived in the worldly entity, that is all of the divine one. Now in the sixteenth verse the Lord by the term 'loke' describes the 'worldly entity'.

The universe (perishable) and the soul (imperishable)—both are 'laukika' (worldly)—'dvāvimau puruṣau loke kṣaraścākṣara eva ca', and God is different from the two and is singular (unique) viz., is 'alaukika' (divine)—'uttamaḥ puruṣastvanyaḥ' (Gītā 15/17). Karmayoga and Jñānayoga—these two paths are also worldly—'loke'smindvividhāniṣṭha'...........(Gītā 3/3). One who attaches importance to the perishable, should practise Karmayoga while he who attaches importance to the imperishable (soul) should practise Jñānayoga but Bhaktiyoga is 'alaukika' (unworldly) (divine) which pertains to God. The 'aparā prakṛti' described in the seventh chapter has been called here 'kṣara', while the 'parā prakṛti' described in the seventh chapter has been named 'akṣara'.

उत्तमः पुरुषस्त्वन्यः परमात्मेत्युदाहृतः।
यो लोकत्रयमाविश्य बिभर्त्यव्यय ईश्वरः॥ १७॥

uttamaḥ puruṣastvanyaḥ paramātmetyudāhṛtaḥ
yo lokatrayamāviśya bibhartyavyaya īśvaraḥ

But, other than these (Kṣara and Akṣara), is the Supreme Person, called the Supreme Soul, Who, as the indestructible Lord, entering the three worlds sustains all beings. 17

Comment:—

'Uttamaḥ puruṣastvanyaḥ'—The Lord, having described two kinds of persons, the perishable and the imperishable, now mentions, that other than these, is the Supreme Person.*

Here the term 'Anyaḥ' (other), has been used for God, in order to explain, that He is not only different, from the imperishable soul, but also possesses a unique character. So the Lord, in the eighteenth verse, declares that He transcends the perishable, and is even higher, than the imperishable. The soul, in spite of being a fragment of God, is attracted towards the perishable. So God, has been called unique, and other than the soul.

'Paramātmetyudāhṛtaḥ'—The term 'Paramātmā, stands for the Supreme Person, and also denotes, attributeless God, the Supreme Soul, the Soul, of all beings. In this verse, both the term 'Paramātmā', and 'Īśvara', have been used, which means that God without attributes, or with attributes, is one and the same, 'Puruṣottama'.

---

* (1) Brahma (the Absolute) is the Supreme Imperishable Person, superior to Brahmā, the creator; unrevealed, limitless in whom both knowledge and ignorance are established. The perishable matter is known as ignorance while the imperishable soul is known as knowledge. The Supreme Lord Who controls both knowledge and ignorance is different from both of them and is totally unique (Śvetāśvataropaniṣad 5/1).

(2) Nature is perishable while the soul, the embodiment of nectar Which enjoys Nature is imperishable. The Lord controls these two (the perishable and the imperishable) (Śvetāśvataropaniṣad 1/10).

'Yo lokatrayamāviśya bibhartyavyaya īśvaraḥ'—That Supreme Person permeates (enters), the three worlds equally.

Here the term 'Bibharti', means that God sustains all beings, but the soul by an error, having assumed Its affinity for the world i.e., people etc., as their own, takes responsibility upon itself that It sustains beings, and then It has to suffer in vain.*

The Lord is called 'Avyayaḥ' (a + vyayaḥ = no spending or expenditure), because in spite of sustaining, all the world He incurs no expenditure; He has no shortage. He ever remains, uniform.

The term 'Īśvaraḥ', stands for God with attributes, and it means, the controller.

A Vital Fact

Though parents, sustain or nourish a child, yet the child, does not know this fact. Similarly, God nourishes all beings, yet an ignorant person (not having an eye on God), does not realize, this fact. But a devotee, who has taken refuge in Him, knows it very well, that only God sustains, all beings.

As far as sustenance of beings is concerned, God is impartial to a devotee and non-devotee, the sinner and the virtuous, the believer and the non-believer, etc., equally.† It is very well, known to all, that in the universe created by God, the sun equally provides heat and light to all beings, the earth provides space to all beings, the gastric fire, equally digests food of all beings,

* The question of sustenance arises only in the path of devotion rather than in the path of knowledge because in the former path a man (the soul) is regarded as different from God. Therefore, this topic should be regarded as the topic of devotion.

† God showers His grace equally on all beings without any distinction of caste, form, riches and age of beings and without thinking whether they deserve praise or blame.

This great cloud in the form of the innerself is the enjoyer of the inner feelings. Does a cloud while providing rain think whether the receiver is the tree Mimosa catechu or Michelia champacca (Prabodhasudhākara 252-253)?

air is equally available to all beings, for breath, food and water satisfy all beings equally and so on.

Appendix—The Lord calls the Supreme Soul as other because the perishable (world) and the imperishable (soul)—both are laukika (worldly) but 'Puruṣottama' (the Supreme Person) is different from the two and is unique viz., unworldly (divine). Therefore the Supreme Soul (God) is not the subject to be reflected upon but is the subject of faith and belief. In believing the existence of God; devotees, saints, exalted souls, the Vedas and the scriptures are the authority. The term 'anya' has been explained by the Lord in the next verse.

'Yo lokatrayamāviśya.........'— In this expression there is the idea (gist) of the topic described from the twelfth to the fifteenth verses. A man has to perform his duty in the human world but the Lord's field of activities comprises all the three worlds. In fact the Lord has no duty to discharge, yet He is engaged in activities for the welfare of all beings (Gītā 3/22—24).

Link:—The Lord having described His identity, with the Supreme Person, now discloses His secret, when He declares:—

यस्मात्क्षरमतीतोऽहमक्षरादपि चोत्तमः ।
अतोऽस्मि लोके वेदे च प्रथितः पुरुषोत्तमः ॥ १८ ॥

yasmātkṣaramatīto'hamakṣarādapi cottamaḥ
ato'smi loke vede ca prathitaḥ puruṣottamaḥ

As I transcend the perishable and am above the imperishable, I am declared as Puruṣottama (Supreme Person) in the world, as well as in the Vedas. 18

Comment:—

'Yasmātkṣaramatīto'ham'—The Lord declares, that the perishable (Nature) is kaleidoscopic, while He remains the same, without undergoing any modifications. So, He transcends the perishable.

Senses are superior to a body, superior to the senses, is mind, superior to the mind, is intellect (Gītā 3/42). In spite of the superiority, of one to the other, the body, senses, mind and the intellect are insentient, and belong to the same class. But, God, transcends all of them, as He is sentient, while all of them, are insentient.

'Akṣarādapi cottamaḥ'—Though, being a fragment of God, the soul, (the imperishable) has Its identity with God, yet here the Lord, declares that He is superior even to the soul. How? There are few reasons: (1) The soul in spite of being a fragment of God, assumes Its affinity for the perishable Nature (Gītā 15/7) and is deluded by modes of Nature, while God (being beyond Nature) never gets deluded, (Gītā 7/13), (2) God, subduing His own Nature, manifests Himself (incarnates), (Gītā 4/6) while the embodied soul, being under compulsion by Nature, streams forth into being (Gītā 8/19), (3) God ever remains untainted (Gītā 4/14; 9/9), while the embodied soul, has to attain the state of untaintedness (Gītā 4/18; 7/14).

When the Lord declares, that He transcends the perishable, and is even higher, than the imperishable, He also means to mention, that the perishable and the imperishable, are also different. Had they not been different, the Lord would have declared, "I transcend the perishable and the imperishable, or I am higher than the perishable and the imperishable." It proves that the imperishable, also transcends the perishable, and is higher than it, in the same way as God, transcends the perishable and is higher than, the imperishable.

'Ato'smi loke vede ca prathitaḥ puruṣottamaḥ'—Here the term 'Loke', stand for scripture, in which God is celebrated as 'Puruṣottama', (Supreme Person).

The term 'Veda', means pure knowledge, which is

beginningless. The same knowledge was revealed serially, in the form of the Vedas, such as the Ṛk and the Yajuḥ etc. In the Vedas, God has been declared as 'Puruṣottama'.

The Lord, in the preceding verse, declared, "Other than the perishable and the imperishable, is the Supreme Person." So here He discloses the secret, that He is the Supreme Person, celebrated as 'Puruṣottama'.

An Important Fact

(1) The entire universe is perishable, while the soul, the fragment of God, is imperishable. Though the imperishable transcends the perishable, and is higher than it, yet the former errs, by assuming its affinity, for the latter. The body like running water of a river, is flowing continuously, while the soul like a fixed rock, ever remains immovable and detached. A body of childhood, changes into a body of boyhood, but 'I', ever remains the same. But we cannot say which day, childhood ended and boyhood, commenced. Had the imperishable, been kaleidoscopic and perishable, there would have been no question of its repeated birth and death. But in spite of, being uniform and imperishable, it assumes Its affinity for the kaleidoscopic and the perishable, and so, It is repeatedly born and dies. In order to, get rid of this birth and death, the perishable (body etc., should be used in rendering service to the world, to such an extent, that a body, becomes manure in the world-garden. God has bestowed upon a man, objects such as, human body etc., to render selfless service to others, rather than to lay claim on them. Therefore, it is the duty of a man, to use them in the service of others. To regard them as his own, is a blunder. (2) In the fifteenth chapter, the Lord first described the perishable Pīpala tree in the form of a world. Then He inspired, Arjuna to cut off this tree and take refuge, in the Supreme Person. Afterwards He described the soul and mentioned It, as His fragment. Then

(from the twelfth verse to the fifteenth verse) He explained, that the light (splendour) in the sun, the moon, and the fire, is His; and permeating the earth, He supports all beings and having become gastric fire, He digests food; He is seated in the hearts of all; He is the source of memory, knowledge and ratiocinative faculty; He is to be known by the Vedas; He is the author of the Vedānta, and knower of the Vedas. Having mentioned His supreme power, the Lord in this verse, reveals the secret of secrets, that He, Lord Kṛṣṇa, sitting before him, is the Supreme Person known as Puruṣottama.

Lord Kṛṣṇa, by His special grace, disclosed His identity to Arjuna, like a father who addresses his son of his secret treasure, or like an officer who discloses his identity to a person who is seeking him.

Appendix—The Lord has used the term 'yasmāt' (because) here in order to draw attention of the strivers towards His unworldliness (divinity).

'Akṣarādapi cottamaḥ'—the term 'imperishable' has been used for both the Self and Brahma—'akṣaraṁ brahma paramam' (Gītā 8/3). This term always stands for the sentient, it never stands for the insentient.

The perishable (world) and the imperishable (soul) have no independent existence but God has His independent existence. The perishable and the imperishable—both abide in God. But the imperishable (soul), being attached to the perishable, becomes dependent on the latter—'yayedaṁ dhāryate jagat' (Gītā 7/5). God naturally remains detached, He does not become dependent on the perishable—'yasmātkṣaramatīto'ham'. Therefore God is superior even to the imperishable (soul). If the man (soul) instead of being attached to the world, gets attached to God, he will become one with God—'jñānītvātmaiva me matam' (Gītā 7/18).

In salvation a striver gets established in the imperishable (Self) but in devotion, the Supreme Person Who is superior to the imperishable is attained. The Self is a fragment while the Supreme Person is the whole.

Link:—The Lord, now in the next verse, concludes the topic of unswerving devotion, mentioned in the twenty-sixth verse of the fourteenth chapter, for attaining which, the world, the soul and the Supreme Person, have been described in detail in this chapter.

यो मामेवमसम्मूढो जानाति पुरुषोत्तमम्।
स सर्वविद्भजति मां सर्वभावेन भारत॥१९॥

yo māmevamasammūḍho jānāti puruṣottamam
sa sarvavidbhajati māṁ sarvabhāvena bhārata

He, who undeluded, knows Me as the Highest Person, is the knower of all and he worships Me, with all his being O Arjuna. 19

Comment:—

'Yo māmevamasammūḍhaḥ'—The soul, is an eternal fragment of God. When It realizes Its real affinity for God, it means, that It is, undeluded.

Delusion is a stumbling block, to the real knowledge of the world, or of God. The reality, about a thing can be known, only when a man has neither attachment nor aversion, to it. This attachment or aversion, is delusion.

When a man knows the world in reality, he (the self) realizes his identity with God, and when he knows the reality about God, he realizes, that he (the self), is different from the world. It means that he renounces his assumed affinity for the world, having known the reality about the world, and realizes his real affinity for God, having known the reality about God.

A man, can possess unswerving devotion only, when he does not assume his affinity for the world.

'Jānāti puruṣottamam'—The man, who is totally free from

delusion, knows that God, is the Highest (Supreme) Person.

He, who regarding the Supreme Person as the Supreme Lord Who, transcends the perishable, has an inclination to Him and considers Him as his own, he knows Him, really as the Supreme Person.

He, who comes to know that the whole power or influence or splendour, that is either seen or heard in the world, is God's, his attraction towards the world totally perishes. If there is the least attraction for the world, it means, that he has not firmly admitted the existence of God, or His power.

'Sa sarvavidbhajati māṁ sarvabhāvena bhārata'—For him, who knows God as the Supreme Person, having no doubt or confusion, nothing remains to be known, and so the Lord calls him, the knower of all.*

Nothing remains to be known for the person, who has known God, even if he is illiterate or less educated.

Such a person, who knows the Supreme Person, is the knower of all and he worships God, with all his being.

When a person, knows that God transcends the perishable, his mind (attachment) deviates from the world, and is concentrated on God. When he knows Him higher than the imperishable, his intellect (faith), is absorbed in God.†

Then God is worshipped, through each of his inclinations and actions. Thus worship to God, with all being is 'unswerving devotion.'

So long as a man, is attached to mundane objects, such as the body, senses, mind and intellect etc., he cannot worship God with all his being, because a man has an automatic inclination,

* O gentleman! He who knows God Who is imperishable, is omniscient and such a person enters the Supreme Lord (Praśnopaniṣad 4/11).

†The mind is concentrated on the object or topic it is attached to and the intellect gets absorbed in it if there is faith (belief).

to an object, he is attached to.

When a striver, accepts the fact 'I am God's and only God is mine', God is automatically worshipped by him, with all his being. Then all the activities (sleeping, waking, speaking, walking, eating and drinking etc.,) are undertaken by him, in order to please God, rather than for himself.

As 'knowing' plays an important role in the path of knowledge, so does assumption, play an important role in the path of devotion. Firm assumption, free from doubt, is 'knowing' (knowledge), in the path of devotion. When a devotee, believes that God is the Supreme Person, he worships Him with all his being, (Gītā 10/8).

When a person holds that God, is the Supreme Person, he becomes a knower of all; then there is no doubt, that the person who worships God, with all his being, will know Him, as the Supreme Person.

Appendix—'Yo māmevamasammūḍho jānāti puruṣottamam'—He, who knows God is really undeluded (Gītā 10/3) but he who does not know God is deluded—'avajānanti māṁ mūḍhāḥ' (Gītā 9/11).

'Sa sarvavidbhajati māṁ sarvabhāvena bhārata'—The perishable and the imperishable—both are fragments of the entire form of God, therefore he who is the knower of these two, is not the knower of all (omniscient). But the person who knows the Supreme Person, Who transcends the perishable and is superior to the imperishable, is the knower of all viz., is the knower of the entire form of God. Such an omniscient devotee remains engaged in God in everyway by doing different duties—'sarvathā vartamāno'pi sa yogī mayi vartate' (Gītā 6/31); because from his view-point there is no other entity at all besides God.

In the Gītā, the term 'sarvavit' (knower of all) has been used only for a devotee. A devotee knows the entire viz., the worldly and the unworldly (divine)—both, therefore he is 'sarvavit'. Within the worldly, the unworldly (divine) cannot be included but within the unworldly, the worldly is included. Therefore the knower of the attributeless God (Imperishable) is not the knower of all but the devotee who knows the entire form of God is the knower of all.

Link:—According to the principle of Arundhatī (moving from the gross to the subtle) the Lord, first described the perishable, then the imperishable and finally, the Supreme Person. He also affirmed Himself to be the Supreme Person. Now in the next verse, He explains the purpose of this description.

इति गुह्यतमं शास्त्रमिदमुक्तं मयानघ।
एतद्बुद्ध्वा बुद्धिमान्स्यात्कृतकृत्यश्च भारत॥ २०॥

iti guhyatamaṁ śāstramidamuktaṁ mayānagha
etadbuddhvā buddhimānsyātkṛtakṛtyaśca bhārata

Thus, this most secret Śāstra has been taught by Me, O sinless one. By knowing this essence a man becomes wise and nothing remains to be done and what must be acquired, is acquired by him, O Arjuna. 20

Comment:—

'Anagha'—Arjuna has been called sinless, as he is free from a carping (cavilling) spirit. Cavilling is a sin, which defiles the mind. He who is free from the cavilling spirit deserves devotion.

A secret, is disclosed only to a person, who is free from a cavilling spirit.* If the secret is disclosed to the person who cavils, it may have a contrary effect on him, i.e., he may find fault even in the speaker that the latter eulogises himself and

* In the first verse of the ninth chapter Lord Kṛṣṇa promised Arjuna that He would declare to him who did not cavil the greatest secret. Here in the fifteenth chapter also the most secret doctrine has been taught by the Lord. So here the term 'Anagha' stands for the person who does not cavil.

deludes others. Thus a man, who finds fault may have a fall.

A man cavils, because of his pride. Actually a man suffers from the defect, he is proud of. So he starts seeing that defect, in others. As soon as, a man is proud of his virtue, he starts finding fault with others, and when he finds faults with others, he is proud of his virtues.

If the Lord calls Himself the Supreme Person, before a man who cavils, he will not believe Him. He will rather think, that He is boastful and so He, is praising Himself.

Those who cavil at God have a fall. Therefore God and saints, do not disclose secrets to those who cavil, and who are without faith (Gītā 18/67). In fact profound secrets are not passed on to those, who cavil.

Arjuna has been addressed as 'Anagha', because the most profound secret has been revealed before him who is upright and free from cavilling spirit.

'Iti guhyatamaṁ śāstramidam'—The expression 'Iti, idam' (thus, His), denotes the conclusion of the topic of, the perishable, the imperishable and the Supreme Person, described, from the first to the nineteenth verses of the fifteenth chapter, after describing unswerving devotion, in the twenty-sixth verse of the fourteenth chapter.

In this chapter Lord Kṛṣṇa, having described the perishable (world) and the imperishable (soul), explained His splendour, power and influence, (from the twelfth to the fifteenth verses). Then He disclosed the secret that He is the Supreme Person, Who transcends the perishable and is higher, than the imperishable.

God incarnates, like an actor in a play. He plays the role of a human being, in such a way that ignorant people do not know Him (Gītā 7/24). They think that He is a common mortal, like other ordinary human beings, who is born on account of actions, of the previous birth. Generally, an actor in a play does not disclose his identity. But the Lord in this chapter (in the eighteenth verse), has disclosed His identity by declaring that He is the Supreme Person. Therefore, the chapter has been called, the most secret.

In the 'Śāstra' generally, there is description of the world, the soul and God (the Supreme Person). As there is a description of all these three in the fifteenth chapter, this chapter has been called 'Śāstra.'

Though the Gītā, is the gist of all the 'Śāstras', i.e., the scriptures, only this chapter, has been called 'Śāstra' (the scripture). As in this chapter, there is, preeminently the description of 'Puruṣottama' (the Supreme Person), this chapter has been called the most secret scripture. In this chapter, there is an account of six methods of knowing Him:—

(1) To know the reality, about the world (Verse 1).

(2) To take refuge in God, having renounced the assumed affinity for the world (Verse 4).

(3) To perceive Him, as established in the self (Verse 11).

(4) To know Him, through the study of Vedas (Verse 15).

(5) To worship Him, by all one's being (heart), by regarding Him as the Supreme Person (Verse 19).

(6) To know the essence, of the whole chapter (Verse 20).

It is appropriate to call this chapter 'Śāstra', because easy methods, for God-realization, have been described in this chapter.

'Mayā uktam'—The Lord declares, that this most secret teachings has been taught out of His special grace by Him, the Supreme Person, Who is the illuminator and base of the entire world, Who is seated in the hearts of all, Who is to be known by the Vedas and Who is higher, than the perishable and the imperishable. No one, can describe Him, in the way He has described Himself, because first anyone can know Him by His special grace only, and then he can describe Him to some extent, while, He can give a real description of Himself, as His knowledge is perfect.

In fact, no one else, except God can know Him perfectly, (Gītā 10/2, 15). In the thirty-ninth verse of the sixth chapter, Arjuna said to Lord Kṛṣṇa, "No one else than Thyself, can dispel my doubt." Here the Lord, seems to declare, that there is no question of doubt, about the, teaching which He has taught to him.

'Etadbuddhvā buddhimānsyātkṛtakṛtyaśca bhārata'—In the whole of this chapter, the Lord has described the reality about the world, the nature of the soul and the matchless influence, and secrecy about Himself. So the term 'Etat', denotes all this (or specially what has been described in the nineteenth verse). He, who knows this most secret, teaching, is wise i.e., for him nothing remains to be known, because he has known the Supreme Person, Who is worth knowing.

Having known God, a man's delusion is destroyed.Without knowing Him, even having known, all arts, scripts, sciences and languages etc., a man remains deluded, because all mundane knowledge is perishable and imperfect. All arise from God. So how can they illumine their source, God? Even if a person ignorant of worldly knowledge as described above, realizes God, then he is really, a man of knowledge.

The devotee, who is undeluded, who worships Him, with all his being, and who is a knower of all, as described, in the nineteenth verse, has been called wise.

Here, the term 'Ca' denotes, that nothing remains to be gained (acquired) by the devotee who worships God with all his being i.e., with unswerving devotion, as described in the preceding verse. "There is no gain, equal to devotion" (Mānasa 7/112/4). Therefore, nothing remains to be gained by a devotee, who has attained devotion.

For him who knows God, either through the path of action, of knowledge or of devotion, nothing remains to be done, to be known and to be gained by him, and his human life truly is successful.

Appendix—The Lord in this chapter has revealed Himself in the form of the Supreme Person viz., in His divine entire form, therefore this chapter has been called the most secret Śāstra (scripture).

Nothing remains to be done by a man by Karmayoga, nothing remains to be known by Jñānayoga and nothing remains to be attained by Bhaktiyoga. I have to do nothing for myself—having realized this fact, nothing remains to be done for a man. The body is not mine, I have no possession over it and I have no connection with it—having realized this fact, nothing remains to be known to a man. I need nothing—having realized this fact, nothing remains to be attained by a man. The term 'buddhimān' used in the verse denotes the notion that the striver has known what was to be known. In the preceding verse the expression 'sa sarvavidbhajati māṁ sarvabhāvena bhārata' denotes that he has attained the attainable viz., nothing remains to be attained by him. In this verse by the term 'ca' also the additional meaning—'nothing remains to be attained by him' can be taken. The worldly perishable and the imperishable—both have already been gained, therefore only the unworldly—God is to be attained. This verse gives the idea that a devotee attains the aim which is attained both by Jñānayoga and Karmayoga viz., nothing remains to be known to him and also nothing remains to be done by him (Gītā 7/29-30, 10/10-11).

ॐ तत्सदिति श्रीमद्भगवद्गीतासूपनिषत्सु ब्रह्मविद्यायां योगशास्त्रे
श्रीकृष्णार्जुनसंवादे पुरुषोत्तमयोगो नाम पञ्चदशोऽध्यायः॥ १५ ॥

oṁ tatsaditi śrīmadbhagavadgītāsūpaniṣatsu brahmavidyāyāṁ yogaśāstre śrīkṛṣṇārjunasaṁvāde puruṣottamayogo nāma pañcadaśo'dhyāyaḥ

Thus with Oṁ, Tat, Sat, the names of the Lord, in the Upaniṣad of the Bhagavadgītā, the knowledge of Brahma, the Supreme, the science of Yoga and the dialogue between Śrī Kṛṣṇa and Arjuna, this the fifteenth discourse is designated:—"The Yoga of the Supreme Person."

Having understood the topic discussed, in this chapter in

the right perspective, a striver realizes his eternal union, with the Supreme Person (God). So this chapter has been designated: "The Yoga of the Supreme Person."

Words, letters and Uvāca (said) in the Fifteenth Chapter—

(1) In this chapter in **'Atha pañcadaśo'dhyāyaḥ'** there are three words, in **'Śrībhagavānuvāca'** there are two words, in verses there are two hundred and eighty-eight words and there are thirteen concluding words. Thus the total number of words, is three hundred and six.

(2) In **'Atha pañcadaśo'dhyāyaḥ'** there are eight letters, in **'Śrībhagavānuvāca'** there are seven letters, in verses, there are seven hundred and one letters and there are forty-six concluding letters. Thus the total number of words, is seven hundred and sixty-two. In this chapter, out of the twenty verses each of the second, the fourth, the fifth and the fifteenth verses is of forty-four letters, the third verse is of forty-five letters, while each of the remaining fifteen verses, is of thirty-two letters.

(3) In this chapter **'Uvāca'** (said) has been used once, and that is **'Śrībhagavānuvāca'**.

Metres used in the Fifteenth chapter

Out of the twenty verses of this chapter, the second, the third and the fourth—these three verses are of **'upajāti'** metre; the fifth and the fifteenth— these two verses, are of **'indravajrā'** metre. Out of the remaining fifteen verses in the first and third quarters of the seventh 'ra-gaṇa' being used, there is **'jātīpakṣa-vipulā'** metre; in the first quarter of the ninth verse and in the third quarter of the twentieth verse 'ra-gaṇa' being used there, is **'ra-vipulā'** metre; in the third quarter of the eighteenth verse 'ma-gaṇa' being used, there is **'ma-vipulā** metre, and in the third quarter of the nineteenth verse 'na-gaṇa' being used there is **'na-vipulā** metre. The remaining ten (1,6,8,10—14, 16-17) verses are possessed of the characteristics of right **'pathyāvaktra'**, Anuṣṭup metre.

|| Shri Hari ||

Sixteenth Chapter

INTRODUCTION

Lord Kṛṣṇa, in the fifteenth verse of the seventh chapter, explained in brief, the traits of a person possessing the demoniac nature, by declaring that those evil-doers who are foolish and who have embraced the demoniac nature, do not, worship Him. In the sixteenth verse, He explained in brief that those possessing divine nature such virtuous men, worship Him. In the beginning of the eighth chapter, Arjuna put seven question based on the last two verses of the seventh chapter. The Lord answered those questions, in the whole of eighth chapter.

The Lord at the beginning of the seventh chapter, had promised that He would unfold to him the knowledge, together with realization. So He started the ninth chapter. In the twelfth verse of the ninth chapter, He explains that senseless persons, with vain hopes, futile actions and fruitless knowledge, embrace a nature which is demoniac, while in the thirteenth verse He declared that great souls, who know Him as the prime cause of creation and worship Him, constantly with undivided mind, possess a divine nature. Then the Lord, upto the eleventh verse of the tenth chapter, described the topic of knowledge and of realization.

After the eleventh verse of the tenth chapter, the Lord should have described the divine and demoniac natures in detail, but Arjuna having been influenced by His grace, offered praises to Him and prayed to Him to tell him of His divine glories. While explaining His divine glories, the Lord in the last verse of the tenth chapter declared, "What need is there, O Arjuna, for detailed knowledge? I stand supporting the whole universe with a single fragment of Myself." So Arjuna, at the beginning of the eleventh chapter, out of curiosity prayed to the Lord, to reveal to him, that cosmic form.

Having revealed to Arjuna His cosmic form, the Lord in the fifty-fourth and the fifty-fifth verses of the eleventh chapter, explained the merits of exclusive devotion, and the traits of such a devotee. So, in the first verse of the twelfth chapter, Arjuna inquired "Who are considered to be superior, those who are properly engaged in Your devotional service, or those who worship the Imperishable and the Unmanifested?" Therefore, the Lord, in the twelfth chapter, described the devotees, who are properly engaged in His devotional service, and described the attributeless, supreme Brahma, in the thirteenth chapter and upto the twentieth verse of the fourteenth chapter. In the twenty-first verse of the fourteenth chapter, Arjuna asked, "What are the marks of him, who has risen above the three guṇas (modes)? What is his conduct like? How does he transcend the three modes?" In response to his questions, the Lord explained about exclusive devotion, the means to rise above the three modes i.e., He gave a hint of divine nature, through exclusive devotion and of demoniac nature, through adulterated devotion. He started the fifteenth chapter, in order to explain how to develop that exclusive devotion.

In the third verse of the fifteenth chapter, there is a mention of cutting down Pīpala tree with a weapon of detachment (i.e., renunciation of attachment) which is a mark of divine nature. In the fourth verse, there is description of divine nature in the expression "I seek refuge, in the Primal Person." It means, that those who do not seek refuge in Him, are of demoniac nature. In the nineteenth verse, there is a description of divine nature, when the Lord declares,"The undeluded person who thus knows Me as Supreme Person, worships Me with his whole being." It means, that those who do not worship Him, are of demoniac nature.

Thus, Lord Kṛṣṇa, could not get an opportunity to explain in greater detail, the divine and demoniac natures, because Arjuna went on putting questions. Now He gets an opportunity to explain the divine and demoniac natures in detail, so He starts the topic.

श्रीभगवानुवाच

अभयं सत्त्वसंशुद्धिर्ज्ञानयोगव्यवस्थितिः ।
दानं दमश्च यज्ञश्च स्वाध्यायस्तप आर्जवम् ॥ १ ॥

śrībhagavānuvāca

abhayaṁ sattvasaṁśuddhirjñānayogavyavasthitiḥ
dānaṁ damaśca yajñaśca svādhyāyastapa ārjavam

The Blessed Lord said:

Fearlessness, purity of mind and heart, steadfastness in yoga, for knowledge, charity, self-control, sacrifice (yajña), study of the scriptures (svādhyāya), austerity (tapa) and straightforwardness. 1

Comment:—

[The Lord, in the nineteenth verse of the fifteenth chapter, declared, "The undeluded person, who thus knows Me as the Supreme Person, worships Me with his whole being." It means, that he worships the Lord, with exclusive devotion. Thus when a devotee has only the aim of God-realization, divine nature is revealed in him, naturally. Therefore, the Lord in the first three verses, describes divine nature pertaining to sentiment, conduct and glory.]

'Abhayam'*— Nervous excitement, caused by the thought of losing something which is agreeable, and meeting with something, which is undesirable, is called fear. Total absence of this sort of fear, is fearlessness.

---

* The Lord mentions fearlessness as the first quality because he who worships the Lord with his whole being by taking refuge in Him becomes totally fearless (Vālmīki Rāmāyaṇa 6/18/33).

Fear can be of two types—(1) External (2) Internal.

(1) External:— (a) A man is afraid of thieves, robbers, lions, and snakes etc., because he identifies himself with his body. But when he realizes, that he is different from the perishable body, he has no fear.

Fear caused in giving up bad habits, of smoking and drinking and leaving the company of friends addicted to vice, is because of one's own cowardly nature. This fear, is removed by abandoning cowardice.

(b) A person is afraid, lest he should act against the will of parents, teachers and saints and against the ordinance of scriptures. In reality, this is no fear. This fear, leads to fearlessness. Actually this sort of fear, is desirable for a striver, because it leads him to spiritual progress.

(2) Internal:— (a) When a man, wants to perform forbidden actions, which involve sin, injustice and atrocity etc., he is full of fear. He performs such evil deeds, so long as, he assumes his affinity with the body, and wants to maintain the body and to gain honour, pleasure and prosperity etc.* But, when he realizes, that the only aim of human life is God-realization† he is freed from evil deeds, and forbidden actions, and he becomes totally free, from fear.

(b) When a man is engaged in evil deeds, he is full of fear. For example, human beings, gods, demigods and devils, were afraid of Rāvaṇa but when he abducted Sītā, he was filled with

---

* In mundane pleasures there is fear of diseases, in high family there is fear of downfall, in riches there is fear of the king, in honour there is fear of destitution, in power there is fear of enemy, in beauty there is fear of agedness, in the scriptures there is fear of debate, in virtues there is fear of evil persons and in the body there is fear of death. Thus all the worldly things are full of fear, it is only dispassion which is free from fear (Bhartṛharivairāgyaśatakam).

† The aim of human life is decided before this human life is bestowed upon us. We have to realize that aim, rather than to decide it.

fear. Similarly, there was no effect of the sound of the musical instruments, such as conchs etc., of the eleven Akṣauhiṇī army, of the Kauravas on the Pāṇḍavas army (Gītā 1/13), but, when the musical instruments of the seven Akṣauhiṇī army of the Pāṇḍavas blared forth, their sound rent the hearts of the Kaurava army (Gītā 1/19). It means, that the hearts of those who commit sins, and do injustice, become weak and so they are filled with fear. But, when a person having given up injustice etc., purifies his feelings and conduct, his fear disappears.

(c) So long as a human being, does not do, what is worth doing, does not know, what is worth knowing, and does not gain, what is worth gaining, he cannot be totally fearless, fear subsists in him.

The more, a striver believes in God and the more, he depends on Him, the more fearless, he becomes. He thinks, that he being a fragment of the Lord, is imperishable, and so there is nothing to be afraid of, while the bodies and the worldly objects are decaying and perishing every moment. By having this discrimination, fear perishes and a striver, becomes totally fearless.

By accepting affinity for the Lord, a person, has no attachment to the body and family etc. Having become freed from attachment, a man is not afraid of death, and he becomes fearless.

'Sattvasaṁśuddhiḥ'— Purity of mind, or purity of heart is 'Sattvasaṁśuddhi'. When a person is detached from the world and is attached to the Lord, his heart is purified. As soon as, he decides the aim of his life as God-realization, his heart becomes pure, because, the aim of attainment of perishable things, causes impurity in the form of sin, distraction and obscurity, (ignorance). In the scriptures, actions without desire for their fruit, worship and knowledge respectively, have been said to be, the means to do away with this threefold impurity. The best means, to purify the heart or the mind, is that it should not be regarded, as one's own.

In order to, do away with one's sins, there is no need for

expiation. A striver, should follow, the spiritual path zealously and promptly. By doing so, his sins will perish and his heart, will become pure.

A striver, has a notion that spiritual activities such as devotion and adoration etc., are different from professions, such as business, etc., viz., these are two different divisions. He believes, that foul means, such as falsehood and fraud etc., have to be adopted in practical life, in business etc. This sort of attitude makes the heart very impure. So a striver, does not advance in the spiritual sphere quickly. Therefore a striver, should be cautious, that he does not incur any sin.

When a crime is committed by an error, a striver, holds himself responsible, for it. So his heart, becomes impure. He should determine, never to commit that error again. Similarly, he holds other persons responsible, for doing evil to him. He should forgive those persons voluntarily, and should pray to God to forgive them, because he had received the fruit of his past actions through them, those persons have become only an instrument. By doing so, the heart or the mind, is purified.

'Jñānayogavyavasthitiḥ'—It is inevitable for a striver, to be fixed in Yoga, in order to have true knowledge of God, whether He is endowed with attributes or He is without attribute. Yoga, means equanimity (evenness of mind), in gain and loss, honour and dishonour, praise and blame etc.

'Dānam'— 'Dāna' (charity), consists in giving away (so-called) one's own things in a disinterested manner, as a matter of duty to others, according to place, time and circumstances etc. A piece of land, a cow, a piece of gold, grain and a piece of cloth, can be offered as charity. Out of these the foremost place, goes to the charity of grain. But charity in the form of fearlessness, is superior even to it. It can be divided into two classes.

(1) To make a man fearless, when he is in difficulties and troubles, by helping him according to one's power and resources.

(2) To free an entangled man, from the cycle of birth and death, by narrating the life story of the Lord,* the publication of sacred texts such as the Gītā, the Rāmāyaṇa and the Bhāgavata, their sale at a nominal rate, delivering of divine discourses, to enable him to attain salvation. The Lord, is very much pleased with this sort of service (Gītā 18/ 68-69). Such service, is the best of all the other, charities. But, while holding divine discourses, the speaker should not regard himself, as superior to others. He should think, that the Lord, in the form of audience, is giving him an opportunity, to make proper use, of his time.

A striver, should offer charity with the feeling that the Lord Himself, has offered the charity, by making him a tool. So, he should offer it to the needy persons, with the feeling, that it is his duty to offer gifts, to them.

'Damaḥ'—'Dama' consists in controlling one's senses. One should not perform, any forbidden action with senses, body and mind. Actions should be performed, according to ordinance of scriptures, by renouncing selfishness and pride, for the welfare of others. By doing so, senses are controlled, attachment and dependence, come to an end and one's body and senses act, in a pure manner.

When a striver's aim, is sense-control, he discharges his duty by performing actions, which are sanctioned by scriptures. Thus, he becomes free from pride, attachment and desire etc. Thus he is purified, and his senses are controlled.

'Yajñaḥ'—It means, (yajña) offering daily oblation to sacred fire. Performance of 'Balivaiśvadeva' (offering a portion of the daily meal to creatures), according to one's caste, is also sacrifice.

* O Lord, the nectar of Your life history provides life and peace to the distressed beings. The great souls describe it by heart. It destroys all the sins and causes auspiciousness. The saints have described it in detail. Those who narrate it on the earth, they are specially charitable to the world i.e., they do the greatest good to the world (Śrīmadbhā. 10/31/9).

Besides it, from the view-point of Gītā performance of one's duty, according to one's caste, social order (stage of life) and circumstances, is also sacrifice (yajña), provided it is for the welfare of others, and is free from selfishness and pride. In addition, to these one's profession, daily routine, obedience to parents, teachers and elders, reverence to cows, Brāhmaṇa (the persons of the priest class), gods and the Lord, is also sacrifice (yajña), provided there is no desire for the fruit.

'Svādhyāyaḥ'—'Svādhyāya' includes chanting of the Lord's name, and study of sacred books, such as the Gītā, the Bhāgavata, the Rāmāyaṇa and Mahābhārata etc. In fact 'Svādhyāya', means the proper study of one's dispositions and situation viz., introspection. A striver, should be very cautious. He should not judge his progress, through changing propensities. Actually, these dispositions (propensities), always undergo modifications, they appear and disappear. So should a striver, not purify these? One must purify them. They can be easily and quickly purified, when a striver, ceases to regard them, and the inner sense, as his own. To regard them as one's own is impurity at the root. The self, being a fragment of the Lord, is pure and it has never got tainted. Affinity with dispositions, veils Self-realization. If we do not feel happy, in good dispositions and sad, in evil dispositions, and never treat these dispositions, as our own, by snapping total connection, with these, we can have, Self-realization.

'Tapaḥ'—Austerity, consists in suffering hardships, such as hunger, thirst, cold, heat and rain etc., and knowingly tolerance of hardships happily, while discharging one's duty, and earning one's livelihood, is real austerity* (tapa) because it destroys sins and provides strength for toleration.

A striver, should not use his austerity, in granting boons, in

*The best austerity consists in welcoming the situation according to favourable or unfavourable circumstances which are caused by the past actions.

hurling curses, in doing evil to others and in satisfying desires. But he should use it, happily in developing power, in order to face obstacles, which hinder his spiritual progress. It is also austerity. During the course of spiritual practice, several hurdles come to his notice. He thinks, that in seclusion and congenial atmosphere, spiritual practice can be easily successful. Not to desire such circumstances viz., not to depend on them, is also austerity. A striver, should never deem his spiritual progress, dependent on favourable circumstances. Instead of having a yearning for favourable circumstances, he should make the best possible use of circumstances, that are available, and go on progressing spiritually. He should try to seek seclusion. But if it is not available, he should be engaged in spiritual practice, happily and zealously by regarding, the available circumstances, as God's gift.

'Ārjavam'—A striver, should be straightforward and simple, in his dealings, without attaching importance, to what the people think of him. He should be upright and simple, in order to attain salvation, even though people regard him, as a fool. Such a person free from deceit, attains salvation. He should harmonize his thoughts, words and deeds, because the thoughts, words and deeds of great souls are harmonized, while those of the vile, are not.

अहिंसा सत्यमक्रोधस्त्यागः शान्तिरपैशुनम्।
दया भूतेष्वलोलुप्त्वं मार्दवं ह्रीरचापलम्॥ २॥

ahiṁsā satyamakrodhastyāgaḥ śāntirapaiśunam
dayā bhūteṣvaloluptvaṁ mārdavaṁ hrīracāpalam

Non-violence, truth, freedom from anger, renunciation, tranquillity, aversion to fault-finding, compassion to living beings, freedom from covetousness, gentleness, modesty and steadiness (absence of fickleness). 2

Comment:—

'Ahimsā' (Non-violence)— Infliction of pain or injury, on any being through body, mind, speech or feeling etc., is violence. Non-injury, is known as non-violence. When a person, instead of having an inclination for the world, has an inclination only, for the Lord, he observes non-violence, in the true sense of the term. But, he who has desire and attachment, to enjoy worldly pleasure and also enjoys them, cannot be free from violence. He degrades himself, and also destroys sense-objects, which he enjoys. He, who enjoys limited worldly enjoyment, considering these as his own, does violence. It is also violence, to regard worldly objects which have been bestowed upon us, for the service of the world, as ours. But, a person, who uses available resources and persons, in the service of the world, without having any attachment for them, becomes free, from violence.

When a person enjoys worldly pleasure with a selfish motive, he inflicts pain, on those needy people who suffer shortage, because they feel miserable and agonised, when they notice the former's, enjoyment. Thus he commits violence. It is because of one's selfishness and enjoyment that he does not care, for others. But, the great souls (saints), who satisfy bare necessities of their life, in order to do, welfare to others, commit no sins or violence (Gītā 4/21), though a person may feel aggrieved, because of his mean mentality and evil nature, when he sees those great souls, satisfying their necessities.

A striver, who is devoted to God, never enjoys sense-objects and so he never, commits violence. He never, inflicts the least pain, on anyone through his body, mind or speech. He is, ever engrossed in the welfare of all beings, without causing pain to anyone even mentally. If anyone becomes a stumbling block, in his spiritual path, he is neither angry with him, nor does he think of doing evil, to him. He being sad invokes the Lord, to remove the stumbling block. But, he has neither anger, envy nor jealousy, against the person who was as obstacle, to his spiritual progress. He becomes, rather more prompt and more alert, because of his inclination towards God. If he bears malice towards a person, who creates an obstacle, it is his obstinacy in his discipline and this shows, his lack of promptness in his practice.

In a striver, there are two traits—1-Promptness 2- Insistence. The former, proves that he has interest in spiritual practice, while the latter shows, that he is attached to spiritual practice. Due to relish, he comes to know of his dificiency, and he develops power to remove that deficiency, and makes an attempt to remove it. But, when there is attachment, there is possibility of a feeling of malice, against the person who creates, the hurdle. The fact is, that if anybody creates an obstacle, it is because of the striver's lack of interest. In case his relish is not lacking, nobody will create any hindrance, but he will become indifferent, to the striver, thinking that the latter is obstinate and so, let him do as he pleases.

As a flower, emits sweet fragrance automatically, so do spiritual molecules emanate from a striver and the environment is purified. His feelings and activities, naturally are helpful for the welfare of all beings. Thus, he perpetrates non-violence. But he who pollutes the environment, through evil feelings and bad conduct, commits, the evil of violence.

'Satyam'—Truth, consists in speaking agreeable words, honestly and faithfully, of what has been heard, seen or experienced, for the welfare of others, and by giving up selfishness and pride. A striver, remains true through his mind, speech and actions, because his only aim, is to realize the Truth namely God.

'Akrodhaḥ'—Excitement caused, in mind to do evil to others, is anger. This burning sensation of the mind finds outer expression in the form of a burning sensation, in the body. Freedom from anger, is 'Akrodha'. If there is no feeling to do evil to others tell them it is mere excitement not angers.

A striver, having God-realization as the aim of his life, is not angry, even with those who do him wrong. He thinks that he is receiving the fruit of his wrong actions, in the form of pain or unfavourable circumstances. Such persons become instrumental in purifying him, of his sins. They are, rather his benefactors, who are warning him to be careful, in future. They are just like a surgeon, who performs an operation on a diseased part, to make it healthy.

A striver, is not angry with those who exhaust his virtues, by praising and serving him. He thinks, that he does not deserve praise or service, and it is out of their good and virtuous nature, that they do so. His virtues are not exhausted, because he does not enjoy their praise or service etc., i.e., he does not derive pleasure, out of these.

'Tyāgaḥ'—Real renunciation, consists in having detachment, from the world. A striver, should have external, as well as internal, renunciation. He should renounce sinful, unjust and evil actions, and should not enjoy worldly pleasures. Besides, he should renounce desire for the perishable, worldly things and objects etc., from his heart. Renunciation of desire, from the heart, is superior to outward physical renunciation. Renunciation, leads to immediate peace (Gītā 12/12).

The desire for perishable, is the main obstacle to one's spiritual progress. When a striver, instead of having the aim of gaining worldly pleasures and prosperity, has only an aim for God-realization, his desires go on disappearing. The more, he renounces desire, the more, he advances spiritually.

'Śāntiḥ'—Absence of distractions, which evolve out of attachment and aversion, is tranquillity or placidity. A striver, remains tranquil in unfavourable circumstances, also by thinking, that these destroy sins, and purify his inner sense of favourable circumstances eat away virtues and there is every possibility of degradation, rather than of progress.

If by chance, his tranquillity is disturbed, out of attachment or aversion, he at once becomes cautious, that being a striver, he should not be affected, either by attachment or aversion. Thus tranquillity, is regained and with passage of time, it is fixed.

'Apaiśunam'—Exposing the faults of others, is 'Paiśuna' and total absence of this tendency is 'Apaiśuna'. When a man aims at God-realization, he does not expose, the faults of others. The more and more, a striver advances spiritually the more, his feelings of malice and backbiting, are lessened and pure feelings develop. Feelings of pride, do not haunt him. He does not regard anyone inferior to him, because he knows that no one has any affinity with Matter (Nature), the affinity is only, assumed. So, how can he expose the faults, of anyone?

A striver, following the Discipline of Devotion, beholds the Lord, pervading everywhere, a striver following the Discipline of Knowledge, remains established in the self i.e., beholds the self alone everywhere while a striver, following the Discipline of Action sees the served everywhere. So, how can a striver, find fault with others.

'Dayā bhūteṣu'—The urge to relieve a being of his suffering, is 'Dayā' (compassion). The Lord, saints, strivers and common men, all possess this urge for compassion, but it is of different types.

(1) The Lord's compassion:—The Lord showers His compassions, on all beings, in order to, purify them. The Lord's compassion is of two types—(a) To create unfavourable circumstances, to purge them of their sins is 'Kṛpā' (b) to create favourable circumstances, is 'Dayā.'

(2) The saints' compassion:— The saints are sad, and happy, with the sadness and happiness, of other beings. Their mercy, is pure and holy. In fact, they are neither grieved, through their own suffering nor through the sufferings, of others. They behold the Lord's grace, in their own unfavourable circumstances. They take upon themselves the sufferings of others, in order to make

them happy. Indra, the king of gods, beheaded the innocent sage Dadhīci, out of anger. But, when Indra demanded his bones for his own safety, the latter sacrificed his life, and gave his bones, to the former. Thus, they sacrifice their life, in order to do good, to others even though, other persons do wrong to them. Similarly, Karṇa offered his skin and Śibi offered his flesh, for the welfare of others, like the clouds, which offer their life for the good of others.

(3) Strivers' compassion:— A striver, tries his best to remove the sufferings of other beings. His heart melts, when he sees the sufferings of others. He has a feeling, that all should be liberated, and all should get bliss, no one should suffer. His mind, is filled with these sentiments. He also makes efforts, for the same. But he does not feel elevated and is not proud in anyway, by doing so. When he beholds people, performing sinful actions, he instead of being angry, with them, takes pity upon them, and tries his best to save them, from such sins. He also prays to God, to free them from their sins. He thinks and acts, for their welfare. By finding himself weak, he invokes the Lord, "O Lord, let them be relieved of their sufferings, and be, Your devotees."

(4) Compassion of common men:—A common man, pities other persons with feelings that he is very kind and good. He considers himself superior, to others and expects to receive honour and praise etc., as a reward for his compassion. He shows mercy, with a feeling of vanity. In that mercy, the element of mercy is good, while the feeling of pride, is an impurity.

There are other common men, who pity only those who belong to their family, sect or religion etc. This sort of mercy, is more impure because of feelings of mineness and partiality. Those who pity others, for their selfish motive, are even more inferior to them.

Thus, compassion of common people, is impure.

'Aloluptvam'— The attraction of senses, towards the objects of senses, when they come in contact, or when one sees other beings enjoying them, is 'Loluptvam' (Covetousness), and the total absence of this sort of covetousness, is 'Aloluptvam' (freedom from covetousness).

The means, that to be free from covetousness:

(i) A striver, should neither enjoy worldly pleasures nor be proud, that he has controlled his senses.

(ii) He should always think, that his aim is God-realization. If sometime he feels any attraction or excitement, he should, invoke the Lord, "O Lord, save me, protect me."

(iii) He should not watch the lustful actions of living beings. However if they come to his sight, he should think that they are gateways to hell and eighty-four lac forms, of lives, but he has to be free from the cycle of birth and death, and, to attain salvation. Such thinking is necessary to guard him. It should be kept intact.

'Mārdavam'—Lack of sternness, viz., mildness of mind, even for those, who have feelings of enmity towards him, and who trouble him is 'Mārdavam'.*

A striver, is mild and gentle, even toward the evil-doers. He tries his best to be mild, in feelings and speech, for all beings. Sometimes strivers, following different paths, as of Action, Knowledge and Devotion, may not appear equally mild, in their dealings, but all of them are very mild, at heart.

'Hrīḥ'—'Hrīḥ', is shame or hesitation, felt in the performance of actions, contrary to ordinance of scriptures and society, either in loneliness or in company. When a striver, changes his egoism and accepts that he is a devotee, or a striver whose aim is God-realization, he hesitates, in performing forbidden actions.

---

* 'Ārjavam' is used when there is prominence of the body while 'Mārdavam' is used when there is prominence of the mind.

'Acāpalam'—Absence of fickleness is 'Acāpalam'. If anyone is fickle, it does not mean, that the work is done quickly by him. When a person, of the mode of goodness, performs an action with steadiness, and patience, by giving up fickleness, it is performed, properly and promptly. When work is done well, he becomes free from anxieties, and worries. In the absence of fickleness, there attaches no evil of procrastination. As he has no desire, besides performing his duty, his mind does not get bewildered and volatile (Gītā 18/26).

तेजः क्षमा धृतिः शौचमद्रोहो नातिमानिता।
भवन्ति सम्पदं दैवीमभिजातस्य भारत॥ ३॥

tejaḥ kṣamā dhṛtiḥ śaucamadroho nātimānitā
bhavanti sampadaṁ daivīmabhijātasya bhārata

Radiance, forgiveness, fortitude, purity, freedom from malice and vanity these, O descendant of Bhārata, are the marks of him, who is endowed with divine nature. 3

Comment:—

'Tejaḥ'—The power (vigour), of great men and strivers (endowed with divine traits), whose company enables sinners to renounce their sins and be engaged, in virtuous actions, is called 'Teja'. The evil-doers, hesitate to perform evil deeds before those great men and strivers. These evil-doers, suddenly change their actions and get engaged in virtuous deeds, before men of divine traits. In the face of a man of anger, also, other persons have a feeling of fear, in acting against his will, this is an upshot of anger.

'Kṣamā'—He, who is endowed with the virtue of 'Kṣamā' (forgiveness)* tolerates the offence of others, without having

* What is the difference between 'Akrodha' (freedom from anger) and 'Kṣamā (forgiveness)? When a person is endowed with forgiveness, he has

any inclination to retaliate, although he is strong enough, to take vengeance. A man, may forgive his near and dear ones, because of his attachment to them, but this forgiveness, is not pure. Similarly, a man may forgive a cruel or a strong person out of fear, and he may forgive an officer for the latter's harsh and abusive language, out of selfishness. But, this is not, real forgiveness. A person, who possesses real forgiveness, thinks that the wrong-doer should never be punished, here or hereafter.

A person may ask for forgiveness, in two ways:—

(1) A person asks for forgiveness having done something wrong, in order to escape punishment.

(2) A person asks for forgiveness, having done something wrong, with the intention that he will never do any wrong. This sort of forgiveness, leads to progress.

Now the question arises, as to how to inculcate, forgiveness. The answer is, that if a person does not expect any reward for his actions, from others nor does he wish to do wrong to the wrong-doers, the virtue of forgiveness, develops in him.

'Dhṛtiḥ'—The unwavering steadiness or fortitude, by which one remains balanced, in favourable and unfavourable circumstances, is 'Dhṛti' (Gītā 18/33).

In the mode of goodness, a man possesses the virtue of fortitude, while he loses it, in the mode of passion and ignorance. A striver, who decides the aim of his life, neither gets disheartened in calamities, nor is overwhelmed with joy, in prosperity. He does not divert his attention, by adverse and favourable circumstances. He wants to attain the goal, with unwavering steadiness, like a pilgrim, who on his pilgrimage to Badrīnārāyaṇa, does not care for favourable or unfavourable circumstances, and moves ahead

---

an eye on the offender that he should not be punished, while in 'Akrodha' (freedom from anger) he has an eye on himself that he should be free from anger and burning sensation. Forgiveness includes 'freedom from anger' while 'freedom from anger' does not include forgiveness. Thus both of them are different.

patiently and promptly, to reach his destination.

'Śaucam'—Purity is of two kinds—external and internal.* A striver, having the aim of God-realization, maintains, external purity, because it leads to internal purity, while a person, who has internal purity, cannot tolerate external impurity. Patañjali has said, that a striver, having external purity, hates his body and does not desire to mix with others. It means, that when a striver maintains the purity of his body by clay and water etc., he realizes, that all bodies are impure and so other bodies have no attraction for him i.e., his desire to derive pleasure, out of contact with other bodies perishes.

External purity, is of four kinds:—(1) of the body, (2) of speech, (3) of family, (4) of money.

(1) Physical purity:—Heedlessness, laziness and fashions etc., make a body impure, while promptness, activity and simplicity etc., purify the body. Purity is also achieved, by means of clay and water etc.

(2) Purity of speech:—False, idle, bitter and slanderous talk, makes the tongue (speech) impure. Speech, devoid of these evils, but having true, agreeable, beneficial and necessary words, which lead to spiritual progress of all persons, families, castes, streets and countries, is pure.

(3) Purity of family:—Imparting good education to children, for their welfare, teaching good conduct, impartiality, and discharging one's duty with justice, and sincerity—this is purity of family.

(4) Purity of money:—Money is purified, through just and honest dealings, keeping in mind, the welfare of others, giving it to those who are poor, needy and destitute, and protecting cows, women and Brāhmaṇas. Moreover, it is purified by serving great saints and sages, and by getting sacred books published for the

* Here the term denotes external purity because internal purity has already been discussed in the first verse of this chapter.

sale at a cheap rates, so that there may be easy communication of their teachings.

When a person, has only the aim of God-realization, he himself is purified, and then his body, speech, family and money, are purified. When the body is purified, the atmosphere also becomes pure and then a person realizes, that the body is an abode of impurities and filth, and it is perishable. So, he can easily renounce his egoism, and attachment. Thus, external purity, leads one to God-realization.

'Adrohaḥ'—Absence of malice, hatred or grudge, even towards those, who behave as enemies, is called 'Adroha'.* A person, having a propensity of malice or hatred, wants to take revenge upon, a wrong doer, as and when, he gets an opportunity. But how can a striver, whose aim is God-realization, think of injuring others, by having a grudge against them? A striver, following the Discipline of Action, performs actions for the welfare of all, a striver, following the Discipline of Knowledge, regards everyone as his own self, while a striver, following the Discipline of Devotion, beholds his Lord, in everyone. So, how can he have malice or hatred, for anyone?

'Nātimānitā'—'Mānitā', denotes pride, and 'Atimānitā, denotes excessive pride. A proud man, thinks that he is superior to common people, and so, he is worthy of being honoured by them, while a very proud man, is he who considers himself worthy of being honoured, even by his teachers and parents etc., who should be adored by him. Total negation of this pride, is called 'Nātimānitā'.

This pride or superiority, is of two kinds:—

(i) Mundane:—A man, regards himself as superior to others, in wealth, knowledge, rank, caste, qualities and social order (stage

* There is difference between 'Krodha' (anger) and 'Drohaḥ' (malice). The burning sensation caused in the mind for the wrong-doer is 'Krodha' while the feeling of enmity to take revenge upon him is called 'Drohaḥ'.

of life) etc., and thinks, that he is worthy of being honoured, by others. (ii) Spiritual:—When some divine traits are revealed, in a striver, he considers himself superior to other persons, and other persons also, praise and honour him. But, he considers himself superior, so long as he has some demoniac traits. When he is endowed, only with divine traits, he is not proud of such traits, he becomes free from pride.

So long as, ego persists, a striver perceives some speciality, in him. The more, this egoism is purged, the more, the feeling of speciality, vanishes. In the long run, in the absence of self-conceitedness, divine traits of 'Nātimānitā' (freedom from pride), are revealed, in him.

A striver, should aim to arouse divine nature, fully in him. Due to difference in nature, in different persons, variance in virtues remains. But lack of virtue, pains a striver. So, by depending on God, he should go on making efforts, to root out demoniac traits. By doing so, by God's grace, divine nature, is revealed in him.

'Bhavanti sampadaṁ daivīmabhijātasya bhārata'—These, are the marks of him, who is endowed with divine nature. When a person, fixes his aim as God-realization, divine nature, is revealed in him. Some divine traits, are also aroused, because of latencies of past births. But, a striver, does not regard those divine traits, as his own; he thinks that the Lord has bestowed upon him, those divine traits, by His grace. So he is not proud, of them.

Actually, divine nature, is not personal, it belongs to the Lord. Had it been personal, a person, would have possessed it forever. But it is not so. When a person regards it, as his own, he has pride, which is a mark of a wicked nature. This pride, gives birth, to all the other traits of such nature. If a person, possesses only divine traits, he cannot be proud, of them. He is proud of them, only when he is endowed with bad nature also. Suppose a man is proud of truth in speech, it means, he also tells a lie, besides speaking the truth. Thus a man, is proud of his divine traits, regarding these, as his own, and thereby having demoniac traits in him. When virtues, in totality are inculcated, there cannot be any pride, of those virtues.

Divine nature is the Lord's, own. So when a devotee, depends on Him only, His divine nature, is naturally revealed in him. Lord Rāma in the Rāmacaritamānasa, declares to Śabarī that a man, woman or creature that has anyone of the nine kinds of devotion, to Him is, very loving to Him.

All the mobile and the immobile creatures, such as human beings, gods, ghosts and evil spirits, beasts and birds, moths, insects and creepers etc., have a desire to live, to maintain their life-breath. This desire, denotes a satanic nature.

Even a detached and dispassionate striver, has a latent desire to live. But he has no covetousness, for sense-objects, as his aim is only God-realization, rather than to nourish his body.

But, when he develops his devotion to God, He becomes dearer to him, than even his life-breath and he addresses Him, as 'the Lord of life-breath' or 'Dearer than life-breath' etc. He can even die, for Him because he cannot bear any separation, from God. He sacrifices, even his life happily for Him, in the same way, as a chaste wife, at the death of her husband, burns herself on her husband's funeral pyre willingly and happily. It means, that when a devotee develops exclusive devotion to God, he is, no more attached to his life, his demoniac nature, totally comes to an end, and divine nature is spontaneously revealed, in him. Gosvāmī Tulasīdāsa, has also mentioned in the Rāmacaritamānasa, that hidden traces of internal impurity, can never be removed without, the water of devotion.

Link:—Having described the marks of a person endowed with divine nature, the Lord in the next verse, discusses in brief the marks, of one who hankers after worldly pleasures and prosperity, and is endowed with a demoniac nature.

दम्भो दर्पोऽभिमानश्च क्रोधः पारुष्यमेव च।
अज्ञानं चाभिजातस्य पार्थ सम्पदमासुरीम्॥४॥

dambho darpo'bhimānaśca krodhaḥ pāruṣyameva ca
ajñānaṁ cābhijātasya pārtha sampadamāsurīm

Hypocrisy, arrogance, pride, anger, harshness and ignorance: these are the marks, O Pārtha (Arjuna), of him who has demoniac (asura) nature. 4

Comment:—

'Dambhaḥ'—'Dambha', consists in making a show of one's virtues, in order to gain honour, fame and praise etc., even when, one does not possess, those virtues. It can be of two kinds:—

(i) A person may pose as a righteous, virtuous, scholarly, wise person, even though he has no such virtues. To show more than he possesses, to show himself as an ascetic, in spite of being sensuous and ostentatious in, feelings and actions—this is hypocrisy. (ii) He may conceal his good conduct, eat forbidden food, and perform forbidden actions, in the company of evil persons, in order to, win respect and praise, by pleasing them.

When a person, attaches too much importance, to his body, life-breath, wealth, property, honour, praise and fame, he pretends, to be what he is not and hypocrisy appears in him.

'Darpaḥ'—It means arrogance, pride of possessions of riches, property, family, rank and position etc., is known as 'Darpaḥ'. Because of this feeling, a man is proud of the things, he possesses.

'Abhimānaḥ'—A man, has pride because of his 'egoism'. A person may regard himself superior and exalted, because of superiority of his physical (gross), subtle and causal bodies. He regards himself superior, to others, because of his high caste, high social order (Āśrama), learning, influence and accomplishment, (Siddhis such as Aṇimā, Mahimā and Garimā etc.). Because of this egoism (pride),* he thinks he can put the entire world upside down.

'Krodhaḥ'—Excitement or burning sensation, caused in the mind, in order to do wrong to others, is 'Krodha' (anger). It appears, when one does something, against a man's wishes. There is difference between 'Krodha' (anger) and 'Kṣobha' (agitation, commotion). When a child does a mischief, and does not obey the parents, they scold him out of 'Kṣobha', so that it may not repeat the mischief again, while in anger, there is tendency to do wrong, to the person with whom one is angry.

A man, has to repent for wrong actions which he performs, overpowered by anger. When he is angry, he harms not only others, but also himself. Moreover, he can do wrong to others, only if they have to suffer it, as fruit of their wrong actions. But, he commits a sin, and spoils his nature. His spoiled nature, will lead him to hell and painful forms of lives.

Anger, is the foremost enemy of a person because it, abiding in the body, destroys the body, in the same way as fire abiding in wood, burns the wood. Everyone including the nearest and the dearest one, is afraid of an angry man. In the twenty-first verse of this chapter, anger has been called, as the gateway to hell. When a man's desire is not fulfilled, anger ensues. From anger, arises delusion; from delusion, a confusion of memory; from which comes, loss of reason; and from loss of reason, one goes to complete ruin (Gītā 2/62-63).

'Pāruṣyam'—It means, harshness or sternness, or a total

*Out of the two terms 'Abhimāna' (pride) and 'Darpa' (arrogance) if one is used, it includes the other term also. But when both are used together independently 'Abhimāna' denotes the feeling of superiority, because of the internal qualities (egoism) while 'Darpa' because of the external possessions (attachment).

negation of mildness. Swaggering or walking with an arrogant air, is bodily harshness. Seeing with harsh eyes, is harshness of eyes. Speaking bitter, taunting and harsh words, constitute harshness of speech. Getting pleased by not helping other creatures, in their adversity is harshness of heart. Vengeance, is harshness in dealings.

A man, with a selfish motive, wants to fulfil his desire by fair means or foul, without thinking, of the trouble of others. So there remains, harshness in his mind, speech, body and behaviour. Out of selfishness, he even commits violence, without thinking of its consequences. With the predominance of self-interest, a man even commits violence. Thus he develops cruelty, in his nature. With cruelty, the serenity of his heart goes away. In the absence of serenity, his dealings become harsh. Thus he engages himself, in extorting money, and harassing others, without caring for the result.

'Ajñānam'—Here 'Ajñāna', denotes ignorance or lack of discrimination. An ignorant man cannot distinguish, the real from the unreal, virtue from sin, and duty from forbidden actions, because he hankers after perishable worldly pleasures and prosperity, without thinking of the consequences. Such ignorant people, like beasts, are given to gratify their life. What ought to be done and what ought not to be done—they cannot know and they do not want to know.

They regard momentary pleasures, which are born of sense contacts, as real pleasure and so make effort to enjoy them. But their fruit, is negative. Instead of pleasure one gets pain.* Even then, he is not warned. He performs forbidden actions, in order to get honour, praise, comfort, wealth and property etc. But,

* O King! people bound by husband-wife relationship etc., perform actions in order to derive pleasure and be free from pain. But those who want to cross the illusion, should think that their actions bear contrary fruits. Instead of enjoying pleasures, they suffer pain; and instead of getting rid of the pain, their pain goes on increasing (Śrīmadbhāga. 11/3/18).

their fruit is disastrous for him, as well as, for the entire world.

'Abhijātasya pārtha sampadamāsurīm'—O Pārtha, these are the marks of a person, who is endowed with demoniac nature.* A person, by identifying himself with the body, has desire to remain alive forever, and enjoy worldly pleasure. The marks of demoniac nature, are seen, in such a person.

In the fortieth verse of the eighteenth chapter, the Lord declares, that there is no creature which is free from the three modes of nature. It proves, that every person in spite of being a fragment of the Lord, is born having affinity with nature (prakṛti). He has the affinity of 'I'ness and mineness with the body, an evolute of Nature; and the affinity of 'Mineness', with things, objects and persons etc., evolutes of Nature. This feeling of, 'I'ness or 'Mineness', is the fundamental mark, of demoniac nature.

A man's relationship with prakṛti, is merely assumed. So he can renounce it. The reason is, that he (the self), is sentient and immutable, while prakṛti is insentient and kaleidoscopic. So, there is no real relationship between the two, it is merely an assumed one. As soon as this relationship is renounced, the demoniac nature, is rooted out. A man, is fully capable of rooting out, demoniac nature.

The more, a man is attached to his life-breath, the more, demoniac traits he possesses. When wicked traits, are on the increase, he harms others, in order to maintain his life-breath, and to enjoy pleasure. He does not, even hesitate to commit murder.

When a man regards, the temporary as permanent, and the unreal as real, all the demoniac traits naturally appear, in him without any effort and they having developed a disinclination for God, lead him to degradation.

---

* Here the term 'Asura' (Demon) denotes those persons who are engrossed in the pleasures born of sense-contacts. It means that such persons instead of having the aim of God-realization hanker after worldly pleasures. Such persons are 'Asura' (Demons) and their nature is demoniac nature.

Link:—The Lord in the next verse, refers the fruit of both the divine and the demoniac natures, and cheers Arjuna by declaring, that he is born with divine nature.

दैवी सम्पद्विमोक्षाय निबन्धायासुरी मता।
मा शुचः सम्पदं दैवीमभिजातोऽसि पाण्डव॥५॥

daivī sampadvimokṣāya nibandhāyāsuri matā
mā śucaḥ sampadaṁ daivīmabhijāto'si pāṇḍava

Divine nature, is conducive to liberation and the demoniac leads to bondage. Grieve not, O Pāṇḍava (Arjuna), thou art born, with divine endowments. 5

Comment:—

'Daivī sampadvimokṣāya'—When a striver, is inclined towards the Lord with a firm determination, he develops, a disinclination for the world. With this disinclination, evil propensities of demoniac nature decrease, and good qualities of divine nature, are revealed. So, he gets interested, in the Lord's name, form, sport (pastime), virtues and life history etc.

The firmer a striver, is in his aim, the more, easily his real affinity, which has been since time immemorial with the Lord, is revealed to him, and so his assumed affinity with the world, perishes. Actually, he has no connection with the world, he has assumed his connection through his identification with the body. He regards the body as 'I', and also as 'mine'. As soon as, he renounces this assumed affinity, the divine nature, which leads to salvation, will be revealed in him.

This divine nature, is conducive not only to one's own liberation, but also to the liberation of all beings. The Lord, has bestowed this human body, so that a person may lead all beings to salvation, in the same way, as the head of a family, looks after the entire family. This human being, has been given such a right by the Lord, that by serving Him, he can even control Him. A striver, should perform, virtuous actions, such as austerity, charity, sacrifice, pilgrimage, fast, chanting, meditation, study of sacred books and retain good company, for the salvation of numberless beings of infinite universes, and should pray to God, from the core of his heart, through these words, "O Lord! Grant exclusive devotion and salvation, to all the beings. This is possible only by Your grace. I can only pray to You by the intellect, provided by You," and should offer his body, senses, mind, intellect, wealth and property etc., to the Lord, for the salvation of the world.* By doing so, he will realize the identity of his possessions, with the world and his natural identity with the Lord, will be revealed. This has been termed by the Lord, by the expression, 'the divine nature is conducive to liberation.'

'Nibandhāyāsurī matā'—The demoniac nature, is conducive to bondage viz., the cycle of birth and death. So long as a striver, does not remove his egoism, his virtuous actions, will not lead him to salvation, even these may lead him to higher regions. It means, that so long as, he has the desire to maintain his body, and to enjoy sense-objects, in his ego the divine traits, superimposed on himself, will not lead him to salvation, though they may bear some pleasant fruit.

The seed of a plant grows, into the tree and fruit of the same category. Similarly, virtuous actions performed by a striver, who has past worldly influences, will bear mundane fruit, in the form of accomplishments, such as 'Aṇimā' and 'Garimā' etc., and higher regions, such as the realm of Brahmā, but they cannot lead to, salvation (Gītā 8/16).

Now the question arises, as to how a man, should attain salvation. The answer is, that as a roasted or boiled seed, does not germinate, similarly, when a striver only has the aim of God-realization, all the worldly seeds perish, his

* The feeling that all beings should attain salvation is the Lord's divine nature, it is not one's own. It is only the Lord Who is one's own.

egoism changes, and he attains salvation.

A person, has attachment for his body, and life-breath, so that he could go on living happily and enjoying honour, praise and pleasure etc. It is because of this attachment, that he cannot attain salvation, because attachment to the modes of nature, is the cause of birth, in good and evil wombs (Gītā 13/21). It means, that he being attached to nature (prakṛti), may go even to the realm of Brahmā, but will not be free, from bondage.

A Vital Fact

The Lord, in this chapter, has mentioned three fruits of demoniac nature. Here in this verse, He mentions the first fruit, as bondage. The worldly minded people, who perform actions, with a desire for their fruit, (as described in the verses from the forty-one to the forty-fourth of the second chapter and also in the twentieth and twenty-first verses of the ninth chapter), also belong to the category of those, whose actions are conducive to bondage. The intellect of those, who hanker after worldly pleasure and prosperity, is many branched i.e., their desires are endless. They perform actions, in order to fulfil their desires, which result in rebirth (Gītā 2/41—44). Similarly, those, who perform sacrifices, in order to gain heavenly pleasure, enjoy heavenly pleasure, being purged of their sins, which were obstacles to the attainment of heaven, having enjoyed extensive heavenly world, return to the world of mortals, on the exhaustion of their merits (Gītā 9/20-21).

Now a question arises, that a striver who falls from Yoga (Gītā 6/41), goes by the same path of the dark fortnight, as a person, having desire for fruit of actions, goes (Gītā 8/25); so the path of a striver, who falls from Yoga, should be conducive to bondage. The answer is, that a striver who falls from Yoga, has no bondage, because in the previous human life, his aim has been to realize God and because of some lust (desire) or unconsciousness or excessive pain, he had to go to heaven etc., instead of realizing God. So the term Yogī, has been used for them (Gītā 8/25), otherwise persons who perform actions, for their fruit cannot be called, Yogīs.

The second fruit, is that people of demoniac nature, fall into a foul hell (Gītā 16/16). Those who, being overwhelmed with desire, commit sins and injustice etc., go to hell, such as 'Kumbhīpāka' etc.

The third fruit of demoniac nature, is that those evil-doers, are hurled into the wombs of demons and then they go to most abominable type of existence, (Gītā 16/19-20).

'Mā śucaḥ sampadaṁ daivīmabhijāto'si pāṇḍava'—Divine nature, leads to salvation while demoniac one, leads to bondage. Lord Kṛṣṇa, explains to Arjuna, that he is born with a divine nature, so that he may not doubt, whether he is born with divine nature, or not.

A striver, having attained divine nature naturally follows the path of Action, Knowledge or Devotion. All the sins of a Karmayogī, through actions and those of a Jñānayogī, through the fire of wisdom, are destroyed (Gītā 4/23,37). But the Lord destroys, all the sins of Bhaktiyogī (Gītā 18/66); and delivers him from, the ocean of birth and death (Gītā 12/7).

'Mā śucaḥ'—Lord Kṛṣṇa, in the third verse, addresses Arjuna as 'Bhārata', in the fourth verse as 'Pārtha', and in the fifth verse as 'Pāṇḍava', in order to encourage him. By addressing him as Bhārata, He means to say, that he belongs to an excellent family; and by addressing him as Pārtha, he says that he is the son of Pṛthā (Kuntī), who served even those who had feelings of enmity towards her. And by addressing him as Pāṇḍava, he wants to emphasize, that he is the son of a righteous and noble father, Pāṇḍu. Thus because of his excellent family, noble and virtuous parents, he possesses a divine nature. So he should not, grieve.

In the Gītā, the Lord has used the expression 'Mā śucaḥ' (Grieve not), two times, once here and once, in the sixty-sixth verse of the eighteenth chapter. The Lord, by using it two times, wants to assure him, that he should not worry, either about the means or the end. He possesses the means, as he is endowed with divine nature (16/5) and he need not worry about the end, because He will liberate him, from all sins (18/66). The Lord, through the medium of Arjuna, assures all strivers, that they need not lose heart by thinking that they do not possess virtue, and so they will not be liberated, from the cycle of birth and death.

Persons, who possess divine nature always think of attaining salvation, in favourable, as well as unfavourable circumstances. When Lord Kṛṣṇa, placed the chariot between the two armies, Arjuna, seeing all his relations there, was filled with compassion and sadness, and he expressed his reluctance to fight. He thought, that sin would accrue to him, by killing his kinsmen, in the war. Thus, he was filled with attachment or delusion, for the family which is of demoniac nature and also, thought of the fear of sin, an obstacle to salvation, which is divine nature.

According to Arjuna, it was a sin to resolve to fight (1/45). Time and again he asked Lord Kṛṣṇa, to tell him of his duty, so that he could attain, to the highest good or salvation, as he was confused (2/7, 3/2, 5/1). This shows his divine nature. On the contrary, Duryodhana etc., and the members of the rival army, saw no sin in the destruction of the family (1/38). So Arjuna, possessed divine nature, from the very beginning. Attachment or delusion, the demoniac nature seen in Arjuna was a temporary phase, of his life, which was destroyed through the Lord's grace (18/73). So here, Lord Kṛṣṇa, advises Arjuna not to grieve.

Arjuna, does not feel that he is endowed, with divine nature. So, Lord Kṛṣṇa says, to him, "Grieve not, because you are endowed with divine nature." The reason is, that noble men do not behold virtues in them, when they become totally free, from vices. As collyrium applied to eyes, cannot be seen, by the eyes, because it identifies itself, with the eyes, similarly, those possessing divine nature, become one with it, so divine traits cannot be seen separately from them. Therefore, Lord Kṛṣṇa, assures Arjuna, that he possesses divine nature naturally, so he need not worry.

A Vital Fact

The Lord by His grace, has bestowed a human body, so that a man may attain salvation. This body, is transitory and perishable, and nothing is certain about it, it may die any moment. So a man should develop divine nature, and renounce demoniac nature.

The term 'Deva', in 'Daivī sampadā', denotes God. Being a fragment of God, a man possesses divine nature, naturally. But, when he (soul), having a disinclination for God, has an inclination for prakṛti (nature) i.e., he identifies himself, with the perishable body etc., demoniac nature manifests, itself in him and all evil propensities, such as lust, anger, greed, delusion, hypocrisy, envy and jealousy etc., arise in him. The desire to maintain life-breath happily, is an important mark, of a man of demoniac nature.

Liberated souls, are totally free from demoniac nature, while all other beings possess, both divine and demoniac nature (16/6). Being a fragment of God, every person possesses divine nature, but sometimes, because of predominance of demoniac nature, divine nature, is concealed.

It cannot perish, because the real, never ceases to be. So far as, liberated souls are concerned, they are totally free, from demoniac traits.* Because of his intrinsic nature a person can never be totally cruel, sinful, vile and corrupt. Even the vilest

* The liberated souls being detached from the perishable get established in imperishable God. Being established in the real (God), virtues automatically prevail in them. These perfected souls rise above the divine traits which are ideal for strivers.

sinner, possesses virtue to some extent. As soon as, divine nature manifests itself, demoniac nature, comes to an end, because divine nature, is imperishable, as it belongs to the Lord, while demoniac nature, is perishable as it pertains to the world.

A man, being a fragment of God, Who is Truth, Consciousness and Bliss solidified, and has a desire to live, to know and to be happy. But, he wants to live with the body, wants to know, with the intellect and wants to be happy, with the help of the body and senses. He wants to fulfil these desires, through the perishable world.

Thus because of his attachment to life-breath, he possesses demoniac nature.* There is one vital point, which needs special attention. He has a desire to live, it means that he (soul), can live alive. He (soul), being a fragment of the Lord, is imperishable but by having affinity of 'I'ness and mineness with the body, he assumes the death of body, as his own death. Similarly, he wants to be wise, with the help of the intellect, and he has a desire to be happy, and maintain his name and fame, even after his death by identifying himself, with the body. But the intellect and the body, are perishable and insentient, while he (soul) is imperishable, and sentient. So, how can the perishable (unreal) and insentient, provide knowledge, (wisdom) and happiness, to the imperishable (real) and the sentient? Thus when he is connected with the unreal, he, in spite of being an embodiment of Truth, Knowledge and Bliss, has desire to live, to gain knowledge and to be happy. He wants these desires, to be fulfilled by the perishable world. Thus demoniac nature is manifested, in him. But when he renounces his affinity with the unreal, the demoniac nature perishes, and divine nature, is revealed in him.

* When a man identifies himself with the body he is attached to the life-breath by having the desire to live happily. This identification gives birth to the demoniac nature. Therefore the embodied who are mentioned in the Gītā by the terms 'Dehavadbhiḥ' (12/5) and 'Dehinam' (3/40; 14/5,7), should be included among those who possess demoniac nature.

When a person,wants to develop divine traits in him, by making effort through devotion, meditation, good company and study of sacred books etc., as a part of his duty, he cannot develop these fully, because whatever is gained by effort is not natural, but is artificial. Moreover, he develops pride, that he has developed these virtues, by his efforts. This pride, is a demoniac trait, which is the root of all evils, and which nourishes evil. Pride persists, in spiritual practice, which is done by effort. When he fails to cultivating the divine traits, he accepts, that it is beyond his control. But, when he realizes, that attachment for the perishable, is the root of demoniac nature, he renounces, this attachment. In that case, divine nature reveals itself in him, because he being a fragment of God, automatically possesses it.

There is one more vital point, which needs attention. A man cannot totally renounce, divine traits. How to know this fact? If a man, decides to speak the truth, he could speak the truth, throughout his life. But if he decides to tell a lie, even for a day, he cannot do so. If someone asks him, whether he is hungry, and he tells a lie, by saying that he is not, he will, have to face a lot of difficulty. But if a person takes an oath, to tell a lie, even if he dies, his oath will prove to be true. Similar, is the case with other divine traits, because all of these are eternal, and natural. A striver, has only to renounce his attachment for the perishable, because attachment to it is assumed, not natural.

Demoniac nature, is unnatural, it appears and disappears, while divine nature is natural. If a man has bad conduct, everybody asks him, why he is behaving, badly. But, no one asks him the reason, when his conduct, is good.

Arjuna specially, possessed divine nature. So Lord Kṛṣṇa asked Arjuna, whence this unmanliness came upon him (2/2-3). It means, that this unmanliness (weakness) was not naturally present, in him. So Arjuna asks Lord Kṛṣṇa, the means to attain to the highest good or salvation (2/7; 3/2; 5/1), even in the battlefield.

It shows, that Arjuna, possessed divine nature, otherwise how could he reject the offer of Urvaśī, a heavenly damsel, outright? Therefore, assuring Arjuna, Lord Kṛṣṇa, asks him not to grieve, because he is born, with a divine nature (16/5).

A feeling of egoism, is born out of the identification of the real, with the unreal. A man performs, virtuous or evil actions, having egoism. When he follows the spiritual path, there remains predominance, of the real in egoism, while there is predominance of the unreal, when he follows a mundane path. Divine nature, is revealed in a person, when there is predominance of the self, and demoniac nature goes on aggravating in him, during the predominance of the non-self. This human body, has been bestowed upon him, to enable him to be free, from demoniac nature. Every human being, is independent and strong to get rid of it. It is because of a person's affinity with the perishable, that he cannot get rid of it.

A man (soul), identifies himself with matter. Actually, there is no desire in a man (pure soul), desire abides, only in the unreal portion of ego. But the soul is said to be, the cause of experience of pleasure and pain (13/20). Actually, the soul is not the cause, but the soul seated in nature, becomes an experiencer (13/21). Actually, the unreal (insentient) undergoes modifications, such as pleasure or pain. But, because the real (sentient), has identification with the unreal. So, the real has to experience, pleasure and pain. As, after marriage wife's needs become the husband's needs, similarly, the soul by identification with, body and thus assuming itself, as a doer has to become the experiencer of pleasure and pain, while all actions are performed by nature (3/27, 13/29). In effect, when a man has a desire for God-realization, there is predominance of the sentient (real), but when he has a desire for the mundane, there is predominance, of the insentient. The predominance of the sentient, gives birth to divine nature, while predominance of the insentient, gives birth to demoniac nature. The sentient in spite of its identification with the insentient, has a desire for truth, consciousness and bliss. All the worldly desires, are included in these three desires (to live forever, to know all, and ever to remain happy). But man commits an error, that he wants to satisfy these desires, by the insentient (world).

The sentient, has assumed its identification with the insentient and it has also accepted, the demoniac nature. The sentient, always remains uniform, without undergoing any modification, while nature (the insentient) undergoes, continuous modifications. If the self (sentient), does not assume its affinity of 'I'ness and mineness, with nature, it is free. Thus affinity of the sentient, with matter, and the demoniac nature born of this affinity, are one's own creation. Had the demoniac nature been in the self, it would not have perished, because the self is imperishable. No question would have been raised, to renounce demoniac nature. In spite of being perishable, it appears to be imperishable, because of its affinity with the imperishable. Therefore, a man can renounce, demoniac nature and can realize, God (16/22).

As soon as, a man inclines towards God, sins of his millions of births (the demoniac traits), perish. The reason is, that he has accumulated these sins, by assuming affinity with nature. The result of this assumed affinity, is that he has to take birth, in good and evil bodies (13/21). Actually, he neither acts, nor gets contaminated (13/31).

The realization of this truth means, to see inaction in action, and action in inaction. It means, that he remains detached, while performing actions and performs actions, remaining detached i.e., he remains detached, whether he performs actions or not. Such a man is wise, among men (4/18). He who is free from the notion of doership, and whose intellect is not tainted i.e., he has no desire, though he slays all people, he does not slay, nor is he bound (by his action) (18/17).* Arjuna asked Lord Kṛṣṇa, "By what, is a man impelled to commit sin?" Lord Kṛṣṇa replied, "It is desire" (3/36-37) which impels a man to commit sins. A man, by identifying himself with a body, has a desire for worldly pleasure and prosperity.* So this attachment to the matter is the cause of demoniac nature. If he is not attached to it i.e., he does not attach importance to it, his divine nature is self-evident. So Lord Kṛṣṇa assures all the strivers, through Arjuna, that they should not grieve and worry, if they see demoniac nature in them, because they naturally possess divine nature also (Gītā 16/5).

The Lord means, that a striver should never be disappointed, in the spiritual path, because being a fragment of God he automatically possesses divine nature. When a striver, aims at God-realization, divine nature, is automatically revealed, in him. The Lord has bestowed this human body by His grace, so that human beings may realize Him. So, if they have no will of their own but identify their will, with that of the Lord, they by His grace, attain salvation automatically.

Appendix—On one side of the soul, there is God while on the other side, there is the world. When a man (the soul), has an inclination to God, he is endowed with divine nature; and when he has an inclination to the world, he is endowed with the demoniac nature. In divine nature there is non-atheism while in demoniac nature, there is atheism. Though all the spiritual disciplines (Karmayoga, Jñānayoga and Dhyānayoga etc.,) for salvation are included within the divine nature—'daivī sampadvimokṣāya', yet in the divine nature there is predominance of devotion. Therefore the Lord in the topic of devotion declares—

mahātmānastu māṁ pārtha daivīṁ prakṛtimāśritāḥ
bhajantyananyamanaso jñātvā bhūtādimavyayam

(Gītā 9/13)

---

* No one wants to be a guilty because a guilty is insulted, rejected and blamed by the society here, while hereafter he has to go to hells and take birth in eighty-four lac forms of lives. But a man being overpowered by desire, born of the attachment to the perishable, performs forbidden actions which bear adverse fruit and the man becomes a defaulter and a sinner (against his wish).

"O Arjuna! The great Souls who possess divine nature, knowing Me as the sole and prime cause of creation and as imperishable, worship Me constantly with undivided mind."

Ahead also the Lord declares—'māmaprāpyaiva kaunteya........' (16/20). Within devotion all the means for salvation are included. Those who love their life-breath and look upon the maintenance of the life-breath as their highest goal are endowed with the demoniac nature. But those, who regard God as more loving than their life-breath, are endowed with divine nature.

Performance of actions to comfort others or the desire to comfort others is 'sentience' while performance of actions for one's own comfort or desire for one's own comfort, is 'insentience'. Adoration and meditation also for one's own happiness, for a peaceful life and for honour and respect is also insentience. When there is predominance of the sentience, the man is endowed with the divine nature; but when there is predominance of insentience, the man is endowed with the demoniac nature.

The root-evil is one which gives birth to all demoniac traits and the fundamental virtue is also one by which all the divine traits are revealed. The fundamental evil is—to accept the existence and value of the body and the world and to get attached to them. The fundamental virtue is—to accept the existence and value of God and to be attached to Him. The fundamental evil and the fundamental virtue, appear in different forms because of different situations.

So long as evils persist with virtues, the virtues appear to be valuable and a man is proud of them. If a person gets rid of evils totally, he is not proud of his virtues. Pride is the root of the demoniac nature. It is because of pride that a man feels that he is superior to others—this is his demoniac nature. It is because of pride that even the divine nature intensifies the demoniac nature. When evils don't persist with virtues, then virtues are not valued by him and he is not proud of them. As a striver does not value his virtues, so his attention is not diverted to his virtues and thus he gets non-plussed.* Arjuna's attention was also not diverted to his virtues and so he was perturbed that he did not possess divine traits. In such a situation to remove his grief, Lord Kṛṣṇa asks him not to grieve because he is born with divine nature—'mā śucaḥ sampadaṁ daivīmabhijāto'si pāṇḍava'.

Link:—All beings, possess sentient and insentient portions. Some of them, having a disinclination for the insentient, are inclined towards the sentient (God), while some having a disinclination for God, hanker after the insentient (pleasures and prosperity). Thus, they belong to two different classes, which are described, in the next verse.

द्वौ भूतसर्गौ लोकेऽस्मिन्दैव आसुर एव च ।
दैवो विस्तरशः प्रोक्त आसुरं पार्थ मे शृणु ॥ ६ ॥

dvau bhūtasargau loke'smindaiva āsura eva ca
daivo vistaraśaḥ prokta āsuraṁ pārtha me śṛṇu

There are two kinds of beings, in the world—the divine and the demon-like. The divine, has been described at length. Hear from Me, O Pārtha (Arjuna) of the demon, in detail. 6

Comment:—

'Dvau bhūtasargau loke'smindaiva āsura eva ca'—The Lord declares, that here are two types of beings—the divine and the demon-like. He means to say, that all beings have a sentient portion of Him, and the other insentient one of prakṛti (matter)

* Once a sage being perturbed said to me, "I have no faith in the Gītā, what will happen to me? Because the Lord in the Gītā has declared that he who is devoid of discriminative insight, has no faith, is of a sceptical nature, perishes." I asked him, "In which book is it mentioned that a man who has no faith, perishes?" He replied, "In the Gītā." Then I said, "When you are getting perturbed by reading the Lord's utterance in the Gītā, then is it not your faith in the Gītā?" Hearing this, he was pleased.

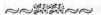

(Gītā 10/39; 18/40). When the sentient has an inclination for the insentient, a person develops demoniac nature, but when he having a disinclination for matter, is inclined towards the Lord, divine nature is aroused in him.

The term 'Deva', denotes God. So all the means, which are conducive to God-realization are known as, divine endowments (nature). As He is eternal and imperishable, so the methods of His realization are also eternal (Gītā 4/1).

The term 'Bhūta, includes—human beings, gods, demons, beasts, birds, insects, moths, plants, creepers, evil spirits etc. But human beings, have a discrimination to renounce, demoniac nature. So they should renounce it, totally. As soon as, they remove it, divine nature is automatically revealed in them.

It is mentioned in the scriptures, that human beings possess both the divine and demoniac natures. Even the cruelest butcher, possesses kindness, because a person being the fragment of the Lord, possesses divine nature automatically; while he develops demoniac nature in him, because of his attachment, for the perishable. Strivers, who follow a spiritual path, from their hearts, feel hurt, when they find demoniac nature, in them and they try to get rid of it. But strivers, who in spite of being engaged in devotion and adoration, hanker after worldly pleasure and prosperity, are not strivers indeed, because even the vilest sinner automatically possesses, both divine and demoniac natures.

A point needs special attention. A person, performs actions according to his egoism and his actions strengthen his egoism. 'I am truthful'—this conviction is centred in man's ego, and so he speaks the truth, and this truth strengthens his egoism, that he is true. Thus, he cannot tell a lie. But a person, who regards himself as worldly and hankers after worldly pleasure and prosperity, tells a lie and thinks, that in the modern world falsehood, is inevitable and indispensable. So, having such feelings in his 'ego', he regards it, impossible to get rid of evil and vice.

A man, being a fragment of God, has virtuous feelings, while having feelings of egoism, and attachment, he develops evils. But evil feelings cannot destroy virtuous feelings totally, because the latter are real and the real, never ceases to be (2/16). On the contrary, evil feelings are born of bad company and whatever is born, is surely to perish, because the unreal has no existence (2/16). A person, whose aim is God-realization arouses virtuous feelings, and performs virtuous actions, and so his evil feelings, disappear. But he, whose aim is, to enjoy worldly pleasure and prosperity, develops evil feelings and performs evil actions, his good feelings are covered.

The term 'Loke'smin', denotes that a person, gets several rights, on this earth. On this earth, particularly, India is the most pious land. Even the gods praise, persons who are born, in India.They are more blessed than the gods, because, the gods, have a yearning for the good fortune of human life, which the Lord having been pleased, has offered human being in India. A man, can attain salvation only, in this human life. So he should arouse divine nature, cautiously. The Lord, by His special grace, has granted this human body. The Lord has also offered men all the resources, including discrimination, to attain salvation. So the term 'Loke'smin', specially denotes human beings. But the Lord, is equally present in all beings (Gītā 9/29). Where there is God, there is His divine nature. So the expression 'Bhūtasargau', has been used. It means, that all beings can follow the spiritual path.

Human beings, who are absorbed in evil actions, are more guilty than those of sinful births—pariah, beasts, birds, insects and moths etc., because the latter, being purified of sins as a result of their past actions are going towards higher births, while the former are degrading themselves, by committing new sins. But the Lord, declares that even such sinners by worshipping Him, with exclusive devotion, can attain eternal peace (9/30-31). Similarly, the most sinful of all sinners, crossing all sins by a raft of knowledge, can attain salvation (4/36). It means, that when even the vilest sinner, can attain salvation, and those of sinful births, can also attain salvation. So the term 'Bhūta' (beings), has been used.

There are several incidents, which show that besides human beings other beings, such as birds and beasts etc., also possess divine nature.* Several dogs, are heard observing fasts. At Gorakhpur, a black dog accompanied a group of devotees, who chanted the Lord's name and sat at place, where divine discourses were held. At Svargāśrama, Ṛṣīkeśa, a snake was seen under a banyan tree. A saint asked it to stay, and he narrated the whole of the Gītā. The snake listened to it calmly. When the text was over, the snake disappeared and was never seen again. Thus birds and animals also possess, divine nature, because of past impressions, but they, unlike human beings, have no

* In Śāntiparva, a section of the epic, Mahābhārata there is a story. Śakunilubdhaka was a hunter, who used to kill birds and beasts. One day he could get nothing to eat, by hunting. Suddenly the sky was overcast and there was a downpour. So he sat under a tree. On that tree, there lived a couple of pigeons. Both of these had flown away to pick up food. The female pigeon flew back earlier, because she got drenched. She was shivering and so she fell down. The hunter put her, into his cage. The pigeon came back and finding his partner missing, began to lament. Hearing his wail she said, "My lord, why are you lamenting? You should discharge your duty, by welcoming a guest by removing his cold and satisfying his hunger. I am lying here in the cage." Hearing her words, the pigeon gathered dry leaves and wood, brought a burning stick and put it on the dry leaves. The hunter got warmth. He said to the pigeon, "I am hungry. What should I do?" The pigeon said, "You are my guest. I shall make arrangement to satisfy your hunger." He thought over it and finding no other remedy, he took three rounds of fire and jumped into it. Seeing his sacrifice, the hunter thought that he was very cruel and sinful, while the bird was virtuous. He determined never to commit such sins, in future. So he freed the she pigeon. She lamented over the death of her husband, and finding herself alone, jumped into the fire. A celestial car, moving in the air arrived, and both of the pigeons, went to heaven.

Seeing both of them going in the celestial car, the hunter threw his weapon away and decided to be engaged in devotion and adoration, which led him to salvation.

discrimination, to develop divine traits.

A human being, has been bestowed upon this human body, so that he may protect all the moving and unmoving beings, such as beasts, birds, herbs, plants and creepers etc., and specially the Sāttvika, animals, birds and herbs etc., because these develop divine nature, in us. The cow is sacred and adorable. Its churned butter, is used in sacrifice (yajña) which causes rain. Rain produces food, from which living beings come forth. Out of those beings, human beings, need bullock for farming. These bullocks are born of cows. Butter and milk of cows, nourish our body and mind. So we should protect the cow as mother. Similarly, herbs remove diseases and nourish the body. So, we should also protect these, so that our life may be pure, here and hereafter.

'Daivo vistaraśaḥ proktaḥ'—Lord Kṛṣṇa, declares that He has described divine nature, at length. In this chapter, He has described the twenty-six signs (nine in the first verse, eleven in the second verse and six in the third verse) of him, who is endowed with divine nature. He has also described it, in the signs of him who has transcended, the three modes of nature (14/22—25), (in the twenty virtues of Jñāna (knowledge or wisdom) (13/7—11), in the marks of a God-realized devotee (12/13—19), in the marks of a Karmayogī (6/7—9) and in the marks of a man of steadfast wisdom) (2/55—71).

'Āsuraṁ partha me śṛṇu'— The Lord, asks Arjuna to hear from Him, in detail, the nature of demoniac beings (Asura), who are given to sensuous life.

Appendix—The divine and the demoniac—the creation of these two kinds of beings is worldly because it is in the human world. In the unworldly entity both these don't exist. The means are both—worldly and unworldly but the end is unworldly only. The unworldly entity is all pervading, endless and limitless. The worldly entity is also within it. In fact the worldly entity has no existence. All is only unworldly. The soul has sustained the world—'yayedaṁ dhāryate jagat' (Gītā 7/5). It means that as long as, from the view-point of the Self, there is existence of the world, the world appears to exist. But when the existence of the world comes to an end, all remains unworldly, as it really is—'Vāsudevaḥ sarvam', 'Sadasaccāham' (viz., 'All is God', 'I am the real as well as the unreal').

Link:—Now the Lord, describes the order of development of demoniac nature, in the next verse.*

प्रवृत्तिं च निवृत्तिं च जना न विदुरासुराः।
न शौचं नापि चाचारो न सत्यं तेषु विद्यते॥ ७॥

pravṛttiṁ ca nivṛttiṁ ca janā na vidurāsurāḥ
na śaucaṁ nāpi cācāro na satyaṁ teṣu vidyate

The demoniac do not know, what to do (pravṛtti) and what to refrain from (nivṛtti). Neither purity, nor good conduct nor truth, is found in them. 7

Comment:—

'Pravṛttiṁ ca nivṛttiṁ ca janā na vidurāsurāḥ'—In the self-willed and unrestrained environment, and due to the influence of modern education and fooding of today people do not know, what to do and what to refrain from. They do not want to know it. If anyone explains it to them, they regard him as a fool, and laugh at him. They think that they themselves are wise. Some people know what to do and what to refrain from. But having

---

* Human beings possessing a demoniac nature, because of lack of fine breeding, do not know, what should be done and what should not be done, what is purity and what is impurity of body, food, speech and behaviour. They do not know the difference, between falsehood and truth. So they become disinclined towards God, What is truth. Then they do not believe in God, righteousness (Dharma), and do not follow their ordinance. They consider the creation to be evolved through mutual contact of men and women, brought about by lust. Thus these atheists, inflict pain on others and themselves, suffer a downfall.

predominance of demoniac nature, they do not translate their knowledge, into practice.

Now the question arises, how to know what to do, and what to refrain from. These can be known through a preceptor, saints, scriptures and thoughts. Discrimination, is also aroused in adversity, as well as, by beholding saints and going on pilgrimages.

Every being possesses discrimination. Human beings, have the ability and opportunity to develop it, while, other beings do not possess ability and get an opportunity to develop discrimination. Birds and beasts etc., possess discrimination, which is confined to their bodily maintenance. Human beings by applying their discrimination, can rear other beings and by renouncing evil conduct and action, can possess good conduct and perform, virtuous actions, as they are free in doing so, while birds and beasts etc., are not free, because they take birth, to bear the fruit of their past actions.

Persons, who believe in the theory 'eat, drink and be merry', do not, realize, what they should do and what they should, refrain from. In them like animals divine nature remains concealed. The Lord has called such persons, also 'Janāḥ (men), because divine nature can reveal itself, in them.

An Important Fact

From the term 'Janāḥ' (men) (16/7), to the expression 'Narādhamān' (worst among men), the Lord has not used any term denoting men, in between. It means, that these men, who in spite of having ability to renounce their demoniac nature, and to possess divine nature, do not do so, and do not deserve to be called, men. They are inferior to beasts and creatures, living in hell, because they are accumulating sins, which will hurl them into hell and the wombs of demons (16/16,19) while beasts and creatures of hell by suffering the fruit of their sins, are moving to higher regions.

The Lord, while describing the signs of persons endowed, with demoniac nature, instead of using the adjectives, beastly etc., has used 'Aśubhān' (impure or inauspicious) and 'Narādhamān' (worst among men), because they are more sinful than beasts etc. The Lord, by using the term 'Naraḥ' (man), in the twenty-second verse of this chapter explains, that only he, who being free from lust, anger and greed, (the three gates to hell), works his own salvation, and deserves to be called, a man. The same fact, has been explained, in the twenty-third verse of the fifth chapter, by the term 'Naraḥ'.

'Na śaucaṁ nāpi cācāro na satyaṁ teṣu vidyate'—Those who are endowed with demoniac nature, have not the least idea, of what purity is. They do not know, how to behave with parents and elders etc. They do not speak the truth and their conduct, is impure. They do not think of truth and purity of conduct, because the aim of their life, is to lead a luxurious life. So, they always hanker after, worldly pleasure and prosperity.

The Lord, in the forty-fourth verse of the second chapter, declares that those, who perform Vedic rites, in order to enjoy pleasure and prosperity, cannot have the determinate intellect, concentrated on God. Then, how can those, having a predominance of demoniac nature i.e., hankering after pleasure and prosperity by foul means, have a determinate intellect, to attain Him?

Appendix—In the order in which men are endowed with the demoniac nature, in the same order light of discrimination disappears. When men endowed with the demoniac nature adhere to pleasures, they can't know what they ought to do and what they ought not to do. Their niṣṭhā (faith) is not even worldly, then no question arises of its being unworldly. Their niṣṭhā paves the way to hells.

The men endowed with demoniac nature look upon the maintenance of their life-breath as the highest goal. Therefore they think only of their own happiness, comforts and self-interest.

They are inclined to perform those activities which provide them comfort and happiness and they don't do any activity which may provide them pain and which do not serve their self-interest. In fact the scripture is the authority in determining what ought to be done and what ought not to be done (Gītā 16/24). But because of deep attachment with their bodies and life-breaths, the men possessing the demoniac nature, don't obey the injunction of the scripture, in what ought to be done and what ought not to be done. Because of their demoniac nature they don't listen to the gospel of the scripture and even if they listen to it, they can't understand it—'yatanto'pyakṛtātmāno nainaṁ paśyantya cetasaḥ' (Gītā 15/11).

Link:—Those, who lack discrimination, purity, good conduct and truth, possess an atheistic outlook, which is described, in next verse.

असत्यमप्रतिष्ठं ते जगदाहुरनीश्वरम्।
अपरस्परसम्भूतं किमन्यत्कामहैतुकम्॥ ८॥

asatyamapratiṣṭhaṁ te jagadāhuranīśvaram
aparasparasambhūtaṁ kimanyatkāmahaitukam

They say, 'The universe is truly unreal having no moral basis, is without God, and born of mutual union, brought about by lust: what else?' 8

Comment:—

'Asatyam'—Persons possessing demoniac nature and atheistic outlook, say that this universe, is without truth and reality. According to them, virtuous actions, such as sacrifice, charity, penance, meditation, study of scriptures, pilgrimage and fasts etc., are unreal and deceptive.

'Apratiṣṭhaṁ te jagadāhuranīśvaram'—The believers, believe in Dharma (righteousness), God and rebirth etc., while atheists do not believe in these. They say, that there is neither virtue nor vice, in this universe. They hold that the universe is without God. They do not believe, in His existence. So, for them there is no question of a creator and controller of the universe.*

'Aparasparasambhūtaṁ kimanyatkāmahaitukam'—They believe, that sexual passion of men and women, is the sole cause, of the entire universe. There is no need of any Lord, or actions of the past etc., in its creation i.e., there is no Lord, Who dispenses the fruit of actions of an individual, according to virtue and vice. According to them, those who regard the Lord, as creator of this universe, are hypocrites and they cheat, the universe.

Link:—The Lord, in the next verse describes the view and the conduct of such atheists.

एतां दृष्टिमवष्टभ्य नष्टात्मानोऽल्पबुद्धयः।
प्रभवन्त्युग्रकर्माणः क्षयाय जगतोऽहिताः॥ ९॥

etāṁ dṛṣṭimavaṣṭabhya naṣṭātmāno'lpabuddhayaḥ
prabhavantyugrakarmāṇaḥ kṣayāya jagato'hitāḥ

Holding fast to this view, these perverted souls of false understanding, and cruel deeds, not believing in the eternal soul, appear as enemies of the world, for its destruction. 9

Comment:—

'Etāṁ dṛṣṭimavaṣṭabhya'—people possessing demoniac nature, do not know what to do and what to refrain from. They do not possess, either purity or good conduct, or truth. They do not believe, that there is a Lord, who dispenses the fruit of actions of an individual, according to virtues and vices. They hold fast, to this atheistic view.

* The term 'Anīśvara' means that they don't believe in the existence of the Lord. It means that the Lord exists but they don't believe in His existence. So they are obsessed with innumerable cares (16/11) while the believers possessing a divine nature remain carefree and fearless.

'Naṣṭātmānaḥ'—They do not believe in the existence of a soul. They are materialists. They believe, that there is no sentient element, as such, it is merely a mixture of materialistic elements, in it sentiency develops in the same way as a mixture of catechu and lime, produces redness. So, they are totally disinclined towards, sentient (soul). Thus they are ruined, and they lose all chances, of attaining self-realization.

'Alpabuddhayaḥ'—Their understanding (discrimination), is weak. Their intellect, is concerned only with sensual pleasures. They believe in 'eat, drink and be merry'. They cannot distinguish, between the real and the unreal, virtue and vice, good and bad conduct. They have no conception of a soul or the Supreme Being, as their understanding in spiritual matters, is clouded. But their intellect is sharp, in amassing wealth, and enjoying worldly pleasures.

'Ugrakarmāṇaḥ'—They perform cruel deeds, such as murder etc., because, they are not afraid of God and scriptural ordinances. But, they are afraid of thieves, robbers and government officers.

'Ahitāḥ'—They are, engaged in doing evil, to others and they derive pleasure out of it.

'Jagataḥ kṣayāya prabhavanti'—They apply their power, prosperity and position etc., for the destruction, of other people. They cannot tolerate the progress, of other people. For their selfish motives, they indulge in violence, murder and usurpation etc., without thinking of the pain, which they inflict upon others. Such demoniac people, kill birds and animals, and eat them.

Link:—The evil ways of such atheists, who are filled with insatiable desires, are described in the next verse.

काममाश्रित्य दुष्पूरं दम्भमानमदान्विताः ।
मोहाद्गृहीत्वासद्ग्राहान्प्रवर्तन्तेऽशुचिव्रताः ॥ १० ॥

kāmamāśritya duṣpūraṁ dambhamānamadānvitāḥ
mohādgṛhītvāsadgrāhānpravartante'śucivratāḥ

Sheltered behind insatiable desires, full of hypocrisy, pride and arrogance, believing false tenets through delusion, they act with impure resolve. 10

'Kāmamāśritya duṣpūram'—These people, endowed with demoniac nature, harbour insatiable desires, in their hearts. They believe that without desire a man, becomes just like a stone and he cannot progress. They do not believe in God, in fortune and in world hereafter.

How to satisfy those desires? The Lord explains:—

'Dambhamānamadānvitāḥ'—They are full of hypocrisy, pride and arrogance. They pretend to be, what they are not, in order to gain wealth, honour, praise and prestige etc. This is hypocrisy. 'Māna' or pride, consists in regarding oneself worthy of honour or adoration, because of one's superiority complex. 'Mada' or arrogance, consists in remaining intoxicated with one's possessions—intellect, merit, learning, wealth and power etc.

'Aśucivratāḥ'—They make impure resolves, such as setting fire to villages cow pens and murdering people etc. They regard, purity of food, conduct, caste and social order (āśrama), as hypocrisy. They resolve that they will not listen to the name and glories of the Lord, and they will not go on pilgrimages and so on.

Robbers also have such resolves, because they do not want to rob people of their riches, without injuring them.

'Mohādgṛhītvāsadgrāhān'—They embrace wrong ideas, through delusion. Delusion consists in conceiving, as right what is wrong, and following a path contrary to truth (Gītā 18/32). They do not follow, the ordinances of the scriptures, the caste and the family. They go contrary, to what is right, good or truthful. Their intellect becomes, so mean, that they do not consider, any duty towards their parents and they indulge in falsehood, fraud and forgery, in order to hoard money.

Appendix—'Kāmamāśritya duṣpūram'—In the third chapter also the Lord declared that desire is the most greedy (all devouring)—'mahāśanaḥ' (3/37) and is insatiable like fire—'duṣpureṇānalena ca' (3/39). Therefore all the desires can never be satiated. Those who have the aim to satiate their desires, can never attain peace. In the satiety of desires, there is much dependence, but the men of demoniac nature regard this dependence as independence because they think that having gained riches etc., they will become independent. They don't believe in the scripture, the preceptor, God and Dharma (righteousness) etc., then in whom besides desire, should they seek shelter?

Link:— The Lord, in the next two verses, explains the feelings, thought and conduct, of such atheists.

चिन्तामपरिमेयां च प्रलयान्तामुपाश्रिताः ।
कामोपभोगपरमा एतावदिति निश्चिताः ॥ ११ ॥

cintāmaparimeyāṁ ca pralayāntāmupāśritāḥ
kāmopabhogaparamā etāvaditi niścitāḥ

Obsessed lifelong with innumerable cares that end only with death, steeped in the gratification of desires and accumulation of wealth as the highest aim, and convinced that, that is the end-all. 11

Comment:—

'Cintāmaparimeyāṁ ca pralayāntāmupāśritāḥ'—They are beset with innumerable cares, worries and anxieties, till they die. So they have to follow, a cycle of birth and death.

The cares or worries, can be of two kinds—the spiritual and mundane. Those, who are worried about their salvation, are noble. But people possessing a demoniac nature, are not beset with spiritual worries. They are obsessed with, such cares and worries, as to how they could maintain honour, praise, fame and prestige etc., how they would live long, what would happen to their family, wealth and property, after their death and so on.

But the fact is, that a man is worried out of ignorance. The Lord, provides the necessities of life to people, according to their fortune.When a person dies, he leaves behind several things and objects, unconsumed. Even a dispassionate saint leaves his loin-cloth and a pot made of hollowed gourd, when he dies, when a rich man dies, his riches are of no avail, to him.

There is an anecdote. There was a very rich man. He built a house of steel, like a safe, because there were so many jewels, ornaments and precious stones etc., in his house. The house, could be unlocked with a key. Once he went into the house and shut it, but the key was left outside. So he died, without food, water and air. Similarly a man suffering from a disease, cannot enjoy delicious dishes, because if he eats such foods, he may die.

Even dispassionate ascetics, who do not possess, even a single penny, get the necessities of life, according to their destiny. So, there is no need for a man to be worried, how he would earn his living. Saint Tulasī declares, "The Lord, first decided the destiny of a being, and then bestowed upon him, this human body. So he need not worry, he should adore Him." Similarly, another saying goes, that the Lord provides cloth, wood and fire, even for a dead body, so if a living man, worries about his livelihood, he is very unfortunate. Saint Rāmadāsa also declares, "An ascetic, has got neither grain nor any animal (for milk or butter etc.,) nor cash, but at meal-time, he receives everything." Those possessing a demoniac nature, do not understand this. They think, that they obtain things, because they worry and make effort and if they do not do so, they may die of starvation.

'Kāmopabhogaparamāḥ'—Those, who look upon the gratification of desires, as their highest aim, hanker after worldly luxuries and pleasures. They are steeped in, enjoying the objects of the senses and in earning money, to enjoy these.

'Etāvaditi niścitāḥ'—They believe, that the only aim of life is to enjoy worldly pleasures* and prosperity and that sensual enjoyment, is the supreme source of happiness. They have no belief, in the happiness of another world. According to them, this sort of belief is a deception. They do not believe in virtues, vices and rebirth etc. So they want to enjoy, as many pleasures here, as is possible.

Appendix—The man, who is steeped in pleasures and prosperity, becomes blind. He can know neither the world nor God. By regarding the unreal world as real, he can't at all cast a glance upon God. He regards the non-existent world as real.

The objects are perishable while he himself is imperishable; then how can the perishable gratify the imperishable?

आशापाशशतैर्बद्धाः कामक्रोधपरायणाः।
ईहन्ते कामभोगार्थमन्यायेनार्थसञ्चयान्॥ १२॥

āśāpāśaśatairbaddhāḥ kāmakrodhaparāyaṇāḥ
īhante kāmabhogārthamanyāyenārthasañcayān

Bound by hundreds of ties of hope, given over to lust and anger, they strive to amass hoards of wealth, by unfair means, for sensual enjoyment. 12

Comment:—

'Āśāpāśaśatairbaddhāḥ'—People endowed with demoniac nature, are bound by hundreds of ties, of hope i.e., they have to amass hoards of wealth, they will win name, fame and honour, and they have to be free from diseases and so on. Even having possessed millions of rupees, they hope to gain more and more

---

* Similarly the unwise people who perform actions in order to reap their fruit hold that there is nothing else beyond the heavenly enjoyments (Gītā 2/42). So they want to enjoy those pleasures which are more attractive than the mundane pleasures.

from the Lord, from saints and even from beasts, birds, trees and creepers etc. Their hopes, are never fulfilled (Gītā 9/12). Moreover, if the hopes are fulfilled, they will die, and even if they live, the things, which fulfil their hopes, will perish or both will perish.

Those who are bound by ties of hope and desire, cannot stay comfortably, at one place, but those who have become free from these ties can live at one place happily.

'Kāmakrodhaparāyaṇāḥ'—They, are given to lust and anger i.e., they harbour in their hearts, various desires for all kinds of sensual enjoyments. When their desires, are not gratified, they become angry and inflict pain, upon others. They think, that desires are inevitable in life, without these a man becomes lifeless, as a stone. Similarly, they think that they can control other beings, through anger and if they are not angry, other people, will get hold of all their possessions.

'Īhante kāmabhogārthamanyāyenārthasañcayān'—Their aim, is to accumulate wealth and enjoy sensual pleasures. In order to fulfil their aim, they adopt foul means, such as dishonesty, cheating, treachery and injustice etc. They do not hesitate even in usurping charity funds and properties of children and widows. They believe that foul means, are indispensable in the world of today. According to them, honesty and justice are merely theoretical assumptions, which cannot be applicable, in real life. If they are honest and just, they will have to suffer, and they will not be able to live, from hand to mouth—such are the beliefs of people of demoniac nature.

Those people, who hanker after heavenly pleasure and prosperity by just means, cannot have a determinate intellect, that they have to realize God (Gītā 2/44). Then, how can those people possessing a demoniac nature, who earn money by foul and unjust means, have a determinate intellect to realize God? But even those people are free, if they so desire through determination, can follow the spiritual path and realize God, because this human life has been bestowed upon them by God, only to realize Him.

Appendix—'Āśāpāśaśatairbaddhāḥ'—Here the term 'śataiḥ' stands for infinite (endless). So long as a man is attached to the world, his desires don't come to an end. In the forty-first verse of the second chapter the Lord declares "bahuśākhā hyanantāśca buddhayo'vyavasāyinām". "The intellect of the undecided (infirm), is scattered in many directions, and is endlessly diverse". The reason is that they, having turned away from the imperishable, have cognised the reality and attached value to the perishable and have been attached to it.

'Kāmakrodhaparāyaṇāḥ'—The people endowed with demoniac nature think that desire and anger are inherent in human nature. They don't perceive anything else beyond desire and anger. These two are their supreme resort.

They hold that they will control a person through anger. But how long will they keep control over the person, who has been under their control because of his helplessness? As soon as he gets a chance, he will take vengeance upon them and harm them. Therefore the result of anger is only bad.

Link:—In the next three verses the Lord gives a description of imagination of the people of demoniacal nature.

इदमद्य मया लब्धमिमं प्राप्स्ये मनोरथम्।
इदमस्तीदमपि मे भविष्यति पुनर्धनम्॥ १३॥

idamadya mayā labdhamimaṁ prāpsye manoratham
idamastīdamapi me bhaviṣyati punardhanam

(Saying) "this has been gained by me today, further that desire I shall fulfil; this wealth is already mine and that wealth, also shall be mine." 13

Comment:—

'Idamadya mayā labdhamimaṁ prāpsye manoratham'— The demoniac people, imagine out of greed, that they have gained so much of money and much more will they gain, by other means, fair or foul. They remain engrossed in such thoughts, that the marriage of their educated son, could bring them so much money; so much money will be saved by evading taxes, and so much money, will be received, through rent and interest.

'Idamastīdamapi me bhaviṣyati punardhanam'—The more wealth, they hoard, the more greedy, they become. They always think, during their daily routine from early morning till late at night, only of means to amass hoards of wealth, and to lead a luxurious life.

But they forget, that they are growing old and one day, they will die a sad death, because they will die thinking of wealth, which they have accumulated and which they will have to leave behind and so wealth will cause, them grief. They, due to greed have to be afraid of their sons and daughters etc. They are also afraid of servants etc., lest the latter should go, on strike.

Question:—Strivers possessing a divine nature also think of earning money. Then, what is the difference between them and the people, who possess a demoniac nature?

Answer:—Though both of them seem to possess the same disposition, yet there is a vast difference, between the two. A striver's aim is God-realization, so he is not engrossed in hankering after pleasure and prosperity, while a person of demoniac nature, gets engrossed, because his aim is to enjoy worldly prosperity and sensual pleasure.

Appendix—Here the Lord explains the expression 'kāmopabhogaparamāḥ' (Those who are given up desire and sensuality) used in the eleventh verse.

असौ मया हतः शत्रुर्हनिष्ये चापरानपि।
ईश्वरोऽहमहं भोगी सिद्धोऽहं बलवान्सुखी॥१४॥

asau mayā hataḥ śatrurhaniṣye cāparānapi
īśvaro'hamahaṁ bhogī siddho'haṁ balavānsukhī

That foe has been slain by Me and others also I shall slay. I am the Lord, I am the enjoyer, I am perfect, mighty and happy. I possess supernatural powers. 14

Comment:—

People of demoniac nature, out of anger, imagine that they have killed a foe and they will kill other people, who are their enemy and act against them. They think, that none is equal to them, because they possess all the luxuries of life, and they are very powerful and happy. They hold, that they are endowed with a prophetic vision, and future events which they foretell, come true. They declare, that they possess accomplishments, such as 'Aṇimā and 'Garimā' etc., and can burn anyone to ashes, in a moment. They ridicule those, who are engaged in adoration, and meditation etc. They regard themselves, as lords of wealth, power and intellect etc., and think that they will always be successful, in their undertakings. They boast of their victory, because they are powerful, but they never talk, of their defeat.

Actually, such people, have an internal fiery sensation, but outwardly, they boast of their power, happiness and achievements.

Appendix—Here the Lord explains the expression 'kāmakrodha-parāyaṇāḥ' (who are given to desire and anger).

The people endowed with demoniac nature feel that they are happy but this is their only pride. In fact they are not happy. Happy are in fact those who are not swayed by favourable and unfavourable circumstances (Gītā 5/23).

The people endowed with demoniac nature, take pride in power of desire and anger. They regard them as powerful because of their affinity with the perishable. Like Hiraṇyakaśipu etc., they regard themselves as the Supreme because other people appear wretched to them.

आढ्योऽभिजनवानस्मि कोऽन्योऽस्ति सदृशो मया।
यक्ष्ये दास्यामि मोदिष्य इत्यज्ञानविमोहिताः ॥ १५ ॥

āḍhyo'bhijanavānasmi ko'nyo'sti sadṛśo mayā
yakṣye dāsyāmi modiṣya ityajñānavimohitāḥ

"I am rich and I have a large family. Who else is equal to me? I shall perform sacrifice (yajña). I shall give in charity. I shall rejoice." Saying thus, they are deluded by ignorance. 15

Comment:—

People possessing pride and demoniac nature, think that they are very rich and hold very high ranks and positions. They boastfully declare, that they have so many kinsmen, friends and followers. They think, that there is none equal to them, in riches, rank and position. They declare, that they will perform such sacrifice and offer such charities, that none can equal to them. Thus they would enjoy their life. They hold, that through great charity and sacrifice they would win name and fame, through newspapers. Their names would be inscribed in hospices, in their memory.

Such people, actually imagine, but they do not translate their thoughts, into practice. If sometimes they do, practice, that is merely a show, in order to get name and fame, as described in the seventeenth verse of this chapter. They remain entangled in the snare of delusion, having vain imaginations, as described, in the thirteenth, the fourteenth and the fifteenth verses.

Link:—The Lord, in the next verse, describes the evil fate after death, of such people, who possess a demoniac nature.

अनेकचित्तविभ्रान्ता मोहजालसमावृताः।
प्रसक्ताः कामभोगेषु पतन्ति नरकेऽशुचौ॥ १६॥

anekacittavibhrāntā mohajālasamāvṛtāḥ
prasaktāḥ kāmabhogeṣu patanti narake'śucau

Bewildered by many a fancy, entangled in the snare of delusion, addicted to the gratification of desire, they fall into a deep and filthy hell. 16

Comment:—

'Anekacittavibhrāntā'— People of wicked nature, are fickle minded. They have innumerable desires, and in order to fulfil them, they make many endeavours and having many a fancy. They do not stick to one idea, and their mind remains confused.

'Mohajālasamāvṛtāḥ'—They remain entangled, in the snare of delusion, as described in the verses thirteenth to fifteenth i.e., they are enmeshed in vain imagination and given to lust, anger and pride, and never get rid of these. They are trapped like an ensnared fish. Entangled in the snare of delusion, they are bewildered, by many a fancy or a thought. They are afraid of harmful consequences, as a result of their various evil thoughts. These thoughts are attended by such fear, as, "We have black money. If somehow, officials come to know of it, or clerks etc., may complain against us, then what will happen? We will harm others, but it may cause harm to us also"—thus engrossed in such thoughts they cannot make any firm resolve. They have to suffer a lot of pain, when their desires, remain unfulfilled.

'Prasaktāḥ kāmabhogeṣu'—Accumulation of wealth and gratification of desires, such as enjoyment of sensual pleasure and winning honour, praise, name and fame etc., are the aim, of their existence.

'Patanti narake'śucau'—While living alive, they live in a hell of delusion, and after death, they are condemned to frightful hell, such as Kumbhīpāka and Mahāraurava, where they have to suffer, the worst torture.*

Appendix—In fact the men of demoniac nature have already been condemned to hells because they have been given over to desire and anger and they are burning in the fire of the feeling of shortages. Consequently they are doomed to dreadful hells.

Attainment of the higher worlds or condemnation to hells depends on a man's thoughts rather than on his actions and objects. Thoughts have special value. Actions are reflections of the thoughts. Therefore the Lord has described the thoughts cherished by men possessed of demoniac nature.

Link:—After describing, the evil fate of the people of demoniac nature, the Lord, in the next four verses describes, the evil feelings born of evil conduct, and disastrous consequences, of those evil feelings.

आत्मसम्भाविताः स्तब्धा धनमानमदान्विताः ।
यजन्ते नामयज्ञैस्ते दम्भेनाविधिपूर्वकम् ॥ १७ ॥

ātmasambhāvitāḥ stabdhā dhanamānamadānvitāḥ
yajante nāmayajñaiste dambhenāvidhipūrvakam

Self-conceited, stubborn, filled with the pride and intoxication of wealth, such devils perform sacrifices (yajña) only in name, with ostentation, disregarding, scriptural ordinances. 17

Comment:—

'Ātmasambhāvitāḥ'—They are puffed up with unbounded pride, of their wealth, honour, praise, name and fame etc. They have a very high opinion, of their caste, social order, intellect, learning, rank and position etc. Regarding themselves as superior to others, they consider themselves worthy of their adoration.

* In the hells a being attains the body which has to suffer tortures. If that body is broken into pieces or boiled in oil or burnt in fire, it does not die so long as the being does not reap the fruit of his evil actions.

'Stabdhā'—They are too arrogant, to behave politely even with saints and an incarnation of God and to bow to these. If under unavoidable circumstances, they have to bow to their superiors, they bow to them haughtily.

'Dhanamānamadānvitāḥ'—They remain intoxicated with, the wine of wealth and pride. They are proud of their acquaintance, with people who hold high ranks and positions. They rely on riches and on their status. They think, that they have such resources, that they can acquire anything they desire, and they can destroy anyone, as they have an approach, with high officials and ministers.

'Yajante nāmayajñaiste dambhena'—They perform ostentatious sacrifices, in order to, win honour, name and fame. They feed people of the priestly class, with meagre food, and show that they have fed them with rich and delicious dishes.

They perform sacrifices, and offer charity, without paying attention to scriptural ordinances, only to influence people. They decorate temples and conduct special religious celebrations, for pomp and show, and self advertisement, when some distinguished dignitaries visit a temple. This sort of worship, in temples is actually, not for adoration but for gaining name and fame, or for pleasing officers, for their own self-interest.

The operaters of cowpens feed the healthy cows properly, but underfeed the crippled, disabled and dry cows. Moreover, they misuse funds, for their selfish motive. They make a lot of collections, but spend only little, to run religious institutions and use such funds for their own family expenses.

Even strivers, observe hypocrisy. They engage themselves in meditation, adoration and telling the beads of a rosary etc., when they see anyone coming, otherwise, they remain engaged in playing cards and worldly gossips etc. All this hypocrisy, is to win honour, name, praise and money.

When there is ostentation, even in strivers, what can be said, about ostentation of people possessing demoniac nature?

'Avidhipūrvakam'—They act against scriptural ordinances. They perform sacrifices, without reverence and faith. Similarly, they offer charity to the, undeserving. They view, all things in a perverted way (Gītā 18/32).

Appendix—The people, endowed with the demoniac nature, are jealous of others and they perform sacrifices in order to show that they are in no way inferior to others, rather they are superior to them. They perform sacrifices in order to win name and fame, they don't believe in its reward. If anyone else performs a sacrifice, they think that he also does it in order to win name and fame. Having no faith in God and in the other world, they disregard scriptural ordinances. Only those people who believe in God and in the next world and also believe that a particular action will bring a particular result, care for the scriptural ordinance.

All the activities of the demoniac natured people are ostentatious. But they take the pride within, that their sacrifice will be far better than that of others. Being proud of their learning they consider themselves as learned and wise and regard others as foolish and ignorant. In fact they live in a fool's paradise.

अहङ्कारं बलं दर्पं कामं क्रोधं च संश्रिताः ।
मामात्मपरदेहेषु प्रद्विषन्तोऽभ्यसूयकाः ॥ १८ ॥

ahaṅkāraṁ balaṁ darpaṁ kāmaṁ krodhaṁ ca saṁśritāḥ
māmātmaparadeheṣu pradviṣanto'bhyasūyakāḥ

Overwhelmed by egoism, brute force, arrogance, lust and anger, these detractors despise Me, Who is seated in their own bodies, and in the bodies of others. 18

Comment:—

'Ahaṅkāraṁ balaṁ darpaṁ kāmaṁ krodhaṁ ca saṁśritāḥ'—

People possessing wicked nature, are given to egoism, force, arrogance, lust and anger. They depend on these propensities, in the same way, as devotees depend on God. They believe, that a person without these propensities, is humiliated and crushed. So, they cultivate these and perpetuate them, so that they may win honour, praise, name and fame, and may keep other people under control.

'Māmātmaparadeheṣu pradviṣantaḥ'—The Lord says, that those people hate Him Who dwells in their own bodies, as well as, in the bodies of others. The ordinances of scriptures and jurisprudence (Smṛtis), are His own ordinances. Those thus disobey Him, and are malicious against Him, are thrown into hell. They despise the Lord, in two ways. First they do not obey the voice of their conscience, which tells them what is right and what is wrong. Secondly, they despise, insult and distress other people, who are none other than, the manifestations of the Lord.

'Abhyasūyakāḥ'—These malicious people, find fault with Him, as well as, with others. They say, that the Lord is partial, because He protects the devotees, and destroys the wicked. They are jealous of saints and ascetics, who are virtuous and they believe, that all saints, ascetics, devotees and strivers, also possess vile propensities, such as attachment, aversion, lust, anger, selfishness and ostentation etc. They oppose, adoration, meditation, fasts and pilgrimages etc., declaring these as futile pursuits, which bear no sweet fruit, because they themselves, have received nothing out of them. They have merely wasted, their time. Thus, those demoniac people, follow a path, contrary to the right one.

Appendix—The men endowed with demoniac nature are very obstinate and they adopt a stubborn attitude in what they believe to be true. This is the principle that only the man who is sad himself, causes sadness to others. The men of demoniac nature remain afflicted with sorrows, so they cause sufferings to others also. They don't perceive virtues in others but perceive evils in them. They hold that all goodness is vested with them. There is no one else in the world who is good or virtuous.

तानहं द्विषतः क्रूरान्संसारेषु नराधमान्।
क्षिपाम्यजस्रमशुभानासुरीष्वेव योनिषु॥ १९॥

tānahaṁ dviṣataḥ krūrānsaṁsāreṣu narādhamān
kṣipāmyajasramaśubhānāsurīṣveva yoniṣu

Those haters, cruel and worst among men, in the world. I constantly hurl such evil-doers, into the wombs of demons, only. 19

Comment:—

'Tānahaṁ dviṣataḥ krūrānsaṁsāreṣu narādhamān'—The demoniac nature, (described in the fifteenth verse of the seventh chapter and the twelfth verse of the ninth chapter) has been explained in detail, from the seventh verse to the eighteenth verse of this chapter. Now, (concluding this topic in the nineteenth and the twentieth verses of the chapter) the Lord declares, that such people who bear malice for other people, and are bent upon doing ill to them, and possessing a demoniac nature, are very cruel. They take delight in, committing violence. They are the worst of men, because the beings dwelling in hell, are becoming pure, after receiving the fruits of their evil deeds, while they by committing cruel deeds, are paving their way to hell. Therefore, in the Rāmacaritamānasa, it is mentioned, that it is better to reside in hell than to have the company of wicked or vile persons, because their company creates such seeds, which are not destroyed even after getting, their fruits in hell and eighty-four lac forms, of lives.

The Lord, has declared that desire is the root of all sins (3/37). When a man has a desire to earn more money, he adopts wrong means, such as falsehood, fraud and knavery and even commits sins, such as smuggling and robbery, and does not even hesitate to commit murder. Thus, he becomes more and more cruel. So, he has to bear pain in the wombs of demons, and also in foul hell.

'Kṣipāmyajasramaśubhānāsurīṣveva yoniṣu'—To call these people, by their name, to see them and to remember them, is very unholy. Such people are called 'Aśubhān' (evil-doers). The Lord, hurls such cruel persons, according to their nature, into the wombs of demons i.e., He sends them, into the wombs of cruel beings such as dogs, tigers, lions, snakes and scorpions etc., not only once, but again and again so that they may be purged of their sins.

Actually every being is a fragment of God, and so man is His. The Lord is a disinterested friend, of all beings. So by regarding these as His own, He despatches them into the wombs of cruel beings, to purify them of all their sins. Thus, being purified they, may attain eternal bliss or salvation. He is different from other friends and kinsmen, who provide comfort and luxuries to a man whom they regard as their own and enable him to get entangled, in worldly pleasures.

As a good teacher, punishes a pupil, so that he may become learned, the most merciful Lord, throws even atheists into wombs of demons, so that they may be purified of their sins, and attain salvation, because He regards them, as His own.

आसुरीं योनिमापन्ना मूढा जन्मनि जन्मनि।
मामप्राप्यैव कौन्तेय ततो यान्त्यधमां गतिम्॥ २०॥

āsurīṁ yonimāpannā mūḍhā janmani janmani
māmaprāpyaiva kaunteya tato yāntyadhamāṁ gatim

Come into the wombs of demons, these deluded beings, move from birth to birth, and do not attain to Me, O son of Kuntī (Arjuna), but they sink down to the lowest state. 20

Comment:—

'Āsurīṁ yonimāpannā mūḍhā janmani janmani māmaprāpyaiva kaunteya'—In the preceding verse, the Lord declared, that He sends persons possessing demoniacal nature, into the lower class of wombs of beasts and birds. Here also, He declares, that in this human life they have got a rare opportunity of God-realization, yet instead of realizing Him, they go into the wombs of demons, and again and again, go on taking birth in demoniacal wombs.

By the term 'Māmaprāpyaiva', the Lord means that He regrets for His act of bestowing that human body, on a being. He had offered the human body, in order to enable him, to attain salvation. But, he had proved treacherous, because he, instead of attaining salvation, sank down, to a still lower plane.

A being, during this human life, even though of the most vile conduct, swiftly may become a soul of righteousness and attain, eternal peace (Gītā 9/30-31) and even at the time of death, may attain the Lord (Gītā 8/5). The reason is, that the Lord is the same for all beings, (Gītā 9/29) and so He has provided an opportunity to all beings, to attain Him. Birds and beasts, because of their undeveloped discrimination, cannot attain Him, but there is no restriction from the Lord, even for them. So the Lord is very sad, when He sees that human beings, instead of availing a golden opportunity to attain salvation, sink to lower planes.

'Tato yāntyadhamāṁ gatim'—'Their sins, do not totally perish even during demoniac births. So, they have to go to still lower planes viz., hells.

Here, a doubt arises as to why the Lord has said, that these deluded beings do not attain Him, but sink down to a still lower plane, when there is no opportunity for them, to realize Him, in the demoniac birth. The clarification is, that the Lord has said so, because man was given an opportunity to realize Him, in the human life, before his demoniac birth, but he did not avail of that opportunity. Hence, he gets a demoniac birth. It means, that human beings, instead of attaining Him, first fall into the wombs of demons, and then sink down to still lower planes of foul hells; such as 'Kumbhīpāka' etc.

An Important Fact

The Lord bestows this human body, upon a being, so that a man may attain salvation. But he being overpowered by desires, selfishness and pride, commits sins, such as robbery, knavery, treachery and violence, which result in outward fruit and inward influence. A person, has to suffer according to evil actions, of the past. But, those, who inflict pain on him, commit new sins, which will bear painful fruits. Moreover, the sins leave their impression on the ego. That is very disastrous, because that impression in the form of evil feelings, instigates him to commit sins, again and again. Therefore, unless and until, a man attains salvation viz., unless he dispels these evil feelings from his ego, these will induce him, to resort to evil actions here, and hereafter, and will lead him to demoniac wombs and foul hell, where he will have to suffer torture.

Among the demoniac beings, such as beasts, birds, ghosts, insects and moths etc., also, it is seen that some of them are more cruel, while others are milder, according to the nature of their previous birth. Even when the Lord by His grace bestows upon them a human body, desire (lust) and anger persist in their ego which are the impressions, of previous birth. The marks of those, who return from hell, are excessive anger, harsh or bitter speech, poverty, enmity towards kinsmen, company of the mean and service, for the mean. Similarly, those who perform virtuous actions, to attain heaven, go to heaven. There, they enjoy the vast heaven, as fruit of their virtuous actions, but their nature does not undergo, any change. The four marks of those returning from heaven, are—(1) inclination towards offering charity, (2) sweet speech, (3) adoration for the gods, and (4) efforts to satisfy members of the priest class. A being, can change his nature, only during this human life.

Link:—The Lord, in the preceding verse, declared that people of demoniac nature, instead of attaining to Him, fall into the wombs of demons and then sink down to a still lower plane. The Lord, in the next verse, gives the reason why, first they fall into the demoniac wombs, and then sink down to a still lower plane.

त्रिविधं नरकस्येदं द्वारं नाशनमात्मनः।
कामः क्रोधस्तथा लोभस्तस्मादेतत्त्रयं त्यजेत्॥ २१॥

trividhaṁ narakasyedaṁ dvāraṁ nāśanamātmanaḥ
kāmaḥ krodhastathā lobhastasmādetattrayaṁ tyajet

Three are the gates of this hell, leading to the ruin of the soul—lust (desire), anger and greed. Therefore, one should avoid these. 21

Comment:—

'Kāmaḥ krodhastathā lobhaḥ trividhaṁ narakasyedaṁ dvāram'—The Lord, in the fifth verse, declared that divine nature is conducive to liberation and the demoniacal, to bondage. Then what is the root of demoniac nature? Desire, for worldly pleasures, prosperity, honour, praise and comforts etc., is the root of demoniac nature, which leads human beings to hell. Desire, anger, greed, delusion, intoxication of wealth (arrogance), and jealousy have been regarded, as the six enemies. Out of these six enemies, in the Gītā, also there is mention of three—desire, anger and greed; while at some place, there is mention of two only attachment and aversion; while at some other place only desire, has been declared, as the enemy of strivers. All the six are practically of the same nature. Out of these, desire is the root which binds a man (Gītā 5/12).

In the thirty-sixth verse of the third chapter, Arjuna asked Lord Kṛṣṇa, "By what, is a man impelled to commit sin, as if by force, even against his will?" The Lord, replied that it is desire, which is later transformed into wrath, and is an all-devouring, sinful enemy. When desire, is not fulfilled, it gives birth to wrath. But, here in this verse desire (lust), anger and greed have been mentioned, as three enemies. It means, that an inclination towards pleasure is desire (lust), and inclination towards accumulation, is greed. Where, only the term 'Kāma' (desire), is given, it also includes desire for pleasure and accumulation of riches. But, when both the terms 'Kāma' (desire) and 'Lobha' (greed), are quoted independently, the term 'Kāma' stands for desire for pleasure, while 'Lobha' stands for desire for accumulation. When, there is any obstruction, in the fulfilment of these inclinations, anger springs. When there is an excess of desire, anger and greed, delusion is born.

From desire, arises anger and from anger delusion (Gītā 2/62-63). If desire is fulfilled, it gives birth to greed, and from greed comes delusion. In fact, it is desire which is transformed into anger and greed. Delusion, leads to the mode of ignorance and then perfect demoniac nature, prevails.

'Nāśanamātmanaḥ'—Desire, anger and greed, degrade a man. Those, who hanker after worldly pleasure and prosperity, regard these three evil propensities, as conducive to their welfare. But, actually a man who falls a prey to these faces degradation or ruination.

'Tasmādetattrayaṁ tyajet'—When a person, comes to know that desire, anger and greed, are three gates to hell, he should renounce, these. How to renounce them? The Lord, in the thirty-fourth verse of the third chapter, has declared that attachment (desire) and aversion (anger) through the feeling of agreeableness and disagreeableness abide, in the objects of senses but a striver should not come under their sway i.e., he should not perform any action, against the ordinance of scriptures, being overpowered by desire, anger and greed. If a man comes under their sway, he is ruined.

Appendix—The sense of enjoying pleasures is 'lust' and the sense of accumulation is 'greed'. If anyone causes an obstruction in the fulfilment of lust and greed, then anger ensues. These three are the root causes of the demoniac nature and they cause all sins.

At the time of death, persons and objects are left behind but the demoniac nature of a man paves his way to hells.

Link:—In the next verse, the Lord explains the glory of a man, who is liberated from these three gates, of hell.

एतैर्विमुक्तः कौन्तेय तमोद्वारैस्त्रिभिर्नरः।
आचरत्यात्मनः श्रेयस्ततो याति परां गतिम्॥ २२॥

etairvimuktaḥ kaunteya tamodvāraistribhirnaraḥ
ācaratyātmanaḥ śreyastato yāti paraṁ gatim

The man freed from the three gates to hell, pursues his salvation and then attains the Supreme Goal, O son of Kuntī (Arjuna). 22

Comment:—

'Etairvimuktaḥ kaunteya tamodvāraistribhirnaraḥ ācaratyātmanaḥ śreyastato yāti paraṁ gatim'—Desire, anger and greed, which were termed the gates of hell in the preceding verse, have been called the gates to darkness, in this verse. Darkness is born of ignorance (Gītā 14/8). A man, swayed by the gates of hell, never thinks "These riches, wife, family and friends, were neither with me, nor will remain in future, and at present also they are separating from me. If I have a sense of mine, with them, I may be damned." It means, that desire for prosperity, pleasure and other worldly things, which are transitory and perishable, leads, a man to darkness. He does not think of the consequences, of his attachment for them. But, he who having been free from desire etc., practises what is good for him, attains the Supreme Goal. So a striver, should be cautious, against desire, anger and greed.

A striver, practises spiritual discipline, to purify himself of evil feelings, and evil conduct, but he does not pay attention to evil propensities, such as desire (lust) and greed etc., which he possesses. So a striver, should be on guard against these. Moreover, he should think of the Lord with form or without form from early morning, till late at night, and from the day he has realized His importance, to the time of death.

The term, 'Etairvimuktaḥ' (liberated from these), does not mean, that a striver after being free from evil conduct, should follow spiritual discipline. But it means, that a striver having the aim of God-realization, should try to be free from desire, anger, greed and other evil propensities. It is because of these propensities, that a striver, commits sins and does not progress spiritually. In fact, a man (soul) being a fragment of God, is sentient, pure and naturally, a store of bliss, but his inclination towards the world, has resulted in impurity in him, so if he develops a disinclination, towards the world, he would naturally, make spiritual progress.

The expression 'Śreyaḥ ācarati' (practises what is good) means, that a striver should perform only prescribed actions, and not prohibited ones. He should not translate, the evil propensities (such as desire or lust and anger), into practice. He should try his best to be free, from them. If he finds that his efforts are going in vain, he should invoke the Lord, and pray to Him to liberate him from these evils. Gosvāmī Tulasīdāsa prays, to God, "O Lord, my heart is Your residence, but several thieves (evils), have settled there. I request them to leave it. But they want to reside there, forcibly" (Vinaya Patrikā 125/2-3). It means, that he is unable to be free, from these evils. So he seeks refuge in Him, so that He may protect him, from these.

Appendix—'Etairvimuktaḥ'—To be free from desire, anger and greed means—to have the aim to renounce them and not to be swayed by them. Even the virtuous action performed out of desire, anger or greed, is not conducive to salvation. So a striver should be very careful to renounce them. Even the virtuous conduct, such as chanting the Lord's holy names and meditating on Him, does not lead to salvation, unless the striver renounces them, because they are the root causes of sins (Gītā 3/37).

It is because of desire, anger and greed that righteousness and ethical propriety of the society are lost; which is very harmful for the world. The men of demoniac nature are steeped in desires, anger and greed. They perform virtuous actions such as religious sacrifice and offer charity for mere ostentation, not for salvation. But the strivers of divine nature, instead of being overpowered by desire, anger and greed, perform virtuous actions for their salvation, which naturally involves the welfare of the world. The men of demoniac nature are envious of such strivers and they think them to be senseless (foolish); but these strivers take pity on those men of demoniac disposition and pray to God to provide them with good sense (moral sense).

Link:—Those, who practise what is good for them, attain the Supreme Goal. But, what happens to those, who act according to their own sweet will, and cast aside the ordinance of scriptures. The Lord, answers in the next verse.

यः शास्त्रविधिमुत्सृज्य वर्तते कामकारतः ।
न स सिद्धिमवाप्नोति न सुखं न परां गतिम् ॥ २३ ॥

yaḥ śāstravidhimutsṛjya vartate kāmakārataḥ
na sa siddhimavāpnoti na sukhaṁ na parāṁ gatim*

He, who having cast aside the ordinances of scriptures, acts in an arbitrary way, according to his sweet will, attains, neither perfection, (purity of inner sense) nor happiness, nor achieve the Supreme Goal. 23

Comment:—

'Yaḥ śāstravidhimutsṛjya vartate'—Those people, perform

* The theme of the twenty-eighth verse of the seventeenth chapter is almost the same.

actions, such as sacrifice, offer charity and do good to others in an arbitrary way, according to their sweet will* disobeying the ordinances of scriptures. The reason, is that they attach importance only to the seemingly good activities. They do not bother to get rid of their evil feelings.

Though they have evil feelings, yet they are proud of their outward good actions. It is because, of their pride, that their virtues are transformed into evil, their glory into blame, and their renunciation into attachment, and pleasure, which lead them to their downfall and ruin. It is because of their internal evil feelings, that they act in an arbitrary way, according to their own sweet will.

A patient, intends to discard unwholesome diet, and plans to take wholesome food. But out of attachment, takes unwholesome diet, which worsens his disease, similarly, people from their own view-point, make an attempt to perform good actions. But evils—desire, anger and greed take them under their sway and they act in an arbitrary way, disregarding the ordinance of scriptures and are thus, damned.

'Na sa siddhimavāpnoti'—Those, possessing demoniac nature, perform supposedly good actions, such as religious sacrifice etc., casting aside the ordinances of scriptures. Thus they may attain benefits, like wealth, and honour etc., but they do not attain perfection, in the form of purity of heart.

'Na sukham'—They do not attain Sāttvika happiness because

* (A) Here in the verse the expression 'Kāmakārataḥ' denotes one's own unrestrained self-will while in the expression 'Kāmakāreṇa' used in the twelfth verse of the fifth chapter there is desire for pleasures. The former looks at the actions while the latter looks at the fruit of the action. But 'Kāma' (Desire) is the root in both of them.

(B) Here a point needs attention that in this chapter from the seventh verse to the twenty-third verse the term 'Kāma' (Desire) has been used nine times in the context of the demoniac nature (16/8, 16/10, 11, 12, 12, 16, 18, 21, 23) (in 12 verse two times each). It means that desire is the root of the demoniac nature.

in their hearts the burning feeling of desire and anger, etc., persists. They may derive pleasure, born of contact with objects, which are only sources of sorrow (Gītā 5/22).

'Na parāṁ gatim'—They do not attain the Supreme Goal, because firstly they do not believe in it. Moreover, their actions, performed out of desire, anger and greed, are not conducive to attainment, of the Supreme Goal.

Their acts are good. So they can attain perfection, happiness and the Supreme Goal. But they do not attain these, because they possess evil propensities, such as desire (lust), anger, greed and pride, which are stumbling blocks, in their attainment. It is because of these evil propensities, that their good actions, generally convert into evil and vice. Therefore, they do not get all these things. Had their activities been evil, by nature, then there would have not been any question of their attaining, perfection, happiness and the Supreme Goal.

Appendix—People of demoniac nature, because of their pride, regard themselves as perfect and happy—'siddho'haṁ balavānsukhī' (Gītā 16/14) but actually they are never perfect and happy—'na sa siddhimavāpnoti na sukhaṁ'. Their hearts burn with the fire of pride and malice.

Link:—Those, who cast aside the ordinances of scriptures, attain neither perfection nor happiness, nor the Supreme Goal. So what should a man do? The Lord, answers the question, in the next verse.

तस्माच्छास्त्रं प्रमाणं ते कार्याकार्यव्यवस्थितौ।
ज्ञात्वा शास्त्रविधानोक्तं कर्म कर्तुमिहार्हसि॥ २४॥

tasmācchāstraṁ pramāṇaṁ te kāryākāryavyavasthitau
jñātvā śāstravidhānoktaṁ karma kartumihārhasi

Therefore, let the scripture be the authority in determining,

what ought to be done and what ought not to be. Having known what is prescribed in the ordinance of scriptures, thou shouldst act accordingly in this world. 24

Comment:—

'Tasmācchāstraṁ pramāṇaṁ te kāryākāryavyavasthitau'— Those, who are attached to their life-breath, do not know what should be done, and what should be refrained from. So, they are specially inclined towards demoniac nature.Therefore, Lord Kṛṣṇa, advises Arjuna to act according to the ordinance of scripture.

The conduct and words, of saints and great souls, are also based on scripture. So obedience to these, is also obedience to the ordinances of the scripture, because they have become saints and great souls, by following the ordinances of scripture. In fact, the ordinances of scriptures are the ideas, precepts, and principles, and acts of God-realized souls.

The expression 'Śāstraṁ pramāṇam', means that a person, who wants to attain eternal bliss, should readily renounce whatever is prohibited by the scripture, and accept what is ordained by it.

'Jñātvā śāstravidhānoktaṁ karma kartumihārhasi'* — People of demoniac nature, do not know, what to do and what to refrain from (Gītā 16/7). So, they do not attain perfection. Lord Kṛṣṇa says to Arjuna, that he should act, according to ordinances of the scripture, because he possesses the divine nature.

First, Arjuna thought, that sin alone would accrue to him, by killing his kinsmen in the battle. So the Lord declared, "Happy are the Kṣatriyas (members of the warrior class), who are called upon to fight, in such a battle that comes of itself, as an open door to heaven" (Gītā 2/32). Here, the Lord says that he should discharge his duty, according to the ordinance of the scripture, because it cannot lead him to bondage. An act, which

* The term 'Iha' here means that a man should avail of the human life which has been bestowed upon him in order to realize God by performing noble actions.

is performed with selfishness and pride, leads to bondage while the action which is performed in an arbitrary way against the ordinance of scriptures, leads to ruin.

One's own duty of fighting in the battle, seems one of cruelty and violence, but actually a Kṣatriya doing his duty incurs no sin (Gītā 18/47). It means, that a person who discharges his duty in accordance with the ordinance of scriptures, incurs no sin. He incurs sin, only when he performs actions, with selfishness and pride, in order to harm others.

Human life, is successful only, when a person without being attached to the body and life-breath, performs actions according to ordinances of scriptures, for God-realization.

Appendix—The Lord in the seventh verse declared that the people of demoniac nature don't know what to do and what to refrain from. Here the Lord declares that their demoniac nature will be wiped out by acting according to the ordinance of the scripture.

Here a doubt may arise how will the people, who have not studied the scripture, know what to do? The clarification is that if they aim at salvation, they themselves will know what to do, because necessity is the mother of invention. But if they don't aim at salvation, even having studied the scripture, they will not know what to do; on the contrary their ignorance will thrive on the assumption that they have a very good knowledge of scriptures.

ॐ तत्सदिति श्रीमद्भगवद्गीतासूपनिषत्सु ब्रह्मविद्यायां योगशास्त्रे
श्रीकृष्णार्जुनसंवादे दैवासुरसम्पद्विभागयोगो नाम षोडशोऽध्यायः॥ १६ ॥

oṁ tatsaditi śrīmadbhagavadgītāsūpaniṣatsu brahmavidyāyāṁ yogaśāstre śrīkṛṣṇārjunasaṁvāde daivāsurasampadvibhāgayogo nāma ṣoḍaśo'dhyāyaḥ

Thus with the words, Oṁ, Tat, Sat, the names of the Lord, in the Upaniṣad of the Bhagavadgītā, the knowledge of Brahma, the supreme, the scripture of Yoga and the dialogue between Śrī Kṛṣṇa and Arjuna, this the sixteenth discourse is designated:

"The Yoga of Division, between the Divine and the Demoniacal."

This chapter is designated 'Daivāsurasampadvibhāgayoga' (The Yoga of Division between the Divine and the Demoniacal), because in this chapter, there is a description of the two contrary natures— the divine and the demoniac. The former nature, leads to salvation, while the latter leads to bondage, low wombs and hell. A striver, who knows the two, in the right perspective, renounces demoniac nature. As soon as, he renounces demoniac traits, divine nature is automatically revealed, in him; and with the revelation of the divine nature, he realizes that he has connection, only with God.

Words, letters and Uvāca (said) in the Sixteenth Chapter—

(1) In this chapter in **'Atha ṣoḍaśo'dhyāyaḥ'** there are three words, in **'Śrībhagavānuvāca',** there are two words, in verses, there are two hundred and eighty-seven words and there are thirteen concluding words. Thus the total number of words is three hundred and five only.

(2) In this chapter in **'Atha ṣoḍaśodhyāyaḥ'** there are seven letters, in **'Śrībhagavānuvāca'** there are seven letters, in verses, there are seven hundred and sixty-eight letters and there are fifty-two concluding letters. Thus, the total number of letters, is eight hundred and thirty-four only.

(3) In this chapter, the term **'Uvāca'** (said) has been used once and that is **'Śrībhagavānuvāca'.**

Metres Used in the Sixteenth Chapter—

Out of the twenty-four verses, of this chapter in the first quarter of the sixth verse, in the third quarter of the tenth verse, and in the first quarter of the twenty-second verse, 'ma-gaṇa' being used there, is **'ma-vipulā'** metre; in the third quarter of the eleventh, thirteenth and nineteenth verses, 'na-gaṇa' being used there is **'na-vipulā** metre. The remaining eighteen verses have the characteristics of right **'pathyāvaktra'** Anuṣṭup metre.

॥ Shri Hari ॥

Seventeenth Chapter

INTRODUCTION

The Lord, in the twenty-third verse of the sixteenth chapter, declared that he, who having cast aside the ordinances of scriptures, acts in an arbitrary way, according to his sweet will, attains neither perfection nor happiness, nor the Supreme Goal. Listening to the Lord's statement, Arjuna thinks that only a few people know those ordinances. A majority of people do not know these ordinances, but they worship the gods according to their caste, social order (āśrama), family tradition and innate faith. Due to their disregard for the ordinances of the scriptures, they should be regarded as demoniac, but due to their faith, they could be considered men of divine traits. So Arjuna wants to know, where such people stand. Therefore, he puts a question to Lord Kṛṣṇa, in the first verse.*

अर्जुन उवाच

ये शास्त्रविधिमुत्सृज्य यजन्ते श्रद्धयान्विताः ।
तेषां निष्ठा तु का कृष्ण सत्त्वमाहो रजस्तमः ॥ १ ॥†

---

* To treat this (seventeenth) chapter as an explanation of the twenty-seventh verse of the ninth chapter (Whatever you do and whatever you offer, do that as an offering to Me) is not reasonable because the twenty-seventh verse of the ninth chapter is included in the topic 'offerings to God' which begins from the twenty-sixth verse and is concluded in the twenty-eighth verse with the result of these offerings. But here is the topic of faith.

† Here the topic is based on the twenty-third verse of the sixteenth chapter because in both the verses there is the mention of 'having cast aside the ordinances of the scriptures'. Instead of 'under the impulse of desire' here the expression 'endowed with faith' has been used; similarly instead of 'acts' the expression 'performs sacrifice' and instead of 'attains neither perfection, nor happiness nor the Supreme Goal' the sentence 'What is their position—Sattva, Rajas or Tamas have been used.

arjuna uvāca

ye śāstravidhimutsṛjya yajante śraddhayānvitāḥ
teṣāṁ niṣṭhā tu kā kṛṣṇa sattvamāho rajastamaḥ

Arjuna said:

Those who not caring for the ordinances of scriptures, perform sacrifice (yajña) in good faith—what is their position, O Kṛṣṇa! Is it sattvic (goodness), rajasic (passion) or tamasic (ignorance)? 1

Comment:—

'Ye śāstravidhimutsṛjya....sattvamāho rajastamaḥ'— The gospel of the Gītā, in the form of the dialogue, between Lord Kṛṣṇa and Arjuna, is for the welfare of all beings. Both of them, had people of the Kali age in view, because the Dvāpara age, was coming to an end. So Arjuna thinking of the people of Kali age, asks Lord Kṛṣṇa, the position of those who have good feelings and are also endowed with faith, but they have not acquired accurate and elaborate knowledge of scriptures.* So, they disregard the ordinances of scriptures, through ignorance. People in general, will have little knowledge, of the scriptures. Moreover, it will be difficult for them to get company of saints and great souls, as they will be rare in Kali age. In spite of their being rare, if anyone wants to get their company, he can have it. But the trouble is, that in Kali age several hypocrites, disguise themselves as saints. Thus, it becomes difficult to recognize them. So it becomes very difficult to have company of real saints, and to derive benefit from them. Therefore, such people neither know the ordinance of scriptures nor have the association of saints and great souls. But, they worship gods and perform austerities, with innate faith. So Arjuna asks, about their position. Is it, of goodness, passion or of ignorance?

'Sattvamāho rajastamaḥ'—The mode of Sattva (goodness),

*The ordinances of the scriptures are neglected by (1) ignorance (2) indifference (3) opposition.

is included in divine nature, while the modes of raja (passion) and tama (ignorance) are included in demoniac nature. The mode of passion, resembles the mode of ignorance, in certain respects.* In the sixty-second and sixty-third verses of the second chapter in the Gītā, it is mentioned, that anger springs from desire, which is a mode of passion, while from anger arises delusion, the mode of ignorance. Similarly, in the twenty-seventh verse of the eighteenth chapter, a doer, who is swayed by sorrow and who is given to violence, is said to be passionate, while in the twenty-fifth verse of the same chapter, violence has been called, a mark of the mode of ignorance, and in the thirty-fifth verse, sorrow, a mark of firmness of the mode of ignorance. Thus several signs of the mode of ignorance and of passion, are similar.

Sāttvika feelings, thoughts and conduct, are included in divine nature, while the rājasika and tāmasika, are included in demoniac nature. A man's position, is decided in accordance with, his nature. Here, by the term 'position', Arjuna wants to know what is the fate of such a man, as he also asked, in the thirty-seventh verse of the sixth chapter.

Here, Arjuna addresses the Lord as Kṛṣṇa (One who attracts). He wants to ask, of what status, He will consider such a man i.e., what is his status and what is his end.

Now a question arises, whether the Lord attracts persons, or whether they are attracted, according to the fruit of their actions. The answer is, that a man receives the fruit of his actions, but the controller of those fruits, is the Lord. He awards the fruits, according to their action. But, being a disinterested friend of all, He throws them into hell, to purify them, of their sins, and then

* Sattvaguṇa (the mode of goodness) is ten times superior to the Rajoguṇa (the mode of passion) while the mode of passion is ten times superior to the Tamoguṇa (the mode of ignorance). It means that the mode of goodness is a hundred times superior to the mode of ignorance.

he attracts all of them, towards Him. So the Lord says, for the people of demoniac nature, that those deluded beings, instead of attaining Him, go down to lower planes (16/20). It means, that the Lord is sad, when he sees that human beings, instead of attaining Him, go down to lower states.

Link:—A man, who does not know the ordinance of the scripture, is endowed with faith, of one type or the other. The three kinds of that innate faith, are described in the next verse.

श्रीभगवानुवाच

त्रिविधा भवति श्रद्धा देहिनां सा स्वभावजा।
सात्त्विकी राजसी चैव तामसी चेति तां शृणु॥ २॥

śrībhagavānuvāca

trividhā bhavati śraddhā dehināṁ sā svabhāvajā
sāttvikī rājasī caiva tāmasī ceti tāṁ śṛṇu

The Blessed Lord said:

The faith of human beings, born of their own nature, is of three kinds—sāttvika (good), rājasika (passionate) and tāmasika (ignorant). Now hear about this. 2

Comment:—

[Arjuna put the question to know, where they stand, while the Lord answers his question, according to their faith, because they stand, as is their faith.]

'Trividhā bhavati śraddhā dehināṁ sā svabhāvajā'— Faith is of three kinds. Now the question arises, whether that faith is born of company, learning of scriptures, or of innate nature. The answer is, that it is born of their nature. By having this faith, people worship the gods etc.

'Sāttvikī rājasī caiva tāmasī ceti tāṁ śṛṇu'— The faith born of nature, is of three kinds—sāttvika (good), rājasa (passionate) and tāmasa (ignorant). Lord Kṛṣṇa, asks Arjuna to hear about these three, from Him.

In the preceding verse, in the expression 'Sattvamāho rajastamaḥ,' the conjunction 'Āho' (Or), has been used, which denotes that according to Arjuna 'sattvam' (good), stands for divine nature, while rajastamaḥ' (passionate-ignorant) stand, for demoniac nature. It means, that according to him, there are only two divisions. As far as bondage is concerned, the Lord also includes both the rajas and the tamas, in demoniac nature, when he declares that demoniac nature is conducive to bondage (Gītā 16/5). But, there is a difference between the two—the rajas and the tamas. The rājasa (passionate) people, perform actions, according to ordinance of scriptures to get their fruit. So having enjoyed, in heaven the heavenly pleasure, they enter (return to) the world of mortals, when their merit is exhausted (Gītā 9/21). But the tāmasa (ignorant) people do not perform actions, according to ordinances of the scripture. So they sink deep (Gītā 14/18). Thus the Lord, divides the faith of people, possessing a demoniac nature, into two parts, the rajas and the tamas, and asks Arjuna to hear from him, of the three kinds of faith— sāttvika, rājasa and tāmasa, separately.

Link:—The Lord, in the preceding verse, explains three kinds of faith. In the next verse, He explains, why it is of three kinds.

सत्त्वानुरूपा सर्वस्य श्रद्धा भवति भारत।
श्रद्धामयोऽयं पुरुषो यो यच्छ्रद्धः स एव सः ॥ ३ ॥

sattvānurūpā sarvasya śraddhā bhavati bhārata
śraddhāmayo'yaṁ puruṣo yo yacchraddhaḥ sa eva saḥ

The faith of each, O Bhārata (Arjuna), is in accordance with

his inner sense. Man is of the nature of his faith; as a man's faith, so is he. 3

Comment:—

'Sattvānurūpā sarvasya śraddhā bhavati bhārata'—Here, the expression 'Sattvānurūpā' stands for 'Svabhāvajā', which was used in the preceding verse. The term 'Sattva', stands for inner sense. So the faith of a man is in accordance with his inner sense. As a man's inner sense is sāttvika, rājasa or tāmasa, so is his faith.

The term 'Sarvasya', denotes 'dehinām' (the embodied), used in the preceding verse. It means, that the faith of each person, whether he knows the ordinances of the scriptures or not, believes in them or not, acts, according to them or not and he may belong to any caste, creed, country, social order, of any tradition but, faith of each and all is of three kinds.

'Śraddhāmayo'yaṁ puruṣaḥ'— A man's character is judged, by his faith. As a man's faith is, so is his character.

'Yo yacchraddhaḥ sa eva saḥ'— As a man's faith, is so is his 'Niṣṭhā', (state of being, conviction) and according to his conviction is his fate. His feelings and actions, are according to his faith. So long as, he maintains affinity with the world, he is the same as is his nature or his inner sense.

A Vital Fact

A man is inclined towards the world by regarding it, as true, while he is inclined towards God, by having faith in Him. Without faith a man, cannot progress in the spiritual sphere, whether he follows the discipline of action, of knowledge or of devotion.

Faith, occupies an important place in a man's life. As a man's faith is, so is he (17/3). He may not be so today, but in the course of time, he will become so.

Today, it is difficult for a striver, to recognize his natural faith, because there are innumerable sects and religions. Having read and heard, different opinions and principles, he finds himself in a fix. He cannot decide, what his aim is, and what he should do. In such circumstances, he should give a serious thought, to his internal feelings which are untainted by any external influences, of association, of a preceptor or scriptures. Thus he comes to know, of his natural inclination or faith.

Every being, has an inclination to be free from all sorrows, and to attain eternal bliss. This inclination, is aroused in human beings, because of their past influences, present education, environment and heredity. They make their decisions, according to their inclination or nature. This resolution, decides their faith. Sāttvika faith, leads to spirituality, while the tāmasa and rājasa ones lead to the mundane world. So, the sāttvika faith is spiritual, while the tāmasa and the rājasa faiths, are mundane i.e., the sāttvika faith is divine nature, while the tāmasa and the rājasa faiths, imply demoniac nature. The seventeenth chapter, has been started in order to enable people to renounce demoniac nature, and to reveal divine nature. The reason, is that those who want to attain salvation, should renounce the demoniac nature and should acquire divine one.

The faith of the people, who want to attain salvation is sāttvika, of those who want mundane pleasures, prosperity and also heaven etc., is rājasa and of those who believe in 'eat, drink and be merry' as well as in indolence, heedlessness and excessive sleep etc., is tāmasa. Faith consists, in the acceptance of the existence of God and in His realization. Where there is faith, love reveals itself naturally, because the soul is a fragment of God. So, as soon as, one develops faith, he is attracted towards Him. When having a disinclination, for the Lord, he remains absorbed in worldly pleasures and prosperity, believing in the mundane. This sort of faith or belief, is not real, it is a misuse of faith. This mundane faith, leads to a downfall. The faith, that he belongs to a particular caste(varṇa) and a particular social order (āśrama), is a higher sort of faith, than mundane faith. But, the best and the real faith, is the faith in God, saints, liberated souls and scriptures. Such faith leads to salvation.*

Those, who have neither knowledge of scriptures, nor company of the great souls, can also have faith in spirituality or God, because of the impressions saṁskāra of the past. Such people naturally believe in God, and are engaged in virtuous actions, such as religious sacrifice, charity, austerity, pilgrimage, fast, good company and study of scriptures etc. Even if they do not perform such virtuous acts, their faith can be recognized, by the sāttvika food, they eat.

All beings, such as human beings, birds, beasts, plants and creepers etc., whether moving or not assumed someone as superior to them and depend upon him or it. When adversity visits them, all take shelter in someone, who is superior to them. He, who has deemed anyone superior to him, and taken shelter in him, he may believe in God or not, he has, in fact accepted God, in principle. He, who goes on viewing superiority of one, over another, in respect of age, learning, quality, wisdom, ability, power and status etc., he will have to accept, finally the most superior One of whom, there is no superior. All superiority, ends in Him and He is God.

'Pūrveṣāmapi guruḥ kālenānavacchedāt'

(Yogadarśana 1/26)

"He is the preceptor of the most ancient ancestors, because He is above, a time limit."

Everybody concedes, someone or the other, as superior to him, from his view-point. This faith in superiority, is according to feelings of his inner sense. These feelings constitute his faith. These feelings, remain different in different persons. So their

* In the mundane faith there is predominance of pleasures, in the religious faith there is predominance of feeling and in the spiritual faith there is predominance of the truth.

faith is also, distinct.

A man's faith is sāttvika, rājasa or tāmasa, according to his nature. All beings, are endowed with the three modes of nature—sāttvika, rājasika or tāmasika (Gītā 18/40). One of them may predominate the other two (Gītā 14/10), in every being. As nature always undergoes changes, so its modes also change. So a striver, whose aim is God-realization, without assuming any affinity, with modes of nature, should remain unperturbed, by them.

The soul is a fragment of God. So when a man, finds predominance of a mode either of passion or of ignorance, he should not regard himself, as mean or low. Being a fragment of God, he (soul), is pure. It is his company or environment, by which one mode of nature predominates, by suppressing the other two. As the nature of a man is, so is his faith—sāttvika, rājasa or tāmasa. So a striver, should keep good (sāttvika) company, should live in good environment, and should study the scriptures. By doing so, his nature and faith, will be sāttvika (good) and these will lead him, to salvation. On the other hand, by bad company, environment and literature, his faith will be rājasika or tāmasika, which will degrade him.

Appendix—Faith is a 'bhāva' (sentiment). As is a man's sentiment, so is his self. The bhāva (sentiment) is of two kinds—'sadbhāva' and 'asadbhāva'. The one which leads to God, is 'sadbhāva' and the one which leads to the world is 'asadbhāva'. In the divine nature there is predominance of 'sadbhāva' while in demoniac nature, there is predominance of 'asadbhāva'.

'I am a striver'—In it if there is the predominance of 'asadbhāva', it causes pride (false pride) and if there is predominance of 'sadbhāva', it causes 'svābhimāna' (Self-respect). Pride causes demoniac nature but Self-respect causes divine nature. If a man thinks that he is superior to others, he becomes proud of his superiority; and if a striver thinks of his duty, he is full of Self-respect that he can't perform any action which is an obstacle to his spiritual progress. Being proud a man can perform an action contrary to his spiritual practice; but if the striver has Self-respect, he will feel shy in performing any action which is contrary to his spiritual discipline. 'Svābhimāna' will lead him to the 'Sāttvika' faith while 'Abhimāna' (pride) will lead him to the 'Rājasika' and 'Tāmasika' faiths.

Link:—The Lord, in the next verse, explains the means of ascertaining the conviction (state of being), of a person by his worship.

यजन्ते सात्त्विका देवान्यक्षरक्षांसि राजसाः ।
प्रेतान्भूतगणांश्चान्ये यजन्ते तामसा जनाः ॥ ४ ॥

yajante sāttvikā devānyakṣarakṣāṁsi rājasāḥ
pretānbhūtagaṇāṁścānye yajante tāmasā janāḥ

Good (sāttvika) men worship the gods; the passionate (rājasika) worship the gnomes (yakṣa) and the demons; the ignorant (tāmasika) offer sacrifices to the spirits and ghosts. 4

Comment:—

'Yajante sāttvikā devān'—The sāttvika (good) people, possessing divine nature, worship the gods. Here, the term 'Devān' denotes the five chief deities—Viṣṇu (the preserver), (Rāma or Kṛṣṇa etc.), Śiva (the destroyer), Gaṇeśa, Durgā (Power) and the Sun, because the term 'Deva', stands for God (Divinity) and His nature viz., divine nature, which is conducive to liberation (16/5). Thus, strivers possessing the sāttvika (good) faith worship, anyone of five chief deities, according to their natural faith. The worship of twelve Ādityas, eight Vasus, eleven Rūdras, and two Aśvinī Kumāras, without any selfish motive, is also regarded as sāttvika worship.

'Yakṣarakṣāṁsi rājasāḥ'—The passionate, worship the gnomes and the demons. They are included among the gods. The gnomes, hanker after the accumulation of wealth, and then guard it, while the demons are bent upon the destruction, of others. The passionate, worship them, to satisfy their own desires and to destroy others.

'Pretānbhūtagaṇāṁścānye yajante tāmasā janāḥ'—The ignorant people, worship spirits and ghosts. Those, who are dead are called 'Preta', while those who are in the forms of the life of ghosts, are 'Bhūta'.

Here, the manes should not be included in the term 'Preta' (spirit), because those, who worship the manes as a part of their duty without any desire for the fruit of their actions (worship), are sāttvika (good). The Lord in the Gītā, has not prohibited the worship of manes (Gītā 9/25). Those who worship the manes, having a desire for fruits, such as their own safety and reward etc., go, to the manes. Such worshippers, regard their manes as their favourite deities, who hold the highest positions. So, they go to the abode of the manes, they cannot go to higher regions, which are beyond the abode of the manes. But, those who worship the manes as a part of their duty, without having any desire for fruits, are sāttvika (good or pure), they are not rājasa (passionate).

Those, who feed dogs and crows selflessly, obeying the ordinance of scriptures, do not attain these. Similar, is the case with those, who worship the manes, without any desire for fruits. Their worship, leads them to salvation. Similarly obsequies, such as Nārāyaṇabali and Gayā-Śrāddha (offering of water, food etc., to the Brāhmaṇas in honour of the manes), which are sanctioned by scriptures, are indispensable. These must be performed, so that the soul of the dead persons, may attain higher states, such as salvation etc. Such actions, are sāttvika.

Those, who while performing (yajña) sacrifice, worship Lord Gaṇeśa and Navagraha (nine planets) etc., according to ordinance of scriptures, without any desire for fruit, actually worship the scripture, in the same way, as a chaste wife of even a demon, attains salvation, not because, she has served her demon-husband but because, she has obeyed the Lord, the saints and the scriptures. In the twenty-fifth verse of the ninth chapter, the worship of gods, has been mentioned to outline the fate of worshippers, while in this verse the worship of gods, has been mentioned to judge, the faith of a worshipper. So the term 'Yajante', has been used here. Thus the Lord, explained that a man worships, a deity according to his conviction, or faith.

Appendix—The 'Sāttvika' persons who worship the gods, go to the gods after death, the Rājasa persons who worship demigods (gnomes) and demons, go to them and the 'Tāmasa' persons who worship ghosts and evil spirits, join the ghosts and evil spirits (Gītā 9/25).

In the Gītā, the term 'Yajña' has a wide range, within which religious sacrifice, charity, austerity, vow and performance of duty etc.,—all are included (Gītā 4/24-25). Therefore here also within the term 'Yajante'—performance of all duties and actions should be included, out of which, Yajña (religious sacrifice) is important. 'Pretānbhūtagaṇāṁścānye'—Our manes are ghosts for others and the manes of others are ghosts for us. Worship to manes is not 'Tāmasika', but worship to ghosts is 'Tāmasika'.

Link:—The Lord in the preceding verses, described those people, who casting aside ordinances of the scriptures, offer worship with faith. They neglect the ordinances because they do not know them. Now He, in the next two verses, describes those who intentionally neglect the ordinances of scriptures, and are also lacking, in faith.

अशास्त्रविहितं घोरं तप्यन्ते ये तपो जनाः ।
दम्भाहङ्कारसंयुक्ताः कामरागबलान्विताः ॥ ५ ॥

कर्शयन्तः शरीरस्थं भूतग्राममचेतसः।
मां चैवान्तःशरीरस्थं तान्विद्ध्यासुरनिश्चयान्॥ ६ ॥

aśāstravihitaṁ ghoraṁ tapyante ye tapo janāḥ
dambhāhaṅkārasaṁyuktāḥ kāmarāgabalānvitāḥ
karśayantaḥ śarīrasthaṁ bhūtagrāmamacetasaḥ
māṁ caivāntaḥ śarīrasthaṁ tānviddhyāsuraniścayān

Those men who perform stern austerities, not enjoined by the scripture, due to hypocrisy and egoism, impelled by desire (lust) and attachment, who torment the elements, in their body, and Me, Who dwell in the body, know these senseless (ignorant) people, to be of demoniacal resolves. 5-6

Comment:—

'Aśāstravihitaṁ ghoraṁ tapyante ye tapo janāḥ'—Those men perform dire austerities which are not sanctioned by the scriptures rather forbidden. It is because of their tāmasika intellect (intellect enveloped in darkness) (Gītā 18/32) that they themselves do not know the ordinance of scriptures. Moreover, they are not prepared to accept those ordinances, and act upon these, even if, those ordinances, are explained to them by some person.

'Dambhāhaṅkārasaṁyuktāḥ'—They, are full of hypocrisy and egoism. They believe, that people who are engaged in adoration, meditation and study of scriptures, are hypocrites. So they also pretend to be, what they are not, and are puffed up with pride, because of their false intelligence, wisdom and knowledge etc. They think that they can bring other people round, to their view-point; and they need not listen to the scriptures, because they possess, enough knowledge.

'Kāmarāgabalānvitāḥ'—The term 'Kāma', stands for lust, for worldly pleasure. They remain engrossed in those pleasures i.e., they remain attached to them. Impelled by the force of desire, they have a thirst for these and so they want to secure and maintain them. Thus, they hanker after worldly pleasure and prosperity and remain engrossed in them, by regarding these, as the only goal of human life. They have the feelings, that if having obtained this human life, they have not enjoyed worldly pleasure, they are just like beasts. If they have not acquired those materials, for enjoyment, what have they gained? Without those enjoyments, their life has gone in vain. They are always given, to sense-enjoyments. They perform austerities, obstinately with a view to acquire material for worldly enjoyment.

'Karśayantaḥ śarīrasthaṁ bhūtagrāmam'—They believe, that austerities consist in tormenting the group of five elements (earth, water, fire, air and ether), in their bodies. According to them, austerity means bodily torture.

In the fourteenth, fifteenth and sixteenth verses of this chapter, there is a description of the austerities of the body, speech and mind. There is no mention of physical torture. Austerity is performed very calmly, without tormenting the body. But the austerities, referred to in this verse, are performed by tormenting the body, against the ordinances of scriptures. So these are called violent austerities.

'Māṁ caivāntaḥśarīrastham'—They, also torment the Lord, Who is lodged in their hearts. As God is seated in their hearts as their very self, so when they torment the self, they torment God. Moreover, they torment Him, by disobeying His teachings.

'Tānviddhyāsuraniścayān'—The Lord, declares that such people should be known to be of demoniacal resolves. Here, the expression 'Āsuraniścayān', does not denote people of ordinary demoniac nature; but those who are extremely demoniac, mean and atheistic.

An Important Fact

In the fourth verse, the term 'Yajante' (worship), has been used, for those people who neglecting the ordinances of scriptures due to their ignorance perform worship, with faith. But here the term, 'tapyante' (practise), has been used for people, who intentionally neglect the ordinances of scriptures and are also lacking in faith. The reason is, that people of demoniac resolve, attach great importance to violent austerities, according to their own fancy and whims. The mark, of their austerity is tormentation of body. They instead of believing in God, and the scriptures, believe in austerities. They perform, violent austerities against ordinances of the scriptures. They remain hungry, for a long time, lie on thorns or nails bare bodied, stand on one leg only, sit facing fire and perform other violent austerities, of such type, to torment their bodies.

In the twenty-third verse of the sixteenth chapter, it is mentioned that those, who having cast aside, ordinances of scriptures, act under the impulse of desire, attain neither perfection, nor happiness nor achieve the Supreme Goal. It means, that they do not secure the full fruit of their actions, because they attach importance to external activities, instead of internal feelings. But, here people of demoniac resolves, go to the lower wombs and hell, because they are given to hypocrisy and egoism, etc. Moreover, they neither have faith, nor want to listen to ordinances of the scriptures and not act upon these.

In the twenty-third verse of the sixteenth chapter, there is reference to disobedience of the ordinance of scriptures through indifference, in the first verse of this chapter, there is disobedience, through lack of knowledge while, here it is, intentional and wilful disobedience. Here the performance of austerities is made having opposition to faith, the ordinances of scriptures and God, and welfare of the people. Such opposition, is not found among the people of the rājasa and tāmasa dispositions, described at places.

Link:—How to know the faith of a man, who does not offer, any sort of worship! The Lord, explains that it can be judged by the food, which is dear to him.

आहारस्त्वपि सर्वस्य त्रिविधो भवति प्रियः।
यज्ञस्तपस्तथा दानं तेषां भेदमिमं शृणु॥७॥

āhārastvapi sarvasya trividho bhavati priyaḥ
yajñastapastathā dānaṁ teṣāṁ bhedamimaṁ śṛṇu

The food, which is dear to all, is also of three kinds. Even so are the sacrifices, austerities and charities. Hear thou, the distinction between these. 7

Comment:—

'Āhārastvapi sarvasya trividho bhavati priyaḥ'—In the fourth verse, the Lord, explained the means of ascertaining the conviction of a person by his sāttvika, rājasa and tāmasa worship. But how to know the conviction of a person who has no faith, and interest, in worship? The answer is, that every person, whether he is a believer or a non-believer, belonging to any sect or religion, has to eat food. So a man's conviction or faith can be known by the food, which is dear to him. By what dishes is a man naturally tempted viz., on hearing, seeing and tasting the food articles, by which the mind is attracted, that will determine, his sāttvika, rājasa or tāmasa, faith.

Some may think that this is a description of three kinds of food. If it is viewed from a gross point of view, the approach may appear correct. But if we ponder over it deeply, it is not correct. This is not description of three kinds of food. But actually it indicates a person's taste for food in order to judge his faith.

The terms 'Sarvasya' (all) and 'Priyaḥ' (dear), have been used to indicate, that each person out of all human beings, wants to eat a particular kind of food—sāttvika, rājasa or tāmasa, which is dear to him. Thus, his nature is inferred from the nature of food he likes and eats. Similarly 'Yajñastapastathā dānam' (sacrifice, austerity and charity)* are also of three kinds. It makes out

*Here the term 'Yajña' stands only for sacrifice, not for all duties or actions that are to be performed because besides the 'Yajña' (sacrifice), austerity

that a person studies books, keeps company, visits places and is engaged in different sorts of activities, according to his sāttvika, rājasa or tāmasa, temperament.

'Teṣāṁ bhedamimaṁ śṛṇu'—Lord Kṛṣṇa asks Arjuna, to note the distinction of sacrifice, austerity and charity, according to a man's temperament. A man, offers charity to a Brāhmaṇa (member of the priest class), while another person offers charity, to a common man. Some keep company with virtuous persons, whose food and conduct etc., are pure, while others keep company with evil persons.*

It means, that people of sāttvika temperament like sāttvika (good) food, company, environment and actions, etc., while people of rājasika (passionate) temperament, have rājasika tastes, and those of tāmasika (ignorant) temperament, like food, company, environment and actions, which are not sanctioned by scriptures.

Appendix—Two kinds of actions are performed by a man according to his temperament—secular and scriptural. Therefore here within 'food', the secular actions (eating, drinking and the way of living etc.,) and within 'austerity, sacrifice and charity' the scriptural actions should be taken (understood).

आयुःसत्त्वबलारोग्यसुखप्रीतिविवर्धनाः ।
रस्याः स्निग्धाः स्थिरा हृद्या आहाराः सात्त्विकप्रियाः ॥ ८ ॥

āyuḥsattvabalārogyasukhaprītivivardhanāḥ
rasyāḥ snigdhāḥ sthirā hṛdyā āhārāḥ sāttvikapriyāḥ

---

and charity are given. Pilgrimage and fast etc., can also be included in them and they may occupy secondary positions.

*As among animals deer accompany deer, cows accompany cows and horses accompany horses, similarly fools keep company with fools and the learned have friendship with the learned because friendship is maintained among persons of the same temperament and conduct.

The foods which promote life, vitality, strength, health, joy and cheerfulness, which are juicy, bland, nourishing and agreeable are dear to the sāttvika type of people. 8

Comment:—

The foods, which promote life, vitality, strength, purity, health, happiness* and peace, which are sweet and juicy (fruit, milk etc.,) which provide strength to the heart and lungs, and which are oily such as butter, ghee, almonds, cashewnut and raisins etc., are dear to the sāttvika type of men. These can be of four kinds—those which are eaten, are drunk, licked, and those which are sucked. A person, who likes such foods is of sāttvika temperament.

कट्वम्ललवणात्युष्णतीक्ष्णरूक्षविदाहिनः ।
आहारा राजसस्येष्टा दुःखशोकामयप्रदाः ॥ ९ ॥

kaṭvamlalavaṇātyuṣṇatīkṣṇarūkṣavidāhinaḥ
āhārā rājasasyeṣṭā duḥkhaśokāmayapradāḥ

Foods which are bitter, sour, saltish, very hot, pungent, dry, scorching and producing pain, grief and disease, are liked, by the rājasika type of persons. 9

Comment:—

Foods which are bitter, such as 'Karelā' and aloe plant, sour, such as tamarind and lemon, saltish, having excessive alkaline and salts, and which are very hot viz., steaming, pungent such as chilies, and dry such as, parched grains (lacking butter, milk etc.,) and which cause burning such as mustard etc.

'Āhārā rājasasyeṣṭā'—Such foods (which are eaten, drunk, licked and sucked), are liked by the rājasika type of persons.

*Though the favourable foods are dear even to the passionate but their love for them will change into poison (18/38). Similarly the ignorant also like them but their liking for them will conduce them to sleep, indolence and heedlessness (entertainment, ill talk and evil habits etc.) (18/39).

Thus a man's faith, is known by the food he takes.

'Duḥkhaśokāmayapradāḥ'—Such foods, produce pain, grief and disease. When a person eats such food, he experiences pain and a burning sensation, in the throat, tongue and palate etc. He is not pleased, but is rather grieved after eating such foods and these cause sickness, in the body.

यातयामं गतरसं पूति पर्युषितं च यत्।
उच्छिष्टमपि चामेध्यं भोजनं तामसप्रियम्॥ १०॥

yātayāmaṁ gatarasaṁ pūti paryuṣitaṁ ca yat
ucchiṣṭamapi cāmedhyaṁ bhojanaṁ tāmasapriyam

That which is, half-cooked or half-ripe, insipid, putrid, stale, polluted and impure, is the food, dear to the tāmasa. 10

Comment:—

'Yātayāmam'—It means half-cooked, half-ripe, overcooked and overripe food and off-season fruit and vegetables etc., kept usable through refrigeration etc.

'Gatarasam'—The fruits etc., which lose their juice due to exposure etc., of which the essence has been taken out through machinery are 'Gatarasam'.

'Pūti—Putrid foods, are those of which the smell is offensive, these are onion and garlic etc. Moreover wine etc.,* which are

* In the scriptures a drunkard has been called a great sinner—He who steals gold, he who drinks wine, he who has sexual intercourse with his preceptor's wife and he who murders a Brāhmaṇa—these four are great sinners and the fifth great sinner is he who keeps their company. It means that drinking is one of the worst evils, worse than even the non-vegetarian diet.

The holy water of the Ganges purifies everything. But the goblet is not purified even with it. So how much impure a drunkard is—one can't imagine.

Its preparation involves a lot of violence. It kills the germs of righteousness i.e., the feelings and impressions of righteousness are destroyed by drinking wine and a man has a downfall.

rendered foul, through fermentation, are also putrid.

'Paryuṣitam'—Cooked food, such as vegetables and 'Capātīs', prepared by mixing water and salt, in them which has been kept overnight, is stale. But sweets, prepared from milk, butter, ghee and sugar do not get stale, as they do not get spoiled, when allowed to stay overnight.

'Ucchiṣṭam'—Food left over on a plate after a meal or food which is either seen, or smelt or partly eaten, by a cow, a cat, a dog or a crow is called polluted (Ucchiṣṭam).

'Amedhyam'—Meat and eggs etc., are impure food, so impure that a man has to take a bath, even if he touches them. The Lord, does not want, even to name articles, of impure food.

'Api ca'—This expression, conveys that besides the above-mentioned foods, all other articles of food forbidden, by the scriptures—such as turnip and carrots etc., are prohibited according to one's stage of life or social order etc., are also included in the tāmasika food.

'Bhojanaṁ tāmasapriyam'— Such food is dear to a tāmasika person. Thus a man' faith is known, by the food, which is dear to him.

Even if sāttvika food, is eaten having attachment for it, becomes rājasika. If it is eaten in excess, it becomes tāmasika. Similarly, dry or stale food offered to a beggar, is rājasika or tāmasika. But if the same food is offered to God, with devotion and it is eaten, less than the appetite* by chanting the name of the Lord, it becomes sāttvika.

An Important Fact Pertaining to the Topic

In this context, it seems as if there is a description of three types of food. But actually, it is a description of a person's inclination, which can be judged by the nature of food, which

*The quantity of the food should be moderate, neither more nor less.

is dear to him. The following points, clarify it.

(1) In the seventh verse of this chapter, the Lord uses the term 'Sarvasya', to indicate that all human beings, like three kinds of food, according to their inclination. That inclination, decides a man's conviction. The term 'priyaḥ' (dear), has also been used in the eighth and tenth verses, and 'Iṣṭa' (dear) in the ninth verse, which indicate a man's inclination, or taste. Had there been a context of food, the Lord, instead of using the term 'priyaḥ' (dear) or 'Iṣṭa', would have said, that these are Sāttvika foods, or the tāmasika ones etc.

(2) The second argument, is that while mentioning the sāttvika food, the Lord first explained the result of taking sāttvika food, and then sāttvika food. It is so, because a sāttvika person, thinks of the consequences of eating a particular food or performing an action, before he eats food, or performs an act.

A rājasika person, first eats food and then thinks, of its adverse effect. So in rājasika food, first there is a description of food and then its result, in the form, the pain, grief and sickness.

As far as the effect of the tāmasika food, is concerned, the Lord has not even mentioned it. It is so, because a tāmasika person, out of delusion does not think of the adverse effect, of the food eaten. He does not think—whether it is earned by fair means or foul, whether it is pure or impure, whether it is sanctioned by scriptures or not. He eats the food, like an animal. It means that he, who eats sāttvika food, possesses a divine nature, while he, who eats either rājasika or tāmasika food, possesses, a demoniac nature.

(3) Had the Lord described the food, He would have described the food in more details, such as that livelihood, should be earned by honest means; the food should he cooked by wearing clean clothes in a well cleaned and pure kitchen; it should first be offered to God, and then eaten by thinking of Him, and chanting His name. This sort of food, is sāttvika.

Similarly, He would have described the rājasa food. Livelihood should be earned by fair means or foul, having predominance of pride and selfishness. The food should be eaten for taste and fashion, and it should be eaten by having attachment, to it. This food is rājasika.

In the same way, food is earned by foul means, such as falsehood, fraud, theft and robbery etc., without any sense of purity and cleanliness, in an impure atmosphere, the food items, may be meat and egg etc., no attention is paid to how the food is cooked. One who takes food, does not wash his hands and feet and takes it with his shoes on. No cleanliness is maintained and it is eaten, in an impure atmosphere. Such food is tāmasika.

But here the Lord, has described the foods, which are dear to the sāttvika (good), the rājasika (passionate) and the tāmasika (ignorant), so that their inclinations, or faith could be known.

(4) Besides this, in the Gītā where there is description of food, there is reference only to the eaters, as 'others restrict their food', (4/30), 'Yoga is not for him, who eats too much, but for him who is temperate, in food' (6/16-17), 'Whatever thou eatest' (9/27) and 'He who eats, but little' (18/52).

Similarly, in the seventh verse of this chapter, the term 'tathā (also), denotes that a man performs sacrifice and austerity, and offers charity according to his sāttvika, rājasika or tāmasika, temperament. Similarly, in this chapter from the eleventh verse to the twenty-second verse, also there is description of the nature of those, who perform sacrifice and austerity, and offer charity.

An Important Thought Over Food

In the Upaniṣads, (Parts of different branches of Vedas) it is mentioned 'As is the food, so is the mind'. As the food, a man eats, so is his mind. So a man should eat pure food, because it purifies his mind. The place, seat, scene and atmosphere where he eats, the food should be pure and holy, as these also effect the mind. Moreover, feelings and thought of a cook should be pure, and good.

Before, having a meal, a person should wash both the hands, both the feet and the mouth. He should sit on a clean and pure seat, with his face towards the east or the north. Then he should offer food to the Lord, by reciting verses—"Whosoever offers to Me with devotion a leaf, a flower, a fruit or water, that offering of love, of the pure of heart I accept" (Gītā 9/26). After this, he should take a little water, on his palm and reciting a verse, "The act of offering is God, the oblation is God. By God, it is offered into the fire of God. God is verily to be attained by him who always sees God in action" (Gītā 4/24), one should drink it. Then, he should put the first morsel of food into his mouth by chanting the name of the Lord. While chewing a morsel, he should recite the sacred mantra (hymn), of sixteen words 'Hare Rāma Hare Rāma, Rāma Rāma Hare Hare, Hare Kṛṣṇa Hare Kṛṣṇa Kṛṣṇa Kṛṣṇa Hare Hare' (or chant the name of his favourite deity), two times. Thus he chews a morsel thirty-two times, because there are sixteen words in the sacred hymn (formula). Thus, the food becomes digestible and nourishing and one remains absorbed, in the adoration of the Lord by chanting His names, which purify, the food.

If a person, while having a meal has evil propensities, such as hatred, envy, jealousy, fear and greed, his food is not digested well, and he suffers from indigestion. So, while eating food, he should be free from all these evil propensities, and should remain calm and pleased. It is heard, that a dog is allowed to run after a calf before a cow is milked. The cow grows angry, after seeing the dog. That milk is offered to soldiers, so that they may become cruel.

An experiment was made on some horses. Some of them were fed with milk of cows, while others were fed with the milk of buffaloes. The former could cross a stream, while the latter could not. Similarly, if there is a fight between a bullock and a buffalo, the buffalo defeats the bullock. But if both of them draw a cart in the heat of the sun, the bullock is more active. The reason is that milk of the cow contains sāttvika nourishment.

As good and evil feelings, have their effect on food, so have looks. If an evil person or a hungry dog, has a look at food, it becomes impure. So what to do? He who wants to eat that food, should think that Lord Himself in that form has come to eat the food. So, first he should offer a part of it to Him, and then eat the remaining food himself. By doing so, the food is purified.

Secondly, those who take a share of the calf from the milk of a cow, make the milk impure. If they milk the cow, after the calf has been well-fed, the milk is pure.

The feelings of a person, who eats, and of the person, who offers food, have also their effect, on food. (i) Food which is offered with great pleasure, is of superior quality. (ii) The food offered with pleasure, but the eater thinks that he has saved some money, by receiving free food—it is considered of medium quality. (iii) Food offered with a feeling of compulsion, that he has been forced to offer the food, because someone has arrived, and the eater eats the food having the feeling of selfishness—that food is, of an inferior quality.

In the Gītā it is mentioned, that good persons are devoted to the welfare of all beings (5/25, 12/4). It means that the things and actions of persons, who are devoted to the welfare of other beings, are pure and holy.

The following verses, should be recited when a meal is over—

"All beings come forth from food, food is produced from rain, rain ensues from sacrifice and sacrifice, is born of action. Action has its origin in Brahma (Vedas), and the Vedas spring from the Imperishable (God); therefore the all-pervading (Brahma), ever rests in sacrifice" (Gītā 3/14-15).

Then, in order to digest food he should recite "Becoming the fire which dwells in the bodies of living beings, and mingling with the upward and downward breaths, I digest the four kinds of food" (Gītā 15/14), and move the navel, with the middle finger slowly.

Link:—Having explained, that the faith of a person can be known by his worship or by the food, which is dear to him, the Lord now explains, the three kinds of sacrifice, by which a man's faith or inclination, is known.

अफलाकाङ्क्षिभिर्यज्ञो विधिदृष्टो य इज्यते।
यष्टव्यमेवेति मनः समाधाय स सात्त्विकः ॥ ११ ॥

aphalākāṅkṣibhiryajño vidhidṛṣṭo ya ijyate
yaṣṭavyameveti manaḥ samādhāya sa sāttvikaḥ

Sacrifice (yajña) which is performed, according to scriptural law, by those, who expect no reward and believe firmly, that it is their duty to offer the sacrifice, is sāttvika (good). 11

Comment:—

'Yaṣṭavyameveti'—Being blessed with human body a man, becomes eligible to perform the sacrifice according to his caste and social order, with a firm belief, that it is his duty to do so, and he should not expect any reward, either here or hereafter. The terms 'eva' (only), and 'Iti' (thus), have been used, to emphasize the fact, that it is his duty and it must be done. He should, have no other consideration, except performance of duty, for duty's sake.

'Aphalākāṅkṣibhiḥ'— A man, expects no reward, either here or hereafter, for sacrifice, which he offers.

'Yajño vidhidṛṣṭo ya ijyate'—The sacrifice, should be offered, according to the ordinance of scriptures.

If he expects no reward, then why should he perform a sacrifice? The Lord, answers 'Manaḥ samādhāya (mind having reconciled), i.e., it is his duty, to perform it.

What is Sāttvika Sacrifice?

The term 'yaṣṭavyam'*, denotes that sacrifices should be offered, as a duty. When a man offers sacrifice having desire of gaining honour, praise and riches here, and heaven and luxuries, in the next birth, he is attached to the sacrifice. But if he performs it, without any kind of reward, his affinity with it is renounced and (in absence of selfishness and pride), his ego is purified.

In it there is a vital point, that when a doer performs an action, he gets affinity with it. An action, is in the image of a doer viz., as is the doer, so is his action. The Lord, in the third verse of this chapter, declares, "As is a man's faith, so is he" and he acts according to his faith. It means, that as affinity of a doer with an action remains, there is every possibility of his getting into bondage. But if he performs an act, as a matter of duty without having any attachment for it, his affinity is renounced and he gets liberated. How is an action to be performed, only for duty's sake? A person, has to do nothing for himself. He should have no affinity, with any object, time and place etc. He should perform his duty, according to the need of the hour. Thus, he will not desire to reap the fruit of action, and will not be bound.

On the other hand, attachment leads him, to bondage. It is declared in the Gītā—"The Yogīs (men of action) perform actions, only with their senses, mind, intellect and body, abandoning attachment" (5/11). It means, that a Karmayogī, should not have any affinity with body, senses and mind. It also implies, that he should not have any affinity, with the ladle, the place and materials for oblation.

Sacrifice, and its fruit, both have a beginning and an end, they appear and disappear, while the soul is imperishable and

* Duty is the action which should be performed, which is according to one's capacity and by which the aim is achieved.

eternal. But, he (the soul) assumes his affinity with actions, and their fruits. Until he renounces this affinity, he gets entangled, in the cycle of birth and death (Gītā 5/12).

Sattvaguṇa, enables a man to renounce his affinity with the world, and leads him to God-realization, therefore, it is called as 'Sat' or transcendental.* All the qualities of the divine nature are Sāttvika. But a person possessing divine nature realizes God, only when he transcends the three guṇas (modes of nature).

अभिसन्धाय तु फलं दम्भार्थमपि चैव यत्।
इज्यते भरतश्रेष्ठ तं यज्ञं विद्धि राजसम्॥ १२॥

abhisandhāya tu phalaṁ dambhārthamapi caiva yat
ijyate bharataśreṣṭha taṁ yajñaṁ viddhi rājasam

Sacrifice, which is offered in expectation of reward or for the

---

* In the Śrīmadbhāgavata in the twenty-fifth chapter of the eleventh section besides the three Guṇas there is also the description of the state which transcends the three Guṇas while in the Gītā there is the description of the three Guṇas only. Why is it so when Lord Kṛṣṇa is the speaker in both of them? The answer is that when the sacrifice is performed as a duty (17/11), gifts are made as a duty (17/20) and an action is performed as a duty (18/9), the person has no affinity with actions and their fruits, and so the Sāttvika actions turn into transcendental ones.

At the end of the seventeenth chapter also the Lord while describing the Lord's name 'Sat' out of the three names 'Oṁ', 'Tat', 'Sat', declares that all the actions which are performed for the sake of the Lord become 'Sat' viz., real (transcendental) (17/27). It means that the actions of a Karmayogī become transcendental when he renounces attachment to the actions and their fruits, while the actions of a Bhaktiyogī become transcendental when they are performed for the sake of the Lord. So there is no description of the state which transcends the three Guṇas.

In the Gītā it is also mentioned the Sattvaguṇa (The mode of goodness) binds (14/6) and those established in Sattvaguṇa rise to the higher regions (14/18). Why? The answer is that it is not Sattvaguṇa which binds but it is attachment to it which binds (14/6, 13/21). Similarly the assumption that one is established in Sattvaguṇa also leads him to bondage (14/18).

sake of ostentation, know, O best of the Bharatas (Arjuna), that such sacrifice is rājasika (passionate). 12

Comment:—

'Abhisandhāya tu phalam'—Sacrifice, which is performed to acquire the desirable and to avert the undesirable, is 'rājasa sacrifice'. If anyone performs a sacrifice, in order to obtain riches, name and fame, honour, obedient servants, sons, family and heaven etc., this is desire, to acquire the desirable. Our enemies should be destroyed; we should never be dishonoured, disrespected and slighted; we should never face unfavourable circumstances—this is desire, to avert the undesirable.

'Dambhārthamapi caiva yat'—Sacrifice which is offered by a man, showing himself off, as a virtuous, good, charitable, righteous and great person for ostentation and for self glorification, is rājasika. It includes sacrifice, offered by people of demoniacal nature, as described in 16/15 and 16/17.

'Ijyate bharataśreṣṭha taṁ yajñaṁ viddhi rājasam'— Sacrifice offered, in expectation of reward or for ostentation, is rājasika.

Such sacrifice is offered, strictly according to the ordinance of scriptures. The reason, is that if it is not performed according to the ordinance of scriptures, it will not bear full fruit. Similarly, if either the method or the action, happens to be contrary, to the sanctioned one, it will bear a contrary fruit i.e., it may be harmful for the performer. But the person who offers a sacrifice only for ostentation does not care much, about the ordinance of scriptures.

By using the term 'Viddhi', Lord Kṛṣṇa, wants to emphasize the fact that mundane attachment (desire), is the root cause of the cycle of birth and death. So, Arjuna should beware of it.

Appendix—The term 'yat' used in this verse expresses the idea that whatever sacrifice or charity or austerity is done in expectation of reward or for the sake of ostentation is 'Rājasa'.

विधिहीनमसृष्टान्नं मन्त्रहीनमदक्षिणम्।
श्रद्धाविरहितं यज्ञं तामसं परिचक्षते॥ १३॥

vidhihīnamasṛṣṭānnaṁ mantrahīnamadakṣiṇam
śraddhāvirahitaṁ yajñaṁ tāmasaṁ paricakṣate

Sacrifice, which is not in conformity with, the ordinances of scriptures, in which no food is offered, no 'mantras' are chanted, no donation is made and which is without faith—that sacrifice, is of the nature of ignorance viz., tāmasika. 13

Comment:—

'Vidhihīnam'—There are different methods, for different kinds of sacrifice, in which there is guidance for the altar, utensils for oblation, direction and seating etc. Similarly, different materials are used, in the sacrifice for different gods and goddesses etc., as in the sacrifice for the Goddess Durgā, the cloth and material of red colour are used. In tāmasa sacrifice, the ordinances are not followed, but are renounced, due to indifference.

'Asṛṣṭānnam'—Tāmasika people, who offer wealth as sacrifice, do not offer food, as charity to Brāhmaṇas, because they think that Brāhmaṇas will become idle, if they get free food and they could not work.

'Mantrahīnam'—In tāmasika sacrifice, sacred hymns are not chanted, as tāmasika people think, that a sacrifice is performed by offering oblation, because it kills germs, and fragrance, spreads. But there is no need for the chanting of sacred hymns.

'Adakṣiṇam'—No sacrificial donations are paid to a priest or Brāhmaṇas, in tāmasika sacrifice, because people of tāmasika temperament, think that they have offered food to them already. If they offer fees to them, they will become idle and lazy, and will create a problem of unemployment, and so on. According to them, such Brāhmaṇas are a burden on the earth. But they do not think that if they do not offer fees or food to the Brāhmaṇas, the Brāhmaṇas may or may not become idle and lazy, but they themselves will become heedless, by renouncing their duty.

'Śraddhāvirahitaṁ yajñaṁ tāmasaṁ paricakṣate'—As far as, offering an oblation into the fire, (yajña) is concerned, the tāmasika people think that it is very foolish*, that food articles, such as grain, churned butter, barley, rice, coconut, date, palm etc., which are useful to maintain the body, should be burnt in a fire. If they perform sacrifice, that is only to gain name, fame, honour and praise, without obeying scriptural ordinances, without distributing food, without chanting hymns, and without paying any donations.

They have no faith, either in scripture, or sacred hymns, or sacrifice or its fruit, out of delusion. They act, contrary to ordinance of scriptures. They are just like, the people of the Kali age, who do not believe in caste and social order, and who are engrossed in activities, contrary to ordinances of the scriptures.

In tāmasa sacrifice, a man having cast aside the ordinance of scriptures, acts according to his own sweet will (Gītā 16/23) and it is offered without faith (Gītā 17/28). These two feelings are involved in it. So, he attains, neither the occult power, nor the highest goal, nor even happiness, here or hereafter. He rather descends into the womb of an insect, a bird or a beast or into infernal regions (14/18). Absence of faith, is the cause of their damnation. As they perform forbidden actions, without faith, they must get punishment for it.

---

* When a farmer mixes the seed in the earth, its production is thousands of times more than the seed sown when the crop is ripe. Similarly the oblation offered by chanting scriptural hymns will certainly bear fruit. So far as the seed mixed in the earth is concerned, it is material as the earth is insentient while the oblation offered into the fire is divine because gods are sentient; and that oblation results in rain which is very useful. Manujī has declared:

"The oblation offered into fire strengthens the rays of the sun and those strengthened rays result in rain (Even the modern scientists accept this fact)."

All beings come forth from food, from rain food is produced (Gītā 3/14) and rain ensues from sacrifice (Gītā 3/14).

In a sacrifice, if the doer, his knowledge, actions, fortitude, intellect, company, the scripture and eatables, are sāttvika, it is sāttvika sacrifice, if they are rājasika, it is rājasika sacrifice, and if they are tāmasika, it is tāmasika sacrifice.

Link:—Having explained the three kinds of sacrifice, in the preceding three verses, the Lord, in the next three verses, explains three kinds of penance of the body, of speech and of mind, their differentiation as Sāttvika, Rājasika and Tāmasika will be explained at a later stage.

देवद्विजगुरुप्राज्ञपूजनं शौचमार्जवम्।
ब्रह्मचर्यमहिंसा च शारीरं तप उच्यते॥ १४॥

devadvijaguruprājñapūjanaṁ śaucamārjavam
brahmacaryamahiṁsā ca śārīraṁ tapa ucyate

Worship of the gods, of the Brāhmaṇas, teachers, elders and the wise (liberated soul) with purity, uprightness, celibacy and non-violence—this is said to be, the penance (tapa) of the body. 14

Comment:—

'Devadvijaguruprājñapūjanam'—Here the term 'Deva', particularly stands for Lord Viṣṇu, Lord Śiva, Gaṇeśa, Goddess Durgā and the Sun-god, the five chief deities of the category of the Lord. So a devotee, should worship his favourite deity, out of the five, without having any desire for fruit.*

Twelve Āditya, eight Vasus, eleven Rudras and two Aśvinīkumāras—these thirty-three gods, are also included in the term 'Deva'. The gods, who are worshipped in sacrifices, pilgrimages, fasts (vows) on special festivals and occasions, such as sacred-thread ceremony and marriages etc., are also included, in the term 'Deva'. Their worship is sanctioned by scriptures.

* The devotees worship their favourite Deity by regarding Him or Her as the Supreme while the others are regarded as gods by them.

So, they should be worshipped, in accordance with ordinance of the scriptures.

Though the term 'Dvija' (twice-born), denotes Brāhmaṇas, Kṣatriyas and Vaiśyas, but here in the context of worship, it stands only for, the Brāhmaṇas.

Here the term 'Guru' (teachers) stand for parents, elders, preceptors and those, who are senior in age, and superior, learning and social order etc. Obedience and service to them, offering flowers, incense, light and food, to them and steps to please them—all these are included in their worship.

Here the term 'Prājña' (the wise), stands for liberated souls. Their worship, consists in carrying out their orders, following their principles and treating them, with reverence from the heart. In fact, Brāhmaṇas and preceptors are venerable, from a worldly point of view. But a liberated soul, is adorable and venerable, from a spiritual point of view. We should respect them from the core of our heart, rather than externally. Respect which comes from one's heart, is real respect.

Śaucam'—Here the term 'Śaucam' (purity) stands for external purity i.e., purity of the body, with water and earth. External purity, causes internal purity. Through purity, a man realizes that filth in the form of excrement, urine, perspiration, phlegm and spit etc., continuously comes out of the body, though it is purified again and again. Moreover, this body consists of impure bones, flesh and marrow etc. This body is nothing but a factory to produce filth and urine. Being conscious of the impurity and filthness of the body, a man rises above the body. Having done so, he has no sense of superiority in him, in respect of social order, stage of life, status and position etc. In order to, inculcate these feelings, purity is observed.

These days, some people complain that those who maintain purity, hate others. It is wrong. Maintenance of purity, does not mean hate for others. It merely means, that this body can never remain pure, though it may be made pure again and again, with water and earth etc.

Learned people regard the body as impure, because it is born of the parent's semen and menstrual discharge, it is nourished by the food eaten, it is full of excrement, urine, spit, saliva and sweat etc., it is mortal, and it is made clean, with water and earth.

'Ārjavam'—It consists, in the absence of crookedness i.e., there should not be any stiffness and twist, in a body. Man who has pride, becomes crooked. So a striver, who wants to attain salvation should renounce pride, by doing so, he develops uprightness.

'Brahmacaryam'—It consists in abstaining from sex. One who observes celibacy, should take the following precautions.

(i) He should not remember past sexual intercourse. (ii) He should not talk to women, with attachment. (iii) He should not joke, with them. (iv) He should not gaze at them. (v) He should not talk to them, in loneliness. (vi) He should not think of sexual intercourse. (vii) He should be determined not to indulge in sexual intercourse. (viii) He should not indulge in sexual intercourse.

A person, in the state of celibacy and in retired order (Vānaprastha), and renounced order (Sannyāsa), must preserve his seminal fluid, in action and thought. A householder, can have sexual intercourse with his wife, after the period of the mense every month, according to ordinance of the scriptures. Such a person, who observes this rule, is considered a celibate, even during his family life. A widow, who controls her sex desire, attains the same goal as a celibate does.

In fact, a celibate is he, who is firm in the vow of celibacy (Gītā 6/14). But if there is seminal emission during sleep or because of a disease etc., when a person does not want discharge of semen, it means that he is, firm in celibacy. So a celibate, should have pure feelings and never allow his mind to be diverted, towards a woman. Even if, by chance it is diverted he should have a firm determination, to observe celibacy.

'Ahiṁsā'—Total lack of violence is Ahiṁsā. A man, commits violence out of selfishness, anger, greed and delusion. Usurpation of others property, is violence out of selfishness, hurting or murdering others is violence out of anger, killing an animal, for meat and leather, or murdering a person in order to get money, is violence out of greed, and striking a dog or plucking a branch of a tree or kicking anyone, is violence out of delusion.

'Śārīraṁ tapa ucyate'—Worship of the gods etc., purity, uprightness, celibacy and non-violence—this is penance (tapa) of the body. Pilgrimage, vows and self-control, should also be included in the penance of body. Penance, in which a body is tortured, is not a noble type of penance, because such a person, who performs violent penance, is known to be, demoniac in his resolve (17/6). Noble penance, consists in following the path of self-discipline, according to ordinance of scriptures and family traditions etc., and also in tolerating the unfavourable circumstances happily. It involves, control over the body, senses and mind.

In Yoga, where there is description of its eight parts, there is description of 'Yama', first of all. Yama (self-restraint), consists of harmlessness, veracity (truthfulness), continence, non-stealing and non-acquisition of property (Yogadarśana 2/30). These are also five Niyamas (religious vows). They are purity, contentment, askesis, study of Vedas and self-surrender to God (Yogadarśana 2/32). Out of these two, more importance is attached to Yama, because in it there is control over body, mind and senses etc., while in Niyama, a man has to follow religious vows.*

A layman may regard, bodily torture as bodily penance. But actually having been detached, from the mundane, one who practises self-restraint or renunciation, is superior to him, who

*The demons such as Hiraṇyakaśipu, Hiraṇyākṣa and Rāvaṇa etc., possessed Niyamas i.e., they practised religious vows but they had no Yamas viz., self-restraint.

tortures his body, because, peace immediately follows renunciation (Gītā 12/12). External penance, does not lead to God-realization, but it can be conducive to God-realization, through internal purity. So a striver, besides practising Yamas (self-restraint), should also practise Niyamas (religious vow), as and when, required.

Appendix—In the penance of the body, renunciation is important; as in worship there is renunciation of one's superiority complex, in maintenance of purity there is renunciation of indolence and heedlessness, in uprightness there is renunciation of pride, in celibacy there is renunciation of sex, in non-violence there is renunciation of one's own comforts. Thus renunciation involves the penance of the body.

अनुद्वेगकरं वाक्यं सत्यं प्रियहितं च यत्।
स्वाध्यायाभ्यसनं चैव वाङ्मयं तप उच्यते॥ १५॥

anudvegakaraṁ vākyaṁ satyaṁ priyahitaṁ ca yat
svādhyāyābhyasanaṁ caiva vāṅmayaṁ tapa ucyate

The spoken words which give no offence, which are truthful, pleasant and beneficial, and the regular study of Vedas—these are said to be, the (tapa) penance of speech. 15

Comment:—

'Anudvegakaraṁ vākyam'—Utterances, which do not cause annoyance and pain, to others, either at present or in future, are called 'Anudvegakaram'.

'Satyaṁ priyahitaṁ ca yat'—Truthful utterance, is that which states the bare facts, in order to, convey to others, the correct idea of what one has actually read, heard, seen or experienced, without having any feelings of selfishness and pride.*

*A man should utter true and pleasant words. He should neither utter unpleasant true words nor pleasant false words—this is eternal Dharma (righteousness) (Manusmṛti 4/138).

Loving, sweet, artless and gentle words, which are free from cruelty, pungency, sarcasm, slander and insult etc., are 'Priya'.

The words, which are altogether free from violence, envy, jealousy and enmity etc., which are full of love, compassion, forgiveness, generosity and good wishes and which do harm to none, at present or in the future, are 'Hita', viz., beneficial.

'Svādhyāyābhyasanaṁ caiva'—A study of the sacred books, such as the Gītā, Rāmāyaṇa and Bhāgavata etc., and explaining these to others, and describing the glories of the characters of the Lord, and His devotees, and narrating these to others, is 'Svādhyāya'.

Recitation of sacred books, such as the Gītā etc., again and again, learning these by heart, and speaking of the names, glories and praises of the Lord again and again, is 'Abhyasana' (practice).

'Caiva'—These two terms, denote the other aspect of penance of speech, such as, not slandering others, not narrating the faults of others, not to indulge in idle talk, and not to study such books, which conduce desire (lust), anger and greed etc.

'Vāṅmayaṁ tapa ucyate'—Speech (words), which has all the above-mentioned indication, is a penance of speech.*

मनःप्रसादः सौम्यत्वं मौनमात्मविनिग्रहः।
भावसंशुद्धिरित्येतत्तपो मानसमुच्यते॥ १६॥

manaḥprasādaḥ saumyatvaṁ maunamātmavinigrahaḥ
bhāvasaṁśuddhirityetattapo mānasamucyate

Cheerfulness of mind, gentleness, calmness and contemplation, self-control, purity of thought—are called, the penance of mind.16

Comment:—

'Manaḥprasādaḥ'—Cheerfulness of mind is called 'Manaḥprasādaḥ'. Cheerfulness, which is caused by contact of

* Sweet (pleasant) words please human beings, beasts and birds. So a man should utter only pleasant words. Why should one show miserliness in speech?

persons, things and circumstances etc., is not permanent, but short-lived. Cheerfulness, which is revealed by giving up evils, remains permanent, and the mind, then becomes serene.

A man's peace of mind is disturbed, when he depends on the perishable worldly persons, such as his wife, sons and other members of the family, as well as, property and riches etc. If, instead of depending on the perishable, he depends only on the Lord, Who is eternal and imperishable, he can never lose, peace of mind.

The methods to remain cheerful—

(i) One should be free, from attachment and aversion, to persons and circumstances etc.

(ii) One should not be partial, out of selfishness and pride.

(iii) One should be full of divine traits, such as compassion, forgiveness and generosity etc.

(iv) One should have feelings for the welfare, of all beings.

(v) One, whose diet is balanced and regular, whose nature favours living in loneliness, who is reserved, who is temperate in sleep and recreation, according to ordinance of scriptures, such a striver, gains cheerfulness of mind, very quickly.

'Saumyatvam'—A person, who remains free from feelings of violence, cruelty, ruthlessness, ferocity, jealousy etc., and who has faith in the Lord's virtues, such as compassion etc., and His omnipresence, possesses gentleness or placidity. His placidity, is not disturbed, even if anyone uses harsh words for him, insults him, accuses him or there is loss in business etc.

'Maunam'—Here, the term 'Maunam', stands for mental penance. Real silence, consists in remaining equanimous in the pairs of opposites, such as favourable and unfavourable circumstances, union and disunion, attachment and aversion, pleasure and pain etc.*

---

* Here the term 'Maunam' does not stand for absence of speech. Had it been so, it would have been included in the penance of speech.

Constant application of the mind, to the words of saints, to the thought of virtues, glories and character, of the Lord as described in the sacred texts, such as the Gītā, Rāmāyaṇa and Bhāgavata as also to the thought of the welfare and salvation of living beings, is also included in the term 'Maunam'.

'Ātmavinigrahaḥ'—When mind becomes thoroughly disciplined and steady, it is called 'Ātmavinigrahaḥ'. Moreover, real self-control, consists in concentrating the mind and diverting it, as and when a person so desires. It means, that he should not be controlled by the mind, rather he should control it.

'Bhāvasaṁśuddhiḥ'—A pure state of mind, free from selfishness and pride, having the thought of welfare of others, is purity of nature. A man's nature, becomes pure when he thinks of the Lord and depends only on Him, and nature becomes impure, when he depends on the perishable world.

'Ityetattapo mānasamucyate'—Thus penance, which has predominance of mind, is called the penance of mind.

Appendix—A man should remain cheerful even in unfavourable circumstances. He should remain unaffected by circumstances. He should remain placid (gentle), even after hearing the undesirable utterances of others. He should not let the mind be free but make it contemplative because by leaving it free, there is enjoyment of pleasure and it does not become contemplative. He should renounce the 'mūḍha' (deluded), 'kṣipta' (volatile) and 'vikṣipta' (sometimes constant, sometimes volatile) inclinations of the mind. He should never think ill of anyone. All this is penance of the mind.

Link:—Now the Lord, in the next three verses, describes

In the Gītā it is seen that Arjuna puts questions attaching importance to actions while Lord Kṛṣṇa answers attaching importance to feelings. In the fifty-fourth verse of the second chapter Arjuna asked "How does the man of stable mind speak?" The Lord replied that he who is neither happy in favourable circumstances nor unhappy in unfavourable ones, is a sage of stable mind.

sāttvika, rājasika and tāmasika penances.

श्रद्धया परया तप्तं तपस्तत्त्रिविधं नरैः।
अफलाकाङ्क्षिभिर्युक्तैः सात्त्विकं परिचक्षते॥ १७॥

śraddhayā parayā taptaṁ tapastattrividhaṁ naraiḥ
aphalākāṅkṣibhiryuktaiḥ sāttvikaṁ paricakṣate

The threefold penance, practised with supreme faith by a man of balanced mind, without the expectation of reward, is called sāttvika (good). 17

Comment:—

'Śraddhayā parayā taptam'—Three kinds of penance, of body, speech and mind, must be performed and this, is a man's foremost duty and it is a panacea, to realize the aim of human life.* By undertaking penance thoroughly, a man gets established in the self, which is the goal of life. So a striver should observe penance with faith, reverence and zeal, facing all obstacles.

'Aphalākāṅkṣibhiryuktaiḥ naraiḥ'—As far as other living beings are concerned, they possess, only a few virtues. Here the term 'Naraiḥ' (men), with two adjectives, denotes that man can inculcate all virtues in him, and can get rid of all evil propensities, such as desire and delusion etc. Moreover, men alone can perform actions, without desire for their rewards.

The Lord, has used the term 'nara' (man), in sāttvika penance, but He has not used it in rājasika and tāmasika, penances. It means, that those men who do not renounce evil propensities, such desire, hypocrisy and delusion, in the human body, which is bestowed, only for God-realization (salvation), do not deserve to be called men. Here the term naraiḥ (men), has been used for those persons, who perform penances, without having any expectation for fruit.

---

* The penance of the body, mind and speech is thoroughly performed only when a person has an aim of renouncing affinity with the perishable.

'Tapastattrividham'—This term 'trividham' (threefold), has been used only in the sāttvika penance, while in the rājasika and the tāmasika ones, the terms 'Yat' 'Tat' (which) have been used. It means, that the threefold penance (of the body, mind and speech) can be thoroughly included, only in the sāttvika penance. In rājasika and tāmasika penances they can be partly included. Out of these two, in the rājasika penance, more marks are included, while in the tāmasika one, only a few marks are found, because the aim of the people who perform tāmasika penance, is to torture others, out of delusion.

Secondly, in the thirteenth chapter from the seventh to the eleventh verses, there is description of the twenty virtues, which make for wisdom (knowledge). Out of these, there are three signs—purity, straightforwardness and non-violence of the penance, of body. There are two marks, of penance of mind namely, self-control and 'maunam' (equanimity). Similarly, there are twenty-six marks of a person, who is endowed with divine nature, in the first three verses of the sixteenth chapter. Out of these, there are three marks of purity, non-violence and straightforwardness of the penance of body and two marks—truth and study of the scriptures, of the penance of speech. So the virtues of wisdom, which lead to self-realization, or divine traits, which lead to salvation, cannot be rājasa (of the mode of passion) or tāmasa (of the mode of ignorance). So rājasika and tāmasika penances, cannot include, the penances of body, mind and speech fully; they can include them, only partly.

Thirdly, a person who studies Gītā, from the beginning to the end, comes to know that its aim is to enable a man to attain salvation. The reason is, that Arjuna asks Lord Kṛṣṇa to tell him what is good for him i.e., by which he can attain to the highest good (2/7; 3/2; 5/1). The Lord, also explains the means by which men, may attain to the highest good. Therefore, in the Gītā out of the three modes of nature, the sāttvika should be accepted while the rājasika and the tāmasika, should be discarded. The reason, is that the former one, is conducive to liberation, while the latter ones, lead to bondage. Therefore, the Lord, has used the term 'trividham' (threefold), in order to explain, that the sāttvika penance, includes the threefold-penance, of the body, mind and speech.

'Sāttvikaṁ paricakṣate'—Penance performed with supreme faith, without expectation of reward, is called sāttvika.

सत्कारमानपूजार्थं तपो दम्भेन चैव यत्।
क्रियते तदिह प्रोक्तं राजसं चलमध्रुवम्॥ १८॥

satkāramānapūjārthaṁ tapo dambhena caiva yat
kriyate tadiha proktaṁ rājasaṁ calamadhruvam

Penance performed, in order to gain respect, honour and reverence and for the sake of ostentation and which yields an uncertain and perishable fruit, is said to be rājasa (passionate). 18

Comment:—

'Satkāramānapūjārthaṁ tapaḥ kriyate'—People of rājasa temperament, perform sacrifice, in order to win respect, honour and reverence, in society. They expect others to respect them, as men of penance, possessing self-control, truth and non-violence. They perform it, so that people may bow to them, wash their feet, offer flowers and garlands to them, wave lights before them, and touch their forehead with the dust of their feet. During their life, and after death, they may have a funeral procession with grandeur, make monument, and offer flowers, sandalwood paste, water and clothes etc., to monuments.

'Dambhena caiva yat'—Though they have no faith in penances, yet they perform these, for the sake of show. They sit cross-legged, start counting the beads of a rosary and worshipping God, by way of ostentation.

'Tadiha proktaṁ rājasaṁ calamadhruvam'—The fruit of rājasa penance, is said to be uncertain and perishable. It means, that a penance which is performed in order to win respect, honour and reverence bears perishable fruit, while penance which is performed for ostentation, may bear fruit or not, and the ostentation may be, a success or not.

The expression 'Iha proktam,' means that a person gets the reward of the rājasika penance, here in the world. Sāttvika people, go to higher regions—heaven etc., the tāmasika, descend to lower regions—hell etc., while the rājasika, remain in the middle regions (Gītā 14/18). Therefore, rājasika penance, bears fruit here, in the form of respect, honour and praise.

Can a rājasika person perform penance of the body, mind and speech? He can worship the gods, by expecting a reward. He can be gentle and can study scriptures. But he cannot observe celibacy and non-violence. He cannot be placid and cheerful, because projection and distraction of the mind, disturb him, because of his desire. Moreover, how can his nature be pure, when he performs penance, in order to win respect, honour and reverence? So a rājasika person, cannot perform, the threefold penance fully.

मूढग्राहेणात्मनो यत्पीडया क्रियते तपः ।
परस्योत्सादनार्थं वा तत्तामसमुदाहृतम् ॥ १९ ॥

mūḍhagrāheṇātmano yatpīḍayā kriyate tapaḥ
parasyotsādanārthaṁ vā tattāmasamudāhṛtam

Penance, performed with foolish obstinacy, with self-torture or causing injury to others, is said to be tāmasika (of the mode of ignorance). 19

Comment:—

'Mūḍhagrāheṇātmano yatpīḍayā kriyate tapaḥ'—In a tāmasika person, delusion predominates. Such a person performs tāmasika sacrifice, out of delusion and obstinacy, by torturing his own self i.e., body and mind etc.

'Parasyotsādanārthaṁ vā'—Such a person, performs penance in order to cause injury to others, and to destroy them, even if he himself has to suffer. Such a person, can perform penance by tolerating excessive heat and cold and observing fasts also, by his own sweet will.

'Tattāmasamudāhṛtam'—Such penance, which is performed, in order to cause injury to others, is called tāmasika.

[A sāttvika person, who performs penance with utmost faith, having no desire for its fruit, deserves to be called, a man. A rājasika person, who performs penance in order to win respect, honour and reverence, does not deserve to be called a man, because even birds and beasts, like respect and honour etc., and they have no show or ostentation. The tāmasika people, are inferior, even to birds and beasts, because they cause injury to others even by self-torture while the birds and beasts, do not cause injury to others, suffering self mortification.]

Appendix—In 'mūḍhagrāheṇa' there is unalloyed 'tamoguṇa' (the mode of ignorance), but in 'parasyotsādanārthaṁ', 'rajoguṇa' (the mode of passion) is also mixed. Delusion is 'tamoguṇa' and selfishness and anger etc., are 'rājasa'. Anger evolves from 'rajoguṇa' and then is transformed into 'tamoguṇa'—'krodhād-bhavati sammohaḥ' (Gītā 2/63).

Link:—Now the Lord in the next three verses, mentions the threefold division of charity (gift).

दातव्यमिति यद्दानं दीयतेऽनुपकारिणे।
देशे काले च पात्रे च तद्दानं सात्त्विकं स्मृतम्॥ २०॥

dātavyamiti yaddānaṁ dīyate'nupakāriṇe
deśe kāle ca pātre ca taddānaṁ sāttvikaṁ smṛtam

A gift, charity which is made, to one from whom no return is expected, with the feeling, that it is one's duty to give, and which is given at a proper place and time and to a worthy person, that gift is held to be Sāttvika (good). 20

Comment:—

Here in this verse, there are two kinds of gifts: (i) A gift is made to one, from whom no return is expected, and regarding it as a duty. (ii) It is made at a proper place and time and to a worthy person.

'Dātavyamiti yaddānaṁ dīyate'nupakāriṇe deśe kāle ca pātre ca'—A person, should offer a gift while regarding it, as his duty. He has to give things in charity to others, because he has wrongly claimed these, as his own. One, who has got possession over some things, has responsibility to give these to others. So, he should make a gift without expecting any return, at all, here or hereafter.

Whom should it be given? The answer is, that it should be given to those, who have neither done good to him, nor there is any possibility of getting return in future. It does not mean, that he should not give to those, who have done him good. But it means, that by doing so he should not regard it, as a gift. He cannot repay the debt of persons, who have done good to him, by merely making a gift. So he must help them, without regarding it as a gift (charity). A gift, which is made with expectation of some return, is called rājasika.

The expression 'Deśe kāle ca pātre ca', has a double meaning and both of these should be taken here in this context.

(i) A gift should be made, at a place, where it is needed i.e., it should be made, in the place which is affected (e.g.,) by drought, flood and famine etc. It should be made at a time, when it is needed. It should be made to a needy person.

(ii) It should be made at a place of pilgrimage, such as the Ganges, the Yamunā, the Godāvarī rivers or Kurukṣetra, Prayāga and Kāśī etc., and on sacred occasions, such as the full moon and the last day of the dark fortnight Saṅkrānti, (the passage of the sun from one zodiacal sign to another) etc., to a learned person, who is well-versed in the scripture, or to a pious and virtuous, hermit or beggar, or to any other deserving candidate.

'Taddānaṁ sāttvikaṁ smṛtam'—Such a gift, is held to be sāttvika. Actually, all things in the universe, are not anyone's personal property, they belong to all the beings. So, a thing should be given to a person who needs it, because he has a claim on it. It should be given to him, because it actually belongs to him. It means that we have assumed, the things which are not ours, as ours. So, we should give these to him, who needs them, with the conviction that actually such things do not belong to us, but they belong to him, who needs them.

Thus a gift, by making which, any connection with the thing gifted, and with its reward, and with the act of making the gift, is totally renounced, is called 'sāttvika'.

Appendix—This 'Sāttvika charity' is in fact renunciation. This is not the charity about which it has been said "If you offer charity, it bears its fruit a thousand times", because in it there is affinity with 'the reward of a thousand*. But in renunciation affinity is cut asunder. The charity which is made with the hope of a return becomes 'rājasa'—'yattu pratyupakārārtham' (Gītā 17/21). In order to negate this 'rājasa' notion, here the term 'anupakāriṇe' has been used.

The mode of goodness in the Gītā has been described 'anāmaya' (flawless) (Gītā 14/6) because it is conducive to renunciation. In 'Sattvaguṇa' (the mode of goodness) affinity is renounced; in 'Rajoguṇa' affinity is established; in 'Tamoguṇa' delusion is caused.

---

* supātradānācca bhaveddhanāḍhyo dhanaprabhāveṇa karoti puṇyam,
puṇyaprabhāvāt suralokavāsī punardhanāḍhyaḥ punareva bhogī.
kupātradānācca bhaveddaridro dāridcadoṣeṇa karoti pāpam,
pāpaprabhāvānnarakaṁ prayāti punardaridraḥ punareva pāpī.

According to the Gītā, performance of action for the welfare of others is 'Yajña'; to remain cheerful everytime is 'Tapa' and to offer the thing to a person with the conviction that 'it belongs to him', is 'dāna'. The performance of sacrifice; penance and charity with a selfish motive is the demoniac or devilish nature.

यत्तु प्रत्युपकारार्थं फलमुद्दिश्य वा पुनः ।
दीयते च परिक्लिष्टं तद्दानं राजसं स्मृतम् ॥ २१ ॥

yattu pratyupakārārthaṁ phalamuddiśya vā punaḥ
dīyate ca parikliṣṭaṁ taddānaṁ rājasaṁ smṛtam

A gift, which is made with the hope of a return or in expectation of a reward, or in a grudging spirit is said to be, rājasika (passionate). 21

Comment:—

'Yattu pratyupakārārtham'—A rājasika gift, is made with the hope of return. Rājasika people, think that if they make a gift to the family priest, of their relatives, the relatives will also give gifts to the former's family priest. Thus, their family priest will get money. Similarly they want to offer a gift to the priest, who is an astrologer, so that he may tell them the lucky moment of the marriage of their sons and daughters, and also of their journey, and business etc. Moreover, they want to make the gift to a priest, who is a physician, so that he may give them valuable medicines. Thus the gift, which is made to expect a return, is called 'Pratyupakārārtha'.

'Phalamuddiśya vā punaḥ'—This gift, is made with a view, that it will bring some unseen reward or heavenly pleasure. Rājasika people, make a gift at places of pilgrimage, (the Ganges, the Yamunā, Kurukṣetra etc., and on sacred occasions, such as the last day of a dark fortnight (Amāvāsyā), the full moon (Purṇimā) and eclipses etc., and to deserving learned priests, who have studied the Vedas. But, because of the desire for reward, it has been called rājasika. So Lord Kṛṣṇa, has not mentioned, that it should be made, at a proper place and time and to a worthy person.

Here, the term 'punaḥ' (then or again), has been used to denote, that such a person first thinks of the man, to whom he is indebted or from whom he expects a reward, and then he makes a gift.

'Dīyate ca parikliṣṭam'—A rājasika gift, is made in a grudging and helpless mood, under compulsion or force. Whatever they give, is given, in a miserly manner, by being grieved, at heart. They believe, that by giving more, the habits of a donee will get spoiled, while they could suffer loss. So, it will be difficult for them, to run their lives smoothly. Thus they make petty gifts, in a higgling way.

'Taddānaṁ rājasaṁ smṛtam'—Such a gift, is said to be rājasika (passionate).

अदेशकाले यद्दानमपात्रेभ्यश्च दीयते।
असत्कृतमवज्ञातं तत्तामसमुदाहृतम्॥ २२॥

adeśakāle yaddānamapātrebhyaśca dīyate
asatkṛtamavajñātaṁ tattāmasamudāhṛtam

A gift, which is made at a wrong place and time, to an unworthy person, without respect or with contempt, is held to be, tāmasika (of the mode of ignorance). 22

Comment:—

'Asatkṛtamavajñātam'—A tāmasika gift, is made without respect, in a disdainful spirit. When a priest, comes to receive the gift, to the house of tāmasika people, they treat him with contempt and say that he did not come to their house, when his presence was required. Another member of the family says, that they should not be ensnared by such priests, they should instead give to the poor and the needy. They regard them as a dog, who should be given a morsel of food, otherwise it will bark. Such a gift is called tāmasa, because by it ordinance of scriptures and the Brāhmaṇas (members of the priest class), are dishonoured.

'Adeśakāle yaddānam'—Out of delusion, the tāmasika people, do not attach any importance to proper place and time. They say, that they have to make a gift, so it could be made, at any place and time. Thus they offer the gift, by dishonouring the ordinance of scriptures, because they instead of attaching importance to the ordinance of scriptures attach importance to the money.'

'Apātrebhyaśca dīyate'—The tāmasika people, give charity (gift), to an unworthy person, arguing that food given as a gift, will satisfy the hunger of that person also, and so it is, also a virtuous action. Moreover, they assume that the people of the priestly class, have made such rules, to earn their livelihood.

'Tattāmasamudāhṛtam'—Such a gift is declared to be tāmasika.

Question:—In the Gītā it is mentioned, that the tāmasika people, go downwards (i.e., into the wombs, of insects, birds and beasts or into infernal regions) (14/18), while in the Rāmacaritamānasa it is mentioned, that charity (gift) given in anyway leads to the good. Thus, the two statements seem to be contradictory.

Answer:—Tāmasika people go downwards, but this rule is not applicable for gifts, because when a person makes a gift, he has to renounce his affinity for the gift. It is because of this renunciation, that even tāmasika charity, is not conducive to hurl one to downward regions. So, a gift has been eulogized, in Śrīmadbhāgavata (12/3/18), in Manusmṛti (1/86) and also in Rāmacaritamānasa (7/103 b). The reason, is that a person who has even little renunciation, cannot have a downfall.

Secondly, in this Kali age, when the hearts of people have become very impure, a concession has been granted by the Lord, that charity (gift) given in any form, leads a man to the good.

By making gifts, a man develops this trait, in his nature and that trait, will lead him to the good. So a gift should be made even without respect. So a saint has interpreted the expression 'Śraddhayā deyamaśraddhayādeyam,' that a gift should be offered with reverence, but it should be offered even, if there is no reverence.

An Important Fact In Connection With Gifts

A gift of food, water, clothes and medicines should be made to a needy recipient, without much thinking, whether he is worthy or unworthy, and whether the place and time, are auspicious or not. Offer food, to a hungry man, water, to a thirsty person, clothes to the naked and medicines to the sick. Similarly, the act of freeing a man from fear and torture etc., is a gift of fearlessness, which should be made. These gifts, are to be made, according to the need of the moment.

One point is to be kept in mind, that an unworthy person, should be given only so much of food and water, that he may not die of starvation or thirst. If he is given more, he may again indulge in sins, such as violence etc.

A devotee, beholds His Lord in all beings. So he worships his Lord, by performing his duty, instead of giving charity (gift), to a person (Gītā 18/46). It means, that a devotee's activities, are connected with God.

Gifts and Their Fruits

In this chapter from the eleventh to the twenty-second verses, the sāttvika sacrifice, penance and gift, are included in divine nature,while the rājasika and tāmasika, are included in demoniac nature.

The fruit of rājasika sacrifice, penance and gift, can be divided into two parts—seen and unseen. The seen fruit, can further be divided into two parts—immediate and future. The immediate fruit of rājasika food, is that it satisfies hunger, while its remote fruit, is that it causes diseases. Similarly, the unseen fruit can also be divided into two parts—here and hereafter. As sacrifice, which is performed for the sake of ostentation (17/12), the penance which is performed, in order to win respect, honour and reverence (17/18) and a gift which is made with the hope of a return (17/21), bear fruit here.* But, if these are performed, in order to attain heaven, they bear fruit, hereafter. Rājasika sacrifice, which is performed for its fruit (17/12), and the gift made for a reward (17/21) can bear fruit, here as well as, hereafter. Out of those, who perform sacrifice, in order to attain heaven (2/42-43; 9/20-21) and those who perform sacrifice, penance and make a gift, for ostentation, respect, honour, reverence and reward, follow the cycle of birth and death.† But the tāmasika people who perform tāmasika sacrifice and penance (17/13, 19) have a fall (14/18), into the foulest hell (16/16), into demoniacal wombs (16/19) and go down, to the lowest state (16/20).

Those, who go to heaven, as the fruit of their sacrifice, suffer from envy, jealousy and vanity there‡. Śatakratu, the king of

---

* The future fruit of the seen and the fruit here of the unseen of the rājasika mode though seem similar yet are different. As the food will bear fruit in the form of diseases, that is future fruit of the seen. But the sacrifice which is performed so that a son may be born bears fruit here in the form of the birth of a son by turning itself into fate. So it is the fruit here of the unseen.

† If the rājasika people's ostentation is excessive (17/12, 18), it may be conducive to hells.

‡ In heaven also there are three categories—high, middle and low. Those who belong to the high category have vanity, because they are superior to the other two types and they are envious of those who are of the same category.

Similarly those of middle class are proud as they consider them superior to those of the low class and have a burning sensation having seen the superior heavenly luxuries of those of the high class.

In the same way those of the low class are envious and jealous of the other two classes as well as of their own class and they are proud when they think of those who have not attained heaven.

gods, is pained, because of atrocities of demons. Moreover, he has a burning sensation, in his heart when he beholds anyone performing penance, because he thinks that the person is doing so, in order to usurp his throne. Now, the question arises, why has he to suffer this burning sensation, when he is purged of those sins, which are obstacles to heavenly enjoyment (9/20). The answer is, that it is the fruit of his violence of animals, which he commits, while performing sacrifice.

Secondly, all actions performed with an interested motive, are tainted with some blemish, as fire is clouded by smoke (18/48). When all action are clouded by defects, there should be many more defects, in the actions which are performed for their fruits. So, in the scriptures, it is mentioned that after performing a sacrifice, the person should express penitence. But through penitence, all the sins do not perish; their signs are left, in the same way, as dirt remains in the threads, even when a cloth is washed with soap. So, even the gods such as Indra, has to suffer, by facing unfavourable circumstances.

Actually, all defects perish, only when a person discharges his duty, without expecting any fruit and surrenders those actions, to God. When he realizes that he is only God's, all his sins of millions of ages immediately disappear.* Lord Rāma in the Rāmacaritamānasa declares, "As soon as, a being has an inclination for Me, his sins of millions of ages, disappear."

Thirdly, Arjuna asked Lord Kṛṣṇa, "By what is a man,

Their residence (of the three categories) in heaven is not permanent because they have to return to the world of mortals when their merits are exhausted (Gītā 9/21) and they remain worried after thinking of it.

*The evils such as envy and jealousy etc., are not the fruit of actions of the past but they develop because of the impurity of heart. When a man performs actions prescribed by the scriptures in order to reap their fruit, his heart is partially purified which leads him to the heaven and heavenly pleasures. But when a man has the only aim of God-realization, his heart is thoroughly purified.

impelled to commit sin, as if by force, against his will?" Lord Kṛṣṇa replied, "It is desire (craving), it is wrath, born of the mode of passion" (3/37). It means, that it is desire born of the mode of passion, which forces a man, to commit, sins. So rājasika sacrifice, which is performed with a desire for its fruit, may involve sins.

Persons, who perform rājasika and tāmasika sacrifice, are of demoniac nature, while persons who perform sāttvika sacrifice have divine nature. But if a person, is attached to traits of divine nature, this attachment too binds him (Gītā 14/6).

Appendix—In the scripture it is related that in Kali age, offering charity is the only 'Dharma' (righteousness), therefore charity given in any way, leads to salvation. It means that in Kali age, performance of virtuous actions such as sacrifice, charity penance and vow (fast) etc., according to the ordinance of the scripture, is difficult; therefore a person should inculcate the habit of giving gifts to others without hoarding them for himself. So charity should be certainly made somehow or the other.

Link:—In the fifth verse of the sixteenth chapter, divine virtues, have been said, to be conducive to liberation, and the demoniac to bondage. Now, the Lord starts the next topic. Those sāttvika persons, who having possessed divine nature, perform sacrifice, penance and offer charity, may commit an error (by feelings, method and action). So what should be done, to rectify that error?

ॐ तत्सदिति निर्देशो ब्रह्मणस्त्रिविधः स्मृतः ।
ब्राह्मणास्तेन वेदाश्च यज्ञाश्च विहिताः पुरा ॥ २३ ॥

oṁ tatsaditi nirdeśo brahmaṇastrividhaḥ smṛtaḥ
brāhmaṇāstena vedāśca yajñāśca vihitāḥ purā

"Auṁ (Oṁ), Tat and Sat"—This has been declared to be the

triple designation of Brahma. By that, were created at the cosmic dawn, the Brāhmaṇas, the Vedas and the sacrifices (yajñas). 23

Comment:—

'Oṁ tatsaditi nirdeśo brahmaṇastrividhaḥ smṛtaḥ'—Oṁ, Tat and Sat—these are the three names of God, (These three names will be explained in the next four verses).

'Brāhmaṇāstena vedāśca yajñāśca vihitāḥ purā'—God at the beginning of the creation, created the Vedas, the Brāhmaṇas (persons of the priest class) and the sacrifices. The methods of performing sacrifices (which also include penance and charity), are explained in the Vedas; those who perform those sacrifices are Brāhmaṇas, and the acts that are performed, are sacrifices.

If there be any defect in the performance of sacrifice and penance or offering of charity, how to rectify the flaw and render it perfect? Utter the name of God (Oṁ or Tat or Sat) the flaw will be rectified, and defect will be rendered perfect. As a cook, while kneading finds more water in the flour, he adds some more flour to it and thus he sets it right. Similarly a person, who performs virtuous actions, such as sacrifice and penance, etc., but finds any defect in those rites, he chants these names of the Lord and that recitation of Names corrects the defect.

Appendix—In 'Mahānirvāṇa tantra' it is mentioned—

oṁ tatsaditi mantreṇa yo yatkarma samācaret,
gṛhastho vāpyudāsīnastasyābhīṣṭāya tad bhavet.
japo'homaḥ pratiṣṭhā ca saṁskārādyakhilāḥ kriyāḥ,
oṁ tatsanmantraniṣpannāḥ sampūrṇāḥ syurna saṁśayaḥ.

(14/154-155)

'oṁ tat sat'—By uttering this sacred text whatever action a householder or a sage begins, with it he gets the desired fruit. All the actions such as utterance of the Lord's holy names, sacrifice, Pratiṣṭhā ceremony and rites etc., become successful by uttering the sacred text—oṁ, tat, sat, there is no doubt about it.

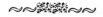

तस्मादोमित्युदाहृत्य यज्ञदानतपःक्रियाः ।
प्रवर्तन्ते विधानोक्ताः सततं ब्रह्मवादिनाम् ॥ २४ ॥

tasmādomityudāhṛtya yajñadānatapaḥkriyāḥ
pravartante vidhānoktāḥ satataṁ brahmavādinām

Therefore, starting with the word 'Oṁ', initiating acts of sacrifice, gift and penance, as enjoined in the scriptures, is always undertaken by followers of the Vedas. 24

Comment:—

'Tasmādomityudāhṛtya yajñadānatapaḥkriyāḥ pravartante-vidhānoktāḥ satataṁ brahmavādinām'—The believers, who specially have faith in the Vedas, attach the greatest importance to the holy name, Oṁ. They perform sacred acts, such as sacrifice, penance etc., which are sanctioned, by scriptures, by uttering this name Oṁ. As a cow cannot become pregnant, without a bull, the recitation of Vedic chants cannot bear fruit, without uttering the holy name, Oṁ.

Why is the holy name Oṁ uttered first of all? The reason is that Oṁ, the Praṇava was revealed first of all. From Praṇava Gāyatrī (the Vedic metre), was revealed. From Gāyatrī, the three Vedas Ṛk, Sāma and Yajuḥ were revealed. So 'Oṁ' is the root of Gāyatrī, and the Vedas. Therefore, all the Vedic rites are performed, by uttering the holy name Oṁ first.

तदित्यनभिसन्धाय फलं यज्ञतपःक्रियाः ।
दानक्रियाश्च विविधाः क्रियन्ते मोक्षकाङ्क्षिभिः ॥ २५ ॥

tadityanabhisandhāya phalaṁ yajñatapaḥkriyāḥ
dānakriyāśca vividhāḥ kriyante mokṣakāṅkṣibhiḥ

With the initial use of the word 'Tat,' the acts of sacrifice, penance and the various acts of charity are performed by the seekers of salvation, without aiming at the rewards. 25

Comment:—

'Tadityanabhisandhāya phalaṁ yajñatapaḥkriyāḥ dānakriyāśca vividhāḥ kriyante mokṣakāṅkṣibhiḥ'—All actions, such as sacrifice, penance and gifts etc., should be performed, in order to please God, without expecting any reward whatsoever. Every action, has a beginning and an end. Similarly, there is union and disunion, of its fruit. But the Lord ever remains the same, without undergoing any kind of change. So, the expression 'Tat' denotes, that the Lord ever remains, the same while the expression 'Anabhisandhāya phalam', denotes that all actions, and their fruits, are perishable. So a striver, should ever remember the everlasting Lord, and he should never aim, at the perishable rewards.

We cannot behold the Lord, Who ever pervades everywhere, because we assume the kaleidoscopic and perishable world, as real. So a striver, by having the aim of God-realization, and renouncing the feelings of 'I'ness and 'Mineness', should perform, the acts of sacrifice, penance and gift, by regarding them as His own, with the power given by Him, for His sake only. This is the real achievement of human life. So a striver, has to realize God, Who is known as 'Tat', and he has to renounce affinity, for the world which seems real.

Devotees of the Lord, uttering other names of the Lord such as Rāma, Kṛṣṇa, Govinda, Nārāyaṇa, Vāsudeva and Śiva etc., begin their acts. All these names also denote the term, 'Tat'.

Seekers of salvation, perform various acts of sacrifice, penance, gift, pilgrimage, meditation, trance, chanting and study of scriptures etc., for the Lord's sake by obeying Him, to please Him. The reasons is, that all bodies, organs, minds, hearts, souls etc., and also we belong, to the Lord. Thus our so-called, property and riches, also belong to Him. So we belong to God and God is ours and with this conviction, all actions, should be performed, to please Him, only.

Appendix—The Lord by the term 'tat' (that) referring to

distance and invisibility means that the Supreme Person is 'alaukika' (unearthly)—'uttamaḥ puruṣastvanyaḥ' (Gītā 15/17). The Supreme Person (God) is not an object to be reflected upon, but is an object of faith and belief.

~~⚜~~

Link:—Having explained the two names, 'Aum' (Oṁ) and 'Tat' of the Lord, in the twenty-fourth verse and the twenty-fifth verse respectively, now He explains, the third name of God 'Sat', in the next two verses, in five different senses.

सद्भावे साधुभावे च सदित्येतत्प्रयुज्यते।
प्रशस्ते कर्मणि तथा सच्छब्दः पार्थ युज्यते॥ २६॥

sadbhāve sādhubhāve ca sadityetatprayujyate
praśaste karmaṇi tathā sacchabdaḥ pārtha yujyate

The word 'Sat' is used in the sense of Existence Absolute and saintliness; and so also, O Pārtha (Arjuna), the word 'Sat' is used, in the sense of a praise-worthy, act. 26

Comment:—

'Sadbhāve'—The existence of God, is known as 'Sadbhāva'. The Lord, Who is without attribute and endowed with attributes, Who is formless and also with form, and His incarnations such as Viṣṇu, Rāma, Kṛṣṇa, Śiva, Śakti (Durgā), Gaṇeśa and Sun-god—all are included with in, 'Sadbhāva'. Thus the Lord, Who ever exists everywhere, and Whose names, forms and sports, are innumerable, is 'Sadbhāva', (reality).

'Sādhubhāve'—The noble dispositions, of the mind, such as compassion and forgiveness etc., which have been described in various spiritual disciplines of different sects and which are conducive to God-realization are included in 'Sādhubhāve', (goodness).

'Sadityetatprayujyate'—The term, 'Sat', is used in the sense of Existence Absolute and goodness. It means that the term 'Sat', is used for the Lord, Who is permanent and unchanging and for, the divine traits such as truth, forgiveness, generosity and renunciation etc., which are helpful in God-realization.

'Praśaste karmaṇi tathā sacchabdaḥ pārtha yujyate'—All noble deeds, which are conducive to God-realization, are said to be praiseworthy. Similarly, all other rites, such as initiation of sacred thread, marriage etc., as well as, charity and construction of wells, temples, hospitals etc., which are sanctioned by scripture, are included in 'Praśaste karmaṇi' (praiseworthy acts). The word 'Sat', is used, in the sense of all these praiseworthy acts.

Appendix—Existence of God is called 'sadbhāva' which never ceases to be—'nābhāvo vidyate sataḥ' (Gītā 2/16). Generally all believers accept that there has always been a singular power which is above all, is the controller Supreme and is also immutable. How can the universe, which is kaleidoscopic and which disappears, be said to be 'is (existent)' or permanent? The reason is that the world, which is perceived and known by senses and intellect etc., neither existed in the past nor will exist in future and at present is also perishing—this is everyone's experience. The senses and intellect etc., by which the world is perceived and known also belong to the same class to which the world belongs. Even then it is surprising that the world in spite of being non-existent ('not') appears to be existent ('is') and permanent (constant). Had the universe really existed, it would have not changed; and when it changes, it means that it is non-existent. Therefore in fact this existence, instead of being of the world and of the body, is of God, in Whose light the non-existent world appears to be existent ('is').

The noble dispositions of the mind are called 'sādhu bhāva'. The term 'sat' has been used for noble dispositions because they are conducive to God-realization. The noble dispositions viz., virtues and good conduct are divine traits (divine nature). The divine nature is 'sat' (real) while the demoniac nature is 'asat' (unreal). All the means which lead to salvation are 'sat' and all the actions which are conducive to bondage are 'asat'. All evils and misconduct are 'asat' while their renunciation is 'sat'. Renunciation of the 'asat' (unreal) is 'sat' and acceptance of the 'sat' is also 'sat'. In fact as much need as there is of the renunciation of the unreal, so much need is not there of owning (adopting) the real. Without renouncing the unreal, the real tacked from outside does not subsist. But by renouncing the unreal, the real is revealed. Therefore by renouncing the unreal, the real is realized.

All the virtuous actions ordained by the scriptures such as sacrifice, penance, charity, pilgrimage, vow or fast, worship and marriage etc., being praise-worthy are 'Satkarma'. But if these praise-worthy actions have no affinity with God, they instead of being called 'sat' (the real), remain merely actions ordained by the scriptures. Though devils and demons also perform virtuous actions such as penance etc. Yet they lead to bondage and become 'asat' actions because they are performed with a selfish motive and are meant to harm others (Gītā 17/19). By those actions even if the Abode of Brahmā is attained, they have to return there from (Gītā 8/16). Men, who work for God-realization, don't meet with an evil end (Gītā 6/40) because its fruit is 'sat' (real). The actions which are performed for the welfare of all beings, by renouncing selfishness and pride, are indeed praise-worthy 'Satkarma'.

यज्ञे तपसि दाने च स्थितिः सदिति चोच्यते।
कर्म चैव तदर्थीयं सदित्येवाभिधीयते॥ २७॥

yajñe tapasi dāne ca sthitiḥ saditi cocyate
karma caiva tadarthīyaṁ sadityevābhidhīyate

Steadfastness in sacrifice (yajña), penance and charity are also called 'Sat', as also, any action for the sake of the Supreme, is called, 'Sat'. 27

Comment:—

'Yajñe tapasi dāne ca sthitiḥ saditi cocyate'—Steadfastness (faith), in praiseworthy action, such as sacrifice, penance and gift etc., is called 'Sat'. So steadfastness in sāttvika sacrifice, sāttvika penance and sāttvika gifts, alongwith, promptness in their performance, is called 'Sat Niṣṭhā' (Real faith).

The term 'Ca' (and), denotes that besides steadfastness, as mentioned above, faith in selfless service, hospitality, obedience, truth, chastity, pilgrimage and performance of one's duty, according to one's caste, creed and social order etc., is known as, real faith.

'Karma caiva tadarthīyaṁ sadityevābhidhīyate'—Besides these noble deeds, there are two kinds of acts—the mundane and the spiritual.

(1) All the acts of earning one's livelihood according to one's caste and social order, such as teaching, business and farming etc., and also eating, drinking, sitting, standing, walking, awaking and sleeping etc., are mundane.

(2) Meditation, adoration, utterance of the Lord's name, loud chanting and listening to the glories of the Lord, and the saints, etc., are spiritual acts.

If both these activities, are performed with reverence and faith, without expecting any reward by giving up one's comfort, only for the Lord's sake, they become 'Sat'. Such acts having affinity with God, Who is Real, are included, in divine nature, which leads to salvation.

If a piece of a pot is put into fire, the fire converts it into its own form. It is the speciality of fire, that the shred takes the form of fire. Similarly action, which is performed for God, becomes Godly i.e., that action leads to God-realization. In fact, an action by itself is insignificant, but because of its performance for God, it has gained significance.

The Lord, by the term 'Tadarthīyam' means to say that all spiritual practice of a striver, who wants only God-realization or salvation, without having any craving even for the highest heavenly enjoyments, becomes 'Sat'. In this connection, the Lord mentions that that none, who works for self-redemption or God-realization meets with an evil destiny (Gītā 6/40). Not only this, but He also declares—the seeker of Yoga of equanimity, also transcends the fruit of actions performed with some motive, as laid down in the Vedas (Gītā 6/44). The reason is, that actions perish by bearing fruit, but the spiritual practice (act) done, for the sake of the Lord, does not perish, rather it becomes 'Sat' (Real).

Appendix—In the twenty-fifth verse of this chapter, there is mention of the performance of actions without aiming at the rewards—'anabhisandhāya phalam'. Now here is mention of the performance of actions for the sake of the Supreme. Those who want to attain salvation, act without aiming at the reward—'mokṣakāṅkṣibhiḥ' (Gītā 17/25) and those who want to attain devotion, perform all actions for the sake of God (Gītā 9/26—28).

The action which is connected with God becomes, 'sat' viz., bears 'sat' fruit and also the action by renouncing affinity with the 'asat' becomes 'sat'.

Link:—In the preceding verse, the Lord declared that acts performed for the Lord's sake, become 'Sat' (Real). Now, the question arises, what is the result of acts which are not performed, for the Lord's sake (i.e., which are performed without faith in Him).

अश्रद्धया हुतं दत्तं तपस्तप्तं कृतं च यत्।
असदित्युच्यते पार्थ न च तत्प्रेत्य नो इह॥ २८॥

aśraddhayā hutaṁ dattaṁ tapastaptaṁ kṛtaṁ ca yat
asadityucyate pārtha na ca tatpretya no iha

Whatever oblation is offered, whatever charity (gift), is given, whatever penance is performed and whatsoever, is done, without faith, is called 'Asat', O Arjuna, it is of no avail here or hereafter. 28

Comment:—

'Aśraddhayā hutaṁ dattaṁ tapastaptaṁ kṛtaṁ ca yat'—If acts of sacrifice, penance and charity, which are sanctioned by scriptures, are performed without faith, these are called 'Asat'. Demoniac people, do not believe, in the next world (hereafter), rebirth, righteousness and God. They act against scriptures. Sacrifice and penance, performed by them, are against the ordinance of scriptures.

Now the question arises as to why they perform sacrifices and penance, when they have no faith in them. The answer is, that they perform these to win praise, regard and honour.

'Asadityucyate pārtha na ca tatpretya no iha'—An action, such as sacrifice etc., which is performed without faith, is called 'Asat'. It is useless in this life, as well as, in the next. If actions are performed, expecting a reward, with faith, according to the ordinance of scriptures, they bear fruit here, in the form of riches, prosperity, obedient sons and chaste wife etc., and hereafter, in the form of the attainment of heaven etc. If they are performed, without expecting any reward, with faith and in accordance with scriptures, these having purified the heart and lead to God-realization. But if these are performed without faith, they are of no avail, either in this world, or in the next world.

Now, a question arises, that sinful acts such as injustice, tyranny, fraud, falsehood and forgery etc., should not bear any fruit, because these are performed, without faith and the person, does not expect any reward. The answer is, that they bear fruit, because whatever action is performed with attachment, bears fruit, even though the doer (agent) does not want it. So, people of demoniac nature, go to demoniac wombs, and to hell.

Any simple and insignificant act, if it is performed, without expecting any reward, for the Lord's sake, becomes 'Sat', and leads to God-realization. But, if an important act, such as sacrifice and penance, is performed with faith, and according to the ordinance of the scriptures in expectation of reward, it perishes, by bearing fruit and does not lead to God-realization. If an act is performed without faith, it becomes 'Asat' i.e., it does not bear any fruit, here or hereafter. It means, that in God-realization it is faith (feelings), not an act, which has predominance.

Sadbhāva (existence of God), Sādhubhāva (noble dispositions of the mind), noble deeds, steadfastness in 'Sat', and actions for the sake of the Supreme—these five are called 'Sat', as these are conducive to God-realization.

Why do acts without faith become 'Asat'? The Lord, by His grace has described virtuous actions, in the scriptures, so that a man by performing these, may attain God-realization. But those actions turn to be 'Asat', when these are performed without faith. Their faithlessness should induce the people to hell etc., but because actions performed by them, are good (virtuous), so their actions are of no avail, i.e., they do not bear any fruit, and this is punishment, for such people.

It is proper, on the part of a man, that he should perform acts of sacrifice, penance, gift and pilgrimage etc., which are sanctioned by scriptures, with faith, having no expectation for fruit. The Lord, by His special grace, has bestowed upon us this human body, so that we may perform virtuous actions, with faith for the Lord's sake. Those actions, will prove to be useful for the welfare of all beings, here as well as, hereafter. So, such noble actions should be performed with faith, in order to please God.

Appendix—In the expression 'kṛtaṁ ca yat', chanting and loud chanting the holy names of God will not be included because in them there is affinity with God, so they are not actions, but they are worship to 'God'.

ॐ तत्सदिति श्रीमद्भगवद्गीतासूपनिषत्सु ब्रह्मविद्यायां योगशास्त्रे
श्रीकृष्णार्जुनसंवादे श्रद्धात्रयविभागयोगो नाम सप्तदशोऽध्यायः॥ १७॥

Oṁ tatsaditi śrīmadbhagavadgītāsūpaniṣatsu brahmavidyāyāṁ yogaśāstre śrīkṛṣṇārjunasaṁvāde śraddhātrayavibhāgayogo nāma saptadaśo'dhyāyaḥ

Thus with Oṁ, Tat, Sat, the names of the Lord, in the Upaniṣad of the Bhagavadgītā, the knowledge of Brahma, the supreme, the science of Yoga and the dialogue between Śrī Kṛṣṇa and Arjuna, this the seventeenth discourse is designated:—

"The Yoga of Division of the Threefold faith.,"

In this chapter, faith has been divided into three kinds—sāttvika (good), rājasika (passionate) and tāmasika (ignorant or dull). One, who knows the threefold faith, in the right perspective, will possess good faith and renounce, the passionate and the dull ones. As soon as, he renounces the two (because of his good faith), he realizes his real and eternal affinity, with God, which is natural. So the discourse has been designated: "The Yoga of Division of the Threefold faith."

Words, letters and Uvāca (said) in the Seventeenth Chapter

(1) In this chapter in **'Atha saptadaśo'dhyāyaḥ'** there are three words, in **'Arjuna Uvāca'** etc., there are four words, in verses there are three hundred and thirty-eight words and there are thirteen concluding words. Thus the total number of words, is three hundred and fifty-eight.

(2) In this chapter in **'Atha saptadaśo'dhyāyaḥ'** there are eight letters, in **'Arjuna Uvāca'** etc., thirteen letters, in the verses there are eight hundred and ninety-six letters and there are fifty-one concluding letters. Thus the total number of letters, is nine hundred and sixty-eight.

Each of the verses, in the chapter consists of thirty-two letters.

(3) In this chapter the term **'Uvāca'** (said) has been used two times—**'Arjuna Uvāca'** and **'Śrībhagavānuvāca'**.

Metres Used in the Seventeenth Chapter

Out of the twenty-eight verses of this chapter, in the first quarter of the third verse 'ma-gaṇa' and in its third quarter 'bha-gaṇa' being used there is **'saṁkīrṇa-vipulā'** metre, in the first quarters of the tenth and twelfth verses and in the third quarters of the twenty-fifth and twenty-sixth verses, 'na-gaṇa' being used there is **'na-vipulā'** metre; in the first quarters of sixteenth and seventeenth verses, 'ma-gaṇa' being used there is **'ma-vipulā'** metre; in the third quarter of the eleventh verse, 'bha-gaṇa' being used there is **'bha-vipulā'** metre; and in the first quarter of the nineteenth verse 'ra-gaṇa' being used there is **'ra-vipulā'** metre. The remaining nineteen verses, have the characteristics of right, **'pathyāvaktra'** Anuṣṭup metre.

|| Shri Hari ||

Eighteenth Chapter

INTRODUCTION

The Lord, in the thirty-ninth verse of the second chapter referred to Sāṅkhyayoga (the Discipline of Knowledge) and Karmayoga (the Discipline of Action). These two very disciplines were mentioned in the third verse of the third chapter as Sāṅkhya Niṣṭhā and Yoga Niṣṭhā. Arjuna wanted to know these two paths (Disciplines). But, as Lord Kṛṣṇa could not get an opportunity to explain divine nature and demoniac nature, from the seventh chapter to the fifteenth chapter, so Arjuna could not express his curiosity, from the third chapter to the seventeenth chapter.

Having mentioned the two paths, in the third verse of the third chapter, Lord Kṛṣṇa in the first verse of the fourth chapter, explained that He taught the imperishable Yoga, to the sun-god. Arjuna asked Him, how he could believe, that He taught the Yoga to the sun-god because His birth, came later, while the birth of the sun-god was earlier. The Lord in response to his question talked of His divine births (incarnations) and the Tattva of Karmayoga. In the thirty-fourth verse of the fourth chapter, He directed him to gain, that knowledge from men of wisdom, by obeisance, by questions and by service to them. Again, in the forty-second verse of the fourth chapter, He commanded him to establish himself in Yoga viz., Karmayoga (in the form of even-mindedness). So Arjuna, at the beginning of the fifth chapter, asked Lord Kṛṣṇa which of the two, the path of knowledge or the path of action (Karmayoga), was decidedly better, for him. The Lord, answered his question, in the fifth chapter and started the sixth chapter on his own.

In the thirty-third and the thirty-fourth verses of the sixth chapter, Arjuna put a question on restlessness (fickleness) of mind. The Lord, answered his question in brief. Arjuna, from the thirty-seventh to the thirty-ninth verses, put the question, "What fate does a striver, whose mind wanders away from Yoga (at the time of death), failing to attain perfection in Yoga, meet with?" The Lord, answered the question in the sixth chapter. In the last verse of the sixth chapter, the Lord declared his devotee the best Yogī among all the Yogīs. The Lord, started the same topic in the seventh chapter, where he described devotion, in particular.

Lord Kṛṣṇa, at the end of the seventh chapter, while describing His entire form, used the terms Brahma and Adhyātma etc. So at the beginning of the eighth chapter, Arjuna put seven questions for the clarification, of those terms. The Lord, answered the first six questions in brief, while He explained the seventh question—how He is to be realized at the time of death, in detail. Then He described the topic, which was left, in the seventh chapter, in the ninth chapter and upto the eleventh verse of the tenth chapter. Arjuna, was very much pleased,when he heard in the ninth, tenth and eleventh verses of the tenth chapter, of the devotees and the Lord's compassion to them. So Arjuna, from the twelfth to the eighteenth verses, praised Him and prayed to Him to tell him in detail about His power of Yoga and His glories. Having described His important glories, at the end of the tenth chapter, He declares,"What need is there, O Arjuna, for the detailed knowledge ? I stand, supporting the whole universe, with a single fragment of Myself."Hearing these words Arjuna, prayed to Him to reveal to him His cosmic form. Having revealed His cosmic form, the Lord declared, that by unswerving devotion He can be seen and known and even merged into.

At the end of the eleventh chapter the Lord explained the merits of devotion and before that also He explained the merits of the worship of His absolute aspect (4/34—37; 5/13—26; 6/24—28 and 8/11—13). So Arjuna at the beginning of the twelfth chapter asked, "The devotees who with their minds constantly fixed in You adore You and again those who worship the Imperishable and the Unmanifested—of these two, who are better versed in Yoga?" In response to his question Lord Kṛṣṇa, explained devotion and devotees, in the twelfth chapter, while worship of the Imperishable and the Unmanifested, in the thirteenth and the fourteenth chapters. In the twenty-first verse of the fourteenth chapter, Arjuna asked,"What are the marks of him, who has transcended the three modes of nature? What is his conduct and how does he get, beyond the three modes?" So the Lord explained the marks and conduct of such a transcendental person, and also explained, exclusive devotion, as the means to attain that state. The Lord, started the fifteenth chapter, in connection with His exclusive devotion. At the end of the chapter, He declared that a person who knows Him, as the Supreme Person worships Him, with his whole being (heart or spirit). He means that persons of divine nature, worship Him. It connotes, that persons of demoniac nature, do not worship Him. Before this chapter also, in the fifteenth verse of the seventh chapter and in the twelfth verse of the ninth chapter, demoniac nature, while in the thirteenth verse of the ninth chapter, divine nature have been described, in brief. So the Lord, started the sixteenth chapter, to explain divine nature and demoniac nature in detail and explicitly.

Arjuna, put the question, at the beginning of the seventeenth chapter, on faith which was in connection with the Lord's declaration, which he made, in the last but one verse, of the sixteenth chapter. The Lord, answered his question by describing the faith, of three kinds in the seventeenth chapter. Now Arjuna, expresses his desire to know severally, the truth about the two paths of knowledge and of action, which were mentioned by Him, in the third verse of the third chapter.

अर्जुन उवाच

सन्न्यासस्य महाबाहो तत्त्वमिच्छामि वेदितुम्।
त्यागस्य च हृषीकेश पृथक्केशिनिषूदन॥ १॥

arjuna uvāca

sannyāsasya mahābāho tattvamicchāmi veditum
tyāgasya ca hṛṣīkeśa pṛthakkeśiniṣūdana*

Arjuna said:

O Mighty-armed, O Inner-controller of all, O Slayer of Keśī, I

*On the basis of what Lord Kṛṣṇa has answered to Arjuna's curiosity, his other curiosities can be guessed. They are as follows—

(a) Sannyāsasya mahābāho tattvamicchāmi veditum:—

(1) What is Sannyāsa?

Freedom from egoistic notion (notion of doership), and untaintedness of reason (18/17).

(2) What are the characteristics (marks), of a Sannyāsī?

He should be free from attachment, non-egoistic, full of resolution and zeal, and unaffected by success or failure (18/26).

(3) What (spiritual) discipline, should a Sannyāsī follow?

He should be endowed with a pure intellect, he should resort to dispassion, dwell in solitude, restrain senses, body, speech and mind and so on (18/51—53).

(4) How should he conduct himself?

He should perform action, without a sense of doership, and being free from attachment, and aversion (18/23).

(5) How does he see beings?

He sees, the one imperishable Being (God) in all beings, undivided in the divided (18/20).

(6) What is its fruit?

To enter into the Supreme (18/55).

(b) Tyāgasya ca hṛṣīkeśa pṛthakkeśiniṣūdana—

(i) What is relinquishment?

Performance of duty by relinquishing attachment to actions and their fruit (18/6).

(ii) What should a relinquisher relinquish i.e., his characteristic?

He should relinquish, the fruit of action (18/11).

(iii) How should he perform his duty or what discipline should he follow?

He should perform his duty, by renouncing attachment and fruit (18/9).

(iv) How should he conduct himself?

Neither aversion to disagreeable action, nor attachment for agreeable action (18/10 first half).

(v) How should he perform his duty?

He should perform it merely, because it should be performed (18/9).

(vi) What is its fruit?

To get established in God (18/10 2nd half).

desire to know severally, the true nature of Sannyāsa (Sāṅkhyayoga) and of Tyāga (Karmayoga). 1

Comment:—

'Sannyāsasya mahābāho tattvamicchāmi veditum tyāgasya ca hṛṣīkeśa pṛthakkeśiniṣūdana'—While addressing Lord Kṛṣṇa as 'Mahābāho', Arjuna means to convey that being omniscient, He is able to explain all the topics. So He should satisfy his curiosity in such a manner, that he may understand the topic easily.

By addressing Him as 'Hṛṣīkeśa,' Arjuna means that He is the Lord of senses, and inner-controller, of all beings. So He should explain to him everything in connection with the nature of 'Sannyāsa', and 'Tyāga', even if he does not demand.

By using the term 'Keśiniṣūdana' he means, that as He frees His devotees, from all troubles and problems, He should also remove his doubts.

Generally, a curiosity is expressed with two purposes, (i) to translate it into practice, (ii) to understand the principle. Those, who want to understand the principle, can become learned by possessing bookish knowledge, and can even write books, but they cannot attain salvation. But those, who after understanding principle, translate it into practice, can attain salvation.*

Arjuna also expressed the curiosity, so that, having known the principle, he may translate it into practice.

The term 'Sāṅkhya' used in the expression 'Eṣā te'bhihitā sāṅkhye' (Gītā 2/39) has been termed 'Sannyāsa', here. The Lord, regards the terms 'Sāṅkhya' and 'Sannyāsa as synonyms—as in the second verse of the fifth chapter, He uses the term 'Sannyāsaḥ', in the fourth and the fifth verses the term 'Sāṅkhya', while in the sixth verse again 'Sannyāsa'. Therefore here also 'Sāṅkhya', has been termed 'Sannyāsa'.

Similarly the term, 'Yoga' used in the expression 'Buddhiryoge

* Having known the unreal as unreal a man cannot attain the real, so long as he does not fix 'Realization of the real' as the topmost aim of his life.

tvimāṁ śṛṇu' (Gītā 2/39) stands for the term 'Tyāga', used here. The Lord regards the terms 'Yoga' and 'Tyāga', as synonyms as—'Saṅgaṁ tyaktvā', in the forty-eighth verse of the second chapter and in the fifty-first verse of the same chapter 'Phalaṁ tyaktvā', in the third verse, of the third chapter 'Karmayogena yogināṁ', in the twentieth verse of the fourth chapter 'Tyaktvā karmaphalāsaṅgam', in the fourth verse of the fifth chapter 'Yogau', in the fifth verse, 'Tadyogairapi gamyate,' in the eleventh verse, 'Saṅgaṁ tyaktvā', and in the twelfth verse 'Karmaphalaṁ tyaktvā', and in the twelfth verse of the twelfth chapter 'Tyāgāt'. All these expression have been used for 'Karmayoga'. Therefore, Arjuna has used the term, 'Tyāga' for 'Yoga' i.e., the Discipline of Action, here.

In fact, Sannyāsa, consists in renouncing one's affinity completely with matter through discrimination, while 'Tyāga', consists in giving up attachment for actions and their fruits. He, who does not get attached to actions and their fruits, is said to have attained to Yoga (6/4).

Appendix—At the beginning of the third chapter, Arjuna in a complaining mood told Lord Kṛṣṇa his confusion between Karmayoga and Jñānayoga; at the beginning of the fifth chapter he wanted to know which of the two Yogas was better and here he wants to know the true nature of the two.

Link:—In response to Arjuna's curiosity, the Lord, in the next two verses, cites four different views of other thinkers, on the subject of Sannyāsa and Tyāga.

श्रीभगवानुवाच

काम्यानां कर्मणां न्यासं सन्न्यासं कवयो विदुः ।
सर्वकर्मफलत्यागं प्राहुस्त्यागं विचक्षणाः ॥ २ ॥
त्याज्यं दोषवदित्येके कर्म प्राहुर्मनीषिणः ।
यज्ञदानतपःकर्म न त्याज्यमिति चापरे ॥ ३ ॥

śrībhagavānuvāca

kāmyānāṁ karmaṇāṁ nyāsaṁ sannyāsaṁ kavayo viduḥ
sarvakarmaphalatyāgaṁ prāhustyāgaṁ vicakṣaṇāḥ
tyājyaṁ doṣavadityeke karma prāhurmanīṣiṇaḥ
yajñadānatapaḥkarma na tyājyamiti cāpare

The Blessed Lord said:

The wise, understand by Sannyāsa, the giving up of all actions, prompted by desire; the learned, declare the abandonment of the fruits of all actions as Tyāga. Some philosophers declare, that actions should be given up as an evil, while others say, that acts of sacrifice, charity and penance, are not to be given up. 2-3

Comment:—

These are the four views of the men of wisdom—

(1) 'Kāmyānāṁ karmaṇāṁ nyāsaṁ sannyāsaṁ kavayo viduḥ'— Some men of wisdom, declare that Sannyāsa means, the giving up of all actions prompted by desire, to gain, the favourable and to get rid of, the unfavourable.

(2) 'Sarvakarmaphalatyāgaṁ prāhustyāgaṁ vicakṣaṇāḥ'— Some learned people, declare that abandonment of fruits of all actions, is relinquishment i.e., 'Tyāga' (relinquishment), consists in performing actions, without desire for fruits.

(3) 'Tyājyaṁ doṣavadityeke karma prāhurmanīṣiṇaḥ'— Some men of wisdom, declare that all actions, should be given up, as an evil.*

(4) 'Yajñadānatapaḥkarma na tyājyamiti cāpare'—Some philosophers declare, that other actions may be given up, but sacrifice, gift and penance, are not to be given up.

The above-mentioned, four views can be divided into two parts—the first and the third divisions are in connection with 'Sannyāsa' (Sāṅkhyayoga), while the second and the fourth

---

*According to the Saṁskṛta grammar, the term 'Doṣavat' has a double meaning—all actions should be given up as an evil and evil actions should be given up. But here according to the men of wisdom, the former meaning is appropriate.

divisions, are in connection with 'Tyāga' (Karmayoga). But in these two similar divisions also, there is a little difference. In the first division, actions prompted by desire, are to be given up, while in the third division all the actions are to be given up. Similarly, according to second opinion, there is abandonment of the fruit of actions, while according to the fourth one, other actions except sacrifice, gift and penance, are to be abandoned.

How is the Lord's view superior to those of other thinkers is discussed as follows:—

(1) **'Kāmyānāṁ karmaṇāṁ nyāsaṁ sannyāsam'**—Here, all actions prompted by desire are given up,* yet there remain obligatory actions, of daily routine and also those that are performed on special occasions or at places of pilgrimage etc. Therefore this view is not perfect, because in it, neither the renunciation of doership, has been mentioned nor has it been mentioned, that one gets established, in the self. But in the Lord's view, both these factors are involved. In the seventeenth verse of this chapter, there is mention of the renouncement of doership, when the Lord declares, "He, who is free from egoistic notion

* Actions are divided into five kinds—

(1) 'Nityakarma' —The daily activities as enjoined by the scriptures such as prayer in the morning, noon and evening known as 'Sandhyā' and recitation of 'Gāyatrī mantra' (the sacred Vedic hymn) etc.

(2) 'Naimittikakarma'—The actions which are performed, on account of some place of pilgrimage or special occasions etc., are called 'Naimittika-karma'. Actions sanctioned by scriptures, at the places of pilgrimage such as Prayāga, Naimiṣāraṇya and Puṣkara etc., and on occasions, such as on the days of eclipses, full moon and dark fortnight (Amāvāsyā) and the eleventh day of every fortnight (Ekādaśī), as well as on the birthday and day of marriage etc., are included in this category.

(3) 'Kāmyakarma'—The religious rites, performed in order to gain praise, honour, son, riches, fame etc., and to get rid of diseases, poverty and other undesirable circumstances etc., are known as 'Kāmyakarma'.

(4) 'Prāyaścittakarma'—Actions which are performed, in order to get rid of the sins of present or the past, are called actions of repentance i.e., 'Prāyaścittakarma'.

(5) Necessary (obligatory) actions—The profession, such as farming, business, service etc., as well as actions as eating, drinking, sleeping, awaking etc., are regarded as necessary (obligatory) actions, of daily routine.

and whose intelligence is not tainted." Similarly, he remains established in the self, has been explained, when he declares, "He may kill all these people, he does not kill, nor is he bound."

(2) 'Tyājyaṁ doṣavadityeke'—In this view of the men of wisdom, it is said that all actions should be given up, as an evil. But all actions cannot be renounced (Gītā 3/5), and even the body cannot be maintained, without action (Gītā 3/8). So the Lord, has called this sort of renunciation of one's duty, as rājasika and tāmasika (18/7-8).

(3) 'Sarvakarmaphalatyāgam'—In this first view of relinquishment, there is relinquishment of fruit i.e., relinquishment of desire.* Relinquishment of attachment cannot be included in it, because by doing so, the view of the men of wisdom and the view of the Lord become one. The Lord declares, "Duties must be performed, relinquishing attachment to action and to its fruit" (Gītā 18/6).

(4) 'Yajñadānatapaḥkarma na tyājyam'—Sacrifice, charity and penance, are not to be given up. But besides these three, there is no mention of other actions, which one performs according to one's caste and social order etc., whether they should be performed or not. So this view is imperfect. According to view of the Lord, all duties and pious acts such as pilgrimage etc., must be performed relinquishing, attachment and fruit (18/5-6).

Link:—Having cited the four views of the men of wisdom, on the subject of Sannyāsa and Tyāga, in the preceding two verses,

* Where there is mention of relinquishment of fruit, there it should be regarded as the relinquishment of the desire for fruit, because the fruit cannot be relinquished. Every action, bears some fruit or the other. When a farmer farms a field, it will bear fruit, either desirable or undesirable. Similarly a businessman, may gain or lose, as fruit of business. Thus success or failure, is the fruit of action. But when a man relinquishes desire, his affinity for fruit, is automatically renounced (Gītā 18/12). Therefore, the Lord, has advised to remain even-minded in success, and failure, and this even-mindedness is called 'Yoga' (Gītā 2/48). This even-mindedness, means that the person should not be attached, to fruits of actions.

the Lord now, in the next three verses declares, the final truth on relinquishment (Tyāga).

निश्चयं शृणु मे तत्र त्यागे भरतसत्तम।
त्यागो हि पुरुषव्याघ्र त्रिविधः सम्प्रकीर्तितः॥ ४॥

niścayaṁ śṛṇu me tatra tyāge bharatasattama
tyāgo hi puruṣavyāghra trividhaḥ samprakīrtitaḥ

Hear from Me the conclusion or the final truth about relinquishment, O best of the Bharatas (Arjuna); 'Tyāga', O best of men, has been declared, as threefold.* 4

Comment:—

'Niścayaṁ śṛṇu me tatra tyāge bharatasattama'—Lord Kṛṣṇa asks Arjuna to hear from Him, His view on relinquishment, first.

'Tyāgo hi puruṣavyāghra trividhaḥ samprakīrtitaḥ'—The Lord addressing Arjuna, as the best of men, says that relinquishment has been declared to be of three kinds—sāttvika (good), rājasika (passionate) and tāmasika (ignorant). According to the Lord, the sāttvika relinquishment, is real relinquishment. But, in order to show the superiority of sāttvika relinquishment, He has mentioned the passionate and the ignorant forms, of relinquishment, also.

In discussing the threefold relinquishment He wants to convey, that a striver should adopt only sāttvika, relinquishment, by giving up the rājasika and the tāmasika, ones.

यज्ञदानतपःकर्म न त्याज्यं कार्यमेव तत्।
यज्ञो दानं तपश्चैव पावनानि मनीषिणाम्॥ ५॥

* The Lord has explained the final truth about relinquishment in the fifth and the sixth verses while the threefold relinquishment has been explained from the seventh to the ninth verses.

As the Lord discriminates between the soul (the real) and the body (the unreal) first of all (2/11—30) because the discrimination is very necessary for a Yogī, similarly here he begins the topic of relinquishment of the desire of fruit and attachment to action regarding it as indispensable for Yogīs.

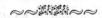

yajñadānatapaḥkarma na tyājyaṁ kāryameva tat
yajño dānaṁ tapaścaiva pāvanāni manīṣiṇām

Acts of sacrifice, charity and penance are not to be given up, but should be performed; for these, (sacrifice, charity and penance) are purifiers of the wise. 5

Comment:—

'Yajñadānatapaḥkarma na tyājyaṁ kāryameva tat'—Here, the Lord has supported the view of the men of wisdom, (18/3). He does not criticize any opinion, in harsh words. He takes the right view of other thinkers, and adds his own belief to it. Here He supports the view of other thinkers, that sacrifice, gift and penance should not be abandoned. He adds His own opinion that these should be performed, because they are purifiers of the wise.

'Yajño dānaṁ tapaścaiva pāvanāni manīṣiṇām'—Here the term 'Caiva', denotes that besides acts of sacrifice, gift and penance, other acts of daily routine, in connection with body and occupation etc., should also, be performed as they are purifiers of the wise. Men, who endowed with equanimity, renounce the fruit of action, are wise (Gītā 2/51). Even such men of wisdom, are purified by acts of sacrifice, gift and penance etc. But the same acts, lead those to bondage, whose senses are not under control, and who perform acts, in order to enjoy pleasure.

In this verse the Lord, in the first half has used the compound expression 'Yajñadānatapaḥkarma', while in the second half, He has given these as separate terms 'Yajño dānaṁ tapaḥ.' Why? He wants to convey in the first half, that acts of sacrifice, gift and penance should not be abandoned but surely performed, while in the second half He means to say, that each of these acts is purifier of the wise.

Appendix—The term 'manīṣī' means thoughtful. The actions which are performed, for the welfare of others, without having any selfish desire, are purifiers viz., they having removed evils, bad conduct and sins etc., are conducive to great Bliss. But if those actions are performed in order to satisfy one's own desire and to do ill of others, they cause impurity viz., cause horrid suffering here as well as hereafter.

एतान्यपि तु कर्माणि सङ्गं त्यक्त्वा फलानि च।
कर्तव्यानीति मे पार्थ निश्चितं मतमुत्तमम्॥ ६॥

etānyapi tu karmāṇi saṅgaṁ tyaktvā phalāni ca
kartavyānīti me pārtha niścitaṁ matamuttamam

But, even these actions also as other duties should be performed, giving up attachment and desire, for fruits. This, O Pārtha (Arjuna), is My decisive and firm belief. 6

Comment:—

'Etānyapi tu karmāṇi saṅgaṁ tyaktvā phalāni ca kartavyānīti me pārtha niścitaṁ matamuttamam'—Here the term 'Etāni', denotes acts of sacrifice, gift and penance, mentioned in the preceding verse, while the term 'Api', denotes other acts in connection with, one's occupation such as business and farming etc., bodily acts, such as eating, drinking, walking, sitting and sleeping-waking etc., in accordance with, scriptural injunctions and other necessary acts, of daily routine. If actions are performed, without having any desire and attachment, for the welfare of others, the flow of actions is towards the world viz., actions are not for one's own self-interest at all, these are totally for the good of others. Thus we get united with God. But if they are performed with attachment and desire, for fruit etc., these lead to bondage and not allow the individuality to vanish.

In the Gītā, in certain contexts, there is mention of relinquishment of attachment, while in others, the Lord talks of relinquishment, of fruit of actions. Here, in this verse, both are mentioned together. It means, that where there is a mention of the one, the other should also be presumed. So a striver, should neither be attached to action, nor to the fruit, of actions. By doing so his attachment for the mind, intellect, senses, body and other possessions, is shaken off (Gītā 5/11).

Attachment is subtle, while desire for fruit of action, is gross.

The attachment of sentient soul, to insentient and perishable world, leads the soul to its birth, in good and evil wombs (Gītā 13/21). As soon as this attachment is relinquished, a striver, realizes his natural detachment.

Philosophers differ, in their views about the universe. Some of them regard it as unreal, like a dream, others hold it, as kaleidoscopic like a body, while still some others believe, in its existence, like water, which always remains in the form of snow, cloud, vapour etc., but never perishes. Thus they hold different views. But they all agree, that perishable matter has no affinity, with the imperishable self. So a striver, instead of being entangled in discussions and arguments, whether matter is real or unreal, or beyond the real and the unreal etc., should give up affinity, with the universe, an evolute of Matter. In fact, the universe including, this body is ever undergoing a change, while the soul ever remains the same, without any modifications. A striver, has to realize this fact.

Whatever circumstances, we are placed in, are the fruits of actions performed, in the past; and actions we are performing now, will bear fruit, in future. So a striver, should neither be attached to persons and things he possesses, nor have a desire for what he expects to receive, in future. He should not have any desire, for fruits.*

Why should, the desire for fruits of actions be given up? The reason is, that actions have a beginning and an end and so has their fruit. So desire and attachment, for the fruit should be given up. Actually, there is no attachment, in the self, it is merely assumed.

In reality we cannot give up, what is ours and also cannot give up, what is not ours. We cannot give up the self, as fire cannot give up heat, and light. We also cannot give up the things belonging to others in this world. We can give up things, which

*The term 'Phalāni' has been used in plural number because such people expect the fruit in the form of comforts, luxuries, praise, honour and fame etc., here and in heaven hereafter. According to the opinion of the Lord, desire for all these fruits should be renounced.

are not ours but we have only assumed these as ours. We have assumed matter and its evolute, and the body as ours. So we have to give up this assumption.

A man, should discharge his duty, very carefully and promptly, by giving up attachment and desire, for fruits, according to the ordinance of scriptures, whether it is significant or insignificant. The reason is, that when we are not concerned with its fruit, no question arises, whether the action is trivial or significant, and whether it bears meagre or rich fruit. An action, appears to be superior or inferior, due to desire for fruit, while in Karmayoga, the desire for fruit, is to be renounced. A follower of the Discipline of Action, performs action to get rid of attachment. In the Gītā, it is mentioned, "Action is said to be the means of the sage, who wishes to attain to Yoga (in the form of equanimity)" (Gītā 6/3), "Not by non-performance of actions does a man, attain freedom from action" (Gītā 3/4). When he performs action for himself, he gets attached to it. So a striver, following the path of action, performs actions for the welfare of others. With his physical body, he does good to others, with his subtle body he thinks, of the welfare of others, and with the causal body his trance, is also meant for the welfare of others. By doing so, his attachment for action, is easily wiped out. Attachment is the only obstacle to God-realization. As soon as a Karmayogī, gets rid of this attachment, he realizes God automatically (Gītā 4/38).

The term 'Kartavya', stands for action which we can perform, which must be performed and which is conducive to perfection. The aim of this human life, is to attain perfection, not to enjoy pleasure or suffer pain. Even other beings, such as birds, beasts, creepers, moths, trees and plants etc., come across favourable and unfavourable circumstances, in the form of pleasure and pain. But they do not know what actions, they must perform. Moreover, they have got no right, to attain perfection. The Lord, declares that this is His decided view, in which there is no room for doubt, and also this is His best view, which is perfect, according to scriptures and which is conducive to perfection.

Appendix—In this verse there is mention of relinquishment of attachment to actions as well as to their fruit—both. Attachment to action and to its fruit is the main bondage, having relinquished which a man attains Yoga viz., becomes Yogārūḍha—'yadā hi nendriyārtheṣu na karmasvanuṣajjate' (Gītā 6/4).

Virtuous actions performed in only a disinterested way lead to salvation. But if virtuous actions are performed with an interested motive, they are conducive to bondage—'ābrahma-bhuvanāllokāḥ punarāvartino'rjuna' (Gītā 8/16).

Link:—The Lord, in the fourth verse of this chapter, declared relinquishment, to be threefold. So, in the next three verses, He describes them.

नियतस्य तु सन्न्यासः कर्मणो नोपपद्यते।
मोहात्तस्य परित्यागस्तामसः परिकीर्तितः॥७॥

niyatasya tu sannyāsaḥ karmaṇo nopapadyate
mohāttasya parityāgastāmasaḥ parikīrtitaḥ

Verily, the renunciation of any duty that be prescribed, is not proper. Its abandonment (tyāga) through delusion (ignorance), is declared to be tāmasika (of the mode of ignorance). 7

Comment:—

[The Lord, describes the threefold relinquishment, because Arjuna wanted to abandon his duty (Gītā 2/5). So Lord Kṛṣṇa, by explaining the threefold relinquishment wanted to warn Arjuna and other human beings, that one should not abandon one's duty, but should abandon attachment to it and also, it's fruit. This abandonment, is called sāttvika abandonment, which leads a man, to freedom from worldly bondage.

Also, the Lord, in the seventeenth chapter described faith and food etc., of three kinds. So here also, He describes abandonment of three kinds.]

'Niyatasya tu sannyāsaḥ karmaṇo nopapadyate'—The Lord in the preceding verse, explained His decisive and firm belief.

But this tāmasika abandonment, is quite contrary and inferior, to that. So the term 'tu' (verily), is used here.

Duty that ought to be discharged, must be discharged. One's profession, according to one's caste and social order, hospitality, sacrifice, prayer and recitation of Gāyatrī mantra (the sacred Vedic hymn) and such other acts, should not be abandoned. Such abandonment if resorted to, is Tāmasika and, is the abandonment of ordained duty (Niyata Karma).

'Mohāttasya parityāgastāmasaḥ parikīrtitaḥ'— Abandonment of any such act, out of delusion (ignorance), is declared to be tāmasika. Not to attend, an urgent meeting or divine discourse, not to attend to sick parents; not to attend the court, at the right time and such other negligence, out of heedlessness, idleness and laziness, are examples of tāmasika abandonment.

What is the difference between 'Vihita Karma' and 'Niyata Karma?' All actions, which are sanctioned by scriptures, are called 'Vihita Karma'. All those actions sanctioned by scriptures cannot be performed, by a person because there is mention of several fasts, on all dates and days. If a man observes all those fasts, when will he have meals? But, out of those action sanctioned by the scripture, the duty that ought to be done, according to one's caste, (social order), stage of life and circumstances, is called 'Niyata Karma'. All the occupations of the four castes (Varṇas)—Brāhmaṇa, Kṣatriya, Vaiśya and Śūdra, are included in the 'Niyata Karma'.

If one's duty is abandoned, out of delusion, it is tāmasika abandonment, and if it is abandoned, in order to gain pleasure and rest, it is rājasika abandonment. But if the duty is discharged by abandoning the desire for fruit and also attachment to it, it is sāttvika abandonment. It means, that a tāmasika person gets entangled in delusion, a rājasika in comforts and luxuries, while a sāttvika person, discharges his duty carefully, without expecting any reward. A person abandons his affinity, with actions and their fruits, because of this sāttvika nature or sāttvika abandonment, not the rājasika and the tāmasika ones. In fact, the latter two, are not abandonment, in the true sense of the word.

A layman regards abandonment of actions, as real abandonment. But according to Lord Kṛṣṇa, real abandonment consists in abandoning attachment, and desire, which lead to bondage (Gītā 13/21).

If external abandonment, is regarded as the real abandonment, every dead person should attain salvation, because he abandons all the worldly possessions, as well as his body and he does not even remember, them. Therefore internal abandonment of attachment and desire etc., is real abandonment, which frees a man, from bondage.

Appendix—A man is more responsible to discharge his prescribed duty than to perform actions sanctioned by the scriptures. As the act of 'watching' by a watchman and 'the supply of water' by a water-hut-man are their duties—'niyata karma' for which they are specially responsible. If a person abandons his duty, he is considered very much guilty for it. Renunciation of one's duty leads to commotion. Therefore a person should not abandon his duty whether he is paid more or less for it or whether it provides him more comfort or less comfort. In these days there is disorder in the society because people don't discharge their duty. If a person does not discharge the duty allotted to him, what will be its consequences for him? If the duty is abandoned, out of delusion, it is Tāmasa abandonment and such a person sinks downwards to lower births and lower regions—'adho gacchanti tāmasāḥ' (Gītā 14/18).

दुःखमित्येव यत्कर्म कायक्लेशभयात्त्यजेत्।
स कृत्वा राजसं त्यागं नैव त्यागफलं लभेत्॥ ८॥

duḥkhamityeva yatkarma kāyakleśabhayāttyajet
sa kṛtvā rājasaṁ tyāgaṁ naiva tyāgaphalaṁ labhet

He, who abandons action, because it is painful or from fear

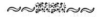

of physical suffering, does not gain the reward of relinquishment by practising such rājasika abandonment. 8

Comment:—

'Duḥkhamityeva yatkarma'— Rājasika people, think that all the acts of sacrifice, penance and charity etc., sanctioned by the scriptures, are painful because in performing these, there are so many restrictions. Moreover, a lot of money has to be spent. They hold this opinion, because they have no faith in the scriptures, the next world, and the actions prescribed by scriptures.

'Kāyakleśabhayāttyajet'—Rājasika people, think that in the performance of actions sanctioned by scriptures, and the social decorum, they have to suffer hardships, by foregoing bodily comfort.* They feel dependent and sad, while discharging their duty, according to their caste (social order), and stage of life, and in obeying their parents, teachers and masters. But, they feel independent and happy, while they work according to their own will. They do not want to be governed, by scriptural ordinances. They want to lead a lazy, idle and carefree life of a Sādhu, or a pensioner, by abandoning household affairs, which involve physical and mental effort.

Here, a doubt arises, that in gaining true knowledge, there is mention of perception, of evil and pain (Gītā 13/8) while, here it is mentioned, that action which is abandoned, because it is painful or from fear of physical suffering, is rājasika relinquishment, and here, relinquishment of action is forbidden. These two statements seem contrary. The clarification is, that these are not contrary, but the topics are different. There, it is mentioned, that one should perceive evil and pain, in pleasure and so should abandon, pleasure. But here, it refers to performing, one's duty. So duty must not be relinquished, rather it must be performed. Perception of evil and pain, in pleasure develops dispassion, which leads to God-realization, while relinquishment of one's duty, because

* A man feels physical suffering because of his attachment to the body and the sense of mine with it.

it is painful or full of physical suffering, leads to bondage (Gītā 3/9). Fruit of both the rājasika and tāmasika relinquishment, is tāmasika, which leads people to sink deeply (Gītā 14/18).

Now a question arises, that a devotee, who attends divine discourses and listens to glories of the Lord, develops dispassions and so he renounces daily duties and is absorbed in devotion, and adoration, should his relinquishment not be regarded as rājasika? No, actually it is not so, because God-realization, is the aim of human life. So if a striver, renounces other action, and is engaged in devotion and adoration etc., he performs his real duty. He cannot indulge in heedlessness, and indolence. But,those who practise rājasika or tāmasika relinquishment, will indulge in evil propensities, such as heedlessness and indolence etc., because they are interested in pleasure.

'Sa kṛtvā rājasaṁ tyāgaṁ naiva tyāgaphalaṁ labhet'— Peace, immediately follows, renunciation. But a rājasika person, does not attain peace, as fruit of his relinquishment, because, his relinquishment is meant to gain rest, comfort and luxuries etc., as this can be seen, even in animals. So, such a person instead of attaining peace, has to receive punishment, as a fruit of neglect, of his duties.

Appendix—Renunciation leads to 'Supreme Peace'—'tyāgācchāntiranantaram' (Gītā 12/12) and the fruit of attachment is 'pain'—'rajasastu phalaṁ duḥkham' (Gītā 14/16). A person possessing the mode of passion does not attain peace, the fruit of renunciation; but certainly suffers pain, the fruit of attachment.

कार्यमित्येव यत्कर्म नियतं क्रियतेऽर्जुन।
सङ्गं त्यक्त्वा फलं चैव स त्यागः सात्त्विको मतः ॥ ९ ॥

kāryamityeva yatkarma niyataṁ kriyate'rjuna
saṅgaṁ tyaktvā phalaṁ caiva sa tyāgaḥ sāttviko mataḥ

But, he who performs a prescribed duty (obligatory action), O Arjuna, because it ought to be done, abandoning attachment

and also the desire for fruit, that relinquishment, is regarded as sāttvika (good). 9

Comment:—

'Kāryamityeva yatkarma niyataṁ kriyate'rjuna'—Here, the particles 'Iti', and 'Eva', have been added to the term 'Kāryam', which denote that the prescribed duty is only to be performed, without any selfish motive, or desire for its fruit. By doing so, the doer's affinity with action, is renounced. So action (duty), does not lead him, to bondage. He is bound, only if he is attached, to action and its fruit, (Gītā 5/12).

All duties, which have been prescribed by the scriptures, according to a person's caste, social order, position and circumstances etc., are included in the 'Niyata Karma'. He should discharge those duties, very promptly and enthusiastically, abandoning idleness, laziness and heedlessness. So the Lord, in the context of the Discipline of Action, has used the term 'Samācara' (perform efficiently), (Gītā 3/9, 19).

'Saṅgaṁ tyaktvā phalaṁ caiva'—He should not be attached to actions, or the means (instruments) of actions, nor should he have desire, for the fruit.

'Sa tyāgaḥ sāttviko mataḥ'*—Sāttvika Tyāga, consists in relinquishing attachment for action, its fruit and also the desire, for its fruit. In rājasika relinquishment, actions are abandoned, because these are painful, and they cause physical suffering; in tāmasika relinquishment, actions are abandoned, out of delusion,

* In the Gītā where there is description of the three modes of nature (7/12; 14/5—18, 22; 17/1-2, 8—13, 17—22 and 18/20—28, 30—35, 37—39) the order is Sattva, Raja and Tama, while here the order is reversed. The reason is—(i) If the Lord after the sixth verse (in the seventh verse) had described Sāttvika relinquishment, there would have been the repetition of the Lord's decided view and Sāttvika relinquishment. (ii) Something is proved superior if the inferior things have already been described. Therefore the Lord in order to prove superiority of the Sāttvika relinquishment first describes the Rājasika and the Tāmasika ones. (iii) In the verses tenth to twelfth there is description of the Sāttvika renouncer. So the Sāttvika relinquishment is given in the ninth verse so that they may be connected.

while in sāttvika relinquishment, actions are not abandoned, but are performed carefully and promptly, according to rules and regulations, without expecting any reward. By sāttvika relinquishment, our affinity with actions and their fruit, is renounced, while in rājasika and tāmasika relinquishment, it seems that we are not at all concerned with actions, but actually internal affinity, is not renounced. The reason is, that in rājasika relinquishment, a man abandons actions, because these are painful and they cause physical suffering. So one remains attached to his comforts. Similarly, in tāmasika relinquishment, when a man abandons action out of delusion, he remains attached, to delusion. Thus even abandonment (relinquishment), leads to bondage, while performance of actions promptly, in accordance with the scriptural injunctions, leads to emancipation.

Appendix—In the mode of ignorance there is delusion (ignorance), in the mode of passion there is selfishness; but in the mode of goodness, there is neither delusion nor selfishness but there is renunciation of affinity. A Sāttvika person performs the obligatory actions (prescribed duty) because they ought to be done. There is a vital point which needs attention, and that is, that when an action is performed as a matter of duty, the affinity with it, is renounced. In the worldly disciplines (Karmayoga and Jñānayoga) the breach of affinity with the body and the world is important. Therefore a striver should perform every action by regarding it as his duty. External abandonment of actions is conducive to bondage but the performance of actions as a matter of duty, without having affinity with them, leads to salvation.*

* In the unworldly discipline (discipline of devotion), affinity with God is important. Therefore a devotee should not practise spiritual discipline such as chanting or loud chanting the Lord's holy names and meditation etc., with the mere sense of duty but should practise it, in a loving manner by regarding it as service or worship to his dearest beloved, in order to please Him. God's everything (His name and Form etc.,) should be loving to him. He should feel delighted while performing actions for God's sake. As a medicine is taken by a patient with the sense of duty but food is not taken with the sense of duty but it is taken in order to satisfy hunger; similarly

Here a doubt may arise that in this verse there is mention of the performance of action rather than Tyāga (relinquishment), then how is it 'Sāttvika tyāga'? The clarification is that in a Sāttvika doer, there is neither delusion, nor selfishness, nor attachment nor desire for fruit; but he performs actions with the sense of duty; therefore as the doer has no affinity with the action, it is 'Tyāga' (relinquishment). Duty remains in the insentient division, in it there is no affinity with the sentient. When a man (the Self) assumes his affinity with the body, then he is connected with the actions performed with the body. If he does not assume his affinity with the body but only discharges his duty, he will not be connected with actions. It is named 'Tyāga' because in it there is renunciation of affinity with the body and the world. In it there is renunciation of affinity with both—the action and its fruit.

Link:—With what sense, should the prescribed acts such as sacrifice, gift and penance be performed, and the prohibited acts and other acts for desire of fruits be relinquished? The answer comes.

न द्वेष्ट्यकुशलं कर्म कुशले नानुषज्जते।
त्यागी सत्त्वसमाविष्टो मेधावी छिन्नसंशयः ॥ १० ॥

na dveṣṭyakuśalaṁ karma kuśale nānuṣajjate
tyāgī sattvasamāviṣṭo medhāvī chinnasaṁśayaḥ

The man, who has no aversion to disagreeable action, and no attachment to an agreeable one, is a man of true renunciation, is intelligent, he who has all his doubts resolved and established in the self. 10

Comment:—

'Na dveṣṭyakuśalaṁ karma'—Pious actions, sanctioned by

a devotee should not chant the Lord's holy names and meditate on Him with the sense of duty and with a view to get rid of them but he should do it in order to arouse his ownship with Him. If he chants the Lord's holy names and meditates on Him with the mere sense of duty, his ownness with God will not be aroused and his love (devotion) to Him will not be revealed.

scriptures, which are performed, with the desire of fruit, and which lead to rebirth (2/42—44; 9/20-21) and the prohibited evil actions, which lead to demoniacal wombs, and hell (16/7—20)—all these actions, are disagreeable. A striver, abandons such disagreeable actions, but has no aversion for them. If he abandons these by having an aversion to them, he gets attached to aversion, and that attachment is worse than action performed with a desire, and also the prohibited evil actions.

'Kuśale nānuṣajjate'—All actions, which are performed according to the ordinance of scriptures, suited to one's caste, social order and circumstances etc., by relinquishing attachment, and fruit and which lead to salvation, are called 'Kuśala', (agreeable). A striver, while performing such actions, has no attachment for them.

'Tyāgī'—The real abandoner (renouncer), is he, who has neither aversion to a disagreeable action, nor attachment to an agreeable one.* His relinquishment, attains perfection, when he is not, in the least, affected by action or inaction (Gītā 3/18; 4/18). Such a man, is said to have attained to Yoga (Gītā 6/4).

'Medhāvī'—He whose actions are performed thoroughly, and are free from desire, and thoughts of the world, and are burnt by the fire of wisdom, him even the sages call, wise (Gītā 4/19). It is great wisdom, if a man is not attached to actions, while performing these. Such a person, has been called wise, among men (4/18).

'Chinnasaṁśayaḥ'—The doubts of such a person, are dispelled, because he remains established in the self, where there is perfection. So, there is no question of any doubt. A doubt, subsists only where knowledge is imperfect i.e., we know something, and we

*The person, who rises above the pairs of opposites in the form of favourable and unfavourable ones, renounces the prohibited actions without aversion; he performs the prescribed actions without attachment. As a crawling baby is engaged in an action and refrains from it without attachment and aversion, a transcendental man also performs actions without attachment and aversion (a child does so out of ignorance while he does so because of his discrimination) (wisdom).

do not know something else.

'Sattvasamāviṣṭaḥ'—When a man, relinquishes attachment etc., he automatically gets situated, in the self. In the nineteenth verse of the fifth chapter, also it is mentioned, that such a person, gets established in the Eternal.

Appendix—This verse means that a striver should renounce attachment and aversion. It is a man's nature that he takes up (performs) the agreeable activities by being attached to them and he renounces the disagreeable ones by having aversion to them. A man gets connected with the world by both—attachment and aversion. The Lord declares that only that man is noble who takes up (performs) the virtuous action but is not attached to it and renounces the evil action but has no aversion to it.

Link:—Why should a man, bother to have no aversion for a disagreeable action, and no attachment for an agreeable action? Why should, he not relinquish actions, altogether? The Lord, clarifies the doubt, in the next verse.

न हि देहभृता शक्यं त्यक्तुं कर्माण्यशेषतः।
यस्तु कर्मफलत्यागी स त्यागीत्यभिधीयते ॥ ११ ॥

na hi dehabhṛtā śakyaṁ tyaktuṁ karmāṇyaśeṣataḥ
yastu karmaphalatyāgī sa tyāgītyabhidhīyate

It is, indeed, impossible for any embodied being to abandon actions entirely. But, he who relinquishes the fruit of action, is verily, called a relinquisher (tyāgī). 11

Comment:—

'Na hi dehabhṛtā* Śakyaṁ tyaktuṁ karmāṇyaśeṣataḥ'—Embodied beings, cannot abandon actions, because the body is an evolute of prakṛti (matter) and prakṛti is ever-active. So how

* Here the term 'Dehabhṛtā' stands for the embodied beings i.e., those who have identified themselves with the body.

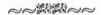

can, an embodied being, abstain from actions? He may relinquish acts of sacrifice, gift, penance and pilgrimage etc., but how could he abandon eating, drinking, walking, sitting, standing, sleeping and waking etc.?

Again, internal relinquishment (relinquishment from the heart), is real relinquishment. External relinquishment, is unreal and temporary. A man, relinquishes external actions, in a trance. But this trance, is also an action, because in trance, affinity with causal body, persists. So there is deviation in trance, also.

No one can remain inactive, even for a moment (Gītā 3/5). Man, does not attain freedom from action, by non-performance of action, nor does he attain to perfection, by mere renunciation of action (Gītā 3/4).

A Vital Fact

A man being sentient, ever remains, uniform and immutable, while Prakṛti is mutable and kaleidoscopic. So long as, a man is attached to prakṛti and its evolute, the body, and identifies himself with it, he cannot abandon actions entirely, because he regards actions of the body, as his own.

Further a man has assumed his affinity with prakṛti, by neglecting discrimination. He has assumed the self, as the body and the body, as his own. It is because of the assumption of egoism, and mineness, that the embodied being cannot abandon actions, entirely.

'Yastu* karmaphalatyāgī sa tyāgītyabhidhīyate'—He, who relinquishes his affinity for action and its fruit, is a relinquisher. So long as he has his affinity with agreeable or disagreeable, good or bad action, he is not a relinquisher. When a man assumes things and actions, as his own, he gets attached to them. Moreover, he is also attached to fruits, of those actions. But, as soon as,

* Here the term 'Tu' denotes that the person who relinquishes the fruit of actions is superior to common mundane people because his aim is God-realization or salvation.

his aim is to relinquish the fruit of action, all his actions are directed, towards the welfare of the world. The reason is, that he realizes, that he has received everything from the world, and so everything belongs to the world. Besides, actions and their fruits, appear and disappear, while he ever remains, uniform and immutable. Having this sort of discrimination, he gives up the fruit of actions, very easily. Such a person, who relinquishes the fruit of action, is called a relinquisher.

There neither was nor is, nor can be, nor is there any possibility, of affinity of the immutable self, with the mutable fruit of action. It is out of ignorance, that man has assumed this affinity. As soon as, this assumed affinity, is renounced, he is called a renouncer. This can be explained by an illustration.

When a person renounces his kinsmen and becomes an ascetic (saint), from his heart, prosperity, adversity or ruin of the family, makes no difference to him. The reason is, that he gives up his assumed affinity, with his family. This was a two-way affinity—from his side, as well as, from the side of the family. But, as far as his affinity with prakṛti is concerned, it is only he, who has assumed this affinity, prakṛti has not assumed it. So, if he wants to relinquish this affinity, he can relinquish it easily, without any doubt.

Appendix—This verse has been uttered from the viewpoint of Karmayoga. In Karmayoga there is renunciation of the desire for fruit while in Jñānayoga—there is renunciation of the sense of doership.

'Relinquishment for the fruit of action' means to relinquish the desire for the fruit of action. The reason is that the fruit for action can't be renounced, as the body is the fruit of action, how will it be renounced? Having eaten food, hunger is satisfied, how will this satisfaction be renounced? Having farmed the land, how will corn be renounced? Therefore in the Gītā, renunciation of the desire for the fruit (of action) has been mentioned as relinquishment for the fruit of action.

In fact the external relinquishment is not real relinquishment but the internal relinquishment is the real relinquishment. If a person, having renounced the world, externally, goes to a solitary place, the body which is the seed of the universe, still remains with him. When a person dies, all things including his body desert him but death does not lead him to salvation. Therefore our desires, the sense of mine and attachment bind us, the universe does not bind us. When we do nothing for ourselves, our affinity with actions is renounced—'yajñāyācarataḥ karma samagraṁ pravilīyate' (Gītā 4/23).

Link:—In the preceding verse, the Lord declared that he who relinquishes the fruit of action, is verily, called a relinquisher. What happens if he does not relinquish fruit of action? The Lord, answers the question, in the next verse.

अनिष्टमिष्टं मिश्रं च त्रिविधं कर्मणः फलम्।
भवत्यत्यागिनां प्रेत्य न तु सन्न्यासिनां क्वचित्॥ १२॥

anisṭamiṣṭaṁ miśraṁ ca trividhaṁ karmaṇaḥ phalam
bhavatyatyāgināṁ pretya na tu sannyāsināṁ kvacit

Pleasant, unpleasant and mixed of three kinds, is the fruit of action, accruing even after death, to those who have not relinquished the fruit, but there is no, here or hereafter, for those who have relinquished the fruit. 12

Comment:—

'Aniṣṭamiṣṭaṁ miśraṁ ca trividhaṁ karmaṇaḥ phalam'—An action, bears three kinds of fruit—pleasant (good), unpleasant (evil) and mixed. In the world generally, a person reaps mixed fruit for his actions. For example, when a man earns money, by working hard, he gets the necessities of life, this is pleasant fruit. But he has to pay income tax, or again, there is loss of money, this is unpleasant fruit. It means, that his pleasure is partial, and in unpleasantness there is a part of pleasantness, because there is no creature, in the world, that is not bound by the three modes of nature (Gītā 18/40). This world, is a place of sorrow or suffering (8/15, 9/33). But no circumstances, are totally pleasant or totally unpleasant. There is predominance of one or the other. In fact, the fruit of actions is mixed, because all actions are clouded by defects (18/48).

'Bhavatyatyāgināṁ pretya'—Common folk, not renouncers, reap these three kinds of fruit. Actually the actions and their fruits, are connected with prakṛti, not with the self, because the body, senses, mind and intellect etc., are evolutes of prakṛti. When a man (self), performs actions, being attached to them, he has to reap pleasant, unpleasant and mixed fruits, in the form of favourable and unfavourable circumstances. These circumstances, make him happy and sad which feelings bind him.

He who feels happy, in favourable circumstances, cannot escape sadness, in unfavourable circumstances. So long as, he enjoys pleasure, he will have to suffer pain. He cannot be free, from worry, sorrow, fear and agitation etc.

By the expression 'Pretya bhavati', the Lord means that those who, do not relinquish the fruit of actions, have to reap pleasant, unpleasant and mixed fruits, after death. But by the expression 'Na tu sannyāsināṁ kvacit' He wants to convey, that those, who have relinquished the fruit of actions, have not to reap the fruit, here or after death. It means, that the non-relinquishers do reap the fruit after death, but they may also reap it here.

'Na tu sannyāsināṁ kvacit'—Renouncers (relinquishers), have not to reap the fruit of their actions, here or hereafter. The favourable and unfavourable circumstances, as the fruit of actions, appear, but they are not affected by them, because they remain neutral. Moreover, they realize the reality, that the self needs, neither action nor anything. They perform all the actions, for the welfare of others. Actions performed, with their physical body, the thoughts possessed, with their subtle body and the trance with their causal body—all are for the welfare of others.

The reason is, that whatever they possess is of the world, and so it is to be utilized for the welfare of the world. They commit an error when they think of their own welfare, only. This is to keep his individuality intact.

Here, in the term 'Sannyāsinām' there is identity between the relinquisher (Karmayogī) and renouncer Sannyāsī (Sāṅkhyayogī). A Karmayogī, remains detached from actions, while a Sāṅkhyayogī, remains totally unconnected with, actions. A Karmayogī, has no desire for the fruit of action i.e., he has no feeling of mineness with it, while a Sāṅkhyayogī, relinquishes his egoism. If the feeling of mineness is renounced, the feeling of egoism, is automatically renounced. Similarly, the feeling of mineness, is renounced, with the renouncement of egoism. So, in the context of Karmayoga, the Lord has first mentioned the abandonment of, the sense of mineness, and then of egoism (2/71) while in Sāṅkhyayoga, he has reversed the order (18/53). In both, there is relinquishment of affinity with prakṛti and its evolutes.

Arjuna asked Lord Kṛṣṇa, that he desired to know severally, the nature of renunciation, (Sannyāsa) and of relinquishment (Tyāga). Therefore, the Lord by using the term 'Sannyāsinām'; wants to convey that a Karmayogī, thinks that nothing is his, nothing is wanted by him and nothing is to be done for him. Similarly, a Sāṅkhyayogī thinks that nothing is his and nothing is wanted by him. A Sāṅkhyayogī does not assume his affinity with prakṛti and its evolute, and so there is no need to say, that nothing is to be done, for him.

Here, the Lord instead of, using the term 'Tyāginām', uses the term 'Sannyāsinām', in order to convey, that state of neutrality which is obtained by men of renunciation, (Sāṅkhyayogī) is also reached, by men of action (Karmayogī) (Gītā 5/4-5). Secondly, till now the Lord explained, that a Karmayogī, remains detached and neutral. Now, by using the term 'Sannyāsinām', He means to convey that, He will explain how to attain that state of detachment, or neutrality by Sāṅkhyayoga.

An Important Fact in Connection with Actions

'Puruṣa' and 'Prakṛti', are two distinct entities. 'Puruṣa' is never subject to change while 'Prakṛti', always undergoes change. When a man, identifies himself with prakṛti, or in other words he identifies himself with the body then the actions done by his body become his actions. Further he develops, a sense of mine, with the objects acquired. In this mineness, the desire for things unacquired, springs. Till these evils, such as desire, mineness, and identification subsist, an activity is called an action. When one renounces this identification, his actions do not bear fruit for him, and turn into inaction. When a liberated soul, realizes the self, actions performed by his body are neutralized actions, (Gītā 4/18). Actually, all actions are performed, by the modes of nature. But, a man by identifying himself with prakṛti (body) thinks, "I am the doer" (Gītā 3/27; 13/29).

Actions are of three kinds—Kriyamāṇa* (actions of the present), Sañcita (accumulated action of the several past human lives, and also of this life till now) and Prārabdha (some of the actions, whose fruit man has to reap, during this life, in the form of favourable and unfavourable circumstances).

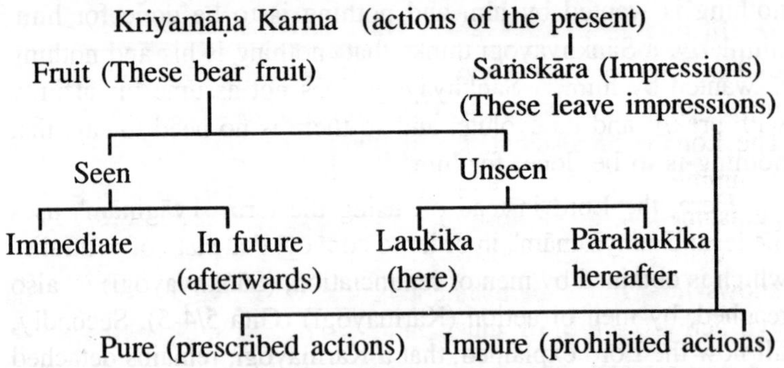

*New actions can be performed only in human life and so are their impressions (Gītā 4/12; 15/2). Other lives such as of birds and beasts etc., are only to reap the fruit of the past actions.

Kriyamāṇa actions are of two kinds— Good and evil. Actions which are performed, in accordance with ordinance of scriptures, are called good, while actions performed against ordinance of scriptures, out of desire, anger, greed and attachment, are evil.

These bear fruits, in two forms—direct fruit, and fruit in the form of impression (influence). Direct fruit is divided into two kinds—seen and unseen. The seen fruit, can further be divided into two—immediate and remote. As the immediate fruit of tasteful food, is that it satisfies hunger and its fruit in future, is that it gives strength. Similarly, he who eats chilli in excess, with food, has a burning sensation, in the tongue, mouth, throat, ears and eyes. That is immediate fruit. It causes disease, in future, and is future fruit.

Similarly, unseen fruit, can either be reaped here, or hereafter. Acts of sacrifice, gifts, penance, pilgrimage and chanting etc., can bear fruit here, in the form of riches, sons, praise and honour etc.,* and hereafter, in the attainment of heaven. Similarly, fruit of evil actions such as theft, robbery and murder in the form of fine, imprisonment and execution is unseen fruit, which is reaped here, while birth as birds, beasts, insects and creepers, and residence in hell is fruit, which is reaped hereafter.

In this connection, a point needs attention. If the fruit of evil actions, is reaped here, in the form of fine, imprisonment, insult and reproach etc., it will not have to be reaped hereafter. The Lord is omniscient. He maintains a record of all the sins, committed by a person, and the fruit, reaped by him. So, whatever punishment is given, to a man is always just, because the Lord is a disinterested friend, of every being. He being omniscient, knows how much punishment he has suffered, as fruit of his evil actions, and how much more he has to suffer. So pain or

---

*Here the future fruit of the seen and the mundane fruit of the unseen seem similar yet are different. The future fruit of the seen is reaped direct without becoming 'Prārabdha' while the mundane fruit of the unseen is reaped by becoming 'Prārabdha'.

punishment, that is inflicted upon a person, is the fruit, of his sinful action.*

*In this connection I heard an anecdote. There was an honest gentleman in a village. In front of his house there was house of a goldsmith. One day some customers gave a lot of gold to the goldsmith, to prepare ornaments. The constable on night duty, came to know about it. So at night he murdered the goldsmith and wanted to run away with the box full of gold. The honest gentleman, saw him going away. He caught him red handed, and challenged him. The constable wanted to pacify him, by offering him a share of the gold. But he did not agree, because he was honest. The constable whistled and having heard the whistle several other constables, came there. They caught the honest man. He was charged with murder and theft. A case was filed against him. When he was presented before a magistrate, he tried to argue, that it was not he, but the constable who was a criminal. But other constables also confirmed, that he had been caught red handed by them, committing a theft, having committed the murder.

The magistrate after listening to the statements of all of them finally gave a judgement, that the gentleman would be hanged to death. The honest gentleman muttered, "In the domain of the Lord there is no justice. I am going to be condemned to death, while the real culprit, is set free."

The magistrate heard his words. He was somehow convinced, that he was speaking the truth. So he made a plan to testify the truth of his words.

Next morning, a person came crying, that his brother had been murdered. So the culprit should be traced. The magistrate, ordered those two men, to bring the dead body. The dead body was lying on a cot, his body was stained with blood and he was covered with a long piece of cloth. When they were carrying the cot, the constable said to the prisoner,"If you had agreed to my proposal, you would have received a share of the gold, and also escaped death." The prisoner said, "There is no justice in the domain of God, because an honest man has to suffer and a criminal, is set free."

The man lying on the cot was listening to their conversation. When the cot was put down the person removing the stained clothes stood up and he narrated the conversation, between the constable and the prisoner, to the magistrate. The magistrate was wonder-struck. He sentenced the constable to imprisonment. The magistrate, was also very honest. He never took a bribe. So he called the gentleman, in loneliness and said, "In this case you are innocent, but tell me frankly whether you have committed any murder, during the life." He replied, "There was a man of immoral conduct, who had illicit relations with my wife. I requested him not to come to my wife, in my absence. One day when I came back home, I found him with my wife. I lost self-control, murdered him and threw his dead body, into the river. No one knew this incident." The magistrate said, "I was perplexed, how I could give the wrong judgement when I always perform my duty, very honestly and sincerely." So the magistrate sentenced him to death, for his past crime and the constable was also condemned to death.

Similarly, if a man reaps the fruit of his virtuous actions here, in the form of riches, honour, praise and freedom from sickness etc., he does not reap it, in the next world. The present actions, leave two kinds of impressions, pure and impure. Prescribed actions leave pure and holy impressions, while prohibited actions, give impure and unholy impressions. These impressions, form a man's nature (habit). When impure impressions are rooted out, a man's nature, becomes pure and holy. But because of past actions, even liberated souls, are found different in their nature, though their actions, are pure and are conducive to salvation, for the entire world.

The nature (habit), which is formed by impressions of the past actions, is very strong and this cannot be easily rooted out.* Similarly, people of different castes perform actions according to nature of their castes, (Varṇa). So Lord Kṛṣṇa says to Arjuna, "That which, through delusion, you don't wish to do, bound by your own acts born of your nature, you will helplessly perform" (Gītā 18/60).

A serious thought, is to be given to this pertinent remark. It is said that the personal nature of a man, sways him and he cannot overpower it. On the other hand, it is said that every human being, is free to do any action, and so he can get, through his efforts, what he likes. The question is, which of the two is more powerful personal nature, or freedom of action. The answer is, that the two are two different matters. They have their own importance and power, in their own context. Nature, described in the sixtieth verse of the eighteenth chapter, is personal nature, pertaining to caste. A human being's nature, is formed according

---

Thus, if a person suffers punishment, for his crimes here, he has not to suffer it, in the next world. Here, in the world the punishment is generally mild, while in the next world, it is more severe (it is with interest). But a person, has to suffer punishment either here or hereafter.

* A tiger remains satisfied, in a dense forest, a lion likes a dense cave; a swan, likes a blooming lotus; an eagle likes a cremation ground, a gentleman wants to live with other gentlemen and a mean fellow, wants to accompany mean persons. It is true that a man does not give up his nature.

to the caste he is born in, and the sperm and ovum his body is constituted with. That nature cannot be changed, and need not be changed. Even scriptures do not advise to change it. A man, is to work under nature's sway. But in personal nature, there is impure part of attachment and aversion. God has given a man, power to wipe out his impure part. He is free to make his nature pure, by wiping out attachment and aversion. Either through the practice of 'Karmayoga', as enunciated in 3/34 or through practice of devotion, by surrendering himself to God, he can make his nature, quite pure (18/62). Thus both the forcefulness of personal nature and independence of a man to act, are proved. It means, that a man is free to purify his nature, while personal (pure) nature, is effective in engaging a man in actions, according to his caste.

The sharp edge of a sword made of steel, turns to gold, if it is touched with the philosopher's stone (Pārasa), but its sharpness, edge and shape do not undergo any change. Similarly, when a man's nature is purified, his actions, are also pure. But he may perform actions, according to his caste (social order), stage of life, religion and beliefs etc., and so his actions, may be different from, others. If a man of the priest class attains salvation, he will maintain more purity, than a man of the labour class, who has also attained salvation. It is so, because of their nature. But this nature, is not defective. So, it need not be wiped out.

A man has to follow a cycle of birth and death, and he is born in good and evil wombs, because of his nature, of assuming affinity with the matter. A man, is free in purifying his nature, by rooting out desire, attachment and identification, with matter. When a man, having renounced his egoism, takes refuge in the Lord, his nature is purified, in the same way, as iron is purified and turns into gold, when it is touched with a philosopher's stone. When a man's nature, is purified, he does not incur sins, by performing actions, ordained by his own nature (Gītā 18/47). When a devotee takes refuge in the Lord, he has no affinity with prakṛti (matter) and the Lord's nature, descends on him. As the Lord is a disinterested friend, of all beings (Gītā 5/29) he also becomes disinterested friend, of all beings (Śrīmadbhāgavata 3/25/21).

Similarly, when a Karmayogī renounces attachment and aversion, his nature is purified. Then, actions by him, are performed for the welfare of the world, automatically. When his actions are performed for the welfare of the world, he gets identified with the power of God, because the Lord, is ever engrossed in the welfare of all beings. Actually, this power of the Lord is open to all human beings. But egoism, attachment and aversion, become the stumbling blocks, in approaching it. As soon as, these are renounced, the Lord's power, starts operating.

Sañcita Karma (Collected actions or accumulated actions)

Fruit — Prārabdha (Destiny)

Saṁskāra (Impressions) — Sphuraṇā (Fleeting Thought)

Actions performed, during past lives and till now, are called 'Accumulated actions' (Sañcita Karma). They consist of two portions—fruit and impressions. These are stored in the inner sense. The fruit-portion, forms 'Prārabdha', and from the impression-portion (Saṁskāra) these are mere fleeting thoughts, (Sphuraṇā). Accumulated actions performed, in the present life are more responsible for inspiration to action. Rarely accumulated actions of past lives, also cause such inspiration.* For example, if in a pot we store onions and then place wheat, gram and barley in it, while taking out these commodities from the pot, what was placed last, comes out first. But sometimes pungency of onions, is also experienced. This example is not fully applicable, as these commodities are manifest, while accumulated actions

* A thought comes to the mind according to the Sañcita Karma as well as the Prārabdha. The thought of the Sañcita Karma can't force a man to perform an action. But if there are attachment and aversion in it, it by becoming a Saṅkalpa (Projection or Pursuit of the mind) can force him to act. The Sphuraṇā of Prārabdha forces a man to act in order to enable him to get the fruit of past actions. But by applying his discrimination he should check himself from performing prohibited actions and he is free in doing so.

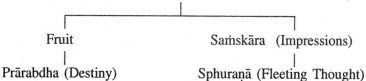

are unmanifest. This illustration, is to bring home the point, that generally there are inspirations to actions, through accumulated actions of the present life, and these are rarely through accumulated actions, of past lives.

In dream (sleep), also the unfulfilled thoughts (ambition) of Sañcita are revealed.* In a dream there is no order and system. You may have a dream and see the city of Delhi in which there is a market of Mumbai and the shops of Kolkata. Similarly, you talk to a man, who is either dead or alive.

In the state of wakefulness, different thoughts come to mind. When one's intellect, loses control over his body, mind and senses etc., his utterances, are non-sensical. In that state, he cannot discriminate, between the right and wrong. In absence of proper functioning of his discriminative faculty, he is called a plain madman. But, when his body, senses and mind are under control, he speaks a sensible language. He is like a wise, madman.

So long as, a man does not realize God, sphuraṇā come to his mind. But when he realizes God, evil thoughts are altogether rooted out. So evil thoughts, never come to the mind of a liberated soul. He never speaks and acts, against the ordinance of scriptures, even in a state of unconsciousness or insanity, because his inner sense, is purified.

---

* In the state of wakefulness also there are three states—wakefulness, sleep and sound-sleep. When a man acts being alert, that is the state of wakefulness. But if any other thought, comes to his mind, that is sleep in wakefulness. But sometimes he is in such a state where he has no inclination to act, that is the state of sound-sleep in wakefulness.

It is because of the momentum to act that in the state of wakefulness, the state of sound-sleep is rarely seen. But if a striver can adopt and maintain this state of sound-sleep in wakefulness, he will quickly progress in the spiritual path because in that state he is identified with God or the self. Though in sound-sleep also his connection with the world is renounced, yet he can't realize the self because his intellect merges in ignorance. But when a man is in the state of sound-sleep in wakefulness, he realizes the self because his intellect remains awake.

This state is superior even to trance because it happens naturally while in trance the mind has to be concentrated through practice and his egoism also persists.

Prārabdha Karma (Destiny)

- Favourable circumstances
- Mixed (Favourable & unfavourable ones)
- Unfavourable circumstances

- self willed action
- action willed by other
- Unwilled action (action willed by destiny)

Out of accumulated actions, actions which are inclined to bear fruit, are called 'Prārabdha' (destiny). Destiny bears fruit, in the form of favourable and unfavourable circumstances, through (i) self-will, (ii) the will of destiny and (iii) will of others. Examples:—

(i) A man buys some goods and makes a profit or sustains loss, as fruit of his 'Prārabdha'. But he buys the goods, by his own will. (ii) A person finds a purse full of gold coins, all of a sudden or he injures his arm when the branch of a tree falls on him. It is the fruit of his destiny, through the will of destiny. (iii) A boy is adopted by a rich man, and the boy, becomes an owner of the rich man's property. Similarly, a man's wealth is stolen by thieves. It is the fruit of one's, destiny by the will of others.

Destiny results, in the form of favourable and unfavourable circumstances, but it does not force a man to perform forbidden actions. If a person is forced to perform prohibited actions, as the fruit of his 'Prārabdha,' the ordinance of scriptures, for the prescribed and prohibited actions, will be of no avail. Secondly, if he goes on performing prohibited actions, according to his destiny, there will be no end to his prohibited actions.

The 'Prārabdha Karma', results in two sorts of fruits—acquired and unacquired. The favourable or unfavourable circumstances, which a person has got now, are called 'acquired fruit'; while during this life, such circumstances which he is going to get, in future, is called 'unacquired fruit'.

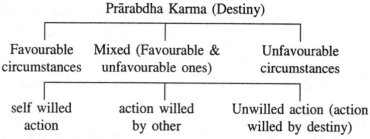

Destiny can bear fruit, in the form of favourable and unfavourable circumstances, either at present, or in future. Actions which are performed at present are added to accumulated actions. So long as, there are accumulated actions, there is destiny, which acts in favourable or unfavourable circumstances. These circumstances cannot force a man, to be happy or sad. It is his affinity, with the circumstances, which makes him happy or sad. If by applying his discrimination, he does not assume his affinity, he can remain equanimous.

Whether favourable or unfavourable circumstances, which a man faces in his life, are the result of 'Prārabdha' (Destiny) or of 'Puruṣārtha' (Present efforts). In this connection, there are many doubts. Before getting a satisfactory answer to this question, it is necessary to understand, what is 'Prārabdha' (Destiny) and what is 'Puruṣārtha' (Effort or labour).

A man has desire of four kinds—for 'Artha' (Wealth), 'Dharma' (Righteousness), 'Kāma' (Passion) and 'Mokṣa' (Salvation).

(1) Artha (wealth)—Wealth is of two kinds, unmoving and moving. Gold, silver, money and property etc., belong to the former kind, while cows, buffaloes, horses, camels, sheep and goats etc., belong to the latter.

(2) Dharma (Righteousness)—Acts of sacrifice, penance, charity, fasts and pilgrimages etc., which are performed with or without desire for their fruits, are included in, 'Dharma.'

(3) Kāma (Passion)—Mundane pleasures, are known as 'Kāma'. They are of eight kinds—Word (sound), touch, form, taste, smell, honour, praise and comfort.

(a) Word (Sound)— Word is of two kinds—form of alphabets (descriptive) and form of sound. Grammar, dictionary, literature, novel, drama and story etc., are all alphabetical,* while musical

*There are ten kinds of sentiments in a descriptive word. These are of conjugal love, humour, pity, wrath, bravery, dread, disgust, wonder, serenity and affection. In all these sentiments, the heart melts. If these sentiments are inclined towards the Lord, these lead to salvation. But, if pleasure is derived out of these, they are degrading.

instruments relate to sound.* A person derives pleasure out of these alphabetical words and sound.

(b) Touch—Pleasure which is born of contact with wife, son and friend etc., and with skin, is pleasure by touch.

(c) Form—Pleasure derived by seeing movies, and other beautiful objects., is pleasure in form.

(d) Taste—Pleasure that a man derives by tasting sweet, salty and sour dishes etc., is pleasure through taste.

(e) Smell— Pleasure derived from the smell of oil, scents and flowers etc., is, pleasure, through smell.

(f) Honour—A man derives pleasure when his so-called body is honoured.

(g) Praise—One derives pleasure, when he is praised.

(h) Comfort— He gets pleasure or comfort out of idleness, laziness and comfort.

(4) Mokṣa (salvation)—Self-realization, benediction, salvation and God-realization, are names, given to Mokṣa.

Out of these four, the two— wealth and righteousness, enhance each other. But, if both of them are utilized to satisfy desire, after satisfying desire both of these perish. Desire devours both these. So in the Gītā, the Lord declares, that desire is insatiable and He asks Arjuna, to kill this enemy viz., desire (3/37—43).

If righteous actions, are performed by renouncing desire, these after having purified the inner sense, lead to salvation. Similarly, if wealth is spent for the welfare of others, abandoning the desire for its reward, it also after having purified inner sense, leads to salvation.

Out of these four in 'Artha' (Wealth), and 'Kāma' (Desire or Passion) there is predominance of destiny. Puruṣārtha is secondary while in righteousness and salvation, there is predominance of

* Drums, tambourines and timbrels etc., made of skin, guitar and mandolin made of wires, harmonium and flute etc., which are blown, and cymbal etc., which are clapped—these are musical instruments.

'Puruṣārtha' destiny is secondary (effort or labour). Their spheres are separate and each has its own predominance in its own sphere. Therefore, it has been declared—

A man should be satisfied with his wife, son, family, food and wealth, but he should never be satisfied with the study of sacred books, adoration, chanting of Lord's name and charity. It means, that a man gains wealth and pleasure, as is destined and so he should be satisfied with them. But he should never be satisfied with, spiritual progress. He should go on labouring, for salvation for which this human body, has been bestowed upon him.

Actions are of two kinds—good (virtuous) and bad (evil). Virtuous actions result, in favourable circumstances, while evil actions result, in unfavourable circumstances. But these cannot make a man happy and sad. It is out of folly, that a man feels, happy and sad. If he gives up his folly, by believing in God* or in destiny† he feels happy, even in the most unfavourable circumstances, as he gets rid of sins by facing painful circumstances. Moreover, he becomes alert, and does not commit sins, in future; and his inner sense is purified when he gets rid of his sins.

A striver, should make the right use of favourable and unfavourable circumstances. In favourable circumstances, he should spend his money and material, for the welfare of others, he should not enjoy these. In unfavourable circumstances, he should abandon the desire for favourable circumstances. He should think, that he is getting rid of his sins, and the Lord by His grace, has caused such circumstances, so that he may be careful not to commit sins, in future, and may progress in the spiritual field. Thus, he should feel happy. This is the proper use

* As a mother remains ever compassionate never otherwise while fondling and scolding her baby, similarly the Lord Who controls the virtues and vices of beings, ever remains compassionate to everyone of them.

† Whatever is to happen must happen and whatever is not to happen, will not happen. A man having such a determinate intellect is never worried.

of unfavourable circumstances, and if he feels sad, in unfavourable circumstances, this is their misuse.

The Lord, has not bestowed upon us this human life, to enable us to enjoy pleasure and to suffer pain. Heaven is the abode for enjoyment and pleasure while hell and eighty-four lac forms, of lives are for suffering pain. But the aim of human life, is to attain salvation by transcending pleasures and pains. Those who remain negligent during human life, follow a cycle of birth and death.

A man, is free in abandoning favourable circumstances but he is not free in abandoning unfavourable circumstances. This can be clarified, by an illustration.

Rāmalāla borrowed a hundred rupees from Śyāmalāla and promised that he would return the amount with interest, in a month. But he could not return it. Śyāmalāla, went to Rāmalāla's house, several times to demand payment as Rāmalāla had promised. But he did not pay the amount. One day Śyāmalāla lost self-control and beat Rāmalāla with his shoes. Rāmalāla filed a case in the criminal court, against Śyāmalāla. A summons, was issued to Śyāmalāla. He presented himself in the court. The magistrate asked him, "Did you beat him with shoes?" Śyāmalāla said, "Yes, your honour. In spite of several promises he did not pay my money. So he compelled me to beat him. I gave him five blows with shoes. Kindly order him to return my money, by deducting five rupees as a fine for five blows (with shoes)."

The magistrate smiled and said, "This is a criminal court. You will have to suffer imprisonment, or fine for your crime. File a law-suit in the civil court if you want to get back your money. The two courts, are different."

Thus, the fruits of evil actions lead to unpleasant circumstances. It is a case of criminal court and a man cannot escape it. But as far as, the fruit of virtuous actions, in the form of pleasant circumstances are concerned, that is a case for a civil court. The two are different. They cannot nullify, each other. Thus sins cannot be counter acted by virtuous actions. The two, are accumulated separately. But if one performs any good act, in order to repent, his sins perish.

Some people complain, that there is no justice in the domain of the Lord*, because in this world, virtuous and good men are suffering, while sinners are enjoying themselves. The answer is, that virtuous persons are suffering, because they are reaping the fruit of their past evil actions; their present virtuous actions, will bear fruit later. Similarly, sinners are reaping the sweet fruits of their past virtuous actions, not of present sins.

Moreover, there is one more point, which needs attention. In favourable circumstances, a man is proud of himself, he hates those whom he regards as inferior to him, and is envious of other persons', better fortune. Thus externally, he seems happy but actually he is not. On the other hand, an ascetic who is dispassionate and a man of renunciation, and who possesses neither wealth nor property, may seem sad, without possessions to worldly people. But, actually his life is very serene and happy. So possessions and riches, do not make a man happy, and their absence does not make him, sad. Real happiness, consists in serenity and happiness of heart, while sadness, consists in burning sensation and sadness of heart.

A man can be free from virtues, by surrendering them to God, without any desire for fruit, but he cannot get rid of sins, by surrendering these to Him. One will have to suffer, the fruit of those sins because actions against the ordinance of the Lord, cannot be surrendered, to Him. This can be made clear by an illustration.

* In the Vana section of the Mahābhārata there is an anecdote. One day Draupadī asked Yudhiṣṭhira, "You are suffering in exile following righteousness while Duryodhana is leading a luxurious life by enjoying the kingdom in spite of his unrighteousness and selfishness. Why?" Yudhiṣṭhira replied, "Those who follow the path of righteousness in order to get pleasures, actually don't know righteousness in the true sense of the term. They are just like animals who hanker after pleasures without knowing righteousness. Therefore humanity consists in following righteousness according to the ordinance of the scriptures without caring either for the favourable or the unfavourable circumstances."

Once a king with many other people, went to Haridwāra. Among the people, there was a wise businessman and a cobbler. The cobbler, thought that he would also act in the same way, as the wise businessman would do. When the priest started the vowtaking-ceremony, the businessman said, "I offer the charity of a hundred rupees, which I lent to that Brāhmaṇa, to Lord Kṛṣṇa." The cobbler, saw that the businessman gained fame, without paying even a single pice. So he wanted to do the same. He said, "I offer to Lord Kṛṣṇa, the gift of a hundred rupees which I borrowed from the trader." By doing so he was very much pleased.

After a few days at the time of harvest, the Brāhmaṇa came to the businessman and requested him to take grain for a hundred rupees and its interest. The businessman said that he had offered that amount to Lord Kṛṣṇa, as charity, so he would not take it back. When the Brāhmaṇa insisted, the businessman asked him to offer it, as a gift to his own sister or daughter. So the Brāhmaṇa had to go home, without making any payment.

The trader, who had lent a hundred rupees to the cobbler, went to him and demanded his hundred rupees. The cobbler said, "I offered those hundred rupees, to Lord Kṛṣṇa as the businessman did." The trader said, "You can't get rid of this debt in this way, you will have to pay me back, the amount with interest." Thus he got grain from the cobbler.

It means that we cannot get rid of our sins and evil actions, by surrendering these to God, we shall have to suffer for them. But, if we surrender ourselves to God and take refuge in Him alone, He liberates us from all sins" (Gītā 18/66).

A second doubt, arises that gaining of wealth does not depend on destiny, because a man saves money, by foul means, such as non-payment of income tax and sales tax etc. But, if he pays full tax, the money is spent. So how does it depend on destiny? The answer is, that if he is destined to gain wealth, he will gain it, by anyother means. But if he is destined to lose it, he will sustain a loss in every case, such as in disease, theft, and litigation etc. Moreover, the impressions of foul means, such as theft of income tax etc., live for so many lives and they instigate one to commit thefts, and for which he has to suffer punishment. Similarly, enjoyment of pleasure is also pre-destined. A man may possess a lot of money, but he may not enjoy pleasure due to illness. He may have to eat very meagre meals as prescribed by a physician. On the other hand, even a man who does not possess much money, may relish tasteful dishes in the company of generous friends, and kinsmen or by anyother means.*

If a man is destined to gain wealth, he may be adopted by a rich man, or he may find it buried in the earth, while digging the earth or by anyother way†. But a man, neither believes in destiny, nor depends on his hard work. So he is inclined to commit sins, such as theft etc., which result in a burning sensation of the heart. Moreover, he is likely to be punished. But, if a man remains satisfied and has faith in destiny etc., his heart remains full of great serenity and bliss, and he also receives the necessities of life. As unfavourable circumstances, such as loss, death, dishonour and insult etc., cannot be avoided, they appear though no one, has a desire for these. Similarly, favourable circumstances, are also inevitable. In the Bhāgavata, it is mentioned—

"O King, as beings receive pain, as is destined to them, having no desire for it, so are pleasures born of sense-contacts, received in heaven and hell. Therefore, a wise man, should have no desire for those pleasures."

As a man, is destined to receive either wealth or pleasures,

---

* It is seen that even to a saint, who renounces the world, people offer so many gifts. Renunciation, has a singularity that a person, who renounces wealth and does not attach any importance to it, develops a new destiny to gain wealth. Saint Rāmadāsa declares, "A saint does not possess either food or animals or cash but when he takes his seat to have meal, he receives all the articles of food."

† A man will receive whatever wealth he is destined to receive, no one can be an obstacle to it. So I am neither grieved nor surprised, because whatever is ours cannot be of others, (Pañcatantra, Mitrasamprāpti 112).

similarly one labours either for righteousness (dharma) or for salvation (mokṣa). In righteousness, importance is attached to things, such as body and wealth etc., while, in attainment of salvation, there is predominance, of feelings and thoughts.

A man, should perform his duty in accordance with, the ordinance of scriptures and social decorum, but he should be satisfied with its fruit. Lord Kṛṣṇa declares in the Gītā, "You have a right to action alone, and never at all, to its fruit" (2/47). He is free in performing actions, but he will receive the fruit, which is destined. How to get rid of fruits, of all the three kinds of actions—kriyamāṇa (of the present), sañcita (accumulated) and prārabdha (destiny).

There are two entities—Prakṛti (matter or Nature) and puruṣa (Spirit or soul). Prakṛti is ever active, while Puruṣa never undergoes any change, in the form of activity. When man (soul), assumes his affinity with matter, he becomes a doer, and an enjoyer. But, when he renounces his affinity with matter, he gets established in the self, and actions do not affect him, in anyway.

Other points in connection with destiny—(i) A man, is destined to come across pleasant and unpleasant circumstances. But they cannot force him to be sad or happy. He becomes sad or happy, out of ignorance. A liberated soul remains equanimous, he does not become, either sad or happy as his ignorance is completely gone. Therefore it is said that no Prārabdha remains for a God-realised soul. (ii) A man's intellect, is guided by his destiny. Being guided by his intellect, a businessman gains, by buying a commodity, while another, loses by selling it. Thus gain or loss, is decided by destiny. But, a man is free to having honest or dishonest dealings, because it is 'Kriyamāṇa' or new action. (iii) A glass, falls down from a hand and breaks into pieces. Does it happen out of negligence or by destiny?

A man should be careful in handling it, but he should consider it as destined, when it is broken. He should learn a lesson, in being more careful, in future. Be cautious while doing and remain always cheerful in happening. (iv) What is the difference in a disease, caused by destiny and disease caused, by harmful diet?

The disease caused by harmful diet, can be cured by taking medicines, but the disease caused by destiny cannot be cured, by medicines. But religious rites such as chanting of Mahāmṛtyuñjaya etc., could cure diseases, caused by destiny.

Diseases are of two kinds—Ādhi (mental) and Vyādhi (physical). Mental diseases can again, be divided into two groups (a) of sadness and worry etc. (b) lunacy. Sadness and worry, are caused by ignorance, while lunacy is caused by destiny. Worry and sadness etc., are given up through wisdom, while lunacy is not abandoned but even during lunacy, a God-realised man cannot perform any improper action, which is forbidden by scriptures. (v) What is the difference between sudden death, and untimely death?

If a man dies of snake-bite, or by falling from a roof or by drowning, heart failure or by an accident, this is sudden death, which is pre-destined. Such a man, dies after completing the duration of his life.

If a man commits suicide, by hanging himself or by jumping into a well or fire or by lying under a moving train or by poisoning himself, this is untimely death. A man commits suicide, without completing his span of life. He who commits suicide, incurs the sin of murder, and this is a new sin. God has bestowed upon us, this human body so that we may realize Him, so it is a deadly sin, if we destroy it by committing suicide.

Sometimes a person, who makes an effort to commit suicide, does not die. The reason is, that his destiny is connected with, the destiny of others. As birth of a would-be-son or good which is likely to be done by him, to the people or any unfavourable or favourable fruit, which is going to be reaped by him, because of his past actions, may save him from dying. (vi) The person who is murdered, dies as a fruit of his past actions, while the murderer takes vengeance, for injuries inflicted upon him, in the previous birth. Then, why is a murderer held responsible, for the crime of murder?

The murderer is guilty. The ruler, has a right to kill a man or hang him to death, for his crime, but a layman, has no right to do so. Suppose a criminal is to be hanged for his crime, and another person murders that criminal, the murderer of the criminal, will be sentenced to death. He was to be executed by the executioners, not by any other person, because executioners, execute by order of the law. So, no one should commit any evil action, such as murder etc., nor think to do so, by disregarding discrimination. If people, go on taking vengeance for their injuries of previous births, this chain will never come to an end, and a man can never attain, salvation.

This human life, is not meant to take vengeance for previous birth; that may be applicable, to the life of a serpent etc. It is possible, that our murderer of the previous birth, is not liked by us naturally. But if we are envious of him and do harm to him, we are performing, a new action which will bear fruit. So we should not be overpowered by envy, jealousy or aversion etc. We should use our discrimination, while performing actions. It is also declared by Lord Kṛṣṇa, in the Gītā, "A man should never come under the sway of attachment and aversion" (3/34).

(vii) What is the difference between destiny, and the Lord's grace?

Whatever a man receives, is by destiny, and that is given by the ruler (manager), God. As a labourer, by working hard in the field, gets his daily wages for the day, but that is given by the landlord. If the landlord is not there, and he does not order the labourer to work in his field, and the labourer works of his own accord, will he get wages? No. He gets wages, only if he carries out the order of the landlord and works, under his guidance and supervision.

If a servant, performs his duty with promptness, skill and enthusiasm, in order to please his master, the master may pay him more than he deserves, and may make him a partner in his farm or factory etc. Similarly, the Lord gives fruit to a man, according to his actions. But if a man performs actions, according to His order to please Him, He may give him even more, than he deserves. But he who works by surrendering himself to God, God becomes a devotee to him (Śrīmadbhāgavata 10/86/59). It is only He, who is so generous and gracious that He makes his devout devotee, His master. So, if a person, instead of surrendering himself at the feet of the Lord, depends on the perishable, it means that his reason, (intelligence) is completely destroyed. He does not perceive, reality.

Link:—As in the Discipline of Action, affinity with one's action is renounced, similarly in the Discipline of Knowledge (Sāṅkhya system), the self has no connection with actions. There are five factors, which contribute to the accomplishment of actions. The Lord declares.—

पञ्चैतानि महाबाहो कारणानि निबोध मे।
साङ्ख्ये कृतान्ते प्रोक्तानि सिद्धये सर्वकर्मणाम्॥ १३॥

pañcaitāni mahābāho kāraṇāni nibodha me
sāṅkhye kṛtānte proktāni siddhaye sarvakarmaṇām

O mighty-armed (Arjuna), learn from Me, these five factors which are contributory to the accomplishment of all actions, as stated in the Sāṅkhya doctrine which prescribes means for neutralizing all actions.

Comment:—

'Pañcaitāni mahābāho kāraṇāni'—These five factors, are contributory to the performance of all actions, whether prescribed or prohibited, according to the Sāṅkhya doctrine. The self, has no connection with actions.

'Nibodha me'—In the Sāṅkhya doctrine, the Lord has used the term 'Nibodha' (Learn), (18/13,50) while in other contexts He uses the term 'Śṛṇu' (Hear) (18/4,19,29,36,45,64). It means that a striver, should learn or understand the Sāṅkhya doctrine well. If he understands it well, he realizes the self, immediately.

'Sāṅkhye kṛtānte proktāni siddhaye sarvakarmaṇām'—These five factors are contributory to the performance of all actions, whether prescribed or prohibited, physical or mental or oral, and whether these are gross, or subtle. When a person regards himself as a doer of actions, he performs actions, and those actions being accumulated, bear fruit for him. But when he renounces doership, those actions are performed, but they do not bear fruit for him i.e., they do not lead him, to sin, virtue or bondage. Then only four factors remain, by which, all actions are accomplished. These are—1. the seat of action (body), 2. the organs (senses), 3. efforts and 4. destiny (Gītā 18/14).

In the Sāṅkhya doctrine, there is predominance of knowledge or discrimination. Then, why has the Lord started the topic of accomplishment of actions? The reason is, that Arjuna belongs to the warrior class and it is his duty to fight. So Lord Kṛṣṇa, exhorts Arjuna to fight, being unattached to it, either through Sāṅkhyayoga or Karmayoga. Arjuna, wants to know the true nature of Sāṅkhyayoga. So Lord Kṛṣṇa, begins the topic of action through Sāṅkhya doctrine.

Arjuna, wanted to abandon actions. So Lord Kṛṣṇa clarifies that neither performance of action, nor abandonment, leads to salvation. But, when a man (the soul), renounces his affinity with the perishable Prakṛti, he attains salvation. That can be renounced, either through Karmayoga (the Discipline of Action), or through Sāṅkhyayoga (the Discipline of Knowledge). In Karmayoga, there is predominance of renouncement of fruit viz., mineness and attachment, while in the Sāṅkhyayoga, there is predominance of renouncement of egoism. But, if a man renounces attachment, his egoism is naturally renounced* and if he renounces egoism,

*A man (the soul) being a fragment of God has identity with Him. But having disinclinations for Him he has the sense of egoism as "I am worldly, I am intelligent, I am learned" etc. He is attached to this egoism. But if he

his attachment and mineness is naturally renounced as mineness depends upon only egoism.

Appendix—The Lord describes the five factors contributory to the accomplishment of all actions in order to explain that the Self is not the doer. Out of these five, when the sense of doership is renounced, then actions totally come to an end viz., affinity with them is renounced.

Link:—The Lord now enumerates these five factors.

अधिष्ठानं तथा कर्ता करणं च पृथग्विधम्।
विविधाश्च पृथक्चेष्टा दैवं चैवात्र पञ्चमम्॥ १४॥

adhiṣṭhānaṁ tathā kartā karaṇaṁ ca pṛthagvidham
vividhāśca pṛthakceṣṭā daivaṁ caivātra pañcamam

The original base of action (body), the doer (agent), the instruments of various sorts (senses), many kinds of efforts and Daiva, impression being the fifth. 14

Comment:—

'Adhiṣṭhānam'—This term stands for both the body and the country (earth's surface), in which this body stays.

'Kartā'—All actions, are performed by prakṛti, not by the self. But, when a man by ignorance, regards actions as his own,

---

performs all actions by thinking, "Nothing is mine, I need nothing and I have to do nothing for me," his attachment is renounced. As soon as his attachment is renounced, his egoism will also be renounced.

A Karmayogī performs all the actions with his physical, subtle and causal bodies for the welfare of others. With his physical body he works for the welfare of other, with his subtle body he thinks for the welfare of others and with his causal body, his trance is for the welfare of others. By doing so his egoism and attachment are renounced and he attains peace.

The peace which is attained after renouncing the world is a means (Gītā 6/3) while the peace which one attains by God-realization is the supreme (Gītā 6/15). So if a striver does not enjoy the peace which is a means, he attains to the supreme peace.

he becomes a doer or an agent.* Such a doer, is contributory to the accomplishment of actions.

'Karaṇaṁ ca pṛthagvidham'—There are thirteen instruments (senses)—the hand, the foot, the mouth (organ of voice), anus and genital organ—these five organs of actions and ear, eye, skin, tongue and nose—these five sense-organs—these ten are external instruments or senses, while mind, intellect and egoism, are internal instruments.

'Vividhāśca pṛthakceṣṭā'—Various kinds of efforts, are made by above-mentioned, thirteen senses, as hands are used for exchange of things, feet for moving, the organ of voice for speaking, anus for discharging excrement, genital organ for discharging urine, ear for hearing, eye for seeing, skin for touch, tongue for taste, nose for smell, mind for thought, intellect for determination and egoism, for pride.

'Daivaṁ caivātra pañcamam'—The fifth factor, for the accomplishment of all actions, is 'Daiva'. Here the term 'Daiva' stands for saṁskāra (Impressions). If a person performs, good actions, they leave good impressions, but if he performs bad or evil actions, their impression is bad. Those impressions instigate him to act. Good impressions, inspire him to perform good actions while evil impressions instigate him to perform, evil actions.

These five factors—body, the doer, instrument, efforts and Daiva or impressions, are contributory to the accomplishment

---

*All the actions are performed by Prakṛti, it has been described in the Gītā in several ways—

(1) All actions are performed by the modes of nature (3/27; 13/29).

(2) The modes are acting on the modes (3/28) and when the seer perceives no agent other than the modes (14/19).

(3) The senses act on sense-objects (5/9).

(4) Here in 18/14 five factors are contributory to the accomplishment of actions.

All these statements mean that actions are performed by nature only and not by the self, but a man by identifying himself with nature assumes that he is a doer (3/27). But a wise man realizes that all actions are performed by nature, so he does nothing at all (5/8).

of all actions. No action can be performed, without the body, which is the base. Without a doer, who will perform actions? Actions can be performed by a doer, with the help of senses, only. There cannot be accomplishment of actions, without efforts. The doer will act, according to the impressions imprinted, on his mind and heart.

Thus, these five factors contribute to the accomplishment of all actions.

Appendix—'Kartā'—Ego is 'aparā prakṛti' and the Self is 'parā prakṛti'. The Soul's affinity is with God but it being identified with ego thinks itself as the doer.

'Daivam'—Good and bad latencies of the past abide in the hearts of all persons—'sumati kumati saba keṁ ura rahahīṁ' (Mānasa, Sundara. 40/3). The company, the scripture and thoughts—these three intensify the good or bad latencies which give inspiration for new actions.

शरीरवाङ्मनोभिर्यत्कर्म प्रारभते नरः।
न्याय्यं वा विपरीतं वा पञ्चैते तस्य हेतवः॥ १५॥

śarīravāṅmanobhiryatkarma prārabhate naraḥ
nyāyyaṁ vā viparītaṁ vā pañcaite tasya hetavaḥ

Whatever action right or wrong a man initiates with his body, speech and mind, these five are its causes. 15

Comment:—

'Śarīravāṅmanobhiryatkarma prārabhate naraḥ nyāyyaṁ vā viparītaṁ vā pañcaite tasya hetavaḥ'—The five factors described in the preceding verse, have been included in this verse also—as the body stands for 'Adhiṣṭhāna,' speech for external instrument (sense), mind for internal instrument (sense), 'Naraḥ' (Man) for the doer and the term 'Prārabhate' (Performs), stands for efforts. As far as 'Daiva' (Impression), is concerned, it also abides in the internal sense, but it is not revealed. It is revealed, through inclination and action, which are performed by inclinations.

Whatever actions a man performs, with the predominance of either, the body or the speech or the mind, whether it is prescribed or prohibited by the scriptures, these five (mentioned in the preceding verse), are its causal factors.

All actions are performed, with body, speech and mind. If they are prohibited, they lead to bondage. So, in the fourteenth, fifteenth and sixteenth verses of the seventeenth chapter, there is description of penances of body, speech and mind, respectively. It means, that if any action is not performed against the scriptures, with body or speech or mind, it becomes a penance. In the seventeenth verse of the seventeenth chapter, it is mentioned that penance which is practised, without expectation of reward, is called sāttvika. Sāttvika penance, leads to emancipation, while the rājasika and tāmasika penances, lead to bondage.

The body, speech and mind, become impure, when a man regards these, as his own. By regarding them as his own, he cannot realize, that he has no connection with actions. So if a striver, does not regard these as his own and does not perform any action for himself, these are quickly purified. Therefore, one should renounce his affinity, with them, either by purifying them, through the Discipline of Action or by applying discrimination, through the Discipline of Knowledge. As soon as, this assumed affinity is renounced, he realizes the self.

All the activities in the world are performed by universal divine power, so is the case with the activities of an individual. But he commits an error by disregarding his discriminating power that he regards himself as doer of actions, such as eating, drinking, sitting, standing, sleeping and waking etc. So these actions bind him. But if he does not assume, that he is a doer, those actions do not bear fruit for him, and he is not bound by them. As actions, such as growth from childhood to youth, breathing, digestion etc., are performed, by prakṛti and if he does not consider himself as doer, they do not bear virtuous or sinful fruits, for him. Similarly, when he has no sense of doership, he realizes that all actions are performed by nature, alone.

Appendix—Presence of attachment and aversion, joy and sorrow etc., in the mind is mental action.

'Nyāyyam'—This term means—'Sāttvika karma', (actions of the nature of goodness), actions ordained by the scripture and virtuous actions. 'viparītam'—this term means—Rājasa-Tāmasa Karma (actions), actions prohibited by scriptures or evil (bad) actions. The expression 'nyāyyaṁ vā viparītaṁ vā' means—all actions.

Link:—Having explained the five factors, which are contributory to the accomplishment of all actions, according to the Sāṅkhya doctrine, the Lord, now criticizes, those, who recognize the self as doer.

तत्रैवं सति कर्तारमात्मानं केवलं तु यः।
पश्यत्यकृतबुद्धित्वान्न स पश्यति दुर्मतिः॥१६॥

tatraivaṁ sati kartāramātmānaṁ kevalaṁ tu yaḥ
paśyatyakṛtabuddhitvānna sa paśyati durmatiḥ

Such being the case, a man of perverse understanding, who, on account of impure (untrained) mind, looks upon his pure self alone, as the doer, does not see right. 16

Comment:—

'Tatraivaṁ sati kartāramātmānaṁ kevalaṁ tu yaḥ paśyatyakṛtabuddhitvānna sa paśyati durmatiḥ'—All actions are performed by body, the doer, the instrument, efforts and Daiva, not by the self. But, he who looks upon his self, as doer, his understanding is untrained i.e., he has not attached importance, to discrimination by which he can realize, that the sentient self is different, from the insentient nature. He is of a perverse mind, because he has not developed his understanding. If he awakens his discrimination, he cannot remain, of perverse mind.

The two terms 'Akṛtabuddhitvāt', and 'Durmatiḥ', seemingly having the same meaning, have some difference. The former term, denotes the cause, why a doer is 'Durmati'. (of perverse understanding), while the term 'Durmatiḥ', is adjective for the doer. The doer, is of perverse understanding, because he has not developed and refined his discriminative faculty. Had he developed it, he could not have been called, a man of perverse understanding.

The self, does nothing (Gītā 13/31). But when man identifies himself, with body, because of his perverse mind, he does not realize, that he is not a doer.

The term 'Kevalam', (merely or only), has been used, both in the Disciplines of Action, as well as of Knowledge. In the Discipline of Action, all actions are performed, merely with body, senses, mind and intellect, and the striver, is not attached to those actions (Gītā 5/11). So, he realizes that all of them have their identity with the world. By realizing this fact he realizes, that he is established, in the self.

In the Sāṅkhya doctrine (Discipline of Knowledge), there is predominance of knowledge or discrimination. Such a striver, realizes that all actions are accomplished by these five factors, not by the self. But, a person whose mind is deluded by egoism, considers himself to be a doer. When his delusion is renounced, he realizes, that he (the self) is not the doer, at all. So the term 'alone', has been used with the self.

Here, a point needs special attention. In the Discipline of Action, the term 'Kevalam', has been used with the body, mind and intellect, to denote that all of these including ego, will be used for service of the universe, and then the self, will remain as it is. But in the Discipline of Knowledge the term 'Kevalam', has been used with the self, which denotes that it is absolutely pure, immutable, enlightened and unattached. But, in this case there remains egoism, in its subtle form, and after sometime, it melts and merges in nature.

Appendix—Of all the 'cases' the nominative case is important. In 'kartā' (nominative) a glimpse of the sentient is perceived which is not perceived in other 'cases'. In fact 'kartā' (the doer) is not the name of the sentient. It is merely assumed one 'ahaṅkāra vimuḍhātmā kartāhamiti manyate' (Gītā 3/27). Therefore the Lord has condemned the person, who looks upon the pure Self as the doer by stating, that his mind is not pure and he is a man of perverse understanding. The reason is that the Self is neither a doer nor an experiencer viz., the Self neither acts nor is tainted—'śarīrastho'pi kaunteya na karoti na lipyate' (Gītā 13/31). In fact senses of doership and enjoyership have no existence, so they can be renounced. 'I am a doer' and 'I am an experiencer'—these assumptions are neither God-made nor nature-made but they are Self-made.

In fact no one is a doer, neither the sentient (the Self) is a doer nor the insentient (non-Self) is a doer. However if we have to assume a doer, only the non-Self is a doer. This fact has been pointed out in the Gītā in different ways—All actions are performed by 'prakṛti' viz., 'prakṛti' is the doer (Gītā 13/29); all actions are performed by the modes; it is the modes which are acting on the modes viz., modes are the doer (Gītā 3/27-28, 14/23); senses are moving among the sense-objects viz., senses are the doer (Gītā 5/9). It means that the doership is in 'prakṛti' rather than in the Self. Therefore an enlightened exalted soul, who remains established in the Self, realizes that he does nothing—'naiva kiñcit karomīti yukto manyeta tattvavit' (Gītā 5/8). The Lord also declares "When a man beholds no other doer than the modes viz., he realizes this fact in all actions there is no doer other than the modes, and knows the Self to be totally disconnected with the modes, which is the reality, then he attains to My Being" (Gītā 14/9).

A striver on reflection and reasoning can easily accept the worldly actions such as eating, drinking, sleeping and waking etc., to be done by 'prakṛti'; but he thinks that chanting the Lord's holy names, meditation, trance and such other spiritual activities are done by himself—this in fact is the stumbling block to a striver. The reason is that from the viewpoint of Jñānayoga, an action may be of the highest standard or of the lowest standard, it is of the same class and is done by 'prakṛti' only. 'Brandishing a lāṭhī' (a long stick) and 'counting the beads of a rosary' are two different activities yet they are in 'prakṛti' only. It means that all worldly actions such as eating, drinking, sleeping, waking and also the spiritual actions such as chanting the Lord's holy name, meditation and trance etc., take place in 'prakṛti' only the performance of an action is not possible without being connected with 'prakṛti'. Therefore a striver should not renounce the spiritual actions but he should not have the sense of doership viz., he should not regard them to be done by himself and for himself. If importance is attached to an action whether mundane or spiritual, it means that importance has been attached to matter (non-Self). If spiritual actions, sanctioned by the scriptures, are given importance, it means that the non-Self is valued which is an obstacle to a striver's spiritual progress.* Spiritual actions aim at God-realization, so they lead to salvation. The more an action is given the secondary importance, the more predominant importance will be attached to the affinity with God, and the more benefit a striver will derive. If there is predominance of a mundane action, then in spite of practising the spiritual discipline for years together, a striver will not get much spiritual benefit. Therefore a striver instead of attaching importance to action, should love God. Love, rather than action, is the real worship to God.

He whose intellect is devoid of discrimination viz., who has not attached importance to his discriminative faculty is 'durmati' (of perverse understanding). For Self-realization, discrimination, rather

*In the worship to God there is predominance of God's grace; therefore a striver has no sense of doership. A Kriyā (which occurs), an action, the worship and the discrimination—these four are different from each other. In 'Kriyā' there is no connection with anyone. In action a person is connected with favourable and unfavourable circumstances (fruit). In worship he is connected with God. In discrimination there is breach of affinity of the Self with the non-Self.

than intellect, is the factor. Intellect is purified by discrimination. In the purification of intellect, virtuous actions are also helpful to some extent, but it is not purified with virtuous actions as much as it is purified by the discriminative faculty. Sins, volatility of mind and ignorance in a striver are not to be blamed so much as the striver is to be blamed, if he does not attach importance to discrimination. Discrimination is beginningless and eternal. Therefore in spite of the persistence of sin, volatility of mind and ignorance, discrimination can be aroused. Discrimination is not destroyed by sin but it is not aroused. A striver does not attach importance to discrimination because he attaches importance to actions and objects. He who attaches importance to actions and objects is a man of perverse understanding.

Link:—In the preceding verse, it has been mentioned that he who looks upon his pure self as the doer, does not see at all. Now the Lord, in the next verse, explains who really sees.

यस्य नाहङ्कृतो भावो बुद्धिर्यस्य न लिप्यते।
हत्वापि स इमाँल्लोकान्न हन्ति न निबध्यते॥ १७॥

yasya nāhaṅkṛto bhāvo buddhiryasya na lipyate
hatvāpi sa imām̐llokānna hanti na nibadhyate

He, who is free from egoism, whose intellect is not tainted, though he may slay other creatures, he slays not, nor is he bound (by actions). 17

Comment:—

'Yasya nāhaṅkṛto bhāvo buddhiryasya na lipyate'—He is free from the egoistic notion that 'I am a doer and his intellect is not tainted, by the selfishness that I shall reap the fruit. As all actions, are performed in light but light is not the doer, similarly the self, is merely a silent witness, of all activities. Thus a striver, realizes that he is not a doer. Similarly, he has no desire of his own i.e., he is free from the pairs of opposites, that it should so happen and it should not so happen, it means, that his intellect is not tainted. Such a striver, remains neither a doer, nor an enjoyer, and he realizes, this fact.

Nature does everything and it always undergoes modifications, while the self, is its illuminator. By knowing this fact, a striver, remains established, in the self. He does not regard himself, as a doer. When he is free from this egoistic notion, his intellect is not tainted, to acquire the fruit of actions.

Egoism is an assumption, and this assumption, is made by an embodied soul, himself. It is he (himself), who assumes a sense of doership or denies, this sense.

'Hatvāpi sa imā̐llokānna hanti na nibadhyate'—Though, he may slay all beings at once, yet he does not really kill, because he has no egoistic notion; and he is not bound, because he has no notion of enjoyership. It means, that he is attached neither to action nor to their fruit. Action and fruits, are within the sphere of Nature. But, due to not realizing this fact, an embodied soul, assumes doership and enjoyership, in himself. When action is performed with a sense of doership, then the three factors, namely, the doer, the organ and the activity, are contributory to the accomplishment of an action. In the absence of doership, all actions are converted into inaction. But, with a sense of doership, any activity, converts into an action. When the sense of doership is extinct, then the cosmic soul (God), Who is the essence and illuminator of all, remains. So, he can neither kill, nor be bound (Gītā 2/19).

He slays all beings—what does it mean? It means that a man who performs his duty, according to his caste (social order) and stage of life, being free from egoistic notion, with his untainted intellect, incurs no sin. For example, a liberated soul belonging to warrior class, while slaying warriors on the battlefield, neither slays nor is he bound, because he is free from egoism, and selfishness.

Here, the context is of war. So, by using the term

'Hatvāpi ' (even having slain), the Lord inspires Arjuna, to wage the war. The term 'Api' (even) denotes—"Such a man, does nothing at all, though he may be ever-engaged in action" (Gītā 4/20), "Being engaged in all forms of activities, he dwells in the Lord" (Gītā 6/31), "The Supreme self, though dwells in the body, it neither acts nor is tainted" (Gītā 13/31). It means, that the Self, remains uniform and fixed, whether a man is engaged in actions, or he does not act. The reason is, that it is nature, which performs all actions.

A man (soul), has his identity with God, but it is because of his egoistic notion, that he becomes separate, from the Lord. Actually, he is neither a doer nor an enjoyer, but by identifying himself with a body he accepts an egoistic notion, and thus becomes a doer and an enjoyer.

This egoism is of two kinds. 'Ahaṁsphūrti', and 'Ahaṅkṛti'. A man, awakes from sound sleep and he realizes that he exists. This is one kind of egoism, which is called 'Ahaṁsphūrti'. But then by identifying himself with the body, he assumes that he belongs to a particular caste, creed and social order etc., this is his affinity with, the unreal. With such affinity (identification), with the unreal (body), he regards actions done by the body, as actions done, by the self. This is another kind of egoism, called 'Ahaṅkṛti'.

There is limitedness, in the self due to ego. Even in 'Ahaṁsphūrti', as mentioned above, individualism remains. But it does not bind. When one accepts 'Ahaṅkṛti', viz., he assumes relationship with someone or something or some action, then dualism of virtue and vice arises in the embodied soul, which induces him to perform good and bad actions. On Self-realization, the limitedness in 'Ahaṁsphūrti', is destroyed. In such a state, actions are done by that liberated soul, in an impersonal state. These do not bind him.

"Na hanti na nibadhyate'—He neither slays, nor is he bound—What does it mean? There are two states of trance temporary and permanent. The temporary state is called 'Nirvikalpa-Avasthā', while the permanent one, is called 'Nirvikalpa-Bodha. The former does not remain uniform, it undergoes change. It can be attained through practice. By remaining detached, from the 'Nirvikalpa-Avasthā', the self-evident 'Nirvikalpa-Bodha, is realized. The latter remains ever uniform without undergoing any change, and it cannot be attained, through practice. In this state, while slaying all beings, a man neither slays, nor is bound by such killing.

How should a man be free, from the egoistic notion and how should his intellect not be tainted?

A man, by applying his discrimination, should realize the fact, that all actions are performed by nature alone, which always undergoes modifications. Moreover, all actions, as well as their fruit, appear and disappear, while the self, as illuminator of all of them, ever remains uniform. By realizing this fact, he can be free from egoistic notion, and his intellect, is not tainted.

Appendix—The expressions—'nāhaṅkṛta bhāva' means to be free from egoism and 'buddhiḥ na lipyate' means to be free from desire, the sense of mine and selfishness.

Arjuna said, "Sin will accrue to us by slaying these desperadoes—'pāpamevāśrayedasmānhatvaitānātatāyinaḥ' (Gītā 1/36) and 'We'll accrue sin by slaying these reverend preceptors and elders—'gurūnahatvā hi mahānubhāvān............' (Gītā 2/5). Therefore here the Lord declares that Arjuna will accrue no sin even though he slays not only his reverend preceptors and elders but also all other creatures because sin will accrue only, if he has the egoistic notion, and if his intellect is tainted. The intellect is tainted by having desire, the sense of mine and selfishness. If a man is drowned in the Ganges, the Ganges accrues no sin; and if anyone drinks its water, bathes in it and irrigates his land and makes it fertile, the Ganges does not earn any virtue. When it rains heavily, several creatures are killed and the life of several other creatures is saved but rain neither accrues sin nor virtue. The reason is that they have neither the egoistic notion nor their intellect is tainted. If a Surgeon performs a surgical operation, being free from desire, the sense of mine and selfishness, in spite of cutting the organs, he incurs no sin. If he is also free from the egoistic notion also, then no question arises at all of his accruing sin.

By Jñānayoga, the egoistic notion is destroyed; and by Karmayoga, the taintedness of the intellect is wiped out. If one of the two is destroyed, the other is also destroyed. It is because of the egoistic notion that in a man (self), the desire for pleasure and salvation evolves. When the egoistic notion is wiped out, then the desire for pleasure is also wiped out—'buddhiryasya na lipyate'. With the destruction of the desire for pleasure, the yearning for salvation is automatically fulfilled because salvation is axiomatic (Self-evident).

Link:—Knowledge and actions in themselves, are not evils. It is the sense of doership, which is an evil. A sense of doership, causes actions—this is explained in the verse, that follows:—

ज्ञानं ज्ञेयं परिज्ञाता त्रिविधा कर्मचोदना।
करणं कर्म कर्तेति त्रिविधः कर्मसङ्ग्रहः ॥ १८ ॥

jñānaṁ jñeyaṁ parijñātā trividhā karmacodanā
karaṇaṁ karma karteti trividhaḥ karmasaṅgrahaḥ

Knowledge, the knowable and the knower, these three motivate action; and the instrument, the action and the agent (doer) are the three constituents (bases) of action. 18

Comment:—

[In the fourteenth verse of this chapter, the Lord explained the body, doer, instruments, efforts and daiva (impressions), these five factors, as responsible for the accomplishment of all actions. Out of these, the most important one, is the doer. So the Lord vehemently criticized, a man, who looks upon his self, as doer, in the sixteenth verse, while He praised one who is free from egoistic notion, in the seventeenth verse. The Lord in the eighteenth verse, clarifies that it is the notion of egoism (doership), which binds a man. The main purpose of this verse is a man should get rid of the notion of doership.]

'Jñānaṁ jñeyaṁ parijñātā trividhā karmacodanā'— Knowledge, the knowable, and the knower, are the threefold incitement to action. Knowledge has been mentioned first of all, because it is knowledge, which motivates a man to action. As a man first knows, that he is thirsty—this is knowledge; and then how he should quench it. It is water, which can quench the thirst. So water is 'knowable', He who knows, is the knower. But all the three—knowledge, the knowable and the knower, together motivate a man to action. If there is absence of anyone of the three, the remaining two cannot contribute, to action.

He who knows the motivation of action, is called 'Parijñātā' (knower only). In this 'Parijñātā' a sense of doership and sense of getting anything for himself, are quite absent. He knows only inspiration (sphuraṇā), of actions. There can be motivation to do an act, only in a particular individual. In respect of different activities, such as eating, drinking, sleeping, hearing etc., the doer of these different activities, can be designated as eater, drinker, sleeper, hearer etc. But the knower of all of these, will be designated by the term 'Parijñātā.'

'Karaṇaṁ karma karteti trividhaḥ karmasaṅgrahaḥ'—The instrument, activity and the agent, are the triple constituents of action. It is the conjunction of these three, which produces action. The means, such as mind, intellect and senses etc., by which he performs actions, are known 'Karaṇa' (Instruments). The acts of eating, drinking, sitting, walking, coming and going etc., are 'Karma' (activities). A person, who having affinity with instruments and activities, performs actions, is called a 'Kartā' (doer). These three, are the constituents of action. Here, the Lord wants to emphasize the fact, that it is a sense of doership, which binds a man. Out of the three constituents of action, the organ (instrument) does not contribute to the accomplishment of action, as it is subservient to a doer. Only that activity, which a doer wants to do, is performed by him. Therefore, an activity is also not, an important contributory factor. According to the branch of learning, known by the name 'Sāṅkhya', it is a sense of doership, which is the chief contributory factor, to action. In the absence of a sense of doership, no action is accomplished. The terms 'Karaṇa', and 'Karma', have been used before, while the term 'Kartā' has been used close to the term 'Karma saṅgrahaḥ', by the Lord, in order to bring home the fact, that it is a sense of doership which gets a man into bondage. If he performs action without a notion of doership, he is not bound because no action is at all accomplished in the absence of the sense of doership. So the Lord has used the term 'Kartā' (doer), close to expression'Karma-saṅgrahaḥ' (constituents of action).

Appendix—Arjuna expressed his desire to know the truth about the path of knowledge and the path of action (Gītā 18/1), therefore the Lord described the path of action upto the twelfth verse. Then the Lord from the viewpoint of the path of knowledge, while describing actions, mentioned five factors which are contributory to the accomplishment of all actions (Gītā 18/13—15). The same fact in a different manner is described here in the form of 'Karmapreraṇā' (incitement to action) and 'Karmasaṅgrahaḥ' (constituents of action).

When a man has the egoistic notion and taintedness, then the knowledge, the knowable and the knower—these three motivate (incite) an action viz., he thinks that if he performs a particular action, it will bear a particular fruit. With the incitement of action, there is 'Karmasaṅgraha' viz., there is accomplishment of sinful and virtuous actions. How the sinful and virtuous actions are performed—this will be described in detail by the Lord ahead from the twentieth verse.

Link:—Now, the Lord from the next verse, classifies them into three kinds so that a striver, by knowing these, may transcend, the three modes of nature.

ज्ञानं कर्म च कर्ता च त्रिधैव गुणभेदतः।
प्रोच्यते गुणसङ्ख्याने यथावच्छृणु तान्यपि॥ १९॥

jñānaṁ karma ca kartā ca tridhaiva guṇabhedataḥ
procyate guṇasaṅkhyāne yathāvacchṛṇu tānyapi

Knowledge (jñāna), action (karma) and the doer (kartā) are declared, in the science of guṇas (Sāṅkhya philosophy), to be of three kinds only, according to differences in the modes. Note these carefully also. 19

Comment:—

'Procyate guṇasaṅkhyāne'—The Lord explains to Arjuna, the three kinds of knowledge, action and agent, as declared in the science of modes (Sāṅkhya philosophy), according to differences in the modes.

'Jñānaṁ karma ca kartā ca tridhaiva guṇabhedataḥ'—In the preceding verse, the Lord explained the threefold incitement, to action and the threefold constituents, of action. Thus he explained six factors.* Out of these the Lord, first discusses three—knowledge from the threefold incitement, while action and agent, from the threefold constituents. Any person, begins an action after possessing knowledge, about it. So knowledge, has been taken first. In the performance of an action, an agent occupies an important place, but action has also been taken with it, because without action, he cannot accomplish (execute), an action. It means, that knowledge occupies an important place, as an incentive to action, while action and agent, are significant, so far as the execution of action is concerned. If these three, are Sāttvika (good), a man is not bound. If these are rājasika (passionate) or tāmasika (ignorant), a man is bound.

Now the question arises as to why the knowable and the knower, have not been taken from the threefold incitement. The

---

*Knowledge, the knowable and the knower—the threefold incitement is subtle material while the instrument, the action and the agent—the threefold constituents of action are gross materials.

reason is, that a knower becomes an agent, when he establishes his affinity, with an action. So, within the three kinds of agents, three kinds of knowers, are included. Moreover, a knower is of three kinds, only when he is attached to modes of nature. If he is not attached to them, he remains merely, a knower, without having a classification of three kinds.

The knowable or the object, to be known is 'Jñeya'. There are different objects to be known, but the aim of knowing these objects, is to derive happiness. So the Lord, has classified the knowable, by the name of happiness into three kinds, further (in 18/36—39).

Similarly the Lord, has not classified the instruments, such as senses and mind etc., into three kinds. Whatever actions, are performed with senses etc., a man performs these by applying his intellect. So the Lord, classifies the instruments by the name of intellect, further (in 18/30—32).

Firmness (steadiness) is necessary, with intellect, in the Discipline of Knowledge. So the Lord, in the Discipline of Knowledge, has used firmness with intellect (6/25, 18/51). He has also classified it into three kinds (18/33—35).

The term 'Tridhaiva', denotes that there are only three kinds, neither more nor less than the three, because the three modes of goodness (sattva), passion (rajas) and ignorance (tamas) are born of nature (Gītā 14/5). So because of connection with these three modes they are of three kinds.

'Yathāvat'—As it has been described in the branch of knowledge, dealing with Guṇas, He is telling him the same, without any addition or substraction.

'Śṛṇu'—Lord Kṛṣṇa asks Arjuna, to hear the topic attentively, because out of the three the sāttvika one, enables a man to realize God, by breaking up his affinity with actions, while the rājasika leads to the bondage of birth and death, and the tāmasika is conducive to degradation, viz., hell and eighty-four lac forms, of lives. So he should adopt the sāttvika mode and abandon the Rājasika and Tāmasika.

'Tāni'—The agent, action and knowledge, have no connection with the self. The self is ever-pure and detached.

'Api'—It is indispensable to know, these three kinds, because by knowing these in the right perspective, a man can realize the fact enumerated in (18/17). 'He who is free from egoistic notions, whose intellect is not tainted, though he slays the people, he really slays not, nor is he bound (by actions)' i.e., he realizes, the self.

Link:—The Lord now begins to describe the Sāttvika Knowledge (knowledge of goodness).

सर्वभूतेषु येनैकं भावमव्ययमीक्षते।
अविभक्तं विभक्तेषु तज्ज्ञानं विद्धि सात्त्विकम्॥ २०॥

sarvabhūteṣu yenaikaṁ bhāvamavyayamīkṣate
avibhaktaṁ vibhakteṣu tajjñānaṁ viddhi sāttvikam

The knowledge, by which one realises the Imperishable Being (Reality) in different beings, as undivided (not separate in separate beings), knows such knowledge to be sāttvika. 20

Comment:—

'Sarvabhūteṣu yenaikaṁ bhāvamavyayamīkṣate avibhaktaṁ vibhakteṣu'—All beings and things etc., are kaleidoscopic, they have no existence of their own. But they seem to exist, in the light of the Imperishable Lord, Who pervades everywhere. A man, out of ignorance sees their existence. As soon as his ignorance is removed, and he gains knowledge, he realizes the existence of God, in all the perishable beings, and things etc.

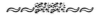

Having gained knowledge a striver, sees the imperishable Supreme Lord, abiding equally in all perishable beings (Gītā 13/27). Though He is undivided, yet He seems to be divided among beings, things, circumstances and incidents etc., (Gītā 13/16). A striver, beholds only imperishable essence, in all the objects, whichever undergo changes. How to know that, he sees only the Lord? He remains free, from attachment and aversion. This is the criterion.

'Tajjñānaṁ viddhi sāttvikam'—This knowledge, is known to be sāttvika. It is called Sāttvika, because of affinity with things and inclinations etc. If this affinity, is renounced, this knowledge is Self-realization, which ought to be known, as stated by Lord Kṛṣṇa. He declares, "I will describe, that which ought to be known and knowing which, one attains immortality" (Gītā 13/12).

A Vital Fact

The universe, is known by senses, the senses are known by intellect, and intellect is known by 'I'. The universe, the senses and the intellect, are known by 'I'. But there is one Illuminator, Who illuminates this 'I' also. That Illuminator is all-pervasive and infinite, while 'I' is limited and finite. 'You' (thou), 'this' and ' that', are also illumined in that light, as 'I' is illumined. That Illuminator, is not subject to illumination. That is Illumination-Incarnate. He is attributeless, the Absolute. He is undivided and He illuminates, everything. His illumination in a particular person, is called sāttvika knowledge.

In other words, Sāttvika knowledge, can be explained, in this way. All the beings, are included in 'I', 'you', 'this' and 'that'. They are diverse, but He who illumines them, is indivisible. They ever undergo changes and are not real, but He ever remains uniform. All the four, 'I', 'you', 'this', and 'that', are not really existent, in that Illuminator. But they get their seeming existence, by that Illuminator only. That Illuminator, illumines all and He Himself is an embodiment of illumination. They are separate (divided), while He as their illuminator, remains undivided. This is sāttvika knowledge. Being pure and illuminating, this knowledge, illumines all divisible, changeable and perishable beings, and objects (Gītā 14/6).

This sāttvika knowledge is said to be the illuminator from

the point of view of the illumined and indivisible from the point of view of the divisible. But when it has no connection with the illumined and divisible objects, it is in fact attributeless, absolute and real knowledge itself.

Appendix—As a common man holds that the Self pervades the entire body, similarly a striver holds that God pervades the entire universe. As the body and the world are one (identical), so are the Self and God one.

From the view-point of a striver, beings also, have their own existence, so his knowledge is 'Sāttvika'. If from his view-point there is no separate existence of beings but there is only one imperishable existence, then it is the transcendental entity viz., Self-realization (attainment of Brahma). That imperishable entity pervades equally everywhere. We have our natural identity with that entity.

Link:—The Lord, now describes, Rājasika knowledge (knowledge of the nature of passion).

पृथक्त्वेन तु यज्ज्ञानं नानाभावान्पृथग्विधान्।
वेत्ति सर्वेषु भूतेषु तज्ज्ञानं विद्धि राजसम्॥ २१॥

pṛthaktvena tu yajjñānaṁ nānābhāvānpṛthagvidhān
vetti sarveṣu bhūteṣu tajjñānaṁ viddhi rājasam

The knowledge, by which one perceives the manifold entities of different kinds, as varying from one another, know that knowledge, to be rājasika (jñāna). 21

Comment:—

'Pṛthaktvena tu* yajjñānaṁ nānābhāvānpṛthagvidhān'—There is predominance of passion, in rājasika knowledge. The Lord declares, "Know thou Rajas to be of the nature of passion" (Gītā 14/7). This passion, causes attachment and aversion.

*The term 'Tu' has been used to denote that the Rājasika knowledge is different from the Sāttvika one.

It is because of this passionate knowledge, that a man sees diversity in different persons, gods, devils, demons, birds, beasts, moths, insects, trees and plants etc., according to their shapes, nature, names, forms and attributes etc. He loses the perception of unity, and does not see the Imperishable Supreme Lord abiding equally, in all the perishable beings, in the form of an imperishable soul.

'Vetti sarveṣu bhūteṣu tajjñānaṁ viddhi rājasam'—The knowledge, by which one sees the manifold entities of different kinds, as varying from one another, according to their different bodies, senses, inner sense, temperaments and life-breaths etc., that knowledge, is rājasika. A man, possessing rājasika knowledge cannot discriminate between, the sentient and the insentient.

Appendix—A man cognises the existence of both—actions and objects and gets attached to them, so he perceives diversity in different beings.

Link:—Now, the Lord describes tāmasika knowledge (the knowledge of the mode of ignorance).

यत्तु कृत्स्नवदेकस्मिन्कार्ये सक्तमहैतुकम्।
अतत्त्वार्थवदल्पं च तत्तामसमुदाहृतम्॥ २२॥

yattu kṛtsnavadekasminkārye saktamahaitukam
atattvārthavadalpaṁ ca tattāmasamudāhṛtam

But, that knowledge which sticks to a single body as the whole, which is without reason, without basis in truth and is trivial, is declared to be tāmasika jñāna. 22

Comment:—

'Yattu* kṛtsnavadekasminkārye saktam'—A tāmasika person, regards a perishable body, consisting of five gross elements, as his own Self. He thinks, that first he was a child, now he is young

* The particle 'Tu' here conveys that the Tāmasika knowledge is different from the Rājasika knowledge.

and then he will grow old. He holds, that he is the enjoyer, he is successful, mighty and happy and there is none else like him. He is entangled, in the meshes of delusion (16/15).

'Ahaitukam'—His knowledge, is irrational and it is against the scriptures. He does not realize, that he (the soul), is imperishable and uniform, while a body is kaleidoscopic and perishable. He identifies the soul, with the body.

'Atattvārthavadalpaṁ ca'—Such a person, does not know the truth, that the soul is different from the body. His knowledge, is very poor and insignificant. So the Lord, has not used the term 'Knowledge', in this verse. A tāmasika person lacks knowledge, he is ignorant. So the Lord instead of using the term 'Knowledge' has used the terms 'Yat' (which) and 'Tat' (that) only.

'Tattāmasamudāhṛtam'—That understanding which is without reason, without foundation in truth, and is trivial, is declared to be tāmasika.

If Tāmasika knowledge, is not knowledge at all, and the Lord hesitates in calling it so, why has it been described? The reason is, that the Lord in the nineteenth verse of this chapter, asked Arjuna to hear three kinds of knowledge, action and agent. So after describing the sāttvika and rājasika knowledge, it was necessary for Him to describe it also as such.

Appendix—In Tāmasa knowledge, demoniac nature is predominant. In this verse the term 'Jñāna' has not been given which means that in fact it is no knowledge at all, it is mere ignorance. It is the intellect of Tāmasa people which has been called 'paśu buddhi' (beastly intellect)—

tvaṁ tu rājan mariṣyeti paśubuddhimimāṁ jahi
na jātaḥ prāgabhūto'dya dehavattvaṁ na naṅkṣyasi

(Śrīmadbhā. 12/5/2)

Śrī Śukadevajī said—'O King! now you, give up this beastly intellect that you will die. The body had no existence in the past, it was born afterwards and then it will die but it is not the case

with you (the Self) that you did not exist in the past, you were
born afterwards and then you will die.'

~~❀~~

*Link:—Now the Lord describes the Sāttvika action (action
of goodness).*

नियतं   सङ्गरहितमरागद्वेषतः   कृतम्।
अफलप्रेप्सुना   कर्म   यत्तत्सात्त्विकमुच्यते॥ २३॥

niyataṁ   saṅgarahitamarāgadveṣataḥ   kṛtam
aphalaprepsunā   karma   yattatsāttvikamucyate

Action which is ordained by the scriptures, that is performed
without a sense of doership and without attachment, or aversion
by one, who seeks no reward, is said to be, sāttvika (karma) (of
the nature of goodness). 23

Comment:—

'Niyataṁ saṅgarahitamarāgadveṣataḥ kṛtam aphalaprepsunā
karma yattatsāttvikamucyate'—Acts ordained by scriptures,
according to a person's caste, (social order), stage of life (Āśrama)
and circumstances, are 'Niyata'.

Here the term 'Niyatam' denotes, that the actions mentioned
above, are to be performed, but actions that are prohibited by
scriptures should not be performed.

Here, the expression 'Saṅgarahitam', denotes freedom, from a
sense of doership. As trees, have no sense of doership when new
leaves sprout, and when they blossom, similarly in the bodies
different activities, such as digestion, development and decay
etc., take place, naturally. So by realizing this fact a striver,
becomes free from doership. Here, the expression 'Saṅgarahitam'
denotes, freedom from doership, because freedom from attachment,
has been mentioned by the term 'Arāgadveṣataḥ' in this verse.
Moreover in Sāṅkhyayoga* it is absence of the sense of doership

*Here in 'Sāṅkhyayoga' the expression 'Saṅgarahitam' denotes freedom
from doership while in 'Karmayoga' the expression 'Saṅgaṁ tyaktvā phalaṁ
caiva' (18/9) denotes freedom from attachments as well as from desire for

which is more important.

The expression 'Arāgadveṣataḥ kṛtam' means, that an action should be performed, being free from attachment and aversion viz., an action should neither be performed with attachment nor renounced, with aversion. Moreover, there should not be attachment or aversion for the instruments (body, senses and mind etc.,) in performing actions.

The expression 'Arāgadveṣataḥ' denotes, freedom from attachment at present, while the term'Aphalaprepsunā' denotes, freedom of attachment, in future. It means, that an action should be performed, without any desire for fruit in future, and there should be detachment from action and objects. It has already been mentioned, that action should be performed, without having either attachment or aversion. Now He declares, that it is to be performed without attachment, in future i.e., without seeking any reward. Such action, is declared to be sāttvika. It is called Sāttvika, so long as, it is connected with prakṛti (nature), in a very subtle form. When its connection is completely renounced, this action becomes inaction or say it has no binding effect.

Link:—Now He describes the Rājasika action (action of the nature of passion).

यत्तु कामेप्सुना कर्म साहङ्कारेण वा पुनः ।
क्रियते बहुलायासं तद्राजसमुदाहृतम् ॥ २४ ॥

yattu kāmepsunā karma sāhaṅkāreṇa vā punaḥ
kriyate bahulāyāsaṁ tadrājasamudāhṛtam

But action, which is performed with great effort by one who seeks to gratify his desires or is done by the egoistic feeling—that

fruit. It means that if a Sāṅkhyayogī has the sense of doership, his affinity with the body will continue which is an obstacle to the Self-realization. But if a Karmayogī has the sense of doership, it is not such an obstacle for him because he acts for others and he has the sense of doership only when he performs actions. When the action is accomplished, his doership merges in the action.

is considered to be rājasika (passionate). 24

Comment:—

'Yattu* kāmepsunā karma'—A passionate person, performs action to seek comfort, pleasure, honour and praise etc.

'Sāhaṅkāreṇa'—He feels boastful of his actions in public, when people praise him, and in privacy, by thinking that he is more prompt, sincere and honest in actions, than other people. Thus action performed with egoistic feeling, is called 'rajas'.

'Vā punaḥ'—The expression 'Vā punaḥ', (or again) has been used to denote, that action either performed for fruit (reward), or again by egoism, becomes rājasika. So, if it is performed both for fruit and impelled by egoism, it surely becomes rājasika.

'Kriyate bahulāyāsam'—While performing action, a man has to make effort and feel strain. But the man, who hankers after physical comforts, feels greater strain. On the other hand, a man who hankers after pleasure and prosperity, does not feel much strain, because he has a yearning for accumulating wealth and enjoying pleasure. So instead of physical rest, he has an eye on prosperity and pleasure.

A rājasika person, while performing action in public, does not feel great strain, because his sense of egoism, is satisfied. But when he performs action in loneliness, he feels much strain, because his sense of egoism is not satisfied, and he is ease loving.

'Tadrājasamudāhṛtam'—Action performed by a person, longing for fruit with egoism, and with much strain, is declared to be rājasika.

Appendix—A Rājasa man has so many demands and so he needs more things when he does any work, and he has to make more efforts in procuring more things. A Rājasa man extends his activities, therefore he has to make more effort. Being attached to

*The term 'Tu' has been used to denote that the Rājasika action is different from the Sāttvika one.

the body, a Rājasa man wants more physical comfort, therefore he feels more strain even while doing a little work.

Link:—Now the Lord, describes the tāmasika action (action of the mode of ignorance).

अनुबन्धं क्षयं हिंसामनवेक्ष्य च पौरुषम्।
मोहादारभ्यते कर्म यत्तत्तामसमुच्यते॥ २५॥

anubandhaṁ kṣayaṁ hiṁsāmanavekṣya ca pauruṣam
mohādārabhyate karma yattattāmasamucyate

Action which is undertaken, from delusion, without regard to consequences, or to loss, one's capacity and injury to others is declared to be tāmasika. 25

Comment:—

'Anubandham'—The person who performs an action for its fruit, performs it well thoughtfully, in order to reap its fruit. But a tāmasika person, undertakes an action without foreseeing its consequences, for himself and for others.

'Kṣayam'—He does not think of the loss of health, wealth, time, honour, fame, praise and ruin, here or hereafter, resulting from the performance of such an action.

'Hiṁsām'—He does not foresee to what extent, it will cause injury to human beings and other creatures and also involve destruction. Moreover, it might pollute the mind, morals and feelings etc., of beings and degrade and ruin them.

'Anavekṣya ca pauruṣam'—He does not consider whether he possesses the requisite ability (or capacity), time, skill, knowledge, and resources etc., or not to perform an act.

'Mohādārabhyate karma yattattāmasamucyate'—A tāmasika person, performs action out of delusion, without thinking of its consequences or loss or injury or his own capacity. Such an action is declared to be tāmasika.

Appendix—A Tāmasa person undertakes action out of

delusion without thinking of his capacity and its consequences etc.* He naturally performs such actions which are obstacles to the affairs of others; as to go on talking on the way and to leave the cycle on the foot-path etc. He does not pay attention to the problems of others.

The Sāttvika nature naturally leads to progress. The Rājasa nature arrests progress and the Tāmasa nature is naturally conducive to a downfall.

Link:—Now, the Lord enumerates the characteristics of a Sāttvika doer (agent).

मुक्तसङ्गोऽनहंवादी धृत्युत्साहसमन्वितः ।
सिद्ध्यसिद्ध्योर्निर्विकारः कर्ता सात्त्विक उच्यते ॥ २६ ॥

muktasaṅgo'nahaṁvādī dhṛtyutsāhasamanvitaḥ
siddhyasiddhyornirvikāraḥ kartā sāttvika ucyate

The doer, (Kartā) who is free from attachment, is non-egoistic, is endowed with firmness and zeal, and who is unaffected by success and failure, is called Sāttvika. 26

Comment:—

'Muktasaṅgaḥ'—As a Sāṅkhyayogī, is free from attachment, so is a Sāttvika doer, free from attachment, desire, lust, necessities and a sense of mine for objects, persons and incidents and circumstances etc. A Sāttvika doer, remains completely detached.

'Anahaṁvādī'—He is free, from the sense of doership and so he never boasts of his actions, like men possessing a demoniac disposition. He is not proud, even of his equanimity or freedom from attachment, to the world.

---

* binā bicāre jo karai, so pāche pachitāya
kāma bigarai āpano, jaga meṁ hota haṁsāya
jaga meṁ hota haṁsāya, citt meṁ caina na pāvai
khāna pāna sanamāna, rāga raṁga mana nahiṁ bhāvai
kaha giradhara kavirāya, karamagati ṭarata na ṭāre
khaṭakata hai jiya māhiṁ, kiyau jo binā bicāre

'Dhṛtyutsāhasamanvitaḥ'—A Sāttvika doer, is endowed with firmness and enthusiasm. A man, possessing firmness performs his duty, without being disturbed by odds, difficulties, obstacles and blame etc., while a man endowed with enthusiasm, discharges his duty with zeal, equally in success and failure, honour and dishonour and in praise and blame etc. Thus a Sāttvika doer, remains endowed with firmness and zeal.

'Siddhyasiddhyornirvikāraḥ'—A Sāttvika doer, remains unaffected in success and failure. He neither feels elevated, when an action is accomplished easily, nor does he feel dejected if it is not accomplished in spite of best efforts. He remains equanimous, in success and failure.

'Kartā sāttvika ucyate'—Such an agent, who is free from attachment, is non-egoistic, endowed with firmness and zeal, and who is unswayed by success and failure, is called sāttvika.

In this verse, there are six characteristics—attachment, egoism, firmness, zeal, success and failure. A sāttvika doer, is free from the first two, he is endowed with the middle two and he remains equanimous, in the last two.

Appendix—In the Gītā equanimity or unaffectedness in success and failure has been mentioned in three verses—'siddhyasiddhyoḥ samo bhūtvā' (2/48), 'samaḥ siddhāvasiddhau ca' (4/22) and here 'siddhyasiddhyornirvikāraḥ'. It means that success or failure is not under the control of a man but it is within his power to remain unaffected by success and failure. Whatever is within his power, that is to be set right.

'Anahaṁvādī'—A Sāttvika man never boasts of himself outwardly that no person can do so well as he can, and does not regard himself to be superior to others inwardly.

Link:—Now, the Lord enumerates the characteristics of a Rājasika doer (passionate agent).

रागी कर्मफलप्रेप्सुर्लुब्धो हिंसात्मकोऽशुचिः ।
हर्षशोकान्वितः कर्ता राजसः परिकीर्तितः ॥ २७ ॥

rāgī karmaphalaprepsurlubdho hiṁsātmako'śuciḥ
harṣaśokānvitaḥ kartā rājasaḥ parikīrtitaḥ

The doer (Kartā) who is passionate, who eagerly seeks the fruit of action, who is greedy, oppressive by nature, impure, who is moved by joy and sorrow—such a doer is said to be, Rājasika (passionate). 27

Comment:—

'Rāgī'—The first characteristic of a passionate agent, is passion or attachment. A rājasika doer, remains attached to action and their fruits, as well as, to persons, things and objects etc.

'Karmaphalaprepsuḥ'—A rājasika person, performs actions to seek their fruit. He offers charity, to gain honour and praise here, and heavenly pleasures hereafter. Similarly, he takes medicines, to keep his body fit and healthy.

'Lubdhaḥ'—A rājasika person, is not satisfied with his possessions. He goes on craving for honour, praise, fame, wealth, sons, and family etc. The more he receives, the more he yearns.

'Hiṁsātmakaḥ'—He possesses an oppressive nature. He inflicts suffering on others, for selfish motive. The more pleasure he enjoys, the more pain, he inflicts on those, who suffer want. Enjoyment of sense-objects, without caring for the miseries of others, is violence. Without violence, no enjoyment is possible.

When the Lord declared, that tāmasa action, (18/25) and tāmasa doer—both are oppressive, He meant to explain, that actions by a tāmasa agent, are not performed with discrimination, because of delusion. So he is oppressive, in his daily life. A rājasa person, enjoys mundane pleasure, then other people who suffer from want have a heart-burn to see them, enjoy such pleasures. It means, that a tāmasa person, does injury to others, through his actions, while a rājasa person, himself is oppressive.

'Aśuciḥ'—A passionate person, makes things and objects, which he amasses, for his enjoyment, impure. He pollutes, the environment. The clothes, which he wears become impure. So no one wants to use the clothes, of a person, who was attached to them, even after his death. One cannot concentrate his mind on God, at such a place, where the dead body of such a man, is cremated. If any person, sleeps there, he has bad and horrible dreams. This passion or attachment for the perishable, makes a body or even bones, impure.

'Harṣaśokānvitaḥ'—He is ever-entangled, in pleasure and pain, attachment and aversion etc., because of success and failure, and pleasant and unpleasant, desirable and undesirable incidents and circumstances etc., which do come across man during his daily life.

'Kartā rājasaḥ parikīrtitaḥ'—The agent, who possesses the above-mentioned characteristics, is called passionate or 'Rajas' .

Appendix—'Hiṁsātmakaḥ'—In the twenty-fifth verse of this chapter in Tāmasika actions also 'hiṁsā' (the oppressive nature of causing injury or suffering to others) has been mentioned, because Rajoguṇa and Tamoguṇa are close to each other, while Sattvaguṇa is far from the two. Rajoguṇa is of the nature of passion while Tamoguṇa is of the nature of delusion. In Rajoguṇa a man remains conscious and careful but in Tamoguṇa he loses consciousness and carefulness. A selfish man having attachment inflicts more sufferings on others than does a deluded man inflict. Therefore in Rajoguṇa there is more violence (injury). A Rājasa man because of attachment and selfishness becomes oppressive (violent). He remains engrossed in violence.

Link:—Now the Lord enumerates the characteristics of a Tāmasika doer.

अयुक्तः प्राकृतः स्तब्धः शठोऽनैष्कृतिकोऽलसः ।
विषादी दीर्घसूत्री च कर्ता तामस उच्यते ॥ २८ ॥

ayuktaḥ prākṛtaḥ stabdhaḥ śaṭho'naiṣkṛtiko'lasaḥ
viṣādī dīrghasūtrī ca kartā tāmasa ucyate

The doer, who is indiscriminate, vulgar, arrogant, obstinate, malicious, indolent, despondent and procrastinative, he is said to be Tāmasika (of the mode of ignorance). 28

Comment:—

'Ayuktaḥ'—Tāmasa (mode of ignorance), deludes, all embodied beings (Gītā 14/8). A Tāmasika person cannot discriminate, between the proper and the improper and between, what should be done and what should be refrained from.

'Prākṛtaḥ'—Prākṛtaḥ or vulgar, is he who has not improved his life through good education, scriptures and good company etc. He possesses a childish nature, having no sense of duty.

'Stabdhaḥ'—An (arrogant) man, remains unbending with his mind, speech and body. He does not bow down to elderly people, parents, teachers etc. He is hard-hearted by nature, having no element of gentleness and humility.

'Śaṭhaḥ'—A tāmasika person, out of obstinacy does not follow good advice and good ideas, of other people. He out of delusion, holds that his own ideas, are good and he sticks to them.

'Anaiṣkṛtikaḥ'—A tāmasika person, does not return good, for the good done to him. He rather returns evil for good. Therefore he is termed as Anaiṣkṛtikaḥ.

'Alasaḥ'—An indolent man, does not perform his duty. He wants to lie down or to sleep or to remain idle.

'Viṣādī'—Such a despondent man, grieves day and night and his worries, disquietude, and sadness, know no end. Therefore all are in him automatic because he has no sense of duty.

'Dīrghasūtrī'—A procrastinating person, does not think how to perform action promptly and thoroughly. He takes a lot of time, in completing the work, which should have been done in a short time. Moreover, he does not complete it, thoroughly.

'Kartā tāmasa ucyate'—An agent who possesses the above-mentioned eight characteristics, is said to be tāmasika.

An Important Fact

In the twenty-sixth, twenty-seventh and twenty-eighth verses, the Lord has enumerated the characteristics of agents. As is, an agent, so are his actions and so are the instruments to perform, those actions. So the sāttvika, rājasika and tāmasika agents, perform actions according to their own nature.

A sāttvika agent, by making his actions and intellect etc., Sāttvika, by rejoicing in Sāttvika happiness, identifies himself with God i.e., reaches the end of sorrow (Gītā 18/36). The reason is, that the aim of a sāttvika agent is God-realization. So, being free from a sense of doership and enjoyership, he identifies himself, with God, because actually he had his identity, with Him. A rājasika or a tāmasika doer, cannot identify himself with God, because he is engrossed in rājasika or tāmasika pleasure and his aim is, not God-realization.

Now, a doubt arises, that an agent can be sāttvika. But how are actions Sāttvika? The explanation is, that when an agent performs action without having attachment for it, without a sense of doership and without expecting any reward, the action, becomes Sāttvika. Such Sāttvika action does good to the doer, as well as, to the entire universe. It makes persons, things, objects, environment to which it is connected, pure (Gītā 14/6) as the purity is the characteristic of the mode of Sattva.

Secondly Patañjali holds Rajoguṇa (the mode of passion) only to be of the nature of activity (Yogadarśana 2/18) while in the Gītā recognising Rajoguṇa as activity also it is predominantly declared to be of the nature of passion (14/7). In fact it is not activity but passion (attachment) which binds.

In the Gītā actions are declared to be of three kinds—Sāttvika, Rājasika and Tāmasika (18/23—25) according to the feelings of the agent. The actions of Sāttvika, Rājasika and Tāmasika agents are Sāttvika, Rājasika and Tāmasika respectively. So the Lord has not considered only an activity to be Rājasika.

Appendix—The term 'viṣādī' (gloomy or sad) should be included in Rajoguṇa but here it has been mentioned in Tamoguṇa. The reason is that the Tāmasa disposition is contrary to discrimination, therefore a Tāmasa person is more gloomy, more grieved than a Rājasa person.

Link:—All actions are accomplished by intellect and firmness. So the Lord now classifies them.

बुद्धेर्भेदं धृतेश्चैव गुणतस्त्रिविधं शृणु।
प्रोच्यमानमशेषेण पृथक्त्वेन धनञ्जय॥ २९॥

buddherbhedaṁ dhṛteścaiva guṇatastrividhaṁ śṛṇu
procyamānamaśeṣeṇa pṛthaktvena dhanañjaya

Hear now, the three kinds of distinctions of Buddhi (intellect) and also of Dhṛti (firmness) O winner of wealth (Arjuna), according to the modes, as I explain these fully and clearly. 29

Comment:—

[In the eighteenth verse of this chapter, the instrument, action and agent have been declared, to be the threefold constituents of action. Out of the instruments, senses are not classified into three kinds. Intellect, predominates senses and it guides them. So the Lord, gives the threefold distinction of Buddhi as three kinds of instrument. It is Dhṛti which does not let a man deviate from his aim. When understanding remains firm to achieve the aim, it is achieved. So, besides intellect, Dhṛti has also been classified into three kinds.*

In the context of incitement and constituents of action, for a

* Intellect and firmness play an important role not only in Sāṅkhyayoga (the Discipline of Knowledge) but in other means of God-realization also. So in the Gītā intellect and firmness have been mentioned together such as 'Let him gain tranquillity little by little, by means of intellect controlled by firmness' (6/25) and 'Endowed with a pure intellect, controlling the self by firmness' (18/51).

striver, knowledge, action and agent, play a very important role. Similarly, in order to follow spiritual discipline and to transcend the three modes of nature, it is indispensable for one to know the three kinds of Buddhi and Dhṛti so that he may rise high, by cultivating the Sāttvika Buddhi and Dhṛti, and give up the rājasika and tāmasika ones.]

'Dhanañjaya'—When Pāṇḍavas performed a sacrifice (yajña) named Rājasūya, Arjuna, collected fabulous wealth, by gaining victory over several kings. So Arjuna is called, 'Dhanañjaya' (winner of wealth). Here Lord Kṛṣṇa explains to Arjuna, that real wealth, consists in transcending the three modes of nature, by cultivating sāttvika Buddhi and Dhṛti. So he should justify his name, by possessing this real wealth.

'Buddherbhedaṁ dhṛteścaiva guṇatastrividhaṁ śṛṇu'— The Lord declares, that though Buddhi is one and Dhṛti is also separate, yet according to predominance of the modes of nature, they have been classified into three kinds—Sāttvika, Rājasika and Tāmasika. He asks Arjuna, to hear attentively, as He is going to explain these fully and distinctly to him.

By using the term 'Caiva', (and also) the Lord declares, that he will explain the three distinctions of Buddhi and also of Dhṛti. Though firmness, seems to be a characteristic of intellect, yet it is different, as well as important. It is because of firmness, that an agent, can make the right use of his understanding. If firmness is sāttvika, a striver's understanding, will remain firm. So in spiritual discipline, there is not so much need of steadiness of mind, as steadiness of understanding (intellect). Steadiness of mind, is required in accomplishments (Siddhis), such as Aṇimā etc. But, in spiritual progress, it is indispensable for understanding, to hold firm to aim.* When a striver's, intellect and firmness—both are sāttvika, he will follow spiritual discipline firmly. So, it is

*'By intellect a striver decides his aim and he holds firm to it through firmness. If even the vilest sinner firmly follows his aim that he has to realize God, all his sins perish and he becomes righteous (Gītā 9/30).

necessary for him, to know the threefold distinction.

'Pṛthaktvena'—He will explain the distinction, of intellect and of firmness, clearly.

'Procyamānamaśeṣeṇa'—Lord Kṛṣṇa says to Arjuna, that He will explain all the important points about intellect and firmness fully, so that nothing else, may remain to be known.

Link:—The Lord defines, the Sāttvika intellect.

प्रवृत्तिं च निवृत्तिं च कार्याकार्ये भयाभये।
बन्धं मोक्षं च या वेत्ति बुद्धिः सा पार्थ सात्त्विकी ॥ ३० ॥

pravṛttiṁ ca nivṛttiṁ ca kāryākārye bhayābhaye
bandhaṁ mokṣaṁ ca yā vetti buddhiḥ sā pārtha sāttvikī

The intellect, which knows the path of action and renunciation, of what ought to be done and what not, of fear and fearlessness, of bondage and liberation—that intellect, is sāttvika (of the nature of goodness), O Pārtha (Arjuna). 30

Comment:—

'Pravṛttiṁ ca nivṛttiṁ ca'—Sometimes, a striver is engaged in work, while at another time, he is engaged in adoration and meditation, by renouncing action. His performance of action and adoration or meditation with desire for fruit, is included in work.* But, if these are performed without a desire for fruit, both are included, in renunciation and lead to God-realization. So, while performing and renouncing an act, a striver, should expect no reward. If both these are performed, to derive pleasure or joy out of them, they are included in work, and lead to bondage. In other words, in both the cases individuality persists, it does not get lost. But, if these are performed, for the good of others,

* When a person devotes his time in adoration and meditation in solitude, he does not possess riches and objects there but he has a subtle desire that he will be honoured and praised by the people as they will regard him as wise because he meditates on God in solitude.

both are included in renunciation. In both cases individuality gets lost. So a striver, should follow a path of renunciation, for Self-realization or follow the path of work (Action), by serving all beings, in order to realize God, the illuminator of the two—on the path of work and that of renunciation.

'Kāryākārye'—Work, which is done according to ordinance of scriptures, consistent with one's caste (Varṇa) and social order (Āśrama), is what ought to be done, while work which is prohibited by scriptures, is that which ought not to be done.

Work which is obligatory and is within our power (capacity), and which leads beings to salvation, is called duty, and it ought to be done. But work which ought not to be done, and which leads to bondage, is not included in duty. We need not do the work, which is beyond our capacity.

'Bhayābhaye'—A man should think, of the root of fear and fearlessness. Action, which may cause harm to one's own self, as well as to others, gives birth to fear. But action which is performed, for the welfare of all beings, is likely to cause fearlessness. When a man performs action, which ought not to be done, he is full of fear, thinking of dishonour, blame and insult. But, when a man works according to ordinance of scriptures for the welfare of all beings, to please God, he remains, fearless. This fearlessness, leads him to God-realization.

'Bandhaṁ mokṣaṁ ca yā vetti'—He, who externally performs, virtuous action such as sacrifice, charity and pilgrimage etc., but internally, has a desire for the unreal and perishable objects, and heavenly pleasure etc., his actions lead him to bondage. But a striver, who has an exclusive devotion to God, attains liberation.

A man thinks that he is dependent, because he does not possess certain things, and he is independent, when those things are available to him. But in fact, he is dependent in both the cases. The difference is, that in the former case, the dependence is seen and felt, while in the latter case, it is not seen because at that time, a man loses his sight. But in fact, both mean dependence, which leads to bondage. The former, is the revealed, bitter poison, while the latter is hidden, sweet poison. But both are poisons, which are fatal.

It means, that all worldly desires lead to bondage while desirelessness, leads to liberation. The need (necessity) for God, also leads to liberation.* If a man has a desire, it is a bondage, whether he possesses the things or not. But if he is free from desire, he is liberated, whether he possesses the things or not.

'Buddhiḥ sā pārtha sāttvikī'—Thus, intellect which knows reality about the path of work and renunciation, what ought to be done and what ought not to be done, fear and fearlessness, bondage and liberation—that intellect is sāttvika. What is reality? Reality is that, we should know, that we have no affinity with the world, we have merely assumed our affinity with it, while our affinity with God, Who is the illuminator and base of the entire creation, is natural. This is reality, which should be known, by the sāttvika intellect.

Appendix—The purpose of knowing the truth of Pravṛtti and Nivṛtti, of what ought to be done and what ought not to be done, of fear and fearlessness, of bondage and liberation, is only to renounce affinity with the world. If affinity with the world is not renounced, that knowledge is not real knowledge but that is mere rot learning.

The Sāttvika intellect mentioned in the Gītā enables a striver to rise above the three guṇas and to renounce his affinity with the world. Therefore the striver possessing the Sāttvika intellect, reflects upon bondage and liberation—'bandhaṁ mokṣaṁ ca yāvetti'. In Sāttviki intellect there is discrimination which is transformed into Self-realization. The discriminative intellect knows that all 'upto the attainment of the abode of Brahmā' is bondage.

---

*There is a difference between 'desire' and 'need' (necessity). There is desire for the worldly things while there is need for God. A desire remains unfulfilled and is to be renounced while a need is fulfilled. If a person gives up worldly desires, God is automatically realized.

Link:—The Lord now defines Rājasika intellect.

यया धर्ममधर्मं च कार्यं चाकार्यमेव च।
अयथावत्प्रजानाति बुद्धिः सा पार्थ राजसी॥ ३१॥

yayā dharmamadharmaṁ ca kāryaṁ cākāryameva ca
ayathāvatprajānāti buddhiḥ sā pārtha rājasī

The intellect, by which one wrongly understands Dharma (righteousness) and Adharma (unrighteousness), what ought to be done and what not, is rājasika. 31

Comment:—

'Yayā dharmamadharmaṁ ca'—Noble pursuits, which are prescribed by scriptures and which lead a man to salvation, are covered by the term 'Dharma', while evil pursuits, which are prohibited by scriptures and which hurls a person into the dark abyss of hell are included in 'Adharma' Service to parents and other elderly people, acts of benevolence, such as construction of wells, hospices, hospitals, offering charity to the poor, the needy, and spending money liberally for the society without expecting any reward—these acts are included in Dharma. But, inflicting pain on others for one's own selfish motive, is Adharma. In fact, that which leads to emancipation is Dharma, while what leads to bondage, is Adharma.

'Kāryaṁ cākāryameva ca'—That which has been sanctioned by scriptures, according to one's caste, (social order) stage of life, at a particular time and place, is 'Kārya' (duty), while what is forbidden by scriptures and which ought not to be done, is 'Akārya' (prohibited action). Some acts, which are worth performing for a particular class, may be worth abstaining from, for people of another. To beg alms, officiating at sacrifices and marriages, and accepting charity and gifts etc., are worth performing, for a Brāhmaṇa (a member of the priest class), while such acts are forbidden for members of warrior class, trading and labouring classes.

A servant, should perform his duty honestly and wholeheartedly, by devoting full time and energy. He should abstain from bribery, idleness and laziness. Similarly, government officers, should work for public welfare, by giving up their selfishness and pride.

The path of work and renunciation, fear and fearlessness, bondage and liberation mentioned in 'Sāttvika' intellect, should also be included in the expression, 'Eva ca' (Even and).

'Ayathāvatprajānāti buddhiḥ sā pārtha rājasī'—Because of passion (attachment), the Rājasika intellect possesses evil propensities, such as selfishness, partiality and inequanimity etc. So it cannot know what is right, and wrong; what is fear, and fearlessness; what ought to be done and what ought not; and what are bondage, and liberation.

Attachment to a person, thing, incident, action and circumstance, causes aversion for other persons, things, incidents, actions and circumstances etc. A man, gets entangled in the world, through attachment and aversion. When he gets attached to the world, he cannot know the reality of world. He can see the reality of world, if he remains indifferent to it. But he can know the Lord, by identifying himself with Him.

In sāttvika intellect, discrimination is aroused, while in rājasika intellect, it is veiled and becomes faint, because of passion. So the intellect, does not remain pure, as water does not ramain pure, when earth is mixed in it. Therefore, a person of rājasika intellect, cannot discriminate, between right and wrong and between what ought to be done and what ought not to be. So, he cannot perform, what ought to be and cannot abstain, from what ought not to be done.

Appendix—He who does not even know Dharma (righteousness) and Adharma (unrighteousness), what ought to be done and what ought to be refrained from properly, how will he know bondage and liberation? He can't know. Because of his passionate intellect, he can't know them in reality as there is predominance of attachment in him, so he can not attach significance to discrimination. Being swayed by the perishable objects, his discrimination disappears.

Link:—The Lord now defines Tāmasika intellect, (intellect of the nature of ignorance).

अधर्मं धर्ममिति या मन्यते तमसावृता।
सर्वार्थान्विपरीतांश्च बुद्धिः सा पार्थ तामसी॥ ३२॥

adharmaṁ dharmamiti yā manyate tamasāvṛtā
sarvārthānviparītāṁśca buddhiḥ sā pārtha tāmasī

That, which enveloped in darkness, is conceived as right, when wrong, and sees all things perverted (contrary to truth), that intellect, O Pārtha (Arjuna), is tāmasika (of the nature of ignorance). 32

Comment:—

'Adharmaṁ dharmamiti yā manyate tamasāvṛtā—Intellect which reproaches God that which acts against ordinance of scriptures, which violates the rules of caste (Varṇa) (social order) and stage of life (Āśrama), which shows disrespect towards parents, teachers and saints, and which regards sinful acts such as, falsehood, fraud, dishonesty, forgery, taking prohibited food and adultery etc., as acts of virtue, is said to mistake 'Adharma' as 'Dharma'.

Obedience and service to parents, study of the scriptures, following decorums of 'Varṇa' and 'Āśrama,' rendering service to others with body, mind and riches, translating saints' teachings into practice, taking pure meals and performance of virtuous actions, which are prescribed by scripture, are regarded, as improper by the people of tāmasika intellect. Thus, they regard 'Dharma' as 'Adharma'.

People of tāmasika intellect, believe that Brāhmaṇas (the people of the priest class), who are law makers, treated themselves as superior to other people, and bound others by different rules and laws. They believe, that India cannot progress, so long as people follow the ordinance of scriptures and the sacred books. According to them, Dharma consists in going against scriptural injunctions, and social decorum.

'Sarvārthānviparītāṁśca'—They regard the body, as the self, and the perishable world, as real. They are non-believers. They regard themselves, more learned than and superior, even to saints. Instead of eternal bliss, they hanker after mundane pleasures, considering these as real. They look upon vices, as virtues, and the wrong, as right. They view all things, in a perverted light.

'Buddhiḥ sā pārtha tāmasī'—Intellect enveloped in darkness, conceives as right what is wrong, bad what is good, and sees all things perverted—such intellect is tāmasika, which leads one to infernal regions (Gītā 14/18). So a person, who wants to attain salvation, should renounce, this tāmasika intellect, totally.

Appendix—He, whose intellect is Tāmasī, in his mundane dealings and in the spiritual field, sees all things perverted. The present time is its living example, as—'butchering animals' is said to be 'the production of meat'. The deadly sin of 'abortion' or the 'destruction of the productive power of a man' is called 'family welfare'. The 'licentious behaviour' of women and the 'destruction of their ethical propriety' is called 'freedom of women'. In the past a woman was the mistress of the house, now she is employed in offices and shops etc., and has to work under the control of males, which is known as 'freedom of women'. Thus 'dependence' is known as 'independence'. 'Moral degradation' is given the name 'progress'. 'Beastly behaviour' is regarded as a 'mark of civilization'. 'Righteousness' is called 'communalism' and what is contrary to Dharma viz., 'unrighteousness' is called 'secularism'. When the time for one's ruin is near, then such a perverted and Tāmasī intellect evolves—'vināśakāle viparīta buddhiḥ', 'buddhināśāt praṇaśyati' (Gītā 2/63).

Link:—The Lord now defines Sāttvika firmness (steadiness).

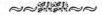

धृत्या यया धारयते मनःप्राणेन्द्रियक्रियाः ।
योगेनाव्यभिचारिण्या धृतिः सा पार्थ सात्त्विकी ॥ ३३ ॥

dhṛtyā yayā dhārayate manaḥprāṇendriyakriyāḥ
yogenāvyabhicāriṇyā dhṛtiḥ sā pārtha sāttvikī

The unwavering firmness equipped with Yoga (equanimity) by which, one controls the activities of the mind, the life-breath and the senses, that is sāttvika firmness, (firmness of the nature of goodness). 33

Comment:—

'Dhṛtyā yayā dhārayate manaḥprāṇendriyakriyāḥ yogenāvyabhicāriṇyā'—Equanimity or even-mindedness in worldly profit and loss, victory and defeat, pleasure and pain, honour and dishonour, success and failure, is called, Yoga.

When a man besides having a goal of God-realization, has desire for success, fame, honour and mundane, as well as, heavenly pleasure etc., his firmness is wavering. But when his only aim is God-realization, his firmness is without swerve.

The faculty of resolutely maintaining one's beliefs, principles, aim, feelings, actions, inclinations and ideas etc., is called 'Dhṛti' (firmness). A man, by unwavering firmness, equipped with Yoga (equanimity) controls the activities of mind, the life-breath and senses.

When the mind becomes free, from different kinds of thoughts that come out of attachment or aversion, and when it gets fixed on one object, where it ought to be fixed, it means control over activities of the mind by unwavering firmness.

When, the process of exhalation and inhalation is regulated, and becomes even, activities of life-breaths, are said to be controlled by unwavering firmness.

When senses of sound, touch, form, taste and smell do not get attached, to the sense-objects but remain under control, the activities of senses are said to be, controlled by unwavering firmness.

'Dhṛtiḥ sā pārtha sāttvikī'—Unwavering firmness by which one controls the activities of mind, the life-breaths and senses, that firmness, is Sāttvikī.

Appendix—The embodied soul is a fragment of God, therefore a man's (the Self's) inclination to anyone else besides God is 'vyabhicāra' (adultery); and to be inclined only to God is 'avyabhicāra' (to be unadultered). The dhṛti (firmness) which has an inclination only to God is unadulterated (unwavering) firmness.

Link:—Now the Lord defines, Rājasika firmness.

यया तु धर्मकामार्थान्धृत्या धारयतेऽर्जुन।
प्रसङ्गेन फलाकाङ्क्षी धृतिः सा पार्थ राजसी॥ ३४॥

yayā tu dharmakāmārthāndhṛtyā dhārayate'rjuna
prasaṅgena phalākāṅkṣī dhṛtiḥ sā pārtha rājasī

That, O Pārtha (Arjuna), by which, because of attachment and desire for reward, one holds fast to dharma (duty), pleasure and wealth—that firmness, is rājasika (of the nature of passion). 34

Comment:—

'Yayā tu dharmakāmārthāndhṛtyā dhārayate'rjuna'—A man, by passionate firmness performs virtuous acts, to reap their fruits, in the form of wealth and pleasure.

On special occasions, he offers charity, goes on a pilgrimage and arranges religious programmes, such as loud chanting etc., of divine names in order to get their reward. So he holds fast to Dharma (Duty) for reward.*

He wants to enjoy mundane pleasure, and believes that a man's life without pleasure, is meaningless. Thus, he holds fast to pleasure.

He believes, that wealth is part and parcel of a man's life.

*If one holds fast to Dharma (duty) for wealth and spends money for Dharma, both of them enhance each other. But if one holds fast to Dharma and spends wealth in order to reap its fruit, after bearing fruit both of them perish.

Without wealth, (money), no virtuous actions (Dharma), are possible. All functions are organised, by spending money. It is money, which gives status and position, to a man. It begets respect and honour. Without money, none is respected. So a man, should hoard as much wealth as he can. According to him, a man wins name, fame and honour because of wealth and nothing is possible, without it. Thus he holds fast to wealth.

'Prasaṅgena phalākāṅkṣī dhṛtiḥ sā pārtha rājasī'—Whatever virtuous actions, out of too much passion (attachment), a Rājasika man performs, according to ordinance of scriptures, he performs these with a desire for reward, in the form of pleasure, honour, name and praise etc., worldly and heavenly enjoyments, hereafter. The firmness of such people, who are too much attached to the world, and who have a desire for reward, is rājasika.

Link:—Now, the Lord defines Tāmasika firmness (Firmness of the mode of ignorance).

यया स्वप्नं भयं शोकं विषादं मदमेव च।
न विमुञ्चति दुर्मेधा धृतिः सा पार्थ तामसी॥ ३५॥

yayā svapnaṁ bhayaṁ śokaṁ viṣādaṁ madameva ca
na vimuñcati durmedhā dhṛtiḥ sā pārtha tāmasī

That, by which a fool does not give up sleep, fear, grief, depression (despair) and conceit (arrogance) that Dhṛti (firmness), O Arjuna, is tāmasika, (of the nature of ignorance). 35

Comment:—

'Yayā svapnaṁ bhayaṁ śokaṁ viṣādaṁ madameva ca na vimuñcati durmedhā dhṛtiḥ sā pārtha tāmasī'—Because of Tāmasika Dhṛti (firmness), a man does not give up excessive sleep, external and internal fear, grief, depression and conceit, but he remains engrossed in these. He is sometimes, addicted to too much sleep, and indolence, he at times entertains fear, because of death, disease, dishonour, defame, insult, ill health and loss of wealth etc., he is off and on grieved and depressed, while other times he is self-conceited, because of favourable circumstances.

Besides the above-mentioned evil propensities, other evils, such as indolence, pride, hypocrisy, aversion, jealousy, violence and usurpation etc., can be included in the expression 'eva ca' (and also).

The Dhṛti (firmness) which does not give up sleep, fear, grief etc., is tāmasika.

In the thirty-third and thirty-fourth verses, the Lord by the term 'Dhārayate' means, that sāttvika and rājasika persons, hold fast to the sāttvika and rājasika Dhṛti (firmness) respectively. But in the case of a tāmasika person, it is not mentioned, that he holds fast to tāmasika firmness, because a Tāmasika person out of ignorance, and delusion, is naturally so much engrossed in sleep fear, grief and despair etc., that he does not give these evils up.

Out of these three kinds of Dhṛti (firmness), in the Rājasika and Tāmasika firmness there is mention of a doer by the terms 'Phalākāṅkṣī' and 'Durmedhā', while the doer has not been mentioned, in the Sāttvika firmness, because in it the doer remains detached, and he has no sense of doership, while, in the rājasika and tāmasika firmness, the doer remains attached.

An Important Fact

This human life, has predominance of discrimination, which is clearly revealed in a Sāttvika person, and so the only aim of his life is to realize God. In a Rājasika person, because of dominance of attachment for mundane things and pleasure, this discrimination, is not clearly revealed, yet by his feeble discrimination, he wants to win pleasure, praise and honour etc., worldly and heavenly pleasure, hereafter, and he does not act, against decorum. But a tāmasika person's discrimination is completely veiled, and he remains engrossed in tāmasika propensities, such as sleep, fear and grief etc.

In spiritual discipline, actions do not play such an important role, as aim does. Actions, thoughts and trance performed, by physical, subtle and causal bodies respectively, are all activities of bodies. But the aim, that he has to realize God, is decided by the self. As is the aim, so are the actions. The aim, can be fixed by Sāttvika intellect, while a man holds firm to it, by Sāttvika firmness. So, from the thirty-third verse to the thirty-fifth verse, the Lord by addressing Arjuna as 'Pārtha' six times, warns him, regarding him as a representative of strivers, that without worrying about mundane persons and objects, he should hold fast, to his aim, by giving up rājasika and tāmasika propensities.

Appendix—The man, who is of the conviction that the evil propensities such as (excessive) sleep, fear, grief, depression and conceit etc., can't be removed, is evil minded. Such type of people don't pay any heed to give up evils, they don't have the courage to give them up but they own them naturally.

Excessive sleep is an obstacle to the progress of a striver. Necessary and moderate (regulated) sleep is not an obstacle (Gītā 6/16-17).

Link:—A man wants to perform actions, to gain happiness (joy). So the Lord, in the next four verses, classifies happiness under, three heads.

सुखं त्विदानीं त्रिविधं शृणु मे भरतर्षभ।
अभ्यासाद्रमते यत्र दुःखान्तं च निगच्छति॥ ३६॥
यत्तदग्रे विषमिव परिणामेऽमृतोपमम्।
तत्सुखं सात्त्विकं प्रोक्तमात्मबुद्धिप्रसादजम्॥ ३७॥

sukhaṁ tvidānīṁ trividhaṁ śṛṇu me bharatarṣabha
abhyāsādramate yatra duḥkhāntaṁ ca nigacchati
yattadagre viṣamiva pariṇāme'mṛtopamam
tatsukhaṁ sāttvikaṁ proktamātmabuddhiprasādajam

And now hear from Me, O Arjuna, of the three kinds of

happiness, in which one rejoices by practice and surely achieves, the end of pain. That happiness, which is like poison at first due to worldly attachment, but as nectar at the end. That which springs from the placidity of mind, brought about by meditation on God, is said to be, sāttvika. 36-37

Comment:—

'Bharatarṣabha'—The Lord addresses Arjuna as Bharatarṣabha, the best of all the persons in the Bharata family, to emphasize the fact, that it is easy for him to overcome the rājasika and tāmasika pleasures. He has overcome, the rājasika pleasure, because he rejected the offer of a beautiful heavenly damsel named, Urvasī. Similarly, he has overcome the tāmasika pleasure of sleep, and he is called 'Guḍākeśa', the conqueror of sleep.

'Sukhaṁ tu idānīm'—Having classified knowledge, action, agent, intellect and firmness, under three heads, the Lord, by using the term 'Tu', declares, that happiness is also of three kinds. A fact needs special attention here. The main stumbling block to spiritual progress or God-realization, is the desire for pleasure.

Even sāttvika happiness, if anyone is attached to it, leads to bondage. If a striver, is attached to happiness which he receives out of adoration, meditation and even trance, it leads him to bondage, by delaying him in God-realization (Gītā 14/6). Now, the question arises, whether eternal bliss of God-realization should also not be enjoyed. In fact, eternal bliss is not enjoyed, it is experienced or felt through self (Gītā 5/21; 6/21, 28). If a striver, does not enjoy happiness derived out of spiritual discipline, he experiences, that eternal bliss, naturally. The Lord has used the term 'Tu', to divert the strivers' attention, to eternal bliss.

Here the Lord by using the term 'Idānīm', means that Arjuna wanted to know the true nature of renunciation (Sannyāsa) and the Discipline of Action (Tyāga); so in response to his query, the Lord, classified abandonment, knowledge, action, agent and firmness each, under three heads. But the aim of all of them, is to derive pleasure (happiness). So, the Lord classifies happiness under three heads.

'Trividhaṁ śṛṇu me'—People remain so much engrossed in rājasika and tāmasika pleasure, that they cannot imagine that sāttvika happiness, transcends them. So the Lord, asks Arjuna to choose Sāttvika joy (happiness), by rejecting rājasika and the tāmasika ones. Sāttvika joy is conducive to God-realization, while Rājasika and Tāmasika pleasure by entangling a man in the world, lead him to a fall.

'Abhyāsādramate yatra'—In Sāttvika happiness, one rejoices by practice. An ordinary man cannot rejoice in it, without practice. In rājasika and tāmasika pleasure, there is no need of any practice. Beings are naturally attracted to rājasika and tāmasika pleasure. The senses, are attracted towards sense-objects, mind and intellect are attracted towards pleasure and prosperity, and there is an inclination towards sleep, in the state of tiredness, naturally. All beings like pleasure, born of sense-contacts, pride, praise and sleep etc. Even dogs get pleased, when they are honoured, and displeased when they are dishonoured.

Now, the question arises, what sort of practice is required to gain sāttvika happiness. Hearing, thinking, study of scriptures and removal of the rājasika and tāmasika inclinations etc., are included in the term, 'practice'.

A striver, should practise adoration and meditation etc., but should not enjoy them. This is the meaning, which the Lord wants to convey, by the expression 'Abhyāsādramate'.

'Duḥkhāntaṁ ca nigacchati'—By practice, as a man develops interest in and attraction for, Sāttvika happiness, his sorrow comes to an end and he gains happiness or joy (Gītā 2/65).

The Lord, by using the conjunction, 'Ca' (and) means to convey that a striver cannot get rid of pain or sorrow, so long as, he rejoices in Sāttvika happiness. The reason is, that even Sāttvika happiness is born of placidity of mind and whatever is born, is perishable. So, how can the perishable, bring sorrow to an end? A striver, instead of being attached to sāttvika happiness, should transcend it. By doing so, his sorrows come to an end.

'Ātmabuddhiprasādajam'—The mind, instead of attaching importance to honour, praise, pleasure and prosperity, thinks only of God. This thinking gives placidity of mind (Gītā 2/64). From placidity of mind accrues sāttvika happiness. It means that when a man being totally detached from mundane contact born pleasure, gets his mind, merged in meditation on God, the happiness experienced is said to be sāttvika.

'Yattadagre viṣamiva'—By the terms 'Yat' (which) and 'tat' (that), the Lord means to convey, that Sāttvika happiness, has not yet been experienced or felt. A striver, has the only aim, to gain it, but he experiences rājasika and tāmasika pleasures. So he faces difficulty in abandoning rājasika and tāmasika pleasure, because he has been enjoying these, since several births. But, he has not yet relished Sāttvika happiness. So having no real experience of Sāttvika happiness, he initially finds it most unpleasant, like poison.

In fact, Sāttvika happiness initially, is not like poison, but it is unpleasant like poison, to abandon rājasika and tāmasika pleasure. As a boy, takes more interest in play and recreation, than in studies in the beginning, because he does not know the importance of studies. But, when he goes on studying and gets success in examination, he becomes interested in studies, and then he attaches more importance to it. Similarly, people, who are attached to tāmasika and rājasika pleasure feel sāttvika happiness, like poison. But to those strivers, who are not attached to mundane pleasure, who have an inclination for the study of scriptures, for good company, loud chanting of divine name, meditation and adoration etc., and whose knowledge, actions, intellect and firmness, are sāttvika, this happiness is like nectar, to them from the very beginning. It is not unpleasant, taxing and irksome to them.

'Pariṇāme'mṛtopamam'—A striver, develops the modes of

goodness through spiritual discipline. When the mode of goodness is predominant, the light of wisdom shines in the mind and senses, and good virtues, such as peace and immutability etc., are revealed.* It is because of these virtues, that it is like nectar, at the end. If this happiness is not enjoyed, a striver, attains eternal bliss (Gītā 5/21). Sāttvika happiness is like nectar, at the end because by gaining it, a man transcends rājasika and tāmasika pleasure and his affinity with matter is renounced, which leads him to God-realization.

'Tatsukhaṁ sāttvikaṁ proktam'—Happiness which is gained by good company, study of the scriptures, loud chanting, meditation and adoration etc., is neither like pleasure gained by honour, praise and prosperity etc., nor like the pleasure which one derives out of heedlessness, indolence and excessive sleep etc., but it is happiness gained by having affinity with God. So it has been said to be, Sāttvika (of the nature of goodness).

Appendix—In the fourteenth chapter, the Lord declared that Sāttvika happiness binds the Self—'sukhasaṅgena badhnāti' (14/6), but here He declares that by Sāttvika happiness, sorrows come to an end. It means that if a striver enjoys the Sāttvika happiness, it binds him (self) viz., does not let him rise above the three modes. But if he does not enjoy it, then by it, his sorrows end. By enjoying happiness, sorrows don't come to an end. Having renounced enjoyment (pleasure), Yoga is attained. He should remain unconcerned and detached from the Sāttvika happiness. The attachment leads the striver to Rajoguṇa which binds him. When Sattvaguṇa is mixed with Rajoguṇa, it is conducive to a downfall (ruin).

The Sāttvika happiness appears like poison initially because a striver does not attach importance to discrimination. A Rājasa person does not value discrimination. Therefore appearance of the Sāttvika happiness initially like poison is because of Rajoguṇa.

* The three modes—of goodness, of passion and of ignorance abide in the mind unrevealed. They are known by their distinctive characteristics as described from the eleventh to the thirteenth verses of the fourteenth chapter.

It means that Sāttvika happiness is not painful but because of the effect of Rajoguṇa in one's intellect, the Sāttvika happiness appears to be painful like poison. He aims at Sāttvika happiness but inwardly he is passionate (Rājasa).

Link:—The Lord now defines, Rājasika happiness.

विषयेन्द्रियसंयोगाद्यत्तदग्रेऽमृतोपमम् ।
परिणामे विषमिव तत्सुखं राजसं स्मृतम् ॥ ३८ ॥

viṣayendriyasaṁyogādyattadagre'mṛtopamam
pariṇāme viṣamiva tatsukhaṁ rājasaṁ smṛtam

Happiness, which is derived from the contact of senses with their objects and which is like nectar at first but as poison at the end—such happiness, is said to be rājasika. 38

Comment:—

'Viṣayendriyasaṁyogāt'—Happiness, which is derived from contact of senses, with their objects, does not need any practice. Every being, including a beast, a bird, an insect or a germ, derives this happiness, without doing any practice. A man, since his childhood has been pleased in favourable, and displeased in unfavourable, circumstances. So, in this passionate happiness, there is no need for practice.

'Yattadagre'mṛtopamam'—The Lord declares, that passionate happiness, is like nectar, at first. It means, that when a passionate man wishes to enjoy such happiness, and when he begins to enjoy it, he derives a lot of happiness, but when he goes on enjoying it, the joy is gradually reduced and then he develops disinclination, towards it. Even then, if he goes on enjoying it, he experiences, a burning sensation and pain. Therefore, it is said that happiness appears like nectar only in its initial stage.

Further, these sensual pleasures seem very pleasant, when people hear of these and when mind is attracted, towards them. But when they are enjoyed, they are not, so pleasant. So in the Gītā, it is declared—When unwise people, hear of heavenly pleasure, they get deeply attached to these (Gītā 2/42) and hanker after them. But when they actually enjoy heavenly pleasure, they do not find these, much pleasant and attractive.

'Pariṇāme viṣamiva'—Sensual pleasures, seem very pleasant at first, but when a person goes on enjoying them, these have bitter and evil consequences, and so those pleasures turn into poison. These sensual pleasures, lead a man to eighty-four lac forms, of lives, prisons, hell and sorrow because the fruit of rājasika action, is sorrow (Gītā 14/16).

It is because of passion (attachment), that people have to suffer pain. A man, who was rich in the past, but has become poor now, has to undergo more suffering, than a person, who has always been poor. Similarly, a person who tasted different kinds of dishes, feels a shortage, when he gets a meagre meal. This feeling of shortage, causes pain.

A man, makes efforts to fulfil his desire. He may either succeed or fail in fulfilling it. If he succeeds, it gives birth to other desires but if he fails, he feels sad and dejected, and again tries to satisfy it. Thus a cycle of desire goes on, without an end their consequences like poison, are bitter.

Now, a question arises here that persons who enjoy passionate pleasure should die, like men who take poison. The answer is, that passionate happiness, does not kill a man, as poison does, but a person develops disinclination for it, as he has for poison. It means, that passionate happiness, is not poison, but is like poison.

Passionate happiness is like poison, because it goes on killing a man for several births, whereas poison, kills only once. A man, possessing passionate happiness cannot get peace, even in heaven, because there also he is jealous of his superiors and equals, and is proud of his achievement, after seeing those, who are inferior to him. Moreover, they have to return to the world of mortals, when their merit, is exhausted (Gītā 9/21). Again, after coming to the mortal world, they perform virtuous actions and reap their fruits, in heaven. Thus, they follow, a cycle of birth and death (9/21). If, because of their attachment, they are engaged in sinful acts, they have to take birth, in eighty-four lac forms of lives and go to hell and then follow a cycle of birth and death, endlessly. So this happiness has been called, like poison, at the end.

'Tatsukhaṁ rājasaṁ smṛtam'—In the thirty-seventh verse, the Lord used the term 'Proktam', for Sāttvika happiness, while he has used the verb 'Smṛtam' here. It means, that a man knows that the result of Rājasika happiness, is sorrow or pain, yet he hankers after it, because of his attachment to it. If he thinks of its consequences, he will not be entangled, in rājasika happiness. Moreover, in scripture and history, there are several examples, which remind that rājasika happiness, results in pain or sorrow. So the term 'smṛtam', has been used to remind him, of its evil consequences.

A man of sāttvika nature, instead of paying attention, to instantaneous happiness, thinks of its result, while a man of rājasika nature, instead of thinking of the result, is engaged in instantaneous happiness. So, he remains entangled, in the worldly snare. The Lord declares, "Pleasures which are born of sense-contacts, are verily, sources of pain, though these appear as enjoyable, to worldly minded people, at first" (Gītā 5/22). So a striver, instead of being entangled in the rājasika happiness, should develop dispassion, for the world.

Appendix—The happiness which is derived from sense-contacts is like nectar at the beginning but is like poison at the end. An indiscriminative person attaches importance to the beginning stage. The beginning does not persist forever but the desire for sensual pleasures ever remains which is the root of all sufferings. But a discriminative person instead of perceiving the beginning, perceives its result, therefore he does not get attached to those pleasures—'na teṣu ramate budhaḥ' (Gītā 5/22). Only a man has got the ability to perceive the result. The man who does not see the result is of a beastly nature.

In fact the beginning (union) is not important but the end (disunion) is important. A man wants the happiness of the beginning but it does not stay because union changes into disunion—this is the rule. The beginning is transient but the end is eternal. The desire for the transient causes sufferings. The disunion of the entire universe is eternal. But because of the Rājasī disposition, union appears to be pleasant. If a man does not relish the pleasure at the beginning, he will ever be totally free from sorrows (sufferings). 'Having an eye on the beginning' is 'bhoga' and 'seeing the consequences' is 'Yoga'.

The pleasure, which appears by the union of the world, is mixed with pain. But by being disunited from the world, there is constant bliss which transcends both pleasure and pain (sorrows).

Link:—The Lord now defines, Tāmasika happiness.

यदग्रे चानुबन्धे च सुखं मोहनमात्मनः।
निद्रालस्यप्रमादोत्थं तत्तामसमुदाहृतम्॥ ३९॥

yadagre cānubandhe ca sukhaṁ mohanamātmanaḥ
nidrālasyapramādotthaṁ tattāmasamudāhṛtam

Happiness which deludes the self both at the beginning and at the end, and which arises from sleep, indolence and carelessness, is declared to be, tāmasika. 39

Comment:—

'Nidrālasyapramādottham'—Excessive attachment, transforms itself into a mode of ignorance, which is called delusion. It is because of delusion, that a man wants to sleep for a long time, even though he does not get sound sleep. Without sound sleep, he ramains lethargic and he goes on dreaming. His time is wasted. But a man, of tāmasika nature, derives happiness out of this sort of sleep.

A man of the mood of ignorance, remains indolent. He wastes

his time in idleness and goes on postponing, even obligatory duties. He derives pleasure, out of this indolence. Being idle his senses and mind etc., become inactive, and he only thinks of futile worldly affairs, which lead him to pain, sorrow, worry and disquietude.

He becomes careless, and the mode of ignorance, is enhanced. He does not perform his obligatory duties, but indulges in idle pursuits, such as smoking, drinking, displays etc., and evil, such as theft, robbery, falsehood, fraud, forgery and in the forbidden food etc.

Such a person, derives pleasures out of indolence, as well as heedlessness. It is because of this nature, labourers want to get full wages, without performing their duty honestly and sincerely, physicians charge fees from patients again and again, without giving them proper treatment, and milkmen, mix water in milk, though they charge the cost of the pure milk. This, sinful heedlessness, leads them to hell.

Heedlessness, veils discrimination, while sleep and indolence, covers the mode of goodness. When discrimination is veiled, heedlessness is revealed, and when light is covered, indolence and sleep are exposed. A tāmasika person, derives pleasure out of sleep, indolence and heedlessness. So tāmasika happiness is said to arise, from these three.

An Important Fact

Sleep is of two kinds—moderate and excessive.

(1) Moderate sleep—sleep provides rest, purity and freshness. It provides strength and zeal, for mundane, as well as, spiritual activities. Sleep is not a defect, it is essential (Gītā 6/17) and provides one freshness and energy to perform mundane and spiritual acts promptly.

Sleep is essential for a striver, for his invigoration. A striver, free from worldly pursuits gets sleep, very soon. He who is engrossed in worldly thoughts, cannot get sleep quickly. This proves, that affinity with the world, does not allow a person to enjoy sleep. In sound sleep, connection with the world snaps, and one gets linked with God. Thus sound sleep, gives vitality and energy to be engaged, in spiritual practice.

Sleep is tāmasika. It contains two elements—unconsciousness and rest. The former, causes delusion which is to be shunned, while the latter, is moderate which is to be adopted. Good strivers, through spiritual discipline, can get much rest and happiness, even during wakefulness, because they remain fixed in God, without thinking of worldly affairs. If they do not get attached, even to rest, and happiness, they attain God-realization.

Strivers, should not go to bed, for rest but they should think that they are going to devote that time, in adoration and devotion, by lying down on a cot, as they adore the Lord, during a day, by performing various duties.

(2) Excessive sleep—Excessive sleep, makes a man indolent and he feels drowsy, all the time. In the eighth verse of the fourteenth chapter, the Lord used first heedlessness, then indolence and finally sleep, while He has reversed the order here. The reason is, that there is a link how they bind all embodied beings, but here the context is, how they degrade, a man. As far as binding force, is concerned, the first and foremost position, goes to heedlessness. It conduces a man to perform forbidden actions, which ruin him. Indolence hinders a man, from performing virtuous actions. So, it has been given, the second place. As far as sleep is concerned, it is only excessive sleep, not a moderate one, which binds a man. So, the third place has been allowed to sleep. But in this verse, the order is changed, because moderate sleep, does not cause harm and it is only excessive sleep, which is conducive to ruin. Indolence leads more to ruin than sleep, while heedlessness contributes the most. Excessive sleep will lead a man to lower births, while indolence and heedlessness, will lead him to hell*

*Heedlessness conduces a man to undertake idle pursuits for the sake of diversion. But when passion (attachment) joins heedlessness, both give

by depriving him, of his discrimination.

'Yadagre cānubandhe ca sukhaṁ mohanamātmanaḥ'—Happiness, which arises, from sleep, indolence and heedlessness, deludes the self both at the beginning, and at the end. Beings lose their discrimination, under the influence of this happiness. So birds, beasts, moths and insects etc., do not think, what ought to be done, at the beginning and also do not think of consequences. Such happiness, is declared to be tāmasika.

An Important Fact

(1) Prakṛti (matter) and Puruṣa (Soul or Spirit), are two different entities, and both of them are without beginning. The knowledge, by which one knows their difference, is also beginningless. Knowledge (discrimination), is possessed by Puruṣa (Soul or Spirit or Self), not by Prakṛti. But, when Puruṣa disregarding this discrimination, assumes affinity with Prakṛti, because of this affinity, attachment arises.*

When attachment, remains in its subtle form, there is dominance of discrimination. But when attachment enhances, discrimination is covered. But if discrimination, is revealed properly, attachment perishes and then, a person is called, liberated. It is because of attachment, that a man runs after worldly pleasure, born of Prakṛti. If he wants to gain sāttvika happiness, he faces difficulty in renouncing rājasika, and tāmasika happiness. But when attachment perishes, the poison-like happiness, turns into nectarine happiness. It is because of attachment, that rājasika (passionate) happiness, seems like nectar at first, but like poison at the end. Attachment to passionate happiness, leads a man to endless pain and sorrow.

birth to desire. It is out of desire that a man commits several sins and crimes whose consequences are very horrible.

* Because of attachment several evils are born in Prakṛti, not in Puruṣa. A man (Self) by identifying himself with Prakṛti (Matter) assumes the evils of Prakṛti in him and so he has to be an enjoyer (Bhogī). But when he realizes that the evils appear and disappear while he remains the same without any modification, he becomes equanimous (a Yogī).

When this attachment is transformed into the mode of ignorance, a man, wastes his time in sleep, indolence, and he indulges in idle pursuits, by giving up his duty. But a tāmasika person, derives happiness out of it. So it deludes the self, both at the beginning and at end.

(2) Actually the kaleidoscopic world, does not exist, while God, Who is Truth, Knowledge and Bliss consolidated, and Who is the base and illuminator of the unreal, always exists. Man (soul or self), being a fragment of God, is also truth, knowledge and bliss consolidated. But, when he has desire for the unreal, his bliss, becomes veiled. But, as soon as, he abandons desire, his natural bliss is revealed.

When sāttvika intellect, merges in eternal bliss, it becomes pure. Natural bliss, which is experienced by pure intellect, is called sāttvika happiness. When man's affinity with this pure intellect, is renounced, there remains, natural bliss, only. Bliss is named sāttvika happiness, because of its affinity with sāttvika intellect, otherwise, it is nothing, besides eternal bliss.

When a man has a desire to gain something, the mind and the intellect get attached to it. But, as soon as, he gains it, his attachment or attraction is abandoned, and he becomes free from pain, which he suffered because of its deficit and he realizes the reflection of the eternal self-evident bliss, immediately. In fact, he does not gain happiness, by acquiring a thing, but by being free from attachment to it. But, a rājasika person, out of ignorance, thinks that it is so, because he has got the thing. Union, with the thing is external, while happiness is, something internal. So, how can external union cause, internal happiness? The fact is, that internal happiness is derived by renouncing internal affinity, with a thing. It means, that when the thing is secured, internal affinity with the thing, is renounced. As soon as, this affinity is renounced, eternal natural bliss, is experienced.

During sleep, when intellect merges with the mode of ignorance, a man forgets all things and objects, of his wakeful state. Their memory, is cause of pain. So, by forgetting these he derives happiness, out of sleep. But, because of the impurity of intellect, he does not experience natural bliss. So, the happiness which arises from sleep, is called 'tāmasika', (of the mode of ignorance).*

It means, that a sāttvika person derives happiness, by having disinclination for the world, when his intellect merges in the self; a rājasika person, by abandonment of attachment to things, while a tāmasika person, by forgetting his duty and indulging in idle pursuits. Thus, natural bliss is veiled, by assumed affinity with, the unreal. But happiness experienced, by all the Sāttvika, Rājasika and Tāmasika people, is nothing, but a reflection of the eternal natural, bliss. So, if we renounce attachment to the three kinds of happinesses, we may progress, spiritually. So a striver should abandon, the three kinds of happinesses.

Appendix—A Tāmasa person is endowed with delusion—'tamastvajñānajaṁ viddhi mohanaṁ sarvadehinām' (Gītā 14/8). Delusion is an obstacle in the use of discrimination. Because of the Tāmasī disposition, discrimination is not aroused. Therefore the discrimination of a Tāmasī person, because of delusion disappears, so he does not see the beginning or the end at all.

Link:—The Lord, classified knowledge, action and happiness, under three heads, characterized by the three modes of nature. In

* During sleep a man's intellect gets deluded i.e., it becomes unconscious. The man derives happiness, by forgetting the world. So this happiness is called Tāmasika. If intellect with senses is not deluded, it becomes a state of trance, which provides rest. A man can transcend the three modes of nature only, if he is not attached to this happiness derived out of trance.

Prakṛti is active and kaleidoscopic, while God is eternal, calm, immutable, flawless, steady and He does not undergo any modifications. During sleep, a man gets established in Him. But as his mind is attracted towards pleasure and prosperity, after waking, he hankers after prosperity and pleasure. Thus because of his attachment to prosperity and pleasure he cannot remain established either in God or the self. If one renounces this attachment, he can remain established, in the self naturally.

the next verse, He winds up the topic, by declaring that all the objects of this creation, are classified under these three heads, characterized by three modes of nature.

न तदस्ति पृथिव्यां वा दिवि देवेषु वा पुनः ।
सत्त्वं प्रकृतिजैर्मुक्तं यदेभिः स्यात्त्रिभिर्गुणैः ॥ ४० ॥

na tadasti pṛthivyāṁ vā divi deveṣu vā punaḥ
sattvaṁ prakṛtijairmuktaṁ yadebhiḥ syāttribhirguṇaiḥ

There is no being on earth nor even among the gods in heaven, that is free, from the three modes, born of nature (prakṛti). 40

Comment:—

[At the beginning of this chapter, Arjuna desired to know severally, the true nature of renunciation (Sannyāsa) and Tyāga (Karmayoga). So the Lord, first described Karmayoga. Winding up the topic the Lord declared, "Pleasant, unpleasant and mixed—threefold, is the fruit of action, accruing to those who have not relinquished the fruit. But there is none whatever, for those who have relinquished the fruit." Having declared so, in the thirteenth verse, by beginning the topic of Sāṅkhyayoga (Discipline of Knowledge), He explained five factors, which contribute to the accomplishment of action. In the sixteenth and seventeenth verses, He decried those, who look upon the self, as doer and praised those, who are free from egoistic notion. In the eighteenth verse, He mentioned the factors, which motivate action and also the constituents of actions, while the self is free, from incitement and constituents. Then, He classified knowledge, action, agent, intellect, dhṛti and happiness into three kinds. While describing the three kinds of happiness, He explained the superiority of sāttvika happiness to rājasika and tāmasika, though all the three are derived by having affinity with Prakṛti. But, the real joy which transcends, the three modes of nature, is unique and supreme (Gītā 6/21).

Even the sāttvika happiness, is not eternal, because the Lord has declared, that it springs from placidity of mind and whatever is born, is not eternal. The Lord means that a striver, has to rise above this sāttvika happiness, also. By transcending the nature and its three modes, he has to realize the real bliss of God or the self. So the Lord declares—]

'Na tadasti pṛthivyāṁ vā divi deveṣu vā punaḥ'—Here, the term 'Pṛthivyām', denotes mortal worlds, as well as, other lower worlds, than the earth. 'Divi' denotes heaven, 'Deveṣu', denotes all beings, such as men, gods, demons, devils, birds, beasts, insects, trees and plants etc., whether moving or non-moving, while the expression 'Vā punaḥ', denotes infinite universes. It means, that either in the celestial world, or in the middle region or in the terrestrial world, in infinite universes, there is no object or being, free from these three modes of nature. All of these are connected with the three modes of nature.

'Sattvaṁ prakṛtijairmuktaṁ yadebhiḥ syāttribhirguṇaiḥ'—Nature and its evolutes, are of three modes and are ever changing. A man, is bound by having connection with these and he is liberated, by renouncing a connection with them, because the self is pure and it undergoes no modifications. Connection with nature, gives birth to egoism, which makes one dependent, though he feels, that he is independent. An egoistic notion gives birth to attachment and desire etc. Therefore, in fact he becomes dependent on persons and things etc. So, one should be free from the modes, of nature.

A striver, first of all should enhance the mode of goodness by abandoning modes of passion and ignorance. In the mode of goodness also, a man should not be attached to happiness and knowledge, because attachment to them, binds him. So he should transcend the mode of goodness, by abandoning attachment. First, he should mould his life, by possessing sāttvika knowledge, action, intellect, dhṛti and happiness etc., because discrimination (wisdom), remains aroused in them. This discrimination induces him to be free from affinity, with 'Prakrti'. But, finally he should transcend them also, by abandoning attachment for them.

Appendix—In the tenth chapter from the devotion (faith) point of view, the Lord declared that all things originate from Him—'na tadasti vinā yatsyānmayā bhūtaṁ carācaram' (10/39). Here from the view point of knowledge (discrimination), the Lord declares that all beings emanate from the modes born of nature. The reason is that from the view point of a discriminative person the real and the unreal—both exist; but from the viewpoint of a devotee only God exists—'sadasaccāhamarjuna' (Gītā 9/19). In the path of discrimination, the renunciation of the unreal viz., of the modes is important but in devotion relationship with God is important.

An ignorant person, rather than an enlightened soul, holds that there is no being in the universe that is free from the three modes. An enlightened soul has an eye on the Self which is by nature free from guṇas (modes) (Gītā 13/31).

Link:—While discussing the nature of 'Tyāga', the Lord declared, "Abandonment of any duty, that ought to be done, is not right. Its abandonment through ignorance, is declared to be, of the nature of ignorance" (18/7). "He who gives up duty for fear of physical suffering, performs 'Tyāga' of the 'Rājasika' kind (18/8), while he who performs a prescribed duty, as a thing that ought to be done, abandoning attachment and the fruit—his Tyāga is regarded as, Sāttvika" (18/9). "In the Sāṅkhyayoga, while explaining the five factors for accomplishment of actions, the Lord declared, "An action which is obligatory, is performed without attachment, or hate, by one who seeks no reward, is said to be sāttvika" (18/23). The Lord, resumes the topic of obligatory actions (duties), allotted to members of four Varṇas (Castes)—Brāhmaṇa, Kṣatriya, Vaiśya and Śūdra, also of Bhaktiyoga.

ब्राह्मणक्षत्रियविशां शूद्राणां च परन्तप।
कर्माणि प्रविभक्तानि स्वभावप्रभवैर्गुणैः॥४१॥

brāhmaṇakṣatriyaviśāṁ śūdrāṇāṁ ca parantapa
karmāṇi pravibhaktāni svabhāvaprabhavairguṇaiḥ

Of Brāhmaṇas; of Kṣatriyas and Vaiśyas, as also of Śūdras, O conqueror of foes (Arjuna), their respective duties are allocated, in accordance with the modes (guṇas) born of their nature (svabhāva). 41

Comment:—

'Brāhmaṇakṣatriyaviśāṁ śūdrāṇāṁ ca parantapa'—Here, the Brāhmaṇas, the Kṣatriyas and the Vaiśyas are included, in one category, while the Śūdras are put in a different category. The former three are 'Dvijas' (Twice born), as they are eligible for initiation, and so they wear a sacred thread, known as 'Yajñopavīta', while the fourth, is not eligible to wear the sacred thread. For the latter different duties have been allotted, according to their caste, as ordained by scriptures.

'Karmāṇi pravibhaktāni svabhāvaprabhavairguṇaiḥ'— Actions, which a man performs, leave their impressions in his mind, and these impressions, determine his nature. Thus nature which is formed by impressions of actions of innumerable life times, give birth to propensities, of the modes of goodness, of passion and of ignorance. The four castes—Brāhmaṇa, Kṣatriya, Vaiśya and Śūdra, and their obligatory duties, have been allocated according to the propensities of those modes (Gītā 4/13), because a man acts, according to propensities, of the mode he possesses.

An Important Fact

(1)

Actions are of two kinds (i) Those, that enable a being to be born, in high and low wombs (ii) Those, which create desirable and undesirable circumstances, and which have been called, good, evil and mixed, i.e., the threefold fruit, of action, in the Gītā (18/12).

A serious thought, reveals that all actions create desirable and undesirable circumstances. A man born in a high family, receives honour, while a man born in a low family, does not.

But, it is not necessary that the former is always honoured, while the latter always dishonoured. So far as the second type of actions, are concerned, they always create, either desirable or undesirable circumstances.

A man is free, in making proper use of both, the desirable and undesirable circumstances. Those who feel happy in desirable circumstances, and sad in undesirable ones, are ignorant, while those who use these as means for spiritual progress, are wise. The reason is, that this human life has been bestowed upon us, so that we may realize God. So, all the circumstances, are the means to realize Him.

Now the question arises as to how the desirable and undesirable circumstances, are conducive to spiritual progress. The answer is, that in desirable circumstances a striver, should serve others, while in undesirable circumstances, he should give up desire for desirable circumstances. Thus, both of these can serve, as means to progress, spiritually.

(2)

In the scriptures, it is mentioned that virtuous actions lead a being to heaven, evil actions to hell, while an equality of virtuous and evil actions, leads him to human life. It shows, that no man, can be either wholly virtuous or wholly evil. Out of those virtuous and evil actions also, in a certain field, virtues may be more, while in other spheres evils may be more.* Similar is the division of modes. Those who have predominance of the mode of goodness, go to higher regions, those, who have predominance of the mode of passion, go to the middle regions, viz., region of

* As in an examination an examinee may obtain poorer marks in a certain subject and better marks in other subjects. But the result is declared on the base of the aggregate marks. Similarly a man's virtuous actions may be more in one sphere while evil actions may be more in other sphere. It is the aggregate of the two which decides his birth. If the virtues and evils of different persons are equal in different spheres, they should receive happy and sad circumstances equally. But it does not generally happen. Similar is the case with the modes of nature as that of Sāttvika etc.

men, while those having dominance of the mode of ignorance, go to the lower regions. Out of those going to a region, they are again divided into different categories, according to their qualities.

Those who have predominance of the mode of goodness, are born as Brāhmaṇas; those, who have predominance of the mode of passion and the mode of goodness, occupy the secondary place, are born as Kṣatriyas; those, who have predominance of the mode of passion, while the mode of ignorance is secondary, are born as Vaiśyas; and those, with the predominance of the mode of ignorance, are born as Śūdra. Out of these four Varṇas (castes) also, there are Brāhmaṇas of the low and high classes according to their birth. Moreover, favourable and the unfavourable circumstances are also different, in different cases. Similar, is the case in other Varṇas (castes) also. So in the Gītā, it has been declared, that there is no being, in the three worlds that is free from the three modes born, of nature (18/40).

Similar, is the case with animals and birds, etc., also. A cow is regarded as superior to a dog, a donkey or a pig. A pigeon, is regarded as superior to a crow, or a kite. All of these do not get, similar desirable and undesirable circumstances. It means, that among the beings of a region also, there is a lot of difference, in their circumstances etc.

Appendix—In the fourth chapter the Lord declared, 'the four-fold caste (order) (varṇa) was created by Me, according to the modes of their nature and actions'—'guṇakarmavibhāgaśaḥ' (4/13); and here He declares that the respective duties of the four castes have been allocated according to the modes born of their nature—'svabhāvaprabhavairguṇaiḥ'. In the fourth chapter there is mention of the creation of the four 'varṇas'; while here is mention of the duties of the four varṇas. It means that in the fourth chapter the Lord explained that people are born in different castes (Varṇas) according to the modes and actions of the previous birth; while here He explains the respective duties of the people of the four castes, according to the performance of their duties they will meet their end (fate).

Link:—The Lord, now mentions the natural duties of a Brāhmaṇa (a member of the priest class).

शमो दमस्तपः शौचं क्षान्तिरार्जवमेव च।
ज्ञानं विज्ञानमास्तिक्यं ब्रह्मकर्म स्वभावजम्॥ ४२॥

śamo damastapaḥ śaucaṁ kṣāntirārjavameva ca
jñānaṁ vijñānamāstikyaṁ brahmakarma svabhāvajam

Serenity, control of the senses, austerity, purity, forgiveness, uprightness, knowledge (wisdom), experience of the proper performance of sacrifice and belief in God and Vedas etc., these are the duties of a Brāhmaṇa, intrinsic to his nature. 42

Comment:—

'Śamaḥ'—'Śamaḥ' means, control of the mind, freeing it from distractions and concentrating it, on the point, where it should be concentrated.

'Damaḥ'—Control of the senses, withdrawing them from external objects and employing these, where they should be employed, is 'Damaḥ'.

'Tapaḥ'—Austerity of the body, mind and speech, has already been described in the Gītā (17/14—16). Here this term means enduring hardships happily, while discharging one's duties.

'Śaucam'—'Śaucam' means, purity of one's mind, intellect, senses and body, as well as of the activities and food etc.

'Kṣāntiḥ'—Total absence of the spirit of retaliation, even when one is insulted or hurt or pained, in spite of having power to take vengeance is called, forgiveness (Kṣānti).

'Ārjavam'—Simplicity, of the body and speech etc., without having any crookedness, fraud and knavery in the mind, is known uprightness (Ārjavam).

'Jñānam'—Study of Vedas, the scriptures and historical records, and fully grasping their teachings and meanings, as well as, the awareness of what ought to be done and what ought to he refrained from, is 'Jñāna'.

'Vijñānam'—The proper method and observance of religious sacrifice (yajña), according to Vedas and scriptures, is known 'Vijñāna'.

'Āstikyam'—Firm belief in God, the Vedas, the scriptures and life after death, and translation of their teachings into practice, is 'Āstikyam'.

'Brahmakarma svabhāvajam'—A Brāhmaṇa's temperament, is naturally suited to the performance of these above-mentioned duties, such as serenity and self-control etc., he experiences no difficulty in performing them.

A Brāhmaṇa who has the predominance of mode of goodness, whose forefathers have been pure and whose actions of the previous birth, are pure, faces no difficulty in possessing the above-mentioned, nine qualities. In his life, the actions of earning livelihood occupy a secondary place. As far as, the people of other three Varṇas (castes), are concerned, because of predominance of the modes of passion and ignorance, their actions, of earning their livelihood also, are included, in natural actions. Therefore, in the Gītā, in the duties of a Brāhmaṇa, only actions which involve these qualities, not those of livelihood, have been included.

Appendix—If the Varṇa tradition has been properly followed, a Brāhmaṇa naturally possesses these qualities. But if a hybrid is born viz., if there is an inter-mixture of castes, then the Brāhmaṇas don't naturally possess these qualities, there is deviation in those qualities.

In the preceding verse the expression 'svabhāva prabhavairguṇaiḥ' was used, therefore here the Lord mentions 'svabhāvaja karma'. In the formation of nature (temperament) the first importance goes to birth and then the company a person keeps, is important. By company, by the study of books (self-study) and by practice etc., the nature changes.

Link:—The Lord now mentions the natural duties of a Kṣatriya.

शौर्यं तेजो धृतिर्दाक्ष्यं युद्धे चाप्यपलायनम्।
दानमीश्वरभावश्च क्षात्रं कर्म स्वभावजम्॥ ४३ ॥

śauryaṁ tejo dhṛtirdākṣyaṁ yuddhe cāpyapalāyanam
dānamīśvarabhāvaśca kṣātraṁ karma svabhāvajam

Heroism, radiance, firmness, resourcefulness (dexterity), not fleeing from battle, generosity, and authoritative, are the natural duties of a Kṣatriya, (a member of the warrior class), inherent in his nature. 43

Comment:—

'Śauryam'—Fighting heroically, and fearlessly, for a just and righteous cause,* on the battlefield, in the face of the most terrible calamity, is 'Śauryam'.

'Tejaḥ'—Moral power of a person by which even sinners, hesitate to commit sins or follow the path against the ordinance of the scriptures and social decorum is, 'Tejaḥ'.

'Dhṛtiḥ'—The unwavering firmness by which a man, does not get unnerved, nor deviates from righteousness, even under the most unfavourable or dangerous conditions is, 'Dhṛtiḥ'.

'Dākṣyam'—Resourcefulness (dexterity) by which one controls, conducts and rules over, the subjects properly and promptly, is 'Dākṣya'.

Yuddhe cāpyapalāyanam'—A Kṣatriya, never turns his back to the battlefield, even in the face of gravest dangers, he never loses heart and never flees from a battlefield.

'Dānam'—Giving away, one's own possessions to deserving persons liberally, is a duty of Kṣatriyas. At present, this charitable nature is seen among the Vaiśyas, but they are not liberal in offering charity. Because of their greedy nature their charity is not sāttvika (Gītā 17/20). But the Kṣatriyas, offer charity,

*The battle which is fought as a duty without any selfish motive and without pre-decision, forced by circumstances, is righteous.

liberally. Therefore, 'Dānam' is mentioned as a natural quality of Kṣatriya.

'Īśvarabhāvaśca'—The Kṣatriyas, have a natural inclination to rule over their subjects. If they behold their subjects going against ethics and righteousness, they check them, from the unrighteous or wicked path, and turn them towards righteous and just path, in a loving manner having no pride.

'Kṣātraṁ karma svabhāvajam'—A Kṣatriya, is he who protects all his subjects, from suffering. The above-mentioned are his natural duties.

Appendix—Kṣatriyas are very heroic and morally radiant. But because of envy, the king, who ruled over the state, tried to discourage other Kṣatriyas who were subordinate to him, he did not let them progress, lest they, being powerful, should usurp the state. It was because of such envy, discord and discouragement among Kṣatriyas that foreigners following other religions were successful in ruling over India.

Link:—The Lord now mentions the natural duties of a Vaiśya, (a member of the trading class) and a Śūdra (a member of the labour class).

कृषिगौरक्ष्यवाणिज्यं वैश्यकर्म स्वभावजम्।
परिचर्यात्मकं कर्म शूद्रस्यापि स्वभावजम्॥ ४४॥

kṛṣigaurakṣyavāṇijyaṁ vaiśyakarma svabhāvajam
paricaryātmakaṁ karma śūdrasyāpi svabhāvajam

Agriculture, cow-rearing and commerce are the duties of a Vaiśya, inherent to his nature, and actions consisting of service, are the duties of a śūdra, born of his nature. 44

Comment:—

'Kṛṣigaurakṣyavāṇijyaṁ vaiśyakarma svabhāvajam'—Agriculture, cattle-rearing and pure trade, are the duties of a Vaiśya born of his nature.

Pure trade consists, in supplying the needs of the, people by transporting the commodities, from one place to another, sincerely and honestly, so that no one may feel a shortage.

Lord Kṛṣṇa, (because of his relationship with Nanda-Bābā), regarded himself as a Vaiśya.* So he himself grazed cows and calves. In the Manusmṛti (the code of Manu) it is mentioned, that the duty of a Vaiśya is cow-rearing. So Lord Kṛṣṇa exhorts Vaiśyas, at least to rear cows, if they cannot raise all cattle. So, the Vaiśyas should bring up cows, by applying all their resources, body, mind, power and riches.

An Important Fact Concerning Cow-Rearing

A cow is to be reared from every point of view. Human beings can attain, four important aims of life, through cow-rearing—these are money (artha), righteousness (Dharma), desire (Kāma) and salvation (Mokṣa). In the materialistic world of today, a cow is very useful. Her milk, churned butter and dung, add to the wealth of a nation. Our country, is an agricultural country. So bullocks, are used to plough the land. The land, can also be ploughed by male-buffaloes, or camels. But bullocks, are superior to them. Buffaloes cannot work so efficiently, as bullocks because the latter have more sāttvika strength, than the former. The latter can work for a longer time, in the sun, than the former. Moreover, the number of the buffaloes is smaller than that of bullocks. As far as camels, are concerned, they cost more than bullocks. If cows are reared, they give birth to bullocks. So bullocks are not to be bought. Bullocks born of foreign cows cannot be used in farming, because ploughs cannot be put on their necks, as they have no withers.

The cow is a sacred animal. The air which touches her body becomes pure. Her dung and urine, check epidemics, such as plague and cholera etc. Houses plastered with dung, are not

*Agriculture, trade, cow-rearing and lending money for interest are the duties of a Vaiśya. But cow-rearing has been our profession since time immemorial (Śrīmadbhā. 10/24/21).

so much affected by bombs, as the cemented houses. Dung eliminates poison. In Banārasa, a saint saved a man, who was supposed to be dead by snake-bite, by smearing his body with dung, two times. Urine of cow, is very useful in heart diseases. A little quantity of urine of a she-calf, as a dose everyday, cures stomach diseases. A saint, suffering from asthma had a lot of relief, by drinking a little urine of the she-calf. In these days, several medicines are prepared from the dung and urine of cows. Gas is also prepared from dung, for cooking purpose.

The grains produced by the dung and urine of the cows as manure, is pure. Dung and urine of cows, make the land more fertile than chemical fertilizers, as was once experimented, on a crop of grapes. Chemical fertilizers, destroy the fertility of land in a few years, and makes it barren, while the manure of cow dung and urine, maintains well its fertility. Cow-dung is being exported to foreign countries, so that the lost fertility of land there, may be restored.

Cows of our country are gentle and sāttvika. So their sāttvika milk sharpens intellect and makes their nature mild. Foreign cows give more quantity of milk, but as they are angry by nature, their milk makes us, cruel. A she-buffalo gives more milk than a cow, but her milk is not sāttvika. Those who drink cows' milk, are more active than those who drink a she-buffalo's milk. Once, an experiment was made on military horses and it was found that horses fed on cow-milk, could cross a river, while the horses fed on buffalo-milk, could not, though the latter seemed stronger. The milk of she-camel, being tāmasika is not useful and its curd and butter, are not prepared. In the Jurisprudence, it is mentioned that camels, dogs and donkeys etc., are untouchable.

Cows occupy an important place in all religious rites. Her milk, churned butter (ghee) and dung etc., are used in rites of birth, tonsure and sacred thread etc. Cow-dung purifies, a place. Cow's milk is used in preparing sweet dishes which are offered to Brāhmaṇas, in honour of manes. A cow is offered as charity, to a Brāhmaṇa, to escape hell. In religious ceremonies a mixture of dung, urine, milk, curd and churned butter (ghee), known as 'Pañcagavya' is used.

Her ghee, is used in religious sacrifices, which are performed to satisfy desires. In the Raghu family, cow had an important place. Her milk and ghee, are nourishing.

Service to the cow without expectation of any reward, leads to salvation and purifies the heart. Lord Kṛṣṇa is known as Gopāla, because He staged a human play, as a cowherd, with bare-feet. In ancient times sages reared cows and their milk and ghee, sharpened their intellect. So they could produce great and rare classics (literature). Cow's milk and butter, provided them longevity, so a synonym of ghee (butter), is 'Āyu'. Great emperors, went to those sages for consultation.

In historical records, there are names mentioned of innumerable persons, who sacrificed their lives, for the protection of cows. But how sad it is, that today thousands of cows are being slaughtered daily, out of greed! If this state of affairs continues, cows will totally disappear. Then cow-dung will not be available. Without cow-dung lands will grow barren, and there will be no production of corn and cotton (cloth). People will be deprived of the bare necessities of life, such as food, water and clothes and they will have to lead a miserable life. The nation, will become dependent and weak. Slaughter of cows, is the main cause of famines, droughts, volcanoes and strifes etc. So it is our first and foremost duty, to stop this slaughter, with might and main.

We should rear cows, use their milk and butter, use cow-dung-gas, for cooking, make cow-pens, in order to protect them, protect the existing pastures (grazing grounds) and press the government to leave more areas of land, free for pastures. The policy of cow-slaughter, should be opposed and government should be forced, through public opinion to enforce a law to stop cow-slaughter immediately, throughout the country, for the protection of the country.

'Paricaryātmakaṁ karma śūdrasyāpi svabhāvajam'—It is the duty of a Śūdra, to render service to the people of the four Varṇas (Castes), with all his resources.

Here, a doubt rises how can a Śūdra, who is born with predominance of the mode of ignorance, endowed with seven evil propensities, such as ignorance, heedlessness, indolence, sleep, unillumination, inactivity and delusion (Gītā 14/8,14,17), render service to others? The clarification is, that it is mentioned in the Gītā, that those possessing the mode of goodness go upwards to the higher regions, the passionate remain in the middle region (mortal world) while those steeped in ignorance, sink downwards (Gītā 14/18). If a being dies, when Rajas (the mode of passion) is predominant in him, he is born among men who are attached to action (Gītā 14/15). It means that all human beings, have predominance of the mode of passion. All these human beings have further been divided into fourfold caste (social order), according to the predominance of their modes—sāttvika, rājasa or tāmasa. So performance of action is important, for all human beings. Therefore, a human birth, has been called 'Karmayoni' (Birth for action). In the Gītā also, while mentioning the duties of the four social orders, the Lord mentions the expressions 'Svabhāvaja Karma' and 'Svabhāvaniyata Karma'. So all men, are inclined to perform actions. Thus, service is the duty of a śūdra, born of his nature and it involves no exertion for him.

The temperament of a Brāhmaṇa, a Kṣatriya or a Vaiśya, is dominated by discrimination and they also possess purity, while because of predominance of delusion, a Śūdra's discrimination, is veiled. It is because of his veiled discrimination, that he has predominance of obedience and service, he has a natural inclination, for service. So service to members of the four Varṇas, by obeying them and by affording them facilities, in carrying out their vocational and daily duties, is his natural duty.

What do natural duties mean?

The nature of the embodied soul which is sentient and

Prakṛti which is insentient, are different. The sentient, never undergoes any modifications, while Prakṛti being kaleidoscopic ever undergoes modifications. The self (soul or spirit), being a fragment of the Lord, is sentient. There is no connection between the sentient and the insentient. But its attachment to the insentient Prakṛti, becomes the cause of Its birth in good and evil wombs (Gītā 13/21). Thus men are born, according to their qualities (modes), because of their attachment with them, as Brāhmaṇas, Kṣatriyas, Vaiśyas or Śūdras. All of them have a natural inclination to their duties, mentioned above. If a person performs these duties, having an egoistic notion for enjoyment, by having a selfish motive, he is bound. But if he performs these without expecting any reward, by giving up selfish motive and egoistic notion, it becomes "Karmayoga", and he is not bound. Through this Karmayoga (Discipline of Action), he worships the Lord, who has manifested Himself, as the entire universe. If one by surrendering himself to God, performs spiritual actions (utterance of His name, meditation, good company and study of the scriptures etc.,) his actions turn into Bhaktiyoga, (The Discipline of Devotion). Then his attachment (affinity to Prakṛti or Nature) is totally renounced, there remains nothing, but the Lord. Thus a striver realizes Him. Then all the actions with his body, senses, mind and intellect are performed, according to his Varṇa (Caste), and Āśrama (Stage of life), as sanctioned by scriptures and he is not attached to them. His actions are, models for others and his love for the Lord, Who is all-bliss, enhances every moment.

Should one's Varṇa (Caste), be decided by birth or actions? A being is born, as a man according to the qualities and actions of his previous birth. So his caste is decided by birth. Thus marriages etc., should be decided by caste. Secondly, for a person whose aim is to receive worldly pleasures, prosperity, luxuries, honour and praise etc., it is obligatory to discharge his duty, according to his caste. If he does not do so, he has a downfall. Even the Vedas, abandon such a demoralized person, at the time of his death, even though he has studied, the six supplementary branches of sacred sciences, (the Vedas) viz., education (Śikṣā), ritual part of the Vedas (Kalpa), an exposition of the Vedāṅgas (Nirukta), metre (Chanda), grammar (Vyākaraṇa) and astrology, (Jyotiṣa). But, he whose aim is God-realization, practises chanting, meditation, adoration, study of scriptures and performs, other spiritual activities, in order to attain his aim. In the spiritual discipline, spiritual feelings and conduct, play a more important role, than Varṇa or Caste. Thirdly, a striver, having the aim of God-realization, attaching more importance to spiritual activities, performs his obligatory duty, according to his caste and stage of life, regarding it as worship to God.

Further, in the forty-sixth verse the Lord explains, that He from whom all beings emanate and by whom all this is pervaded—by worshipping Him through the performance of his own duty, does man attain perfection. Every person, has got the right to perform his duty. The gods, demons, beasts and birds do not possess this natural right, yet it is not forbidden to them, because being a fragment of God, they can attain Him. Every being, can lay full claim, over the Lord. It proves, that there is predominance of feelings, discrimination and action in God-realization, while birth predominates in dealings, such as livelihood and marriages etc. So, in the Bhāgavata it is mentioned, that if a man of a lower caste possesses the virtues of higher caste, he should be regarded noble, though he is born of a low womb. Similarly, in the Mahābhārata it is mentioned, in a dialogue between Yudhiṣṭhira and Nahuṣa, that a Śūdra, whose conduct is noble, should not be regarded, as a Śūdra and a Brāhmaṇa who does not perform the duty of a Brāhmaṇa, should not be regarded as, a Brāhmaṇa. It means, that there is predominance of action, rather than birth.

Scriptures reveal, that even a man of the lowest caste, can possess the virtues of the highest caste and progress spiritually. So he need not get discouraged. Scriptures encourage a man of high caste to perform his duty, if he does not perform it. In

Jurisprudence (Smṛti), it is mentioned that Brāhmaṇas, who eat forbidden food and who are immoral, should not be respected even, by words. But scriptures declare, that a devotee of the Lord in spite of belonging to the lowest caste, is superior to a learned Brāhmaṇa.* A Brāhmaṇa has been called, the voice of the Lord's cosmic form. It means, that he has to impart knowledge and teach and preach to the people of the four Varṇas, with words of mouth because he possesses knowledge.

A Kṣatriya, has been called an arm or hand of the Lord's cosmic form, because it is he, who protects people of the four Varṇas (Castes), from enemies. A hand protects the body from danger and serves it in sickness. Such is the duty of a Kṣatriya. In case of anarchy it becomes the duty of all four castes to protect their kith and kin, as well as their property.

A Vaiśya, has been called the stomach of the Lord's cosmic form. As the stomach, receives and digests food and nourishes all the limbs, similarly, it is the duty of a Vaiśya, to accumulate commodities and to supply these to people, by transporting these from one place to another, according to the need and demand of

*(1) The low caste who chants the name of the Lord is noble. The noble men who chant His name have performed penances, oblations, pilgrimages, deeds of virtuous conduct and have studied the scriptures (Śrīmadbhā. 3/33/7).

(2) I hold that a low caste who has surrendered himself to God with his mind, speech, actions, wealth and life-breath is superior to a Brāhmaṇa endowed with twelve qualities who has a disinclination for the lotus-feet of Lord Viṣṇu because the pariah sanctifies his family while the Brāhmaṇa having a disinclination for the Lord because of the pride of his superiority complex can't sanctify even himself (Śrīmadbhā. 7/9/10).

(3) The low caste who remains engrossed in devotion to God is superior to a sage, while a Brāhmaṇa devoid of devotion to Lord Viṣṇu is inferior to a pariah because such a pariah with his kith and kin attains liberation from the worldly bondage while that Brāhmaṇa is hurled into hells.

(4) A low caste who is a devotee of Lord Viṣṇu is superior to a Brāhmaṇa who is not a devotee of Lord Viṣṇu because such a pariah with his kith and kin attains liberation from the worldly bondage while such a Brāhmaṇa goes to hells (Brahmavaivarta, Brahma. 11/39).

(5) If a Śūdra is a devotee of God, he is not a Śūdra, he is the noblest Brāhmaṇa. In fact out of all the Varṇas (Castes) a Śūdra is he who is devoid of devotion to God (Mahābhārata).

the people. It is he, who offers charity to Brāhmaṇas, pays tax to the Kṣatriyas, brings himself up and remunerates, the Śūdra for his labour. By agriculture, trade and cow-rearing he supplies, the need of the four Varṇas.

A Śūdra, has been called the foot of the cosmic form of the Lord. As feet carry the weight of the entire body, from one place to another, a Śūdra renders service, to the people of all four Varṇas (Castes).

These are the natural duties, of the persons of four castes, and involve no difficulty or exertion, for them. For duties, in more detail, refer to the books on Jurisprudence (Smṛti) and follow those duties (Gītā 16/24).

Though at present the four Varnas (castes), are mixed, yet Brāhmanas possess virtues, such as serenity, self-control and austerity etc., more than people of the other three castes. Similarly, heroism, vigour and firmness are specially found in the Kṣatriyas, while Vaiśyas are more well-versed in agriculture, cattle-rearing and trade, than the other three castes. In the same way, a Śūdra has more inclination to render service, than people of other three castes. Thus the people of different castes, have a natural inclination, for their duties, which are born of their nature, even today.

Some ignorant people, who have not studied the scriptures seriously, blame the Brāhmaṇas (persons of the priest class) that they have established their superiority in writing the scriptures. They hold, that the second position or place went to the Kṣatriyas, because of the authority and the third to the Vaiśyas, as they supplied the needs of the people. The people of these three castes, trampled on the Śūdras, out of selfishness and pride and asked them to render service, to persons of the three castes.

The clarification is, that it is written nowhere that Brāhmaṇas are superior to the people of the other three castes, and so they should lead a luxurious life. Their life is full of renunciation, hardship and penance. Even in the household life, a Brāhmaṇa should not accumulate wealth. He should not hoard grain more than a full jar and be not attached to mundane pleasures. He should accept charity, only after performing his religious sacrifices, oblations and other religious rites etc. If he accepts the gift of a cow, he should observe expiation.

When a Brāhmaṇa, is invited in order to offer water and food etc., (as a 'Śrāddha') in honour of manes, the Brāhmaṇa invokes the hosts' manes, by observing continence and self-control. He performs the rites of offering oblation, to the manes according to scriptural injunction. Then he takes a meal in the house of the host. Afterwards he recites a sacred formula of Gāyatrī (a mantra of the Ṛgveda, which is to be recited daily by the twice-born), to purify himself. It is not something creditable, for a Brāhmaṇa to take a meal on the occasion of 'Śrāddha', or to accept charity. The credit lies in his renunciation. He accepts the host's meal and gift, to enable the host's manes, to attain emancipation, rather than for his selfish motive.

A Brāhmaṇa, can earn his living, by five means according to Manusmṛti (Code of Manu)*—

(i) When crop is harvested, a few grains remain scattered here and there. A Brāhmaṇa picks these. Similarly, in the grain market, where grain is weighed, grains scattered on the earth, are picked by him. The former is known as 'Śiloñchavṛtti', while, the latter as 'Kapotavṛtti'. This sort of livelihood, called 'Ṛta' is regarded as the best for him.

(ii) If a host offers him a gift, without his request, it is called 'Amṛtavṛtti' or 'Ayācitavṛtti'.

(iii) Getting a gift as a reward, by explaining people of auspicious time for marriage and other rites etc., is called Mṛtavṛtti.

(iv) Earning a living through, business is 'Satyānṛtavṛtti'

* Ṛta, Amṛta, Mṛta, Pramṛta and Satyānṛta—these are the five means of earning a Brāhmaṇa's livelihood. He should never earn his living by rendering service to others.

(v) If he is unable to earn his livelihood by anyone of the above-mentioned means, he can earn it, by agriculture by following the ordinance of scriptures, as he should not plough land with one bullock, nor in scorching heat of the sun and so on. It is called 'Pramṛtavṛtti'. He should eat food, after performing five daily ceremonies, (the study of the scriptures, offering sacrifice to gods, hospitality to guests, offering water to manes and casting of food, on ground for insects etc.).*

In the Gītā, there is mention of nine natural duties of a Brāhmaṇa, and none of these is, for earning his livelihood. In the case of a Kṣatriya, out of the seven natural duties, the two—war and lordliness, are partial means of earning his living. In the case of a Vaiśya, all the three natural duties—agriculture, cattle-rearing and trade, are the means of earning a living. Similarly, is the case of a Śūdra, whose only natural duty is service, which is a source of earning and for him there are not many restrictions, on his food and source of livelihood.

The Lord, in the Gītā, declares, "Devoted to his own duty, man attains perfection" (Gītā 18/45). It means that a śūdra can attain perfection, merely by service, a Vaiśya, by agriculture, cow-rearing and trade, a Kṣatriya, by seven duties, such as heroism and vigour etc., while a Brāhmaṇa, by performing nine duties, such as serenity and self-control etc.

Then He declares, "By worshipping Him through the performance of his own duty, man attains perfection" (Gītā 18/46). In fact, a man attains perfection by performing duty, as worship to Him, without expecting reward. As far as rendering service, is concerned, it is a sort of worship. So a śūdra worships God through service. Thus his worship is doubled. So he can attain perfection, more easily than a Brāhmaṇa. Secondly the responsibility fall on the eldest son, while the youngest receives

* It is forbidden for a Brāhmaṇa or a Kṣatriya to earn his livelihood by rendering service to others (Manusmṛti 4/4, 4/6). But it does not mean that he should not render service to others. He should serve others even the Śūdra. But he should not earn his living by service.

the greatest love, without having any responsibility. Here, the eldest son is a Brāhmaṇa, while the youngest one, is a Śūdra.

In fact, a man of a high caste, has to face difficulty in obeying scriptural injunctions thoroughly, and so he attains salvation with difficulty, while a man of lower caste attains Him easily. In this context, there is a story in the Viṣṇu Purāṇa. Once several sages went to Vedavyāsa, in order to know his decision about the relative superiority of castes (Varṇa). Vedavyāsa received them cordially and went to take a bath in the Ganges. While bathing he uttered three times "Kaliyuga (Kali age), you are lucky; Women, you are lucky; Śūdras, you are lucky." When he came back, the sages asked him how Kali age, women and śūdras were lucky. He answered, "In the Kali age, women and Śūdras by performing their duties, can attain salvation quickly, and easily."

One more point needs attention here. A man who works for his selfish motive, does not deserve respect either in the family, or society. So, is the case with Brāhmaṇas. They have not praised themselves in the scriptures, in order to prove their superiority. Noble men always praise and respect, other people. Brāhmaṇas are respected and praised, for their virtue of renunciation. So everyone, should give a serious thought to this topic, and should not accuse saints, sages and Brāhmaṇas, who wrote the scriptures.

The fourfold order, of society (viz., Brāhmaṇa, Kṣatriya, Vaiśya and the śūdra) was created, according to divisions of quality and work (Gītā 4/13). But even if a being, has to be born in either a high womb, because of a boon etc., or low womb, because of a curse etc., he acts according to the nature of the previous birth. It is because of this factor, that persons such as Dhundhukārī etc., in spite of being born in high wombs, perform evil actions while persons, such as Vidura, Kabīra and Raidāsa etc., in spite of being born, in low wombs perform virtuous deeds and become great men.

Today, we should try to get rid of personal and social evils, which are against ordinances of scriptures, by discrimination, good company and study of scriptures. We should make our life pure and holy, so that we may attain, the aim of human life.

Link:—The Lord in the next two verses, explains why a man should perform, his natural duties.

स्वे स्वे कर्मण्यभिरतः संसिद्धिं लभते नरः।
स्वकर्मनिरतः सिद्धिं यथा विन्दति तच्छृणु ॥ ४५ ॥

sve sve karmaṇyabhirataḥ saṁsiddhiṁ labhate naraḥ
svakarmanirataḥ siddhiṁ yathā vindati tacchṛṇu

Devoted to his own inherent duty, man attains perfection (God-realization). How he, devoted to his own duty, attains perfection, that thou hear now. 45

Comment:—

'Sve sve karmaṇyabhirataḥ saṁsiddhiṁ labhate naraḥ'—A study of the Gītā reveals, that a man's nature, may lead him to salvation if he remains free from attachment and aversion, as well as fruit of action. If a man performs his natural duties scrupulously, without self-interest and attachment, the impetus to action calms down, and he becomes detached from objects and actions etc. So a striver, gets established in the self, which is natural. Then, he is naturally attracted towards the Lord. A man, should perform his duty promptly and enthusiastically, for the welfare of others. By doing so, he experiences a sort of pleasure, called, 'Abhirati', for action. But if an act is done with attachment, having an eye on its return—this is called 'Āsakti', for action. The former leads him to perfection (salvation), while the latter leads him to bondage.

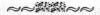

In this context in 'Sve sve karmaṇi', 'Svakarmaṇā tamabhyarcya', 'Svabhāvaniyataṁ karma' and 'Sahajaṁ karma' etc., the term 'Karma' (action) has been used, in singular number. It means that if a man performs an action or several actions promptly and enthusiastically, in order to realize God, and all his actions merge, in that aim of God-realization. It means, that all of these are conducive to God-realization. The Ganges having risen in the Himālayas, flows to the Gaṅgā-Sāgara. On the way several streams, drains and small rivers, join it and they become the Ganges. Similarly, all the actions of a person, whose aim is to attain God, join that aim. But, he who is attached to action and who has a desire for several rewards, by performing action or several actions, instead of God-realization, the intellect of such an undecided person, is scattered in many directions, and is endlessly diffused (Gītā 2/41) and he cannot attain, perfection.

'Svakarmanirataḥ siddhiṁ yathā vindati tacchṛṇu'—The Lord, exhorts Arjuna to hear from Him and grasp properly, how a man, who is devoted to his duty, attains perfection (God-realization).

An Important Fact

Even a servant, who is paid wages, renders service to his master, even when his service is limited to actions and fixed hours. But it cannot be called, real service. When a man considers others venerable, either through birth, learning, caste or stage of life, capability, status or virtues, he has only one central idea, how they should get comfort, and how they should be pleased. To render service to them, according to their will and taste, for their pleasure is called, real service. The servant, in such service has no self-interest and ego. He looks, only at the interest of the people, he has to serve—this is real service. Real service involves the feelings, of a devotee. His only aim is to please the Lord, keeping in mind only His taste. The same service, if rendered with hearty devotion, becomes adoration. Smearing the forehead with sandalwood paste, offering flowers, garlanding and offering of prayers, and praises and such other activities of devotion, are included in adoration. When a devotee, either beholds his master, or the Lord, touches His feet, his body is thrilled, and he feels much delighted. When he is thrilled, there may be a bit of slackness in his service to his master, (preceptor or the Lord), but it purifies his heart and enables him to behold the Lord or to realize Him. When, this devotion enhances, a devotee attains God-realization immediately. Such a devotee, always thinks how to provide happiness and comfort, to his master, preceptor or God, without thinking of his own happiness and comfort, at all. By doing so, he is highly delighted.

All the activities of such a devotee, whether these are performed, with his physical, subtle or causal body, become worship of the Lord. Even his daily routine, and his eating, drinking etc., becomes the material for his worship.

As a follower of the Discipline of Knowledge, always thinks, that he does nothing, similarly a staunch devotee worships, God by performing several duties, only for God's sake, and in that state, his egoistic notion, is renounced.

Appendix—Besides the inherent duty according to one's Varṇa (social order), whatever other duties have been accepted by a man, all of them should also be included within 'sve sve karmaṇi'. As a man adopts the profession of a lawyer, a servant, a teacher or a physician etc., the discharge of that duty justly in a loving, respectful and selfless manner is also 'svakarma' (own duty) for him.

When a man performs an action with the sense of selfishness, partiality and desire etc., it is called 'āsakti' (attachment). But if he performs an action in a loving manner, without the desire for fruit and for the welfare of others, it is called 'abhirati'. The Lord has negated 'attachment' in actions—'na karmasvanuṣajjate' (Gītā 6/4). If a man has neither the superiority complex nor the inferiority complex, on the basis of his caste, but performs his duty properly, just like the part of a machine (watch), and does not blame and humiliate others, and is not proud of himself, then it is 'abhirati'.

In fact an action (duty) is not important but it is the 'attitude' which is predominant. If the doer of an action has the pure feeling, it will lead him to salvation, though he may belong to any 'varṇa'. In performing an action there is predominance of 'varṇa' while in 'feeling' there is predominance of the divine nature or the demoniac nature. Therefore all the people can be endowed with the divine or the demoniac nature without the distinction of 'varṇa'. Divine nature leads to salvation and the demoniac nature is conducive to bondage. Therefore even if a Brāhmaṇa is boastful of his hight varṇa, he will be endowed with the demoniac nature viz., he will have a downfall—

nīca nīca saba tara gaye, rāma bhajana lavalīna
jāti ke abhimāna se, ḍūbe sabhī kulīna

(The people of low castes who remained engrossed in the worship to God attained salvation while all the people belonging to the high caste because of their pride were ruined).

यतः प्रवृत्तिर्भूतानां येन सर्वमिदं ततम्।
स्वकर्मणा तमभ्यर्च्य सिद्धिं विन्दति मानवः ॥ ४६ ॥

yataḥ pravṛttirbhūtānāṁ yena sarvamidaṁ tatam
svakarmaṇā tamabhyarcya siddhiṁ vindati mānavaḥ

He from Whom all beings emanate and by Whom all this is pervaded—by worshipping Him, through the performance of one's own duty, man attains perfection. 46

Comment:—

'Yataḥ pravṛttirbhūtānāṁ yena sarvamidaṁ tatam'—The Lord, from Whom the entire universe emanates, Who conducts it, Who is the creator, base and illuminator of all beings, and objects, Who pervades all, Who existed, before the creation of infinite universes, and will exist, when all the universes perish and Who pervades infinite universes, should be worshipped, through the performance of one's own duty, according to one's Varṇa (Caste).

'Svakarmaṇā tamabhyarcya'—According to Manusmṛti (code of Manu), the six duties of a 'Brāhmaṇa, are—study, teaching, performance of religious sacrifice, performing it, for others as a priest, accepting charity and offering charity. Out of these, teaching, performing religious sacrifice for others as a priest, and accepting charity—these three are the means of his living, while study, performance of religious sacrifice and offering charity, are his duties. Through these six duties, as well as through the nine duties mentioned in the verse forty-two of this chapter, and also through other activities such as eating, drinking, going, sleeping etc., he should worship, the Lord Who pervades all beings. It means, that he should serve all beings, regarding them as the manifestation of the Lord, to please Him, without expecting any reward.

Similarly, protection of subjects, offering charity, performance of religious sacrifice, study and detachment from sensual pleasures—these five, are the duties of a Kṣatriya, mentioned in the code of Manu. A Kṣatriya, through these five duties, and seven duties, mentioned in the forty-third verse of this chapter, as well as through the activities of daily routine, such as eating, drinking etc., should worship the Lord, Who has manifested himself, as beings.

A Vaiśya, through religious sacrifice, study, offering charity, charging interest, agriculture, cattle-rearing and trade, and all other activities, should worship the all-pervading Lord. Similarly, a Śūdra through service and all other activities, should worship the all-pervading Lord, without expecting any reward.

All the duties of men, mentioned in the scriptures, according to their Varṇa (Caste or Social order) and āśrama (stage of life), are meant, to worship the cosmic form of the Lord. If a striver, while performing his activities, thinks that he is worshipping the Lord, with his activities, all those activities are included in the worship of the Lord. Grandfather Bhīṣma, on the battle-field worshipped Lord Kṛṣṇa, with arrows, through his duty of a warrior. With his arrows Lord Kṛṣṇa's armour was broken,

He was injured and it became difficult for Him, to hold the bridle of the horse of the chariot. At the last moment of his life, Bhīṣma thinks of the same Lord and concentrates his mind on Him—"Let my mind and intellect, concentrate on Lord Kṛṣṇa, Whose armour was broken, with my sharp arrows, Whose body is injured, Whose face is adorned with perspiration, because of exertion, and Whose beautiful curl, is stained with dust raised by the gallop of horses."

A striver, should worship the Lord, through mundane and spiritual activities, but he should not be attached, either to the activities or the instruments and means, by which they are performed because attachment (a sense of mineness) makes things impure and polluted, and so they cannot be offered to God; they can't be used for His worship. So a striver, should think that whatever he possesses, belongs to the omnipresent Lord, and he as His instrument, has to worship Him with the resources bestowed upon him, by Him. Thus all his activities, become worship to the Lord, otherwise not.

'Siddhiṁ vindati mānavaḥ'—It means, that a person who worships the Lord, through the performance of his own duty, by being free from his connection with Prakṛti (Nature), gets established, in the self. Then because of past influence, of his surrender to the Lord, his exclusive devotion to the Lord, is aroused. In that case, nothing further remains to be achieved by him.

Here, the term 'Mānavaḥ' (man), stands not only for Brāhmaṇas, Kṣatriyas, Vaiśyas, Śūdras, or for celibates, householders, people of retired order, and renounced order, but also for, all the people of different religions and sects etc., such as Hindus, Muslims, Christians, Bauddhas, Parsees and Jews etc. As a mother becomes pleased with the different activities, of her sons, similarly the Lord is pleased, with the activities of men, by regarding those activities as worship to Him.

Lord Kṛṣṇa, in the seventieth verse of this chapter declares, "He who studies this sacred dialogue of ours, by him, I shall be worshipped through the sacrifice of knowledge (wisdom), so I hold." It shows that if a person studies the Gītā, the Lord considers it, as His worship. Similarly, when a person, by having a disinclination for the perishable world, has an inclination for the Lord, He accepts it as worship, to Him.

An Important Fact

Through Karmayoga (the Discipline of Action), a devotee is detached from matter, while through Bhaktiyoga (the Discipline of Devotion), he has an inclination for God. A Karmayogī, serves the world with his body, senses, mind and intellect by abandoning his selfishness, pride and desire. By doing so, the flow of his actions is towards the world and the impetus to act, calms down, his assumed attachment, to these things is renounced, and his natural detachment, is revealed.

A devotee, following the Discipline of Devotion, worships the Lord through the performance of his natural duties, as well as, the spiritual duties, such as chanting His name, meditation and adoration etc. Thus, he develops an inclination for God, having a disinclination for Matter, and his love for Him enhances.

A devotee, from the outset surrenders himself to God exclusively. So all his mundane and spiritual activities, are automatically surrendered to Him. Outwardly, mundane activities seem different, from the spiritual ones, but actually, there is no difference between the two.

At last, a Karmayogī and a Jñānayogī, also become one. As a Karmayogī, becomes detached by serving the world, having no selfishness, pride and desire, so does a Jñānayogī, through knowledge (wisdom), offer all his activities to prakṛti (nature) and become, detached.* Thus, both of them become

* It is inevitable for all the strivers whether they follow the Discipline of Action or that of Knowledge or of Devotion to get detached from the world. In the Gītā there is mention of this detachment for a Karmayogī in 5/11, for a Jñānayogī in 18/26 and for a Bhaktiyogī in 11/55.

free from the bondage of actions. The actions of a Karmayogī, are dissolved entirely (Gītā 4/23) while the fire of knowledge, reduces all actions of a Jñānayogī, to ashes (Gītā 4/37). Thus he gets freedom. If he does not enjoy this freedom, he becomes totally indifferent to this freedom. Then by God's grace, divine love can be revealed in him.

Appendix—Here the meaning of the term 'pravṛttiḥ' used in the expression 'yataḥ pravṛttirbhūtānāṁ' should be taken as 'origination' (emanation) because all beings do originate from God but actions do not emanate from God. An action (activity) emanates from the mode of passion—'lobhaḥ pravṛttirārambhaḥ' (Gītā 14/12). The term 'pravṛtti' in the fourth verse of the fifteenth chapter also has been used in the sense of origination—'yataḥ pravṛttiḥ prasṛtā purāṇī'.

This universe is the first incarnation of God—'ādyo'vatāraḥ puruṣaḥ parasya' (Śrīmadbhā. 2/6/41). Therefore this world is an idol of God. As in an idol we worship God, we offer flowers, we apply sandalwood paste viz., we instead of worshipping the idol, worship God; similarly we have to worship God in the form of this world with each and every action of ours. The audience should worship the orator by listening to Him, the orator should worship the listener by his speech or by his spiritual discourse—thus all beings should worship one another through the performance of their duty. They should have an eye on God rather than on 'varṇa' such as Brāhmaṇa and Kṣatriya etc. The sages and saints did obeisance to Lord Rāma by regarding Him as God rather than a Kṣatriya when he was sent into exile. The important fact in worship is—all is God's and it is only for Him. As we worship the holy Ganges with the Ganges-water, similarly we have to worship God with the things bestowed upon us by Him. In fact performance of all actions is worship only to God, we have to rectify our error of regarding it for us. Having offered the God's things to Him, our selfishness, pleasure-seeking nature, and desire for fruit, will be wiped out; and having accepted our power (strength) as only God's, our sense of doership will also be destroyed and we shall attain God.

The worship to the world by regarding it as the manifestation of God, is highly prized than the worship to an idol of God. The reason is that if an idol of God is worshipped, the idol does not appear to be pleased, but if service is rendered to beings, they clearly appear to be pleased.

If human beings are served by regarding them as the manifestation of God with actions and objects, the universe will disappear and only God will remain viz., 'All is God'—it will be realized, As in a rope when the illusion of a snake is wiped out, the snake ceases to be but the rope certainly remains; similarly when in God, the illusion of the existence of the world is wiped out, then the world in the form of the world disappears, and it remains as the manifestation of God. The reason is that the existence of the world is merely an assumption but 'God exists'—this is reality.

In Śrīmadbhāgavata, the Lord declares—

nareṣvabhīkṣṇaṁ madbhāvaṁ puṁso bhāvayato'cirāt
spardhāsūyātiraskārāḥ sāhaṅkārā viyanti hi

(Śrīmadbhā. 11/29/15)

"When a devotee regards all women and men as My manifestation and he beholds Me in them*, then very quickly evils such as envy, fault-finding, contempt etc., including egoism are removed."

The Lord in the Gītā declares—'ahamātmā guḍākeśa sarvabhūtāśayasthitaḥ' (10/20)—"I am 'the Self' seated in the hearts of all beings." Therefore if we serve any being, respect him, and greet him with pleasure and hospitality, by regarding him as the manifestation of God, it will be service to God.

* The reason of beholding God in men and women is that we mostly perceive virtues and vices in men and women, so we don't perceive that they are the manifestations of God. Therefore when we instead of perceiving virtues and vices in them, will behold only God in all beings and objects, we'll easily regard them as the manifestations of God.

Similarly if we disrespect and humiliate any being, it will be disrespect and humiliation to God only—'karśayantaḥ śárīrasthaṁ bhūtagrāmama cetasaḥ' (17/6).

As in the path of knowledge, the modes are acting on the modes ('guṇā guṇeṣu vartante'), similarly in the path of devotion, God is being worshipped by God's things. But there is a vast difference between the two. In 'guṇā guṇeṣu vartante' there is predominance of matter (non-Self) which a striver, following the path of knowledge, disowns but in 'svakarmaṇā tamabhyarcya', there is predominance of the sentient (the divinity) which the striver, following the path of devotion, owns. Therefore in the path of devotion, inertness is wiped out, the universe in the form of the universe is concealed, and it is revealed as God because in fact it is only God. If the universe appears as the universe to a striver, he should serve it, and if it appears as the manifestation of God, he should worship Him. He should do nothing for himself. Performance of action for one's own sake, is 'bondage'; for the sake of the world, is 'service' and for God's sake, is 'worship'.

Link:—The Lord, in the next two verses, explains that a striver, need not lose heart, while worshipping the Lord through the performance of his duty, even if there remains any defect, in his performance.

श्रेयान्स्वधर्मो विगुणः परधर्मात्स्वनुष्ठितात्।
स्वभावनियतं कर्म कुर्वन्नाप्नोति किल्बिषम्॥ ४७॥

śreyānsvadharmo viguṇaḥ paradharmātsvanuṣṭhitāt
svabhāvaniyataṁ karma kurvannāpnoti kilbiṣam

Better is one's own duty (dharma), though devoid of merit than the duty (dharma) of another even if well-performed. He who carries out the duty ordained, by his own nature, incurs no sin. 47

Comment:—

'Śreyānsvadharmo viguṇaḥ paradharmātsvanuṣṭhitāt'— Here, the term 'Svadharma', denotes one's duty according to one's Varṇa (Caste).

A man, having an aim of God-realization, has to perform his duty, according to what he thinks, himself to be. If he thinks that he is a man, he has to perform his duty as a man. If he thinks that he is a teacher, or a student, he has to teach or study. Similarly if he holds, that he is a striver, a devotee, or a seeker of knowledge, he has to practise spiritual discipline, devotion or seek knowledge, whole-heartedly.

Similarly, a man has to perform his duty, according to his varṇa (caste) and āśrama (stage of life). A Brāhmaṇa's duties, are—performance of religious sacrifice accepting charity, and teaching etc., in order to earn his living. For a Kṣatriya, fighting and authority, for a Vaiśya agriculture, cow-rearing and trade, and for a Śūdra service, are the duties to earn their living. One's own duty, even though devoid of merit, is better than the duty of others. The duties prescribed by the scriptures, for persons of a particular Varṇa, is 'Svadharma' (one's own duty), while the same duty for people of other Varṇas, castes is, Paradharma (Duties of others). Performing religious sacrifice, for others as a priest, and taking charity etc., are a Brāhmaṇa's own duties, as these are sanctioned by scriptures for him, but the same duties are Paradharma, for the Kṣatriyas, the Vaiśyas and the Śūdras, as these are forbidden by scriptures, for them. But, at the time of extreme distress, duties which are forbidden, by scriptures, become duties, for people, of all varṇas (castes). For example, a Brāhmaṇa can earn his living by agriculture, and trade etc., which are duties of a Vaiśya, at the time of extreme distress.*

*At the time of distress a Brāhmaṇa can earn his living through the profession of a Kṣatriya and at the time of extreme distress through the profession of a Vaiśya. But a Brāhmaṇa should plough the land with two bullocks instead of one and work in the field in the morning and evening when it is cool. Moreover, he should not deal in sugar, butter, oil and salt etc.

As far as the natural duties, such as serenity and self-control etc., of a Brāhmaṇa, are concerned, these are duties, for all members belonging to the four Varṇas, because they are prescribed by scriptures, for all of them.

God-realization, is the only aim of human life. So every human being is a striver, therefore he has to cultivate all the divine traits, in him by renouncing demoniac ones. Everyone is free and strong, enough to abandon demoniac traits, and to develop divine ones. No one is dependent, weak and ineligible, in it. According to their temperaments, different persons may possess different divine traits. A person may have predominance of forgiveness, in his nature, in another, person there may be forgiveness only, on asking for it. In some other person, there may be predominance of compassion, while in another there may be compassion, on thought. Such differences may exist.

'Svabhāvaniyataṁ karma kurvannāpnoti kilbiṣam'—In scriptures, two kinds of actions, are mentioned—prescribed and prohibited. Out of the prescribed actions, those actions which are performed according to one's caste (Varṇa), or stage of life (Āśrama) time, and circumstances etc., are called 'Niyata Karma'.

One's nature, is formed according to three modes of nature—of goodness (sattva), of passion (rajasa) and of ignorance (tamasa). Actions which are performed according to that nature, are called 'Svabhāvaniyata Karma'. These are also known as natural duties—duties born of nature, one's own duties and innate duties etc.

A being is born, in a particular varṇa (caste) according to qualities and actions, of his previous birth. Though actions perish, but their impression (saṁskāra) continues. So in life one is born with that nature, which he inherits. The Lord (in Gītā 18/48) declares, that though all undertakings are tainted with blemish, yet a person should perform his duty, according to his Varṇa

---

Similarly a Kṣatriya can earn his living through the profession of a Vaiśya and a Vaiśya through the profession of a Śūdra.

(caste) as sanctioned in the scriptures, for the welfare of others, by giving up his selfishness and pride. By doing so, he incurs no sin. Similarly he, who performs actions, for the maintenance of the body alone, incurs no sin (Gītā 4/21).

An Important Fact

Now a doubt arises, whether a person born in the family of a butcher, should not abandon his duty of slaughtering animals? Does a butcher not incur, sin? Can he attain salvation, by performing such a forbidden action?

The explanation is, that natural duty is that which is not forbidden, and which is not harmful to anyone. The actions which are harmful or injurious to others, cannot be called, one's natural duties. These are performed out of attachment and desire. A forbidden action, is always evil and so it must be abandoned, because it is a demoniac trait, while virtuous actions, are divine traits. A man, may have a mere thought of committing evil, because of past impressions, but that thought cannot compel him, to perform evil actions. That inclination, can be rooted out, through discrimination, virtuous thoughts, good company and study of scriptures etc. Reasoning also reveals, that no one wants to be injured and slaughtered. So none has a right to injure and slaughter, others. If a person wants other persons to do good to him, he should also do good, to others. The scriptures also reveal, that any sin or unjust action, is not natural, it is born of an evil. In the third chapter, Arjuna asked Lord Kṛṣṇa, "Impelled by what does a man, commit sin, even involuntarily as though driven by force?" The Lord replied, "It is desire, it is anger, born of the mode of passion, which impels a man to commit sins" (3/36-37). Actions which are performed, out of desire, wrath, selfishness, and pride, are not pure, but are impure.

Actions, which are performed, in order to attain God, are not defective, even though they may be different, for people of different castes. Having realized God, a Brāhmaṇa will observe purity and sanctity in the preparation of food, and in having it. But a person of a low caste, having realized God, will not observe purity and sanctity, like a Brāhmaṇa. He will eat food which is left on the plate, after a meal while a Brāhmaṇa, will not eat it. So actions of the liberated souls, are faultless. Their nature is pure, because they are free, from either attachment or aversion.

A man, is born in the family of a butcher, in order to reap the fruit of his sinful actions. He is not born there, to commit sins. In the Yogadarśana (one of the six schools of Hindu philosophy), sinful action bears fruit, in the form of caste, age and suffering, but it does not force that man to perform new sinful actions, (2/13). He is free in performing actions. If his heart becomes pure, he cannot slaughter animals. A person, asked a saint, "What should a butcher, who considers slaughtering animals his profession, do?" The saint replied, "If he goes on chanting the name of the Lord, with sanctity, for three years, he will find himself unable to perform, his duty as a butcher. He will scorn his action and then, he will give it up." He will not be able to slaughter animals, if he wants to realize God, from his heart, because his heart will change and virtues, will be revealed in him.

In the Rāmacaritamānasa Lord Rāma says, to Śabarī, "Listen to the nine kinds of devotion which I am going to describe" (3/35/4). Afterwards He declared, "You very well possess, all kinds of devotion" (3/36/4). It means that Śabarī did not know the nine kinds, of devotion, though she possessed all of them. Through adoration, meditation and good company, we develop virtues, which we are not aware of. So a man, should make his nature pure, and he is capable, of making it pure. He finds himself incapable, because of his attachment to mundane pleasure and prosperity. Those who hold discourses to preach others, can't be virtuous, unless they themselves translate those preachings, into practice, by making their nature pure, having the aim of God-realization.

The Lord, has bestowed this human body, so that human beings may attain salvation, by purifying their nature. They can purify their nature, it is neither impossible nor difficult. This human body, has been called the gateway to salvation (Mānasa 7/43/4). Had it been impossible, to purify nature, how could this human body have been called, the gateway to salvation? There is no use of this human life, if a man cannot purify his nature.

Appendix—By performing one's own duty there can be sin but the striver cannot incur this sin—'kurvannāpnoti kilbiṣam'. In incurring sin the main cause is the 'feeling' rather than an 'action'. Therefore sin is incurred, not by actions but by selfishness and pride.

सहजं कर्म कौन्तेय सदोषमपि न त्यजेत्।
सर्वारम्भा हि दोषेण धूमेनाग्निरिवावृताः॥ ४८॥

sahajaṁ karma kaunteya sadoṣamapi na tyajet
sarvārambhā hi doṣeṇa dhūmenāgnirivāvṛtāḥ

One should not abandon, O Arjuna, one's innate duty, even though it may have flaws, for all undertakings are clouded by defects, as fire is by smoke. 48

Comment:—

[In the preceding verse, the Lord declared, " He who performs his duty ordained by his own nature, incurs no sin." It means that duty ordained by one's own nature, also involves sin. Therefore, the Lord declares, "The natural duties, even though defective, should not be abandoned, because all of these are clouded by defects, as fire by smoke."]

'Sahajaṁ karma kaunteya sadoṣamapi na tyajet'—The duties ordained by one's own nature, are called innate duties. A Brāhmaṇa's innate duties, are serenity and self-control etc., a Kṣatriya's heroism and vigour etc., a Vaiśya's agriculture and cattle-rearing etc., and a Śūdra's, service.

Duties ordained by one's own nature, have the following defects:—

(1) God and the soul, His fragment, both are one's own (Sva), while Prakṛti (Matter) and its evolute, body etc., are different (Para). But the self, a fragment of God, being overpowered by Prakṛti, becomes a slave to it. In other words, all activities are taking place in nature. But, the self by assuming affinity with Nature holds, that they are taking place in him. Thus, he becomes a slave to it. To be such a slave, is a great mistake.

(2) Every action involves violence, in one way or the other.

(3) Action which is desirable to one, is undesirable to someone else. This undesirability, is a defect.

(4) An action may not be performed well, because of heedlessness or error.

A person, should not abandon his innate duty, even though it may be defective. For example, a Kṣatriya's or a Vaiśya's actions, are not to be as virtuous and polite, as those of a Brāhmaṇa. But the Kṣatriyas or the Vaiśyas are not held responsible for those defects and for violence, which their activities involve. They derive benefit by performing these, because these are sanctioned by scriptures and are easily performed, as they suit their temperament.

Alms, is the means of a Brāhmaṇa's livelihood. It may seem free from any defect but it is not. Suppose a beggar is standing at the door of a householder, and another comes there. He is a burden on the householder. There can be jealousy between the two beggars. If food materials are not ready, the householder feels sorry. Suppose, a householder does not want to offer anything, so he suffers pain, after seeing the beggar. If he offers something, he has to incur expenses. But, if the beggar or Brāhmaṇa, returns empty-handed, the householder incurs sin. So he gets entangled, in a dilemma. Thus, though alms involve a blot, yet a Brāhmaṇa, should not abandon it.

A Kṣatriya, has to kill warriors of the army of an enemy.

But he incurs no sin, because it is his innate duty, which is prescribed by scriptures. Similarly, in agriculture, the duty of a Vaiśya involves, violence of several insects and germs. But a Vaiśya, incurs no sin, as it is his innate duty, which is sanctioned by scriptures. So innate duties, should not be abandoned.

Though men, by performing innate duties, incur no sin, how will those duties, lead to salvation? In fact, these are evil propensities, such as desire, attachment, selfishness and pride, which bind a man and because of which, a man incurs sin. So if he performs duties for God's sake, by abandoning evil propensities, without expecting any reward, he will not be bound.

'Sarvārambhā hi doṣeṇa dhūmenāgnirivāvṛtāḥ'—As, there is smoke at the beginning, when fire is burnt, similarly, all undertakings are enveloped by defects, as their performance depends on incidents, circumstances and occasions etc., and these may be undesirable for others. So, a man who performs these duties without expecting any reward, incurs no sin. Therefore, the Lord is saying to Arjuna, "Brother! It is thy duty, to wage war, which you regard as dreadful, for there is nothing more welcome, for a man of the warrior class, than a righteous war" (Gītā 2/31).

Appendix—Because of the attachment to forbidden actions or because of the enjoyment of pleasure against the ordinance of the scripture, performance of actions, sanctioned by the scriptures, seems difficult. In fact actions sanctioned by the scriptures are innate and natural, they need no labour. From the forty-first verse upto this verse the terms 'svakarma', 'svadharma' and 'sahaja karma' have been used. It proves that the Gītā regards 'svakarma' (one's own duty), 'sahaja karma' (innate duty) as 'svadharma' (one's own duty).

Actions which are sanctioned by the scriptures, are certainly tainted with blemish; but if a striver has no desire, he does not hanker after pleasures, then he is not tainted with blemish. It means that whether the doer is tainted with blemish or not, depends on his intention; as—if a surgeon has good intention, wants to serve the patient rather than to earn money, while performing a surgical operation, he cuts the part of the patient's body, yet he is not tainted with blemish, but his act is regarded as virtuous because he performs the operation selflessly for the good of the patient.

Link:—Now, the Lord while introducing the topic of Sāṅkhyayoga, describes a man who is qualified to practise, Sāṅkhyayoga.

असक्तबुद्धिः सर्वत्र जितात्मा विगतस्पृहः ।
नैष्कर्म्यसिद्धिं परमां सन्न्यासेनाधिगच्छति ॥ ४९ ॥

asaktabuddhiḥ sarvatra jitātmā vigataspṛhaḥ
naiṣkarmyasiddhiṁ paramāṁ sannyāsenādhigacchati

He, whose intellect is unattached alround, who has subdued his body, and from whom desire has fled—he, attains the supreme state of non-action, through Sāṅkhyayoga, (the Discipline of Knowledge). 49

Comment:—

Sannyāsa (Sāṅkhyayoga), is the means to attain, the supreme state. Now, the Lord describes the three factors in the first half of the verse which enable a man to practise Sāṅkhyayoga (the Discipline of Knowledge).

(1) **'Asaktabuddhiḥ sarvatra'**—His intellect remains unattached, to incidents, circumstances, things, actions and persons etc.

(2) **'Jitātmā'**—He has conquered his body i.e., he is not overpowered by heedlessness and indolence etc., rather he overpowers these. He performs prescribed duties promptly, and abstains from forbidden actions.

(3) **'Vigataspṛhaḥ'**—He has no subtle desire, even to get the bare necessities of life, such as water, food, clothes and shelter. He is satisfied with, whatsoever, he gets.

It means that a striver, who wants to follow the Discipline of Knowledge (Sāṅkhyayoga), has to renounce his attachment to matter and then he is endowed with, the above-mentioned, three qualities. If he is unattached, his body, senses and mind are subdued, and when these are subdued, he becomes free, from desire. Then, he becomes qualified to practise Sāṅkhyayoga, (The Discipline of Knowledge).

'Naiṣkarmyasiddhiṁ paramāṁ sannyāsenādhigacchati'—Such a man, whose intellect is unattached, everywhere, who has subdued his self, from whom desire has fled—he by Sāṅkhyayoga, attains the supreme state viz., God-realization. The reason is, that actions take place in prakṛti (matter), not in the self. When a striver (the self), has not the least attachment for that action, the action or its fruit, does not affect him at all. So the natural state of detachment, and actionlessness, is revealed.

Appendix—'Naiṣkarmyasiddhi' means that an action should become totally inaction, there should not remain the least affinity with action; while performing an action; the striver should remain untainted (detached)—'karmaṇyakarma yaḥ paśyedakarmāṇi ca karma yaḥ' (Gītā 4/18). Non-performance of actions is not 'naiṣkarmya' (actionlessness) (Gītā 3/4), but it is necessary for a striver to perform action (Gītā 6/3).

'Asaktabuddhiḥ sarvatra jitātmā vigataspṛhaḥ'—This is attainment of perfection (peace) by Karmayoga (Gītā 2/71), having attained which a Karmayogī follows the path of knowledge (Gītā 5/6) and attains the state of actionlessness by this path. In this way by Karmayoga, only actionlessness (naiṣkarmyasiddhi) is attained (the striver becomes free from the bondage of action) (Gītā 3/4) but by devotion he attains the supreme state of actionlessness (parama naiṣkarmyasiddhi). Karmayoga and Jñānayoga are the paths (niṣṭhās)—'loke'smindvividhā niṣṭhā' (3/3) but the supreme state (parā niṣṭhā) of Karmayoga-Jñānayoga will be attained only by devotion—'niṣṭhā jñānasya yā parā' (18/50). It means that both 'parama naiṣkarmyasiddhi' and 'parā niṣṭhā'—both are attained only by devotion.

Link:—Now, the Lord promises to discuss the process, through which man attains the supreme state of actionlessness.

सिद्धिं प्राप्तो यथा ब्रह्म तथाप्नोति निबोध मे।
समासेनैव कौन्तेय निष्ठा ज्ञानस्य या परा॥५०॥

siddhiṁ prāpto yathā brahma tathāpnoti nibodha me
samāsenaiva kaunteya niṣṭhā jñānasya yā parā

Know from Me, in brief, O Arjuna, how he, who has attained perfection, (purification of the inner sense) attains Brahma (the Eternal or the Absolute), that supreme state of knowledge (jñāna). 50

Comment:—

'Siddhiṁ prāpto yathā brahma tathāpnoti nibodha me'—Here, the term 'Siddhim' (perfection), denotes purification of the inner sense (viz., mind and heart), which was discussed in the preceding verse, by the expressions 'Asaktabuddhiḥ' (unattached intellect), 'Jitātmā' (subdued body) and 'vigataspṛhaḥ' (freedom from desires). Such a person, whose inner sense is purified, has no desire or attachment for anything, circumstance, or person. Nothing, remains to be achieved by him. So it has been said, that he has attained perfection.

A worldly person, thinks that he has attained perfection, if his desires are satisfied, and he has attained accomplishments (Siddhis), such as aṇimā (that which makes a Yogī infinitely small and invisible) etc. But in fact, this is not perfection, because satisfaction (fulfilment), of one desire, gives birth to other desires. These desires prolong and they bind him. Real perfection, consists in total freedom, from desires.

A striver, who has attained perfection in the form of purification of the inner sense, attains Brahma. Lord Kṛṣṇa, exhorts Arjuna, to hear from Him of the important factors, in brief, because these are indispensable for a striver, who wants to practise, the Sāṅkhyayoga.

The term 'nibodha' (Know), denotes that in the Discipline of Knowledge, action and material, are not so important, as is knowledge. So the term 'Nibodha,' has been used here, as well as in the thirteenth verse of this chapter, in connection with a 'Sāṅkhyayogī'.

'Samāsenaiva kaunteya niṣṭhā jñānasya yā parā'— 'Parāniṣṭhā', is the final stage of Sāṅkhyayoga (the Discipline of Knowledge). Lord Kṛṣṇa asks Arjuna, to know after hearing from Him in brief, how a striver following the path of Knowledge, attains Brahma (the Eternal), that supreme state of knowledge.

Appendix—Here the term 'siddhiṁ' means complete purification of the inner sense, having attained which a Karmayogī can follow either the Path of Knowledge or the Path of Devotion—

tāvat karmāṇi kurvīta na nirvidyeta yāvatā
matkathā śravaṇādau vā śraddhā yāvanna jāyate

(Śrīmadbhā. 11/20/9)

"Actions should be performed by the time, there is detachment (dispassion) from mundane pleasures or until there is faith in listening to My pastime and divine strories and in their loud chanting etc."

If a striver does not insist on anyone of the three disciplines of Karma, Jñāna and Bhakti, then these are the 'means' as well as the 'end'. As means, these three are different but as an end all the three are one. Therefore in the Gītā, the Lord in certain references declared devotion as a means to achieve an end which is knowledge (Self-realization)—'mayi cānanyayogena bhaktīravyabhīcāriṇī' (13/10), 'māṁ ca yo'vyabhicāreṇa..... brahma bhūyāya kalpate' (14/26); and in other references He declared Jñāna as a means to achieve Bhakti which is an end—'sanniyamyendriyagrāmaṁ sarvatra........sarvabhūta hite ratāḥ' (12/4), 'brahmabhūtaḥ prasannātmā.........madbhaktiṁ labhate parām' (18/54).

The Lord by the expression 'svakarmaṇā tamabhyarcya siddhiṁ

vindati mānavaḥ' (18/46) declared the attainment (perfection) of devotion by Karmayoga; and here He declares the perfection of Jñānayoga viz., Self-realization through Karmayoga by the expression 'siddhiṁ prāpto yathā brahma'. In the fifth chapter also by the means of Karmayoga, quick perfection of Jñānayoga viz., 'attainment of the Absolute' has been declared—'yoga yukto munirbrahma nacireṇādhigacchati' (5/6).

Link:—The Lord in the next three verses, describes the virtues with which a striver, should be endowed, in order to attain Brahma (the Eternal or the Absolute).

बुद्ध्या विशुद्धया युक्तो धृत्यात्मानं नियम्य च।
शब्दादीन्विषयांस्त्यक्त्वा रागद्वेषौ व्युदस्य च॥५१॥
विविक्तसेवी लघ्वाशी यतवाक्कायमानसः।
ध्यानयोगपरो नित्यं वैराग्यं समुपाश्रितः॥५२॥
अहङ्कारं बलं दर्पं कामं क्रोधं परिग्रहम्।
विमुच्य निर्ममः शान्तो ब्रह्मभूयाय कल्पते॥५३॥

buddhyā viśuddhayā yukto dhṛtyātmānaṁ niyamya ca
śabdādīnviṣayāṁstyaktvā rāgadveṣau vyudasya ca
viviktasevī laghvāśī yatavākkāyamānasaḥ
dhyānayogaparo nityaṁ vairāgyaṁ samupāśritaḥ
ahaṅkāraṁ balaṁ darpaṁ kāmaṁ krodhaṁ parigraham
vimucya nirmamaḥ śānto brahmabhūyāya kalpate

Endowed with a pure intellect, firmly restraining the senses, turning away from sound and other objects of senses, casting aside attraction and aversion, dwelling in solitude, taking light diet, controlling speech, body and mind, ever engaged in meditation and concentration, resorting to dispassion, having abandoned egoism, violence, arrogance, desire, anger, covetousness (accumulation), devoid of the notion of mineness and tranquil in mind—such a

man, becomes qualified to attain Brahma. 51—53

Comment:—

'Buddhyā viśuddhayā yuktaḥ'—A striver of Sāṅkhyayoga, who wants to realize God, should be endowed with a pure or Sāttvikī intellect, (Gītā 18/30). There should be no doubt in this intellect. In the Discipline of 'Sāṅkhya', buddhi' (intellect), is given priority. Discrimination, which is very essential for a striver, is revealed in pure intellect. It is by this discrimination, that he severs his connection with matter.

'Vairāgyaṁ samupāśritaḥ'—As worldly people depend, on objects and persons, out of attachment or passion, a striver, of Sāṅkhyayoga, remains detached. He has no attachment for worldly persons, and places etc., worldly and celestial pleasures, have no charm for him.

'Viviktasevī'—Such a striver, has a natural inclination to live in solitude.This inclination is, praiseworthy. But if a striver, does not get such an opportunity to live in solitude, he should not be perturbed. This perturbation, shows the importance of worldly things, in his mind. This importance, causes further perturbation of the mind, which is an obstacle to meditation. He should remain equanimous, both in solitude, and at a crowded place.

Solitude, is conducive to concentration, meditation and purification, of heart. But, it also provides a good opportunity to drowsiness and relaxation. Moreover, a striver derives pleasure, out of praise and honour, won through his residence in a lonely place. These are stumbling blocks, to the progress of a striver. So, he should be on guard, against them.

'Laghvāśī'—A striver, should take regulated diet. He should eat, those articles of food, which suits his body. Moreover, he should not take too much food, he should eat, as much as, is indispensable for the body. It should not be taken to nourish the body, but only to satisfy hunger, like medicine. He should take such food as is easily digestible and is suitable for spiritual practice. It should also be pure or Sāttvika.

'Dhṛtyātmānaṁ niyamya ca'—He should firmly restrain, the intellect from worldly temptations, and should not allow it to deviate from the aim of God-realization. By such unswerving or Sāttvika firmness, (Gītā 18/33) he should control his senses, and should not let them run after worldly enjoyments, any time.

'Yatavākkāyamānasaḥ'—He should control his body, speech and mind (Gītā 17/14—16). He should not indulge his body, in any futile pursuit, such as lottering here and there, and journey, for pleasure etc. His speech, should be truthful, agreeable and necessary, free from reproach and scandal etc. The mind, should be utilized, in the thought of the Lord, rather than of the world.

Śabdādīnviṣayāṁstyaktvā'—A striver, should withdraw the senses of sound, touch, form (sight), taste and smell from their respective objects, because a striver whose senses are not turned away from their objects, cannot practise meditation. If he enjoys sense-objects, in an attached spirit, he will dwell on sense-objects, during meditation, and he will not be able to meditate.

'Rāgadveṣau vyudasya ca'—A man, is attached to persons and things regarding these, as useful for him. If anyone creates an obstacle to the attainment of any worldly object, he automatically hates him. If he is attached to something desirable, he has an automatic aversion, to the undesirable one. A man, is bound both by attachment and aversion, because he goes on thinking of the two. So, he should cast aside attraction (attachment), and aversion.

'Dhyānayogaparo nityam'—A striver, should be ever engaged in meditation, and concentration. During fixed hour of meditation, he should practise meditation, while during the time he discharges his professional and other practical duties, he should believe that nothing else exists, besides, the Lord (Gītā 18/20).

'Ahaṅkāraṁ balaṁ darpaṁ kāmaṁ krodhaṁ parigraham vimucya'—A person, has egoistic notion, by regarding himself as superior to others, because of his virtues. It is called 'Ahaṅkāra'. The force to bring others under one's sway in a wrongful manner, is called 'bala' (power). Vain consciousness, of one's property and riches etc., is known as 'Darpa' (arrogance). The desire for obtaining worldly pleasures, prosperity and favourable circumstances, is 'Kāma'. The feeling of excitement or provocation, (a kind of hot sensation) to do wrong to others, because these have been a stumbling block to our selfishness, and pride is 'Krodha' (anger). Covetousness and accumulation of things and objects, for enjoyment, is 'Parigraha'.* A striver, abandons the above-mentioned egoism, force, arrogance, desire, anger and covetousness.

'Nirmamaḥ'—'Nirmamaḥ', is he who renounces a notion of mineness, in things, body, mind and senses etc. In fact, things, persons and our so-called bodies, were not ours, a hundred years ago and will not remain ours, after a hundred years. We can assume the persons as ours, in order to serve them, and we can make the right use of the things, but it is wrong to regard these as ours, forever. If we do not regard these as ours, we become free, from the notion of mineness.

'Śāntaḥ'—Tranquillity of mind, is disturbed by assuming affinity with, the world. If this affinity is renounced, a striver, will remain tranquil in mind, because attachment or aversion, disturbs peace of mind.

'Brahmabhūyāya kalpate'—A striver, who is devoid of the notion of mineness, and is tranquil in mind, becomes qualified to attain Brahma i.e., as soon as his affinity with the unreal, is renounced, he becomes worthy of attaining, Brahma. The reason is, that this affinity with the unreal, is an obstacle, to attainment of Brahma viz., God-realization.

Link:-The Lord in the next verse explains the marks of such a striver who becomes qualified to attain Brahma and also

---

* A celibate, a person of the retired order (Vānaprastha), and a man of the renounced order (Sannyāsī) must not accumulate objects and things. If a householder accumulates objects and money etc., to render service to others, that is also not 'Parigraha'.

points out what he attains further.

ब्रह्मभूतः प्रसन्नात्मा न शोचति न काङ्क्षति।
समः सर्वेषु भूतेषु मद्भक्तिं लभते पराम्॥५४॥

brahmabhūtaḥ prasannātmā na śocati na kāṅkṣati
samaḥ sarveṣu bhūteṣu madbhaktiṁ labhate parām

Having become one with Brahma, and being tranquil (cheerful) in mind, he neither grieves nor desires, and regards all beings as alike, he acquires supreme devotion for Me. 54

Comment:—

'Brahmabhūtaḥ'—When, mind does not attach importance to the perishable, its evil propensities, such as egoism and pride, etc., are renounced. Then man has no feeling of 'mine', for them. Then, he does not accumulate or hoard things, for pleasure. When, he is not attached to pleasure and prosperity etc., naturally the mind becomes tranquil.

Thus, when a striver transcends the unreal, he becomes qualified to attain Brahma. Then from his point of view he becomes, one with Brahma and he realizes this fact, that he is Brahma. This state is called 'Brahmabhūtaḥ' here and in 5/24.

'Prasannātmā'—When mind attaches importance, to unreal things, man desires to obtain those things. This desire, disturbs peace of mind. But, when importance is not attached to unreal things, a striver's mind, remains calm and cheerful. The reason is, that in the eyes of such a Yogī, the world ceases to exist, only Brahma exists.

'Na śocati na kāṅkṣati'—Such a Yogī, who has attained oneness with Brahma, does not grieve at the heaviest loss, nor does he crave for favourable circumstances. It means, that he remains unruffled in perishable circumstances, because he does not behold anything, other than Brahma.

'Samaḥ sarveṣu bhūteṣu'—So long as, a striver does not become free, from the pairs of opposites, such as pleasure and pain, attachment and aversion etc., he cannot realize his identity, with God. Without realizing his identity with Him, he cannot regard, all beings as alike. But, as soon as, he becomes free from the pairs of opposites, he realizes his oneness, with God. Then, he has no separate personality or existence of his own,* and he becomes one, with Him. Thus, he regards all beings as alike, in the same way, as the Lord is alike to all beings (Gītā 9/29). As in a dream, everything is created by the mind, there is nothing except mind. The mind exists in creation and creation exists, in the mind. Similarly, God as Self, abides in all beings, and all beings, exist in the Self (God) (Gītā 6/29). This is, what the Lord means, by 'Samaḥ sarveṣu bhūteṣu'.

'Madbhaktiṁ labhate parām'—When a Yogī having realized his identity with God, regards all beings alike, he has a unique attraction, towards God and it enhances every moment. That attraction has been called here 'Parābhakti', (Supreme devotion).

As, in the twenty-fourth verse of the fifth chapter, there is mention that a Sāṅkhyayogī, identified with Brahma, attains Brahma Who is all Peace, similarly, a Yogī having realized his identity with Brahma, attains supreme devotion, to Him.

Appendix—The striver, who follows the Path of Knowledge, has latencies of devotion, does not insist on his opinion, does not regard salvation the ultimate end, does not refute and censure devotion, he is not satisfied with the attainment of salvation. Therefore having attained salvation, he also attains devotion (love).

He who from his viewpoint holds that he is Brahma, though actually he has not attained Brahma, for him the term 'brahmabhūtāḥ' has been used. Being 'brahmabhūta' the Self becomes identical in attributes with Brahma viz., he enters into the Lord's Being—'mama sādharmyamāgatāḥ' (Gītā 14/2). To be identical in attributes with Brahma is salvation. Then he merges (surrenders) himself in the all-pervading Lord of infinite universes, the Supreme Soul and becomes verily the Lord's own

* When a man accepts his separate existence, it leads him to bondage.

Self (inseparable with Him)—'jñānī tvātmaiva me matam' (Gītā 7/18). This intimate relationship in which the devotee becomes the Lord's own self viz., inseparable with Him, is the attainment of 'parā bhakti' (love which increases every moment).

In the Path of Knowledge, renunciation of matter is important which is done by discrimination. When the matter is renounced in the light of discrimination, the objects renounced may leave their latent impression, which causes philosophical differences of opinions. But having attained love, there is no latent impression of the objects renounced, because a devotee renounces nothing but he regards all objects and beings etc., as the manifestation of God—'sadasaccāham' (Gītā 9/19). Love is not attained by the use of discrimination but is attained by faith. In faith there is dependence only on God's grace. Therefore the striver who has the latent impression of devotion, the God's grace, does not let him be satisfied with salvation, the relish of salvation (integral relish) becomes insipid for him and by God's grace the relish of love (infinite relish) is bestowed upon him.

The affinity with the world causes disquietude; therefore by Karmayoga, with the breach of affinity with the world, 'serene bliss' is attained. By Jñānayoga a striver by getting established in the Self, attains Bliss of the Self. In Bhaktiyoga by becoming one with God, the devotee attains the Supreme Bliss viz., infinite Bliss (love which enhances every moment).

Link:—In the next verse, the Lord points out, the reward of supreme devotion.

भक्त्या मामभिजानाति यावान्यश्चास्मि तत्त्वतः ।
ततो मां तत्त्वतो ज्ञात्वा विशते तदनन्तरम् ॥ ५५ ॥

bhaktyā māmabhijānāti yāvānyaścāsmi tattvataḥ
tato māṁ tattvato jñātvā viśate tadanantaram

Through devotion he comes to know Me in essence (tattva),

what and who I am; then having known Me in reality, he forthwith merges unto Me. 55

Comment:—

'Bhaktyā māmabhijānāti'—When a striver, is attracted towards God, he surrenders himself to Him and becomes one with Him. He, has no separate existence of his own, his egoism, in its subtle form also disappears. He attains supreme devotion, and then he knows God, in truth.

When he realizes his identity with God, his affinity with the world is renounced, but he has egoistic thoughts, in its subtle form, by thinking, "I am Brahma, I am tranquil, I am free, from modifications." Because of this subtle egoistic notion, his individuality and dependence persist, because egoistic thought is an evolute of prakṛti (nature) and prakṛti is different, from the self. This egoism perishes after attaining supreme devotion. As soon as, this egoism completely perishes, he knows God, in truth.

'Yāvān'—At the beginning of the seventh chapter, the blessed Lord said to Arjuna, "Listen how, practising Yoga, with mind attached to Me, with complete dependence on Me, thou shalt know Me, in full, without any doubt." The same fact, was pointed out, at the end of the seventh chapter, when He declared, "Those who, having taken refuge in Me, strive for deliverance from old age and death, know Brahma (the Absolute), Adhyātma (the entire self), entire field of action (i.e., they know Him as attributeless) and also My integral being, comprising Adhibhūta (material field), Adhidaiva (Brahmā) and Adhiyajña (the unmanifest Divinity dwelling in the hearts of all beings as their witness) (i.e., they know Him endowed with attributes)."

Besides knowing Him, as attributeless and endowed with attributes, they also know Him in His other forms, such as Rāma, Kṛṣṇa, Śiva, Gaṇeśa and Sun etc. Thus he knows what He is.

'Yaścāsmi tattvataḥ'—A devotee, comes to know, that God is one, but He manifests Himself in different forms, again and again, according to the feelings of devotees. Thus, though a devotee calls a particular form of the Lord, his favourite Deity, He is one and the same in all the different forms.

'Tato māṁ tattvato jñātvā viśate tadanantaram'—Having known the Lord in reality he immediately enters into Him i.e., attains Him and knows the truth, about Him. This is perfection, and this is, the fruitfulness of human life.

An Important Fact

A man (soul), is automatically attracted towards God. But, when he assumes his affinity with prakṛti (matter), he is disinclined from God, and is inclined to the world. Then this very attraction is called lust, desire, hope or ambition etc.

The thing that is desired, is perishable and kaleidoscopic, while the self is, eternal and unchanging. But he by identifying himself with prakṛti, is attracted towards the changeable. This attraction or attachment, leads him to the cycle of birth and death. But, if he practises anyone of the disciplines of Action, Knowledge or Devotion, he can be free, from this cycle of birth and death. If serious thought is given to these three disciplines, it is found, that in all the three, there is devotion for God. In the Discipline of Action, there is devotion to duty (18/45). (This devotion to duty, is at last changed into devotion to the self (2/55, 3/17) and in the case of a man, who has past impressions (saṁskāra) of devotion for God, his devotion to duty, is transformed, into his devotion for God.) In the Discipline of Knowledge, this devotion is to the self (5/24) and in the Discipline of Devotion, this devotion is for God (10/9).* Though in all the three disciplines, there is devotion to duty or self or God but in Gītā devotion for God, has been specially glorified.

* When a man regards a thing as his own, he is automatically attracted towards it. God has been ours, since time immemorial. If we realize this fact, we shall be automatically attracted, towards Him. That attraction will provide eternal and unique bliss to us. Then, we shall be free from all evil propensities, such as desire, anger, greed, pride and envy etc. All evils are born, because spiritual bliss, has not been attained.

A Yogī (who is equanimous), is superior to ascetics, men of knowledge and men of rituals (Gītā 6/46). It means, that a Yogī, who has links with prakṛti (matter), in spite of observing austerities, possessing knowledge of scriptures and performing Vedic rituals, such as holy sacrifice, offering charity and going on pilgrimages, etc., receives a perishable reward, while a Yogī, attains spiritual realization. Therefore, he is superior to the other three. The Lord, further points out, that even among Yogīs, the greatest is a devotee (bhakta), (Gītā 6/47). In this context, a Bhaktiyogī, knows Him fully. A Sāṅkhyayogī, through supreme devotion, knows Him, fully. The same description of His full form is represented by the term, 'Yāvān.'*

At the beginning of this topic, the Lord promised to explain, how a man endowed with pure intellect, attains Brahma. He explained, that a striver engaged in meditation and concentration, resorts to dispassion. Then, being free from egoism and mineness, he attains tranquillity. One, who is tranquil in mind, becomes qualified to attain Brahma. In that state, the pairs of opposites, such as attachment and aversion, pleasure and pain, born of his affinity with the world, totally perish. Then, he regards, all beings alike and afterwards that he attains, supreme devotion.

A man (the soul), has developed a disinclination for God, by having attachment for perishable things and persons etc. But, still he has an inclination for Him, as in distress and adversity, he invokes Him for help and protection.

*The term 'Yāvān' (what He is) has been explained, in 7/19 with the declaration 'All this is God.' The same eternal Lord has been explained by distinguishing the real from the unreal, higher and lower natures, spirit (soul) and nature (Prakṛti), the knower of the field and the field and also beyond the real and the unreal (11/37). The same eternal Lord, has been explained giving three forms—higher, lower natures and 'I' (7/5-6), the knower of the field, the field and 'Me' (13/1-2), the imperishable, the perishable and the Supreme Person (15/16-17). Again each of these three, has been divided into two—lower nature, into actions and things, higher nature into spirit and Brahmā (the creator) and 'I' into attributeless, and endowed with attributes.

It can be explained by an illustration. Water can have six different forms—atom as attributeless Brahma, vapour as God with attributes, cloud as Brahmā, drops as common embodied soul, rain as action of creation and ice as element (earth, air, water and fire etc.).

That supreme devotion, is true love. Through that supreme devotion or true love, he knows Brahma fully and forthwith enters into Him.

A striver, through exclusive devotion can know Him in essence, can see Him, and can even, enter into Him (Gītā 11/54) while a Sāṅkhyayogī, can know Brahma in essence, can enter into Him, but the Lord is not bound to reveal His vision before Him, because he has no desire to behold Him. But it does not mean that he is in anyway inferior to the striver who through exclusive devotion can behold Him.

Here, entrance into Him, is that attachment to love which is inexpressible and which is said to enhance, every moment.* This love, is the state of perfection, in which nothing remains to be known, nothing remains to be done, and nothing further to be achieved. So, such a Yogī, has neither attachment for action, nor curiosity to know, or hope to live, or fear to die, nor greed, to receive.

Until he attains supreme devotion even having become one with Brahma, he possesses, a subtle egoistic notion, that he is Brahma. But this notion does not lead him, to the cycle of birth and death, unless he is attached to modes of nature. Attachment to the modes, is the cause of his birth, in good and evil wombs (Gītā 13/21). For example, when a man awakes from sound sleep, first of all he thinks 'I am'. Through this thought he is attached to his name, form, caste, place and time etc. This egoistic notion, becomes the cause of his good and evil actions. Thus, he follows a cycle of birth and death. But, when he attains supreme devotion, this subtle egoistic notion, is renounced. A striver, of high rank, who has become one with Brahma, sees the one Imperishable Being, in all existence (18/20). But, so long as, he has affinity with the mode of goodness, after awaking from sleep, he thinks 'I am Brahma' or 'All is God'. It means, that

*This love is free from attributes and desires, it enhances every moment, it cannot be divided, it is the subtlest and it can only be experienced.

during sleep, he forgets this fact and he remembers it, when he awakes. When he transcends, the three modes of nature, he realizes, that he is free from the state of sleep and wakefulness, because both of these take place in nature, while he (the self) ever remains, the same. So, such a liberated soul, is neither attached to illumination (wakefulness) and delusion (sleep), nor has an aversion, for them (14/22).

Appendix—'What (as much) I am and who I am' (yāvān yaścāsmi)—this statement pertains only to God endowed with attributes because 'yāvān-tāvān' cannot be applicable to attributeless Brahma, it can be applicable only to God endowed with attributes. In 'catuḥślokī' (consisting of four verses) Bhāgavata also the Lord while using the term 'yāvān' said to Brahmā—

yāvānahaṁ yathābhāvo yadrūpaguṇakarmakaḥ
tathaiva tattva vijñānamastu te madanugrahāt

(Śrīmadbhā. 2/9/31)

"As much I am, of what feeling I am, of what forms, attributes (qualities) and actions I am; by My grace you should exactly realize the reality of My entire form as it is."

The expression 'yāvān yaścāsmi' has been described by the Lord in the thirtieth verse of the seventh chapter by the expression 'sādhibhūtādhidaivaṁ māṁ sādhiyajñaṁ ca ye viduḥ'. It proves the speciality and significance of God endowed with attributes.

The striver following the Path of Knowledge, after Self-realization, attains devotion, then he knows Brahma in essence and also enters into Him, but he does not behold Him; nothing lacks in him but he has no desire for God's vision while the striver who follows the path of devotion from the beginning, knows God in essence, enters into Him and also beholds Him (Gītā 11/54). Therefore when there is mention of the saints who followed the Path of Knowledge, it is said that they loved God viz., had devotion to Him but there is no mention that they beheld Him.

As people coming by different paths, having entered the

gate, meet together, so do the strivers following different spiritual paths, having entered into God, become one viz., without having even the subtle trace of ego, they become free from differences of opinions.

There are two states of love—(1) When a devotee is engrossed in love, then the lover and the beloved don't remain two but they become one. (2) Sometimes in a devotee there is an overflow of love, then the lover and the beloved in spite of being one, become two in order to stage the drama of human life. Here the term 'viśate' has been used to indicate the first state.

Link:—In the first verse of this chapter, Arjuna expressed his desire to Lord Kṛṣṇa, for explaining the true nature of renunciation (Sannyāsa), and the Discipline of Action (Tyāga). In response to his question Lord Kṛṣṇa, from the fourth to the twelfth verses, explained abandonment (Tyāga—Karmayoga) and from the forty-first to the forty-eight verses, again He explained Karmayoga, as well as in brief, Bhaktiyoga (Discipline of Devotion). From the thirteenth to the fortieth verses, He explained renunciation (Sannyāsa or Sāṅkhyayoga) while, from the forty-ninth to the fifty-fifth verses He explained Sāṅkhyayoga (Discipline of Knowledge), with the predominance of the tranquillity of mind and also in brief the supreme devotion. Now Lord Kṛṣṇa, exhorts Arjuna to perform actions, by taking refuge in Him.

सर्वकर्माण्यपि सदा कुर्वाणो मद्व्यपाश्रयः।
मत्प्रसादादवाप्नोति शाश्वतं पदमव्ययम्॥ ५६॥

sarvakarmāṇyapi sadā kurvāṇo madvyapāśrayaḥ
matprasādādavāpnoti śāśvataṁ padamavyayam

Performing continually all actions whatsoever, taking refuge in Me, by My grace, My devotee, attains the Eternal imperishable State. 56

Comment:—

'Madvyapāśrayaḥ'—Such a devotee, instead of depending

on actions, their fruits, incidents, things and persons etc., and surrendering himself to Him, depends only on Him. He does not regard anything or person, as his own. Such a devotee, has to make no effort to be free from the bondage, of cycle of birth and death. The Lord Himself, straightway rescues him, from the ocean of birth and death (Gītā 12/7). One has not to worry about his living or spiritual progress. The Lord, takes over full responsibility to attend to his needs (Gītā 9/22). According to His rule, even the vilest sinner by taking refuge in Him, not only satisfies the needs of life, but also attains the supreme goal (Gītā 9/30—32).

'Sarvakarmāṇyapi sadā kurvāṇaḥ'—The Lord, by using the term 'Sarva' with 'Karmāṇi', and the term 'Sadā', with 'Kurvāṇaḥ', means to say that the state which is attained, by a meditative Sāṅkhyayogī, through meditation by controlling his body, speech and mind, is attained by a Karmayogī devotee, while performing mundane, social, physical and spiritual actions, on having taken refuge, in Him by His grace.

Generally, people think that a devotee living in solitude and engaged in devotion, adoration and meditation, attains salvation. But how can a man, who is ever engaged in activities, like a machine, attain salvation? The Lord, clarifies the doubt, by announcing "Matprasādāt (by My grace)". It means, that he who has taken refuge in Him, attains salvation by His grace. Who can check Him from blessing His devotee with beatitude?

The Lord, regards every human being, as His own and so the Divine grace is axiomatic, and is always showered. But, so long as, a man depends on the world, having a disinclination for God, His grace, does not bear fruit, for him. But, as soon as, he starts giving up his dependence on the world, he starts feeling His grace. When he totally depends only on God, he fully realizes, His grace.

'Avāpnoti śāśvataṁ padamavyayam'—The supreme eternal imperishable state, cannot be attained, through action, effort and spiritual discipline. It can be attained, only by His grace. The same state, is named Paramadhāma (Supreme Abode), Satyaloka (the Abode of Brahma, the uppermost of the seven worlds), Vaikuṇṭhaloka (the Abode of Lord Viṣṇu), Goloka (the Abode of Lord Kṛṣṇa) and Sāketaloka (the Abode of Lord Rāma), in the path of devotion while emancipation, salvation or Self-realization, in the path of knowledge the supreme abode or state attained is one and the same but it is named differently from the viewpoint of different strivers following various paths of discipline (Gītā 8/21; 14/27). Where there is God there is His Abode, because both of these are, one and the same. As God is omnipresent, so is His Abode. As soon as, a devotee develops an exclusive devotion for Him, no trace of individuality or limitedness remains, and he can behold His Divine sport and His Abode, everywhere. But, a devotee who holds that the Lord resides, in a particular Abode, as Goloka or Sāketaloka etc., he is carried to that Abode, either by the courtiers of God, or sometimes even by God, after the death of his physical body.

Appendix—About a Jñānayogī the Lord declared, that he having renounced all sense-objects, controlling his senses, ever being engaged in meditation and having abandoned egoism, mineness, desire, anger etc., becomes qualified to attain Brahma (18/51—53). But here the Lord declares for a devotee that he by performing all prescribed actions according to his order of life and stage of life, by His grace, attains the Eternal Imperishable state, because he has taken refuge in Him—'madvyapāśrayaḥ'. It means that a devotee by taking refuge in the Lord's holy feet, easily attains Supreme Abode. A devotee himself has not to attain salvation, but without having the least dependence on his power and knowledge etc., he has to take refuge in God, by having faith in Him. Then only God's grace leads him to salvation—'matprasādādavāpnoti śāśvataṁ padamavyayam'. The Lord sees that His devotee has taken refuge only in Him,* so He takes no

* Ye yathā māṁ prapadyante tāṁstathaiva bhajāmyaham

(Gītā 4/11)

heed of his flaws. In the Rāmacaritamānasa it is mentioned—

rahati na prabhu cita cūka kie kī, karata surati saya bāra hie kī.

(Bāla. 29/3)

'The Lord does not mind the errors committed by a devotee but he remembers the good feelings of his heart a hundred times.'

jana avaguna prabhu māna na kāū, dīna bandhu ati mṛdula subhāū.

(Uttara. 1/3)

'The Lord does not take heed of the flaws of His devotees, because He is the friend of the poor and is of a very tender (sweet) heart.'

'madvyapāśrayaḥ'—It means—'Exclusive refuge in Me without having the least dependence on anyone else.'

'eka bāni karunānidhāna kī, so priya jākeṁ gati na āna kī.

'This is the habit of the all-merciful God that the devotee, who does not depend on anyone else besides Him, is loving to Him' (Mānasa, Araṇya. 10/4).

Link:—By explaining to Arjuna, His general rule in the preceding verse, the Lord now instructs guidelines specially for Arjuna.

चेतसा सर्वकर्माणि मयि सन्न्यस्य मत्परः।
बुद्धियोगमुपाश्रित्य मच्चित्तः सततं भव॥५७॥

cetasā sarvakarmāṇi mayi sannyasya matparaḥ
buddhiyogamupāśritya maccittaḥ satataṁ bhava

Mentally dedicating all actions to Me, with Me as the Supreme Goal, resort to the Yoga of equanimity, and have your mind, constantly fixed on Me. 57

Comment:—

[In this verse the Lord has laid emphasis on four points:—

(i) Mentally surrender all actions to Me.

(ii) Regard Me, as the Supreme Goal, (Surrender yourself to Me).

(iii) Renounce your affinity, with the world through equanimity.

(iv) Have your mind constantly fixed, on Me.]

'Cetasā sarvakarmāṇi mayi sannyasya'—A man, mentally should regard the body, mind, senses, intellect, things, incidents, actions and persons etc., as belonging, only to God. Due to egoism, he regards them, as his own, which is sheer foolishness. The Lord, has appointed him, as an agent, to make proper use of things, persons, body, senses and mind etc., given to him. All actions, whether mundane or spiritual, which are sanctioned by scriptures, are performed by His will. So he should surrender, all of these to Him, without having any sense of mineness.

'Matparaḥ'—A devotee, should think that the Lord is his only Supreme Goal, none else besides Him is his, and so he should surrender himself, to Him. He has nothing to do at all, with worldly affairs, things and persons etc., as they are different from him. If he regards wealth, family, body, senses and mind etc., as his own, he has to depend on them, and thus he becomes a slave to them, though he thinks, that he is their master.

In fact, the Lord is one's own, and He has the greatest regard, for His devotee. He becomes a servant of him and makes him a jewel of His crown, while worldly people try to suppress and making him their slave. Therefore, a person surrendering himself to Him, should regard Him, as his Supreme Goal.

'Buddhiyogamupāśritya'—In the Gītā, great importance has been attached to equanimity. If a man becomes equanimous, he becomes a man of knowledge, of meditation, a Yogī and a devotee. But, if he is not equanimous, the Lord does not regard him as perfect, even though, he possesses several other virtues. Equanimity is naturally found, in man. But, he becomes happy and sad, by identifying himself with happy and sad circumstances. So a man should not identify himself, with given circumstances. He, in fact remains, the same while circumstances appear and disappear. So, one should remain established, in the self. By remaining established in the self, he will have equanimity.

Equanimity is worship of God (Viṣṇu Purāṇa 1/17/90). So the Lord, exhorts Arjuna, to resort to the Yoga of equanimity.

'Maccittaḥ satataṁ bhava'—The mind of a devotee, who surrenders himself to God, is obeisant at His feet. Then his natural claim over the Lord, is revealed and He takes His seat, in his mind. This is fixing of the mind, on Him.

The Lord uses the term 'Satatam' (constantly) with 'Maccittaḥ', to exhort Arjuna to have his mind constantly fixed, on Him. When a devotee knows the fact, or even assumes, that he is God's, his mind is automatically fixed, on Him. When a disciple accepts his relationship with his preceptor, he constantly thinks of him. Even when, he does not think of his preceptor, a thought remains established in him, because he (the self) has accepted the relationship. As far as his relationship with God is concerned, it has been so since time immemorial. But, by assuming his affinity with the world, he has forgotten the real relationship. So, in order to remind him, of his real connection with Him, He exhorts him, to have his mind constantly fixed, on Him.

While performing mundane activities, a striver, should not allow his heart to be affected, by being completely absorbed in these. He should keep his heart rigid. But, while performing spiritual activities, such as chanting, the Lord's name silently or loudly, adoration and meditation etc., the heart, should be absorbed, in these activities. By doing so, his mind will be quickly fixed on Him.

An Important Fact Pertaining to Love

When a striver, mentally surrenders all actions to God, he realizes his real disunion, from the world* and when he surrenders

* In fact, a man can never be united with the world. He ever remains disunited from it. When the thought of a thing, which he lacks, comes to mind, it is his assumed union, with that thing. The lack of thing makes him sad. But when he receives the thing, it goes out of his mind and this disunion makes him happy. Similarly, when a thing is lost or destroyed, a man is sad,

himself to God, he is eternally united, with Him i.e., the Lord becomes, the dearest object of his love. As far as, a mental state, in love (union and disunion) is concerned, it can be of four kinds—union in eternal union, disunion in eternal union, eternal union in disunion, and disunion in disunion. These, can be explained by an illustration:—

When there is union of Lord Kṛṣṇa and Śrī Rādhā, that is union, in eternal union. When they are united, Śrī Rādhā thinks that Lord Kṛṣṇa, has gone away from her and so she cries, "O dear, where have You gone?" This is disunion, in eternal union. Lord Kṛṣṇa is not with Śrī Rādhā, but she constantly thinks of Him and feels that He is with her. This is eternal union in disunion. Lord Kṛṣṇa, has gone out of sight. But Śrī Rādhā thinks that she has not met Lord Kṛṣṇa, for a long time. She has a desire to meet Him. This is disunion in disunion.

In fact, in all the above-mentioned four states, there is ever an union of the devotee with the Lord, and there is no possibility of disunion. This union is called love, in which the lover and the beloved, both remain united. This sport of union and disunion, goes on between a devotee and the Lord, in order to exchange love.

This love enhances every moment. When a devotee meets the Lord, he is afraid lest, He should again disappear.* So he is never satisfied, he is attracted more and more towards Him, by thinking lest He should disappear again. Thus love enhances.

In love (devotion), a devotee can have four kinds of sentiment—of service, of friendship, of affection and of conjugal

---

because he has internal union with it. But if through disinclination he realizes, that it was not his and it could not be his, he is not sad. It means that there is external disunion in assumed internal union, and there is internal disunion, in assumed external union. Thus in fact, there is no union of man with the world, he assumes his union with it, by an error of judgment.

* Both union and disunion enhance love. If there is ever-union of the two, love will not enhance, it will remain the same. Therefore the Lord disappears (conceals Himself) in order to enhance love.

love. Out of these four, the sentiment of friendship is superior, to that of service, the sentiment of affection, is superior to that of friendship, while the sentiment of conjugal love, is superior to that of affection because the thought of His glories, majesty and supremacy goes on decreasing from the first sentiment, to the fourth one. But, out of these four, even if one sentiment attains perfection, the remaining three are, also included in it. The reason is, that the Lord is perfect, and so is love for Him and so is man (soul), being a fragment of the Lord. He remains imperfect, because of his affinity with the world. If he develops his love for Him, in anyway, this love will become perfect.

In the sentiment of service, a devotee regards himself as a servant of the Lord, who is his master. So, the Master has full control over him and can use his service in anyway, according to His own sweet will, without consulting him.

In the sentiment of friendship, the Lord is a friend of the devotee. The Lord is loving to the devotee, while the devotee loves God. God has full claim on the devotee, and the devotee also on God. So, if a devotee satisfies the desire of the Lord, the Lord is also expected to fulfil a devotee's desire.

In the sentiment of affection, a devotee thinks that he is the parent or preceptor of the Lord, Who is a child and so it is his duty, to bring Him up and to look after Him, lest he should hurt himself. When Kṛṣṇa, went to a forest, Nandabābā and Yaśodā, sent Balarāma to look after Him.

In the sentiment of Mādhurya (conjugal love)* a devotee

* In the sentiment of Mādhurya (conjugal love) generally people think that it is the relationship between a man and a woman. But in fact it is not confined to a husband and a wife. 'Mādhurya' means sweetness and that sweetness develops by becoming one with the Lord. The more a devotee identifies himself with the Lord, the more sweetness develops. So if there is perfection in anyone of the sentiments either of service or friendship or affection, there will be perfect sweetness.

There is a difference between 'Abheda' (Non-duality) and 'Abhinnatā' (identification). In non-duality a devotee regards himself as the Lord while in identification there is internal intimacy in spite of being two as are two intimate friends. The more intimacy a devotee develops, the more sweetness

does not remember the Lord's supremacy. He thinks, that he is one with Him, because of his intimacy. He longs to provide Him, with every comfort.

Love is divine and spiritual. Only the Lord, deserves its bliss. The lover and the beloved, both are spiritual. In this sentiment of love, sometimes a lover becomes the beloved, while the beloved becomes a lover. In fact, it is the Lord Himself, Who becomes two, in order to relish love.

Some worldly ignorant people, do not understand the true nature of love. They regard lust, as love. But lust can be seen in all beings, and specially among ghosts, devils, demons and fiends etc. But, only the liberated souls, deserve love.

In lust, both the persons want to receive something or the other, from each other, while in love, a devotee wants to offer everything to the Lord. In lust, a person wants to satisfy his senses, while in love he wants to serve the Lord, without any desire for reward. Lust is physical, while love is spiritual. Lust involves delusion and pain, while love is totally free from delusion and pain, and involves emancipation and infinite bliss. In lust, there is attachment and dependence, while in love, there is relinquishment and independence. Lust is selfish while love is selfless. A lustful man, becomes a slave to others, while the Lord Himself becomes a slave, to a devotee, who possesses love. Lust changes into insipidity, while love enhances every moment, and provides bliss. Lust is born of depression, while love is revealed out of the happiness, of the beloved. In lust, a man wants to derive pleasure, while in love a devotee, wants to please the Lord. Lust leads to hell, while love leads to the abode of God. In lust, man and woman ever remain two, while in love, the devotee and the Lord, become one and the same.

Appendix—In the preceding verse the Lord, having declared the attainment of the eternal imperishable state, now tells the

---

is revealed. This is known as sentiment of love. The Lord reveals Himself in different forms to taste this love.

method how to attain that state. For a striver there are two important duties—to renounce affinity with the world and to have affinity (love) with God. In the term 'madvyapāśrayaḥ' used in the preceding verse, there is predominance of the affinity with God; while in the verse in the term 'buddhiyogamupāśritya' there is predominance of the renunciation of affinity with the world.

The Lord by the term 'buddhiyogamupāśritya' means that there should not persist even the subtle affinity with the world—'dureṇa hyavaraṁ karma buddhiyogāddhanañjaya' (Gītā 2/49); the striver should be totally free from attachment and aversion.

By fixing the mind constantly only on God equanimity (buddhiyoga) is naturally attained, therefore the expression 'maccittaḥ satataṁ bhava' has been used.

Link:—The Lord, in the next two verses, points out to Arjuna the reward of obeying His command, and the harm which would befall him, if he did not obey Him.

मच्चित्तः सर्वदुर्गाणि मत्प्रसादात्तरिष्यसि।
अथ चेत्त्वमहङ्कारान्न श्रोष्यसि विनङ्क्ष्यसि॥५८॥

maccittaḥ sarvadurgāṇi matprasādāttariṣyasi
atha cettvamahaṅkārānna śroṣyasi vinaṅkṣyasi

Fixing thy mind on Me, thou shalt by My grace, overcome all obstacles; but if, from egoism, thou wilt not listen to Me, thou shalt perish. 58

Comment:—

'Maccittaḥ sarvadurgāṇi matprasādāttariṣyasi'—The Lord declares, that by fixing his mind on Him, Arjuna will by His grace, overcome all obstacles and sorrows, without making any other effort.

When a devotee surrenders his action and himself to the Lord, and has no attachment for the pleasures, which are born of sense contacts, the Lord shoulders the responsibility, to do away with his evils, if these remain in their subtle form, and enables him to realize God. So He declares, that Arjuna will overcome all obstacles, by His grace. It means, that a devotee by having a disinclination for the world, should have an inclination for God. He has committed an error, that he has attached himself to the world. If he renounces this attachment and has an inclination for God, the Lord by His grace, removes all his obstacles and leads him to perfection.

When a man accepts his affinity, with body etc., which are evolutes of prakṛti, he has to perform his duty, according to his caste and order of life, as sanctioned by scriptures. It is because of this affinity, that he incurs sin or performs virtuous deeds, and has to receive reward in the form of pain or pleasure. If he develops a total disinclination for prakṛti, and its evolutes, and an inclination for God, he is not bound to perform his duty, in accordance with his caste and stage of life. Prohibition and prescription, do not apply to him, because they have their predominance in the domain of prakṛti. In the domain of the Lord, there is predominance of surrender, to Him.

Man (self), is a fragment of God (Gītā 15/7). If he proceeds towards Him, he becomes free from indebtedness of gods, sages, creatures, parents and grand parents (manes)* etc., because the self or the soul, has never taken or borrowed anything, from them. The self, being a fragment of God, is perfect. But when it assumes its affinity with a body, it feels a lack otherwise not—'The real, never ceases to be' (Gītā 2/16). When he does not feel a lack (want), how could he be indebted to them? This is, overcoming all obstacles.

A striver, who follows a spiritual path, observes the Lord's grace, in all obstacles, such as poverty, diseases and also other disturbances, in the spiritual path. The Lord, removes the obstacles

*'O King, he who abandoning all actions, takes refuge in the Lord, becomes free from the debt of gods, sages, kith and kin and manes and does not remain a servant to them.

of such a striver, who depends only on Him, and enables him to attain Him. There is possibility of hurdles being created, in the spiritual discipline and in God-realization. Therefore, the Lord declares, that He will remove such hurdles and will lead him to His realization.

'Atha cettvamahaṅkārānna śroṣyasi vinaṅkṣyasi'—The Lord because of His abundant grace upon Arjuna, says to him, that if he, because of egoism does not listen to Him, and does not act according to His advice, he will perish. If he does not hear Him, out of ignorance or by an error, it is pardonable. But if he does not listen to Him out of egoism, he will perish, because this egoism will enhance his pride, which is the root of a demoniac nature.

In the fourth chapter, the Lord said to Arjuna, "You are My devotee and friend" (4/3). Again in the ninth chapter, He said to him, "Know it for certain, Arjuna, that My devotee never perishes" (9/31). It shows, that Arjuna is a devotee to the Lord, so he can never have a disinclination for God, and he can never perish. But if even he does not listen to the Lord, he will have a disinclination for Him, and therefore he will have a downfall i.e., follow the cycle of birth and death (Gītā 9/3; 16/20).

An Important Fact

In the fifty-sixth verse of this chapter, Lord Kṛṣṇa declares, "Taking refuge in Me, by My grace, a devotee attains, the eternal imperishable state." Again here, He declares,"O Arjuna, by My grace, you will overcome all obstacles." It means, that the Lord's grace, is more powerful, than any spiritual discipline. But, it does not mean that Arjuna should not practise spiritual discipline, he should make it a part of his duty, to practise it as the only aim of human life, is God-realization. A person, who does not realize God, he even on reaching the highest world as that of Brahmā, will have to return from there (Gītā 8/16).* Therefore, having

* O lotus eyed! Those who have not taken refuge in Your feet and whose

received this human body, a man should realize God, and be free from the cycle of birth and death. For a Karmayogī also Lord Kṛṣṇa has declared, "Endowed with equanimity, a person casts away, in this life, both good and evil" (Gītā 2/50). It means that the only aim of human life, is to be free from bondage viz., the cycle of birth and death.

In the eleventh verse of the tenth chapter, the Lord declared, "By My grace, I dispel darkness, born of ignorance, by the shining lamp of wisdom", while in the forty-seventh verse of the eleventh chapter, He said, "By My grace, I have shown you this Universal Form." By laying emphasis on His grace, here He declares, that by His grace the eternal imperishable state, will be attained (18/56) and by His grace, all obstacles will be overcome, (18/58). Having attained the eternal imperishable state, there is no possibility of any obstacles. But the Lord, lays emphasis on this point, to remove Arjuna's fear, who thought that he would incur sin by waging war, the manes of his race would fall, and the age-long caste traditions and family customs, would get lost. He also thought, that if the sons of Dhṛtarāṣṭra, armed with weapons, killed him in battle, while he was unarmed and unresisting, it would be better for him (Gītā 1/36—46). So the Lord declares, that by His grace he will overcome all obstacles i.e., he will neither, incur sin in the least, nor be bound. But, by His grace being purified, he will attain the Supreme State.

Appendix—The only duty of a devotee is to take refuge in God and to think of Him only, then the Lord shoulders his full responsibility. The Lord, by showering His special grace on the devotee, enables him to overcome all obstacles and leads him to His attainment—'yogakṣemaṁ vahāmyaham' (Gītā 9/22). Therefore in the 'Brahmasūtra' it is mentioned—'viśeṣānugrahaśca' (3/4/38)—'By devotion to God, God showers His special grace

intellect has not been purified because of being devoid of Your devotion, though they regard themselves emancipated, yet they are really bound. They even if, through laborious spiritual discipline, reach high seat, but they fall from there.

on His devotee.' In fact God has already bestowed his mercy upon every human being but when a devotee takes refuge in God, he specially realizes that mercy.

यदहङ्कारमाश्रित्य न योत्स्य इति मन्यसे।
मिथ्यैष व्यवसायस्ते प्रकृतिस्त्वां नियोक्ष्यति ॥ ५९ ॥

yadahaṅkāramāśritya na yotsya iti manyase
mithyaiṣa vyavasāyaste prakṛtistvāṁ niyokṣyati

If filled with egoism, thou thinkst: ' I will not fight,' vain is this resolve, as your Kṣatriya nature will compel thee to fight. 59

Comment:—

'Yadahaṅkāramāśritya'—Cosmic intelligence, is born of prakṛti and egoism, is born of cosmic intelligence. Out of egoism, a man thinks, "I am body." One who is given to such egoism, can never be actionless i.e., free from actions, because prakṛti is ever active and subject to change. He, who has assumed affinity with it, can never remain actionless (Gītā 3/5).

When a man due to his ego, is swayed by ever active prakṛti, he cannot remain actionless. Sometimes, he may seem doing physical actions, while at times abstaining, from them. But, in both states, he does action, as his affinity with the body, is intact. When, he renounces his affinity with prakṛti (body), then irrespective of his activity or not, he is quite actionless viz., detached. Then, nothing remains to be done by him. If a devotee takes refuge in the Lord, and thus renounces all his connection, with the body, he is not helplessly driven, to action.

'Na yotsya iti manyase'—In the second chapter, Arjuna having taken refuge in the Lord, prayed to Him, "I am your disciple. Instruct me, who has taken refuge, in You" (2/7). Then Arjuna bluntly said to Lord Krṣṇa, "I will not fight" (2/9). It was undesirable, of him to say so, if he really sought refuge in the Lord. It was desirable for him to say, that he would act according to the Lord's bidding. So the Lord, thought that instead of taking refuge in Him, he was taking refuge in egoism. Hearing Arjuna's words full of egoism, Lord Kṛṣṇa could not help smiling (2/10). But He had abundant love and grace, for Arjuna. So He started preaching, the sermon, in the second chapter. Otherwise, He would have said then and there, which He has said now, in the eighteenth chapter 'Do as you wish' (18/63). Further, the Lord warned him, that if he had taken refuge in Him, he would not have said, "I'll not fight." These words, pricked the Lord's mind. Through the very same words, "I'll not fight" the Lord said to him, that his words proved, that he had taken refuge in his egoism, not in Him. Moreover by taking refuge, he would not have been helplessly driven, to action by prakṛti (Gītā 7/14) as prakṛti (nature) compels only that person, to action who has not taken refuge in Him (Gītā 7/13).

There is a vital point, which needs attention. By having attachment for the objects of nature, a man thinks, that he is their master. But in fact, he becomes a slave to them, as he depends on them. But he does not become a slave, to those objects, which he does not regard, as his own. So, he should not regard the objects as his own, as these are not his own. He should hold, that only the Lord, is his. By having this belief, he should take refuge, in Him. Having taken refuge in Him, he becomes totally independent. But those, who take refuge in egoism, circulate in the path of the world of death (9/3). So the Lord says, 'Prakṛtistvāṁ niyokṣyati'—that his, nature of being a member of the warrior class, will compel him to fight, and he will not be able to refrain himself, from war.

'Mithyaiṣa vyavasāyaste'—Resolve, is of two kinds—real and unreal. The resolve of our affinity with God is real, while the resolve of our affinity with prakṛti (nature), is unreal. In the former, there is predominance of the self, while in the latter, there is predominance of prakṛti or inner sense. So the Lord, says to Arjuna that his resolve of not fighting, is in vain, as he is a member of the warrior class. He should depend on the Lord, not on prakṛti (nature) and its evolutes, the world.

If a being resolves, that he belongs to the Lord and so he has to worship Him, with exclusive devotion, his resolve is real, true and eternal. The Lord, explaining the merit of such a resolve, declares in the thirtieth verse of the ninth chapter, "Even if the vilest sinner worships Me, with exclusive devotion, he should be considered a saint; for he has rightly resolved." The right resolve, is that he is God's and so he will adore Him.

'Prakṛtistvāṁ niyokṣyati'—By this expression, the Lord means to say, that his nature as a warrior, will compel him to fight. The nature of a Kṣatriya (the member of warrior class) is chivalry, and not to flee from a battlefield (Gītā 18/43). So, he cannot restrain himself from fighting, in a righteous war.

Appendix—In the preceding verse it was mentioned that the 'fruit' of egoism would be adverse; while in this verse it is mentioned that out of egoism the 'duty' will not be performed properly. The Lord means to say that Arjuna's listening to Him or not listening to Him, will not conduce him to a downfall but out of egoism he will be ruined. Performance of an action or its non-performance is not an obstacle, but egoism is the main stumbling block.

The Lord told Arjuna that by His grace, he would attain Him and also overcome all his obstacles (18/56, 58). But in spite of the Lord's such utterances, Arjuna did not respond, while he should have said, "I shall act, according to your bidding." Then the Lord declares, "If out of ignorance you don't listen to Me, it matters little, but if out of egoism, you don't listen to Me, you will be ruined." The Lord means to say that as He shoulders the full responsibility of a devotee about his means and end, so should a devotee wholeheartedly take refuge in Him. But if he takes refuge in egoism, it means that he has not taken refuge in Him but he has taken refuge in 'aparā prakṛti' viz., egoism. On the one hand the Lord inspires him to perform his duty to fight; and on the other hand his Kṣatriya nature compels him to fight. If he does not obey the Lord, his Kṣātra nature will force him to fight. If his nature compels him to fight, he himself will have to shoulders the responsibility; and if by listening to the Lord, he performs his duty, the responsibility will be shouldered by Him. If he himself shoulders the responsibility, it will lead him to bondage; but if the Lord shoulders the responsibility, it will lead him to salvation.

Link:—In the previous verse, the Lord described that nature would compel Arjuna, to perform action. In the next verse, He explains the same point.

स्वभावजेन कौन्तेय निबद्धः स्वेन कर्मणा।
कर्तुं नेच्छसि यन्मोहात्करिष्यस्यवशोऽपि तत्॥ ६०॥

svabhāvajena kaunteya nibaddhaḥ svena karmaṇā
kartuṁ necchasi yanmohātkariṣyasyavaśo'pi tat

O Arjuna, that action which through delusion you do not want to do, bound by your own acts born of your nature, you will helplessly perform. 60

Comment:—

'Svabhāvajena kaunteya nibaddhaḥ svena karmaṇā'— Svabhāva (nature), consists of a total sum of actions and inclinations of the previous birth, the influence of parents of this birth, the environment and the education, he receives. The same nature has been called Svadharma (own duty)—"Considering your own duty, you should not waver" (Gītā 2/31).

'Kartuṁ necchasi yanmohātkariṣyasyavaśo'pi tat'—Lord Kṛṣṇa says to Arjuna, that endowed with martial qualities, such as prowess and valour etc., of the warrior class, being bound by your Kṣatriya nature, you will have to do irresistibly, what you do not want to perform, out of delusion. The scriptures have also sanctioned the duties, according to one's own nature. Lord Kṛṣṇa declared, "One's own duty, though devoid of merit, is preferable to the duty of another, well performed" (Gītā 3/35; 18/47). So, he is bound to perform the act of fighting, born of his nature. It is out of delusion, that he is thinking not to fight.

The nature of liberated souls, is perfectly pure. So, they are not driven to action, by their nature. But still, they perform actions, according to their nature. Common people are driven to action, under the sway of their nature (3/33). So Lord Kṛṣṇa tells Arjuna, that he will also have to perform action of fighting, according to the nature of a member of the warrior class, and that will not bear good fruit. As if he fights, by obeying either the scriptures or the saints or Him, it will lead him to salvation, because this action, will be free from attachment and aversion. When a man performs actions, in accordance with ordinances of scriptures, or His order, his attachment and aversion for actions, automatically melt away, as he has an eye on the ordinance or the order. Thus, he is not swayed, by attachment and aversion.

An Important Fact

In the Gītā, it has been mentioned several times, that men act, as swayed by their own nature (3/5; 8/19; 9/8). And it has been specially mentioned in 3/33 and here in 18/59.* This proves, the predominance of one's own nature. A being's nature, accompanies him to his birth, in good and evil wombs. If he is pure of nature, having no attachment to persons and things etc., he will not be reborn. It is attachment, to the modes of nature, which is the cause of birth of the soul (self), in good or evil wombs (Gītā 13/21).

* In Jñānayoga (the Discipline of Knowledge) the man of wisdom renounces his affinity with Prakṛti (Nature) and so he is not compelled to perform actions by Prakṛti (Nature).

Now, a question arises, when a man is compelled to perform actions according to his nature, how will prescription and prohibition of scriptures be applied? How will the preaching of preceptors, be translated into practice? How will strivers inculcate virtues, by discarding evils and vices?

The answer to the above questions is that, as a man cannot stop the flow of the Ganges, but can redirect it, similarly he cannot renounce the duty of his caste (Varṇa), but can purify his nature, by being free from attachment and aversion, by having the aim of God-realization. It means, that a man is powerful and free, in purifying his nature.

In the Gītā the Lord, has described two disciplines—of action and of devotion, to improve one's nature.

(1) Discipline of Action:—In the thirty-fourth verse of the third chapter, the Lord declared, "Attachment and aversion are a man's foes. So a man, should never come under their sway." It means, that instead of performing actions out of attachment and aversion, he should perform these according to the ordinance of scriptures. If a disciple, carries out the behest of his preceptor, with zeal and pleasure, his attachment and aversion get obliterated. Similar, is the case with a son in relation to his parents, a wife to her husband and a servant in relation to his master. By doing so happily, a man becomes free from attachment and aversion. But, if he performs action according to his own sweet will, attachment and aversion are firmly established. When he performs only prescribed actions happily though his mind misguides him to do otherwise, his attachment is rooted out. When one is prompted not to do some action but if he does it according to the ordinance of the scripture his aversion vanishes.

(2) Discipline of Devotion:—When a man takes refuge in God, and becomes merely an instrument in His hand, he performs actions, as sanctioned by Him and so attachment and aversion of his nature, are rooted out.

It means, that in the Discipline of Action, when a striver does not come under the sway of attachment and aversion, his nature is purified (Gītā 3/34). In the Discipline of Devotion, when a striver takes refuge in Him, his nature is purified (Gītā 18/62). When nature is purified, there remains no ground for bondage.

A man performs actions, either after being swayed by attachment and aversion, or by following scriptural injunctions. Attachment and aversion, are strengthened if he performs these under the sway of attachment and aversion. Thus, his nature becomes impure. But, if he acts according to the set principles, his nature, is purified. Strivers, who act according to ordinance of scriptures, advice of great men and liberated souls, having only an aim of God-realization, set examples and standards, for others. So do, great men and emancipated souls (Gītā 3/21).

Appendix—Nature is of two kinds—(1) Nature of performing prescribed actions (2) Nature of performing forbidden actions. Out of these, the nature of performing prescribed actions, being natural, is 'sva'—one's own nature; while the nature of the performance of forbidden actions, being 'āgantuka' (visiting nature) is 'para' (not one's own). The nature of the performance of prescribed actions, being natural, is not 'janya' (born); but the nature of the performance of forbidden actions being alien is 'janya' (born of attachment, born of bad company). A man's main duty is to improve and purify his nature viz., he should give up the nature of performing forbidden actions and he should conduct himself well according to the nature which he has formed by performing the prescribed actions. The Lord has ordered Arjuna to perform his prescribed duty according to his 'varṇa' (order of life) (caste) sanctioned by the scripture.

The Lord says to Arjuna that either as a matter of duty, or as obedience to His order, he will have to fight. Without taking refuge in Him, his egoism will persist by which even the prescribed actions will lead him to bondage. But if he takes refuge in Him, he will get rid of egoism. It is egoism which leads to bondage. When even a wise man, who is not swayed by nature and whose nature is perfectly pure, acts in accordance with his nature, then how can a man, who is swayed by his nature and whose nature is impure, act contrary to (against) his nature?

Link:—Soul (the self) is a fragment of God, and is sentient, while nature is self-made and insentient. So how does soul, come under the sway of nature? The Lord answers the question, in the next verse.

ईश्वरः सर्वभूतानां हृद्देशेऽर्जुन तिष्ठति।
भ्रामयन्सर्वभूतानि यन्त्रारूढानि मायया॥ ६१ ॥

īśvaraḥ sarvabhūtānāṁ hṛddeśe'rjuna tiṣṭhati
bhrāmayansarvabhūtāni yantrārūḍhāni māyayā

The Lord dwells in the hearts of all beings, O Arjuna, causing them by His illusive power, to revolve, in accordance with their nature, as if they are mounted on a wheel of the body. 61

Comment:—

'Īśvaraḥ sarvabhūtānāṁ hṛddeśe' rjuna tiṣṭhati bhrāmayansarvabhūtāni yantrārūḍhāni māyayā'—The Lord, Who is an impartial controller, sustainer and conductor, of all beings, causes those beings to revolve like wooden dolls, mounted on a wheel, who have assumed their body, as 'I' or 'mine'.

Just as, a man boarding a train goes only to stations, where it arrives and when he gets off it, he has not to go to those other stations where the train further goes; similarly, so long as a man assumes his affinity of 'I'ness and 'mineness', with this body, the Lord conducts him, according to his nature* and he revolves, following the cycle of birth and death.

This affinity of 'I'ness and mineness, gives birth to attachment and aversion, which make the nature impure. This impurity of

* Nature dwells in the causal body. The same nature is revealed in subtle body and physical body.

nature, compels him to perform actions. But when he renounces his affinity with his body, his nature becomes purified, by being free from attachment and aversion, and he is not helplessly driven, to action. In that case, he is not conducted, by the illusive power of the Lord.

Now, a doubt arises whether a man is free to act, according to his will or does he depend for his actions, on any other agency? If he depends on any other agency, how can he perform, only those actions which are prescribed by scriptures?

The answer is, that as ice is frozen in a refrigerator, and heat is produced by a heater, according to their own mechanism, though both of the machines are run by electricity. Electricity, has no will and insistence of its own, that it would run only a particular machine. But, it works every machine. In the same way, all beings revolve, according to their own nature, by drawing inspiration and energy, from the Lord. It means, that persons of good nature, perform virtuous deeds, while persons of evil nature, perform evil deeds. Thus, one's own nature, is responsible for the performance of good and evil deeds. But, a point needs special attention. A man is free in purifying his nature, or in sullying it, while other creatures such as birds, beasts and even the gods are not free, in improving their nature. The Lord by His grace, has bestowed upon us this human body, so that we may attain salvation. So a man, should attain it by improving his nature.

When the Lord declares, that He dwells in the hearts of all beings, He means to say, that just as water pervades everywhere under the earth, but can be received from a well, similarly, the Lord pervades everywhere, yet a heart is His special residence. Similarly, in the third chapter it has been declared, that the all-pervading Lord, is always present in sacrifice (Yajña) (Gītā 3/15).

An Important Fact

A striver, generally commits an error, when he assumes that during adoration, loud-chanting of divine names and meditation etc., God is far away from him, and He will not be revealed there and then. Similarly, he may think that he does not deserve, God-realization. God is not merciful to him, and so on. So he strengthens the belief, that God is far away from him. But he should have the conviction, that as God pervades everywhere, He is in him and in his body, mind, breath and intellect and chanting also. There is no one nearer, than He is. By having this conviction a striver, should practise adoration, chanting and meditation etc.

Now a doubt arises, that if we assume that the Lord is in us, the Lord and we, will be different. The clarification is, that it is our egoistic notion, which makes us seem different from God. If we accept Him as ours, we become one with Him and love is revealed.

When the Ganges is flooded, water overflows its banks and is filled in pits etc., which are away, from the river. When again it flows in its normal course, the water of the pits, is separated from the main course. This water is considered defiled, like wine. It is dirty. Several germs and insects are born in it and cause diseases. When it is again mixed, with the main stream of the Ganges, its impurity, limitedness and unholiness, go away and it again becomes pure and the holy water of the Ganges.

Similarly, when a man out of his egoistic notion, develops a disinclination for God, he is full of several impurities, such as dependence, hatred, enmity, shortage, disquietude, unevenness, limitedness, inertness and unholiness etc. But, when again he has an inclination for the Lord, and takes refuge in Him, Whose fragment he is, all his impurities, as his separateness from and slavery for the world, perish. The reason is, that he himself being a fragment of the Lord, is free from defects. It is because of his egoistic notion, that defects develop in him.

Appendix—The term 'bhrāmayan' means that the entire universe is conducted by God's power—'mattaḥ sarvaṁ pravartate' (Gītā 10/8). The Lord inspires beings to act according to their nature but He does not insist on it. It is because of God's non-insistence, that a man, being swayed (driven) by desire, sense of mine and attachment, performs virtuous and sinful actions; and in order to reap their fruit he goes to the heavenly world or to hells and lower wombs. But he, who takes refuge in God, God inspires him specially. Being devoid of egoism, whatever he does, he does it according to God's inspiration.

Link:—The Lord, in the preceding verse, said that the Lord dwelling in the hearts of all beings, causes them to revolve as if mounted on a machine. In such a case, what should a man do, to get rid of this bondage? The answer comes now.

तमेव शरणं गच्छ सर्वभावेन भारत।
तत्प्रसादात्परां शान्तिं स्थानं प्राप्स्यसि शाश्वतम्॥ ६२॥

tameva śaraṇaṁ gaccha sarvabhāvena bhārata
tatprasādātparāṁ śāntiṁ sthānaṁ prāpsyasi śāśvatam

Take refuge in Him, alone, wholeheartedly, O Arjuna. By His grace, you shall attain supreme peace and eternal abode. 62

Comment:—

[A tendency is generally found, among people, that they do not have full faith, in great personalities, because of much familiarity with them. But when those great persons, leave this mortal world, people repent at their past actions. Similarly, Lord Kṛṣṇa acts as a driver of Arjuna's chariot, and obeys him. When Lord Kṛṣṇa says to him, that a devotee who takes refuge in Him, by his grace obtains supreme peace and eternal abode and fixing his mind on Him, he will overcome all obstacles, Arjuna does not respond. It may mean that Arjuna has not full faith in the words of Lord Kṛṣṇa. So Lord Kṛṣṇa exhorts him to take refuge in the unmanifest Lord, Who dwells in the hearts of all beings.]

'Tameva śaraṇaṁ gaccha'—Lord Kṛṣṇa exhorts Arjuna, to 'seek refuge in the omnipresent Lord, Who dwells in the hearts of all beings and Who directs them.' It means, that instead of depending on perishable things, incidents, circumstances and persons etc., he should depend, only on the imperishable Lord.

In the preceding verse, the Lord mentioned that He causes the beings, who assume affinity of 'I'ness and 'mineness' with the body, to revolve as if mounted on a machine. Here by using the term 'eva' (even) Lord Kṛṣṇa, exhorts Arjuna not to have the least affinity of 'I'ness and 'mineness' with body, but seek refuge in God alone.

'Sarvabhāvena'—It means, that Arjuna should think of Him with his mind, should worship Him with his body, and should remain pleased in (all happenings through) His sweet will, whether desirable or undesirable, for him. He should be specially happy with undesirable circumstances, by thinking that the Lord has created such circumstances, against him for his welfare even against his will without consulting him in order to, enable him to attain salvation.

'Tatprasādātparāṁ śāntiṁ sthānaṁ prāpsyasi śāśvatam'— Lord Kṛṣṇa, announced, "By My grace, one attains the eternal state" (18/56) and "By My grace, thou shalt overcome all obstacles" (18/58). The same fact, has been pointed out here, when He declares, "By the grace of the Lord, Who dwells in the heart, you will obtain, supreme peace and eternal abode." In the Gītā, supreme peace has been called, eternal abode. But here, the Lord has used both these expressions together. So here 'Parā śānti' (Supreme peace), should mean total disinclination, for the world, while Śāśvata sthāna (eternal abode) should denote the eternal divine abode.

Here, Lord Kṛṣṇa has exhorted Arjuna to take refuge in the all-pervading God. So a doubt arises, whether Lord Kṛṣṇa, is not the all-pervading God.

The clarification is that the refuge (shelter) in the all-pervading Lord has been called more secret, than all secrets (18/63) while refuge in the person of Lord Kṛṣṇa, has been called the most secret of all. It shows that Lord Kṛṣṇa is greater than, the all-pervading God.

Lord Kṛṣṇa also declared, "Though unborn and imperishable and also the Lord of all beings, I manifest Myself through My power, (Māyā)" (4/6); "Having known Me, as the Enjoyer of sacrifices and austerities, the Great Lord of all the worlds, and the Disinterested Friend of all beings, My devotee, attains Me" (5/29); "But those who do not regard Me, as the Enjoyer and the Lord of all the worlds, fall" (9/24). It also proves by positive and negative inference, that Śrī Kṛṣṇa is the Supreme Lord.

In this chapter it is mentioned, that the Lord dwells in the hearts of all beings (18/61) and in the fifteenth chapter, it is mentioned that He (Lord Kṛṣṇa) is lodged in the hearts of all (15/15). It means that the all-pervading Lord, and Lord Kṛṣṇa are not two, but both are, one.

Then why did Lord Kṛṣṇa say to Arjuna, "Take refuge in Me alone." The reason is, that in the fifty-sixth verse Lord Kṛṣṇa said, "By My grace, one attains the eternal imperishable state"; in the fifty-seventh and fifty-eighth verses He said, "Surrender to Me. By My grace you will overcome all obstacles." But Arjuna did not speak viz., he did not express his acceptance by words or demeanour. It means, that Arjuna did not believe in what Lord Kṛṣṇa said. Then Lord Kṛṣṇa scolded him, "If filled with egoism, thou thinkst; 'I will not fight,' vain is this, thy resolve. Nature will compel thee" (18/59). Arjuna did not respond even to this scolding. So Lord Kṛṣṇa had to say, "If you don't want to take refuge in Me, seek refuge in the Lord, Who dwells in the hearts of all beings."

In fact, Lord Kṛṣṇa and the Lord Who dwells in the heart of all beings, are one and the same.

Appendix—The Soul (Self) is a fragment only of God. Therefore Lord Kṛṣṇa exhorts Arjuna to seek refuge in only God. When a man takes refuge in God, he gets rid of egoism. So long as a man (the Self) is not under the control (refuge) of

God, he is swayed by 'prakṛti' (nature). The more he is inclined towards the inert matter (non-Self), the more he is endowed with the demoniac nature; and the more he is inclined towards pure consciousness, the more he is endowed with the divine nature.

Link:— In the preceding verse, Lord Kṛṣṇa ordered Arjuna to take refuge in God, Who dwells in the hearts of all beings. But Arjuna did not respond. So Lord Kṛṣṇa, in order to warn him asks him to do, as he wishes.

इति ते ज्ञानमाख्यातं गुह्याद्गुह्यतरं मया।
विमृश्यैतदशेषेण यथेच्छसि तथा कुरु॥६३॥

iti te jñānamākhyātaṁ guhyādguhyataraṁ mayā
vimṛśyaitadaśeṣeṇa yathecchasi tathā kuru

Thus has this knowledge (jñāna) (more secret than all secrets), been imparted to thee by Me. Having reflected over it fully, do as you think best. 63

Comment:—

'Iti te jñānamākhyātaṁ guhyādguhyataraṁ mayā'—The term 'Iti' (thus), stands for refuge, in the omnipresent Lord, Who dwells in the hearts of all beings. This teaching is more secret* while the

* Wise men endowed with equanimity, renouncing the fruit of actions, attain the blissful supreme state (2/51); the perfection which is attained by Jñānayoga is also attained by Karmayoga (4/38); a Karmayogī attains to the Absolute, in no time (5/6); abandoning attachment to the fruit of actions, the Karmayogī attains peace (5/12). Thus Karmayoga (Discipline of Action), has been declared to be an independent means, to realize God. So it is said to be a secret.

By renouncing affinity with the world, seeking refuge in God, Who is formless, is more significant, than Karmayoga. Therefore it is called more secret.

I am imparting to you the ancient Yoga which I taught to sun-god (4/3); all this world is pervaded by Me (9/4); I surpass the perishable and am higher even than the imperishable, I am known as the Supreme Person (15/18). In these statements the Lord has shown His lordliness. So this is called the greatest or sovereign secret.

Abandoning all duties seek refuge in Me alone, I shall release thee from

teaching of Karmayoga (Discipline of Action), is a mere secret.

'Vimṛśyaitadaśeṣeṇa'—The Lord, having told Arjuna, the more secret knowledge, in the form of surrender tells him, that the topic of refuge, is full of devotion. So Lord Kṛṣṇa asks Arjuna, to reflect over this topic of surrender, refuge or devotion, fully. The term 'etat', denotes the topic of refuge, described in the fifty-sixth and fifty-seventh verses of this chapter, while the term 'aśeṣeṇa' denotes the topic of devotion, described in the whole of Gītā.* Through the expression 'Vimṛśyaitadaśeṣeṇa', the Lord expresses His special grace, in a secret way. The Lord, wants that he should not have a disinclination for Him. If he ponders

---

all sins; grieve not (18/66). This is called His supreme word, the most secret of all.

That Yogaśāstra is said to be the supreme secret in which all the disciplines of Action, of Knowledge and Devotion are described (18/68,75).

* In the Gītā the topic of devotion has been described in the following verses—Among all the Yogīs, he who full of faith worships Me, is deemed by Me to be the most devout (6/47); those who take refuge in Me alone cross this Māyā (divine potency) (7/14); such a great soul, who realizes that all this is God, is very rare (7/19); I am easily attainable to the Yogī who constantly thinks of Me with undivided mind (8/14); the Supreme Person is attainable only by exclusive devotion (8/22); great souls possessing a divine nature worship Me constantly with undivided mind (9/13); the devotees of firm resolve, constantly chanting My names and glories, and bowing to Me, worship Me with single-minded devotion (9/14), I secure what is not already possessed and personally attend to the needs of those devotees who worship Me alone (9/22); whosoever offers to Me with devotion a leaf, a flower, a fruit, or water, that offering of love, I accept (9/26); whatever you do, whatever you eat, whatever you offer in sacrifice, whatever you give, whatever you do as penance, offer it all to Me (9/27); you will be freed from the bonds of action yielding good and evil fruits (9/28); fix your mind on Me, be devoted to Me, adore Me, bow down to Me (9/34); I dispel the darkness born of ignorance of My devotees so that they may attain Me (10/9—11); through single-minded devotion I can be seen and known and even entered into (11/54); the devotee who regards Me as his supreme goal reaches Me (11/55); those who worship Me with supreme faith are the best in Yoga (12/2); I rescue those from the ocean of birth and death who worship Me with single-minded devotion (12/6-7); by fixing your mind on Me and your intellect in Me alone, thereafter you will abide in Me (12/8); He who worships Me with exclusive devotion transcending the three modes becomes eligible for attaining Brahma (14/26); he, who worships Me with his whole being, is the knower of all (15/19) and so on.

over His gospel, he will realize the reality, that none is superior to, more loving and more merciful, than Him.

'Yathecchasi tathā kuru'—Lord Kṛṣṇa advises Arjuna, to reflect fully over His teaching and then do, as he best wishes. It shows, Lord Kṛṣṇa's manifest intimacy, grace and benevolence, for him.

In verse (7/2) when the Lord declares, that He will unfold to him in its entirety, this knowledge with realization and in (9/1), when He states that He will declare knowledge with realization, and in (10/1) when He asks him to listen to His supreme word, these show His common grace, for Arjuna. But, in (18/58) when He says to Arjuna, that if he does not act according to His advice, he will perish, it is His special grace.

When Lord Kṛṣṇa asks Arjuna, to do as he wishes, Arjuna is very much perturbed by thinking, that the Lord is abandoning him. A devotee, can tolerate his chiding, but cannot bear his separation from the Lord. Arjuna, was not so much perturbed, when he was admonished by the Lord, with the words that he would perish if he did not act according to His advice, as he was now. He thinks, that he committed a blunder, that in spite of the Lord's loving advice warning, and exhortation to taking refuge, in the all-pervading God, he did not respond favourably. So at last the Lord, had to say "Do as thou wishest." By thinking so Arjuna, feels miserable to express himself to the Lord. He now feels very sad and dejected. So the Lord utters the most secret words, of his own accord, in the next verse.

Appendix—'Yathecchasi tathā kuru'—The Lord asks Arjuna to do as he best wishes—Lord Kṛṣṇa does not make this utterance in order to abandon him but in order to attract him towards Him specially; as when a ball is thrown towards a wall with force, it is done to catch it again, rather than to abandon it. It means that the Lord in the preceding verse, having mentioned that Arjuna should take refuge in immanent formless God, now wants to attract Him towards Himself viz., towards God Who is endowed with attributes and with form so that Arjuna may not be deprived of the attainment of the Lord's entire form. The formless God (Brahma) does not comprise God endowed with form, but God endowed with form comprises formless God (Brahma).

Link:—In the preceding verse, Lord Kṛṣṇa ordered Arjuna, to reflect over His teaching fully and over its gist. But Arjuna could not grasp the gist of His teaching, because the purport of the teaching is not known, as much to a listener, as to speaker. Secondly, Lord Kṛṣṇa asked him to do as he wished. Hearing these words, he got despondent. So Lord Kṛṣṇa, giving him the quintessence of His teaching consoles him.

सर्वगुह्यतमं भूयः शृणु मे परमं वचः।
इष्टोऽसि मे दृढमिति ततो वक्ष्यामि ते हितम्॥६४॥

sarvaguhyatamaṁ bhūyaḥ śṛṇu me paramaṁ vacaḥ
iṣṭo'si me dṛḍhamiti tato vakṣyāmi te hitam

Listen again to My supreme words, the most secret of these all. Well beloved art thou of Me, therefore, I shall tell thee, what is good for thee. 64

Comment:—

'Sarvaguhyatamaṁ bhūyaḥ śṛṇu me paramaṁ vacaḥ'—In the sixty-third verse, the Lord told Arjuna, the wisdom which was more secret (refuge in God) than the teaching of Karmayoga, which was secret, while in (9/1) and (15/20) He imparted the most secret teaching (Guhyatamam—His glory). But He did not convey, His supremely secret word (Sarvaguhyatamam), before. It is only here, that He unfolds it to him.

He also warns Arjuna, that this supreme word, should not be disclosed to a man who is without austerity, nor to one, without devotion, because it is the most secret, of all the other secrets, disclosed so far.* (This is—Abandoning all duties, seek refuge in

*At the beginning of the tenth chapter Lord Kṛṣṇa said, "Hear once

Me alone). This is the supremely secret teaching, of the Gītā.

In the seventh verse of the second chapter, Arjuna said, "Being tainted by the vice of faint-heartedness, and my mind puzzled, with regard to duty, I ask you. Tell me that which is decidedly good; I am your disciple. Pray instruct me, who has sought refuge in you." So Lord Kṛṣṇa (in 18/66) says, "Abandoning all duties, seek refuge in Me alone. I shall release you from all sins; grieve not." This is Lord Kṛṣṇa's supreme word, the top secret of all secrets.

By the expression 'Bhūyaḥ śṛṇu,' (listen again) Lord Kṛṣṇa means to say, that He also imparted His teaching to him, even before, but at that time he failed to take special note of it. So, He was conveying the mystery of all mysteries again, and expected that Arjuna would listen to it, with rapt attention.

This gospel was imparted to him in (18/57) when the Lord said to him, "Have your mind constantly fixed on Me," and also in (18/58) when He declared, "Fixing your mind on Me, you will by My grace, overcome all obstacles." But He did not use the expression 'Sarvaguhyatamam' (the supreme secret of all) before, and Arjuna did not take any special note of it. So,

---

again My supreme word, O mighty-armed,"while here He says, "Hear again My supreme word, the most secret of all." The difference is that there He used the words 'mighty-armed' while here 'the most secret of all.' There in (10/9) He used 'Maccittāḥ' (with their minds wholly fixed on Me), while here He uses in (18/57-58) the term 'Maccittaḥ' (with thy mind fixed on Me). The difference is that the former teaching is for the general people while the latter is specially for Arjuna as He uses the second person for him. There He declared that by His grace his ignorance would be dispelled while here He says that by His grace he will overcome all obstacles.

There in (10/1) He said, "I shall speak to you, who are so loving out of solicitude for your welfare" while here He says, "I shall tell you what is good for you." There in 9/34 having said 'Fix your mind on Me' He said, "O mighty-armed, hear once again My supreme word" (10/1), while here having said, "Hear again, My supreme word, the most secret of all" (18/64) He said, "Fix your mind on Me" (18/65).

As the expression, 'Sarvaguhyatamam' (the supreme secret of all) has been used once, so has the sentence, "Abandoning all duties, take refuge in Me alone" (18/66).

in order to divert Arjuna's attention to His supreme word, the supreme secret of all, Lord Kṛṣṇa uses this expression.

'Iṣṭo'si me dṛḍhamiti'—The Lord, in the preceding verse admonishing him, asked him to do, as he wished. What can be a more severe punishment, to an obedient devotee, than these words of indifference? Arjuna having heard these words, is perturbed, by thinking that the Lord is abandoning him. In order to remove his fear He consoles him by saying, "well beloved art thou of Me." Had Arjuna not been perturbed, there would not have been any need for Lord Kṛṣṇa, to tell Arjuna, that he was well beloved of Him.

Moreover, Lord Kṛṣṇa uses the term 'Iṣṭa' (favourite), because He considers His devout devotee as His favourite deity. As a devotee, with exclusive devotion, regards the Lord as his favourite deity, so does the Lord, as He declares, "Howsoever men approach Me even so do I seek them" (Gītā 4/11). In the Bhāgavata, Lord Kṛṣṇa says to Uddhava, "O Uddhava, neither Brahmājī nor Lord Śaṅkara, nor Balarāmajī, nor Lakṣmījī, who reside in My body nor My soul, is so much loving to Me, as a devout devotee like, you."

By using the term 'Dṛḍham', the Lord means to say to Arjuna, that he should be free from fear, because he has accepted "I have sought refuge in You" (Gītā 2/7). The reason is, that anyone who having sought refuge in Him, says from his heart even once, "I am only yours,"the Lord grants him security, from all beings such is His vow.

'Tato vakṣyāmi te hitam'—Lord Kṛṣṇa says to Arjuna, that he is His loving friend and therefore, He will impart to him the teaching of taking refuge in Him, which is the supreme secret of all. Further, He will unfold it to him, to do good to him, without hoping for any reward, from him. It proves that a man's welfare or good, lies in taking refuge, in the Lord, without depending on anyone else.

The man (soul), is a fragment of God, and so he should

depend only on God, and he should take refuge in him, only. If he depends on things, incidents, circumstances and persons etc., he will have to be sad and worried, because all of these are perishable. As coal ignites in the fire, but it becomes black, when it is separated from fire, similarly, if a man (soul) (self), has an inclination for the Lord and takes refuge in Him, he shines, by becoming one with the Lord and may lead the world to salvation. But, if he has a disinclination for the Lord, he has to suffer and follow a cycle of birth and death.

Appendix—In 'tameva śaraṇaṁ gaccha' (18/62), 'take refuge in Him alone'—there is refuge in formless God and in 'māmekaṁ śaraṇaṁ vraja' (18/66), 'take refuge in Me alone'—there is refuge in God endowed with attributes. By taking refuge in the formless Brahma, a striver attains salvation, but by taking refuge in God endowed with form, a striver besides attaining salvation also attains love (devotion). Therefore refuge in God endowed with form is 'sarvaguhyatama' viz., the Supreme Secret of all. The Lord in the reference of only devotion, uses the expression 'Supreme word'. In the first verse of the tenth chapter also the Lord asked Arjuna to listen to His Supreme word—'śṛṇu me paramaṁ vacaḥ'.

Arjuna said to Lord Kṛṣṇa, "I am your disciple"—'śiṣyaste'ham' (2/7), but the Lord says to him, "you are my beloved friend"—'iṣṭo'si'. It means that the spiritual guide (preceptor) initiates the pupil but the Lord, instead of having the teacher-pupil relationship, makes a devotee his friend.

Every activity of the Lord is for the welfare of others but in this reference special welfare is solicited, so the Lord says 'tato vakṣyāmi te hitam'.

मन्मना भव मद्भक्तो मद्याजी मां नमस्कुरु ।
मामेवैष्यसि सत्यं ते प्रतिजाने प्रियोऽसि मे ॥ ६५ ॥

manmanā bhava madbhakto madyājī māṁ namaskuru
māmevaiṣyasi satyaṁ te pratijāne priyo'si me

Fix thy mind on Me; be devoted to Me; worship Me; prostrate thyself before Me; so shalt thou come unto Me. I promise thee truly, for thou art dear to Me. 65

Comment:—

'Madbhaktaḥ'—A striver, first of all should change his egoistic notions ('I' ness), by accepting, that he belongs to the Lord. Without changing the ego, he cannot make speedy progress. By doing so, his progress in the spiritual path, becomes easy and natural. Hence first of all a striver should be devoted to Me.

A disciple accepts a person as his preceptor, and then he becomes of his preceptor. A girl after her marriage accepts her husband as hers, by changing her egoism and so she becomes attached to the family, of her husband. Similarly, a striver should accept that he is of the Lord only, and only the Lord is his; he does not belong to the world, and the world does not belong to him (when egoism changes, mineness also naturally changes).

'Manmanā bhava'—When a striver, assumes that he belongs to the Lord and the Lord belongs to him, He becomes naturally loving to him as He is his own and then his mind is naturally fixed on Him. In that case, he naturally thinks of His name, glory and sport etc. Moreover, he recites His name and meditates on Him, very promptly and affectionately.

'Madyājī'—When a striver, becomes of the Lord, by changing his egoism, he serves Him by performing actions. The more his intimacy with the Lord develops, the more devoted, he becomes in rendering service, to Him. That service, changes into adoration. So whatever worldly, household or bodily work he does, becomes worship of the Lord. He has a firm conviction, that he has to do nothing, except worship God.

'Māṁ namaskuru'—A striver, by prostrating himself before the Lord, should totally surrender himself, to Him. In that case, he should be extremely happy, both in favourable and unfavourable circumstances, by regarding it, as gracious divine dispensation.

He holds, that whatever God does is, for his welfare, whether he understands it or not, as He is a disinterested friend of all beings. So, he should think, that the Lord, by creating desirable or undesirable circumstances, is absolving him of his good deeds and sins, and making him pure, so that he may be attracted towards His feet. This is prostration, before the Lord.

'Māmevaiṣyasi satyaṁ te pratijāne priyo'si me'—Lord Kṛṣṇa, promises truly to Arjuna, that by fixing his mind on Him, by being devoted to Him, by worshipping Him, by prostrating himself before Him, he will come to Him* because he is dear to Him.

By the term 'Priyo'si' (thou art dear), the Lord means that every being (soul), is very dear to Him, because it is His fragment. He may, send it to eighty-four lac forms of lives or even to hell, but His aim is to purify it. This gracious dispensation of the Lord, towards all beings, reveals His loving nature. So Arjuna here, represents all beings.

Every being (soul), is very loving to God. A human being, having a disinclination for God, assumes worldly perishable things, such as wealth, property, family, body, senses, mind, intellect and life-breath etc., as his own, while the world has never accepted him, as its own. All the worldly things, are kaleidoscopic and perishable, while he himself is unchanging and imperishable. But he commits an error, by assuming his affinity, with the changing world, as eternal. This is the reason, that this affinity with a person persists, even when a person is dead. This assumed affinity, is the cause of his fall. He is free, whether he accepts this affinity or he does not accept it. So, by renouncing this assumed affinity, he should realize his real and eternal affinity with God and should take refuge, in Him.

Appendix—God is already attained to Arjuna; therefore

*If a devotee either fixes his mind on Him or is devoted to Him or worships Him or bows to Him—by practising one fully, the remaining three are naturally practised.

here the Lord by using the term 'māmevaiṣyasi' means that he will know Him in His entirety, about which the Lord at the beginning of the seventh chapter said, "asaṁśayaṁ samagraṁ māṁ yathā jñāsyasi tacchṛṇu." Then Arjuna will have deep intimacy with Him viz., he will become the Lord's own self, about which the Lord said in the seventh chapter 'jñānī tvātmaiva me matam' (7/18); 'priyo hi jñānīno'tyarthamahaṁ sa ca mama priyaḥ' (7/17) (viz., 'exceedingly dear am I to the wise, and he is exceedingly dear to Me').

Link:—Having consoled Arjuna, in the preceding two verses, the Lord in the next verse, unfolds the supreme secret of all secrets.

सर्वधर्मान्परित्यज्य मामेकं शरणं व्रज।
अहं त्वा सर्वपापेभ्यो मोक्षयिष्यामि मा शुचः ॥ ६६ ॥

sarvadharmānparityajya māmekaṁ śaraṇaṁ vraja
ahaṁ tvā sarvapāpebhyo mokṣayiṣyāmi mā śucaḥ

Abandoning dependence on all duties (dharma), take refuge in Me, alone. I shall liberate you from all your sins; therefore grieve not. 66

Comment:—

'Sarvadharmānparityajya māmekaṁ śaraṇaṁ vraja'—Lord Kṛṣṇa, exhorts Arjuna to take refuge, in Him by abandoning dependence on all duties and determination of his duty i.e., what to do and what not to do. Refuge in the Lord, is the quintessence, of the gospel of the Lord. When a devotee takes refuge in Him, like a chaste wife, he has to do nothing, for himself. As a chaste wife, performs every action, in order to please her husband, without thinking of her own taste and inclination, and her husband's Gotra (sub caste) becomes hers, similarly, a devotee who takes refuge in Him, surrenders everything to Him and becomes, free from worry, fear, sorrow and doubt.

Here the term 'Dharma,' stands for duty. The reason, is that from the forty-first verse to the forty-fourth verse, the terms 'Svabhāvaja Karma' (duties born of their natures) have been used. In the first half of the forty-seventh verse, the term 'Svadharma,' (one's own duty) has been used. Again, in the second half of the forty-seventh verse and also in the forty-eighth verse, the term 'Karma' (Duty) has been used. It means, that in this context at the beginning and the end the term 'Karma,' has been used, while in the middle the term 'Svadharma,' (one's own duty) has been used. So the term 'Dharma,' stands for duty.

Now a question arises, whether one's duties should be practically abandoned. The answer is that it is not proper to abandon one's duties, because in response to the order of Lord Kṛṣṇa, Arjuna says, "I shall act according to Your word" (18/73). Then he carried out His order, and waged war. Moreover, in the sixth verse of this chapter, the Lord declared, "Acts of sacrifice, gift and penance and all other duties, must be performed."*

* In the third chapter there is description that a man should not abstain from actions. "Not by non-performance of actions does a man reach actionlessness, nor by mere renunciation does he attain to perfection" (3/4)."None can remain inactive even for a moment" (3/5). "He who restraining the organs of action, thinks of the sense-objects, is called a hypocrite" (3/6). "He who controlling the senses by the mind engages himself in action, he excels" (3/7). "Perform your allotted duty because desisting from action, you cannot even maintain your body" (3/8). "Perform action for the sake of sacrifice alone" (3/9). Having created mankind at the beginning of creation, the creator, Brahmā said to them, "By this shall ye propagate; let this be the milch-cow to provide you necessities for sacrifice"(3/10). "You and the gods fostering each other shall attain to the supreme good " (3/11). "He who enjoys the gifts without giving to the gods in return is a thief" (3/12). "Those who partake of what is left after sacrifice, are absolved of all sins while those who cook for the sake of nourishing their body alone, eat only sin' (3/13). "He who does not perform his duties, lives in vain" (3/16). "A man by performing actions without attachment attains the supreme." (3/19). "It is through action alone that Janaka and other wise men reached perfection. You should perform action with a view to the maintenance of the world" (3/20). The Lord says, "If I don't perform actions, I should be the creator of confusion of castes and destruction of these people" (3/23-24). "The wise should act without attachment as the unwise act with attachment" (3/25). "Let no wise man unsettle the mind of ignorant people attached to action, but should get them to perform all their duties, duly performing them

After studying the Gītā, it becomes clear, that a man should not renounce his duties, under any circumstances. Arjuna thought that it was better to live on alms, than to perform his duty, in slaying the honoured teachers in the war (2/5); but Lord Kṛṣṇa, exhorted him to wage such a righteous war, by saying that there is nothing more welcome for a man of the warrior class, than a righteous war (2/31—38). It proves, that one should not renounce one's duty, which has been prescribed for him, according to his caste, stage of life and circumstances etc.

Then, why does Lord Kṛṣṇa say to Arjuna, to abandon all duties? The Lord means to say that all duties, must be offered to Him. By doing so, a striver, will not depend on duties, but will depend on God. The Lord, declares, that those who depend on duties, (actions) are subject to birth and death (Gītā 9/21). By depending only on Him, one need not decide, what ought to be done and what ought not to be done. It practically happened, in Arjuna's life.

Arjuna was fighting against Karṇa. The wheel of Karṇa's chariot, got stuck in mud. Karṇa was trying to push it out. So he said to Arjuna, "You are in the chariot but I am not in a chariot. You possess knowledge of scriptures, and you are well-versed in the science of arms, like Sahasrārjuna. You also know the science of ethics. So it is not proper on your part to shoot arrows, at me". So Arjuna did not shoot any arrows. Then Lord Kṛṣṇa said to Karṇa, "It is righteous, rather than sinful, to kill such a desperado, as you.* Six chariot-warriors, including you have murdered Abhimanyu, who was alone. Therefore, there is no use for you to support righteousness. It is fortunate, that you are reminded of righteousness, at this moment. But he who himself, does not translate righteousness into practice has no

himself" (3/26). Thus the Lord has laid great emphasis on the performance of one's duty in the third chapter.

* A desperado who is bent upon doing harm to anyone should be killed. Such a killer does not incur any sin (evil).

right to preach it, to others." Having uttered these words Lord Kṛṣṇa, ordered Arjuna to shoot arrows. By obeying Him, Arjuna began to shoot these.

If Arjuna, had taken the decision about his duty, by applying his intellect, he would have committed an error of judgment. But he left it to the Lord and it was He, Who took the right decision.

Arjuna, was in a dilemma whether to fight or not to fight (2/6). He thought, that if he fought, there would be destruction of his family, and sin would overtake the entire family. The women of the family, would become corrupt, and there would ensue an intermixture of castes. Thus, age-long, caste-traditions and family customs, would die (1/39—44). On the other hand, there was nothing more welcome, for a man of the warrior class, than a righteous war. Therefore, Lord Kṛṣṇa asks Arjuna, to entrust Him with the task of taking the decision, about his duty, without being confused about it.

'Māmekaṁ śaraṇaṁ vraja'—Here the term 'ekam' (alone), stands for exclusive or undivided. In (3/2) and (5/1) also Arjuna by using the term 'ekam' (one) asked Lord Kṛṣṇa, to tell him definitely, the one discipline by which he might attain bliss. So Lord Kṛṣṇa in response to his question, says that exclusive (undivided) refuge is the best discipline, to attain bliss or God-realization.

In the Gītā, Lord Kṛṣṇa has laid, time and again, great emphasis on the merit of, exclusive devotion. 'Those who take refuge in Me alone, get over this divine delusion of Mine' (7/14); 'I am easily attainable to the Yogī (ascetic) who always and constantly, thinks of Me, with undivided mind' (8/14).* For those men who worship Me alone, I provide, what is not possessed and preserve what they already possess' (9/22); 'Through single-minded devotion, I can be seen and known and even entered into' (11/54); 'I speedily deliver, from the ocean of birth and death, those who

* 'Undivided mind' stands for exclusive devotion or exclusive dependence.

meditate on Me, with single-minded devotion' (12/6-7); 'Those who worship Me with exclusive devotion, transcend the three modes of nature' (14/26). Thus, having described the merit of exclusive devotion, the Lord gives the quintessence of the entire gospel, of the Gītā by declaring, "Take refuge in Me alone." It means that the Lord, is the means as well as, the end.

The sentence 'Māmekaṁ śaraṇaṁ vraja' means, that a striver, should take refuge in Him, not by mind and intellect, but by the self. When he himself takes refuge by the self, his mind, body, senses and intellect etc., automatically take refuge, in Him.

'Ahaṁ tvā sarvapāpebhyo mokṣayiṣyāmi mā śucaḥ'—It may be thought, that Lord Kṛṣṇa allured Arjuna to liberate him, from the sin, as he was afraid of, in the first chapter. But, it is not reasonable, because, as soon as a man seeks refuge in the Lord, his sins of millions of births perish. If the Lord wanted to allure him, that he would liberate him from all sins, He would have done it earlier, before he took refuge in Him.

When the Lord declares, that He will liberate him from all sins, He means to say, that having taken refuge in Him, if he finds that he has not got rid of evil propensities, has not developed devotion to God, and has not beheld Him, he need not worry. It is the Lord's responsibility, to free him from all defects. If he himself wanted to shoulder the responsibility, it shows that he has not yet taken refuge. When he has taken refuge in Him, he should be free from worry, sadness, fear and doubt. If these evils, crop up in him, they will prove to be obstacles in refuge and the responsibility (burden) will remain his. This responsibility, is a blot on refuge. After he has taken refuge in Him, his shortcomings are the Lord's, and his whole responsibility, goes to the Lord.

When Vibhīṣaṇa took refuge in Lord Rāma, Rāma shouldered his full responsibility. Once in a village named Vipraghoṣa, a Brāhmaṇa (a member of the priest class), was killed by him. First, he was badly beaten up and then he was chained and imprisoned. When Lord Rāma came to know of this incident, He flew to Vipraghoṣa by the airy vehicle, named Puṣpaka. The villagers, extended a cordial welcome to Lord Rāma, and said to Him, that Vibhīṣaṇa had murdered a Brāhmaṇa and so they gave him a severe beating, but he was not killed. Lord Rāma said, "Oh, people of the priest class, I have granted him an age of a Kalpa (consisting of 4,32,00,00,000 years of mortals), and also a kingdom. How can he be killed? Moreover, he is My devotee. The responsibility of the crime of a servant, goes to his master, and the master deserves punishment. Therefore instead of Vibhīṣaṇa, punish Me." The Brāhmaṇas, having perceived the affection of Lord Rāma for a person who has taken shelter in Him, were wonder-struck and all of them sought refuge in Him.

It means that 'I am the Lord's and the Lord is mine;' this is the quintessence of all spiritual disciplines. Nothing, such as eligibility, capability, qualification and virtue, is equal to a sense of mine, with the Lord. A weeping child, awakens all the members of a family at midnight and they try their best to please the child. Why? Because, the child is theirs. So a devotee, who has taken refuge in the Lord, should hold that he is the Lord's and only the Lord is his.

'Mā śucaḥ' means—

(1) Having taken refuge in me, if you grieve, it is out of your pride and it is a crime and it is a blot, on refuge.

When you have taken refuge in Me, you should totally depend on Me. If you do not totally depend on Me, it is a crime. If you worry after thinking of your shortcomings, it means that you have pride of your own strength because you want to get rid of these by your own power.* If you have defects, you should be sad, but not worried, like a child who starts weeping without

* In the assembly of the Kauravas when an effort is made to strip Draupadī, she holds the Sārī with her hands and teeth. But then finding herself helpless, she invokes Lord Kṛṣṇa and totally depends upon Him. Then Duḥśāsana gets totally tired but is unable to strip the Sārī from her body, because the Sārī becomes endless to strip her.

worrying, when he sees a dog coming towards him. But if you worry, the people will laugh at you, and at Me. They will think that a devotee of God is worried, and the Lord does not rid him of it. It means that your lack of faith in Me, brings a blot on Me, and My refuge. Therefore, abandon your worry.

(2) Do not worry, even if your thoughts and feelings, have not been purified. It is My responsibility, to purify these.

(3) In the seventh verse of the second chapter, Arjuna says to Lord Kṛṣṇa, that he has taken refuge in Him. But in the eighth verse, he says that even on obtaining undisputed sovereignty, and an affluent kingdom on the earth, and lordship over the gods, he does not see any means, that can drive away the grief, which is affecting his senses. At this, the Lord seems to say to Arjuna, that he is right because a man cannot be free from grief, so long as he is attached to perishable persons and objects. But, it is a blunder on his part, if he grieves even after having taken refuge in Him.

(4) A devotee, having taken refuge in the Lord, should not worry what will happen to him, here or hereafter. In this connection a devotee said, "O slayer of Narakāsura, you may provide me residence, either in heaven or hell or on the earth and behave towards me, in anyway according to Your sweet will. But I have only one demand, that I may go on thinking of your most beautiful feet, which excel the beauty of an autumn-lotus of season, even at the time of my death.

An Important Fact Pertaining to Refuge

When a devotee, assumes that he is the Lord's and the Lord is his, his defects such as worry, fear, sadness and doubt, are rooted out. The reason is, that all defects are based on his dependence on the world, including the body, and on his disinclination, for the Lord. As soon as his affinity, with the Lord gets a firm footing, all his defects perish.

The criteria of one's firm affinity, with the Lord are the following:—

(1) Fearlessness:—The devotee who takes refuge in the Lord, becomes free from external fear, as that of poisonous snakes, and scorpions, and wild beasts such as lion etc., and also from internal fear, of evil propensities etc. A striver, should not have such a fear, that his tendencies may be of evil nature, as by God's grace, he becomes saturated with divine mercy. So, there is no question of any such fear, for him. He could not purify his evil thoughts, as he regarded these as 'mine'. To regard these as one's own, is impurity. He also becomes totally free, from the greatest fear of death, from which even great scholars cannot escape. He perceives the Lord's grace, everywhere.

Now, a doubt may arise, that when a devotee worships God with exclusive devotion, it means that he regards himself as different from God and as fear arises in duality so he should be afraid of Him. But this doubt is baseless, because the devotee becomes so much intimate with the Lord, that no question arises of his being afraid, of Him. He being the Lord's fragment, having taken refuge in Him, becomes fearless, forever, like a child, who becomes fearless in the lap of his mother. He is different from prakṛti (nature), not from Him. The Lord and he (self), are sentient, eternal, imperishable and unchanging, while prakṛti is insentient, transient, perishable and everchanging. So he can be afraid of nature, but not of the Lord. Actually, a devotee (self) has his identity with God, but he forgets it. And when he takes refuge in the Lord, he realizes this fact.

(2) Freedom from sadness (sorrow):—A person, grieves over what has passed. To grieve over the past, is a blunder. A devotee, believes that whatever is allotted, cannot be blotted, and every action, incident or circumstance, destined by the Lord, is for his good. By thinking so, he remains free from sadness.

(3) Freedom from worry:—When a devotee takes refuge in God, he is not at all worried, about the necessities of life, here or what will happen to him, in future. If he surrenders himself to God, how can any worry remain? Worry is contrary

to surrender. If there is worry, actually there is no surrender. The Lord declares, "I'll release you from all sins." What efforts does he need then? He is least worried, whether his mind and intellect, are purified or not. If sometimes evil propensities, get hold of his mind, he may invoke the Lord to save him, but he does not, at all worry or grieve. He becomes a yesman of His will, because the Lord, shoulders his full responsibility. If sometimes, he feels that body, senses, mind, life-breath and intellect, are his, it is his error. He prays to God to deliver him, from this error and becomes free from worry.

(4) Freedom from doubt:—He does not doubt, whether he is of the Lord or not, and whether the Lord has accepted him or not. He believes, that he has been of the Lord since time immemorial, and he will remain His. He holds, that it was an error on his part that he had regarded himself as separate, from the Lord. But it is impossible, because the Lord declared, "He (the self) is a fragment of My own self" (Gītā 15/7). Thus, he has a belief that he is of the Lord and the Lord is his, without doubt.

(5) Not to put to a test:—The devotee, who takes refuge in the Lord, does not put his surrender to a test, that he should possess such virtues; and if he does not possess them, it means that he has not taken, true refuge. He has a firm belief, that he has taken refuge in the Lord, and so he is surprised, when he perceives that the signs of a devotee, who is dear to the Lord (Gītā 12/13—19), are missing from him.* By thinking so, he

* In order to make the point clear there is an anecdote. At the death of the mother, the two elder brothers asked the younger brother to take the ash of the dead mother's body and cast it into the Ganges. The distance of the Ganges from their house was six hundred miles. He got tired after covering a distance of three hundred miles. So he threw the ash and filled the metal mug with rainy water in order to show that he had gone to the Ganges and brought its holy water. When he came back home, his elder brothers knew the fact because he had come back earlier than he should have returned. When they asked him, he told a lie.

Next day one of the elder brothers said to the younger brother that he

develops the marks of an enlightened devotee, without making any effort.

(6) Not to have a contrary resolution:—Such a devotee, has no contrary resolution, that he is not of the Lord. He has a firm belief, that his relationship with the Lord is permanent and eternal, and he is only His. He was not conscious of this. It was his blunder. This relationship is axiomatic. Now this blunder is no more. So, how can he have a contrary belief?

One who heartily accepts refuge in God, he becomes free from evil, such as fear, grief and worry etc., and his belief in surrender, is intensified automatically.

A girl after her marriage regards her husband's house, as her own. This relationship is so much strengthened, that when she becomes a grandmother or great grandmother, she almost forgets, that she belonged to another family. When the wife of her grandson or great grandson misbehaves, towards any other member of the family, she scolds her by uttering the words, that a girl born in another family has spoiled, the environment of her family. It means, that when such an assumed affinity, is so strengthened,why should the real affinity of a man, with the Lord, not be strengthened? His assumed affinity, with the world, is the only obstacle to it.

If such a devotee, lacks anything in devotion or conduct; if he has contrary tendencies and his conduct is not according to the Lord's will, there will be a feeling in his heart. God by His

had a dream in which the mother said to him that he had thrown the ash on the way, not into the Ganges. The younger brother replied if the mother instead of coming in this direction having covered a distance of three hundred miles, had gone in the opposite direction, she would have reached the Ganges.

This anecdote shows that a devotee should not have a contrary resolution like the younger brother who said why the mother came in the opposite direction and if she had gone the other side, she would have reached the Ganges.

A devotee should think why he lacks the marks of an enlightened devotee when he has taken refuge in the Lord. By thinking so he will inculcate those virtues (marks) and become enlightened. But if he has the contrary resolution, he will be cheated by his own self.

grace, will purge him of all sins and will make up his deficiency and he need not make any amends.

The Lord, perceives the feeling of 'mineness', of a devotee for him. He cannot behold his defects, because he is His fragment permanently, while defects are temporary, as these appear and disappear. When a child, soiled with mud comes to his mother and seeks her lap, the mother is ever prepared to put him in her lap, without thinking whether he is dirty or clean. All this happens, due to a feeling of mineness. The child, does not mind whether it is dirty or not or whether the mother cleans it or not. Instead of seeing the mud, it only beholds the mother. Draupadī had evil feelings of enmity and anger, for Duḥśāsana, and she resolved that she would not dress her hair, unless she stained it with Duḥśāsana's blood. But as soon as she called, Lord Kṛṣṇa, He appeared before her, because of her closeness with Him.

Regarding the feeling of 'mineness', one may consider (i) 'The Lord is mine' (ii) 'I am the Lord's'. In the former case a devotee may lay a claim over the Lord, and thus may wish that his desires should be fulfilled by Him. But in the latter, he surrenders himself to the Lord and thus becomes a puppet of His sweet will. A striver, should never lay claim on God. He should rather accept God's lordship, over him. If the Lord does something according to his will, he feels hesitation, that the Lord has to satisfy his will. If he feels satisfied and happy in any happening according to his will, it means that there is some deficiency, in his surrender.

Such a devout devotee, has nothing to do for him. He has already offered himself and his possessions to the Lord, which were really the Lord's. Whatever, he does, does only God's work. In such a situation, even in the most adverse and horrible circumstances, he remains enamoured of Divine grace, in abundance. So a striver, who takes refuge in the Lord ever remains pleased, with His will, without having any desire of his own, even in the most undesirable circumstances like that of Kākabhuśuṇḍi.

Kākabhuśuṇḍi narrated the life story of his previous birth, that he was a Brāhmaṇa, (a member of the priest class). The sage named Lomaśa put a curse, upon him. So he took birth, as a crow. But he was not sad, because he thought that it happened by Lord's will (Mānasa 7/113/1). Sage Lomaśa saw, that he was still happy. So he called him and preached him how to meditate on Lord Rāma, because he was a loving devotee of God. Moreover, he narrated to him the life story of Lord Rāma, and gave him blessings, "You will become dear to Lord Rāma. You will possess all virtues. You will be able to transform yourself, into any form, you like. Your home with its surroundings will remain totally untouched, by any deluding potency of the Lord (Māyā) and so on." Just then there was an oracle, "O sage, whatever you have said will prove true, this crow is a devotee of Mine, by thought, word and deed." So in the Rāmacaritamānasa, it is said that the sage's curse proved to be a blessing for it, because of adoration and such a blessing is seldom granted, even to an ascetic.

Here, adoration stands for being pleased by the Lord's sweet will, even in most unfavourable and undesirable circumstances. The more unfavourable the circumstances, are, the more pleased, a devout devotee becomes, because love enhances every moment.

As a rule, if a thing is ours, it is dear to us. All the beings are the Lord's and so they are very dear to Him (Mānasa 7/86/2), and the Lord is also naturally loving to them. But they have a disinclination for Him, by an error regarding the kaleidoscopic world and the bodies, as their own. Still the Lord does not renounce them, as these are a fragment of the Lord. He ever loves them. So, for the protection of the virtuous, for the destruction of the wicked and for the firm establishment of righteousness, He is born in every age (Gītā 4/8). What is the Lord's own purpose, which is served through these three objectives of His incarnation? It is because of His love for people, that he comes into being for their welfare. His incarnation proves His sense of mineness, mercy, lovingness, benevolence and disinterested and impartial magnanimity. It is because of disinclination of beings for Him, that they have to suffer and follow the cycle of birth and death, So the Lord, asks them to fix their mind on Him, to be devoted to Him, to worship Him and to prostrate themselves before Him, so that they may have an inclination for Him, and a disinclination, for the perishable world.

Whatever the Lord designs, it is only for the welfare of all beings. If people, pay attention to this fact, nothing remains to be done, by them. The Lord, has a keen desire to do good, to beings. So He discloses the secret of all secrets. "Abandoning all duties, take refuge in Me alone." The reason is, that He regards Himself as a disinterested friend of all beings (5/29). He has given them freedom to attain Him, by anyone of the Disciplines of Action, Knowledge or Devotion and get rid of worldly sufferings forever.

In fact, a being attains salvation, only by God's grace. So He and the liberated souls, who know Him in reality, have revealed the different disciplines—of Action, Knowledge, Devotion, Aṣṭāṅgayoga, Layayoga, Haṭhayoga and Rājayoga etc., because both of them think of the good of all beings, without any selfish motive (Mānasa 7/47/3). The Lord by His grace, by making a striver, just an instrument, enables him to attain perfection.

A devout devotee, who takes refuge in the Lord, does not worry, that he has not yet had a vision of the Lord, he has not developed true devotion for Him and that his inclinations have not been purified and so on. If he worries, he is like a monkey's young one, who by holding its mother, shoulders the responsibility itself. A devout devotee, like a kitten, which totaly depends upon its mother, depends on the Lord, without worrying whether He appears before him or not, whether He bestows love upon him or not, and whether He purifies his propensities or not. A kitten folds its limbs and remains ready for its mother to carry it anywhere. Similarly a devotee withdrawing himself from the world, beholds the Lord by meditating upon Him, reciting His name and perfoming such spiritual activities. He remains fully satisfied and happy with whatever happens to him, regarding it as the Lord's, sweet will.

A devotee is like clay, which leaves itself to a potter's will. The potter, mixes water in it, kneads it, crushes it, pats it, puts it on his wheel, moulds it, and makes pots, such as pitcher, jar and plates etc. Similarly, a devotee leaving himself at the Lord's will, becomes free, from worry and fear etc. Then, the Lord's grace, showers on him incessantly. The more free he is from worry and fears, the more Divine grace, is showered on him. The more he is worried and prides in his capability, the more impediments, he puts in, Divine grace. The Lord's uncommon, unique, incessant and continuous grace, is showered on a devout devotee, who takes refuge, in Him.

When a fisherman casts his net, in order to catch fish, all the fish which come within the net, are trapped. But the fish which come closer to his feet, is not trapped. Similarly, beings having been attached to the world, get entangled and follow a cycle of birth and death. But those, who take refuge in Him, get over the deluding potency (Māyā) of the Lord (Gītā 7/14). There is an important difference, between the attitude of the fisherman and the Lord. The fisherman wants to trap the fish, but the Lord wants beings to be liberated from illusion, by taking refuge in Him. So He declares, "Take refuge in Me, alone." A person gets entangled in illusion, by being attached to worldly pleasure.

As in a moving mill, all the grains are ground but which are those near the rivet are not pulverised. Similarly in the grinding-stone of the world, people are crushed i.e., they suffer and follow a cycle of birth and death. But those, who take refuge in Him, escape suffering and the cycle of birth and death. However, there is a difference between, grain and devotees. The grains remain near the rivet, without making any effort, while devotees themselves, by having a disinclination for the world, take refuge at His feet. It means, that if a man (soul), even being a fragment of the Lord, accepts his affinity with the world, and wants his desire to be fulfilled by it, he has to suffer, by following the cycle of birth and death.

A man's affinity with the world is an assumed, one, while with the Lord it is real. Affinity with the world makes him a slave to the world, while the affinity with the Lord, makes him a Lord, even to the Lord. If a person, regards himself superior to others, because of learning, riches, power and even renunciation and dispassion, it means, that he is a slave to them, because in fact he is not superior, but these possession have made him feel superior. So there is superiority of these possessions, rather than his real own. He is inferior to them. But if a devotee takes refuge in the Lord, and depends only on Him, the Lord makes him a jewel of His crown, or considers him, His Lord. But, even then he has no superiority complex, no pride of his virtues. In that case, the Lord's uniqueness descends on him and sometimes even their bodies, senses, mind and intellect bocome divine, as their earthliness is completely gone. Such devotees, with their bodies merge in God. Mīrābāī merged in His idol. Only a piece of her Sārī, was left in the Lord's mouth. Similarly, saint Tukā Rāma went to the Abode of Lord Viṣṇu, with his body.

In the Discipline of Knowledge, body does not become divine, because a Jñānī (wise man), by renouncing his affinity with the unreal, becomes established in the divine essence. But, when a devotee, develops an inclination for God, his body, senses, mind and life-breath etc., are also inclined towards the Lord. It means, that those who behold only divine essence everywhere, divinity descends on their bodies, though they appear as gross, to the worldly people.

When a devotee takes refuge in the Lord, He with Goddess Lakṣmī, showers on him so much of affection and grace, beyond description. When the Lord saturated with love, comes alongwith His consort Lakṣmī on His vehicle Garuḍa, to behold His devotee, hymns of Sāmaveda are sung, by its wings. But if a devotee, instead of worshipping Lord Viṣṇu, the preserver, worships only

Goddess Lakṣmī (the goddess of wealth), whose vehicle is an owl, he receives wealth and is intoxicated with, pride, and then falls. The reason is, that he looks at Mother Lakṣmī with deceptive eyes, as he wants to enjoy himself, with her help. Thus, he is very mean. Moreover, if a person has a desire only to obtain wealth by adoring Her, he may not get it. But if he adores the Lord, Goddess Lakṣmī also certainly appears with Her husband, Lord Viṣṇu and blesses him with wealth.

In this connection, there is an anecdote of Hanumān, the monkey-god. Once Lord Rāma, Goddess Sītā and devotee Hanumān, were sitting under a tree, in a garden. A creeper vine, was creeping over the branches of a tree. It looked very beautiful with its flowers and leaves. Lord Rāma said to Hanumān, "Look, how beautiful this creeper is! It is enhancing the beauty of the garden and specially this tree, over which it is creeping. Moreover, it is because of it that beasts and birds seek shelter under this tree. How blessed it is! Is it not so?"

Hearing praise from the Lord, Goddess Sītā said, "Dear son Hanumān, the beauty of this creeper depends, on the tree. Its base or support, is the tree. Where can it creep without a tree? So the credit for its beauty and shelter, goes only to the tree, truly! Hanumān?"

Hanumān said, "There is something more meritorious, than these two."

"What is that?" said Sītā.

Hanumān said, "Mother, how fine the shade of the tree and the creeper is! I relish the shade of the two". Similarly, the Lord and His power of bliss, enrich the glory of each other. Some devotees consider both of them supreme, others declare only the Lord, as supreme, while still others regard His power of bliss, as supreme. However, for a devout devotee, refuge in both of them, is desirable.

Once, a blind saint was going along the bank of the Yamunā, with a stick in his hand. The river was flooded. Suddenly he fell into the river and also lost his stick. He remembered the Lord's declaration, pertaining to refuge. So, he surrendered himself to the will of God. Then he felt, as if someone had pulled him out on to the bank and provided him with a stick as well. Thus a devotee, is ever happy, with what God destines for him.

Once a goat got astray from its herd, at dusk. It saw the footprint of a lion, and sat near it by taking refuge in it. When beasts, such as jackals and wolves, etc., came to attack the goat, it said that it had sought refuge, at the feet of the lion. So being afraid of a lion, all of them fled. Finally, the lion came and asked why, the goat was sitting there, all alone. The goat said, that it had taken refuge in the lion, whose footprint was there. The lion saw that it was his footprint. So he assured it, that it need not be afraid of anyone, as he would offer protection.

At night, when an elephant came to drink water, the lion asked him to put the goat on his back, and feed it with green leaves. The elephant carried out his order, and the goat, ate green leaves and remained carefree.

Similarly, when a man seeks refuge in God, he gets rid of all obstacles and becomes fearless, like the fish which swims against the flow of a river, while even an elephant cannot move, in that direction.

Affinity with the Lord out of love, desire, fear and envy, leads a man to salvation*. But those who have no affinity with

* Not only one, but so many people out of desire, envy, fear and love by concentrating their mind on God and being purged of the sins, have realized God as a devotee realizes Him, through devotion. The cowherdesses, out of desire, Kaṁsa out of fear, the kings such as Śiśupāla and Dantavaktra, out of envy, members of the Yadu clan out of family relationship, and you (Yudhiṣṭhira etc.,) out of love, and we (Nārada etc.,) out of devotion, have concentrated our minds on God (Śrīmadbhā. 7/1/29-30).

Lord Kṛṣṇa says, 'O sinless Uddhava! In all the ages, by good company i.e., affinity with Me, demons and devils, birds and beasts, celestial musicians and damsels, snakes, perfect souls and demi-gods, have attained Me. Among human beings, persons of trading and labour classes, women and even persons of the lowest class, who are endowed with the mode of passion and ignorance, have attained My Supreme State. Vṛtra, Prahlāda, Vṛṣaparvā, Bāli, Bāṇa, Maya,

him, but remain indifferent, are deprived of God-realization. Those who take refuge in God, are dear to Him and become of the 'Acyuta' (Infallible), Lord's caste and creed, though they are of different sexes, castes, creeds, colours, calibres etc.* They become one with Lord 'Acyuta'. So their 'Gotra' (sub-caste), also becomes 'Acyuta.'

The Secret of Refuge

It is only the Lord, Who really knows the secret of refuge, in Him. I am trying to explain this according to my own understanding, and request that, the reader without grasping the deep and abstract meanings, should not take a contrary view. They should reflect upon the topic, because it is something very vital and rare.

In the Gītā, pertaining to refuge Lord Kṛṣṇa has pointed out two factors—

(i) 'Seek refuge in Me alone' (18/66).

Vibhīṣaṇa etc., of the demon class; Sugrīva, Hanumān, Jāmbavān etc., of the monkey class, beasts and birds, such as the Gajendra and Jaṭāyu. Tulādhāra of the trading class; Dharma, a hunter, Kubjā of the low caste, cowherdesses of Vraja; wives of the people of priest class who performed sacrifices, and other people, because of good company, have attained Me.

Those people neither studied the Vedas, nor obeyed the great personalities as sanctioned by scriptures, nor observed any fast, nor performed any penance. But only by good company i.e., affinity with Me, they attained Me.

* In My adoration, there is no distinction between men and women, and between persons having different names, and belonging to different stages of life, the only important factor is, devotion to Me (Adhyātma. Araṇya 10/20).

What is the use of being born in the upper most caste (Brāhmaṇa)? What is the utility of the deep study of all the scriptures? It means, that there is no utility. Who can be more blessed in the entire universe, than the being whose heart is full of devotion to God?

Was the hunter a man of good conduct? Was Dhruva aged? Did Gajendra (lord of elephants) possess any learning, or art? Did Vidura belong to an upper caste? Was Ugrasena belonging to the Yadu clan, heroic? Was Kubjā beautiful? Was Sudāmā rich? No. Yet all of them realized God, because devotion is the only virtue, which is loving to God and He gets satisfied with devotion, not with virtuous conduct and learning etc.

(ii) 'An undeluded person, knowing all worship me with his whole being (heart)' (15/19); 'Seek refuge in Him, alone with all your being' (18/62).

How to take refuge in Him? A devotee without paying any attention to His virtues, glories, names, abode, beauty and lordliness etc., and having no desire of his own, should surrender himself to Him. He should believe, that he is only the Lord's and only the Lord, is his. But anyone should not assume a contrary meaning. The contrary implications, is that he stops listening to the virtues and glories etc., of the Lord, and does not go to His birthplace etc.

A devotee holds, that the Lord is his, whether He possesses virtues, such as grace, beauty, glory, influence etc., or not. If the Lord is more hard-hearted and unkind than anyone else, in the entire universe, still He is his.* If a person respects a rich man or a powerful man, or a man holding a high post, he in fact, does not respect him but he respects his riches or power or post. Similarly, if a devotee adores the Lord because of His virtues, glories, beauty and lordliness etc., he in fact, does not adore the Lord, but he adores those qualities. So a striver, instead of setting eyes on His qualities, should behold Him purely.

Seven sages went to Goddess Pārvatī, and described the vices of Lord Śiva, and virtues of Lord Viṣṇu, and requested her to renounce her affinity, with Lord Śiva. In response to their proposal she said, "Even if Lord Śiva is a sea of vices and Lord Viṣṇu a sea of virtues, but anyone who has set mind on someone, is only connected with him" (Mānasa 1/80).

A similar message was conveyed by the cowherdesses to

---

* My most loving Śrī Kṛṣṇa, whether ugly or handsome, without virtues or most virtuous, envious of me or most gracious to me, howsoever He treats me, He is my only resort.

Whether He delights me by embracing or crushes me, under his feet while I cling on to his feet or breaks my heart without appearing before me, that Śrī Kṛṣṇa of the free will may treat me in anyway, He likes, but He is the only Lord of my life, (Śikṣāṣṭaka 8).

Uddhava, when he brought Lord Kṛṣṇa's message, to them.

Those, who have an eye on the Lord's virtues and glories etc., can attain salvation and glory etc., but cannot have vision of God. But, a devout devotee who beholds Him only, can have His vision, bind Him and even sell Him. The Lord holds such devotees in high esteem. Those, who see His glory and influence, etc., have regard for His glory and influence, etc., and it shows, that they have a desire to receive something. But if a devotee beholds only the Lord, it means, that he has taken refuge in Him and he is only the Lord's.

An ogress named Pūtanā, by applying poison to her teats put these into Lord Kṛṣṇa's mouth, so that while drawing milk He might be poisoned. But the merciful Lord, enabled her to attain salvation, treating her as his mother. Who can be more gracious than He* ? He awards salvation to an ogress, who wants to poison Him. How should He award His mother, who feeds Him with milk everyday? He gives himself to her, He submits to her. When His mother shows a stick to Him, He starts to weep.

A devotee, who has taken refuge in the Lord, does not think whether his body, senses and mind etc., are under his control, or not. He does not think of his honour, praise, virtues and conduct etc. He does not think, that his eyes should be filled with tears, and throat be choked with delight, when he chants the Lord's name and glories, or listens to divine discourses. He regards all these items as trivial. The reason, is that if he finds virtue and characteristics of enlightened devotees (Gītā 12/13—19) in them, he will feel proud. But, if he finds that he misses them, he will be dejected. So a devotee, should not worry about these. But He should not take the contrary meaning that he may bear enmity or malice or have a possessive spirit. Divine propensities, are naturally developed in devotees who take refuge, in God. He

* Oh! This sinful Pūtanā having applied the deadly poison to her teats, wanted to feed Kṛṣṇa in order to kill Him, while He awarded her salvation, which should have been awarded to a nurse. Who can be more merciful than He in whom one may seek refuge (Śrīmadbhā. 2/3/23)?

looks neither at his own virtues, nor at the virtues of saints, and liberated souls, that he should possess these.

People complain, why a devotee falls ill, why he suffers, why he becomes poor and why he is insulted and dishonoured, why his son may expire, why his riches are lost and so on. But such complaints or thoughts are futile. Those, who put a devotee to such a test, do not know anything, either about good company, devotion or refuge. But it does not mean, that such a devotee is always poor, sick or is insulted, dishonoured or blamed. He is not the least concerned with health and sickness, praise and blame, or honour and dishonour etc. He beholds, the Lord only. He does not think, even of the glory of the Lord, that He is creator, preserver and destroyer, of the entire universe.

Someone asked a saint, whether he was a devotee of the Lord, Who creates the universe, or one Who preserves it or one Who destroys it. He replied, "This is nothing special about our Lord, this is a phase of His life and glory." A devout devotee, should never look at His glory.

At Ṛṣikeśa, on the bank of the Ganges, a saint was holding a discourse, during the summer season. A cold wind out of cold wave came to that side. A striver said, "What a cold wind!" Another striver said, "How could you divert your attention to the cold wind, from a divine discourse?" Therefore, so long as a striver, pays attention to these outwardly temptations etc., it means that he is not devoted, to the Lord.

In this connection, there is an anecdote, relating to a depraved woman. Her conduct is bad, but it teaches a good moral. She wanted to meet her lover. On the way, there was a mosque where a learned muslim was offering his prayer, to God. She unknowingly put her foot on the arm of the learned person, and went away. When she comes back, he was very angry with her, and he scolded her by saying, that she was very foolish, as she did not see that he was offering his prayer to God. She replied that she was so much absorbed by her passion, for that man, that she could not see him. But, how could he behold her, when he was engrossed in offering his prayer, to the Lord? According to her, there was no use of such a prayer, and study of the Kurāna. He should have devoted himself, heart and soul, to the Lord, otherwise he cannot be called a devout devotee, and it means, that he has not taken refuge in Him.

When the Kauravas and the Pāṇḍavas, learnt archery, their preceptor gave them, a test. An artificial bird, was perched on the branch of a tree. Each of them was asked to hit the throat of the bird. But before shooting, each was asked, what he was beholding. Other persons said, that they saw a branch, a bird, wings and the beak etc. The same question, was put to Arjuna. He answered that only the throat, was visible to him. So he was ordered to shoot the arrow. Arjuna hit the throat of the bird with his arrow, because he saw the aim, to achieve. Thus a devotee should have only the aim of Divine love. This is called unswerving devotion (Gītā 13/10) or exclusive devotion, to Him.

Someone told saint Gosvāmī Tulasīdāsa, "Your Lord Rāma, Whom you worship, is partly divine, as He possesses only twelve divine traits (Kalā), while Lord Kṛṣṇa is fully divine, as He possesses all the sixteen divine traits." Having heard these words, Gosvāmī Tulasīdāsa bowed to him and said "You have been very kind to me, by explaining that Lord Rāma is an incarnation, having twelve Kalās (divine traits). I worshipped Him, regarding him as Daśaratha's loving baby son, only." He did not pay attention to the fact, that Lord Kṛṣṇa was a complete incarnation of God, as He possessed all the sixteen Kalās (divine traits).

Several devotees worship Lord Rāma, or Lord Kṛṣṇa, regarding Him as a small boy, a son of Daśaratha or Nanda. So they request saints, to bless their favourite Deity, boy Rāma or Kṛṣṇa. The Lord, likes such a devotee and such a blessing, very much. It means, that such devout devotees, do not pay any attention, to His glories.

If a person touches the dust of a courtyard, where Kanhaiyā

(Kṛṣṇa) played, this dust enables him to attain, all the four kinds of salvation. But mother Yaśodā, regarding it as dirt, threw it into a dustbin, because she beheld Kṛṣṇa only her son, without paying any attention to His glory and qualifications etc.

Saints, have declared that if a person wants to have a vision of the Lord, he should have nothing with him because the dependence on anything, such as mind, intellect, learning, riches or kith and kin etc., are veils, which are obstacles to His vision. As soon as, this veil of dependence on the material world, is removed, a devotee beholds the Lord really.

Once a saint, met a rustic peasant of Vraja. The peasant said that he worked only for his loving Kṛṣṇa. The saint said, that he had an exclusive devotion to him. The peasant said that he had the most exclusive devotion, to Him. The saint said to him, "What is the most exclusive devotion?" The peasant said, "What is exclusive devotion?" The saint said, that in exclusive devotion a devotee has undivided devotion, to his favourite Deity, without worshipping the Sun-god, Gaṇeśa, Durgā and Brahmā etc. The rustic peasant said, "O Grandpa, I have the most exclusive devotion, because I don't know any damn name besides my Kanhaiyā (Kṛṣṇa)." Thus, a devout devotee, does not meditate on, what is the Absolute, what is soul, whether God is endowed with form and attributes or is without attribute and formless, and so on.

Once a saint, in Vraja was discussing spirituality, with someone. A cowherdess, heard their discussion. She asked her companion, about the terms God and soul etc. The latter said, that these should be the other names of their loving Kanhaiyā (Kṛṣṇa) or His neighbours, or relatives, because these saints are bent upon attaining Him. So they always talk about Him. Similarly, the cowherdesses also believe that only Kanhaiyā is theirs, and they are His. But they have no desire to receive, anything from Him.

Mother Yaśodā says to Dāū (Balarāma), the elder brother

of Lord Kṛṣṇa, "Look after this Kanhaiyā, because he is very innocent. He should not go into dense woods etc." Balarāma replies, "Kanhaiyā is very carefree. He puts his hand into the holes of snakes and does such other mischiefs. He may be bitten by poisonous snakes etc." So Balarāma and other cowherds, look after Kanhaiyā, lest he should do any mischief, They do not believe, when anyone says that He rears and preserves the entire world, because according to them, He is only a loving kid.

Once, a saint began to narrate the glories of Lord Kṛṣṇa, to the cowherdesses, while talking to them. The cowherdesses said, "The key of the treasure of His glories is with us. He has nothing. So how can he grant anything to anyone?" Anyone who nurses any desire should never approach Him. So, one who wants nothing from Him, even in adversity or at the time of death, should go to Him.

Sage Vālmīki says to Lord Rāma in the Rāmacaritamānasa, "You reside in the heart of a person who loves, You, naturally without expecting any reward, because that is Your own seat" (2/13).

When a devotee has no desire of his own, the Lord, becomes loving to him and He resides in him. A devout devotee, loves him for His sake, not for his own sake. If he loves Him, to get his desire fulfilled, it means that there is no true love, there is attachment, lust or delusion. Therefore, the cowherdesses gave a warning to travellers, say, "O travellers, do not go by that street, because that is very deadly and dangerous. There a naked boy, having a dark complexion like black catechu tree, is standing with his hands on his buttocks. In appearance, he is like an ascetic, but he robs travellers, of the treasure of their hearts, without any exception".

He is called Kṛṣṇa, because He attracts everyone towards Him. One who is attracted towards Him, becomes His forever and he remains of no use to anybody in the world. Such a man, who is of no use to anybody, is really useful to, everyone. But, he has no self-interest, to be served by anyone. When a devotee takes refuge in Him, he has not to adore Him. Adoration like breathing, becomes a natural part and parcel of his life. A devotee, cannot forget Him, he becomes restless, without remembering Him, even for a moment (Nāradabhaktisūtra 19). Such a noble devotee, shuns the Kingdom of the entire universe which if offered to him, as a substitute for forgetfulness of the Lord, for even a fraction of a moment (Śrīmadbhā. 11/14/14).

In the Bhāgavata it is mentioned—Excellent devotees, are those who cannot renounce the Lord's lotus feet, which are scarcely available to the gods, not even for half a moment (Śrīmadbhāgavata 11/2/53).

It is declared by Lord Kṛṣṇa in the Bhāgavata, "Devotees who have surrendered themselves to Me, have no desire to attain the seat, either of Brahmā or Indra (the lord of the gods), or the kingdom of this world, or the underworld or all yogic perfection or even salvation," (Śrīmadbhāgavata 11/14/14).

Bharata, the brother of Lord Rāma also declares in the Rāmacaritamānasa, that he has no desire, either for riches or for righteousness, or for lust or even for salvation, but he wants to be blessed with the boon, that he should love (adore) Lord Rāma's feet, in all births (2/204).

Appendix—A Karmayogī has his 'nitya' (eternal) affinity with God, a Jñānayogī has Tāttvika unity, while the devotee, who has taken refuge in God, has 'ātmīya affinity', ownness with God. In 'nitya' affinity there is renunciation of the transient relationship with the world; in 'tāttvika' unity there is realization of the Self (Self-realization); and in 'ātmīya' affinity there is oneness with God. In 'nitya' affinity there is 'śānta rasa' (peaceful relish or bliss); in 'tāttvika' unity there is 'akhaṇḍa rasa' and in 'ātmīya' affinity there is infinite relish (bliss). Without attaining infinite relish, a man's hunger is not fully satisfied. The infinite relish can be attained by taking 'refuge' in God. Therefore 'seeking refuge in God' is the Supreme Secret and the best spiritual discipline.

'Sarvadharmānparityajya' does not mean physical abandonment

of all duties but it means abandonment of dependence on all duties. Thus a striver should not depend on duties. As in the first chapter, it is mentioned 'ta ime'vasthitā yuddhe prāṇāṁstyaktvā dhanāni ca'—here 'prāṇāṁstyaktvā' does not mean abandonment of lives but it means abandonment of the desire to live because by abandoning the life, how will a warrior be arrayed on the battlefield? It is impossible. Similarly in the ninth verse of the first chapter, it is mentioned—'anye ca bahavaḥ śurvā madarthe tyaktajīvitāḥ'—it does not mean that many other heroes are arrayed by abandoning their lives. It means that those heroes have given up hope to live alive viz., they don't care for their lives. Therefore here the expression 'sarvadharmānparityajya' should mean 'abandonment of dependence on duties'. As heroes don't care for their lives, similarly devotees don't care for duties. They don't attach importance to duties. The reason is that they attach more importance to 'refuge in God' than to duties. In duty there is connection with the insentient, while in 'refuge' there is affinity with the sentient. The duty is discharged according to one's 'varṇa' (order of life) and 'āśrama' (stage of life), therefore in it there is significance of the body. But a devotee takes refuge in God himself, therefore in it there is significance of God.

'Māmekaṁ śaraṇaṁ vraja'—In mundane life a devotee should have fair dealings with love, respect and courtesy with others but as he needs nothing from others, he does not depend on anyone else but he totally depends on God only.

yaha binatī raghubīra gusāīṁ
aura āsa-bisvāsa-bharoso, harau jīva-jaḍatāī

(Vinayapatrikā 103)

'O Lord Rāma! I pray to you to free me from the stupidity of my hope, belief and dependence on the matter (world)'.

eka bharoso eka bala eka āsa bisvāsa
eka rāma ghana syāma hita cātaka tulsīdāsa

(Dohāvalī 277)

"As a 'cātaka' bird lives only on rain drops (it does not drink even Ganges-water), similarly Tulasīdāsajī wants to have trust, hope and belief only in Lord Rāma and he wants to depend only on His power."

In fact only God grants full refuge. As a baby raises its hand to go to the lap of its mother, the mother raises it up by catching its hand, similarly when a devotee, by applying his power, is inclined to God and prepares himself for taking refuge in Him, God grants him full refuge.

Arjuna wanted to get rid of sins, therefore the Lord said that He would liberate him from all sins because it is God's nature that howsoever a devotee seeks Him, so does He meet him—'ye yathā māṁ prapadyante tāṁstathaiva bhajāmyaham' (Gītā 4/11). In fact liberation from sins is not the fruit of refuge. By exclusive refuge a man being inseparable with God, can attain infinite bliss. Therefore a striver, without having the desire to be liberated from sins or sufferings, should take refuge in God. If a striver has some desire, he gets something (perishable) but if he is totally free from desire, he gets all (imperishable or endless). God offers Himself to the devotee, becomes submissive to him who takes refuge in Him and feels indebted to him.

This refuge is the gist of the Gītā which the Lord has related by showering His special grace. In this 'refuge' only, the gospel of the Gītā attains perfection. Without it the gospel of the Gītā would have remained incomplete. Therefore when Arjuna surrendered himself totally to God, by declaring, that he would act according to the Lord's bidding 'kariṣye vacanaṁ tava', after that the Lord did not sermonize.

Link:—In the next verse, Lord Kṛṣṇa forbids Arjuna, to unfold the supreme secret gospel of all the other secrets, as mentioned in the preceding verse, to those who are undeserving.

इदं ते नातपस्काय नाभक्ताय कदाचन।
न चाशुश्रूषवे वाच्यं न च मां योऽभ्यसूयति॥६७॥

idaṁ te nātapaskāya nābhaktāya kadācana
na cāśuśrūṣave vācyaṁ na ca māṁ yo'bhyasūyati

This is never to be mentioned by you, to anyone who performs no austerities, or has no devotion, nor who is unwilling to hear, or who finds fault with Me. 67

Comment:—

'Idaṁ te nātapaskāya'—Here, the term 'idaṁ' (this), stands for the supreme secret 'abandoning all duties, take refuge in Me, alone' unfolded in the preceding verse.

Austerity, consists in tolerating pain and unfavourable circumstance, happily, while performing one's duty. The mind is not purified without austerity, and without purity useful advice cannot be accepted. So the Lord declares, that this supreme secret of all secrets, should not be revealed to a person, who is devoid of austerity. This secret of all secrets, should not be unfolded to one, who is devoid of austerities i.e., who is intolerant. This tolerance is of four kinds:—

(1) Tolerance in the pairs of opposites:—He should be free, from the pairs of opposites, such as attachment and aversion, pleasure and pain, honour and dishonour, praise and blame etc. Men of virtuous deeds are free from delusion, in the shape of pairs of opposites (Gītā 7/28); "The undeluded ones, are free, from the pairs of opposites, known as pleasure and pain" (15/5).

(2) Tolerance of impulses:— One resists impulses of lust, anger, greed and aversion, etc., (Gītā 5/23).

(3) Tolerance for religions (doctrines) of others:— He does not doubt his own doctrine, nor does he criticize and condemn, the doctrines of others. He realises, that the discipline of renunciation and of action, are one (Gītā 5/5).

(4) Tolerance, in the progress of others:—He is not jealous and envious of others, when they progress or when they are praised and honoured (Gītā 4/22, 12/15).

A perfected soul, possesses these four kinds, of tolerance. One who aims at these, is austere, while he who does not aim at them, is not austere.

This most profound secret, should not be unfolded to one, who is not austere, because he will not believe it, and he will find fault with it and thus have a downfall. Secondly, a man whose aim is not to purify his propensities, conduct etc., may think that he need not grieve, because the Lord will liberate him, from all sins. By thinking so, he may be indulging in evil and may have a fall. So, the Lord directs Arjuna, not to impart this secret gospel to one, who is devoid of austerities, otherwise, he may misuse it.

'Nābhaktāya kadācana'—He, who is devoid of devotion and has no faith in God, should not be imparted this supreme secret, because he may see things in a perverted way (contrary to the truth), by thinking that the Lord brags, Who wants others to carry out His order, for His selfish motive. Such an unbeliever by belittling such teachings, would have a downfall. So this supreme gospel, should not be conveyed to such a man.

'Na cāśuśrūṣave vācyam'—This supreme gospel, should not be imparted to one, who is unwilling to listen to it, because he will turn a deaf ear, to it. Thus, he will commit a sin, which will be harmful for him.

'Na ca māṁ yo'bhyasūyati'—This most secret teaching, should not be imparted to one who finds fault with Him. He finds fault because his heart is very impure. By finding fault with him, he is deprived of the gain and rather has a downfall. This defect is sometimes, found even in devotees, who have faith in God. So strivers, should be aware of this defect. Such men who are free from criticism, are released from the bondage of actions (Gītā 3/31). Moreover, He also declares that a man who listens to this gospel with faith, being free from cavil, shall attain to the divine immortal abodes such as Vaikuṇṭha, Goloka etc., (Gītā 18/71).

When the Lord declares, that this supreme secret is not to be spoken to such a person, He does not want him to be deprived of this gospel. But he, without having faith in the Lord and His words, may regard Him, as boastful and selfish and thus by accusing Him may have a fall. So it should not be spoken, to such a person.

Appendix—The Lord has laid special emphasis on the point that the Supreme Secret word should not be mentioned to anyone who has no devotion or who finds fault with Him. If it is mentioned to anyone who has no devotion or finds fault with God, it is more blame worthy than if it is related to one who performs no austerities or who is unwilling to hear, because the intellect of the people, who are without devotion and who are of a fault finding nature, is perverted.

'Abhakta' means the person who opposes devotion. He, who lacks devotion, has not been called here 'abhakta'. Even in devotees, out of ignorance, this defect of fault-finding can be perceived* but because of devotion this defect naturally perishes.

'Aśuśrūṣave' means the person, who is unwilling to hear, out of egoism. He who, out of ignorance, is unwilling to hear, has not been called 'aśuśrūṣave' here.

Link:—In the next two verses, the Lord explains the reward of propagating this gospel of the Gītā, among his devotees and declares, that such a person is the most loving to Him.

य इमं परमं गुह्यं मद्भक्तेष्वभिधास्यति।
भक्तिं मयि परां कृत्वा मामेवैष्यत्यसंशयः ॥ ६८ ॥

* In spite of having faith, in a person the carping defect may persist; therefore the Lord has mentioned that a person should have faith and should also be free from the carping nature.

ya imaṁ paramaṁ guhyaṁ madbhakteṣvabhidhāsyati
bhaktiṁ mayi parāṁ kṛtvā māmevaiṣyatyasaṁśayaḥ

He who, with supreme devotion to Me teaches this supreme secret to My devotees, shall doubtless, come to Me alone. There is no doubt about it. 68

Comment:—

'Bhaktiṁ mayi parāṁ kṛtvā'—The supreme devotion means that the person does not impart this gospel of the Gītā, in order to receive praise, honour, fame and gifts etc. But his aim is to develop devotion to Him, to meditate on Him, to propagate His teachings, to liberate the people, from sorrow and suffering and to lead them, to salvation.

There is a difference between the devotion mentioned in the fifty-fourth verse of this chapter, and in this verse. There, a Sāṅkhyayogī having become one with Brahma (the Absolute), attains supreme devotion to the Lord i.e., he realizes his real affinity with God, which he has had since time immemorial. But here, a striver without having any worldly desire, for praise and honour etc., in the least, yearns for devotion to Him.

'Ya imaṁ paramaṁ guhyaṁ'—The teaching of the Gītā as imparted in the whole Gītā, in the form of a dialogue between Lord Kṛṣṇa and Arjuna, is the supreme secret. The expression 'Supreme secret, also includes whatever is secret or more secret, or the most secret.

'Madbhakteṣvabhidhāsyati'—A devotee, is he who has faith in the Lord and His words and who wants to listen to His teaching. One who declares this teaching to His such devotees, attains Him.

In the preceding verse, in the expression 'Nābhaktāya'—singular number was used, while here in 'Madbhakteṣu'—plural number has been used. Why? The reason is, that if there is only one person, who is devoid of austerities or devotion or who is unwilling to hear or who cavils, among many others, the speaker, should impart the gospel of the Gītā, because it will be beneficial to all of them, except one. When a man feeds sparrows with grains, sometimes even a crow comes, to pick some grains, though the man wants to feed the sparrows only. Similarly, a preacher (speaker) imparts the teaching of the Gītā only to those, who are qualified and deserving to listen, to it.

'Māmevaiṣyatyasaṁśayaḥ'—If a person, teaches this supreme secret to His devotees, aiming at God-realization, he will doubtlessly, attain Him. The reason is, that according to Gītā when a man, worshipping Him through the performance of his own duty, attains perfection (18/46) and also through the offer of bodily actions attains, Him (9/27-28); why should he not attain Him by propagating the gospel of the Gītā, having an aim of supreme devotion to Him?

न च तस्मान्मनुष्येषु कश्चिन्मे प्रियकृत्तमः।
भविता न च मे तस्मादन्यः प्रियतरो भुवि॥ ६९॥

na ca tasmānmanuṣyeṣu kaścinme priyakṛttamaḥ
bhavitā na ca me tasmādanyaḥ priyataro bhuvi

There is, none among men who does more loving service to Me than he; nor shall there be, another on earth, dearer to Me than him. 69

Comment:—

'Na ca tasmānmanuṣyeṣu kaścinme priyakṛttamaḥ'—A person, who wants to receive and secure material things, and attaches importance to them, cannot be said, to be endowed with supreme devotion. But he, who without having any desire in the least for mundane things etc., having only the aim of God-realization or God's vision, or God's devotion, wants to translate the teachings of the Gītā into practice, can be said to be endowed, with supreme devotion. Such a person, is qualified to propagate the gospel of the Gītā. If sometimes, he happens to have a desire to receive honour and praise etc., that desire cannot last much longer, because it is not his aim.

There is, none dearer to Him, than he who propagates the gospel of the Gītā among men, because there is no other job more loving, to Him, than propagation of this gospel. Moreover, he does so only for the Lord's sake, without expecting any reward, in the form of praise, honour, name and fame etc. As far as, mundane desires are concerned, they can be satisfied, in other births, such as of gods, birds, beasts, insects, trees, plants and creatures of hell also. But the success of human life, lies in God-realization and in becoming beloved, of Him.

'Bhavitā na ca me tasmādanyaḥ priyataro bhuvi'—A devotee, who has some desire to win praise, honour, name and fame, without having the only aim of God-realization and without practising the teachings of the Gītā, but propagates the gospel of the Gītā, through adoration, recitation, publication, memorization and cheap sale and getting these done by others, is dearer to the Lord, while he who propagates the teaching of his own sect or religion, is only dear to Him.

A striver, can translate most of the teaching of the Gītā into practice, very easily. Every person, without any distinction of caste, creed, colour, country, stage of life etc., who performs his duty for the welfare of others without expecting any reward, and without having any desire, while performing professional and physical activities (eating, drinking, sleeping etc.) can attain God-realization and supreme bliss (Gītā 6/22).

The gospel of the Gītā, does not force anyone to change his caste, creed, colour, country and actions etc. But, it imparts the teachings that a man should purify his thoughts, sentiments and aim. A person, by imparting the gospel of the Gītā to His devotees, will remove their doubts and obstacles, and enable them to realize God, easily and quickly. So, such a person will be most loving to God, because He is very much pleased with those people, who help others in realizing Him. The Lord, feels very happy and satisfied, with salvation of human beings.

Appendix—The gospel of the Gītā can easily lead every person under every circumstance to salvation; therefore the Lord mentions the special glory of its propagation. The Gītā declares that even a warrior, while fighting in the war, can attain salvation by treating pleasure and pain alike—'sukha duḥkhe same kṛtvā' (2/38), by dedicating this action of fighting to God—'yat karoṣi yadaśnāsi' (9/27) and by worshipping the Lord through the performance of his duty—'svakarmaṇā tamabhyarcya' (18/46) and so on. When even such a circumstance (horrid action) as war can lead to salvation, then how will other circumstances not lead to salvation?

The man, who becomes loving to God, attains the three Yogas—Karmayoga, Jñānayoga and Bhaktiyoga.

Link:—What should a striver do, if he is not qualified to propagate the gospel of the Gītā? The Lord, answers this question in the next verse.

अध्येष्यते च य इमं धर्म्यं संवादमावयोः ।
ज्ञानयज्ञेन तेनाहमिष्टः स्यामिति मे मतिः ॥ ७० ॥

adhyeṣyate ca ya imaṁ dharmyaṁ saṁvādamāvayoḥ
jñānayajñena tenāhamiṣṭaḥ syāmiti me matiḥ

And, he who contemplates this sacred dialogue of ours, he shall be worshipping Me, through the sacrifice (yajña), of knowledge (wisdom)—such is my conviction. 70

Comment:—

'Adhyeṣyate ca ya imaṁ dharmyaṁ saṁvādamāvayoḥ'— Lord Kṛṣṇa says to Arjuna, that this dialogue is the gist of scriptures.

Though they had been living together for years, yet they could not have such a rare dialogue. This sort of dialogue takes place on rare occasions.

Real curiosity, is not aroused, so long as a man does not get disenchanted of mundane affairs, and is not dispassionate. When he becomes restless, in the mundane maze, to find out the way, he has a heart-to-heart talk with a person, from whom he expects right guidance. He becomes his pupil, takes refuge in him and puts questions to him freely.

The more curious a pupil is, to satisfy his curiosity, the more enthusiastic the preceptor is to satisfy it, with new explanations and arguments. When a cow feeds a calf with her milk, the more hungry the calf is, with more force he pulls the udders and so the whole milk of the cow comes to her udders, from other areas. Similarly, when an inquisitive striver, asks questions again and again, new ideas and answers crop up, in the mind of the speaker. Then, a dialogue between the speaker and the listener, becomes excellent.

The real dialogue, between Lord Krṣṇa and Arjuna, begins with 2/54 when Arjuna curiously asks Him "What are the marks of the man, who has steady wisdom?" Before this, Arjuna never asked a question with such curiosity, nor did the Lord so spontaneously express His views, before. This dialogue is the gist of the Vedas and the scriptures. It can lead a man to salvation, very easily, even in the most adverse circumstances, if he translates this gospel into practice. In adverse circumstances, he instead, of losing heart should make the best possible use i.e., he should renounce, the desire for favourable circumstances, because unfavourable circumstances destroy his sins, and enable him to renounce desire, for desirable circumstances. The more desire, a man has for favourable circumstances, the more fearful are the unfavourable circumstances. As soon as, he starts renouncing his desire for desirable circumstances by degrees, to that extent his attachment to the agreeable will be renounced, and his fear of the disagreeable, will perish. When he becomes totally free from attachment and fear, he will become equanimous. This equanimity, has been called Yoga and those who are established in equanimity, are established in God. In the Gītā, different disciplines, as of action, of knowledge, of Devotion, of Meditation, as means to realize God, have been described.

The term 'Adhyeṣyate' (will study), denotes that the one who studies the dialogue, in the form of the Gītā, learns it by heart, tries to understand its gospel, will develop a curiosity to know this gospel, more and more. The more curious he is, the more clearly, it will be unfolded to him. When its secret is revealed to him, he will translate it into practice. By thoroughly practising its teachings, he will become the very image of the Gītā. By seeing him, people will be reminded of the Gītā, in the same way as people of Ayodhyā, were reminded of Lakṣmaṇa, by seeing Guha, the chief (king), of the primitive tribe called 'Niṣāda'.

'Jñānayajñena tenāhamiṣṭaḥ syām'—Sacrifice is of two kinds—of wealth and of knowledge. In the former, there is predominance of things and actions, while in the latter, there is predominance of knowledge. In the sacrifice of knowledge, a striver, puts questions to a saint or a preceptor, in order to know the real essence, and the saint or preceptor explains it. A striver, reflects seriously upon it. Then he realizes, where he stands. Having known the real essence, nothing remains to be known by him. This is called the sacrifice of knowledge. But here, Lord Kṛṣṇa says to Arjuna, that He will be worshipped through the sacrifice of knowledge, by him who studies this secret dialogue, between them. The reason is, as a loving devotee is pleased and thrilled, when he is reminded of the Lord by someone, similarly, when the Lord sees anyone studying the Gītā, He is reminded of his devotee, having exclusive devotion to Him, and the teaching imparted by him to others. So he gets pleased, and thrilled and by assuming this study, as the sacrifice of knowledge, He is worshipped. By studying this gospel, knowledge, specially wells forth, in his mind.

'Iti me matiḥ'—When the Lord declares, that it is His conviction, He means to say that, He listens to the gospel of the Gītā, when anyone studies it, because He pervades everywhere (Gītā 9/4) and His ears are everywhere (Gītā 13/13). Having heard this gospel, He is overwhelmed with knowledge, love and grace, and His intellect, is immersed in his memory. Thus, though he does not worship Him, he merely studies the Gītā, yet He accepts it as worship to Him, i.e., He by His grace awards him, the fruit of the sacrifice of knowledge.

Secondly, while one studies the Gītā or learns it by heart, he has a sweet memory of this dialogue, so He assumes, that he is rendering a great service, to Him.

Once, a boy was brought by a priest. The priest had trained him in the art of oration, and had given him a written speech. The boy had learnt it by heart. When the boy delivered the speech, with right gestures and expressions, the chairman and the audience were so much pleased with him, that they showered money on him and congratulated him from their hearts. But in fact, that boy did not understand the subject matter of the speech, as he was not well educated. He had merely learnt it by heart, without understanding it. Similarly, when a person recites the verses of the Gītā, even without understanding these, the Lord is worshipped through the sacrifice of knowledge, because the Lord understands them well, in the same way, as the chairman and the audience understood, the speech of the boy. Moreover, He Himself resides at such a place; and as an audience was present at the speech of the boy, at the place, where Gītā is studied, all sacred-places (places of pilgrimage), such as Prayāga etc., as well as gods, sages, divine snakes, cowḥerds, cowherdesses and ascetics, such as Nārada and Uddhava etc., also reside there.

Appendix—The Lord regards the knowledge—sacrifice as superior to material sacrifice—'śreyān dravya mayādyajñāj jñāna yajñaḥ parantapa' (Gītā 4/33). When there is so much glory of the study of the Gītā, then how much glory should be thereof translating the gospel of the Gītā into practice?

Link:—There are some people who are unable, even to study the dialogue. What should they do? The answer comes, in the next verse.

श्रद्धावाननसूयश्च शृणुयादपि यो नरः।
सोऽपि मुक्तः शुभाँल्लोकान्प्राप्नुयात्पुण्यकर्मणाम्॥ ७१॥

śraddhāvānanasūyaśca śṛṇuyādapi yo naraḥ
so'pi muktaḥ śubhāllokānprāpnuyātpuṇyakarmaṇām

And, the man who listens to it with faith and without cynicism, even he, being liberated from sins, shall attain to the happy world of the righteous. 71

Comment:—

'Śraddhāvānanasūyaśca śṛṇuyādapi yo naraḥ so'pi muktaḥ śubhāllokānprāpnuyātpuṇyakarmaṇām'—'Sraddhāvān', is he who has faith in the Gītā and holds it in reverence while 'Anasūyaḥ', is he who does not find fault with the Lord or His utterance, in the least. Such a person who listens to the gospel of the Gītā, with faith and without finding fault, with it, being liberated from all sins, attains to the worlds of the righteous.

The Lord, by using the term 'Api', twice means to say, that not to talk of the person who propagates and studies the Gītā, even he who listens to it, being liberated from sins, attains to the happy world of the righteous.

In a man's speech, generally there are four defects. These are—doubt, heedlessness, desire and incapability. But the Lord's gospel, is totally free from all these defects, because the Lord is the ultimate purity, where there is not even an iota of impurity. Therefore, there is no possibility of any doubt, in this gospel. If any person, is unable to understand this gospel, or he doubts any fact, he should think that he is unable to have a thorough grasp of the subject, because of his imperfect intellect. By having such a belief, his critical attitude comes to an end. Devotion with faith, also destroys a critical state of mind.

There was a disciple of Caitanya Mahāprabhu, who while studying the Gītā, got so much engrossed in it, that sometimes there was a burst of laughter, while at the next moment there was a burst of tears, in him. But his pronunciation, was not correct. Someone complained to Caitanya Mahāprabhu, that his disciple was a hypocrite, as he shed tears while studying the Gītā, though he could not pronounce the verses correctly. Caitanya Mahāprabhu asked the disciple, "Do you understand the verse, while studying the Gītā?" He said, "No". "Then why do you burst into tears?" He replied, "When I study the Gītā, I behold Lord Kṛṣṇa and his devotee, Arjuna sitting and talking. So I am overwhelmed with emotions, by beholding them and listening to their dialogue." Hearing his answer, Caitanya Mahāprabhu was very much pleased, with him. If such a devotee, listens to the gospel of the Gītā with faith, he attains salvation, without any doubt. He being liberated from all sins, attains, to the happy worlds of the righteous.

Here, the expression 'Puṇyakarmaṇām', does not stand for those righteous persons, who perform righteous deeds, such as sacrifice etc., to receive their fruit, because they have to return to the world of mortals (Gītā 9/21), again and again. Here, persons of righteous deeds, are those devotees who attain to Vaikuṇṭha, the Abode of Lord Viṣṇu; Sāketa, the Abode of Lord Rāma; Goloka, the Abode of Lord Kṛṣṇa; Kailāsa, the Abode of Lord Śiva, according to the worship, of their favourite Deity. All of them realize, God merely by listening to the gospel of the Gītā, with faith and without derision.

Appendix—'Śubhām̊llokānprāpnuyātpuṇyakarmaṇām'—The listener who listens to the gospel of the Gītā with faith and devotion becomes authorized to attain to the higher worlds such as heaven and even to the Abode of God, viz., if he is endowed with more faith and devotion, he will attain to the Abode of God; and if he has less faith and devotion, he will attain to other worlds.

Not to speak of the study of the Gītā and listening to it, but there is a great glory of even having a copy of the Gītā. There was a constable who was going home at night. On his way he saw a beautiful lady under a tree in the moon light. He talked to that woman, that woman asked him, if she could accompany him. He consented and so the woman, who was indeed a witch, followed him. That witch daily at night came to him, slept with him, had sensual intercourse with him and departed in the next morning. Thus she began to exploit that constable viz., began to suck his blood and so he became very weak. One night when they were lying in bed, he asked her to switch off the light. She while lying, by lengthening her arm, switched off the light. So the constable came to know that she was not a common woman but she was a witch. He was much frightened. The witch warned him that, if he disclosed her identity to anyone, she would kill him. Thus she came daily at night and went back in the morning. He was reduced to a skeleton. The other people asked him the reason of his weakness and thinness. But being frightened of the witch, he did not disclose the secret. One day he brought some medicine from a shop. The shopkeeper (chemist) gave him the medicine in a small paper packet. The constable put the packet into his pocket and came back home. At night when the witch came to him, she remained standing at a distance and asked the constable to throw the paper packet from his pocket down. The constable believed that there was some miracle in the paper packet, so the witch did not dare to come to him. The constable bluntly refused to throw the packet. The witch insisted on it again and again but the constable didn't agree to her proposal. When she thought that he was beyond her control, she went away. The constable took out the paper packet and saw that it was a torn piece of paper of the Gītā. Since then the constable, having known the glory of the Gītā, began to keep the Gītā in his pocket every time. That witch never came to him again.

Link:—Having glorified the hearing of the Gītā in the preceding verse, the Lord, in order to reveal the significance of the hearing of the Gītā, to all the person, puts Arjuna a question, in the next verse, although He knew everything.

कच्चिदेतच्छ्रुतं पार्थ त्वयैकाग्रेण चेतसा।
कच्चिदज्ञानसम्मोहः प्रनष्टस्ते धनञ्जय॥७२॥

kaccidetacchrutaṁ pārtha tvayaikāgreṇa cetasā
kaccidajñānasaṁmohaḥ pranaṣṭaste dhanañjaya

O Pārtha (Arjuna), has this been heard by you with one-pointed mind? O winner of wealth (Arjuna), has your delusion, born of ignorance, been destroyed? 72

Comment:—

'Kaccidetacchrutaṁ pārtha tvayaikāgreṇa cetasā'—The term, 'etat' (this) denotes much nearness. So Lord Kṛṣṇa asks Arjuna, whether he has heard what He explained, in the seventy-first verse, that a man should listen to the gospel of the Gītā with faith and without derision. The Lord means to say, whether he has listened to this gospel with faith, and with an uncarping spirit.

By the expression 'Ekāgreṇa cetasā', the Lord means to ask Arjuna, whether he has listened to His supreme word, the most secret of all of taking refuge in Him alone, (18/66), which was promised by Him, in the sixty-fourth verse and which was forbidden for one, who is devoid of austerities, in the sixty-seventh verse.

'Kaccidajñānasammohaḥ pranaṣṭaste dhanañjaya'—Lord Kṛṣṇa puts the second question to Arjuna, whether his delusion, born of ignorance, has been destroyed. If his delusion has been destroyed, it means that he listened to the gospel preached by Him, otherwise not, as it is a fact, that the delusion of a person who listens to this gospel with faith and without scoffing, is dispelled.

Lord Kṛṣṇa addresses Arjuna, by the term 'Pārtha' (son of Pṛthā viz., Kuntī), in order to show His affection for him. He addressed him, by this term in the twenty-fifth verse of the first chapter, when He asked him to behold all the kinsmen, to arouse the delusion of kinship, and to make him restless, to be free from this delusion. So Lord Kṛṣṇa here again, addresses him as 'Pārtha', to ask him whether his delusion of kinship has been destroyed.

By using the term 'Dhanañjaya, Lord Kṛṣṇa says to Arjuna, that he is called the conqueror of wealth, by conquering the wealth of kings. But real wealth, consists in the destruction of delusion. So he should become a conqueror of wealth, in the real sense of the term.

Link:—Arjuna in the next verse, answers the question put, in the preceding verse.

अर्जुन उवाच

नष्टो मोहः स्मृतिर्लब्धा त्वत्प्रसादान्मयाच्युत ।
स्थितोऽस्मि गतसन्देहः करिष्ये वचनं तव ॥ ७३ ॥

arjuna uvāca

naṣṭo mohaḥ smṛtirlabdhā tvatprasādānmayācyuta
sthito'smi gatasandehaḥ kariṣye vacanaṁ tava

Arjuna said:

O Acyuta (Kṛṣṇa), my delusion is destroyed and memory is gained through Your grace. I stand firm, with my doubts dispelled and I shall act, according to Your word. 73

Comment:—

'Naṣṭo mohaḥ smṛtirlabdhā tvatprasādānmayācyuta'—Arjuna addresses the Lord as 'Acyuta', to emphasize the fact that, He never deviates from His divine nature, while a man turns away from one's own Self and has a fall. The term 'Acyuta', has been used three times in the Gītā by Arjuna. First (in 1/21), he asked him to place his chariot between the two armies. Second, (in 11/42) he prayed to His cosmic form. There was no change in His state. At last (in 18/73) he uses this term here, when he says that he will act according to His word. Thus there are three kinds of states of mind, of Arjuna at the beginning, the middle and the end, but the Lord remains the same, without any change, in his state.

In the second chapter, Arjuna surrendered himself to the Lord by declaring, "I am your disciple. Do instruct me, who have taken refuge in you" (2/7). In this verse, that refuge, attains perfection.

At the end of the tenth chapter, Lord Kṛṣṇa said to Arjuna, "What need is there for detailed knowledge? I stand supporting the whole universe, with a single fragment of Myself." Having heard this declaration, Arjuna could realise the Lord's singularity and received a kind of enlightenment, which forced Arjuna to utter the words, "My delusion has been dispelled" (Gītā 11/1). But having seen the fearful cosmic form of the Lord, when Arjuna was confounded with fear, He asked him, neither to be afraid nor bewildered (11/49). It proves, that Arjuna's delusion, was not destroyed by then. But, here in response to Lord Kṛṣṇa's question, Arjuna answers that his delusion is destroyed, and he has gained knowledge (memory).*

---

* Here Arjuna's both kinds of delusion— the mundane (Gītā 2/52) and Vedic textual (Gītā 2/53) have been destroyed.

There is a vast difference, between the memory of the mind and that of the self. The reality of a thing is established through the proof of senses and mind, while the existence of God cannot be established, through this proof i.e., God cannot be confined within the range of the proof of senses and mind.* God is beyond all proofs. But the entire universe, is within the sphere of proof, while proof comes within the sphere, of the knower.

The knower is one, while proof can be of different kinds. Some scholars regard proof (Pramāṇa) of three kinds—evident, by guess, and of the vedas, while others regard it as of four kinds—evident (Pratyakṣa), by guess (Anumāna), that with which something is compared (Upamāna), and word (Śabda), while some others besides these four, regard it of three more kinds—reasoning (Arthāpatti), in apprehension (Anupalabdhi) and traditional theory (Aitihya). Thus scholars, differ in their opinions, as far as kinds of proof are concerned, but all of them agree, that the knower, is one. Proof is a kind of inclination, while the knower (self), is a kind of realization.

As far as the term 'smṛti' (memory), is concerned, it has been explained—(1) The revelation of something already experienced. (2) Memory means the knowledge born of past influences (impressions), Saṁskāras.

---

*We can know the world through (proof). But God Who is the base and illuminator of knowledge, cannot be known by knowledge, because the illumined cannot illuminate the illuminator. So He can be known by having faith in Him.

Those who have faith in scriptures, accept the existence of God, by regarding these as authority, while those who have faith in the liberated souls, accept His existence according to their word. But the mind and senses, cannot prove His existence. Therefore, the believers believe in his existence, through scriptures and liberated souls, by having faith in them while the non-believers cannot accept the existence of God, by regarding scriptures and liberated souls as authority. It means, that whatever is known through senses and mind, is direct proof, while the proof of assumption etc., is the argumentative proof, the progenitor of direct proof. But as far as, proof of saints and scriptures is concerned, that can be gained, through faith.

This memory, is an inclination of mind. This inclination, can be of five kinds—proof (Pramāṇa), error (Viparyaya), alternate (Vikalpa), sleep (Nidrā) and memory (Smrti), and each of these kinds can further be subdivided into two parts—difficult and easy. Inclination for the world, is difficult i.e., it binds a man, while inclination for the Lord is easy, as it frees a man, from bondage and suffering. Ignorance, is the cause of these inclinations. But the Lord is free, from ignorance. So He can be known by the self, not by any inclination or cause. When his memory is once gained, He can never be forgotten, while in the inclination of mind there is sometimes memory, while at the other time, there is forgetfulness.

A man, forgets the Lord when he accepts the existence of the unreal world, and attaches importance to it. Though this forgetfulness, has been since time immemorial, yet it comes to an end. When it comes to an end, the memory of one's self, is aroused which is called 'Smṛtirlabdhā' i.e., the veil is removed, and the reality is revealed.

This memory, according to the inclination (taste) of strivers, can be divided into three kinds—(1) Discipline of Action i.e., memory of the performance of action, without expecting any reward. (2) Discipline of Knowledge i.e., memory of the self. (3) Discipline of Devotion i.e., memory of one's relationship, with God. Thus the memory of these three disciplines is aroused, because though all the three disciplines, are self-evident and eternal, a man forgets them.

When a man, accepts the existence of worldly things and attaches importance to them, he is attached to them—this is forgetfulness (veil) of the Discipline of Action. When he is attached to the unreal, he has a disinclination for the self—this is forgetfulness of the Discipline of knowledge. The man (self), is a fragment of God. But he, having a disinclination for God, has an inclination for the world, and is attached to it. It is because of this attachment, that his devotion is veiled—this is forgetfulness, of the Discipline of Devotion.

Here, destruction of forgetfulness (disinclination) for the self is smṛti (memory). This gaining of memory (knowledge), of the self is real memory, which when once gained, cannot be lost, because the self ever remains uniform, without undergoing any modifications. The memory of the mind, can be lost, because being an evolute of prakṛti (matter), it is changeable.

It means that, when a man identifies the self with the world and the body, it is called 'vismṛti' (forgetfulness). But, when by separating himself from the world and the body, he realizes the self, it is smṛti (memory or knowledge). The memory of the self, is one's own memory, without the help of any other means, such as senses and mind etc., while the memory of the mind, is an inclination of the mind. As a man, has knowledge of his entity without any proof, without the help of any organs through his own self, similarly, self-realization, is through one's own self. It is beyond all organs and instruments etc.

The memory of the self, is gained instantly, without any effort. Karṇa, was the son of Kuntī, but when he was abandoned by Kuntī after his birth, he was brought up by Rādhā, the wife to a charioteer named Adhiratha. So he took Rādhā to be his mother. But when he came to know from the sun-god, that his mother was Kuntī, he gained memory, without any effort.

The self, being a fragment of God, is desireless, pure and liberated. But a man having forgetfulness (disinclination), of the self, has desires, becomes impure and is bound. But, when he has no affinity, at all with mind etc., his memory (knowledge), is automatically aroused, without making any effort and without any practice. When once it is aroused, it is not lost, so is not to be aroused, again.

Memory (knowledge), is aroused by God's grace. His grace

is showered upon, a man, when he has an inclination for Him. He has an inclination for Him, when he has a disinclination for the world. As Arjuna said to Lord Kṛṣṇa, that he would act according to His word, similarly, a devotee without depending on the world, should declare that he will act according to His word, only.

It means that this memory (knowledge), is gained by the Lord's grace, when a striver has an inclination for Him. So Arjuna says that he has gained knowledge (memory), through His grace. The Lord continuously showers His limitless grace upon all beings, but a man realizes His grace, when he has an inclination for Him.

By the expression 'Tvatprasādānmayācyuta' Arjuna wants to say to Lord Kṛṣṇa, that He by His grace has disclosed to him the most secret essence. So it is only by His grace, that he has gained knowledge (memory). First, he requested Him to instruct him who had sought refuge in Him, but then he said that he would not fight. Till he got Self-realization, the Lord goaded him. It was only His divine grace. Even unasked, He disclosed the supreme secret, the topic of surrender to him (18/64—66). Thus, by His grace, he could know the reality, and his delusion was dispelled.

'Sthito'smi gatasandehaḥ kariṣye vacanaṁ tava'—Arjuna says to Lord Kṛṣṇa, that his doubt whether he should wage the war or not (2/6) is dispelled totally, and he is now established in reality. It means, that he has no desire of his own, he will act, according to His word.

Here a point needs attention. First, Arjuna had delusion because of his attachment, to his kith and kin. There, the Lord declared the process, "When a man thinks of the sense-objects, attachment for them arises; from attachment springs up desire; from desire ensues anger; from anger arises delusion; from delusion loss of memory; from loss of memory, the destruction of discrimination;

from destruction of discrimination, he perishes (Gītā 2/62-63). Arjuna by reminding the Lord of that process, declares that his delusion is dispelled, and he has gained memory, which was destroyed by delusion. In response to the statement, that from loss of memory, there is destruction of discrimination, Arjuna says, that his doubt is dispelled. In response to the statement, that from destruction of discrimination, one perishes, Arjuna declares that he stands firm. By saying so, Arjuna wants to explain to Lord Kṛṣṇa, that he has listened to the gospel of the Gītā and so he remembers it. But as far as the destruction of his delusion is concerned, it is only because of His grace. Thus the description of delusion, as described there and here, is one and the same.

In the second chapter from the sixty-first to the sixty-third verses, the Lord declared that wisdom of a person, whose senses are under control, is steady. It means, that when a person having a disinclination for the world, depends only on God, his intelligence is firmly set. If he does not depend only on Him, his mind thinks of sense-objects and then the process of attachment, desire, anger, delusion etc., follows. These ruin a man, because they are demoniac propensities. But here, is the description of his progress. When he, having a disinclination for the world, has an inclination for God, his delusion is dispelled, because he possesses a divine nature. It means, that a person goes to ruin, if he, having a disinclination for the Lord, is overpowered by his senses, is described there. But here, when a man has an inclination for God, it is by His grace that he gains memory (knowledge), of his real affinity with God.

In the spiritual sphere, God's grace is a more effective means, than hearing of texts, cognition, constant musing, meditation and trance etc. The reason is, that when a striver follows any spiritual discipline, by depending on his own effort, he maintains subtle egoism, which perishes, only when the striver totally depends on the Lord's grace, without regarding it as fruit of his effort.

A Vital Fact

Arjuna said that he had gained memory. The question arises why had he lost it. When a man (soul), by identifying himself with the unreal attaches importance to it, he forgets, the self. By forgetting the self, he thinks that the shortage of the unreal, is shortage in him. Similarly, by identifying himself with the body, he regards the death and birth of a body, as his own death and birth, and he regarded his father, rather than the Lord, as his creator. So he became forgetful of the Lord.

If a question is raised here as to whether the mistake was made prior or affinity with the non-self, was assumed, earlier. In other words, whether through ignorance, he assumed affinity with the non-self first, or through affinity with the non-self, there was ignorance. The answer is, that the Lord bestows the human body, so that man (soul) may be free from a cycle of birth and death, which he has been following since time immemorial and may attain infinite bliss, viz., God-realization. God felt bored all alone (Bṛhadāraṇyaka 1/4/3). The Lord created the human being, in order to play with him. The game can be played smoothly and freely, when both the players are free. So the Lord gave him freedom, as well as discrimination, so that he could distinguish the real from the unreal. If the Lord, had not bestowed upon him, freedom and discrimination, he might have been like a beast, without any speciality. But man, misused this freedom and got attached to unreal pleasure and prosperity. This was his error of judgment. Now the question arises, why is he attached to the unreal? The reason is, that he wants to enjoy transitory pleasure without thinking of their result (Strivers are those who think of the result, while the worldly people are those who do not think of the result). Attachment to the unreal, is the cause of error. How to know it ?

When a man, having renounced his attachment to the unreal, has an inclination for God, his error is rectified and his memory, is gained. This proves, that attachment to the unreal, is the real cause of error. This error is not natural, it is man-made. As he has created it, so it is his responsibility, to rectify it. The Lord, has given him power, to rectify this mistake. As soon as, this mistake is rectified, the memory (knowledge); of the self, is automatically regained and then nothing remains to be done, to be known and to be achieved by him.

Till now, man has taken birth many times, and he has had his union and again disunion with things, persons, states, circumstances and incidents etc., many times, but he himself has remained, the same. Union is surely to be turned into disunion, while disunion is not definitely to be changed into union. In fact, there is only disunion, there is no union This process of disunion, has been going on since time immemorial. What seems union, is continuously turning into disunion. The realization of total disunion, from the world is Yoga—'This disconnection from union, with pain is called Yoga' (Gītā 6/23) (Yoga—union with the self or with God). This union, is self-evident and eternal.* But this union is not realized, because we assume our union with the world and the body. As soon as, this assumed union is renounced, the real union is realized. Assumption of union with the world, is forgetfulness (ignorance) and realization of the fact, that a man can never have union with the world, is memory (knowledge).

Appendix—The worldly memory is a relative term, which is contrary to forgetfulness; but the memory of the divine entity is not of that kind but it is—a state of realization. The independent of this 'Tattva' experience has been called here 'smṛtirlabdhā'.

In fact there is never forgetfulness of that divine entity but

* In the Disciplines of Action and Knowledge there is eternal union with the self while in the Discipline of Devotion there is eternal union with God.

there is only turning away from it. It means that first there was knowledge and then it was forgotten—this sort of forgetfulness is not applicable to the divinity.* If we accept it as this sort of forgetfulness, then after memory again it will sink into oblivion. Therefore it has been declared in the Gītā—'yajjñātvā na punarmoham' (4/35)—viz., having gained this knowledge of the Self, a man does not get deluded again. Having assumed the non-Existent (unreal) as existent and according significance to it, a striver has disinclination for the real—this is known as forgetfulness. These—disinclination and inclination are from the view-point of a striver rather than from the view-point of the Self. The real Self ever remains the same, whether we have inclination to it or disinclination for it. If we assume the non-Existent (unreal) as non-Existent, the existent entity (the real Self) will naturally reveal itself the same as it is.

The thought is of two kinds—one is that we think of something and the second type of thought wells up. The former thought is an action but latter is not an action. In the former there is predominance of intellect but in the latter there is breach of affinity with the intellect. Therefore the Self is not realized by former type of thought but it is realized by the revelation of the thought. It means that when a striver, having the aim of Self-realization, goes on differentiating the real and the unreal using his discrimination, and the unreal is renounced, then "the world neither existed, nor exists, nor will exist nor can exist"—this thought is revealed. With the revelation of this thought, discrimination gets transformed into Self-realization viz., the world disappears

---

* Having gained knowledge (Self-realization) there appears nothing new viz., it does not appear that first there was ignorance and then the knowledge was gained. Having gained knowledge a striver realizes that he was ever endowed with knowledge, only he had not an eye on it. If it is assumed that first there was ignorance, then the knowledge was gained, it means that knowledge has a beginning while it is beginningless. Anything, that has a beginning, ends and that, which is beginningless, is endless.

and the divinity is revealed; the assumed existence comes to an end and the reality remains. The revelation of thought has been mentioned here as 'smṛtirlabdhā'.

'Aparā Prakṛti' (the lower nature) belongs to God. But we have committed an error that we have been connected with the lower nature viz., we have assumed it as ours and for us. We are responsible for this connection, so it is our responsibility to renounce it also. Because of the assumption of our affinity with the lower nature, we have forgotten our real affinity with God and we are bound. Therefore only renunciation of affinity with the lower nature will lead us to salvation. In order to renounce affinity with the lower nature—"the body is neither mine, nor it is for me'—importance should be attached to this discrimination. By attaching significance to this discrimination—"the lower nature is neither mine nor for me"—the memory is gained.

Arjuna has not realized the dualistic or non-dualistic entity but he has realized the real entity which transcends both dualism and non-dualism. The reason is that dualism-non-dualism is delusion* while Arjuna's delusion has been destroyed.

A man (the Self) naturally belongs to God from time immemorial, he has to renounce only the dependence on the world. Arjuna has predominantly gained the memory of Bhaktiyoga, Karmayoga and Jñānayoga are the means but Bhaktiyoga is an end. Therefore the memory of Bhaktiyoga is real. The memory of Bhaktiyoga is—'vāsudevaḥ sarvam' viz., "All is God". The realization of 'vāsudevaḥ sarvam' is 'smṛtirlabdhā'. This realization is possible only by God's grace—'tvatprasādāt'. Words (utterances) are limited but the Lord's grace is limitless.

Reflection involves the sense of doership but in memory there is no sense of doership. The reason is that reflection (thinking) is done with the mind; the intellect is superior to the mind, ego is

* 'dvaitādvaita mahāmohaḥ' (Māheśvara tantra)
'aho māyā mahāmohau dvaitādvaita vikalpanā' (Avadhūtā 1/61)

superior to the intellect, the Self is superior to ego, the memory is gained by the Self. We reflect upon something but in memory only the eye is cast there. At the time of forgetfulness also the divinity remains the same. In divinity there is no oblivion, therefore as soon as a glance is cast, the memory is dawned.

'Sthito'smi gatasandehaḥ'—At first from the view-point of a Kṣatriya, Arjuna thought that it was justified to fight in the war; then having seen his teachers and elders arrayed on the battle-field, he thought that sin would accrue to him by slaying them; but as soon as the memory was gained, all the problems were solved. His doubt whether he should wage the war or not, was totally dispelled. Then Arjuna said to Lord Kṛṣṇa that nothing remained to be done by him but he would carry out His order only—'kariṣye vacanaṁ tava'. This is surrender.

Link:—In the twentieth verse of the first chapter, the gospel of the Gītā in the form of the dialogue between Lord Kṛṣṇa and Arjuna began, with the term 'Atha' (now). In the next verse, by using the term 'Iti' (thus), Sañjaya concluding the message reveals to his master, the glory of this dialogue.

सञ्जय उवाच

इत्यहं वासुदेवस्य पार्थस्य च महात्मनः।
संवादमिममश्रौषमद्भुतं रोमहर्षणम्॥ ७४॥

sañjaya uvāca

ityahaṁ vāsudevasya pārthasya ca mahātmanaḥ
saṁvādamimamaśrauṣamadbhutaṁ romaharṣaṇam

Sañjaya said:

Thus, have I heard this wonderful dialogue between Vāsudeva (Kṛṣṇa) and the high souled Pārtha (Arjuna) which caused my hair to stand, on end. 74

Comment:—

'Ityahaṁ vāsudevasya pārthasya ca mahātmanaḥ'—Sañjaya says, that he heard the dialogue between Kṛṣṇa and Arjuna, which is wonderful, singular and thrilling.

Here the term 'Iti' (thus), denotes the conclusion of the dialogue, which was started by the term 'Atha' (Now) in the twentieth verse of the first chapter.

Arjuna, is addressed as high souled, because Lord Kṛṣṇa, carries out his direction. When he orders Lord Kṛṣṇa to place his chariot between the two armies, He places it there (1/21,1/24). Moreover He answers all the questions, put by Arjuna in detail, in a loving manner. Thus Sañjaya heard the dialogue between the high souled Arjuna and Lord Kṛṣṇa.

'Saṁvādamimamaśrauṣamadbhutaṁ romaharṣaṇam'—What is wonderful and thrilling in the dialogue? It is generally mentioned in the scriptures, that a man can follow a spiritual path and attain salvation, by renouncing the world. People in common, have the same belief that a person, having renounced the world, and by becoming a recluse, can attain salvation. But, according to the gospel of the Gītā, a man can attain salvation by making proper use of the circumstances, he is placed in. The circumstances may either be the sweetest, and the most favourable or the bitterest and the most unfavourable, like massacre in war, they can lead to salvation.* The reason is, that attachment to the world, is the cause of one's birth in good and evil wombs (Gītā 13/21). Proper use of circumstances, is the means to root out, that attachment

*A man can attain salvation under all circumstances through non-attachment. In fact it is non-attachment to the world which leads to salvation. This non-attachment can be developed by any means as that of the Discipline of Action or Knowledge or Devotion. But it is the attachment which is the stumbling block to salvation. When attachment is renounced, aversion also disappears. When a man becomes free from attachment and aversion, he attains salvation, because liberation from them is called salvation.

In fact a man is emancipated but he has assumed (accepted) that he is bound. As soon as he abandons this assumption, he becomes free.

i.e., he who performs his duty, being free from attachment and aversion, is easily set free, from bondage (Gītā 5/3). This is something wonderful in this dialogue.

The Lord, having incarnated, disclosed his identity and asked Arjuna to take refuge in Him. This disclosure of His supreme secret, causes Sañjaya's hair to stand on end and thrills him with bliss.

Appendix—In the Gītā the term 'mahātmā' (the exalted Soul) has been used only for devotees. Here Sañjaya has addressed Arjuna as 'mahātmā' because he regards Arjuna as a devotee. The Lord has also declared 'bhakto'si me' viz., 'O Arjuna! thou art My devotee'.

Link:—A striver, feels grateful to a person by whom he is guided, in the spiritual sphere. Therefore, in the next three verses, Sañjaya feels obliged to Vedavyāsa.

व्यासप्रसादाच्छ्रुतवानेतद्गुह्यमहं परम्।
योगं योगेश्वरात्कृष्णात्साक्षात्कथयतः स्वयम्॥ ७५॥

vyāsaprasādācchrutavānetadguhyamahaṁ param
yogaṁ yogeśvarātkṛṣṇātsākṣātkathayataḥ svayam

By the grace of Vyāsa, I come to hear this supreme and most secret Yoga, direct from Kṛṣṇa Himself, the Lord of Yoga, declaring it. 75

Comment:—

'Vyāsaprasādāt śrutavān'—Sañjaya was very much delighted, after hearing the dialogue between Lord Kṛṣṇa and great souled Arjuna. This supreme secret, was heard by him, by Vyāsa's grace. The Lord Himself addressing Arjuna, declares that He will speak to him His supreme word from a desire to do him good (10/1); He asks him, to listen again to His supreme word, the most secret of all, as he is very dear to him (18/64); He truly promises that he will come to Him, for he is dear to Him (18/65); He asks him not to grieve, as He will release him from all sins (18/66). Sañjaya could get this golden opportunity of listening to the Lord's secret gospel, only by Vyāsa's grace.

'Etadguhyaṁ paraṁ yogam'—This gospel of the Gītā, is the supreme and the most secret Yoga, because it has been imparted by the great Lord of all Yogas. The eternal affinity of the embodied soul, with the Lord is Yoga. In order to realize that union, a striver, has to practise the Disciplines of Action and Knowledge etc. This set of Yogas (Disciplines), described in the Gītā, has been called the scripture of the Yoga (yogaśāstra).

'Yogeśvarātkṛṣṇātsākṣātkathayataḥ svayam'—Sañjaya's joy knew no bound. Therefore overwhelmed with delight Sañjaya declares that he has heard this Yoga (Gospel), direct from Lord Kṛṣṇa, Himself declaring it. What was the need to Sañjaya to use the five words 'Yogeśvarāt, Kṛṣṇāt, Sākṣāt, Kathayataḥ and Svayam' here? Sañjaya by using these five words, wants to say that he has not heard this dialogue, by way of tradition or through any other person, but he has heard it direct from the holy lips of the Lord Himself.

Appendix—Arjuna said to the Lord 'tvatprasādat' viz., 'by Your grace' (18/73), while Sañjaya feeling obliged to Vedavyāsa here says, "vyāsaprasād" viz., 'by the grace of Vyāsa'. The Lord by His grace bestowed upon Arjuna the divine eye while Vyāsajī by his grace bestowed upon Sañjaya the divine eye.

राजन्संस्मृत्य संस्मृत्य संवादमिममद्भुतम्।
केशवार्जुनयोः पुण्यं हृष्यामि च मुहुर्मुहुः ॥ ७६ ॥

rājansaṁsmṛtya saṁsmṛtya saṁvādamimamadbhutam
keśavārjunayoḥ puṇyaṁ hṛṣyāmi ca muhurmuhuḥ

O, King, as I repeatedly recall this dialogue, wondrous and

sacred; of Keśava (Kṛṣṇa) and Arjuna, I am thrilled with joy, again and over again. 76

Comment:—

'Rājansaṁsmṛtya saṁsmṛtya saṁvādamimamadbhutam keśavārjunayoḥ puṇyaṁ hṛṣyāmi ca muhurmuhuḥ—Sañjaya says to Dhṛtarāṣṭra, that the dialogue between Lord Kṛṣṇa and Arjuna, is so wonderful and thrilling, that it can lead a man to salvation, even when engaged in the horrible activity of killing people, in a war. Remembering this dialogue Sañjaya, rejoices again and again, by thinking that a man can attain salvation, under all circumstances.

This dialogue is a, unique one. Though Lord Kṛṣṇa and Arjuna, lived together for a long time, yet there was never such a wonderful and thrilling conversation, between them. When Arjuna was puzzled with regard to his duty, on the one hand, he did not want to fight, due to his attachment to the family and on the other hand, as a member of the warrior class, it was his first and foremost duty to fight. When a person does not adhere to a belief, he becomes confused finding himself restless.* Arjuna was in a dilemma.

It was his restlessness, which enabled him to be attracted towards the Lord. It was because of his inclination, exclusive devotion and curiosity, that the Lord having forgotten His supremacy, was so much engrossed in love for Arjuna, that He disclosed the most profound and the supremely secret, gospel of the Gītā to him. No one, can describe the merit of this dialogue.

Appendix—The dialogue between Lord Kṛṣṇa and Arjuna is full of so much profound and secret truth which has neither

* These days people don't seem to be curious and restless to know the reality about God and the world because they are satisfied with the transitory mundane pleasures, prosperity, praise and honour etc. They are so much engrossed in them that their restlessness to know the reality is suppressed.

been mentioned in a treatise nor has been narrated by any exalted soul in his spiritual discourse. This is a very singular dialogue between the Lord and His devotee. Such clear facts are available neither for study nor for listening. In this dialogue it is mentioned that even such a horrible activity as war can lead a man to salvation. This dialogue explains that a man of every Varṇa (order of life), Āśrama (stage of life) and Sect etc., under every circumstance, can attain salvation. Therefore this dialogue is very marvellous—'saṁvādamimamadbhutam'. When this dialogue is so unique, then how much unique it will be, if the gospel of this dialogue is translated into practice!

The gospel preached by Lord Kṛṣṇa is very wonderful*, and the Lord preached the gospel of the Gītā by getting established in Yoga†, so how wondrous and singular this gospel should be! The political speech delivered by Lord Kṛṣṇa in the Kauravas assembly was so singular that hermits and sages went there to listen to His speech‡; then this Gītā is the spiritual dialogue. In Śrīmadbhāgavata also when Uddhavajī perceived that the Lord

---

* vācaṁ tāṁ vacanārhasya śikṣākṣarasamanvitām
aśrauṣamahamiṣṭārthāṁ paścāddhṛdayahāriṇīm
(Mahābhārata, Udyoga. 59/17)

Sañjaya said—'After that I listened to the gospel of Lord Kṛṣṇa Who is well-versed in conversation, whose each and every word was educative. That gospel presented the derived import and attracted the mind.'

† dharmārthasahitā vācaḥ śrotumicchāma mādhava
tvayocyamānāḥ kuruṣu rājamadhye parantapa
(Mahābhārata, Udyoga. 83/68-69)

Paraśurāmajī said :—O Mādhava, scorcher of the enemies! We want to listen to the speech delivered by You, which dealt with the topic pertaining to 'Dharma' (righteousness) and 'Artha' (money matters) in the assembly of Kauravas and other kings.

‡ na śakyaṁ tanmayā bhūyas tathā vaktumaśeṣataḥ
paraṁ hi brahma kathitaṁ yogayuktena tanmayā
(Mahābhārata, Āśva. 16/12-13)

Lord Kṛṣṇa said, "It is beyond My control (power) to repeat the entire gospel in the same form. At that time I, being established in Yoga, described the Supreme Reality."

answered the questions in a very singular manner, then he put thirty-five questions altogether (Śrīmadbhā. eleventh canto, nineteenth chapter, twenty-eighth to thirty-second verses).

'Hṛṣyāmi ca muhurmuhuḥ'—Sañjaya could never get a chance to listen to such facts pertaining to actions, knowledge and devotion any other where, therefore Sañjaya was thrilled with joy again and again after listening to this dialogue.

Sañjaya knew the Lord in reality. When Dhṛtarāṣṭra asked Sañjaya about it, Sañjaya answered—

māyāṁ ca seve bhadraṁ te na vṛthā dharma mācare,
śuddha bhāvaṁ gato bhaktyā śāstrād vedmi janārdanam.

(Mahābhārata, Udyoga. 69/5)

O King! may you live happily! I am never fraudulent. I don't indulge in hypocrisy. My heart has been purified by God's devotion; therefore I know Lord Kṛṣṇa in reality as He is mentioned in the scripture.

Thus first Sañjaya knew Lord Kṛṣṇa in reality, by studying the scripture; but afterwards he knew Him in reality, having directly heard the dialogue between Him and Arjuna.

तच्च संस्मृत्य संस्मृत्य रूपमत्यद्भुतं हरेः।
विस्मयो मे महान् राजन् हृष्यामि च पुनः पुनः ॥ ७७ ॥

tacca saṁsmṛtya saṁsmṛtya rūpamatyadbhutaṁ hareḥ
vismayo me mahān rājan hṛṣyāmi ca punaḥ punaḥ

And recapitulating again and again, that most wonderful cosmic form of Hari (Keśava), great is my astonishment, O, King; and I am overwhelmed and thrilled with joy over and over again. 77

Comment:—

'Tacca saṁsmṛtya saṁsmṛtya rūpamatyadbhutaṁ hareḥ vismayo me mahān rājan hṛṣyāmi ca punaḥ punaḥ'—In the preceding verse, Sañjaya declared the dialogue between Lord

Kṛṣṇa and Arjuna to be wonderful, while here he declares His cosmic form, to be the most wonderful. Why? The reason is, that the dialogue can be studied even now but His cosmic form cannot be beheld now.

In the ninth verse of the eleventh chapter Sañjaya called Lord Kṛṣṇa the great Lord of Yoga, while here he declares that remembering again and again that most wonderful form of Hari (Kṛṣṇa), great is his astonishment. It is natural to be astonished, beholding the cosmic form of the Lord of Yoga. Further Lord Kṛṣṇa, revealed to Arjuna His cosmic form out of compassion, while Sañjaya was able to behold that cosmic form, by great sage Vyāsa's grace.

Though the Lord revealed, His cosmic form to mother Kausalyā, when he incarnated as Rāma, to mother Yaśodā and also to Duryodhana etc., in the assembly of the Kaúravas. When He incarnated as Lord Kṛṣṇa, yet those cosmic form were not so terrifying and wonderful as that was seen by Sañjaya, because in the latter form, principal warriors were rushing head-long into the Lord's fearful mouth, set with terrible tusks and some were seen stuck between His teeth with their heads crushed. In the latter form, it was seen that both the armies were being slaughtered. Remembering such a wonderful form of Lord Kṛṣṇa, Sañjaya was thrilled with joy, again and again and he declared, that it was only by great sage Vyāsa's grace, that he could behold His cosmic form.

Appendix—The Lord revealed to Arjuna His Cosmic Form which was within limits. Had Arjuna not been confused with fear, the Lord would have revealed His Cosmic Form in more details. But Sañjaya was wonder-struck after beholding even that Cosmic Form.

Sañjaya first knew the glory of the Lord, having studied the scripture; then he listened to the wondrous dialogue between Lord Kṛṣṇa and Arjuna; and then he beheld the most wonderful Cosmic

Form of Lord Kṛṣṇa. It means that the dialogue between the Lord and Arjuna was more wondrous than what he had studied in the scripture; and more wonderful than the dialogue, was His Cosmic Form. Therefore Sañjaya has mentioned the dialogue as wonderful—'saṁvādamimamadbhutam' (18/76) and the Cosmic Form as very much wonderful—'rūpamatyad bhūtam'.

Link:—At the beginning of the Gītā, Dhṛtarāṣtra indirectly wanted to ask the consequences of the war i.e., he wanted to know, whether his sons or those of Pāṇḍu, would win. Sañjaya answers the question in the next verse.

यत्र योगेश्वरः कृष्णो यत्र पार्थो धनुर्धरः।
तत्र श्रीर्विजयो भूतिर्ध्रुवा नीतिर्मतिर्मम॥ ७८॥

yatra yogeśvaraḥ kṛṣṇo yatra pārtho dhanurdharaḥ
tatra śrīrvijayo bhūtirdhruvā nītirmatirmama

Wherever, there is Kṛṣṇa, (the Lord of Yoga) and wherever, there is Arjuna, (the wielder of the bow); there rest prosperity, victory, glory and righteousness; such is my conviction. 78

Comment:—

'Yatra yogeśvaraḥ kṛṣṇo yatra pārtho dhanurdharaḥ'— Sañjaya says to Dhṛtarāṣṭra, addressing him as the king, that where there is Lord Kṛṣṇa the protector, the adviser of Arjuna, the Lord of all Yogas, possessing great power, prosperity, learning and wisdom; and where there is Lord Kṛṣṇa's obedient and loving friend, Arjuna, the archer, there are prosperity, victory, glory and righteousness—such is his conviction.

When Lord Kṛṣṇa bestowed upon Arjuna, divine vision, Sañjaya addressed Him as 'Mahāyogeśvaraḥ' (the great Lord of Yoga). Now reminding Dhṛtarāṣṭra, of the same great Lord of Yoga, he uses the term 'Yogeśvaraḥ' (the Lord of Yoga). The Lord is the inspirer, who inspires archer Arjuna, who is obedient to Him.

The Lord has been called the Lord or the great Lord of Yoga, because He is the master of all Yogīs. He possesses, all virtues such as omniscience, prosperity, beauty and gracefulness, naturally in a bondless quantity. These virtues, are eternal and axomatic. All virtues culminate in Him.

When the war was declared, Bhīṣma was the first to blow his conch to declare the war, on behalf of Kaurava-army. It was proper on his part to do so, because he was the chief commander. But on behalf of Pāṇḍava-army, it was Lord Kṛṣṇa, the chariot-driver Who declared the war, by blowing the conch. From the worldly point of view, the Lord was only a charioteer. So what right had He to declare the war, by blowing a conch? But he did it and nobody resented it. It means that He was the chief of the Pāṇḍava-army, while Arjuna stood next to Him. So here Sañjaya mentions their names, in order to show their importance.

Throughout the gospel of the Gītā, the Lord addressed Arjuna as 'Pārtha' thiry-eight times, more than any other name. Similarly Arjuna has addressed the Lord as Kṛṣṇa nine times, more than any other form of address. Thus the term 'Pārtha,' is more loving to Lord Kṛṣṇa, while the term 'Kṛṣṇa' is more loving to Arjuna. Therefore, while concluding the Gītā Sañjaya, also uses these two terms.

'Tatra śrīrvijayo bhūtirdhruvā nītirmatirmama'—Wealth, splendour and prosperity, are included in the term 'Śrī'. Where there is Lord Kṛṣṇa, the husband to the goddess of wealth, there wealth is naturally in abundance.

The term 'Vijaya', denotes Arjuna, as well as bravery and valour etc. Where there is valorous Arjuna, there such characteristics, as heroism and vigour etc., naturally prevail, as these are the characteristics of members of the warrior class.

Similarly, where there is Lord Kṛṣṇa, the Lord of Yoga, there are glory, nobility, influence, competence and such other virtues; and where, there is righteous Arjuna, there are morality, righteousness and firm policy etc. The fact is, that all virtues, such as prosperity, victory, glory and righteousness etc., are always present in Lord Kṛṣṇa, as well as, in Arjuna. This division has been done according to predominance of the virtues, of the two. Otherwise, all divine traits, such as prosperity, gracefulness, modesty, generosity and beauty etc., are naturally found, in boundless quantity, in both of them.

Sañjaya answers the question of Dhṛtarāṣṭra, which he asked indirectly, by declaring that the victory of Pāṇḍu's sons, is certain without any doubt.

ज्ञानयज्ञः सुसम्पन्नः प्रीतये पार्थसारथेः।
अङ्गीकरोतु तत्सर्वं मुकुन्दो भक्तवत्सलः॥
नेत्रवेदखयुग्मे हि बहुधान्ये च वत्सरे।
संजीवनी मुमुक्षूणां माधवे पूर्णतामियात्॥

ॐ तत्सदिति श्रीमद्भगवद्गीतासूपनिषत्सु ब्रह्मविद्यायां योगशास्त्रे श्रीकृष्णार्जुनसंवादे मोक्षसन्न्यासयोगो नामाष्टादशोऽध्यायः॥ १८॥

oṁ tatsaditi śrīmadbhagavadgītāsūpaniṣatsu brahmavidyāyāṁ yogaśāstre śrīkṛṣṇārjunasaṁvāde mokṣasannyāsayogo nāmāṣṭādaśo'dhyāyaḥ

Thus with the words Oṁ, Tat, Sat, the names of the Lord, in the Upaniṣad of the Bhagavadgītā, the knowledge of Brahma, the Supreme, the science of Yoga and the dialogue between Śrī Kṛṣṇa and Arjuna, this the eighteenth chapter (discourse) is designated:—

'The Yoga of Liberation by Renunciation'.

This discourse has been designated as 'Mokṣasannyāsayoga,' because in this discourse there is predominance of the description of devotion, in which even liberation or salvation, is renounced.

Words, letters and Uvāca (said) in the Eighteenth Chapter

(1) In the chapter in '**Athāṣṭādaśo'dhyāyaḥ**, there are three

words, in **'Arjuna Uvāca'** etc., there are eight words, in verses, there are nine hundred and eighty-nine words and there are thirteen concluding words. Thus the total number of the words, is one thousand and thirteen.

(2) In this chapter in **'Athāṣṭādaśo'dhyāyaḥ'** there are seven letters, in **'Arjuna Uvāca'** etc., there are twenty-five letters, in verses there are two thousand, four hundred and ninety-six letters and there are forty-eight concluding letters. Thus the total number of the letters, is two thousand, five hundred and seventy-six. Each of the verses in this chapter, consists of thirty-two letters.

(3) In this chapter the term **'Uvāca'** (said) has been used four times—**'Arjuna Uvāca'** twice, **Śrībhagavānuvāca'** once and **'Sañjaya Uvāca'** once.

Metres Used in the Eighteenth Chapter

Out of the seventy-eight verses, of this chapter, in the first quarters of the twelfth, forty-sixth and fifty-second, verses 'ma-gaṇa' being used there, is **'ma-vipulā'** metre; in the first quarter of the twenty-third, thirty-second, thirty-seventh, forty-first, forty-fifth, fifty-sixth and seventieth verses 'na-gaṇa' being used there, is **'na-vipulā'** metre; in the first quarter of the thirty-third, thirty-sixth, forty-seventh and seventy-fifth verses 'bha-gaṇa' being used there, is **'bha-vipulā'** metre; in the third quarter of the thirteenth verse 'ma-gaṇa' being used there is **'ma-vipulā'** metre; in the third quarter of the twenty-sixth verse 'ra-gaṇa' being used there is **'ra-vipulā'** metre; in the third quarter of the thirty-eighth and sixty-fourth verses 'na-gaṇa' being used there is **'na-vipulā'** metre; in the first quarter of the forty-ninth verse 'ma-gaṇa' being used there is **'ma-vipulā'** metre, while in the third quarter 'bha-gaṇa' being used there is **'bha-vipulā'** metre. The remaining fifty-nine verses have the characteristics of right **'pathyāvaktra'** Anuṣṭup metre.

APPENDIX ONE

Bird's-Eye View on the Gītā

The eighteenth chapter of the Gītā, is the gist of the whole Gītā, and all the topics discussed in the previous seventeen chapters have been summed up here. In this chapter, there are three important points which need attention—(1) A topic, which has been touched upon in brief in other chapters, has been discussed in detail, in this chapter, (2) a topic, which has been examined in detail in other chapters, has been concluded here, briefly and (3) topics dealt with in other chapters, have been elucidated in a different manner in this chapter.

In the gospel of the Gītā there is particular reference to two disciplines about which the Lord has mentioned thus, "This has been presented to you from the view-point of Jñānayoga; now hear the same from the stand point of Karmayoga" (2/39) also. "Two courses of spiritual discipline were enunciated clearly by Me to the world, in the past—the discipline of knowledge to the discerning and the discipline of action to, the people of action" (3/3). Arjuna, at the beginning of the eighteenth chapter, puts a question to the Lord, to understand the reality about the two disciplines. So reference to disciplines has been concluded, in the eighteenth chapter, either in brief, or in detail or in a different manner, as necessary.

The subject of devotion, which has been dealt with specially from the seventh to the twelfth chapters is a secret of the Lord's heart, is totally different from the other two disciplines and is unique. In the discipline of devotion, a devotee depends only on God and is dedicated only to Him. The Lord concludes the gospel, commending persons to depend on Him or surrender to

Him, or taking refuge in Him.

From the thirty-ninth verse of the second chapter upto the end of the second chapter, and also in the third chapter, there is predominant description of the discipline of action. In the sixty-first verse of the second chapter, the term 'Matparaḥ' has been used for "dependence on God", which has been described in a little more detail in the thirtieth verse of the third chapter. Thus there is also some description of devotion, with the discipline of action. In the fourth chapter, the Lord while mentioning how the discipline of action was handed down from generations, describes the divine character of His birth and activities and then the discipline of action, while explaining that His actions are models for others. In the fifth chapter, there is a comparative discussion on the two disciplines and finally the Lord briefly defines devotion and concludes the chapter. Thus the discipline of action discussed from the second chapter to the end of the fifth chapter, has been explained in a different way from the fourth to the twelfth verses, of the eighteenth chapter.

The discipline of knowledge, dominated by discrimination, is examined from the thirteenth to the twenty-sixth verses of the fifth chapter, and from the nineteenth to the thirty-fourth verse of the thirteenth chapter, has been interpreted in a differently manner from the thirteenth to the eighteenth verses of the eighteenth chapter.

The allotted (obligatory) duty mentioned in the eighth verse of the third chapter, has been expounded in detail, from the forty-second to the forty-eighth verses, of the eighteenth chapter.

The discipline of devotion detailed from the seventh to the twelfth chapter has been touched upon briefly and in a different manner, from the fifty-sixth to the sixty-sixth verse, of the eighteenth chapter.

The description of the four social orders, which is given in brief, in the thirteenth verse of the fourth chapter has been amplified from the forty-first to the forty-fourth verse of the eighteenth chapter. Here (in 18/41—44) it can also be assumed as the conclusion of the innate faith, mentioned in the first and the second verse of the seventeenth chapter.

While describing the discipline of knowledge, the Lord declares that all actions are performed by nature and its modes (guṇa) (3/27, 13/29). He also states that the seer perceives no agent, other than the modes (14/19), He in addition explained that the senses move among the sense-objects (5/9) etc. The same topic has been developed further, from the thirteenth to the eighteenth verses of the eighteenth chapter in brief, and in a different way.

The modes of nature have been described from the fifth to the eighteenth verse, of the fourteenth chapter, and from the twentieth to the fortieth verse, of the eighteenth chapter in detail, differently.

Meditation on God, described in detail in the sixth and the eighth chapters, has been described in brief and differently from the fifty-first to the fifty-third verses of the eighteenth chapter. Here (in 18/51—53) this topic can be regarded as the conclusion of twenty virtues of the discipline of knowledge, described from the seventh to the eleventh verse of the thirteenth chapter.

Sañjaya, has in brief concluded his recital, in the seventy-eighth verse of the eighteenth chapter, the divine glories of the Lord, from the eighth to the twelfth verse of the seventh chapter, the sixteenth to the nineteenth verse of the ninth chapter, the twentieth to the thirty-eighth verse of the tenth chapter and from the twelfth to the fifteenth verse of the fifteenth chapter.

The Lord's Cosmic-Form, described in the eleventh chapter has been concluded by Sañjaya in the form of a recollection, in the seventy-seventh verse of the eighteenth chapter.

The faith, described in the thirty-first verse of the third chapter, in the thirty-ninth verse of the fourth chapter and the third verse of the seventeenth chapter, has been summarised by the Lord in brief, in the seventy-first verse of the eighteenth chapter.

The duties of a member of the warrior class, included from the thirty-first to the thirty-eighth verse of the second chapter has been described in brief, in the forty-third verse of the eighteenth chapter.

The fact, that all living creatures act according to their own nature, as mentioned in the thirty-third verse of the third chapter, has been enlarged in the fifty-ninth and the sixtieth verse, of the eighteenth chapter, conclusively.

Infatuation or dejection are described from the thirty-first verse to the forty-sixth verse of the first chapter, and ended in brief in the seventh, the sixtieth, the seventy-second, and the seventy-third verses, of the eighteenth chapter.

The marks of a man of steadfast wisdom (stable in mind), are described from the fifty-fifth to the seventy-second verse of the second chapter, and topic concluded in the tenth and the eleventh verses, of the eighteenth chapter.

The topic of remembrance of God, at the time of one's death, is dealt with in the fifth verse of the eighth chapter, in the fifty-seventh, the fifty-eighth and the sixty-fifth verses, of the eighteenth chapter, and the Lord assures man of his help.

Divine traits, described in the first three verses of the sixteenth chapter, have been defined differently from the forty-second to the forty-fourth verse, of the eighteenth chapter.

Demoniac traits, described earlier, from the seventh to the twentieth verse of the sixteenth chapter, have been explained in brief in the sixty-seventh verse of the eighteenth chapter, when the Lord points out the marks of a person unqualified for listening to the gospel of the Gītā.

The knowledge-sacrifice (Yoga) achieved through the study of sacred books, as against sacrifice of wealth etc., described in the twenty-eighth verse of the fourth chapter, has been concluded, in the seventieth verse of the eighteenth chapter.

The Lord from the eleventh to the thirtieth verse of the second chapter, exhorts Arjuna not to grieve about death, when the soul does not die. The same topic has been concluded in the sixty-sixth verse of the eighteenth chapter when the Lord exhorts Arjuna not to grieve by the words, 'mā śucaḥ' after surrender to God.

Thus, the eighteenth chapter is the gist or quintessence of the Gītā. If we contemplate over this chapter seriously, we come to know the core and essence of Gītā.

The Vedas are the gist of all the scriptures, the Upaniṣads the gist of the Vedas, the Gītā the gist of the Upaniṣads and the most profound secret, of surrender to God (refuge in God) for man's salvation described in the sixty-sixth verse of the eighteenth chapter, is the core of the Gītā.

APPENDIX TWO

Methods of Recitation of the Gītā

It is a man's nature that when he performs an act with great interest, he is dedicated to it and absorbed in it; yet he cannot identify himself with prakṛti (Nature) and its evolutes, (objects and pleasures etc.,) because he is always different from them. But, if he remains absorbed in chanting the Lord's name, in thinking of Him and in meditating on His principles (teachings), he is identified with Him, because then he is one with Him. Therefore, when a devotee recites His name, thinks of Him and studies the sacred books, such as the Gītā, the Rāmāyaṇa and the Bhāgavata etc., he would be absorbed in them. The method of the recitation of the Gītā is given hereunder:

In order to recite the Gītā, there should be a seat of Kuśa grass, or of a woollen cloth or of sack cloth and then a person facing the east or the north, should sit on it.

At the beginning of the recitation of the Gītā, the following sacred text (verses) should be recited—

"Oṁ asya śrīmadbhagavadgītā mālā mantrasya bhagavān vedavyāsa ṛṣiḥ, anuṣṭup chandaḥ, śrī kṛṣṇaḥ paramātmā devatā', aśocyānanvaśocastvaṁ prajñāvādāṁśca bhāṣase iti bījam, sarvadharmān parityajya māmekaṁ śaraṇaṁ vraja iti śaktiḥ, ahaṁ tvā sarvapāpebhyo mokṣayiṣyāmi mā śucaḥ iti kīlakam."

The explanation of this text is as follows:—

As there are many beads in a rosary or flowers in a garland, so are the verses recited by the Lord, like the beads of the rosary of the Gītā. The first seer to understand the significance of these verses, was divine Vedavyāsa—'Oṁ asya śrīmadbhagavadgītā mālā mantrasya bhagavān Vedavyāsa ṛṣiḥ'.

There is much use of the metre 'anuṣṭup' (a verse of thirty-two letters in Saṁskṛta), in the Gītā. The Gītā begins with this metre, (Dharmakṣetre.....) and the gospel also begins with and, (Aśocyān anvaśocastvaṁ.....) ends with the metre (Yatra yogeśvaraḥ...), the same metre. The gospel also begins (Aśocyānanvaśocastvaṁ) and ends with it (sarvadharmānparityajya). The metre used is 'anuṣṭup'.

Lord Kṛṣṇa, who is the Supreme Goal, to be attained by all human beings is its God (Lord).

The gospel is preached to the ignorant, and they deserve the same gospel, Arjuna is also talking about righteousness but he is grieved because of attachment (infatuation) to his family. So his mind is confused, with regard to his duty. Therefore, he takes refuge in the Lord and prays to Him to instruct him what is decidedly good for him. So, in order to remove his grief, the Lord starts preaching the gospel of the Gītā, which is the seed of the Gītā—'aśocyānanvaśocastvaṁ......bījam'.

Self-surrender to God (refuge in God), is the quintessence of all spiritual disciplines and all gospels, because no other discipline is as easy, excellent or powerful, as taking refuge in Him. So it is best for a man to take refuge in Him, by renouncing dependence on all other spiritual disciplines—'sarvadharmān-parityajya.....śaktih'.

The Lord promises that He will liberate the being, who takes refuge in him, from all sins. The Lord could never deviate from this promise, as it is a 'Kīlaka' (a pivot)—ahaṁ tvā sarvapāpebhyo...kīlakam.

Thus after reciting the text 'Oṁ asya śrīmadbhagavadgītā mālā mantrasya......iti kīlakam', the activity of 'Nyāsa' (touch of hands and fingers together; and of heart, known respectively as 'Karanyāsa' and 'Hṛdayādinyāsa') should be performed. The significance of this activity of 'Nyāsa' is explained as follows:—

In the scriptures it is mentioned that a devotee should worship gods and study the sacred books to becoming divine viz., by being pure and holy. That divinity, purity or holiness is embraced by vesting the holy texts, in the body and its parts (any). The holy text or the hymn, which is to be recited, should be absorbed by the devotee in the body. This is known as 'Nyāsa' (Nyāsa of hands and his fingers and Nyāsa of the heart).

Karanyāsa (Touch of hands-fingers)

Karanyāsa, means the touch of the ten fingers together or the touch of both the palms together or the touch of the outer surfaces of the hands together, in reciting the sacred text—

(1) 'Nainaṁ chindanti śastrāṇi nainaṁ dahati pāvaka ityaṅguṣṭhābhyāṁ namaḥ'—By reciting this sacred text, the thumbs should be in touch, together.

(2) 'Na cainaṁ kledayantyāpo na śoṣayati māruta iti tarjanibhyāṁ namaḥ'—By reciting this sacred text, the forefingers of the two hands should be in touch, together.

(3) 'Acchedyo'yamadāhyo'yamakledyo'śoṣya eva ca iti madhyamābhyāṁ namaḥ'—By uttering this sacred text, the middle fingers should be touched together.

(4) 'Nityaḥ sarvagataḥ sthāṇuracalo'yaṁ sanātana ityanāmikābhyāṁ namaḥ'—By reciting this sacred text, the ring-fingers should be touching together.

(5) 'Paśya me pārtha rūpāṇi śataśo'tha sahasraśa iti kaniṣṭhikābhyāṁ namaḥ'—By uttering this sacred text, the little fingers should be touched together.

(6) 'Nānāvidhāni divyāni nānāvarṇākṛtīni ca iti karatalakarapṛṣṭhābhyāṁ namaḥ'—By reciting this sacred text, the palms and the outer surfaces of the two hands should be in touch.

Hṛdayādinyāsa (Touch of the heart etc.)

Hṛdayādinyāsa means touch of the heart etc., with the five fingers of the right hand, on reciting the sacred text—

(1) 'Nainaṁ chindanti śastrāṇi nainaṁ dahati pāvaka iti hṛdayāya namaḥ'—on uttering this sacred text, the heart should be touched with five fingers of the right hand.

(2) 'Na cainaṁ kledayantyāpo na śoṣayati māruta iti śirase swāhā'—on uttering this sacred text, the forehead should be touched, with the five fingers of the right hand.

(3) 'Acchedyo'yamadāhyo'yamakledyo'śoṣya eva ca iti śikhāyai vaṣaṭ'—on reciting this sacred text the tuft of hair on the top of the head should be touched with the five fingers of the right hand.

(4) 'Nityaḥ sarvagataḥ sthāṇuracalo'yaṁ sanātana iti kavacāya hum'—on reciting this sacred text, the left shoulder should be touched with the five fingers of the right hand while the right shoulder with the five fingers of the left hand.

(5) 'Paśya me pārtha rūpāṇi śataśo'tha sahasraśa iti netratrayāya vauṣaṭ'—on reciting this sacred text, both the eyes and the middle part of the forehead (where the third eye of wisdom is supposed to be) should be touched with the front part of the five fingers of the right hand.

(6) 'Nānāvidhāni divyāni nānāvarṇākṛtīni ca iti astrāya phaṭ'—on reciting this sacred text the right hand should first be taken to the back of the head from the left hand side, and then should be brought to the front side of the head, from the right hand side and should clasp the left palm with the forefingers and the middle finger of the right hand.

After 'Karanyāsa' and Hṛdayādinyāsa', one should utter the text—'Śrīkṛṣnaprityarthe pāṭhe viniyogaḥ' viz., 'I want to recite the Gītā only to please God.'

There are three methods of the recitation of the Gītā, 'śṛṣṭikrama' (from the beginning to the end), 'saṁhārakrama' (from the last verse of the eighteenth chapter to the first verse of the first chapter) and 'sthitikrama' (from the first verse of the sixth chapter, to the last verse of the eighteenth chapter and then from the last verse of the fifth chapter to the first verse of the first chapter). A celibate may recite the Gītā, through śṛṣṭikrama, a renouncer, through saṁhārakrama, and a householder, through sthitikrama. But it is not a hard and fast rule. The recitation of Gītā, in whatever way done, is always beneficial.

The Gītā recited with 'Sampuṭa' (recitation of a verse at the beginning of each verse), with 'Sampuṭa vallī', (recitation of a verse two times at the beginning of each verse) and without 'Sampuṭa'. Any verse can be selected as 'Sampuṭa'. In recitation with 'Sampuṭa' the verse of 'Sampuṭa' is first recited and then the verse of the chapter. Again, the verse of the 'Sampuṭa', is first recited, then the verse of the chapter is recited. Again the verse of the 'Sampuṭa' is recited and then the second verse of the chapter. This process should continue. This is done either from the beginning to the end of the Gītā or from the end to the beginning (from the first verse of the first chapter to the last verse of the eighteenth chapter or vice versa). In 'Sampuṭa Vallī recitation of the verse selected as 'Sampuṭa' is recited two times. If the Gītā is recited with 'Sampuṭa' or with 'Sampuṭa Vallī', uncommon power is gained. If the gospel of the Gītā is specially reflected upon, the heart is purified, peace is attained and the devotee becomes qualified for God-realization.

The Gītā is also recited without the recitation of the verse of 'Sampuṭa'. A striver can recite all the eighteen chapter either everyday; or nine chapters the first day and the remaining nine chapters the next day; or six chapters each day for three days; or three chapters each day for six days; or two chapters each day for nine days. If he wants to recite the whole Gītā in fifteen days, one should recite one chapter each day, from the first date to the eleventh date, on the twelfth date he should recite the twelfth and the thirteenth chapters, on the thirteenth date he should recite the fourteenth and fifteenth chapters, on the fourteenth date, the sixteenth and the seventeenth chapters and on the fifteenth date, the eighteenth chapter. If there is an increase or decrease of date, in the fortnight according to the Hindu calendar, the sixteenth and the seventeenth chapters, can be recited for two days or the seventh and the eighth chapters, both, can be recited, in one day only.

If a striver has learnt the whole Gītā by heart, he should recite the first verse of all the eighteen chapters, then the second verse of all the eighteen chapters and then the third verse of all the chapters and so on. Thus he should recite the whole Gītā. Similarly he can recite the last verse of all the chapters beginning from the last chapter to the first and then the last one verses of all the chapters from the last chapter, to the first. Thus he should recite the whole Gītā from the last chapter, to the first chapter.

आरती

जय भगवद्गीते, जय भगवद्गीते।
हरि-हिय-कमल-विहारिणि सुन्दर सुपुनीते॥ जय०॥
कर्म-सुमर्म-प्रकाशिनि, कामासक्तिहरा।
तत्त्वज्ञान-विकाशिनि विद्या ब्रह्म परा॥ जय०॥
निश्चल-भक्ति-विधायिनि, निर्मल, मलहारी।
शरण-रहस्य-प्रदायिनि सब विधि सुखकारी॥ जय०॥
राग-द्वेष-विदारिणि, कारिणि मोद सदा।
भव-भय-हारिणि, तारिणि परमानन्दप्रदा॥ जय०॥
आसुर-भाव-विनाशिनि, नाशिनि तम-रजनी।
दैवी सद्गुण दायिनि, हरि-रसिका सजनी॥ जय०॥
समता-त्याग सिखावनि, हरि-मुख की बानी।
सकल शास्त्रकी स्वामिनि श्रुतियोंकी रानी॥ जय०॥
दया-सुधा बरसावनि मातु कृपा कीजै।
हरि-पद-प्रेम दान कर अपनो कर लीजै॥ जय०॥

|| Shri Hari ||

Terminology (Glossary)—according to Hindi alphabet

		Chapter-Verse
adhidaiva	Brahmā, the creator	8-1
adhibhūta	perishable world	8-1,4
adhiyajña	Lord Viṣṇu	8-2,4
ananya (cetāḥ)	exclusive (mind)	9-22
aparā (Prakṛti)	lower (Nature)	7-5
avyakta	unmanifest	2-25, 8-18,20,21; 12-5
avyabhicāriṇī	unswerving	13-10, 18-33, 14-26
aśraddadhānaḥ	faithless	4-40
asaktaṁ	unattached	9-9, 13-14
asat	unreal	9-19, 11-37, 13-12, 17-28
asammūḍhaḥ	undeluded	5-20, 10-3, 15-19
asvargyam	excluding-heaven	2-2
ahaṅkāra	egoism	3-27, 16-18, 18-53, 59
ātmā	Self (soul)	6-5,6; 7-18, 9-5, 10-20, 13-32
ādideva	Primal Deity	11-38
ābrahmabhuvanāt	upto the world of Brahmā (the creator)	8-16
āsurī	demoniac	16-5
āstikyam	belief in God	18-42
icchā	desire	13-6
indriyasya	sense	3-34
iṣṭaḥ	beloved (worshipped)	18-64 (18-70)
īśvaraḥ	the Lord	4-6
uccaiḥśravasam	Indra's vehicle, the king of horses	10-27

		Chapter-Verse
ucchiṣṭam	refuse	17-10
udāsīnaḥ	unconcerned (indifferent) (neutral)	12-16, 6-9
uparamate	quietude	6-20
uśanā	Śukrācārya, the learned preceptor of the demons	10-37
ṛk	One of the four Vedas, a collection of the aphorisms of sacred formulas	9-17
ṛddhaṁ	affluent (rich, prosperous)	2-8
ṛṣayaḥ	sages, holy men	5-25, 10-13
ekākṣaram	One syllabled	8-13
airāvatam	Indra's elephant, born at the time when the ocean was churned	10-27
Oṁ	sacred one syllabled Aum, Brahma (the Absolute)	8-13,17-23,24
Oṅkāra	sacred one syllabled Aum, Brahma (the Absolute)	9-17
karmaṇaḥ	action	3-1,9; 4-17, 14-16, 18-7,12
karmaphale	fruit of action	4-14
karmabandhanaḥ	bound by action	3-9
karmayogam	Discipline (path) of Action	3-7
karmasaṅgena	attachment to action	14-7
karmasaṅgrahaḥ	constituents (basis)	18-18
kāma-krodha	desire (lust)-anger	16-12
kārya-karaṇa-kartṛtve	effect, instrument and agent	13-20
Kuntībhojaḥ	Kuntī's brother	1-5
Kuntīputraḥ	Kuntī's sons (Arjuna, Bhīma & Yudhiṣṭhira)	1-16

		Chapter-Verse
kurukṣetre	land of the Kurus (Kuru family)	1-1
kṣatriyāḥ	a warrior (a member of the warrior class)	2-32
kṣaram	perishable	15-18
kṣetra	field (body) (Nature)	13-1
kṣetrajña (Kṣetrī)	knower of the field (Soul) (Spirit)	13-1
gatiṁ	end	6-37
gatiḥ	ways	4-17
gatī	path	8-26
gandharva	Gandharvas are celestial singers & musicians	11-22
gāṇḍīvaṁ	Arjuna's bow	1-30
gāyatrī	most important of all the metres contained in the Vedas (The Vedas have emanated from it)	10-35
guṇa	modes (attributes) of Prakṛti (Nature)	3-28, 29
guṇasaṅgaḥ	attachment to the modes	13-21
guṇātītaḥ	rise above (transcend) the modes of nature	14-25
guruḥ	teacher (preceptor)	11-43
gṛhastha	householder	
cāturvarṇyaṁ	fourfold caste (order)	4-13
citraratha	the most prominent celestial singer	10-26
cekitānaḥ	A Yādava (a member of the Yādava family who fought on the side of the Pāṇḍavas)	1-5

		Chapter-Verse
chandasāmaham	of the metres (Vedic verses)	10-35
jātidharmāḥ	caste religious rites (traditions)	1-43
jitasaṅgadoṣā	victorious over the evil of attachment	15-5
jitātmā	subdued the self (body etc.)	18-49
jitendriyaḥ	subdued the senses	5-7
jīvabhūtaḥ	having become a soul	15-7
jīvaloke	in the world of life	15-7
jñāna	knowledge (through the study of scriptures)	6-8
jñānacakṣuṣaḥ	eye of wisdom (knowledge)	15-10, 13-34
jñānatapasā	penance of wisdom (knowledge)	4-10
jñānadīpena	lamp of wisdom (knowledge)	10-11
jñānayajñena	knowledge sacrifice (wisdom-sacrifice)	9-15
jñānayogena	path (Discipline) of Knowledge	3-3
jñānī	man of wisdom (wise)	7-16, 17, 18
jyotiṣāṁ	among lights (luminaries)	10-21
tattvadarśinaḥ	the wise (seers of truth)	4-34
tattvavittu	knower of truth	3-28
tattvam	true nature (truth or essence)	18-1
tapasā (tapaḥ)	penance (austerity)	(7-9)
tapasviṣu	ascetics	7-9
tamasaḥ	darkness of ignorance	8-9
tamasā	darkness	18-32
daivī	divine	7-14, 16-5
daivīm	divine	9-13, 16-3, 5

		Chapter-Verse
dravyayajñāḥ	wealth-sacrifice	4-28
drupadaputreṇa	Dhṛṣṭadyumna, the son of Drupada	1-3
droṇam	name of the teacher of the Pāṇḍavas	2-4, 11-34
dvandvaḥ	dual	10-33
dvandvātīto	free from the pairs of opposites	4-22
dvijottama	best of the twice-born	1-7
dhanurdharaḥ	wielder of the bow	18-78
dharmakṣetre	holy field (field of righteousness)	1-1
dharme	pious traditions (pious conduct)	1-40
dharmam	duty	2-33
dharmyāmṛtam	immortal wisdom (law or doctrine)	12-20
dhātā	supporter	9-17
dhārtarāṣṭrasya	(Duryodhana) the son of Dhṛtarāṣṭra	1-33
dhyānaṁ	meditation	12-12
namaskuru (namaḥ)	bow down, prostrate	9-34, 18-65
narake	hell	1-44, 16-16
(narakasya)	hell	16-21
navadvāre	nine gates (two ears, two eyes, two nostrils, mouth, genital organ, anus)	5-13
naṣṭātmānaḥ	ruined soul	16-9
nāmayajñaiḥ	sacrifice in name	16-17
nityayuktasya	always absorbed (even steadfast)	8-14
nityasannyāsī	perpetual renouncer (ascetic)	5-3

		Chapter-Verse
nidrālasya pramādotthaṁ	sleep, indolence, heedlessness	18-39
nidhānaṁ	store house	9-18
nibaddhaḥ	bound	18-60
nimittamātraṁ	merely an instrument	11-33
niyatamānasaḥ	subdued (controlled) mind	6-15
niyatātmabhiḥ	person of steadfast mind	8-2
tāmasaḥ (tāmasī)	mode (nature) of ignorance	8-9,13-17,14-16,17; (17-2, 18-32, 35)
tejaḥ	glory (splendour)	7-10, 10-36, 15-12
tejaḥ	vigour	16-3, 18-43
tyaktasarvapa-rigrahaḥ	giving up all possessions	4-21
tyāgaḥ	renunciation (relinquishment)	16-2, 18-4,9
tyāgī	relinquisher	18-11
traiguṇya	three modes (attributes)	2-45
traividyā	knowers of the three Vedas	9-20
dakṣiṇāyanam	six months of the southern passage path of the Sun	8-25
dambho	hypocrisy (ostentation)	16-4
dayā	compassion	16-2
darpaḥ	arrogance	16-4
dānaṁ (dāna)	charity (gift)	10-5,16-1,17-7, 20-22, 25; 18-5, 43
divyāḥ	divine	10-16,19
dīrghasūtrī	procrastinating	18-28
durbuddheḥ	evil minded	1-23
durmatiḥ	man of perverse under-standing	18-16
duḥkhayonayaḥ	sources of pain	5-22
duḥkhālayam	abode of pain	8-15
dṛḍhaniścayaḥ	unshakable in determination	12-14

		Chapter-Verse
dṛḍhavratāḥ	firm resolve	7-28
devadeva	God of gods	10-15
devayajāḥ	worshippers of gods	7-23
devarṣiḥ	celestial sage	10-13
dehabhṛtā	embodied being	18-11
dehavadbhiḥ	by the embodied	12-5
dehī	the embodied	2-22,30; 5-13,14-20
daityānām	among demons	10-30
daivaḥ	the divine	16-6
niṣṭhā	firm state of discipline	3-3
nistraiguṇyo	free from the three attributes (modes)	2-45
niḥśreyasakarau	lead to salvation	5-2
niḥspṛhaḥ	free from thirst for enjoyment	2-71
nīti	righteousness (firm or wise policy)	10-38, 18-78
naiṣkarmyasiddhiṁ	the Supreme State consisting in freedom from action	18-49
naiṣkarmyaṁ	actionlessness	3-4
naiṣkṛtikaḥ	malicious	18-28
naiṣṭhikīm	everlasting (final)	5-12
nyāyyaṁ	right	18-15
nyāsaṁ	renunciation	18-2
paṇavānaka-gomukhāḥ	tabors, drums, cowhorns	1-13
paradharmaḥ	duty of another	3-35
paramātmā	the Supreme spirit (God)	6-7, 13-22,31; 15-17
parameśvara	Lord Supreme (Supreme Lord)	13-27
pitaraḥ	manes	1-34, 42
purāṇaḥ	ancient (primeval)	2-20, 11-38
puruṣaḥ	self (soul)	15-17

		Chapter-Verse
prakṛtiḥ (mūla)	Nature (Primordial Matter)	7-4, 9-10, 13-20, 18-59
prajāpatiḥ	the creator (Brahmā)	3-10
praṇipātena	prostration (humble reverence)	4-34
prapadye	take refuge	15-4
Prabhuḥ	Lord	5-14, 9-18, 24
pramādaḥ	heedlessness (negligence)	14-13
prayāṇakāle	at the hour of death	7-30, 8-2,10
pralaya	dissolution, annihilation	7-6, 9-18, 14-14,15
pravṛttiḥ	activity	14-12, 15-4, 18-46
prasaktāḥ	addicted	16-16
prasāda	placidity (Serenity or purity) of mind	2-64,65
prāṇāpāna	ingoing and outgoing life-breaths	4-29, 15-14
prāṇāyāma	breath restraint	
pretān	gnomes	17-4
phala (hetavaḥ)	(seekers after) fruit (reward)	2-49
badhyate	bound	4-14
bahudaṁṣṭrākarālaṁ	many terrible tusks	11-23
buddhiḥ	mind, intellect (intelligence)	2-39, 41,44,52, 53,65, 66
brahma	the Absolute (God)	4-24
brahmacaryam	celibacy	8-11, 17-14
brahmanirvāṇam	beatitude of God (Brahmic bliss)	2-72, 5-24,25,26
brahmabhūtaḥ	identified with Brahma (the Absolute)	5-24, 18-54
brahmabhūyāya	for becoming Brahma (the Absolute)	14-26, 18-53
brāhmaṇakṣatriyaviśāṁ	the three Varṇas (castes) known as Brāhmaṇa, Kṣatriya and Vaiśya	18-41

		Chapter-Verse
brāhmī	Brahmic state (eternal state of beatitude of God)	2-72
bhaktaḥ	devotee	4-3, 7-21, 9-31
bhaktiḥ	devotion	13-10
bhagavan	the blessed Lord (Lord)	10-14,17
bhajatāṁ	worshipping	10-10
bhāvaiḥ	things and feelings	7-13
bhūtānām	beings	4-6, 10-5, 20,22, 11-2, 13-15, 18-46
bhoktā	enjoyer, experiencer	9-24, 13-22
bhogaiśvarya-prasaktānāṁ	attached to pleasures and prosperity (man cembodied soul) is a fragment of God)	2-44
manaḥ (manasā)	mind	1-30,2-60,(3-6,7; 5-11,13)
madhyastha	mediator	6-9
manaḥprasādaḥ	cheerfulness of mind	17-16
manīṣiṇāṁ	the wise (philosophers)	18-5,3; 2-51
mantraḥ	hymns	9-16, 17-13
maharṣayaḥ	sages	10-2,6
mahātmā	great soul	7-19, 11-50
mahābhūtāni	the five great (subtle) elements	13-5
mātrāsparśaḥ	sense-objects	2-14
māyā	divine illusion	7-14
mārgaśīrṣaḥ	a month of the Hindu calender	10-35
muktam (muktaḥ)	liberated	18-40,5-28,12-15, 18-71
muniḥ	sage	2-56, 5-6,28; 10-26
mumukṣubhiḥ	seekers of liberation	4-15
mūḍhaḥ (mūḍhāḥ)	deluded (ignorant)	7-25, 7-15, 9-11, 16-20

		Chapter-Verse
mṛtyusaṁsāra-sāgarāt	ocean of death bound existence	12-7
mokṣam	liberation (salvation)	18-30
mohaḥ	delusion	11-1, 14-13, 18-73
maunī	(silent) he who thinks of God only	12-19
yakṣarakṣasām	genies and demons	10-23, 17-4
yajur	one of the four Vedas	9-17
yajñadānatapaḥ	sacrifice, gift, penance	18-3, 17-25
yatacittasya	disciplined (controlled) mind	6-19
yatacetasām	those who have subdued (controlled) their minds	5-26
yatavākkāya-mānasaḥ	speech, body, mind subdued (controlled)	18-52
yatātmavān (yatātmā)	self-controlled	12-11,14
yantrārūḍhāni	mounted on a machine	18-61
yamaḥ	god of death	10-29, 11-39
yuktacetasaḥ	steadfast mind	7-30
yuktatamaḥ	most devout	6-47
yuktatamāḥ	most perfect (best versed) in Yoga	12-2
yuktaḥ	a Karmayogī (a Sāṅkhyayogī)	5-12, (5-8)
yuktātmā	established in god	7-18
yogakṣemaṁ	gain and security	9-22
yogabhraṣṭaḥ	He who has fallen (deviated from Yoga)	6-41
yogaḥ	equanimity (evenmindedness)	2-48
vijñāna	Wisdom (Self-realization)	6-8
vyaktayaḥ	manifest	8-18
vyavasāyātmikā	determinate (resolute) (one pointed)	2-41, 44
vyāsaprasādāt	by the grace of Vyāsa	18-75

		Chapter-Verse
vaiśya	trading class	18-44
vānaprastha	retired order	
śaṅkhaṁ	conch	1-12,13,14
śabdabrahma	the fruit of actions as the Vedas	6-44
śaraṇam	refuge	2-49,9-18,18-62,66
śarīravāṅmanobhiḥ	body, speech, mind	18-15
śarīrasthaṁ	dwelling (seated) in the body	17-6
śāntiḥ (śāntim)	peace (tranquillity)	(2-70,71 etc.) 2-66, 12-12, 16-2
śāstravidhānoktam	said in the ordinance of the scriptures	16-24
śāstravidhi	ordinance of the scriptures	16-23
śuklakṛṣṇe	the bright and the dark	8-26
śūdrasya	one of the four Varṇas (caste) (service class)	18-44
śraddhā	faith	17-2,3
śradhāvān	man of faith	4-39
śreyaḥ	salvation	1-31,2-5,7;3-2 etc.
ṣaṇmāsā (śuklaḥ)	six months of the northern path of the sun	8-24
ṣaṇmāsā (kṛṣṇaḥ)	six months of the southern path of the sun	8-25
saṅgaḥ	attachment	2-47, 62
sataḥ	real	2-16
samatā (samattvam)	equanimity (even-mindedness)	10-5, 2-48
samabuddhayaḥ (samabuddhiḥ)	alike, even-minded	12-4, 6-9
sarvagataḥ	all-pervading	2-24
sarvaguhyatamaṁ	most secret	18-64
sarvadehinām	all embodied beings	14-8
sarvadharmān	all duties	18-66

		Chapter-Verse
sarvabhutahite	seeking good (welfare) of all beings	5-25, 12-4
sarvaloka-maheśvaram	Great Lord of all the worlds	5-29
sarvasaṅkalpa-sannyāsī	renounced all thoughts of the world	6-4
sarvārambha-parityāgī	renounced doership in all actions	12-16, 14-25
savijñānam	with real knowledge of manifest Divinity-i.e., in the world there is nothing else besides the manifestation of God	7-2
savyasācin	Arjuna who could shoot arrows with his left hand also	11-33
sahajam (karma)	innate (duty)	18-48
saṅkarasya	confusion of castes	3-24
sannyāsa (sannyāsī)	renounced order (renouncer)	
sannyāsaḥ	renunciation	5-2, 6
sannyāsī	renouncer	6-1
sampadaṁ	gift	16-3,4,5
sādhaka	striver (aspirant)	
sādhanā	spiritual practice or spiritual discipline	
sammohaṁ	delusion	7-27
saṁśuddhakilbiṣaḥ	purified from sins	6-45
saṁsiddhim	highest perfection (God-realization)	3-20, 8-15, 18-45
saṁsparśajā	born of contact (with objects)	5-22
sāttvika	nature (mode) of goodness	17-11, 18-9, 26 etc.
sādhuḥ (sādhūnām)	Saint (good)	9-30, (4-8)
sāṅkhyayogam (sannyāsa)	the Discipline (path) of Knowledge	5-4

		Chapter-Verse
sāma	One of the four Vedas	9-17
siddhānām	Those who have attained perfection	7-3, 10-26
siddhiḥ (asiddhiḥ)	success (failure)	4-12, (2-48, 18-26)
sukṛtaduṣkṛte	good (virtue) and evil (vice)	2-50
sukhaduḥkhe	pleasure and pain	2-38
sudurācāraḥ	vilest sinner	9-30
suviruḍhamūlam	firm rooted	15-3
suhṛdam	disinterested friend (well-wisher)	5-29 (1-27)
suhṛnmitrāry-udāsīnamadhya-sthasdveṣya	well-wishers, friends, neutrals, mediators, hateful	6-9
sūkṣmatvāt	because of its subtlety	13-15
sūtaputraḥ	Karṇa (Karṇa was brought up by a charioteer)	11-26
saumadattiḥ	Bhūriśravā, the son of Somadatta	1-8
sthitaprajñasya	a man of steadfast (stable) wisdom	2-54,55
sthitadhīḥ	Do	2-54,56
spṛhā	craving	4-14, 14-12
smṛtivibhramaḥ (smṛtibhraṁśād)	loss of memory	2-63
svargaṁ	heaven	2-37
svādhyāyajñāna-yajñāḥ	study of the scriptures and knowledge as sacrifice	4-28
harṣaśokānvitaḥ	moved by joy and sorrow	18-27
hitakāmyayā	wishing welfare	10-1
hṛddeśe	in the heart	18-61

Gita Press, Gorakhpur

Our Publications, Kalyan and Kalyana-Kalpataru available at :

Gorakhpur — 273005	Gita Press—P.O. Gita Press	© (0551) 2334721; 2331250; Fax (0551) 2336997
	website:www.gitapress.org /e-mail:booksales@gitapress.org	
Delhi — 110006	2609, Nai Sarak	© (011) 23269678; Fax 23259140
Kolkata — 700007	Gobind Bhavan-Karyalaya, 151, Mahatma Gandhi Road e-mail : gobindbhawan@gitapress.org	© (033) 22686894; Fax 22680251
Mumbai — 400002	282, Samaldas Gandhi Marg (Princess Street) Near Marine Lines Station	© (022) 22030717
Kanpur — 208001	24/55, Birhana Road	© (0512) 2352351; Fax 2352351
Patna — 800004	Ashok Rajpath, Opposite Women's Hospital	© (0612) 2300325
Ranchi — 834001	Cart Sarai Road, Upper Bazar	© (0651) 2210685
Surat — 395001	Vaibhav Apartment, Opposite Nutan Niwas, Bhatar Road e-mail : suratdukan@gitapress.org	© (0261) 2237362, 2238065
Indore — 452001	G-5, Shree Vardhan, 4 R.N.T. Marg	© (0731) 2526516, 2511977
Jalgaon — 425001	7, Bhim Singh Market, Near Railway Station	© (0257) 2226393; Fax (0257) 2220320
Hyderabad — 500095	41, 4-4-1; Dilshad Plaza, Sultan Bazar	© (040) 24758311
Nagpur — 440002	Shriji Kripa Complex, 851, New Etawari Road	© (0712) 2734354
Cuttack — 753009	Bhartiya Towers, Badam Badi	© (0671) 2335481
Raipur — 492009	Mittal Complex, Ganjpara Telghani Chowk	© (0771) 4034430
Varanasi — 221001	59/9, Nichibag	© (0542) 2413551
Haridwar — 249401	Sabjimandi, Motibazar	© (01334) 222657
Rishikesh — 249304	Gita Bhawan, P.O.-Swargashram	© (0135) 2430122, 2432792
Coimbatore — 641018	Gita Press Mansion, 8/1M, Racecourse	© (0422) 3202521
Bangalore — 560027	#15, 4th 'E' Cross, K.S. Garden,Lalbagh Road	© (080) 22955190, 32408124

Station-Stalls

Delhi (Platform No. 5-6); **New Delhi** (No. 16); **Hazarat Nizamuddin** [Delhi] (No. 4-5); **Kota** [Rajasthan] (No. 1); **Bikaner** (No. 1); **Gorakhpur** (No. 1); **Kanpur** (No. 1); **Lucknow** [N.E. Railway]; **Varanasi** (No. 4-5); **Mughal Sarai** (No. 3-4); **Haridwar** (No. 1); **Patna** (Main Entrance); **Ranchi** (No.1); **Dhanbad** (No. 2-3); **Muzaffarpur** (No. 1); **Samastipur** (No. 2); **Howrah** (No. 5 & 18 Both); **Kolkata** (No. 1); **Sealdah Main** (No. 8); **Asansol** (No. 5); **Cuttack** (No. 1); **Bhubaneshwar** (No. 1); **Ahmedabad** (No. 2-3); **Rajkot** (No. 1); **Jamnagar** (No. 1); **Bharuch** (No. 4-5); **Indore** (No. 5); **Vadodara** (No. 4-5); **Aurangabad** [Maharashtra] (No. 1); **Secunderabad** [A.P.] (No. 1); **Guwahati** (No. 1); **Kharagpur** (No. 1-2); **Raipur** [Chhattisgarh] (No. 1); **Bangalore** (No. 1); **Yesvantpur** (No. 6); **Hubli** (No. 1-2); **Sri Satya Sai Prashanti Nilayam** [South Central Railway] (No. 1) and **I.S.B.T. (Delhi)**

Retail Counters

Churu — Rishikul-Brahmacharyashram, Purani Sarak, **Rishikesh** — Muni Ki Reti, **Tirupati** —Shop No. 56, T.T.D. Mini Shopping Complex, **Berhampore**—Municipal Market Complex, Block-B, Stall No. 57 to 60, I[st] Floor, **Gujrat**—Santram Mandir, Nadiyad.